Motif-Index
of
Folk-Literature
Vol. VI

MOTIF-INDEX

OF

FOLK-LITERATURE

A Classification of Narrative Elements in
Folktales, Ballads, Myths, Fables, Mediaeval Romances,
Exempla, Fabliaux, Jest-Books, and
Local Legends

REVISED AND ENLARGED EDITION BY

STITH THOMPSON
Indiana University

VOLUME SIX
INDEX

INDIANA UNIVERSITY PRESS
BLOOMINGTON & LONDON

Manufactured in the United States of America

ISBN 0-253-33886-7

3 4 5 6 7   80 79 78 77 76

ALPHABETICAL INDEX[1]

An asterisk before a number indicates that cross-references to related matters will be found immediately following the item. Numbers followed by "ff." indicate that the item is general and introduces specific examples not always recorded in this index. Plurals always immediately follow the singular number of nouns.

Aaron's censer (pistol) J1446; rod F971.1. — Miracles cease at A's death F900.3.1.

Abandoned castle F771.4.3; child aided by seagulls, doe, angel T611.7; child joins parents in game (recognition) H151.9; child receives magic sight D1821.6; child rescued by dog B549.3; children accidentally discovered N768; or murdered children S300—399; maiden helped by nurse P361.5; queen entertains in forest, recognized H155; son exposed to tiger H105.5.4; souls feed on spiders E752.7.1; wife recognized H152.3. — Child born of woman a. in pit T581.2; father reinstates a. son N731.3; ghost of one a. by lover E334.3; girl a. in tree H151.14.1; girl rescued, then a. R111.6; parent seeks famine relief from a. child H154; rescue of a. persons R130ff.; waves break caul of a. child N655.

Abandoning. — Mortal a. world to live in fairyland F373; mother a. beautiful baby F575.1.1.

Abandonment to avoid fulfillment of prophecy M371.0.1; on cliff submerged at high tide (punishment) Q466.2; and exposures S140ff.; in forest as punishment Q435; of hero at birth A511.2.1; of hero in lower world *K1931.2; of integrity brings devil G303.6.2.5; on stretching tree K1113; in water *S142. — Step-sisters cause girl's a. in jungle K2129.3.

Abandonments and exposures S140ff.

Abbess caught in sin permits nuns to sin K1274; secretly delivered of her child by Virgin T401.1; and washerwoman (flea and fever) J612.1. — Nun hidden by a. from pursuing knight betrays own hiding place V465.1.2.1; nun rewarded, made a. Q87.3.

Abbey. — Ghost prevents box's removal from a. E299.2; looking for keys of a. J703.1.

Abbot burns mouth, excuses crying J1478.1; caught in sin permits monks to sin K1274; escapes from paramour's husband K521.6; and king

---

1 For invaluable aid in the preparation of this index I am indebted to Miss Clara L. Little and Mrs. Sue Lena Hickam. The new and enlarged index had the expert help of Mrs. Nancy MacClintock and Mrs. Marjorie Congram, and was prepared under special grants of the American Philosophical Society and Indiana University. For all this I am most grateful.

H561.2; cannot find needle J1651; receives guest in rags J916. —
Angel chastizes a. V235.3; fat a. cured by starving K1955.1.1; fire
consumes woman slandering a. Q552.13.3; God as surety: a. pays
J1559.2; luxury of a. and cardinal J1263.4.1; monk who did not ask
for the position made a. Q61.1; self-righteous monk rebuked by a.
L435.1.1; sham a. K1961.5; thievish a. to be eaten by wolves Q556.12.1;
virgin becomes monastery a. K1837.7.

Abdicating. — Father a. in son's favor P16.1.4; king a. after queen's
adultery P16.1.2.

Abducted bride hidden in fairyland F322.4; wife brought back by fakir
R165.3; wife leaves needle sign H119.2. — Druid discovers a. wife
D1816.5.1; girl a. by fairy F324; girl a. by fairy accidentally drowns
N339.9; hero's wife a. N391.0.1; man a. by devil G303.9.5.6; quest as
punishment by a. girl's father H1219.3; sacrifice for return of a. person
V17.7; statue left instead of a. queen K661.4; thieves carry a. woman
on bier, drown out her wailings K419.8; woman a. by giving medicine
K1364; youth a. by fairy F325.

Abduction *R10ff.; by animal for breaking tabu C986; of Christianized
fairy F389.2; by devil *G303.9.5; to fairyland *F320; by man disguised
as woman K1321.2; by masking as husband K755.1; by mountain-men
*F460.4.4.1; by ogre G440ff.; punished Q213; by taking aboard ship
to inspect wares K1332. — Banishment for a. of bride Q431.5.2.

Abducting child by calling self "her husband" K361.1.1; woman after
asking her for fire K762. — Demons a. men G302.9.2; fairy a. men with
whom in love F302.3.1.4; fairy a. mortal's wife F301.6; false accusation
of a. wife K2127.1; king a. woman P19.2.1; lover a. beloved K1371.4;
lover in disguise for a. K1831.2.2; moon a. woman A753.1.1; ogre a.
new-born babe G442.1.

Abductor in disguise R24; induces magic sleep D1964.3; pretends lover
sent him to princess K1914. — Burning to punish a. Q414.0.4.2; lover
rescues his lady from a. R161.1; magic sleep induced by a. D1964.3.

Abel slain with camel bone F839.3. — Animals refuse to avenge murder
of A. B591.0.1; Cain drinks blood of A. D1812.3.3.7; cry of blood of A.
A1344.1.

Abersetus as guardian of door of heaven A661.0.1.4.

Abiding. — Vow on a. laws M185.

Ability. — God dislikes offerings beyond one's a. V10.2; person transformed to animal recognized by a. to read H62.2; recognition by unique
a. H31; reward for a. to keep secrets Q62; test of a. *H500; test of
wife's a. to keep secret H472ff.

Abnormal features or growth of changeling F321.1.2.1.

Abnormally born child has unusual powers T550.2.

Aboard. — Capture by taking a. ship K775.1; man magically appears
a. ship D2121.11.

Abode, see also **Dwelling, Home;** of the dead *E480ff.; of devil (between hoofs of swine) G303.8.7; of evil spirits (north) G633; of unpromising hero (heroine) L130ff.

Abortion T572.2; placed in innocent woman's bed K2112.2.4. — Ghost of a. E225.1; origin of a. A1351.2; punishment for a. Q251.1.

Above. — Creator from a. A21; deceptive crop division: a. the ground, below the ground K171.1; dwarfs have homes a. the ground F451.4.2ff.; emergence of gods from a. A115.5; the Lord a., the lord below K1525; region a. the three worlds A651.1.1.2; vehicle travels a. and below ground *D1533.2ff.

Abraham learns to worship God (cumulative tale) Z42.2; as prophet M301.7.3. — Angel's visit to A. H828.

Abraham's — Land of dead in A's bosom E489.10.

Abridgement of freedom as punishment Q430ff.

Abroad. — Do not marry a girl from a. J21.4; wild hunt a. until cock-crow *E501.11.1.2.

Abscess breaks when patient laughs at foolish diagnosis N641. — Birth from a. T541.2; tigress grateful for opening of a. B386.

Absence. — Feigned a. tests wife H466.1; in god's a. his function ceases A173.1; obedient husband given leave of a. J2523.

Absent person seems to be present K1881. — Why certain animals are a. from countries A2434.2; bending bow of woman's a. husband (suitor contest) H331.4.2; cannibals advised to be a. while hero is being cooked K619.1; present servant girl preferred to a. mistress J326; sleeper not to be awakened, since soul is a. E721.1.1; body in trance while soul is a. E721.2; wraith looks after a. person E723.4.6; youth a. when entire family wiped out N659.2.

Absent-minded nurse puts child down well J2175.3.

Absent-mindedness, absurd J2000—J2049.

Absolution. — Unquiet dead sinner taken to priest for a. E411.0.2.

Absorption in charms of beloved causes cut finger T26.1.

Abstinence from wine by deer after breaking leg J133.3.

Abstract. — Wanting to see a. quality J2488.

Abstractions, gods of A460ff.; personified Z110ff.

Absurd contest won by deception K60ff.; tasks H1010—H1049ff.; truth discredits husband J1151.1.2. — King makes a. statement J817.3; wife agrees with husband's a. statements H474.

Absurdities based upon false assumptions J2210ff.; cause fool to laugh U15; rebuke another absurdity *J1530ff.; of tight-rope walker's performance J156.2. — Lies: logical a. X1700.

Absurdum, reductio ad (of judgment) J1191, (task) H952, (riddle: stallions of Babylon) H572.

Abundance in otherworld F169.8. — Fairy promises a. to mortal F349.4.

Abuse of dwarfs by mortals F451.5.11; of fairy gifts tabu F348.7.1; of hospitality punished Q292.3; of live stock by fairies F366; of mother punished (devils carry off girl) Q281.1.1; of property by witch *G265;

of stepchildren punished by return of dead mother *E221.2.1; of women, children tabu C867.1. — Ears stopped to avoid hearing a. J672.2.

Abuses. — Repartee concerning clerical a. J1263ff.; twelve a. of world Z71.8.2.

Abused and pampered horses B316; son becomes hero L10.2; step-daughter L55.1; youngest daughter L52.

Abusive speeches drive ogres away G571. — Woman's a. lover T232.4.

Abyss at end of Milky Way A778.10. — Bodies of water in primitive a. sink A910.3; tree appears to save saint from a. V222.10.

Access to lower world F90ff.; to other world F150ff.; to upper world *F50ff.

Accident. — Animal warns against a. B521.2; ghost haunts a. scene E275, E334.2.2; injury from reënacting a. J2133.14; knockers' appearance as a. warning F456.1.2.2.4; luring victim by feigning a. K833; magic object protects from a. on journey D1384; mountains from a. to primeval lizard A 961.3; plant characteristics from a. to original plant A2741; sounds of a. reënact tragedy E337.1.2; treasure discovered by a. N534; who is guilty of a.? Z49.11.

Accidents. — Birds fight, cause series of a. Z49.6.1; bungling fool has succession of a. J2661; lucky a. *N400ff.; unlucky a. N300ff.

Accidental action of ancient animal produces animal characteristics A2211; arrival in lower world *F102; calling on god's name held to outweigh a life of wickedness V91; cannibalism (man eats the dried meat of a Jew on shipboard) X21; death of woman scorned in love T71.1; discharge of gun kills much game X1124.3; discovery of crime N610ff.; discovery of riddle answer H575; drinking of love philtre produces mutual love *T21; encounters N700—N799; and intentional fire J1175.2; killing as bad omen D1812.5.1.23; success in hunting or fishing N620ff. — Detection by a. remark N275.2; recognition through a. encounter H152; victim of a. death cannot rest in grave E411.10.

Accidentally. — Bride wounded a. on way home T152; cobold a. acquired F481.0.1.4; hasty condemnation of man who a. becomes suspected of crime N342; magic a. found D841; objects a. picked up used to overawe ogre N691; princess defeated in repartee by means of objects a. picked up H507.1.0.1; sham wise man a. unmasks robbers K1956.1; villain a. killed by own order K1612.1; youth a. knocks old woman over M301.2.1.

Acclamation of saint by miraculous manifestation *V222.

Accompanying. — Animal a. man on journey B579.1; marvelous light a. saint V222.1; sea dragon in serpent form a. hero D659.4.2.

Accomplishment of quests H1230ff.; of tasks D753, H950ff.; of vigilance test H1480ff.

Account book of dead E481.8.1; book of mistakes J1371; of common experiences demanded as identity-test H15. — Giving a. of what happened in princess's bedchamber H344.1.

Accounts squared by shaving the wife J2082; straightened by ignorant steward L144.1. — Cutting paper of a. J2489.4.

Accountants. — God's a. tally human acts A189.8.

Accounting to be given afterward J1627.

Accoutrements. — Disguise by carrying other's a. K1810.1.

Accursed, see also **Cursed;** dancers C94.1.1. — What are most a. things? H659.18.

Accusation admitted and accuser discomfited J1162; admitted but fool pleads mistakes in the details J2499.3; of murder from blood smeared on innocent person K2155.1. — Bishop's nose bitten off for false a. Q451.5.3; criminal in church mistakes service as a. N275.5; quilty man sentenced for false a. J1141.12; reductio ad absurdum of a. J1191.5.

Accusations, false *K2100—K2199.

Accused. — Benefactor falsely a. of theft W154.13; criminal confesses because he thinks himself a. N275; congregation a. of sins by devil G303.24.1; falsely a. maiden dies F1041.1.3.1; falsely a. man's suicide N347.6; foster brother falsely a. of seduction P273.2.3; heavenly voice test: lying for a. H216.2.

Accuser, envious J1351.2. — Proverb on winning over a. J171.3.2.

Accusing conspirators to confiscate their estates K487. — Thief a. companion of mutual theft K401.0.1.

Accustomed. — Longing for a. living V135.

Achikar *H561.5.

Achilles, see *K1836; heel Z311.

Acid bath for unwelcome lover K1227.4.1.

Acknowledgement of son brings disenchantment of monster D741.1.

Acorn crop (payment to be made at harvest of first crop) K221.

Acorns. — Magic a. D985.4, D1667.2; pseudo-magic a.: protect pigs K119.2.

Acquisition of culture A1400—A1499; of familiar spirit F403.2.1; of helpful animal B310; of food supply for human race A1420ff.; of magic objects D810ff.; of magic powers *D1720ff.; of magic strength D1835; of strength by strong hero F611.3; of extraordinary skill by brothers *F660.1; of treasure or money (accidental) N630ff.; of wisdom (knowledge) J0—J199.

Act of truth H252. — Respite from death until performance of certain a. *K551.

Acts of charity bring forgiveness for sin Q171.1; performed for changing luck *N131. — Clever a. J1100ff.; short-sighted a. J2050ff.

Acteon transformed to deer and eaten by dogs Q415.1.1.

Action. — Confession induced by bringing unjust a. against accused J1141.1; continuous a. started by breaking tabu C916; extraordinary a. explained H591; inappropriate a. from misunderstanding J1820ff.; magic statue of archer put into a. by picking up precious object from ground D1620.1.5.1.

Actor *P471; forgets and speaks in his own person J2041ff.

Adam names all animals A2571.0.1 named from first letters of four stars A1577.1; learns animal languages from Eve B217.8; names male animals, Eve, female A2571.0.2; at first nameless A1281.6; spat on tobacco plant A2854; story false since skeleton has all his ribs J1262.8. — First walk by A. A1392; five devils created by A. create other devils in same manner G303.1.5; God sends A. to earth to father mankind A1285.1.1.; Mother Earth pregnant with A. A401.1; ravens show A. how to bury dead D2223.7; riddles concerning A. H706, H812, H813; Satan jealous of A. A63.5.1; souls presented to A. E755.0.3; tears of A. and Eve leaving paradise become trees A2612.1; why Eve not made with A. A1275.8.

Adam's Apple, origin of A1319.1; body made of eight things A1260.1.3; burial place N774.3.1; clothes of light F821.7; corpse talks with God E545.22; disobedience blamed H1557.2; tears of repentance bring flood A1012.1; wisdom D1811.0.1; work destroyed by devil by night G303.14.1.1. — Earth created from A's body A831.9; fairies not A's children F251.10; heavenly bodies mourn A's death F961.0.3.1; tree from Christ's crucifixion planted by A's son A2632.2.

Adaptability J800ff.

Adder grows in heart of man F559.7.2; kills bird hunter just as he is shooting bird N335.1; transformed to blindworm *A2145.5.

Adder's — Why a's tail tastes like liver A2378.9.4.

Adders in hell A671.2.1.1.

Address of fool (a big high house) J1742.2. — Modesty has no a. J91.

Addressing the dead E545.19; saints to win contest K18.1.2; spirit compels it to speak F404.1; woman in verse betrays changeling's maturity F321.1.1.3. — Pardon for a. courtier as king P15.1.2; use of second plural in a. anyone A1599.5.

Adhesion of blood test of paternity H486.1; for breaking tabu C994. — Magic a. *D2171ff.; (to object as punishment) Q551.2.1.

Adhesive stone (magic) D1413.17.

Admiration of beautiful things causes thief's capture J2136.5.1.

Admirers. — Poet vaults away from a. J1224.1.

Admission of accusation discomfits accuser J1162; of theft by many, real thief concealed K415.1; to heaven Q172; to heaven (faultfinding forbidden) *F13; denied to both heaven and hell *Q565, A1942.1; of sale of kisses provoked by rival's overstrict conduct K1275.1; to woman's bed brings disenchantment of animal D734; to woman's room bought T45. — Test for a. to warrior band H1566.

Adopted son plots parents' death S22.1.1. — Abandoned child a. by queen S354.1; hill as a. child A969.6; mermaid ruins her a. daughter's seducer B81.13.9; mortal god's a. son A189.11.

Adoption of children J21.27, *T670ff.; as sister by dwarfs F451.5.1.2; by fairies F311; of hero by king *N836.1; by old couple N825.1; of own son by king N731.1.1; by rich man K2015; by transforming self to child D646.2.

Adrift. — Ghost sets boats a. E299.5; imposter casts foster brother a. on seas K1931.1.1; punishment: setting a. in boat Q466.0.2.

Adult transformed to child D55.2.5.

Adulterer can't rest in grave E411.2; causes sun to stand still D2146.1.1.2; killed Q411.0.1.1; punished by madness Q555.2. — Magic cup sticks to a. H411.4.2.

Adulteress betrayed by child J125.2; blackmailed by lover K1582; charges pair of shoes as fee, prepares for old age J761.3; chooses loathly paramour T232.2; on death-bed reveals children's illegitimacy T238; discredits scorned suitor's testimony J1151.4; ejected into street clad only in shirt Q432.2; escapes in old-woman's disguise K521.4.5; explains child born by suggestion J2338; feigns unusual sensitiveness K2051; forced to wear symbolic dress Q487; hurled from high rock escapes injury: she may not be punished again J1184.1; kills lover K2231.1; lures husband to his death K778.5; outwits husband K1510ff.; and paramour outwitted by husband *K1550ff.; and paramour outwitted by trickster K1570ff.; and paramour plot against her stepson S31.1; persuades husband she has not been away J2315.1; plots own abduction R10.2; rebuked for absurdity J1532; tells lover, "I can see whole world" K1271.4; tricks husband into killing lover K2111.4. — Animal as confederate of a. B598; "chaste" woman an a. K2063; paramour exposes a. naked K1213.1; veiled a. flees with paramour K1821.3.1; wife as a. K1500ff.; woman slandered as a. K2112; woman slandered as a. is thrown into lion pit: lions do not harm her B522.3.

Adulterous love changed into chaste one T372; person cannot rest in grave E411.2; wife. plots own abduction R10.2. — Animal as confederate of a. wife B598; coarse living sends a. king back to wife V146.1; devil as messenger to the a. G303.9.4.5.2; god from a. union A112.8; whimbrel's a. mate sent to death K813.1.

Adultery *T230, *T481ff., see also **Infidelity;** among the gods A164.2; betrayed by riddling answers H582.2; detected by spit marks J1142.3; in primeval family A1556.3; punished *Q241ff.; revealed by child in mother's womb T575.1.1.2; tests H400ff.; tabu C115. — Animal reveals mistress's a. *A2237.1, J551.1; the bag of lies: threat to tell of queen's a. K1271.1.1; deception connected with a. *K1500ff.; fairy banished for a. F252.4.1; fairies commit a. F254.5; father causes death of son innocent of a. N344.2; fool discloses woman's a.; killed J2365; foster son commits a. with foster father's wife P275.1; husband as God behind tree forces his wife to confess a. *K1971.5; husband refuses to believe in wife's a. J2342; husband relates wife's a. in dream J1147.1; husband takes wife's place and receives punishment for her a. T261.1; husband's jealousy forces wife to a. T257.7; king abdicates after queen's a. P16.1.2; man dies at wife's a. F1041.1.3.5; overlooking a. for reputa-

tion's sake J221.1.1; princess disguised as man accused of a. with
queen K2113; queen commits a. with husband's foster son P29.2; rich
woman accuses ascetic of a. K2113.2; senator overlooks wife's a. rather
than impair his reputation J221.1.1; sun-god commits a. A220.0.1; unwitting a. with blood-brother's wife N766; wife's a. to aid husband in
battle T455.2.1.

Advancement. — Worshipping devil to secure a. V55.

Advantage temporarily gained by pretending to yield in combat K2378.

Advent. — Time of Messiah's a. tabu C428.

Adventure told as dream J1155. — Animal cries recall ancient a.
A2275.4; casting lots for a. N126.1; going home before a. completed
tabu C756.3; quest for a. H1221; vow not to eat before hearing of a.
M151.

Adventures, experiences leading to N770ff.; of kings P15ff.; related by
old robber frees his three sons R153.3.3; result from promise to dying
father M258.1; of thumbling F535.1.1. — Clever wife advises husband
how to succeed on a. J1112.3.

Adventurers, twin T685.1.

Adversary pushed into ground F942.2.1. — Animal overcomes man's a.
B524; ground cut from under a. F942.2; quest for strong a. H1225.

Adversity genius appears to king C14; personified Z135. — Spirit of a.
brings bad luck N134.1.4; sultan tries to avoid a. J2488.2.

Advice, see also **Counsel;** from animals *B560ff.; from bird B122.1; from
bodily members D1312.1; to bride T137.1; of cock proves disastrous to
himself K1633; from dead mother E323.4; from dervish J152.2; of devil
to human beings G303.9.7; from distant sage H1393; from dream
D1814.2; from druid P427.3; of your enemy to be disregarded J646;
after event valueless J756; from excrements *D1312.1.1; from fairy F347;
from God D1814.3; from grateful objects D1658.3.1; from magic object
D1312; to marry own daughter secured from priest by unnatural father
T411.1.1; sought by Palamides from Ulysses who has injured him
J646.1; from supernaturals seen in dreams K2035; from thief for owner
to go away K343; from wife behind tree K1971.4.1; of wife scorned
leads to disaster J155.3; from a woman in bed T453. — Brother's false
a. causes death K991.1; "don't take woman's a." J21.37; giant gives
reward for a. Q111.5; god gives king a. A182.3.4.1; hero gets a. from
peasant P411.4; king sends wise man to give rival a. K1944; magic a.
*D1814; prostitute gets a. from customer T453.2; reward for good a.
Q113.1; saint gives a. V223.1; spendthrift's a. to thrifty J1363; taking
woman's a. tabu C195.

Adviser. — Beware of following an interested a. J758; creator's a.
A40ff.; foster brother as a. P273.1.3; gifts made to a. Q114.0.1; wife
as a. J155.4.

Advising. — Animals a. men B569ff.; god a. mortal A182.3.5; heads
of slain a. hero E545.21; mortal a. fairy F394.1; trickster a. intercourse
K1354.1.1; wife a. husband J1112.3.

Advocate, devil as G303.22.11, M215.

Adze. — Magic a. D1601.14.2, origin of a. A1446.4.

Aegeus and Theseus N344.

Aerial journey, seduction on K1334.

Aesculapius as magician D1711.6.2.

Aesop with lantern J1303; with unbent bow J553.1.

Affection shown by frightened wife so rare that husband pardons robber T284.

Affiancing. See **Betrothals, Engagements.**

Afire, see also **Fire.** — Building with enemies inside set a. K925.1; dupe's house set a. K812.1; enemies' forest set a. K2364.1; house seems a. K1889.1; magic object sets things a. D1566.1; murder by setting house a. S113.2.3.

Aforesaid as title J1749.1.

Afraid, see also **Fear.** — Sun a. to wander at night A722.6.

African. — Origin of A. tribes A1611.3.

Africans. — Why A. have bad feet A1665.1.

After. — Advice a. event valueless J756; before, during, and a. J1343.2; dead returns third day a. burial E586.2; devil works with man who continues to work a. night G303.22.9; devil appears when woman looks at herself in mirror a. sunset G303.6.1.4; dwarfs come a. giants have almost died out F451.1.3; ogres powerless a. cockcrow G636; peace before rather than a. war J156.1; prophecy: death a. certain time M341.1.6; tabu: action a. certain time C752ff.; wandering a. death as punishment Q503, E501.3.7; whistling a. sunset brings devil G303.16.18.

Afterbirth. See **Placenta.**

Afterworld. Creator goes to make a. A78.

Again. — "Shall I tell it a.?" Z49.4.

Agaria are cultivators A1689.10; eat rats A1681.4; not afraid of fire A1689.2.

Agartree a transformed magician A2731.4.

Agates. — Water becomes a. D475.4.8.

Age of dwarfs F451.3.11; of giants F531.6.4; of owl causes it to be killed K1985; is relative J1352.2; of trolls F455.2.10; and youth in love T91.4. — Adulteress prepares for old a. J761.3; changeling calculates his a. by age of forest F321.1.1.5; changeling deceived into betraying a. F321.1.1; effects of a. and size absurdly applied J2212; god of a. A474.2; gods' great a. A191.1; guessing unknown propounder's a. H521.1; finding a. of monster C821; magic change in a. D56; magic object produces immunity from old a. D1349.2; magic peach gives immunity from a. (eternal youth) D1338.3.2; man claims same a. for many years J1218; old a. personified Z114; old a. must be planned for J761; in old a. spirits become gods A117.3; secret a. overheard by eavesdropper N475.1;

suffering in youth or old a. J214; trees of extraordinary a. F811.21; youth and a. are alike J2214.2.

Ages of animals B841.2; of the world (four) A1101.

Aged, see also **Old;** man as hero L101.1; people abandoned S140.1; people killed in famine S110.1; person eaten G76. — Disenchanted children a. D799.1.

Aging retarded D1338.0.1. — Magic a. D1890ff.; premature a. F126, Q551.12.

"Agnus dei" as a prayer for money J1741.2.

Agreeing. — Flatterer always a. with king J814.2; wife a. with all husband's statements H474.

Agreement, see also **Bargain.** — Deceptive a. to kill wives K944; marital continence by mutual a. T315.1; refusal to perform part in mutual a. K231.1.

Agriculture. — Acquisition of a. A1441; god of a. A432, A541.2; goddess of a. A432.1; sacrificial rite for a. S274.

"Ah me!" (ogre's name) C21.

Aid, see also **Help;** of animal summoned by using part of its body as talisman *B501; to children brought by dead mother *E323.2; from deer, opossum, and snake J461.4; from ghost to living E363ff.; of God not used in creating devil G303.1.3; of hidden informant in solving riddle H573.1; to ogre brings about hero's capture G411; from ogre's relative G530ff.; of owner's daughter to capture castle K781; of supporting forces not asked J1169.3; to thief by owner J1392; from wild man released from captivity G671. — Asking king for military a. H1224; call for a. heard from distance D1827.2; fairy offers a. for marriage F302.3.2.1.

Ailments, see also **Diseases.** — Eclipses due to sun's a. A737.11.

Air fragrant at Nativity V211.1.1; magically made fragrant D1599.2. — Angels fill a. above druid's grave V238.4; castle in a. F771.2.1, H1133.2; climbing into a. on magic rope D1582; dupe takes prisoner's place in a. K842.1; eagles carry castle in a. F982.1, F771.2.1.2; extraordinary flights through a. F1021ff., (by magic) *D2135, (on animal) B542ff., (on geese — lying tale) X1258.1, (dwarf on wooden horse) F451.6.2.2, (inflated giant) F531.6.17.2, (god on wind-swift horse) A171.1, (girl being rescued) *R111.3.1, (mountain-folk on horses) F460.2.2, (Wild Hunt) E501.14.1; fairies take persons into a. F329.3; fairies travel through a. F282; god rides through a. A171.1; god of the a. A216; gods nourished by a. A153.9; image flies through a. D1626; object magically raised in a. D2135.0.2; object rises into a. *F1083; object thrown into a. causes enemies to fight over it K1082.2; magic shears clip garments from a. D1601.12.1; paradise in a. over mountain F132.1.1; refuge in a. R324; same a. at home as abroad J2274.2; spirits in a. E587.4, F407.2, F411.2, F418, F966; voices from the a. F966; witch rides through a. G241.3.2.

Air-castles J2060ff.

Airship. — Magic a. *D1118; person killed from magic a. K988.

Aladdin D845, D1662.2, D1470.1.16.

Alarm by cackling geese B521.3.2; from bells rung backward P651.3; given by captured animal which asks respite K551.7; given by magic bell *D1317.7; of king by flea's bite B521.3.3; raised in order to cheat *K484; raised puts cheater out of countenance J1216; raised by stolen magic object D1612.5ff.; sounded foolishly J2199.1.

Alba. — Prophecy: death between Erin and A. M341.3.2.

Albatross. — Bad luck follows killing a. C841.10.1, N250.1; mythical white a. B30.1.

Albino twins cannibals G11.11.1.

Alcestis dies so that husband's death may be postponed T211.1. — Death postponed if substitute can be found for A. *D1855.2; Hercules fights with "Death" and rescues A. R185.

Alchemist K1966; fox as B121.2.

Alder. — Magic a. tree D950.11.

Ale, magic D1045.1; serves itself D1601.23. — Acquisition of a. A1426.3; brewing a. from milk H1021.10; consecrated a. as magic cure D1500.1.10.5; inexhaustible barrel of a. is fairy gift F348.9; making a. from single grain H1022.6.1; poison flows from a. vessel F1092; saint purifies poisoned a. V229.6.2; transformation: water to a. D478.2; wives compete in a.-brewing T145.3.

Alehouses. — Devil sings in a. G303.13.4; tabu for chief to enter a. C564.1.

Alexander carried by two birds B552.1; drinks cup poisoned by friend P317.1; orders feast for those who have not known sorrow N135.3.1. —Cynic praises reason to A. J1442.1.1.

Alexius K1815.1.1.

Alfred the Great (bakes cakes) K521.4.1.2, (punished for late rising) P15.1.

Ali Baba and the forty thieves K312.

Alibi by thief who plays all night for dance K411. — Thief cuts off own arm as a. K407.2.1.

Alike. — Brothers so a. wrong one killed P251.5.2; twins look exactly a. T685.3.

Alive. — Dead made to appear a. K1885; dog buried a. to prevent ghosts from walking E431.8; hero still a. A570ff.; hero taken to heaven a. D1856.1; man kept a. by consecrated sword E163; marriage to man a. only at night T113; person dead during day, a. at night E155.4.

All depends on how you take it J555.1, H588. — Cruel father puts to death a. children S11.3.4; murderers kill a. coming to certain spot S110.5; queen copulating with a. men T492; treasure finders must not take a. money N553.3; tree bearing a. fruits F811.7.

All Saints' Day. — Death for worshipping idols on A. A558.12.

Allah. — Escaping A. by moving away from Moslem land J1823.4.

Allegorical quests H1376ff.; riddles H767; visions V515. — Prophetic dream a. D1812.3.3.5.
Allegory, see **Symbolism, Symbolic.**
Allerleirauh K1815.
Allies erroneously slain at night N349.1; and possessions of the devil G303.10ff. — Animal a. B267ff.; demigods fight as mortals' a. A536; foolishness of attacking real a. J683; foxes desert their a., the hares J682.1.
Alligator. — Enmity of jackal and a. A2494.5.4; friendship of jackal and a. A2493.11.1; man becomes a. D194.1; prophecy: death by a. M341.2.24.
Alligator's rough back A2356.2.11; scales A2315.2; stripes A2413.5; short tongue A2344.1.2.
Ally. — Former a. helps king in disguise K1812.18; mortal as a. of gods A189.1ff.
Almond tree, transformation to D215.7.
Alms obtained thrice by disguised ubiquitous beggar K1982; to be returned hundredfold so parishoner steals them J1262.5. — Arm grows from giving a. F1095; ghost asks a. as before death E599.4; giving a. in God's name brings tenfold return J1262.5.1; man to marry first woman giving him a. T62.1; nurse begs a. to keep child R131.0.1; poor people given a. H152.1; pupils eat a. given master W125.4; refusal to accept a. from barren woman V436; saint refuses pearls as a. V462.2.2.1; seven to whom a. are given Z71.5.6.11; tabu misuse of money in a. box C51.1.4; tabu not to give a. to Brahmins C94.1.2; three reasons for not giving a. J2225; women giving a. to each other reincarnated as wells H1292.1.1; wager: woman can be forced to give a. N67.
Almsgiving. — Practical retorts connected with a. J1580ff.; reward for a. Q44; saint saves a. king from hell V229.15.
Aloes, island of F732.2.
Aloft, magic object bears person *D1532ff.
Alone. — Animals that live a. A2433.2.3; animal or object expected to go a. J1881; are you a. at home? H583.1.1; bathe a. and not in common bathing place J21.33; "don't go a. on journey" J21.36; "don't rob women a." J647.2; eating a. tabu C284; escaping sin by living a. J495; hero fights whole army a. F614.10; husband frightened into sleeping a. K1514.17.2; king's traveling a. tabu C563.1; "I am not a.!" W211.3; magic sight by standing a. D1821.10; rescue a. from shipwreck chosen over drowning with goods J222; sleeping children not left a. A1579.1; symbolism shows not good to fight a. Z161; why leopard walks a. A2433.2.3.1; woman a. in house makes Indians think men are home K548.1.
Aloof. — Jews keep a. A1689.13.
Alp (nightmare) F471.1.
Alphabet to be said to restrain anger J571.1; written on cake learned

by eating it D1819.4.2. — Magic a. D1273.6; origin of a. A1484.2; reading without learning the a. F695.1.

Altar V116; as best of stones H659.3.1; bleeding F991.4.1; casts away host with louse baked in it V31.4; cloths F962.12.2, V135; floats in air F1083.0.1.1; magic D1166; in otherworld F166.5; as refuge R325; shakes at unworthy F1009.3; smoke from sacrifice tabu for chief C564.5. — Celibacy at the a. J1264.2; chalice on a. tests guilt H233.1; devil won't stoop to a. V298; drop must not fall on a. C51.1.8; false swearer not allowed to approach a. M101.1; Jinns frequent sacrificial a. F499.3.3; leaf falls on a. F962.12.5; olive branch laid on a. of Mercy V15; Satan entangles ram's horns on a. G303.9.9.20; tabu: using a. for secular purposes C51.1.1; transformation: man to a. D261.

Altarcloths V135; from heaven F962.12.2.

Altered letter of execution gives princess to hero *K1355.

Alternate biting and caressing of hares by dog K2031; punishments of sinners in hell Q562. — Fairies become birds in a. years D624.2.

Amalekites as magicians D1711.10.6.

Amaranth. — Contest between rose and a. J242.1.

Amazon bride T173.1; overcomes enemies singly K778.1; sets task for hero H1149.5.

Amazon's curse M411.11.1; daughter loves hero T91.6.4.1.2.

Amazons F565; control river issuing from cave D915.5; kill all male children F565.2. — Fear test: fighting with a. and horrible spirits H1423.

Ambassador from dogs to Zeus A2232.8; from Turkey misunderstands Christian ceremonies J1825. — Disguise as foreign a. K1839.7; queen makes lowly man a. Q56.3.

Amber originates in poplar trees A2755.3.1. — Island of a. F731.5.

Ambergris made from bitumen eaten by fish F826.2.

Ambiguous oath K1513; oracle M305; questions trick dupe K493.

Ambition as ever-increasing paradox answer H1075. — Prudence in a. J510ff.; overweening a. punished *L420ff.

Ambitions. — Father's a. transferred to child at conception T597.

Ambrosia A153; pond F713.1. — Resuscitation by a. E102.2.

Ambush revealed by bird's movements J53. — Attacking animal killed by another in a. N335.6.1; murder from a. K914; transformation to escape a. D642.4.

Ambushed enemy deceived into declaring himself K607; trickster killed by intended victim K1641.

Amen. —Stones say "A." V229.2.10.

American. — Origin of A. Indian tribes A1611.1.

Ammunition saved till enemy uses his K2378.4.

Amonites as magicians D1711.10.6.

Amorous, see also **Love;** intrigue observed and exposed K1271. — Transformation for repulsing a. advances D661.1; woman restrains a. king J816.4.

Amour of bishop preached about by truth-telling peasant J1211.1.

Amours of king with great men's wives teach him secrets J155.2.

Amphibia. — King of a. B245; magic a. B177; origin of a. A2160ff.

Amphibian vehicle D1533. — Devil as a. G303.3.3.7; helpful a. B493ff.; marriage to person in a. form B645ff.; reincarnation as a. E615; soul in form of a. E736; witch as a. G211.6.

Amphibious monster G346.3. — Why tortoise is a. A2214.5.

Amputated. — Root restores a. hands, feet D1518.2.

Amulet against attack D1381.16; brings love T11.4.7; enlarged to become cloak D489.2; of leaves for menses C146.1; preserves chastity D1387.1; rendered efficacious by charm D1577.2; renders invulnerable D1344.3. — Identification by a. H96; magic stone as a. D931.0.4; magic a. D1070ff, D1273ff, D1392.1.

Amyous defeated in boxing match K13.

Ananias Z71.1.5.

Añan's. — Stealing A.s bait H1151.17.

Anatomy, fatal disregard of J1910ff.

Ancestor of gods A111.3; worship V1.3. — Creator as a. of heaven and earth A75; culture from tribes' a. A1405; giant ox a. of all animals A1791; magic knowledge from mythical a. D1810.11; quest for news of a. H1252.1.1; quest to other world for a. H1252.1.

Ancestors claimed to want hero rewarded K362.11. — Ancient and modern a. (from Troy and Nuremberg) J1357; barber killed: king's a. need him in heaven K964; bribed judge's a. J1192.3; dwarfs are a. of mortals F451.5.3; game with bones of a. P203; gods as a. of mankind A188.2; robber innocent: follows traditions of his a. J1179.4.

Ancestress. — Prophecy: woman as a. of David and Messiah M363.2.1.

Ancestry boasted of by lowly J954. — Tracing a. brings recognition H11.1.4.

Anchor catching in submarine monastery N786; falls on fairies F285; floats on water F1047; stolen by fairies F365.2; of wood would hold if only large enough J2212.3.

Anchors. — Needles and a. as fox's excuse J1391.8.

Anchorite, see also **Hermit;** consumes tree D2082.2; falsely accused of murder K2116.2.1; immune to magician's powers V228.2; prophesies at childbirth M301.5.1; saved by dove T331.5; tempted by money V475.5. — Beast-like a. F526.4; body of a. rises from river E379.2; lover disguised as a. K1826.3; scorned lover becomes a. T75.5; treacherous a. K2285.2; vow concerning dead a. M151.5.1; woman wagers that she can seduce a. T337.

Anchorite's curse M411.14.2; son hero L111.6. — Conception after a. blessing T514.1; dove flies out of a. mouth V345.

Anchorites under temptation *T330ff. — Is town too full of a.? H607.4.

Anchovies. — "Spoiled" a. K344.1.2.

Ancient and modern ancestors J1357. — Animal characteristics from change in a. animal A2210ff.; treasure buried in a. settlements N511.1.2; wild huntsmen in a. costume E501.8.4.

Androcles and the Lion B381.

Andromeda B11.11.

Angel *V230; assigns task H927.2; assists childbirth T584.0.4; of the bush A419.1.1; causes earthquake D2148.1; confers power of self-transformation D630.2.1; as creator A17; of Death's sword F833.11; of the deserts A419.2.1; for each animal B1.1; of earth A400.2; forbids armies to fight F1097.1; gives soul information E759.2; guards treasure N583; of hell A302; helpers in religious tests H1573.0.1; helps find lost pin N211.3; helps perform task H983; holds mass in church V49.2; holds nose when handsome sinner passes V119.3; of lightning A285.0.1; of love compels falling in love T10.2; of mountains A418.1; names child T596.1; rescues abandoned child R131.16; reveals relics V140.1; suckles children T611.5.3; takes form of certain person K1811.4.2; takes mortal to heaven F63.2; of thunder A284.0.1; warns of Christ's danger V211.2.3.0.1; works, prays as lesson to monk H605. —Ability to see a. of God D1825.3.4.1; captive protected by a. R85; cloud-a. A283.1; contest between man and a. H1598.1; cure by a. D2161.5.5; devil becomes white a. G303.8.1.2.1; disguise as a. K1828; disguise as a. of death K1828.1; girl's face resembles an a. D1865.3; locality sanctified against pestilence by a. as result of prayer and fasting D2162.3; magic from A. of Death D1725.1; magic object from a. D812.10; man transformed to a. D44.1; marriage of mortal and a. T111.6; mortal deceives a. of death R185; otherworld journey with a. F7; seduction by alleged orders from a. K1315.1.2.1; suitors as corpse, a., and devil K1218.4; tabu for a. to remain on earth too long C761.4.3; wind-a. A282.0.2; wisdom from a. J158.

Angels *V230ff.; accompany sun's chariot A724.1.2; appear where saint is born V222.0.2; arrange course of heavenly bodies A703; battle Leviathan and Behemoth A1082.7; change size D631.4.2; of the day A1171.3; of death cannot bring soul to heaven E754.2.2.1; defend road to heaven V511.1.2; feed exposed child S353.2; as God's messengers A165.2.3; oppose man's creation A1217.1; in otherworld F167.13; as rescuers R168; of Satan G303.10.18; set over clouds, winds, rains A1130.1; separate souls for heaven, hell E755.0.2. — Creation of a. A52ff.; demons partly like a. G302.4.1; figtree stays with a.: rewarded A2711.7; god dealing with a. A195.1; humility of a. J902; journey with speed of a. D2122.4; magic invisibility of a. D1981.6; magic knowledge of a. D1810.0.6; man created by a. A1291.1; man's strength equals a. D1830.1; planets supervised by a. A780.1; rebel a. A54; riddle about a. visiting Abraham H828; sight of a. over heads of the good D1825.3.2; souls of pious as a. E754.7; stars supervised by a.

A769.3; time of creation of a. A52.2ff.; wings of a. protect earth
A1128.1; worship of a. V1.2.4.

Anger aroused so master may win fight J1682; bargain K172, F613.3;
as cure for sickness F950.2; of God A102.17; is sin J153.2. — Animal
bursts from a. F981.1.1; army faces enemy rather than a. of their king
J216.1; when in a. say the alphabet J571.1; avoiding punishing in a.
J571.4; "control your a." J21.2.6; dwarfs in a. F451.6.8; explanation
of a. from hermit J153.2; extraordinary nature phenomena at saint's
a. F960.4; extraordinary physical reaction to a. *F1041.16; hero's contortions in a. A526.6; incurring animal's a. H1156; king quick to a.
P12.13; king struck in a., life saved N656; minister in a. leaves king
H1385.12; ogre's a. at killing his livestock G614; pretended a. K1772;
quest for the a. of God H1376.3.1; quest: learning what a. is H1376.3;
sign of a. (nudity) Z181, (red garment) Z141.1; strong man bites,
powders brass in a. F639.10; test of valor: rousing servant's a. H1561.4.

Angleworm B491.4.2.

Animal aids abandoned child(ren) S352; army B268; behavior as evil
omen D1812.5.1.12; behavior teaches man what to avoid J134; betrays
thief K427; -birth slander K2115; bride B600ff.; brothers-in-law B314;
buried alive to cure disease D2161.4.6; burned to cure disease D2161.4.7;
cannot change his nature J512; captor appeased by being fed captive's
family K614; characteristics A2200—A2599; comes to life E3; as creator
A13ff.; as creator's companion A33; cries misunderstood J1811; as
culture hero A522; by day, man by night D621.1; -descent slander
K2115.1; disguises as human being K1822; indicates election of ruler
H171; escapes by shamming as another K521.7; escapes by slipping out
of skin F1088.4; executed for crime B275.1; faithful B301ff.; fight as
suitor contest H331.15; foot on human being F551.1; ghosts *E520ff.;
helpful B300ff.; hides sun behind body, causes eclipse A737.6; husband C36ff.; horns bloom, bear man as fruit A1263.5; in human form
recognized H48; killed from within K952; kills ogre G512.9; king
B240ff.; kingdom (community) *B220ff.; languages B215ff.; languages
learned *B165ff., *B217ff.; learns to fear men J17; magically paralyzed
D2072.0.2ff.; with unusual members B15; as messenger *B291ff.; mistaken for something else J1760ff.; nurse B535; offspring from marriage
to animal B632; ogres *G350ff.; overawed K1710ff.; paramour B610ff.;
parliament B230ff.; performs spinning task H1092.1; punishes broken
promise M205.1; raises future hero L111.7; recognizes his returned
master first H173.1; reincarnated as god E657; reincarnated as man
E656; reports master wealthy and wins girl K1917.3; rescuer B540ff.;
retains other animal's powers E780.2; reveals substitution of false bride
*K1911.3.1; saved from pit B301; sent to go by itself J1881.2; serving
only certain man H172; sinks into earth F949.1; skin grows on man's
back Q551.2; statue F855.3; substituted for child served at meal
K512.2.1; substituted for human sacrifice A1545.2; suckles strong hero

F611.2.1; suitor B620ff.; swallowed F911; swallows man (not fatally) F911.3; thought to be a person J1762ff.; transformed to god D43.1; transformed to object D420ff.; transformed to person D300ff.; warfare B260ff.; wedding B280ff.; wounds self to blame other animal for eating young K2153.1. — Abduction by a. R13; adventure from following a. to cave N773; adventures from pursuing a. N774.3; animal characteristics: change in ancient a. A2210ff.; ascent from lower world on a. F101.6; attacking a. killed by another in ambush N335.6.1; bringing a. heads H1154.0.1; bringing the devil an unknown a. K216.2; capture by hiding in artificial a. *K754; child born with a. head T551.3; child promised to a. S215; conception from eating a. T511.5; cooked a. comes to life E168; creation of a. life A1700—A2199; criminal confesses because of misunderstood a. cries N275.1; cure by transferring disease to a. *D2161.4.1; curse by a. M411.19; dead a. comes to life E3; death as a. Z111.3.1; unexpected death at hands of an a. N335; deity takes form of a. to visit mortals K1811.5; demon as a. G303.3.2; demons on a. feet F401.3.0.1; descent to lower world on a. F98; detection through aid of a. J1145; the devil in a. form G303.3.3ff.; divination from a. activity D1812.5.0.8; dragon as compound a. B11.2.1ff.; earth from body of slain a. A831.6; entrance to woman's room in hollow artificial a. K1341; fairy in form of an a. F234.1; fairy as giant a. F234.1.0.1; faithful a. B301ff.; familiar spirit in a. form F403.2.2.1; fettered monster as ferocious a. A1072.2; flesh of a. reveals guilt D1318.7.1; foolish imitation by a. J2413; fools and the unknown a. J1736; free a. saves captured friend F642; ghost a. guards treasure E291.2.2; ghost transformed into a. E453; giant as a. F531.1.8; gift or sale to a. J1850ff.; god in a. form *A132; gods with a. features A131; the great a. *X1201; helpful a. B300ff., (acquisition) B310ff., (reward) B320ff., (death) B330ff.; helpful a. aids fugitives R243; hero follows a. into lower world F102.1; hero son of a. A511.1.8; human and a. offspring from marriage to animal B633; illusory a. shapes on hilltops K1886.6; injury to a. kills witch G275.12; journey to underground a. kingdom *F127; killing a. in refuge tabu C841.0.3; killing an a. revenged Q211.6; lame a. magically cured D2161.3.7.1; life bound up with that of a. E765.2; looking at certain a. tabu C316; magic adhesion to a. *D2171.3ff.; magic a. proof against burning D1841.3.1; magic a. proof against drowning D1841.6.1; magic a. proof against hound D1841.7; magic a. proof against weapons D1841.5.2; magic image of a. relieves from plague D1586.1; magic object teaches a. languages *D1301; magic object found on grave of slain helpful a. D843.3; magic power from christening an a. D1766.4; magic powers from baptising an a. *D1766.3; magic skin of a. D1025; magic strength from helpful a. D1834; magic treasure a. killed D876; man by day: a. by night D621.1.1; man disguised as a. sent among enemy K2358; man disguises as a. K1823; man transformed to a., kept as pet by heroine T33; mankind from human-a. mating A1221.6; marriage of person to a. *B600ff.; mountain-man in a. shape F460.1.1; mountains from primeval a. A961; mysterious a. punishes penitent Q554.5; offending a. wife tabu C35; ogre captured while transformed to a. G514.4; one a. mistaken for another J1750ff.; origin of a. sacrifice A1545.3; origin of a. worship A1546.7; person with a. face F511.1.3; person returns to original a. form when tabu is broken C963.1; person has small a. within his body F529.4; person thought to be a. J1765; person transformed to a. refuses human food D686.1; pestilence in a. form F493.0.1; poisoned food fed to a. instead of to intended victim K527.1; prophesying through knowledge of a. languages M302.1; pursuing certain a. forbidden C812; pursuit of a. leads to ogre's house G402.1; quest to a. realm H1289.1; quest assigned because of hero's knowledge of a. languages H1214; quest for remarkable a. H1331; quest for unknown a. H1383; recognition by overheard conversation with a. H13.1; recognition of person transformed to a. H62; reincarnation as a. *E610ff.; reincarnation: a. to man E656; resuscitation by passing helpful a. over corpse E79.1; revealing help of a. tabu C427; revealing knowledge of a. languages forbidden C425; revenant in a. form *E423ff.; riddles on a. qualities H842; runner captures two of every a. F681.8; sacrifice to a. V11.7; secret remedy revealed by departing a. N452.2; secrets overheard from a. conversation *N451; seduction disguise as a. K1328; separable soul kept in a. E715; sickness transferred to a. D2064.3; simultaneous birth of a. and child T589.7.1; small a. overcomes large L315; soul in a. form E730ff.; spirit in a form F401.3; spirit protects each a. species F419.3; automatic statue of a. D1620.2; stolen a. returns to owner K423.0.1; task: capturing pair of every wild a. in the land H1154.9; task: selling an a. and keeping him H1152; test: guessing unknown a. H522ff.; theft by trickster's trained a. K366; thief disguised as a. K311.6; transformation to act as helpful a. D659.4; transformation to a. (devil) D102, (god) D101, (man) D100ff., (object) D440ff., (another animal) D410ff., (for breaking tabu) C962, (to seduce woman) *D658.1; transformation by helpful a. D684; transformation by magic a. D684.0.1; transformation: fern to a. D441.4.1. transformation for nourishing a. D518; troll in a. form F455.2.8, G304.1.1ff.; true bride in a. form reveals false K1911.3.1.1; ungrateful a. returned to captivity J1172.3; wife flees a. husband R227.1; wish for a. husband realized C26; witch in a. form G211ff.; witch burned by burning bewitched a. G275.3.1; witch rides unusual a. G241.1ff.; woman gives birth to a. T554; wounding a. without killing it tabu C841.0.2; youngest a. overcomes adversary L72.

Animal's characteristics acquired by eating it D1793.1; extraordinary death F981; extraordinary growth F983; extraordinary protection F984; size changed at will D631.2. — Attention drawn by helpful a. theft of food from wedding table: recognition follows H151.2; earth rests on a. back A844; eating courageous a. heart makes courageous D1358.1; eating ferocious a. heart makes person cruel D1357; magic a. heart renders invisible D1361.29; soul leaves man's body and enters a. E725.1. **Animals** B (entire chapter); abused to cause person's death D2061.2.2.7; advise men B560ff.; in the ark A1853.1, A2031.2, A2145.2, A2214.3, A2232.4; attacked under illusion that they are men K1883.2; as attendants of gods A165; avenge injury Q597; blessed for good services at crucifixion A2221.2; borrowed by fairies F391.1; build road A2233.1; buried with the dead V67.5; called magically D2074.1; carry extra-ordinary burden F982; carry men B550ff.; change color F985; climb on one another's backs and cry out: frighten robbers K335.1.4; compete as messengers to call father of newborn child H483; created by magic D2178.4; cursed M414.8; cursed by saint M411.8.4; die for desecrating holy place Q558.14.1; duped into fighting each other K1082; eaten by fairies become whole again *F243.3.1; enticed over precipice K891.5.1; exchange duties J512.7; escape when forbidden basket is opened C915.2; as extraordinary companions F601.7; fear men J17; follow wild hunts-man *E501.4ff.; friendly B300ff.; gigantic B870ff.; give power of in-ducing love D1903; glowing B19.4; gnaw on moon A755.4.3; of the gods A155ff.; as gods' messengers A165.2.1; grateful *B350ff.; grateful and ungrateful men W154.8; headless B15.1.1; help hero on quest H1233.6; help man in contest K2; help men at task H982; help in military victory K2351; helpful B300—B349; helpless in sea-voyage together J1711.1; in human form retain animal ways D682.3.1; with human traits B200ff.; hybrid B1114; journey together B296; in legal relations B270ff.; magic B100ff.; magically shriek, frighten enemy D2091.12; magically stricken dead D2089.3; miraculously multiplied D2106.1.2; mistaken for ghosts, killed J1782.4; mythical *B0ff.; nourish men B530ff.; oracular *B150ff.; with jeweled ornaments F826.1; in other-world *F167.1; in otherworld pass in and out of church and become human beings *F171.5; overcome man's adversary by strategy B524.2; preying on one another teach death's universality J52.1; produced when forbidden drum is beaten C916.2; give prophecy of future greatness M312.0.2; prophetic *B140ff.; pull up trees F621.1; pursued in wild hunt E501.5.5; ransom themselves B278; rejoice at Christ's birth B251.1; religious B250ff.; retort concerning their dangers J1420ff.; reveal how to become saint V229.25; as sacrifice V12.4; sacrificed so that dead have food on way to otherworld E433.3; save person's life B520ff.; speak to one another at Christmas B251.1.2; speaking B210ff.; steal back magic D882.1; stolen from saint miraculously replaced V224.3; swallow animals F911.2; thought to be devils J1785; transformed to stones D471.8; treacherous K2295; bear treasure *B100ff.; treated as if human J1850—J1899; truth-telling B130ff.; unjust decision against man J1172.3.2; war between wild and domestic B262; wisdom-giving *B160ff.; wise B120ff. — Abode of dead a. E480.1; absurd sympathy for a. or objects J1870ff.; absurdities concerning birth of a. J1533ff.; assignment of edible a. A1422; bargains between men and a. M244; bridge to otherworld guarded by a. *F152.0.1; captured a. avenge themselves Q385; capturing a. (task) H1154; catching wild a. as suitor task H336.2; chain tale: a. killing each other in man's field provide meat Z43.6; covenant of friendship between a. M246.1; creation of a. A1700ff.; cruelty to a. S481; cruelty to a. punished Q285.1; curses on a. M471; deception into killing own a. K940ff.; descent of man from a. A1224; devil's a. G303.25.15; the devil's a. and God's *A1751; devil's a. devour God's A2286.2.1; devil and God create a. *A63.4; division of the a. (riddle) H841; domestic a. fight as owners compete H1588.2; dupe's a. destroyed or maimed K1440ff.; entrance to otherworld guarded by a. F150.2; extraordinary occurrences concerning a. F980ff.; fairies' a. F241; fanciful traits of a. *B700ff.; father rescues son stolen by a. R153.3.2; festival of a. B299.7; fighting a. seen in otherworld F171.4; food kept for a. tabu C248; fool makes shoes for a. J1873.1; foolish attempt of second man to overhear secrets from a. *N471; former friendship between domestic and wild a. A2493.0.1; formerly a. talked A1101.2.3; game a. magically made overwary D2085; giant's enormous a. F531.4.11 giants' a. F531.6.7.1.1; giants' a. help him in fight F531.6.16.2; god of a. A440ff.; goddess protects a. from hunters A189.12; healing by a. B510ff.; helpful a. lost in wager W2.4; hero's extraordinary a. A524.1; hidden a. attack owner of house K1161; images of a. ridden (driven) D1631; magic invulnerability of a. D1840.2; kindness to a. rewarded Q51; kinds of helpful a. B400ff.; king of a. B240ff.; magic control over a. D2156ff.; magic dominance over a. D2197; magic knowledge of a. language D1815.2; magic object gives power over a. D1440ff.; magic power from a. B500ff.; magic sight as gift of grateful a. D1821.11; man rules all a. H1421.1.1; men and a. readjust span of life A1321; origin of domesticated a. A1443; pairs of a. in ark *A1021.1; parts of slain a. as token of slaying H105; pestilence sent upon a. D2094; princess brought to laughter by small a. H341.2; punishment of lazy a. A2233.1; punishment: being eaten by a. Q415; miraculous punishment through a. Q557; quest for dangerous a. H1360ff.; quest for devastating a. H1362; quest over path guarded by dangerous a. H1236.2; rakshasa eats domestic a. at night G369.1.3; recognition by overheard conversation with a. H13ff.; rescue from ogre by helpful a. G552; resuscitation by a. E122; resuscitation of a. devouring each other E32.2; sacrifice of a. to dragon B11.10.0.1; sale of worthless a. K130ff.; secret remedy overheard in conversation of a. N452; services of helpful a. B500ff.; short pregnancy in a. T573.0.1; small a. dupe larger into trap L315.15; souls of a. E730.1; strong hero sent for wild a. F615.2; strong man kills a. with own hands F628.1; sun, moon carried by a. A728.4; sun's a. A732; tabu to eat live a. C221.5; tabu to kill sacred a. C92.1; talkative a. incense master J2362; taming wild a.

H1155 tasks contrary to the nature of a. H1024; theft of fire by a. A1415.2; topographical features caused by a. A903; troll's a. G304.3.2; unique survivor from destruction of a. Z356.1; what a. are to be eaten by man A1422.0.2; why a. serve man A2513; why a. sources of food A1422.0.1; why certain caste is kind to a. A1599.13; wisdom acquired from a. *J130ff.; witch brings death, disease to a. G265.4; witch causes a. to behave unnaturally G265.6; witch causes a. to die G267; witch transforms her lovers into a. G263.1.

Animation of body by soul E726; of jar beneath banyan tree A199.1; of statues by water or wind F855.2.

Ankles of exposed child pierced S333; tied to lay ghost E442.1. — Deluge reaches giant's a. F531.2.1.3.

Annihilating army single-handed (task) H1135.

Anniversaries, royal P13.7.

Announcement of own death by dead E545.3; of death of Pan F442.1; of prohibition by mysterious voice C601; of time for sunrise and sunset by bird B122.4. — Wraith as a. of death E723.6.

Annoyance. — How can people be freed from a.? H1292.19; when will animal be freed from a.? H1292.9.

Annual resuscitation of a god E155.2.

Annulment of witch's spells by drawing her blood D1741.2.1.

Anointing with honey protection against ghosts E439.10; of kings P13.5.1; for magic invulnerability D1846.1. — Quest for a. oil H1265.

Another. — Animal characteristics: obtaining qualities of a. A2240ff.; betrothed girl can never marry a. T65.1.1; devil enters body of a. G303.18; fairy in likeness of a. F234.2.4; punishment: carrying corpse of murdered man until a. can be induced to take it Q511.2; reincarnation in a. human form E605; sacrifice of child to save a. life S260.1.4; shrew tamed by setting a. shrew against her T251.2.1; transformation: one animal to a. D410ff.; transformation to likeness of a. person *D40ff.

Answer to cry mandatory C681; to all foreigner's questions: "I don't understand" J1802.1; rewarded with gold ring Q91.4; to three questions in rhyme secures devil's help G303.22.3. — Animal characteristics: punishment for discourteous a. to God (saint) A2231.1ff.; child born in a. to prayer T548.1; cobold avenges uncivil a. F481.1; finding a. to certain question (test) H508; plant punished for ungracious a. to holy person A2721.3; princess gives right a., monkey, wrong H343.2; princess's a. to all questions is "No" K1331; quest: a. to certain question H1388; quest for riddle a. H1278; ridiculous a. at end of each tale Z13; soft a. turneth away wrath J817; tabu: uncivil a. to holy (or supernatural) being C94.1; unwelcome a. given by man hidden behind image K1971.8; wall of snow around hut in a. to prayer D2143.6.2.

Answers to devil's riddle permit escape H543; in foreign language C495.2.2; found in other world to questions propounded on the way

H1292, (riddles) H544, (to questions) given magic object D1311ff., (coconut shell) D1311.9, (mirror) D1311.2, (sun) D1311.6.3. — Baffling malice with ready a. J1251; deaf men and their a. X111; king and peasant vie in riddling questions and a. H561.6; lady a. queen so straightforwardly she gets light punishment J751.1.1; magic object gives a. for fugitive *D1611ff.; prearranged a. bring comic results C495.2, J1741.3, X111.9; quest to morning star for a. to questions H1282; quibbling a. J1252; riddling a. H583ff.; oracular images occupied by spirits or priests who give the a. K1972; woman who asked for news from home gets many impossible a. J2349.4.

Answering call when asleep tabu C811.3; fool's questions next day J571.7; only "yes" and "no" J1255; questions only when on throne J1189.1; questions just like woman settles her ownership J1153.2. — Hero not a. questions until dressed P644; man a. all questions F645.1; single speech a. many questions H501.2.

Ant bites as punishment Q453.1; bites tongue, voice made smooth F556.1.2; carries load as heavy as himself A2251.1; collects incense and myrrh for Christ A2221.4; and lazy cricket (grasshopper) J711.1; grateful for preventing destruction of nest B365.2.1; helpful B481; keeps stored grain in sun J711.5; keeps house with animals J512.7.1; language B215.6.1; neither man, beast nor bird (riddle) H862; oracular B154.2; pinching frog causes accidents N381.1; thieving K366.3; thrown from heaven: hence narrow waist A2214.2. — Beetle makes immoderate request, a. modest: inverse awards A2232.3; child taken to defecate over a. hole K1461.2; creation of a. A2011; devil as a. G303.3.3.8; dupe persuaded to sit on a. hole K1023.3; enmity of bear and a. A2494.8.2; enmity of elephant and a. A2493.11.3; fairy as a. F234.1.16.3; friendship between a. and pheasant A2493.29; giant a. B873.4; grasshopper builds no house for winter; a. strikes him blind A2233.4; man becomes a. D182.2; man hears a. leave nest fifty miles away F641.2; man transformed as a. N453; little a. finds a penny (cumulative tale) Z32.3; reward to a. for industry Q86.1; man rides on a. F535.2.5; speaking a. B211.4.1; spider hands box to a. and refuses to take it back A2243.1; spirit in a. form F401.3.4.2; transformation: a. to person D382.2; transformation: man to a. D182.2; transformation: monkey to a. D411.5.3; transformation to a. to gnaw bow-strings of enemy D651.4; wedding of a. B285.1; why a. collects resin A2453.1; why a. has small waist A2355.1.2; why a. lives in ant-hill A2432.1.

Ants ask God for wings: wind blows them away A2232.9; burrow into elephants' brains B524.1.8; carry silk thread to prisoner R121.4; overcome serpent L315.14. — Creation of man from a. A1224.7; dupe persuaded to pick up biting a. K1023.2; giant man-eating a. B16.6.1; gold-digging a. B756; helpful a. sort grains H1091.1; how a. can secure longer life H1292.11; king of a. B246.1; kingdom of a. B224.1; man kills nest of a. J96; nest of a. thrown on ogre K621.1; war between elephants and a. B263.2; why a. carry large bundles A2451.1; why a. fall upon every man A2479.7; why a. don't live on hare's back A2584.2; why a. are lords of the bush A2433.5.5; why black a. are everywhere A2434.1.4; why small a. live in houses, driver ants in bush A2433.2.1.1; why white a. are a pest A2522.3.

Ant-bear eats insects A2435.3.8.

Ant-hill. — Boy lives in a. F562.5; digging alleged treasure from a. K1125, K1388.1; man becomes a. D287.1; rainbow from a. A791.8; transformation to a. C961.5; why ant lives in a. A2432.1.

Antaeus invincible in wrestling K12.3.

Anteater created A1896; deceives jaguar K1721.2.

Anteater's proboscis, origin of A2355.3.1.

Antediluvians. — Wisdom from a. J166.2.

Antelope becomes goat D411.4.2; hostile to other animals A2494.1; sends leopard for fire, eats game K345.4; transformed (to another animal) D411.4, (to nut) D421.2.1, (to dog) D411.4.1. — Fool tries to shoot dead a. until it will come to him J1909.2; friendship between a., woodpecker and tortoise A2493.32; helpful a. B443.2; killing a. tabu C841.8.1; many-eyed a. B15.4.1; mythical a. B19.8.

Antelope's. — Origin of a. long neck A2351.4.3; why a. antlers reach backward A2326.3.3.

Antelopes. — King of a. B241.3.13.

Anthony crosses river on cape D1520.6. — Fish come to hear A. of Padua preach B251.2.7.1.

Antichrist a one-eyed monster A1075; uproots trees F621.2.1.

Antichrist's coming prophesied M363.1.1; flat body F525.4. — Signs before A. birth A1075.1.

Anticipatory whipping J2175.1.

Antidote. — Magic a. for poison *D1515; moly as a. to spells and enchantments D1385.2.

Antigone buried alive as punishment for disobedience Q456.0.3. — Funeral rites forbidden A. V62.1.

Antimony D1331.3.3.

Antipathies, see also **Dislike, Enmity;** of giants F531.6.11; of trolls G304.2.4.

Antique. — Spirits dressed in a. clothes F401.1.

Antler. — Deer with giant a. B15.3.3.

Antlers. — How stag got long a. A2326.3.2; magic transportation on a. D1520.32; stag with golden a. and silver feet B101.4.1; stag proud of a. L461; suitor contest: splitting a. H331.8; why antelope's a. reach backward A2326.3.3; why deer has a. A2326.1.1.1.

Anus. — Dupe puts hand up animal's a. K1036.1; golden a. F521.3.3.2; monster swallows people through a. F917; resuscitation by pricking a. E29.3.

Anuses. — People without a. F529.2.

Anvil driven into ground by strong man F614.1; salvager to be king
H1574.3.1; to which one sticks D1413.10; swims river (lie) X1741.4. —
Bewitched child struck on a. G271.9; dispute of hammer, a. J461.6;
hill from a. A963.6; magic a. *D1202, D2143.1.6; shower of fire from
magic a. D1566.1.5; shower of gems from magic a. D1469.3.

Anxiety, see also **Worry;** of dwarfs to speak F451.2.0.4; prevents resuscitation E186.1.

Ape, see also **Monkey;** creation of A1862; plucks feathers from heron
who has carried him across water W154.5.1.3; pretends to louse heron,
but plucks out his feathers K874.1; throws away nut because of its
bitter rind J369.2; tricked into jumping on to stakes K891.2; tries to flee
with favorite child: neglected child saves himself L146.1. — Ass tries
to jump on the roof like a. J2413.2; dispute of elephant, a. J461.8;
fight between a. and tortoise B264.5; flying a. B49.2; fox spoils food
rather than divide with the a. W152.1; helpful a. B441.1.1; man transformed to a. D118.1; man-a. B29.9; person with a. face F511.1.3.1;
why a. has red back A2411.1.5.1.1.

Apes. — Army of a. B268.1; liar rewarded by the a. J815.1; raven killed
by a. who will not receive his teachings J1064.1.

Aper K836.

Apertures of animals' bodies closed up F998.3.

Aphrodisiac given naked woman in stream K1395. — Magic a. D1355.

Aphrodite. — Plants from tread of A. A2621.2.

Aphrodite's team of sparrows (doves) A136.2.1.

Apia (bird) is flat-chested A2353.1.

Apostacy. — Punishment of Jew for a. Q232.2.

Apostles of Christ V292.

Apparent injustice over greater wrong J225; and real values J230ff.

Apparitions, see also **Ghosts.** — Owner frightened from goods by a. of
the dead K335.0.5; punishment: meeting frightful a. Q552.11.

Appeal of dying lawyer X315.

Appearance of angel V231; of brownie F482.1; and disappearance of
garment in reply to command D2188.1.1; of devil G303.3ff.; of dwarf
F451.2; of fairies F230ff.; of Fortuna N111.2; of giant F531.1ff.; of
the gods A120ff.; of mermaid B81.9; of mountain-men F460.1; of
object when tabu is broken C917; of revenant E420ff.; of spirits F401;
of trolls F455.2, G304.1; of wild huntsmen E501.7ff.; of witches G210ff.
—Causes of animal a. A2400—A2499; choice between worth and a.
J260ff.; circumstances of the devil's a. G303.6; disguise by changing
bodily a. K1821; friends identical in a. F577; hero (heroine) of unpromising a. L112; magic a. D2188.1; magic change to different a.
*D52; person changes a. at will *D631.1.1; personal a. of various
peoples A1660ff.; professions according to bodily a. A1650.3.2; time
of a. of wild hunt E501.11ff.; vows concerning personal a. M120ff.

Appearances deceive U110ff.; kept up to deceive suitors as to girls' undesirability K1984.

Appearing before king unsummoned tabu C563.5. — Banished devil a. on earth A106.2.1.1; demons a. at stated times G302.6.1; house a. overnight to shelter priest V229.21; person a. many places at once D2031.18.

Appeasing enemies with women's breasts K774.1; giants by feeding them G582; ogre by calling him uncle Q41.1.

Appetite magically diminished D1927. — Curse: a. of twelve men M416.1; prospective bride shams small a. K1984.2; two monks renew their a. J1606; strong hero's enormous a. F612.1; unnaturally large a. cured by saint V221.10.

Applauding music when told W116.6.

Apple as chastity index *H434.1; as chastity test *H411.14; divided and eaten as love charm D1905.2; extraordinary *F813.1ff.; followed to otherworld F159.3; slays Cain F839.3.1; test (worthiness for friendship) H1558.0.1.1, (innocence) H256, (obedience of sons) H1557.1, (suitor) H316, (unknown father) H481.1; thrown in race with bride *H331.5.1.1; tree grateful for being shaken D1658.1.5; trees bear after saint's blessing D2157.3.1. — Bride test: thrifty peeling of a. H381.2.1; conception from eating a. T511.1.1; disenchantment by eating a. D764.4; fatal a.-throwing game K864; first man born from a. A1253.1.2; golden a. as prize in beauty contest H1596.1; golden a. thrown to remind merman's wife not to forget to return to him C713.4; infant indicates his unknown father by handing him an a. H481.1; love letter hidden in a. K1872.3; magic a. *D981.1, (as fairy gift) F343.15; magic a. tree D950.10, F162.3.4; man becomes a. D211.5; murder with poisoned a. S111.4; pomegranate and a. tree dispute J466.1; pursuit of rolling golden a. H1226.3; quest for marvelous a. H1333.3.1; recognition by unique ability to break iron a. with first stone cast H31.6; resuscitation by magic a. E106; resuscitation by removal of poisoned a. E21.1; skillful marksman shoots a. from man's head F661.3; soul in golden a. E711.8; soul hidden in a. in salmon E713.1; statue of infant Jesus takes a. V128.1; suitor test: a. thrown indicates princess's choice H316; tabu: touching a. C621.2.1; test of innocence: a. and gold offered H256; throwing a. to test sex H1578.1.4.1; transformation: man to a. tree D215.5.

Apples at Christmas F971.5.2; immovable D1654.2; impaled on stiff hair F555.8; transformed to grain D451.3.1; transformed to pig bristles D451.3.4; of youth D1338.3.1. — Ash tree bears a. F971.4.1; bridge of a. F842.1.3; demon formed from charmed a. F402.5.1; fugitives sustain selves on a. R257; magic a. cause horns to grow on person D1375.1.1.1; magic a. under sea F162.3.4.1; recovery of magic object by use of magic a. D881.1; souls as golden a. E745.5.1; stealing magic healing a. H1151.20; task: stealing golden a. H1151.1; test of girl masking as man: nuts and a. offered H1578.1.5; three golden a. as identification H91.3.

Appraisal. — Trickster's a. sells worthless glass as diamond K451.4.

Appraiser of horse a one-eyed man X122.

Apprentice receives magic D829.1. — Devil promises to help mistreated a. G303.22.12; hungry a. attracts master's attention by telling lies on him J1341.5; magician's a. D1711.0.1.

Approach. — Brass (copper) statue at city gates blows on trumpet at stranger's a. *D1317.9.1; escape by falsely reporting a. of rescuers K545; fairy prevents mortal's a. F395; ghostly warner of wild hunt's a. E501.6; too familiar a. to danger J655.

Appurtenances. — All a. demanded on buyer J1293.5.

Apricot. — Transformation by eating a. D551.1.2.

Apron. — Devil drops stones from a. A977.3.1; hero formed from mother's a. A511.1.4.2.

Aquatic. — Hero kills a. animal F628.1.4.

Aquila, origin of A779.2.

Arabia. — Gold appears in A. at Christ's birth N529.1.

Arabians as liars X661.

Arachne transformed to spider A2091.1.

Arbitrator. — Don't be a. without being asked J21.45; tree appealed to as a. D1311.4.1.

Arch. — Sea waters a. over people F931.9.1; stream forms a. over otherworld isle F162.2.9.

Archangels drive Satan from heaven G303.8.1.2; as porters of heaven A661.0.1.3. — When a. created A52.2.4.

Archbishop. — Fool asks a. about his family J1747; man magically made to believe himself a. D2031.5.

Arched. — Why cat has a. back A2356.2.3; river a. over saint's body like a vault F932.2.

Archer. — Magic statue of a. D1620.1.5; mighty a. F638.

Archer's skill in shooting eggs F661.4.1; skill as suitor test H326.1.2.

Architect kills pupil surpassing him W181.2.1. — Hawk as sky palace a. J2060.3; king kills a. after completion of great building, so that he may never again build one so great W181.2; thief enters treasury through passage made by him as a. of the building K315.1.

Argo, origin of A779.3.

Argonauts H1332.1.

Argument. — No a. good without witness K1655.1; princess offered to man who can defeat her in a. H507.1.1; princess skillful in a. J1111.1; queen banished for defeating king in a. S416; trickster steals during a. K341.27.

Argus has eyes all over body F512.2.2, D1961.

Ariadne abandoned on an island S145; rescues lover R162.

Ariadne-thread given as a clue out of the labyrinth R121.5.

Ariel. — Archangel A. as porter of heaven A661.0.1.3.

Arion B551.1.

Aristotle and Phyllis K1215; rises from sick bed to battle for country P711.7.

Aristotle's. — Cause of A. wife's death K987.

Ark as God's home A151.10.1; suspended in air F1083.0.1.2; of the temple V112.0.1. — Animals in the a. (flies) A2031.2, (griffin) A2232.4, (mouse) A1853.1, (snake) A2145.2, (unicorn) A2214.3; deluge: escape in a. A1021; the devil and the a. *G303.23ff., K485, C12.5.1; dove returns to a. in obedience to Noah A2221.7; the giant on the a. F531.5.9; helpful animal stops leak in Noah's a. *B527.2; magpie refuses to get into a., sits outside jabbering A2542.1.1; raven does not return to a.: black color as punishment A2234.1.1; those excluded from Noah's a. build another A1021.0.1.

Arm broken by Christ's image J1823.1.2; to fall off (curse) M431.4; grows from giving alms F1095; shortened for breaking tabu C946. — Birth from an a. T541.6; companion's a. allowed to be cut off so as to prevent detection K407.2; compulsion to bend a. D2069.2; earth rests on God's a. A849.2; giant's a. pulled off G512.6.1; god's marvelous a. A123.5.2; man carries his head under his a. F511.0.4; monster's a. token of dog's innocence H105.3; new a. from another's arm bone F668.5; new moon with old moon in her a. a sign of storm D1812.5.1.5.1; ogre's long a. thrust down chimney G369.5; pressing hundreds beneath a. H599.4; return from dead to punish theft of golden a. from grave E235.4.1; magic sight by looking under a. D1821.3.1; substituted a. E782.3.1; sun at night lowers a. A722.5; thin a. indicates desire for human flesh G95; wife sacrificing a. for husband's safety T211.1.3; wild huntsman carrying skull under a. E501.7.4; witch withers a. G269.11.2.

Arms, see also **Weapons;** cut off as punishment Q451.1.5; of fairy F231.1; restored E782.3. — Bringing a. to capital tabu after sunset C752.1.1; cutting off a. for sleeveless sweater J2131.3.1.1; falling in love at seeing woman's a. T16.1; fighting with opponent's a. P643; giant peculiar as to a. F531.1.6.7; giving a. in pledge tabu C855.6; god with many a. A123.5; identification by coat of a. H126; keeping the measure by stretching out the a. J2036; learning feats of a. from woman in bed T453.1; magic causes a. to fall from shoulders D1403.3; magic flaming a. D1645.8; magic drink restores a. D1518.1; man with luminous a. F574.2; men with seven a. F526.5; mutilation: cutting off a. S161; no ransom of captured without a. P557.1; oath taken on a. M113; person unusual as to his a. F516; spirits with heads under a. F401.4; test of sex of man masking as girl: a. placed among baskets H1578.2; woman instructs in art of a. P461.4.

Arm-pit as hiding place F1034.4. — Fairies' hole in a. F232.1.1; familiar spirit acquired by carrying egg under left a. F403.2.1.1; god born from mother's a. A112.7.2; vagina in a. F547.5.7.

Arm-pits. — Lightning from hero's a. A526.9; man vulnerable only in a. N476.2, Z311.4.

Arm-ring transformed to serpent D444.7. — Recognition through a. H94.6.

Arm-tassel compels woman to follow ogre D1427.2.

Armadillo as creator's companion A33.4.1; with silver plate over forehead B119.3. — Creation of a. A1897; giant a. B871.2.9; horned a. B15.3.4.2; sacred a. B811.7.

Armageddon A1080ff.

Armed vagina F547.1.1. — Combat with one-a. opponent P557.4.4.1; devil is a. G303.9.6.0.1; man must enter spirit world a. E480.3; one-a. hero L112.10; poorly-a. hero overcomes well armed L311.2.

Armless deity A128.3; people F516.1; revenant E422.1.2.

Armor ordered thin in front and thick in back J673; rattles as owner dies E761.7.1.0. — Air-tight a. F824.1; child born with complete a. T552.5; disenchantment by ripping a. D712.8; dwarf's magic a. D838.7; extraordinary a. F824; hero buried in a. V61.3.0.1; husband in a. establishes mastery T251.2.2; husband traps wife and paramour with magic a. K1563; magic a. *D1101, (protects from attack) D1381.10; quest for a. from a grave mound H1392; warrior buries oversized a. to prove prowess K1969.2; widow in a. routs would-be ravisher T320.2.1.

Army P551; of animals B268ff.; appears like forest K1872.1; of cannibal monsters G11.16; destroys giant F531.6.12.6.1; drowned by unnoticed tide N339.7; extraordinary F873; faces enemy rather than anger of king J216.1; of the gods A165.7; of half-animals, half-men B20.1; intoxicated and overcome K871.1; leaders in single combat for victory H217.1; origin of A1596; saved from ambush by observation of birds' movements J53; of spirits, ghosts F403.2.3.7; stopped by saint's curse D2091.13; of strong men F628.2.4. — Animals from Pharaoh's drowned a. A1715.1; arrow indicates attacking a. D1314.1.7; birds from Pharaoh's drowned a. A1901; creation of sandpiper: Pharaoh's cook calls drowned a. to dinner A1944.1; enchanted a. tabu C549.2; fairy a. F252.3; fairy a. on Hallowe'en F255.4; groom has to fight bride's a. H332.4; helpful bees (hornets) sting opposing a. B524.2.1; hero fights a. alone F614.10; magic a. of snakes, frogs D2091.2.1; magic oath stops invading a. D1400.1.11.1; magic object summons a. for rescue D1421.5; making broth for a. H1022.5.1; phantom a. attacked K1883.1; phantom a. created out of puffballs and withered leaves F585.1; river rises to prevent a. from crossing F932.8.2; saint drives away a. with cloud V229.7.1; soldiers of magic a. resuscitated E155.1.2; sleeping a. *E502; task: annihilating a. single-handed H1135; task: clothing an a. from one hank of flax H1022.2; task: feeding a. from one measure of meal H1022.5; task: making ladder which whole a. cannot set up H1147; transformed soldiers of fairy a. disenchanted when overcome F383.5; treasure hidden by retreating a. N511.1.7; Virgin Mary's shift as banner causes blindness to opposing a. D1331.2.3; witch's a. of dragons, lions, bears G225.5.

Armies like seeds and peppercorns J1625; miraculously separated F1097; separated by magic illusion D2031.8.

Aroma of God A139.7.

Around. — Riding three times a. the hill to free captive confined within R112.2; tabu: looking a. C332; walking a. by magic (circumambulation) *D1791.

Arrested farmer maligns sons H581.4; men tell who they are H581ff. — Silence wagerers a. as thieves J2511.2.

Arrival. — Accidental a. in lower world *F102; rejoicing at a. of rich man in heaven E758.

Arrogance comes with wealth J1085.2; repaid L430ff.; toward deity tabu C53.2. — Peacock given ugly feet so as to prevent too great a. A2232.7; world-fire from a. A1031.5.

Arrow accidentally grazes woman's breast N331.1.2; accidentally makes prize shot N621.1; accidentally slays man in church M381; as boomerang F661.11; extraordinary *F831; falls at death E761.7.1.2; kills one-eyed giant G511.1; made to appear crooked D2031.9; magic *D1092; as man's message shows lion how terrible man himself must be J32; shoots sky rope F51.0.1; shot to heaven returns bloody F1066; shot into leg of sun's horse A732.2.1; splits khijur leaves A2741.5. — Ascent to upper world on a. F65.1; ascent to upper world on a. chain *F53; dragon swallows a. (thunderbolt) intended for hero B529.2; eagle killed with a. made with own feather U161; god with a. of flames A137.14.1.1; island created by shooting a. A955.2; lucky shot with a.: foot and ear of deer N621; luring man by securing his a. K1399.4; magic a. flight D1526.1; mighty feats with a. F638; murder by burning a. K955.3; one a.-shot kills many tigers F679.5.3; pursuit of magic a. leads to adventures H1226.2; resuscitation by shooting a. E61; resuscitation by striking with a. E11.2; riddle about a. H751; shooting a. through iron H1562.13; shooting a. to win race deceptively K11.8; shooting game: blind man's a. aimed K333.1, K863; soul in a. E711.13; spring from sacred tree shot by a. A941.7.2; Virgin Mary intercepts an a. in battle D2163.3; woman wins a. contest F610.0.1.1.

Arrows darken sky J1453; of fire F831.2, (as punishment) Q552.13.0.1; from magician's fingers D2091.14; invisible D1655.1.1; substituted *K1617; turn aside for king H71.10.7. — Chain of a. transformed to bridge D469.3; Cupid with a. of lead and gold A475.0.1; god's a. A157.2; numskulls try to kill mosquitoes with bows and a. J2131.0.1; origin of bows and a. A1459.1.1; people choose bows and a. instead of guns and horses A1614.4.3; precocious hero demands bows and a. F611.3.3.0.1; shooting rope of a. F661.7.3; splintering a. with sword

F667.2; stars from a. shot at sky A763.1; victim's a. made harmless K818.3; wind returns a. shot against Christians F963.2; wounds from poisoned a. D2161.4.14.1.1.

Arsenic. — Devil chased by a. fumes G303.16.14.2.

Arson. — Judgments concerning a. J1175; thieving innkeepers guilty of a. J1149.9.

Art. — Fantastic beasts, birds, etc. in a. B5; origin of decorative a. A1465; possessing an a. admits one to king's hall P14.7; wanting to learn a. of love T4.

Arts taught to man by angel A1460.1. — God of the a. A465; god of many a. A450.1; culture hero teaches a. and crafts A541; origin of literary a. A1464.

Artemis goddess (of hunting) A452.1, (of chastity) A476; as leader of wild hunt E501.1.8.2. — Flesh of A. eaten as quail or bear V30.1.1.

Arteries severed instead of feeling pulse K1017.

Arthur and Excalibur D813.1.1, D878.1.

Articles, see also **Objects.** — Household a. act at command D1601.9; magic a. made during mass D1766.5.2; magic household a. answer for fugitive D1611.9; recovered magic a. dropped by rescuing animals into the sea D882.2.

Artificial heavens F792; paradise and hell to punish and reward F705; whale made as strategem K922. — Capture by hiding in a. animal *K754; child of a. impregnation abandoned S312.4; flight on a. wings *F1021.1; oracular a. head *D1311.7.1; recognition by a. hands H57.5.

Artificers, dwarfs as F451.3.4.1.

Artillery. — Sound of a. simulated to overawe enemy K2368.1.

Artisan blinded to prevent duplication S165.7.

Artisans P440ff.

Artisan-god A451.

Artist hoodwinks king: cuckold can't see picture J1492; loses results of labor in moment of procrastination J1071.1; punished for foul portrayal of Jesus Q222.3. — Why a. painted too few birds J1491.

Aryan. — Baptismal water vanishes before A. bishop V325.

Ascending. — Dragon king a. to sky H1292.14; god a. to heaven A171.0.2; hero a. to heaven A566.2; male sun-god while a., female while setting A227.1.

Ascent of mankind from under the earth A1232; to sky on cloud *F61.1; to stars A761; to upper world on arrow chain *F53.

Ascetic aids quest H1233.3.1; carries woman in his hair F1034.2.1; imitates Brahmin, goes to hell J2415.5; kills son born after seduction T338.1; plows field, it turns to gold D2102.2.1; sees scorpions as gold D1825.8; as villain K2285.1. — Austerities of a. sacred C94.9; birds mock a. B787; elephants look after a. in jungle B530.2; disguise as a. K1826.2; domestic vs. a. life H659.21; hospitality to a. rewarded Q45.3; lovely a. (disguised girl) wins rich woman's love K1322.1; magic object from a. D812.14; magic power through a. practices D1733.3; rich woman accuses a. of adultery K2113.2; villain disguised as a. or nun K2285.

Ascetics beg alms of own mother N735.1. — Chastity methods of a. T302; women disguised as a. K521.9.

Ascetic's. — Seven rooms in a. house F771.11.

Asceticism *V462ff.; rewarded Q39.1.

Aschenputtel L52, L55.1, L131.

Ash pole appears at death E767.1; stakes driven through slain S139.2.2.7. —Sacred a. V1.7.1.2; snake avoids white a. B765.18.1; transformation: a. to hazel D451.1.2; white a. stick protects against snakes D1447.3.

Ash-tree bears apples F971.4.1; becomes hazel D451.1.1; late at distribution of qualities at creation: therefore buds last A2725.1, A2771.1. — Magic a. *D950.6; man transformed to a. D215.3.

Ashen. — Driving horses over a. yoke tabu C833.4.

Ashes become gold D475.1.1.1; blown into face of scoffer Q554.3; of corpse put through sieve S139.2.2.8; of dead dog speak E521.2.1; of dead thrown on water to prevent return E431.9; dissolve animals F981.5; as eye remedy K1011.2; falling form path K321.1; form trail R267; of hero revive E174.1; as hero's abode L131.1; on moon's face A751.5.2; sold as gold K121; transformed into animals D441.6.1; transformed into insects, snakes protect hero K2351.2.2. — Blowing a. in animals' faces K621.2; burning houses to sell a. K941.3; burning and scattering a. (punishment) Q414.3; detection by strewing a. J1146; dupe burns house because trickster reports high price paid for a. K941.2; falling to a. for breaking tabu C927.2; ghost detected by strewing a. *E436.1; heart's a. cast into river F932.7.1; hot a. poured by gods on kingdom Q552.13.0.3; magic a. *D931.1.2; magic glance reduces tree to a. D2082.1; man created from a. A1268; man transformed to a. D286; milky way as a. A778.8; money turns to a. D475.2.3, (devil's) G303.21.1; mosquitoes from a. of bad woman A2034.3; mustard-seed reduces man to a. D1402.16; ogre's a. cast on stream cause rapids to stop G655; person magically reduced to a. D2061.1.1, (hunter by heroine's chastity) *D2061.2.5; punishment: eating a. Q478.5; resuscitation from a. E42; resuscitation of cremated man by blowing on the a. E66.1; resuscitation through a. thrown on funeral pyre E132; serpent's gaze reduces man to a. B765.14.1; sham miracle: rupees turn to a. K1975.2; sugar transformed to a. D476.2.4; sun throws hot a. on moon's face A751.5.2.1; thief learns location of dupe's food supply by strewing a. *K321; trail of a. R135.0.6; transformation by throwing a. D575.1; wind raised by throwing traitor's a. on lake D2142.1.4.1; women throw a. in eyes of attacking soldiers K2356.

Ashore. — Crab comes a.: killed by fox J512.1; giant mermaid cast a. B81.13.13.

Asinus vulgi J1041.2.

Asking costs nothing J1338; questions (counseled against) J21.6, (forbidden) C410ff., (rewarded) Q85. — Effects of wild hunt remedied by a. the huntsmen E501.19.2ff.

Asleep, see also **Sleep, Sleeping.** — Answering call when a. tabu C811.3; boy learns lesson while a. in saint's lap V223.4.1; castle in which everyone is a. F771.4.4; cuckold feigns to be a. K1501.2; culture hero a. in mountain *A571; death respite until victim a. K551.27; "don't fall a. in strange place" J21.41; falling a. on rock which shoots upwards N314; hero a. while sweetheart marries another T92.4.1; importunate lover put a. in street Q473.4; lover a. at rendezvous D1972; undesired suitor killed a. Q411.2.1; victim killed while a. K834; when one is a. the soul is wandering E721.1ff.; witch recognized by seeing wasp enter her mouth while a. *G251.1.

Asmodeus F402.2.1.

Aspen cursed for serving as cross A2721.2.1.1. — All trees except a. refuse to make Christ's cross Z352; devil throws sand at a.: hence rough bark A2734.1, A2751.2.1; why a. leaves tremble A2762.1.

Ass associates with lion, disdains own family W165.2; beheaded (first thing king meets) J1169.4; betrays deity's secret: hence ugly bray A2239.3; brays on hearing conch shell J2211.4; brays to warn of thieves J2413.1.1; tries to caress master J2413.1; who carried divine image thinks people bow before him J953.4; claims to have killed cow, frightens tiger K1715.10; consulted about the loan J1552.1; has cross on shoulders from being struck by Baalam A2239.6; deprived of his saddle (punishment) J1862; determines road to be taken B151.1.1.2; envies horse in fine trappings J212.1; falls into water and catches fish in his ear N626; follows after lion and is punished J952.2; avoids food eaten by animals before being slaughtered J12; foolish to kick against the pricks J833; -god A132.3.3; gold-producing *B103.1.1; good living but not dead (riddle) H841.1; thought to be hare J1754; without a heart K402.3; helpful B402; is not at home when man wants to borrow him J1552.1.1; with human intelligence B22.2; indifferent to enemy's approach U151; insults dying lion W121.2.1; is jealous of the horse until he learns better L452; tries to jump on the roof J2413.2; knows where to find hidden wind B133.0.1.1; laughing J1169.5; in lion's skin unmasked when he raises his voice J951.1; loaded and commanded to go home J1881.2.1; tries in vain to play lyre J512.4; with magic wisdom B121.4; gets progressively worse masters N255.2; as mayor J1882.2; who has worked with ox thinks himself equal to ox J952.4; in the potter's shop J973; predicts weather B141.3; punished for stealing mouthful of grass U11.1; refuses to drink after it has enough J133.2; as sacrifice V12.4.8; with silver nose hunts hares (lie) X961.32; speaking B211.1.3.1; as tollkeeper B292.13; thought to be devil J1785.3; transformed into horse D412.6; transformed to person D332.1; turns on his driver who would save him from falling over the precipice J683.1; insists upon payment of tithes B259.1; "of twenty older than man of seventy" J1352.2; carries usurer's body to the gallows B151.1.1.2.1; worship V1.8.10. — Baalam's a. V237, (advises that angel is barring way) B151.1.1.2.2, (perceives angel) B733.1; boar refuses to fight with lowly a. J411.1; body of man, hoofs of a. B22; breeding fine horses from an a. J1909.4; buyer returns a. which has associated with lazy companions J451.1; person calls another an a. J1352; camel and a. together captured because of ass's singing J2137.6; camel with a. on his back dances J2133.1; St. Christopher and the a. J1269.9; how much the a. cost J1601; death respite for teaching a. to speak K551.11; devil rides away on an a. G303.7.2; what is difference between you and an a. (counterquestion) H571.1; enmity of hyena and a. A2494.3.1; fairies steal a. F365.1; ferocious animal frightened by a. braying K2324.1; numskull cannot find a. he is sitting on J2022; fool thanks God that he was not sitting on the a. when it was stolen J2561; fox leads a. to lion's den but is himself eaten *K1632; friendship between wolf and a. A2493.15; frogs reprove a. for lamenting when he falls into morass J2211.1; guests call each other ox, a.: given appropriate food J1563.4; hard-hearted horse allows a. to be overburdened W155.1; king's capriciousness censured: the a. in the stream J1675.3; the lazy a. loaded with sponges J1612; lion as king makes a. his lieutenant J421.1; lost a. offered as reward to the finder J2085.1; marriage to person in a. form B641.4; miller, his son, and the a. (trying to please everyone) J1041.2; mourning dead a.: cumulative tale Z32.5; numskull knocks figure of Jesus from the a. J1823.1.4; old lady reminded of a. by priest's singing X436; peasant ashamed of being thrown off by a. J411.4; pseudo-magic money-dropping a. K249.3; teaching an a. to read H1024.4, *K491; red pepper for the slow a. (man tries it on himself) X11; revenant as a. E423.1.4; rider relieves the a. of his burden J1874.1; man scolds his a. and frightens robber away N612.1; shepherd taken to be a. J1765.1; "stick fast": fool seizes a. J2489.9; strong man lifts a. F624.1; the tailless and earless a. J2373; thief claims to have been transformed into a. K403; monster three-legged a. B15.7.2; tiger frightened off by threatening with a. K547.8; tiger mistaken for a. J1758.3; transformation to a. Q551.3.2.6; man transformed to a. D132.1, (by putting on bridle) D535, (plays lyre) *D693; truth-telling a. B133.0.1; wager: will jackal howl or a. bray first? N92; wedding of a. B281.7; why a. does not have cloven hoof A2376.1.1; why a. has cross on back A2356.2.7; why a. smells his own excrements A2495.2; why a. is stupid A2537.2; why dung of a. is triangular A2385.1; wild a. envies tame ass until he sees his burdens L451.2; why a. has long ears A2325.3.

Ass's behavior predicts the weather B141.3; charter in his hoof J1608; jawbone supplies water D1472.1.24.2; magic jawbone kills D1402.3.4. — Deduction: horse drinks a. milk J1661.1.5; person with a. ears F511.2.2;

girl bewitched into thinking lover has a. head G269.22; magic a. head
*D1011.0.2, (fulfills wishes) D1470.1.7; man's body, a. head B22.1;
pumpkin thought to be an a. egg J1772.1; too much a. flesh eaten
(foolish diagnosis) J2412.4; vampire with a. ears E251.4.2.

Asses. — The burden of two a. J1352.1; Egyptians fond of a. A1689.12;
lies about a. X1242.0.1; lions despise what a. admire V149.1.

Assailant. — Girl slays brother's a. P253.4.

Assailants. — Man pardons his a. W11.5.1.1.

Assassin. — King frees would-be a. P15.5; moon warns of a. F961.3.3;
sun warns of a. F961.1.4; suspected a. given murder opportunity
H1556.3.

Assassination. — Father orders son's a. S11.3.7; king takes measures
against a. J634.

Assassinator's friend asks to die with him P319.2.

Assaulting. — Animals punished for a. women A2239.5.

Assembly of fairies at milestone F217.2; of gods A167; or group transformed to animals D103. — Don't uncover weapon in a. J21.2.4; tabus
concerning entry into a. C853.

Assignation. — Lovers' a. by symbolic messages Z175.2; maid substitutes
for mistress at a. H1556.4.3.

Assigners of tasks H920ff.

Assignment of bride to another T141; of crafts and professions by
creator A1440.1; of edible animals A1422; of food to animal A2435.1;
of quest H1210ff.; of superhuman task to determine true husband of
woman J1176.5; of tasks H900ff., (to suitors) H335.0.2.

Assistance, see **Aid, Help.**

Assistant. — Thief's numskull a. prevents theft J2136.5.4.

Associates, choice of *J400ff.

Association of dwarfs with mortals F451.5.8; with fools J1710ff.; of
equals and of unequals J410ff.; of great and lowly J412; with those
of another faith punished Q431.18.

Assumption by divine beings of their own shape in sleep D796; of human
forms by demons in order to deceive F402.1.4; of various shapes by
wandering soul E721.5.

Assumptions. — Logical absurdity based upon certain false a. J2210ff.

Astonishment of God that I sit on horse and king on ass H797.2. —
Dumbness magically cured by a. D2025.4; expressing a. at marvel
(forbidden) *C491, (causes transformation) D512.

Astray. — Fairies lead travelers a. F369.7; importunate lovers led a.
K1218; people led a. (by mermaid) B81.3, (by mists) K1886.2, (by
spirit) F402.1.1, (by Will o' the Wisp) F491.1.

Astride. — Exposure a. wood in river S141.3; giant a. a church-roof
F531.3.3.

Astrolabe, divination by D1311.6.0.1.

Astrologer P481; -magician D1712.0.1. — Devil as a. G303.3.1.22;

disguise as a. K1825.8; magic object from a. D818; man deriding faith in stars becomes a. N186; sham a. K1964; treacherous a. K2299.1.

Astrology M302.4.1. — Origin of a. A1487.1.1.

Astronomer shoots down falling star J2275.1. — Farmer surpasses a. in weather prediction L144.2.

Astronomers P429.1.

Astronomy. — Absurd theories in a. J2270ff.; origin of a. A1487.1.

Asunder. — Corpse drawn a. S139.2.2.6; life token: ring springs a. E761.5.3.

Atalanta's race *H331.5.1.1, *R231.

Atheists V323.

Athena chooses olive tree J241.1. — Why raven sacrifices to A. J821.1.

Atlantis A692.

Atlas supports earth on shoulders A842.

Atonement V315.

Attack on hare (crayfish) J2612; by hypocrite who pretends friendship K2010ff.; on intruders by ogre G475ff.; on soldier by dwarfs F451.5.2.11; on saints by Satan G303.9.6.2. — Amulet against a. D1381.16; animal's means of a. A2463; animals warn against a. B521.3; girl aids brother against a. P253.4; magic a. against enemy D2091; magic object protects from a. D1381ff.; retreat in return for cessation of a. M263; wandering ghost makes a. E261.

Attacker. — Escape by making a. believe there are many defenders K548; moon interferes between a. and person attacked A737.5; witch impervious if she looks at a. G221.4.

Attacking. — Advice on not a. hastily J21.2.1; bears a. men A2524.3; demons a. men G302.9.1; fish a. anything they find A2524.4; foolishness of a. real allies J683; hospitality repaid by a. enemy Q45.5; "kill man a. you" J21.52.6; vow on a. enemy M161.1; wise man considers whom he is a. J612.

Attar river in otherworld F162.2.5.

Attempts (vain) to circumvent theft of fire A1415.4; to escape fulfillment of prophecy M370ff.; of fettered monster to reach sword A1074.2; to kill hero *H1510ff.; of devil to vivify creations A1217.

Attendance of dwarfs at weddings F451.5.1.7; of human midwife on fairies F372.1; at mass outweighs evil deeds V44. — Reward for a. on holy man Q38.

Attendant. — Animal as constant a. of man B575; dead arises when shroud bursts and pursues a. E261.2; hero's faithful a. A515.4.

Attendants around God's throne A152.4; disenchanted D799.3; of the gods A165; of silver king F576. — Giants' a. F531.6.16; wife's a. chase wrong man, miss lover K1549.6.

Attention attracted (king's in clever ways) J1675.1, (recognition follows) H151ff., (by telling lies) J1341.5, (by trickery) *K477, (by magic object) D1420ff., (by magic) *D2074ff., (of sweetheart) T56, (of men by women) A1373; distracted (by sight of beloved) T26, (by repeating strange action till it becomes commonplace) J1075.1, (from misgovernment by beginning war) K2381; to warnings J1050ff. — Attracting girl's a. by breaking her head J2461.9; cleverly attracting king's a. J1675.1; enchanted person attracts a. of rescuer D794; gambler's a. distracted by women N8; ogre attracts a. by whistling G653.

Attractiveness to men tested H1596.0.1.

Attributes. — Recognition by physical a. H50ff.; sun's a. A738.

Auction in hell draws Jews from heaven X611. — Owner bids up goods at a. K465.

Auctioneer praises worthless cow till owner buys her back J2087.

Audacious water bolder than continent husband T315.2.1.

Audhumla (cow) B19.2.1, B715.

Audible. — Giant a. to man only when resting on elbow F531.2.10; ghost a. only to person summoning him E389.2.

Audience of one hired to hear bad singer X145.1; secured with the pope by rudeness K477.1. — Escape by pleading for larger a. K579.8; using lamb to get a. J1653.

Augean stable H1102.

Auger, magic D1187.1.

Augurer, see **Divination, Oracle.**

Auk. — Darkness from a. swallowing sun A721.2.1; giant a. B872.4.

Auks. — Stones become a. D565.9.

Aunt P294; marries nephew T421. — Cruel a. S72.

Aunt's. — God Vishnu torments a. lover K1578.

Aurora Borealis as bridge to otherworld F152.1.8. — Origin of a. A795; souls of dead as a. E742.3.

Ausgelohnt F451.5.10.9.

Auspicious days N127. — Delaying birth until a. day T589.8; wager: it is a. day N53.

Austerities. — Magic object acquired by religious a. D855.2; reward for a. of hermit Q34; vow to destroy kingdom by a. M193.

Authenticity. — Deity attests a. of sacred writings A1996; testing a. of relics V140.4.

Author, see also **Writer;** believes his book stupid, fools praise it J1714.4.

Automata. — City of wooden a. D1628; God makes a. and vivifies them A141.1; magic a. *D1620ff.

Automatic oar D1523.2.1; object *D1600ff.; service in otherworld F183.1. —Alleged a. object K119.1; constructing a. peacock H326.1.1.

Automaton. — Jewish a. will not work on Saturday V71.1.

Automobile, see also **Car.** — Ghost rides in a. E332.3.3.

Autumn is richest (riddle) H636.1. — Goddess of a. leaves A430.1.2; sitting on sepulchral mounds tabu in a. C755.5; why days shorten in a. A1156.

Avalon as abode of gods A151; as happy otherworld where dead are healed *E481.4.1; journey to *F111.

Avarice punished *Q272.

Avaricious man given gift of benevolence by fairies F343.4; man transformed to ant A2011.2.

Ave on the tongue V254.3. — Flower with A. on leaves E631.0.2.1.

Aves. — Efficacy of saying A. V254ff.; Virgin Mary refuses to help wife against her rival who has always said her A. T285.

Avenging bride's former fiancé H335.1.1; father's brother P293.5; murder (bride's father's as suitor task) H335.1, (faithful animal at grave) B301.2, (magic horse) B184.1.7, (warning by God's voice) M348; by nearest blood relation P525.3; scorned love (by fairy) F302.3.3; self by feigning dullness J1675.7; uncivil answer (by cobold) F481.1. — Animal a. injury B857; blood-brethren a. each other P312.2; brothers a. each other P251.3.1; external soul a. murder E710.2; faithful servant a. master P361.6; foster brothers a. each other P273.1.1; friends a. each other P310.2; girl in man's clothes a. father K1837.4; god a. self on giant A162.5; prophecy on a. own death M322; quest a. king H1228.1; return from dead for a. E234.3; sister a. brother's death P253.5; son a. father P233.6; tournament a. king P561.2; woman a. scorned love T71.2.

Aversion of Evil Eye D2071.1ff.; of fairy spell by turning coat F385.1; of woman to marriage T311.

Avis J1154.1.

Avoidance of devil's power G303.16ff.; of evil spirits at childbirth T582.1; of fatigue by magic D2032; of men by young sparrows J13; of others' power J640ff.; of places which have been fatal to others J644; of all pronouns in tale Z15; of prophecy fulfillment M391.1; of punishment J1180ff.; of religious ceremonies by witches G285; of things harmful by nature J656; of shrewish wife T251.1; of wild hunt E501.17.5ff.

Awake. — Driving insane by keeping a. S191; "he who lies a. gains" J21.41.3.

Awakening of dead after three days E489.1; of fearless hero by cold water H1441; in morning by magic ring D1317.5.2; of sleeper forbidden since soul is absent E721.1.1; of sleepers prevented by hand-of-glory D1575.1. — Friar a. girl for seduction K1354.3.1.

Away. — Guardian enticed a. K629.2; impregnation from far a. husband T539.5; ogre vulnerable only if face turned a. Z315.

Awkward servant J2665.

Awl, magic *D1187.

Axe becomes golden D475.1.17; dropped in water: modest choice Q3.1; in stump removed by finger F614.2.3; thrown at one animal misses, kills another N337.3; turns into tiger D1594.5. — Boot mistaken for a. sheath J1772.11; breaking iron with wooden a. H1116.2; cat in wood-pile prevents a. from cutting D2186; cutting rocks with brass a. H1116.1; extraordinary a. F837; finger becomes a. handle D457.9; two giants with one a. G151; god with a. A137.1.1; identification by a. H131; iron a. becomes silver D475.3.4; magic a. *D1206; man invulnerable from a. D1841.5.3; milk transferred from another's cow by a. handle D2083.3.1; murder by a. S139.4; origin of the a. A1446.2; quest for a. which sticks in beam outside a tower H1338; man searches for a. which he carries on shoulders J2025.1; sight of wild hunt causes one to stick a. or knife in food E501.18.9; soul in a. E711.14; squaring lumber without blunting a. H1199.13; teeth like a. heads F531.2.12; tooth becomes a. head D457.8; tree cut down with a. for which it has furnished a handle U162.

Axes ground on rolling boulders X1012.1; thrown away J2171.4. — Animal killed by a. left in tree K897.2; father ties a. to fool abandoned daughter S338.

Axeman, skillful F666ff.; (lie) X986.

Axle. — Carrying a wagon a. which has broken a wheel (task) H1183; crooked a. accused H659.18.1.

Ay ay. — Buying eggs and "a." H1185.1.

Ayikha bush. — Why a. is firmly rooted A2774.1.

Baalam as magician D1711.1.3. — Ass has cross on shoulders after struck by B. A2239.6.

Baalam's ass B151.1.1.2.2, B733.1, V237; family as magicians D1711.11.1.

Baarlam and Josaphat M351.

Babe. See **Baby.**

Babes in the wood S300ff.

Babel, tower of *C771.1, D2004.9.1, F772.1.

Baboon as shepherd for man B292.1.1. — Color of b. A2411.1.5.2; creation of b. A1863; enmity between b. and fox A2494.9.1; where b. got tail A2378.1.1; why b. has bare place on back A2317.10; why b. has crooked tail A2378.9.2; why b. walks on all-fours A2441.1.2.

Baboons abduct boy R13.1.1. — Birhors eat b. A1422.2.

Baby, see also **Child, Infant;** drags mill-stone F64.3.2.2; finds mother, goes to her for suckling H495.1; giants' size F531.2.14; ordered killed for pulling father's beard S327.2; son hurled into battle to punish mother Q469.11; swallowed by tigress, comes out F914.3. — Dead mother returns to care for neglected b. *E323.1.2; fairy-mortal b. with long hair, beard F305.3; house-spirit as b. F480.4; man kills giant's b. F531.5.14; maternity test: producing b. within year H494; nature of a b. misunderstood J1911; newborn b. reveals secret N468; ogre abducts newborn b. G442.1; revenant as woman carrying b. E425.1.4; saintly b. holds arms in form of cross V229.2.1; stolen sheep dressed as b. in cradle K466.2; transformation: man to b. at will D55.2.5; why eagle cries like a b.: tortured baby became eagle A2426.2.15.

Baby's cry imitated to distract owner K341.7.0.1.

Babies exchanged P313.1. — Devil appears to girl who prays over b. she has killed G303.6.2.7; stone substituted for newly-born b. K2115.2.1; why b. die easily A1326; why b. have soft spots in head A2875.

Babyhood. — Friendship starts at b. P313.1.

Babylon, stallions of H572.

Babylonians don't keep oaths M108.1. — Why B. are roundheaded A1663.1.

Bacchic. — Refusal to take part in B. rites C57.2; woman performing B. rites C312.2.4.

Bacchus A481; personifies wine Z139.3.1.

Bachall, magic *D1277. — Christ leaves b. V211.2.2; saint transfers disease to his bell (b.) D2161.4.2.2; saint's b. defaces idol V356.3; saint's b. used in cursing D2175.2; swearing by saint's b. M116.1.

Bachalls. — Friends exchange b. P311.0.1; saints exchange b. P311.7.

Bachlach, disguise as K2357.14.

Back. — Alligator's rough b. A2356.2.11; birth through b. T541.15; bringing b. person from the dead F81.1; breaking witch's b. H1562.8; brown man with white b. F527.4; carrying child on one's b. into house tabu C875; counting hairs in pig's b. H1118; devil carries away a lord on his b. G303.9.5.2; disenchantment of girl by carrying her on b. D732.1; dupe rides trickster's b., captured K726; earth rests on animal's b. A844; eyes in b. of head F512.4; fairy's b. rough F232.1.2; fearless hero awakened by eels down his b. H1441.1; flight carrying another on b. F242; fool given the truth on his b. J551.2; giant carries man on b. F531.5.1.1.2; ghost carries coffin on b. E592.2; ghost rides on man's b. *E262; huckauf jumps on man's b. *F472; image cut into man's b. by flaying, salting S114.2; loathly bridegroom carried on b. in basket by wife T216; looking b. forbidden C331; marvelous sensitiveness: blister on b. from lying in rose leaves F647.9; murder by breaking b. S116.3; mutilation: skin cut from b. S166; ogre jumps on one's b. and sticks there G311; ogre tricked into carrying his prisoners home in bag on his own b. G561; one eye in b. of head F512.1.3; origin and nature of animal's b. A2356ff.; person without b. F525.6; plea for stabbing in chest, not b. W45.1; punishment: animal skin grows on man's b. Q551.2; punishment: thong of leather cut from b. Q451.8; slave bathing mistress's b. in stream pushes her into crocodile hole K831.1; reincarnation of b. into hoe handle E649.3.1; straw on horse's b. restrains him D1442.2; trickster pretends lameness and is taken on woman's b.: violates her K1382; why camel's b. humped A2356.2.13; witch begs man to scratch her b.: kills him *G269.1; wife carries mutilated husband on her b. so that he may beg T215.1.

Backs. — Animals climb on one another's b. and cry out: frighten robbers K335.1.4; fairies have hollow b. F232.1; images at church turn b. D1639.3; wild huntsman makes people carry him on their b. *E501.15.3.

Backbone for horse made from stick X1721.1; of ogre's mother broken G512.7.

Backwards. — Why antelope's antlers reach b. A2326.3.3; bells rung b. P651.3; devil notes people looking b. in church G303.24.1.7.2; devil works b. G303.13.2; devil's knees are b. G303.4.5.6; dwarf's feet twisted b. F451.2.2.1; hero can turn feet, knees b. A526.8; invisibility by reciting formula b. D1985.2; knees b. F517.1.5; mutilation: turning feet b. S162.5; numskull rides b. J2024; power of prophecy by crawling b. around grave D1812.2.1; reading Bible b. reveals witch G275.2; resuscitation with head on b. E34.1; riding b. on donkey as punishment Q473.5.2; runner runs b. F681.7; spirits' fingers, toes point b. F441.4.4; walking b. around church gives witching power G224.8; walking b. to leave false trail K534.3; walking b. to obey oath K2312.2; wild huntsmen with heads on b. E501.7.3.

Backwoods couple found "living in darkness", cut window J1738.6.

Bacon changed to iron D476.3.2. — Fish promised in return for b. K231.11; numskull drags b. on string J2461.1.1; skating with b. to grease huge griddle X1031.4.1; "Take yourself to hell with the b." K419.4; turnips called b. J1511.2.

Bad character shown by the eyes H1550.1; dream as evil omen D1812.5.1.2; luck put into a sack N112.1; man (i.e. devil) *G303ff.; omens D1812.5.1ff.; rearing causes son to bite father's nose off Q586; ruler, bad subject U210ff. — Associating with b. friend fatal J429.2; black stars seen over heads of the b. D1825.3.2; boy behind the tree complains of b. food K1971.3; breaking b. news to a king J1675.2; crickets as b. omens B147.3.2.1; "don't keep b. company" J21.25; father drives away b. son P233.2.1; father in vineyard doing good and b. (pruning vines) H583.2; good and b. in all books J174; good and b. culture heroes *A525; good, b. fairies battle F277.0.3; the house is burned down — that is too b. Z51.1; peacock a b. king J242.4; persistent b. luck N250ff.; persons bring b. luck N134.1; revenant with b. breath E422.1.5; revolt of b. gods against good *A106.1; no b. tidings given king P14.9; why certain animals b. B792.

Badger transformed to person D315.3. — Helpful b. B433.2; man becomes b. D124.4.

Badgers slain in violation of pledge K2023. — Capturing b. H1154.10.

Bag, see also **Sack;** conjuring *D1274.1; laid by fence-hole for hares X1114; of lies threat to tell queen's adultery K1271.1.1; magic *D1193; in the moon A751.9.2; with rice for the road K444.3; of tricks J1662; of winds C322.1; wishing D1470.1.27. — Burial of cut-up body in b. E431.18; cake b. full of cobras K444.2; captor's b. filled with animals or objects while captives escape K526; child born in b. T561.3; clothes b. cut in two with sword F667.3; deception into entering b. K711; detection of theft by finding b. repairer J1141.5; eating contest: hole in b. K81.1; evil eye covered with b. D2071.0.1.1; ghost as b. E426.1; giving away the old water b. in which the money is hid J2093.1; hiding in b. in order to be carried K1892.1; looking into b. forbidden C322; ogre carries victim in b. G441; ogre tricked into carrying his prisoners home in b. G561; pseudo-magic wealth-providing b. K111.3; quest for b. of truths H1376.4; rain from emptying b. D2143.1.8; reincarnation as b. of water E636.1; resuscitation by magic b. E64.14; sacred hosts fill b. in coffin V35.2; spirit in b. as helper F403.2.2.4; stabbing b. of blood *K1875; taking prisoner's place in a b. K842; thief hides in money b. K307.1; transformation to be put in food b. D657.1; wife carried up tree to the sky in b. in husband's teeth J2133.5.1.

Bags. — Negligent priests buried under b. filled with words omitted from service V5.2; new b. for old K266.

Bagpipe as devil's bellows G303.10.14. — Death respite while playing b. K551.3.5; fairies teach b. playing F262.2; playing b. frightens robber K335.1.5.

Bailing out pond with thimble H1113.1; out stream J1967.

Bait. — Getting b. from trap by luring in another animal K1115.1; human eyes as fish b. S165.6; stealing Añan's b. H1151.17; tiger gives man food for dear b. K361.3; unique fish b. Z312.4.

Bakali. — Quest for b. flower H1333.5.3.

Baker P442; substitutes for imprisoned princess R83. — Cuckoo a transformed b. A1993.1; dwarf as b. F451.3.4.5; giant as b. F531.3.7; lover disguised as b. woman K1214.1.1; witch as b. G246.

Baker's. — King called b. son J816.2; owl is b. daughter who objected to dough given Jesus A1958.0.1.

Baking without fire D2158.1.5.2. — Dwarfs b. F455.3.5; fairies b. bread F271.10; fugitive king disguised and set to b. K521.4.1.2; how husband knows wife b. J1713.1; lie: remarkable b. X1031.4; mother is b. the bread we ate last week H583.4.2.

Balance. — His faith into the b. V512.1; ordeal by b. H226; religious exercises weighed in b. V4.1.

Balcony. — Chickens thrown from b. J2173.5.

Bald cow H1331.3.1; daughter as accursed H659.18.1; man aims at a fly J2102.3; man and the cynic J1442.9; man finds comb J1061.2; man tries to sell hair-restorer J1062.2.1. — Origin of b. heads H1315.2; swallowed person becomes b. F921; why certain animals are b. A2317.

Balder's death K863.

Baldness from breaking tabu C949.2; magically cured D2161.3.4. — Magic helmet prevents b. D1389.8; wife exposes second wife's b. T257.2.1.

Balky. — Trading b. horse K134.6.

Ball falling into water puts person into ogre's power G423; of fire haunts murderer E530.1.2; game in lower world E494; of human brains F839.5; thrown indicates princess's choice H316.3. — Animal killed by forcing b. into throat K951.5; Apple (or b.) containing man's soul can be split only by man's own sword D1651.10; conception from putting b. into bosom T532.6; counselor killed in own treacherous b. game K1626.2; dead persons play b. E577.1; devil as b. of fire G303.3.4.2.1; devil as a black b. G303.3.4.2; disenchantment by crystal b. D771.12; dropped b. leads to adventures when recovery is attempted N777; fiends play b. with soul E752.1.2; head used as b. S139.2.2.4.1; heroine's three-fold flight from b. R221; lucky cast of b.: kills dog through mouth N623.2; magic b. *D1256, (of thread) *D1184.1, (of hair) D991.3; magic b. of string to which one sticks D1413.18; marvelous b. player F697; origin of b. game A1495.1; power of chaste woman: making b. of water H413.2; prince sees heroine at b. and is enamored N711.6; pursuit of rolling b. of yarn H1226.4; reincarnation as b. E637; seduction by seeking lost b. K1349.9; soul in golden b. E711.9; test of sex of girl masking as man: b. thrown into lap H1578.1.4; tabu: letting b. fall into water *C41.2; tabu: staying too long at b. C761.3; throwing b. to princess as suitor test H331.16; thunder as gods play b. A1142.6; witch-b. kills G262.4.

Balls. — Mines found where b. fall N533.5; sun and moon as b. of feathers A738.1.1.

Balm. — Giant has wound-healing b. F531.6.5.3; magic b. *D1244; thirteen rivers of b. in otherworld F162.2.7.

Balsam rivers in otherworld F162.2.5. — Bath of b. F872.7; water becomes b. D478.8; witch kills b. plant G265.9.1.

Bamboo goddess A435.1; to be returned exactly as it is K196.3; stalks as life token E761.3.1; transformed to person D431.10. — All seeds in b. cut by hero A1425.1; alleged oracular b. cup K114.4; butterfly becomes b. D424.1; contest: bringing grain from closed b. K69.1; iron in b. in deceptive contest K44.1; magic b. tree D950.15; origin of b. A2681.6; soul in b. E711.2.6; why b. has nodes A2756.

Ban on trolls F455.9; on tournaments rescinded P561.1. — Person under religious b. cannot rest in grave E412.

Banana large as elephant's tooth F813.6.1; leaf becomes fish D441.5.2. — Fool eats wrong part of b. J1732.2; meat transformed to b. D457.5.2; origin of b. A2687.5; speaking b. tree D1612.1.2; touching b. tabu C621.2.2; why b. bears fruit from crown of tree A2771.4.

Bananas distract pursuing fairies F381.2.1; hide when stone is thrown D1641.16; ripen from bottom up E761.3.1.1; magic b. *D981.13; monkey cheats fox of b. K171.9.

Band, see also **Bracelet.** — Iron b. forged round a man's waist Q522.5.

Bands. — Iron b. around heart to keep it from breaking F875.

Bandage. — Identification by b. H118.

Bandicoot as children's nurse B535.0.2. — Helpful b. B437.1.1; man transformed to b. D117.3.1.

Bangle, magic *D1075.

Bangles. — Man exchanges b. for son M101.3.2.

Banished minister found indispensible and recalled P111; wife or maiden S411; wind A1122.3; youth becomes king L111.1.1. — Actors b. along with vagabonds P471.1; bad luck b. N250.4; brother b. S73.2; fairies b. from fairyland F252.4; fairy mistress insists wife be b. F302.5.4; man b. into moon for theft A751.1.4; misunderstood wife b. by husband S411.1; mother b. to stables by king S21.4; nobleman b. by king coveting his castle P12.8; poets b. P427.7.9; rain-god and wind-god b. by sun-god A287.0.1; revenants b. E437; revolting devil b. to hell A106.2.1; son b. by father S11.5, S322.1.5.1; wife b. S411; youngest son b. for telling king truth J551.6.

Banishment for breaking tabu C955; caused by dream of future greatness L425; as punishment Q431; tests suitor's sincerity H314.2. — Inverted shoes indicate b. Z174.1; magic b. D2099.2.

Bank. — Murder revealed to thieves climbing into b. N615; trickster gets money from b. by raising alarm K484.1.

Banks. — Dwarfs live in high b. of seashore F451.4.1.8; separation by being on different b. of stream N315.

Banker's ability to recognize honest merchant J1661.1.9.

Bankrupt father sells his daughters in marriage to animals S221.1.

Banner. — Large b. gives away jackal king J951.5; magic b. gives victory D1400.1.16; Virgin Mary's shift as b. causes blindness to opposing army D1331.2.3.

Banners appear like flock of birds K1872.5.

Banquet of the dead E499.1. — Drunken enemies slaughtered in b. hall K871.2; enemies invited to b. and killed K811.1f.; magic b. D1030.2; magic healing b. D1500.1.30.

Banquets of the gods A153.3.

Banshees as prophets M301.6.1.

Banyan leaves become gold D475.1.3.1; tree on moon A751.6.1. — How b. got its milk A2791.3; jar beneath b. tree animated A199.1; offending spirit of b. tree C43.1; origin of b. tree A2681.10; why b. roots hang down A2791.13.

Baptism, see also **Christening;** *V81; of animal gives magic powers *D1766.3; of children lays ghost E443.6; by druids P427.1.3; of heathen V332; as magic cure D2161.4.9; rescues man from devil G303.16.6; of saint by angel V241.4. — Heretical b. V322; king demands b. of guests P337.1; phenomena accompany b. of wonder child V229.2.4; resuscitation for b. E176; transformation by b. D587; water miraculously produced for b. D925.1.0.1.

Baptismal water (as magic object) *D1242.1.1, (vanishes before Aryan bishop) V325. — Man enabled to read b. service by washing in holy water K1819.4.1; ring as b. token H82.4.

Baptized wine J1312.3. — Disenchantment of monster child when b. D741.2; stone on which saint b. D931.0.3; why magpie hybrid: not b. during flood A2382.1.

Baptizer. — Magic power from b. D1722.1.

Bar. — Devil strikes man dead with iron b. G303.20.3; ogre killed with own iron b. G519.2.

Barber P446; alone praises usurer X511; becomes king L113.8; clever J1115.3; cured by telling secret D2161.4.19.1; discovers secret physical peculiarity N465; ghostly E571; hired to cut king's throat sees warning on the bottom of the basin J21.1; killed: king's ancestors need services in heaven K964; kills child: blames thin skin J1166.1; leaves inexpensive village for high wages in city J342.1; makes demands while wielding razor J625; as matchmaker T53.5; passes for a Brahmin K1827.0.2; rescues abandoned boy R131.8.8; shaves wife's beard (lie) X1727.1; skillful F665; suggests task H919.1.1; tries to become trader J513.2; unskillful J1484. — Before b. great incline head and give blood and money H581.1; customer agrees to demands of b. while razor is at his throat J625; disguise as b. K1825.3; one-eyed b. sees thread stretching to sea F642.6; thief disguised as b. K311.13; treacherous b. K2253.

Barber's contest in shaving H504.2; and jackal's common garden K171.8.

Barbers. — Jokes about b. X252.

Bard P427.7.5; rescues child R131.19; vows against making requests M164.

Bare, see **Bald, Barren.**

Barefoot. — Neither b. nor shod H1055; salamander enters b. person B784.1.8.

Bargain in anger F613.3, K172; is deceptive *K100ff.; is foolish J2080ff.; is lucky *N421. — Dead return to fulfill b. E342; devil made sick of his b. K262.1; drinking only after a b. K236.2; family carried away to fairyland as part of b. F327; immortality gained from b. with death D1851.2; love-compelling man sickens of b. K837; payment precluded by terms of the b. K220ff.; priest dies from deceptive b. F1041.1.3.4; touching head as sign of accepting b. P675.

Bargains and promises *M200ff. — Chain tale: progressively worse b. Z41.5; trickster undertakes impossible b. and collects his part M291.

Bargaining sends family off to fairyland F327. — Lover b. with husband K1581.10.

Bark of plant A2751ff. — Animals from b. thrown on ground A1714.2; disguise in birch b. K1821.9.1; land made from b. D476.1.4; magic b. D952; tanning shoes with b. from saint's tree Q551.6.2.1; why tinsa tree has no b. at bottom of trunk A2751.2.3.

Bark-cloth for chiefs alone C564.4; origin of A1453.5.

Barking. — Dogs' b. causes forgetfulness D2004.10; dog driven away from other animals because of b. A2494.4.0.1; dog b. to dog in moon K1735; how dog's b. began A2425.1; man's b. D2063.6; why dog b. at thief A2426.1.5.

Barley plant droops if prince is in trouble D1310.4.3; in wounds as false remedy K1016. — Magic b. D965.15, D973.2; origin of b. A2685.4; wheat becomes b. D451.2.2.

Barmecide feast P327.

Barn. — Birds magically confined to roofless b. D2072.0.2.2.1; burial in b. as punishment Q491.1.2; cleaning manure-filled b. H1102.2; destructive bird killed, b. found full of gold B103.7.1; fairies dance in b. F261.3.5; feathering b. H1104.1.1.

Barnacle goose B712.

Barrel of ale fairy gift F348.9; filled miraculously with penitent's tears F1051.1. — Building b. around a bunghole W152.14.1; casting into water in b. as punishment Q467.1; descending sea in glass b. J52.2; devil as rolling b. G303.3.4.5; fatal game: rolling down hill on b. K866; forbidden b. C624; fox and noisy but empty b. J262.1; king in glass b. to study fishes P15.6; look! look! she cries from the b. W136.1; man can stand on b. rolling down hill F679.4; man in b. grabs wolf by the tail and is drawn out of danger X1133.3; magic b. D1171.9, (supplies drink) D1472.1.18; naked lover as devil in sooty b. K1555.2; thief in oil b. K312; wind raised by putting cat under b. D2142.1.5.

Barrels. — Lie: b. of tears shed over lying X909.1.1.

Barren hillside turns to wheat at Christ's presence V211.1.8.3; trees as punishment for Fall of Man A2721.8; wife banished S411.3; wife conceives in time to prevent husband's leaving N681.2; wife exposed by husband S62.3; wife gives husband handmaid T282; wife makes child by magic K1924; woman assigns quest for dusty cloth H1377.4; woman pretends to bear child K1923.3. — Land made magically b. *D2081; dragon's shriek makes land b. *B11.12.2; magic chain renders orchard b. D1563.2.1; magic song makes b. land fruitful D1563.1.2; refusal to accept alms from b. woman V436; river b. of fish D2085.1; second wife taken because first b. T145.2.

Barrenness induced by magic T591; magically cured D2161.3.11; removed (by blood) D1347.2, (by charms) D1501.1, (by eating or drinking) D1925.1, (by prayer) D1925.3, (by sacrifice of child) S271; as result of fright F1041.17.1.

Barrier to otherworld (river of fire) *F142, (water) *F141.

Barrow as home (of dwarf) F451.4.1.9, (of troll) F455.1.1. — Magic object from b. D838.5.

Barrows. — Dead live in b. E481.3.1.

Bashful dwarfs F451.5.19; suitor wooes oak T69.4.

Basil, the pot of T85.3.

Basilisk B12ff.

Basin, magic *D1171.12; to which one sticks *D1413.7. — Tale of the b. *K1217; warning on the bottom of the b. J21.1.

Basket of things becomes iron D479.5; tied to wolf's tail and filled with stones K1021.2. — Air-castle: b. of glassware to be sold J2061.1.1; air-riding b. D1118.1; bride in b. C169.1; coin left in b. borrowed to measure money betrays secret wealth N478; dropped b. leads to adventures N777; dupe enters trickster's b. and is killed K814; escape from

deluge in b. A1029.5; escape by leaving pursuers in b. K676; exposure
of child in b. S141; future hero found in b. L111.2.1; god with b.
A137.4; hair tied to b. causes dupe's death K1021.1.1; insect asks to
be put in loosely-woven b. K581.6; light kept in b. A1411.1; looking into
b. forbidden C327; magic b. *D1171.11; magic b. (box) furnishes livestock D1477.4; magic b. (box) furnishes slaves D1476.3; man drawn
up into female apartments in b. *K1343.1; monkey instead of girl in
floating b. K1625; ogre carries victim in b. G441; one b. of wit better
than carloads J1662.1; paramour pretends to be returning winnowing
b. K1517.11; prince finds girl floating on water in b. N711.5; sky b.
F51.2; soul hidden in fish b. E712.6; thief enters city in b. K312.2;
trick exchange: b. of stones for bread K149.1; trickster's b. for tiger
partner K2033; trickster hides in b. K1892.1.2; Vergil in the b. K1211;
victim suspended in b. over filth and thrown in Q474; victim tricked
into entering b. K714.4; weapons concealed in food b. K929.11; wife
has husband carried off in b. K1514.6; woman dupe puts thief in
food b. K359.3.

Baskets. — Animals escape when forbidden b. opened: origin of animals C915.2; capture by hiding in food b. K758; lies about b. X1756;
origin of b. A1446.5.5, A2828; resuscitation by magic b. E64.20; sunlight carried into windowless house in b. J2123.

Basket-makers. — Why some men are good b. A1650.3.1.

Bastard, see also **Illegitimacy;** hero L111.5, Z255. — The cynic and the
b. stone-thrower J1442.7; deduction: the king is a b. J1661.1.2;
prophecy: princess to marry b. M369.2.1.2; slander: prince is b.
K2128.

Bastards, tabus of C575.

Bat created A1895; diver, and thornbush shipwrecked A2275.5.3; falls
due to sun's extreme heat: hence peculiar feet and nose A2214.6; giant
B31.4; helpful B449.3; lifts stone before rescue H1562.2.2; makes sun
smile, ends eclipse A1046.1; rescues man from height B542.1.2; sleeps
in day: curse for being asleep when devil tempted man to eat forbidden
fruit A2236.3; in war of birds and quadrupeds B261.1. — Eight-eyed
b. B15.4.1.4; friendship of b. and owl A2493.2; soul in form of b.
E731.7; witch as b. G211.2.10; woman reborn as b. E692.1; why b. is
bald A2317.8; why b. flies by night A2491.1; why b. sleeps by day
A2491.1.1.

Bat's body made larger A2301.4.

Bats in house a ghost sign E436.3; keep fireflies B788. — Eternal b.
B19.9; why b. cry as they fly A2426.1.6.

Bath of blood as cure for leprosy F955.1; of blood of beloved to cure
love-sick empress T82; in blood of king as cure for mange D1502.5.1;
extraordinary F872ff.; in magic milk rejuvenates D1338.4; in milk of
white, hornless cows as antidote for poison D1515.3. —Acid b. for
unwelcome lover K1227.4.1; blood b. causes woman to be carried off

by a bird N335.2; boiling water poured on master in b. K1462.1; bride's garments stolen in b. K1911.1.8; cynic at b. J1442.2; escape by pretended b. K551.4.7; good b. (cat to mouse) J1422; helpful mare cools boiling b. for master B526.2; king in the b. D2012.1; lover put off till after girl's b. K1227.1; muddy b. for blemished king J815.3; only person in b. J753.1; poisoned b. accidentally used N332.1.1; tabu: going into b. on return from serpent kingdom C711; victim killed in b. K831; weekly b. taker comforted by yearly taker J882.3; wounds healed by marrow b. F959.3.3.

Baths. — Fool at b. believes he's someone else J2012.6; public b. as adulteress's tryst K1587.

Bathhouse of fairies F265.1.

Bather's. — Abduction by stealing b. clothes R32; bird carries off b. garments N352.2.

Bathing in boiling water as suitor test H328.5; in common place tabu J21.33; fairy F265; in fairyland lake tabu F378.2; forbidden C721; girl visited by devils G303.10.4.2; hair in buffalo milk makes it unusually long D1337.1.3.1; infants in milk T601; pool reserved for royalty P92; in waters compulsory C663; witch G245. — Abortion by long b. T572.2.6; blindness cured by b. F952.7; compulsion: b. in certain waters daily C663; conception from b. T523; dead person b. E599.13; death respite for b. K551.4.4; disenchantment by b. (in milk) D766.4, (in water) D766.1; enemy surprised while b. R4.1; escape by b. guard in boiling water K629.1; eyes restored by b. in spring F952.7; fairies b. in enemy's blood F259.2; falling in love with b. person T16; lover first sees beloved b. N716; magic cure by b. D2161.4.14; magic results from b. *D1788; men tricked into b. in "disease-water" K1077; ogress b. in pool becomes beautiful G264.0.1; punishment of b. people in hell remitted Q578; races dark-skinned from b. after white men A1614.2; resuscitation by b. E80.1; ritual b. V96; seduction (or wooing) by stealing clothes of b. girl K1335, R32; sight of mermaid b. makes man immortal B81.13.3; slave b. mistress's back in stream pushes her into crocodile hole K831.1; speaking while b. tabu C401.6; spirit in hell endlessly b. people Q501.9; substitute products used in b. rich man: his substitute pay J1511.2.1; suitor b. in boiling water H1023.24; sun b. in stream of fire A722.5.1; tabu: b. without straining stream afterwards C 721.3; tabus concerning b. fairy child F378.6; transformation by b. D562; tree maidens b. at midnight F441.2.1.4; women meet when b. P611.

Bathroom in minaret J2237. — Attempt to suffocate king in b. P16.3.1.1; suffocating in b. S113.2.2.

Batting. — Sham dead detected by b. eyes H248.5.

Battle P551, see also **Army;** captives sold as slaves P173.3; carnage personified Z132.0.1; at end of world A1080ff.; of fairies and the gods F277; of giants, dwarfs F535.5.1.1; of the gods at world's end

A1081; of islands F748; between lice of Strassburg and of Hungary X651; noise precipitates birth T581.6; rage *F873.0.1, N349.2; reactions of warriors F1041.16.6; as suitor contest H331.2.1. — Adultery to aid husband in b. T455.2.1; angel as helper in b. V232; baby son hurled into b. to punish mother Q469.11; cairn marks b. site A989.4 capture on field of b. R5; certain person to fight particular b. M369.3; cohabiting with woman after b. C664.0.1; dead buried after b. V69.1; dead king carried into b. P12.5.0.1; defeat in b. at world's end A1084; demons b.: hills torn up A964.3; devil as helper in b. G303.22.14; devil interrupts mass by pretended b. G303.9.9.2; escape from b. by flying in air R324.1; extraordinary nature phenomena during b. F960.3; fairy aids mortal in b. *F349.2; fairy offers man change of form and feature for aid in b. F343.11; fairies b. F277.0.3; faithful animal killed in b. B335.5; father kills son in b. rage N349.2; furious b. *F1084; god helps mortal in b. A185.1; gods intervene in b. A172; good king never retreats in b. P12.5; hero aids followers in b. A581.2; hero sleeping during first of b. K2378.5; king in disguise flees b. K1812.10; king pretends going to make peace: really b. K1774; land changes from b. between gods A901.1; leaving b. while lord alive cowardly W34.3; lost memory recovered in b. N645; magic defense in b. *D2163; men go mad in b. F1041.8.6; messenger sent is only b. survivor N693; mock b. scares off enemy K2368.2; prayer before b. brings victory V52.3; prophecy: death in b. M341.2.18; prophecy: loss of b. M356.1.1; rather death in b. than in bed M161.6; recurrent b. A162.1.0.1; relics carried into b. V144.1; scolding contest introduction to b. H507.5; spirits hover in air over b. F418; substitute in b. K1845; suitor contest: bride offered to the one distinguishing himself most in b. H331.2.1; tabu: going to b. without being clothed in silk C878.2.1; transformation to another form to persuade men to go to b. D659.9; Virgin Mary intercepts an arrow in b. D2163.3; vow to become Christian if b. won M177.1.1; waves reverberate at preparation for b. F931.4.1; warrior refuses to delay b. W33.2; wild hunt appears in old b. field E501.12.6.1; witch in b. G275.10.

Battles. — King loses b. for plundering church Q556.6; oath concerning b. for Jesus M177.1.2.

Battle-axe D1097, F837.

Battle-pen P552.1.

Battle-shouting A1341.1.

Battlefield. — Birds hover over b. F989.14; ghostly voice heard on b. E401.0.1; soldier's ghost haunts b. E334.5.

Battling. — Hero b. under lake F691.0.1; rival lovers b. T92.7; woman b. demons for husband's soul E756.5.

Baucis and Philemon Q1.1.

Bauerntochter, die kluge H561.1.

Bavarian language X652.

Bawds, see also **Prostitutes;** T452.

Bay leaves protect against witches G272.2.4.

Baying dogs in wild hunt E501.4.1.10, E501.13.4. — Hounds' b. indicates nature of quarry F679.5.2.

Bazaar, advice on going to H588.18.

Bazaars, fairy frequents F234.2.8.

Beach. — Child born on b. T581.9; mermaid is washed up on b. B81.13.2; why turtle lays eggs on b. A2433.6.1.2.

Beacon, origin of warning A1599.1.

Beads break ice jam D1549.11; cling together E761.4.8; sorted as task H1091. — Besiegers scatter b. in protecting K2367; flowers become b. D451.4.0.1; magic b. *D1071.1; man becomes b. D263.4; witch's knees b. G229.4.4.

Beak, see also **Bill.** — Bird with b. of iron B15.7.13.1; bird with fiery b. B15.7.13; crow's b. and tail alternately stick to tarred bridge Z39.3; disenchantment from bird when queen milks own milk into bird's b. D759.2; hawk hard to hold by b. H659.2.1; man with bird's b. F514.2; monster's b. as slaying proof H105.5.3; origin of bird's b. A2343; why bird's b. is colored A2343.2; why kingfisher's b. is long A2343.1.5; why starling's b. is split A2343.3.1; why woodpecker has sharp b. A2343.3.2.

Beam across door protects from witch B272.7.1; breaks at giant's glance F531.3.14. — Falling b. in cave kills travelers K1172; quest for axe which sticks in b. outside a tower H1338; strong man carries huge b. F631.6; trying to get a b. through a door crosswise in otherworld *F171.6.3; trying to stretch the b. J1964.1.

Beams of light tie sun to earth A733.4. — Beard projected over b. of hall F545.1.2; builder's throw away b. from the scaffolding J2171.3; two b. of fire shoot from devil's eyes G303.4.1.2.3.

Bean split from laughing sewed together F662.3; straw and coal F1025.1. — Hospitable fire of b. merchant sought H581.2; magic b. *D983.1; why b. has black stripes A2741.1, A2793.1.

Beans. — All b. cooked, fill room J1813.9; black b., white soup J1291.1; I boil those which come and go (b. rising and falling in water) H583.6; coins thought to be red b. J1772.3; eating b. forbidden C224.1; the meal of b. X754; origin of b. A2686.6; task: sorting b. H1091.

Bean-goose E423.3.11.

Bear abducts girl, makes her his wife B601.1.1, R13.1.6; asks boy to stay with her cubs B299.4; becomes goose D411.10; bites the seemingly dead horse's tail K1047; boasts of having eaten horses J2351.4; builds house of wood: fox of ice J741.1; could formerly lift mountain B746; thought to be dog J1753; fears man, who falls out of tree on him J17.1; fishes through ice with tail A2216.1, K1021; frightened by sneezing K2354.2; frightens off robbers K335.1.9; -god A132.5; as grandfather (bluff) K12.2; hard to hold by claws H659.2.1; heplful B435.4; husks millet for man B571.4; in human form B651.7; keeps human wife captive in cave R45.3.1; killed from ambush K914.1; as king of animals B240.1; knows if person looks at his track K1813.0.1; learns how to catch crabs with his hairy claws J102; mistaken for log J1761.9; mistaken for man, strangled J1762.8; paramour *B611.1; plays games with heroine H1537.1; on haywagon thought to be the preacher J1762.2; put off guard by listening for hunters K832.4; put to sleep by rubbing, killed K836; riding horse lets paws fall on horse's flanks J2187; says he is boy's father, asks food B635.1.3; serves saint B256.6; sold as watch-dog K133.2; substituted for woman in box: kills villain K1674; summoned by magic D2074.1.1.3; as suitor B621.1; throws hens to the fox K1022.3; and trainer K1728; transformed to bow D421.6.1; transformed to man D313.3. — Alleged gold-dropping b. K1252.1; bird-b. B44; blood of b. venomous B776.5.5; bridling a ferocious b. (task) H1154.3.2; coward boasts of frightening b. K1953.1; creation of b. A1836; culture hero's pubic hair thought to be b. hair J1772.4; devastating b. killed B16.2.5; devil as b. G303.3.3.8; eaten meat of b. lover causes unborn son to have b. characteristics B635.1.1; enmity of b. and ant A2494.8.2; enmity of tiger and b. A2494.10.3; escape from b. takes from summer to winter X1133.2; first parents b. all children they wish A1277.2; flesh of Artemis eaten as b. V30.1.1; food of b. A2435.3.3; fool releases b. while master is away J2191; fox persuades b. to lie in hay, sets it afire K1075; frightened b. falls out of tree at cat's shriek K2324; giantess kills monstrous b. F531.3.12.3; ghost in form of b. sneezes E552; ghost of b. E522.2; godless man attacks b. as saint J1762.2.1; why b. has hump on back A2356.2.6; joke on man chased into camp by b. X584.1; why b. lives where he does A2433.3.17; lion, b., and wolf resuscitate master B515; log becomes b. D441.3.2; magic b. B182.2; magic hair of b. D1023.1; man accidentally killed by b. trying to chase away flies N333.2; man-b. B29.7; man and b. in hay-rick B855; man crawls inside b., cuts way out K952.2.1; man disguised as b. K1823.4; man, lion, and b. in pit J685.1; man sets dogs on b. who rescued him W154.25; man transformed to b. D113.2; marriage to b. B601.1; mother ape burns b. L315.4; one b. child escapes death, ancestor of all A1006.8; origin of the Great B. (Ursa Major) A771; ox-demon transformed to b. D412.2.5; why grizzly b. is peaceable A2531.2; reincarnation as b. E612.8; revenant as b. E423.2.1; robber disguised as b. K311.6.1; she-b. as false bride K1911.1.6; soul as b. E731.8; speaking b. B211.2.3; strong man kills b. F628.1.1.4; tame b. rings church bells X412; tiger, jackal, and b. each learn to fear man J17.1; troll has b. in stable G304.3.2.3; how b. lost tail A2216.1, A2378.2.4; why b. has short tail A2378.4.2; strong man son of b. who has stolen his mother F611.1.1; what the b. whispered in his ear J1488; witch in form of b. G211.2.1; witch transforms man to b. G263.1.1; woman in b. form D743; woman reveals husband's whereabouts to b. T244.1.

Bear's den A2432.6; enemies A2494.8; food C25; foster child B635.1.2; son B635.1. — Escape by dressing in b. skin K521.1.2; hare causes pursuing b. death K929.13; helper in b. skin aids escape K649.7.2; man threatens to cleave b. skull with penis K1755.1; quest for b. milk H1361.2; tricksters eat b. food K361.2; woman rescued from b. cave R111.1.13.1.

Bears devour the wicked Q415.6; as giants' dogs F531.4.11.1; as God's messengers A165.2.1.1.4. — Deceptive game: b. sway in tree K855.1; female b. have no breasts: young suck paws B725; grizzly b. A2367.2.1, A2524.1; lies about b. X1221; strong man captures b. F615.2.4; trolls afraid of b. G304.2.4.2; why b. attack men A2524.3; why b. do not have breasts A2353.4; why b. hibernate A2481.1; why b. have short, crooked legs A2371.2.4; why grizzly b. have three stripes on inside of stomach A2367.2.1.

Beard of dwarfs F451.2.3ff.; as path to heaven F57.3; shaved as punishment Q497; on she-goat does not make a male U112. — Baby killed for pulling b. S327.2; barber shaves wife's b. (lie) X1727.1; catching fish in b. F634.1; child born with b. T551.13.2; custom of wearing b. A1597; dead body incorruptible (b. and fingernails continue to grow) E182; devil's b. G303.4.1.3; devil fastened to hell's door by b. G303.17.3.2; disguise by dying b. K1821.1; disguise by shaving off b. K521.2.1; dwarf caught by b. F451.6.1; fairy-mortal baby's b. F305.3; giant with long b. F531.1.6.4; how goat got his b. A2322.4; god with red b. A125.2; god with white b. A137.18; had a good b. (only word of praise) X511; grain to grow without b. J2072.2; green b. F545.1.1.1; why hair is gray before b. H771; helper's b. and eyebrows cut N810.2; how much is king's b. worth? (riddle) H712; Jesus's long red b. V211.2.1.2.1; a long b. and sanctity J1463; magic strength of b. D1831.2; magic b. D991.1; maid given b. T321.1; man suddenly acquires long gray b. on scaffold F1044; monster's b. proves visit H105.4.1; numskull's b. cut off (does not know himself) J2012.1; ogre's b. caught fast K1111.1; origin of b. A1315.3; pulling b. as insult P672; quest for three hairs from devil's b. H1273.2; philosopher spits in king's b. J1566.1; remarkable b. F545.1; singeing b. to avoid assassination J634.1; transformation: grass to b. D451.5.4; vow to kill anyone touching b. M166.3; wife persuaded to cut hair from husband's b. K1085; witch with b. G219.2.

Beards. — Dwarfs' b. in three strands F451.2.3.1.1; first men without b. A1597.1; fur made from b. of conquered kings P672.1; lies about b. X1727; only brave may wear b. P642; youths wear false b. K1821.4.

Bearded woman F545.1.5; woman ghost laid by shaving E451.7. — Gray-b. fairy F233.10; tabu: b. man (going dirty to bed) C891.2, (abusing women or children) C867.1.0.1, (laughing when shaken) C461, (refusing combat) C835.1.1, (refusing request) G871.0.1, (sleeping at sunrise) C735.1.1; tabus for b. men C565ff.

Beardless hero Z257; man F545.1.0.1; villain K2275.

Bearer. — King will kill b. of bad tidings J1675.2.

Bearers of God's Throne A152.7.

Bearing. — Budding and b. of plant A2771ff.; dead wife b. children for husband E322.1; flower from grave b. letters E631.0.2; magic object b. person aloft *D1532ff.; miraculous blossoming and b. of fruit F971; woman transformed to animal b. animal T554.0.1.

Bearskin F821.1.3.1; creator clothed in A18.4.

Beast forced to bring back stolen child D2156.3; furnishes omens B147.1; -giant B871ff.; invokes saint's protection B251.4.1; -men B20ff.; paramour B611ff.; as suitor B621; wedding B281. — Abduction by wild b. R13.1; adventures from seeking domestic b. N774.2; beauty and the b. D735.1; domestic b. transformed to person D330ff.; exposed child carried off by wild b. S355; feeding ravenous b. to satisfaction (task) H1123; ghost of wild b. E522; guardian b. overcome by mirrors K335.1.7; killing ferocious b. H1161; man transformed to wild b. D110ff.; marriage to b. in human form B651; marriage to b. by day and man by night *B640.1; marriage to person in b. form B641; marriage of person to b. B601ff.; mother kills son thinking him a wild b. N325.3; playing game with ferocious b. H1537; separation of twins through being carried off by b. N312; wild b. transformed to person D310ff.; witch as wild b. G211.2.

Beasts and fishes exchange places: fatal to both V136.2; guard castle F771.5.1; helpful B400—B449; hostile B17.1; with magic wisdom B121ff.; in otherworld F167.1.1. — King of b. B241ff.; man given dominion over b. A1421.1; mythical b. B10ff.; passing among b. as fear test H1408.

Beast-man. — Stone becomes b. D432.1.2.

Beaten, see also **Pounded.** — Allowing self to be b. as bride test H386.1; changeling b. F321.1.4.6; husband b. by paramour K1514.4.1; importunate lover b. K1218.8; king in disguise b. by own men K1812.0.1; numskull b. J2131.1; priest b. to death J1786.4; returning husband b. by servants K1514.4; person b. (by magic club) D1401.1, (by magic whip) D1401.3, (by whips for breaking tabu) C982; Peter b. at inn K1132; lazy wife is b. by husband W111.3.4; wife b. for refusal to bring warm water T254.6.1; wild huntsman has his horse b. E501.15.2; will work when b. J1545.1; witch bound and b. G275.7.

Beating arouses sham sick man K1676; bewitched object G271.4.5; brings about recognition H182; to death as punishment Q422.0.1; the devil G303.16.19.19; gift bearers W154.20; own foot J1867.1; wife before food purchased so she will cook it right J2175.1.1; wife daily M134. — Creator b. his wife A32.3.2; creation of animals as punishment for b. forbidden drum *A1731; daily b. of transformed dogs D691; disenchantment by b. D712.5; father b. son with shoes H36.1.1; friends agree to b. wives K1394; ghost b. man with whip E261.5; ghost laid by b.

body E446.3.1; husband b. wife in paramour's place K1569.4; incognito prince, receives b. for his courtesy and realizes his folly J18; resuscitation by b. *E11; the soldier receives a b. promised the boy K187; thanks long-dreaded b. is over J2568; thunder-spirit b. his children A1142.5.1.2; torture by b. S186; wife b. husband daily T251.8; wisdom acquired from b. J18.

Beatings. — Daily b. as punishment Q458.1.

Beatrice, Sister K1841.1.

Beatus prayer for condemned souls V51.4.

Beautification by magic *D1860ff., *D1337. — Miraculous b. upon conversion to Christianity V331.3.

Beautiful fairy woman exhibits self F397; giantess F531.1.0.1.1; goddess A125.4; mantle F821.4; land of dead *E481.4; princess's look kills F574.1.3; wife as enemy J2462.3; witch G229.5; woman in disguise K1821.7; woman married to hideous man T268. — Death from sight of b. woman F1041.1.6; disguised flayer tightens skin to look b. K1941.1; fairy as b. woman F234.2.5; fairy-mortal child b. F305.2; fairies give b. clothes F343.5; flame indicates presence of b. woman F1061.1; fool wins b. woman L161.2; heroine in menial disguise discovered in her b. clothes H151.6; hideous person magically makes self seem b. D2031.4; hideous youth becomes b. D682.4.2; madness from seeing b. woman *F1041.8.1; magic object makes b. *D1337ff.; mermaid half-b., half-monstrous B81.9.3; ogre eats b. girl G13.2; otherworld people ever young, ever b. F167.9; ogress bathing in pool becomes b. G264.0.1; planting b. garden H1199.1; quest for the most b. bouquet H1302; quest for the most b. of women H1301; quest for b. girl H1214.1; quest for most b. ring H1319.3; rakshasa in form of b. wench G369.1.5; serpent's b. wife J155.1.1; trickster exacts b. wife from curious K443.6.1; useful preferred to b. J242, J245; visitors to island become b. F129.4.3; what is most b.? (riddle) H641; which most b.? luck or ill-luck? N141.3; wooing the strong and b. bride T58.

Beauty and the beast D735.1; contest H1596.1, (between goddesses) A163, (between peacock and crane) J242.5, (between swallows and crows) J242.6; contest dependent on first greeter K176.1; contest won by deception K98; doctor K1013, J1062.1; of giant F531.1.0.1; of various peoples A1664. — Animal tamed by maiden's b. B771.1; apparent b. of least importance J264; cause of animal's b. A2401; fainting from seeing a b. T24.2.3; fairy queen's b. temporarily destroyed by intercourse with mortal F304.2; geese tell of b. of their mistress and bring about recognition H151.12; goodness preferred to b. J244; god of b. A462; choice: loss of b. or speech J213; hero's irresistible b. spot A526.3; hero spared for his b. F1088.1; magic object gives b. D1337ff.; prophecy: b. for girl M312.4; remarkable b. F575; seduction by sham b. test K1339.4; sinful b. converted V229.12; sleeping b. D1960.3; waiting many years to see a b. T24.7; wife granted b. wish, elopes J2075.4;

woman's b. lights up the dark F574.1; woman's b. reported to king causes quest T11.1.1.

Beaver borrows muskrat's tail and never gives it back A2241.10; and muskrat exchange tails A2247.6; and porcupine trick each other K896.1; sacrifices scrotum to save life *J351.1. — Color of b. A2411.1.4.2; dwelling of b. A2432.3; why b. lives along rivers A2433.3.12; where b. got tail A2378.1.6; why b. has flat tail A2378.7.1; why b. splashes his tail in water and dives when attacked A2462.2.

Becalmed. — Witch aids b. boat G283.1.2.2.

Bed changes size D631.3.7, D1620.3.2; fatal to all his ancestors J1474; heating in hell for certain person Q561.1; of totem-tree tabu C848. — Advice from woman in b. T453; beggar buys right to sleep before girl's door, at foot of b., in b. K1361; bride and groom conducted to b. T137.2; capture in trap b. K735.4; cuckold husband hides under b. K1514.4.2.1; death cheated by moving b. *K557; death at head or foot of b. forecasts progress of sickness D1825.3.1; disenchantment by admission to woman's b. D734, D759.7, K1361.1; disguised man takes wife's place in b. K521.4.1.4; "don't sit on b. without touching it first" J21.34.2; dupe sleeps on "king's b.": falls into well K1078; dwarfs plan to dig underground b. for Rhine F451.5.22; entrance into girl's b. by trick *K1340ff.; equal share of chief's b. J2526; extraordinary b. F787, F846; friar's trousers on adulteress's b. K1526; ghost in b. with living E472; ghost leaves body mark on b. E568.1; giant's enormous b. F531.4.10; girl takes impostor's place in marriage b. K1611.3; goddess's b. of snakes A155.6; going to b. with Odin (task) H1199.11; going to b. for sorrow F1041.9.1; guest forces host into his b: host killed K1611.2; guest keeps calling for more b. clothes J1563.1; gullible husband under the b. K1532; Judith kills Holofernes in b. K872; king buys spendthrift's b. J1081.1; knife in b. as protection against witches G272.3; knife left in innocent person's b. K2155.1.1; learning a trade in b. W111.5.9; leper laid in queen's b. K2112.2; literal penance: not to lie in b. (sleeps on eider down) J1161.5; lover's gift regained on refusal to leave b. K1581.8; lovers in b. only kissing H1556.4.1; magic causes b. wetting D1379.4; magic b. *D1154.1; magic b. and pillows as chastity test H411.10; magic restlessness in b. D2063.2; maidservant given to lover's companion as b. partner T484; make the b. but do not make it (task) H1068; man carried off on b. escapes R219.1; man pinned in b. by weapon caught in quilt N386.2; man will not move in b. when water drops in his eyes W111.1.3; murderer strangles companion in b. K951.0.2; ogress killed in bridal b. G519.1.3; old maid in b. X752; owner tells thieves to come back later, not yet in b. J1392.2.1; paramour hidden in b. K1521.4; Procrustes makes men fit his b. G313; recognition by describing unique b. H16.4; robber stabs at clothes in b., misses victim K437.1; sham figures of wife, paramour in b. K525.1.1; servant lays skin of dead dog in the b. of his mistress and master K2134; sleeping on feather b. tabu C735.2.7; sleeping in saint's b. forbidden C93.1; stealing sheet from b. under person (task) H1151.3; substituted object left in b. K525.1; substitutes in b. (forgotten wife for false bride) D1978.4, D2006.1.4, (goat for disgusted wife) K1223.1, (old woman for girl) K1317.2.1, (strong servant for husband of strong bride) K1844.1, (wife for mistress) K1843.2; talking b. reveals king's identity N617; to whom princess turns in b. H315; vow not to go to b. with wife until enemy killed M152; hero wakened from magic sleep by wife who has purchased place in his b. from false bride *D1978.4; wraith goes to b. at home, real body away E723.4.1.

Beds exchanged with ogre's children K1611; in otherworld F166.8. — Glowing b. of dead E487; object set between b. of couple T353; trickster exchanges b., gets food K499.8.

Bed-legs. — Magic b. *D1154.1.1; speaking b. overheard N454.1.

Bed-ticks H1129.2, H1129.7.

Bedbug. — Reincarnation as b. E616.5; terrapin from b. eggs J1772.1.1; why b. is flat A2305.2; woman reborn as b. to annoy husband E693.2.

Bedbugs, lies about X1291.

Bedclothes. — Ghost pulls b. from sleeper E279.3; spirits pull off person's b. F470.1.

Bedcover of chastity T351.1; stolen J2672. — Ear used as b. F542.2.

Bedding. — Feast of "b. and handspreading" T162; prince feels hair on b. F647.9.1.

Bedside. — Death at b. of dying sweetheart T81.1.

Bedstead warns of danger of snake D1317.11. — Legs of b. talk D1610.17.1; magic b. legs kill dangerous animals D1402.17; magic b. protects D1380.12; magic transportation on flying b. D1520.17.1.

Bee fetches balm from heaven to restore hero's speech B514.2; as God's spy A33.3.1; helpful B481.3; as matchmaker B582.2.4; as messenger from heaven to earth B291.4.1; rests on water lily which closes over it at night and kills it J2137.3; sting damages king's son; swarm destroyed J1179.14; transformed to person D382.1; vitalizes tiger D1594.3; as witch's familiar G225.1: — Charm calls down b. swarm D1441.2; creation of b. A2012; dungbeetle thought to be b. J1751; great b. (lie) X1282.1; the hunt for the lost b. (lie) X1861; marriage to b. in human form B653.1; origin of color of b. A2411.3.1; Pleiades as b. swarm A773.6; recognition of disguised princess by b. lighting on her H162; reincarnation as b. E616.1; sleeper's soul leaves body as b. E721.1.2.4; speaking b. B211.4.2; why b. is sacred A2541.1; separable soul in b. E715.3.1; soul in form of b. E734.2; man transformed to b. D182.1; victim asked to catch b. nest: gets clubbed K815.19; Wash B. Day J1743.3; why b. is blind A2332.6.9; witch as b. G211.5.2.

Bee's. — Dupe strikes b. nest: bitten K1023.5; fools see b. nest reflected in water: try to carry off the well J1791.9; man escapes from b. nest on bear's tail X1133.4; shape of b. body A2300.1; why b. sting not fatal to man A2346.2.

Bees born from carcass of ox B713.1; and bugs can't eat same food J1565.2; build church of wax to contain consecrated host B259.4; caught in sack which is opened at home J2131.2.1; drop honey into woman's mouth F561.6; feed infants B531.1; leave honey on infant's lips B147.3.1.2; mistaken for Jutlanders J1762.5; in otherworld F167.1.3.1; sting honey-thieves Q597.3; thrown into redoubt drive out enemies K2351.2. — Charm calls down swarm of b. D1441.2; creation of honey-b.: transformed man A2012.0.1; first b. in Ireland A2012.2; garden with golden, silver b. F818.1; god sends stinging b. to punish men A2012.3; helpful b. sting opposing army B524.2.1; honey as excrement of b. A2385.3; king of b. B246.3; lies about b. X1282; riddle about b. and honey in lion's carcass H804; saint sends b. against enemy B524.2.1.1; sound of swarming b. disguised as children's singing K1023.4; why b. eat their own children A2435.5.1.1; why b. die after they sting A2346.1, A2232.2; why b. may not get honey from red clover A2435.5.1, A2231.3.2.

Bee-hive changes to wasps (sham miracle) K1975.1; hoax K1023; in troublemaker's bed K2138. — Consecrated host put into b. C55.3; honey from royal b. H1332.7; thief in b. K335.1.6.3; who gets the b. J1451; witch rides on b. G241.4.4.

Beef. — Task: furnish b. neither male nor female H1074.

Beer becomes wine D477.3; brewed in egg-shell F451.5.17.1; foams (life token) E761.6.4; let run in cellar J2176; magically kept from brewing *D2084.1; returned for bread, neither paid for K233.4. — Drinking b. without touching pot H1046.3; leek in b. poison protection D1383.5; magic b. *D1045; sign of cross protects b. D1766.6.4; stingy innkeeper cured of serving weak b. J1341.7; well of b. D925.0.2.

Beetle as creator A13.3.2; created A2021; cursed for betraying Holy Family: now has eyes always on ground A2231.7.1.1. — Enmity between hen, b., and duck A2494.13.10.2; hum of b. A2426.3.1, A2231.11; over-hasty b. X1862; sacredness of b. A2021.1; soul as b. E734.6; why b. creeps on ground A2441.3.1; A2232.3; witch as b. G211.5.3; witch recognized by seeing b. enter mouth while asleep *G251.1.

Beetles mistaken for food, eaten J1761.7; in wounds as false remedy K1016. — Why b. live in manure A2433.5.4.

Before. — Dwarfs in land 1000 years b. mortals F451.1.4; escaping b. enemy can strike J641; foolish demands b. death J2174; make peace b. rather than after war J156.1; people in otherworld hitch horses both b. and behind wagon F171.6.4; prophecy: death b. certain age M341.1.3; eating b. certain time forbidden C231; doing things b. certain time forbidden C756; three blasts on horn b. sunrise to rescue prisoner from mound R112.1; wine wished b., during, and after meal J1343.2; witch powerless when person speaks b. she does G273.2.

Befouling. — Maidens b. selves to escape rape T327.4.

Begetting by earbox J1919.7. — Disguised queen b. child with husband K1812.8.3; fairy b. son with human queen K1844.4; pseudo-magic charm for b. child K115.1.4; guest b. child with host's daughter P32.5.1.

Beggar asks goldsmith for goldplate J1338; with small bag surpasses the one with the large L251; buys right to sleep before the girl's door K1361; claims to be emperor's brother J1337; on cross in place of Christ L435.4; in disguise spits at queen Q471.2; disguised as gentleman *K455.3; gets little no matter how long he begs N264; refused hospitality escapes from fire N177; frightens lawyer into giving by telling him of lawyers in hell X312; with horse, wife, or dog considered rich by poorer beggar U65; laid in queen's bed K2112.2; overlooks money N351.2; refused payment for standing in tank all night K231.14; returns to his mother child stolen by fairies F321.4; rewarded for poem P163; served coals for food K492.1; transforms wedding party into wolves T155; treacherous K2291; ubiquitous K1982. — Ascetic's life as b. V462.9; Christ disguised as b. V211.2.1.2; defeated king as b. L410.4; devil as b. G303.3.1.23; father-in-law disguised as b. *K1817.1, H384.1; enigmas concerning b. H594; forgotten wife recalled as she gives b. food D2006.1.10; help from b. N826, N 825.3.1; infertile rajah marries b. T121.8.1; king becomes b. L419.2; magician as b. frees prisoners D2031.4.3; poverty as diseased b. Z133.1; princess sent to b. in trunk N712.1; persistent b. invited upstairs J1331; protean b. D611; reward for sharing food with b. Q42.1.2; saint gives little to b. J225.6; "save it for the b." C490.1.1; seduction by posing as b. K1315.10; suitor as b. tests bride H384.1.1; sultan as b. tests friends H1558.7.1; thief disguised as b. K311.17; wife substitutes calf for b. husband abuses K1846; witch poses as b. K764.

Beggar's curse M411.2; ghost laid by pig E451.6. — Blind b. money stolen from stick K333.4; burning b. clothes yields gold K245; confederate in b. disguise aids escape K649.7.1; dead b. stick will not stay until back in b. service D1651.5; treasure in b. hat N524; man as b. bride K1911.4.

Beggars P160ff. — Ghost laid by giving b. money E451.5.1; gods disguised as b. K1811.1; jokes on b. X530ff.; newly rich enjoy giving to b. U130.1; repartee concerning b. J1330ff.; trickster gets coins from blind b. K1081.1.1.

Beggaring. — Man b. self by charity V432.

Begging ghost E599.4; man to scratch witch's back *G269.1; before stone statues H1553.1; from wife's new husband L432; from wife's suitors K1568. — Ascetics b. from own mother N735.1; dead b. food E541.5; origin of b. A1599.15; relative b. from one he's formerly abused L432; vow to answer b. M172.1.

Beginning formulas Z10.1; of social relationships A1470ff. — Date with b. like its end, its top like its bottom (1691) H707.1; warrior b. combat may desist P557.4.2.

Begun. — Thing b. must be kept up all day J2073.1.

Beheaded criminal calls "Ave" V254.7.1; man carries his head under arm F511.0.4; man swims F1041.14; man's head laid at feet to prevent return E431.7; man's head replaced crooked F511.0.6; sailor swims F1041.14.1; simpleton's head replaced backwards J27. — Ass b. J1169.4; drunken man thinks he is b. J2311.10; eyes of b. person gouged out S165.1; head of b. witch mends if rubbed with salt G223; king b. in bed by wife K873.1; man to be b. for watching fight J21.51; man asks to be b. in water tank, ducks K558.2; witch b. G275.7.1.

Beheading, see also **Decapitation;** bargain M221; for breaking tabu C929.3; giant to escape prison R211.8; giants one by one K912; as punishment Q421; witch as task H1191.1. — Chief b. sentinel who does not recognize him F1041.16.9; murder by b. S133; St. Cecilia lives after b. D1840.1.3.

Behemoth: mythical gigantic animal B18. — Animals changed through fear of B. A2294; angels battle B. A1082.7.

Behind me night and before me day (formula for girl fleeing) R255. — Bought b. the village J1169.2; cooking what is b. you J2485; the devil creates devils by casting water b. himself G303.1.4.1; murder from b. K959.4; people in otherworld hitch horses both before and b. wagon F171.6.4.

Beholding woman fatal G264.1. — Man b. angels V230.1.

Bel surrounded by the priests like king and nobles (riddle) H825.

Belches. — Lakes originate from b. A920.1.5.1, D921.2.

Belching. — Sham magician b. fire K1963.4.

Belfagor T251.1.1.

Belfruit. — Woman becomes b. D211.3.

Belief in approach of husband secures confession from adulteress *K1572; in Christianity tested H1573.1; in own greatness induced in pupil by magician as test of gratitude H1565.1. — Erroneous b. as to own identity J2013; never believe what is beyond b. J21.13; prophet never secures b. M301.0.1.

Beliefs, religious V300ff.

Believing. — Father kills self b. that son is dead N344; liar b. own lie X902; lover kills self b. mistress dead N 343; two persons b. each other deaf X111.3.

Bell breaks and priest's patron whistles at mass X442; on magic dog dispells grief D1359.3.1.3; rings to indicate location of well D1314.4.1; to be rung when child is born T583.3; sounds at saint's approach V222.6; from underwater monastery F725.6. — Angel brings b. as drinking utensil for child T611.7; animals ring b. and demand justice B271.3; cow wears church b. X1235.1.1; dead hear saint's b. E545.14; devil exorcised with b. G303.16.14.4; disenchantment by ringing b. D789.10;

fox rings the b. K1114; ghost laid by burying church b., clapper separately E459.6; ghostly b. E533; hiding from ghosts under church b. E434.1; homage to saint's b. C94.8; little b. says "he's here" J1812.3; magic coin fills b. with money D1452.5; magic b. *D1213; magic healing b. D1500.1; mother ties b. on child, cat cuts it off, etc. Z39.6; raising sunken church b. C401.4; ringing b. tabu C756.0.1; ringing b. to announce chess win: fire alarm disregarded J2199.1; ringing of church b. causes devil to lose his power G303.16.12; ringing church b. as fear test H1412.1; ringing of church b. by nun tabu C94.7; saint transfers disease to his b. D2161.4.2.2; saint's b. heard, never found K1887.3.1; spring from water in saint's b. F933.1.1; stolen b. refuses to sound D1602.8.1; sunken b. sounds *F993; supernatural wife summoned by b. T111.0.2; swearing by saint's b. M116.2; tabu: looking under certain b. too soon C326; tree grows through saint's b. F979.6; water poured from saint's b. produces fountain D1567.3.

Bells hung at every corner of ship P651.1; on horse's mane P651.2; ring at saint's birth F960.1.4; rung backward as alarm P651.3. — Church b. *V115ff.; dress of gold, silver, and diamond b. F821.3; dwarfs dislike church b. *F451.5.9.3; enemies flee as church b. ring D1400.1.9.1; origin of church b. A1466; saints curse by ringing b. M411.8.1; saints exchange b. P311.7.1; tame bear rings church b. X412; wild hunt heralded by ringing of b. E501.13.1.4.

Bell-ringing the sweetest sound H635.1.

Bellerophon H918.

Belling the cat J671.1.

Bellowing of bull heard over entire land B741.4; of cow defeats army B741.3.

Bellows. — Bagpipe is devil's b. G303.10.14; beast with human head, shape of smith's b. B96; origin of b. A1447.1; strong man carries b. F624.10.

Belly, see also **Stomach;** and the members J461.1, A1391. — Animal with men in its b. playing cards F911.3.3; animals hide boy in their b. B529.1; man builds boat and sails about in giant's b. F911.5.1; escape under ram's b. *K603; flood from b. A1013; fool thinks b. is speaking to him: stabs himself J1817; needle in elk's b. L391; origin and nature of animal's b. A2354ff.; ogre kills self when he sees crumbs lying on his b. G523; ogres who have no b. G366.1; person with enormous b. F529.6; rescue from swallower's b. F913; thumbling in animal's b. persuades latter to go to his father's house K565; true bride lives in b. of fish K1911.2.2.1; wee cock: "Get into my b." K547.1; why salmon has purple b. A2412.4.2.1; why women have marks on b. A1310.4.

Bellies. — Landlords have biggest b. J1289.17.

Beloved. — Man scorned by his b. T75; quest for unknown b. H1381.2.1.1; what is the most b. (riddle) H647ff.

Below. — Confinement b. earth M372.1; creator from b. A25; emergence of gods from b. A115.5; girl seduced b. ground K1344.1; vehicle travels above and b. ground *D1533.2ff.

Belt transformed to bridge D454.3.3. — Child unwittingly promised: "What your wife has under her b." S242.1; fairy has b. F236.3; fairy's magic destroying b. F302.5.5; giant with gigantic chain as b. F531.4.2; magic b. *D1057, K525.8.1; power of dwarf in his b. F451.3.1; stealing b. from queen (task) H1151.5; tightening b. to counteract hunger F1076; wild huntsman has b. E501.8.5.

Beltane festival A1535.5, V70.1.1.

Benares. — Penance until spires of B. reduced, rebuilt Q521.7; pilgrimage to B. V533.

Bench, see also **Chair, Seat;** to which person sticks D1413.5. — Bride b. T136.4.1; magic b. *D1151.1.

Bender of pines G314. — Remarkable b. X947.

Bending bow as test D1651.1, H31.2, H331.4.2; the tree K1112. — Bird escapes hunter b. his bow J641.1; reeds b. before wind save themselves J832; stake miraculously b. F1093; tree b. to certain person D1648.1.

Benediction. — Merman's wife not to stay till church b. *C713.1; punishment for not giving b. Q223.13.2.

Benefactor falsely accused of theft W154.13. — Reincarnated b. helped E601.2.

Benevolence of witches G220.0.1. — Devil's b. to impious people G303.22.5; fairies give avaricious man gift of b. F343.4.

Bent. — Why buffalo's horns are b. A2236.3.4; murder by springing b. tree S135, H1522.1; return from lower world by being slung by b. tree F101.2.

Beowulf fights dragon B11.11; found in boat L111.2.1.

Bequeathing of animal characteristics to man B592; of helpful animal to hero B312.3; soul to devil M211.3. — Father b. four symbolic pots to sons J99.2.

Berry picker identified by scent F652.1. — Blowing on b. disenchants D778.1; conception from eating b. T511.1.2; magic b. D981.10; magic tree from b. D951.1.

Berries. — Bringing b. in winter H1023.3; hero returning with b. sent back for tree H1241.1.1; magic b. cause horns to grow on person D1375.1.1.10; man too lazy to pick b. W111.1.6; origin of b. A2687.3; quest for b. from tree guarded by giants H1333.3.3; why wren eats no b. A2435.4.11.1.

Berserk F610.3. — Curse by b. giant M411.10.

Berserks banished after defeat Q431.14.

Bertha F475.1.

Besieged city set afire by birds K2351.1; women's dearest possession J1545.4.1. — Enemy chief vows to marry b. city's princess M146.7; enemy induced to give up b. city K2365.

Besiegers crushed by treasure cast on them K2353.

Besieging. — Only one way of b. city Z316.

Besom. — Extraordinary b. (broom) F857.

Best. — Each likes his own children b. T681; "it is for the b." W25.2; quest for b. cap H1319.2; quest for b. meat H1305.1; truth the b. policy J751.1; what are b. and worst stones? (riddle) H659.3; what is b.? (riddle) H648ff.; what do you like b. J171.2.2.

Bestiality T465; punished Q253.1.

Bestowed. — Gifts b. on living by ghosts E373; immortality b. D1851.

Bestriding. — Giant b. mountain F531.3.5.1; giant goddess b. entire land A133.2.

Betel. — Extortion of b. leaf addict W193.1; origin of b. A2691.5.

Betel-nut grows on person as punishment Q551.1.1; as weapon F839.6. — Magic b. D985.5, D1524.11.

Bethlehem. — Star of B. D1314.13.1.

Betrayal of brothers' hiding-place by fool J2668; of clandestine visit of princess to hero by token H81.2; of devil by his goat hoofs G303.4.5.4.1; by dwarfs F451.6.11; of each other by thieves K307; of fox by peasant's pointing K2315; of fugitive by magic objects *D1612ff.; of hero by extraordinary companions F601.3; of husband to father-in-law K2213.7; of husband's secret by his wife K2213.2ff.; into ogre's power G410ff.; of parents' misdeeds by children J125; of person's rank by habitual conversation H38ff.; of secret by magic speaking reed *D1316.5; of self by fugitive compelled by magic object D1612.2; of self to enemies by talkative animal J2351; of thief by clever animal K427; of thief by breaking of stick with money in it H251.3.4.

Betraying. — Animal cursed for b. holy fugitive A2231.7.1; captain not b. king's secret P361.7; changeling deceived into b. his age F321.1.1; child b. own illegitimacy T644; lover b. woman K2232.1; mortal b. dwarfs' secrets F451.5.1.6.1; plant cursed for b. holy fugitive A2721.4.

Betrothal, see also **Engagement;** of children T69.2; of young man to statue T376. — Punishment for breaking b. Q252, Q416.0.1.

Betrothed, see also **Fiancée.** — Hero returns rescued princess to her b. R111.4.

Better things at home K1952.2. — Let me catch you b. game K553.1; maid behind statue of Virgin advises the mistress to give servants b. food K1971.3.1; making b. from good (hedging field) H583.2.3.

Betting, see also **Gambling;** contest between two kings N1.3. — Advice against b. J21.8.1.

Between two thieves (dying like Christ) X313. — Boy sleeps b. couple to safeguard virtue T352; cross b. shoulders as sign of royalty H71.5; magic sight by looking b. dog's ears D1821.3.4; path b. monsters (Scylla and Charybdis) G333; pig carrying scissors, comb, and razors b. ears H1154.1.

Bewailing a calamity that has not occurred J2198. — Weeping man turned into owl: still b. A2261.5.

Beware of following an interested adviser J758; of man (precept of the lion to his sons) J22.1.

Bewitched fairies F254.3; objects G265.8. — Cows b. by dwarfs to give no milk *F451.3.3.5; people b. by dwarfs F451.3.3.5.1; witch burned by burning b. animal G275.3.1.

Bewitcher. — Killing queen's b. H346.1.

Bewitching, see also **Witches;** *D2070ff.

Bhuiya yoke cow and bullock together A1689.1.

Bible V136; exorcises witch G271.2.5; nullifies fairy power F382.4; texts as magic spells D1273.3; under doorstep detects thieves D1817.0.1.5. — Devil cheated of his victim by boy having a b. under his arm K218.2; devil unable to read b., loses bargain K211.1; ghost laid by b. E443.8; gold in b. H261; reading b. backwards reveals witch G275.2; riddles based on the b. or legend H810ff.; weighing witch against b. H234.

Biblical figure as magician K1711.1; heroes as wise men J191.2; worthy as giant F531.0.1; worthy as prophet M301.7. — Levity about b. passages J1262.4.

Bier. — Enchanted person on b. D5.2; physician forced to carry patient's b. P424.3.1; remarkable b. F788; thieves carry abducted woman on b. K419.8.

Bifrost F152.

Big, see also **Great, Large;** ears F542.2; trees' small fruit A2771.9. — Choice: b. piece of cake with my curse or small piece with my blessing J229.3; frog tries in vain to be b. as ox J955.1; giant with eyes as b. as cauldrons F531.1.1.2.1.

Bigger. — Magic animal grows b. B195; thief hoping for b. booty, loses smaller K421.1.

Bija. — Why b. tree often struck by lightning A2791.12.

Bill (bird's beak), see also **Beak.** — Crane will not weep at crucifixion: must suffer thirst in August and break b. A2231.2.1; crossbill's b. from aiding Christ at crucifixion A2221.2.4.2; crow must wash his b. in order to eat with other birds Z41.2; disenchantment from bird by cutting off b. D711.3; the hawk frightened at the snipe's b. J2616; hornbill borrows tomtit's b. A2241.9.

Bill (reckoning) of sale written on sandal F1015.3. — The other man to pay the b. K455.4; b.-paying hat sold K111.2.

Billygoats. — Three B. Gruff K553.2.

Bilskilnir. — Five hundred forty rooms in B. F781.2.1.

Bin. — Filling grain-b. through bottom hole H1023.2.3.

Binding, see also **Bound;** by magic *D1411ff., D2072ff.; together sand and string Q512.2; waves of the sea (task) H1137. — Fairies b. man to ground F361.2.3; man b., marrying fairy F302.4.4; transformation by b. with string around neck D585; vow: not b. hair till enemy is conquered M122; witch's hair has power of b. G221.1.1.

Bindweed, origin of A2655.

Birch. — Disguise in b. bark K1821.9.1; magic b. tree D950.12; magic b. twig D953.2; origin of b. trees A2681.4; revenant with hat of b. E422.4.1; why b. is cursed A2776.1; why b. has white bark A2751.4.1.

Bird advises man to treat his lazy children as she does her young Z24.1.2; avenges caged mate Z52; -bear B44; betrays hiding-place of the Virgin B131.6; boasts of capturing the rabbit J2173.3; brings flower F982.4; call enables trickster to escape K648; calls as evil omen D1812.5.1.12.2; cares for blinded master B536.1; carries food from deserted child to starving parents S361; carries a grain of sand from a mountain, etc. (measure of eternity) H701.1; carries off magic horn D861.7.1; carries off magic ring D865.1; carries man across water B551.2; carries person to upper world *F62.1; carries off persons R13.3; carries off ring (lovers become separated) N352; catches fishes by imitating friend K756.3; with changing color B731.13; characteristics from flying contests A2254; as child's nurse; has new clothes made: flies away without paying K233.1; coloring as reward for obedience to deity A2221.6.1; controls off-springs' sex, appearance F987.1; council assigns coats to different birds B238.2; council assigns place and work to all B238.1; as creator A13.2; as creator's companion A33.2; as culture hero A522.2; deity A132.6; determines road to be taken B151.2; as devil's messenger G303.10.17; as domestic servant B292.2.2; feathers sink as hero dies E761.7.7; without feathers on tree without leaves (riddle) H764; feeds young to threatening fox K1788; with fiery beak B15.7.13; flies into large animal's ear and kills him L315.1; flies with man to safety B542.1; as god's ancestor A111.3.3; with gold head, silver wings B15.7.3, B101.1; grateful for being saved from serpent B364.4; grateful for release B375.3; grateful for rescue of its young B365.0.1; as guardian of primordial fire A1414.6; in the hand J321.1; has red spot on tail as reward for moving woman's organ A2229.6; heals man B511.5; helper on quest H1233.6.2; calls out the hours F989.3; of ill-omen B147.2.2; indicates election of king H171.2; indifferent to pain Z49.3; having injured man avoids reconciliation J15; with iron beak B15.7.13.1; kills snake attacking master's family B524.1.6; language B215.1; as magician B191.6; as messenger B291.1; gives milk B735; must bring orphan to king H901.0.2; nests on top of one in morning, of another in evening (riddle) H725.1; as ogre G353; overcareful about food killed by eagle J2183.3; overpowered by stepping on his shadow D2072.0.4; from paradise B39.1; paramour B614; pecks hole in sky-roof F56.2; plays timpan B297.1.1; pleads with bow for life F836.5; plucks another bird's feathers out K2382.1; prevents mother from killing babe B524.4; of prey catching quarry a good omen D1812.5.2.4; protruding from king's stomach J1842.3; puffs up until it dies J955.1.2; punished by being thrown into air K581.4; as reincarnated girl resumes original form E696.1; rejuvenates person B594.1; rescues man from sea B541.3; rests on person's shoulders B575.2; running before sun bears golden letters

B7.3; as sacrifice V12.4.11; scouts sent out from ark A1021.2; sent daily to tell of hero's condition (life token) E761.7.6; as shadow of god A195.3; gives shelter with wings B538.1; shows way by singing B151.2.0.3; with silver wings B101.1.1; sold as messenger K131.2; steals island B172.11; stepmother feeds young thorns S31.3; substituted for stone in throwing contest K18.3; as suitor B623ff.; without tail K402.2; with tail of fire B15.7.14; tears out feathers in grief F1041.21.6.2; sheds tears B736.1; tears restore sight D1505.5.1; thinks he must support sky J2273.1; trained to cling to trapped paramour K1574.1; transformed to animal D413; transformed to person D350ff.; is transformed youngest brother N733.4; of truth B131; shows way by dropping feathers every seven steps *B151.2.0.1; warns against adultery, killed J551.1.1; wedding B282ff.; whistling leads searcher B157.1; with magic wisdom B122ff. — Adventures from pursuing b. N792, N774; alleged oracular b. skin sold K114.2; angel in shape of b. V231.1; animal criticized by b.: nest destroyed B275.4; aquatic b. carries man across water B551.2; origin and nature of b. beak A2343ff.; book-satchel becomes b. D444.5; breath of b. withers B777; building a lodge of b. feathers in one night (task) H1104.1; cannibal b. as ogre G355; capture by hiding in artificial b. K754.3; capturing b. H1154.7; captured b. bargains for freedom M244.2; child follows b. and loses its mother N313; clever b. J1118; color of b. A2411.2ff.; conception from eating b. T511.5.4; counting feathers in b. (task) H1118; cow sold to b. J1852.1; origin of b. crests A2321ff.; cries of b. *A2426.2ff.; dead father returns as b. E327.5; daughter promised to monster as bride to secure b. she has asked for S228; dead wife returns in form of b. E322.4; deaf man with b. in tree X111.8; destructive b. killed, barn found full of gold B103.7.1; devil as b. G303.3.3.3ff.; disenchantment from b. (when queen milks own milk into bird's beak) D759.2, (by cutting off bill) D711.3; disguise as b. tender K1816.5.1; drink this wine which a b. took to nest (riddle) H806; magic b. dung D1026.1; dupe strikes at b. on child's head and kills child K946; dwarf with b. feet F451.2.2.2; nature of b. eggs A2391ff.; enmity between b. and lizard: latter muddies water A2494.16.4; magic b. entrails D1015.3.1; escape from lower world on b. F101.6.1; evil eye sets b. on fire D2061.2.1.1; red eye of b. cooks meat F989.2; fairy as b. *F234.1.15; fairies with b. feet *F231.2.1; man can transplant feather from one b. to another F668.3; origin of b. feathers *A2313ff.; forgotten fiancée remembered by b. D2006.1.7; fox persuades b. to show him how she acts in a storm K827.1; friendship between b. and crab A2493.27; ghost of b. E524; girl as b. visits lover D641.1.1; god rides b. A136.1.4; goldmaking b. B103.1.5; golden b. B102.1ff.; golden b. stolen from fairies F359.2; hearing b. cry good omen D1812.5.2.5; hills from flopping of primeval b. A961.1; identification by feather taken from hero transformed to b. H78.2; identification by hair dropped by b. H75.2; immortal b. B37; jealous husband kills b. which wife falsely says she has been listening to Q587; magic jewel carried off by b. D865; killing murderous b. H1161.1; king refuses to quarrel with b. J411.9.1; lazy woman sees how b. pecks hole in stone J1011; little b. as large bird's mate J1293.1; magic b. liver D859.4.2, D1015.4.1; lover as b. visits mistress D641.1; magic b. *B172ff.; magic b. head D1011.0.1, (produces treasure) B113.2; magic b. heart D859.4.1, *D1015.1.1; magic b. nest *D1292; magic horn carried off by b. D861.7.1; magic leaves turn white b. black D1337.2.1; magic object pointed out by b. D849.2; making many kinds of food from one small b. (task) H1022.6; man transformed to b. D150ff., G263.1.5; man waits for b. shot eight days ago F638.3; mankind from featherless b. sent from sky A1231.1; marksman shoots b. through eye F661.5.2; marriage to b. B601, (in human form) B652; marriage to person in b. form B642; mother b. searches for root entangling young D839.1; mouse, b., and sausage keep house together J512.7; murder discovered through knowledge of b. languages N271.4; the oldest b. A1904; one b. escapes as hunter bends his bow: other remains and is shot J641.1; prediction by b. that girl will have dead husband M353; princess catches rajah's golden b. N713.1; procuring b. out of season H1024.6; prophecy: b. to become king M369.4.1; prophetic b. B143ff.; pursuit of b. leads to ogre's house G402.1; quest for b. of truth H1331.1.1; quest for lost b. H1386.3; quest for marvelous b. H1331.1, (caused by sight of one of its feathers) H1213; quest for princess caused by sight of one of her hairs dropped by b. H1213.1; reincarnation as b. *E613ff.; reincarnation: boy to b. to boy E610.1.1; resuscitation by b. flying over dead E79.1.1; revenant as b. E423.3ff.; secret overheard by masking as b. G661.2; separable soul in b. E715.1; hero sewed up in animal hide so as to be carried to height by b. K1861.1; shepherd transformed to b. still calls sheep *A2261.1; sick queen under red satin carried off by b. N335.2.1; sky measured by b. A702.6; soul in form of b. E732ff.; soul leaves body as b. E722.1.4; speaking b. B211.3, (tells where treasure is buried) N537; speech magically recovered when certain b. is caught D2025.2; stealing eggs from under b. H1151.12; storm because of b. singing D2141.0.6; tabu to eat b. C221.1.2; tabu to kill sacred b. C92.1.6; tame b. and wild b. L451.1; tardy b. alone succeeds at b. convention L147.1; tears on sight of b. H14.1; theft of fire by b. A1415.2.1; thieving b. K366.2; fool thinks b. reflected in water is gold J1791.10; three teachings of b. *K604; three-headed b. B15.1.2.2.1; transformation to b. C962.2; treasure carried by b. to nest N527; treasure-producing b. killed B192.3; treasure-producing parts of b. B113ff.; twelve-legged b. B15.6.3.3.2; voices from eggs plot against b. mother J646.2; water b. takes dupe to sea K1042; well throws up b. bones F933.8; wind a b. dwelling in mountain-hole A1122.2; witch as domestic b. G211.3; witch as wild b. G211.4; woman bears b. T554.10; woman transformed into b. D11.2, Q551.3.2.2; years seem moments while man listens to song of b. D2011.1.

Bird's breath withers B777. — Chain tale: b. pea stuck Z41.6; eaten b.

head teaches animal languages *D1301.4; river in b. ears D915.2.1; spirit in b. form F401.3.7; trickster hides in tree, eats b. food K1971.1.1; talisman found in b. stomach N527.2; why b. head is large A2320.5.

Birds beat waters with wings to welcome saint B251.2.5; build canoe for master B572.2; call at canonical hours B252.2; captured by imitating their song K756.1; of Cirencester K2351.1; cling to sky in flood A2211.7; cursed M414.8.4; of different habits unfriendly J416.1; discuss the trap J655.1; drip blood at Judgment Day B259.5; drop quill for man's pen B159.1; drop stones on enemy D2163.5.1; get drunk A1427.0.1; exchange eggs A2247.4; enticed into bag K711.0.1; take back their feathers from ungrateful wolf Q597.2; fight, cause accidents Z49.6.1; fill sea with dirt, end flood A1028.2; set fire to besieged city K2351.1; flee from cuckoo J645.1; fly away with net K687; forced from nest by mother J65; frighten enemy's horses K2351.5.1; of the gods A155.3; hatched from broken eggs repaired by skillful tailor have red line around necks F662.1.1; hover over battlefield F989.14; indicate building site for church V111.3.1; indicate where town to be built B155.2.3; lament saint's departure B251.2.9; lift greyhound into air F982.1.1; lighting on heads cause men to kill one another K1082.3; made of iron in hell A671.2.11; magically called D2074.1.3; magically confined to roofless barn D2072.0.2.2.1; as messengers of the gods A165.2.2; mock ascetic B787; in net fly away with it K581.4.1; not to sing around goddess' home C481.1; furnish omens B147.2; in otherworld F167.1.2; in otherworld sing religious songs B251.3; perch on cow's ears B853; perch on saint B256.1.1; point out road to hero B563.2; of prey A2494.13.10.6; promised feast, led into trap K730.5; who aspire to blackbird's coat punished A2232.6; nest in saint's hand B256.1; save man from hunger by pitching themselves into his fire B531.5; as scouts B563.6; seeking richer lands are nearly all killed J513.1; serve saint B256.5.1; singing ceases at revelation B251.8.1; in snare fly out endlessly Z11.2; spit fire B742.2; swallow each other (lie) X1204.2; take part at saint's funeral B251.2.12; talk taught man K1068.1; tear ogre to pieces G512.9.2; throw their feathers to hero, he flies off B540.1; warn of enemy's approach B521.6; weep when man cuts self B303.1. — Abandoned person in woods comforted by b. S465; adventure from pursuing thieving b. N774.1; Alexander carried by two b. with meat held in front of them B552.1; allowing b. to nest in one's hair Q541.5; ambush betrayed by movement of b. J53; army of b. B268.5; banners appear like flock of b. K1872.5; boy eating raw b. G36.2.1; why certain b. may not drink out of river A2435.1.1; cow with two bags: one-legged and twelve-legged b. in them B15.7.9.1; creation of b. A1900ff.; cumulative tale: carpenter releases caught b. Z49.7; devastating b. B33; dwarfs resentful that mortals shoot at b. F451.4.4.1; earth supported on b. legs A844.10; eating food b. have pecked at forbidden C245; election of king of b. B236.1; extraordinary swarms of b. F989.16; fight between one-legged,

twelve-legged b. H619.5; fairy minstrel's b. sing accompaniment
F262.3.2; fairies become b. D624.2; flight of b. A2442.1; food of b.
A2435.4ff.; fool gives gifts to b. J1851.2; formerly b. talked A1101.2.3;
fruit transformed to b. D441.2.1; giant b. B872ff.; god cheats b. of
tamarind K499.6; grain trail eaten by b. R135.1; grains sorted by helpful b. H1091.2; haunts of b. A2433.4ff.; helpful b. *B450ff.; helpful b.
demand food B322.2; how b. began to lay eggs A2486.4; hunting b.
forbidden C841.2; island of b. F743.1; king of b. B242ff.; king brought
to sense of duty by feigned conversation of b. J816.1; kingdom of b.
B222; lies about b. X1250; magic b. cause hosts to sleep by shaking
wings B172.9; magic b. chained together B172.7; magic b. die when owner
is killed B192.0.1; magic b. keep falling off perch D1649.1.2; magic spell
causes b. to roost D1442.6.2; man looking at b. pulled into pool K832.6;
markings on b. *A2412.2ff.; men with beaks of b. F514.2; mythical b.
B30ff.; nests of b. A2431ff.; numskull tries to shake b. from tree
J1909.3; omens from flight of b. D1812.5.0.2; parliament of b. *B232;
resuscitation by cutting off b. heads E29.5; silver, gold, and diamond b.
B731.5; souls await Judgment as b. E751.2; tabu: b. feeding on hero's
land C566.2; tabu: listening to fluttering of b. after sunset C885.1;
tabu: swimming with b. C858; thorns planted to kill b. when they light
K959.5; trees with green b. hanging by claws F811.9; unusual migration
of b. as Doomsday sign A1002.2.4, A1091.4; war of b. and quadrupeds
B261; war between b. and reptiles B263.4; war between groups of b.
B263.5; warning b. B143.1ff.; why artist painted too few b. J1491;
why b. do not live in societies A2492.2; why b. are everywhere
A2434.1.1; wonderful b. guarded by monster G375.

Bird-beast B40ff.

Bird-heart. — Magic b. eaten unwittingly D859.4.1.

Bird-liver. — Magic b. eaten unwittingly D859.4.2.

Bird-men B50ff.

Birhors eat monkey, baboon flesh A1422.2.

Birnam wood comes to Dunsinane K1872.1.

Birnli will nit fallen Z41.

Birth of child with chain around neck: sign of royalty H71.7; of child
as cannibal G33; delayed by magic T574; of fated child retarded
M376.4; of gods A112; of magic object with hero *D857; of moon
from first couple A745.1; prevented until mother confesses slander
Q559.5.1; rites confer royalty P37; of saint predicted by miracles
V222.0.1; same day as conception T573.1; of strong man F611.1; of
sun from first couple A715; trees *T589.3. — Absurdities concerning
b. of animals J1533ff.; all sins since the b. of Christ J1743.1; conception and b. *T500ff.; culture hero incarnated through b. from virgin
A511.1.3; culture hero speaks before b. A511.1.2; curse given at b.
of child M412.1; curse: monstrous b. M437; origin of customs con-

nected with b. A1560ff.; diseases cured at holy man's b. D2161.6.3; extraordinary nature phenomena at b. of holy person F960.1; fairy predicts b. of child *F315; fairy presides at child's b. F312; false bride takes true bride's place at b. of child *K1911.1.2; fate decided before b. N121; giant immortal so long as he touches land of his b. D1854; god swallows his pregnant wife to prevent b. of son M376; king of fishes prophesies hero's b. B144.1; lovers mated before b. T22.1; mentioning land of person's b. forbidden C442; miraculous b. *T540ff.; monstrous b. (as punishment for girl's pride) *T550ff.; mother assists at b. (riddling answer) H583.4.1; hero has lain motionless since b. F583; offspring of fairy and mortal has long hair and beard at b. F305.3; old woman prophesies at child's b. M301.2.2; woman who has prevented b. of children casts no shadow Q552.9; preventing b. of enemies J622; prophecy: death at child's b. M341.1.7; prophecy: hero's b. at certain time, place M311.0.2; prophecies about b. M369.7; twins quarrel before b. A511.1.2.1; release from curse with b. of child M421; roads appear at hero's b. *F1099.2.1; simultaneous b. of predestined lovers T22.4; soul forgets everything at b. E705; soul received at b. E726.1; star indicates b. of holy person F961.2.1; new star for each b. E741.1.1.1; shooting star signifies a b. E741.1.2; supernatural b. of culture hero A511; tabu imposed at b. C901.2; no time, no b., no death in otherworld F172; b.-control punished *Q251; trees grow to honor hero's b. F979.11; weeping at child's b. P617; woman pretends has given b. to aid fugitive K522.1.1.

Births. — Monstrous b. from incest A1337.0.7; royal b. occur in special place P10.1.

Birth-rate. — Determination of relation between b. and death-rate A1322.

Birthday. — Pious die on their b. F1099.7.

Birthmark. — Dead man's hand touches b. and thus removes it E542.2; recognition by b. H51.1.

Birthmarks T563. — Test: guessing princess's b. *H525.

Birthright. — Father transfers b. from oldest son P233.11; older brother has b. P251.7; younger brother given elder's b. L41.

Biscayans put medicine into rice J2134.2.1.

Bishop absurdly given military mission J1536; disguised as priest K1826.5.1; exchanges places with prisoner W16; fond of lawsuits J552.2.1; forced to ordain ignorant priest U41; foretells saint's birth M364.7.3; and prince J1289.2; refuses to eat small fish as he did when abbot J703.2; struck for breaking the peace J1823.2; wishes all monks castrated X457.1. — Deaf b. and drunken priest X111.13; father wants grandchild to be b.: allows seduction K1398; four-footed b. J2283; girl falsely accuses b. K2111.6; ghosts attack b. who has suspended pious priest E243; greedy b. dies at peasant's death D1715.2; incognito princess travels as b. K1812.8.2; man magically made to believe himself b., archbishop, and pope D2031.5; nose of falsely accusing b. bitten off Q451.5.3; oil bursts forth as saint made b. V222.5; paralysis for scorning b. Q573.2; plowing as test for b. H1573.2.3; priest catches b. in incontinence J1211.1.1; princess disguised as b. to flee man T323.1; sham b. K1961.4; treacherous b. K2281.

Bishop's. — Bad associates cause b. death J45.2; numskull thinks the b. snoring is his death rattle J1833; peasant preaches about b. amour J1211.1; reptile leaps into unjust b. throat V229.2.11.1; symbolic interpretation of points on a b. hat H608.1.

Bison as child's nurse B535.0.1.1. — Creation of b. A1878; devastating b. B16.2.9; helpful b. B411.4.1.

Bitch eats wheat dough: origin of noblemen A165.6.1. — Ghosts cannot near spayed b. E439.6; woman transformed to b. *D141.1; weeping b. K1351.

Bitches transformed to women D341.1. — Magic b. B182.1.2; magic b. enchanted by fairy music B182.1.7; women transformed to b. B297.2.1.

Bite causes series of accidents Z49.6.2; of wild huntsman's dogs drives other dogs mad E501.15.6.3. — Amorous b. T467; charms as antidote for b. of snake D1515.1.1; cure for snake b. F959.5; death from b. of stone lion (prophecy fulfilled) M341.2.10; serpent's b. produces treasure B103.6.1; snake b. for broken tabu C992; snake b. test H1517; snake sucks poison from b. D2161.4.10.2.2; spider b. cured by Virgin Mary D2161.5.2.5.

Biting fingers to see if one is dreaming F1041.13; the foot K543; off corpse's finger for ring leads to cannibalism accusation N342.6; off of parent's nose by son on gallows Q586; off own tongue K825.3; off victim's tongue K825.1.1; metal in anger pulverizes it F639.10; relative instead of kissing K2021.2; on stone as toothache remedy K1015.1. — Chain tale: b. grain in half Z49.8; contest in b. a stone K63; corpse b. off woman's nose E259.1; dog alternately b. and caressing hares K2031; indentions on plants from b. A2732; magic air journey from b. an ear D2135.2; metaphor on b. the ear J2489.3; nut falls and prevents snake from b. man N652; paramour b..off mistress's nose S172.1; resuscitation by b. victim's bone E29.1; riddle on b. the ear H588.15; serpent b. a file J552.3; severed head b. earth F1096.3; sleeping in shoes to avoid b. insects J2102.1.

Bitten. — Animal characteristics: members b. off A2216ff.; god's head b. off A179.4; husband lets self be b. to death to save wife T211.1.2; punishment: being b. by animal Q453; woman b. by own watchdog K1651.

Bitter water drunk as chastity test H411.4.1; water grateful for being praised D1658.1.3. — Ape throws away nut because of b. hull J369.2; dupe induced to eat b. fruit K1043; impious man's head turns well water b. F933.4; sweet and b. fountain in otherworld garden F162.1.2.1; when sweet fails, try b. J1088; why tree has b. fruit A2771.8.

Bittern. — Creation of b. A1965; song of b. A2426.2.3, A2261.1.

Bitumen. — Ambergris made from b. eaten by fish F826.2.

Black beans, white soup J1291.1; berserk F610.3.2; birds B172.10; dog good omen D1812.5.2.10; dogs in wild hunt E501.4.1.5; Donald (name for devil) G303.2.4; dummy indicates banishment Z174.1.1; giant F531.1.7.3; god A123.7.2; is guard against Evil Eye D2071.1.4; horse in wild hunt E501.4.2.2; as magic color D1293.4; man becomes white D57.2; man *F527.5; man changes color by prayer V52.11; nipples reveal virginity loss T494; as raven, red as blood, white as snow Z65.1, T11.6; sheep turn white F985.1; spots on moon A751.9.1; as symbolic color Z143; tribe because woman put on fire A1614.8; and white horses chasing each other (riddle) H722.2; witch *G219.7. — Why b. bears are better eating than grizzly bears A2511.1; body turns b. from anger F1041.16.8; body turns lake b. F934.5; demons as b. birds F401.3.7.2; devil called "the b. one" G303.2.2; devil dressed in b. G303.5.1; devil has b. horses G303.7.1.1, G303.7.3.1, G303.17.2.9; devil as b. wench G303.3.1.12.3; devil's face b. G303.4.1.7.1; dwarf wears b. F451.2.7.9; why tip of ermine's tail is b. A2378.8.4; excommunication makes host turn b. V84.2; fairies b. F233.9; Fortuna half white, half b. N111.2.3; Frederick the Great drives dwarfs across B. Sea F451.9.1.13; ghost b. E422.2.4; the gray and the b. hairs J83; "have a b. look" J2489.7; hero in disguise of b. knight rescues lady R169.1; idol turns b. at unchaste woman H411.9.1; magic leaves turn white bird b. D1337.2.1; mirror becomes b. (life token) E761.4.3; negro so b. that he makes whole garden somber F573; numskull tries to wash b. hen white J1909.6; objects on one side of palisade in otherworld garden b., on other side white F162.1.2.3; pasturing b. sheep until they become white Q521.4; picture turns b. (life token) E761.4.2; planet in b. chariot pursues sun, moon A735.2; pot calls the kettle b. J1063; why raven is b. A2411.2.1.5, A2218.1; raven does not return to ark: b. color as punishment A2234.1.1; revenant b. E422.2.4; rivers of b. water in hell A671.2.2.4; silver object turns b. (life token) E761.4.5; soul as b. entity E722.1.2; soul as b. or white spirit over coffin E722.1.1; spirit as b. dog F401.3.3; spirit as small b. man F403.2.2.6; transformation to b. man D57.4; trolls b. F455.2.3; troops of b., white, and red soldiers F873.1; washing b. wool white H1023.6; white field, b. seed (riddle H741; white sheep comes to upper world, b. to lower F67; white woman bears b. child T562; why the b. clothes J1304; why center of eye is b. A1319.7; why ebony is b. A2751.4.2; why ebony tree has b. wood A2772.4; why sky is b. A702.8; why tip of weasel's tail is b. A2378.8.3; wild huntsmen dressed in b. E501.8.1; wild huntsman with b. fur cap and white staff E501.8.6; witch rides on b. cat G241.1.4.1.

Blackbeetle reproduces inside person B784.1.5.

Blackberries. — Why b. red when green J1291.1.1.

Blackbird avenges wife's capture K481.1; to be caught alive yearly C684.1; as creator A13.2.1; orders ants to burrow into elephant's brains B524.1.8. — Capturing b. yearly H1154.7.2; color of b. A2411.2.1.9; creation of b. A1924; devil in form of b. G303.3.3.3.3; giant b. B31.6.1; how the b. received its name A2571.1; man becomes b. D151.7.

Blackbird's wedding B282.11. — Birds who aspire to b. coat punished A2232.6.

Blackbirds destroy crops B33.1.3. — Quest for fat of water b. H1331.1.5; saint's bell rung against b. D1385.12.1.

Blackening. — Woman b. face as disguise K1821.7.1.

Blackmail of adulteress by lover K1582; of careless watchers K443.3. — Money acquired by b. K443; threat to tell of amorous intrigue used as b. K1271.1.

Blacksmith, see also **Smith;** chants Dante J981. — God as b. A142.0.1; origin of b. work A1447.2.

Blacksmith's and horse-trader's dreams J1622.

Blackthorn branch under cloak H527.

Blade of grass transformed to horse D451.5.1. — Witch in form of b. of straw G212.1.

Blades in food kill ogre G519.4; to wound and detect wife's lover K1565.

Blame for theft fastened on dupe K401. — Misfortune with oneself to b. the hardest U160; shifting b. to another J1166.

Blamed. — Devil always b. G303.9.3.4; devil b. by monk who takes what does not belong to him G303.25.10; evidence of crime left so that dupe is b. K2155; image b. for unwelcome answer given from behind image K1971.8; image b. by suppliant for misfortunes V123; object foolishly b. J1891.

Blaming supernatural wife forbidden C31.4.

Blandishments. — Resisting b. of leader's fiancée W34.1.

Blanket. — Child divides b. for cruel father's old age J121; embroidering b. in one day (task) H1093; ghost pulls b. off sleeper E544.2; resuscitation by magic b. E64.11; short b. must be patched J1179.3.

Blason populaire X681.

Blasphemer paralyzed except for tongue saying "Ave" V254.3.1; stricken dead Q558.4. —Knight fights b. J1164; man who has received sacrament overcomes b. V34.3; Satan as b. G303.9.8.11.

Blasphemer's. — Blood flows from b. mouth Q551.6.5.1.

Blasphemy prevents church bell's raising V115.1.3.2; punished Q221.3. — Dumbness punishment for b. Q451.3.4; phantom driver wanders for b. E512.

Blazing. — Devil disappears amid b. fire in river G303.17.2.4; god with b. eye A124.1; witch's b. eyes G213.4.

Bleaching. — Devil's grandmother b. (snow) *G303.11.4.2; fairies b. linen F271.4.1.

Bleating of goat frightens animals assembled for fight K2323.2. — Calf's b. as accusation J1895.

Bleeding animal exorcises witch G271.4.4; bone F991.2; from breaking tabu C949.4; heavens F961.0.6; image D1624; lance F991.1; rock F809.4; trees A2766, E631.0.4, F811.20; wood as Doomsday sign A1002.2.2, A1091.2; wounds do not deter hero H1507. — Absence of b. reveals witch G229.4.3, G259.3; corpse b. when murderer touches it D1318.5.2; cure by fall which causes b. N644; mouth b. as death omen J2311.1.2; murder by b. K923; opening own veins and b. to death Q427; stone b. before being skinned (task) H1023.10.1; stone b. before church plundered D1317.12.1.

Blemish tabu on king C563.2. — Foster parents fined for b. on child P270.1; reproach of b. punished Q284; secret b. revealed N465.0.1.

Blemished children born of monstrous parent T550.5. — Muddy bath for b. king J815.3.

Blessed plants A2777. — Animals b. for good services at crucifixion A2221.2ff.; animal b. for helping holy fugitive *A2221.5; animal b. for honoring infant Jesus *A2221.1; iron b. by saint incapable of wounding D1674; land of the b. F701.2; liquor b. by saint causes magic sleep D1364.7.1; paradise of the b. F111.4; plant b. for pious act A2711ff.; water b. by saint as love-philtre D1355.2.1; whomsoever demons curse is b. M493; why certain plants and trees are b. A2777.

Blessing not worth a penny J1261.4. — Barrenness removed by saint's b. D1925.4; brother secures b. due another K1988; child's b. fills countries with what they are famous for M393.1; curse magically changed to b. D2175.5; dead saint gives b. E367.2; devil's power avoided by b. G303.16.2.3; ghost laid by b. grave E443.1; disenchantment by b. D781.1; disguise as older brother to obtain b. K1839.11; fairy wounded by mortal is healed only by obtaining mortal's b. D2161.4.10.2.1; god b. mortal A182.3.3; god changes curse to b. M425; not b. mountains gives mountain-men power F460.4.6; big piece of cake with curse or small piece with b. J229.3, L222; saint's b. to descend from generation to generation M321.1; saint's b. renders man skillful F660.2; saint's b. makes stone oracular D1311.16.0.1; saint causes b. by druids D2076; transformation to obtain b. D659.5.

Blessings as hospitality reward Q45.1.1; as reward Q195. — Prince forfeits b. if he fails to claim throne P38.

Blest, Islands of the *A692.

Blighted garden magically restored D2195.

Blind ancestress guides hero to heaven A566.2; comforted by soul's inner eyes J893.1; and deaf cure each other by blows N642.1; dupe K333.1; fiancée betrays self K1984.5; giant F531.1.1.3, G121; girl marries lame man T125.2; god A128.1; lame, and deaf as witnesses in court X141; leading blind falls into pit J2133.9; man carries lame man N886; man who feels young wolf recognizes his savage nature

J33; man's exchange with devil G303.25.16.1; man's extraordinary
perception F655; man's magic sight D1820.1.1; man's robber detected
J1149.5; man carrying lame man treasure guardians N577; man
recovers treasure by deceiving thief K1667.1; man sees unborn rats
F642.3.3; man as soothsayer D1712.2; man steals from neighbor K306.4;
man and the bull X123; man's arrow aimed (Balder's death) K863,
(slain game stolen) K333.1; men duped into fighting K1681; men accidentally hurt each other N388; men's conclusions about elephant
J1761.10; poet unintentionally kills friend N337.1; poets P427.7.3;
promise M223; thief killed by rope slipping on withered date tree
K436; town X1503.2; villain K2273.1; wife, deaf husband happy T202;
wives bear children in pool T581.2.2; wildboar in wild hunt E501.4.3.2.
— Behavior of the b. U170; devil b. G303.4.1.2.7; flower visible only
to b. F814.5; Fortuna b. N111.2.1; how b. men get about J2387;
hunchback leads b. man N886.1; husband says that good food will
make him b. K1971.1; infant born b. drowns self T585.3; king goes b.
from overweeping F1041.3; lake bursts forth where b. king plucks
rushes A920.1.12; man fishes up two b. women from a well F1065;
man stricken b. as punishment Q559.2; men originally b. A1316.3.3;
princess rescued by b. man restores his sight R161.2; prophecy: unborn
child to be b. M355; rescuer impersonates captive and deceives b.
guardian while captive escapes R121.2; saint cures b. hyenas B384;
sham b. man throws suspicion on real b. K2165; theft from b. person
K333; thief robs b. miser: gives tenth to charity K2096.2; trading b.
horse K134.5; trickster gets coins from b. beggars K1081.1.1; why bee
is b. A2332.6.9; why certain animals are b. A2332.6; why leech is b.
A2332.6.8; wind is b. A1129.3; witch renders b. G263.4.5.

Blinded ogre G511; slave's revenge K1465; trickster directed by trees
*D1313.4. — Abandoned queen b. S438; artisan b. to prevent duplica-
tion S165.7; bird cares for b. master B536.1; greedy man magically b.
J514.3; man b. trying to heal girl N395.

Blindfolded emperor traveling to paradise J2326.3. — Drinkers cheat
b. bartender K233.2; husband b. by adulteress K1516.5; man washes
clothes b. F1017.

Blinding with dust, then robbing K2356.1; the guard *K621; by magic
D2062.2; by needles in eyes S165.3; opponent to win race K11.7; as
punishment Q451.7ff.; a witch (task) H1191. — Capture by b. K783;
choice between emasculation or b. J229.12; man b. brother S73.3;
mother b. son S12.4; murder by b. K957; son b. father S21.2.

Blindman's Buff. — Bear plays B. H1537.1.

Blindness in animals A2332.6ff.; cured by killing snake D2161.4.10.5;
magically cured D2161.3.1; miraculously cured F952; from sight of
holy person D2062.2.2. — Angel of b. A478.6; fairies cause b. F362.1;
how to cure snake of b.? H1292.4.2; husband feigns b. and avenges
himself on his wife and her paramour K1553; magic object causes b.

D1331.2ff.; magic object causes both supernatural sight and b. D1331.3; magic object cures b. *D1505ff.; magic b. as punishment remitted Q571; origin of b. A1339.1; saint cures b. V221.12; sight of wild hunt causes b. E501.18.7; vulture cures b. B511.5.1; water-spirits cause b. F420.5.2.11.

Blindworm has no eyes A2332.6.1, (borrowed by nightingale) A2241.5.
— Adder harmful to holy person transformed to b. *A2145.5.

Blink. — Why men b. A1316.2.

Blister on back from lying in rose leaves F647.9.

Block dressed as child, saves child from death K525.1.3.

Blocked. — Road b. by spirit F402.1.2.

Blocksberg (witch's sabbath) G243.

Blood of animal considered venomous B776.5; of certain animal said to be sweet A2236.1, K961.0.1; bath causes women to be carried off by bird N335.2; bath as leprosy cure F955.1; -brotherhood P312; and brains (escape by shamming death) K473, K522.1; of brother and sister refuses to mingle F1075; catches fire F964.3.2; of scourged Christ on certain spiders A2221.2.3; covenant M201.1; from cross on robin red-breast A2221.2.2; of dragon B11.2.13; on end of each hair F555.6; as evil omen D1812.5.1.1.1ff.; flowing from Jesus' image converts V331.1.1; flows from desecrated building Q222.0.2; flows from blasphemer's mouth Q551.6.5.1; indicates guilt or innocence *D1318.5ff.; as life token *E761.1ff.; as magic drink *D1041; as sacrifice V12.1; shed in battle pollutes D1563.2.2.1; smeared on innocent person brings accusation of murder K2155.1; stops flowing from wound E761.1.13; streams from angry warrior's head F1041.16.6.1; in spittle as test of subjection H252.2; sucking chafer B16.6.2; transformed to another object D457.1; transformed to animal D447.3; turns black D492.2; from wizard becomes red grain of cedar A2731.3. — Adhesion of b. (test of paternity) H486.1; all living things from Jesus' spattered b. A1724.3; animal's b. venomous B776.5ff.; bath of b. F872.3; bath of b. of beloved to cure love-sick empress T82; bath in b. of king as cure for mange D1502.5.1; betrothal by lovers' drinking each other's b. *T61.1; birds drip b. at Judgment Day B259.5; birth from b. T541.1; brother about to drink b. of seemingly guilty sister P253.1; brownie murders, catches b. in cap F363.2; carrying murdered man's b. (ordeal) H227; child sacrificed to provide b. for cure of friend S268; child's b. makes earth red A1277.3; Christian child killed to furnish b. for Jewish rite V361; church stone sheds b. Q222.0.1; cock's b. substituted for sacrificial human's K525.9; conception from b. T534; cry of b. of Abel A1344.1; curse: hero not to stand sight of b. M438.2; deception by sham b. *K1875; deep streams of b. flow during battle F1084.1; disease caused by menstrual b. A1337.0.4; disenchantment by drawing b. D712.4; disenchantment by drinking b. D712.4.1; "don't shed women's b." J21.2.5; dragon's b. B11.2.13; drawing witch's b. annuls her spells D1741.2; drawing b. renders witch powerless G273.6; drinking b. teaches animal languages

D1301.2; dwarfs have b. F451.3.5.4; earth created from b. of gods' victim A831.8; earth reddened with b. of human sacrifice A1241.4; enemy tricked into first spilling b. K2358; executioner substitutes animal's b. for victim's K512.1.1; fairies bathing in enemy's b. F259.2; flaming spear must be cooled in noxious b. D1645.8.1.1; flood from b. A1012.3; ghost as b. E422.1.11.5; ghost summoned by pouring b. of sacrifices into trench E382; girl's b. examined to see if she is pregnant T579.2; god with body of b. A123.1.6; gods have no b. A1399.2; ground defiled by menstrual b. C144; ground dries up when first woman's b. drips on it A856.2; hero to drink dying monster's b. M257; horse shall wade in b. at Armageddon A1080.1; horse weeps tears of b. B301.4.2; human b. accidentally tasted brings desire for human flesh G36.2; human b. makes leaky tanks waterproof S261.0.1; husband nourishes starving wife with his own flesh and b. T215.3; insect fries human b. to eat A2435.5.2; insects from b. of slain animal A2001.1; lake of b. F713.6; magic b. (human) *D1003, (of animal) *D1016, (healing) *D1500.1.7.3; magic lost with b. D1741.2; magic object stanches b. D1504ff.; magic power from shedding b. D1766.2.3; magic rod turns waters to b. D1549.9; maidens befoul selves with b. T327.4; man created from b. A1263.1; man created from game animal's b. A1263.1.2; man dies from drop of killed hound's b. Q582.4; man made from animal's b. A1241.4.1; man sweats b. and absorbs hair into head on exertion of strength F1041.10; man's b. made of water A1260.1.5; man sweats b. F1041.10; mandrake from b. of person hanged on gallows A2611.5; milk becomes b. D457.2, D476.2.3.1; moon turns to b. F961.3.1; ocean made from b. A922; ogre says he smells human b. G532; ogre sucks victim's finger and drinks all his b. G332.1; ogre with monstrous b. G367; origin of b. A1319.6; origin of serpent's b. A2367.3.1; pact with devil signed in b. M201.1.2, (sealed in b.) M218.1; person with remarkable b. F554; Pisācas drink b. and eat human flesh G312.1; plant from b. of slain person E631.0.3; quest to hell for b. of sorceress H1277; rain of b. F962.4; rain produced by spitting b. toward sky D2143.1.4; rakshasa can be defeated by hero who has rakshasi b. in veins G369.1.2; rakshasa's mistress lying in pool of b. G369.1.7; red as b., white as snow Z65.1; red sky from b. A1147.1; resuscitation by b. *E113; river of b. F715.2.1, (in hell) A671.2.2; river from b. of sick mortals F162.2.13; rose from b. of slain of War of Roses A2656.2; rue from drops of Christ's b. A2611.7; saint's tears of b. V229.2.6.1; secret escapes with man's b. N481; seed mixed with b. as love charm D1355.3.1; serpent sucks man's b. B16.5.1.2.1; snake from b. of slain monster A2145.1; soul (life) in b. E714.1; ghost bursts into spray of b. H175.5; springs from innocent king's b. A941.5.8; streams of b. magically drawn down on foe D2091.3; stars as moon's b. A764.2; streams of battle b. F1084.1; substitute specimen in b. test K1858.2; sun b. color F961.1.8; shower of b. F962.4; sun, moon animated by human b. sacrifice A714.8;

sun, moon vivified with b. A717.1; sun's children turn into b. in daytime A736.5.2; tabu: marriage with person whose b. one has drunk
C165; tears of b. F541.9; tears of b. as evil omen D1812.5.1.1.1; tears
of b. from excessive grief F1041.21.1; tears of b. as sign of royalty
H71.8; tests for noble b. H1574.1; toad sucks b. B766.3; transformation
by applying b. D595; treasure found by sprinkling ground with b.
of white cock D2101.1; tree from innocent man's b. E631.0.5; trees grow
from b. F979.12; using b. tabu C893; vampire sucks b. E251.3.3; waters
transformed to b. F930.4; well of b. F718.8; unwitting adultery with
wife of b.-brother N766; why gods accept only b. A153.6; why leech
feeds on human b. A2435.6.3; wife drinks b. of slain husband P214;
witch feeds animal familiar with her own b. G225.0.1; witch sucks b.
G262.1.

Blood-clot. — Birth from b. T541.1.1; man created from b. A1263.1.

Blood-oranges, origin of A2687.1.

Blood-test for inheritance J1176.3.

Bloodhounds decapitate victim B17.1.2.1.

Bloodstain ineradicable E422.1.11.5.1.

Bloodthirsty animal by trickery admitted to fold: kills peaceful animals
K828ff; revenants E250ff.

Bloody key as sign of disobedience C913; knife F1066.1. — Arrow shot
to heaven returns b. F1066; cows made to give b. milk D2083.2.1;
object becomes b. (life token) E761.1ff.; transformation: objects become b. D474.

Bloody Cap murders travelers F363.2.

Blooming staff *F971.1, H331.3; staff as chastity index H432.4. —
Animal horns b. bear man as fruit A1263.5; flower b. when touched
D2195.1; flowers b. in winter F971.5; garden b. in winter H352;
marriage dependent on cut branch b. M261.1.1; sexual promise dependent on garden's b. in winter M261.1; tree b. nightly F811.13;
tree b. out of season D2145.2.2.2.

Blossom, see also **Flower;** *D975.

Blossoms, singing F979.21.

Blossoming staff *F971.1. — Miraculous b. and bearing of fruit F971;
trees magically b. D2157.3.

Blotches on face punish satirist Q265.2.1. — Magic poem raises facial
b. D1403.1; successful suitor to be without b. H312.1.

Blow on the ears J2494, K2376; at end of year (labor contract) F613.1;
recalls memory of mother's milk Z61.4; from spirit causes paralysis
E265.1.1; of staff brings water from rock *D1567.6. — Accepting b.
in face to show patience H1553.4; first b. must kill C742.1; giant's b.
makes cleft in rock F531.6.6.4; not flinching under b. (test) H1561.3;
insane man accidentally cured by b. on head N642; mountain opens at
b. of divining rod D1552.1; second b. resuscitates *E11.1; seven at

a b. (boast) K1951.1; value of a b. J1193.2; villain killed by b. intended for victim Q581.2; vow not to give more than one b. M166.1.

Blows aimed at others strike donors D2184.1; shared K187. — Chapel endowed with b. for friar X454; dog receives b. K2171; giant b. to prevent approach of ship F531.3.1.4; Peter receives the b. twice K1132; three b. for every one given J2213.2.

Blower slows down princess in race H331.5.1.1.1; turns mill F622. — Lie: remarkable b. X935.

Blowing contest won by deception K26; the house in Z81; magic into ears D1721.3; mountain away by magic D2152.3; serpent B743. — Devil b. skin off man G303.18.3; disenchantment by b. on victim D778; elf-knight produces love-longing by b. on horn F301.2.1; ghosts b. smithy into air E279.7; lion b. life into cubs B751.4; person b. poison on another is himself poisoned K1613.1; resuscitation by b. trumpet E55.3; resuscitation of cremated man by b. on the ashes E66.1; transformation by b. D588; wild huntsman b. horn E501.15.1; wind raised by b. into tobacco pipe D2142.1.6.1; witch keeps winds from b. G283.2.

Blubber. — Tabu to eat b. C221.3.4.

Blue beard F545.1.1; dogs and cats B731.6.2; -eyed horse H1331.4.1; fortunate in love matters T3.1; lights follow witches G229.7; man F527.3; ox: lie X1237.2; red, yellow horses in fairyland F241.1.1.3; snow X1653.2; as symbolic color Z144.1; teeth F544.3.3; tooth identifies man H79.8. — Devil dressed in b. clothes G303.5.4; fairies in b. clothes F236.1.2; half-red, half-b. man F527.6; magic b. ribbon D1078.1; magic b. stone D1382.12; one eye brown, other b. F541.6.1; transformation: stone to b. man D432.1.1; water-spirits dressed in b. F420.1.6.6.5; why sea is b. A1119.1; why sky is b. A702.4.

Bluebeard S62.1.

Bluebell as model for church bell A1466.1.

Bluebirds. — Why b. are everywhere A2434.1.2.

"Bluecap" mining spirit F456.2.

Bluejay as culture hero A522.2.1. — Flight of b. A2442.2.4.

Bluffing frightens owner away from goods K335.0.4. — Deception through b. *K1700—K1799.

Blunt — Chopping down large tree with b. instrument (task) H1115.

Blushing. — Women b. in presence of male statue F647.4.

Bo-tree, sacred V1.7.1.4.

Boar as confederate of adulterous wife B598.1; with golden bristles B101.2.1; guards holy man's swine B256.6.1; licks holy man's wounds B256.6.3; makes music for holy man B256.6.2; with nine tusks in each jaw B15.7.8; refuses to fight with lowly ass J411.1; sings song B211.1.4.1; in spider's web F989.18; in wild hunt E501.4.3; wins duel with tiger K97.1. — Capturing, binding b. (task) H1154.3.3; cuckold's knife cannot carve head of b. H425.1; dupe tricked into measuring b. with poisoned bristles K898; earth made of mud shaken off primeval b. A822; enmity of tiger and b. A2494.10.2; fairy in form of wild b. F234.1.3; falcon and heron eaten by wild b. recovered alive from his body X1723.2; ferocious b. fed and put to sleep by rubbing K836; giant b. B871.1.2; giant devastating b. B16.1.4.1; great wild b. X1233.1.2; helpful b. B414.1; hero accidentally wounded by wild b. N337.2; lion and wild b. make peace J218.1; magic b. B184.3.1; magic b. slain F98.1.8; man rides b. F989.4; man transformed to b. D114.3.2; origin of wild b. A1871.1; prophecy: hunters will encounter b. M397; quest for marvelous b. H1331.2; reincarnation as wild b. E611.3.1; self-luminous artificial b. D1645.7; singing b. B214.1.2; slaying thieving b. H335.3.3; venomous b. B776.4.2; vow to kill wild b. alone at night M155.1; why tiger does not attack wild b. A2257.1; wild b. hunted by man, once faithless wife A1422.3; wild b. as ogre G352.2; wild b. obeys saint D2156.4; yoking together lion and wild b. (task) H1149.1.

Boars. — Army of b. B268.12; king of b. B241.2.12.

Boar's bristles remarkably long X1233.1.1. — Cobold from b. testicle F481.0.1.1; earth supported on b. tusk A844.9; inexhaustible b. flesh D1652.1.9.1.1; obtaining wild b. lard H1154.11; wild b. haunt tabu C619.2.

Boards from forest endure forever F812.7. — Coffin-making b. announce death D1322.1.2.

Boast of bird about capturing the rabbit J2173.3; forces warriors to face enemy H945.1. — Foolish b. of ancestry by lowly J954; freedom abridged till b. confirmed Q433.12; king overhears girl's b. as to what she should do as queen N455.4; king's b. about wife brings about death T295; overheard b. about hidden money brings about robbery N455.1; pardon given if hero produces the lady about whom he has made b. M55; poor boy's b. concerning fate made good N234; quest assigned because of hero's b. H1215; tasks assigned because of b. H915.1; tasks imposed because of wife's foolish b. H916.1.

Boasts. — Foolish b. bring trouble J2353.1; ogre overawed by hero's b. about marvelous relatives K1718.

Boaster hurls back flung stone H1562.5; of victory over a weaker person reprimanded J978.

Boastfulness W117.

Boasting after danger over J2626; coward J2631, K1837.1, K1951.4; flykiller K1951.1; forbidden *C450ff.; at home safe J552.6; numskull in unimportant post J2331; of sexual prowess P665; of supernatural wife forbidden *C31.5; woman casts ring into sea L412.1. — Sham warrior intimidates soldiers with his b. K1951.3; son to be killed for b. S327.1; tasks assigned because of mother's foolish b. H914.

Boat, see also **Ship;** F624.7; drawn by swans B558.1; expected to grow into ship J2212.7; journey to otherworld F157; to land of dead *E481.2.2; to lower world F93.0.1; lured to land, wrecked in vengeance K815.12; made invisible D1982.5; race as suitor test H331.5.4; stopped by magic D2072.0.3; of the sun A723; gets tired J1884; towed by dog B541.4.1; transforms self at will of master D632. — Angel carries b. to water V232.2.0.1; child abandoned in b. rescued R131.15; crocodile as b. R245.1; cut-throat terrorizes b. passengers N695; dead drag b. to strand E543; dead placed on b. V61.1; deity departs in b. A192.2.2; disembarking from b. from other world C524; dupe makes b. of mud J2171.1.3; embarkation in leaky b. Q466; escape from deluge in b. A1021; escape by rowing b. stern foremost K534.4; exposure in b. *S141; exposure in b. as sin test H263.1; extraordinary b. *F841ff.; fairy b. F242.2; fairy harper in bronze b. F262.3.1.3; father abandoning children in b. S141.2; fools make b. go over precipice J2129.1; future hero found in b. L111.2.1; giantess almost sinks b. F531.2.13; giant's stone b. F531.4.8; girl enticed into b., abducted R12.4; girl with treasure in b. N572.3; hedgehog and crab jump from b. after turtle J2133.11; hero arrives in b. A513.2; hole in b. to let water out J2119.4; journey to otherworld in crystal b. F157.1; leaf as b. D1524.8; looking at certain b. forbidden C315.1; luminous b. of witches G222.2; magic b. *D1121ff.; magic b. to fairyland F213.1; magic b. keeps thief at sea Q559.10; magic sod as b. D1524.7; magic stone serves as b. D1524.3; making b. from splinters of a spindle and shuttle (task) H1022.7; man builds b. and sails about in giant's belly F911.5.1; man transformed to b. D255; man's long legs steady b. F517.0.2.1; many-oared b. mistaken for animal J1772.14; marking place on b. J1922.1; mermaid asks b. blocking her dwelling be moved B81.13.1; mouse sails in b. of bread-crust *B295.1; ogre tars hero's b. J2171.1.2; quenching burning b. J2162.3; rapid b.-builder F671.1; river-god stops b. for sacrifice S263.4; rowing contest in sawed b. K14; rowing in b. which is tied up J2164.2; sailing in leaky b. without sinking D2121.13; saint changes course of b. in answer to prayer T321.6; seduction by enticing aboard b. to inspect wares K1332; self-sacrifice to save b. S264.1.2; selling soul for b. sailing in sky M211.6; shell transformed to b. D452.2.1; skillful tailor sews together scattered planks of capsizing b. F662.2; strong man breaks b. F614.4; strong man as rower: rows one side of b. against many people at other F614.4.1; strong man tears b. apart with hands F639.6; tabu: disembarking from b. C524; tabu: grumbling at narrowness of certain b. C881.1; tabu: pointing b. towards god's island C51.9; vow to recover loose b. or go to hell Q221.4.2; winged serpent as b. (passengers within) F911.3.2.

Boats, see also **Ships;** of skin unsuccessful C841.0.1. — Bridge of b. F842.2.3.1; ghost sets b. adrift E299.5; holes bored in enemies' b. prevent pursuit K636; lies about b. with light draft X1781.

Boat-building. — Origin of b. A1445.1; shortsightedness in b. J2171.1.

Boatman ignorant of bookman's work J251.1. — Transformation to b. D23.1.

Body, see also **Corpse;** dismembered so soul cannot return E721.1.2.3.1; of dwarf F451.2.1ff.; of fairy F232ff.; of living corpse E422.1ff.; magically saved from corruption after death D2167; thrown in lake turns water black F934.5. — Animal with b. of horse, legs of hound B14.2; animal guards master's dead b. F576.4; animals distribute parts of man's b. in accordance with prophecy F989.10; animals from different parts of b. of slain giant *A1724; animal gives part of b. as talisman *B501; animals from transformed parts of b. A1724; child born without b. T550.7; child removed from b. of dead mother T584.2; concealment in another's b. *F1034ff.; cynic asks b. be exposed J1442.4.1; dead b. incorruptible E182; dead b. not to be moved E411.0.3.1; debate of b. and soul E727; devil enters b. of another G303.18; devil can touch b., not soul G303.25.18; exchanging parts of own b. for food M225.1; fairy women take b. of dead hero to fairyland F323; flood from b. fluids A1012; food from b. of slain food-goddess A1420.1; ghost carries man with half a b. E261.1.3; ghost carries own dead b. E592.1; gods born from various parts of creator's b. A112.3; headless b. sings D1615.8; headless b. vital E783.6; insects from b. of slain monster *A2001; interred b. of saint performs miracles K1685; lover's b. kept embalmed for years by grieving mistress T85.4; lucky marks on b. N135.4; magic b. of water *D910ff.; magic passes from b. to b. D1751; magic object speaks from inside person's b. *D1619.2; man made from creator's b. A1211ff.; man's b. of clay A1260.1.5; minerals from b. of dead culture hero A978.1; mountains from part of deity's b. A962.1; one animal jumps through b. of another F916; origin of animal's b. A2300ff.; origin of fire: found in person's own b. A1414.2; own b. as stake N2.1; parts of b. as hiding place F1034.3ff.; parts of human b. furnish treasure D1454; person enters animal's b. X1723.3; person with flat b. F525.4; person with mouths all over b. F513.0.2; person with transparent b. F529.5; plants from b. of slain person or animal A2611ff.; power of mind over b. U240ff.; relation of b. to soul E727; saint's b. remains unspoiled in earth V229.2.8; scalding mush scatters on heroine's naked b. H1503; self-returning b. D1602.12.1; soul cannot enter heaven till b. buried E750.0.1; soul in form of heavenly b. E741; soul kept in special part of b. E714ff.; soul leaves b. at death E722ff.; soul leaves or enters the b. E720ff.; soul as replica of b. E747.1; soul of witch leaves b. *G229.1; speaking from swallower's b. F915; taking a stick from the b. (task) H1021.7; two wives each claim part of husband's b. T145.4; universe from b. of slain giant A642; universe from parts of creator's b. A614; wife refuses to give up husband's dead b. T211.4.2.1; witch carries her children in her own b. G229.2; witch's b. injured while witch is away G275.14; woman's b. used as still F891.1.

Body's. — River rises to prevent b. passage across F932.8.1.

Bodies of victims in front of ogre's house G691. — Animal with one head, two b., six legs B15.7.11; artificial heavenly b. F793; cannibals cut off parts of children's b. G86; demons without b. G302.4.3; devil appears to girl who prays over pit where she has thrown the b. of her babies G303.6.2.7; extraordinary behavior of heavenly b. F961;

extraordinary b. of water F710ff.; giants with shaggy hair on b. F531.1.6.3; goddess with three b. A123.1.7; magic object controls heavenly b. D1546; rakshasas have power of extending b. eighty miles G369.1.1; sun, moon as divine b. of gods A718.2; two persons with b. joined F523.

Body-dirt. — Animals from b. of deity A1725.2; girl's b. golden F521.3.3.1.

Bodily members as advisers D1312.1. — Animal pressed: hence b. marks A2213.2; arrangement of man's b. attributes A1310ff.; curse: b. injury M431; fanciful b. members of animal *B720ff.; lie: persons with remarkable b. parts X916; magic b. members *D990ff., (animal) *D1010ff.; magic object restores b. members D1518; professions according to b. appearance A1650.3.2; recognition by b. marks or physical attributes H50ff.; vital b. members E780ff.

Bog becomes flowery mead D479.1. — Saint's journey over b. D2125.0.2.

Bogey imitates mother, kills child K2011.1.2.

Boil transferred to a post D2161.4.2.1; on youth for keeping a secret F1041.9.2.1.

Boils. — Magic object cures b. D1502.8.

Boiled. — Numskull feeds hens hot water so they will lay b. eggs J1901.2; pig can be b. only after true stories H251.3.11; suit for chickens produced from b. eggs J1191.2; hatching b. eggs (task) H1023.1; unchaste woman's skin b. away H411.11.1.

Boiling blood as life token E761.1.5; to death in pitch or oil S112.1; horse's heart releases curse M429.2; liquid as life token E761.6.3; lover's hair fetches him D1355.3.5; oil doesn't harm compassionate woman Q151.12; in oil as punishment Q414.1; pot seen as threat, broken J1813.10; of river from magic trousers D1549.3.3; those which come and go (beans rising and falling in water) H583.6; water for master's bath K1462.1; water meant for hero, used on man preparing it K1626.3; water to wash in J2465.4.1. — Bath of b. oil F872.2; bathing in b. water H328.5; bathing in b. water without cooling it H1023.24; beautification by b. and resuscitation *D1865.2; cool and b. fountain in otherworld garden F162.1.2.2; escape by bathing guard in b. water K629.1; escape from b. oil R215.2; man proof against b. water D1841.2; murder by b. victim's gloves D2061.2.2.5.1; oath on b. oil H412.4.2; ogress falls into b. spring G519.1.4; ordeal by b. water H221.4; rejuvenation by b. D1885; resuscitation by b. *E15.1; ring makes b. water cold D1566.2.5; river b. F932.7; saint unhurt by b. water D1841.2.1; water b. when angry warrior immersed F1041.16.6.6; water not b. until fish returned to well V134.3; witch drinks b. oil G525.1; witch keeps water from b. D2137.1; witches b. wizardry cauldron G249.5.

Boldness of the blind U170ff.; of dogs K2524.6; punished Q333.

Bole. — Swine shaking tree b. H1199.6.

Bolster. — Waiting for thief to return b. J2214.3.2.

Bolt from heaven kills animal F981.4.

Bolts. — Three b. left on hell by Christ V211.7.3.

Bombax. — Why b. tree has thorns A2752.1.

Bon mot. — King rewards scullion for b. Q91.2.

Bonbons. — Inexhaustible vase of b. D1652.5.5.

Bond woman girded with rope P171.2. — Debt with worthless b. repudiated K231.5.

Bonds cannot be loosed save by man who fettered them D1651.9. — Abandonment in b. S148.

Bondmaid. — Man weds his b. T121.6.

Bondo women not to wear clothes C181.6.

Bone of man jumps from fire E15.0.1; transformed to dog D447.8; transformed to other object D457.12; transforms self to person D437.1; in wolf's throat removed from crane W154.3. — Accidental death from flying splinter of b. N335.4; alleged resuscitating b. sold K113.1; animal grateful for removal of b. lodged in its throat B382; animal with head of b. B15.1.3, cannibal crunching human b. says noise is only eating of peas G87; captive sticks out b. instead of finger to cannibal G82.1.1; conception from smelling b. dust T532.1.4.1; death from fish b. in throat N339.12, F363.1; giant with enormous b. weapon F531.4.5.3; gnawed b. as weapon F839.1; human b. in demon's stomach becomes boy E149.1; magic b. (of animal) *D1013, (human) *D1007; magic object heals broken b. D1518.4; man created from animal b. A1263.7; prophecy: death by means of b. M341.2.14; resuscitation by biting victim's b. E29.1; return from dead to punish theft of b. from grave E235.4.3; swallowed b. causes woman to appear dead N694.1; swelling b. as forgiveness sign F991.2.1; vivification by hitting with b. D1594.0.2; witch b. G224.11, D1442.8.

Bones of dead collected and buried E607.1; of dead thrown into river E607.1.1; of birds constantly thrown up from well F933.8; wrapped in holy sheepskin revive E174. — Animal born from b. B716; animal characteristics: b. A2367.1ff.; bird with magic b. and feathers *B172.4; breaking b. of eaten animal forbidden C221.3.2; bringing quantity of mosquito b. H1022.9; climbers temporarily remove b. F1054; devil leaves sinner's body, only b. remain G303.18.0.1; disenchantment by assembling b. D717; dwarfs from giant's b., blood F451.1.1.1; earth created from b. of gods' victim A831.8; fish b. mistaken for peas J1772.6; in fish division dupe gets b. K171.6; game with ancestor's b. P203; ghost takes b. from grave E593.4; ghost's b. brought home from foreign soil E459.2; goddess scatters pubic hairs on fish: why he has so many b. A2211.15; heroes born from swallowed b. A511.1.4.3; house of b. F163.3.2.2; house-spirit without b. F480.5; insects from b. of slain animal A2001.1; jinns without arm b. F499.3.1; king's b. sent back so people will know of their freedom M14; ladder of b. up slippery mountain F848.3; lost husband's b. found among cannibals G691.4; man's b. made of stone A1260.1.5; mankind from b. of dead brought from underworld A1232.1; modest choice of parting gift: b. instead of meat L222.2; mountains from b. of slain giant A961.5; mosquitoes from b. of slain demon A2034.2; person reduced to pile of b. D2061.1.1.1; pillars of dead chief's b. A151.4.4; planting b. to produce young J1932.4.2; prophecy: miraculous removal of saint's b. M364.8; puppies' b. as evidence woman ate own child K2116.1.1.1.1; rejuvenation by burning and throwing b. into tub of milk D1886.1; relic b. jump away from flame V140.4; resuscitation by rubbing b. on ground E29.2; saint's b. for lack of worship remove themselves from church V143; sex tabu broken: child born without b. C101; singing b. reveal the crime *E632ff.; son recovers father's b. R154.2.2; sorcerers use marrow of corpses' b. D1278.2; stepmother feeds children fish b. S31.4; strong man breaks man's b. F614.6.1; tabu to lie on ancestors' b. C541.4; tabu: touching b. of murdered person C541.3; talking b. advise hero E366.3; vessel of human b. F881.2; vision of dry b. V515.1.5; when devil leaves dead sinner's body, only b. remain G303.18.0.1; why animal b. sacrificed A1545.6; woman exchanges a horse for a sack of b. J2099.1.

Bone-powder changed into cheese D476.1.10.

Boneless man turned over to produce seasons A1152; person F529.7. — Swallowed person becomes b. F921.1.

Bonga, see also **Fairies;** F201, F365.4; girl as flame F234.3.2; house full of animals F221.2; lends dishes to mortals F343.6; lives in tree F216.2; made village headman F347.1; mistress F302.0.1; pegged to ground, placed under stone F386.3; returns stolen goods for man F302.3.1.1.

Bonga's namesake first daughter F302.5.1.1.

Bonito. — Origin of b. A2122.

Bonnet. — Ghost with pulled-down b. E422.4.2.

Boo. — Tale-teller yells "b." Z13.1.

Book brought back from fairyland F379.2.1; dropped in water by saint not wet F930.1; of fate N115; magically preserved D2167.2; by marvelous memoried man D1910.0.1. — Account b. of dead E481.8.1; alleged idol to pay for b. K1971.13; angel dictates b. V246.0.2; author of b. against heretic honored by Virgin Mary and angels V327; carrying saint's b. insures victory D1381.25; cow swallows b.: cause of maniplies in stomach A2219.2; devil exorcised with b. G303.16.14.4; divination from sacred b. D1311.14; extraordinary b. F883.1; fools praise b. so author finds it stupid J1714.4; ghost steals b. from priest E593.2; illiterate's sham weeping over b. K1795; magic b. *D1266, (conjured away by throwing it on stream) D2176.4, (furnishes wealth) D1469.6, (removes itself) D1641.11.1; man believes himself wise because he owns b. J2238; mountain men give children a b. F460.4.2.4; murder with poisoned b. S111.5; oath taken on sacred b. M114.1; otter recovers lost b. from water B548.3; prophecy from b. M302.8; reading from b. makes fallen tree stand D1571.3; sacred b. does not burn D1841.3.3; spring breaks forth where animal delivers b. left behind by saint A941.5.4; unique ability to read magic b. H31.7.2; value of b. depends on appreciation of it J1061.5.

Books in church read without man's tongue F1055; sorrow for owner, fall from shelf F994.1. — Curse makes b. illegible D2089.5; devils two b. for noting sins G303.24.1.9; divine inspiration of sacred b. D1811.2.1; good, bad in all b. J174; magic dew destroys b. D1599.6; many b. do not make a scholar U111; origin of medical b. A1487.2; origin of worship from holy b. A1546.5; recognition through b. H134; sacred b. received from Buddha in person V212.1; saint curses hidden b. M411.8.5; sanctity of b. tested in fire H221.1.3, (in water) H222.4; sham wise man burns up b. K1956.8; sorcerer and b. in mountain F721.2.3; Sibylline b. J166.1; wisdom from b. J166; witches' power from b. G224.3; youth tricks mother by carrying many b. U111.1.

Book-satchel transformed to bird D444.5.

Bookholder. — Deer's horns as saint's b. B256.3.

Bookkeeper. — Cheating b. excused: gave money to poor V416.1.

Boomerang. — Arrow as b. F661.11; saint causes missiles to b. D1093.1.

Boon granted, son released from prison R123. — Any b. desired J1593; ingeniously worded b. asked of God K2371.3; reward: any b. that may be asked Q115.

Boorish. — Fairy's b. clothes F236.5.

Boot mistaken for axe-sheath J1772.11.

Boots sent by telegraph J1935.1. — Catching fish in b. while wading X1112; detection for theft of bull escaped by putting b. on the bull *K412; judge's bad-luck b. N136; large supply of b. for journey H1231; lie: remarkable b. X1021.1; magic b. *D1065.1ff.; magic b. render invisible D1361.38; Puss in B. B582.1.1; shoemaker's apprentice greases b. as he would grease a fowl J1631; seven-league b. D1521.1; taking off undesired lover's b. K1227.4; thief undetected cuts soles off b. F676.2; trickster cheats pair of b. from two cobblers K233.3; water enters into giant's b. from above F531.3.1.1.

Booty. — Clever thief, having seen his victim in a disgraceful position, may keep b. J1211.2; dupe loses b. through singing J2351.3; effects of wild hunt remedied by asking to partake in b. of hunt E501.19.4; king gets first choice of b. P13.9.1; lion divides the b. J811.1.1; thief hoping for bigger b., loses smaller K421.1; wolf as commander orders all b. divided, but keeps his own U37.

Boring as animal's occupation A2456; hot irons through ears Q469.9; way out of prison R221.2. — Flood from animal's b. into ground A1016.1.

Border. — Inn at b. of otherworld F147.4; wood at b. of otherworld F143.

Born, see also **Birth.** — Beings b. in hell A671.6; child b. too soon J1276; children b. on same night betrothed T61.5; divination as to which son to be b. first D1812.5.0.17; earth b. of chaos A801; eldest god b. in front, younger at back A161.5; friends b. at same moment P311.4; hero b. three times A511.1.7; prophecy: child to be b. M311.0.3; vow to marry one b. under same circumstances M146.2; what not yet b., given life? H832.

Borrowed bread (that we ate last week) H583.4.2; feathers *K1041; horse deceptively wins tournament K28. — Comb b. by fairy from Christian maid to comb hair of changeling bride F322.1.1; dwarfs return b. goods F451.5.10.4; eyes b. by animal *E781.3; money b. from fairies F358; object b. for a day retained K2314.1; stomach b. by animal E787; witness claims the b. coat: discredited J1151.2.

Borrower's absurdities J1531; and lender's (practical retorts) J1550ff.

Borrowing friend's money, coat to teach lesson J21.38; money from fairy F342.2; from mortals by dwarfs F451.5.10.3; from mortals by fairies F391; from peasant by mountain-men F460.4.5. — Animal characteristics: b. and not returning A2241ff.; chain b. brings huge amount on little credit K455.10; girl b. from fairies, abducted F324.1; lover's gift regained: b. from the husband and returning to the wife K1581.3; spirits b. from mortals F417.1; trolls' b. F455.6.2.

Bosom. — Conception from putting ball into b. T532.6; giant carries man in his b. F531.5.1.1; mother's b. (softest) H652.2.

Both? K1354.1, K437.

Bottle becomes gold D475.1.14; hidden in thigh F1034.3.2. — Alleged inexhaustible b. sold K117; burying b. prevents witch's urinating G271.4.7; coin noisy in empty b. J262.2; complaint about the empty b. K455.6; creator distributes b. A1440.1; death enclosed in a b. Z111.1; deception into b. (vessel) K717; demon enclosed in b. *D2177.1, (released) R181; filling water-b. with spout downward H1023.2.2; ghost corked up in b. E464; jinn escapes b. to kill captor J339.17; magic b. *D1171.8, (supplies drink) D1472.1.17; opening b. tabu C625; saint throws ink b. at devil D2176.3.3.3; soul hidden in water b. E712.7; spirit as fly going into b. F401.3.4; spirit in b. as helper F403.2.2.4; stopped b. as protection against witches G272.10; ten serving-women carried in b. D55.2.4; test of strength: breaking heavy b. over a loaf of rye bread H1562.3; thief hides in b. K439.11.

Bottlefly finds stolen woman in sky B543.1.

Bottom. — Earth brought up from b. of primeval water A811, A812; quest for the b. of the sea H1371.2.

Bottomless lakes (pools) H713.2; tub magically holds water D2199.1. — Filling b. water tube H1023.2.4; filling leaky vessel with water from a b. jar Q512.1.

Bough does not burn F979.5. — Fire bends b. to shape of crozier F964.1; magic b. *D954.

Boughs. — Tree grateful for having b. trimmed D1658.1.5.1; twelve cypresses with thirty b. each (riddle) H721.3.

Bought, see also **Buying;** game used to prove hunting prowess K1968.1. — Admission to woman's room b. T45; child b. to serve as sacrifice to demon S273; chest containing hidden paramour b. by trickster as sham-magician K1574; good counsels b. *J163.4; dream of treasure b. N531.3;

eyes b. back and replaced *E781.2; flower (enchanted girl) b. from her mother by prince T52.1; place in husband's bed b. by forgotten fiancée D2006.1.4; woman's hair b. by devil G303.25.13.

Boulder. — Ogress pegged to b. G514.5.1; strong man lifts mighty b. F624.2.

Bound, see also **Binding.** — Devil b. with chain A1070ff., G303.8.4.1; life b. up with light *E765.1; pestilence spirit b. by magic F493.3.2; thief b. as family god K439.8; vow against being b. M166.2; witch b. and beaten G275.7.

Boundary. — Dead returns to replace b. marks he has removed E345.1.

Boundaries, god of A414; of the otherworld F140ff.; spirit of F494.2. — Elephant draws plow to mark empire's b. B599.3; origin of b. A997; origin of erection of monuments to mark b. A1599.2.

Bouquet. — Flower b. leads to brothers' recognition H16.3; love through seeing b. T11.4.3.1; quest for b. of all flowers (bee-hive) H1377.2; quest for the most beautiful b. H1302.

Bovine, see also **Cow.** — Transformation: b. animal to person D314.1; transformation: man to b. animal D114.1.

Bow, see also **Arrow;** brings luck to king D1812.5.2.9. — Aesop with the unbent b. J553.1; Amazons cut off left breast of daughters so that they can handle b. F565.1.1; baby hands disguised father a b. H481.1.1; bear becomes b. D421.6.1; bending b. of woman's absent husband (suitor contest) H331.4.2; child born with magic b. T552.5.2; conception from god's b. T532.9; death by rebounding b. N335.3; divine twins make b. A527.1.1; extraordinary b. F836; girl makes enormous b. F624.9; god with b. of fire A137.14.1; god's b. A157.6; magic b. *D1091; magic musical b. D1233.1; magic transportation on musical b. D1520.33; one bird escapes as hunter bends his b. J641.1; prince born with gold b. H71.7.2; rainbow as b. of thunder god A791.1; recognition by unique ability to bend b. H31.2; witch eats b. G269.6.

Bows. — Numskulls try to kill mosquitoes with b. and arrows J2131.0.1; origin of b. A1459.1.1; peoples choose b. and arrows or guns and horses A1614.3; precocious hero demands b. F611.3.3.0.1.

Bow-string. — Remarkable b. F836.0.1; wolf tries to eat b. J514.2.

Bow-strings. — Mice gnaw enemies' b. and prevent pursuit K632; transformation to ant to gnaw b. of enemy D651.4.

Bowed. — Why certain fish have b. backs A2356.2.4; why sheep walk with b. heads A2221.9.

Bowel. — Auguries from b. movements D1812.5.0.8.1.

Bower. — Captivity in b. R41.2.2; crystal b. for fairy's mistress D2185.1; crystal b. in otherworld F165.3.5.1; shining b. for fée F224.

Bowing. — Cloud b. to female mountain A969.2; crucifix b. as sign of favor D1622.1; image b. to indicate favor D1622.2; king selected by elephant's b. to him H171.1; magic object b. D1648; tree b. before prince H71.10.1.

Bowl mistaken for helmet J1772.5; transformed D454.6.1. — Devil as round b. G303.3.4.8; magic b. *D1172.2, (restores strength) D1519.1.1; sun a golden b. with peacock on rim A724.2; washing in magic b. produces immunity from old age D1349.2.2.

Bowling. — Dead persons b. E577.3.

Box connection of poor to rich man J1561.6; on the ears J2494, K2376; opened by right person D1651.12; swallowed by dragon leads to underground kingdom F721.3.2; transformed to carriage D454.1.1. — Attempt to keep wife chaste by carrying her in b. *T382; bear substituted for woman in floating b. K1674; children abandoned in potter's b. S152; compressible magic b. D491.2.1; descent into ocean in glass b. F1022.1; disease brought to man in b. A1337.0.1.1; escape from deluge in b. A1029.5; ghost prevents removal of b. from abbey E299.2; heroine in b. which is bought by prince K1342.1; husband carries off b. containing hidden paramour K1555; impostor demands b. K1944; impostors carry hero in b. K1942; light kept in b. A1411.1; looking into b. forbidden *C321; magic basket (b.) furnishes livestock D1477.4; magic basket (b.) furnishes slaves D1476.3; magic b. *D1174; (furnishes money) D1452; moon kept in b. A754, A755.1; ogre trapped in b. G514.1; pope tests women's obedience: not to look into b. H1557.4; prince first sees heroine as she comes forth from hiding-b. N712; purchase of b. without knowledge of its contents N91; river contained in b. D915.3; soul hidden in b. E712.4; spider hands b. to ant and refuses to take it back: hence ants carry huge loads A2243.1; sun a bowl in crystal b. A724.2; sun kept in b. A721; touching magic b. tabu C533; treasure b. filled with trash: owners quarrel K2131.4; trick into entering b. K714.2; trickster hides in b. to be carried K1892.1.1.

Boxes ordered placed in temple by captive general cause relaxed vigilance and permit his escape K536.

Boxing-match: fatal boxer defeated K13.

Boy borrows python's hands and feet A2241.8; corps P551.5; as helper N832; hero Z251; kills his animal father B631.0.2; lives on ox F562.1; and the mantle H411.7; overhears witches, gets their magic D838.9; persuades father not to plow up crop, saves own life J92; resuscitated by lie H252.4.1; says "I know", gets into difficulties; now says "I don't know" J21.52.7; shot from cannon X1852; slays ogre G512.8.3; twitted with illegitimacy seeks mother H1381.2.2.2.1. — Adulteress disguised as b. elopes K1593; angels help b. prince V232.1.1; animals hide b. in their belly B529.1; bone in demon's stomach becomes a b. E149.1; chain tale: b. changes self to nut Z43.5; clever b. *J1113; delivery b. frightened, gives up chickens K335.0.9; devil enters the body of dead b. G303.18.1; hero's exploits as a b. Z231; ogre as small b. G376; persecuted b. hidden in mare's belly K551.3.6.2; reincarnation: b. to bird to b. E610.1.1; seven-year-old b. begets child T579.3.1; small b. overcomes gorilla L311.5; spirits teach b. how to sing F403.2.3.3; substitution of low-caste b. for promised child H38.2.5; supernatural mother to return if b. born M272;

taking b. to enemy's tent as fear test H1418; tasks assigned because of foolish boast of b. H915; water-spirits take mistreated b. F420.5.2.2.2; woman seduces b. by feigning illness K1393.

Boy's golden body royalty sign H71.2.1. — Oath taken on b. head H252.4.

Boys as hostages P533.1.1. — Disenchantment by drinking milk of queen who has borne two b. D764.1; little b. help hero win girl T66.2; living b. transformed into plants A2617.1; ogress invites b. to live with her G414; resurrected b. return to heaven E755.0.1.

Bracelet gift from river goddess N815.0.2.1. — Magic b. *D1074; magic wishing b. D1470.1.39; recognition by b. H95.

Bracelets, extraordinary F827.6.

Braggart. — Drowning punishment of b. Q552.19.0.1.

Brahma as creator A1.4; cursed by other gods: has no temples A162.4; takes men to Siva F12.3; -world A697.1. — Reward: birth in B.-world V526.

Brahmin forced to pay cow's burial fee K499.5; gives servant polluted fish K344.1.1; in love with washerwoman T91.7.1; may marry from any caste T131.9; punished for killing animal Q231; in rags treated as beggar; steals to feed guests W11.4.1; takes shape of prince K1952.0.1; teaches king wisdom J179.1; ungrateful to goose rescuer W154.12.2; unwittingly kills calf N361.1; wins discussion on religion V351.1.1. — Absurdity of turning king into B. J1293.3; ascetic imitates B. J2415.5; barber passes for a B. K1827.0.2; chain tale: why B. worships himself Z42.3; curse of B. M411.14.3; fate takes form of pupil of B. K1811.4.1; honest B. spared by tiger Q151.10; king can't execute B.; brings about his suicide J1181.0.1; penance: inviting B. to dinner Q527; stupid B. J1705.2; treacherous B. K2284.2; wells as B. women H1292.1.1.

Brahmins. — Almsgiving to B. C94.1.2.

Braiding. — Dwarf b. hair for sleeping maids F451.5.1.13; transformation by b. hair D577.

Brain of forgetfulness D1365.11; transformed to serpent D447.10. — Clouds from Ymir's b. A1133.1; magic animal b. D1011.7; magic b. *D997.2; magic b. assures heaven for man who dies upon it D1588.1; magic dog b. cures D1502.8.1; removable b. F557.1.

Brains as snakebite cure D1515.4.6. — Ball of human b. kills enemy N623.3; compassionate executioner: substituted b. K512.2.0.1; eating own b. K1025.1; enemies' b. used as balls S139.2.2.4.2; human b. as ball weapon F839.5; insects from b. of slain animal A2001.1; pottle of b. as metaphor for clever girl J163.2.1; sham blood and b. K473, K522.1.

Brain-fever bird's cry A2426.2.16.

Bramble chosen king of trees P11.0.2.1. — Devil has not been seen since he created b. G303.17.3.4; lake rises from b. bush F934.2; ogress reincarnated as b. bush E631.4.

Brambles heaped to halt enemy K2369.12. — Forced dancer in b. N55.1.

Branch dries up water in river D1542.3.3; leaps from hand to hand D1641.6; of tree transformed to animal D441.3. — Ambitious b. chosen king of trees J956; bringing b. of tree guarded by ghosts (task) H1151.10; doing penance till green leaves grow on dry b. Q521.1; dry b. on innocent man's grave blossoms E631.0.5.1; magic b. *D954, (musical) *D1615.2; magic b. produces rice harvest D1563.1.6; man kills son thinking that he is cutting a b. N325.1; tree b. transformed to palace D451.1.0.1; youth asks for b. of tree H611.

Branches of tree guarded by dragon H1333.6; turn upward to avoid idolators F979.20; of world-tree H619.3. — Capture between b. K742; numskull sticks his head in the b. of a tree J2131.5.3; tree b. prove journey H84.1; tree with musical b. F811.6; tree with silver b. D1461.0.2; tree with twelve b. (riddle) H721.1; twining b. grow from graves of lovers E631.0.1.

Branching tree as roadway for souls E750.2.3.

Brand. — Life bound up with burning b. E765.1.2; strong hero engendered from burning b. F611.1.10.

Branding person makes him one's slave for life P171; as punishment Q472; of sacred animals H55.2. — Ghost b. drunkard E279.5; recognition through b. H55.

Brandy. — Acquisition of b. A1427.1; making a knot of spilled b. (task) H1021.4; sea people give ogre b. G525.

Brass, see **Brazen;** apple F813.1.4; clothes F821.1.2; seeds pave city F761.5.3; serpent as snakebite antidote D1515.4.5; statue at city gates blows on trumpet *D1317.9.1. — Acquisition of b. A1432.3; city of b. F761.2; ship b. within, steel without F841.1.6; tree with b. leaves F811.2.1.1.

Brave. — Only b. wear beards P642; sham b. man K1953; why lion is b. A2524.5.

Bravery W32; as tribal characteristic A1676. — Deed of b. required before feast W213.1; money received from ghosts as reward for b. E373.1; origin of b. A1381.

Bravest know to wait J572.1.

Bray. — Ass betrays deity's secret: hence his ugly b. A2239.3.

Braying of ghost donkey E402.2.2. — Ferocious animal frightened by ass b. K2324.1.

Brazen, see **Brass;** tower F772.2.1. — Earthen and b. pots in river J425.1; magic b. dog B182.1.8; oracular b. lion D1311.7.2.

Brazier of the gods A142.1.

Bread accidently dropped from tree on bear's nose kills bear N331.2; baked with onions for undesired guest J1563.3; becomes cake D476.4; dropped in mud: messenger returns for more K343.1.1; of fairies F243.1; made from mud D476.1.1; made by a sick woman (deduction) J1661.1.3; made from tree leaf D476.1.2; stolen by saint restored V412.1; transformed to another object D454.2, D471.1; transformed to serpents D444.4;

tree springs from crumb D454.2.2. — Badly baked b. for father-in-law
S54.1; beer returned for b., neither payed for K233.4; beggar wants b.,
not you J1332; baking b. we ate last week H583.4.2; bleeding b. F991.3.1;
consecrated b. *D1031.1.1; cutting both ends of b. loaf brings devil
G303.6.2.13; deceptive bargain: as much b. as he wants to eat K173;
devil makes amends for stolen b. G303.9.3.1.1; devils disappear when
priest blesses b. G303.16.2.3.3; devil eats unblessed b. V31.5; dream b.
K444; dwarf bakes b. F451.3.4.5; dwarfs dislike b. baked without salt
F451.3.7.2; dwarfs emigrate because mortals put caraway seeds into b.
F451.9.1.1; fairies give mortals fairy b. F343.19; fairies baking b. F271.10;
fatal b. J1824; identification by ring baked in b. H94.2; lazy wife
throws b. out of window W111.3.3; lies about b. X1811; literal host:
b. and salt J2476; long-staying guest given black b. J21.9.1; magic b.
*D1031.1, (inexhaustible) D1652.1.1, (furnishes treasure) D1465.1; "may
your b. turn to stones" M411.2; misusing b. forbidden C535; murder
by feeding with b. full of pins K951.2; murder with poisoned b. S111.1,
K951.3; not to step on sacred b. C55.1; not to wipe children with b.
C851.1.1; ordeal with b. and cheese H232; peasants fed white b. demand
rye b. U135.3.2; pig becomes b. D422.3.1; quarrel over b. eaten by
invisible man K1883.6; quest for the best of b. H1305; rejected b.
resought J1923; respite from death gained by tale of the preparation
of b. K555.1.2; riddle: always eat b. with honey H588.11; rubies baked
in b. J1655.2; scraping b. tray as bride test H381.2.2; task: eat b. but
bring it back whole H1071; task: eating mountain of b. H1141.1;
test of strength: breaking a heavy glass bottle over a loaf of rye b.
H1562.3; transformation by eating b. D551.4; two loaves of b. as
parting gift N782; why he did not eat the b. J1345; wild hunt avoided
by holding b. E501.17.5.6; witches bake b. G246; witches lack b. and
salt G229.3; wolf who wanted to make b. Z49.5.2; woman gets b. by
prayer D1766.1.8.

Bread crumb. — Abandoned children find way back by b. clue R135ff.

Bread crust. — Mouse makes boat of b. *B295.1.

Breadfruit. — Origin of b. tree A2681.11; resuscitation by b. wood
image E53.2; tabu to eat b. C224.3.

Breadmaking as bride test H383.1.

Breaker of iron (strong man) F625. — Lie: remarkable b. X946.

Breakfast. — Enigmatic request for chickens for b. H599.6; evil eye
before b. causes death D2071.0.3; farmer's b. for help: glass of water
and lantern W152.12.1; groom invited to wedding b. with bride T137.3.

Breaking of bargains M205; girl's head to attract her attention J2461.9;
of glass occurs by threes D1273.1.1.2; heavy glass bottle over loaf of
rye bread as test of strength H1562.3; of goddess into five parts causes
river's five branches A934.11.3; mirror as evil omen D1812.5.1.3; of
object as life token E761.5ff.; of promises M205; huge rock to pieces
(task) H1116; of stick with money in it betrays thief H251.3.4; twig

forbidden C513; upon a wheel Q423. — Banishment for b. water pots
Q431.16; cannibal b. wind as attack G93; continued b. wind D2063.5;
devil causes noise of b. wind G303.6.2.15.1; disenchantment by b. lamp
D789.2; disenchantment by b. tabu D789.4; disenchantment from flower
by b. stalk D711.4; disenchantment from leaf by b. it from tree D711.5;
dwarf b. wind so hard canoe collapses F451.3.13.3; earth from egg b.
A814.9; girl summons fairy lover by b. tabu *F301.1.1; origin of rocks
from b. of God's sieve A971; punishment for b. betrothal Q252; trained
deer b. leg by drinking wine thereafter abstains J133.3; transformation
by b. tabu D510ff.; witch b. limbs G269.12; witch causes b. wind in
public G269.21.1.

Breast, see also **Bosom, Pap.** — Amazons cut off left b. of daughters
F565.1.1; conception from fruit thrown against b. T532.3; giant with
lips hanging onto b. F531.1.4.2; ghostly horse puts hoofs on b. of
sleeper E281.2; headless person with eyes and mouth on b. F511.0.1.1;
husband becomes cannibal from eating wife's b. G36.1; maid cuts off
b. to heal man's serpent wound D1515.4.1; milk suddenly appears in
woman's dry b. T592; mother's b. (is softest) H652.2, (is sweetest) H633.3;
ogress with one b. G369.6; origin and nature of animal's b. A2353ff.;
person with ears on b. F511.2.1; person with mouth in b. F513.0.4; princess wins wrestling match with suitor by revealing her b. H331.6.1.1;
punishment: burial alive up to b. Q456.1; remarkable b. F546; robin
steals fire, has b. scorched A2218.5; severed b. regrows when woman
bears child E788; snake sucks from woman's b. A2435.6.2.1; turf laid
on b. of dead to prevent return E431.6.

Breasts. — Date palm's fruit like old woman's b. A2791.11; elephant
loses its b. A2353.3; female bears have no b. A2353.4, B725; giantess
(fairy, mountain-wife) throws her b. over her shoulder *F531.1.5.1,
*F232.2, *F460.1.2, *G123; loom of woman's b. F856.1; magic b. of
woman D1009.3; maiden sends to her lecherous lover her b. which
he has admired T327.1; mermaid has large b. B81.9.2; origin of women's
b. A1313.4; punishment: snake sucks woman's b. Q452; punishment:
woman's b. cut off Q451.9; recognition in bed by large b. H79.6; recognition of son by gushing up of milk in mother's b. H175.1; sun, moon
from b. of mother earth A715.4; vision of seals sucking chieftain's b.
V515.2.1; wife offers starving husband milk from her b. T215.2; witch
sucks blood from b. G262.1.2; woman's b. dry up as punishment C942.4;
woman suspended by b. Q451.9.1; women's b. on foreheads A1313.4.1.

Breastplate, magic *D1101.3, D1079.3.

Breath in the cold thought to be tobacco smoke J1801; of dragon kills
man B11.2.11.2; of dragon renders hideous D1337.2.2; of magic horse
blows off or sucks in those he pursues B184.1.5; slows down princess
in race F622.1, H331.5.1.1.1. — Anchorite's b. consumes tree D2082.2;
angry warrior's b. heats adversary F1041.16.6.8; bad b. magically cured
D2161.3.9; bad b. reveals disguised snake's identity K1822.3; birds

wither everything with their b. B33.1.1; cat sucks sleeping child's b.
B766.2; catching a man's b. (task) H1023.13; cauldron warmed by b.
of nine maidens F686.1; complaint about bad b. K2135; foul b. from
breaking tabu C985.3; ghost searches for b. E599.1; ghost sucks people's
b. E251.3.4; inducing bad b. to escape man's lust T320.4.1; magic b.
*D1005; man created from b. A1262.1; man's bad b. proves wife's
fidelity T221; man's b. made from wind A1260.1.5; men live by gods'
b. A1394; revenant with bad b. E422.1.5; soul in the b. E714.6; thumbling
in danger of being sucked in by man's b. F535.1.1.4; wishes repeated in
one b. granted D1761.0.2.1.

Breathing on enemy causes death D2061.2.9; magically lights lamp D1933;
nine days under water F691; on sacred fire forbidden C51.1.3; tree
X1116. — Animal b. fire *B742; creator's b. causes the winds A1121;
doctor cures heart: patient stops b. X372.1; horse in wild hunt b. fire
*E501.4.2.4; resuscitation by b. on corpse E66; sponge in corpse's mouth
causes illusory b. K1885.1; tide caused by b. of sea monster A913.2.

Breeches, see also **Trousers.** — Jumping into the b. J2161.1; magic b.
*D1055; rascals pull off judge's b. and leave him exposed K1285;
thieving contest: first steals eggs from under bird, second meantime
steals first's b. K305.1; why Russians wear their shirts outside their b.
A1683.1.

Breviary. — Priest uses cook-book for b. V467.

Brewing ale from milk H1021.10; beer by means of magic song D1045.0.1;
in eggshell F451.5.17.1, F481.4; magically prevented *D2084.1. — Introduction of b. A1426.3.1.

Briars. — A fleeing fox loses an eye in the b. J2182.

Briar-patch punishment for rabbit K581.2.

Bribed boy sings wrong song *K1631; executioner releases culprit K513;
guards let prisoner escape R211.9; judge J1192ff., (punished) Q265.1;
witness nonplussed: wrong question asked J1157. — Animal b. for help
B325; death's messengers b. Z111.6.1; demons b. with food G582.1;
priest b. to betray confessional V468; witch b. for secrets G275.5.1.

Bribery of courtiers by smith to protect wife T257.9. — Escape by b.
K626; murder induced by b. K986; priest refuses small b. J1263.2.3; upright judge refuses b. W35.2; wisdom lost by b. J186.

Brick. — King works at b. building P15.7; magic b. *D935.4.

Bricks transformed to gold D475.1.7. — Gold hidden in b. N518; palace
of gold, silver b. F771.1.1.2.

Bricklayer P455.

Bridal, see also **Bride, Marriage, Wedding;** couple seized by tiger for
religious failure Q557.7; party will not pass over bridge for fear of
water-demon G424. — Bad omen for two b. processions to meet
D1812.5.1 8; dangers to husband in b. chamber T172ff.; husband driven
from b. chamber T171; ogress killed in b. bed G519.1.3; throwing fruits
on b. couple A1555.1.1.

Bride, see also **Marriage, Wedding;** abducted by fake carpenters K1825.7; accidentally kills husband N331.1.3; in basket C169.1; enchanted by witch loses organs D2062.4.1; fetched by groom after wedding T137.5; given away T135.7; has maid sleep in husband's bed to conceal pregnancy *K1843.1; helps suitor perform his tasks H335.0.1; like moon Z62.2; magically provided D1595; offered to correct guesser H511; offered to man who can defeat her in repartee H507.1; offered to man who can find answer to question H508.2; offered to man who can out-riddle her *H551; purchased T52; resuscitates hero E121.1.3.1; saves self from ravisher T320.3; stealing K1371; substitutes picture, escapes groom K525.1.2; tests *H360—H399; whose kissing annoys husband says she did not know it was he J1485; wounded accidentally on way home T152.
— Abducted b. hidden in fairyland F322.4; casting sheep's eyes at the b. J2462.2; changeling b. F322.1; choosing b. by horoscope T54; choosing smallest possible b. J229.10; covenant to get friend a b. M246.3; devil tries to get man to kill his b. G303.9.4.3; divided b. (Solomonic judgment) J1171.2; dividing the winnings: half of the b. demanded M241.1; eagle seeks king's b. D647.2; faithful servant accompanies b. to new home T133.1; false b. unable to finish true one's weaving H35.3.1; false death message to secure another's b. K1864.1; favorite performs task to win b. for king K1848.2; foolish b. J2463; foster brother steals b. K1371.1.2; ghost substituting for b. E363.1.1; hero wakened from magic sleep by wife who has purchased place in his bed from false b. *D1978.4; ignorant b. castrates groom J1919.5.1; keeping questionable b. for fear of worse J229.9; king mourns disappeared b. F1041.9.1.2; king's son woos father's b.: both killed K1094; leaving earthly b. for service of Virgin T376.1; magic arrow shot to determine where to seek b. D1314.1.3; man drowns b. S62.2; murderous b. T173; ogress's daughter as b. H305; ornaments b. wore in former birth H1371.4; otherworld journey to get b. F87; oversensitive b. K2052; quest for b. *H1381.3.1; quest for b. for king H1381.3.1, T11.1.1; quest for the most beautiful b. *H1301.1; quest for b. richest and poorest H1311.2; real wife thwarts husband's acquiring b. J1112.1.1; recognition of maidservant substitute b. by her habitual conversation H38.2.3; runaway horse carries b. to her lover N721; rescue of b. from mysterious perils by hidden faithful servant R169.4.1; smallest woman best b. J1442.13; substituted b. *D1911ff.; substituting false b. for father K1094.1; suitors put to severe tests by prospective b. or father-in-law *H310—359; thief disguised as b. K311.16.2; thieves abduct b. from palace K315.3; umbrellas welcome b. A1555.3.

Bride's instinctive expertness in love J64. — Disguised man takes b. place: leaves goat for bridegroom K1836.3; giant b. equipment F531.1.13; testing b. chastity H452.

Bride-race. — Loser in b. must die H331.5.0.1.

Bridebench. — Gifts on b. T136.4.1.

Bridegroom T137.3ff.; abducted by giantess R10.4.1; alone plucks flowers from bride's grave H31.12.1; attacked in bride's apartments K778.4; bribes thief to leave wedding J1392.5; buys widow cloth for bride Z140.4; castrated by ignorant bride J1919.5.1; chosen from pictures T131.1.2.2; dies from joy F1041.1.5.1; driven from bridal chamber by magic T171; killed by lightning on wedding night N339.4; to meet disaster on elephant M340.4; and men come for bride T133.5; murdered while bride asleep K873.2; permits visit to lover H1552.1; prisoner in giantess' room R41.4; propounds riddles H540.5; slain on way to bride T153; substitutes bedmate to overhear her secret K1844.3; like sun Z62.2. — Betrothal token to parents of b. T61.4.4; cowardly b. W121.7; dangers to b. in bridal chamber T172; disguise a b. to enter girl's room K1349.1.4; false b. K1915; foolish b. follows instructions literally J2462; god as b. A137.12; ignorance of b. on wedding night J1744.1; literal b. drowns bride J2489.11; loathly b. D733; man gets b. drunk, enjoys bride K1371.5; numskull b. unwittingly detects thieves N611.3; oath to marry daughters only into family with b. for each M149.5; princess brings ill luck to b. K443.12; quest for unknown b. H1381.7; robber b. K1916; shirt for father of b. H383.2.3; substitute b. K1915, (to save husband from poison maiden) H1844.2; swine b. disenchanted D733.2; thief disguised as bride robs b. K311.16.2; thief disguised as b. K311.8.3; trickster masking as b. K1354.3.2; witch breaks leg of b. G269.12.1; woman engages false b. for daughter K1624.

Bridge-building contest K48; connecting earth, heaven A657.1; -crossing as righteousness test H1573.6.1; cut from under sinner, he falls into hell Q417.3; of the Gods A986; of heaven A661.0.5; to land of dead *E481.1.2.1; made by magic *D1258.1; to otherworld *F152; tests souls H210.1; of untouchable tree's wood M172.2. — Animals as b. across stream B555; animals build b. B299.8; bargain with devil evaded by driving dog over b. first S241.1; belt becomes b. D454.3.3; blind man crosses a narrow b. which his guide is afraid to attempt U171; bridal party will not pass over b. for fear of water-demon G424; building a b. of cattle K1441; building enormous b. (task) H1131; crossing stream on an ashen b. (by use of staff) H586.6; the crow on the tarred b. Z39.3; deaf man on the b. X111.5; devil builds b. G303.9.1.1, H1131.2; devil builds b. minus one stone G303.14.2; do not cross a b. without dismounting from your horse J21.7; dragon guards b. to otherworld B11.6.6; dragon makes b. across steam for holy man B549.2; dream of treasure on the b. N531.1; dupes lured onto tree-trunk b.; fall to death K983.2; extraordinary b. *F842ff.; fugitives cut support of b. R235; ghost frightens people off b. E272.3; stubborn goats meet each other on a b. W167.1; ghosts gathered on a b. E496; long tongue cut out and used to b. a stream F544.2.2.1; magic b. *D1258; maiden at b. to hell A672.2; monkeys construct b. across the ocean B846; ogre attacks intruders on b. G475.2; perilous trap b. *F842.2.1; rainbow as gods' b. A791.3; recognition by overheard conversation with b. H13.2.1; secrets overheard from b. N451.1; self-folding b. prevents pursuit D1642.1; smoke becomes b. D469.2; soul-b. A661.0.5.1; soul crosses on scythe blade as b. E721.6; stone b. appears for fugitives, disappears for pursuers R246.1; tabu: crossing sacred b. C93.4; wand becomes b. D451.6.1.1; if witch grabs horse's tail on b. man is safe from her G273.4.1.

Bridges, lies about X1817.

Bridle goes with horse when horse is brought P621. — Bewitching with magic b. G241.2.1.1; disenchantment by taking off b. *D722; fortune from informing foreign king of use of saddle and b. N411.3; horse losing b. tabu C884.2; loosing b. in selling man transformed to horse tabu C837; lost ass, saddle and b. offered as reward to the finder J2085.1; magic b. *D1209.1; transformation to horse by putting on b. *D535.

Bridling a wild animal (task) H1154.3.

Bright, see also **Gleaming, Glowing, Luminous, Shining;** eyes as sign of royalty H71.6; star indicates birth of holy person F961.2.1. — Devil wears a b. green coat G303.5.2.3; dwarf king has b. torch F451.7.4; extraordinarily b. sword F833.3; saint's hand made b. V222.1.2.

Brightest stars are sun's children A764.3. — What is b.? (riddle) H651ff.

Brigit, festival of V70.6.

Brimstone. — Water becomes b. D478.13.

Brine becomes wine D477.2.

Bringing back person from the dead F81.1; documents from distant city in one day H1107; as many horses as there are days in the year (task) H1117; an ogre to court H1172; water from distant fountain more quickly than a witch H1109.1.

Bristles. — Boar's b. poisoned K898; boar's b. remarkably long X1233.1.1; hog with silver b. H355.2.

Broad and narrow road in otherworld F171.2; path to hell F95.2. — Breast b. and made of metal F546.1; extraordinarily b. spear F834.2; giantess more b. than tall F531.2.5.1; remarkably b. men F532.

Broken leg saves man from fatal fight N178.1; objects restored by saint V229.10; vessel leads to adventure N783. — Boat b. by strong man as rower F614.4; cup given by fairy not to be b. F348.2; death from b. heart F1041.1.1; devil has b. foot G303.4.5.2; earth made from b. ground A824; emeralds from b. vase A978.3; enemy's sword b. by magic wand D1414.1; fixing the two pieces of a b. sword (task) H1023.8; identification through b. ring H94.5; identification by b. weapon H101; lover's gift regained: the b. article K1581.1; mending a b. jug (task) H1023.9; money from the b. statue J1853.1.1; mountain-men leave b. implement for man to mend F460.4.3; object miraculously b. F1098.0.1; promise to dying man b. M256; punishment for b. oaths M101; recognition by b. tooth H57.1; sewing together a b. mill-stone (task) H1023.7; skillful tailor sews up b. eggs F662.1.

Bronze boat F841.1.2; fairy boat F242.2.2; fortress in otherworld F163.5.1;

man (Talos) F521.3.1; palisade around otherworld F148.4; pillars in otherworld F169.1.1; sail F841.2.5.

Brooch. — Lost b. found in fish N211.1.5; magic b. D1072.3; raths marked out with b. A1435.2.1.

Brood. — Dove disregards experience and loses b. J16; dove's pride in her large b. linked with fear for their loss U81.1.

Brook, see also **Stream;** spirit F424.1. — Gathering all stones from b. (task) H1124.

Broom across door protects from witch G272.7.2; strikes sky, raises it A625.2.3; transformed into porcupine drives away ravisher B524.5. — Extraordinary b. F857; golden b. F857.1; lion's tail as b. H1151.11; magic b. D1209.8; origin of b. A1446.5.1; sweeping with a stick instead of a b. J1822; wife with b. frightens devil K212.1; worn-out b. at head of wild hunt E501.10.2.

Brooms. — Devil summoned by spitting on castaway b. G303.16.19.2.

Broom-corn. — Why b. is covered with blood-red spots A2751.4.5.

Broomstick. — St. Peter's wife meets him with a b. T251.3; witch flies through air on b. G242.1.

Broth, see also **Soup.** — Making b. for army H1022.5.1; saint cheated of b. without butter K499.2.1.

Brothel. — Adulteress's tryst in b.: scares off husband K1514.13; bull-keeper accused of maintaining a b. J2521.1; king's daughter put into b. to catch thief K425; saint accused of evil in entering b. N347.2.

Brother accused of impregnating sister K2121.1; aids task H981; causes brother's death by sending him to robbers K991.1; chosen rather than husband or son P253.3; Dead (ogre) pursues G323; in disguise aids quests H1233.2.2; eats brother G73.2, S73.1.2; flogs unchaste sister to death Q458.2.1; kills brother in duelling game K867; kills sister's husband J482.1.2; rescues brother from ogre G551.4; rescues sister(s) R156; secures blessing due another K1988; and sister arrange marriage of their unborn children M146.4; -sister incest M365.3, *T415; -sister marriage Q520.3, (of first parents' children) A1552.3; of the gods A164.1; throws away what he catches and what he does not catch he carries with him H583.3; transforms self to deer, seeks sister D647.1; wins sister's suitor test H310.2. — Angry b. mistakenly kills sister's husband N342.5; beggar claims to be emperor's b. J1337; blood of b. and sister will not mingle *F1075; burial of living man with dead blood b. S123.2.1; cruel b. S73; culture hero fights with his elder b. A525.1; culture hero's blood b. A515.3; disguise as older b. to obtain blessing K1839.11; dying man assigns bride to his b. T141.1; earth from murder of first b. and sister A831.4; eldest b. as hero Z221; escape by substituting b. K527.2; enigmatic counsels of a b. H596.1; false boasting of having killed foster b. K1766.1; foolish b. prays, acquires clever brother's property V52.12; foster b. steals bride K1371.1.2; ghost reminds b. of will E236.4.2; girl flees incestuous b. R224; girl getting child by b. D45.4;

girl seduced by b. becomes cannibal G37; god issue of b.-sister marriage P3; helpful animal foster b. B311.1; his b. cannot pray either J2352.1; husband, wife disguised as b. and sister K1839.14; impoverished youngest b. seeks work from elders L432.4; incestuous b. burned to charcoal D1865.2.1; insects from b.-sister incest A2006; is that you or your b.? J2234; king slays b. and brother's son S11.3.5; lecherous b. T415.1; lost b. recognized by modeling palace H16.1; lover kills his rival b. T92.5; man tricked into being sworn b. K2384; man's anger at eating with b. F1041.16.10; mild b. triumphs over warlike L353; money to good b., poison to bad D1663.6; moon, sun are sister and b. A736.1.1ff., A736.1.4.2; moon as sun's younger b. A745.3; prophecy: youngest b. to rule M312.2.2; punishment for killing foster b. Q211.9.2; queen in love with own b. K2213.3.4; quest for lost b. H1385.8; rescue from ogre by b. G551.1; resuscitation by b. E125.3; sham death to stab b. K911.2; sister and b. *P253; sister treacherous to b. K2212.0.1; treacherous b. *K2211; vow not to fight with b. M166.4; white b., black sister (riddle) H722.1; woman deceived into sacrificing honor for release of b. K1353; younger, preferred b. substituted by mother for elder K1855; youngest b. alone succeeds on quest H1242; youngest b. helps elder L31; youngest b. shares wealth with older ones W11.14.

Brother's consent for sister's marriage needed T131.1.1. — Clever younger b. property choice J242.8; dead b. return E226, (friendly) E326; madness over b. death F1041.8.10; nipple from b. caress J1833.1.1; troll's life in his b. forehead E714.3.1.

Brothers *P251; as creators A15.2; deceive sister swimming to her lover T83.1; die at sight of brother they sold into captivity N384.13; eat their sister G73.1; flee being sacrificed S272.1; as heroes *Z210ff.; identical in appearance F577.2; killing each other over paternity slander K1092; pose as princes K1952.3; rescue abandoned sister S357; rescue brothers R155; settle quarrel J552.5; and sisters do not marry A1552.1; having extraordinary skill *F660.1, (rescue princess) R166; and sisters *P250ff. — Accidental meeting of b. N733; berserk b. F610.3.3.1; combat of unknown b. brings about recognition H151.10; cruel b. forced to beg from abused sister L432.1; culture heroes are b. A515.1ff.; curse: all b. to be killed by single man M441.1.1; disenchantment by sewing shirts for enchanted b. D753.1; dream reveals death of b. D1813.1.4; elder b. impose task H934.4; enemy b. unite against common enemy J624.3; extraordinary companions are b. F601.5; flower bouquet brings recognition of b. H163; fool betrays his b. J2668; four b. construct a woman — whose is she? Z16.1; gifts from the b. J1283; hundred b. seek hundred sisters as wives T69.1; king's b. as joy, woe H1378.2; king's foster b. banished Q431.2.3; magic fish talk so that ogre thinks hero has many b. with him D1613.1; magic object stolen by b. D861.3; maiden will not give her troth to two b. successively T65.1; moon is wife to twelve sun b. A753.1.4.2; orphan b. as heroes L111.4.3; seven b. and one sister

Z71.5.1; seven b. marry seven sisters Z71.5.8; sun b. each work for one
month, play for eleven A739.3; sun and moon as b. A736.3; tasks assigned
at suggestion of jealous b. H912; three b. contest in wishing H507.3.1;
three b. take turns using mule J1914.2; three hunchback b. drowned
K2322; two b. at ogre's home G401.1; undesired combat between sworn
b. N731.2.2; weak son condemned to be servant of b. M438.5; witch
estranges b. G269.7.

Brother-in-law *P263; made king's inferior by holding his sword K1292;
seduces sister-in-law T425. — Magic object received from animal b.
B505.1; murder of b. punished Q211.9.1; suitor in contest with b. H332.2;
treacherous b. K2211.1; wisdom from b. J177.

Brothers-in-law. — Helpful animal b. *B314.

Brows. — Giant three spans between b. F531.2.2.

Browbeaten husband shown by cock how to rule his wife T252.2.

Brown horse in wild hunt E501.4.2.3; man with white back F527.4;
patches on soil where marvelous cow lay A989.1; as symbolic color
Z146. — Dwarf wears b. F451.2.7.8; one eye b., other blue F541.6.1;
fairies b. F233.8; mermaid's b. skin B81.9.5.2.

Brownie murders travelers for their blood F363.2.

Brownies F482.

Bruidhen as otherworld F135. — Smith as lord of b. P447.3.

Brunhilde T173.1.

Brush transformed to mountain D454.7. — Diving match won by deception: breathing under b. K16.1; man in moon burns b. as punishment
for doing so on Sunday A751.1.1.

Brushwood at a distance mistaken for a ship K1886.4.

Bubble. — Devil created out of a b. G303.1.3.2; transformation: doe to
b. of water (enchanted woman) D421.2.2; water b. becomes person
D439.3.

Bucket dropped in well leads to adventures N777.2. — Children in moon
with yoke and b. A751.7; drawing b. of well water without rope
H1023.20; magic b. *D1171.10; ordeal by stone from b. H233; wolf in
one b. and fox in the other K651.

Buckets. — Inexhaustible b. as source of lakes A920.1.1.

Buckeye as repository for fire A1414.7.1.

Buckwheat. — Why b. produces twice a year A2793.9.

Buds A2771ff. — Extraordinary tree b. F811.17; mankind emerges from
b. on trees A1236.1; trees bear first b. to commemorate reign of primitive
hero A2771.5.

Buddha V212. — Casting of image of B. delayed until a maniac's mite
is thrown into the furnace V125; ceremony of the proclamation of a B.
V88; journey to B. F12.4; punishment for doubting religion of B. Q225.3;
saint's relics assume form of B. D457.16.1; slander: B. killed woman
K2155.2.

Buddhist otherworlds A697.

Buddhists slaves of Taoists V355.

Buffalo as animals' king B240.7; eating up turban J1192.1.1; magically called D2074.1.1; helps tiger quench fire: white mark left on buffalo's neck where tiger held on while being ducked in water A2211.12; as king of animals B240.7; refuses tiger's dinner invitation J425.2; sucks up hero, releases him F914.2. — Bathing hair in b. milk D1337.1.3.1; boy as housekeeper for b. herd N832.1; blind man mistakes woman for b. X124.1; bride as reward for b. killing T68.2; cannibal devours b. raw H46.1; creation of b. A1878; custom of eating b. flesh A1515.1; deity rides b. A136.1.6; devastating b. G357; duel of b. and tiger B264.3; fools try to use b. tongue as knife J1971; flying b. B43.1; friendship of tiger and b. A2493.3; giant b. B871.1.1.3; helpful b. B411.4; horse sewed in skin of b. F984.1; how b. got hair under chin A2322.1; Indra sends down b. whose milk offered to saints B184.2.3.3; man becomes b. D112.5; man catches b. by rope and is dragged to death J2132.1; man transformed to b. D114.1.4; marriage to b. in human form B651.2; origin of b. A1878.1; origin of hide of b. *A2311.6, A2247.1; overcoming savage b. H1161.2; porcupine and b. K952.1; punishment: reincarnation as b. Q560.1.1; reincarnation as b. E611.2.4; sacred b. B811.3.1; sale of dead b. by making him seem alive K136; skinning b. alive X983; speaking b. B211.1.5.2; sun sits on back of b. A722.8; tabu to slaughter b. in temple C935.5; trickster puts on b. skull J2131.5.1; transformation to b. so as to eat grass D655.1; why horns of b. are bent A2326.3.4; why tiger eats b. A2435.3.9.4; wild b. herd used by trickster to steal K335.0.13.

Buffalo's eyes turn into protecting dogs D699.1; fate in bamboo growing from head N119.2.

Buffaloes emerge from earth, first man holding tail A1714.3.1; fail to come at god's leavetaking: now killed by tigers A2231.12; give hero horns to summon them B501.1; grateful for being cleaned B395.1; grateful for care of their calves B395; sacrificed for ghosts E433.4.1; save hero from tiger B524.1.5.1; tramp hero's enemies to death B524.1.5. — Blood of b. vitalizes tiger D1594.4; bringing much mud without b. H1129.1.1; cheese from white b. milk H1361.6; creator of b. A84.1; fighting b. as task H1165; gate takes twelve b. to open F776.1.1; god's b. A155.7; goddess of b. A441.1.1; thief serves king lost b. J1289.15; quest for devastating b. H1362.1; riding b. H1155.5; transformation to milk b. D659.13; treasure appears on horns of b. N549.1; wind drives b. for god A199.4.

Buffoon. — Disguise as b. K1818.3.1; reward for generosity to king's b. Q42.5.

Bugle. — Alleged resuscitating b. K1138.

Bugs, bees can't eat each other's food J1565.2. — Creation of b. A2052; dog-eating b. J1531.2.1; why b. smell bad A2416.6.

Builder. — Careful b. outside when storm comes is killed: careless b. saved N174; devil (giant) as a b. G303.9.1ff., F531.6.6.

Builders throw away beams from the scaffolding until it all falls down J2171.3. — Fairies as b. F271.2.

Building causeway as suitor test H359.1; enormous bridge (task) H1131; castle (task) H1133, (in one night) H1104; falls because of breaking tabu C931; home one wattle at a time J67.1; too large a structure forbidden C771; nests learned by bird A2431.1; sinks into earth F941; site determined (by halting of animal) B155.1ff., (by magic arrow) D1314.1.2, D1314.1.4, (by magic staff) D1314.2.5; village in one night H1104.2. — Acquisition of b. craft A1445; animals b. palace for man B572.1; devil builds b. G303.9.1.13; dwarfs b. tower F451.3.4.1.1; enchanted b. D6; escape from deluge on floating b. A1021.0.6; fairies b. for mortal F346.2; friendly ghost haunts b. E338; ghost laid inside b. E437.6; ghost-like b. E531; god b. temple A141.2; great b. X1033; magic b. provides treasure D1457; magic discovery of place for b. D1816.6; magic object produces b. D1483; man becomes b. D268; man learns b. from wasp A1445.2.2; man sells soul to devil in return for devil's b. house M211.2; magic lyre charms stones into their places in b. D1565.2; omen at laying foundation of b. D1812.5.2.8; prophecy: child to build religious b. M311.2; strong man pulls down b. F627; treasure hidden in b. N517.

Buildings bewitched G265.8.5; in otherworld F163. — Dwarfs destroy b. F451.5.2.5; extraordinary b. F770ff.; giants by night move b. built by men in day F531.6.6.1; ghosts haunt b. E280ff.; lie: remarkable b. X1030ff.; magic b. and parts *D1130ff.; religious b. *V110ff.

Built. — Castle (hell) b. by devil G303.8.3.2; devil destroys by night what is b. by day G303.14.1; devil in each stone of church b. with ill-gotten wealth G303.8.4.2; fires b. by dead persons E578; palace b. by mountain-spirits F460.4.2.1; road b. by devil for farmer in one day G303.9.2.2; soul wanders and demands that a temple be b. for him E419.1.

Bulbul. — Chain of killings: from b. to boy Z49.13.

Bull, see also **Steer;** in the china shop J973; determines road to be taken B151.1.2; draws one hundred carts for master's wager B587.3; -god A132.9; with human hands, feet B15.6.4; lows musically B297.0.1; with man's head B23.2; melts away after evil spirit has issued from him F981.2; mistaken for horse J1759.4; Nandia, provides warrior's equipment D2107.1; paramour *B611.4; recognizes princess H162.3; refuses to fight goat J371.1; survives plague F989.6; with three cranes A137.7; transformed to person D333.1; worship V1.8.1.1. — Arrow shot at b. returns F831.4; beating calves to punish b. J1863.1; bewitched man believes dead b. chasing him G269.24; blind man and the b. X123; brazen-footed, firebreathing b. B19.1; bellow of b. heard over entire land B741.4; deceptive division of shared b. K171.7.1; devastating b. B16.1.5.3; devil as white b. G303.3.3.1.4; divinity reincarnated as b. E611.2.1; earth supported by b. A844.2ff.; enmity between dog and b. A2494.4.8; escape by riding on sacred b. K551.6.1; fairy in form of cow (b.) F234.1.1; frogs fear defeated b. J613.2; fugitive b.-calf returns, defeats father L111.1.2; ghost as fiery b. E421.3.4; giant b. B871.1.1.2; gnats apologise for lighting on horn of b. J953.10; god rides a b. A136.1.3; heifers impregnated by supernatural b. T539.4; helpful b. B411.1; hornless b. B15.3.0.1.1; jackal makes lion suspicious of b. K2131.2; killing fierce b. H1161.2.2; lifting b. over fence J2199.3; magic b. B184.2ff.; making a b. bear a calf (task) H1024.1.1; man transformed to b. D133.2; marriage to god in b. form *B641.3; milking a b. (task) H1024.1; mouse torments b. who cannot catch him L315.2; prophetic dream induced by eating meat of b. D1812.3.3.6; punishment: riding through streets on b. Q473.1; "Rain" as ogre in b. form G372; raven on horns thinks he has led b. J953.10.1; sacred b. B811.3.2; soul as b. E731.13; stealing two horns of savage b. (task) H1151.7; sun as black b. A728.3; taming the b. by cutting off his horns J2107; winged b. B43.

Bull's bellow B741.4; eye transformed to hornets D457.11.1; magic legs D1012.1.1; tail exterminates army D1400.1.21; urination thought to be bleeding J1818.1. — Dragging to death by b. horns Q416.2.2; magic supplies from b. belly D1470.2.6; palace from b. legs D1483.1.

Bulls. —Fight of lions and b. J1022; sick man offers deity more b. than he owns K231.3.5; shadows of b. given to imaginary owner J1551.7.

Bullet. — Magic b. D1096.3; silver b. injures devil G303.16.19.14; silver b. protects against giants D1385.4.

Bullets cannot hit devil G303.4.8.11; ineffective on serpent B765.17. — Dupe wastes b., then seized K724; sheet protects army from b. D2163.9; witch catches, sends back b. G229.4.2; witch's familiars impervious to b. G225.0.4; witch throws b. back G265.8.3.1.2.

Bullfight as suitor contest H331.15.2; as task H1165. — Why man picked as b. judge W35.1.

Bullfinch's wedding B282.7.

Bullfrogs can not swim: never in water X1643.1.

Bullock mistakes cotton pods for own fat J1772.8; struck on hindquarters to kill it J1906.1. — Cow and b. yoked together A1689.1; deceptive b. wins swallowing contest K82.4; frog abuses b. J952.5; helpful b. B411.5; lion divides slain b. Q3.2; magic b. wins master's fight K1.1.1; master's horse exchanged for vicious b. K1456; old b. left to die W155.1.1; reincarnation as b. E611.2.1.1; speaking b. B211.1.5.3; wager on b. defeating elephant N77.

Bullocks. — Lie: two b. go where one cannot X1743.2.

Bulrushes. — Moses in the b. L111.2.1; trickster joins b. in a dance J1883.

Bumblebee, see also **Bee.** — Helpful b. B481.3.1; man becomes b. D182.1.1.

Bumblebees crossbreeding with mosquitoes X1280.1.1.

Bundle of wood magically acts as riding-horse D1523.3. — Bringing b. of faggots without rope H1023.19; dead person sails over sound on b. of straw E581.7; devil as b. G303.3.4.10; fairy as b. of rags F234.3.3; large b. identifies chief H41.10; making sails for a ship from one b. of linen H1022.3; quarreling sons and b. of twigs J1021; writing tablets become b. D454.11.

Bundles. — Why ants carry large b. A2451.1.

Bunghole. — Building barrel around a b. W152.14.1; looking into b. of fairy barrel tabu F348.9.

Bungholes. — Eating b. X1761.2.

Bungling barber P446.1; fool J2650—J2699; host J2425.

Bunkhouse. — Lie: great b. X1033.

Burbot, color of A2411.4.3, A2218.

Burden of two asses J1352.1. — Animals carry extraordinary b. F982; ghost carries b. E592; relieving the beast of b. J1874.

Burdens. — Animal useful for bearing b. A2515; largest b. laid on smallest asses U12.

Bureaucrats debate who shall put out fire J2532.

Burial, see also **Burying;** alive *S123, (as punishment) *Q456, (of aged mother) S21.1, (to banish plague) S266; in certain ground assures heaven E754.3; in church wall cheats devil of soul K219.4; mounds as fairy dwellings F211.0.1; in old grave to deceive angel J2212.2; places as homes of dwarfs F451.4.1.9; service for fairy queen F268.1; service read into hat to prevent dead walking E431.1; among underworld folk F268. — Angel directs saint's b. V241.1.1; animal determines b. place of saint B155.3; arrow shot to determine b. place D1314.1.5; aversion to b. in foreign soil P711.8; cairn marks b. place A988; cow's b. fee K499.5; the cynic's b. J1442.4; dead grateful for b. E341.1.1; dead head grateful for b. E783.8; dead returns on b. day E586.1; dead returns third day after b. E586.2; disgraceful b. as punishment Q491.1; escape by dire prophecy on b. K575; escape by shammed b. K522.5; ghost enforces b. wishes E419.8; ghost haunts b. spot E334.2; ghosts prevent b. of corpse E273.1; ghost returns to demand proper b. E235.2; leek under tongue b. protection D1389.12; magic as reward for b. D812.4.2; origin of b. A1591; saint directs own b. E545.15; saint's b. place unharmed by sea F931.3; singing at b. P617; special b. exorcises witch G271.7; spirit disturbs b. vault F473.6.9; spring breaks forth to commemorate place of heroes' b. A941.4.1; usurer refused b. Q273.2.

Buried ghost E231.4; object found by magic D1816.4; treasure N511ff. — Animal b. alive to cure disease D2161.4.6; blind man recovers b. treasure K1667.1.1; bones of dead collected and b. E607.1; captive b. alive freed after struggles with jackal R212.1.2; corpse begs sinner not be b. on top of it E545.9; dog b. alive to prevent ghosts from walking E431.8; earth rejects b. body E411.0.6; everyone b. in saint's soil to go to heaven M364.11; fool has himself b. because he stinks J2193; ghost laid when leg is b. E441.1; ghost returns because not properly b. E235.2.2; gospels b. with saint V136.1; lights show where saint b. V222.1.4; live person b. by mistake J1834; lovers b. in same grave T86; man b. alive escapes tomb when it is robbed R212.1.1; man b. in sea F931.3.1; moon b.

in pit A754.1; mountain from b. giant A969.1; no one b. in saint's church shall go to hell Q174.1.1.2; ogre persuaded to go into hole: b. alive G512.4; persons b. with dead king P16.4; promise to be b. with wife if she dies first M254; raising a b. treasure (task) H1181; soul cannot enter heaven till body b. E750.0.1; storm from calling up spirits to help find b. treasure D2141.0.2; swindler b. on dungheap Q491.1.1; tail b. K1021.1; test of wife's ability to keep secret: the b. sheep's head H472.1; wheel b. in doorstep to prevent deviltry D1385.10; Virgin Mary has dissolute monk b. in consecrated ground V255.

Burlesque of church services K1961.1.2.1, (in witch's sabbath) G243.

Burned clothes restored by saint V229.10.1. — Clothes b. by magic D2089.8; clothes b. to rid them of insects J2102.6; colored face after being b. F1082.1; corpse b. to prevent return E431.13; country b. up by magic sphere D1408.1; coyote b. when hay is set afire: hence yellow patch behind his ears A2218.4; criminal's house b. down Q486.1; desecrated church b. through saint's power Q222.5.5; dupe persuaded to be b. in order to go to heaven K843; enemy lured into house, b. up K811.4; fairies' palace cannot be b. F222.1.1; fires b. in streets to ward off witches G272.4; giantess with b. arms F531.1.6.7.3; hair b., victim dies D2061.2.2.4.1; harlot b. as punishment Q243.1.1; heretic b. in bed by insane man V321; house b. down (to deliver man imprisoned in it) R121.3, (to rid it of insects) J2102.4, (when trickster reports high price paid for ashes) K941.2; how was town b.? J2062.3; invulnerability by being b. D1846.1; ogre b. to death G512.3; onlooker b. by woman's beauty F574.1.1; paramour b. in barrel of tow K1554.1; person b. up by magic object D1402.0.1; priests b.: dying woman wished cauterization J1511.18; ravisher's grave and body miraculously b. Q414.0.4.1; rescue from being b. R117; sky prevents earth being b. A651.1.1.1; souls in hell alternately b., drowned Q562.2; tree in which eagle has his nest b. by fox L315.3; uxorious king b. to death N339.5; victim b. (in building) K745, (in his own house) K812; victim b. up under dry-leaves covering K1010.1; witch b. by furrows G273.5.1; witch causes person to be b. G269.14; wizard b. as saint saved H1573.3.4; world b. as fire poured on A1031.4.1; world would be b. up if all sun brothers work together A739.3.

Burner. — Charcoal b. drives fairies off with fire F389.1.

Burning animal husband C36.1; animal in straw to release curse M429.3; bodies vomit F1099.5; caterpillars C841.3; cut hair to prevent witchcraft D2176.5; to death *S112ff.; to death after bringing devil's fire Q582.2; down house for seduction access K1349.7; dupe who gets into grass to learn new dance K1055; food test H1511.2; house quelled by stone cast F679.6; land after sowing seed J2460.1; by magic D2144.4; magically evaded *D1841.3; to make wife beautiful K1013.2.1; object forces witch to reveal self G257.1; oil thrown on ogre G572.1; pillar reaching heaven F774.2; as punishment for breaking tabu C927; river F715.6; saja wood tabu C514; stones F809.6.1; thatch protection against

witch G272.17; wasp nest J2102.5. — Animal characteristics from b.
*A2218ff.; animal saves man from death by b. *B526; cat leaps through
man, b. him to ashes B16.1.1.2; changeling returns child when threatened
with b. F321.1.4.5; changeling told house b., leaves F321.1.4.9; color of
flame indicates what is b. F1061.2; cure by b. grain where man has died
D2161.4.8; deceptive game: b. each other K851; devil exorcised by b.
wood G303.16.14.2.1; disenchantment by b. magic hair D771.1; enemies'
feet magically b. D2091.10; evil spirit exorcised by b. fish D2176.3.1;
fairy's look b. mortal F363.4; fakir's imperviousness to b. H1576.2; fire
b. up whole tree at once H1129.5; flood from b. hot liquid A1016.2; fool
tries to purify cotton by b. it J1974; ghost laid by b. body *E446.2; ghost
laid by b. hair E446.2.1; giant rescues woman from b. at stake R151.2;
girl beautified by b. D1865.2.1; house b. for no reason F473.2.4; husband
rescues wife from b. N658, R151.2; jackal's b. tail K581.5; kingdom b.
at night H1292.20; life bound up with b. brand E765.1.2; literal fool b.
down house J2516.3.4; magic object b. animals D1445.6; magic object
protects against b. D1382ff.; magic results from b. D1787; man b. to
death, too lazy to put out fire W111.1.1.1; miraculous b. as punishment
Q551.9.1; murder by b. *K955ff, N657; ogre killed by b. soul G512.5;
ogre tricked into b. his throat K1033; old man b. self with gunpowder,
burns self worse with hot water N255.6; ordeal by b. H221ff.; punishment: b. alive Q414; quenching the b. boat J2162.3; rabbit b. self when
stealing ember A2218.7; release from curse by b. vomit M429.1; sham
wise man b. down own house K1956.8; son rescues mother from b. at
stake R154.1.1; son tries b. up mother S112.7; secret learned by b. hand
N482.1; soul of sleeper prevented from returning by b. the body
E721.1.2.3; sparrow carries b. straw to desecrated church Q222.5.5;
strong hero engendered from a b. brand F611.1.10; unconsumed b. bush
F979.5.1; victim kills swallower from within by b. F912.1; whose duty
to put out fire? meanwhile town b. up J2183.6.1; witch burned by b.
bewitched animal G275.3.1; witch exorcised by b. stick G271.1.

Burns. — Charm for b. D1503.3.1; magic cure of b. D2161.2.3; man in
moon b. brush as punishment for doing so on Sunday A751.1.1; tempted
man b. himself to avoid temptation T333.5.

Burr-woman G311.

Burrow of mole A2491.3; of rat into enemy city K2351.8. — Why crabs
b. in sand A2433.6.3.2; why hyena stays in b. A2433.3.4.

Bursting buttons from violent emotion F1041.6; of frog when he swells
to be big as ox J955.1; of ogre who tries to drink pond dry G522; of
stone as sign of unjust judgment *D1318.1.1; of sword in son's hand
when he is about to kill his father *D1317.6.1; of troll when sun shines
on him G304.2.5; of vessels reveal disobedience D1318.12.1. — Dead
arises at b. of shroud and pursues attendant E261.2; miraculous spring b.
forth for holy person F933.1; object b. as life token E761.5ff.; origin

of culture hero from b. stone A511.1.4.1; river b. from well in pursuit A934.7; serpent b. asunder F981.1.

Burying, see also **Burial;** bewitched animal alive G271.4.10; dupe's hair to catch him K1021.1; the mole as punishment K581.3. — Deity b. mortal A185.4; disenchantment by b. victim and sowing grain over him D719.1; ghost laid by b. church bell, clapper separately E459.6; money received for b. sham-dead person K482; ogre suitor b. woman's murdered lover K912.3; promise on b. father in homeland M258.3; ravens teach Adam b. of dead A2223.7.

Bus. — Ghost rides b. E581.4.

Bush by day, woman by night D621.2.1; loses clothes in shipwreck: hence catches passerby's clothes A2741.4; mistaken for elephant J1771.4. — Angel of the b. A419.1.1; god speaks from b. A182.3.0.1; lake rises from bramble b. F934.2; magic b. D964; self-burning b. D1672.2; spurge-laurel is devil's b. G303.10.11; unconsumed burning b. F979.5.1; why ants are lords of the b. A2433.5.5; why b. holds on to passerby A2792.1, A2275.5.3; why hare lives in b. A2433.3.3.

Bushes. — Eavesdropping wife hidden in b. killed unwittingly by husband N322.2; future hero found in b. L111.2.1; hero an abortion thrown into the b. T572.2.3.

Bush-buck, red color of A2411.1.6.3, A2219.1.

Bush-cat, cry of A2426.1.1.

Bush-rat bites off tortoise's tail A2216.4.

Bushel. — The level b. K223; wind raised by putting cat under b. D2142.1.5.

Bushmen, origin of A1611.3.1.

Bushy. — Why animal has b. tail A2378.6.

Business relations of dwarfs and mortals F451.5.10ff. — Animals in b. relations B294ff.; hero made b. partner of rich man Q111.1; lucky b. ventures *N410—N439; modest b. plans best L250ff.; not in his line of b. J1354; paramour pretends to be coming on b. K1517.10; thanks for being out of b. J2569; worldly-minded learn to pray by thinking of their usual b. V51.2.

Bustard hatches but two eggs A2486.2, A2284.2.

Busy. — "Cease being king if too b. to hear me" J1284.2; executioner kept b. until rescue comes K555; peasant always b. A1655.1; pretending to be b. K1773.

Butcher *P448. — Prophecy: son will be killer; parents make him a b. M306.2; queen is placed in kitchen and abused by b. Q482.2; sheep killed by b., who, they are persuaded, will spare them J2137.5; treacherous b. K2249.4.1.

Butcher's. — Heads of b. family demanded by buyer J1293.5.

Butchers. — Jokes on b. X230ff.; oxen decide not to kill b. since inexpert killers might replace them J215.2.

Butter becomes bloody D474.5; made from nettles D476.1.5; magically kept from coming D2084.2; transferred from another by magic D2083.4; weighed with the bread K478. — Boy with hat of b. X914; charms to make b. come D1573; clarified b. recognized as leavings F647.11; curse: milk will not turn to b. M471.1.1; deceptive b. loan J1556.1; fairy prevents b. coming F369.6; filling cracks with b. J1871; fool squeezes sixteen pounds of b. from dog J1919.3; giants like b. F531.5.13; man made of b.: it melts A1226.1; meat disguised as b. during Lent K498; mountain-man has stack of b. before his door F460.2.4; mud sold as b. K144.3; parson smears his hand with b. X417; pot deceptively sold as b. K144.2; saint makes b. D1573.1; stingy man only looks at b., doesn't eat it W152.5; water becomes b. D478.11; woman created from b. A1275.5.

Butterby Church Z61.3.

Buttercask stolen by playing godfather K372; thought to be a dead man J1783.1.

Butterfly transformed to bamboo D424.1. — Creation of b. A2041; dress becomes b. D444.10.1; friendship between moose and b. A2493.28; man becomes b. D186.1; monkey jumps into water after a b. J2133.10; reincarnation as b. E616.2; soul in form of b. E734.1; wasp twits b. with coming from ugly crysalis J312.1; wedding of b. B285.6.

Butterflies. — Origin of marks of b. A2412.3.2; thieving b. K366.7; transformed b. are rainbow's origin A791.9; why b. haunt urine A2433.5.6.

Butting. — Deceptive game: b. one another like rams K868.

Buttocks. — Bare b. as mock sunrise K1886.3.2; goddess with one and a half b. A123.8; magic b. D1006; ogre cutting off own b. G528; origin of animal's b. A2362; stinging of b. as cough cure N643.

Buttons burst as consequence of violent emotion F1041.6.

Buyer and deaf seller X111.11. — Attempt to cheat the b. J2083.

Buying, see also **Bought;** forbidden C781; off masked thief K152; same article several times K258.2. — Dwarfs b. peas for more than they are worth F451.5.10.5; drunk man tries b. island X812; ignorant youth b. medical degree K1955.8.1; numskulls b. things in common: paying full price J2037; wife b. husband T296.

Buzzard hatched by hawk ejected for fouling nest Q432.1; steals coyote's eyes K333.3; transformed to door flap D423.4. — Food of b. A2435.4.5; origin of crest of b. A2321.7; why b. is bald A2317.3; witch as b. G211.4.5.

Buzzards. — Lassoed b. rescue man from hole B547.2.1.

Cabbage. — Carrying wolf, goat, and c. across stream H506.3; the great c. (lie) X1423.1; transformation by eating c. D551.2.1.

Cabbages, meat fed to J1856.1.

Cabinet-maker P444.

Cackling geese spread alarm B521.3.2; of guinea hen A2426.2.13.

Cadaver arm trick renders insane N384.0.1.1.

Caesar's scorn of his wife's advice leads to disaster J155.3.

Caesarean childbirth a custom T584.3.

Cage, see also **Prison.** — Adulteress confined in a c. Q433.1.1; enormous c. F899.3; ogre trapped in c. G514.1; soul in bird c. E711.15; thief hidden in c. K312.1.

Cages. — Captivity in c. R41.7.

Cain drinks Abel's blood in dream D1812.3.3.7; slain with apple F839.3.1; slays Abel with camel bone F839.3; stole ducks from Eden A2426.4.1.1. — Animals refuse to devour C. B591.0.1; Formorians descended from C. A1659.1.1; giants as descendants of C. F531.6.1.9; mark of C. Q556.2; pygmies as descendants of C. F535.0.1.

Cairn marks battle site A989.4; marks burial A988. —Battle-c. P554.

Cake bag full of cobras K444.2; becomes bloody D474.3; vendor robbed on way to fair K475.3. — Alphabet written on c. learned by eating it D1819.4.2; bleeding c. F991.3; bread becomes c. D476.4; eating c. in famine if there is no bread J2227; enemy cured by poisoned c. F959.6.1; identification by ring baked in c. H94.1; magic c. *D1031.2ff.; magic c. restores speech D1507.5; magic rolling c. D1313.1.2; man worships a c. which from time to time he eats V1.10.1; planted c. grows cakes F1005.1; pseudo-magic c. tree K112.3; pursuit of rolling c. leads to quest *H1226ff.; single c. for Lent made large *K2311; tiger-shaped c. fulfills death prophecy M341.2.10.1; why c. not eaten during Lent V73.6.3; wolf bringing c. from the window-sill beaten K1022.4.

Cakes. — Alfred and the c. K521.4.1.2; charging thirty c. for cooking twenty-five K255.1; coins mistaken for c. J1772.3.1; guest of stingy host brings along c. to eat J1575; how he knew she was baking c. J1713.1; poisoned c. intended for husband eaten by thieves N659.1; pupil eats c. given as alms to master W125.4; rhymes about c. wife has stolen K435.1; throwing c. into uncles' faces H35.5; tree of c. D2106.3, F811.1.10; wall of c. separates enemies D2163.6.2.

Calabash. — Animals escape from forbidden c. C915.2.1; child born carrying c. T552.3; goddess with c. in moon A751.8.3; life bound up with c. E765.3.2; looking into c. tabu C324.1; magic c. *D965.2; man transformed to c. D221; origin of sea from overturned c. A924.1; recognition by c. H133; soul in c. E711.2.1; universe created from c. A617.2.

Calabashes magically broken D2099.4. — Flood from broken water c. A1016.4.

Calamity, see also **Catastrophe, Disaster.** — Bewailing a c. that has not occurred J2198; crow's maxim on flying away from c. J171.3.1; devil's presence presages c. G303.15.1; ghost light indicates impending c. E530.1.5; ghost as c. omen E575; wraith as c. omen E723.8.

Calamities at hero's birth T583.2; of the world A1000ff.

Calculation of changeling's age by the age of the forest F321.1.1.5; of time and the seasons A1485. — Interrupted c. J2035; riddles of difficult c. H680—H719.

Calendar, Russian A1689.7.

Calf all one color belongs to devil G303.10.9; asks for respite until he grows up K553.0.2; mistaken for colt J1759.4.1; pitying draft ox is taken to slaughter L456; as sacrifice V12.4.4.2; -sheep B14.3; transformed to person D333.2; weeps B736.6. — Brahmin unwittingly kills c. N361.1; devil as c. G303.3.3.1.4; did the c. eat the man? J1815; eating c. forbidden C221.1.1.2; forgotten fiancée reawakens husband's memory by serving as milkmaid and talking to c. *D2006.1.2; ghost of c. E521.4; ghost as c. E423.1.8.1; god assumes form of c. D133.4.1; golden (silver) c. B102.5ff.; golden c. entered by Satan G303.18.4; golden c. moves D1639.5; hatching out a c. from a cheese J1902.2; helpful c. B411.3; Holy Ghost has just had a c. X435.4; image of golden c. vivified D445.3; islands from transformed cow and c. A955.5; line drawn by saint's bachall separates c. from its mother D1574; magic c. B184.2.5; magic knowledge of unborn c. D1819.8; making a bull bear a c. (task) H1024.1.1; man named "C." frees veal thief K579.7; man transformed to c. D133.4; origin of c. sacrifice A1545.3.2; parson made to believe that he will bear a c. J2321.1; prophecy: death from c. M341.2.22; punishment for flaying live c. Q211.6.1; quest for golden c. H1331.3.3; reincarnation as c. E611.2.3; riddle about golden c. H832; saint gives c. to wolf W10.2; slain c. alive next day *E155.5.1; speaking c. B211.1.5.5; swift when only a c. J2212.5; tabu to kill sacred c. C92.1.2; transformation to c. Q551.3.2.8; why is cow beaten by c.? H1292.16; wife substitutes c. for beggar husband abuses K1846; wolf substitutes for c. D2156.8; worship of golden c. V1.11.1.

Calf's bleating as accusation of stealing J1895; head to death's head D465, (punishment) Q551.3.3. — Cow punished for c. misdeeds J1863; getting the c. head out of the pot J2113; person with c. head F511.0.9.2; tail in ground betrays c. killing K1686; water on the c. back J1903.1.

Calves kept from cows to commemorate death V65.1; kept from cows during fast P623.0.7. — Beating c. to punish bull J1863.1; fairies admit c. to cows F366.1.2; fairies ride c. F366.1.3; four c. to one cow at birth T586.4.1; men must have been c., fond of milk J2214.6; "why dost thou frighten the silly c.?" K1784.2.

Calf-shed. — Future heroine found in c. L111.2.1.1.

Calf-statues, origin of A1546.0.3.

Call: Dord fían R187.1; for help from distance D1827.2. — Magic object comes at owner's c. D1649.2; treasure found when obeying c. of nature N534.6.

Called. — Animals c. together by magic object D1441; devil becomes powerless when c. by name G303.16.19.9; devil's castle c. hell G303.8.3.2; king's sons c. kings P30.1; girl not to eat before being c. by father C231.1; man c. for help by animal B383; mortals c. to by fairies F276.

Calling on devil makes him come *G303.6.1.2. — Fairy c. victim only once F363.5; ghost c. E402.1.1.1; ghosts summoned by c. E386.3; sham c. to helpers frightens off robbers K548.3; tabu: c. (on ogre or destructive animal) C20ff., (on God) C94.4, (on spirit or devil) *C10ff., (on supernatural wife) C31.6; wind raised by c. on devil D2142.1.3; wood-spirit c. in woods F441.6.4.

Calm when wind-spirit sleeps A1128.2. — Making weather c. H335.6; quiet c. brings man fortune Q6.1.

Calming of whirlpool D2151.4.

Calumniated princess's corpse fails to rot H251.3.14; wife reunited with husband N741.3.1; woman intercedes for accusers W11.5.9.1. — Feigning sleep with c. hero H1556.5.

Calumniators try to make friendly kings fight K1084.4.

Calypso, isle of F131.1.

Camel as animals' king B240.11; and ass together captured because of ass's singing J2137.6; bone slays Abel F839.3; and donkey trade un-deserved compliments J867; determines road to be taken B151.1.5; determines road to be taken B151.1.5; helpful B405; induced to offer self as sacrifice K962; and jackal exchange food J512.11; killed by lion in game K869.3; lures wolf, crushes him K839.5; mistaken for religious holiday J1738.7; tries in vain to dance J512.3, J2133.1; wishes long neck J2072.5. — Creation of c. A1873; goat eats while c. talks H334.2; jackal puts head in anus of sham-dead c. K1036.1.1; man overloads, starves c. W155.1.2; mice overcome c. L315.10; one-eyed c. (deduction) J1661.1.1; men at first frightened at c. take him into their service U131.2; speaking c. B211.1.6; tabu: touching resting c. C537.1; treacherous c. K2295.5; why ears of c. are such A2325.4, A2325.7, A2232.1; why neck of c. bends upwards A2351.1; winged c. B47.

Camel's tail cut off, turns to grass R231.2. — Jackal demands c. tongue K255.4; rat imagines self c. owner J953.17; why c. back humped A2356.2.13; wolf puts head in c. mouth J2131.5.5.

Camels fall from sky into girl's eyes F615.3.1.2. — Copulation of c. A2496.3; giant roasts c. G171; lie: tying up c. in sheet X942.1; loading ferocious c. H1154.3.5; man, c. rise into air F1083.2; thank God that c. have no wings J2564.

Camouflage K1872ff.

Camp. — Disguise to enter c. K2357; enormous army c. F873.2; trans-formation to gain enemy's c. D641.2.

Campfires. — Pursuit by following c. R272.

Camping. — Leaping a c. place tabu C876; warrior reveals c. place J2366.

Camphor, island of F732.3; tree of F811.1.5.

Camrösh B35.

Can, magic D1171.5.

Canaanites go nude A1683.4; have curly hair A1661.3; have red eyes A1666.1.

Canal dug by saint on tree D2121.14. — Bluff: digging c. instead of bringing water in skin K1741.3.1; "where did dirt go when c. dug?" J1309.3.

Canary. — Color of c. A2411.2.1.14; why eggs of c. are yellow A2219.1, A2391.1.

Cancer from ghost's slap E234.1, E542.1.4.1. — Magic cure for c. D1502.10.

Candle becomes stone D471.9; burning quickly as holiness test H257.1; of human fat K437.2; kept at right so as to tell one's right hand in dark J1735.1; light protection against ghost E434.9; light used to examine sun dial J1943; put in the stove to dry J2122; stuck with pins as love charm J1355.3.6. — Animal with c. mistaken for ghost J1782.5; adulteress sends husband out for c. K1521.4.1; burned c. causes death D2061.2.2.6; cat and c. J1908.1; chaste woman can blow out c. with one puff and relight with another H413.1; devil exorcised with c. G303.16.14.4; each drop of innocent blood turns to c. D1318.5.3; ever-burning c. D1652.11; let me live as long as this c. lasts *K551.9; life bound up with c. E765.1.1; magic c. *D1162.2ff.; minister swallows c. to outwit devil G303.12.5.4; miser dies rather than buy c. W153.11; pope's c. lights itself H41.3; resuscitation by c. E64.6; sailor offers saint c. as large as mast K231.3.1; soul as c. E742.1; substitute for c. repaid with substitute for money J1551.5; trespass betrayed by dripping c. C916.1.

Candles. — Creation of bee to provide wax for c. in church A2012.1; deer with c. atop antlers B253.6; disenchantment by maidens walking with lighted c. in procession D759.6; holy c. V133; thief places c. on crabs K335.0.5.1.

Candle-moth. — Monkey transformed to c. D411.5.2.

Candlemas, festival of V70.6.

Candlestick, jewelled F789.2.1.

Cane as evidence of robbery N614. — Giant c. for strong man F612.3.1; thrown c. becomes child T549.2.

Canes. — Origin of c.: from whip in ground A2825.

Canidae, creation of A1830ff.

Canine animal transformed to person D313ff. — Man transformed to c. animal D113ff.

Canis B331.2.

Canister. — Heart breaks at third drink from silver c. F1041.1.1.1.

Cannibal *G10ff.; bird G353.1; bird as ogre G355; gods A153.8; killed by wife's relatives G551.5; nature of woman recognized when she devours dead buffalo raw H46.1; offers wealth for life G683; ogre G312. — Cutting toenails of c. woman G519.1.2; husband rescues wife from c. R151.3; normal man transformed to c. D91; person becomes c. G30ff.; quest to land of c. giants H1289.3.1; sun as a c. A711.2; witch's familiar a c. G225.0.7.

Cannibals G0—G99; persuaded to take snuff and killed K827.2. — Culprit eaten by c. Q429.1; ghormuhas: c. half-horse, half-man B15.7.5; lost husband's bones found among c. G691.4.

Cannibalism *G10—G99, (accidental) X21, (occasional) G50—G79, (regular) G10—G49; out of vogue C227.1; of Pisācas G312; punished

Q215. — False accusation of c.: biting off corpse's finger to get ring N342.6; threatened c. frightens off robbers H335.1.10.

Cannon. — Boy shot from c. X1852; nobody can move c.: guard quits J1849.4; treasure buried in c. barrel N511.1.8.

Canoe hauled over dead man's body causes return from dead E607.3; island D1524.4; of sand J2171.1.3.1; transformed into coconut tree A2615.3; transformed into rock D454.10.2. — Birds build c. B572.2; clam swallows c. party F911.4.1.1; cocoanut c. F841.1.4.1; compressible c. D631.3.1; enormous c. F841.3.3; fairies build c. F271.2.3; god as c. builder A451.2.1; hibiscus blossom becomes c. D451.4.2; magic c. *D1122; man becomes c. D255.1; merman lays hands on side of c. B82.7; phantom c. E535.3.1; stone c. D1524.3.1; women in c. tabu C181.10.

Canoes formerly self-propelling A1346.2.4.

Canoe-bailer transformed to person D434.3.

Canonical hours V48. — Birds call at c. hours B252.2.

Canons compared to stew J81.3.

Canopy. — Wedding c. over bride and groom T135.14.

Canopies in otherworld F166.9.

Canute vainly forbids tide to rise L414.

Canvas. — Ship wrapped with feather-beds and c. F1031.

Cap of invisibility F455.5.3, K1349.10; o' Rushes K521.4.3, K1815, R221. — Ghost of man buried without c. E412.3.1; ghost in red c. E422.4.6; huldra-woman's c. F460.1.4.3; magic c. *D1067.2; permission to pick up c. gives entrance to heaven K2371.1.1; quest for best c. H1319.2; trolls' c. of invisibility F455.5.3; wild huntsman with black fur c. E501.8.6.

Caps of dwarfs F451.2.7.1, F451.2.7.6, F451.3.3.8; of mountain-men F460.1.4.1ff. — Devils' c. from man's nail parings G303.25.5.1; fairies with red c. F236.3.2; substituted c. cause ogre to kill his own children *K1611.

Capaneus. — Zeus smites C. while he is climbing a ladder L472.

Cape, see also **Cloak, Mantle.** — Magic transportation by c. D1520.6.

Capital punishment Q410ff. — Bringing arms to c. after sunset tabu C752.1.1; leaving c. ninth night tabu C751.6; parishoner glad to get back c. J1583; wager: fortune made from c. or from working at vocation N66.

Capon and the hen J1269.6.

Capriciousness of luck *N170ff. — King's c. censured: ass in stream J1675.3.

Captain buried with his crew V67.4.1; hangs own son for violating order M13.2; will not betray king's secret P361.7. — Mermaid asks c. to move boat B81.13.1.

Captive freed for having kept word Q54.2; king's children made slaves P173; in ogre's house helps hero G535; sends token of safety H85; released because of ability to recite story J1185, V151.1; spirits of dead H972.1. — Animal rescues c. *B544; former c. recognizes chieftain

H173.2; god protects tormented c. A185.2.2; magic object enables c. to escape D1395ff.; man's love for c. wife rewarded Q56.1; mountainmen chain c. peasant F460.4.4.2; rescue of c. *R110—R199; woman c. in elephant's ear H1151.18.

Captive's. — Cannibal cuts c. finger to test fatness G82.1; magic as c. ransom D859.8; recognition of c. voice brings about rescue from ogre G556.

Captives and fugitives R (entire chapter); re-blinded if they cross steppingstones without stumbling H1575.1; as slaves P173. — Journey to disenchant c. H1385.0.1; mortals c. in fairyland *F375.

Captivity *R0—R99; preferred to death J217. — Animal grateful for ransom from c. B366; crab sings about his c. B214.1.8.1; daw fleeing from c. caught by thread around foot N255.5; death preferred to c. J227.1; fettered monster's c. A1074; ogre in animal form lures victim into c. G403; transformation to escape from c. D642.1; ungrateful animal returned to c. J1172.3; wild man released from c. aids hero G671.

Captor beguiled *K500—K699; contributes to captive's ransom W11.5.8; persuaded into illusory punishment K580ff. — Escape by overawing c. *K540ff.; joining c. out of gratitude R71; magic object helps overawe c. D1613; princess rescued from c. R111.1; punishment which proves fatal to c. K582; rescue by daughter of c. R162.

Capture of animals A2465ff., as task H1154ff.; of castle by feigning death K2362; by deception K700—K799; by magic object *D1430ff.; of moon J2271.4; by ogre G420ff.; of town by boy-hero F611.3.2.6; of two of every animal F681.8. — Numskull brings about his own c. J2136; selling soul to escape c. M211.7.

Captured animals avenge themselves Q385; fairy's promises for her release F341.2.1; queen commits suicide P26. — Demon sees image in mirror, thinks he is c. J1795.1; dwarfs promise to emigrate if c. dwarfs are released F451.9.1.5; fairy c. F387; fairy c. by mortal escapes F329.4.3; father rescues son c. by enemy R153.3.1; hero c. by man he has rescued N763; maiden c. by mermaid B81.4; mermaid c. B81.13.11; ogre c. G514ff.; person aids ogre and is c. G411; soul of sleeper c. in animal form E721.1.2.1; souls c. on leaving corpse E752.1.3; sultan's daughter in love with c. knight T91.6.4.1.

Car, see also **Automobile, Carriage.** — Fairy c. F242.1; man before whom riderless c. stops chosen king H171.4.

Caraway. — Dwarfs dislike c. seed in food F451.3.7.1, F451.9.1.1.

Carbuncle, incandescent D1645.1.

Carcass. — Animal born from c. B713; animal caught in c. J2136.6; bees born from c. of ox B913.1; capture by hiding in animal c. K751.1; haunted house where horse c. drops down chimney H1411.1.1.

Carcasses. — Eating one hundred c. as suitor test H331.17.

Card. — Ghost scares c. players E293.2; magic c. *D1267; magic object stolen in c. game D861.6; magic wishing c. D1470.1.48; picking up c.

fallen to ground forbidden C525; soul won from devil in c. game E756.2; spirit summoned by writing on c. D2074.2.4.

Cards. — Dead persons play c. E577.2; devil appears when c. are played G303.6.1.5; devil plays c. N4; Krishna plays c. with wives A164.3.1; men in animal's belly playing c. F911.3.3; parson plays c. N5, N71; playing c. with devil in church (fear test) H1421; power of winning at c. N221; sermon begun with illustration from c. N71; symbolic interpretation of playing c. H603; trickster cheats clerks at c. J1115.1; weighted order c. J1382.2.

Cardinal. — Color symbolism of c. points Z140.2.1; treacherous c. K2282.

Cardinal's decision on monks' sounding matins J1179.13; luxury J1263.4.1.

Care against future tyranny J643; of children *T600—T699; of favorites by deity A185; in selecting the creature to carry one J657. — Crown brings too much c. J347.2; inscription on home of riddle-solver: "I have no c." H562; will take c. of the thirst J1322.1.

Carelessness causes thief's capture J2136.5. — Husband made to believe that yarn has changed to tow through his c. J2325.

Caressed. — Hares (sheep) treacherously c. by dog K2031, K2061.3.

Caresses. — Son disenchants animal father by enduring his c. without fear D735.4.2.

Caretaker. — Sun as c. of the poor A739.8.

Caribou becomes person D314.1.2. — Creation of c. A1876.1; how c. got antlers A2326.1.2, A2247; looking at c. tabu C316.2; man becomes c. D114.1.6; why c. migrated A2482.2; why c. has no teeth A2345.7.3; why c. has small eyes A2332.3.3.

Carnage. — Battle c. personified Z132.0.1.

Carnal. — No c. sin in otherworld F167.10.

Carnation transformed to person D431.1.2. — Hero's power to transform girl to c. brings about recognition H151.7; man (woman) transformed to c. D212.1.

Carnivora, creation of A1810—A1839.

Carols. — Knockers sing c. at Christmas time F456.2.3.2.

Carp. — Man transformed to c. D171.

Carp's wedding B283.2.

Carpe diem (advice from fool) J2197.

Carpenter P456; blames the nails J1891.2; of the gods A143; makes magic horse D853.1; races wooden horse D1719.1.4. — Animals as c. B572; cumulative tale: c. releases caught birds Z49.7; disguise as c. K521.2.5, K1816.11, K2357.12; ingenious c. F675; remarkable c. X994; magic c. constructs expandable bed D1620.3.2.

Carpenters. — God of c. A451.2; men disguised as c. abduct bride K1825.7; why c. are everywhere: flood scatters them A1445.2.1.

Carpentry. — Origin of c. A1445.2; shortsightedness in c. J2171.

Carpet. — Countryman's avoidance of c. J1742.5.1; extraordinary c. F783; half a c. to keep father warm in old age J121; incendiary c. of

giants' cave set afire K812.1.1; magic c. *D1155; magic c. takes hero
to girl's room K1346.1; magic shuttle makes c. D1485.1; paramour rolled
into c. K1521.7; quest for most beautiful c. H1319.3.

Carriage as swift as thought D1521.4. — Animal characteristics: c.
A2440ff.; animal drives c. B295; box transformed to c. D454.1.1; devil
disappears into c. drawn by four black horses G303.17.2.9; devil's c.
drawn by white horses G303.7.3.4; extraordinary c. F861; fairy hangs
onto c. F366.5; forgotten fiancée magically stops wedding c. of new
bride D2006.1.5; ghost on c. ride E332.3.2; magic c. *D1111f.; man
throws c. with horses, driver on haystack F624.3.1; pumpkin transformed
to c. D451.3.3; woman has worn out c. load of shoes with walking
F1015.1.2.

Carried. — All that can be c. as wages K1732; burden c. by ghost
E592; castle in air c. by eagles F771.2.1.2; church c. across a stream
by giants F531.3.6; curse: to be c. off by evil spirit M432; dead wife c.
with man E322.5; death feigned in order to be c. K1861; dupe c. aloft
and dropped *K1041; exposed child c. off by wild beast S355; extraordinary burden c. by animals F982ff.; fée c. off by mortal F304.6;
giant c. to eagle's nest F531.6.17.3; giant load c. by strong man F631ff.;
giant so large he cannot be c. by horse F531.2.7; girl c. off because of
broken tabu C951; head c. under arm F511.0.4; hero c. by bird to
mistress's chamber B582.2.1; hero c. over water by magic salmon *B175.1;
king always c. by slaves P14.5; man c. in giant's pocket F531.1.5.1; men
c. by animals B550ff.; lover c. on mistress's shoulders: no footprints
K1549.3; mortal c. by dwarf F451.3.8.1; owner c. with magic object
thrown ahead D1526; paramour c. off in box K1555; people c. away to
fairyland *F320ff.; person c. off by wild hunt E501.18.4; person c. off
to otherworld for breaking tabu C954; person c. to or from upper
world by bird *F62; souls c. to heaven by doves E754.2.1; stolen goods
c. to dupe's house so that he is accused K401.2; ten serving women c.
in bottle D55.2.4; thorn stick c. by devil G303.4.8.5; Thumbling c. up
chimney by steam of food F535.1.1.2; trees c. by giants F531.3.10;
trickster hides in bag to be c. K1892.1; ungrateful ape plucks feathers
from heron who has c. him across water W154.5.1.3; victim c. in bag
by ogre G441; wild huntsman c. on people's backs *E501.15.3; witch c.
off by devil G275.1.

Carrier. — Lie: remarkable c. X942; river c. throws passenger off to
drown S131.1.

Carrion as vulture's food A2435.4.5.1.

Carrying child on back tabu C875; corpse of murdered man (punishment)
Q511; each other and shortening the way (telling tales and amusing)
H586.3; ever-increasing burden up mountain H1114.2; off huge quantity
of money (task) H1127; hundreds of sheep across stream one at a time
(task) H1111; large load identifies chief H41.10; many water jugs as

suitor test H331.10; mountain on head H1146; murdered man's blood (ordeal) H227; person to remedy instead of opposite J2214.8; water in a sieve (task) H1023.2. — Angel c. mortal V232.2; animal c. man across water B551ff.; animal characteristics from contest in c. A2251; dead try c. off living E266; devil c. off people G303.9.5; disenchantment of girl by c. her on back D732.1; fish c. man shakes him off when struck M205.1.1.1; flight c. friend on back R242; familiar spirit acquired by c. egg under left arm-pit F403.2.1.1; giant c. prodigious burden F531.3.13; god c. siblings on back A137.4.1; impostors tricked into c. hero in box K1942; king c. off subject's wife P15.2.1; king to be succeeded by person c. his body P17.12; man marries fairy c. him off F302.3.1.3; ogre tricked into c. his prisoners home in bag G561; revenant as woman c. baby E425.1.4; reward for c. Christ across a stream Q25; servant c. master, drops him in stream J2133.5.1.1; servants c. master to search for dog J2163.2; tabu: unseemly acts while c. divine image C56; trial by ordeal subverted by c. magic object D1394.1; trickster c. girl across stream, leaves old woman K1339.7; trolls c. off people F455.6.6; vow against c. a woman M142.

Cart, see also **Carriage, Wagon;** as back legs for crippled pig X1202.1. — Devil in c. G303.7.4; extraordinary c. F861ff.; flying c. F861.2.1; ghost rides in c. E272.1; magic c. D1112; phantom c. driver E512; strong hero lifts c. F624.3.

Carts to shade roof J1879.1. — Man draws sixty c. of wood X953.1.

Cartridge. — Magic c. kills D1402.7.4.

Cartwheel. — Cauterizing sick c. J2412.7; devil helps man place c. G303.22.4.

Carving boar's head impossible for cuckold H425.1. — Magic c. knife *D1173; origin of wood c. A1465.5; recognition by c. H35.4f.; wise c. of the fowl H601.

Case. — Sun kept in a c. A721.0.3.

Cash payers favored J1382ff.

Cashel, vision concerning V515.1.3.2.

Cask. — Devil to fill c. full of money K219.3; escape from deluge in c. A1021.0.2; exposure in c. *S141; ghost as rolling c. E426.2; magic c. D1171.9; odor of the wine c. J34; punishment in spiked c. Q463; resuscitation by assembling members and leaving in c. for nine days E37; sea issues from marvelous c. F711.1; treasure buried in c. N511.1.8; treasure found in c. N525; water sold as wine in partitioned c. K476.3.

Casks. — Chaste wife tricks suitors into c. K1218.1.1; thieves hidden in oil c. K312.

Casket with Good Luck in it given to men by Zeus N113.1; lid furnishes money D1452.3. — Children in c. floating down river H157.

Caskets, three H511.1, L211, D1658.3.2.

Cassandra destined never to be believed M301.0.1.

Cassawary. — Man becomes c. D169.4; tabu to eat c. C221.1.2.1.

Cast. — Divine child c. out at birth A112.11; disposal of c.-off wife
S430ff.; evil spirit c. out of person E728.1; hills from stones c. by giants
A963.5; lucky c. of weapon N623; ogre's ashes c. on stream cause
rapids to stop G655; no shadow c. by ghosts E421.2; c.-forth wife must
sit at horseblock of palace Q482.4.

Caste of supernatural husband C32.2.3; tabus C551. — Falling in love
with different c. T91.7.2; god enamored of low c. woman T91.3.3.1;
princess cannot marry into low c. P41; quarrel of dog and cat over
which has higher c. A2281.1.2; untouchables are certain c. whose touch
is considered a pollution C551; woman curses her c. M464; why certain
c. is kind to animals A1599.13.

Castes. — Origin of c. A1651; tabu to eat with certain c. C246.

Casting animal's eyes K1442; in graveyard tabu after sunset C752.1.5;
lots as truth test H245. — Devil creates devils by c. water behind himself G303.1.4.1.

Castle, see also **Palace;** disenchanted D705.1, D789.8; in magic box
D1174.1; magically made smaller D491.5; magically transported D2136.2;
in lower world F80.1.1; sinks into earth F941.1. — Building c. (task)
H1133, (in one night) H1104, (suspended between heaven and earth)
H1036; building wax replica of c. H1133.6; captivity in c. R41.1; capture
of c. (by feigning death) K2362, (by pretending to surrender and entering)
K777; destruction of iron c. H1562.12; devil builds himself a c. and
calls it hell G303.8.3.2; devil prophesying in enchanted c. H1411.3;
disenchantments concerning c. D759.4, D759.5; dragons live beneath c.
B11.3.4; dwarfs in underground c. F451.4.1.2; dwarfs move mortal's c.
F451.5.1.12; drawfs' gold c. F451.4.3.6; fairy c. F222; friendly ghost
haunts c. E338.1; eagles carry c. in air F982.1; enchanted c. D6; extraordinary c. *F771ff.; ghost at c. every seven years E585.2; ghosts haunt
c. E282; giant lives in c. in air G162; giant ogres possess c. G111;
hedgehog builds c. B191.5; key to enchanted c. D791.4; king angry at
hero entering c. without permission P14.11; king banishes nobleman
whose c. he wants P12.8; magic object found in magic c. D846; maiden
found in magic c. N711.2; objects found in deserted c. where hero is
served by unseen hands H1239.2; outcast's c. like king's H153; owner
disguised as monk enters own captured c. K2357.0.2; quest for c. of
jewels H1343; troll's c. G304.3.1; wild hunt appears at c. E501.12.8;
woman in c. gives guest directions H1232.3.

Castles. — Dog between two c. J2183.1; giants live in ruined c. F531.6.3.1.

Castor and Pollux A116.

Castrated. — Bishop wishes all monks were c. X457.1; friar accused of
rape c. K2111.3; joker asks to be c. N334.3; Virgin saves life of c. man
V256.4.

Castration bargain (wife sent) K241; by magic D2062.4.2; as mutilation
S176.1; of paramour by husband K1558.1; as punishment Q451.10.1;
of self by beaver to save own life J351.1; to test wife H492.3; through

ignorance J1919.5. — Choice between c. or blinding J229.12; husband prepares for c. of crucifix K1558; making the dupe strong by c. K1012.1.

Cat aids confession of debt J1141.1.11; alleged to fish for master K341.11.1; as beast of ill-omen B147.1.2.2; beaten for not working W111.3.2; and candle J1908.1; carries person B557.7; carrying lantern K264.2; castle F771.4.2; causes enmity between animals K2131.1; ceases catching rats as soon as he is given home in monastery U271; chooses rat meat at feast U135.1; commanded to pray so as not to slay man: why he purrs A2236.8; crawls to steeple and tries to fly J2133.3; crossing path ghost sign E436.2; curses woman eating fish cat has caught Q281.3; and devil G303.3.3.1.2, G303.10.1, J1785.5; of divine origin: is praying when it purrs A1811.3; drives away, doesn't eat, rats J766.1; fails to be beguiled into releasing mouse K561.1.1; garbles message from man to tiger A2281.1.1; grows large as cow F983.3; to guard cheese J2103.1; guards imprisoned beauty T50.1.4; hangs on wall pretending to be dead K2061.9; harms dead and dying B766.1ff.; invites hens to a feast and kills them K815.4; as judge between sparrow and hare K815.7; kills attacking rat B524.1.3; leaves house when report is made of death of one of his companions *B342; lures foxes with music K815.15; made to mew, distract owner K341.7.2; makes truce with mice, then eats them K815.13; offers to act as doctor for cock and hen K2061.7; as ogre sucks blood G351.2; omits teaching tiger all he knows A2581; and parrot cheat each other at dinner J1565.3; as sacrifice V12.4.2; scratches out bear's tongue (lie) X1211.1; as servant B292.6ff.; shrieks and the frightened bear falls out of the tree K2324; skin sold as mink K261.1; steals sausage from table but dog receives blows K2171; sucks sleeping child's breath B766.2; as thumbling's horse F535.1.1.6; trained for gambling N7; transformed to person D342; transformed to maiden runs after mouse J1908.2; transformed to other animal D412.1ff., A1945.1; unjustly accuses, eats cock U31.1; in warehouse J1175.1; and witches D1766.4, G211.1.7, G224.11.12, G241.1.4, G225.3, G243.2.2, *G252, G262.1.1, G262.3.2; witness to betrothal punishes violator M205.1.2; in wood-pile prevents axe from cutting D2186. — Abduction by c. R13.2.3; animal thought to be a giant c. J1756; association of rat (mouse) with c. ceases as soon as mutual danger has passed J426; belling the c. J671.1; boy to see whether there is fire in the house feels of c. W111.2.5; creation of c. A1811; why c. eats first A2545.2; dead c. better than crown to crow J242.7; devastating c. B16.1ff.; fat c. Z33.2; food of c. A2435.3.2; fortune to go in direction c. jumps K2.1; ghost of c. E521.3; giant c. B871.1.6; giant ogre as c. G126.1; giant tricked into becoming mouse and eaten by c. K722; helpful c. *B422, (borrows measure for his master's money) K1954.1, (wins wife for master) B582.1.1, (helps steal back magic stolen object) *D882.1.1; horse used by mortal under fairy spell changes to gray c. F234.4.1; humans with c. characteristics B29.4ff., F511.2.2.1 (ears),

F512.1.4 (eyes), F514.3 (snout); hare escapes galloping c. K562.2; hostile
c. B17.1.5; how c. was domesticated A2513.2; husband reincarnated as c.
H1385.4.1; killing c. tabu C841.11; lifting a certain c. (task) H1149.2;
is the big c. still living? K1728; why c. keeps chimney-corner A2433.3.1.1,
A2223.1; magic c. B181.1ff.; magic object received from c. woman
D825.1; man transformed to c. D142; man reincarnated as c. E611.5;
mouse created by Lucifer, c. by Michael to destroy mouse A1751.1;
mouse transformed to c. D411.6.2; moving dead c. tabu C537.3; poor
boy said by helpful c. to be dispossessed prince K1952.1; revenant as c.
E423.1.2; getting rid of c. J2101; sacred c. B811.4; sea-c. B73; singing c.
B214.1.3; speaking c. B211.1.8; stolen meat and weighed c. J1611; tabu:
resurrecting c. for trifling purpose C96.1; talking to c. obtains serving
for student J1341.10; truth-telling c. B135; turnips called bacon: c. called
rabbit J1511.2; tying c. to horse's tail K2383; Whittington's c. N411.1;
why c. hides its excreta A2385.4, A2495.1; why c. keeps chimney-corner
A2433.3.1.1; why mouse does not defend self against c. A2462.3.

Cat's bodily characteristics A2325.6 (jagged ears), A2326.2.1 (lack of
horns), A2356.2.3 (arched back), A2365.2.0.1 (penis), A2441.1.10 (walk);
curse causes woman to bear cats M437.1; enemies A2281.1ff., A2494.1ff.;
friendships A2493.9ff., A2493.18; marriage B281.9ff., B282.4.2, B601.12;
only trick J1662; paw cut off (woman's hand missing) D702.1.1; supernatural qualities B121.3 (magic wisdom), D1032.2 (magic flesh),
D1840.2.1 (invulnerable), D2071.1.2 (averting Evil Eye), D2142.1.5 (raises
wind), E731.2 (as soul), G283.2.1 (prevents wind), N542.2 (locates treasure); tail mistaken for worm J1759.5. — Curse: god to live c. life
M414.13.1; deity with c. head A131.3.1; giant as black c. son *F531.6.1.3;
lighting the c. tail J2101.1; milk overheated to break c. taste for it
K499.4; ogre with c. head, tail G369.4; origin of c. skin A2311.2.

Cats crossing one's path sign of ghosts E436.2; infest haunted house
H1411.2; unite against wolf J1025.2. — Army of c. B268.11; country
without c. F708.1; dance of c. B293.1; fear test: night watch with magic
c. H1411.2ff.; four c. carry coffin F982.2; king of c. B241.2.3; lies about
c. X1211; magic fishhook catches c. D1444.3; how mice can rid themselves of c. H1292.10; mouse teaches her child to fear quiet c. J132; rats
cause c. to be killed K2172; saint kills king of c. F981.7; scratching c. in
hell A671.2.13; slain c. hung up and covered with grain (penance) Q523.6;
tiger-cubs mistaken for jungle c. J1758.6.

Cataclysm. — Leviathan produces c. by striking earth with tail B16.4.1.1;
vow binding unless c. occurs M117.

Cataclysms. — Succession of creations and c. A632.

Catapult-hurled stones thrown back at enemy F636.4.2.

Cataract. — King's death spear cast into c. P16.5.

Cataracts, origin of A935.

Catarrh. — Wife cures c. F950.2.1.

Catastrophe, see also **Calamity, Disaster.** — Escape by announcing c. K686; mermaid as omen of c. B81.13.7; world c. A1000ff., M357.

Catch tales X903, Z13. — Great c. of fish X1150.1.

Catcher. — Hero as marvelous c. F698.1; lie: remarkable c. X944.

Catching, see also **Caught;** animal devil G303.9.9.7; the devil G303.16.19.18; a noise (task) H1023.12; huge fish without nets or tackle (task) H1154.4; wild animals as suitor task H336.2. — Bird of prey c. quarry a good omen D1812.5.2.4; dwarf driven away by maid c. and kissing him F451.5.19.1; first man c. woman in snare A1275.10; resuscitation by c. in snare E23; transformation to fish by c. in fish-trap D533.

Caterpillar. — Burning c. tabu C841.3; god with body of c. A123.1.5; helpful c. B484.1; man becomes c. D192.1; marriage to person in c. form B643.3; why hairy c. is venomous A2532.2.

Caterpillars. — Why c. climb trees A2479.6.

Catfish transformed from children carry marks of knife holder A2261.3.1; transformed from woman carries woman's tatoo marks A2261.3. — Giant c. B874.7; man becomes c. D177; origin of c. A2127.

Cattle bewitched G265.6.2; formerly ate rice and pulse A1101.2.2; killed as punishment Q595.2; let loose so as to distract owner's attention K341.7.1; magically disappear D2087.3; as men's masters A1101.2.1; produced by magic D2178.2; and sheep of the sun (riddle) A732.1; step on lobster, flatten it A2213.2.4; of the sun A155.1; thief struck by lightning Q552.1.8.1; tied so tightly they strangle K1447. — Building bridge of c. K1441; enmity of c. and snails A2494.12.3.1; fairy c. F241.2ff., F356; fairy gives man horses, c., etc. F343.9; fairies steal c. F365.6; faithful c. at master's death B301.6ff.; first c. in Ireland A1877.1; forbidden direction while tending c. C614.1.0.1; ghost stampedes stolen c. E234.2; ghostly reenactment of c.-driving sounds E337.1.4; giant cane holds fifty c. F612.3.1; giant eats a thousand c. F531.3.4.1; herd of c. put into magic cup D491.1.1; herd of c. transformed to wolves D412.2.1; horse takes c. out to pasture X1241.2.1; hostile c. B17.1.3; huldra c. F460.2.9; huldra as c. traders F460.4.2.5; innocent boy hanged for c. theft N347.3; killing more c. than necessary tabu C766.1; man-eating c. B16.1.5; merman demands c. as offering B82.2; monk brings back all stolen c. possible J2499.4; murrain upon c. as punishment Q552.3.7; pasturing witch's c., her daughters H1199.12.2; people choose c. A1614.4.3; quest for marvelous c. H1331.3; sacred c. of sun god B811.3.3; saint's bell keeps c. from straying D1446.1; servant must keep horns and hide of his c. that are slain P622; stealing c. which are guarded by a marvelous dog (task) H1151.8; thirsty c. fight over well B266.1; trolls ride on c. F455.3.3.3; two-footed c. demanded: silly pundits sent J1717; when cow calls calf, all c. graze B852; washing black c. white (task) H1023.6; why flies sit on eyes of c. A2494.14.3; witch rides on c. G241.1.6.

Caught, see also **Catching.** — Animal c. by magic object D1444; animal's habits when c. A2466ff.; dwarf c. by beard in cleft of tree F451.6.1; ogre c. in noose and killed G514.3; speech magically recovered when certain bird is c. D2025.2; sun c. in snare A728; transformation to be c. D646.

Caul. — Child born with serpent in c. T551.8; exposure of child with c. S325.0.1.1; murder by showing man his c. D2061.2.7; waves break c. of abandoned child N655; worm from c. born with child B714.

Cauldron of greed W151.0.1; magically sticks to wall D2171.4.2; of regeneration E607.5; on water-monster's head K2314.2.1. — Bluff: huge c. called hero's kitchen-pot K1718.3; gigantic c. F881.1.1; magic c. *D1171.2, (in otherworld) F166.4.2, (received from lake spirit) D813.1.2, (reveals guilt) D1318.13; theft of c. detected J1661.1.10; witches boil wizardry c. G249.5.

Cauldrons. — Giant with eyes as big as c. F531.1.1.2.1; origin of c. A1439.4.

Cauliflower, children said to come from T589.6.5.

Caulker, pope disguised as K1816.2.

Causeway. — Building c. as suitor test H359.1; building c. as task H1129.6; fairies build c. F271.2.2; underwater c. to otherworld F842.2.4.

Cauterized. — Priests burned: dying woman asks to be c. J1511.18; sick cartwheel c. J2412.7.

Caution, wisdom of J580ff.

Cavalcade, fairy F241.1.0.1.

Cavalry of dogs B268.2. — Mice and hogs let loose put elephant c. to flight K2351.3; runaway c. hero K1951.2.

Cave call K607.1; entrance to lower world F92.6, A671.0.3; opens to hide fugitives D1552.5; as refuge R315; as repository of fire A1414.7.3; of winds A1122. — Abandonment in c. S146.2; adventure from following animal to c. N773; animal rescues from c. B549.4; beam in c. kills travelers K1172; captivity in c. R45.3; covering of giants' c. set afire K812.1.1; deer lures victim into demon's c. K714.7; dwarf c. F451.4.1.1, F451.4.3.1, F451.6.14; escape from deluge in c. A1024; extraordinary c. F757; gods' home in c. A151.1.2; hunter discovers girl being reared in c. N724; magic deer reveals c. entrance D1552.9; magic in giant's c. D845.1; ogress keeps princesses in c. G334.1; origin of c.-digging A1435.0.1; ogre kept in c. G514.2.1; princess rescued from giant's c. R111.2.3; river issuing from c. controlled by race of Amazons D915.5; rock at c. entrance falls D2153.2; spending night in c. as penance Q524.1; statue in c. entrance frightens giantess K1726; sun and moon from c. A713; sun hides in c. A734.1; travelers taken from c., eaten G94.1; treasure in underground c. N512.

Caves. — Chiefs buried in hidden c. V61.8.1; giants enchanted in c. F531.6.13.1; giants live in c. F531.6.2.1; habitable c. in otherworld

F164; huts replace c. as dwellings A1435.3; mankind emerges from c. A1232.3; rocks enter c. F1006.4; spirits live in c. F402.6.4.1.

Cecilia. — St. C. lives after beheading D1840.1.3.

Cecrops F526.6.

Cedar. — Blood from wizard becomes red grain of c. A2731.3; magic c. tree D950.18; origin of c. tree A2681.13; iron created to punish pride of c. A978.2.

Cedars. — Temple c. bear fruit F811.7.2.1.

Ceiling. — Chamber with crystal c. (in otherworld dwellings) F165.3.1.1, (in dwarf cave) F451.4.3.3.

Celebrations of dwarf weddings and christenings F451.6.3.2; of marriage T130ff. — Deer lost through premature c. J2173.4; prisoners released in c. of victory P14.1; religious c. *V0—V99.

Celestial, see **Heavenly.**

Celestial spheres, see **Heavens.**

Celibacy and chastity *T300—T399; and continence *T310ff.; at the altar J1264.2. — Origin of c. A1556.2; peoples practicing c. F566.

Cellar. — Familiar in magician's c. G225.0.5; fool lets wine run in the c. J2176; penance: being locked in c. and key thrown into water Q544; treasure in c. of ruined house N511.1.6; wine c. entered by removing lock K317.2; wolf overeats in c. K1022.1.

Celtic fairy mistress dominant F302.6.1. — Pagan C. otherworld like Christian paradise A694.1.

Celts, origin of A1611.5.4.

Cemetery, see also **Graveyard.** — Cannibals live at c. G18.1; dead move when c. is moved E419.4; light moving toward c. as sign of death D1322.2; looking over c. walls tabu C334; parson thinks he hears devil in c. cracking nuts X424; sleeping in c. tabu C735.2.5; shooting man to start c. X1663.2.

Cenn Cruaich, festival of V70.8.

Cenotaph. — Woman thinking lover dead erects c. and mourns before it T85.1.

Censer. — Aaron's c. J1446; sulphur in the c. J1582.2.

Censure. — Miracle saves saint from unjust c. V229.2.11.

Census. — Taking c. tabu C897.2.

Centaur B21; befriends abandoned man R143; rescues man from jungle B547.3. — Blood of c. as love philtre D1355.2.2.1; ghost as c. E423.6; man transformed to c. D199.1.

Center. — Determination of world c. A1181; mountain at c. of earth A875.1.1; person (giant, wood-spirit) with one eye in c. of forehead *F441.4.1, F512.1.1, F531.1.1.1; what is c. of earth? (riddle) H681.3.

Centipede kills ogre B524.1.10; magically enlarged D2038.1; plays with pearl B109.2. — Devastating c. B16.6.5; helpful c. B491.4.1; magic c. aids captive D1395.9; man becomes c. D192.2; poisoned sting of c. brings death to world A1335.13.

Centurion wants to be killed rather than converted Q151.8.

Century. — Bird carries a grain of sand from a mountain each c. (measure of eternity) H701.1; treasure reveals itself each c. N541.2.

Cerberus *A673, B15.7.1. — Quest for C. in hell H1271; sop to C. B325.1.

Cereal thrown on floor in anger F1041.16.10. — Magic c. D1033.

Cereals, origin of A2685ff.

Ceremonial continence T310.1; friendship P311.6.

Ceremony of the proclamation of a Buddha V88; of sacrifice V18. — Betrothal c. T61.4; eating during c. C231.5; evil spirit exorcised by religious c. D2176.3.2; fairies disappear when c. of church is used F382; magic results produced by religious c. *D1766; other religious c. as magic cure D2161.4.9.1; parody of church c. at witch's sabbath G243.2; prayer as c. V58; repeating the c. J2498; wedding c. T135; witch's power from altering religious c. G224.5.

Ceremonies used at unearthing of treasure N554. — God ordains c. A176; misunderstanding of church c. causes inappropriate action J1823; religious c. *V0—V99; witches avoid religious c. G285.

Certain. — Fairies visible only at c. times F235.2; ghost finds rest when c. thing happens E451; ghosts walk at c. times E587; invulnerability from c. things D1841; otherworld dwellings open only at c. times F165.2.

Certificate. — Cat loses dog's c. A2281.1.

Cesspool. — Paramour falls in c. K1517.4.1.

Chafer. — Blood-sucking c. B16.6.2; fierce black c. B16.6.2.1.

Chaff sky-rope F51.1.4. — Making a rope of c. (task) H1021.2.

Chagrin. — Death from c. because man cannot answer question F1041.1.3.10; laughter from c. F1041.11.1.

Chain, see also **Series;** around neck tests truth H251.3.6; of arrows transformed to bridge D469.3; of borrowings bring huge amount K455.10; of punishments Q401; tales Z20. — Ascent to upper world on arrow c. *F53; breaking of c. in anger F1041.16.3.1; child born with c. around neck H71.7; disenchantment by putting c. around neck D723.1; dragon keeps maiden tied with golden c. B11.10.1; devil bound with huge c. G303.8.4.1; drop of honey causes c. of accidents N381; extraordinary c. F863; filing away c. with teeth R121.10; forging of c. for fettered monster A1071.2; giant with gigantic c. as belt F531.4.2; gold c. as otherworld support F169.6; hind with gold c. on neck B105.1; iron c. hangs from heaven F51.1.6; magic c. (ornament) *D1078, (iron) D1251, (renders orchard barren) D1563.2.1; magic c. protects D1381.19, D1388.0.3; magic power in c. lost when it is stolen D1561.2.3; origin of mountain c. A965; quest for animal with golden c. H1332.4; recognition of twins by golden c. under their skin H61.1; thieves stretch c. across road and evade pursuers K413; tying sun with stone c. H1023.23.

Chains. — Castle suspended on four c. F771.2.1.1; disenchantment by putting c. around neck D723.1; fettered monster's weakened c. renewed by supernatural power A1074.7; fiery c. in hell A671.2.4.7; ghost sounds c. E402.1.4, E565; mountain-men put peasant in c. F460.4.4.2; noise of c. leads to buried ghost E231.4; quest for the finest of c. H1303; souls in c. in hell E755.2.2; transformation by removing c. from neck D536; wild hunt heralded by rattle of c. E501.13.1.2.

Chained. — Animals c. in couples B845.2; girl c. to wall by giant R111.2.3.1; magic birds c. in couples B172.7; pregnant queen c. to king T579.7; prisoners c. R51.2; soldiers c. together to prevent flight P551.2.

Chair moves toward pope A171.6; over fiery pit as figure of precariousness of life J85; rocked by spirit F473.2.1. — Death glued to c. Z111.2.2; devil's c. in hell made from thrown-away nail parings G303.25.5; extraordinary c. F786; ghostly c. E539.4.1; heaven entered by sitting in St. Peter's c. K2371.1.4; heavenly music caused by columns under Lord's c. A661.0.2.1; horse's forehead as golden c. F874.2; magic c. *D1151.2; man lured into mechanical c., killed K984; person killed by spike magically made to appear on c. D2061.2.6; recognizing sweetheart's sedan c. H324.1; ring prevents person from rising from c. D1413.2; salt prevents witch's rising from c. G254.2; self-rocking c. D1601.28; weeding garden from rocking c. W111.5.13; witch cannot rise from c. with four-leaf clover under it G254.

Chairs in heaven A661.0.3, H619.1, V515.1.1, Z71.1.2. — Origin of peoples according to choice of c. A1614.4.2; witches rock empty c. G249.11.

Chalice used in guilt test H233.1. — Magic c. D1171.6.4; priest throws c. at owl J1261.2.7.

Chalk marks identify mistress H58.1; transformed into oil tins D454.13.

Challenge to battle P556; at otherworld entrance F150.3; to revenant to combat E461.1. — Hero's c. to warriors in his land C566.5.

Challenger. — Customs concerning c. to combat P557.4.4; small child beats giant c. F611.3.2.5.

Chamber with crystal ceiling in otherworld F165.3.1.1. — Forbidden c. *C611; suitor test: entering princess's c. *H344; underground treasure c. F721.4.

Chamber-pot, magic *D1171.13.

Chameleon duped by elephant K1042.1; plays xylophone B297.1.2; saves hero's life: may change color A2223.8. — Creation of c. A2148.1; enmity of c. and lizard A2494.16.2; movement of c. A2441.4.4; why c. can change his color A2411.5.6.1.

Champion test H1568; vindication by H218.0.1. — King's c. enforces respect P14.15; valor as bird hovering over c. Z124.1.

Champions of gods A145. — Queen pours liquor for c. P29.3.

"Champion's portion" of meat P632.2.1.

Chance and fate N (entire chapter).

Chandelier of crystals in dwarf home F451.4.3.4.

Changes of bodily appearance so as to escape K521.2; in bodily form at fall of man A1310.1; in color of blood (life token) E761.1.6; of color not to be attempted J511; in the earth A850ff.; of form impossible for devil G303.3.6. — Attempted c. of animal nature absurd J1908; magic c. in man himself *D50ff.; magic object effects c. in persons D1300—D1379; magic object works physical c. D1330ff.; reincarnation with c. of sex E605.1; simulated c. of sex to baffle Evil Eye D2071.1.3; yearly c. in hyena's sex B754.1.1.

Changeableness W175.

Changed message K1851; remarks K1775. — Adulterous love c. into chaste one T372; angel c. into the devil G303.1.1.3; animals' dwelling-place c. A2433.1.2; animal's color c. F985; clothes not to be c. till a certain time M125; horse used by mortal under fairy spell c. to gray cat F234.4.1; person's disposition c. by magic object D1350ff.; person's size c. by magic object D1377; sea's place c. F931.1; size c. at will D631; transformation: material of object c. D470ff.; voice c. by work of silversmith F556.2.

Changeling *F321.1ff., F451.5.2.3. — Eagle prefers own offspring to c. J497; mother casts out c. P231.6.

Changelings, trolls as F455.6.7.

Changing of luck or fate N130ff.; places or caps in bed K1611. — Cow with c. colors B731.4; disguise by c. bodily appearance K1821; princess c. clothes with maid to flee man T323.1.1; punishment for c. faith Q232; rejuvenation by c. skin D1889.6; transformation by c. clothes D537; wives c. clothes with imprisoned husbands R152.3.

Channel. — Underground c. to otherworld F153.1.

Channels. — Lies about underground c. X1545; origin of sea c. A920.2.

Chanticleer believes that his crowing makes the sun rise J2272.1.

Chanting of saint kills animal D1445.3; of spell over shadow D2061.2.2.2. — Future poet c. in womb T575.1.4; heavenly bodies c. God's praise F961.0.4; Satan c. God's praises G303.9.8.9.

Chaos. — Earth born of c. A801; evil spirits born in c. G302.1.2; first deity grows out of primeval c. A115.1; creator comes out of c. A22; primeval c. *A605.

Chapel endowed with blows for friar X454; in otherworld F163.2; remarkable F773. — Stones in c. from transformed salmon A977.5.2.

Chaplain administers sacrament and saves woman's soul from devil G303.16.5.1. — Treacherous c. K2284.1.

Character of kings P12ff. — Tests of c. H1550—H1569; traits of c. W (entire chapter).

Characters. — Mysterious c. on fire rock F809.6.2.

Charcoal burner P458, (drives fairies off with fire) F389.1, (treacherous) K2262; sack magically multiplies D2106.2. — Expensive wood burned to make c. J2094; origin of c. making A1452; raised treasure turns into

c. N558; transformation: handkerchief with three knots to clod, potsherd, and c. D454.3.2.1.

Chargers. — Faggots become c. D441.3.1.

Chariot of fire A13.6.3.1; of the gods A156.5; horses spring at one unentitled to throne H71.10.4; invisible D1982.3; of light carries souls to heaven E754.5; magically collects flowers D1601.33; of the sun A724; tilts under false royalty H41.9.1; wheels throw up wall R5.1. — Angel guides c. V232.5.1; crossing water in c. D2125.3; dead persons draw c. E583; deceptive grant: land c. travels K185.7.3; divination from c. wheels' sound K1812.5.0.12; driving c. over displeasing person Q227.3; entering c. tabu after certain food C756.4; escape to sky in magic c. R323.2; fairy c. F242.1; fairy c. pulled by pole through horse F241.1.6; god drives c. over waves A171.0.1; god rides in c. A171.1.1; god's c. goes through air A136.3; god's c. bears bodies to heaven E722.2.10.1; goddess's c. drawn by one-footed horse A136.2.2; heavenly c. takes couple to sky A761.2; journey to upper world in c. F66.1; magic c. *D1114; moon c. A757.1; planet in black c. pursues sun, moon A735.2; pregnant woman crushed beneath c. S116.2; race won by deception: c. disabled K11.4; saint's resurrection where c. breaks down M364.4.1; stealing c. from king H1151.13.3; swans harnessed to c. B558.2; tabu to proceed after c. mishap C833.7; winged c. F861.2; winged serpents pull c. B558.7.

Chariot's. — Turning c. left side tabu C643.

Chariots join in keen F994.2. — Stars melt iron c. F961.2.6.

Charioteer faithful to death P361.1.3; killed instead of saint N338.1; of the sun *A724.1; taunts master, arouses him J1682.

Charioteers. — Hero refuses to slay c. W11.5.12.

Charitable man's death postponed Q151.1.

Charity *V400—V449; rewarded by birth of child T584.4. — Admittance to heaven for single act of c. Q172.2; devil frustrated by c. G303.16.19.11; double return for c.: savings given away J2489.6; heaven entered by demanding back the c. gift K2371.1.2; hypocrisy concerning c. K2096; intemperance in c. J562; trickster takes goods given in c. to his family K461; what is the greatest? c. H659.7.3.

Charm, see also **Spell**; against theft of children by fairies F321.2; around neck transforms D585.1; causes horns to grow on person D1375.1.3; dries (life token) E761.4.6; makes root bitter D479.3; to win cases in law court D1406.1; written in blood has magic power D1273.0.1. — Alleged c., fly, escapes: damages claimed K251.3; ghost summoned by c. E386.2; impregnation by use of c. T527; magic c. (formula) *D1273ff., (fetish) *D1274, (medicine) *D1241, (ghoulish) *D1278, (writings) *D1266.1; ogress seduces with c. G264.3; ogre's c. stolen G613; rain c. sold to aid eloping couple D2143.1.10; witches c. causes paralysis D2072.2.1; witch's c. opposite of Christian *G224.1; word c. gives witch power G224.12.

Charms cause witch to reveal self G257. — Dead mother called up from grave to give her son c. E323.3; finger cut because of absorption in the c. of beloved T26.1; origin of c. for pregnant women A1562.1; pseudo-magic healing c. sold K115.

Charming. — Fairies c. prince into sleep F302.3.4.5; wife c. husband back R152.4.

Charnel. — Fetching skulls from c. house (fear test) H1435.

Charon A672.1. — Fee of C. A672.1.1, E489.3, P613.

Charter. — Ass's c. in his hoof J1608.

Charybdis and Scylla G333.

Chasing devil away G303.16.11.3; mutilated man into forest S143.3; night by day A1172.3; ogres away by fire G581. — Fairies c. man who dares them F361.17.8; fairies c. overseer F361.3.2; ghost c. pedestrian E272.4; priest c. devil away G303.16.14.1; wife's attendants c. lover K1549.6.

Chasms mark leaps of giants A972.5.2.

Chaste sleeping together T350ff.; woman deceives gallant with a substitute in bed K1223.4; woman has magic power *D1714.1; woman promises herself to her lover when the rocks leave the coast *M261; woman refers lover to her husband for permission K1231; woman surprised in adultery K2063; maiden at prayer vanishes from would-be ravisher's embrace D1714.1.1; wife tricks importunate lovers K1218. — Girl with c. mother chosen as wife J482.3; wild animal will not harm c. woman B771.0.1.

Chastity *T300—T399; tests *H400—H459; wager *N15. — Adulteress makes pretense of c. K2051.4; cut-off finger proves wife's c. K1512.1; demon has to serve girl whom he cannot persuade to break vow of c. G303.16.19.5; magic object preserves c. *D1387ff.; message of c.: uncooked meat left behind T386; sword of c. T351; promise to sleep in c. with woman broken J1174.2.1; transformation to preserve c. D664; wife's heavy c. belt T373.

Chastizing. — Son c. father for scorning mother P233.9.

Chasuble. — Hairs on saint's c. release souls from hell Q174.1.1.1; sinners going to heaven numbered by hairs in saint's c. M364.3.1; white c. becomes red D454.3.1.1.

Chasubles. — Maidens unharmed by fire in c. D1841.3.2.4.

Chateaux. — Devil as builder of c. G303.9.1.5.

Chattering dwarfs F451.3.13.2; squirrel in the earth-tree A878.3.3.

Cheap price country J342.1.1. — King and c. slippers J829.1.

Cheated. — Devil c. (at card playing) N4.0.1, (in race) K11.0.1, (of his promised soul) *K210ff., (by dismissing mass early) G303.16.16; farmer who trades horses with the devil is c. G303.25.12; numskull talks and allows himself to be c. J2355; scornfull mistress c. by scorned lover posing as rich man L431.2.

Cheater cheated *J1510ff.; discovered by fishing in the street J1149.2; as hero L114.4; put out of countenance by raising alarm J1216. — Virgin pardons repentant c. V261.2.

Cheaters *K300—K499; examined apart J1141.3; sell each other valueless articles K148; visited by god in animal form Q554.6. — Trickster masks as doctor and punishes his c. K1825.1.3.

Cheating by illusory transformation of animals D612.1; as suitor test H331.13. — Clever girl c. robber K434; deer's antlers reward for not c. A2326.1.1.1; dupe's casual words used in c. K1155; fairies revenge for c. F361.13; foolish attempt at c. buyer J2083; ghost slaps c. son: cancer grows E234.1; magic object acquired by c. K830ff.; man c. god in dice A189.3; rogues c. each other J1516; thief c. other thieves K307.2; two cheats c. one another K421.3; Virgin Mary reveals c. V252.1.

Check. — Leaving c. on coffin K231.13.

Cheek bitten K2021.1, (as death warning) D1812.0.1.1. — Devils leave hermit who turns other c. when struck G303.16.15; mutilation: c. cut off S166.2; ointment cures left c., not right D1663.2; remarkable c. F545.3.

Cheeks like blood as suitor test H312.5; stuffed with food operated on for swellings X372.4.1. — Giant's peculiar c. F531.1.6.8; husband disapproves of wife painting c. Q331.2.1.3; mouth full of food: c. cut open for abscess J1842.2; vain woman's c. burned Q331.2.1.2.

Cheese from buffalo milk H1361.6; -covered dung sold as cheese K143.1; smeared on crab lures giant K827.5; transformed to stone D471.4; thrown down to find way home J1881.1.1. — Bone-powder changed into c. D476.1.10; cat to guard c. J2103.1; diving for c. J1791.3; getting a sword to lift the c. J2173.2; grindstone's picture mistaken for c. J2685; magic c. *D1036.1; numskull tries to hatch out a calf from a c. J1902.2; one c. sent after another J1881.1.2; ordeal by bread and c. H232; raven with c. in mouth K334.1; sowing c. to bring forth a cow J1932.2; thrifty cutting of c. (bride test) H381.2; trickster squeezes a c. K62.

Cheeses concealed from saint turned to stone Q552.16.1.2. — Rolling c. to scare off Indians K548.1; stones are transformed c. A977.5.1.

Cherry tree has lotus flowers F811.7.2.3. — Healing with c. tree J2412.5; magic c. *D981.4; magic c. tree *D950.4.

Cherries. — Father shares c. with sons J1341.9.

Chess game as test H509.3. — Gods play c. A163.1.1; invention of c. A1468.1; king playing c. when important news arrives P14.3; monkey plays c. B298.1; origin of c. (cumulative tale) Z21.1; parrot advises queen playing c. B565; skill at c. F679.8; unique ability to play c. H31.10.

Chessboard made from slain enemy S139.2.2.4.3. — Divination with c. D1311.23.

Chest, see also **Box;** of murdered child becomes moon A1277.3. — Animal in the c. K1515; cuckolded man shuts wife's paramour in c. and lies on the c. with the latter's wife K1566; dying woman lures paramour into c.: asks for it to be buried K1555.0.1; entrance into woman's room by hiding in c. K1342; exposure in floating c. S141, S331; girl catches thief in c. K434.3; husband takes off c. containing paramour K1555.0.2; lover hidden in c. with feathers K1517.4; magic c. *D1174; man hiding in c.

9*

catches thief K751.2; money exacted from watchers who permit c. to be stolen K443.3.1; moon from c. of sacrificed youth A741.2; murder by slamming down c. lid S121; paramour hidden in c. K1521.2, (frightens off robbers) K335.1.6.1, (and carried off) K675.1, (priest) K1218.1.4; queen lures husband into c. K2213.15; seduction by having maiden placed in floating c. K1333; sham-magician buys c. containing hidden paramour K1574; soldier asks to be stabbed in c. J216.4; supposed c. of gold induces children to care for aged father P236.2; thrall cursed to sit on c. M455.3; treasure buried in c. N511.1.8; treasure found in c. N525; unjust banker deceived into delivering c. of money K1667; victim tricked into entering c. K714.2.

Chests. — Worthless c. as security for credit K455.9.

Chestnut. — Magic c. *D985.2, (as food) *D1035.1.

Chewed. — Magic charm of c. flesh D1273.0.3.

Chewer. — Lie: remarkable c. X933.

Chewing of spruce gum by Indians A1681.1. — Devil c. up church papers G303.24.5; goat pretends to be c. rock K1723; magic results from c. D1799.5.

Chicken, see also **Cock, Hen;** feet of spirits *F401.3.5; as laborer B292.9.2; picks out attacker's eyes B524.8. — Arrows rubbed with c. fatal D1402.7.5.1; blindness cured by c. dung F952.6; creation of c. A1988; enmity of civet cat and c. A2494.1.8; enmity of fox and c. A2494.9.2; helpful c. B469.5.1; husband in the c. house K1514.1; hypocrite will not share in stolen c.; only takes gravy K2095.2; magic c. B171; magic c. thigh D1013.1; magic warmth of c. wing D1481.1; man transformed to c. D166.1; peasant's share is the c. J1562.2; priest's guest and eaten c. K2137; speaking c. B211.3.2.1.

Chickens. — Automatic hen and c. of gold D1620.2.2; educated c. tell of woman's adultery K1271.1.3; enigmatic request for c. for breakfast H599.6; enmity between birds of prey and c. A2494.13.10.6; fool kills c. by throwing them off a balcony J2173.5; fox is promised c.: is driven off by dogs K235.1; guarding c. from the fox by weighting them down in water J2125; mother kills c. (cuts off heads of the well) H583.4.3; old woman gives c. to devils G303.25.6; stolen c. turn to stone D471.8.1; strong hero asks that c. stop scratching F615.3.1.1; teaching c. to talk J1882.1; thieves' funeral for c. K375; trickster buys c., says priest will pay K455.4.1; why wildcats eat c. A2435.3.15.

Chief asks another for yam cutting (daughter) H611.3; of dead frightens visitors H1401.1; recognized by large bundle H41.10. — Creator appoints a c. for each class of things A1187; first man made world's c. A1285.1; high-spitting as test of a c. H41.2; men buried with dead c. V67.4; storm heralds newborn c. F960.1.1.3; unknown prince chosen c. of children in play *P35.

Chief's. — Tabu not to eat c. food C241.2; warriors surrender after c. death R75.2.

Chiefs buried in hidden caves V61.8.1. — Tabus of c. C564ff.

Chieftain recognized by swineherd H173.1. — Deceptive land grant to wounded c. K185.7.3.

Chieftainess fans mist off river A937; preparing food tabu C564.8; of too high rank to be wooed P281.1.

Chieftainship as reward Q112.1.

Child, see also **Baby, Infant;** adopted by rich man in order to get rid of him K2015; born as cannibal G33; born with objects indicating fate N121.1; borne off by tiger, which is caught by griffin, which is killed by lioness, who rears child with her whelps N215; in cradle guesses devil's riddle H543.2; cursed by father cannot rest in grave E412.4; of deity visits earth F31; of demon king marries mortal F402.2.3; develops from man's urine T512.2.1; feeds snake from milk-bottle B391.1; follows bird and loses its mother N313; forced to cry till magic given D835; found on deserted island A1234.3; as foundation sacrifice smiles and wins freedom S261.1; as helper N827; killed by one left to care for it K1461; of moon and mortal A753.1.5; and mountain people F460.4.1.2.1, F460.4.2.4; mystically recognizes mother H175.2; plays with magic object *D861.10; as prophet M301.20; recognizes relative's flesh when it is served to be eaten G61.1; as result of prayer Q192, T548.1; reveals murder N271.6; sacrifice S260.1.1, S268; saved from death by dressed-up block K525.1.3; sick from witchcraft struck on anvil G271.9; -stealing demon G442; threatened with ogre actually abducted *C25.1; throws down a kid (lie) X1856.1; throws millwheels from one town to another (lie) X1856.2; in womb gives guest directions H1232.5. — Abandoned c. joins parents in game: recognition follows H151.9; adult becomes c. D55.2.5; animal rescues c. B549.3 (dog), B522.4 (eagle); animals with human c. as slave B292.0.1; beautiful c. F575.3; cast-off wife and c. exposed in boat S431.1; compassionate executioner: substitute c. K512.2.2; cooked c. revived by saint E121.4.1; criminal detected by having c. hand knife to him H211; crocodile goes after second c. J2173.6; crying c. ceases only to gather strength W182; devil as c. G303.3.1.16; devil c. born with horns G303.4.1.6.2; disguise as c. K1839.12; distress over imagined troubles of unborn c. J2063; "don't adopt a c." J21.27; dragon hears cry of c. B11.12.6; dupe cares for c. while robbed K345.3; dwarf makes return of c. dependent upon guessing of riddle F451.5.15.2; dying c. assigns task H937; earth from c. (children) A831.5, A831.3; exposed or abandoned c. rescued R131ff.; fairy c. kept by mortals F329.4.1; fairy gives mortals a c. F343.13; fairies adopt human c. F311; fairies help forgotten c., strangle another J2415.4; false bride makes c. demand mother's clothes K1911.1.8.1; false bride takes true bride's place when c. is born *K1911.1.2; father of illegitimate c. must walk in front of cross J1515.1; father's ghost rebukes c. E327.4; fool kills c. J1842.2, J2465.3f., J2661.1, K946; fool thinks he has given birth to a c. by letting wind J2321.2; friendly return of dead c. E324; ghost of murdered c. E225;

ghost of unknown c. passes over parents H175.5; giving a c. a name
tabu C437; god punishes man by killing his c. A1335.15; healing power
of saint as c. V221.0.3; heart of unborn c. renders person invisible
D1361.8; hill as adopted c. A969.6; human c. of sky-mother longs for
earth father D2006.2.1; impostor claims to be father of c. of princess
K1936; innocence of c. tested H256.1; journey to hell to circumcise c.
F81.3; light-giving c. H1396; like parent, like c. U121; lovers' c. sent
with token H82.3.1; magic object received from c. D828; magic object
for service to c. D817.1ff.; magic placates crying c. D883; man as God
behind the tree forces the girl to admit having illegitimate c. K1971.5.1;
magic calabash cooks and cares for c. D1601.1; magic sight given to
abandoned c. D1821.6; offending supernatural c. (tabu) C33; people
eating c. become supernatural G55; pious c. able to carry water in
sieve H1023.2.0.2; posing as relative to kill c. K2011; prophecy on killer
of c. M306.5; protection from devil by holding three-year old c. through
the night G303.16.19.6; rakshasa eats c. G369.1.4; reincarnation as c.
E605.7f.; reincarnation of murdered c. as bird *E613.0.1; retort from
underfed c. J1341ff.; revenant as c. E425.3; sham physician predicts sex
of the unborn c. K1955.3; small c. beats giant F611.3.2.5; Solomon's
judgment: the divided c. J1171.1; soul as c. E747; stolen c. found in
hollow tree R311.3; stolen c. rescued by animal nurse B543.3; tabu to
carry c. on one's back C875; touch of c. resuscitates E149.3; transformation to c. to be adopted D646.2; transformation: salmon to c. D376;
transformed mother called by her c. D792; transformed mother suckles
c. D688; trolls size of twelve-year-old c. F455.2.1; ugly husband placates
wife, says he wants handsome c. J1541.3; unborn c. affected by broken
tabu C993; unknown parent of c. sought H1381.2ff.; victorious youngest
c. *L0—L99; why can't c. talk? H1292.15; wisdom of c. decides lawsuit
J123; wolf defends master's c. against serpent B524.1.4; wolf waits in
vain for nurse to throw away c. J2066.5; woman seeks unknown father
of her c. H1381.2.1.

Children abducted R10.3; ask too difficult questions J2370.1; born during
husband's long absence J2342.2; in casket floated down river H157;
devoured by ogress come from fire F913.2; disenchanted after long period
are aged D799.1; of the East J192.1; envious of money given by deceased
father to bishop have vision V415; prefer father they know to real
father they do not yet know J325; flee from father who turns cannibal
G31; not left alone when asleep A1579.1; lured into ogre's house
G412; play hog-killing N334.1; of polygamous marriage A1576; punished
for parents' offenses Q402; refused food leave home R228; rescue parents
R154; sold or promised S210ff.; of the sun A736.5; transformed into
horsemen D98; unwittingly promised (sold) S240ff.; wander into ogre's
house G401; and wild hunt E501.2.7, E501.5.4, E501.18.1.3.1. —
Abandoned c. identified by rice H49.1; abandoned or murdered c.
*S300—S399; abusing c. tabu C867.1; animals care for c. B535ff.; beggar's
many c. P161; betrothal of c. T61.5; blood of c. as cure for leprosy

D1502.4.2.1; boasting of c. forbidden C452; burning c. to give them fawn's spots K1013.2.2; care of c. *T600—T699; catfish transformed from c. carry mark of children's knife holder A2261.3.1; close resemblance of two c. F1072; criminal's wife and c. sold into slavery Q437.1; cruel c. S20ff.; cure by putting c. on roof D2161.4.11; curse: c. will be sick M460.1; dead mother returns to aid persecuted c. *E323.2; dead wife returns and bears c. for husband E322.1; death of c. for breaking tabu C920.1; death of c. as punishment Q553.4f., Q559.9; deception by substitution of c. K1847; deceptive agreement to kill c. K944; demons strangle c. G302.9.4; devil's c. G303.11.2.2; dishonor to c. for breaking tabu C930.1; dog and hog dispute over their c. J243.1; dragon devours c. B11.10.3; dumbness as punishment for hiding c. Q451.3.1; dwarfs and c. F451.3.5.3, F451.3.5.5, F451.5.2.3, F451.5.21; dying woman's wraith visits c. E723.4.4; each likes his own c. best T681; encounter with clever c. dissuades man from visit J31; enemy's c. H1397.2 (quest), K930ff. (murder); fairies and human c. F310ff., F321, F326; father unwilling but mother willing to sell c. H491.1; father mutilates c. S11.1; first couple bring in c., clothe them A1277.4; first parents bear all c. they wish A1277.2; first parents c. of god A1271.3; folly of father's giving all property to c. before his death P236.1; friends and their c. P310.4, (become enemies) P312.4.2; giants' c. F531.6.8.6; innocent woman accused of killing her new-born c. K2116.1.11; legitimacy of c. tested by dipping them in river H222.1; living c. buried with dead mother S123.3; magic power of c. D1717ff.; male c. killed by Amazons F565.1.2; man betrayed into eating own c. K940.1; as many c. as holes in a sieve (formula) Z75; many c. at a birth T586.1; monkeys from c. hidden by Eve when God visited her A1861.1; mortal saves fairy's c. F337.1; mother who devours her c. when they grow up (riddle) H734; mountain with c. F755.5; mountain men give c. a book F460.4.2.4; murder of c. punished Q211.4; murderer's c. become dwarfs F451.1.2; ogre kills noisy c. G478; ogre steals c. G305; origin of c. (explanations to c.) T589.6; origin of relation of mother and c. A1575; parents and c. *P230ff.; playing with c. helps great man J25; poisonous toad sits on food of undutiful c. Q557.1; prophecies about birth of c. M311.0.3, M369.7; punishment for refusal to have c. *Q251; rank among c. P632.3; reduced number of c. as punishment Q553.3.7; repartee concerning parentage of c. J1270ff.; rescue of c. from ogre by brother G551.3; return from dead to demand stolen c. E236.2; river formed where seven c. place stones A934.2; shark-ogre eats c. G308.5; shortsightedness in dealing with c. J2175ff.; song of c. incriminates thief K435; stars as c. of sun, moon A764.1, A764.3; stolen mother returns from fairyland each Sunday to minister to her c. *F322.3; substituted c. K1920ff.; suckling c. rock mother in cradle (lie) X1856; sun, moon and darkness as god's three c. A700.8; treacherous c. K2214; true bride's c. thrown away at birth K1911.2.3; two c. in moon A751.7; unbaptized c. (as fairies) F251.3, (in wild hunt) *E501.2.7, (pursued by

fairies) F360.1, (pursued in wild hunt) *E501.5.4, (reincarnated as birds)
E613.0.2; underworld people from c. which Eve hid from God *F251.4;
undutiful c. P236; ungrateful c. punished *Q281.1; unknown prince
chosen chief of c. in play *P35; unnatural c. eat parent G71; unnatural
parents eat c. G72ff.; various c. of Eve *A1650.1; wagers on unborn c.
N16; walling up as punishment for murder of c. Q455.1; water-spirit
drags c. into river F420.5.2.1.5; why bees eat their own c. A2435.5.5;
why c. learn to walk late A1321.1; why prince plays with c. J1661.1.7;
wisdom learned from c. J120ff.; witch carries her c. in her own body
G229.2; witch steals c. *G261; woman with three hundred sixty-five c.
L435.2.1.

Children's — Cannibals cut off parts of c. bodies G86; mutilation of c.
bodies for identification H56.2; power of flying from eating c. hearts
D2135.1.

Childbed. — Intercourse with woman in c. S185.2.

Childbirth, see also **Birth** T580ff.; bell sounded falsely: not heeded in
need J2199.1.2; magically delayed T574. — Banishment till rose grows
from table for preventing c. Q431.4; charms make c. easy D1501.2;
despite c. pain women become pregnant H659.13.1; dead father helps
daughter in c. E327.2; fairy aid to queen in c. F312.3; goddess of c. A477;
husband abandons wife in c. S143.4; husband looking at supernatural
wife in c. forbidden C31.1.4; letter alleged to aid c. K115.1.1; origin of
c. A1351; painful c. as punishment Q553.3.6; sacrifice at c. V17.9; tabu
connected with c. C150ff.; tabus following c. C154; tree bows to help
Virgin Mary in c. D1648.1.2.1; Virgin Mary helps abbess in secret c.
T401.1.

Childless couple adopt hero N825.1; couple promise devil a child S223;
woman lost while fugitive woman burdened with child is saved N185;
woman reborn as fish E694.4; woman rescues boy R169.9. — Prophecy:
child to be born to c. M311.0.3.1; seduction by giving c. man's wife
medicine K1315.2.4; unlucky to look at c. person T591.2.

Childlessness, curse of M444.

Chili plant causes dumb man to speak F954.4. — Enemy blinded with c.
powder K783.1; jealous woman reborn as c. E692.4; rattlesnake harmful
because earth worm feeds him c. pepper A2211.11; soul in c. plant
E711.2.3.

Chimera B14.1.

Chimney. — Why cat keeps c. corner A2223.1, A2433.3.1.1; corpse drops
piecemeal down c. H1411.1; devil descends c., spoils pudding C12.5.5;
devil goes up c. in smoke G303.17.2.1; fairies descend c. F275; intruder
captured in c. K732; intruding wolf falls down c. and kills himself
J2133.7, K891.1; looking up c. tabu C337; magic object found in c. D847;
ogre's arm thrust down c. G369.5; paramour hidden in c. K1521.1; theft
through c. K316; Thumbling carried up c. by steam of food F535.1.1.2;
witch steals child with hand through c. G261.1; witches come, go by c.
G249.3.

Chimpanzee, see also **Monkey;** leads lost hunter home B563.1.2. — Enmity of c. and man A2494.12.9; origin of body hair of c. A2322.6; why c. has large teeth A2345.9; why c. lives in forest A2433.2.1.2; why c. lives with men A2433.2.4.1.

Chin. — How buffalo got hair under c. A2322.1; mutilation: c. cut off S166.2; woman so old her c. reaches her knee F571.3.1.

China first land in world A802. — Bull in the c. shop J973.

Chips from tree return to their places as cut D1602.2.2; of wood become animal D441.10. — Magic feather (song) causes c. from tree to return as fast as cut D1565.1; recognition by unique manner of carving c. H35.4; remarkable thrower of c. makes forest F636.2.

Chipmunk. — Lies about c. X1224; stripes of c. A2217.2, A2413.2.

Chirping. — Annoyance of swallows' c. less than sandpipers' J215.1.4.

Chisel. — Creator with hammer and c. in hands A18.5; why magpie's tail like c. A2378.7.2.

Chittagongs formerly braver A1676.1.

Choice, see also **Choosing, Chosen;** of kings P11; between life or heaven V311.3; of dangerous road tests valor H1561.9; of magic object from worthless D859.5; of weapons alternates P557.4.3. — Animal or object indicates c. of ruler H171; apple thrown indicates princess's c. H316; criminal allowed c. of method of execution P511; first at combat field gets c. of weapons P557.4.1; girl to wed man of her c. T131.0.1.1; girl must marry father's c. T131.1.2.1; grateful objects help in c. of caskets D1658.3.2; Hobson's c.: take what is offered or get nothing J201; modest c. best L210ff.; origin of death from unwise c. A1335.3; princess's unrestricted c. of husband T131.0.1; starved lover given c. of lady or food K1218.1.3.1; tribes from c. Sun offers A1610.5.

Choices *J200—J499; by chance N125. — Little gain, big loss in c. J340ff.; origin of tribes from c. made A1614.4.

Choir imitates apologizing minister J2498.1. — Angel c. responds to saint V234.1.3; mermaid sings in c. B81.3.2.

Choked. — Departing husband c. by deserted wife K951.0.1; lord who robs poor widow of her cow c. on first mouthful Q552.6; scoffer c. to death by mysterious stranger who blows ashes into his face Q554.3; woman's undutiful son c. by serpent Q557.2.

Choking lawyer with smoke Q469.5. — Death by c. for breaking tabu C922.1; murder by c. K951ff.

Cholera. — God of c. A478.3; man mistaken for c. J1786.3; origin of c. A1337.2.

Choosing, see also **Choice;** correctly from three caskets H511.1; flowers as test of sex of girl masking as man H1578.1.3; princess from others identically clad H324; tree on which to hang K558.

Choosy. — Too c. princess married to idiot J2183.5.

Chopping. — Deceptive contest in c. K44; marvelous sensitiveness: fracture from hearing man c. wood F647.8.1; task: c. down large tree with blunt implements H1115.

Chopsticks. — Seven pairs of c. H1199.16; younger twin unthinkingly hands c. to elder H255.

Choral singing accompanies saint V222.3.

Chosen, see also **Choice, Choosing;** people V317. — All three gifts c. by trickster J1202; brother c. rather than husband or son P253.3; early death c. rather than long life without lady M366; remaining transformed to mule c. rather than living with shrewish wife T251.1.3; remaining in Purgatory c. rather than returning to shrewish wife T251.1.2; unpromising magic object c. *L215.

Christ (Jesus) *V211; accused of trying to fool the people J1823.1.1; appears to St. Martin after charity V411.8; carries water in cloak F866.7.2.1; causes animal characteristics A2287ff.; changes stones to peas D452.1.6.1; creates fire in hell from his blood A671.0.2.1; in desert overcomes devil by fasting V73.0.1; in disguise as leper Q25.1; grants immortality to Nephites D1856.2; has too many debts J2477; kills man plotting murder J225.4; magically ages one of the magi D1897; as matchmaker T53.2; not having married, knew nothing about suffering T251.0.2; puts knots in wood A2738; prophesies people will live "till coming of Patrick" M300.1, M363.1.2; releases soul from hell E754.1.6. — Actor does not want to be C. J2495.3; all living things from splattered blood of C. A1724.3; all sins since the birth of C. J1743.1; animals blessed for honoring infant C. *A2221.1; animals lick C. child B251.10; animals worship infant C. B251.1.1; beggar on cross in place of C. L435.4; crossbill's bill from aiding C. A2221.2.4.2; devil appears as C. G303.3.2.1; devil tries to pass for C. K1992; dialogue between C. and souls in hell E755.2.8; dog created as watch-dog for C. A1831; dying like C. — between two thieves X313; five wounds of C. Z71.3.2; hot springs arise where C. bathed feet A942.1; image of C. wounds nun V122.1; indentions on rocks from footprints of C. A972.1.1; infant C. shown to nun D1766.1.2; Jews crucifying C. punished in Cornish mines F456.1.1.1; like C. on Palm Sunday J1265.1; leopards guide C. to Egypt B563.5; likeness of C. criticized V124; man behind the crucifix says "Good Evening" to drunk man who thinks C. is speaking to him K1971.7; numskull knocks figure of C. from ass J1823; oath concerning battles for C. M177.1.2; owl is baker's daughter who objected to dough being given C. A1958.0.1; in Passion Play C. says, "I am thirsty": thief on left speaks up, "I too" J2041.1; pilgrimage to roads C. walked V531.1; pike helps C. cross stream: made king of fishes A2223.4; plant blessed for help at birth of C. A2711.1; plant cursed for disservice to C. A2721.1; punishment for foul portrayal of C. Q222.3; punishment for opposition to C. at crucifixion *Q221.2; return from dead to prophesy coming of C. E367.3; riddle about C. in thirtieth year H826; spider steals thread from C. A2231.6; springs rise where C. bathed his feet A942.1; seven whistlers are souls of Jews who crucified C. A1715.3; shoemaker cursed for spitting at C. P453.1; standing up for C. as friendless J1738.5; statue of infant C. takes apple V128.1; swallows torment C. on cross A2231.2.2;

three whom C. raised from dead Z71.1.11; tree protects C. from rain: is green all year A2711.4.

Christ's coat of mercy protects Pilate from punishment D1381.4.1; forty-days' fast V73.6.1; height as magic measurement D1273.4; image has broken his arm J1823.1.2; image wounds nun V122.1; letter protects *D1381.24.1. — Animals rejoice at C. birth B251.1; animals speak at C. nativity B211.0.1; all locks opened at C. nativity D2088.0.1; appearance of C. body to prove transformation of host V33.1.1; blood from C. wounds restores sight D1505.8.1; children speak in wombs at C. birth T575.1.5; death at news of C. crucifixion F1041.1.3.9; dead prophesy C. coming E367.3; devil exorcised at C. nativity G303.16.19.10; diseases cured at C. birth D2161.6.1; eight miracles of C. body Z71.16.1.3; fetters loosed on C. nativity D1395.8; giant whale cast ashore on C. nativity B874.3.2; gold appears in Arabia at C. birth N529.1; hero born at C. nativity T589.7.2; indentions on plants from C. biting them at crucifixion A2721.2.2; Jews rubbed C. body with garlic A1662.1; markings on animals as recollections of C. life and sufferings A2221.3; Romans hate C. poverty V385; rue from drops of C. blood A2611.7; swallows lift C. crown of thorns from his brow A2221.2.4; spring flows at C. command F933.1.2; tree for C. crucifixion A2632.2; treasure found at C. nativity N541.4; wells break forth at C. birth A941.5.0.2; wild huntsman released from wandering by mould from C. grave *E501.17.7.1; woman taught that it is better to pray before C. image than before a saint's V51.4.

Christened. — Oath not to be c. until Christian battles fought M177.1.2.

Christening, see also **Baptism;** V87. — Animal c. B299.10; dwarfs celebrate c. feasts of their own F451.6.3.2; dwarfs invisibly attend c. feasts of mortals F451.5.1.7; magic power from c. an animal D1766.4; troll bluffed away from c. K1736; witches c. cat G243.2.2; wolf kept at door until c. is finished K551.8.

Christian burial service for fairy F268.1; fairy F243.0.1, F389.2; frees poor from sacrifice K1603; king demands baptism of guests P337.1; laws profitless J1825.1; paradise A694; paradise and pagan otherworld F160.03; traditions cencerning Jews *V360ff. — Devil can't approach C. girl G303.16.19.12; druid's spells kill C. king D1402.13; druids kill C. king F402.1.11.1; fairy borrows comb from C. maid to comb hair of changeling bride F322.1.1; fairies disappear before name or ceremony of C. church F382; magic spells mixed with C. prayers *D1273.0.2; oath literally obeyed: to tell no C. K2312.1; origin of C. worship A1546.3; prophecy that youth shall abandon his religion and become C. M351; runes protect against curse of dead C. D1385.20; vow to become a C. M177.1; what is best religion, C. or Mohammedan? H659.5.1; witch's charm opposite of C. *G224.1.

Christians crushed in cave R315.2; and giants F531.5.8; prohibited from whistling in dark lest the devil appear G303.16.18.1. — Arrows shot against C. blown back F963.2; coffins of C. V61.6; foul disease for persecuting C. Q570.1; Jew thinks C. have merciful God J1263.3; mountain-men make sausage of C. F460.4.4.4.

Christianity. — Belief in C. tested H1573.1; conversion to C. V331; dead convert to C. E367.4; dwarfs and C. F451.5.9ff.; dwarfs emigrate because C. offends them F451.9.1.6; fairy demands lover deny C. F302.8; fairy professes C. F251.8; first Irish convert to C. A1546.3.1; giants converted to C. F531.5.8.3; giants hostile to C. F531.5.8.1; pagan punished for conversion to C. Q232.1; power of C. tested H1573.3; setting house on fire rather than accept C. V328; trolls and C. F455.7.

Christmas *V72. — Animals speak to one another on C. B251.1.2; apples at C. F971.5.2; cows kneel on C. Eve B251.1.2.3; devil in woods to gather nuts on C. Eve G303.8.13.3; fernseed gathering on C. Eve C401.5; flowers blooming at C. F971.5.3; giants and men fraternize at C. F531.5.1.2; knockers' C. Eve mass in mines F456.1.2.3.1; man attacked on C. night by dancing ghosts E261.3; Schlaraffenland lies three miles beyond C. X1712; treasure reveals itself only on C. midnight N541.1; trolls steal fish at C. F455.6.3.1; trolls visit people C. Eve F455.6.5.1; twelve days (gifts) of C. Z21.2.1; water to wine on C. D477.1.1, M211.1.1; wild hunt appears between C. and Twelfth Night E501.11.2.2.

Christopher and the ass J1269.9; and Christ child Q25.

Church built by usurer's money collapses Q273.4; built where giants throw stones F531.3.2.1; desecrator cannot rest in grave E412.5; dignitaries *P120ff.; in otherworld F163.2; produced by magic D1134.1; as refuge R325; services burlesqued in witch's sabbath G243; services of the dead *E492; sinks underground F941.2; spared in flood because of prayers D2143.2.1; stones sheds blood Q222.0.1; supernaturally moved at night D2192.1; which refused to bury saint burned Q552.13.2.2. — Angel abides in c. V242.2; angel holds mass in c. V49.2; angel tells where to build c. V246.1; angels build c. V232.10; animal burns neglected c. B596; animals in otherworld pass in and out of c. and become human beings *F171.5; burial in c. wall cheats devil K219.4; Butterby C.: no c. at all Z61.3; cleaning the c. by moving it J2104.1; contest in jumping from the c. tower K1.7.2; criminal in c. mistakes service as accusation N275.5; curse for plundering c. Q556.6; cursed c. clock runs incorrectly H252.6; dead arise when one plays organ for first time in c. E419.5; devil in c. G303.8.4, G303.24ff.; devil in each stone of c. built with ill-gotten wealth G303.8.4.2; devil may be escaped by going to c. daily G303.16.13; devil disguised as man goes to c. to confess K1987; devil makes mischief on c. G303.24.4 (destroys steeple), G303.24.1.7.1 (disturbs worshippers), G303.9.9.18 (moves seats), A977.2.2 (throws stones); destruction, rebuilding of c. prophesied M364.10; discontinuing use of a c. forbidden C51.1.6; dog lets devil into c. to steal A2229.2; dwarfs hold c. services F451.6.3.6; dwarfs live in a c. F451.4.2.4; dwarf seeks to enter c. F451.5.9.5; fairies disappear when some name or ceremony of Christian C. is used F382; friendly ghost haunts c. E338.2; ghost effects return of stolen c. plate E236.7; ghost rebukes those withholding c. money

E415.2; ghosts haunt c. E283; giants carry a c. across a stream F531.3.6; guarded maiden first seen by hero in c. T381.1; heat prevents c. theft D1389.2.1; images at c. turn backs as mark of disfavor D1639.3; lightning strikes excommunicated person who enters c. V84.1; lime used in building c. as cure D1500.1.10.6; magic arrow indicates place to build c. D1314.1.4; magic c. D1134.1; magic stone protects c. from oppression D1389.1; man becomes c. D268.0.1; man whose death prophesied takes refuge in c. M381; man promises to build c. if he is saved at sea M266; mermaid sings divinely in c. B81.13.6; merman's wife not to stay till c. benediction *C713.1; misunderstanding of c. customs or ceremonies cause inappropriate action J1823; mountain gives stones for c. D1552.7; mountain men throw person over c. roof F460.4.4.3; mountains and hills from stones thrown by giant at c. A963.5; moving c. tower J2328; numskulls buy c. in common J2037.1; parody of c. ceremony at witch's sabbath G243.2; prophecy: saint to found c. M364.1.1; punishment for desecrating c. Q222.5; books in c. read without man's tongue F1055; person to live as long as c. stands E765.3.1; playing cards with devil in c. H1421; prince sees maiden at c. and is enamored N711.4; punishment for scoffing at c. teachings *Q225; neglect to attend c. punished Q223.5; radiance fills c. when saint dies V222.1.1; remarkable c. F773; repartee based on c. or clergy J1260ff.; robber or dog in c. thought to be a ghost J1782.1; speechless vigil in c. (test) H1451; spending night in c. H1412; stealing from c. punished by hanging Q411.11.2; stone bleeds before c. plundered D1317.12.1; symbolism of c. and image H619.2; thief reveals self in c. J1141.15; threat to build c. in hell K1781; turf from c. roof gives clairvoyance D1323.7; vision concerning state of Irish c. V515.1.3.1; walking backward around c. gives witch power G224.8; wedding ceremony in c. T135.9; white mare thought to be c. J1761.2; his wife the c. J1264.1; wild huntsman wanders for disturbing c. service E501.3.8; witch marks c. steeple G241.3.3.

Churches *V111. — Devil as builder of c. G303.9.1.6; giants throw stones after c. F531.3.2.1; half of Irish c. to be named for Ciaran M364.9.

Church bells *V115ff., ring selves at holy person's death V222.6.1, rout enemy D1400.1.9.1, speak D1610.15.1, cannot be raised because silence is broken V115.1.3.1, rung as protection against storm D2141.1.1. — Dwarfs dislike c. F451.5.9.3; ghost laid by burying c., clapper separately E459.6; hiding from ghosts under c. E434.1; mermaid prevents raising of sunken c. B81.13.10; origin of c. A1466; trolls cannot endure c. G304.2.4.1; what c. say V115.4.

Churchdoor. — Recognition by overheard conversation with c. H13.2.4.

Churchman. — Disguise as c. K1826; seduction by posing as c. K1315.6; sham c. K1961ff.

Churchmen in wild hunt E501.2.5. — Animal c. B252; treacherous c. K2280ff.; wild hunt powerless against c. E501.17.1.2.

Churchyard ghosts E273, (friendly) E333. — Dancing in c. forbidden

C51.1.5; magic c. mould *D1278.1; tabu to dig in c. C93.3; wild hunt appears in c. E501.12.2.

Churl. — Disguise as c. K2357.14; transformation into c. D29.1.

Churn. — Breaking spell on bewitched c. G271.4.11; coin in c. releases curse M429.6; fairies bathing in c. F361.17.5; fox struck with c.-dash: hence white tail A2215.5; salt in c. protects against witches G272.16.1.

Churning. — Dwarfs c. F451.3.4.7; fairies c. F271.7; origin of c. A1439.5.1; origin of c. stick A2823.

Ciaran. — Irish churches to be named for C. M364.9.

Cicada. — Man transformed to c. D183.1.

Cicadas ordered to sing God's praises D2156.7.

Ciconiiformes. — Creation of c. A1960ff.; transformation to c. D155ff.

Cicuta. — Transformation by eating c. D551.2.2.

Cider as man's enemy J1319.1.

Cigar, magic D1261.

Cimmerians, voyage to land of F129.3.

Cinderella L102; male L101.

Cinderella's three-fold flight from ball R221.

Cinders. — Man created from c. A1268.

Cinnamon, origin of A2686.8.

Circe transforms lovers into animals G263.1.0.1.

Circle. — Devil cheated by having priest draw a sacred c. about the intended victim K218.1; dwarfs cannot harm mortal with c. drawn around him F451.3.2.3; magic c. *D1272; magic c. keeps devil out G303.16.19.15; sitting in c. of feasts P338; saints' land surrounded by fiery c. A661.0.10; warriors fight in c. P552.1.

Circles. — Sun, moon as animated wooden c. A714.8.

Circular house rotating on cock's claw F771.2.6.1.

Circuit. — Earth scattered on c. of four directions on primeval water A814.6.

Circuitous path quickest J2119.2.2.

Circumambulations. — Magic power by c. *D1791; repeated c. with prayer V58.3.

Circumcised. — Child born c. T585.9; first man created c. A1281.5.

Circumcision V82. — Dust on c. wound A1567.1; journey to hell for c. of child F81.3; magic c. blood D1003.2; mother suckles all babies at c. H495.3; neglect of c. punished Q223.11; origin of c. A1567.

Cirencester, sparrows of K2351.1.

Cistern. — Cleaning enormous c. in one day (task) H1097.2.

City built by magic D2178.1; buried in sand F948.5; burned with all inhabitants S112.0.1; of demons F402.3; founded on spot (where cow lies down) B115.2, (where arrow falls) D1314.1.2; of gods A151.5; hurled down precipice in punishment Q552.22; infested by jinns, deserted G307.4; of king opposing saint burned Q552.13.2.1; person ignorant of farm J1731; populated by wooden automata D1628; saved from disaster as reward Q152; sinks in sea F944; without provisions but with much money starves J712.1; of women F112.2. — Bringing documents from distant c. in one day (task) H1107; building c. as task H1133.5; conqueror spares c. W11.5.5; countryman misunderstands c. comforts J1742.5; covenant: c. not to be taken from inhabitants without their consent M293; curse on c. M475; defeated surrender their c. R75.1; deity to restore c. A185.8; dragon encircles c. B11.2.8.1; earth swallows heretical c. Q552.2.3.2.2; enduring insults to enter c. gate H1553.3; fairy gains entrance to locked c. D2088.1; faithless widow offers c. to husband's killer T231.3.1; god of c. A412; illusory c. separates companions K1886.5; inhabitants of c. transformed to fish D692; magic object protects a c. D1380.0.1; man ordered to number fools in c. J1443; monkeys decide not to build c. J648.1; old man contented till forbidden to leave c. H1557.3; only one way of besieging c. Z316; philosopher saves c. from destruction J1289.10; pious man renders c. invulnerable D1846.5.2; reward: being saved from destruction of c. Q150.1.1; righteous save sinful c. from destruction M294; ruler delivers c. to enemy K2369.3; sage curses c. M411.24; sinful c. burnt as punishment Q486.1.1; strong man carries off c. gates F631.2; truth leaves c. because there is no place left for her Z121.1; voice from heaven curses c. Q556.0.2.; wild hunt appears over c. E501.12.9.

Cities, extraordinary *F760ff.; of refuge P518, R345; submarine F725.2. — Jokes concerning c. X680; origin of c. A995; remarkable c. X1560; three c. in heaven A661.1.2.

Civet. — Enmity of c. and chicken A2494.1.8; hare tricks c. into being eaten by lion K813.2.

Civilization personified Z136.

Clad, see **Clothed.**

Claim. — Devil asserts c. to soul offered in jest G303.6.1.3; false c. to powers of a god forbidden C51.6; impostors' c. of reward earned by hero K1932; property c. based on lie X905.3; thief shows up owner's unjust c. J1213; thief's successful c. that stolen goods are his own K405; why a mother has prior c. on her children A1575.1.

Clairvoyance given by magic object *D1323ff., D1331.1; from prayer D1323.18.

Clam swallows canoe party F911.4.1.1; test H1521. — Giant c. B874.6; great c. fights hero's pursuer B523.3.

Clams. — Giant c. in otherworld F167.1.4.1.

Clam-shell lures man into sea G308.7. — Animal preserves fire for abandoned children in a c. S352.1; creation of universe from c. A617.

Clan gods A415, M119.2.

Clans. — Marriage within c. sanctioned T131.5.1.

Clandestine lover recognized (by tokens) H81ff., (by paint marks) H58, (by scratches) H58.2; paramour *T475; visit of princess to hero betrayed by token H81.2.

Clapper. — Ghost laid by burying churchbell, c. separately E459.6.

Clapping hands when dangling from tree fatal J2133.13. — Magic from c. hands D1799.2.

Clarifying. — Nut c. waters F930.8.

Clarinet. — Gun mistaken for c. J1772.10; magic c. *D1223.

Clashing rocks D1553, H1525; swords herald wild hunt E501.13.1.3.

Class tabu C550—C599. — Transformation to person of different social c. D20ff.

Classes. — Humor of social c. X200—X599; origin of different c., social and professional A1650ff.; stupid c. J1705.

Claw. — Circular house rotating on cock's c. F771.2.6.1; transformation by putting on c. of helpful animal D532.

Claws caught in tree cleft K1111; on dragon's feet B11.2.4.2. — Animal characteristics: c. and hoofs A2376; bear hard to hold by c. H659.2.1; bear learns how to catch crabs with his hairy c. J102; child born with c. T551.9; devil has c. G303.4.4; devil puts c. through girl's hands G303.10.4.5; giant with nails like c. F531.1.6.1; how crab got its c. A2376.4; lion suitor allows his c. to be cut J642.1; men with iron c. cannibals G88.1; monster's c. as slaying proof H105.5.3; person with c. on feet F517.1.4; priest separates girl from devil's c. G303.16.14.1.1; trees with green birds hanging by c. F811.9.

Clay dropped from sky forms hill A963.9; model causes king to recognize lost brother H16.1. — Boat of c. J2171.1.3.2; carrying water in a leaky vessel by repairing it with c. H1023.2.1.1; consecrated c. as remedy D1500.1.6.2.1; covering with c. to escape K521.3.1; hardened c. is hard to mold J21.52.3; magic c. D935.2; man made from c. A1241.4.1; man's body of c. A1260.1.5; origin of c. A998; tribes from creator's c. models A1610.6.

Clean. — Food denied until hands c.: impossible task K278; salt to keep people c. A1372.10; seduction access by waiting for c. clothes K1349.6.

Cleanest girl to be eaten K619.1.1.

Cleaning Augean stable H1102; child by removing intestines K1461.1; church by moving it J2104.1; dagger on robe's inside A1599.7; enormous cistern in one day (task) H1097.2; horse with boiling water K1443; houses with cow-dung C536. — Four places c. soul Z71.2.4; magic power from c. D1799.1; rancher unrecognizable after c. up W115.3; reward for c. loathsome person Q41.2.

Cleanliness. — Lice as c. test H1585.

Cleansing fountain in heaven A661.0.4.

Clearing land (axe broken) K1421, (as task) H1129.6; out manure by digging hole K1424; out the room (throwing out the furniture) J2465.5. — Fairies c. land F271.5; god c. plains A181.1; strong man c. plain F614.9.

Cleaving boulder frightens witch K547.13; horse and rider in two F628.2.10.

Cleft. — Cure by passing patient under c. of tree D2161.4.5; dwarf caught by beard in c. of tree E451.6.1; female overpowered when caught in tree c. K1384; giant's blow makes c. in rock F531.6.6.4; magic imprisonment in c. tree Q435; mankind from c. rock A1245.3.

Clement V duped into abdicating K2282.1.

Clergy *P426. — Curse of c. causes death D2061.2.4.2; giants exorcised by c. F531.5.8.2; repartee based on church or c. J1260ff.

Cleric, see also **Monk, Priest;** goes with saint whom his cow follows B159.3; as helper N846; as riddle-solver H561.8; robbing grave K335.0.8; as saint's successor D1812.5.0.7.2; son realizes mother's incest H582.2.1; tempted by devil G303.9.4.4; tempts self with women Q537.2. — Angel in form of c. V231.4; animal leads c. to holy place B563.4.1; dead saint exonerates c. E376.1; fly buzzes when c. returns B251.2.4; fly, wren, fox live with c. B256.10; imprisoned c. answers saint's prayer D2074.2.5.1; transformation into c. D25.2.

Clerics exempted from military service P551.3; fast for revelation P623.0.1.1; fishing F986.1; mistaken for fairies F234.2.4.1; sail in skin boats C841.0.1; saved from drowning F1088.3.1. — Debtor c. punished Q499.5; devil's book for sins of c. G303.24.1.9; fairies hate c. F399.3; horses travel unguided between c. B151.1.1.0.1; mutinous c. expelled P226.2; whale helps voyaging c. land B256.12.

Clerical virtues and vices V460ff. — Neglect of c. duties punished Q223.13; repartee concerning c. abuses J1263ff.

Clerk who enters tavern arrested with others for murder N347.1; mistranslates order, gets pie K362.8.

Clever daughter-in-law defeats wealthy J185.1; Elsa J2063; peasant girl asked riddles by king H561.1; person deceives robbers, summons help K432; persons and acts J1100—J1699; person's defeat pleases inferior J885; queen P20.1; remark wins jester's pardon by prince J1181.3; retorts J1250—J1649; sister saves brother's wife P253.8; wife in disguise wins husband H461.1; youngest daughter L61. — Encounter with c. children J31; foolish person becomes c. J1116; husband's c. remark discomfits adulterers K1569.8; king and c. youth H561.4; quest for c. woman H1381.3.3; sham magician exposed by c. girl K1963.1; stupid fear c. J423; stupid youngest son becomes c. L21; sun as moon's c. brother A736.3.2.

Cleverness *J1100—J1699; as bride test H388; rewarded Q91; as suitor test H327. — Falsely accused minister reinstates himself by his c. K2101; king pleased with thieves' c. J1198.1; strength preferred to c. J246; tests of c. *H500—H899; tasks performed by c. H961.

Client, the lawyer's mad *K1655.

Cliff from lover's leap A968.2; ogre thrown to his children G519.3. — Abandonment on c. Q466.2, S147.1; child falls from c.; uninjured N653; child's falling over c. to punish mother Q559.9; climbing extraordinary c. H1199.14; demons live in white c. F402.6.4; dwarfs live in a c. F451.4.2.1; extraordinary c. F808; fatal game: throwing from c. K854;

fright into falling down a c. J2611; murder by pushing off c. K929.9; murderess forced to leap from c. Q417.1; magic c. D932.1; ogre kicks victims over c. G321; owl saves man from plunging over c. B521.5; rejuvenation by jumping over c. D1889.11; stretching c. D482.4; throwing moon over c. J2271.3; victim pushed off c. as he looks for tree K832.5; witch dwells on c. G231.

Cliffs. — Origin of c. A968; trolls live in c. F455.1.2.

Climate, see also **Weather;** same at home and abroad J2274.3. — Lies about c. X1660.

Climax of horrors Z41.10.

Climber. — Marvelous c. F684.1; stealing from tree c. K341.4.1.

Climbers. — Tree c. temporarily remove bones F1054.

Climbing into air on magic rope D1582; down as he climbed up J2244; extraordinary cliff H1199.14; glass mountain (task) H1114; the mast (bluff) K1762; match won by deception K15; red hot rod (punishment) Q469.2; on roof prohibited women C181.4. — Attempt at c. to heaven L421.1; disenchantment by c. D753.4; dupe c. rope for food injured K1034; hero c. up girl's sari killed N339.11; souls c. pillars to heaven E754.6; tribe c. down from sky to earth A1631.2; wolves c. on top of one another to tree J2133.6.

Clinging. — Beings born in hell c. to walls A671.6; journey to otherworld by c. magically to an object *F155; magic object c. to guilty person *H251.3.8.

Clink. — Payment with c. of money J1172.2.

Clitoris. — Extraordinary c. F547.4; origin of c. A1313.2.1.

Cloak, see also **Mantle;** dipped in water as false proof of storm K1894; fits all sizes D1692; from fur of all animals F821.1.3.2; given to a stone to keep it warm J1873.2; transformed to other object D454.3.4. — Abduction by giving soporific and rolling up in a c. R22.1; amulet becomes c. D489.2; carrying coals in c. without harm H221.1.1; devil in a black c. G303.5.1.1; devil in fold of knight's c. G303.8.9.1; devil steals knight's c. G303.9.9.3; fairy gives magic c. F343.5.1; identification by feather c. H111.2; magic c. *D1053; magic c. makes person old D1341.2; putting head under saint's c. reveals rewards in heaven D1329.1; transformation by donning c. D537.2; thief steals c. left as surety K346.5; thief borrows c. to carry food, steals it K351.2; "what is under my c.?" H526.

Clock as reward for passing curiosity test H1554.2; stops at owner's death E766.1; ticking thought to be gnawing of mice J1789.2. — Cursed church c. runs incorrectly H252.6; magic c. flies D1651.14.

Clod. — Murder by putting c. in person's windpipe K951.4; transformation: handkerchief with three knots to c., potsherd, and charcoal D454.3.2.1.

Clods from horse's hoofs appear like birds K1872.5.1.

Clog. — Dog proud of his c. J953.1.

Cloister haunted by ghost E284. — Devil seduces monk from c.

G303.3.1.12.4; friendly ghost haunts c. E338.3; girl to be king's bride kept in c. T381.0.1; warrior retires to c. Q520.6.

Closed. — Dwarf cave c. by iron doors F451.4.3.1; magic journey with c. eyes D2121.2.

Closing the door tight with iron nails K1417. — Images with opening and c. eyes D1632; miraculous opening and c. of magic object *D1550ff.; opening and c. tree to give saint passage F979.2; waters magically dividing and c. *D1551ff.

Closet. — Lazy servant looks into dark c. to see if it is yet light W111.2.1; skeleton in the c. V115.

Clot of blood, birth from T541.1.1.

Cloth on back protects against being eaten H119.1; becomes bloody (life token) E761.1.8; causes magic sleep D1364.13; as chastity index H431; for chiefs alone C564.4; large or small at will D631.3.6; as long as river H1149.8; sold to statue J1853.1; transforms D572.3; working as bride test H383.2. — Animals from transformed c. A1714.1; boy born in c. wrapping T581.11; covering with white c. disenchants D777.1; dwarfs spin, weave c. F455.3.4; earth from couple dancing on c. A825; eating food without untying c. H506.7; fairies work on c. F271.4; goddess's c. spread on ground: spring flows A941.5.6; guessing nature of devil's c. H523.2; how much c. would it take to make God's coat? J1291.3.1; identification by c. H110ff.; ignorant priest forces rolls of c. instead of bread down a dying man's throat J1738.1; imaginary coler of c. J1551.8; king orders piece of c. shown after his death J912.1; lover's gift regained: piece of c. as gift K1581.5; magic c. *D1051; origin of bark-c. A1453.5; origin of designs on c. A1465.3.2; origin of raffia c. A1453.7; quest for dusty c. H1377.4; quest for marvelous c. H1355; rat and serpent imprisoned together in a sevenfold c. covering K1182; resuscitation by wet c. over corpse E80.2; stingy woman's c. stolen K341.13; thief advises c. be left out overnight: steals it K343.2.2; thief throws needle containing stolen c. K341.13.1; thievish tailor sews the stolen piece of c. on the outside of his coat X221; tying c. between legs tabu C181.5; washing black c. white H1023.6; weaving c. from two threads (task) H1022.1; widow c. J2301.2.

Cloths, altar V135.

Cloth-making, origin of A1453.

Clothed. — Coming neither naked nor c. H1054; naked person made to believe that he is c. J2312ff.; nude woman c. in own hair F555.3.1; ogre c. in rock G371.1; parents c. from palm-tree A1420.5.

Clothes, see also **Garments;** auctioned in hell attract Jews X611; burn when owner dies E767.2; burned magically D2089.8; burned to rid them of insects J2102.6; changed so as to escape K521.4; confer invulnerability D1845.2; carry owner over water D1524.2; from magic nut D1470.1.6; magically clinge to body D2171.6; hung on sunbeam *F1011.1; of knight who kneels in mud before host as it passes miraculously kept clean V34.4; producing tree K118.1; put into nutshells F1053; thrown into the cooking food J1561.1. — Abduction by stealing c. R32; beggar's c. burned, yield gold K245; boy with c. of paper X1853; bride test: wearing deceased wife's c. H363.1; bringing c. soonest in bride contest H375.2; burial in c. of one's murderer V68.3; capture by using enemy's c. K761; correct wearing of c. as suitor test H312.6; creator paints c. on models of men A1453.6; dead grateful for c. E341.4; devil hides in c. of running people G303.6.2.1.2; disguise in killed enemy's c. K2357.7; disguise by wearing other person's c. K1810.1; disguise of woman in man's c. *K1837; diving for c. K1051.2; dupe fights bear, c. stolen K1252.1; dupe's c. stolen K343.5; emperor's new c. *K445; escape by arranging captor's c. so as to delay him K634; exchange of c. between master, servant K527.3; extraordinary c. F821ff., (in otherworld) F166.3; fairy leaves when he is given c. F381.3; fairies give beautiful c. F343.5; fool in new c. does not know himself J2012.4; giant's c. F531.4.7; heroine in menial disguise discovered in her beautiful c. H151.6; king changes c. with thief K346.1.1; magic c. *D1050ff.; magic object furnishes c. D1473; magic power from donning magician's c. D1721.0.1; magic sight by turning c. inside out D1821.9; man gulled into giving up his c. K330.1; man to be judged by his own qualities, not his c. J1072; man's c. identify werwolf H64.2; miser wants to enter heaven in gold-filled c. W153.15; no c. needed for Day of Judgment J1511.7; paramour steals husband's c. K1549.1; polluted c. J2184; princess changing c. with maid T323.1.1; profaning hallowed c. and vessels forbidden C93.2; recognition by exact fitting of c. H36; respite from death until c. are changed K551.4.1; respite from wooer while he brings c. all night K1227.3; serpent's bite produces ornaments and c. B108.6; sewing c. onto skin H1505; saint restores burned c. V229.10.1; shame for nakedness appears to first woman (leaves for c.) H1383.1; spirits dressed in antique c. F401.1; stealing c. from ghosts (fear test) H1431; touching certain c. tabu C545; transformation by changing c. D537; tribe wears c. like dogs A1683.2; thief in owner's c. K311.8.4; trickster permitted to try on c. K351; vow not to change c. till a certain time M125; washing enormous number of c. (task) H1096; wearing all his c. J1289.5; welcome to the c. J1561.3; what were the c. of Adam and Eve? H812; why the black c. J1304; wives change c. with husbands in prison R152.3; woman sells favors for beautiful c. T455.3; wooing by stealing c. of bathing girl H1335.

Clothing bewitched G265.8.2; of brownie F482.2; as chastity index H431; with embroidery as tokens H86.2; of gods A158; the servant J2491; transformed to other object D454.3.1; tabu to Bondo women C181.6; of wild huntsmen E501.8ff. — Deity c. his father, the sky A625.2.4; devil is in green c. with hat G303.5.2.1; disenchantment by covering with deliverer's c. D789.1; extraordinary c. and ornaments F820ff.; first couple c. children A1277.4; food does not spoil saint's c. F1091; forethought in provision for c. J730ff.; girl hides lover under c. K1892.2; god c. self with lightning A179.7; identification by c. H110ff.; lie: remarkable c. X1021; magic c. furnishes treasure D1455; murder by abuse of victim's c. D2061.2.2.5; otherworld c. never wears out F166.3.1; plants from c. of deity A2625; poisoned c. test H1516; return from dead to demand c. stolen from grave *E236.1; selling used c. forbidden C782.1; stealing witch's beautiful c. H1151.23; spirit slashes c. F473.6.2; swallowed person bereft of c. F922; tabus concerning c. C878.

Cloud bears dying man's message D1715.3; bows to female mountain A969.2; folk visit earth F33; gives crops rain or drops it in ocean J88; god A283; magically made to cover sun D2147.1; marks Nativity site V211.1.3; obstructs view of man promised all he can see Q552.15; obstructs vision in deceptive land grant K185.12; symbol of misfortune Z156. — Ascent to sky on c. *F61.1; black c. blown upon enemy D2091.11; cannibal recognized by c. of dust raised H46; dead's c. house E481.8.4; fairy disappears in form of c. F234.3.1; fool seeks the ears of grain in the direction of the c. toward which he has sowed them J1922.2.1; god in c. A137.11; magic c. *D901; magic journey in c. D2121.7; marking the place under the c. J1922.2; prisoner carried off in c. R122.2; saint drives away army with c. V229.7.1; soul as c. E744.2; soul borne away on c. E722.2.1; throwing contest: golden club on the c. K18.2; trickster threatens to throw weight into c. K1746; troll in form of c. G304.1.2.1.

Clouds above and below earth A873; beaten for not watering crops X1642; as props of the sky A702.7. — Absurd theories about c. J2277; animals drop from c. A1795; bird wants sunshine, worm c. U148.1; colored c. as evil omens D1812.5.1.11; divination from c. D1812.5.0.10; extraordinary behavior of c. F967; extraordinary c. F795; god with c. as shields A137.14.3; mad warriors fly up into c. F1041.8.7; magic control of c. D2147; origin of c. A705.1, A1133; origin of Magellanic C. A778.0.1; origin of thunder c. A1142.4; stars are trees growing on c. A769.1.

Cloudland. — Gods live in c. A151.1.4; tabu to sleep before seven days in c. C735.2.1.1.

Clove, origin of A2663.

Cloven hoof (of cow) A2376.1, (of dragon) B11.2.4.2.

Clover (four-leaf) brings good luck D1561.1.5; gives clairvoyance D1323.14; makes fairies visible F235.4.6. — Magic c. *D965.7; witch unable to rise from chair with c. under it G254.

Club strike kills ogre G512.8.1. — Devil has c. foot G303.4.5.8; extraordinary c. F835; giant's huge c. F531.4.4; god with c. A137.2; magic c. *D1094, (gives victory) D1400.1.7.1; magic transportation by c. D1520.27.1; thief-catcher caught by own c. K1605; throwing contest: golden c. on the cloud K18.2.

Coach. — Devil in c. drawn by headless horses G303.7.3.3; hay on shaft urges c. horses on J1671; phantom c. E535.1.

Coal of fire offered in innocence test H256.1; jumps, gurgles in bin
E539.5; transformed to person D439.2. — Bean, straw, and c. go journeying F1025.1; lazy girl on live c. W111.1.1.5; magic c. *D931.1; ordeal
by burning c. H221.1; origin of c. A1431; wild huntsman's dog when
seized becomes black c. E501.15.6.7; woman puts live c. in lover's cloth
K1581.5.1.

Coals transformed to gold D475.1.1. — Beggar served c. for food K492.1;
devil picks up live c. G303.4.8.12; eyes of live c. F541.1.3; fairies give c.
that turn to gold F342.1; murder by live c. in garments S112.4; sack of c.
as fairy gift F343.20; saint invulnerable to glowing c. D1841.3.2.2; saint's
breath kindles c. D1566.1.4.1; swallowing hot c. because husband unfaithful T81.8.

Coat. — Boy in church calls out that rich man has taken his c. to hell
with him X435.5; compassionate executioner: bloody c. K512.1; Christ's
c. of mercy protects Pilate from punishment D1381.4.1.; devil wears a
bright green c. G303.5.2.3; fairy spell averted by turning c. F385.1; foul-
smelling skin-c. to repel lover T323.2; frightened robber leaves his c.
behind K335.1.0.1; harlot weeps to think that she has left impoverished
lover his c. W151.1; identification by c. of arms H126; light c. fits in
palm F821.2.1; magic c. protects against attack D1381.4; the marked c.
in the wife's room K1543; saint exchanges c. with beggar V411.2; thief
tricked into robbing himself by changing the place of his c. K439.3;
thievish tailor cuts a piece of his own c. X221.1; witness who claims borrowed c. discredited J1151.2; wooden c. F821.1.4.

Coats. — Bird council assigns c. to different birds B238.2; dwarfs wear
red c. F451.2.7.5; servants would not have left the c. J1179.5.

Cobbler, see also **Shoemaker;** gives shoes to poor boy, rewarded later
Q42.9; reforms shrewish queen T251.2.4. — Disguise as c. K1816.10;
the minstrel repays the c. J1632; monkey imitates c. J2413.4.3.

Cobblers. — Jokes about c. X240ff.; trickster cheats boots from two c.
K233.3.

Cobold avenges uncivil answer F481.1; made to surrender booty F480.3.1.

Cobra carries person B557.8; grateful for milk B391.1.1; grateful for ulcer
cure B388; grateful for thorn removal N647; writes letter on prince's
tongue B165.1.3. — Back scratching stick changed into c. A1335.14; conception from hiss of c. T532.10; earth rests on head of c. A84.4.8; enmity
between c. and viper A2494.16.3; friendship between crab and c.
A2493.19; light from shield of c. A1412.1; man falling into well kills c.
N624; prophecy: death from c. M341.2.21.1; resuscitation by removing c.
flesh E21.1.1; starting fire near abode of c. H1156.1.

Cobras in boxes as punishment gift Q415.3.1. — Cake bag full of c.
K444.2.

Cobwebs as medication X252.1.

Cock advises of coming enemy B122.7; as ambassador of god A165.2.2.1;
believes his crowing makes sun rise J2272.1; calls the dawn B755; carries

god to upper world F62.3; crows, "Christus natus est" B251.1.2.1; crows at church and the sexton awakes and begins to sing X451; and dog enemies A2494.4.11; with elixir to lighten people B739.1; with enormous ears F989.19; feigns death to overhear hens H1556.1.1; -god A132.6.3; hears inaudible voice of dying man B733.2.1; of hell A673.2; and hen build pyre B599.1; killed by his captors in spite of his plea of usefulness to man U33; with horns on feet, knob on head (riddle) H746; and others gain possession of house K1161; persuaded to crow with closed eyes K721; persuaded to cut off crest and spurs K1065; persuades fox to talk and release him K561.1; under pot crows for guilt H235; prefers single corn to peck of pearls J1061.1; shows browbeaten husband how to rule his wife T252.2; to sing for fox, asks dog to listen K579.8; as suitor B623.5; in Valhalla awakens the gods A661.1.0.4. — Alliance of c. and seafowl B267.4; cat offers to act as doctor for c. and hen K2061.7; cat unjustly accuses, eats c. U31.1; chain tale: c. strikes out hen's eye Z43.2; continent husband reproved by seeing c. and hens T315.2.2; dead c. rises, crows, and spatters scoffers so that they become leprous Q552.8; death of the c. Z31.2.1.1; demons' c.-feet G302.4.5.1; devil disappears when c. crows G303.17.1.1; devil flees when c. is made to crow G303.16.19.4; devil in form of c. G303.3.3.3.5; "each c. crows in his own barnyard" J552.6; eaten grain and c. as damages K251.1; egg becomes crowing c. F989.20; fox confesses to c., then eats him K2027; fox persuades c. to come down and talk to him, kills him K815.1: friendship between c. and dog A2493.16; ghost of c. E402.2.1, E524.2; ghost demands body: given c. E459.1; golden c. in earth-tree A878.3.6; golden c. warns of danger D1317.15; golden c. warns against attack B143.1.5; helpful c. B469.5; Indra carried by c. B552.3; lion comforted for his fear of the c. J881.2; magic c. carries great loads in ear B171.1.0.1; magic from christening c. D1766.4.1; magic power from sacrificing (christening) a c. D1766.2.2; man transformed to c. D166.1.1; mythical c. B30.2; one c. takes glory of another's valor J972; origin of c. sacrifice A1545.3.3; originally c. had horns A2326.2.3; person simulates c. crow K1886.3.1; prophecy on c. fight D1814.1.1; quest for jeweled c. H1331.1.3.1; roasted c. comes to life and crows E168.1; sacrificing of c. is at last carried out K231.3.3; silver c. crows D1620.2.2.1; series: white c., red c., black c. Z65.2; sheep, duck, and c. in peril on sea voyage J1711.1; speaking c. B211.3.2; thread made to appear as a large log carried by a c. D2031.2; treacherous c. K2295.3; treasure found by sprinkling ground with blood of white c. D2101.1; treasure to be found by man who ploughs with c. and harrows with hen N543.2; village founded where c. crows B155.2.1; wedding of c. and hen B282.22; wee c. overawes beasts K547.1; why c. scratches for food A2435.4.8.1; why c. crows to greet sunrise A2489.1.1; why c. crows on roof with neck stretched out A2426.2.18.1; why c. does not speak A2422.10; why c. lives in town A2433.4.2, A2250.1; why c. is vain and selfish A2527.1; why c.

wakes man in morning A2489.1; why elephant flees when c. crows A2531.3.1; witch as c. G211.3.1.1; woman crowing like c. K1691.2.

Cock's advice proves disastrous to himself K1633; blood substituted for sacrificial human K525.9; crowing interpreted J1811.4; cry "cock-a-doodle-do" A2426.2.18; escape from fox K561.1; food A2435.4.8; second mate lets stepchildren starve J134.1; whiskers (cumulative tale) Z41.3. — Basilisk hatched from c. egg B12.1; circular house rotating on c. claw F771.2.6.1; cobold hatched from c. egg F481.0.1.1; devil has c. feet G303.4.5.9; dragon from c. egg B11.1.1; lions fear c. crowing J2614.3; nut falls on c. head *Z41.4; origin of c. red crest A2321.10; preserving the c. freedom J1892; river contained under c. wings *D915.2; why c. comb becomes white A2321.10.1.

Cocks who crow about mistress's adultery killed J551.1; kept from intercourse have tender meat B754.5. — Mouse teaches her child to fear quiet cats but not noisy c. J132; why c. crow A2421.6.

Cockaygne, land of X1503.

Cockcrow. — Between midnight and c. best time for unearthing treasure N555.1; disenchantment at c. D791.1.7; ghost (fairy, witch, dwarf) laid at c. *E452, E587.3; stone moves at c. D1641.2.3; witch's familiar disappears at c. G225.0.6.

Cockfight as suitor contest H331.15.1.

Cockle. — Marriage of mountain and c. shell T126.2.

Cockroach. — Creation of c. A2061; enmity of fowl and c. A2494.13.3; magic whistle vitalizes c. D1594.6; wedding of mouse and c. B281.2.2; wedding of c. and rat B285.8, B281.11.1.

Cockscomb plant used to kill sun A1156; whitens D492.1. — Devil avoids c. flowers G303.16.14.5; man becomes c. plant D213.1; reincarnation as c. E631.1.4.

Coconut canoe F841.1.4.1; shoots restore sight D1505.18.1; transformed to philosopher's stone D451.3.2; tree from head of slain monster A2611.3; tree is tall A2778.1. — Canoe transformed into c. tree A2615.3; creation of woman from c. A1253.2.1; fish struck by c.: hence flat tail A2213.5.2; magic c. (as food) *D1035.2; magic c. shell *D985.1; magic c. water restores sight D1505.5.5; origin of c. A1423.3, A2681.5.1; soul in c. E711.2.5; springs from c. shell F718.12.

Coconuts. — Light and dark skinned peoples made from light and dark c. A1614.3; monkeys attack by throwing c. B762; people who live on c. F561.3; why c. absent from certain island J2031.3.

Cocoon's. — Making large shawl from one c. silk H1022.4.3.

Codfish, markings on A2412.4.3.

Coffee. — Dead husband asks for c. E321.3; magic c. pot *D1171.1.1; origin of c. A2691.1.

Coffer. — Adulteress throws c. out window to distract husband K1514.15; wrecked man saved on c. of jewels becomes rich N226.

Coffin buried upright V61.3; bursts, dead arises E261.2.1; carried through hole in wall to prevent return of dead E431.4; cover transformed to person D434.4; with iron band prevents tiger ghost's return E431.20; lands at burial site D1314.12; moves itself D1641.13; what one buys who does not want it or use it H878. — Bursting c. of one sold to devil E411.9; corpse in c. refuses to be moved in wagon D1654.9; corpse makes room in c. for friend E477; devil removes disciple's body from c. M219.2.5; dowry in c. E228; extraordinary c. F852ff.; fairies borrow tools to make c. F391.3; four cats carry c. F982.2; ghost carries c. on back E592.2; glass c. F852.1; hinge of c. as remedy D1500.1.15.2; king's c. sunk into river P16.9; leaving money on c. K231.13; magician carries woman in glass c. *D2185; pole for c. rests appears at death E767.1; sacred hosts in c. V35.2; soul as black or white spirit over c. E722.1.1; spectral c. E538.1; tiger enticed into c. K714.2.2; tools announce death D1322.1; victim tricked into entering c. K714.2; wraith selects c. lumber E723.7.5.

Coffins. — Christians' c. V61.6; reward for providing c. for poor Q42.2; spirit disturbs c. F473.6.9.

Cohabitation, see also **Sex, Sexual intercourse;** of hero with sleeping girl and leaving of identification token with her H81.1; of living person and ghost E474; brings change of luck N131.1; among lunatics X541; with first woman met C664.0.1. — Moon's c. with man A753.1.3; moon's c. with woman A753.1.2.

Coil, magic D1282.

Coin in churn releases curse M429.6; left in money scales betrays secret wealth N478; multiplies self D2100.2; placed in mouth of dead to prevent return E431.11. — Chapperbands c. false money A1689.8; contest: c. first attracting fly wins K92.1; devil holds molten c. in mouth G303.4.8.2; as dwarfs emigrate each deposits a c. into kettle for mortals F451.9.4; fish with c. in mouth B105.4.1.; little c. noisy in bottle J262.2; magic c. *D1288; perspiration-covered c. believed weeping J1875.4; philosopher forgets to put c. in mouth before death (Charon's fee) E489.3; putting c. in dead person's mouth P613; short weight c. for charity K2096.1; "you must pay in better c. than is your wont" K1228.

Coins concealed in jar J1655.3; mistaken for cakes J1772.3.1; thought to be red beans J1772.3. — Crushing c. in fingers F614.12; deceptive bargain: the ogre and the copper c. K183; dividing four c. among three persons J1241.2; fool leaves c. lying on roadside J1836; murder by slipping c. into meat K929.5; origin of gold c. A1433.1; silver c. from pumpkin A1433.2.1; stones transformed to gold c. D475.2.1; trickster gets c. from blind beggars K1081.1.1; what workman does with four c. he earns H585.1.

Coition, see also **Sexual Intercourse;** as illness cure *F950.4, J1149.4.

Cold personified Z139.4; produced by magic D2144.1; test (attempt to freeze hero to death) H1512; water magically warmed D2144.3.1; in

winter A1135.1; before theft of fire impedes speech: explanation of
difficulty of certain languages A1616.1. — Alternate heat, c. in hell
A671.3.3; breaking window to let c. out J1819.2; contest in enduring c.
H1541; contest of heat and c. D2144.2; do not discard clothing till c.
weather is over J731; dog swallowing up the c. K135.1.1; flight so high
that eyelids drop from c. F1021.2.2; giants in region of c. F531.6.2.6;
god sends c. to prevent stones from growing A975.1; land of c. F704;
lies about c. weather X1620; magic control of c. D2144ff.; magic object
protects against c. D1382ff.; man in c. consoles himself thinking of rich
man in hell J883.2; marvelous withstander of c. F685ff.; origin of illness
from c. A1337.8; origin of c.: sun turns upward A1135.1.1; porcupine as
controller of c. D2144.1.1; primeval c. A605.2; punishments by c. in hell
Q567; revenant with c. (hands) E422.1.3, (lips) E422.1.4; sleeping naked
in c. as test H1504; taking c. in effigy J1628; why toad lives in c. place
A2433.6.7.

Coldest. — Which is c. season? J1664.1.

Coldness in hell A671.3.1; of otherworld F169.7. — Scorned woman complains of man's c. T71.2.1.

Coleoptera, creation of A2020ff.

Colic, demon of F493.1.2.

Collar. — Crow causes serpent to try to swallow stolen c. and thus be
accused of theft K401.2.1; deception into putting on a c. K713.2; ghost
steals c. of priest E593.1; magic c. *D1068; magic c. indicates falsehood
by squeezing throat, truth by falling to ground D1316.8; magic hunting
c. D1068.1, (insures death of game) D1449.2; sheep with fiery c. B19.4.3;
strong man attacked with millstone puts it on as c. F615.3.1.

Collecting as animal's occupation A2453; debt in hell through help of
dwarf F451.5.1.14; enormous amount of material H1149.4; for impossible
bargain M291.

Collier P415; and fuller cannot live together U143.

Color of dragon B11.2.2ff.; of fairy F233; of fairy's (clothes) F236.1,
(cows) F241.2.1, (horses) F241.1.1; of flame indicates what is burning
F1061.2; of ghostly dog E423.1.1.1; of giant F531.1.7; formulas Z65;
magically changed D492; of revenant E422.2ff.; of plants A2772ff.;
symbolism *Z140; transformed D682.4; worn signifies rank P632.4. —
Animal's c. as reward for piety Q149.1; animals change c. F985; attempt
to change one's c. foolish J511; barber paid to change c. of woman's
face burns her with acid J1161.6; blood changes c. (life token) E761.1.6;
chameleon saves hero's life: may change c. A2223.8; change in person's
c. D57; city of extraordinary c. F741; creator establishes twelve winds,
each a different c. A1129.1; custom of differentiating social classes by c.
of dress introduced A1650.2; dress c. of sun, moon, and stars F821.1.5;
each world corresponds to different c. A659.4; earth's c. from slain
child's blood A1277.3; eyes remarkable as to c. F541.6; fanciful c. of
animal B731; handkerchief c. of sun, moon, and stars F822.1; imagined

c. of cloth J1551.8; islands of extraordinary c. F741; magic c. *D1293f.;
man cursed with c. of the dead Q556.4; origin of c. of animal *A2411ff.,
*A2219.1; origin of c. of animal's (back) A2356.3, (eyes) A2332.5ff.,
(legs) A2371.4f., (tail) A2378.8ff., A2286.2.4, (tongue) A2344.3f.; origin
of bird's c. A2221.6.1; origin of sea's c. A925.2; person changes c. F1082;
person of unusual c. F527; praying man's c. changed V52.11; river
given c. D1658.1.6; rock of extraordinary c. F807; sea changes c. F931.7;
skin changes c. because of broken tabu C985; skin c. A1614.6; stone's
c. indicates guilt or innocence H233; tree of extraordinary c. F811.3;
turning c. from emotion F1041.11.2; why chameleon changes c.
A2411.5.6.1.

Colors of otherworld F178. — Cup of three hundred c. F866.1; origin
of c. at sunrise and sunset A797; rainbow's three c. A791.4.

Colored traitor K2260ff. — Artificially c. horses B731.2.2; many-c. god
A123.7.1; multi-c. hair F555.5; ogres' blood many c. G367.1; origin of
c. races A1614; why bird's beak is c. A2343.2.

Colt, see also **Foal, Horse;** mistaken for devil, addressed J1785.4.1. —
Real mother of c. will swim to it J1171.4; reductio ad absurdum: the
decision about the c. J1191.1; starving c. fierce with hunger J2214.10;
treasure found if one goes with one-night old c. on to one-night old ice
N542.1; untrained c. result of master's neglect J143; wolf thought to
be a c. J1752.

Colter. — Heating plow's c. to release curse M429.4.

Column, see also **Pillar;** to upper world F58. — Fool thankful that God
has built a palace without a c. J2565; four-sided c. in otherworld
F169.1.3; man transformed to a marble c. D231.2; wild hunt disappears
in c. of fire E501.16.4.

Columns under lord's chair cause music A661.0.2.1. — Fiery c. in hell
A671.2.4.11; four c. around otherworld fire F165.7.1; huge rock c. combat
each other, form landmarks A901.2.

Comb drips blood (life token) E761.1.7; transformed to mountain D454.7.1.
— Adventure from returning for c. N773.2; baldheaded man finds the c.
J1001.2; escape by sending for forgotten c. K629.1.1; fairy borrows c.
from Christian maid for changeling bride F322.1.1; girl borrows c. from
fairy F324.1; golden c. F827.5; harrow as hero's c. K1718.4; magic c.
*D1072.1; magic pig carrying scissors, c., and razors between its ears
H1154.1; man transformed to c. D263.3; murder with poisoned c. S111.3;
picking up c. tabu C543; quest for c. H1347; resuscitation by removal of
poisoned c. E21.3; why cock's c. becomes white A2321.1.0.1; why crab's
legs like teeth of c. A2376.5; woman goes back for c., robbed K346.3.

Combs, iron S187.2.

Combed. — Children's hair c. by fairies F313; dead's hair c. V68.2; gold
and silver c. from hair D1454.1; sleeping maid's hair c. by dwarf
F451.5.1.13; woman's hair c. by devil G303.9.5.5.

Combing hair of fairies (task) H1192; hair forbidden C723f. — Devil c.

witches makes sparks fly G222.1; fatal c. of victim's hair K875; horse's magic strength from hair c. D1835.2; magic sleep by c. hero's hair D1962.3.1.

Combat, see also **Contest, Fighting;** between god of light and dragon of ocean A162.2. — Army leaders in single c. H217.1; customs concerning single c. P557.4; disenchantment by c. D763.2; eagerness for c. W212; huge columns c. each other, form earth's features A901.2; refusing c. forbidden C835; revenant challenged to c. E461.1; single c. between gods A162.7; single c. to prove valor H1501.2; tabu: going to (leaving) certain place without c. C866f.; transformation c. D615; undesired c. between sworn brothers N731.2.2; unwitting c. (of brothers) H151.10, N733.1, (of father and son) *N731.2, (between sons of friends) H767; trial by c. H218; wild hunt in c. E501.17ff.; wit c. H507.

Combats. — God of single c. A485.3.

Combatants become sworn brethren P311.1. — The two c. without hands or feet or words (bull and buffalo) H861.

Combustible. — Why wood c. A2782.

Comedian, equanimity of W25.

Comet. — God in form of c. A124.5; impregnation by c. T525.2.

Comets, origin of A786.

Comfort. — Words of Christian c. cause devil to vanish G303.16.4.

Comforted. — Abandoned person in woods c. by prophet and birds S465; devotee of Virgin c. at death V267; repentant sinner c. by angel V235.2.

Coming. — Butter magically kept from c. D2084.2; riddle about girl's c. and flood H583.10.

Command, see also **Order;** to use only one phrase J2516.3.3; would become permanent J1521.3. — Magic results produced by c. *D1765, D2102.2; one c. as test of wife's obedience H473.2.

Commands. — Enigmatic c. to girl H580.1.

Commandments. — Twenty c. better than ten J2213.5.1.

Commemoration of death V65. — Lakes burst forth in c. of hero A920.1.4, A934.3; spring as c. of hero's experiences A941.3.2, A941.4.1.

Commemorative religious meal A1549.1; trees F979.11.

Commended. — Demons powerless over souls c. to God before sleep E754.1.1.1; poor miller c. by priest X212.1; wife c. to devil guarded till man's return C12.4.

Commerce, origin of A1471.

Commiserated. — Robbers c. J1392.2.

Common citizen saves country's honor P711.3; man transformed into exalted personage D22; names for dwarfs F451.8.1. — Friendship between prince and c. man P311.8; king mingles with c. people J914; must drink from the c. cup J1467; prince refuses to play with c. children J411.3; recognition through c. knowledge H10ff.; uniting against c. enemy J624, J145.

Commonplace. — Time renders all things c. J1075.

Communication with god fatal C52.1; of lovers T41; by pouring milk into stream K1549.5.

Communion, see also **Eucharist, Excommunication, Sacrament;** feast to placate dead A1541.1.2; table dust breaks spell G271.2.6. — At c. witches spit out wine over shoulders G285.1; misunderstandings of c. J1824.1; woman eating before c. can't swallow wafer V39.9.

Compact, see also **Bargain, Contract.** — Luck in gambling from c. with devil N6.1.

Companion, see also **Ally, Comrade;** tries foolishly to imitate good luck J2415. — Coming neither with nor without a c. H1061; horse as witch's c. G225.2; impostors abandon c. and usurp place K1931; incognito king rewards c. strangers K1812.13; labor contract: as much money as my c. (strong man) can carry F613.2.1; magic wisdom possessed by extraordinary c. D1719.4; talkative man betrays his c. J2352; thief accuses c. of their mutual theft K401.0.1.

Companions arrive as hero is about to be killed N699.3. — All children born same day as prince are his c. P32.1; animals as creator's c. A33; creator's c. A30ff.; divinity's c. A195; extraordinary c. *F601ff.; fool objects to fools as c. J1715; hero with animal c. Z235; skillful c. create woman: to whom does she belong? *H621; origin of devil and his c. G303.1ff.; riddling remarks of traveling c. interpreted by girl at end of journey H586ff.

Company. — Curse: lack of good c. M443.1; "don't keep bad c." J21.25; eating in c. tabu C285; educated men as choice c. J146.

Companies. — Heaven's inhabitants divided into c. A661.1.1.

Comparison, riddles of H660ff.

Compassionate executioner K512; woman unharmed by boiling oil Q151.12; youngest daughter L54.

Compelling, see also **Forcing;** innocent man to write treasonable letter K2156; person by magic book to do evil D1678. — Magic object c. person (to dance) *D1415ff., (to follow) D1427f.; woman drives away the hungry, c. the filled to eat H583.4.4.

Compensation, see also **Pay, Payment.** — Reincarnation as c. E694.

Competition in friendship between prisoner and jailor P315.1; between student and master P342.

Competitors. — Misinforming guest c. about country's water, wood supply H1239.4.

Complacency, wife's H474, *N11.

Complaint about bad breath K2135; of dissatisfied rivers against the sea W128.3; of snake to Zeus that people step on him J623.1.

Complexion. — Disguise by dyeing c. K1821.5.

Compliments tabu C499.2. — Donkey, camel trade c. J867.

Compound. — Dragon as c. animal B11.2.1ff.; person with c. body F526.

Compressible objects *D491ff., D631.3ff.

Compulsion. — Image under c. V123.1; magic c. to make journey D2121.15.

Compulsions, unique *C650—C699.

Comrade, see also **Companion;** slain, believed to be enemy K1883.5. — Devil cheated of his promised soul when the victim sells his to a c. K219.2; jumping into the river after their c. J1832; loyal friends won't fight disgraced c. W34.2.

Comrades. — Bonds can be loosed only by c. of man who tied them D1651.9.1.

Concealed wife awaits favorable moment to come forward N741.1. — Fugitive c. by opening tree D1393.1; ghost c. with dwarfs F451.5.4.1; magic power to see c. things D1825.4; person c. in another's body *F1034ff.; pregnancy c. by having maid sleep in husband's bed *K1843.1; weapons c. in basket kill opener K929.11.

Concealing boys' identity by scolding K649.3. — Clever c. of jewels J1655; fairies' c. mist F278.2.

Conceived. — Christ c. on same day crucified V211.0.2; last born twin c. first T587.3; magically c. children to marry M146.3; where were you when your mother c.? J1291.4.

Conception and birth *T500—T599. — Belief in Immaculate C. V312; evil enters body with c. A1384.2; father's ambitions transferred to child at c. T597; immaculate c. of hero A511.1.3.3; magic c. of hero Z216; prophecy: hero's c. at certain time M311.0.2.1; woman talks to her child before its c. T575.2.

Concern. — Whose c. it is J1353.

Concert by hogs J1675.5.

Concessions. — Wisdom of c. to power J811ff.

Conch. — Ass brays on hearing c. shell J2211.4; child born in c. shell T561.1; ghost sounds c. shell E402.1.3.1; man issues from c. shell D621.6; magic c. shell furnishes money D1452.4.

Concoction. — Magic c. causes evil eye D2071.0.2.

Concubinage *T450ff.

Concubine, see also **Courtesan, Prostitute.** — Devil's c. haunts E411.2.2; father's counsel on c. H588.10; friar steals from c. K1839.5; jealous c. plots against real wife's children S322.3.2; priest's c. cannot rest in grave *E411.2.1; priest's c. unable to rise from stone Q551.2.7; punishment for taking c. Q243.3; treacherous c. *K2222.

Condemnation because of death without confession V22. — Hasty c. or killing *N340ff.

Condemned friend tests friendship H1558.13; man revealed as king's son N731.4; soul as black E722.1.2; soul recovered E754.1ff. — Beatus prayer for c. souls V51.4; devil as advocate of falsely c. man G303.22.11; queen intervenes for c. courtiers P21; rich man who does not repent until ready to die c. by devil Q271.2; substituting self for one c. K528.2; woman who saved his life c. to death by suitor W154.14.

Condemner. — Punishment escaped by discomfiting c. J1182.

Conduct of bridal couple before ceremony T134. — Decisiveness of c. J1040ff.; man refuses to follow friend in wicked c. P318; origin of code of c. between husband and wife A1571; taking a pattern (picture) of c. J2471; wise and unwise c. J200—J1099.

Conductor of the dead A311. — Devil shepherd's c. to hell to collect debt from nobleman F451.5.1.14.

Coney. — Squirrel borrows tail of c. A2241.7; stripes of c. A2413.6; why c. lives among rocks A2433.3.5.

Confederate persuades captor to throw away trickster K649.12. — Escape by help of c. K640ff.; ghost as man's c. E379.4; lie corroborated by a c., who poses as a newly-arrived stranger K455.7; theft by c. K365.

Conferred, see also **Bestowed.** — Invisibility c. on person D1983.

Confessed. — Ghost laid when crime has been c. E451.1; recognition when parents come to son to be c. H151.3.

Confession of all treachery wins bride H331.11; discredited by declaring it all a dream J1155; made easy for peasant J1263.7; obtained by a ruse *J1141; of sins *V20ff.; without giving up sin punished V25.2. — Complacent judge disregards the c. P521; death respite until c. K551.1.1; devil is made impotent by c. G303.16.9; after c. of sins fox is immediately ready to steal again K2055; ghost causes murderer's c. E231.5; husband as God behind tree forces c. of adultery from wife *K1971.5; of misdeeds by ghost E376; pretending not to hear in c. X441.1; reward for c. of sins Z36.1; seduction by priest during c. K1339.6; weather changes on deed's c. D2140.3.

Confessional. — Neglect to hear c. punished Q223.4; punishment for betraying c. Q224; priest induced to betray secrets of c.: money then exacted from him for silence K443.8, V468.

Confessor duped into being go-between for adulteress and lover K1584; and penitent exchange confidences V29.7. — Ghost laid by c. E443.2.3; live c. better than dead martyr J1261.9; man without c. like body without head V20.1.1; ruler wants lying c. J1263.6; search for c. V29.1.

Confidence. — Excess of c. punished Q330ff.; pretended exchange of c. about one thing that can kill K975.1; wealth gained by seeming to be in king's c. K1782.

Confinement to keep child in ignorance of life J147; of girl during menses C141; of girl at puberty C131; in tower to avoid fulfillment of prophecy M372; of wicked son on island Q433.9.

Confines. — Quest to c. of hell for blood of sorceress H1277.

Confirmed. — Dwarfs listen to singing by c. children F451.5.21.

Confiscating conspirators' estates K487; goods after failure to consummate relations with princess P616. — Mortals c. dwarfs' property F451.5.10.7.

Conflagration, see also **Fire.** — General c. as punishment C984.6.

Conflict of good and evil creators *A50ff. — Flood from c. of gods A1015.1; revenants in c. E460ff.; weak overcomes strong in c. L310ff.

Conflicts of the gods A162; between religions *V350ff. — Forethought in c. with others J610—J679.

Confounding. — Poet c. student J1684.

Confucius, sacrifices to V11.4.

Confusion caused to aid escape K649.9; of tongues *A1333. — Hero causes c. in enemy camp K2369.10.

Congenital helpful animal *B311.

Congregation. — Church and c. sink to bottom of sea F941.2.2; the devil accuses c. of sins G303.24.1.

Conjugal, see **Marital.**

Conjurer, see also **Magician;** P483; brands sacred animals H55.2; must leave before sunrise C752.2.2; restores lost wife R133.2. — Man wishing to be c. fears devil's help C12.1.1; reincarnation as c. E605.9.

Conjuring bag *D1274.1; away evil spirits in name of deity *D1766.7.1.1; away quest obstacles H1237. — Power of prophecy from c. D1812.2.2; rejuvenation by c. D1889.10.

Conquered. — Animal helpful after being c. B315; enemies c. by magic object D1400.1ff.; magic object vomited by c. monster D826.1; quarrelsome wife c. by silent husband T256.1; tribute required of c. foreigners T531.1.1.

Conquering gambler N1.2. — All-c. spear F834.4.

Conqueror returns defeated man's family W11.5.4; rewarded by revenant E465. — Chaste woman resists c. T325; warriors enter service of c. R74.

Conquest. — Prophecies concerning c. M369.5.

Conscience as judge's tribunal W35.2.

Conscientiousness W37.

Consecrated bread as magic object *D1031.1.1; healing ring D1500.1.15.1; host put into beehive C55.3; objects cure D1500.1.10; wine *D1046.1, (used to discover treasure) N533.4. — Animals refrain from spoiling c. food B259.4.1; bathing in c. water D2161.4.14.2; man kept alive by c. sword E163; princess sick because toad has swallowed her c. wafer *C55, D2064.1, V34.2; shepherd's c. staff keeps cow from straying D1446.3; surrendering life for c. land V463.1.

Consecration of ignorant priest J1263.1.2; price J1263.2.1.

Consent of brother for sister's marriage needed T131.1.1; of spear to combat F834.7. — Relative's c. to marriage necessary T131.1.

Conservative but absurd ways kept U139.2.1.

Consider the end: counsel J21.1.

Consolation in misfortune J850—K899. — Husband's c.: seeing greater shrew than wife T251.9.

Consoling message from the dead E361.2. — God c. mortal A182.3.1; philosopher c. woman J152.4.

Consort. — Promise to have but one c. M262.

Consorting with princess without sleeping (test) H347; with woman tabu C193. — Punishment for c. with lower class Q243.5.

Conspiracy. — Magic detection of c. D1817.0.4.

Conspirators frighten boastful coward K1951.4. — Accusing c. to confiscate their estates K487.

Constancy as bride test H387. — Wife's c. resuscitates husband T212.1.

Constant hunger caused by magic object D1373ff.; replacement of fighters E155.1.1.

Constantine's vision of the Cross V515.1.4.

Constantinople. — Virgin Mary destroys army beseiging C. V268.3.

Constellations bewailing death F961.2.5.1; origin of A766.

Consummation of marriage J1306; *T160ff.; of marriage to own mother N681.3.1.

Consumption demon F493.1.1.

Contact. — Conception from casual c. with man T531; disenchantment by physical c. D782; magic results from c. with water D1788.1; magic results from c. with earth *D1778; tabu: c. (with the dead) C541ff., (with the supernatural) *C0—C99, (with things belonging to a king) C501, (with women at childbirth) C153.

Contagiousness of bad company J451; of yawns J1448.

Container. — Extraordinary c. for fluids F866.7; rain from c. in sky A1131.4; relics kept in c. so as to prevent pestilence J762.1.

Contemplation. — Comfort in the c. of impossible pleasure J864; transformation by c. D584.

Contempt. — Hand cut off for c. of court Q451.1.2.

Contentiousness W188; punished Q300ff.

Contentment of old man till forbidden to leave city H1557.3; with what you have J346.

Contest arranged by Virgin Mary A1372.7; in beauty H1596, (between goddesses) A163, (between peacock and crane) J242.5, (between swallow and crow) J242.6; of dogs H1588; between god of fire and god of rain A975.2.1; in generosity H1552.2; of heat and cold D2144.2; in hunting H1592; in laziness W111.1; in magic D1719.1; between rose and amaranth J242.1; between runner swift as thought and one swift as sight F681.3.1; in shooting H1591; over souls E756; in stealing K305; between sun, moon A736.11; of wisdom and wealth J185; won by deception *K0—K99. — Animal characteristics result of c. A2250ff., (between God and devil) A2286.2; animal haunt established by c. A2433.1.1; animal king chosen as result of a c. *B236.0.1; animal wins c. for man B587; animal characteristics from c. in watching A2256; betting c. between two kings N1.3; boasting scares opponent from c. K1766; bride c. H375; deceiver in swinging c. killed *K1618; decision made by c. H217; devils and angels c. for man's soul E756.1; disenchantment by magic c. D785; disenchantment by overcoming person in c. D716; giant in c. with man F531.5.11; giants, dwarfs in c. F451.10.2; king chosen by c. P11.2.1;

magic animal used in c. B195; moon-god loses c. to mortal A182.3.6; mountain from ancient c. A964; mowing c. with household spirit F488.2; rock-casting c. D1731.3; strong woman wins arrow c. F610.0.1.1; transformation c. between magicians D615.1; useful wins c. over beautiful J242.

Contests in endurance H1540ff.; in lying X905; in riddling H548. — Witch makes man enter dangerous c. G292.

Contestant who circles stones wins J2119.2.2.

Contesting. — Flaying alive as punishment for c. with a god Q457.1; rivals c. for girl T92.11.

Continence *T310ff.; vow until enemy killed M152.

Continent. — Islands originally a c. A955.11.

Continually falling in love T10.4. — Firewood c. swept away from swimming man H1129.5.1; journey to upper world by keeping thoughts c. on heaven *F64.

Continuing magic acts *D2172ff., (hurting selves) D2184, (sneezing) D1372, (what one starts in morning) D2172.2. — Man c. work after night joined by devil G303.22.9; princess hangs up weapons of dead lover as c. reminder T85.2; wisdom from c. reminder of foolishness in the past J167.

Continuous fighting F1084.0.3; winter destroys the race A1040ff.; action started by breaking tabu C916; prayer sustains man through frightful vigil V52.2. — Fool locked in dark room made to believe that it is c. night. J2332.

Contortions in anger A526.6, F1041.16.5.

Contraband gold discovered K447.

Contract, see also **Bargain;** with the devil destroyed M218; in blood M201.1. — Journey to hell to recover devil's c. F81.2, H1273.1; strong man makes labor c. F613ff.

Contracts P525.

Contraction of person into smaller space D55.2ff. — Serpent's dilation and c. B91.5.1.

Contradictions. — Chains involving c. or extremes Z23; tales with c. Z19.2.

Contrary. — Life in land of dead c. to ours E489.2; magic object works in c. fashions D1663; objects behaving c. to their nature F473.2; tasks c. to laws of nature H1020ff.

Contrasts found in otherworld garden *F162.1.2. — Peasant and wife c. to king and queen P411.1.1; two brothers as c. P251.5.4.

Control. — Fairies have c. over mortal's destines F312.2; magic c. (of the elements) *D2140ff., (of fires) *D2158ff., (of seasons) *D2145ff., (of waters) *D2151ff.; magic object has c. D1300—D1599, (over disease) *D1500ff., (over the elements) *D1540ff., (over fire) D1566ff., (over person's will) D1379.1f.; moon under deity's direct c. A759.6; witches have c. over weather G283; youth trusts self to horse over which he has no c. J657.1.

Controller. — Man as c. of sun's rising and setting A725; porcupine as
c. of cold D2144.1.1.
Conundrum. — Recognition by answer to c. H19.2.
Convent, see also **Nun;** guest put to needle-threading test H509.1. —
Disguised prostitutes take wife to "c." K1592; man acts as statue of
saint in order to enter c. K1842.1; man disguised as gardener enters c.
and seduces nuns K1323; seducers in disguise enter c. K1321.4.
Convention of long-nosed people X133; of trees F979.13.
Conversation between clouds F967.3; between the dead E545.1; with dead
E545.7; of fire-spirits F497.1; of lovers T42. — Animals' c. reveals how
to become saint V229.25; fox holds c. with his members J2351.1; forgotten
fiancée reawakens husband's memory by c. of magic doves D2006.1.3;
king brought to sense of duty by feigned c. of birds J816.1; rank betrayed
by habitual c. H38ff.; recognition by overheard c. with animals or
objects H13ff.; secrets overheard from animal c. *N451; slave recognized
by his c. H38.3; treasure information from overheard c. N534.4; thieves
deceived by prearranged c. J1517.
Conversations, formulistic Z18.
Conversing. — Soul c. with dead E721.8.
Conversion by dead E367.4; of fairy wife into woman F302.5.2.1; of Jew
by Virgin Mary V266; of King to Hinduism absurd J1536.2; from one
religion to another V330ff. — Miraculous beautification upon c. to
Christianity V331.3; saint to succeed in c. M364.3.
Convert. — First c. to Christianity A1546.3.1.
Converts. — Reward for securing c. Q23.
Conveyances, magic *D1110ff. — Fairies' c. F242; ghost-like c. E535.
Cook as helper N842. — Devil as c. G303.3.1.13; lie: remarkable c. X1005;
poor man wants high office: made c. L427; thief disguised as c. K311.12.1;
treacherous c. K2254.
Cook-book. — Priest uses c. for breviary V467.
Cooked animal comes to life E168; child revived by saint E121.4.1; cock
crows E524.2.1; human flesh speaks out G64. — Animals already c. for
eating X1208.1; beating wife so food will be c. right J2175.1.1; cannibals
advised to be absent while hero is being c. K619.1; flesh of stolen animal
cannot be c. D1318.7.1.1, Q212.4; gods like c. food A153.7; hills flat
where gods c. A972.5.5; magic fruits c. D866.1; meat c. by bird's red eye
F989.2; numskulls sow c. grain J1932.1; people c. in kettle by devil
G303.25.4; planting c. food K496; quest for best-c. dish H1305.2; sowing
c. grain *H1023.1.1; tiger formerly c. its food A2435.1.2; unsuccessful
imitation of being c. without harm J2411.6.1; why food is c. A1518.
Cooking as bride test H383.4; food on hot breasts F546.5; griddle cakes
as bride test H383.1.2; by magic calabash D1601.1; interrupted G475.1;
processes misunderstood J1813; rice with fire far away J1191.7; rice
without fire H506.9; spit recovered from sea H1132.1.6; what is behind
you J2485; without fire D2158.5.2. — Corpses used as c. fuel S139.2.2.5;

escape by pretended c. K611.2; exorbitant charge for c. K255.1; fairies steal c. F365.7; firelike river used for c. F932.11; foolish thief c. wakens house J2136.5.5; glutton eats all meal while c. it W125.2; leaven tabu for c. C888; lie: remarkable c. X1031.3; literal fool c. wrong amounts J2461.1.4.1; magic c. pot obeys only master *D1651.3; magic porridge-pot keeps c. C916.3; miser doesn't want wife c. too much W153.2.1; origin of c. A1455; recognition by unique c. H352; servants touch c. pot J1563.5.2; sun c. for saint D2149.3; sun's rays c. saint's meat V222.13; tiger lives on self-c. food F989.22.2; woman c. for paramour K1549.8.

Cookstove, witch as G212.2.

Cooled. — Scout sees whether earth has c. after fire A1039.1.

Cooling ears by breaking vessel on head J2469.4; off sick by hanging in well J2412.6. — Sun c. off at night A722.5.2.

Cooperation. — Creation of a person by c. of skillful men F1023; man created by c. of the gods A1218.

Cooperative birth T589.1.

Copper apple F813.1.3; castle F771.1.3; -colored house F165.8; horseman indicates road *D1313.3; statue at city gates blows on trumpet at stranger's approach *D1317.9.1; transformed to gold D475.1.9; tree F811.1.3. — Acquisition of c. A1432.4; bow of gold, silver, and c. F836.1; golden boat with c. rudder F841.1.8; magic c. *D1252.2; pygmies dressed in c. F535.3.1; two c. vessels are steaming over fire under earth A857.1; water becomes c. D478.9.

Copperhead guides rattlesnake to prey B765.13.

Copulation, see also **Sexual Intercourse;** of animals A2496; of devil as queen with horses G303.3.1.12.5. — Sham-death for c. with divine maidens K1325.0.1; universe from c. of objects A615.2.

Coraciiformes, creation of A1950ff.

Coral. — Goddess as c. reef A139.8.2; man becomes c. D237; why c. is soft A2872.

Cord. — Penance: wearing friar's c. on bare skin Q522.7; umbilical c. tabu C531.1.

Cordelia H592.1, M21.

Cordon. — Monk's c. saving him from hell J1261.8.

Corduroy. — Wagon run over c. bridge to simulate artillery K2368.1.1.

Cormorant's color A2411.2.5.1; tongue pulled out by putting louse on it *K825.1.

Corn from body of slain person *A2611.1; carried away grain at a time Z11.1; comes up with black ears after mud flood Q552.14.2; grows so fast it pulls up own roots X1532.1; roots in hair F1099.4; transformed to person D431.8. — Deceptive grain division: the c. and the chaff K171.2; devil gives Eve two grains of c. G303.9.4.1; dwarf groans while carrying ear of c. F451.3.9.1; fairies snip c. from stalks F369.5.1; god of c. A433.1; inexhaustible c. D1652.1.3.2; lazy man: "Is c. shelled?" W111.5.10.1; lies about c. X1455; magic c. *D965.8; magic c. turns to gold D2102.5; making ale from single grain of c. H1022.6.1; man from ears of c. A1255.2; mule carrying c. escapes while one carrying gold is robbed L453; so hot c. pops X1633.1; soul of c. E701.5; why c. does not yield in the middle A2793.10; witch's spells blight c. G269.7; woman threshing c. in moon A751.8.2.

Cornelia shows children as her jewels T256.

Corners. — Spider transformed for greediness: now occupies dark c. A2261.2.

Cornish. — Jews' ghosts punished in C. mines F456.1.1.1.

Cornucopia, god with A137.5.

Coroner. — Ghosts disappear for c. E599.2.

Corps sans âme F963.4.

Corpse, see also **Body, Ghost;** bleeds when murderer touches it D1318.5.2; burns of own accord F964.3.3; cannot be moved D1654.9.1; to be cut in two: feigned death revealed J1545.8; drops piecemeal down chimney H1411.1; exclaims over miracle E545.10; with his feet cut off X422; handed around K2151; leaps up as saint passes E597; lost, live person buried J1834; magically saved from corruption D2167; set up to frighten people K2321; spits out Host V39.7; thrown among robbers frightens them from treasure K335.1.2.1; transformed to serpent D449.2; watched over before burial E752.10.1; of woman dying in childbirth C153.1. — Adulteress's c. drawn through streets Q473.0.2; animal prevents anybody coming near master's c. B301.1.2; animals eat c. of holy man, die B275.3; arm of husband's c. catches wife, drowns her N339.14; curse: c. to be cut in three M453; dead grateful for treatment of c. E341.1.1; demon's c. turns to worm H47; demon enters c. E121.6.1; devil (beats wicked man's c.) Q491.3, (follows lawyer's c.) G303.25.8. (hidden in c.) G303.8.15; drowned c. found by magic D1816.4.1; eyes, ears, fingers of c. substituted for those of demanded victim K512.2.0.3; flames issue from mouth of c. E421.3.7; ghost watches own c. E599.3; ghosts (eat c.) E256, (flay c.) E255, (prevent burial of c.) E273.1; gratitude for having c. ransomed *E341.1; grieving man goes to die near wife's c. T211.9.2.1; hand of c. as remedy D1500.1.6.1; head of c. thrown on water to prevent return E431.9.1; indignity to c. S139.2.2, (as punishment) Q491; joke involving girl's c. causes priest's death N384.8; live man thought to be returning c. K2151.1; the living c. *E422; magic object saves c. from corruption *D1585; mare not to draw c. C181.11; marvelous sensitiveness: meat (wine) tastes of c. E647.1; money tied on c. thrown overboard from ship in order to secure burial V64; monk digs up sweetheart's c. T334; mother does for another what the latter cannot do for her (lays out a c.) H583.4; multiplication of saint's c. D2106.1.4; murdered man's c. sticks to murderer Q551.2.4; murderer's c. mutilated Q491.6; only prostitutes can carry the c. of a prostitute X521; opening c.-wrapping tabu C328; penance: lying with every c. Q524.2; praying over c. saves soul from devil K218.7; precautions to keep evil spirits from getting c.

E752.10; pretending to address c. as heir K451.5; punishment: carrying c. of murdered man Q511; resuscitation by (breathing on c.) E66, (licking c.) E17; return from dead to punish indignities to c. or ghost E235ff.; ring to put on finger of c. K362.2; river flows from c. A511.1.1.1; saint's c. sits up in grave E235.8; servant in master's c. K1969.3.1; shooting at father's c. test of paternity H486.2; sitting up with c. H1461; sleeping with c., thinking it alive J1769.2.1; soul wanders till c. decays E722.3.2; souls captured on leaving c. E752.1.3; spirits put c. into river F402.1.8; spouse's c. kept after death T211.4f.; substitute for the c. J1959.2; suitors as c., angel, and devil K1218.4; tabu: leaving c. at shrine C51.1.14; taking down c. of hanged man tabu C541.5; thief disguised as c. K311.1, (detected) J1149.7; thief frightens away c. guards K335.0.7; thing thought to be c. J1783; toads and snakes devour c. of rich man in his grave Q491.4; trickster throws c. in river and accuses princess of murder K1383; two devils extracted from c. G303.1.8; only usurers can carry the c. of the usurer X514; water thrown on c. to prevent return E431.2; witch's c. heavy G259.4; woman substitutes c. in lover's bed K1223.4.

Corpses. — Cat mutilates c. B766.1; escape by prophesying c. will ruin city K575; foes' c. dismembered P555.2; giants keep c. on hand to eat G691.1; hurling-match for c. H1436; monster made from parts of c. G377; room heated by crowded c. F686.2; speaking c. J2311.9; test for demons in c. E431.0.1; vampires eat c. E251.3.1; wives killed: large price for c. K941.1.1.

Correct wearing of clothes as suitor test H312.6. — Ogre's c. guess wins princess G463.

Correcting. — Animal c. examination paper for rescuer B579.3; man blames master for not c. him in youth J142.2; stingy dead woman c. laundress's overcharge W152.3.

Corroborating ghost's appearance E421.5. — Second liar c. first X907.1.

Corroded. — Skin c. by hydra's poison F1041.5.

Corruption of maids in household by faithless menservants P365.1. — Corpse magically saved from c. D2167; loss of c. as reward Q150.2; magic object saves corpse from c. *D1585.

Corset — Murder by lacing c. tight K953.1; resuscitation when strangling c. lace breaks E21.2; tight c. stifles woman to death Q331.2.2.

Cosmic egg *A641.

Cosmogony A600ff.

Cosmology A600ff.

Cost price of stolen coat recovered (nothing) J1397. — Points of view on c. of wine J1315; what the ass c. J1601; sickle bought at great c. given back J2514.

Costliest. — What is c.? (riddle) H638.

Costumes. — Hero wearing so many c. taken for many K1883.9.

Cot, golden D846.1.

Cottage. — Fairies' neat c. F221.4.

Cotton as best flower H659.23; in ears J672.2; at first already spun A1346.2.1; pods mistaken for fat J1772.8; transformed to leaves D451.2.4; transformed to snake D441.8; tree on moon A751.6. — Adventures from running after blown c. N777.1; leaves become c. D451.8.1; magic c.-wool D1299.4; origin of c. plant A2684.3; purifying c. by burning it J1974; quest for c. driven by wind H1355.5; why hares have c. tail A2378.9.3.

Cottonwood cursed for serving as cross A2721.2.1.3.

Couch. — Avoiding sitting on foot of c. H506.6; magic c. *D1154.

Couches for men of high rank P632.1.

Cough as soul re-entering body E721.3.1. — Dead man identified by his c. J1937.1; stinging buttocks as c. cure N643.

Coughing tabus C484.1; universe into being A618.1; up magic object K331.4; thief blinds watchmen D2062.2.6. — Origin of c. A1399.4.

Council of animals assigns place and work to all B238; of gods A167.1.

Councillors, old men preferred as J151.2.

Counsel, see also **Advice, Precept.** — Brothers scorn brother's c. P251.4; listening to mother's c. forbidden C815; return from dead to give c. E366; reward for giving c. Q43; spirit gives c. F403.2.3.6.

Counsels chosen for parting gift L222.1; proved wise by experience *J21ff. — Enigmatic c. of a father H588; good c. bought *J163.4; porter's revenge for wise c. J1511.6; proverbial wisdom: c. J171ff.

Counselor killed in own treacherous game K1626.2. — Angel as c. to mortal V246; court c. P14.15.1; treacherous c. K2298.

Counselors. — King seeks bride only because c. insist T64.

Count (numerical) only waves before you J311.1. — Absurd inability to c. J2030ff.; literal following of c. J2466; man forgets to c. self, dies E791; numskull throws money to frogs so that they can c. it J1851.1.1; so many leaves on the tree and if you don't believe it go c. them H705.2.

Count (personage) in disguise K1812.20. — Impostor impersonates dead c. K1936.

Counted. — One tiger-cub c. many times deceives tiger K933; stones cannot be c. F809.1; swine cannot be c. accurately B184.3.0.5; years not c. before monk entered monastery J181.

Countenance, see also **Face.** — Parson put out of c. X434; clever man puts another out of c. J1210—J1229.

Counteraccusation follows admission of robber's false plea J1162.2.

Countercharm exorcises witch G271.6.

Counterfeit money burned up J1511.10. — Money turns to c. C939.2; prostitute paid with c. K1581.11.

Counterfeiting. — Burning as punishment for c. Q414.0.6.1; ghost foils c. of will E236.4.1.

Countermagic against Evil Eye D2071.1.5.

Counterquestions H571, J1291.

Countersunwise circuit for ill luck D1791.2.

Countertasks *H951. — Payment evaded by setting c. K248.

Countess. — Dwarf follows c. around like dog F451.5.8.1.

Counting fairy gifts tabu F348.6; hairs in pig's back (feathers in bird) H1118; out pay with hole in the hat and hat over a pit K275; possessions forbidden C776; tabus C897; tasks H1118ff.; the waves H1144.2.

Country, see also **Land;** where everything is cheap J342.1.1. — Forbidden c. C617; king returns to rescue native c. R191; magic object devastates c. D1480ff.; magic sight of whole c. at once D1825.2.2; man who saves c. rewarded with princess T68.2; prophecies concerning destiny of c. M356; town mouse and c. mouse J211.2; wolves of his own c. dearer than dogs of another P711.1; why ptarmigan lives in c. A2433.4.3.

Countries. — Why animals live in certain c. A2434.3ff.

Countryman in the great world J1742.

Couple, see also **Pair.** — Boy sleeps between c. to safeguard virtue T352; earth made by first c. dancing A825; earth by sacrifice of children of first c. A831.3; estranged c. each pay for reconciliation K441.4; first c. parents of (moon) A745.1, (sun) A715; primeval human c. A1270ff.; sinless c. H1381.4.; stone from sky kills all but one c. A1009.3; wicked c. to be killed by own child M343.4

Couples placed to establish tribes A1610.2. — All animals created in c. A1704; animals chained in c. B845.2; magic birds chained in c. B172.7.

Couplets. — Recognition by matching c. H12.2.1.

Courage conquers all U243. — Dragon wants to see "c." J2488.1, K722.1; mother kills sons lacking c. P231.4; wine gives c. to face Pope J1318.

Courageous. — Eating c. animal's heart makes c. D1358.1; magic spell makes person c. D1358.2.

Course of wild hunt E501.1.4ff. — Angels arrange c. of heavenly bodies A703.

Court, see also **Law;** keeps the change J1193.2.1; orders bride to consummate marriage T166; in otherworld F177.1. — Bluff in c.: the stone in the purse K1765; bringing an ogre to c. (task) H1172; cleverness in law c. J1130—J1199; contempt of c. punished Q451.1.2; exposed infant reared at strange king's c. S354; expulsion from c. saves counselor's life N178.3; ghosts tried in c. E573; girl in disguise at lover's c. K1816.0.2; hero takes refuge at king's c. R331; jests on unfavorable c. decision J835; magic object helps win in law c. D1406ff.; not leaving God's c. for king's J1269.13; poor girl masks as doctor and is made c. physician K1825.1.2; robbers' secret used in c. against them N455.2.1; swallow killed in c. house by snake laments injustice in house of justice U27; unknown son returns to father's c. N731.1; women disqualified as c. witness A1589.1.

Courtesan, see also **Concubine, Prostitute;** pursued in wild hunt E501.5.1.2; as thief K302.1. — Capture in house of c. K778.3; newborn girl fated to be c. N121.3; priest's c. cannot rest in grave *E411.2.1; queen forced to become c. L410.7.

Courtesans in wild hunt E501.2.4.

Courtesy. — Deed of c. forbidden C740ff.; disguised king taught c. by peasant P15.1.1.

Courtier in love with queen T91.6.1.1; rewarded for resisting princess Q87.2; shields king's love affair J1211.3. — Boor transformed to c. by love T10.1.2; princess loves c. T55.1.1; princess marries c. T121.3.

Courtiers. — Queen intervenes for condemned c. P21; riddle of king and c. H731.

Courting another man disguised as a woman K1321.3. — Boy c. his mother T412.4; silence in c. ugly woman J1074.2; trickster rides dupe c. K1241.1.

Courtship of stork and crane B282.23. — Jokes on c. *X760ff.; origin of customs of c. and marriage A1550ff.

Cousins P295. — Accidental meeting of c. N746.

Couvade T583.1.

Covenant, see also **Bargain, Contract;** with animals B279; between god and mortal A185.9; of friendship A1599.12, P311.5. — Blood c. M201.1; rainbow as c. between creator and man A791.10.

Covering with cloth disenchants D777.1; face instead of putting out lamp W111.2.9. — Disenchantment by c. with deliverer's clothing D789.1; disenchantment by removing (destroying) c. of enchanted person D720ff.; long hair as c. for girl F555.3.3; origin of animal characteristics: body c. A2310ff.; person with unusual c. F521; resuscitation by c. body E134.1; why certain animals are bare of c. A2317.

Coverings. — Soul hidden in a series of c. E713.

Covetous goldsmith P447.8; wish to the enemy J2074.

Covetousness punished Q277. — Wealth refused, c. feared J347.1.

Cow, see also **Calf;** Audhumla B19.2.1; the animal that is good living and dead H841.3; bears man child B631.5; with breeches on reveals witch G257.5; and bullock yoked together A1689.1; with changing colors B731.4; climbs to roof (lie) X1235.4; as creator A13.1.1; determines road to be taken B151.1.2.1; disappears New Year's night D2087.3.1; has foaled: explanation for lover's horse K1549.4; follows saint B159.3; gives marvelous milk for saint B597; gives twelve measures of milk for twelve apostles B251.2.10; god A132.9.1; grants all desires B184.2.1.3; grateful for being milked B394; imprisoned, had eaten men R9.5; with inexhaustible milk D1652.3.1; killed to get all milk at once J1905.6; licks saint's feet B251.2.6.2; licks stone, discovers saint's relics V140.3; lowers ocean by drinking F989.11.1; mistaken for devil addressed J1785.4; as nurse cares for children B535.0.1; partly brown after resuscitation E33.1; punished for calf's misdeeds J1863; puts bread in oven (lie) X1255.5; with red ears B731.4.2; refuses to move in grief for master B301.6.2; refuses to help stepdaughter, killed B335.7; as sacrifice V12.4.4.1; with silver horns B15.3.2.3.1, B101.8, H355.1; springs from rime of universe's creation B715; strikes at flies while boy eats B579.2; supplies saint, disciples with milk D2156.2.1; survives plague F989.6; swallows book: cause of maniplies in stomach A2219.2; taken to roof to graze J1004.1; with tallow liver B15.7.9, H1331.3.2; thief grabs tiger by mistake N392; touched by arrow becomes pregnant T532.4; transformed to another animal D412.2ff.; with two bags: bird in each B15.7.9.1; with white ears B731.4.1; worship V1.8.1. — Advising buyer c. is thief J2088.2; bald, white-headed c. H1331.3.1; bellowing of c. defeats army B741.3; buying c. in common: each paying full price J2037.2; buying monkey instead of c. J2081.4; color of c. A2411.1.6.4; creation of c. A1877; cross marked on bewitched c. breaks spell G271.2.1.1; curse: c. will give red milk M471.1; deceptive division of shared c. K171.7.1; destructive c. possessed by demons B16.1.5.2; devil as c. G303.3.3.1.4; devil drives c. mad G303.7.8; divided ownership of c. J1905.3; divine c. descends to earth F35.1; dwarf home is beneath c. stable F451.4.1.5; dwarfs request that c. stable be moved F451.4.4.3; enmity of dog and c. A2494.4.10; enmity of hyena and c. A2494.3.4; fairy in form of c. F234.1.1; fairy warns owner that c. is choking F339.1; fish guards c. B576.3.1; fool does not milk c. for month so that she will give plenty for a feast J1005.1; fool interested only in how c. could have got on the pole where he finds c. dung instead of his purse J2382; foolish bargains: horse for c., c. for hog, etc. J2081.1; four calves to one c. at birth T586.4.1; friendship between c. (and tiger, calf and cub) A2493.24, (and lioness) A2493.30.2; giant c. B871.1; ghost rides c. E581.3; gold-dropping c. B103.1.2, (exchanged for common) D871.1.1; gold hoard found by c. N534.2; helpful c. *B411; hornless c. B15.3.0.1, (milk from) J1512.1; indentions on rock from footprints of saint's c. A972.3.1.2; islands from transformed c. and calf A955.5; jester takes c., tells king people have milk U67; magic c. B184.2; magic c. dung *D1026.2; man can't drive c. he refused to share Q589.1.0.1; man kills c. with hand F628.1.2.1; man transformed to c. G263.1.3; mankind born from c. A1224.4; marvelous c. and calf leave patches on soil A989.1; marvelous c. offended, disappears C918.1; milk from the hornless c. J1512.1; milk of hornless single-colored c. renders wife fruitful T591.1.2; milking c. directly into mouth J2173.8; milking unruly c. H1155.2; miraculous increase of milk from c. D2156.2; money exacted from watcher who permits theft of wooden c. supposed to be real K443.4; nectar-yielding c. B19.2; numskull sells c. to bird J1852.1; numskull ties the rope to his leg as the c. grazes on the roof J2132.2; offending sacred c. tabu C94.3.1.1; old woman gives only c. to God; sent back a hundred Q21.1; only crippled c. spared by robbers N178.4; pasturing c. which runs all day H1112.2; pearl-dropping c. B103.1.2.1; pouring water over c. J2465.1.1; prophetic c. B141.5; quest for bald, white-headed c. H1331.3.1; rabbit thought to be c. J1757; recognition by conversing with c. H13.1.3; recognition of own c. in huge herd H163; refusal to eat fifth descendant of stolen c. F647.10; reincarnation as c. E611.2; revenant as c. E423.1.8; rich man seizes poor widow's c. U35; Sabbath-keeping c. B259.2; sacred c. B811.3; sea c. B72; settlement site where c. stops, milk flows by itself

B155.2.2; shepherd's consecrated staff keeps c. from straying D1446.3, singing c. B214.1.1; sowing cheese to bring forth c. J1932.2; speaking c. B211.1.5; spring breaks forth where saint's stolen c. is found A941.5.5; steaks cut from live c. who heals herself by magic D2161.2.1; substituting common c. for magic one K476.8; tabu to eat c. C221.1.1.1; tabu to kill, cook sacred c. C221.1.1.1.3; thieving c. K366.1; tiger eats c. friend J427; "to every c. belongs its calf" P526.1; transformation to c. *D133.1; transformed c. advises daughter D688.1; trickster steals farmer's c. and then sells her to the farmer K258.1; truth-speaking c. B132; tying c. with stones to keep from blowing away J2119.8; vampire milks c. dry E251.3.2; when c. calls calf, all cattle graze B852; white c. comes to be milked for infant saint B251.2.10.1; why c (has cloven hoof) A2376.1, (has so few teats) A2363.1, (is always eating) A2231.1.1; why black c. eats green grass, gives white milk, yellow butter J1291.1.1; why c. has no upper teeth A2345.7.1; why is c. beaten by calf? H1292.16; witch as c. G211.1.3.

Cow's feet provide wealth D1469.7; milk with remarkable tastes D1665.2. — Child with c. head T551.3.4; dog rescues c. teats from fire: origin of his black muzzle A2229.1; huldra with c. tail F460.1.5; milker ties c. tail to himself and bees sting cow J2132.3; origin of c. and buffalo's hides A2311.6; riddle: four hang, four walk, two show the road, one wags behind (c. teats, feet, eyes, tail) H743; trickster evades paying c. burial fee K499.5; prophesying sex of c. offspring H528.1; white c. flesh as magic cure *D1500.1.33.2; why c. body hollow on one side A2356.2.12; witch curdles c. milk D2083.2.2.

Cows in church thought to be ghosts J1782.1.1; come up mountain for herdsman's call F679.1; die of shock at being fed W152.13.1; grateful for hero's housekeeping B396; killed for their hides when large price is reported by trickster K941.1; kneel on Christmas Eve B251.1.2.3; lose milk at king's death B301.6.3; magically made dry D2083.1; magically multiply (reward) Q141; to make curds before milking J1905.5; meek H659.21; speak to one another on Christmas B251.1.2.2; of the sun B19.6.1; white-headed during good king's reign Q153.1. — Army of c. B268.10; bath in milk of white, hornless c. as antidote for poison D1515.3; birds perch on ears of c. B853; calves kept from c. (in commemoration) V65.1, (during fast) P623.0.7; cast-off wife sent to herd c. S437; charm makes c. give plenty of milk D1449.1; color of devil's c. changed while he sleeps so that he does not know them A2286.2.4, K483; devil's c. one-horned: God gives them two A2286.2.3; dwarfs bewitch c. to give no milk *F451.3.3.5; fairies milk c. F271.1; fairies milk mortal's c. dry F366.1; fairies' c. F241.2; grazing c. at night render fairies visible F235.9; grazing c. eat same amount B854; jackal covers up clumsiness in catching c. J873.2; king demands milk from all hornless c.: given poison from wooden K839.4; lies about c. X1235; magic bag sucks milk from c. D1605.2; milk gushes from c. in deity's presence· H45.2; milk from saint's c. forms lake F989.9; quest for demon-owned c. H1364; recognizing milk of stolen c. F647.5.3; roads marked out by supernatural c. A989.2; skillful milker milks c. incessantly F678.1; snake milks c. at night B765.4; spirits tangle up peasant's c. F402.1.3; stolen c. cause war K300.1; why c. have two horns A2326.3.1; why c. ruminate A2472.1, A2231.1.1; witch transforms self to hare so as to suck c. D655.2.

Coward boasts of frightening bear away K1953.1; boasts when there is no danger W121.2; gloats over robber slain by another person W121.2.5; hiding from adversaries J2631. — Boastful c. frightened (by conspirators) K1951.4, (by his wife) K1837.1.

Cowards. — Tailors c. as warriors X223.

Cowardice W121; most shameful H659.12.1. — Men shamed for their c. by woman standing naked before them J87.

Cowardly duelers K2323; fool *J2600—J2649; to leave battle while lord alive W34.2.

Cowbell. — Capture by ringing c. K756.2.2.

Cowboy shoots injured wife J1919.9; stands up for friendless Jesus J1738.5. — Ghost of slain c. E337.1.4.

Cowdung goes on warpath F1025.2.1. — Jewels in c. cakes J1655.1; oath taken on c. M114.5.

Cowherd disappears New Year's night D2087.3.1; as foster father N856.2; hero L113.1.6; looking for cattle thief recognizes him in the lion J561.2; rescues abandoned child R131.3.3.

Cowhide falls, robbers flee K335.1.1.2. — Alleged oracular c. sold K114.1; magic c. D1025.5, (assures heaven for man who dies upon it) D1588.2.

Co-wife cruel to pregnant woman S185.1; transforms other wife D665.3 — Jealous c. kills woman's children S322.3; persecuted sons of c. S471; punishment for murder of c. Q211.10; task assigned at suggestion of jealous c. H911.1, H913.1.2; treacherous c. *K2222; younger son of c. a hero L10.2.

Cowl as saint's ransom burns Q552.18.1.1; in thornbrake symbol of Christ V124.1. — Magic c. *D1067.3.1, (protects from fire) D1382.9; monk who dies without his c. cannot rest in grave E411.7; saint's anger sets c. afire F1041.16; saint's c. (protects fox from hounds) D1447.2.1, (untouched by sea) F930.1.0.1.

Cowrie-shell turns into men D432.2.1.

Cowshed. — Cleaning c. H1102.1; tabu to enter c. during menses C141.2.

Cowslip pulled, girl dies E765.3.4.

Coyote as culture hero A522.1.3; as marplot at creation A61; persuaded to break leg: therefore has thin right leg A2284.5; rescues child R131.7; rides with sun A724.1.0.1; throws eyes in air: they are stolen K333.3; as trickster J1117.2; tries to fly J2133.3.1; wears fox's rattle J2136.1. — Color of c. A2411.1.3.2; creation of c. A1834; enmity of rabbit and c. A2494.6.2; enmity between c. and meadowlark A2494.12.4; why c. has (long muzzle) A2213.4.1, A2335.4.4, (long teeth) A2345.2, (yellowish eyes) A2332.5.1, (yellow patch behind ears) A2218.4, A2412.1.3.

Coyote's body made larger A2301.3.

Cozening K347.

Crab beats deity's forbidden drum: eyes lift out of body *A2231.10, A2332.4.2; carried by crane, cuts off his head K953.3; carries animals in ear F982.8; as child's nurse B535.0.13; comes ashore: killed by fox J512.1; cuts heron's neck J631; hunts hare (lie) X1344.1; mistaken for tailor J1762.1.2; prefers death to imprisonment J216.3; pulled first living creatures from his side A1211.8; saves from crocodile attack J21.36; saves hero from snake B524.1.12, B549.5; shape of husband D719.2; thought to be the devil J1785.2; thrown to ground: breaks into pieces, hence small size A2214.4; on tiger's tail J1762.3; transformed to man D375; tries to lay eggs in boiling water pot J2415.3; walks backward: learned from his parents U121.1. — Bungling rescuer caught by c. J2675; cheese smeared on c. lures giant K827.5; creation of c. A2171.2; discourteous answer: why c. has eyes behind A2231.1.3, A2332.4.2; dolphin and whale scorn c. as peacemaker J411.6; enmity of c. (and jackal) A2494.5.3, (and spider) A2494.16.5; friendship between c. (and cobra) A2493.19, (and bird) A2493.27; giant c. B876.2.1; god becomes c. D175.1; golden c. B102.8; hedgehog and c. jump from boat after turtle J2133.11; helpful c. B478, B495.1; how c. got its claws A2376.4; magic c. B178.1; man transformed to c. D175; marriage to person in c. form B647.1.1; mother c. blames her children for not walking straight J1663.1; mythical c. B94.1; reincarnation as c. E629.2; singing c. B214.1.8; trickster pinched by c. J2136.4; tricky potter reborn as c. E692.3; what is in the dish: "Poor C." N688; why c. is afraid in dark A2534.1; why c. is cunning A2525.2; why c. has no head A2320.4; why c. lifts eyes out of body or has eye behind A2332.4.2.

Crab's exorbitant lending price to frog K255.2; haunts A2433.6.3; offspring born through chest B754.7.1; wedding B283.1. — Cause of c. walk A2441.4.2; cross on c. back A2412.4.4; origin of dents in c. shell A2312.3; why c. legs like teeth of comb A2376.5.

Crabs take moonlight walks, eaten K772.1. — Bear learns how to catch c. with his hairy claws J102; lies about c. X1344; tabu to eat c. C221.1.3.3; tiger's fear of c. exploited K1715.13; thief places candles on c. K335.0.5.1; why c. burrow in sand A2433.6.3.2; why c. live in water A2433.6.3.1.

Crack. — Dupe caught in c. in ground K1111.2.

Cracks. — Animals hop over c. in ground A2441.1.0.1; filling c. in ground with butter J1871; origin of c. in tortoise's shell A2312.1.1.

Crackling. — Deceptive land purchase: fields c. when burnt to be his K185.9.

Cradle. — Betrothal of children in c. T61.5.1; child in c. guesses devil's riddle H543.2; deliverer in the c. D791.1.3; devil takes an upbaptized child out of the c. and substitutes a wooden log G303.9.9.4; disguise as

child in c. K1839.12; dwarfs exchange children in c. F451.5.2.3; Evil Eye
averted by swinging cat over child's c. D2071.1.2; fairy steals child from
c. F321; flame illuminates sacred person's c. V200.1; goddess of c. A477.1;
hero leaves c. for war T585.7; old man sleeps in c. F571.4; stolen sheep
dressed as baby in c. K406.2; suckling children rock mother in c. (lie)
X1856; tale of the c. K1345.

Craftiest. — Wolf is the devil's c. enemy G303.25.1.

Crafts acquired A1440ff.

Craftsman, God as A141.

Craftsmen, fairies as F271.0.1.

Craftsmanship bestowed by saint D1926.

Cranberry, magic *D981.10.1.

Crane bridge (fugitives helped across a stream) *R246; as child's nurse
B535.0.7.2; minister to lion king B240.4.1; outwits, eats fish J657.3; pecks
out spy's eye Q557.5; pecks out tiger's eyes S165.2; pulls bone from
wolf's throat: wolf refuses payment W154.3; recognizes princess H188;
gets resevoir emptied, eats fish J758.2; as suitor B623.1; tricks fish into
being carried, eats them K815.14; tries to catch fish like hawk J2413.7;
will not weep at crucifixion: must suffer thirst in August A2231.2.1,
A2435.4.2. — Conception from c. dung T511.8.5; courtship of stork and
c. B282.23; crab carried by c., cuts off his head K953.3; creation of c.
A1968; fox and c. invite each other J1565.1; helpful c. B463.3; man
marries c. in human form B652.2; man transformed to c. D162; marriage to c. B602.5; peacock and c. in beauty contest H242.5; reincarnation
as c. E613.9.1; skin of c. becomes magic bag D1193.1; soul in c. E715.1.4;
tiger, c. quarrel J428; woman bears c. T554.3.

Cranes carry away girl B522.4.1; disregard warnings and are killed
J1052; fighting together defeat all J1025.1; of Ibycus N271.3. — Bull
with three c. A137.7; stork killed along with c. J451.2; war of pygmies
and c. F535.5.1.

Crash, ghostly E402.1.6.

Crater. — Giant cooks on volcano c. G171; skillful bowman shoots c. of
Vesuvius open F661.6.

Crawling, see also **Creeping;** on all-fours (neither on horse nor on foot)
H1053.6. — Magic power by. c. through ear of magic horse D1733.2;
penance: c. on knees (to Rome) Q523.1, (and watering dry staff until
it blooms) Q521.1.1; power of prophecy induced by c. backward around
grave D1812.2.1.

Crayfish. — Attack on c. J2612; fools ignorant as to what c. is J1736.1;
friendship of c. and pike A2493.33; origin of c. A2171.

Crazed. — Person c. by Echo D2065.6.

Creaking limbs held apart by fool J1872; wagon dies J1872.0.1; of wheelbarrow frightens J2615. — Cauterizing wheel to stop c. J2412.7.

Cream protected from witch G272.16.1. — Breaking spell on bewitched c.
G271.4.11; fairies' c.-colored horses F241.1.1.4; lie about cow's c. supply

X1235.2.1; sea of c. F711.2.2; water becomes c. D478.11; woman created from c. A1275.5.

Created. — Animals c. by devil and God *A63.4; house c. by magic D1133.1; other devils c. by devil G303.1.4; men c. by God A179.6; rock in sea c. by magic D2153.1; woman c. (from cream) A1275.5, (by skillful companions) *H621.

Creation of animal life A1700—A2199; of devil from God's shadow G303.1.1.1; of devil when God strikes stone with his whip G303.1.1.4; of the earth A800—A899; of the heavenly bodies *A700—A799; of hell A671.0.2; interrupted since God must go to a fire A2286.1; of the moon *A740ff.; of man A1200—A1299; of a person by cooperation of skillful men F1023; of souls E703; of the stars A760ff.; of the sun A710ff.; of the universe A600ff. — All miracles created at c. F900.2; devil has not been seen since c. of bramble G303.17.3.4; hare runs away at c.: almost loses tail A2215.2; waters created on first day of c. A910.1.

Creations. — Trickster's false c. fail him J2186.

Creative. — Self-mutilation with c. purpose S160.1.1.

Creator, see also **God, Lord;** A0—A99; in anger creates man-eaters G312.5; appoints chief for created things A1187; commands ants become men A1224.7; creates (earth) A830ff., (man) A1210ff., (the universe) A610ff.; establishes twelve winds, each a different color A1129.1; lives in sky beneath us A651.2.0.1; opens shop, assigns crafts and professions from it A1440.1; of rivers A930.1; sent for water: meantime animals assume their present forms A1713; separates sun and moon to prevent birth of more stars A736.1.4.3; sent down insects to plant plants A2601. — Creation of animals by c. A1702; supreme god as c. A101.1; topographical features of the earth arranged by c. A902; years seem moments to c. D2011.3.

Creator's breathing causes the winds A1121; voice makes the thunder A1142.1. — Culture hero c. son A512.2; giant as c. servant F531.0.2; hero completes c. work A530.1; man created in c. image A1212; opening of c. eyes causes day A1171.

Creators. — Joint c. A37; male and female c. beget gods A112.2; two c. go by different route to establish features of the earth A902.1.

Creatures. — Magic power to see invisible c. D1825.3; marvelous c. *F200 —F699; seeing supernatural c. forbidden C311.1; supernatural c. propound riddles H540.1.

Credential tests H242.

Credit. — Deception into giving false c. K455; false articles used to produce c. K476.2; money borrowed on c. of old beggar disguised as gentleman *K455.3; refusing c. to god forbidden C53; saint gives c. for good deeds to another, rewarded Q42.8; three reasons for refusing c. J1552.2.

Creditor captures Sun, Moon R9.1.2; falsely reported insane when he demands money K242; in former existence confiscates goods in next

Q554.7. — Arresting c. to postpone debt payment K238.2; debtor's wraith seeks c. E723.4.3.

Creditors. — Trickster summons all c. at once, precipitates fight, and escapes payment K234.

Creek. — Magic bark sets c. afire D1408.1.1.

Creepers, origin of A2682.

Creeping, see also **Crawling.** — Magic by c. through a hole *D1795; ordeal by c. under sod H228; penance: c. naked through thorns Q522.3.

Cremated. — Daughter has father c. with husband K2214.1.1; dead wagon c. J1872.0.1; heart c. to lay ghost E441.3; resuscitation of c. man by blowing on the ashes E66.1.

Cremation, origin of A1592.

Crepitation, magic D2079.1.

Crescentia K2112.

Crests. — Origin of bird c. A2321; origin of family c. A1578.1.

Crevasse, origin of A969.8.

Crevice. — Ghost comes through c. E445.1.

Crew. — Captain buried with his c. V67.4.1; sick c. accused as magician K2129.2; witch carried off by devil's c. G275.1.1.

Cricket hears water hiss on hot iron: learns his song *A2272.1.2; lights on king's head H162.2. — Ant and lazy c. J711.1; creation of c. A2063; friendship between frog and c. A2493.20; helpful c. B486.2; man transformed to c. D183.2; owl invites c. to share his nectar: kills him K815.5; soul in form of c. E734.5; wedding of c. B285.2.

Cricket's chirp A2426.3.4, A2272.1.2; wings in fox's excrement betray his plans K2061.10. — Ass tries to get a c. voice J512.8.

Crickets as good omens B147.3.1.1; as bad omens B147.3.2.1.

Cries, see also **Cry.** — Animal c. misunderstood J1811; nature and meaning of animal c. *A2426ff.; origin of animal c. *A2425; three c. allowed maiden about to be murdered K551.3.3; three c. of the world Z71.1.17; three first c. to God A1344.1; why eagle c. like baby A2426.2.15.

Crime inevitably comes to light *N270ff.; less serious if committed for lady P517; personified Z139.2; unwittingly committed M360ff. — Accidental discovery of c. N610ff.; animal tried for c. B272.2; child in mother's womb reveals c. T575.1.1; detection of c. through knowledge tooth D1817.3; evidence of c. left so that dupe is blamed K2155; ghost haunts scene of c. E334.1; ghost laid when c. has been confessed E451.1; innocent man accidentally suspected of c. N347; magic detection of c. *D1817ff.; saints magically detect c. D1817.2; severed finger as sign of c. H57.2.1; statue laughs and reveals c. D1639.4.

Crimes punished *Q210ff. — Small trespasses punished: large c. condoned U11.

Criminal allowed to choose his method of execution P511; confesses because he thinks himself accused N275; detected by having child hand knife to him H211; going to death predicts that his judge shall soon

meet him M341.4; may fight against odds rather than be judicially
executed P513; saved from fire at stake by Virgin Mary V252.2.

Criminal's property destroyed Q486; wife and children sold into slavery
Q437.1.

Criminals buried at crossroads E431.17. — Virgin Mary comforts repentent
c. V275.

Crimson rock F807.1; sheep F933.3; tree F811.3.3.

Cripple healed by distributing knowledge H1292.4.3; marvelously cured
F953.

Cripples hurry away from shrine lest they be healed and lose their livelihood X531; of shrine frightened and run away without crutches V113.1.
— Origin of c. A1338.1.

Crippled mortals of dwarf ancestry F451.5.3; saint receives horse, chariot
V221.0.2.1; villain K2272.

Crippling. — Witch c. G263.4.3.

Critic. — Gift of property silences c. U21.2; king honors poet and c.
J811.3.

Croaking of frogs at prince's command H71.10.3.

Crocodile as animals' king B240.15; -boat R245.1; carries burden F982.5;
carries man across river B551.3; cheated by old man K499.3; dance
A1542.2.1; goes after the second child J2173.6; grants boy death respite
K551.22.3; masking as log obeys suggestion that he move upstream
K607.2; as ogre G354.2; opens mouth, monkey escapes K561.3; paramour B613.2; in strawstack burned to death K1055.1; swallows water-
snake, which kills him J2137.4; tells dog to drink in river without fear:
plan detected K2061.8; transports saint B557.4; as wooer B622.2. —
Bird with c. head B49.1; crab saves from c. attack J21.36; creation of c.
A2146; devastating c. B16.5.2; enmity of c. and (dog) A2494.4.2, (elephant) A2494.11.2; fox outwits c., escapes K543.1; friendship of jackal
and c. A2493.11; giant c. B875.2; hero kills c. F628.1.4.1; helpful c.
B491.3; magic causes c. to go ashore D1449.5; man transformed to c.
D194; marriage to c. B604.3; marriage to person in c. form B645.2;
origin of c. worship A1546.7.1; reincarnation as c. E614.3; sham-dead c.
quivers flesh H248.2.1; thief as c. K311.6.4; trickster employed to teach
c.: eats him K931.1; wer-c. D194.0.1; why c. has (marks of water pot on
head) A2320.6, (no tongue) A2344.1.1.2, (half a tongue) A2239.7,
A2344.1.1.1, (short tongue) A2344.1.1, (rough skin) A2311.7; witch as
c. G211.6.2.

Crocodiles. — Journey to land of c. F127.3; monkey in danger on bridge
of c. pretends that king has ordered them counted K579.2; ordeal by c.
H224.

Crooked. — Giant with c. nails F531.1.6.1.2; giant with c. nose
F531.1.6.6.1; luck determined by c.-necked demigod N125.2; person's c.
nose F514.4; why flounder's mouth is c. A2341.1.

Crop burned to rid it of insects J2102.7; division between parrot, cat

J1565.3; spirits F445.1. — Boy saves life by showing father foolishness
of plowing up his c. (killing his child) J92; deceptive c. division K171.1;
fairy steals c. F365.4; harvesting early for half c. J1932.6; magic c.
produces stone F809.3; mortal fosters fairy child to prevent c. destruction M242.1; payment to be made at harvest of first c. (acorns) K221;
planting, growing c. overnight H1103.2.2; plow animals determine c.
share J1179.11; separable soul in c. of sparrow E715.1.2; why munia
wears c. on back of neck A2351.7; witches ruin c. G265.9.

Crops burned as punishment Q595.2; stolen by magic *D2087.1. — Absurd
practices connected with c. J1932; black birds destroy c. B33.1.3;
dwarfs interfere with mortal's c. F451.5.2.5; extraordinary growth of c.
in paradise F815.3; failure of c. during reign of wicked king Q552.3;
fairies destroy c. F369.5; fairies promise abundant c. F349.4; gods or
goddesses of special c. A433; highest ranking man in land to be
sacrificed for good c. S263.1; loss of c. as punishment C934.1; magic
control of c. D2157ff.; magic growth of saint's c. D2157.2.1; magic spell
destroys c. D1563.2.4; menstrous woman will ruin c. C141.1; nobles ruin
peasant's c. U35.2; owl advises where to plant c. B569.2; sacrifice for
good c. V17.1; saint's bell starts c. growing D1563.1.4.

Crósan. — Demon (c.) causes disease F402.1.5.

Cross between shoulders as sign of royalty H71.5; on breast F546.3; of
Christ made of four kinds of wood V211.4.1; on crab's back A2412.4.4;
magically raised in air D2135.0.2.1; protects against ghosts E434.8.1;
renders invisible D1361.41. — All trees except aspen refuse to make
Christ's c. Z352; angel gives saint a c. V232.7.1; appearance of c. causes
conversion V331.1.2; why ass has c. on shoulders A2239.6, A2356.2.7;
beggar on c. in place of Christ L435.4; blood from c. on robin redbreast
A2221.2.2; Constantine's vision of the c. V515.1.4; deer with c. between
horns B253.5; disenchantment by sign of c. D788; dwarfs fear the c.
F451.5.9.1; devil's power avoided by the c. G303.16.3; earth supported
on wooden c. A843.1; elder tree used in making the c. A2711.2.1; fairies
fear c. F382.1; father of illegitimate child must walk in front of c.
J1515.1; finding of the c. V211.3; ghost cannot pass c. E434.8; magic c.
*D1299.3, (removes itself) D1641.9; magic power of holy c. D1719.6;
magic results from sign of the c. *D1766.6; runaway cavalry hero grabs
c. from graveyard K1951.2; sign of the c. *V86ff., (intimidates Jews)
V342; stone c. (indicates treasure) N535.1, (rises into air) F1083.1; saintly
baby holds arms in form of c. V229.2.1; sign of c. breaks witch spell
G271.2.1; temple about to be taken over by pagans saved by appearance
of a sign of the c. V344; tree cursed for serving as c. A2721.2.1; tree
blessed that made the c. A2711.2; troll helpless before sign of c.
F455.7.2; vigil with hands in shape of c. V462.4.2; windmill thought to
be holy c. J1789.1.

Crosses on certain trees A2751.3.2.

Cross-eyes miraculously straightened F959.2.

Crossing river except at source forbidden C833; river impossible for mortals F141.1.2; river on scythe-blade E721.6; stream impossible for witch (ghost, ogre) *G273.4; water by use of magic object *D1524ff.; water when spirits are offended forbidden *C41.3. — Wearing shoes only when c. river F1015.2.

Crossbill's bill from aiding Christ at crucifixion A2221.2.4.2.

Crossbow to shoot guilty J1141.10; spares bird F836.5. — Loaded c. kills wife opening forbidden chest T254.4.

Crossbreeding. — Lies about c. insects X1280.1.

Crossroads. — Magic power at c. *D1786; parting at c. N772; suicide buried at c. E431.16.3; why dogs leave droppings at c. A2473.1.1.

Crosswise. — Tree-trunks laid c. of the sledge J1964; trying to get a beam through a door c. in otherworld F171.6.3.

Crow, see also **Raven;** accepts owl's hospitality, burns him to death K2026; alighting on a falling tree thinks his weight made it fall J953.11; appropriates sparrow's nest J684.2, K354.1; befriends pigeon, steals from his home K359.4; as bird of ill-omen B147.2.2.1; chooses dead cat over crown J242.7; claiming swan wife J1293.1.1; demands young swan in payment K255.3; drops filth on king L410.3; drops pebbles into water jug so as to be able to drink J101; drops stolen necklace in snake's hole, snake killed K401.2.2; fat remedies king's wounds F959.3.5; hatches cuckoo's egg A2431.2.1.1; kills dove singing to save her brood U31.2; learns owls' secrets, defeats them K2042; as messenger B291.1.2; must wash bill in order to eat with other birds (cumulative tale) Z41.2; on the tarred bridge Z39.3; refuses to marry titmouse B282.22.1; releases deer from snare K642.1; sacrifices self to save king of crows P361.9; searches three worlds for happiness J136; sits on sheep's back W121.2.3; slain as he goes to wash mouth K551.4.6; as suitor B623.4; thinks harvesters are stealing his grain J953.7; tied to jackal's tail J2132.3.1; tries to imitate partridge's walk J512.6; tries to prophesy like raven J951.3. — Alliance of raven and c. B267.3; cawing of c. A2426.2.6; color of c. A2411.2.1.6; creation of c. A1919; creator sends c. to scout for earth nucleus A812.3; cumulative tale: louse eats c. Z33.4.1; demon as c. F401.3.7.1; devil as c. misleads travelers G303.9.9.17; enmity of c. (and owl) A2494.13.1, (and kite) A2494.13.2, (and prairie-dog) A2494.13.5; falcon and c. as joint creators A37.1; friendship between c. and (louse) A2493.23, M246.1.2, (snake) A2493.25f.; frog escapes c. by telling him to sharpen bill K561.1.2; ghost as c. E423.3.8; ghost driven into dead c. E437.3; giantess as c. F531.1.8.4; goose mates with c. B671; helpful c. B451.4; magic fat of c. *D1017.1.1; man transformed to c. D151.4, G263.1.5.1; otherworld "where no c. flies" Z91; person simulates cock c. K1886.3.1; prophetic c. B143.0.8; soul in form of c. E732.2; speaking c. B211.3.9; swan blamed when c. drops filth J429.2; swan outlasts c. in flying L394; tiger flatters c., kills her K815.9; troll as c. G304.1.1.4; warning c. B143.1.1; wedding of c. and titmouse B282.8; where c. got

voice A2421.3; why white c. is dumb A2422.3; why c. eats excrement
A2435.4.7.1; why c. cannot enter sparrow's nest A2431.3.6.1; why c.
has short tail A2378.4.7; why c. is disliked A2522.5; witch in form of c.
G211.4.1.

Crow's house full of wren's eggs H1129.9; maxim on flying away from
calamity J171.3.1; nest A2431.3.6ff. — Young c. alertness: man and
stone J1122.1.

Crows mow meadow (lie) X1252.1; reveal mare's killing B131.1. — Contest in beauty between swallows and c. J242.6; devils in form of c.
G303.3.3.3.2; fox shams death, catches c. K827.4; king of c. B242.2.1;
kites, c. quarrel over wounded fox J581.5; lies about c. X1252; owls and
c. dispute over day or night vision B299.2.1; queen made to scare c.
away Q482.5; war between c. and owls B263.3; what do c. do when they
are five years old? (start their sixth year) H865; why c. peck at human
flesh A2435.4.7; why elephant flees when cock c. A2531.3.1.

Crowbar. — Wall accuses c. J1966.

Crowded. — Dupe c. into the water K892; dupe c. over precipice K891.5.2.

Crowding together of animals seasonally A2484.

Crowing, see also **Cockcrow;** of cooked cock E524.2.1; of demi-coq in
king's body *B171.1.1; of ghost rooster E402.2.1; of resuscitated roasted
cock E168.1. — Chanticleer believes that his c. makes sun rise J2272.1;
cock's c. at sunrise A2489.1.1; cocks c. about mistress's adultery, killed
J551.1; cock c. with closed eyes seized K721; devil disappears at c. of
cock G303.16.19.4, G303.17.1.1; imitation of cock c. deceives devil
G303.16.19.4.1; woman c. in place of rooster, killed K1691.2.

Crown exposes infidelity of husbands H422.1; fits only true king H36.2.1;
from heaven (quest) H1261; of the sun A731.2; of thorns given Joseph
V211.1.6. — Christ born from c. V211.0.1; dwarf king wears costly c.
F451.2.7.7; extraordinary c. F828; fairy king's c. stolen F355; father
wears c. but is no king J1264.3; fool wears c. K1810.1.1; god's c. A156.2;
king cannot judge without c. P13.1; king's c. in well F166.4.1; king
rejects c.; too many cares J347.2; magic c. D1079.1, (of serpent)
*D1011.3.1; man becomes c. D263.5; recovering c. from sea H1132.1.7;
serpent's c. teaches animal languages B165.1.2; serpent's life in its gold
c. E714.2; snake lays aside his c. to bathe B765.2; taking off c. in
penance Q523.9; treasure-producing serpent's c. *B112.

Crowns as reward Q193. — Fairies with gold c. on heads F236.4.

Crowning of kings P13.5.

Crozier from heaven F962.12.1; in sod reveals gold N534.3. — Fire bends
bough to c. shape F964.1; magic c. *D1277.1.

Crucifix bows as sign of favor D1622.1; wounds bleed D1624.2. — Devil
as c. G303.3.2.1.1; ghost leaves c. E544.1.1; how much is c. worth? H716;
husband prepares to castrate c. K1558; living c. chosen J1738.2; man
behind c. says "Good Evening" K1971.7; punishment for indignities to
c. Q222.2; reward for offering food to c. Q32, Q172.1.

Crucifixion V211.2.3; of captured woman S139.3; as punishment Q462; of self as penance Q522.1. — Animals blessed for good services at C. A2221.2ff.; animal characteristics: punishment for hostility at C. *A2231.2ff.; crossbill's bill from aiding at C. A2221.2.4.2; curse for participation in C. Q556.1; death at news of Christ's c. F1041.1.39; feats on hearing of C. F1041.16.3; gypsy helpful at C. A1674.1; origin of tree for C. of Christ A2632.2; plant cursed for disservice at C. A2721.2; punishment for opposition to Christ at C. *Q221.2; stone rent at C. A979.1.

Cruel king invited to execution, killed K811.3; punishments Q450ff.; relatives S0—S99; sacrifices S200—S299; woman reborn as firefly E692.5. — Kind foster parents chosen rather than c. parents J391; magic object makes person c. D1357; maiden abducted from c. father R10.1.2; phenomena at c. treatment of innocent F960.7.

Cruelty to animals punished Q285.1; conquers monk's lust T317.6; punished Q285; tabu C867. — Enemies won more by kindness than c. J26; Flying Dutchman sails because of c. E511.1.1; sea foolishly accused of c. J1891.3; unnatural c. S (entire chapter); wild huntsman wanders because of c. E501.3.1.

Cruet. — Magic c. D1171.8.1; self-returning c. D1602.13.

Crumbs. Ogre kills self when he sees c. lying on his belly G523.

Crunching. — Cannibal c. human bone G87.

Crushed. — Besiegers c. by falling treasure K2353; Christians c. in cave R315.2; thief c. to death by fragments of own boring N339.15; why mouse c. in crossing road A2239.9.

Crushing coins to powder with fingers F614.12; of house by magic D2099.3; iron walls as baby F611.3.2.3; in rice mill as punishment Q414.3.1. — Murder by c. S116, (in false embrace) K953.4; mutilation by c. S167; strong man c. ribs of embracer F639.9; water-spirit c. boat F420.5.2.7.1.

Crustacean. — Flying c. B48; magic c. B178; mythical c. B94.

Crustaceans, origin of A2171.

Cry, see also **Cries;** of the blood of Abel A1344.1; of giant ox impregnates all fish B741.1. — Animal's c. imitated to distract owner's attention from his goods K341.7; baby's c. imitated to distract owner K341.7.0.1; compulsion to answer c. C681; compulsion to regard hunting c. and follow hounds C681.1; dragon hears child's c. B11.12.6; foolish mother does not understand baby's c. J1911.2; spirits answer war c. F418.1.

Crying child (stops to renew strength) W182, (used to obtain magic) D835; induced by magic D2034. — Abbot's excuse for c. J1478.1; animals c. out frighten robbers K335.1.4.1; child c. because father unknown T646.1; to come laughing and c. at once H1064; fox c. out in sleep H48.1; ghost c. E402.1.1.3; laughing and c. at same time *F1041.11; laughing or c. fruits D1619.3; man c. at friend's death F1041.21.4; stolen animal c. out from thief's stomach Q552.4.1.

Crystal boat F157.1; bower in otherworld F165.3.5.1; ball disenchants
D771.12; bower for fairy's mistress D2185.1; bridge F842.1.1; castle
F771.1.6; column F774.1.1; tree F811.1.6. — Chamber with c. ceiling in
otherworld dwellings F165.3.1.1; fence of metal or c. in otherworld
F169.5; house of gold and c. in otherworld *F163.3.1; marble cup be-
comes c. D475.5; magic c. renders courageous D1358.3; moon lives in
c. house A759.4; sun a bowl in c. box A724.2; tree with c. buds F811.17.1;
tunnel of c. four miles long F721.1.1; walls of c. in otherworld *F169.2.
Crystals. — Dwarf home has chandelier of c. and gems F451.4.3.4; magic
c. automatically heat for cooking D1649.5.
Crystal-gazing D1821.3.7.3, K1965.
Crystalline island F731.2.
Cubs give hero lion's milk H1361.0.1. — Man helps animal's c. B383.
Cuchulinn prophesies women's birth M301.5.2. — Battle rage of C.
F1041.16.5; why C. abjured kingship P16.1.3.
Cucking-stool as punishment Q474.
Cuckold loses luck N6.2; recognizes wife's ring in friend's possession
H94.0.1; weeps at child's funeral, real father sings U119.1.1. — Artist
hoodwinks king: c. can't see picture J1492; hidden c. reveals his presence
by rhymes K1556.
Cuckolds, tests for H425.
Cuckolded "as per instructions" J2342.2.2. — Man with unfaithful wife
comforted when he sees jealous husband who guards wife carefully c.
J882.2; teacher instructs pupil in love, c. K1692.
Cuckoo borrows food from other birds A2241.4; delivers other birds from
their cruel king: agree to hatch out cuckoo's young A2229.5. — Birds
flee from c. lest he later become a hawk J645.1; creation of c. A1993;
why c. had red eyes A2332.5.2; father killed by son returns to life as c.
A2275.6; fence built to pen c. J1904.2; why c. flies with difficulty and
sings with wings spread A2442.2.2; hearing c. call a good omen
D1812.5.2.5; hedging in c. so summer will stay year round J1904.2.1;
helpful c. B469.8; man transformed to c. D156; why c. has no nest
A2231.2.1, A2431.2.1; numskull climbs tree to help c. J1872.1; procuring
c. to sing in winter H1023.3.1.1; reincarnation as c. E613.5; resuscitation
by c. E122.1; serf in tree shot as c. K1691.1; woman as c. on tree shot
down K1691.
Cuckoo's color A2411.2.6.10; feathers A2241.6, A2313.1; food A2435.4.1;
song A2426.2.5; voice A2423.2.2; wedding B282.3.2, B282.19. — Crow
hatches c. egg A2431.2.1.1; saint causes c. call D2156.9.
Cuckoos cry when asleep: weasels kill them K815.10.
Cuckoo-clock (bird calls out the hours) F989.3.
Cucumber, enormous F816.1.
Cudgel, magic *D1094, D1401ff.
Cuirass, magic *D1101.2.
Cukasaptati (seventy tales of a parrot) K1591.
Culm-borers help win contest K69.1.

Culprit exposed to sinning condition to repent H1573.7.1. — Magic knowledge of offense of c. D1810.0.12.

Cultivated places become desert F969.5. — Origin of c. plants A2684.

Cultivation, magic D2157.6.

Cultivator, god as A181.2.

Cultivators, Agaria as A1689.10.

Culture. — Acquisition of human c. *A1400—A1499; king prefers primitive to civilized c. J245.2.

Culture hero, see also **Demigods, Hero;** A500—A599; creates useful animals A1703; departs A560ff.; establishes law and order A530ff.; expected to return *A580ff.; nature of A520ff.; origin of A510ff.; removes world-props A1058. — Race of c. with ostrich: ostrich loses beautiful feathers A2252.3; origin of minerals from body of dead c. A978.1.

Cumulative, see also **Chain, Kettenmärchen, Series, Succession:** tales *Z0—Z59; tasks H941.

Cunning. — Barbers' c. P446.2; why crab is c. A2525.2.

Cup or contents has greatest gravity? J2391; as feast token H84.2; full of milk symbolic offering to unwanted saint H607.4; given by fairy not to be broken F348.2; made of single ruby J21.49; to be repaired given to thief K362.3; with two and three handles J2605.1. — Alleged oracular bamboo c. K114.4; angel takes c. from old man J225.3; bridal couple drink from same c. T135.11; extraordinary c. F866; guessing nature of devil's gold c. H523.3; hole in c. avoids intoxication K82.1.2; horse accidentally poisoned instead of master when attempt is made to give hero poisoned c. N332.3; identification by c. H121; identification by ring dropped in c. H94.4; knights drink from huge nine-gallon c. F531.1.4.3; loving-c. at betrothal T61.4.2; magic c. *D1171.6, (of bamboo) N455.10, (tests truth) H251.3.13, (protects) D1380.17, (protects against loss of strength) D1389.3; marble c. becomes crystal D475.5; monk loses temper at c. W185.4, (overturned) H1553.5; new c. protection against witch G272.8; one traveler to another: is this c. valuable or not? H586.7; recognition by c. in sack H151.4; skull used as drinking c. Q491.5; theft of c. from fairies when they offer mortal drink F352.1; trading silver for worthless c. J2096; troll's c. stolen F455.6.4.1; were merely measuring king's c. J1391.7; riddle about value of c., daughter's marital status H586.7.

Cups. — Dove sees painted c. of water and dashes into them J1792.1; earthen c. replaced by golden H262.1; monkeys' magic c. K311.6.2; rainbow from gods' emptying their drinking c. A791.6; recognition by overheard conversation with c. H13.2.5.

Cupbearer abducted from Finns P50.4; of the gods A165.3.

Cupid with arrows of lead and gold A475.0.1. — Venus jealous of C. and Psyche's love W181.6.

Cupidity, punishment for Q551.2.8.1.

Curds. — Animal shows c. as spit K1715.12; cows to make c. before

milking J1905.5; earth sets like c. A826; woman created from sour c.
A1275.5; woman sells poisoned c. to man A1335.12.

Cure of diseases by Sacrament V34.1; for leprosy by drinking from
opposite lip of horn from that which caused it D1783.2; by physician's
imitating of sick man's actions F957; of sick by cutting off heads of the
well (chickens) H583.4.3; by threatening patients with death K1955.1;
yourself before doctoring others J1062. — Banishment of children as c.
for feigned illness S322.4.1; bath of blood of beloved as c. for love-
sick empress T82; blood of saint as c. D1500.1.7.3.2; child sacrificed to
provide blood for c. of friend S268; coition as illness c. J1149.4;
deceptive c. by illusion K1889.2; dipping into cold water as fever c.
J2214.9; drunkard refuses c. of fever if it is to take away his thirst
J343.1; fairies' white powder c. F344.3; flesh of certain animal (person)
alleged to be only c. for disease K961ff.; magic c. for specific diseases
D2161.1; marriage to prince as reward for c. H346, T67.2; miraculous
c. for leprosy F955; reward for c. *Q94; search for c. for prince H1292.4;
seduction by asking for sham c. K1326.1; sham c. by pretended extraction
of object from patient's body K1871.2; strenuous c. for madness J1434;
wife travels for years seeking c. for husband T215.7.

Cures by transferring disease to dead E595. — Marvelous c. F950ff.

Cured. — Promise to have but one consort if c. M262.

Curfew. — Ghosts walk after c. E587.3.

Curing incurable ulcer H1199.2.2; illness of children kills them J2175.6;
with waters of saint's fishpool D1242.1.3; wound by treating object
causing it D1782.2. — God disguised as doctor c. mortal K1811.3; price
for c. ogre's wound G682; quest for only person c. sickness H1319.1;
saint c. blind hyenas B384.

Curiosity *W137; punished *Q341; about secret enables animal to be
tied K713.1.4; tests H1554. — Animal trapped through c. as to what
the trap is K730.1; child's c. exposes thief K433; quest as punishment
for c. H1219.8.

Curious wife: wait and see T258. — Trickster exacts wife from c. people
K443.6.1; wild hunt harmful to c. E501.18.1.3.

Curlew. — Why c. has red legs A2371.4.1.

Curling. — Upper lip c. over nostril: lower hanging down to neck
F544.1.1.

Curly hair holds nuts F555.9. — Canaanites' c. hair A1661.3; straightening
a c. hair (task) H1023.4.

Currants. — Reincarnation of eyes into c. E649.5.

Current. — Magic root floats against c. D1547.1.

Curse by disappointed witch *G269.4; evaded by guessing magic names
H517; laid by untold stories C672.1; magically changed to blessing
D2175.5; by mermaid B81.13.8; of mother on unborn child S223.2; by
ogres G269.4.1; as punishment Q556ff., (for broken promise) M205.2,
(remitted) Q576. — Accidental meeting with person involved in over-

coming c. N718; army stopped by saint's c. D2091.13; big piece of cake with my c. or small piece with my blessing J229.3; devil's name used in c. (appears) C12.5; dwarfs emigrate because mortals c. F451.9.1.10; fairy lays c. on child F316; magic results from c. *D1792; mother's c. on son causes eclipse A737.2; punishment for undeserved c. Q265.4; runes protect against c. D1385.20; unique exceptions from c. Z357; witch's c. causes illness G263.4.0.1; why elephant hurts self in grass: mouse's c. A2239.10; why mouse is crushed: elephant's c. A2239.9.

Curses *M400—M499. — Old woman's c. inform abandoned hero of his parentage and future S375.

Cursed church clock never runs correctly H252.6. — Why animal is c. A2231.7, A2542; body c. by soul E727.1.1; Brahma c. by other gods A162.4; child c. by father cannot rest in grave E412.4; dancers rude to holy man c. and must keep dancing till Judgment Day C94.1.1; giant c. F531.6.12.1.2; horse owner c. by clerics B133.4.1; king c. by dwarf-smiths P15.4; presence of c. person brings disaster to land M491; sun c. by moon A736.9; tortoise c. for going under water while ferrying goddess A2231.7.3; tree on which Judas hanged himself c. A2721.5; why certain plants are c. A2721, A2776; will-o-the-wisp is girl c. for gathering plants on Sunday A2817.2.

Cursing contest K91; by magic D2175. — Damnation by c. D2061.2.4.1; death by c. *D2061.2.4.1; drinking holy water facilitates c. V132.3; dwarfs c. forced gifts F451.5.2.13; man c. sun and wind for burning L351.2; man put in moon for c. Q235.1, (God) A751.1.2; masses used along with other magic for c. D1766.5.1; prince penalizes c., although he himself curses W133.1; serfs c. master by mistake J1845; son c. father indirectly P236.3; tabu: sailor c. the wind C41.4; teacher c. disobedient pupils P343; wife c. husband who forces her T288.1.

Curtain. — Contest in lifelike painting (mare and c.) H504.1.2, (grapes and c.) H504.1.3; falling in love when c. pulled aside T29.1; heavenly c. around God's throne A152.5; jewelled c. F789.3.1; skillful marksman throws rushes into a c. F661.7.1.

Curtains in otherworld F166.7. — Looking behind c. tabu C336.

Customs *P600—P699; connected with kings P13; connected with unique compulsion C650.1; of giant ogres G130ff. — Culture hero establishes c. *A545; marriage c. *T130ff.; military c. P557; origin of c. A1500—A1599, (connected with birth) A1500ff., (of courtship and marriage) A1550ff., (of eating) A1510f., (of hunting) A1520ff., (religious) A1540ff., (social) A1530ff.

Cut hand gives away thief's complicity J1149.8; off parts of body restored (by saint) V221.9, (by holy man) V229.10.2. — Animal characteristics: members c. off A2216ff.; burning c. hair to prevent witchcraft D2176.5; cannibals c. off parts of children's bodies G86; captive's finger c. to test fatness G82.1; cat's paw c. off: woman's hand missing D702.1.1; ground c. from under adversary F942.2; identification by c. garment

H117; long tongue c. out and used to bridge a stream F544.2.2.1; moon
c. in two by sun A755.4; mortal wins fairies' gratitude by letting them
c. his hair and shave him F331.2; naked woman pursued and c. in two
by rider E501.5.1.1; primeval woman c. in pieces A642.1.

Cuts. — Barber uses hair to stanch c. X252.2; ground dries up when first
woman c. her little finger A856.2.

Cuticle. — Earth from creator's c. A833.

Cut-throat terrorizes boat N695.

Cutting off arm as alibi K407.2.1; off arms for sleeveless sweater
J2131.3.1.1; off child's ears: fool takes threat as order J2465.11; clothes
bag in two F667.3; devil's fingernails (fear test) H1422; down tree tabu
C518; off giant's foot G512.6; hair as punishment Q488; off ogre's head,
hands G512.1.2.1; off part of own body J213.3.2; into pieces as punishment Q429.3; at plow: fool cuts bullock's legs J2465.8; off son's head
to marry fairy H313.2; steer in two to test sword F611.3.3.1; table reveals
witch G257.3; things by magic object D1564; thread by shooting arrow
F661.12; certain trees tabu C43.2; tree (branches tabu) C513.1, (with one
stroke) H1562.1.1, (as unique ability) H31.5. — Abandoned child thinks
father c. wood S338; boy c. down trees bribed to spare one N699.5;
bride test (thrifty c. of cheese) H381.2, (c. up fish) H383.5; cat in wood-
pile prevents axe from c. D2186; deceptively c. off victim's hand K825.4;
disenchantment by c. off and reversing bodily members D712.1; disenchantment by c. person in two D711.2; escape by c. fetters K649.11; fortune told by c. sand D1812.3.2; man c. off own head F511.0.4.1; murder
by c. S118; ogre c. off own buttocks G528; peasant c. wood as guests
arrive P411.2; penis c. down trees F547.3.6; sword c. everything F833.5;
suitor task: c. open magic gourd H335.2; threats on c. corpse in two
reveal feigned death J1545.8; task: c. firewood from rocks with brass axe
(rock struck to splinters by lightning used) H1116.1; trickster c. up
partridges with "executioner's" knife K344.1.3; victim kills swallower
from within by c. F912.2.

Cuttlefish. — Man transformed to c. D174.

"Cutty Soams" mining spirit F456.3.

Cutworm A446.2, A2182.4.

Cycenus cuts off heads of strangers in order to build temple of heads
G315.

Cyclone. — Lie: man rides c. X1004.2.

Cyclops F512.1.1. — Proof of slaying C. H105.5.2.

Cynical philosopher lives in tub J152.1; retorts J1442ff.; retorts concerning honesty J1370ff.

Cypresses. — Twelve c. with thirty boughs each (riddle) H721.3.

Cyrus L111.2.1.

Daddy-long-legs. — Why d. has long legs A2371.2.12; why d. has long
life A2578.1.

Daedalus flies on artificial wings *F1021.1; puts thread through coils of snail shell H506.4.

Dagger cleaned on inside of robe A1599.7; indicates ogress dead or alive E761.7.15; in wall above bed falls and kills girl N331.1. — Infallible d. D1653.1.9; magic d. *D1083.1; marriage of girl to a d. T117.1.

Daily beating of men transformed to dogs necessary unless hero himself is to be transformed D691; beatings as punishment Q458.1; course of the sun A726; life of angels V247; life of the gods A150ff.; transformation D621; visit to saint compulsory C687.1. — Dead find no rest since someone d. knocks at grave E419.2; devil may be escaped by going to church d. G303.16.13; ghost visits earth d. E585.3; human being devoured d. G15; injunction: to perform certain act d. C687; magic sword slays man d. D1402.7.1.1; pilav as d. food (father's counsel) H588.2.

Dainty. — Food has taste of any d. desired D1665.

Dainties. — Refusal to eat d. V462.2.2.

Dairy-god A411.3. — Evil magic in d. *D2083; magic d. products *D1036.

Dairies. — God's d. A155.7; origin of d. A1439.5.

Dairyman. — Lie: remarkable d. X1082.2.

Daisies. — Tears of Mary at Annunciation become d. A2612.2.

Dal, wheat, rice dispute superiority T461.5.

Dam builder punished for defying God Q221.4.1. — Devil builds d. G303.9.1.2, H1131.2; spear used to d. stream F834.5.

Damage. — Deceptive d. claims K251.

Dame Berchta F475.1.

Damming. — Flood from d. rivers A1019.2; riddle about d. up outlets H588.9.

Damn. — Ram says "D." on Sabbath B211.1.1.1.1.

Damnation by cursing D2061.2.4.1.

Damned souls E752ff.

Damocles. — Sword of D. F833.2.

Damsel, see also **Maiden;** as wager N2.6.3. — Divine d. converts fairy wife into woman F302.5.2.1; poison d. F582; serpent d. F582.1.

Dance, see also **Ball;** of the dead E493; with the dead E238.1. — Backwards and forwards d. K153; camel tries in vain to d. J512.3; changeling's wild d. F321.1.1.2.1; devil haunts d. halls G303.10.4.0.1; devil punishes girl who loves to d. Q386.1; devils come to a d.-loving maid and play when she bathes G303.10.4.2; dupe lured to supposed d. and killed K816; dupe persuaded to d. on trickster's body K827.3; dupe persuaded to get into grass in order to learn new d. K1055; escape by pretending to d. and thus be untied K571; fisherman fails to make fish d. to his flute J1909.1; freemasons forced to d. till they sweat blood Q388.1; frog causes deer to d. into snare K730.2; god of d. A465.4; goddess of d. A112.1.1.1; magic object compels person to d. *D1415ff.; making ducks d. with closed eyes K826; making pigs d. (task) H1186; mortal wins fairies' gratitude by joining in their d. F331.1, F331.4; persons magically caused to d. selves to death *D2061.1.2; resuscitation by nine-day d. E63.2; thief plays all night for d. while confederate commits theft K411; trickster joins bulrushes in a d. J1883; trolls' d. F455.6.6.1; wife's d. charms husband back R152.4; witch harnesses man and leads him to d. G269.3; witch rides man to d. G269.3.1.

Dances. — Devil d. on grave G303.9.8.3; origin of religious d. A1542.

Dancer stabs spectator K916. — Disguise as d. K1825.6; lightning as torches of invisible d. A1141.7.1; marvelous d. F699.1.

Dancers cheated: one coin payment K231.2.1; as followers of the devil G303.10.4; of the gods A166; upon whom icicles hang F572; rude to holy man cursed C94.1.1. — Devil appears invisible among d. G303.6.2.1; hoodwinked d. K826.

Dancing in afterworld E489.5; alps F471.1.1.2; animals B293; automata D1627; brownies F482.5.1; in churchyard forbidden C51.1.5; to death in red-hot shoes (punishment) Q414.4; ducks K826; dwarf F451.6.3.4; of enchanted person D794.1; fairies F261; giants F531.6.17.1; girl outwits robbers, brings strong men K551.3.6.1; mare rescues boy K551.3.6.2; men defeat captors K551.3.6.3; mountain-folk F460.3.1; naked in church punished Q222.5.3; night spirits F470.2; pigs G265.6.1.1; punished Q386; self to death D2061.1.2, (to repay devil for clothes) K1227.3.1; on sharp instruments as test H1531.1; shoes to pieces daily F1015.1.1; teacher a thief K374; thief directs robbery K341.21; trolls F455.3.2; at wedding T136.3.1; witches G247. — Breaking legs for prowess in d. K1013.6; celestial nymphs d. F642.5; dead lover d. at sweetheart's wedding E214.1; death respite while d. K551.3.6; deceptive d. lesson K153; devil d. with a maid till she dies G303.10.4.1; dog d. on hind legs G265.6.4.1; dwarfs emigrate because they dislike peasants' d. and loud music F451.9.1.9; earth made by couple d. on cloth A825; escape by d. K571.1; escape from d. captors K606.2; fairies d. with child F321.5; fairies d. with youth till he dies F302.3.4.2; girl fond of d. curses C12.5.3; girl shows herself naked in return for youth's d. hogs *K1358; girl sinks into earth for d. in church Q552.2.3.1; girls d. in heaven A661.4; lives spared as reward for d. Q151.13; long d. as endurance test H1501; magic d. *D2174; magic d. object D1646; man attacked on Christmas night by. d. ghosts E261.3; mortal beats drum for d. fairies F302.6.2.1; origin of d. A1462; origin of particular d. A1542.1; pillars d. to magic guitar D1599.1; pixies' d. contest F302.3.4.2.1; providing d. fairies as suitor task H1177.1; quest for d. apple H1333.3.1.2; quest for d. water H1321.4; religious d. V93; small man d. in spider web F535.2.3; stealing food from d. children K341.17; Saora wave axes, shout while d. A1689.4; victim enticed into d.: captured K772, K826.

Dandy tailored by devil, left naked G303.9.9.11.

Danger averted by dream warning K1810.8.3.2; warning restores speech

F954.5. — Agreeing to demands while in d. J625; animal warns of fatal d. B521; approaching d. too familiarly J655; association of rat with cat ceases as soon as mutual d. has passed J426; boasting after d. is over J2626; choice: plainness with safety or grandeur with d. J212; coward boasts when there is no d. W121.2; disregard of d. to objects (or animals) J2120ff.; dream reveals d. D1813.1.6; escape from d. by deception *K500ff.; foolish disregard of personal d. J2130ff.; horse warns hero of d. *B133.1; inattention to d. J651; lie: hunter in d. X1133; magic object warns of d. *B133.1; man sells child in order to save himself from d. S222; no time for minor fights when life is in d. J371; prediction of d. M340.5; red wards off d. D1381.15; sacrifice to get help in d. V17.3; saint incurs another's d. P319.8; shrewish wife reforms after d. T251.2.5; Thumbling in d. of being sucked in by man's breath F535.1.1.4; voice warns of d. in mine V542; witch places man in d. G292.

Dangers to husband in bridal chamber T172. — Animals retort concerning their d. J1420ff.; brothers deliberately seek d. they have been warned against *Z211; fanciful d. from animals B766; forest of d. F812.3.

Dangerous animals unnamed C433.2; husband T181; penances Q525. — Animal rescues man from d. place B547ff.; curse: undertaking d. quest M446; dupe goes to d. place, killed K991; falsely accused hero sent on d. mission K2102; house filled with d. animals J347.5; quest for d. animals H1360ff.; quest for d. bride H1381.3.1.2.3; quest over path guarded by d. animals H1236.2; questions to the dead are d. E545.5.

Danmar tree. origin of A2681.8.

Dante abuses lowly blacksmith chanting Divine Comedy J981; accused of religious negligence J1261.2.5; puts teasing ruler out of countenance J1224.2; unrewarded while minstrel is J1364.

Dao. — Chain tale: man sharpening d. bitten Z49.6.3.

Darby ram X1243.1.

Dark haired people as magicians D1711.9; traitor K2260ff. — Banished devil appears on earth only on day of d. moon A106.2.1.1; dwarfs fear the d. F451.3.6.5.1; fairies seen as d. shadows F235.7; fool cannot tell his right hand in the d. J1735; hungry parson hunts porridge in d. X431; life token: milk turns d. E761.4.5; seduction theme: God can't see in d. V465.1.2.2; why not to eat in d. A1512; why some nights are d. A1174.2; witches see in d. G249.10.

Darkening. — Bird swarms d. sun, moon F989.16.2; magic spell d. sun D1546.1.2.1; object d. as life token E761.4ff.; sun d. at death of holy person F965.2; tree d. whole world F811.14.1.

Darkness as god's child A700.8; of lower world F80.1.2. — Deity arises from shell of d. A115.6; giants in region of d. F531.6.2.6; god dwells in d. A151.13; gods of d. and of light A107; great d. from awk swallowing sun A721.2.1; island of d. F129.4.5; impenetrable d. F965.3; land of d. F706; magic d. D908; miraculous d. as punishment Q552.20.1; premature

d. F965; primeval d. A605.1; slaying under cover of d. K914.3; sun thrown on fire: period of d., rain A1068.

Darknesses. — Tabu: drinking from river between two d. C263.

Dart, recognition by H125.4.

Dashing. — Dropping and d. to pieces as punishment Q417; miraculous d. to death Q551.10.

Date (fruit). — Blind thief's rope slips on withered d. tree K436; magic d. *D981.9.

Date palm. — Why fruit of d. looks like old woman's breasts A2791.11.

Dates. — Ignorance of d. J1743; riddle of d. H707.

Daughter bears son, father dies E765.4.3; encouraged by dead mother E323.6; insulted by father's offer of new husband K2052.4.3; must be named for fairy F302.5.1.1; promised to animal suitor B620.1; punished by marriage to poor man T69.5; rescues father R154.3; succeeds on quest son failed L152; unwittingly turns parents out of doors N367; as wager N2.6.2; wooed, mother dies E765.4.2. — Accidental meeting of (father and d.) N732, (mother and d.) N736; captive king's d. enslaved P173.1; clever d. solves riddles H561.1.1.1; creator's d. A32.2; dead father helps d. in childbirth E327.2; death vowed if another d. born M184; devil wooes an innkeeper's d. G303.12.1; devil's d. G303.11.5; dwarf promises money and property to mortal father for hand of d. F451.5.18.1; false d. accepted as resurrected child K1926; fascination with ogre's d. G455; father and d. *P234; father rescues d. R153.5; father takes his d. to cannibal to be eaten G75; father will die when d. marries E765.4.1; father's deceptive advice to inhospitable d. J1561.5; formerly I was d., now I am mother (riddle) H807; ghost appears to d. E321.5; giantess d. of giant, maiden F531.5.7.1.2; help from ogre's d. *G530.2; with help of captor's d. prisoners slay many of his soldiers at a banquet K811.1.1; hero's d. bears boy A592.2.1; hero's virgin d. A592.2; impoverished father begs from abused d. L432.2; king promises d. she may choose mate Q115.2; king's d. tabu in marriage C196; magic object from d. D815.6; magic object stolen by d. D861.8.1; man made to believe d. has borne child K1923.2; man palms off elder d. as younger K1911.1.5.1; mother abandons remarkably beautiful d. F575.1.1; mother and d. P232, (as rivals in love) T92.6; mother haunts d. E222.0.1; mother wishes lazy d. may marry devil C12.4.1; mother's ghost tries to tear d. to pieces E222.1; murder of wild huntswoman's d. E501.3.10; numskull praises his d. as being pregnant J2427; ogre's d. (burned in his own oven) G512.3.2.1, (killed with father) G512.0.2; old woman loses willingness to die for d. H1556.4.5.1; parent to die same day as d. E765.4.3.1; prostitute claims to be victim's d. K347.1; quest for vanished d. H1385.2; rescue by captor's d. *R162; sacrifice to find abducted d. V17.5.1; second d. won by saying first dead K1366; seventh d. to be magician N121.4; son of abandoned d. becomes hero S371; tabu to look on d. for twelve years C312.3; toad exchanges ugly d. for lizard's K476.5; treacherous d.

*K2214.1; treasure to be found by man who marries original owner's d.
N543.3; trickster's d. a dupe J1111.2; troll's d. after being cooked in
kettle recognized by golden fingernail H79.1; victorious youngest d.
*L50ff.; vow to marry none but d. of certain man M146.5; witch as d.
of fairy, man G203.1; woman substitutes for her d. in dark K1317.5;
yam cutting symbol for marriageable d. H611.3; youth in court for kissing prince's d. pleads his love for her J1174.1.

Daughter's good fortune discovered by beggar father N732.2.1; intercession saves father wronging her W11.5.9.2; sickness after father breaks
tabu C940.2. — Cup's value compared to d. marital status H586.7; dead
father stops d. weeping E327.1; death upon d. marriage M341.1.1.3;
father opposed to d. marriage T97; man unwittingly causes d. death
N320.1; mermaid ruins her d. seducer B81.13.9; tabu: younger d. marriage before elder C169.2.

Daughters meek H659.21; of men and sons of God F531.6.1.1; sacrificed
to avert famine S263.2.2; seducing father T411.2.1. — Choice between
foolish son or wise d. J226.3; doctor prescribes sexual intimacy to mother:
d. follow treatment K2052.4.1; husband leaves home after fourteen d.
born N231; lakes as d. of the gods A920.1.14; mountains as d. of gods
A962.9; oath to marry d. only into family with bridegroom for each
M149.5; seven d. of Humility J901; sun and moon as skygod's d. A736.4;
threat to marry d. to first comers N455.12; vow to marry off d. to first
men seen M138.1; witch's cattle her d. H1199.12.2.

Daughter-in-law tabu C173. — Bad relations of mother-in-law and d.
P262.1; clever d. J1111.3; cruel d. S54; enigmatic permission to d.
H588.0.1; lazy d. learns work W111.3.6; mother-in-law humiliated as
cure for malady of d. K1945.1.1; mother-in-law plots death of d. S51.1;
sour-faced d. H659.18.1; treacherous d. K2214.2; wise d. defeats wealthy
J185.1; woman eats d. G79.2.

David as prophet M301.7.2. — God punishes D. for his pride L415; King
D. mingles with common people J914.1; prophecy: woman as ancestress
of D. M363.2.1; what says D.? X435.1.

Daw as bird's king B242.1.6; fleeing from captivity caught in trees by
thread around foot N255.5; tries to carry off lamb like eagle J2413.3;
tries to swallow glowworm sparks J1849.2; waits in vain for the figs to
ripen in winter J2066.2.

Daw's food A2435.4.10.

Daws. — Kind words for d. but driving them off K2090.1.

Dawn reflection of roses of paradise A1179.2.1. — Animal calls the d.
*B755; at d. sun plays with moon A722.9; animal punished for not
heralding d. A2236.5; bird of d. B34; day as son of night and d. A1171.4;
fairy house disappears at d. F221.1; ghost laid at d. *E452; god of d.
A270ff.; gods flee at approach of d. C311.1.8.1; goddess of d. A270.1;
phantom house disappears at d. F771.6; wolf announces d. prematurely
to collect debt *K494.

Day controlled by magic D2146.1; husband: night husband T482; as mortals' period A189.17; and night as formula Z73; produced by magic D2146.1.3. — Angels of the d. A1171.3; appointing king by d., slaying him by night P13.6; artist's children by d. and by night J1273; the auspicious d. N127; coming neither by d. nor by night H1057; dead quiescent during d. E452.1; dead returns third d. after burial E586.2; devil builds road for farmer in one d. G303.9.2.2; during d. dwarfs appear in form of toads E451.2.0.5; devil destroys by night what is built by d. G303.14.1; during d. moon stays under earth A753.3.3; dwarfs emigrate because mortals desecrate holy d. F451.9.1.11; dwarfs regard D. of St. John the Divine F451.5.9.4; emperor thinks d. lost when he gives no gifts W11.2.1; ghost invisible during d. E452.2; god's d. one thousand years A199.5; if it is d., give me food: if it is night, let me sleep W111.2.3; inexorable fate: no d. without sorrow N101.1; invulnerability for single d. K1845.1; kingdom well by d. burns at night H1292.20; long d. (if the clock is still striking it must be 50 o'clock) J2466.3; magic control of d. and night D2146; magic power to continue all d. what one starts D2172.2; man can stand all d. on one foot F682; marriage to beast by d. and man by night *B640.1; object borrowed for one d., night, retained K232.2; ointment makes night seem d. D1368.1.1; one d. from happiness to misfortune H685.1; one shape by d.: another by night D621.0.1; one sun-god for night, another for d. A227.2; origin of night and d. A1170ff.; origin of custom of catching fish by d. as well as by night A1457.2; owl as watchman goes to sleep: does not see by d. A2233.3; person dead by d., alive at night E155.4; profaning sacred d. forbidden *C58; prognostications from d. of week and first d. of year D1812.5.0.7.3; promise not to kill on "any d.": night killing K929.3; quest to be accomplished in one d. H1245; riddle of the d. and night H722ff.; sending for beef when neither d. nor night H1074; soldiers of fairy king are trees by d. and men by night F252.3.1; souls at Judgment D. E751; sowing and reaping same d. F971.7; tailor occupies God's throne for d. P441.1; wife in heaven by d., with husband by night E322.3; windows and doors for every d. in year F782.1; woman alive by d., dead at night E155.4.1; work of d. magically overthrown at night *D2192; year and a d. Z72.1.

Day's journey from earth to heaven H682.1.1; journey from one end of the earth to the other H681.1.1. — Sun earns d. wages for his daily work H715.1.

Days. — Bringing as many horses as there are d. in the year H1117; dead awaken after three d. to new life and great wisdom E489.1; diminishing number of sacred d. forbidden C58.1; February's shortage of d. A1161; how many d. have passed since the time of Adam (riddle) H706; magic weakness for five d. each year D1837.1.1; mortal wins fairies' gratitude by naming d. of week F331.3; resuscitation by assembling members and leaving in cask for nine d. E37; speaking during seven d.

of danger forbidden C401.2; why d. lengthen in spring A1155; why d. shorten in autumn A1156; why there are more d. than nights H772; years thought d. *D2011; years are d. in Tusita world A697.2.1.

Day of Judgment, see **Doomsday.**

Daybreak. — Servant who is to call his master at d. looks into dark closet to see if it is yet light W111.2.1; truest dreams at d. D1812.3.3.1.

Daydreamer breaks pots, loses future profits J1493.

Daydreaming toad run over J2061.4.

Daylight renders fairy prince mortal F383.4.1. — Acquisition of d. A1412.3; ogre who cannot endure d. G632; supernaturals tricked into d. exposure K839.6.

Daytime. — Darkness comes in d. in order to save life of maiden about to be executed F965.1; star shines in d. F961.2.3.

Dazzling. — Magic d. shield D1645.5.

Dead E (entire chapter); beggar's stick will not stay until back in beggar's service D1651.5; body becomes god A104.2; cannot rest because of a sin E411; dog transformed to money D422.2.1; fish reveals guilt D1318.2; girl frightens father and lover J2621; heads necessary to drinking C281; king carried into battle P12.5.0.1; leaves transformed to gold D475.1.3; and living go together to gate of heaven E754.2.3; lover's return (friendly) E310ff., (malevolent) E210ff.; made to appear alive K1885; man mistaken for living J1769.2; man not killed by weapons tabu C319.2; man stretches forth hand to honor saint V222.7; man tries to come back to life E162.2; men try to carry kettle from hell to heaven A1433.0.1; mother's breasts nourish baby for two years T611.9; opposes return of living from land of the dead F105; place net across river to prevent living man from returning to earth F93.1.1; quarrel with living, hence own land E481.0.2; relative's return (friendly) E320ff., (malevolent) E220ff.; Rider (Lenore) E215; tree comes to life *E2; man's tooth as cure for toothache D1502.2.1; wife marriage test H363. — Abode of the d. *E480ff.; absurd ideas about the d. J1937; adulteress returns from d. as devastating dragon E263; alleged return with gold from d. J2411.5; animal searches for d. man B546; apparently d. woman revives K426, N694; bird reveals d. rider B131.4; captive spirits of d. H972.1; cat hangs on wall pretending to be d. K2061.9; chief of d. frightens visitors H1401.1; child born to apparently d. mother T581.2.1; child born of d. mother T584.2.1; child speaks from d. mother's womb T575.3; conductor of the d. A311; corpse not entirely d. who has left good property H586.5; curse: hero to remain as d. until curser dies M438.4; dance of the d. E493; death feigned to enter land of d. K1866; descent to lower world of d. *F81; devil in d. man's shape G303.3.1.20; devil enters the body of d. boy G303.18.1; devil in place of d. man in shroud G303.18.2; dinner with the d. E238; escape from land of d. R219.2; failure of crops for mistreating d. Q552.3.0.4; fairies as souls of d. F251.2; falling d. at lover's return T211.7; falling in love with

d. body T16.2; Flying Dutchman has d. men as sailors E511.2.1; food placed out for returning souls of d. E541.1; fool tries to shoot d. antelope until it will come to him J1909.2; footsteps in manure proof d. man walked H264; fortune's wheel turned by d. king in mountain N111.3.1; friendly return from the d. E300—E399; girl marries lover who thought her d. K1839.2; god of the d. A108.1; god of the world of the d. *A310ff.; gods are spirits of d. A117.5; grateful d. man *E341ff.; good d. but not living (riddle) H841.2; intercourse with d. human body T466; island in otherworld garden inhabited half by d. and half by living F162.1.2.5; journey to land of the d. E374; kindness to orphans repaid by d. parents Q47; king raised from d. P19.5; light as souls of d. A1412.2; magic d. fish *D1281; magic d. man's tooth *D1009.2.1; magic knowledge from d. D1810.13; magic received from d. D812.4.1; malevolent return from the d. E200—E299; man forced to eat d. father's heart goes mad G91.1; man at grave pretends to be d. speaking K1974; man returns from d. to protest against priest who had been too easy with him at confession V25.1; man wants to be d. one day J2188; mass said for d.: they arise and say "Amen" V45; mould put on table for the d. E433.1; mountain spirits as souls of d. F460.0.1; origin of feast for the d. A1541.1; owner frightened from goods by apparitions of the d. K335.0.5; path to world of d. F95.0.1; people flee man reported d. J1786.8; person d. during day, alive at night E155.4; person made to believe that he is d. J2311ff.; physician forced to carry d. patient's bier P424.3.1; power of seeing whether d. go to heaven or hell B161.4; prayer for journey to land of d. V52.9; pretending man d. to test saint Q591.1.1; punishments in land of d. Q560.1; rescue by grateful d. man R163; resuscitation by frightening d. E25; return of contract sought from d. man H1273.1.1; return from the d. E0—E199, (to do penance) E411.0.2.1, (to reveal murder) *E231; riddle on house full of d. H831; robbers frightened from goods by the d. K335.1.2; room in hell for the d. A678; sacrifice to the d. V11.6; saint commands return from d. V229.1; servant lays skin of d. dog in bed of his mistress and master K2134; sham d. claim reward for information about their death J2511.1.2; sham d. man deceived into making gesture K607.3; sleeper answers for d. man J2618; soul leaves body to converse with d. E721.8; speaking to the d. tabu C497; stingy d. woman raises her head to correct account of laundress W152.3; summoned d. prophesies M301.14; sun's night journey in land of d. A722.3; contact with the d. forbidden C541; tabu: offending the d. C16; tabu: stripping d. and slain C877; tasks accomplished with help of grateful d. H972; thunder drums of the d. A1142.9.1; trading d. horse K134.7; treasure hidden in pillow under d. man's head N522; tree in hell made of living heads of the d. A671.2.3; two d. men struggle over living man E467.1; unquiet d. sinner taken to priest for absolution E411.0.2; vigil for d. father H1462; voices of d. heard from graveyard E401; voyage to Isle of the D. F129.4.4; ways of disposing of d. V61; why opposum plays d. when caught A2466.1; witch calls up d., makes them walk on water G299.1; witch revives d. G263.5; woman playing d. to spy on husband killed N384.12.

Dead Sea's origin A920.1.15.

Deadly. — Unique d. weapon Z312.

Deaf and dumb man can see soul taken to happiness or punishment D1821.7; and dumb speak F1041.22; blind, and lame as witnesses in court X141; dumb, blind, and lame man catches hare (lie) X1791. — Blind wife, d. husband happy T202; blind and d. cure each other by blows N642.1; deception by playing d. K1981.

Deafness caused by magic object D1332.1; magically cured D2161.3.5. — Feigning d. to lure enemy K911.5; humor of d. X110ff.; magic object cures d. D1506; trickster cheats by pretending d. K231.15; trickster feigns d. and gets hospitality from miser K1981.1.

Dearer. — Mother love d. than gold (riddle) H662.

Dearest. — Exiled wife's d. possession J1545.4.

Death in battle preferable to bed M161.6; caused by (ascetic devotions) V462.2.3, (broken heart) F1041.1.1, (cannibalism) G91.2, (chagrin) F1041.1.3.10, (cursing) *D2061.2.4, (fire from heaven) Q552.13.1, (fairies) F363, (glance) D2061.2.1, (grief) T211.9.1, (grief over death) F1041.1.2, (intercourse) T182, (excess of women) T99.1, (love) T81, (magic charm) D806.2, (meeting ghost) E265.3, (opposing dogma of Immaculate Conception) V312.2, (saint's breath) D1500.4.2.2, (sleepiness, anger, and greed) H803, (speaking with pestilence) F493.2.1, (spirit) F402.1.11, (sight of Wild Hunt) E501.18.10, (waterspirits) F420.5.2.12; cheated by moving bed *K557; of children as punishment Q553.4; as curse M451; of dwarfs F451.3.5.1; escaped through disguise, shamming, or substitution *K520ff.; exposes hypocrisy K2065; of faithful servant for his master P361.1; of father fated at daughter's marriage E765.4.1; feigned (to be carried) K1861, (to meet paramour) K1538, (to live with mistress) K1538.2, (husband's discovered) J1545.8, (to capture) *K751, (to test debtor friends) H1558.5, (to seduce) *K1325, (to steal) K341.2, (to join lover) K1538.1; forestalls evil fates N121.2; of friends for each other P315; fulfills grief prophecy M340.1; follows loss of magic object D860.0.1; of the gods A192.1; is the hardest (riddle) H637.2; of helpful animal *B330ff.; of hero Z292; on horseback E492; from joy F1041.1.5; kills only those whose time it is to die A487.0.1; through lack of foresight J2137ff.; of little hen (cumulative tale) Z32.2; of loving couple from separation T212; -machine's inventor uses it K1681.1; by magic *D2060ff.; message softened by equivocation K2313; omens (through dream) D1813.1.4, (ghost light) E530.1.6, (ghost) E574, (magically heard noises) D1827.1ff., (overly generous gift) W11.13, (snow on house) D1812.5.1.18, (seeing own wraith) E723.2, (dry river bed) D1812.5.1.16.1, (blood) D1812.5.1.1.4, (foreknowledge of hour) D1812.0.1; order evaded K510ff.; as penalty or punishment *Q411ff., Q582, (for losing footrace)

13*

H1594.0.1, (for broken oath) M101.3, (for broken tabu) *C920ff., (for losing bride-race) H331.5.0.1; personified *Z111ff.; postponed (if substitute can be found) *D1855.2, (by saint) D1855.3; preferred above God and Justice J486; prophesied M341; prophecy fulfilled M370.1; preferred to captivity J227.1; preferred to marriage with unwelcome suitor M149.2; preferred to other evils J227; as rescuer R169.16; sends man back to earth E121.13; sentence escaped by propounding riddle king (judge) cannot solve *H542; of snake encircling world A1082.3.1; of snake only after sunset B752.2; of strong man F615.0.1; from sudden realization N383; suspended until god's return A173.1; thought sleep E175; vegetable C662; of witch G278; as wife's paramour J2349.2. — Accidental d. N330ff.; angel of d. A52.1.1, V233; angels of d. cannot bring soul to heaven E754.2.2.1; animal saves man from d. sentence B522; animal's behavior at d. A2468ff.; announcing d. directly tabu C499.1; beautification by d. and resuscitation D1865; burning witch to d. G275.3.0.1; captivity preferred to d. J217; cat leaves house when report is made of d. of one of his companions *B342; charitable man's d. postponed Q151.1; city inaccessible to d. F767.3; condemnation because of d. without confession V22; conversion to Christianity on pain of d. V331.2; creator's d. A76; cumulative tales involving a d.: animal actors Z31; daughter of king of d. E121.1.3.1; deception by feigned d. *K1860ff.; disappearance or d. of giants F531.6.12; discontented ass longs for d. but changes his mind when he sees skins of dead asses at fair J217.2; disguise as angel of d. K1828.1.1; dog caresses sick sheep: shepherd knows that he hopes for sheep's d. K2061.3; dogs howling indicate d. B733.2; escape from d. or danger by deception *K500ff.; extraordinary d. F901, F1041.1, (of animal) F981ff.; extraordinary phenomena at d. *F960.2; extraordinary three-fold d. F901; evil spirits exorcised by saint's d. D2176.3.3.0.1; fairies dance youth to d. F302.3.4.2; faithfulness to marriage in d. *T211ff.; fanciful behavior of animal at d. B752; flogging to d. as punishment Q458.2; foolish demands before d. J2174; god of d. A487; god of d. replaced in forged letter K1851.1; god's kiss causes painless d. A185.6.1.1; grieving to d. over childrens' fate after death J2063.1; Hercules fights with D. R185; hosts refrain from telling guest of d. in household P323; humiliating d. as punishment Q499.2; husband sends d. message after sleeping with disguised wife K1843.2.1; if he does not live, d. may have him J1513.1; illusion of d. K1884; immortality from bargain with d. D1851.2; inviting only those never touched by d. J1577.1; judge's temper leads to unjust d. sentence W185.5; kernel tries to escape d. J1875.1; kinds of d. produced by magic D2061.1; king grows lean from fear of d. U241; learning what d. is H1376.1; learning fear of d. H1376.2.1, J27; magic object (causes d.) D1402ff., (saves owner from d.) D1392; (disappears at owner's d.) D867, (warns of d.) D1322; magic power of seeing D. at head or foot of bed D1825.3.1; magic power from D. *D1724; magic power to see d. circumstances D1825.5; man converted to belief in future life on d.-bed V311.1; man longing for d. changes mind when Death appears J217.0.1.1; man promises child in order to save himself from d. S222; man's spirit prophesies own d. E489.4; message of d. K978.1, (fatal to sender) K1612; messenger of d. imprisoned R6; moon's phases caused by watchers' d. A755.2; Moses' staff has eaten after its d. (riddle) H824; murdered boy still sings "Ave" after d. V254.7; mysterious d. as punishment Q558, (remitted) Q574; mysterious voice announces d. of Pan F442.1; no mortal escapes d. E361.3; no time, no birth, no. d. in otherworld F172; nobleman after d. must serve as menial Q482.3; numskull catches buffalo by rope and is dragged to d. J2132.1; numskull laughs at his child's d. J2461.3; numskull thinks the bishop's snoring is his d. rattle J1833; object sought brings quest assigner's d. H1248; ogre gives riddle on pain of d. G681; ogre stoned to d. G512.2; old man and D. C11; one man prays either to keep friend from d. or for both to die E165.1; origin of d. A1335; origin of the d. chant A1543.1; originator of d. first sufferer K1681; otherworld journey after d. F6; persons magically caused to dance selves to d. *D2061.1.2; promises connected with d. M250ff.; prophecy: immunity from certain types of d. M367; quest: learning what fear of d. is H1376.2.1; riddle propounded on pain of d. H541.1; roof taken off above sick man that d. may come E722.2.3; saint sanctifies against d. D2176.0.1; sea ghost predicting d. E271.2; sham physician cures people by threatening them with d. K1955.1; singing at approach of d. J2461.1.2.4; slave recommended as immune to d. J1455; slaying king's son to prevent father's d. H1162.2; soul leaves body at d. E722; souls wander after d. E750.1; staff of life and d. E64.1.1; storm at d. of (wizard) D2141.0.4, (wicked person) D2141.0.5; strong man evades d. F615ff.; suitor task: avenging bride's father's d. before marriage H335.1; suitor's sincerity tested by reporting girl's d. H314.1; sun darkened at d. of holy person F965.2; sun does not rise after d. of hero F965.2.1; sun shines day and night after holy d. F961.1.5.1; supernatural manifestations at d. of pious person Q147; swan saves self by singing d. song N651; sword of Angel of D. F833.11; tasks imposed on pain of d. H901; test of d. H248; test of friendship: to go with one to d. H1558.3; tidal wave marks person's d. place A913.1; time of d. postponed D1855ff.; transformation to escape d. D642.2; two persons informed of each other's d. K2142; uncharitable pope wanders after d. V425; understanding of d. from watching animals at prey J52.1; Virgin Mary prevents (retards) d. so as to save sinner's soul V251; vow not to flee in fear of d. M161; wandering after d. as punishment Q503; wands of life and d. D1663.1; water of life and d. *E82; white rose the symbol of d. Z142.1; why men no longer know time of d. A1593; wicked flatter d. J814.4; wife dies so that husband's d. may be postponed T211.1; wife threatens husband with d. if he will not tell secrets T252.3; wild huntsman wanders (because of unshriven d.) *E501.3.4, (because he wished to continue hunting after d.) E501.3.7;

willingness to die for mate disappears at d. H1556.4.5; wise man humble in d. J912; witch causes animal d. G265.4.1; woman d. of all who behold her G264.1; woman dies on hearing of lover's d. T81.7; wraith announces d. E723.6; wraith tells of d. in family E723.4.5; youth saved from d. sentence R169.6.

Deaths come in threes D1273.1.1.3. — Choice of d. J216; mountain-man's six d. F460.2.12; riddle involving d. of elephant, snake, jackal H803; tragic d. on certain days of week N128.0.1.

Deathbed promise will be kept M251. — King prevented from d. disinheritance J1521.2.1.

Debate of animals as to which is the elder B841; of body and soul E727.1. — Listening to d. J1486; wise man beats heretic in d. K3.4.

Debating. — Escape by d. K622.1; senseless d. about usefulness J466; thief caught while d. theft J2136.5.1.1.

Debt confessed with cat's aid J1141.1.11; "if it is promised" P525.0.1. — Beheading as punishment for d. Q421.0.1; dead returns to repay money d. E351; deception in payment of d. K200ff.; debtor refuses to pay his d. *K231; dwarf conducts shepherd to hell to collect d. from nobleman F451.5.1.14; imaginary d. and payment J1551; lawyer tries to evade d. payment K1623; literal payment of d. (not real) K236; no return from dead until d. paid Q271.3; pretence of taking trip to return penny d. K2054.1; three thousand-year old d. J1384; wife demanded as d. payment T52.8.

Debts. — Christ has too many d. J2477; cutting wood burnt last year (paying old d.) H583.2.4; dead cannot rest until d. paid E415.4; notary invents d., collects them K441.2.1; paying unowed d. to save reputation J221.3; retorts concerning d. J1380ff.

Debtor clerics punished Q499.5; punished *Q271; gives self away J1141.1.3. — Insolvent d. drawn through streets Q473.0.1; man behind the tree threatens his d. K1971.2.

Debtor's corpse flogged Q491.2; wife demanded as payment T52.8; wraith seeks creditor E723.4.3.

Debtors do not forgive J2495.2. — Death feigned to test d. H1558.5.

Decalogue. — Words of d. legible on both sides F883.1.3.

Decapitated. — Ghost laid by d. body *E446.3; hero resuscitates d. princess E149.2; ogre d. G512.1.2.

Decapitation to prevent ghost's return E431.7.2; of princess by ogre G335; of victim by bloodhounds B17.1.2.1. — Beautification by d. and replacement of head *D1865.1; disenchantment by d. D711ff.; resuscitation by d. *E12; transformation by d. D566.4.

Decay. — Fish resist d. for year F986.4; magic d. of persons D2061.1.4; magic preservation from d. D2167ff.; reciting martyrology prevents body's d. V52.14; soul wanders until d. of corpse E722.3.2.

Decayed. — Earth from d. matter on primeval water A814.3.

Decaying. — Punishment: body not d. after death Q559.7.

Deceitful person's brains as cure D1515.4.6. — Why women are d. A1372.5.

Deceived. — Changeling d. into betraying his age F321.1.1; ghost d. E432; ogre d. into self-injury *G520ff.; ogre d. into releasing prisoner G560ff.

Deceiver falls into own trap *K1600—K1699. — To be beaten by d. of husband J1182.1; cynic and d. J1442.10; serpent as d. in paradise B176.1.1.

Deceiving. — Demons assume human form for d. F402.1.4; girls keep up appearances for d. suitors K1984; hireling d. master J1114.1; moon d. sun A753.3.1; prophecy: man d. many women M345.2; queen d. husband as revenge K2213.14; repeated transformations for d. wives D616; vow against d. benefactor M168.1; wife not d. husband for man she loves T211.8.

Deception K (entire chapter); by disguise or illusion K1800—K1899; punished *Q260ff., Q451.11.1; revealed in dream D1819.2. — Boy's d. of uncle and climbing tree X905.4.1; self-d. of the lowly J953.

Deceptive nocturnal noises K1887.2. — Repaying d. loan J1556; why animals are d. A2525; appearances d. U110ff.

Decision of lawsuit by child's wisdom J123; left to first person to arrive M92; made by contest H217. — Clever judicial d. J1170ff.; deity changes d. A196.2.1; senseless judicial d. M1.

Decisiveness of conduct J1040ff.

Decoration of house as wife test H473.5. — Origin of tribal d. A1687; stars hung as d. in heavens A763.2.

Decorative. — Origin of d. art A1465.

Decorators. — Thieves disguised as interior d. K311.7.

Decoy. — Capture by d. G514.7, K750ff.; magic objects as d. for pursuer D672.1; transformation to deer d. D643.2.

Decreasing. — Increasing-d. paradox task H1075.

Decree of gods irrevocable A196.2. — Child exposed to avoid death d. S329.1; favorable d. as reward Q116.

Decrees and judgments *M0—M99.

Deduction. — Extraordinary powers of d. H505.

Deductions, clever J1661.

Deed. — Only good d. unintentional V512.2; promise kept in d., not spirit M205.0.1; reward fitting to d. Q101.

Deeds of brownies F482.5; of the devil G303.9ff.; of dragons B11.6ff.; of evil spirits F402.1; of familiar spirits F403.2.3; of the gods A170ff.; of pygmies F535.5; rewarded *Q10—Q99; of vampires E251.3. — Evil d. of witches G260ff.; fairy minstrel lives among mortals to learn of their heroic d. F393.1; magic results from good d. D1799.6; magic reward for good d. D855.5; one wrong and five hundred good d. J1605; saint gives credit for good d. to another man Q42.8.

Deep. — Angel of the d. A421.0.1; extremely d. water F713.2.1; riddle: how d. is (the sea) H681.4, (the earth) H681.2; why hare's eyes are set d. A2332.4.1; why some fish swim d., others shallow A2238.3, A2444.1; wife shows husband d. water J1545.9.

Deepest. — What is d.? H643; wren goes d. into earth K17.1.1.

Deer aids man J461.4; becomes woman D314.1.3; belled and enclosed J1904.2.2; with candles atop antlers B253.6; captured in bird-net, water flows upstream J1534; as confederate of adulterous wife B598.2; with cross between horns B253.5; foster parent resuscitated E138.1; furnish bier and bear saint's corpse to church B256.3.1; with giant antler B15.3.3; with gold and silver horn B15.3.2; of gold and jewels possessing life D1620.2.3; hitched to wagon B558.4; in human form B651.6; lick saint's tomb daily B251.2.6; lures victim into demon's cave K714.7; lost through premature celebration J2173.4; in net freed by animals B545.1; offers herself instead of captured mate T211.1.4; paramour B611.5; with pearls around neck B105.2; persuaded to butt head into tree *K1058; pursued in wild hunt E501.5.5.2; steps on kitten (cumulative tale) Z49.6; summoned by singing D2074.1.1.2; thief keeps counting pieces J2136.5.3; thought to be man J1762.4; transformed to object D421.5; in Valhalla fills fountain A661.1.0.4. — Air-castle: to sell hide of sleeping d. J2061.3; brother transforms self to d. D647.1; capturing d. from herd watched by giant H1154.2; child of mortal and d. B635.3; color of d. A2411.1.6.5; crow, rat release d. from snare K642.1; destructive d. B16.2.7; devil as d. G303.3.3.2.8; dog's horns stolen by d. A2326.2.2; dragon as modified d. B11.2.1.10; enchanted d. reveals cave entrance D1552.9; enmity between d. (and leopard) A2494.2.4, (and terrapin) A2494.12.7; fairies have herds of d. F241.5; fancifully colored d. B731.7; first d. in Ireland A1875.0.1; friendship between d. (and tiger) A2493.17, (and fish) A2493.5; fruit tree grows from d. shot with fruit pits X1130.2; ghost as d. E423.2.6; girl transformed to d. D114.1.1.1; golden d. B102.5, (entices away guardians) K341.7.3; gold-making d. B103.1.4; helpful d. B443.1; hero licked by d. mother B635.3.1; hero son of d. A511.1.8.1; horns of d. as saint's bookholder B256.3; jackal persuades d. to steal K2037; journey on magic flying d. D1620.2.3.1; killing d. tabu C841.8; king of d. B241.2.10; lie about d. bag X1119.2; magic charm binds d. D1411.4; magic d. B184.4; man becomes d. and marries d. B648; man carried by d. B557.3; man transformed to d. D114.1.1; marriage to d. B601.10, (in human form) B651.5; marriage to man in d. form B641.2.1; marriage to woman in d. form B641.2; obstacle race between d., hare K11.9; origin of d. A1875; rain-withholding d. B192.2; reincarnation as d. E612.5; Satan disguised as d. K1823.5; Satan liberates caught d. G303.9.9.21; soul as d. E731.14; soul in d. E715.4.1; story told about d.: fool starts chase J1849.1.1; three-horned d. B15.3.1.1; trained d. drinks wine till he breaks his leg but thereafter abstains J133.3; transformation to d. (decoy)

D643.2, (which is devoured by dogs) Q415.1.1; treasure-d. B105.2; truth-telling d. B136; white markings on d. A2412.1.1; why d. has antlers A2326.1.1.1; why d. has white mark on nose A2335.2.1; why d. run, stop, and run on again A2461.4; why d. scent people from distance A2475.1; why d. tail tastes like liver A2378.9.4; witch as d. G211.2.4; witches drive herds of d. G249.1; woman begs hero for mercy for d. W133.2; woman flays running d. F664.1.1; woman's scented hair attracts d. T257.5.1; wrestling between porcupine, d. K12.5.

Deer's. — Monkey borrows d. tail A2241.11; Rakshasa in d. head swallows men G369.1.6; resuscitation by wax from d. ear E115.

Deer-heads. — Wild huntsmen with d. E501.7.2.

Defeat in battle P555, (as sign of world's end) A1084; personified Z132.2. — Clever person's d. pleases inferior J885; granary now haunted because of devil's d. G303.15.2; lance foretells owner's d. D1311.17.3; princess offered to man who can d. her in repartee H507.1; transformation to d. enemies D651ff.; trickster pretends d.: enemy attacked at ceremony K2366.1.

Defeated, see also **Conquered;** enemy turns friend P310.5; giant gives daughter to victor G510.1. — Enemy d. by storm D2141.2; enemies d. by magic object D1400.1ff.; ogre d. *G500—G599; witch d. G275ff.

Defeating a certain old woman (task) H1149.3; enemies as suitor task H335.4; or ridding oneself of fairies F380ff. — Disenchantment by d. enchanter in single combat D763.2.

Defecating. — Captor d. on smaller animal K683; child d. over ant hole K1461.2; crow d. on king L410.3; escape by d. ruse K551.16; tabu: d. while carrying divine image C56.1.

Defects. — Magic cure of physical d. *D2161.3; origin of physical d. A1338.

Defendant. — Riddle assigned d. in suit H542.1.

Defendants. — Animals as d. in court B272.

Defence against ghosts and the dead E430ff.; when one needs it most J673. — Animal's means of d. A2461ff.; eunuch's d. J1471; man killed in d. of sweetheart's honor T326.2; robber's d. for stealing from rich J1269.8; self-d. against many ships, men H1199.8; trumpeter's false d. J1465.

Defences. — Forethought in d. against others J670ff.; logically absurd d. J2233.

Defiling. — Fairies d. waters F369.2.

Deflowering. — King d. all twelve year old girls T161.0.1.

Deformed child exposed S325.0.1; child as hero L112.3; villain K2270ff. — Disguise as d. men to secure entertainment K1818.4; father kills d. children S11.3.2; man with d. head slays barbers K974; prophecy: unborn child to be d. M355; sight of d. witches causes man to release wife from spinning duty J51; three d. witches invited to wedding in exchange for help *M233; three witches d. from much spinning *G201.1; wealthy girl marries d. philosopher T121.5; woman deserts husband for d. lover T232.

Deformity cured by waves of sea F959.2.1; as punishment Q551.8. — Curse of d. M442; magic poem causes d. D1403.1.1; person cured by repairing image that has same d. D2161.4.4; reproach of physical d. punished Q284; witch causes d. G269.11; woman takes on lover's d T24.4.

Defying. — Flying Dutchman sails because of d. storm E511.1.3; seaman d. God shipwrecked Q221.4.

Degraded gods become angels A52.0.2.

Deification as reward Q172.9.

Deity, see also **Divinity, God;** *A100ff.; abducts person R14; aids quest H1233.5; bestows immortality D1851.5; creates valleys from mountains F756.2.2; creates magic objects D803; cursed M414.13; in disguise tests saint H1573.2.2; forces dwarfs to flee F451.9.1.14; in frightening guises H1401; as ghostly rider E332.3.3.2; gives advice in dream J157.0.1; gives hero great powers L103; gives persecuted child flock of sheep S464; has power of self-transformation D630.4; as helper N817; humbled L410ff.; induces magic sleep D1964.6; makes king, wronged subjects change places Q7; orders islands created A955.0.1; performs tasks H975; rears abandoned child S353.1; rescues child R131.11.4; rewards animal for bringing him water A2221.11; saves person to be sacrificed S255; sends woman to tempt anchorite T332.1; settles disputes between races M4; transformed to jackal D113.4.1. — Animal characteristics established by d. A2286ff.; animals from parts of body of d. or saint A1725; attacking d. tabu C62; child of d. visits earth F31; cure by d. D2161.5.3; curse by disguised d. M411.21; disguise as d. K1828; insect points out d. by settling where he is H162.1; journey to see d. *F12; lightning produced by d. A1141.6; magic power from d. D1726; magic results produced in name of d. D1766.7.1; magic stolen from d. D861.0.1; mortal in guise of d D43; night from d. wrapping self in dark mantle A1174.4; plants from clothing of d. A2625; quest of a d. H1266; quest to see d. H1289.4; recognition of d. H45; sacrifice to d. V11.9; sham d. K1969.4; tabu to look at d. C311.1.8; tabu: neglect of service to d. C57ff.; tasks set by d. H927; topographical features caused by experiences of d. A901; woman rejects d. for human lover T75.0.2.

Deity's name breaks witch's spell G271.2.3. — Bird carries d. daughter A2223.2; moon under d. control A759.6; resuscitation by writing d. name E75.

Deities push sun at solstices A1157; test king H1574.3.0.2.

Delay. — Dying lawyer asks d. X315.1; long d. in punishing nobleman U34.1; magic object causes d. of pursuit *D1611ff.

Delaying birth until auspicious day T589.8. — Lover d. gift K1581.7.1; warrior refuses bribe for d. battle W33.2.

Deliberation, wisdom of J570ff.

Delicate girl lives only on perfume F647.12.

Deliverer in cradle D791.1.3; of curse M411. — Prophecy: child to become nation's d. M311.5.

Deliverer's. — Disenchantment by covering with d. clothing D789.1.

Delivery, see also **Birth, Childbirth;** boy frightened into giving up chickens K335.0.9.

Deluge, see **Flood.**

Demands of pregnant woman C152.2, T571. — Agreeing to d. while in danger J625; excessive d. to prevent marriage H301; impossible d. rebuked J1512; haughty mistress makes extravagant d. of lover L431.1; king's d. on guests P337; prudence in d. J530ff.

Demi-coq *B171ff., K481.

Demigod of underworld A305. — Luck determined by crooked-necked d. N125.2; topographical features caused by experiences of d. A901.

Demigods and culture heroes A500—A599; transform things at will so that they assume present form D683.1.

Demijohn. — Ghost rides d. E581.6.

Democratic. — Prince of d. tastes chosen J412.1.

Demon aids quest H1233.4.4; allowed on earth four times a year A106.2.1.2; becomes animal D102.1; becomes larger D486.1; cats infest castle F771.4.2.1; of consumption F493.1.1; drinks river dry J1791.3.2.1; eats sand in otherworld F171.8; enclosed in bottle *D2177.1, (released) R181; enters person and refuses to leave until wishes have been fulfilled K2385; as familiar spirit F403.2.2.5; frightened by own reflection K1715.1.3; gives self-transformation power D630.1.1; as guardian of treasure N571; guide to otherworld F159.4; lover F471.2.0.1; mistaken for goat J1769.3; -owned cows H1364; steals rescued woman R111.8.1; terrorized by small hero's bluff K1715.7. — Abduction by d. R11.2.2; being eaten by d. as punishment Q415.0.1; cannibal d. G11.15; corpse of d. turns to worm H47; eating food of d. forbidden C242; devastating d. kills and eats people G346.2; fury as d. entering man's heart Z123.1; house haunted by d. H1411.4; impregnation by d. T539.3; magic cloth pacifies d. D1409.2; magic herb keeps off d. lover D1386.2; magic knowledge of d. language D1815.3; magic power from d. D1721.1.2; magic strength from d. D1835.6; mortal as d. D47.1; nun eating unblessed lettuce eats d. G303.16.2.3.4; placenta becomes a d. T584.6; princess's loathsome disguise to avoid d.-lover T327.6; resuscitation by d. E121.6, (entering corpse) E121.6.1; soul carried off by d. E752.2; thief disguised as d. K311.5; transformation: d. (in human form) to worm D192.0.1; transformation: man to d. (spectre) D95; witches worship d. G243.4; woman gives birth to d. T556.

Demon's members cut off to prove killing H105.5. — Bone in d. stomach becomes a boy E149.1; resuscitation according to d. instructions E181.2.

Demons, see also **Spirits;** F402, *G302; on animal feet F401.3.0.1; assume human form for revenge D651.1.2; battle: hills torn up A964.3; bribe trickster to leave their skins K1715.9; burn heretics at stake Q414.0.8; carry off king's soul F402.1.5.1; cause fog D1361.1.0.4; change size D631.4.3; guard marvelous garden F818.2; haunt castle F771.4.5; imprisoned by magic D2177.1.1; plague souls in hell E752.1.2.1; powerless over souls commended to God before sleep E754.1.1.1; propose hide and seek game to kill hero K869.2; set world on fire A1031.3; sleep twelve years F564.3.6; spread pestilence F493.4; in stone images exorcised D2176.3.3.1; as watchmen of the gods A165.4.1. — Death from fear of d. F1041.1.11.2; disenchantment by winning contest with d. D785.1; dream d. F471; drunken man left to temple d. K776.2; earth from saint's grave expels d. D1385.1; evil d. possess gamblers N1.0.1; foolish attempt of second man to overhear secrets from d. *N471; four d. in ring aid task H973.2; holy water disperses d. V132.2, D1385.15.1; invulnerability from d. D1841.9; journey to land of d. F124; Lucifer appointed chief for d. A1187; magic bell disperses d. D1385.12; magic left by frightened d. D859.7; magic sinks d. D1400.1.23.1; magic from temple d. D812.5.1; saint wrests soul from d. E756.4; slander: woman possessed of d. K2125; whomsoever d. curse is blessed M493.

Demonic. — Ground swallows d. wasp F949.1.1; madness from d. possession D2065.1.

Den. — Animal lured into lion's d. K714.6; fox sees all tracks going into lion's d. but none coming out J644.1; imprisonment in lion's d. R45.2; man unharmed in d. of animals B848.

Denial. — Devil tempts youth into d. of Virgin G303.9.4.8.

Dentist duped to pull out two teeth for one J2213.7.

Deo volente J151.4.

Departed, see also **Dead;** race A1401. — Girl masks as doctor to find d. lover K1825.1.4; gray hair the symbol of d. usefulness Z155; the Lord has d. (reports numskull on Palm Sunday) J1823.1.3.

Departing animal counsels man J135; house F1063; husband assigns his wife tasks H922. — Castle stands when all else d. F771.10; fairies d. F388; secret remedy revealed by d. animal N452.2; task left by d. husband for wife to accomplish H1187.

Departure of gods A192.2ff.; of wild hunt forced E501.17.8. — Culture hero's d. A560ff.

Dependence on self J1030ff.

Dependent. — Dwarf makes return of child d. upon guessing of riddle F451.5.15.2; life d. on external object or event *E765; one person's life d. on another's E765.5; strength of witches d. on their touching earth G221.2; why limbs d. on body A1391.1.

Deposed. — Gods d. for a time A173; father d. by son P236.4.

Depositors. — Three joint d. may have their money back when all demand it J1161.1.

Deposits. — Unjust banker deceived into delivering d. K1667.

Dervish as helper N844; who stops work shown his mistake J702.1. — Advice from d. J152.2.

Descendant. — Mule as d. of king's war-horse J954.1; refusal to eat fifth d. of stolen cow F647.10.

Descendants. — Curse: d. of nine robbers never to exceed nine M461; curse: d. not to multiply M461.1; curse: d. to be unshapely M442.1; fairies as d. of early race of gods F251.1; man meets his future d. F1099.8; man's d. shall serve brother's P251.5.6; prophecy: preeminence of man's d. M310.1.1; royal d. as reward Q112.0.7; sacrifice so d. may be kings W215.3; tribe d. of one woman survivor A1006.7.

Descending. — Demigods d. from heaven A513.1; god d. from heaven A171.0.3; god awaits spirits d. to hell A317.

Descent of chimney by fairies F275; of first man to earth A1230ff.; to lower world of dead *F81; of man from animals A1224; of star as human being A762; from tree impossible D1413.1. — Animal d. slander K2115.1; extraordinary d. into ocean F1022; shooting stars' d. to earth A788.

Description. — Love from d. T11.1; recognition by d. of object H16.

Desecrated altar bleeds F991.4.1; well overflows F933.6.1.

Desecration of God's name tabu C51.3.1. — Dwarfs emigrate because of d. of holy day F451.9.1.11; punishment for d. of holy places *Q222; transformation of lovers into lion and lioness because of d. of temple Q551.3.1.

Desecrator. — Church d. cannot rest in grave E412.6.

Desert demons' abode G302.5.1. — Abandonment in d. S144; cultivated places become d. F969.5; fire pillar protects in d. D1380.1.1; following luminous tree in d. K1886.1.1; miracles in d. cease F900.3.1; monk goes into d. to avoid women T334.1; origin of d. A957; river at d. travelers' prayer D2151.2.5.1; treachery punished by banishment to d. isle Q431.2.2; wild hunt appears at d. spot E501.12.7.

Deserts. — Angel of the d. A419.2.1.

Deserted city F766ff.; daughter's good fortune discovered by accident N732.2; wife chokes departing husband K951.0.1. — Adopted child d. when own child born T674; maiden disenchanted, d., and refound D795; man d. by fairy mistress F302.2.1, F302.3.4.3; objects found in d. castle H1239.2; poor boy finds treasure in d. city N534.5; unseen hands serve in d. castle H1239.2.

Deserting. — Lover d. woman K2232.1; man d. wife for fairy F302.5.0.1; punishment for d. fairy mistress Q247; soldiers d. to enemy king K2365.3; vow on d. wife on wedding day M149.4.

Designated. — Favorite for election to office d. by Virgin Mary V261; pope d. by sound of bell D1311.12.1.

Designs. — Origin of d. on cloth A1465.3.2.

Desire, see also **Sex;** for adultery punished Q241.1. — Chaste sleeping with girl to signify d. T356; choice between d., duty J233; conception after reciprocal d. T514; punishment for d. to murder Q211.8; sexual d. induced by magic D1355, D1900; what women most d. (quest) H1388.1.

Desires, see also **Wishes.** — Cow grants all d. B184.2.1.3; sea yields people's d. F931.9.2; telling story to allay woman's d. K2111.0.1.

Despair. — Fool kills himself in d. because a sparrow has taken one grain from his field J2518.1; man in d. digging his own grave finds treasure N545.

Dessert. — Countryman's ignorance of d. J1742.3.1; maid forced to whistle as she brings in d. W152.12.3.

Destination of emigrating dwarfs F451.9.2; of the soul E755ff. — Angels mark saint's d. V238.3.

Destined hero Z254. — Treasure opens itself for d. hero N552.1.

Destiny better than work, show, or speculation N142. — Deity ascertains baby's d. A189.7; fairies control mortal's d. F312.2; fates allot d. A463.1.2; giant as clerk to God of D. N111.5; prophecies concerning country's d. M356; stone of d. H171.5.

Destitute parents abandon children S321.

Destroyed. — Contract with the devil d. M218; criminal's property d. Q486; druid d. by saint's power V229.6.3; dupe's property d. K1400—K1499; fairy queen's beauty temporarily d. by intercourse with mortal F304.2; home of dwarfs is endangered or d. F451.4.4ff.; magic object d. D866; treacherous priests prolong mass while city is d. K2354.

Destroying festivity purchases by mistake J1846. — Disenchantment by d. covering of enchanted person D720ff., (by d. enchanter) D763, (by d. skin) D721.3; dungbeetle keeps d. eagles' eggs L315.7; numskull d. own property J2461.1.8; objects' attempt at d. humanity A1009.2; philosopher stops king from d. city J1289.10; tabu: d. animal skin of enchanted person too soon *C757.1.

Destruction of an alp F471.1.2.2; by devil at night of what is built by day G303.14.1; of enemy's weapons J621; of fish and nets by strong man as fisherman F614.5; of friendship by marriage T201; of hunting party by devil with terrible wind G303.20.2; of mortal's work by dwarfs F451.5.2.5; of obstacles by magic staff D1562.1; of plants by strong man as gardener F614.3; of property as punishment Q595. — Angel of d. A521.5; curse of d. on city Q556.0.2; fitting d. of property as punishment Q585; god of d. A488; hospitality of a citizen saves a city from d. Q152.1; reward: being saved from d. of city Q150.1.1; upon d. of pestilence-spirit plague ceases F493.3.1; transformation by d. of enemy's property D651.3.

Destructive fairy drink F367; magic object tried out on inanimate object K525.8; magic powers *D2050—D2099.

Details. — Fool admits crime but pleads mistakes in d. of accusation J2499.3; quarrel and fight over d. of air-castles J2060.1; witness discredited by inability to tell d. J1154.

Detaining. — Forgotten fiancée reawakens husband's memory by d. lovers through magic D2006.1.1; ghosts d. wandering soul E721.4.

Detected. — Criminal d. by having child hand knife to him H211; devil d. by his hoofs G303.4.5.3.1; devil, d., goes up chimney in smoke G303.17.2.1; ghost d. E436; poison d. by magic object *D1317.0.1; thief d. *K420ff., (by psalter and key) H251.3.2, (by sieve and shears) H251.3.3.

Detection of hypocrisy K2060ff.; of perjury by magic spring H251.3.9; through ruse J1141.11; and wounding of wife's lover by broken glass K1565. — Cleverness in d. of truth J1140ff.; magic d. of crime *D1817ff.; thief escapes d. *K400ff.; transformation to escape d. D671.0.2.

Detective. — Thief believes d. is mind-reader J1141.1.9.

Determination of luck or fate N120ff.; of the months A1160f.; of night and day A1172; of seasons A1150ff.; of span of life A1320ff.; of world center A1181; of world quarters A1182.

Determined. — King's successor d. by questions asked H508.1; reincarnation in form d. at death E602.

Dethronement. — Prophecy: king's d. by grandson M311.1.

Detonation hurls ships out to sea F1078. — Wild hunt heralded by d. E501.13.1.1.

Devas. — Riddle about king of D. H827.

Devastating animals B16, G350.1, *H1362; monster G346, H1471; swine sent by demon B16.1.4. — Adulteress returns from dead as d. dragon E263; bolt from heaven kills d. animal F981.4; fairies as d. animals kill flocks F366.3; fairies exile d. host F349.3; hero overcomes d. animal G510.4; magic object d. country D1408; vow against d. country M168.

Device. — Noblemen quarrel over a d. J552.1.

Devil (Satan) *G303ff. See, in addition to the following, the extensive list of motifs assembled at G303. — Devil and the ark *G303.23f., *K485; betrays self to woman paramour D1386.2.1; broods over woman A1371.4; chases ghost into chapel R325.1; claims debtor when inscription rots K231.12.1; comes to rendezvous instead of lover K1317.10; decides to leave possessed man of his own accord J829.2; drops stones A977.3; exorcised by "Ave" V254.4; finishes stones D2066.1; in form of dragon B11.1.4; gets shadow instead of man F1038.2; gives smith lantern to light way between heaven and hell A2817.1; gives wishing power D1720.1.1; gives witch familiar G225.0.2; and God torment each other A63.4.1; goes to confession V29.8; hidden in cup of liquor B483.0.1; as husband eats corpses G20.1; impersonates woman's maid at toilette Q331.2.1.1; knows how far it is from heaven to earth for he has fallen this distance H682.1.10; prophesies in enchanted castle H1411.3; runs hands through hair, coins fall D1454.1.1.1; says that his deeds are strong even if not fair J246.1; in serpent form tempts first woman (Satan and Eve) A63.6; sows stones A975.1; substitutes himself for new-born child T684; as suitor assigned tasks H335.0.3; as suitor must build bridge, dam H1131.2; takes man waiting for water to become wine D477.1.1; throws stones A977.2; transformed to animal D102; turns object to stone A977.4; "won't take me" Q333.1. — Allegorical game of witch, d., maiden, church Z178; baker and d. walking together P442.1; banished d. appears at dark of moon A106.2.1.1; bargain with d. *M210; combat between Thundergod and d. A162.3; creation of mouse by d. in ark A1853.1; dead priest saves gambler from d. E341.5; dog lets d. into church to steal: rewarded with dog-skin A2229.2; eavesdropping man in disguise as d. killed unwittingly by daughter's lover N322.1; fasting against the d. P623.0.2; formula-tale saves girl from d. K555.2.1; girl refuses to dance with d. until well dressed K1227.3.1; gnats created by. d. to worry God A2033.0.1; god cheats d. at mowing K42.2.1; god plagues d. with fleas A2032.4; hermit deceived by the d. kills his own father K943; journey to hell to recover contract from d. F81.2; lakes made by d. A920.1.10; liar escapes from d. H1318; magic circle protects from d. D1381.11; magic journey: man carried by d. D2121.5; magic object recovered with help of d. D885; man sells soul to d. *M211; man thought to be d. J1786; marriage ring protects from d. D1385.3; monk leaves monastery after seeing d. there; sees scores of them in world U230.0.1; naked lover as d. in sooty barrel K1555.2; owner frightened away by thief disguised as d. K335.0.12; payment of money to the d. refused, since debtor hears that the d. is now dead K231.4; punishment for yielding to temptation by d. Q233; putting the d. in hell: seduction trick K1363.1; quest to d. for riddle answer H1278; revolting d. banished to hell A106.2.1; Robert the D. kills wet-nurses T614; saint binds d. with her hair D1831.1; soul carried off by d. E752.2; suitors as corpse, angel, and d.K1218.4; tabu: offending d. C45; thief disguised as d. K335.0.12; thief masked as d. bought off by owner K152; three-night watch over grave to guard man from d. H1463; Virgin forbids d. to take robber saying "Aves" V254.8; Virgin Mary rescues man attacked by d. V264; Virgin Mary substitutes for woman whom husband has pledged to d. K1841.3; wheel buried in doorstep to prevent work of d. D1385.10; witch carried off by d. G275.1; witch struggles with d. G299.2; witches dance with d. G247.1; witches in league with d. G226; worship of d. V1.2.2.

Devil's cows one-horned A2286.2.3; footprint A972.2.2; likeness insulted, punishment C45; likeness kills beholder Q338.2. — Ghost of d. concubine E411.2.2; marks on fish from d. fingerprints A2217.3.2; vision of earth in d. snares V513.2.

Devils instead of angels visit woman who has forgotten God in her prosperity Q559.1; tormenting sinners in hell E755.2.7. — Creation of d. A63; foreigners' heads exchanged with d. A1610.1.1; holy men keep d. under control G315; indentions on rocks from footprints of d. A972.2; magic horseshoe keeps off d. D1385.9; man deceives, escapes d. K611.4; saint dispels pagan d. V356.1; seven d. wives attempt resuscitation ritual K113.0.1; youth who had never seen a woman: "the d." T371.

Devotions. — Stream becomes hot in which saint performs his ascetic d. F932.3.

Devoured. — Infant's flesh d. by maddened women N325.2; lover d. by Lamia G262.0.1.1; offspring d. by first parents A1277.1; whoever breaks devil's pact d. M219.4.

Devouring, see also **Cannibals.** — Cat d. flesh of man's legs B16.1.1.3; creator tries d. his son, the culture hero A71; dragon d. children B11.10.3; dogs d. souls in hell A689.8.1; eclipses caused by monster d. sun or moon A737,1; ghosts d. girl E251.3.1.1; giant d. people G11.2.1; mother d. her children when they grow up (ocean and rivers) H734; resuscitation of animals d. each other E32.2.

Devout. — Priest dreams all d. women in hell X438.1.

Dew of blood F962.4.2; in footprints reveals trail R268. — Absence of d. identifies woman-flower H63.1; Adam creates five devils by wetting five fingers with d. G303.1.5; celestial d. transforms D572.7; conception by drinking d. T512.7; cure by washing in d. D2161.4.14.3; filling pot with d. H1129.4; magic d. *D902.2; resuscitation by d. E80.4.1; snake sucks poisonous d. from grass B765.3; origin of d. A1132; sweet d. F962.7.1.

Dextrotsum circuit D1381.25.1, D1791.1.

Diabetes. — Rascals sew man's trousers leg till he thinks that he has d. J2317.1.

Diabolical, see also **Devil;** person never sleeps F564.1.

Diadem, magic D1079.2.

Diagnosis. — Extraordinary d. F956; imitation of d. by observation: ass's flesh J2412.4; patient laughs so at foolish d. that he gets well N641; physician killed for fatal d. P424.3; pretended d. entirely from urinalysis K1955.2.

Dialect. — Criminal confesses because of misunderstanding of d. N275.2; girl possessed by ghost speaks in unknown d. E725.2.

Dialects. — Parable on learning d. J98.

Diamond castle F771.1.5.1; charms serpents D1442.11; kingdom F707.3; in meat carried to eagle's nest N527.1; reveals underground palaces D1551.7.1; -toothed ogre G363.3; tree F811.1.8; works by being pressed D1662.3. — Clusters of d. and emerald grapes F813.2.1; dress of gold, silver, and d. bells F821.3; inscribed d. recalls lover T56.3; magic d. opens tank passage D1551.7; magic d. reveals palace D1557.3; mountain formed of d. F752.3.2; stealing d. from elephant's forehead H1151.6.1; unbreakable d. penetrates iron F826.3; witnesses make image of d. J1154.2; worthless glass sold as d. K142, K451.4.

Diana as leader of wild hunt E501.1.8.

Dice made from graveyard bones N1.2.2; split so saint wins soul E756.4.1. — Charm aids d. game D1407.4; defeating bride at d. H332.1.2.1; game won with loaded d. K92.2; girl plays d. with suitors K1237; magic d.

*D1284; man cheats god at d. A1893; soul in d. E711.12; throwing certain number on d. proves chastity H413.5.

Die. — Broken d. save man at gambling N1.2.1.

Dick Whittington M312.

Dieb, zögernder J2136.5.1.

Diet. — Origin of d. during confinement A1565; people of unusual d. F561ff.

Difference in animal natures overlooked J2211. — Counterquestion: d. between you and cushion H571.1; the d. between poor man and rich (riches) H875.

Different. — Birds of d. habits unfriendly J416.1; dog leader fears defeat because his forces are of d. breeds J1023; king in red: courtiers in d. colors (riddle) H731.3; porridge eaten in d. rooms J2167; transformation to d. (race) D30ff., (sex) *D10ff., (social class) D20ff.

Differentiation of peoples A1600—A1699.

Difficult. — Riddles of d. calculations H680—H719; transformation to reach d. place D641; transformation to escape d. situation D642; treatment of d. guests J1563ff.; why certain languages are d. A1616.1.

Difficulties. — Consider d. of course you are about to undertake J751.

"Dig here!" inscribed on (image with pointing finger) F855.1, (stone over treasure) N535.

Digger, mighty F639.1.

Digging child from ground T545; first wells A1429.3.1; forbidden *C523; magic object D848; a pond quickly (task) H1105; underground bed for Rhine F451.5.22; without hands X1725. — Angel aids d. for water V232.3.1; buried man d. self out X1731.2.1; disenchantment by d. D789.8; dupe dies of exhaustion from d. K1061; dwarfs d. for treasure F451.6.9; fairies d. for treasure F244.5; lakes from d. of primeval ox A920.1.2; man in despair d. his own grave finds treasure N545; murder discovered while d. house N271.7; numskull d. up a well J1933; rivers from d. of primeval ox A934.1; sky window from d. plant in upper world *F56.1; springs' origin: deity's d. A941.5.7; tabu: d. in churchyard C93.3; thieves d. field for gold K2316; treasure found while d. N534.7.

Dilating. — Sea-serpent d. and contracting B91.5.1.

Diminishing number of sacred days forbidden C58.1. — Goods magically d. D2089.7.

Dining. — Lie: great d. quarters X1032; sun, moon and wind d. with thunder, lightning A153.3.2.

Dinner with the dead (Festin de Pierre) E238. — Fairies' yearly d. to haymakers F343.17; prince preparing giant d. K567.1; why d. time comes soon in mountains J2276.1.

Diocletian. — Earthquake in palace of D. V222.9.

Dipping out sea with spoon (task) H1143; rod D1314.2; water without wetting dipper H1046.1. — Legitimacy of children tested by d. them in river H222.1.

Directed. — Blinded trickster d. by trees *D1313.4; fugitive d. but enemy misdirected by (tree) D1393.4, (crane) R246; hero d. on journey by princess J155.1; mortals d. to treasure by dwarfs F451.5.1.9.

Direction of river's flow magically reversed D2151.2.1. — Bird shows d. by singing B151.2.0.3; forbidden d. of travel C614.1ff.; hero in womb indicates d. for mother to take A511.1.2.2; looking in certain d. forbidden C330ff.; magic object obtained by reaching in certain cardinal d. D859.3; reed as d. finder D1313.5.2; saint's girdle causes tree to fall in right d. D1549.2; wild hunt courses in particular d. E501.14.2.

Directions for getting pay given in return for directions for healing J1551.4; on quest given by sun, moon, wind, and stars H1232. — Child promised to devil for d. out of woods when father is lost S226; "don't start from here" (d.) J1648; earth scattered in a circuit or in four d. on primeval water A814.6; formula: cardinal d. Z71.2.1; land of dead in one of the cardinal d. E481.6.

Dirk stuck into thigh in order to keep from sleeping H1482.

Dirt transformed to pepper D452.4.1. — Birds fill sea with d. A1028.2; magic d. protects D1380.9; man from d. mixed with creator's blood A1211.1; man from d. rubbed from creator's body A1211.5; "where did d. go when canal dug?" J1309.3.

Dirtiness punished *Q322.

Dirty boy as hero L112.4. — Numskulls' efforts not to get d. J2163.1; pretending pants are d. to steal them K344.3; riding d. on horse tabu C891.1; too d. to eat K553.6.

Disability. — Fairies' physical d. F254.1; humor of d. *X100—X199.

Disagreeable child surpasses likeable one L155; tasks set hero H931.2; youth favorite of Fortune N173.

Disappearance of devil G303.17; of fairy gift when tabu broken F348.0.1; of fairy house at dawn F221.1; of fairies when some name or ceremony of the Christian Church is used F382; of fairy in form of a cloud F234.3.1; of fish from sea as punishment for woman's having washed a child with a fish F931.2; of giants F531.6.12.1; of helpful animal when tabu is broken C935; of ill-gotten gains Q552.18; of person caused by magic object D1405; of phantom house at dawn F771.6; of supernatural wives T111.0.1; of trees at sunset F811.11; of treasure C401.3, D1555.3, N553.2, N557. — Appearance and d. of garment in reply to command D2188.1.1; extraordinary underground d. F940ff.; fitting d. of property as punishment Q585; magic d. D2095, *D2188; phenomena at d. of wild hunt E501.16ff.

Disappearing lake F934.4; otherworld island F134.2; sword F833.9. — Animal d. into lake F989.13; magic object d. D867; men d. every night D2087.4.

Disappointed lover becomes a wild man in the woods T93.1; lover induces magic sleep D1964.2. — Curse by d. witch *G269.5.

Disappointment with religious order V475.3. — Clerical vows after d. in love V472; prostitution after love d. T450.2.

Disar, worship of V1.2.3.

Disarming of officer by sentry J1526.1. — Escape by d. K630ff.; prevention of hostilities by d. suspect J626; victim lured into d. K818.

Disaster, see also **Calamity, Catastrophe;** because tabu broken C984; from following instructions J2465ff. — Caesar's scorn of his wife's advice leads to d. J155.3; devil appears to warn of impending d. to a house G303.6.2.6; immunity from d. as reward Q150ff.; presence of cursed person brings d. on land M491; wild hunt as omen of d. E501.20.1.

Disasters from fool's lack of forethought J2661.4. — National d. occur at same date N128.1.

Disbelief. — Tabu: d. in religious teachings C61.

Discarding, see **Disposal.**

Disciple stays in cheap-price country T342.1.1. — Body of devil's d. removed from coffin M219.2.5; greedy d. ignores warning, condemned as thief N347.7; judge becomes prophet's first d. J1169.8; master rescues d. R167; master tests d. by river plunge H1561.10.

Disciples. — Dying hero's promise to d. M257.1; wild animals as saint's d. B251.2.7.

Discomfiting. — Husband d. wife K1569.4; punishment escaped by d. condemner J1182; rivals d. each other T92.11.1.

Discomfiture, humor of *X0—X99.

Discomfort. — Magic d. *D2063; magic object protects from d. on journey D1384ff.

Discontent of pine-tree: cause of pine needles A2723.1. — Plant punished for d. A2723ff.

Discouragement. — Absurd extreme of d. J2518.

Discourtesy to God punished A2231.1ff., Q221.1; punished Q327; toward priest tabu C94.1.3. — Animals from men transformed for d. to God (Jesus) *A1715.2.

Discovered. — Devil d. by his hoofs G303.4.5.3.1; heroine in menial disguise d. in her beautiful clothes: recognition follows H151.6; treasure magically d. D2101; secret of strength treacherously d. *K975.

Discovery of abbot's (abbess's) incontinence brings permission to monks (nuns) to do likewise K1274; of devil by God G303.1.2ff.; of gold by saint's bachall *D1314.3; of new wonder before eating C287; of ring thief H1199.9.1; of treasure N530ff.; of treasure brings luck N135.2.1; of wife's adultery by husband K1550.1. — Accidental d. of crime N610ff.; lover's gift regained: accidental d. of identity K1581.4; magic d. of desired place D1816ff.

Discrediting. — Clever d. of testimony *J1151ff.

Discretion J500—J599.

Discussion by symbols H607ff. — Demons at academic d. G302.5.3; repartee based on doctrinal d. J1262ff.

Disdainful. — Devil marries d. girl G303.12.5.2; fleeing wolf d. of dog J953.5; man put in moon for d. sacrifice A751.1.3; speaking to king makes man d. of own family W165.1.

Disease, see also **Illness, Sickness;** healed as reward Q161.2; transferred to object D2161.4.2ff. — Bathing in "d.-water" K1077; cure by transferring d. to animal *D2161.4.1; cures by transferring d. to dead E595; death from d. for breaking tabu C929.2; death, return to life rids d. E598; demon causes d. F402.1.5; devil strikes dead with d. G303.20.4; fairies cause d. F362; foul d. for persecuting Christians Q570.1; god of d. A478; Leviathan's gorge spreads d. B16.4.1; magic control of d. D2162; magic cure for specific d. D2161.1; magic mouse causes d. B183.1.2; magic object controls d. *D1500ff.; origin of d. A1337; particular d. caused by breaking tabu C941; punishment: death from unknown d. Q551.6.0.2; relics of saint cure d. V221.0.1; remedies worse than the d. J2100ff.; sacrifice as protection against d. S276; spirits of d. F493.1; taking clerical vows heals d. V471; why d. created L482.5; woman prays for d. to repel lover T327.2.

Diseases to combat overpopulation P721; cured at particular time D2161.6.

Diseased child exposed S325. — Ascetic prays to become d. V462.5.0.1; queen's illicit passion for d. man T481.2.

Disenchanted. — Cannibal d. by overcoming it G33.1; enchanted heroine recognized when seen temporarily d. H151.6.1; person d. from animal retains tail H643; recognition of d. person by ornaments under his skin H61.2; transformed fairy warriors d. F383.5; transformed person d. upon admission to girl's bed K1361.1.

Disenchanting. — Fairy d. mortal wife F302.3.2.2; hero d. vanished wife R133.1; journey for d. captives H1385.0.1; treasure from d. N591.

Disenchantment D700—D799; for breaking tabu C968; by dwarfs F451.3.3.4; fails D791.3; by faithfulness of others D750ff.; by removing (destroying) covering of enchanted person D720ff.; by rough treatment D710ff.; by submission D730ff.; as task H1199.5; and transformation at will D630ff. — Marriage to prince as reward for his d. T67.1.

Disfavor. — Images at church turn backs as mark of d. D1639.3.

Disfiguration of perjurer by spring H251.3.9; for speaking falsely H244; by witch's kisses G264.2.

Disgorged, see also **Vomited.** — Animal's broken heart d. F981.6.1; swallowed person d. F914, F912.3.

Disgorging. — Cows d. rice K366.1.4; saintly babe d. unclean food V229.2.2.

Disgrace. — Fairies freed of d. by blood bath F259.2; foolish priest pushed into the water wishes he had drowned so that congregation would have been in d. J2185; "shame and d." C929.1.

Disgraceful journey through streets as punishment Q473.

Disguise as girl to avoid execution K514; as man to escape lover K1236;

as pilgrim to enter enemy's camp K2357.2. — Beggar in d. obtains alms three times from same person K1982; brother in d. aids quest H1233.2.2; capture by d. as dead *K751; confederate in d. helps escape K649.7; deception by d. *K1810ff.; deity in d. tests saint H1573.2.2; devil in d. hunts souls E752.1.1; examine strange country in d. J21.43; father feigning death returns in d. and seduces daughter T411.1.2; fairies in d. F237; guest in d. P322.2; herdsman in d. as abbot answers questions H561.2; heroine in menial d. discovered in her beautiful clothes H151.6; king in d. (to observe subjects) P14.19, (to learn subjects' secrets) N467; loathly husband god in d. D733.3; lover in d. abducts beloved K1371.4; man knowing of murder plot against his friend assumes d. and is killed in his place P316.1; princess's loathsome d. to avoid demon-lover T327.6; recognition through imperfect d. H151.6.2; scorned lover in d. as rich man cheats his scornful mistress L431.2; seduction by d. *K1310ff.; theft by d. as master of the house K362.4; thief's d. as woman K419.2; vanquished ruler in d. gets audience with victor J829.3; woman in d. (becomes pope) K1961.2.1, (overcomes enemies) K778.1.

Disguises. — Escape by successive d. K533; hero in successive d. rescues lady R169.1.

Disguised flayer dresses in skin of his victim K1941; hero attacks enemy at feast K913; hero's hair discovered H151.13; husband visits his wife K1813; god chosen as husband T111.1.1; king punished by peasant P15.1; king recognized by habitual speech H38.1; man recognized by dog H173; man steals back magic object D882.4; mistress identified by chalk marks left on back by lover H58.1; trickster beaten by man he is trying to frighten K1682; wife helps husband escape from prison R152.1; wife thwarts husband J1112.1.1. — Bull recognizes d. princess H162.3; capture by hiding in d. objects K753; Christ d. V211.2.1.1; combat of d. friends P314; father-in-law d. as beggar to test bride's kindness H384.1; devil in form of woman introduces men d. as women for seduction of impious nuns G303.3.1.12.1; fool d. as king, killed N338.2; husband tempted by wife d. in fine clothes T224; lover d. in humiliation K1214.1.1; man d. as woman enters princess's room K1343.2; owner frightened away by thief d. as devil K335.0.12; princess d. to flee man T323.1; one lover d. and carried out of house by other K1517.1.1; princess d. as man accused of adultery with queen K2113; recognition of d. princess by bee lighting on her H162; rescuer d. as officer saves prisoner K649.2; stolen animal d. as person so that thief may escape detection K406; trickster d. to escape notice of creditors K237; villain d. as ascetic or nun K2285; voice d. to lure victim G413; wise men d. as peasants J31.1.

Disgust. — Dumbness from d. F1041.19.

Disgusting. — Hero with d. habits L114.5; woman has d. lover T232.

Dish which husband detests and wife keeps serving him T255.5. — Deaf husband orders deaf wife to prepare certain d. X112; magic d. *D1172;

man transformed to d. D251; quest for best-cooked d. H1305.2; reincarnation as d. E633; silver d. becomes wooden D475.3.5; society like a d.: must be mixed J81.1; what is in the d. (poor Crab) N688.

Dishes become jewels D475.4.3; of the same flavor J81. — Bonga lends d. to mortals F343.6; numskull throws the d. out J1831; securing d. locked in vault H1199.15; trolls' d. golden F455.4.2.2.

Dishonesty W157ff.; habit can't be broken U138.

Dishonor. — Death preferred to d. *J227.2; fairies revenge for d. F361.9; seduction by threatening d. K1397.

Disinheriting. — King prevented from d. adopted son J1521.2.1.

Disintegration (man eats himself up or dismembers himself) F1035.

Disliked child surpasses likeable one L155. — Why animal is d. A2522ff.

Dislodge. — Recognition by unique ability to d. sword H31.1.

Dislodged. — Wild huntsman's dog cannot be d. from house it has entered E501.15.6.5.

Dismembered corpse E422.1.10. — Body d. so soul cannot return E721.1.2.3.1; bones of d. person assembled and buried V63; foes' corpses d. P555.2; perjurer d. by lion H251.1.1; slain person d. S139.2; tabu to look at d. woman C312.2.3.

Dismemberment before burial V61.4.2; of self F1035. — Rejuvenation by d. D1884, D1885.1, resuscitation by d. *E14.

Dismissal with a pittance after years of service W154.1; of mass early cheats devil of reward G303.16.16.

Dismounting from horse forbidden *C521; from magic sack tabu C521.1. — Do not cross bridge without d. from your horse J21.7; shortsightedness about d. J2171.6.

Disobedience *W126ff.; forbidden C31.3, C836; to God punished Q221.5, V245.1; of helpful animals injunctions brings disaster B341; punished *Q325. — Adam's d. blamed H1557.2; animal characteristics as punishment for d. A2234ff.; banishment because of d. Q431.3; burial alive as punishment for d. to king Q456.0.3; flogging as punishment for d. to rulers Q458.0.2; permanent sign of d. for breaking tabu *C910ff.; plant punished for d. A2722ff.; transformation for d. D517; vessels burst and reveal d. D1318.12.1.

Disobedient child burned S326.1; children cast forth S326; wife T254. — Dead mother appears and makes d. child eat fatal serpent Q593; teacher curses d. pupils P343.

Displaced. — Proud king d. by angel L411.

Display of murdered man's head before his own house S139.2.1. — Plain people become rulers, put on d. W116.3; woman's vain d. punished Q331.2.1.

Displaying self as punishment Q473.6. — Seduction by d. obscene likeness K1385.

Displeasure. — Transformation to show d. D659.3.

Disposal of cast-off wife S430ff.; of clothing before winter over unwise

J731; of changeling F321.1.4. — Reward for d. of purchased cobold F481.0.1.2.1; treacherous d. of true bride by false K1911.2.

Disposition of animals A2520ff. — Magic object changes person's d. D1350ff.

Dispute at creation of sun A716; won by wise men disguised as peasants J31.1. — Angel settles d. between saints V229.18; pagan in d. with Christian stricken dumb V352; saint's d. with devil G303.16.11.5; settling dowry d. J1678; unjust umpire decides a religious d. K451.1.

Disputes. — Deity settles d. between races M4.

Disregarding advice of your enemy J646; facts J1850—J1999. — Thunder slays those d. him Q552.1.0.2.

Disrespect to God brings death A1335.6.1; punished Q395; for the sacrament J1261.2.

Disrobing woman outwits robber K551.4.3. — Hero attacked by d. female's confederate K832.3; men d. report they have been attacked K1087.0.1; woman d. to attract enemy's attention Q411.4.2.

Dissatisfaction *W128ff.

Dissatisfied fir-tree finds its own needles best A2723.1; workmen exchange work U136.1. — Fairy d. with fairyland leaves to live among mortals F393.0.1.

Dissolute. — Devil in church fills his sack with d. songs G303.24.1.5.

Dissolving. — Ashes d. animals F981.5.

Distaff sticks to hand as punishment Q559.5.

Distance of otherworld F137. — Animal travels extraordinary d. B744; cooking rice, warming man at long d. J1191.7; devil kept at d. by answering his riddles H543.1; fairy mistrel's music heard at d. F262.3.3; false judgment of d. in mountains J2214.12; formula of d. Z92; giant steps prodigious d. F531.3.5; magic journey by making d. vanish D2121.4; ogress extends limbs any d. G365.2; person sees great d. F642.8; riddles of d. H680ff.

Distant. — Bringing documents from d. city in one day (task) H1107; bringing water from d. mountain more quickly than witch (task) H1109.1; fox in swollen river claims to be swimming to d. town J873; magic knowledge of events in d. place D1813ff.; magic power to see d. objects K1825.2; quest to d. sage for advice H1393.

Distilling learned from devil A1456; of sustenance for saint by magic lime tree D1472.1.3.1.

Distorted. — Punishment: face d. Q551.8.7.

Distracting. — Girl d. opponent, lover wins game K92.3; priest sells d. donkey J357.

Distress. — Alleged messenger from relatives in d. given goods J2326.4; don't lean on relatives in d. J21.44; friend helps friend in d. N455.8.

Distribution and differentiation of peoples A1600—A1699; of man's body by animals F989.10; of tribes A1620ff.; of wit by Hermes L301.

Distrusted. — God d. when he can be brought by a man J1261.2.2.

Disturbing of grave punished E235.6. — Devil d. churchgoers G303.24.1.7.1; wild huntsman wanders for d. church service E501.3.8.

Ditch. — Devil digs d. G303.9.1.8; food lures victim into d. K811.5; ghost throws man into d. E542.3; jumping ocean d. F1071.2; king in battle hides in d. P12.5.1; miserly friar stays in d. W153.5; sun will lock moon in deep d. A1066.

Ditches. — Fairies dance in d. F261.3.4.

Divan. — Magic d. D1154.4; speaking, walking d. *D1310.8.

Diver, see also **Diving;** robbed K341.4. — Creation of d. (bird) A1975; nest of d. A2431.3.2, A2238.4; earth d. A812; mighty d. F639.2; lie: remarkable d. X965; why d. (loon) holds legs backward A2215.6, A2371.2.9; why d. always looks at sea A2275.5.3, A2471.4.

Divided blanket J121. — Booty d. by lion J811.1.1; identification by matching parts of d. token H100ff.; money d. into three parts: (1) for the poor, (2) for pilgrims, (3) for himself and family W11.3; spoil d. for animals by hero B392; Solomon's judgment: d. (child) J1171.1, (bride) J1171.2; waters magically d. D1551.

Dividing after God's fashion: little to poor, much to rich U61; all they have by cutting beds and houses in two J2469.3; which favors the divider J1241; the oyster (one shell to each) K452.1; all winnings M241. — Brother clever in d. property J242.8; clever d. J1230—J1249; fox d. dying man's gifts B294.1; magic stick d. waters D1551.6.

Divine, see also **Divinity, Gods;** beings assume their own shape in sleep D796; intervention prevents lover's suicide T75.6; nurse T605; voice points out magic D849.7. — Choice of kings by d. will *P11.1; conception from d. impregnation T518; plants created by direct d. agency A2634; saints have d. visitors V227; sun and moon as d. hero's wedding presents A759.2; test of d. favor H1577; thief threatened with d. punishment J1141.14.

Diviner D1712. — Man becomes d. D1720.2; resuscitated man becomes d. E564; tribal customs established by d. A1501.

Diviners, origin of A1654.2.

Diving for cheese J1791.3; match won by deception K16; for reflected enemy J1791.5; for sheep K1051. — Animal d. into lake and disappearing F989.13; dupe d. for alleged jewels K1051.1; otherworld reached by d. into water (of well or lake) F153; thief persuades owner of goods into d. for treasure K341.4; woman d. for man's reflection J1791.6.0.1.

Divining D1812.5ff.; bones reveal guilt D1318.6; rod locates hidden treasure D1314.2. — Magic object used for d. *D1311; mountain opens at blow of d. rod D1552.1; soothsayer's d. methods D1712.1.

Divinity, see also **Deity, God, Gods;** reincarnated as (bull) E611.2.1.0.1, (cow) E611.2.0.1. — Gods give d. to mortal A189.16; head of d. as protection of land D1380.3; symbols of d. Z184.

Division of the animals (riddle) H841; of goddess's time between upper and lower worlds A316; of power among gods A161.1; of river's flow

D2151.2.1.1; of all winnings (bargain) *M241. — Beginning of d. of labor A1472; deceptive d. of profits K171; devil and his son fight over d. of earth G303.11.2.1; threefold d. of king's day P14.16; wise d. of the fowl H601.

Divorce given wives before battle P557.7. — Origin of d. A1558.

Djun, river animal B877.3.

Doce palabras retorneadas, las Z22.

Doctor, see also **Physician;** accidentally saves rajah N688.1; loses a horse for the sake of the truth J551.3; ridicules Christian belief V382; snake B765.21; unable to cure himself scorned J1062.2; with unusual skill F668. — Asking d. where it hurts J2021.1; cat offers to act as d. for cock and hen K2061.7; dragon fly as snake's d. B765.24.1; farmer surpasses d. in choosing food L144.2; father calls d. son a murderer H581.4; god disguised as d. K1811.3; malicious wife reports that her husband is a famous d. H916.1.1; paramour poses as d. K1517.2; quack d. a hero L113.7; seduction by posing as d. *K1315.2; sham d. *K1955, (kills his patients) K824, (makes king's army ill) K2368.3; though d. is no longer needed fool goes to tell him so J2241; transformation to d. D25.1; why trip to d. futile J2241.2; wolf as sham d. looks at horse's foot K1121.1.

Doctor's expressions misunderstood J1803.2. — Accidental cure by d. ruse N648; establishment of d. fees A1594.1.1.

Doctors. — King questions six d. J171.2; repartee concerning d. and patients J1430ff.; wager: more d. than men of other professions N63.

Doctoring. — Cure yourself before d. others J1062; deception through false d. *K1010ff.

Documents. — Bringing d. from distant city in one day (task) H1107.

Dodging. — Escape by d. K631.1.

Dodici parole della verità, le Z22.

Doe, see also **Deer;** becomes water bubble D421.2.2; furnishes milk (for abandoned child) T611.7, (for man) B292.3. — Fairy as d. F234.1.4.1; helpful d. B443.1; one-eyed d. outwitted by approaching from her blind side K929.2; woman transformed to d. D114.1.1.2.

Does magically give milk D2156.1.

Dog allowed to warm self in house begins to bark U126; alternately bites and caresses hares K2031; as animals' king B240.9; asks raven why he sacrifices to Athene J821.1; sent ahead so as to avoid seeing husband transformed K2371.4; barking to dog in moon K1735; between two castles J2183.1; bewitched G265.6.4; buried alive to prevent ghosts from walking E431.8; buried with enemy S139.2.2.3; buried instead of foster son K525.6.1; burned in jumping contest over fire: enmity between dog and hare A2253.1; caresses sick sheep hoping for sheep's death K2061.3; as child's nurse B535.0.4; chooses between opposing tribes B134.4; in church thought to be a ghost J1782.1; as culture hero A522.1.1; defends master's child B524.1.4.1; dies on mistress's grave B301.1.2; in disguise to frighten tiger K1810.2; driven away from other animals because of his barking A2494.4.0.1; driven out of dining room claims to be drunk J874; with droppings of gold B103.1.3; drops meat for reflection J1791.4; has eaten 14 pounds of butter but fool squeezes 16 pounds from him J1919.3; exposes host hiding meat J1562.3; with fire in eyes *B15.4.2.1; follows lion but flees at lion's roar J952.3; follows master's corpse into river B301.1.1; follows washerwoman, hopes bundle is meat J2066.6.1; friendly to guest, barks on street K2031.1; frightened into giving up eating men K1721.1; -god A132.8; granted patent of nobility A2546.1; as guardian of treasure B292.8; guards imprisoned beauty T50.1.4; guards master's life and wealth: may eat before other animals A2223.5; guards master's wife's chastity K1591.2; -headed man with horse's mane B25.1.1; will not help build house: must remain out of doors A2233.2; and hog dispute over their children J243.1; with human head B25.2; imitates wolf, wants to kill horse J2413.5; indicates (hidden treasure) *B153, (pregnant woman) B152.1, (road to be taken) B151.1.6; kills would-be murderer B524.7; language *B215.2, leader fears defeat because his forces are of different breeds J1023; lets devil into church to steal: rewarded with dog-skin A2229.2, A2311.1; looks for most powerful master: stays with man A2513.1.1; loses his patent right and seeks it (why dogs look at one another under the tail) A2275.5.5, A2471.1; made king B292.10; with magic (sight) B141.4, (wisdom) **B121ff.; magically paralyzed D2072.0.2.6; in the manger W156; as messenger B291.2.2; mistakes mussel for an egg and cuts his mouth J1772.2; offered as security for debt B579.6; as ogre G351.1; paramour B611.2; Parsley in the soup J2462.1; and pig's plowing contest K41.2; plows for man B292.4.3; prophesies enemy's coming B141.4.1; proud of his clog, thinking it a decoration J953.1; receives the blows when cat steals K2171; refuses to help wolf K231.1.3; replies to man's remarks B210.1; rescues (cow's teats from fire: origin of his black muzzle) A2229.1, (abandoned child) B549.3, (drowning man) B541.4; returns from dead, clears master B134.5; as sacrifice V12.4.1; who has saved child from serpent killed by father who sees his bloody mouth B331.2; saves man from ghost E439.3; scares fox away from cock K815.1.1; to scent the rice J1341.3; sells rotten peas B294.3; as shepherd B292.1.2; so old head is skinless B841.3; as totem B2.1; transformed to object D422.2; tries to bite man rescuing him from well W154.5; tries to catch fate in its own tail N119.1; transformed to person D341; transformed to another animal D412.5ff.; turned into god D43.1.1; turns water to wine B119.1; vomits gold and silver B103.4.3; waits to be hit with meat J2066.6; warns of pursuit B521.3.4; weeps B736.3; as witch's familiar G225.6; as wolf's shoemaker eats up the materials K254.1; worship V1.8.3; as worthless, faithless lover H587.1. — Adulteress compelled to eat with d. Q478.2; alliance of d. and (sheep) B267.2, (wolf) B267.1; antelope transformed to d. D411.4.1; ass tries to caress his master like the d. J2413.1;

automatic statue of d. D1620.2.8; bear thought to be d. J1753; black d. good omen D1812.5.2.10; boat towed by d. B541.4.1; boy gets back d. from man claiming bugs ate it J1531.2.1; boy to see whether it is raining calls d. in and feels of his paws W111.2.4; carrying master to search for d. J2163.2; cat becomes d. D412.1.3; claim that d.-head captured game J1214.1; creator's d. A33.1.1; crocodile tells d. to drink in river without fear K2061.8; daughter unwittingly promised to d. rescuer S247; dead d. set up to trap woman K2152.1; devastating d. B16.1.2; devil in form of d. G303.3.3.11, (kills people) G303.20.6, (chews up church books) G303.24.5; disdain of the wolf for the d. J953.5; disguised man recognized by d. H173; divination from d. howling D1812.5.0.9; devil invoked through black d. G303.6.1.6; dwarf follows countess around like little d. F451.5.8.1; eaten magic d. howls from eater's belly D1619.2.1; why d. eats first A2545.3; enmity between d. (and cat) A2281.1, A2494.1.2, (and leopard) A2494.2.5; escape, leaving d. as substitute K525.6; fairy as d. F234.1.9; fairy kills d. in revenge F361.17.6; fairies give hunter a d. F343.2; faithful d. (to be killed) B842, (killed by overhasty master) B331.2.2, (threatened with death proves worth and is spared) Q151.4; food of d. A2435.3.1, A2545.4; fool dragged by d. tied to him J2132.2.1; foolish d. finds treasure and dies rather than leave it J1061.3; fox feigns to be playing with sheep when d. drives him off K2061.2; friendship between d. and (cock) A2493.16, (elephant) A2493.31, (man) A2493.4; ghost of d. E521.2; giant d. B871.1.7; girl removes d. from lion's claws B848.2; golden d. B102.7; why d. has hairy paws A2375.2.3, A2245; headless d. B15.1.1.1; healing with hair of d. that bit one D2161.4.10.3; helpful d. *B421; hostile d. B17.1.2; house d. blames master for teaching him lazy habits J142.1; how d. (began to bark) A2425.1, (got its tail) A2378.1.7; hungry wolf envies fat d. until he sees marks of his collar L451.3; hunter beats d. which has grown old in his service W154.4.4; hunting d. tested as puppy by gripping hide H1588.1; indentions on rock from paws of King Arthur's d. A972.5.3; injunction to give sample of food to d. before eating C685; island mistaken for d. J1771.5; king escapes giving d. to hostile tribes K234.1; why d. lacks restraint A2526.1; the lawyer's d. steals meat K488; lazy d. wakes only for his meals W111.5.4; leopard and crocodile both sent for the d. K978.1.1; why d. (is always looking) A2471.6, (looks back at person who has beaten him) A2471.6.1; magic d. B182.1, (brain cures) D1502.8.1, (carries owner in his ear) B557.6, (protects) D1380.16, (shrinks) D491.1.3, (shrinks at night) D621.4.1; man kills giant d. F628.1.5; man made to believe that he is a d. barks at people J2013.2; man reincarnated as d. E611.6; man suckled by d. T611.10; man transformed to d. D141; marriage to d. B601.2, (in human form) B651.4; marriage to person in d. form B641.1; master sets serf as watch-d. J1511.12; mitten becomes d. D444.10.2; monster with huge d. tracks F401.3.3.1; mother feeds child to d. S12.2.1; moving dead d. tabu C537.3; murderer detected by actions of murdered man's d. J1145.1; my d. picked up a string, but did not wish to give it to me unless I gave her bread (cumulative tale) Z41.4.2; origin of d. sacrifice A1545.3.1; part man, part d. B25; peasants persecuted by d.-headed savages B25.1.2; peddler scolds d. who is waiting J1475; place to live given as patent right to d. A2433.1.3; procurer of wildest d. to be king P11.2.2.1; pseudo-magic d. sold K135.1; punishing the d. by feeding him J2108; quarrel of d. and cat over which was higher caste A2281.1.2; quarrel over d. starts feud N387.1; quest for marvelous d. H1331.6; rakshasa eats d. G369.1.4; recognition by overheard conversation with d. H13.1.2; reed pricks d. urinating on it L391.1; remedy for mad d. bite D1515.5; resuscitation by mummified d. E53.1; revenant as d. E423.1.1; robbers frightened by d. B576.1.2; saint controls mad d. V221.4.0.1.1; sexton's d. steals sausage from parson's pocket X411.1; sheep becomes d. at night D621.5; sheep jealous of d. because he does nothing W181.1; sign of cross kills d. D1766.6.5; singing d. B214.1.4; son of d. B635.4.1; soul in form of d. E731.1; speaking d. B221.1.7; spirit as black d. F401.3.3; stag's horns borrowed from d. A2241.1; stealing cattle which are guarded by marvelous d. (task) H1151.8; stolen magic ring stolen back by helpful cat and d. *D882.1.1; going home before d. precedes forbidden C756.1; tabu to eat d. C221.1.1.4; tabu: fire, weapon, d. together C887; tabu: touching hairless d. C537.2; tame d. prefers food basin to fleeing hare J487; testament of the d. who has been given Christian burial J1607; thief tries to feed watch d. and stop his mouth K2062; thieving d. K366.4; tiger thought to be d. J1758.2; too watchful d. killed B332; tortoise and d. partners as thieves B294.7; transformation to d. Q551.3.2.7, (d. to another animal) D412.5ff., (stone to d.) D442.1; transformed man as hostile d. B17.1.2.3; transformed man as d. prophesies coming of enemy B141.4.1; trickster eating own d. K1664; troll rides on d. F455.3.3.1; truth-telling d. *B134, (killed to hide murder) B339.1; two-headed d. B15.1.2.1.4; unwitting bargain with devil evaded by driving d. over bridge first S241.1; venomous d. loosed against saint B776.3.1; village founded where d. barks B155.2.1; waste of time to make a bed for a d. J562; why can't d. bark? H1292.15; why d. is bald A2524.6; why d. barks after thief A2426.1.5; why cat and d. fight A2281.3; why d. follows animal's scent A2512.1; why d. has no horns: stolen by deer A2326.2.2; why d. howls at night A2427.2; why d. lost speech A2422.1; why d. snaps at fly A2479.8; why lion does not attack d. A2464.1; wife forces husband to kill d. B335.1.1; wife's former incarnation as d. E601.1; wild huntsman's d. when seized becomes stick E501.15.6.7; witch in form of d. G211.1.8; witch rides on d. G241.1.3; witch transforms husband into d. G263.1.4; wolf as God's d. A1833.3; wolf proposes abolition of d. guards for sheep K2061.1.1; woman bears d. T554.2; woman in moon with d. A751.8.2; worm becomes d. D418.2.2.

Dog's characteristic haunt A2433.3.2; claws as grains under paws A2376.2; enemies A2494.4ff.; flesh magic *D1032.3; head soup as cure

D1508.4; head used for divination D1311.8.1; licking of man produces forgetfulness D2004.2.1; tail mistaken for gun J1772.12; tail wagging raises wind D2142.1.1. — Adulteress compelled to eat a d. leavings Q478.3; cat loses d. certificate A2281.1; cause of d. walk A2441.1.3; child with d. head T551.3.1; Eve created from d. tail A1224.3; magic d. (bell dispells grief) *D1359.3.1.3, (breath burns dead bodies) D1566.1.6; magic sight by looking between d. ears D1821.3.4; magic stone in d. forehead B722.2; magician, giant, contest over d. tail D1719.1.3; man with d. feet F551.1.3; making d. tail straight H1023.4.1; monster's arm token of d. innocence H105.3; oil in black d. ear brings rain D1542.1.6; origin of d. skin A2311.1; origin of d. service to man A2513.1; quest for wild d. milk H1361.4; why red d. excrement contains hair A2385.2; wolf as d. guest sings J581.1; wolf prefers liberty and hunger to d. servitude with plenty L451; marvelous sensitiveness: meat is d. flesh F647.5.1; woman's organs like d. F547.5.10.

Dogs born of woman D601; break bonds, kill master's attacker B524.1.2.1; with eyes like plates and tea-cups B15.4.3; as fairy gifts F343.2.1; flee from their master because in time of famine he has killed his cattle J2211.3; of gold and silver F855.3.2; handed over as hostages to the wolves by sheep K191; in hell A673.1; howling as bad omen D1812.5.1.12.1; howling indicate death B733.2; in human shape: friends seducing wife H592.4; incited to devour souls in hell A689.3.1; kill attacking cannibal *B524.1.1; kill ogre G512.9.1; large or small at will D631.2.1; listen to wolves' hypocritical words K815.3; in otherworld F167.1.1.1; protect from spirits F405.5.1; pulling on leash (life token) E761.7.5; rescue fleeing master from tree refuge *B524.1.2; by river try to get food in river by drinking the river dry J1791.3.2; scare away fairies F381.9; tear up lion skin but fear living lion W121.2.4; track down law-breakers B578; warn against witch B521.3.1; in wild hunt E501.4.1; of wolf color join the wolves J2137.2. — Behavior of wild huntsman's d. E501.15.6; bones thrown to d. permit escape L222.2; buffalo's eyes turn into protecting d. D699.1; cavalry of d. B268.2; contest of d. H1588; daily beating of men transformed to d. D691; deduction: animal drinks d. milk J1661.1.5.1; dwarfs fear d. F451.3.6.5.2; eating food offered to d. as penance Q523.3; fairy d. F241.6; fire-breathing d. B742.4; ghost visible to d. E421.1.3; ghosts as d. with glowing tongues and eyes E421.3.6; helpful d. purchased B312.4.1; hero's marvelous d. A524.1.1; hostile d. made friendly by having them fight common enemy, the wolf J145; why d. howl, looking at sky A2471.6.2; why d. hunt A2452.1; keeping four d. in herd (task) H1112.1; king of d. B241.2.7; lean d. envy arena-dog his fatness L455; lies about d. X1215; why d. lift their legs A2473.1; why d. look at one another under tail *A2471.1; magic d. B182.1ff.; magician claims he can make d. grey K1677; names of d. literally interpreted J2493; polychromatic d. B731.6.0.1; power of wild hunt evaded by sacrificing to huntsman's d. E501.17.4.3; being eaten by

d. as punishment Q415.1; quest for the smallest of d. H1307; sheep-d. unite to hunt wolf J624.2; snow transformed to d. D449.4; why d. do not speak A2422.1.1; sorceress's toes become d. D447.5; tribe wears clothes like d. A1683.2; war-d. B268.2.1; why d. get stuck in copulation A2496.1; why d. howl when man is dying A2427.2.1; why d. leave droppings at crossroads A2473.1.1; why d. sniff at one another A2471.1.1; why tigers eat d. A2435.3.9.1; wild animals kept as d. *B575.1; witch allows self to be coursed by d. G211.2.7.1; witch overcome by helpful d. of hero G275.2; wolves as God's d. A165.2.1.1.1; wolves of his own country dearer than d. of another P711.1; Zeus has embassy of d. punished for fouling his court A2232.8, Q433.3.

Dogs' barking causes forgetfulness D2004.10; names give warning K649.5.

Dogfish act like dogs X1316.

Dogflesh: "food you've never eaten" J2469.5.1; is magic *D1032.3.

Dog-headed man has mane of horse (cattle) B25.1.1.

Dogmas V310ff.

Dogskin, magic D1025.6, (transforms) D565.7.

"Doing as I say, not as I do" J1433.

Doll. — Automatic d. D1620.0.1; forgotten fiancée remembered by means of d. D2006.1.6; magic d. D1268, (answers for fugitive) D1611.11, (freeing from clutches of) T67.3.1, (freeing king from) H1196, (furnishes treasure) D1469.2, (stolen) K331.4; marriage to d. T117.8.

Dolls become fairies D435.1.2.

Dolorous tower F772.2.5.

Dolphin paramour B612.2; and whale scorn crab as peacemaker J411.6. — Helpful d. B473; man transformed to d. D127.5.

Dolphins seek King Solomon's ring A2275.5.4. — Why d. swim up and down A2444.2.

Domestic vs. ascetic life H659.21; beast transformed to person D330ff. — Animal as d. servant B292.2, B574; bride test: d. skill H383; devastating d. animals B16.1; devil as d. beast G303.3.3.1; god of d. animals A441; helpful d. beast B400ff.; helpful d. fowls B469.5; how animals made d. A2513; man transformed to d. beast D130ff.; origin of d. animals A1443; reincarnation as d. animal E611; revenant as d. animal E423.1ff.; war between d. and wild animals B262; witch as d. beast G211.1.

Domination by fairy mistress F302.6.1. — Magic d. over animals D2197.

Dominion over world as reward Q112.0.6. — Man given d. over beasts A1421.1.

Donald. — Black D. (name for devil) G303.2.4.

Donating, see **Giving.**

Donkey, see also **Ass, Mule;** and camel trade undeserved compliments J867; gift to ruler J2415.1.1; and ox not to plow together C886. — Ghost d. E402.2.2; immortal d. B843.2; mythical d. B19.11; ogress as d. G351.5; priest sells distracting d. J357; reincarnation as d. E611.1.2; trickster accuses woman of lying with d. K2112.2.1; unjust king compared to d. H592.5; woman will not follow d. on safe path: attacked by robbers J133.4.

Donkey's — Child with d. head T551.3.3; jewel found on d. neck N534.8; striking off d. head to punish it J2113.1; why d. penis is large A2365.2.1.3.

Donkeys ask immediate reward from God: eat their own excrements A2232.11; Genoese compared to scattering d. J1021.2; punishment: humiliating ride on d. Q473.5; repartee on d. not smoking J1289.20; why d. urinate when others begin A2495.3.

Donning. — Magic power from d. magician's clothes D1721.0.1; transformation by d. hood D537.1.

Doom. — Saint made judge of d. Q173.

Doomsday (Day of Judgment) A1002; a long way off J1261.7; resurrection E178. — Bird describes D. B143.2; birds drip blood at D. B259.5; bleeding wood as D. sign A1091.2; fifteen signs of D. Z71.16.11.3; moon by day D. sign A1053.1; no clothes needed for D. J1511.7; sinners to be burnt on D. M341.2.7.1; souls at D. E751; sun at night D. sign A1052.2; talking stone at D. A1091.3; unusual migration of birds at D A1091.4.

Door entrance to lower world F91; to fairyland opens once a year F211.1.1; falls on robbers from tree K335.1.1.1; hung backwards as protection against ghosts E439.9; to otherworld F156; transformed to stone D471.2.1. — Church d. opens magically, proves priest's innocence H216.3; closing the d. tight with iron nails K1417; concealed d. leads to woman's room K1349.8; devil cannot enter house with horseshoe over d. *G303.16.17; devil fastened to hell's d. by his beard G303.17.3.2; devil stands in church d. and writes down names on sheep skin G303.24.1.4; entrance to fairyland through d. in knoll F211.1; forbidden d. (all may be entered except one) C611.1; ghost cannot cross new d. sill E434.10; ghost slams d. E402.1.7; golden d. to troll's castle G304.3.1.1; guarding the d. K1413; he who opens palace d. to be king P11.4.1; horse's head nailed over d. F874.1; kicking through d. F639.5; magic charm opens d. *D1557; magic d. *D1146, (holds person fast) D1413.16; monster guards d. of habitable hill F721.2.2; mountain-man has stack of butter before d. F460.2.4; object across d. protects from witches G272.7; opening mouth makes d. open D1782.1.1; palace with d. at each end for sun's journey A151.4.2; passing through d. guarded by hound as fear test H1423.1; pointing at d. causes fall D2069.1.1; recognition by overheard conversation with church d. H13.2.4; servant to close d. at night leaves it open so that he will not have to open it next morning W111.2.2; slamming d. on exit from mountain otherworld *F91.1; snapping d. K736; trying to get a beam through a d. crosswise in otherworld *F171.6.3; wife and paramour rebuked for not shutting d. K1569.2; wind opens locked church d. F963.3; wraith opens, closes d. E723.7.3.

Doors fly open at death E722.2.6; of heaven guarded by rivers of fire A661.0.1.1.1; in otherworld F165.1. — Dog will not help build house:

must remain out of d. A2233.2; dwarf cave closed by iron d. F451.4.3.1; dwarf cave has large square room with little d. F451.4.3.2; extraordinary d. and windows F782ff.; fairy house without d. F221.5; gods of d. A411.1; hair from fox's tail opens all d. D1562.2; locked d. open for ghosts E599.11; many d. in prison R41.5; power to go through closed d. D2121.12; saint passes through closed d. F694; slamming d. grateful for being fastened D1658.1.4; sun at night closes d. A722.4; Valhalla has 540 d. A661.1.0.1; why fowls never shut d. at night A2433.4.6; wild hunt goes through houses when front and back d. are on a line E501.14.6; witches open d. G249.8.

Doorbell. — Wraith rings d. E723.7.2.

Doorflap. — Buzzard becomes d. D423.4.

Doorframe. — Strong man carries off d. F631.2.1.

Doorkeeper of the gods A165.5; of hell A671.1; with one human eye, one cat's eye F512.1.4.

Doorkeepers, automata as D1639.1.

Doorpost rises for holy person F1009.1.

Doorstep. — Bible under d. detects thieves D1817.0.1.5; magic d. D1146.1; wheel buried in d. to prevent deviltry D1385.10.

Doorway. — Breaking down d. instead of dismounting J2171.6; weaver outwits d. tax J1289.13.

Dord fían R187.1.

Dormitory. — Children sleep in village d. T688; village d. A1559.1.

Double bribe to judge J1212.1; dealers K2030ff.; reward successfully claimed K441ff. — Music teacher charges d. to those who have taken music before X351; rascal claims to be only simple not d. fool J1393; wife who saw d. X121.

Double-meaning verse aids theft K232.1.

Doubling. — Dragon d. his demands B11.11.8; king d. reward to knight W11.12.1; servant d. master's boasts J2464.

Dough. — After three weeks the fiancée still has d. under nails H383.1.1; bitch eats wheat d.: origin of noblemen A1656.1; dropping d. thought to be a ghost J1782.2; giant comes to bake too soon and spills d. F531.3.7; serpent kneaded into d. H1407; snake in d. troll child test F455.10.1; sound of fermenting d. J1812.3; wild huntsman's dogs eat d. E501.15.6.6.

Dove disregards experience in nest-building J16; flies out of anchorite's mouth T331.5, V345; helps deity draw wife into net B582.2.5; and magpie's exchange of eggs A2247.4, A2486.3; as messenger B291.1.3; returns to ark in obedience to Noah: receives raven's sheen A2221.7; sees painted cups of water and dashes into them J1792.1; transformed to person D354.1. — Cooing of d. A2426.2.8; creation of d. A1948; crow kills d. singing to save brood U31.2; devil cannot change into a d. G303.3.6.2; dog becomes d. D412.5.1; fairy as d. F234.1.15.2; fox masks as d. J512.10; golden d. F855.3.3; helpful d. B457.1; magpie as

hybrid of d. and raven A2382.1; man transformed to d. D154.1,
G263.1.5.2; monogamous life of d. A2497.1; Noah fails to pay d. for
bringing back olive branch: hence its mourning A2291; parson is to let a
d. fly in church X418; prophetic d. B143.0.6; raven and d. fight over
man's soul E756.3; raven imitates d. J2413.9, (punished) A2232.10; reincarnation as d. E613.6; revenant as d. E423.3.1; soul in form of d.
E732.1; speaking d. B211.3.5; tabu to eat d. C221.1.2.3; thrush teaches d.
to build nest A2271.1; why d. has two eggs A2247.4, A2486.3.

Dove's graceful step A2441.2.2; nest A2271.1, A2431.3.1; pride in her
large brood linked with fear for their loss U81.1. — Origin of markings
on d. head A2330.7.

Doves in net console selves J869.1; show monk treasure B562.1.3; tear
up wolf (lie) X1256.1. — Aphrodite's team of d. A136.2.1; forgotten
fiancée reawakens husband's memory by having d. converse D2006.1.3;
king of d. B242.2.2, K815.8; lies about d. X1256; maltreated children
transformed to d. S365.1; Mohammed lures d. to his ears K1962.1;
souls carried to heaven by d. E754.2.1; tame d. close wild ones in trap
and thus help common enemies J683.2.

Down. — Corpse buried face d. S139.2.2.3.1, V61.4.1; garments of
mountain d. H1054.4; unnecessary choice: to go uphill or d. J463; what
is softer than swan d. (riddle) H672; why animals always look d. A2471.9;
wife carried with head d. drowns J1916.

Downfall of ascetic V229.20. — Animal characteristics as punishment for
planning man's d. A2236ff.

Dowry in coffin E228; given at marriage T52.4. — Combat among sisters
for d. H507.4; foolish bride gives away d. J2463.1; monk helps friend
get d. K1915.1; monk appropriates d. K361.4; peacock on king's temple as
d. C655.1; settling d. dispute J1678; village as part of d. T52.9.

Draft-animal, unusual B558ff.

Dragged. — Bacon d. on string by literal numskull J2461.1.1; boat d. to
strand by dead E543; death by being d. behind horse Q416.2, S117; fool
d. by tying dog to himself J2132.2.1; mill d. by strong man F631.1;
numskull d. J2132; rain from waterskin d. along sky A1131.4.1.

Dragging. — Demon d. victims beneath water G336.1; rivers from god
d. his staff A934.4; water-spirit d. children into river F420.5.2.1.5.

Dragon *B11ff.; as creator's companion A36; enticed into pot K722.1;
festival A1541.4.2; god A139.3; haunts lake G308.4; king advises hero
B560.1; makes bridge across stream for holy man B549.2; mistaken for
log, sat upon J1761.8; parts as identification between lovers H105.6; as
power of evil B11.9; as power of good B11.8; as rain-spirit B11.7ff.; seen
in sky F796; swallows, releases magic box F721.3.2; swallowing arrow intended for hero B529.2; tongue proof H105.1; wants to see courage
J2488.1; worship V1.8.8. — Animal languages learned from d. B217.6;
bridal chamber invaded by magic d. T172.2; bringing d. leg as suitor
test H322.3; conception from d. rays T521.3; drinking horn becomes d.

D444.6; deeds of d. B11.6ff.; why d. dies by means of fire A2468.3; fight with d. *B11.11ff.; fettered monster as d. A1072.4; form of d. B11.2ff.; giant with d. scales for feet F531.1.3.1; girl offers self to d. to save parents S262.4; habitat of d. B11.3ff.; habits of d. B11.4ff.; killing d. before princess sacrificed H335.3.1; magic circle of saliva kills d. D1402.14; magic d. heart *D1015.1.2; magic d. statue D1345.2; magic tree guarded by d. *D950.0.1; marriage to d. B605; marriage of d. girl, orphan boy T118.2; origin of d. B11.1ff.; overcoming d. as task H1174.2; powers of d. B11.5ff.; prophecy: fiery bolt from d. to kill world M357.1; sacrifice of human being to d. *B11.10f.; sight of d. punishes neglect to fast Q223.9.1; snake transformed to d. D418.1.2; supernaturally impregnated woman bears d. T554.1; transformation: d. to stone D429.2.2; tree guarded by d. H1333.6; why d. king can't ascend to sky H1292.14; witch as d. G211.9.1.

Dragon's breath renders hideous D1337.2.3; heart-blood as remedy D1500.1.7.3.3. — Animal languages learned from eating d. heart B217.1.2; creator with d. head A18.1; devil in d. head on a shield G303.8.10; earthquake at d. death F960.2.5.3, Q552.25.1; eating d. heart makes courageous D1358.1.1; invulnerability through bathing in d. blood *D1846.4; men created from sown d. teeth A1265; quest for d. liver, heart H1332.6; sowing d. teeth (task) H1024.5.

Dragons in hell A671.2.5. — Devil as d. G303.3.2.4; king of d. B248; man kills d. with own hands F628.1.3.1; pigs become d. D412.3.5; witch's army of d. G225.5.

Dragon-fighter. — Identity of d. not to be revealed C422.1.

Dragonfly as snake's servant B765.24.

Dragonsblood as love charm D1355.3.8.

Draining land in one night H1097.

Drake and devil carry waters of English Channel G303.9.2.4.

Draught. — Quest for healing d. H1324.2.

Draughts (game). — Fairies steal d. pieces F365.5; falling in love while playing d. T34.2.1.

Drawbridge partially cut, giant falls K924. — Slamming d. to otherworld *F152.2.

Drawing asunder by horses as punishment Q416ff.; witch's blood annuls her spells D1741.2.1. — Disenchantment by d. blood D712.4; transformation when one expresses astonishment at smith d. water in an egg shell D512.1.

Drawn. — Chariot d. by dead persons E583; corpse d. asunder S139.2.2.6; devil in coach d. by headless horses G303.7.3.3; golden wagon d. (by moles) F861.1.1, (by four golden elephants) F861.1.2; man d. to girl when her heart is magically removed and fed to him D1905.1; magic fire d. down on foe D2091.1; person d. (attracted) by magic object D1420ff.; person d. in by magic object D1412ff.; ship d. by loadstone *F806.1.

Dreadnaughts seek dangers they have been warned against Z211.

Dream bread K444; contests K66; demons F471; of fairy kiss J2345; of future greatness causes banishment L425; interpretation answered by another J1527; of marking the treasure X31; reveals sin to saint D1817.2.1; that all parsons are in hell X438; shows events in distant place *D1813.1ff.; of treasure bought N531.3; of treasure on the bridge N531.1; warning against marriage C168; warns emperor of wife's unfaithfulness *D1813.1.1. — Accidental death through dodging blow in d. N336; advice from d. D1814.2; conception through d. F460.4.1.2.1, F611.1.13, T516; consummation of marriage postponed until revelation by d. of future of family T165.1; cure follows d. instructions D2161.4.0.1; deception revealed in d. D1819.2; detection through feigned d. J1147; devil appears in d. G303.6.1.6; disenchantment by obeying d. D753.3; future revealed in d. *D1812.3.3ff.; imagined ownership derived from d. J1551.7; information received through d. D1810.8.2; journey to otherworld as revealed in d. *D1812.3.3ff.; location of fountain revealed in d. D1816.1; love through d. T11.3; magic knowledge of king's d. D1819.7; magic object received from lady in d. D812.8; magic power received in d. *D1731; magic sword received in d. D812.12.1; man discredits his confession by declaring it all a d. J1155; mine discovered through d. N596.1; monkey saves condemned birds through feigned d. K645; quest assigned because of d. H1217, (feigned) H1212.1; quest for girl seen in d. H1381.3.1.2.2; quest for marvels seen in d. H1229.3; quest for things seen in d. H1320.2; realistic d. F1068; recalling someone else's d. H1042; recognition from d. H24; sham wise man interprets girl's d. K1956.6; snake turns to gold in answer to d. N182; souls seen in d. E720.1; tailor's d. of flag made of stolen cloth J1401; treasure discovered through d. N531; trickster explains d. as dead father's demand for gift J2326.2; wisdom (knowledge) from d. *J157.

Dreams. — Blacksmith's and horse-trader's d. J1622; demons fool men in their d. G302.9.6; god of d. A499.5; interpreter of d. D1712.3; magic object induces d. D1584; marvels seen in d. D1731.2; origin of d. A1399.2; prophecy through d. M302.7; symbolic interpretations of d. H617; supernatural persons seen in d. give advice K2035.

Dreamer. — Greedy d. willing to accept nine coins J1473.

Dreaming. — Biting fingers to see if d. F1041.13.

Dregs. — Fraud detected by measuring wine d. J1176.2.

Dress, see also **Clothes;** of dwarf F451.2.7; of fairies F236; so fine it goes through ring H355.6; of mountain-men F460.1.4; of pygmies F535.3; of revenant E422.4; transformed to animal D444.10. — Adulteress forced to wear symbolic d. Q487; bride test: making d. from wasted flax H381.1; conspicuous d. of maid pledged to devil S223.0.2; custom of differentiating social classes by color of d. introduced A1650.2; disguise of man in d. of woman *K1836; disguise of woman in d. of man *K1837;

extraordinary d. F821ff.; lazy wife in soiled d. thinks husband is bringing her a new dress from market W111.3.1; origin of leaf d. A1453.4; overzealous visitor cannot wait to d. J2517; trail of d. shreds R135.0.4; touching d. tabu C545.3; tribal characteristics: d. A1683; wife's d. symbolic of sexual generosity H492.2.1.

Dresses of giants, giantesses F531.1.11. — Changing d. to take king's place K1810.1.3.

Dressed. — Drunken man d. as a rich lord J2322; girl refuses to dance with devil until well d. K1227.3.1; how the devil is d. G303.5ff.; spirits d. in antique clothes F401.1.

Dressing. — Lover d. as woman K1214; married man helps bridegroom's d. T134.3; monkey d. in dead mistress's gown K1839.3; self-d. image D1623; shortsightedness in d. J2161.

Dressmaker P452.

Drills. — Fire d. (do not function) D2089.10, (invented) A1414.1.1.

Driller. — Lie: remarkable rock d. X991; oil well d. drills for fifty years W37.1.

Drink, see also **Drunk;** of devils G303.25.14; has taste of any liquor desired D1665.1; irresistible H659.20; from magic cup deprives man of legs D1410.6; magically furnished D2105.4; magically supplied D1040.1; poured out to gods V12.9; refused saint disappears Q552.18.2. — Angel tricked by d. into telling woman how to enter heaven K2371.1.6; animals refuse to help dig well: may not d. from river or spring A2233.1.1; ascetic faster increases sufferings by placing food and d. before himself V462.2.1; ass refuses to d. after it has had enough J133.2; brother about to d. blood of seemingly guilty sister P253.1; crocodile tells dog to d. in river without fear K2061.8; crow drops pebbles into water jug so as to be able to d. J101; dwarfs steal d. F451.5.2.2.2; dying monster requests hero to d. his blood M257; falling in love while d. being poured T34.1; food and d. appear and disappear in otherworld D1982.4; food and d. from magic object *D1472ff.; health as reward for d. Q145.1.1; heart breaks at third d. from silver canister F1041.1.1.1; house without food or d. J2483; liking for food and d. J1343; lover refuses d. T24.6; magic d. *D1040ff., (causes arms to fall from shoulders) D1403.3, (gives immortality) D1346.1, (potion) *D1241, *D1242ff.; magic glass supplies d. D1472.1.16; metaphors about d. J2489.1; must d. from the common cup (the sea) J1467; ogre persuaded to d. pond dry bursts G522; one d. leads to drunkenness, condemnation N340.3; parson takes d. of liquor during the sermon X445.1; person lives without food or d. for a year (or more) F1033; Pisācas d. blood and eat human flesh G312; drunkard's wife should have brought him d. J1323; poison magically separated from d. D2168.1; poisoned d. test H1515.2; sword so heavy that hero must take d. of strength before swinging it F833.1; transformation: water to marvelous d. D478.4; trickster gets strong d. deceptively K231.6.2;

truth in d. U180ff.; vampire brought to life by being fed human food and d. E251.2.3; water becomes marvelous d. D478.4; wolf tries to d. well dry to get cheese J1791.3.1.

Drinkable. — Gods provide d. water A1429.3.2.

Drinker. — Animal as mighty d. F989.11; flask imparts magic strength to d. D1335.7; lie: remarkable d. X932; mighty d. F633.

Drinkers cheat blindfolded bartender K233.2. — Devil's stream kills d. G303.16.2.3.5.

Drinking beer without touching pot H1046.3; blood, milk and wine as pledge P312.1; blood teaches animal languages D1301.2; -bout assembly of animals B237; enormous amount (task) H1142; from fairyland well tabu F378.4; festival in memory of dead V65.2; forbidden *C250ff.; ghost E556; from golden vessel disenchants D771.5; hole in pot lets gruel run out J2176.2; holy water facilitates cursing V132.3; the moon J1791.1; only after a bargain K236.2; up river to get all the fish K231.11; as road to heaven J1314. — Absurd ignorance concerning animal's eating and d. J1903; adulteress d. from paramour's skull Q478.1.2; animal warns man against d. B521.1.2; betrothal by lovers' d. each other's blood *T61.1; bride and groom d. from same cup T135.11; clever deductions by d. J1661.2; compulsory d. at feast A1514; conception from d. T512; cure for leprosy by d. from opposite lip of horn from that which caused it D1783.2; death respite while d. K551.2.1; deceptive d. contest H82; devil d. church well dry G303.9.9.14; devil in d. contest G303.9.8.5; disenchantment by (d. blood) D712.4.1, (eating or d.) D764; doctor d. himself after he forbids it J1433; dogs try to get food by d. river dry J1791.3.2; fear test: eating and d. from skulls H1434; giant d. prodigiously F531.3.4; giant god d. lake dry A133.1; hero treacherously slain at d. bout K929.8; Hindu d. from Mohammedan's vessel V383.2; idol d. milk D1633.1; magic results from eating or d. *D1793; man too lazy for d., loses voice W111.1.5; marriage by d. festival T135.6; mutual love through accidental d. of love philtre *T21; no teeth as excuse for not d. J1391.6; ogre sucks victim's finger d. all his blood G332.1; permission for d. water refused W155.5; though old woman believes she is in hell she calls for d. companions J1321.2; rejuvenation by d. D1889.9; respite from death until prisoner has finished d. his glass K551.2; revenants d. E541.4; spirit d. water supply dry G346.4; stones d. D1641.2.5; transformation by d. D555; trickster d. from another's flask K499.9; victim enticed into d. by over-salting food K839.3; witch prevents person from d. D2072.0.5.1.

Drinking-horn found by stumble N223; transformed to dragon D444.6. — Cure for leprosy by drinking from opposite lip of d. D1783.2; death from d. E765.4.5; dwarf forced to swim in d. X142.2; forbidden d. C622; huldra d. F460.2.10; magic d. *D1171.6.3, D1889.9, (as chastity test) H411.4, (supplies wine) D1472.1.24; self-pouring d. D1601.26; theft of d. from fairies F352.

Drinking-tube as chastity index H439.2.

Dripping clothes of drowned person's wraith E723.7.8. — Comb d. blood (life token) E761.1.7; sound of d. water thought to be ghost J1782.2.1.
Driven. — Anvil d. into ground by strong man F614.1; cannibals d. from land G11.18.1; cobold d. away by brewing in eggshell F481.4; creditor d. away K235; devil shows how he can be d. away G303.13.5; devils *d.* away by cross G303.16.3.1; devil d. from heaven G303.8.1; dwarfs d. out of land by three sevens in 1777 F451.9.1.3; giant d. by girl F531.5.10.1; giants d. away by men F531.6.12.7; hungry hens d. away and geese stuffed H583.4.4; herds d. off by mountain-men F460.4.4.6; herds of deer d. by witches G249.1; horses d. by dead person E582; images of animals d. D1631; ogres d. away by oaths G571; sinner d. from graveyard by other dead E411.0.5; wagon d. by thumbling sitting in horse's ear F535.1.1.1; two he-goats d. by troll G304.3.2.2.
Driver told to put his shoulder to the wheel J1034. — Ass turns on his d. who would save him from falling over a precipice J683.1; why d. ants live in bush A2433.2.1.1.
Driving off birds after kind words K2090.1. — Father d. away bad son P233.2.1.
Droll dwarfs F451.3.10.
Dromedary. — Horse of d. family B710.2.2.
Drop from magic cauldron gives supernatural information D1310.2. — Each d. of innocent blood turns to burning candle D1318.5.3; "fair d." falls on saint V222.1.0.2; tabu: allowing a d. to fall upon altar C51.1.8.
Drops of water become angels A52.0.7. — Collecting all d. of water H1144.1; how many d. in the sea (riddle) H704; humans from creator's d. of wine A1211.6; magic blood d. impersonate fugitive D1611.6; magic d. *D1242.3; two d. of blood indicate two deaths D1812.5.1.1.2; water d. wear stone hollow J67.
Dropped tub unharmed F1081. — Apparently dead woman revives when d. N694.1; axe d. in water: modest choice Q3.1; book d. in water by saint not wet F930.1; clay d. from sky forms hill A963.9; identification by hair d. by bird H75.2; identification by ring d. in wine H94.3ff.; quest for princess caused by sight of one of her hairs d. by bird H1213.1; recovered magic articles d. by rescuing animals into the sea D882.12; rope cut and victim d. *K963.
Dropping and dashing to pieces as punishment Q417; of fox's tail frightens animals K2323.1. — Animal characteristics from d. ancient animal from air A2214; animal d. magic food B531.4; birds d. stones on saint's enemies D2163.5.1; corpse d. piecemeal down chimney H1411.1; death for d. on emperor's coat Q411.15; devil d. stones A977.3; treasure-d. animals B103.1ff.
Droppings. — Why dogs leave d. at crossroads A2473.1.1.
Drosselbart T76.
Drought produced by magic D2143.2; as punishment Q552.3.3; at world's end A1065. — Farmer as fisherman goes hungry in d. J345.2; goddesses

produce d. A189.10; magic d. against enemy D2091.8; magic object causes d. D1542.2; rivers from saint's prayer during d. A934.5; star deity and d. demon fight A255.

Drowned corpse found by magic D1816.4.1; girl reborn as leech to avenge murder E693.1; man's ghost leaves water puddles E544.1.3; person cannot rest in peace E414; woman's hair speaks E545.20.1. — Adulterers tricked on to thirsty mules, d. K1567; animal d. relieving bee stings K1023.4; army d. by unnoticed tide N339.7; besiegers d. by diverting river K2369.5; dream leads to d. body D1810.8.2.2; female rabbit d. in Flood B754.4; foal d. by witch G265.2; giant d. F531.6.12.8; girl d. in well as river's origin A934.10; infant allowed in river, d. J2175.4; king, foster son jumping into sea, d. F1041.16.7; loaf of bread locates d. man D1314.6; lover d. as he swims to see his mistress T83; man has bride d. S62.2; man d. on mountain (lie) X1857; ogre d. G512.11; reincarnation of d. persons as birds E613.0.4; souls of d. in heated kettles in hell *E755.2.1; souls in hell alternately d., burned Q562.2; Virgin restores life to d. man V256.5; wife carried head downwards in water, d. J1916; wife d. while throwing husband's corpse into river N339.14; wraiths of d. appear in dripping clothes E723.7.8; youth d. gazing at own image N339.10.

Drowning escape by drying up waters D2165.2; of girl abducted by fairy N339.9; man rescued by siren B53.1; princess rescued R131.2.1; as punishment Q428, (for breaking tabu) C923, C927.3, (for drowning) Q581.3.1, (for turtle) K581.1; to save treasure J2146.2; self after beset by elves F324.2; self as sacrifice to water-gods to save husband's boat from capsizing T211.1.1; selves to save virginity T326.1; shipboard rivals K527.4; son to test goddess's favor H1577.2; in swamp as punishment Q467.3; test H1538. — Animal d. out of sea-water H842.1; animal grateful for rescue from d. B362; animal saves man from death by d. B527; captors lured into d. selves K656; curse: death by d. M451.2; death by d. while drinking water M341.2.3; devil plans d. of God at time of creation A63.2; druid's spells cause d. D1402.13.2; escape by shammed d. K522.6; fatal game: d. K853; fathers d. rescuing sons R153.3.5; fish saves hero from d. B175.2; fox attempts d. jug, gets drowned J2131.5.7; ghost causes d. E266.1.1; ghost rescues from d. E379.1; girl d. as she swims to lover T83.1; immunity from d. D1841.6; infant born blind d. self T585.3; king's d. in bath follows literal instructions J2516.3.3; lake bursts forth d. evil doer, A920.1.3, A920.1.8; lover rescues lady from d. R161.3; magic boar d. hound pack B184.3.1.1; magic chain protects from d. D1388.0.3; magic object (causes d.) D1402.0.2, (protects from d.) *D1388ff.; man inattentive to d., drowns J651.2; mermaid's singing causes d. B81.11; miraculous   d. as punishment Q552.19; monkey tricked into d. self K891.3; murder by d. K958, S131; owl saves man from d. B527.3; parents meet daughter they tried d. N732.3; prophecy: d. in particular stream M341.3.3; punishment by d. Q467; rescuing d. man forbidden C41.1;

river d. victim F932.8.4; scolding d. child instead of helping him J2175.2; self-sacrifice by d. S264.1.2; slaves spare infant from d. K512.0.1; spring miraculously breaking forth and d. wrongdoer F933.6; wager involving d. self N13; water d. girl filling pitcher D1432.1; water saves prophet from d. F930.3; waters d. wrongdoer F930.2; water-spirit allows d. body to come up thrice F420.5.2.1.4; water-spirits save man from d. F420.5.1.10; wife encourages husband's proposed d. J1545.9; wind raised by d. cat. D2142.1.5; woman d. in attempt to push husband into water K1652.

Drug, see also **Medicine;** hidden in enemy's fingernail K873.4; of invulnerability T325.1. — Magic d. renders invulnerable D1344.2; origin of fish d. A2834.

Drugs. — Seduction by use of d. K1339.5; use of d. to usurp lover's place K1317.6.

Drugged. — Burial alive of d. person S123.1; husband d. by wife on way to paramour K1514.17.1; undesired lover d. T322.3.

Druid *P427; aids task H985; assigns tasks H939.1; causes sun to stand still D2146.1.1.1; converted to Christianity V331.0.1; directs fairies F394.1.1; directs king's death F363.1; interprets dream D1812.3.3.0.1; as magician D1711.4; makes self ugly on one side, beautiful on the other D2031.4.1. — Air above grave of converted d. full of angels V238.4; Christ called d. V211.0.5; demons coerced by d. tabus G583; fairy leaves after d. spell F381.6; magic contest between d. and saint D1719.1.1; no sunshine on d. island F961.1.6; resuscitation by d. E121.7.1; saint in conflict with d. V229.6; transformation by d. D683.9; transformation by saint as proof of Christianity before d. H1573.3.3.

Druid's circumambulation D1791.1.1; hedge prevents attack D1381.1; spells cause drowning D1402.13.2; spells kill Christian king D1402.13. — Fairy defeated by d. magic F389.5.

Druids attempt to poison H1515.1; bereave men of senses D2065.3; bless instead of curse D2076; can pass through trees D1932; cause illusions D2031.0.4; cause magic thirst D2063.3.1; come to adore infant Jesus V211.1.7; direct fairies F394.1.1; guard magic spring D927.2.1; have knot magic D1282.1.1; magically detect crime D1817.1; prophesy saint's coming M364.7.1; as prophets M301.3; raise storms D2141.0.8; send spirits to kill Christian F402.1.11.1; teach immortality V311.0.1; as teachers P340.0.1; turn men into dogs D141.0.2; undergo ordeal (by hot iron) H221.2.2, (by water) H222.0.1; use mistletoe D965.4.1. — Demons coerced by geasa of d. G583; fairies are d. F251.12; funeral rites by d. V60.2; images and d. V120.1; magic hymn protects against d. D1385.16.1; magic invisibility of d. D1981.3; monks as converted d. P426.3.2; sacred groves of d. V114.1; saint magically causes d. to bless instead of curse D2076; spirit sent by d. causes death of Christian king F402.1.11.1; tabu: king speaking before his d. speak C402.1; white robes of d. V131.2.

Druidess. — Chant of d. causes drowning Q467.3.1.

Druidic mist D902.1.1. — Bird reveals d. secrets B122.1.2.

Druidism. — Death for disbelief in d. Q558.13.2.

Drum. — Animals produced when forbidden d. is beaten *C916.2; bees in d. fly out, defeat army K2351.2.1; deity's special d. A159.2; demon-skins for d. K1715.9; dupe allowed to guard king's d. (wasp nest) H1023.1; escape from deluge in wooden d. A1021.0.2; foolish thief beats stolen d. J2136.5.7; ghost summoned by d. E384.1; huldra d. F460.2.8; magic d. *D1211; man inside d. believed to make noise J2026; marriage of girl to a d. T117.3; mortal beats d., gets fairy wife F302.6.2.1; ogre imprisons victim in d. G422.1; ogre keeps girl in d. R49.3; origin of d. A2824; sound of d. followed into ghost town F102.2; stealing ogress's d. H1151.24; tabu: heeding persuasive d. C811.1; toad plays d. B297.1.2; woman not to touch husband's d. C181.1.

Drums announce gods' approach A199.7; beaten before bride T133.3. — Beating d. scares off robbers K548.2; island with nightly noise of d. F745; thunder d. of the dead A1142.9.1.

Drummer drums for own wedding W152.10. — Elephant as d. J1882.3.

Drunk, see also **Drink, Intoxicated;** dancers punished Q386.2; elephant sent against enemy K2351.4; enemies slaughtered K871.2; king sentences unjustly J816.3; man calls judge very wise J1289.12; man made to believe that he has been to heaven and hell J2322; man makes king think him rich K1954.2; man thinks he's beheaded J2311.10; man makes sport of another man for being drunk J1063.2; man thinks Christ is speaking to him from behind crucifix K1971.7; murderers reveal crime N271.11; philosopher's foolish wager J1161.9. — Birds get d. A1427.0.1; creator d. A87; devil cheated of his promised soul by making the intended victim d. K219.1; dog driven out of dining room claims to be d. K874; escape by making watchman d. K625.2; man gets bridegroom d., enjoys bride K1371.5; man made d. left to demon's mercy K776.2; ogre made d. and overcome G521; St. Andrew gets d. A1372.10; saint's breath makes men d. D1500.4.2.1; theft by making owner d. K332; thief feigns pursuit by d. husband K314.

Drunkard cannot drown J2282; cured of seeing double J1623; refuses cure of fever if it is to take away his thirst J343.1; rides lion, thinks it a donkey J1758.5; unrepentant J1321. — Disguise as d. K1839.9; ghost brands d. E279.5.

Drunkenness, see also **Intoxication.** — Condemnation of d. after one drink N340.3; hermit chooses d.: other sins follow J485; humor based on d. X800—X899; magic object cures d. D1511; origin of d. A1386; repartee concerning d. J1320ff.

Dry branch on innocent man's grave blossoms as proof of innocence E631.0.5.1; feet tabu over river C833.5; river bed as bad omen D1812.5.1.16; rod blossoms F971.1; spring restored by removal of certain stone F933.2. — Causing d. spring to flow again (task) H1193; cows magically made d. D2083.1; fairy remains d. in rain F259.3; fountain magically goes d. D1647; lies about d. weather X1640; magic medicine causes streams to go d. D1542.3.1; magic wand keeps outdoor sleeping place d. D1542.4; man magically keeps d. D1841.4ff.; man sells d. snow for salt X1653.3; ogre persuaded to drink pond d. bursts G522; skillful fencer keeps sword d. in rain F667.1; spring goes d. (life token) E761.7.2, (after fratricide) D927.5.

Dryad F441.2.2.

Drying up lake in one night H1097.1; up of rivers D2151.2.3. — Death respite for d. self K551.12; drowning escape by d. up waters D2165.2; earth d. up D2081.1; earth made by d. up of primeval water A827; ground d. up when first woman bleeds on it A856.2; river d. up for day F932.6.1; sun d. out earth A733.5; woman d. hair scares ghost E432.3.

Dryness. — Goddess of d. A431.4.

Dualism of animal creation A1757.

Ducats. — Rich man shakes d. into pope's lap J1263.2.2.

Duck as ogre G353.3; persuades cock to cut off his crest and spurs K1065; recovers key from sea B548.2.2.2; sheep and cock in peril on voyage J1711.1; transformed to person D365; transformed to precious stone D423.3. — Creation of d A1983; enmity between hen, beetle, and d. A2494.13.10.2; friendship of hen and d. A2493.34; ghost as d. E423.3.10; helpful d. B469.4, (wild) B469.4.1; killing golden d. tabu C841.6; man transformed to d. D161.3; wagon drawn by d. F861.4.2; why d. quacks A2426.2.10; reincarnation as d. E613.1; separable soul in d. E715.1.1; why wild d. has red eyes A2332.5.7; witch in form of d. G211.3.2.

Duck's color A2411.2.6.4; feet A2375.2.8; food A2435.4.12; sandals become his feet D444.10.3. — Creation from d. eggs A641.2.

Ducks in pool in church V134.4; recover lost object B548.4. — Frogs were d. stolen from Eden A2426.4.1.1; "how often do you kill d.?" "Only once" J1309.2; if d. can ford river why not man? J1919.2; man shoots ram-rod full of d. X1111; remarkable d. X1261; roast d. fly (by magic) D2191, (lie) X1208.2; treasure becomes d. D449.3; trickster induces d. to dance with closed eyes K826; witches as d. G269.19.

Ducklings take to water instinctively J64.

Duel with bride as suitor test H332.1.1; with father-in-law H332.3; to prove which religion is better V351; as task H1166; won by deception K97. — Animal characteristics from d. A2257; challengers agree to sham d. K1771.4; fatal d.: brother kills brother in game K867; in d. with long poles the ogre is forced into the pigsty K785; sham d. to bring about recognition K1791; sinking into mud in d. F943; song d. H503.1.

Dueler. — One d. fights with God's help, the other with his brother's J1217.1.

Duelers. — Animals as cowardly d. K2323.

Dueling customs P677. — Giant d. over girl F531.5.7.0.2; origin of d. A1341.2.

Dug, see **Digging.**

Duke's — Lover in disguise as d. son K1831.2.2.

Dulled. — Sword cannot be d. D1081.2; sword magically d. D2086.1.

Dullness. — Feigning d. for vengeance J1675.7.

Dumb hero L124; man recovers speech in order to confess V23.2; person brought to speak F954; person's speech restored by gold D1507.8. — Deaf and d. (man can see soul taken to happiness or punishment) D1821.7, (speak) F1041.22; formerly men d., animals talked A1101.2.3; Jews protesting against marriage of Jewess and Christian stricken d. V343; man who cuts off tongue of swallow has d. children Q552.5.1; man eats father's heart, struck d. G91.1.1; pagan disputant with Christian stricken d. V352; person struck d. by Echo D2065.6; saint cures d. person V221.11; saint restores d. man's speech V221.2; sham d. man wins suit K1656; suitor test: bringing d. princess to speak F954.2.1; witch strikes d. G263.4.4.

Dumbness from disgust F1041.19; feigned to escape unwelcome marriage K523.0.1; magically cured D2161.3.6; as punishment (for breaking tabu) C944, (for hiding children) Q451.3.1; for surly speech Q583.2. — Magic d. *D2020ff.

Dummy set up as corpse K2321.2. — Black d. indicates banishment Z174.1.1.

Dumplings. — Sheep's head has eaten d. J1813.8.

Dung, see also **Excrement, Manure;** bursts into flames D1649.4; drops on washing hands D2194; on moon's face A751.5.2; from rich man's mules coveted P151; transformed to other object D457.13. — Blindness cured by chicken d. F952.5; cleaning with cow d. C536; conception from crane's d. T511.8.5; cow drops gold d. B103.1.2; dog alleged to excrete sweet d. K135.1.3; dropping d. on bribed judge's ancestors J1192.3; dupe induced to eat d. K1044; hero's head smeared with d. F531.5.12, P672.3; magic d. of animal *D1026ff.; magic supplies from bull's d. D1470.2.7; opposing witness's pockets filled with d. K1291; oracular pill is really dog's d. K114.3.1; "pick up everything!": fool collects d. J2516.2.1; sale of d. K143; resuscitation from bird d. E64.19; shooting stars are star-d. A788.4; spoiling the rice-field with d. K344.2; why d. of ass is triangular A2385.1; why fly lives on d. heap A2432.9; witch's rosary consists of goat d. G243.2.1.

Dungbeetle eaten J1761.11; helpful B482.2; keeps destroying eagle's eggs L315.7; prefers his dunghill to all other smells U122; thought to be bee J1751. — Friendship between grasshopper and d. A2493.21.

Dungeon. — Captivity in d. R41.3; children born in d. T581.2.3.

Dunghill. — Changeling is left on d. F321.1.4.4; dwarf's d. home F451.4.4.3.1; swindler buried on d. Q491.1.1; wife washes face in d. puddle H473.4.

Dunmow, ham as prize at T252.4.

Dunsinane. — Birnam wood comes to D. K1872.1.

Dupe cutting off part of own body J2131.3.2; gives trickster horses as dead father's demand J2326.2; loses booty through singing J2351.3. —

Blame for theft fastened on d. K401; blind d. deceived in shooting arrow K333.1; culture hero is d. A521; evidence of crime left so that d. is blamed K2155; god as d. A177.1; property of d. destroyed K1400—K1499; trickster rides d. courting K1241.1.

Duped, see also **Tricked.** — Husband d. into taking wife to paramour K1583; priest dies at being d. F1041.1.3.4.

Duplicating feat on journey C833.6.

Durham's. — Bishop of D. fool J1369.4.

Dust from communion table breaks spell G271.2.6; storm blows eyes shut J1158.1; strewn on circumcision wound A1567.1; of Tabernacle as chastity test H411.18. — Another kind of d. if the wolf's tail breaks X1133.3.2; cannibal recognized by cloud of d. raised H46; conception from smelling bone d. T532.1.4.1; food becomes d. D476.2.1; magic d. *D935.3, (kills snake) D1402.27; person turned to d. C927.1; removing d. from adulterous wife's clothes J2301.3; resuscitation from d. E42.1; rope of d. X1757.1; serpent subsists on d. B768.4; skull of suicide must roll in d. until it has saved a life Q503.1; stones become d. D452.1.12; transformation into d. D294; wolf does not mind d. J352.1.

Dusty. — Quest for d. cloth H1377.4.

Dutchman, Flying E511.

Duty. — Choice between desire, d. J233; filial d. rewarded Q65; king brought to sense of d. by philosopher J816.1.1; knight's d. to perform lady's bidding P52.1; when will ferryman be released from his d.? H1292.8; wraith doing person's d. E723.3.

Duties. — Exchange of d. brings disaster J512.7; king's four d. to subjects P12.6.1; lazy servant gets others to perform his d. W111.2.0.1.

Dwarf falls in love with girl seduced by magic K1672; as foster father P271.3; gods A134; hero of superhuman strength F610.2; as human D49.1; king falls into porridge pot X142.1; king laughs at absurdities about him U15.0.1; punishes for breach of tabu C905.1; as underground spirit *F451ff.; waits for ram, lamb escapes K553.2.1. — King cursed by d. smiths P15.4; magic object from d. *D812.12, (for kindness to child) *D817.1.1; marriage of mortal and d. T111.5; quest for bride for d. H1381.3.1.3; treacherous d. K2277.

Dwarf's beard caught fast K1111.1; magic armor D838.7; magic objects D801.1. — Headache from d. cursing M424.

Dwarfs battle giants F535.5.1.1; change size D631.4.1; and giants friendly F531.6.15.3; from Ham's curse A1614.1.1; and human beings F451.5ff.; magically keep ghosts from rising E439.2; in otherworld F167.2; perform tasks H973.3. — Appearance of d. F451.2ff.; cannibal d. G11.1; characteristics of d. F451.3ff.; during the day d. appear in form of toads or other vermin F451.2.0.5; emigration of d. F451.9ff.; fallen angels become d. V236.1; four d. support sky A665.2.1.2; gift of d. turns to gold F451.5.1.4; helpful d. F451.5.1ff.; home of d. F451.4ff.; human midwife for d. *F451.5.5; magic object summons d. D1421.3; magician and queen

as d. D2031.4.2; malevolent d. F451.5.2ff.; names for d. F451.8ff.; origin
of d. F451.1ff.; possessions of d. F451.7ff.; pygmies also called d. F535.

Dwarf-deer pastes other animals' eyes shut and pretends that hunters
are coming K2382.2.

Dwarfed. — Why certain trees are d. A2721.2.1, A2775.

Dwelling, see also **Home;** of demons F402.6; of fairy F220ff.; of Fortuna
N111.1, (on lofty mountain) F132.2; of god A151ff.; of helpful spirit
warriors in rocks and hills F450.1.1; of witches G230ff. — Animal
characteristics: d. and food A2430ff.; tabu: woman being in one's d.
C193.1.

Dwellings. — Characteristics of otherworld d. F165; huts replace caves
as d. A1435.3.

Dye blessed by saint D1684. — Husband drops d. on adulteress's dress
K1550.1.1; magic d. D1297.

Dyes. — Girl gathers plants for d., is cursed A2817.2; origin of d.
A1439.2, A1453.3; saint causes d. to malfunction D2084.3.

Dyeing beard as disguise K1821.1. — Disguise by d. complexion K1821.5;
man's presence unlucky during d. N134.1.1.

Dying, see also **Death;** child assigns task H937; culture hero A565; from
fright after prophecy M392; lover sends sweetheart his ring T61.4.5.1;
man assigns bride to his brother T141.1; man's curse M411.3; miser tells
son to extinguish candle as soon as he dies W153.11.1; and reviving (fatal game) K856; woman lures paramour into chest K1555.0.1; woman's
wraith visits children E723.4.4. — Birds d. when owner is killed B192.0.1;
cock hears inaudible voice of d. man B733.2.1; devil appears to d. man
G303.6.2.8; entire household d. same night F1099.1; fairy d. of longing
F259.1.3; fox as divider of d. man's gifts B294.1; friends d. shortly after
each other P310.6; faithful horse d. with master B301.4.7; fate prohibits
man's d. N101.3; father and daughter d. together P234.2; magic power
of d. man's words *D1715; man d. of pretended illness Q591.3; man
goes to heaven without d. F11.2; newborn child kisses d. mother T585.6;
observation of d. people for a year takes a man's thoughts from lust J62;
river rises to prevent body's being carried over it against d. man's wish
F932.8.1; shooting star signifies that someone is d. *E741.1.1; translation
to otherworld without d. F2; treasure buried by d. man N511.1.0.1;
visiting friends take everything from house of d. man W151.2; woman
falls in love with d. warrior T89.1; warrior d. faces foe P557.6; why
dogs howl when man is d. A2427.2.1.

Dynamite. — Knockers tamper with d. F456.1.2.1.3; lie about hog eating
d. X1233.2.1.

Dynasty. — God founds royal d. F32.1.

Eagle as bird of ill-omen B147.2.2.5; cares for baby while mother works
B535.0.12; carries (off condemned child) B522.4, (off ill-gotten gain)
Q557.3, (giant to its nest) F531.6.17.3, (man to safety) B542.1.1, (off
youth) R13.3.2; catches newborn gazelle B754.7.2; as creator of man

A13.2.2; -down rope to sky F61.2.2; eats tortoise J657.2; as god's bird
A165.1.2; killed with arrow made with his own feather U161; king of
birds B242.1.1; as messenger B291.1.9; as ogre G353.2; as omen of
victory B147.2.1.2; prefers own offspring to changeling J497; preys on
Prometheus's vitals Q501.4; regains throne for king B589.1; released:
grateful B375.3.1; renews youth B758; saves man from falling wall
B521.2.1; statue gives wealth D1469.13.1; takes revenge on man B299.1.1;
tests eaglets by having them gaze at sun B751.3; transformed to person
D352.2; with twelve wings, three heads B15.7.16; warns shepherds that
wolf is eating sheep and thus imperils own food supply J715.1. — Cat
brings suspicion between e. and sow K2131.1; cat from transformed e.
A1811.1; chain tale: man shoots e. Z49.10; daw tries to carry off lamb
like e. J2413.3; dragon as modified e. B11.2.1.11; falcon defeats e.
L315.9; fight between e. and fish B264.2; food of e. A2435.4.4; fox
burns tree in which e. has his nest L315.3; giant e. B872.1; giant as e.
F531.1.8.3, F531.1.8.7; gorilla transformed to e. D411.9; helpful e.
B521.2.1; man transformed to e. D152.2; marriage to e. B602.1; monkey
transformed to e. D411.5.1; mother e. casts out changeling, rears bold
son P231.6; mother e. distinguishes between stupid, intelligent eaglets
B122.5; prophetic e. B143.0.7; reincarnation as e. E613.3.1; return from
lower world on e. *F101.3; soul as e. E732.6; tabu to eat e. C221.1.2.4;
tortoise carried by e. J657.2; transformation to e. (to carry hero to
safety) D659.4.3, (to seek king's bride) D647.2; treacherous e. K2295.2;
war between birds and e. B263.5.1; wedding of e. and kite B282.2.1;
why e. cries like a baby: tortured baby became eagle A2426.2.15; why
e. has long life A2578.2; wise e. B122.0.5, (in earth-tree) A878.3.4;
woman pregnant after e. sits on head T532.7.

Eagle's body made smaller A2213.1, A2302.4; flight A2442.2.8; nest as
refuge R322. — Why e. back is brown A2356.3.1; diamond in meat
carried to e. nest N527.1; dungbeetle keeps destroying e. eggs L315.7;
prince grows up in e. nest B535.0.5; recognition through gold found
in e. nest H91.1; resuscitation by e. touch E79.3.

Eagles carry castle in air F771.2.1.2, F982.1.

Eagle-owl turns head around A2351.2.

Ear cornucopia B115.1; of stolen animal protrudes from thief's mouth
Q552.4; tips transformed to pelts D457.19. — Bird flies into large animal's e. and kills him L315.1; birth through e. T541.14; "bite the e."
H588.15, J2489.3; boy asks sister for an eye and e. T415.7; child born
with one e. T551.7; conception through e. T517.3; crab carries animals
in e. F982.8; disenchantment by water in e. D766.1.3; dog carries owner
in his e. B557.6; dwarf groans while carrying e. of corn F451.3.9.1;
flesh struck from ravisher's e. F304.4.1; god born from mother's e.
A112.7.1; husband concealed in wife's e. F1034.1; judge saves one e.
for other litigant J1289.8; magic air journey from biting an e. D2135.2;
magic e. of animal *D1011.2; magic power by crawling through e. of

magic horse D1733.2; murder by hot lead poured into e. S112.3; murder
by stabbing in e. S115.1; plucking e. of grain forbidden C512; removing
pea from e. J1115.2.2; resuscitation by wax from deer's e. E115; ribbon
long enough to reach from e. to e. K195; skillful marksman grazes e. of
sleeping person F661.9; slave's e. bored P171.1; testing the evidence by
experiment: biting the e. off J2376; thumbling drives wagon by sitting
in horse's e. F535.1.1.1; transformation by twisting e. D565.4.1; twins
born with one e. in other's mouth T587.2.

Ears cut off as punishment Q451.6ff.; not to be cut off twice J1187.2;
of demons cut off as proof of killing them H105.5; stopped with wax to
avoid Siren's song J672.1. — Animal languages learned by having e.
licked by serpent B165.1.1; animals' e. like elephant's until hare bites
them off A2216.7; ass's e. on king discovered by barber N465; bird
language learned by having e. magically cleansed B217.5; birds perch
on e. of cows B853; boring hot irons through e. Q469.9; box on the e.
returned K2376; camel asks for horns: punishment, short e. A2232.1; why
cat has jagged e. A2325.6; cock with enormous e. F989.19; cooling e. by
breaking vessel on head J2469.4; cutting off e., hat falls over eyes,
can't see J2721; fairies with unusually large e. F232.3; flies try to drink
water from elephant's e. J971; flowers on e. protect against fairies
F384.4; giant's e. six hundred feet long F531.2.2.2; herbs in e. as protection D1385.2.1; house with neither eyes nor e. H583.8; literal fool
cuts off child's e. J2465.11; magic blown into e. D1721.3; magic sight
by looking between dog's e. D1821.3.4; Midas with ass's e. *F511.2.2,
N465; mutilation: tearing off e. S168; origin of animals' e. A2325ff.;
origin of e. A1316.4; person without e. F511.2.4; person unusual as to
his e. *F511.2ff.; power of soothsaying from serpents' licking e. B161.1;
reincarnation of e. into mussel shell E649.4; remarkable e. *F542ff.; ripe,
unripe e. in allegorical dream D1812.3.3.5.1; river in bird's e. D915.2.1;
sound of wild hunt avoided by sticking fingers in e. E501.17.5.8;
stopping e. to keep in wisdom J1977; transformation by seizing e. D565.4;
vampire with ass's e. E251.4.2; what makes your e. so big? Z18.1; why
camel has no e. A2325.7; why serpent has no e. A2325.8; wind caused by
flapping of e. of a giant A1125.1.

Earache. — Magic object cures e. D1502.7.

Earbox. — Begetting child by e. J1919.7.

Ear-wax. — Why e. inside the ear A1319.3.

Earl P50.1; imprisoned for hunting in king's forest Q433.10; killed in
combat with man he wants killed K1626.1; throws water at messenger
F1041.16.11. — Appointment to e. as reward Q113.1.

Earl's daughter given as reward T68.2; daughter rescued from giant
R111.2.3.1; son seduces foster brother's sister P273.2.2. — Impostor
claims to be e. son K1952.4.

Earlier universe opposite of present A633. — Maids must rise even e.
K1636; "rise e." J21.23.

Earlking G305.

Early death with fame preferred J216.5; pupil finds the gold N633. — Prophecy of e. death M341.1.2; riddle on starting work e. H588.12; start journey e. in the day J21.19.

Earnest. — Sham threat: "In e. or in jest?" K1771.1.

Earning. — Animal e. money for master B579.7; man e. as much as he gave away for charity in former life V411.5.1.

Earnings. — Giving all e. to poor as penance Q542.

Earrings tabu to Saora women C181.9. — Live-bird e. F827.1; peasant demands e. as price of silence after seducing priest's wife K1582.1; recognition by e. H94.11; woman promises marriage for e. K2338.

Earth, see also **Ground;** A800—A899; becomes silver D475.3.1; cursed M414.12; disturbances at end of world A1060ff.; Diver A812; at foot of stairs to swallow up man M341.2.25; gives birth to woman A1234.4; as God's footstool A133.2.2; made by cups of earth placed on spider's web A823; magically dried up D2081.1; opens at command F942.3; opens to rescue fugitive R327; punished for disobedience at Fall of Man A2721.8; red from child's blood A1227.3; rejects buried body E411.0.6; as remedy D1500.1.28; from river bed saves soul E754.1.7; rises F969.2, (from water so saint can cross) D2125.0.1; sinks into sea at end of world A1061; speaks D1610.19; spirit F494.3; subsides beneath flood A1019.1; swallowings as punishment Q552.2.3; swallows up impious horsemen Q221.4.3; swallows up overproud man C770.1; swallows, then vomits, children R142; transformed to (animal) D442.2, (gold) D475.1.8; -tree *A878; trembles at Crucifixion V211.2.3.1; under umbrella A653; as virgin mother of Adam A1234.1. — Absurd theories about the e. J2274; animal born from e. B717; animals created from e. A1714.3; Archangels drive Satan from heaven to e. G303.8.1.2; at beginning people start to eat the e. A1420.6; castle at middle point of e. F771.3.4; Cerberus to be brought to e. H1271; creation of e. A610.2; cure by passing through e. at crossroads *D2161.4.3; curse on everybody on e. evaded by person in earth M427; dead person visits e. periodically E585; devil in interior of e. G303.8.5; disenchantment by touching e. D782.2; distance from e. to heaven (riddle) H682.1ff.; fairy gift not to be taken to e. F348.1; ghost lives midway between heaven and e. E481.5; ghost shakes off e. when he rises from grave E410.2; giant with lower lip reaching e. F531.1.4.1.1; giant's stride spans e. F531.3.5.2; god of e. A400ff., J1441; god issues from e. A115.2; god lays foundations of e. A141.4; heathen swallowed by e. H1573.1.1; heaven and e. (connected by navel string) A625.2.1, (from egg) A641.1, (touch each other) A657.2; heaven mother, e. father A625.1; hiding in the e. K515.6; hills from e. wrinkling up feet A969.4; inhabitant of upper world visits e. F30ff.; journey inside the e. F114; king never touches e. P14.5; kissing the mother (e.) first J1652; magic aging by contact with e. after other-world journey D1896; magic e. *D935, (heals wounds) D1503.12, (protects) D1380.9; magic e.-mould holds person fast D1413.20; magic e.-slip D2091.15; magic results from contact with e. *D1778; magic sight of e. from otherworld D1825.2.1; magic of stones fixed in e. D931.0.2; man becomes pillar of e. D287.2; man from e. reddened with blood of human sacrifice A1241.4; man made from e. A1241, (from four different places) A1241.5; man thanks e. for saving his life but if he had fallen into well he would have blamed Fortune N111.4.1; man with e. in his shoes says he is standing on his own land J1161.3; marriage of e. and sky A702.5, T126.3; marriage of Mother E. and ogre T126.1; marvelous runner can run round the e. in five minutes F681.5; Mother E. *A401; new race made of red e. after world calamity A1006.3; nine days' fall from heaven to e. A658.1; object sinks into e. F948; ocean the son of E. and Heaven A921; planting the e. A2602; riddles about e. (most beautiful) H641.2, (costliest) H638.1, (distances) H681ff., (fattest) H653.1, (parents separating and mixing) H583.4.5, (strongest) H631.3, (weight) H691.2; river connecting e. and upper and lower worlds A657; sea like e. at man's burial F931.3.1; sinking into e. F942; sinking of e. as punishment Q552.2; sinner wanders between heaven and e. E411.0.4; snake created to suck poison from e. A2145.3; soul of the e. E701.1; speaking e. reveals murder D1318.16; strength is renewed with each contact with e. K12.3; strength of witches depends on their touching e. G221.2; tabu: goddess eating on e. C211.3.1; topographical features of the e. A900—A999; wax turned into e. D479.6; why waters do not engulf the e. A915; wild hunt avoided by throwing self to e. E501.17.5.4; wild hunt goes around the entire e. E501.14.5.

Earthenware pots in river J425.1. — Toad swallows e. F911.6.1.

Earth-mother. — World parents, sky-father and e. A625.

Earthquake accompanies holy man V222.9; at death F960.2.5; as giant falls down F531.3.8.5; at hero's return F960.9; kills giant F531.6.12.5; magically caused D2148; as punishment Q552.25; saves fugitive R236.3; spirit F438. — Extraordinary e. F969.4; fool's fear of e. J2634; god with body of e. A123.1.4.

Earthquakes caused by hungry old woman shaking A843; at world's end A1061.1. — Cause of e. A1145; magic object controls e. D1544; why people do not fear e. A1381.1.

Earthworm with light in tail B722.4; thought to be snake J1755. — Enmity of e. and rattlesnake A2494.16.6; origin of e. A2182.3; rattlesnake harmful because e. feeds him chili pepper A2211.11; why e. is red at one end A2411.5.5.

Earthworms killed whenever earth dug A1599.6.

Easiest. — Riddle: what is e.? H659.14.

East. — Castle e. of sun and west of moon F771.3.2; divinity's departure for e. A562; fairies live in e. F219.3; giants live in e. F531.6.2.3; male god invoked in e. A183.1; otherworld in e. F136.1; prayer with face toward e. V58.2; sun travels from west to e. F961.1.2.

Easter V75. — King in anger punishes misdeed on E. day J571.3; putting fish aside for E. J2124; whale helps clerics celebrate E. B256.12.

Eastern. — Most e. castle in world F771.3.3; taprobane at e. end of world A871.0.1.

Eastward. — Star moves e. F961.2.8.

Eaten god V30.1; grain and cock as damages K251.1; heart *Q478.1, (gives one the owner's qualities) *E714.4.1, (produces magic strength) D1335.1.2; object speaks from inside person's body *D1619.2; person resuscitated E32.0.1. — Ambergris made from bitumen e. by fish F826.2; apple divided and e. as love charm D1905.2; bones of e. man advise hero E366.3; breakfast, dinner, and supper e. one immediately after the other W111.2.6; cloth on back guarantees against being e. H119.1; corpses e. by (ghosts) E256, (vampires) E251.3.1; crumb trail e. by birds R135.1; dead souls e. by spirits E752.8; devil e. by wolf G303.17.3.3; earth e. by early people A1420.6; enemies frightened away by making them think they will be e. K1715.4; god killed and e. A192.1.2; hare and man contest: loser to be e. A2256.1; king e. daily E155.6; magic object e. D859.4; magic bird-heart when e. brings man to kingship D1561.1.1; magic nuts e. produce love D1355.12; milk and bread e. with child by snake B765.6; peasants think that the calf has e. man all but feet J1815; person's entrails e. by witch G262.2; priest's guest and e. chickens *K2137; prodigious amount e. by giant F531.3.4ff.; punishment: being e. by animals Q415; resuscitated e. animal *E32; sick stag's provisions e. up by visitors W151.2.1; spirits believe they will be e. K1715.4.1; weak animal (man) makes large one (ogre) believe that he has e. many of the large one's companions K1715.

Eater of magic bird-heart will become rich (king) M312.3; of magic fish to spit up treasure M312.3.1. — Lie: remarkable e. X931; mighty e. F632; notorious e. J1468.

Eaters of stolen food detected J1144. — Voyage to land of Lotus E. *F111.3.

Eating, see also **Devouring, Food;** continually interrupted X12; courageous animal's heart makes courageous D1358.1; in the dark unwise since devil eats from plates A1512; "death vegetable" compulsory C662; of dough by wild huntsman's dogs E501.15.6.6; enormous amount (task) H1141; entire goat without leaving scrap H1141.4; fish intestines next morning when hungry J1606.1; ferocious animals heart makes person cruel D1357.1; food offered to dogs (penance) Q523.3; gluttonously W125; from hands of menstruating woman tabu C143; before hearing of adventure tabu M151; horseflesh punished Q499.6; human flesh, see **Cannibalism;** of human hearts as cure for insomnia D2161.4.13; a hundred onions J2095; magic food looses magic D1741.9; like man impossible to person once an animal H64.4; the moon (task) H1035; one hundred carcasses as suitor test H331.17; one's own newborn child L71; oneself up F1035, G51.1; pomegranate without letting seed fall H326.2;

after satisfied tabu C766; from skulls as fear test H1434; tabu *C200—
C299; tabus for pregnant women C152.3; way out of frozen animal
X1723.3.1; what is stolen without sin H1151.19. — Abortion by e.
T572.2.2; absurd ignorance concerning animal's e. and drinking J1903;
advice on e. before going to bazaar H588.18; animal wounds self, blames
other one for e. young K2153.1; animals agree against e. umpire M222;
animals e. corpse of holy man die B275.3; animals e. saint's body
stricken Q558.11; animals' extraordinary e. F989.22; best time for e.
H659.17; brother e. brother S73.1.2; caution in e. J585; clever deductions
by e. J1661.2; conception from e. *T511ff.; contest in e. iron K63.1;
continual e. of certain animals A2478, A2231.1.1; covenant confirmed
by e. together M201.2; cumulative tales involving e. of an object Z31.3;
custom of e. buffalo flesh A1515.1; customs connected with e. P634.0.1;
deceptive e. contest *K81ff.; deceptive e. game: lion kills camel K869.3;
demons e. enormously G302.9.7, F402.4; devil never e. in an inn
G303.4.8.4; disenchantment by e. D764ff., (enchanter's heart) D763.1;
dog e. before other animals A2223.5; dragon e. ox each meal B11.6.7;
dragon e. people for rent B11.10.2; dupe e. stones K1043.2; effects of
wild hunt remedied by e. part of flesh thrown down by it E501.19.5;
fat giant e. self J2119.5; father e. own children K940.1, S11.3.8; forced
e. of frightful meal S183; giants keep corpses for e. G691.1; grief prevents e. F1041.21.3; hart e. the earth-tree A878.3.2; hero bluffs demon
with e. threat K1715.7; husband becomes cannibal from e. wife's breast
G36.1; innocent woman accused of e. her new-born children K2116.1.11;
Jewish child burned for e. consecrated Christian bread V363.1; lie: animals e. each other up X1204; madness from over-e. F1041.8.5; magic
results from e. or drinking *D1793; magic weakness from e. D1837.5;
make-believe e., make-believe work J1511.1; man before dying e. up his
money W151.7; man-e. god A135; man e. sweets calls self "B" K602.2;
monster e. people G346.2; mortals not e. fairy food F361.15; mother forces
child to break e. tabu S12.2.3; mothers e. own children Z215; mountain
spirits e. raw food F460.2.14; nun e. unblessed lettuce eats a demon
G303.16.2.3.4; origin of e. customs A1510ff.; person e. only tobacco
F561.4; pilgrim rebuked for e. too much J1346; poor host closes eyes
not to see e. guest P336.3; punishment: e. ashes Q478.5; punishment for
splitting head and e. man's brains Q211.7; rakshasa e. domestic animals
at night G369.1.3; revenants e. E541; secret meat-e. betrayed N478.1;
secret for not e. foreign food overheard N475.2; serpent inside man e. his
food G328.1; servant plans to deceive his master by not e. J2064; sham
e. K81; shark-ogre e. swimming children G308.5; spirit e. food F473.6.4;
spirit e. person F402.1.11.2; strong hero engendered by e. fruit F611.1.8;
sun e. up its children A736.1.4.1, A764.1.2; sun e. up stars A1066; tabu:
e. from offerings to gods C57.1.3; talker keeps person from e. J1564;
thief e. from plate without detection F676.1; transformation by e.
*D551ff.; transformation to buffalo for e. grass D655.1; tribal charact-

eristics: e. A1681; trickster e. own dog K1664; victim enticed into e., killed K839.1; vow against e. until secret learned M151.1; wife banished for e. by stealth S411.4; wife e. up husband's earnings T251.10; wisdom from e. fox's heart B163.1.1; wolves e. each other up so that only tails are left X1204.1; woman e. before Communion can't swallow wafer V39.9.

Eavesdropper overhears secret name *N475; unwittingly killed N322.

Ebb-tide goes to great whirlpool A913.3.

Ebony. — Island of e. F732.1; why e. tree is black A2751.4.2; why e. tree has black wood and smoke-colored leaves A2772.4.

Ecclesiastical. — Quest for lost e. rule H1382.3; seven e. orders Z71.5.6.3.

Echidna B29,2.

Echo A497; abducts person D2065.6; answers K1887.1; as dwarfs' voice F451.2.8; of giantess's song F531.3.8.4; invisible A497.1; as wood-spirit F443. — Abduction by E. R11.2.2.1; evil spirits from e. G302.1.2; magic e. answers for fugitive D1611.15; origin of e. A1195.

Eclipse in God's proximity F961.0.2; as punishment Q552.20; of sun at historical event F961.1.9; after Sun, Moon captured R9.1.2. — Continuous world e. A1046; origin of e. of moon A737.0.1; sun hides face in shame: hence e. A737.8.1.

Eclipses as evil omens D1812.5.1.4. — Causes of e. A737.

Economy. — Shortsighted e. J2199.4.

Eddies. — Fairies travel in wind e. F282.1.

Eden. — Frogs were ducks stolen from E. A2426.4.1.1; souls pass through E. E755.1.3.

Edible substance changed to inedible D476.2. — Assignment of e. animals A1422; inedible substances become e. D476.1.

Edification. — Sacrifice at temple e. V12.4.0.1, V17.8.

Edifices. — Religious e. *V100—V199.

Edric as wild hunt leader E501.1.7.3.

Educated men as choice company J146.

Education of hero A511.3. — Foolish attempt at e. of animals J1882; lack of proper e. regretted J142; strange language used to show e. W116.7; wisdom (knowledge) through e. J140ff.

Eel burned by torch, hence red eyes A2218.8; with fiery mane B15.7.12; -god A132.12; as king of fishes B243.1.2; paramour B612.1; transformed (to object) D426.1, (to person) D373. — Creation of e. A2131; fairy as e. F234.1.10; ghost as e. E423.9; giant e. B874.2; god becomes e. D173.1; helpful e. B476; hostile e. attacks hero B17.2.1.2; magic charm hooks e. D1444.1.4; magic e. pursues man R262; magpie tattles about the e. J551.5; man transformed to e. D173; marriage to e. B603.2; mythical e. B64; tabu to eat e. C221.1.3.2; why e. (has no tongue) A2344.2.2, (is slippery) A2306.1.

Eels killed with snakes in pond J2114. — Fearless hero frightened by being awakened by e. put down his back H1441.1; god of e. A445.2; king of e. B243.2.2; leaves become e. D441.5.1.

Effigy. — Punishment in e. Q596; taking cold in e. J1628.

Egg becomes bloody D474.4, (as sign of disobedience) C913.1; becomes crowing cock F989.20; creature changes size at will D631.4.4; as reward of appropriate saying K444.1; as shinny ball F878; transformed (to house) D469.1.1, (to mist) D469.1, (to person) D439.4. — Basilisk hatched from cock's e. B12.1; birth of human being from e. T542; breaking e. on castle parapet H1149.6; champion does not break e. upon which he sits H1568.1; choice of one e. or none J201.1; conception from eating e. T511.7.2; cosmic e. *A641; creator born from e. A27; deity in shape of e. A114.2.1; dog mistakes mussel for an e. J1772.2; dragon from cock's e. B11.1.1; earth from e. (breaking on primeval water) A814.9, (from bottom of sea recovered by bird) A812.2; enormous e. X1813; familiar spirit acquired by carrying e. under left arm-pit F403.2.1.1; general hatches out e. K1253; goose that laid golden e. D876; god born from e. A114.2; goose e. becomes hen's D479.4; guess what I have in my hand and I will give it to you to make e.-cake with J2712.1; hero born from e. A511.1.9, F611.1.11; horse born of e. B19.3; magic e. *D1024, (furnishes livestock) D1477.3, (furnishes slaves) D1476.2, (produces soldiers) D1475.7; making an invisible knot with an e. (task) H1021.5; man becomes e. D276; man created from e. formed from sea-foam A1261.2; marooned e.-gatherer *K1616.1; marriage with woman coming from e. T111.3; obstinate wife and the third e. T255.4; origin of sky from e. brought from primeval water *A701.1; pale sun restored with e. A721.4; person returns to original e. form when tabu is broken C963.2; pumpkin thought to be an ass's e. J1772.1; quest for vulture's e. figured with golden letters H1332.2; roc's e. B31.1.1; scholar given third e. J1539.2; seven-headed witch defeated by throwing e. at each head G275.4; sewing together broken e. H1023.7.1; shepherdess born of red and blue e. T542.1; soul in e. E711.1; stream changed to e. D476.1.8; three horses from dove's e. on last day A1091.1; wager: to swallow e. in one gulp N75; witch killed as e. G275.4.1; woman lays e. T565; world as e. A655.

Eggs from eggplant X1495; stolen from fairies F359.1. — Absurd ignorance concerning the laying of e. J1901; air-castle: basket of e. to be sold J2061.1.2; animal thief of e. detected when he comes to a spring to drink J1144.2; why animals lay e. as they do A2486ff.; boy punished for stealing bird's e. Q285.1.2.1; buying e. and "ay, ay" H1185.1; cobold likes scrambled e. F481.0.1.3; crab's attempt to lay e. in pot J2415.3; crow's house full of wren's e. H1129.9; crushing e. tabu C544; dividing the e.: one man's hand in pot at time J1241.5; dividing five e. equally between two men and one woman J1249.1; dove and magpie exchange e. A2247.4, A2486.3; dungbeetle keeps destroying eagle's e. L315.7; first thief steals e. from under bird (second meantime steals first's breeches)

K305.1; goose e. bewitched G265.8.4.2; guess how many e.? you have all seven J2712.2; how birds began to lay e. A2486.4; killing hens to get all the e. at once J2129.3; mankind originate from e. A1222; marksman's skill in shooting e. F661.4; nature of bird's e. A2391; numskull sits on e. to finish the hatching J1902.1; potatoes as e. of the earth J1722.1.2; securing e. from atop glass tower H1114.1; sitting on e. without breaking them H962.1, H1568.1; skillful tailor sews up broken e. F662.1f.; snake e. D551.6.3; soul in three separate e. E711.1.1; stealing e. from under bird H1151.12; suit for chickens produced from boiled e. J1191.2; tabu to eat birds' e. C221.3.3; task: hatching boiled e. *H1023.1f.; trickster hides e. in breeches to avoid tax, made to sit K1693; two e. given tailor to eat so as to stop his singing J1341.4; voices from within unhatched e. J646.2; walking on e. H225.2; wise man destroys serpent's e. J622.1; woman lays, hatches e. F569.1.

Eggplant goes on warpath F1025.2.1. — Eggs from e. X1495; magic e. D983.5; reincarnation as e. E631.5.3; riddle about e. garden H583.2.5; speaking e. D1610.3.4.

Eggshell. — Brewing in e. to drive away cobold *F481.4; smith drawing water in an e. D512.1.

Eggshells. — Witches travel in e. G241.4.2.

Egg-white. — Payment of e. K249.2.

Egypt as demons' abode G302.5.2. — Animals from frogs sent as plague to E. A1734; storks become men in E. in winter D624.1; wisdom from E. J192.2.

Egyptian. — Satan slays first-born E. G303.20.9.

Egyptians fond of asses A1689.12; as magicians D1711.10.3. — Bloody waters for E. F930.4.

Ehod mi yodea Z22; saves girl from devil K555.2.1.

Eight-armed giant F531.1.6.7.2; -eyed bat B15.4.1.4; -eyed giant F531.1.1.5.1; -eyed person F512.2.1.2; as formulistic number Z71.16.1; handfuls of food in ceremony C231.5; heavens A651.1.5; paradises A661.2. — Adam's body made of e. things A1260.1.3; death as e.-headed monster Z111.3; flood lasts e. months A1010.2; man's body from e. sources A1260.1.

Eighteen. — Prophecy: death before e. years M341.1.3.2; prophecy of greatness if boy lives to be e. M312.0.3.

Eighty as formulistic number Z71.16.6.

Eighty thousand as formulistic number Z71.16.8.

Eighteen hundred. — Dwarfs emigrate New Year's Eve of 1800 to return New Year's Eve of 1900 F451.9.3.

Eighteen thousand. — Giants live to be 18,000 years old F531.6.4.2.

Einherjar A165.7.

Eisenhammer, gang nach dem K1612.

Eisenhans G671.

Either .... or (sham threat) K1771.2.

Ejaculation guess N688.

Ejectment as punishment Q432.

Eland. — Man transformed to e. D114.1.2.

Elastic. — Man with e. reach F516.4.

Elbow. — Giant must rest on e. to be heard F531.2.10.

Elbows. — Indentions on rock from e. of hero's enemy A972.5.4; women kill with their e. G341.

Elder brother leads to ogre's home G401.1; brother rescues younger R155.2; brother threatens to kill unborn younger S73.1.3; brothers banished for treachery Q431.2.1; brothers impose task H934.4; brothers unwittingly aid youngest N733.3; children to protect younger P250.1. — Animals debate as to which is the e. B841.1; treacherous e. (brother) *K2211, (sister) *K2212; youngest brother helps e. L31; youngest brother rescues his e. brothers R155.1.

Elders. — Animal e. B1; Susanna and the e. J1153.1.

Elder (tree) cursed for serving as cross A2721.2.1.4; twigs reveal witch G257.6. — Tree-spirit in e. F441.2.3.2; why e. bleeds when cut A2766.1; why e. is never struck by lightning A2711.2.1.

Eldest brother as hero Z221; daughter will marry man only if he will marry all her sisters too T131.3; god born in front A161.5.

Election of fairies' king F252.1.1; of fox B239.1; of king in animal parliament B236. — Animal or object indicates e. of ruler H171ff.; bells sound e. of pope D1311.12.1; Virgin Mary designates favorite for e. for office V261; Virgin pardons e. cheater V261.2.

Electric shock scares away treasure diggers N561; storm breaks island F962.1; storm kills a thousand F968.1.

Elements silent, motionless at Nativity V211.1.5. — Death by e. as punishment M101.3.1, Q552.0.1; deity controls e. A197; four e. Z71.2.2; giants control e. F531.6.5.4; god reduces e. to order A175; magic control of e. *D1540ff., *D2140ff.; primary e. of universe A654; swearing by the e. M119.1.

Elephant accidentally poisoned N332.2.1; as animals' king B240.14; called "earth egg" J2671.3; carries person B557.11; cuts own leg to escape theft accusation K407.3; described by blind men J1761.10; determines road to be taken B151.1.4; draws plow to mark empire's boundaries B599.3; as drum beater J1882.3; eats poison man intended for self N627; frightened by moon's reflection J1791.12; as god's messenger A165.2.1.1.3; keeps house with other animals J512.7.1; killed by cutting off trunk K825.2; killed by mouse smearing poison L315.5.1; lets jackal enter stomach F929.1; loses its breasts A2353.3; offers chameleon ride on oiled tail K1042.1; put in pocket to show friends X941.3; rescues stolen girl B543.3.1; selects king's wife H171.1.1; transformed to object D421.3; transformed to person D314.3; -wrestler F617.1. — Abduction by e. R13.1.10; abduction by e.-man R16.5; airgoing e. B45; beautiful girl holding e. in each hand X943.1; bridegroom to meet disaster on e.

M340.4; bush mistaken for e. J1771.4; capture by hiding in artificial e. K754.2; capturing wild e. H1154.3.4; caring for mad e. H1155.4; creation of e. A1887; damages for broken pot: pay for e. K251.5; devastating e. B16.2.6; devil as e. G303.3.3.2.10; dispute of e. and ape J461.7; divine e. descends to earth F35.2; dragon as modified e. B11.2.1.6; drunk e. sent to attack enemy K2351.4; dwarf draws entrails from e. F451.3.4.11; earth rests on tortoise, serpent, and e. A844.6; enmity between e. and thousand-leg A2494.11.1; false boast: e. killed at one blow K1951.1.1; false claim: killed e. with hand K1787; firewood of e. tusks F811.22; fly jeers at king's e. J211.2.1; fool thinks God in e. J2499.5; friendship between e. and (dog) A2493.3.1, (jackal) A2493.11.2, M246.1.1, (monkey) A2493.14ff.; giant e. B871.5; giant uses e. as fish bait F531.3.12.1; god rides flying e. A136.1.5; god's e. A155.5; helpful e. B443.3; hired e. dies, owner wants live one back J1191.4; how can e. eat with tails at both ends? J1903.4; how e. got its tusks A2345.6; jackal cheats animals of mutually-killed e. K171.0.2; king selected by e. bowing to him H171.1; lark causes e. to fall over precipice L315.5; why e. does not live in town A2433.3.15; why e. lives in Nigeria A2434.3.3; magic jewel from e. B103.0.7; man disguised as e. K1823.2; man with e. head B28; man transformed to e. D114.2; marriage to e. B601.5; mice and hogs let loose put e. cavalry to flight K2351.3; mouse destroying e. H1161.3.1; numskull bribed to keep silent in e. sale N613; overcoming e. as task H1161.3; ox-demon transformed to e. D412.2.6; why e. is peaceable A2531.3; princess's husband selected by e. T63; rabbit and e. partners on trading expedition B294.6; reincarnation as e. E612.11; respite given while captive teaches e. to speak K551.11; riddle about deaths of e., snake, and jackal H803; savage e. lulled to sleep by virgin D1964.1; singing e. B214.1.12; sparrow intervenes in e. quarrel J2143.1; special power of chaste woman: raising fallen e. H413.4; stranger accidentally picked up by sacred e. and chosen king N683; strong man throws e. across sea F624.1.1; tame e. not accepted by wild brethren B261.1.1; test of resourcefulness: weighing e. H506.1; why e. has testicles inside A2284.4, A2365.1; tortoise leads e. into trap K730.4; vampire with e. face E251.4.1; wager on bullock defeating e. N77; white e. controls rain D2143.1.13; with rat transformed to white-winged e. D411.2.1; why e. flees when cock crows A2531.3.1; why e. has white marks A2412.1.5; why e. hurts self in grass: mouse's curse A2239.10; why e. lives without a hut A2432.10; why e. sees half-blindly A2332.6.7.

Elephant's enemies A2494.11. — Cause of e. walk A2441.1.7; animals' ears like e. until hare bites them off A2216.7; ascent to heaven by e. tail F75, J2133.5.2; earth rests on e. back A844.7; flies try to drink water from e. ears J971; god with e. face A131.2; jackal in e. belly eats liver, kills him K952.1.1; jackal imprisoned in e. dead body K1022.1.1; jackal in e. carcass K565.2; lie: child throwing e. carcass X943.1.1; man's ears like e. F531.2.12; princess rescued from e. captivity R111.1.12; person with e.

feet F517.1.7; stealing diamond from e. forehead H1151.6.1; stealing of e. tail (tusks) as task H1151.6; tortoise breaks e. back N335.7; why e. penis is large A2365.2.1.2; why mouse crushed in crossing road: e. curse A2239.9; woman captive in e. ear H1151.18.

Elephants B801; bring rain B791; fear swine's grunting J2614.3; have sexual desire only after eating mandrakes B754.2; lean from fairy music F369.8; look after ascetic in jungle B530.2. — Ants burrow into e. brains B524.1.8; captured e. pull together, escape J1024.1; city of e. F769.3; giant roasts e. G171; golden wagon drawn by four golden e. F861.1.2; hero fells maddened e. F628.1.6; journey to Land of E. F127.2; king of e. B241.2.11; land of e. B221.4; punishment: trampling by e. Q416.3; quest to land of e. H1289.1.1; war between e. and ants B263.2; war-e. B268.3.

Elevating. — Ground e. itself for saint V229.13.

Elevator. — Magic e. (stone on which one steps carries one underground) D1539.1.

Eleven as formulistic number Z71.7; portals to otherworld F156.5; rivers spring from well in midst of earth A875.2.

Elf, see also **Elves, Fairies;** knight entices maiden away and kills her F301.5; produces love-longing by blowing on horn F301.2.1; sets tasks for maid F301.4.

Elfland. — Girl from e. must eat earthly food in order to remain C661.

Elf-mound. — Magic bitches from e. B182.1.2; magic swine from e. B184.3.0.1.

Elfshot *D2066.

Elias drives devils from heaven G303.8.1.1; having had father and mother, is not dead (riddle) H814.

Eligius J2411.2.

Elijah passes to heaven alive D1856.1.1.

Elixir. — Cock's e. lightens people B739.1; conception from drinking e. from goat's horns T512.1; magic e. D1242ff., (to procure a child) T548.3.

Elk. — Capturing e. (task) H1154.5; color of e. A2411.1.6.6; creation of e. A1876; man-e. B29.6; needle kills an e. L391; why e. lives in woods A2433.3.13.

Elk's ears provide food D1472.1.24.3. — Magic e. head keeps falling down D1649.1.1.

Elopement R225; with wrong lover T92.4ff. — Fiancée forces e. with another man T157; man takes lover's place in e. K1317.9.

Eloping girl recaptured by parents R355; with king's daughter tabu C567.1; with woman who desires it obligatory C192. — Cave as e. lovers' refuge R315.1; forest as refuge of e. lovers R312.1; hero e. with king's fiancée slain K929.8; maid e. with pretended lover is forced by him to strip T72.1; princess e. with wrong man N318.2; rain charm sold to aid e. couple D2143.1.10; wooing emissary e. T51.1.1.

Eloquence, god of A465.3ff.

Elsa, Clever J2063.

Elusive. — Why game animals are e. A2552.

Elves, see also **Fairies;** *F200—F399; get stones from fairies D2066.1; have half thumb F232.7; have old men's faces F239.5; set country afire C934.3. — Woman beset by e., drowns self F324.2.

Elysium A151.

Emaciation caused by envy Q551.6.6.

Emasculation, see **Castration.**

Embalmed. — Lover's body kept e. for years by grieving mistress T85.4.

Embalming tabu C541.6.

Embarkation in leaky vessel as punishment Q466.

Embassy. — King imprisons another king's e. R3; royal bride conducted by e. to husband's kingdom T133.2; Zeus has e. of dogs imprisoned for fouling his court *Q433.3.

Embers transformed into animal D441.6. — Maidens unharmed by glowing e. D1841.3.2.4.

Embrace. — Disenchantment by enduring animal's e. D735.4; murder by crushing in false e. K953.4.

Embracing at village gate tabu C194.1. — Devil takes place of girl man is e. G303.9.9.16; lover dies from e. beloved T81.5; man e. other feels for gold K2021.3; princess e. teacher on wedding day M261.2.

Embroidering blanket in one day (task) H1093.

Embroidery on clothing as token H86.2. — Origin of e. A1465.2; recognition by e. H35.3.2.

Embryo, see also **Foetus.** — Soul of e. wanders E721.9.

Emerald box by well H1348.1. — City of e. F761.4.1; clusters of diamond and e. grapes F813.2.1.

Emeralds from broken vase A978.3.

Emergence of first man to earth A1230ff.; of stone from primeval water A816.1; of tribe from lower world A1631. — Witches at e. of mankind F203.2.

Emergency. — Ghost aids in e. E363.1.

Emetic. — Eaters of stolen food detected by e. J1144.1.

Emigration of dwarfs F451.9ff.

Emissary. — Kindness of e. saves girl's virginity T324; ruler pardons murdering e. W11.5.2; wooing by e. T51; wooing e. wins lady's love for himself T51.1.

Emissions. — Night e. from lusting bring near death T24.1.1.

Emotion. — Buttons burst as consequence of violent e. F1041.6; turning color from e. F1041.11.2.

Emotions. — Animals with human e. B773; divinity's e. A194.

Emotional reactions bring recognition H14. — Flood to satisfy e. need A1017.

Emperor blindfolded on ass traveling to paradise J2326.3; friendly to everyone W21; punished for murders Q211.0.3; rebukes overzealous servant as being a nuisance J554; thinks day lost when he gives no gifts W11.2.1. — Devil carries off murdering e. R11.2.1.1; dream warns e.

of wife's unfaithfulness *D1813.1.1; execution evaded by wishing to be e. J1181.2; girl flees lecherous e. T320.5; horse indicates election of e. H171.3; imaginary clothes for e. K445; punishment for deceiving e. Q236; servant plays at being e. J955.2.

Emperor's. — Death for dropping on e. coat Q411.15.

Empire personified Z116.1. — Elephant draws plow to mark boundaries of e. B599.3; prophecy of e. for fugitive hero M314.4.

Employed. — Sham-warrior e. at palace K1951.3.1.

Employees. — Tricks on new e. J2347.

Employment. — Don't work yourself out of e. J766; eavesdropping servant realizes misery of his e. N455.11.

Empousa B15.6.2.

Empress sews to show humility J918.

Empty shoe follows wild hunt E501.10.1. — Devil's shoes e. G303.4.5.1.2; noisy things often e. J262; sleeping in e. hut forbidden C735.2.2.

Emptying lake with pail in one day H1143.1. — Rain from e. bag in road D2143.1.8; rainbow from gods' e. their drinking cups A791.6.

Emu. — Why e. has no wings A2284.1, A2377.1.

Enamored. — Girl e. of monster T118; woman e. of unknown knight in tournament loses interest: he is her husband T236.

Enchanted heroine seen temporarily disenchanted H151.6.1; pear tree K1518; person *D5ff.; princess lives with dwarfs F451.5.4.3; snow K236.3. — Children e. by stepmother S31.2; city of e. people F768.2; giants e. in caverns F531.6.13.1; helpful animal an e. person B313; ordeal by e. water H222.3; person e. by witch's salve so as to be ridden by witch G241.2.2; soldiers of e. army tabu C549.2; stepdaughter e. by cruel stepmother on eve of wedding T154; tabu: destroying animal skin of e. person too soon *C757.1; transformation by plucking flowers in e. garden D515; witch has persons she has e. as servants G263.2.

Enchanter. — Disenchantment by destroying e. D763.

Enchantment by witch *G263. — Dwarfs free people from e. F451.3.3.4; magic object keeps off e. D1578; magic salve protects from e. D1385.6; seduction by feigning e. K1315.3.1; silence under punishment breaks power of e. *D1741.3; sleeping off e. period D1973.

Encircling by circumambulation *D1791, V58.3. — Disenchantment by e. D787; dragon e. city B11.2.8.1; seven seas e. world A872.1; snake e. world A1082.3.1; transformation by e. object thrice D563.

Enclosed. — Death e. in a bottle Z111.1; demon e. in bottle *D2177.1; enemy magically e. by walls D2091.16; fairy harper e. in yew tree F386.1.1; recognition by means of ring e. in wound H61.3; series of e. coffins F852.4.

Encounters, accidental H152, *N700—N799; unlucky N553.2.

Encouraging. — Dead mother e. daughter E323.6.

End formulas Z10.2; of the gods A1085; of king's reign P16; of world A1050ff. — Bringing deluge to e. A1028; castle at world's e. F771.3.1;

cock thinks world is coming to an e. Z43.3; "Consider the e." J21.1; date with beginning like e., (1691) H707.1; distance from one e. of earth to other (riddle) H681.1; divinity retires to e. of world A567; quest for the world's e. H1371.1; riddling remarks of traveling companions interpreted by girl at e. of journey H586; strong man's labor contract: blow at e. of year F613.1; wise man before entering a quarrel considers how it will e. J611.

Ending. — Enigmatic e. of tale H620ff.

Endless tales Z11.

Endogamy, origin of A1553.

Endurance contest won by deception K50ff.; of frightful experiences by youngest son in vigil for dead father H1462.1; of hardships with menial husband L113.1.0.1; powers as suitor test H328. — Contests in e. H1540ff.; tests of e. H1500—H1549; test of wife's e. H465; vampires power overcome by e. and prayer E251.1.1.

Endured. — Churchbells not e. by trolls G304.2.4.1; cross made by straps of knapsack not e. by devil G303.16.3.2; daylight not e. by ogre G632.

Enduring and overcoming curses M420ff. — Fame more e. than life L212.3.1.

Endymion given endless sleep M433.

Enema. — Murder by e. punished Q426.1.

Enemy attempts to kill helpful animal B335.3; chief vows to marry besieged city's princess M146.7; cured by poisoned cake F959.6.1; horses captured by lion join forces and become friends J891; invited for marriage, attacked K2013. — Army faces e. rather than the anger of their king J216.1; avoiding power of future e. J645; bringing best friend, worst e. H1065; bringing e. without weapon M234.2; defeated e. turns true friend P310.5; disregard advice of your e. J646; diving for reflected e. J1791.5; generosity toward e. W11.5; head of slain e. tabu C845.1; heart of e. eaten produces magic strength D1335.1.2; helpful animal killed by hero's e. B335; hostile dogs made friendly by having them fight the common e., the wolf J145; incognito king aids e. K1812.12; liquor as man's e. J1319.1; magic attack against e. D2091; magic object taken from e. D838.12; man keeps word to return to e. M202.2; owner frightened away from goods by report of approaching e. K335.0.1; princess in love with father's e. T95.0.1; prophecy: unborn child to kill e. M359.3; saint heals e. V441.1; saint's e. tries to induce his seduction T337.1; singing friendly song to e. K606.0.3; storm raised to defeat e. D2141.2; transformation to animal killing e. D651.1.1; transformation of e. D665; treacherous priests prolong mass to let e. destroy city K2354; tree points way to fugitive but misdirects e. D1393.4; uniting against common e. J624; vow against eating until e. killed M151.4; vow to attack e. or die M161.1; vow concerning fallen e. M166.1; wolf is the devil's craftiest e. G303.25.1.

Enemy's servant as helper N857; sex organs prove slaying H105.7. — Avoid e. revenge J647.1; capture by putting on e. clothes K761; death preferable to e. service M161.5; deceptive entry into e. presence K477.3; destruction of e. weapons J621; disguise in killed e. clothes K2357.7; falsely announcing e. approach as fear test H1405; killed e. son enslaved P173.2; lover disguised in e. clothes K1810.1.2; magic wand breaks e. sword D1414.1; prayer brings e. death V52.8; shooting at e. reflection in water J1791.5.1; taking boy to e. tent H1418; women spread shawls in e. path and entangle them K2352.

Enemies buried alive S123.6; caused to lose sight of each other K1886.2.1; duped into fighting each other K1082.0.1; make peace rather than slay each other *J218; won more by kindness than cruelty J26. — Animal betrays himself to his e. by talking J2351; why certain animals are e. A2494ff.; defeating e. as suitor task H335.4; foolishness of noise-making when e. overhear J581; friends' children become e. P310.4.2; god has e. kill him A179.3; god's e. A189.14; helpful buffaloes tramp hero's e. to death B524.1.5; hero tells e. how he may be killed K975.1.1; horse kills master's attacking e. B524.1.7; illusory e. K1883; magic causes e. to fight among selves *D2091.4; magic illusion protection against e. D2031.6.1ff.; magic object conquers e. D1400.1ff.; magic sack furnishes mannikin who cudgels owner's e. D1401.2; magic writing makes foster brothers e. P273.2.4; monk's e. quarrel and thus save him J581.3; preventing the birth of e. J622; quest for e. H1397; riddle: what are the two fixed .. the two eternal e.? H851; saint's bachall (brings down mountain on heads of e.) D1549.4, (keeps off e.) D1381.12; sham magician identifies e. as all dishonest K1956.10; transformation to defeat e. D651ff.; trolls as humans' e. F455.6.9.

Energy personified Z126.

Engagement, see also **Betrothal;** by trickery K1372. — Ring broken as token of broken e. Z151.

Engendered. — Strong hero marvelously e. F611.1.8.

Engendering, see also **Begetting.** — Pseudo-magic charm for e. offspring K115.1.4.

England must be full of widows J2214.11.

English. — Devil and Drake carry waters of E. Channel G303.9.2.4; why E. more powerful than Hindus A1689.11.1.

Engraved. — God's name e. on sun A733.2.

Engraving upon fire rock F809.6.2; shield with unique pattern H1199.4.

Engulfing. — Waters of heaven e. earth A810.2.1; water-spirits e. boy F420.5.2.2.2; why waters not e. earth A915.

Enigmas, see **Riddles.**

Enigmatic counsels of a father valuable H588; ending of tale H620ff.; happenings in otherworld F171.0.1; prophecy M306; quests H1377; smile (laugh) reveals secret knowledge N456; statements H580ff. — Daughter construes e. sayings H561.1.1.1.

Enjoying. — Disease to prevent man e. himself A1337.0.6, L482.5; woman e. enemy's ravishings T458.

Enjoyment preferred to wealth J484. — Devil advises e. and not thinking of God G303.9.7.2; husband objects to wife's e. of intercourse T257.8.

Enlarged. — Objects e. D480ff.

Enmity, see also **Enemies;** between animals from original quarrel *A2281ff.; between fisherman and dweller on the river U141; between giants F531.6.8.3; between priests and monks (chickens and eggs) X428. — Inherent e. between members of a family P201; liar brings e. between friends K1084.2; magic writings produce e. D1379.3.

Enoch Arden decision J1179.10.

Enormous, see also **Gigantic, Huge.** — Building e. bridge H1131; cleaning e. cistern in one day H1097.2; collecting e. amount of material H1149.4; dragon of e. size B11.2.12; strong hero sent from home because of e. appetite F612.1.

Enough. — Let well e. alone J513.

Enslaved, see also **Slave.** — Choice: free poverty or e. wealth J211; equanimity of the e. W25.1; ruler e. L410.6.

Entangled. — Enemy e. by women's shawls K2352.

Entering body of dead parrot or rajah K1175; fairyland through well F212.1; house after sunset tabu C752.1.3. — Devil e. another's body G303.18; means of e. house or treasury K310ff.; soul e. body E720ff.; suitor test: e. princess's chamber *H344; tabu on e. woman's quarters C182.2; vow against e. house other than own M182; wise man before e. quarrel considers how it will end J611.

Entertained. — Mortal e. by disguised god K1811.0.1; strangers e. by family to whose hitching-ring they happen to tie their horses P328.

Entertainer. — Trickster as e. steals meat K341.19.

Entertaining strangers tabu C745. — Woman e. every traveler H152.1.1.

Entertainment. — Inappropriate e. repaid J1565; king demands e. from guests P337.

Enticing guardian away K629.2. — Fairies e. to fairyland F301ff., F328; fairies e. by stopping ship F302.3.1.2; seduction by e. aboard ship to inspect wares K1332; wolf tries e. goat down from high place K2061.4.

Enticements. — Fatal e. of phantom women F585.1; rival suitors sleep with princess and vie in e. so that she will turn to them H315.

Entrails substituted for meat K476.1. — Boar's e. torn out F981.8; dwarf draws e. from elephant F451.3.4.11; eating his own e. K1025; excreting own e. Q559.11; fettering with own sons' e. Q469.7.1; hero pretends to eat own e. K1721.1; magic e. of animal D1015.3; man's e. visible when he laughs F594; pigeon's e. fetch lover D1355.3.4; punishment: twisting e. from body Q469.7; soul in e. E714.11; why Santals eat e. of hare A1422.1.1; wild huntsmen with e. stringing from open bodies E501.7.5; witch eats person's e. G262.2.

Entrance to dwarf home leads through filthy place F451.4.1.7; to fairy land underground F211.1, F211.2, into girl's (man's) room (bed) by trick *K1340ff.; of house impossible (for devil if horseshoe is over door) *G303.16.17, (for mountain-man before light is put out) F460.2.3; to lower world F91ff.; to otherworld F150ff.; to upper world F50ff. — Capture by closing e. to victim's home K737; castle revolving at night so that e. cannot be found F771.2.6.2; death on e. to marriage chamber M341.1.1.4; dupe lured into hole, e. closed K737.1; dwarf seeks e. to church F451.5.9.5; lions placed in city to prevent e. B847.

Entrapped suitors K1218.1. — Ogre e. in cage G514.1.

Envious jackal makes lion suspicious of his friend the bull K2131.2; man sets out to kill generous one W18. — Accuser e. of harlot J1351.2; children e. of money given by deceased father to bishop V415; covetous and e. J2074; prince e. of hero's wife assigns hero tasks H931.1; wild ass e. of tame ass until he sees his burdens L451.2.

Environment. — Acquisition of livable e. A1410ff.; animal "punished" by being placed in favorite e. K581.

Envoys debate which due greatest honor W161.1. — Mutilation of e. S160.4.

Envy W195; punished Q302. — Death from e. F1041.1.10; no e. in otherworld F172.1.

Ephesus. — Matron of E. K2213.1; seven sleepers of E. D1960.1.

Epic remembered from one hearing F692.1. — Quest for unknown e. H1382.2; return from dead to repeat e. E371.2.

Epicureans as atheists V323.1.

Epidemic. — Eating cure becomes e. J1511.3; owners frightened away from goods by report of deadly e. K335.0.2; saint ends e. *D2162.1ff.

Epilepsy remedy D2161.3.8.1. — Origin of e. A1337.3.

Epiphany. — Wild hunt appears between Christmas and E. E501.11.2.2.

Epistle. — Magic e. assures wearer will utter truth D1316.9.

Epoch. — New sun starts new e. A719.2.

Equal share of chief's bed J2526. — Association of e. and unequal J410ff.; hero seeks his e. H1381.5; marriage with e. or with unequal J414; princess to marry her e. T50.2.1; wife as one's e. J21.31.

Equals. — Friendship possible only between e. P310.8.

Equanimity of comedian when his house is carried off by flood W25.

Equivocal inscriptions at parting of three roads N122.0.1; oath K550.1, K1513, M105; prophecy of immunity M367.1. — Theft by assuming e. name K359.2.

Equivocation. — Cheating through e. K475ff.; deception by e. *K2310ff.

Erbsenprobe H41.1.

Eric fines P535.

Erin. — Prophecy; death between E. and Alba M341.3.2.

Eriu. — King's espousal to E. P11.6.

Ermanrikr sends sons, nephews to death K948.

Ermine. — Color of e. A2411.2.2; man becomes e. D124.2; why tail-tip of e. is black A2218, A2378.8.4.

Erotic scenes on bedroom walls reform continent husband T315.2.2.1.

Errand. — Escape by pretending to perform e. for captor K567; fool's e. J2346; owner sent on e. and goods stolen K343.1; taking year to do e. J2461.4.

Esau as magician D1711.1.2.

Escape by deception *K500—K699; from deluge A1020ff.; from devil by answering his riddles H543; on flying horse B542.2; from lower world by magic F101.4; from one misfortune into worse N255; from prison by use of magic fiddle D1395.1; from sea on fish's back B541.1; to the stars R321; of trickster without paying K233; on tree R311; from undesired lover *T320ff., (by deceptive respite) K1227; from witch G276ff. — Children e. to sky and become thunder A1142.3; disguised wife helps husband e. from prison R152.1; easy e. of weak (small) *L330ff.; flight of maiden to e. marriage T311.1; fettered monster's e. at end of world A1070ff.; knockers prevent trapped miners' e. F456.1.2.1.4; leave a loophole for e. J762; magic circle prevents e. D1417.1; magic object maintains quiet so that fugitive may e. D1393.2; sack from which one cannot e. D1413.9.1; tasks assigned prisoner so that he may e. punishment H924; transformation to e. difficult situation *D642ff.; transformation to old man to e. recognition D1891; troubles e. when forbidden casket is opened C915.1; vain attempts to e. fulfillment of prophecy M370ff.; wife swims to husband, arranges his e. T215.6.

Escapes *R210ff.; by magic *D2165ff. — Accidental e. N660; extraordinary e. *F1088.

Escaped lamb delivers himself to shepherd rather than to slaughter J217.1. — Detection e. by thief *K400ff.; devil's power may be e. G303.16ff.; execution e. by use of special permissions granted the condemned *J1181; witch overcome or e. *G270ff.

Escaping before enemy can strike J641. — Gods tricked into help in e. one's fate K2371.2; prisoners e. by asking leave K475.2; selling oneself and e. K252; victim e. executioner makes substitution K512.2.2.1; witch e. from locked room G288.

Escort. — Devil as girl's e. to dance G303.10.4.4.

Esdras chain: stronger and strongest (cumulative tale) Z41.2.1.

Eskimo, origin of A1611.1.2.

Establishment of animal life A1700—A2199; of human life A1200—A1699; of natural order A1100ff.; of plant life A2600—A2799.

Estate. — Ghost protects his e. E236.6; post falls when owners lose e. E766.3.

Estranged couple pay trickster for reconciliation K441.4. — Brothers e. by witch G269.7.

Eternal bats B19.9; ferryman P413.1; god A102.6; life without eternal youth as curse M416.2; youth D1883. — First men had e. life A117.1; two e. enemies (riddle) H851.

Eternity. — Seconds in e. (riddle) H701ff.

Ethereal music E402.4.

Etiquette. — Social e. A1537.

Eucharist, see also **Communion, Consecrated bread, Sacrament.** — Jewish child thrown into oven by father for taking e. V363.

Eumenides A486, C433.

Eunuch visits augurer to see whether he is to be a father J1271; says that his ill fortune is no shame J1471. — Widow rejects e. as estate-manager husband K2052.4.2.

Eunuchs, origin of A1313.0.1.

Europe. — Slaughter from wheel rolling over E. M341.2.20.

Europeans know more than natives A1667.1. — Origin of E. A1611.5.

Eustacius pursued by misfortune N251.

Evaded. — Death e. (person enters on the next life without dying) D1856, (by strong man) F615ff.; death order e. K510ff.; direct answer e. J1254; execution e. by using three wishes J1181.1; guardian animals e. B576.1.1; law e. by marriage for a night T156; ogre's power e. G534; task e. by subterfuge H950ff.; wild hunt e. E501.17ff.

Evangelist. — Seduction on promise issue will be fifth E. K1315.1.2.

Evangelium secundum Pergamum J1741.1.

Eve dreams of Cain, Abel D1812.3.3.7; names female animals A2571.0.2. — Adam learns animal languages from E. B217.8; devil appears to E. G303.6.2.11; devil gives E. two grains of corn G303.9.4.1; devil tempts E. A63.6; disobedience of E. blamed H1557.2; monkeys from children hidden by E. when God visited her A1861.1; new E. (mouse in jug) H1554.1; riddles concerning E. H811, H812, H813; Satan's intercourse with E. G303.12.7.1; tears of E. leaving paradise become trees A2612.1; underworld people from children which E. hid from God *F251.4; various children of E. *A1650.1; why E. not made with Adam A1275.8.

Eve's clothes of light F821.7.

Evening. — Four legs in morning, two at midday, and three in e. (riddle) H761; god of e. star A252; monster comes out of hole in e. G346.0.1.

Evenings. — Lower world people drink, dance in e. F108.2.

Events, extraordinary F900—F1099.

Ever-blooming garden in otherworld F162.1.1; -burning lamp D1652.6.

Evergreen. — Why leaves are e. A2765.

Everyman tests friends H1558.3.

Everyone asleep in castle F771.4.4; falls in love with princess T15.1.

Everything to turn to gold (Midas's touch) J2072.1. — First people have e. they wish A1346.2.2; "pick up e.!": fool picks up dung J2516.2.1.

Evidence of crime left so that dupe is blamed K2155. — Cane as e. of robbery N614; cleverness connected with the giving of e. J1150ff.; ghost leaves e. of appearance E544.

Evil ascetic misuses magic V462.13; deeds of witches G260ff.; demons set world on fire A1031.3; effects of meeting wild hunt E501.18ff.; magic in the dairy *D2083; man cast from grave E411.0.7; omens D1812.5.1ff.; predictions concerning journeys M358.1; spirits *F402ff., G0—G699, (born of echo) G302.1.2, (cast out of person) E728.1, (conjured away in name of deity) *D1766.7.1.1, (exorcised) *D2176.3, (hold back river) D2151.2.3.1, (possess person) E728, (prevented from using body) E752.10. — All e. will have an end J171.2.3; why animal is e. A2523; association of good and e. J450ff.; bull melts away after e. spirit has issued from him F981.2; conflict of good and e. creators A50ff.; culture hero spares certain e. spirits A531.1; devil originates from e. man's spittle G303.1.1.2.1; dragon as power of e. B11.9; father makes an e. greater H583.2.1; horse unable to draw e. dead man E411.0.3; huntsmen cannot die until e. righted E501.3.9; Jesus drives e. spirits into hogs: hence short snouts A2287.1ff.; land without e. F111.6; left hand for e. *D996.0.2.1; loss of all e. as reward Q150.2; magic book compels person to do e. D1678; magic journey during which one must not think good or e. D2121.6; magic object protects from e. spirits *D1385ff.; man speaks no e. W24; "may God spare you from e. man or woman" J21.38; north as abode of e. spirits G633; numskull believes self e. spirit J2013.4; opposition of good and e. gods A106; present e. preferred to change for worse J215; prophecy: unborn child to bring e. on land M356.3; putting out of countenance by telling e. stories J1211; revealing hiding place to e. spirits J2367; revolt of E. Angels against God A106.2; room in hell for e. spirits A678; storm from calling on e. spirit D2141.0.1; to be carried off by e. spirit M432; tree of knowledge of good and e. F162.3.5; transformation by e. spirits D683.6; wisdom from e. spirits J176.

Evils, choice between J210ff.

Evil Eye *D2071ff.; sets bird on fire D2061.2.1.1. — Counter magic against E. D2071.1.5; god with E. A128.2.1; islands transformed by E. of one-eyed god A955.5; magic paralysis by E. D2072.1.

Evolution. — Creation of man through e. A1220ff.; creation of universe through e. A620.1.

Ewe's hide grafted to man's head E785.1.1.

Ewes. — Fairies cause e. to have two lambs F339.3.2.

Ewige Jude Q502.1.

Exaggeration. — Humor of lies and e. *X900—X1899, K657.

Exaltation of the lowly L0—L499, (riddle) H797.1. — Spiritual e. from eating human flesh *G13.

Exalted person rescues abandoned child R131.11. — Wish for e. husband realized *N201.

Examination of strange country in disguise J21.43. — Animal corrects e. paper for rescuer B579.3; Christ's disciples did not pass e. J1263.1.4; separate e. of witnesses discredits testimony J1153.

Example. — Animal gives wise e. to man J133ff.; king's e. makes merchant wealthy N415.

Excavated. — Passage e. by fairies F271.2.1.

Excavation. — Sea from earth e. A924.4.

Excelling. — Man e. woman A1376.

Exception. — Dissolute wife only e. to man's happiness J1355.

Exceptions, unique *Z300—Z399.

Excess. — Death from e. of women T99.1.

Excessive demands to prevent marriage H301; use of magic power C762.1, D877.

Exchange, see also **Bargain;** of clothes between master and servant K527.3; of duties brings disaster J512.7; of forms by persons D45ff.; of gold-filled loaf for common N351. — Animal characteristics from e. of qualities *A2247ff.; betrayal through e. of stolen goods K439.1; deceptive e.: useless for magic object K140.1; devil to help gambler in e for one task yearly M214; female slaves as medium of e. P170.0.1.1; helpful animal obtained by e. B312.2; magic object acquired by e. (no trick) *D851, (trick) D831; man and wife e. duties J2431, *K1687; plant characteristics from e. of qualities A2742; pretended e. of confidences as to the one thing that can kill K975.1; theft of fire by trick e. A1415.3.

Exchanges. — Series of trick e. Z47.

Exchanged. — Children e. in cradle by dwarfs F451.5.2.3; children e. by parents K1921; eye e. for wisdom J163.3; eyes e. for food M225; foetus e. from one woman to another T577; immortality e. D1853; magic object e. for worthless D871.1; organs e. with animal E789.1; wives e. T141.2.

Exchanging objects with the devil G303.9.9.10; soul for witch powers G224.4. — Animal languages learned by e. tongues with helpful dragon B217.6; confessor and penitent e. confidences V29.7; dissatisfied workmen e. work U136.1; men e. duties: each cheated J2431.1; men e. jobs: each thinks other's easier K1687; mothers e. children S216; trickster e. beds, gets rival's food K499.8.

Excitement. — Death from e. F1041.1.3.9.

Excommunicated person cannot rest in grave E412.1. — Hog will not accept food from e. men B259.3; tabu to aid e. C95.

Excommunication V84; of animal B275.2; as punishment Q436.

Excrement, see also **Dung, Manure.** — Birth from e. T541.8.1; deceptive e. exchange K1721.2; extraordinary e. F559.3; horse trade involves eating e. K198; magic e. as cure for cancer D1502.10.1; why red dog's e. contains animal hair A2385.2; resuscitation from e. E41; rope of e. J2133.12; why crow eats e. A2435.4.7.1.

Excrements as advisers *D1312.1.1; of animals A2385; cause approaching animals to fall dead D1402.18; eaten by mistake J1772.9; thought to be berries J1772.9.1; transformed to person D437.4. — Animal's treatment of its e. A2495; doll's gold e. D1469.2; donkeys ask immediate reward: eat own e. A2232.11; magic e. *D1002; man finds cat's e. after he dreams he is rich X31.1; origin of e. A1317; speaking e. D1610.6.4; treasure from e. D1454.5; trickster creates men from his e. J2186; why pigs feed on e. A2435.3.14.1.

Excreting own entrails as heresy punishment Q559.11. — Dog e. sweet dung K135.1.3; power of e. jewels D1561.2.1; worm e. earth A828.1.

Excuse. — Thief makes a lame e. J1391.

Excuses. — Lovers' absurd e. for intrigue K1271.2.

Executed. — Animal e. for crime B275.1; blood of e. man as remedy D1500.1.7.3.1; fox e. for thefts B275.1.2; ghost of unjustly e. man E234.4; innocent man e. because he is right size J2233.1; man whose neck rope fits to be e. P14.18; ravisher e. Q244.0.1; whoever e. one day destined to become king in next birth J1189.3; witch e. for witchcraft G291.

Execution escaped by use of special permissions *J1181; release by marrying woman P512.1. — Altered letter of e. gives princess to hero *K1355; at e. man revealed as king's son N731.4; criminal allowed to choose his method of e. P511; delay in pardon allows deserved e. N394; escape from e. *R215; fat man chosen for e. N178.2; foolish demands before e. J2174; friend saved from e. P319.3; helpful animals quench e. fire *B526.1; husband's letter protecting wife altered to e. order K2117.1; identity established just in time to avert e. N686; king lured by e. invitation, killed K811.3; king sends regrets for e. K2098; long gray beard suddenly acquired on scaffold at e. F1044; loss of eye saves man from e. N178; making a good e. J2233; man carries written order for his own e. *K978; magic manifestation at e. proves innocence H215; magic object saves person from e. *D1391ff.; sham e. fatal to jester N384.7; speech magically recovered on e. stake D2025.1; substitute for e. obtained by trickery K841; wind blowing flag causes prisoner's e. N394.1.

Executioner miraculously blinded and condemned man saved R176; persuaded another victim ordered K511.1. — Compassionate e. K512ff.; sword magically changes to wood when e. is to decapitate innocent person H215.1; trickster calls self e., gets all food K344.1.3.

Exercises, religious J2495, V4.

Exhibiting. — Fairy woman e. self to warriors F397; person e. own nude figure T55.6.

Exhilarating. — Magic fruit e. D1359.3.3.

Exile returns and is successful L111.1; for seven years Z71.5.5. — Brothers follow each other into e. P251.3; prince chooses e. in honor J347.3.

Exiled king teaches ruler wisdom J55; wife's dearest possession J1545.4. —Accidental meeting of seeker of e. prince with prince at meal N745; devastating host e. by fairies F349.3; subject e. for trivial remark U38.

Existence of animals depends on man's e. A2513.0.1. — Vow fulfilled in next e. M107.

Exit. — Slamming door on e. from mountain otherworld *F91.1.

Exits. — How many e. from paradise? H682.3.

Exogamy T131.5; origin of A1553.

Exonerating. — Dead saint e. cleric E376.1.

Exorbitant price demanded, received K255.

Exorciser torments spirit F405.14.

Exorcising devil by "Ave" V254.4; ghosts E443; giants F531.5.8.2; by magic *D2176ff.; Will o' the Wisp F491.3; witches *G271. — Man killed for e. ghost E247; priest e. demon mistaken for demon J1786.4; spirit gives e. powers D1721.1.3.

Expelling demons from saint's grave D1385.1. — Magic object e. animals D1443; magic object e. person from land D1587; mother e. child S12.5; saint e. devil to hell G303.16.11.4; trickster e. owner from his house K354.

Expenses. — Kingdom's e. outweigh gains J342.2.

Expensive living along with high wages J342. — Child every two months too e. J1276.2; is wine e. or cheap? J1315.

Experience. — Counsels proved wise by e. *J21ff.; enigmatic statement made clear by e. H592; plants originate from e. of holy person A2620ff.; riddle expounded from chance e. H565; wisdom (knowledge) acquired from e. J10ff.

Experiences during magic sleep D1976; leading to adventures N770ff. — Identity tested by demanding account of common e. H15; marital e. of the devil G303.12; revealing e. in otherworld forbidden C423.3.

Experiments. — Man created after series of unsuccessful e. A1226.

Experimental. — Decisions based on e. tests J1176.

Explanation of natural phenomena A1200—A2899. — Quest for e. of dream H1217.1; riddles of e. H770ff.

Explanations. — Three e., last true Z64.

Exploits. — King chosen for e. P11.4; tears at recital of own e. H14.2; tokens of e. H84.

Explosion. — Witch causes gun e. G269.16.

Exposed child rescued R131ff. — Amorous intrigue observed and e. K1271; children e. S301; honey-covered victim e. to flies Q464; impostors e. K1935.1; infidelity of husbands e. by crown H422.1; mistress e. naked to her husband Q476; prince in love with girl e. in jungle T91.6.3.1; queen e. in leather in market Q483.1; sham magician e. by clever girl K1963.1; sheep, oxen protect e. child B535.0.10.

Exposure in boat *S141, (as sin test) H263.1; of infant to avoid fulfillment of prophecy M371; of own baby instead of tyrant's P361.4; to sunlight forbidden C842; astride wood in river S141.3; to ridicule when wig snatched off X52.1. — Cruel e. S140ff.; ordeal by e. H236; punishment: unseemly e. Q495.

Expression. — Allusive e. for gods' incest A1599.16; forbidden e. C498.

Expressions. — Commonplace e. scare off wife's suitors J2461.2.2.

Expulsion from court saves counselor's life N178.3; of devil from heaven

G303.8ff.; from fairyland for breaking tabu F378.0.1. — Fairy mistress demands e. of wife F302.5.4.

Extending. — Giant e. across whole island F531.2.1.4; ogress e. limbs any distance G365.2; rakshasas e. bodies far G369.1.1.

Extermination of mice infesting city H1109.4. — Expensive e. of rodents J2103.

External soul *E710ff. — Animals help man overcome monster with e. soul B571.1; escape by alleged possession of e. soul K544; life dependent on e. object or event *E765ff.; secret of e. soul learned by deception K975.2.

Extinct. — Why griffin is e. A2232.4.

Extinguishing, see also **Quenching;** fire by spitting H221.5. — Miraculous rain e. fire *D1391.1.

Extortion W193; by confessor V29.9.

Extraordinary, see also **Unusual;** actions explained H591; behavior of trees and plants F970ff.; bodies of water F710ff.; buildings and furnishings F770ff.; cities F760ff.; clothes in otherworld F166.3; clothing and ornaments F820ff.; companions F601ff.; cures F950ff.; islands *F730ff.; mountains and valleys F750ff.; nature phenomena F960ff.; occurrences F900—F1099, (concerning seas or waters) F930ff., (concerning animals) F980ff.; persons F500—F599; places and things F700—F899; rocks and stones F800ff.; sights in otherworld F171; sky and weather phenomena F790ff.; swallowings F910ff.; trees and plants F810ff.; underground disappearance F940ff.; weapons F830ff. — Asking questions about e. things inadvisable J21.6; brothers acquire e. skill *F660.1; conception from e. intercourse T517; finding e. object as suitor test H355; horse's head for e. use F874; persons with e. powers F600—F699; quest for e. plants H1333; recognition by e. prowess H32; treasure buried in e. topographical formations N511.1.3; witch with e. members G213ff.

Extravagant wife J1701.1. — Haughty mistress makes e. demands of lover: repaid L431.1.

Extremes. — Cumulative tales involving e. Z51. — Foolish e. J2500—J2549.

Eye bursts from voice overstrain F1085; drops prescribed for stomach ache X372.3; juggler J2423; lost waiting for water to become wine D477.1.2; remedy (for blinding) K1011; transformed to other object D457.11; in vulva F547.5.3. — Bird's red e. cooks meat F989.2; birth from an e. T541.7; boy asks sister for an e. and ear T415.7; cat's luminous e. *B721; charm for diseased e. D1505.11; child born with one e. T551.11, Q556.4.1; crane pecks out e. of spy Q557.5; "crookedness in e." from curse D2062.2.1.1; curse: loss of e. M431.1; demon with one e. G369.7; devil inflames saint's e. G303.9.6.2.1; disguise by cutting one e. out D1821.6; fleeing fox loses e. in briars J2182; foolish lover does not know that his mistress lacks e. J1737.1; fork in e. from breaking tabu

C943.1; fortune has one e. N111.2.1.1; giant with one e. blind G511.1; ghost as an e. E422.1.11.1; god with blazing e. A124.1; horse with blue e. H1331.4.1; hot onion to e. J2412.1; husband's one e. covered K1516ff.; islands transformed by evil e. of one-eyed god A955.5; king gives away his only e. W11.16; left e. only vulnerable spot Z311.1; loss of e. (for breaking tabu) C943.2, (saves man from execution) N178; magic e. D993; magic sight by putting ointment into e. D1821.4; magic watchful e. remains awake while other eyes sleep D1961; man condemned to lose his e. allowed to choose the instrument P511.2; man made from creator's e. A1211.4; man so small he can go through e. of needle F535.2.2; nightingale borrows blindworm's e. A2241.5; one e. exchanged for wisdom J163.3; one e. recedes, other protrudes when angry F1041.16.2; one wishes that he may lose an e., so that other will be blind J2074; parson with one e. marries wrong couples X413; persons blown into woman's e. X941.4; pulling out e. so that pain will cease J2412.2; reward for tearing out e. Q42.6; returning e. to one-eyed man J1512.2; saint plucks out e. to avoid marriage T327.3; saint's prayer restores opponent's e. V52.15; skillful marksman shoots animal through e. F661.5ff.; skillful surgeon removes speck from midge's e. F668.2; soul leaves body through e. E722.2.11; sun's all-seeing e. A739.7; three persons with one e. *F512.1.2, *G121.1ff., G612, *K333.2; throbbing of right e. as favorable omen D1812.5.2.1; watch mistaken for the devil's e. J1781.2; water-spirits' one e. F420.1.1.5; why center of e. is black A1319.7; why soldiers with one e. good J1494; wood spirit gigantic with one e. in center of forehead *F441.4.1.

Eyes of animal substituted as proof for children's K512.2.0.2; burst forth for urging saint to marry Q551.8.4; fall out of blasphemer's head Q551.6.5.2; of giant F531.1.1ff.; exchanged for food M225; lost from looking at forbidden well C623.1; magically replaced D2161.3.1.1; successfully replaced *E781ff.; as sacrifice V12.7; size of brass pots F531.2.12; of stone lion become bloody D474.9; the swiftest (riddle) H632.2, H661; treated for the stomach ache J1603; of various peoples A1666; which can see heaven D1820.3; wagered N2.3.3. — Adulteress binding husband's e. K1566.1; animals with unusual e. B15.4ff.; bad character shown by e. H1550.1; beetle cursed for betraying Holy Family: now always has e. on ground A2231.7.1.1; blind comforted by soul's inner e. J893.1; blindness cured by rubbing sand on e. F952.3; bright e. as sign of royalty H71.6; buffalo's e. turn into protecting dogs D699.1; casting sheep's e. at the bride *J2462.2; cock persuaded to crow with closed e. K721; cross-e. miraculously straightened F959.2; devil's e. G303.4.1.2ff.; devil gives horse four e. but God reduces to two A2286.2.2; discourteous answer: why crab has e. behind A2231.1.3; dogs with e. hanging out over mouth in wild hunt E501.4.1.4; dogs with fiery e. in wild hunt E501.4.1.3; dwarf-deer pastes other animals' e. shut and pretends that hunters are coming K2382.2; eating own e.

K1025.2; eel burned by torch: hence red e. A2218.8; fairy's red. e.
F233.3.1; fairies made visible through use of magic stone on e. F235.4.3;
fright at animal's e. in the dark J2624; genie sleeps with e. open G634;
ghosts as dogs with glowing tongues and e. E421.3.6; god with unusual
e. A123.3ff.; goddess born from mother's e. A112.7.3; goddess of
thousand e. A475.1.1.1; hare instructs his sons to use their e. to advantage J61; headache cure: removing e. K1011.1; headless person
with e. on breast F511.0.1.1; hero's different colored e. A526.5.1;
hero's e. would pop out if washed B521.1.1; horse originally had e. on
feet A2262.1; horse with fiery e. in wild hunt *E501.4.2.5; host,
hostess, and cat have but three e. among them J551.4; house lined with
human e. F163.3.2.1; house with neither e. nor ears (enigma) H583.8;
images open and close e. D1632; lemur looks where forbidden: has big
e. A2234.3; magic journey with closed e. D2121.2; maiden sends to
her lecherous lover her e. T327.1; mother's e. the brightest (riddle)
H651.2; mutilation: putting out e. *S165; necklace of human e. F827.4;
numskull puts out his e. J2131.4; opening of creator's e. creates day
A1171.1; origin and nature of animals' e. A2332ff.; origin of e.
A1316.3; pepper or tobacco thrown into e. of guard *K621; person
transformed to animal recognized by his e. H62.1.1; person unusual as
to his e. F512ff.; person without e. F512.5; poor host closes e. not to
see guest eat P336.3; putting out wife's e. J2462.3; raven plucks out
men's e. B17.2.3.1; reincarnation of e. into currants E649.5; remarkable
e. F541ff.; scorpion scoops out men's e. B17.2.4.1; seeing without e.
X1724; serpent demands human e. for drink S263.3.2; servant cheats
master boasting of e. in back of head J1511.9; severed head opens
e. E783.4; sham dead detected by batting e. H248.5; skillful marksman shoots both e. of an ogre F661.5.4; sun and moon (placed for e.
in the sky) A714.1, (as Rama's e. torn out) A714.7; tempted rabbi tears
out e. T333.3.1; toad trades his tail for mole's e. A2247.5; vampire
with e. of owls E251.4.3; washing e. to keep awake H1484.1; where owl
got his e. A2332.1.5; why caribou has small e. A2332.3.3; why frog's e.
bulge out A2332.4.3; why rats don't stick their e. out in the straw
J2371.3; why zabi's e. narrow: laughs so hard A2332.3.2; wife puts out
one of her e. to show sympathy with her husband T215.4; wife's e. invulnerable to sea water D1841.4.5; wild huntsmen with fiery e. E501.7.6.2;
witch with extraordinary e. G213; witches use animals' e. at night
G249.10.1; witness claims e. were blown shut J1158.1; woman with
bad e. J1169.1; women throw ashes in e. of attacking soldiers so that
they are defeated K2356.

Eyeballs transformed to torches D457.11.2. — Sucking snake's e. T611.11.
Eyebrow. — Magic hair in man's e. kills all who see it D1402.2; poisonous
e. causes death to beholder F555.7.
Eyebrows so heavy must be on back to see F441.4.5. — Devil has no e.
G303.4.1.2.6; hardest to hold wolf by e. H659.2.1; helper's beard and e.
cut N810.2.

Eye-hole. — Giant's skull so large that fowl can pass through e. F531.2.3.1.

Eyelashes. — Origin of e. A1315.6; path to sun on sun's e. (rays) F154.

Eyelid. — God with handle through e. A128.2.2; heavy e. F541.7.

Eyelids. — Flight so high that e. drop from cold F1021.2.2; ogre so old that his e. must be propped up G631; old man with hanging e. F571.1.

Eyesight lost by spying on holy cloak D1410.8; regained with stolen eyes E781.1.1. — Humor of bad e. X120ff.; magic object affects e. *D1331ff.; plea to God for riches, issue, restoration of e. K2371.3; youngest wife's son restores e. to rajah's wives L13.1.

Face of angry warrior aflame F1041.16.6.4; chilled for breaking tabu C948.7; of dwarf F451.2.5; must be wiped dry after washing A1599.4; of saint radiant F574.3.1. — Corpse buried f. down S139.2.2.3.1, V61.4.1; demon with black f. G342; devil's f. G303.4.1.7; fish with human f. B83; ghost as f. E422.1.11.2; ghost with glowing f. E421.3.3; ghost strikes man's f. E542.1.4; girl's f. becomes angelic at death D1865.3; giant's f. elbow-length wide F531.2.2.1; god unusual as to f. A123.2ff.; ill-omened f. of king N119.3; luminous f. as sign of royalty H71.6.1; lips on side of f. F544.1.4; magic f. D992.3; man disfigures f. to remove temptation T333.3; man's destiny read in his f. M302.2.2; mask mistaken for f. J1793; naked Indian not cold: "Me all f." J1309.1; origin of animal's f. A2330ff.; person killed by hitting fly on f. *N333.1; person unusual as to his f. F511.1ff.; punishment: f. distorted Q551.8.7; rat persuades cat to wash f. before eating K562; red, black f. after being burned F1082.1; satire causes f. ulcers D1402.15.3; slap turns man's f. around F1041.24; sun hides f. in shame: hence eclipse A737.8.1; sun turns fiery f. upward A1135.1.1; vampire with elephant f. E251.4.1.

Faces. — Elves' f. like old men's F239.5; fire, hail as sun's f. A733.3; Fortuna with two f. N111.2.2; god with many f. A123.2.1; man born at first with two f. A1316.0.1; men with two f. F526.5; spirits allow people with f. to ground to pass F406.3.

Facial features F545; (of goddess reversed) A282.0.1.1. — Animal pressed: hence f. or bodily marks A2213.2ff.; origin of f. features A1316.

Facing. — Prayer f. east V58.2; warrior dies f. foe P557.6.

Facts, absurd disregard of J1850—J1999.

Fading of spirit into air F407.2; of tree (flower) as life token *E761.3.

Fáfnir a dragon from transformed man B11.1.3.

Faggot. — Magic f. D957, (drips to indicate rising tide) D1324.2.

Faggots transformed to chargers D441.3.1. — Bundle of f. held together by snake H1023.19.

Failure in all efforts (as curse) M441, (as punishment) Q553.6; to bless mountains gives mountain-men power F460.4.6; of crops during reign of wicked king Q552.3; of devil when he tries to wall in too large a piece of ground in a night G303.13.3; of false bride when husband tests her K1911.3.3; in resuscitation because of premature disturbance of members E37.1. — Continual f. to find treasure N550.1; ghosts punish f. to provide for their wants E245; riddle propounded with penalty for f. H541; wild huntsman wanders for f. to keep fast day E501.3.5; wood-spirits cause f. F441.6.1.

Faint. — Deception by pretended f. K1818.6; woman in sham f. revived by beating K1676.1.

Fainting brings recovery of speech F954.3; from fright for lover T24.2.2; away for love T24.2.1; from noise of wooden pestle and mortar F647.8; at sight of goddess F1041.1.6.1. — Pretended f. when husband strikes adulteress with a rose K2051.2.

Fair by night and ugly by day D621.3. — Fairies f. F233.6; fairies hold a f. F258.1; forbidden horse f. C619.3; man on island of F. Women overcome by loving women F112.1; why go all way to f.? vendor robbed en route K475.3.

Fairs. — Animals hold f. B294.4; origin of f. A1535.2.

Fairest thing in the garden J1472. — Love through prophecy that prince shall marry the f. T12; prize to the f. H1596.1; quest for the f. H1301.1.

Fairy assigns quest H1219.4; assigns task H938; becomes monster D49.3; confers invisibility D1983.2; converses with dead E545.8; curses village M411.16; in disguise lends death-bringing horse K985; dwellings F220ff.; enters locked city D2088.1; in foot-race with mortal H1594.1; as helper N815; helps overcome witch G275.8.2; in husband's form visits queen, begets son K1844.4; imposes tabu C901.1.5, C999.1.1.4; -like witch G264.4; loses stronghold through loan K232.2.1; as magician D1711.5; marrying mortal tabu C162.1.1; mist mistaken for enemy smoke K236.9.9; mistress F302ff.; mound G233, P17.0.3, R121.8; music evil omen D1812.5.1.13; offers warrior long life, happiness D1857.2; otherworld confused with land of dead F160.0.2; parent confers transformation power D630.3; as phantom F585.0.1; performs tasks H973.1, H977; as physician P424.4, (abducted to heal mortals) R33; rescues abandoned child R131.12; seen in dream D1731.2.1; stronghold riddle answer H768; suckles child T611.3; will marry king cutting off son's head H313.2; wins kiss in game K786; wounded by mortal D2161.4.10.2.1. — Child divides last loaf with f. Q42.1.1; dreaming of f. kiss J2345; first man marries a f. A1275.9; flood caused by loosing f. horses A1012.2.1; horse used by mortal under f. spell changes to gray cat F234.4.1; impostor kills f., wears its clothes K1911.1.10; king's family from f. prince A1653.2; lake quells f. war A920.1.7.1; magic beautification of f. D1860.0.1; magic contest of druid, f. D1719.1.2; magic object (received from f.) D813ff., (summons f.) D1421.6; magic power from f. *D1723; magic sword protects woman from f. lover in husband's absence D1386.1; mortal fosters f. child to prevent crop destruction M242.1; mysterious housekeeper f. mistress N831.1.1; pagans flee into f. mounds P426.0.1; pig-f. transformed to fish D412.3.1; power of prophecy from f. D1812.1.1; punishment for desertion of f.

mistress Q247; rescue from f. stronghold R112.3; rejuvenation by f. D1882.2; resuscitation by f. E121.8; returning home after marrying f. tabu C644; saint's horse miraculously preserved as proof of power of Christianity before f. H1573.3.2; spring breaks forth where f. horse lies down A941.1.2; tabu to dig in f. ring C523.2; tabu to offend f. C46; transformation by f. D683.7; transformation by offspring of f., mortal D683.7.1; wife chosen instead of f. mistress J414.1; woman abducted by f. R16.3.

Fairy's knowledge of mortals D1813.0.2; magic power D1719.5. — Bathing f. clothes and magic stolen D838.10; bower for f. mistress D2185.1; magic from f. door D1811.1.1.1; magic weakness from f. curse K1837.3; witch as f. daughter G203.1.

Fairies *F200—F399; aid quest H1233.4.1; in animal form lured into own shapes, killed K821; become birds every other year D624.2; blamed for theft K419.10; cause illusions D2031.0.2; cause sound from many directions K1887.3; as coal miners F456.4.1; in goaling match with mortals H1593; converted to Christianity V331.8; create magic tree D950.14.1; get stones from mermaids D2066.1; help forgotten child, strangle imitator J2415.4; and human children F310ff.; live in range of hills F214; and mortals F300—F399; must not eat mortal food C211.3.2; mutilate mortals S160.3; as prophets M301.6; pursued in wild hunt E501.5.2; transformed to animals fight D615.4.1. — Appearance of f. F230ff.; battle of f. and gods F277; behavior of f. F260ff.; bringing f. to court H1177; combing hair of f. (task) H1192; defeating f. F380ff; dolls become f. D435.1.2; fallen angels become f. V236.1; fasting against f. P623.0.3; indentions on rocks from footprints of f. A972.2; lakes created by f. A920.1.7; magic knowledge of f. D1810.0.4; malevolent f. F360ff.; possessions of ᶜ F240ff.; kissing f. forbidden C122; looking at f. forbidden C311.1.2; quest for queen of f. H1381.3.8; race with f. N775; sleeping king abducted by f. N661; tabu: spying on f. C51.4.3; theft from f. F350ff.; vow to marry queen of f. M146.1; witches married to f. G287; worship of f. V1.2.1.

Fairyland *F210ff.; inhabited by women only F112.0.1. — Eating in f. forbidden C211.1; escape to f. R326; escape from f. R218; fairy leaves f. for mortals F393.0.1; fairies carry people away to f. *F320ff.; giant lives in f. F531.6.3.2; hell confused with f. A671.0.4; hero fights f. giant F176.1; magic tree springs from f. berry D951.1; mortal abandoning world for f. *F373; mortal goes to f. and marries fairy F302ff.; musical rock in f. F803; objects brought home from f. F379.2; ogre tyrannizes over f. G464; quests to f. H1286; return from f. F379.1; silence in f. C405; speaking tabu in f. C715.1; staying too long in f. forbidden C712.1; transformation to lure hunters to f. D659.10; transportation to f. B542.2.1; visit to f. F370ff.

Faith put into the balance V512.1. — Absolute f. as clerical virtue V461.7; lack of f. loses magic D1741.4; magic reward for f. D855.4;

punishment for associating with those of another f. Q431.18; punishment for changing f. Q232; reward for f. Q22, Q27; twelve articles of f. Z71.8.1.

Faiths. — Three true f.; God's and his children's J1262.9.

Faithful animal B301ff.; brother P251.1; old dog (to be killed) B842, (proves worth and is spared) Q151.4; falcon killed through misunderstanding B331.1; foster brother P273.1; servant *P361ff. — Girl cursed so no man f. to her M438.3; girl f. to husband despite lover's return T211.7; sister f. to transformed brother P253.2; what is most f.? H659.25; wife's oath to be f. J2301.1.

Faithfulness in marriage *T210ff.; as suitor test H338; to Virgin Mary, even if not to Christ, rewarded V253. — Disenchantment by f. of others D750ff.; parting lovers swear f. T61.2.1; test of f. of husband and wife H492; tests of wife's f. H460ff.

Faithless, see also **Unfaithful;** foster brother P273.2; servants P305. — Dead sweetheart haunts f. lover E211; disguised husband wins f. wife's love K1813.1; ghost of f. lover's victim E334.3; riddle involving ruby, nectar, f. creature H587.1; what is most f.? H659.26; wife in disguise wooed by her f. husband K1814; wife tries to cure f. husband by furnishing fine accommodations for him at poor mistress's J1112.1.

Faithlessness in marriage *T230ff. — Impalement as punishment for f. Q461.1; ring springs asunder when f. of lover is learned *D1318.9.1; woman as pilgrim learns of lover's f. K1837.2.

Fakir aids quest H1233.3.2; brings back abducted wife R165.3; as helper N844.2; prefers jungle life to luxury W34.4; thankful for shrewish wife T251.11. — Disguise as f. K1817.1.1; god in form of f. A182.3.4.1; rich girl marries f. T121.5.2; wife disguised as f. K1814.3.

Fakir's foreknowledge of guests' coming D1812.0.2.3; skill tested by beat H1576.2. — Loosing sandals destroys f. power D1782.3.1.

Fakirs. — Full pot sign city full of f. J1293.4.

Falcon and crow as joint creators A37.1; defeats eagle L315.9; eaten by wild boar recovered alive from his body X921.9; as messenger B291.1.4; not so good as represented J1826; saves master from poisoning B143.1.4; of Sir Federigo N345; transformed to person D352.3. — Cock has never seen a f. roasted J1423; enmity between f. (and fowl) A2494.13.12, (and hen) A2494.13.10.4; faithful f. killed through misunderstanding B331.1; giant f. B872.3; girl becomes f. D152.4; god as f. has tail cut off: hence falcon's short tail A2216.6; helpful f. B455.2; king strangles f. when it kills eagle Q424.1; kings try to save dying f. N836.2; magic f. brings hero water B172.5; retrieving king's f. H1154.7.1; soul as f. seen in dream E732.9; transformation to f. for rescue D643.1.

Falconiform. — Transformation: man to f. D152ff.

Falconiformes. — Creation of f. A1930ff.

Fall from breaking tabu C996. — Cure by f. causing bleeding N644; holy man's f. from horse evil omen D1812.5.14; lark causes elephant's

f. over precipice L315.5; leaves f. from tree as life token E761.7.3;
magic needle makes everything f. to pieces D1562.4; man lets one lip
f. to stomach F544.1.2; nine days' f. from heaven to earth A658.1;
person magically caused to f. D2069.1; saint's image lets golden shoe
(ring) f. as sign of favor to suppliant D1622.3; Satan's f. from heaven
A106.2.2; things accidentally f. and kill person N331; witch causes f.
G269.13; why monkeys do not f. from trees A2576.

Fall of Man. — After f. first parents fed from tree A1420.5; animal
characteristics as punishment for planning f. A2236ff.; earth punished
for disobedience at f. A2721.8; Lucifer causes f. A63.5; plants as punishment for f. A2631.1.1.

Fallen angels V236; king in disguise helped K1812.18. — Special power
of chaste woman: raising f. elephant H413.4.

Falling after attempt to fly with witches G242.7; furniture threatens
bridal couple T175.1; into hell Q417.3; into ogre's power G400—G499;
in love T10ff.; star shot down by astronomer J2275.1; of trees reveals
Savior's will D1311.4.0.2. — Death from f. on own weapon N339.8;
dupes f. over precipice K891.5.4; lies about f. X1731; magic help from f.
D2166; magic object keeps f. down D1649.1; man f. from tree frightens
off tiger N696.1; man f. underground F949.2; object f. on robbers, they
flee K335.1.1; origin of f. stars A788; perilous f. gate *F776.2; rising
and f. sky F791; saint prevents rocks' f. D2149.4.1; squirrel's markings
and immunity from f. as reward A2221.8.

Falls. — Bridge which f. when mounted F842.2.2; building f. because of
breaking of tabu C931; dupe persuaded to climb tall tree, f. K1113.1;
life token: staff stuck in ground f. E761.2.2; marvelous picture f. from
sky in storm F962.12.3; numskull f. J2133; origin of f. A935; payment
to be made when last leaf f. K222; person f. into ogre's power *G400ff.

False accusations *K2100—K2199; alarm of robbery causes cheated man
to be imprisoned K484.3; beauty doctor K1013; bride *K1911ff.; bridegroom K1915; claim of reward K442; dragon-head proof H105.1.1;
judging punished Q265; pride of son ashamed of his peasant father
W165; prophet K1962; swearer not allowed to approach altar M101.1;
swearing of oath forbidden C94.2; witnesses cannot describe stolen
jewel J1154.3. — Devout possessor of f. relics miraculously receives
authentic ones V142; dwarfs emigrate because mortals are f. F451.9.1.2;
escape by f. plea *K550ff.; hero awakened from magic sleep by wife
who has purchased place in his bed from f. bride *D1978.4; repartee
concerning f. reform J1400ff.; sale of f. treasure K120ff.; seduction by
bearing f. order from husband or father K1354; service under f. name
K1831; trickster's f. creations fail him J2186.

Falsehood personified Z131. — Fairy banished for f. F252.4.2; horse
refuses to carry f. speaker B133.4; magic lamp indicates f. by lighting
D1316.2; red as symbol of f. Z141.3; wager that f. is better than truth
N61.

Falsehoods. — Prophecy: person to tell three f. M369.1.

Falsely. — Devil as advocate of f. condemned man G303.22.11; nose of f. accusing bishop bitten off Q451.5.3.

Falsified message A2276, *K1851.

Fame chosen over long life M365.1; is greatest (riddle) H659.7.1. — Early death with f. preferred J216.5, L212.3; future f. prophesied M310.1; goddess of f. A466; wasp seeking f. stings courtiers W116.5.

Familiar. — Acquisition of f. spirit F403.2.1; demon as f. spirit F403.2.2.5; devils f. spirit M219.3; witch's f. spirit G225.

Familiarity takes away fear U131.

Family *P200—P299; carried to fairyland F327; of demons F402.7; of gods A168; of good man rewarded Q191; resuscitated E181.2; of thieves K301.2. — Animal captor appeased by being fed captive's f. K614; beetle cursed for betraying Holy F. on way to Egypt A2231.7.1.1; conqueror returns defeated man's f. W11.5.4; creator's f. A32; devil founds f. G303.12.4; don't injure yourself to insure future of your f. J322; escape by posing as member of murderer's f. or tribe K601; fairy gift not to leave possession of mortal's f. F348.3; fairy f. lives in cottage F221.4; faithless wife kills f. K2213.3.1; fool asks archbishop about his f. J1747; ghost f. visits grave E324.2; groom becomes member of bride's f. T137.4; king breaks promise to care for f. M205.4; man buried at home so may watch f. V61.3.0.3; man disdains own f. after speaking to king W165.1; master of seven liberal arts begs from wagoner who with his one art supports his f. X371; members of dupe's f. killed K1460ff.; moon's f. A745; mutual agreement to sacrifice f. members in famine K231.1.1; not recognizing own f. J2014; origin of king's f. A1653.2; origin of regulations within the f. A1570ff.; prayers of f. comfort prisoner V53; property division within f. A1585; prophecy: f. will die M359.6; quarrels among f. of dead X113; quest for lost f. H1385.9; saint's vision of king's f. V515.2.2; suitor in contest with bride or member of her f. H332; sun-god's f. A220.2; tree supports pious f. F979.19; unknown member of f. immediately and magically recognized H175; wry-mouthed f. X131; youth absent when entire f. wiped out N659.2.

Famine F969.7; prophesied M359.9; as punishment Q552.3.1. — Arrogant advice to f. sufferers J2227; cake and herrings as cure for f. J2227; cannibalism during f. G78.1; children abandoned in f. S321.1; daughters sacrificed to avert f. S263.2.2; goddess causes f. A431.1.3; king fasts during f. years P14.23; man mistaken for F. J1786.3; old people killed in f. S110.1; recognition of abandoned child when parents come to him for relief from f. H152; storing grain against f. J711.4.

Famished wolf asks sheep to bring him water K2061.5.

Famous. — Blessing fills countries with what they are f. for M393.1.

Fan, magic *D1077, (bears person aloft) D1532.10.

Fanaticism, religious V383.

Fanciful traits of animals *B700—B799.

Fang. — Detached snake f. kills B765.19.

Fangs. — Snake and turtle exchange head for f. A2247.2.

Fanning. — Devil f. fire with tail G303.4.6.2; faithless widow f. husband's grave T231.2.

Faraway. — Quest for f. princess H1301.1.2.

Farewell. — Dead returns to say f. E364.

Farm. — Animal as f. laborer B292.9; child unwittingly promised: what is born on your f. S245; city person ignorant of f. J1731; ghost light on f. indicates pending move E530.1.4; grateful fairies do f. work F339.3.1; nisser belong to particular f. F482.3.3; wild huntsman lives in room on f. E501.15.8.

Farmer kills anyone riding his horse L434; seeks laborer ignorant of sex K1327; sleeping through harvest time Q585.3; surpasses astronomer, doctor in weather prediction and food choice L144.2; who trades horses with the devil is cheated G303.25.12; unable to rid himself of brownie F482.3.1.1. — Arrested f. maligns sons H581.4; devil aids f. in reaping contest G303.19.2; devil appears to claim soul offered to devil by f. in jest G303.6.1.3; devil builds road for f. in one day G303.9.2.2; devil hires out to a f. G303.9.3.1; escape disguise as f. K521.2.4; gift of f. to incognito king rewarded K1812.9; misfortune follows f. N271.7.

Farmers. — "Skinning" f. J2472.

Farming left for fishing J345.2. — Dwarfs do f. F451.3.4.3; lies about f. on mountain X1523.2.

Farrowed. — Obtaining fat from swine not f. H1025; quest for pig not f. H1331.2.2.

Farting, see **Breaking wind;** continued D2063.5.

Fast-growing plants X1402. — Horse so f. fly cannot light on him B184.1.1.1; king wants f. answers P14.8.1; saint as baby refuses nurse on f. days V229.2.3.1; "stick f.": fool seizes ass J2489.9; tree with extraordinary f. life cycle F811.13.1.

Fasts. — Origin of religious f. A1541.7; wild huntsman wanders for failure to keep f. E501.3.5.

Fastened. — Continually slamming doors grateful for being f. D1658.1.4; devil dies when he is f. in hell's door by his beard G303.17.3.2; world columns f. by gods with mother's hair A841.0.1.

Fasting P623; on eleventh day abandoned H313.2; the first month J2135.1; invokes angel V235.0.2; as penance Q535.4; in sackcloth and ashes Q523.10; tabu on holidays C634; women tempted D2031.16. — Abortion by f. T572.2.4; animals f. B251.4; ascetic f. V362.2; beautification by f. D1866.3; contest in f. H1545; deceptive bargain: f. together K177; deceptive contest in f. K53; eight unprofitable types of f. Z71.16.1.4; ghost laid by f. E443.7; hermit f. to death for fame E754.4; intemperance in f. J565; lust repressed through f. T317.4; magic power by f. D1733.3.1; magic results from f. *D1766.8; neglect of f. punished

Q223.9; reincarnation by f. E607.4; resuscitation by f. E62.1; reward for f. Q26; saint ends epidemic by f. D2162.1; strength from f. F611.3.0.1; wisdom from f. J179.4.

Fastrada, ring of T85.4.1.

Fat abbot cured by starving K1955.1.1; cat (cumulative tale) Z33.2; of crow prevents burning D1382.2; giant wants to eat self J2119.5; and lean kine in otherworld F171.1; man chosen for execution M178.2; rendered from daughter's corpse Q478.4; troll (wolf) (cumulative tale) Z33.4; woman with beard F545.1.5.2. — Captured person (animal) persuades his captor to wait till he gets f. K553; crow f. remedies F959.3.5; division of f. and lean fowls J1241.4; extremely f. giant F531.2.5; hungry wolf envies f. dog until he sees marks of his collar L451.3; magic f. of animal D1017.1; quest for blackbirds' f. H1331.1.5; resuscitation by animal f. E116; sun a f. woman walking across sky A738.1.2; tabu to eat animal f. C221.3.4.1; witch smears f. on brooms in preparation for flight G242.1.1.

Fatal bed where his ancestors have died J1474; deception *K800—K999; enticements of phantom women F585.1; imitation J2401; kiss from dead E217. — Accidental f. ending of game or joke N334; avoiding places which have been f. to others J644; basilisk's f. glance B12.2; fairy's kiss f. F302.3.4.1.1.

Fate controls gods A196.1; takes form of Brahmin's pupil K1811.4.1. — Chance and f. N (entire chapter); deceiving f. K2371; fairy prophesies lover's f. in battle F302.7; gods tricked into help in escaping one's f. K2371.2; man's f. written on his skull M302.2; nature of luck and f. N100ff.; ways of luck and f. N100—N299.

Fates A463.1. — Three f. prophesy at childbirth M301.12.

Fated hero M361.

Father bequeathes four symbolic pots to sons J99.2; casts daughter forth S322.1; causes death of son innocent of adultery N344.2; confined at time of childbirth T583.1; and daughter *P234; -daughter incest T411, (prophecy) M344.1, (punished) Q242.2; will die when daughter (marries) E765.4.1, (bears son) E765.4.3; feels son in danger D1813.0.3; forced to share cherries J1341.9; -god A103; of gods A111.2; guards girl from suitors T50.1.2; with handsome son and hideous daughter J244.1; hides wealth to keep son from gambling N94; of illegitimate child must walk in front of cross J1515.1; imposes tabu on son C901.1.1; of incestuous children punished Q242.4; kills child S11.3; kills daughter lest she become prostitute T314; kills self believing that son is dead N344; kills son in battle rage N349.2; leaves sons three jewels, all to be used J462.3.1; of Noah's sons J2713; opposed to daughter's marriage T97; orders son's luck-bringing animal destroyed N251.6; prefers daughter P230.1; promises girl to wed man of her choice T131.0.1.1; rebukes son dragging him past threshold J121.2; reinstates abandoned son N731.3; rescues children R153.2; has been to Rome, hence resemblance to

18

emperor J1274; saves self, forgets children S141.2; and son *P233, (as culture heroes) A515.2, (as love rivals) T92.9, (in mortal combat) *N731.2; takes his daughter to cannibal to be eaten G75; tests H480ff.; throws son in oven H165; tricked into giving away daughter in marriage K1371.2; wants to marry own daughter T411.1; wears a crown but is no king J1264.3; went five years ago to measure depth of earth (died) H681.2.2. — Accidental meeting of f. and daughter N732; Adam and Eve having neither f. nor mother are dead H813; Adam as f. of mankind A1285.1.1; birth from wound or abscess on body of f. T541.2.1; boy kills his animal f. B631.0.2; boy shows f. foolishness of plowing up crop J92; bride's monster f. T172.3; child begs mother name him good f. J1279.1; child cursed by f. cannot rest in grave E412.4; child miraculously suckled by his f. T611.2; children choose f. they know to the real father they do not yet know J325; children flee from f. who turns cannibal G31; cruel f. S11; cruel foster f. S36; dead girl frightens f. and lover J2621; death of f. as punishment Q411.3; deity clothes his f. the sky A625.2.4; dwarf king prevents a f. from shooting his son F451.5.1.16; Elias, having had f. and mother, is not dead H814; enigmatic counsels of a. f. H588; fairy f. abducts child F326; fairy foster f. F311.2; fish was my f., man was my mother H791; fool advises buyer that horse is worth little or his f. would not sell it J2088.1; ghost f. summoned to get sword E387.2.1; god from f.-daughter incest A112.1.1; goddess's f. as cannibal G11.0.1.2; grandfather as foster f. P291.1; hermit kills his own f., supposing him to be the devil K943; hero locked up while f. murdered R54; inconvenience of having a f. J2222; impostor claims to be f. of princess's child K1936; impoverished f. begs from banished daughter L432.2; incapacitated f. magically restored as lost son returns D2161.4.10.4; king helps revenge f. N836.3; king sends message to dead f. H1252.4; in large family f. unwilling but mother willing to sell children H491.1; Lot's wife, having had f. and mother, is not dead like other mortals H815; lots cast to determine f. of illegitimate child N126.2; lovers' meeting: hero in service of lady's f. T31.1; magic object received from f. D815.2; maiden abducted from cruel f. R10.1.2; man accidentally fed bread which his f. has poisoned N332.1; mother lets daughter marry own f. P232.2; mother sends son to find unknown f. H1216; mother's brothers as foster f. P293.1; promise to dying f. leads to adventures M258.1; prophecy: son will tie f. to horse, strike him M312.0.5; quest assigned by f. H1210.1, (as punishment) H1219.3; quest for lost f. H1385.7; quest to see if f. in heaven or hell H1252.1.2; quest for unknown f. H1381.2ff.; slaying son so f. will not die H1162.2; son blinds f. S21.2; son kills f. who returns to life as cuckoo A2275.6; son rescues f. R154.2; son slays f. in self-defense J675.1; stepfather as foster f. P281.1; suitors contest with bride's f. (in shooting) H331.4.1, (race) H331.5.2; suitor is put to severe tests by his prospective bride or her f. H310ff.; supposed chest of gold induces children to care for aged f. P236.2; sword bursts in son's hand when he is about to kill his f.

*D1317.6.1; sword from summoned dead f. E373.2; tasks assigned by jealous f. *H913.2; tiger f. of human child U128.1; transformation through thoughtless wish of f. D521.1; trickster masking as f. advises intercourse K1354.1.1; unexpected meeting of f. and son N731; unwitting f.-daughter incest N365.2; vigil for dead f. H1462; "What does your f. say when you begin to eat?" X434.2; "Where did the f. stay?" X435.2; wife incites sons to war on f. K2213.9; wise words of dying f. J154; youngest son refuses to shoot at corpse of f. H486.2; youth accidentally takes poison intended for f. N332.4.1.

Father's ambitions transferred to child at conception T597; consent to marriage necessary T131.1.2; dream of bloody sons, omen of their murder D1812.5.1.1.3. — Man forced to eat dead f. heart goes mad G91.1; saint bestows f. goods on poor V437; breaking f. first counsel causes breaking all J21.25; dead f. friendly return E327ff.; fight with f. friend as valor test H1561.2.2; grief at hearing of f. death *F1041.21.5; infant eats murdered f. corpse G25; son avenging f. death H1228.2; magic on f. grave D842.2; queen persuades husband to claim her f. kingdom P23.2; son's acts of charity save his f. soul V413; son on gallows bites off his f. nose Q586; suitor task: avenging bride's f. death before marriage H335.1; swearing by f. life M119.8.2; tricksters feign f. death to collect rent K356; unknown son returns to f. court N731.1; vow against eating until f. death explained M151.3; wife chooses f. side in feud P211.

Fathers have eaten sour grapes, children affected U18; wagering over mastery of unborn children's house N16.2. — Child of three f. born with three stripes T563.1; prophecy: boys to be f. of saints M312.6; twin heroes sired by two f. A515.1.1.1.

Father-in-law *P261; angers strong man F631.2.1; gives enigmatic permission H588.0.1; requires suitor visit foreign country H336.1; sued for not dying as predicted W151.5. — Bride's kindness tested: f. disguised as beggar H384.1; cruel f. S52; duel with f. H332.3; feeding f. badly baked bread S54.1; God as f. J1261.1.1; magic object received from f. D815.5; suitors contest with f. in shooting H331.4.1; sun f. A226; treacherous f. K2218.2.

Fatigue. — Charm prevents f. D1384.4; magic avoidance of f. D1924, D2032.

Fatigued, see also **Tired.** — Guards f. by trickster so that they sleep while goods are stolen K331.2.2.

Fatness, humor of X151; repartee concerning J1410ff.

Fattening girl before wedding T132.1; louse *F983.2; pig by underfeeding J1903.3. — Cannibal f. victim *G82ff.; swine magically kept from f. D2089.3.1.

Fattest goat taken from demon H1423.3. — Riddle: what is the f.? H653.

Fault. — Finding f. punished Q312ff.; finding f. with wife J1701.1; husband finding f. nonplussed J1545.3; man admitted into heaven but must not find f. *F13.   18★

Faults. — Devil writes f. of man on goat-skin G303.24.1.2.

Favor with royalty induced by magic D1900.1. — Child sacrificed to gain f. of gods S263.2; divine f. withdrawn as punishment Q553; fox asking f. set on by dogs J871.1; God's f. lost for breaking tabu C937; image indicates f. to suppliant D1622ff.

Favors. — Dividing the winnings: f. from man's own wife M241.2; dwarfs thwart efforts of mortals to get additional f. F451.5.12; sacrifice to obtain deity's f. V17.0.1; woman sells f. for particular purpose *T455ff.

Favorable omens D1812.5.2ff.; prophesies M310ff.; traits of character W0—W99; wind caused (by magic fountain) D1543.1, (by magic stone) D1543.2. — Clever division f. to divider J1241; time f. for unearthing treasure N555.

Favorite performs task to win bride for king K1848.2; youngest daughter L51; youngest son L12. — Deity cares for f. individuals A185; heroes sons of wife not king's f. L111.8; neglected surpasses f. child L146; spurned f. makes rajah laughing-stock K1670.

Fawn, see also **Deer;** with golden lustre B731.7.2; in spite of his fine horns, runs from the dog U127. — Burning children to give them spots of f. K1013.2.2; prophecy: son catching f. will be king M314.1; wild f. sent to disrupt army K2351.7.

Fear, see also **Fright;** of husband for wife makes him leave behind boots he has won T252.4.1; of mountain-folk for thunder F460.2.1; as sickness cure F950.5; tests H1400. — Abortion caused by f. T572.2.5; angel of f. A489.3.1; animal characteristics from great f. A2212ff.; animal learns through experience to f. men J17; death from f. F1041.1.11; devils' f. of St. Isaac G303.25.2; dwarfs' f. of cross F451.5.9.1; extraordinary result of f. F1041.17; fairies' f. of cross F382.1; giants' f. of lightning F531.6.11.1; girl disenchants animal husband by enduring his embraces without f. D735.4.1; good enter otherworld without f. E750.2.1; hero feigns f. when looked at K1777; illness from f. W121.8; king grows lean from f. of death U241; learning of f. H1440ff.; learning f. of Death J27; magic plant banishes f. D1389.13; origin of f. A1382; plaintiff insists that judge shall put some f. into the defendant debtor J2492; prevention of hostility by inspiring f. in enemy J623; quest: learning what f. is H1376.2; tests of f. H1400—H1449; tabu: f. of threatening animals while treasure is being raised N553.5; thief confesses from f. J1141.10.

Fearing. — Animal rewards man for not f. it Q82.2; weak f. strong J425, J613.

Fearless traffic with devils H1420ff. — Men are f.: tiger made to frighten them L482.4.

Fearlessness. — Boasting of f. tabu C455; reward for f. Q82.

Feast of "bedding and handspreading" T162; at beginning of adventures N770.0.1; for those who have not known sorrow N135.3.1. — Animal characteristics: obtaining for f. and not returning A2242; Barmecide f. P327; bride chosen from f. guests H362; calamity from f. of John the

Baptist A1002.1; cat invites hens to a f. and kills them K815.4; charm prepares f. D1472.2.4; coming to f. tabu after sunset C752.1.4; communion f. A1541.1.2; compulsion to invite singer to f. C682; compulsory drinking at f. A1514; consuming f. without discovering a new wonder C287; cup as f. token H84.2; day after F. Day disputes importance with F. Day F976; deed of bravery required before f. W213.1; disguised hero attacks enemy at f. K913; dwarfs f. mortals in their home F451.6.3.1; fairies f. F263; fairy takes revenge for not being invited to f. F361.1.1; feigned wedding f. to deceive cuckold K1527; fool does not milk cow for a month so that she will give plenty for a f. J1905.1; fountain gives wine on f. days F716.1; hideous food at devil's f. G303.25.14.1; how many dead mice go to a f.? (riddle) H881.1; laws made at yearly f. P541.2; leaving f. tabu C282.1; murder by luring to f. S113.2.3; no room left for f. J2178; prophecy on first participant of f. D1812.5.0.7.1; punishment for working on f. day Q559.4; refusing a f. tabu C282; Satan at f. where poor are absent G303.15.4.3; sleeping trickster's f. stolen J2173.1; Tara f. A1535.4; tabu: partaking of certain f. C286; Thyestian f. *G61; tribe not attending f. must send gift P531.1; trickster's interrupted f. revenged J1564.1; wedding f. T136.1; wild hunt appears on f. days E501.11.2.3; wolves have annual (church) f. B253.2.

Feasts P634; to honor certain god A1541.2. — Devils' f. G303.25.17; dwarfs invisibly attend wedding or christening f. of mortals F451.5.17; origin of secular f. A1535; perpetual f. in otherworld F173.3; religious f. A1541, *V70ff.; seven years between f. Z72.3; sitting in circle of f. P338.

Feasting by night tabu C237. — Stingy man's children f. in his absence J1522.2; tabu: f. for week C230.1; tabus on f. visitor C616; witches f. G248; woman, beasts f. on human flesh G11.6.3.

Feat on spear point H1149.5. — Duplicating f. of skill on journey C833.6; performer of greatest f. to be king P11.2.2.1.

Feats. — Father orders illegitimate boy sent to him when he can perform certain f. T645.3; Gargantuan f. F531.3ff.; hero's remarkable f. A526.7; quest to undertake f. of valor H1223; learning foreign f. of arms as suitor task H336.1.

Feather bed tabu C735.2.7; over door: if girl who enters blushes she is not a virgin H412.3; transformed to person D437.3; transformed to tree D457.7; used as mast F841.2.2. — Burning f. containing ogre's life G512.5.1; descent from upper world on magic f. (life ladder) F61.2.1.1; eagle killed with arrow made with his own f. U161; identification by f. cloak H111.2; magic f. *D1021; magic sight by looking through f. D1821.3.10; man can transplant f. from one bird to another F668.3; ogre's life in parrot's f. in man's pocket E715.1.3.1; one f. makes a hard pillow J2213.9; recognition by f. H78; sacred f. V1.10.3; ship wrapped with f. beds and canvas and pitched F1031; soul as f. E745.1; transformation by putting on f. of helpful animal D532.

Feathers. — Bird tears out f. F1041.21.6.2; bird without f. flies on tree without leaves (riddle) H764; bird f. sink in river (life token) E761.7.7; bird plucks out another bird's f. K2382.1; bird shows way by dropping f. every seven steps *B151.2.0.1; birds throw f. to hero who flies off B540.1; borrowed f. *K1041; building a lodge of bird's f. in one night (task) H1104.1; conception from f. falling on woman T536; counting f. in bird (task) H1118; dragon with golden f. B11.2.2.1; dress of f. F821.1.6, (magic) D1069.2; filling twelve bedticks with f. (task) H1129.2; flight by putting on bird f. K1041.1; gods covered with f. A139.9.3; lecherous king glued with f. K1218.1.8; lost soul in raven f. E752.4; magic causes f. to grow on person D1375.6; man can keep together f. in great wind F673; origin of bird's f. A2313; origin of peacock's brilliant f.: made by culture hero to please woman A2411.2.6.7; how ostrich lost beautiful f. A2252.3, A2402.2; peacock's f. ruffled in presence of poison B131.5; people with f. F521.2; quest for remarkable bird caused by sight of one of its f. H1213; quest for three f. of marvelous bird H1331.1.2; quest in hell for three dragon f. H1274; ravens show Adam how to bury dead: are born with white f. A2223.7; snow from f. or clothes of a witch (Frau Holle) A1135.2.1; sun and moon as balls of f. A738.1.1; tar and f. as punishment Q475; thatching roof with f. H1104.1.2; "thief's f. on head" detects crime J1141.1.5; trail of f. blown away R135.1.1; why bird has two beautiful f. in his tail A2378.8.7; why swallow has black f. and only two A2378.8.6; why young ravens have white f. A2313.5.

Features. — Cannibal with extraordinary f. G11.11; changeling has abnormal f. F321.1.2.1; gods with animal f. A131; ogres with monstrous f. G360ff.; person retains animal f. D702.2; person without f. F511.0.1; physical f. of underworld F80.1.

February's shortage of days A1161.

Fecundity, see **Fertility.**

Fed, see also **Feeding.** — Animal familiar f. with witch's own blood G225.0.1; animal lured by being f. K811.0.1; death passes by man who has f. his stepmother Q151.2; girl's heart f. to man draws her to him D1905.1; guests f. before being questioned P324.2; own flesh f. to helpful animal by hero *B322.1; parents f. from palm-tree A1420.5.

Federigo. — The falcon of Sir F. N345.

Fee used up before main question is reached K265. — Charon's f. A672.1.1; husband collects f. from paramour K1569.1; lawyer asks double amount of damages as f. K488; present or retaining f. J1559.1.

Fée carried off by mortal F304.6. — Shining bower for f. F224.

Fee-fi-fo-fum (cannibal exclamation) *G84.

Feebleness. — Giantess's son scorns father's f. P233.3.1.

Feeding, see also **Fed;** army from one measure of meal (task) H1022.5; the child steaming food J2465.3; mother: fool stuffs, kills her J2465.3.2; ravenous beast to satiation (task) H1123; sheep without fattening them H1072; stolen money in flour to animal K366.0.1; visitors dog flesh

J2469.5.1. — Birds f. on hero's land tabu C566.2; disenchantment by f. enchanted animals D745; disenchantment by f. transformed creature D775; dragon f. on treasure B11.6.3; giants appeased by f. them G582; giant's help secured by f. him N812.0.1; goat f. other animals from its body B535.1; man not f. animal rescuer W154.24; mother f. child to dog S12.2.1; murder by f. sharpened pieces of wood K951.6; thief tries f. watch dog and stopping his mouth K2062.

Feet, see also **Foot, Legs;** cut off as punishment Q451.0.1, (for theft) Q451.2.2; of dragon B11.2.4; of dwarf F451.2.2ff.; of giant F531.1.3; magically fixed to pavement D2171.7; seized in supplication P676; of various peoples A1665; wagered N2.3.2.1. — Animals with unusual legs or f. B15.6; beheaded man's head laid at f. to prevent return E431.7; why birds' f. are bare A2317.9; bishop with four f. J2283; clever girl comes sitting on animal but with f. reaching ground H1053.2; cold hands and f. for the dead man J2311.7; corpse with his f. cut off X422; cow's f. provide wealth D1469.7; devil has claws on his f. G303.4.4.2; devil's f. and legs G303.4.5ff.; devil's horse has human f. G303.7.1.2.1; demons' f. G302.4.5; dry f. tabu over river C833.5; earth to rest God's f. on A5.1; enemies' f. magically burned D2091.10.1; explanation of duck's f. A2375.2.8; fairy's f. F231.2; false bride's mutilated f. K1911.3.31; fire to burn hands and f. (curse) M431.3; ghost's f. backwards E422.1.6.1; giant's large f. F531.1.3.6; giants sit on mountain and wash f. in stream below F531.3.9; god with goat f. A131.5; hanging up by f. as punishment Q462.2; hero's f. backwards A526.8; hills from earth wrinkling up f. A969.4; hurting f. to save shoes J2199.4.1, W152.11; island supported on four f. F736.1; "keep f. warm" J21.29; magic animal f. D1029.3; magic salve restores severed f. D1500.1.19.1; magician's f. must touch ground D1719.10.1; man originally without hands and f. A1225.2; mankind begotten by giant's two f. A1221.1; medicine on f. permits man to walk on water D1524.1.1; murder by driving iron through f. S112.2.2; mutilation: (cutting off f.) *S162, (turning f. backward) S162.5; ogre monstrous as to f. G365; origin of hands and f. A1311; origin and nature of animal's f. A2371ff., A2375ff.; person unusual as to his f. F517.1; person with wings on f. F522.1; person without f. F517.1.1; pins stuck in soles of dead man's f. to prevent return E431.12; pricking f. exposes false corpse J1149.7; pygmies with upturned f. F535.4.2; rabbits freeze f. fast to ice at night (lie) X1115.1; raven singes f.: why its wings clap A2218.6; reincarnation of f. into hoe E649.3; remarkable f. F551ff.; revenant with chicken f. *E422.1.6; shoemaker offers to trim peasant's f. to fit shoes K1783; size of f. as bride test H365; sparks come from man's f. F683; spirit with f. turned wrong way F401.9; springs rise where Christ bathed his f. A942.1; stag with golden antlers and silver f. B101.4.1; suitors chosen with f. as only part seen H312.3; tokens on f. identify god H45.4; transportation by putting magic ointment on f. D1520.26; why guinea fowl's f. red: hot oil poured on them A2375.2.10;

wild hunt throws horses' f. on persons who see it E501.18.3; witch with extraordinary f. G216; wood-spirit without f. F441.4.2; yellowing soles of f. death omen J2311.1.5.

Feigned, see also **Sham** and **Illness** (feigned); death leads to exiled lover's death N343.3; death to test wife's faithfulness H466; ignorance of person's identity K1792; madness unmasked by threatening man's child J1149.1; capture by f. death *K751, K2362; death f. in order to be carried K1861; death f. to escape unwelcome marriage K522.0.1; death f. to meet paramour K1538; deception by f. death (sleep) *K1860ff.; detection through f. dream J1147; king brought to sense of duty by f. conversation of birds J816.1; ogre deceived by f. ignorance of hero G526; quest assigned because of f. (illness) H1212, (dream) H1212.1; seduction by f. death *K1325.

Feigning *K2000ff.; death to kill enemy K911. — Capture by f. illness K757; death as punishment for f. sleep Q558.10; adulteress f. unusual sensitiveness K2051; test of fidelity by f. death H1556.1; trickster f. deafness gets hospitality from miser K1981.1; trickster quarrels with owner of goods and frightens owner away by f. death K335.0.3.

Feline, see also **Cat;** animal transformed to person D312. — Creation of f. animals A1810ff.; man transformed to f. animal (wild) D112.

Felled tree raises itself again at night *D1602.2; tree restored by reassembling all cut parts E30.1. — Pleiades from hunters who f. world-tree A733.5.

Felling forest in one night (task) H1095; tree (deceptive bargain) K178, (with one blow) F614.8; wood with sword F1041.16.3.

Felt. — Resuscitation by piece of f. E64.10.

Female, see also **Woman;** creator A15.1; eater of corpses G21; master thief K302; physician P424.5; revenant E425.1ff.; right to land P61; servant forbidden to priest J1539.1; slaves P170.0.1. — Beef neither male nor f. H1074; cloud on male mountain bows to f. mountain A969.2; Eve names f. animals A2571.0.2; ghost in f. dress E422.4.4; ghosts may eat only f. animals E259.2; male and f. (creators) A12.1, (creators beget gods) A112.2, (waters) A918; origin of f. sex organs A1313.2; transformation to f. to seduce D658.3.

Fence. —Cutting f. down instead of fixing it K1432; metal, crystal f. in otherworld F169.5; thief, "Don't throw me over f." K584; thorn f. around food-plants K1038; throwing f. stakes away J2516.8.

Fences. — Suitor climbs eight f. T46.1.

Fenced. — Land purchase: as much as can be f. in a certain time K185.8; riddle: thorns f. with thorns H583.2.5.

Fencer treacherously cuts off opponent's head K832.2; skillful F667ff.; yields to opponent with pestle J676.

Fencing. — Student challenges f. master P342.1.

Fenris Wolf. — Fetter for F. F864.1; gods battle F. A1082.2.1; Odin battles F. A1082.2.

Fermenting dough's sound J1812.3.

Fern transformed to animal D441.4.1. — Magic f. blossom D965.14.

Ferns. — Devil as bunch of f. G303.3.4.3.

Fernseed gathering on Christmas Eve C401.5; magic *D971.3.

Ferocious animal flees victim K547.5; animal frightened by ass braying K2324.1; animals loosed against attackers B17.1.1; sow G351.3. — Bridling f. bear (task) H1154.3.2; dupe substitutes for trickster when f. animal attacks K846; eating f. animal's heart makes person cruel D1357.1; killing f. animal as suitor task H335.3; killing f. beast as task H1161.

Ferocity. — Why wild animals lose their f. A2294, A2531.0.1.

Ferried. — Dwarfs pay for being f. across water F451.5.10.6; emigrating dwarfs are f. across water F451.9.5; fairies f. across stream F213.2.

Ferry. — Charon's fee to f. souls A672.1.1; pushing f. as strength test H1562.10.

Ferryman P413; to lower world F93.0.1.1; on river in lower world (Charon) A672.1, E489.3, P613; setting people over a stream until relieved by another (penance) Q521.5. — Question (on quest): when will a f. be released from his duty? H1292.8.

Fertile. — Charms make soil f. D1563.1.1, D2157.1; giant's fields f., others arid G112.

Fertility test H1572. — In absence of goddess of f. no reproduction of life A431.1.1; god of f. A431; magic object produces f. *D1347ff.

Fertilized. — Earth f. by magic springs D1563.0.1.

Ferule. — Only one f. fits staff Z322; quest for f. to fit staff H1344.

Festin de Pierre *C13.

Festival of animals B299.7; compulsion C684.4. — Beltane f. A1535.5; intercourse during f. tabu C119.1.4; marriage by drinking f. T135.6; marriages made at f. T147; sudden love at f. T34.1; wedding, funeral f. on same day V65.3.

Festivals. — Sacrifice at religious f. V16.

Festivities of dwarfs F451.6.3; of giants F531.6.8.4.

Fetched. — One object f. by another D1428; skull f. from a charnel house H1435.

Fetching, see also **Bringing.** — Devil f. contracted souls M219.2.

Fetish worship V1.10. — Magic f. *D1241, *D1274; resuscitation by f. E53; slave going near f. forbidden C561.1.

Fetters loosed at Christ's Nativity D1395.8; as punishment Q434; of underground monster *A1071. — Angel looses man's f. V232.4; escape by cutting f. K649.11; rescue from prison by saint, who enters and breaks f. R121.6.

Fettered, see also **Chained;** Fenris Wolf F864.1; monster as dragon A1072.4; monster's escape at end of world A1070ff. — Abducted princess f. in giant's room R41.5; deception into allowing oneself to be f. K713; limbs of dead f. to prevent return E431.5; man f. with own sons'

entrails Q469.7.1; mother rescues f. son R153.4.1; princess f. to chair
by hair R111.2.3; sea f. F931.8.
Feud within family P201.1; over trifle N387. — Wife chooses father's
side in f. P211.
Feudal tribute P533.
Fever personified Z112.1. — Dipping into cold water to cure f. J2214.9;
flea and f. exchange night-lodgings J612.1; magic cure for f. D1502.3,
D2161.1.2; origin of f. A1337.4; sickle with f. J1959.1.1; wrestling match
of f., stone image K12.4.
Fevers, god of A478.4.
Fiachna's incest H582.2.1.
Fian P551.0.1; calls for aid R187.1.
Fiana, origin of A1658.1.
Fiancé. — Avenging bride's former f. H335.1.1; deceived f. may sleep
with seducer's wife J1174.21.
Fiancée, see also **Betrothed;** falls in love with another man at betrothal,
elopes T157. — Blind f. betrays self K1984.5; forgotten f. D2003ff.,
(reawakens husband's memory) D2006.1ff., (recalls lover) T56.3; lover
returns to find f. married N391; magic stolen by f. D861.5.1; man resists
blandishments of leader's f. W34.1; slovenly f. W115.1.
Fictitious. — Fool appointed to f. office boasts of it J2331.2.
Fiddle. — Devil plays f. at wedding G303.9.8.2; dupe wishing to learn
to play f. has finger caught in cleft of tree K1111.0.1; magic f. *D1233;
man becomes f. D254.1; respite from death while one plays the f.
K551.3.1; spirit plays man's f. F473.6.8; wolf-captor scared by f.-playing
of captive ram K2327.
Fiddler in hell breaks strings, must return to earth for repair K606.1.3.
— Devil abducts f. for hell G303.9.5.8.
Fidelity, see also **Faithfulness.** — Forcing attentions on friend's sweetheart
as f. test K2297.1; husband learns of wife's f. N455.6; oft-proved f.
T320.1; olive branch insures f. of husband D1355.8; tests of f. H1556;
reward for marital f. Q83.1; transformation to test f. D659.8; woman's
naiveté proves her f. T221.
Field at borders of otherworld F144; lying across road accursed H659.18.1;
magically cultivated D2157.6; -spirits F445; sprouts wheat at Christ's
presence V211.1.8.3; turns to gold D2102.2.1. — Addressing f. of reeds
J1883.1; carrying plow horse so as not to tramp up f. J2163; damages
for the f. devastated by a flock J1179.1; extraordinary f. T885; father
makes better from good (hedges his f.) H583.2.3; gathering all stones
from f. (task) H1124; plowing the f.: horse and harness destroyed K1411;
plowing f. of vipers (task) H1188; spoiling the rice-f. with dung K344.2;
uncut f. is already harvested (belongs to spendthrift) H586.4; white f.,
black seed (riddle) H741; wild hunt appears in a f. E501.12.6.
Fields set afire, men lured to death K812.2. — Giant's f. fertile, others
arid G112.

Fiend, see also **Devil.** — Man tempted by f. in woman's shape T332; tribute taken from fairies by f. at stated periods F257.

Fiends play ball with soul E752.1.2.

Fiery, see also **Fire, Luminous;** aspects of hell A671.2.4ff.; columns rise before warrior F1041.16.6.3; dragon B11.12.3; excreta T559.3.1; pillar guides person to church D1314.10; pillar sign of Christ's visit V211.2.1; serpent B19.4.2; sword F833.4; temple F163.2.2. — Beasts with f. eyes B14.4.2; bird with f. beak B15.7.13; demon as f. pillar G302.3.1; devastating serpent with f. breath B16.5.1.1; devil kills man with f. sword G303.20.1; dogs in wild hunt with f. (eyes) E501.4.1.3, (tongues) E501.4.1.2; eel with f. mane B15.7.12; ghost as f. bull E421.3.4; horse with f. eyes in wild hunt *E501.4.2.5; leaping into f. furnace unharmed H1573.1.4; men put to f. test ask pious man to join them K528.3; sun turns f. face upward A1135.1.1; wild huntsmen leave f. tracks E501.7.6.3.

Fifteen as formulistic number Z71.16.11. — No rainbow for f. years A1002.3; prophecy: child shall hang before f. years M341.1.3.1; witch with f. tails G219.8.1.

Fifth of land's production belongs to king P13.9.2. — Man refuses to eat f. descendant of stolen cow F647.10.

Fifty-feet tall giant F531.2.1.2; -two as formulistic number Z71.16.9; -three as formulistic number Z71.16.15; -six as formulistic number Z71.16.16. — Fox had rather meet one hen than f. women J488; giants f. feet tall with footprints six feet long F531.2.1.2; giant cane holds f. cattle F612.3.1; giant with f. heads F531.1.2.2.7; king with f. sons (daughters) T586.2.1; man can hear ant leave nest f. miles away F641.2.

Fig. — Creation of man from f. A1253.1.1; extraordinary f. F813.7; magic f. *D981.5; stolen f. in mouth, cheek lanced W111.5.8; why flower of wild f. unfindable A2791.4.

Figs. — Clever girl refrains from eating f. which would bring on magic sleep J585.1; daw waits in vain for f. to ripen in winter J2066.2; magic cake of f. D1031.2.2; rain of f. J1151.1.3.

Fig-tree is chief priest of trees A2777.1; from which one cannot descent D1413.1.3; as god A435.2; helps cross river F1071.1; stays with angels: rewarded with sap of all other trees A2711.7. — Magic f. D950.8; why f. is evergreen A2711.4, A2765.1; wife hangs self on f.; friends ask for shoot J1442.11.

Fight of animal and houndpack B264.1; brought about by trickster K1082, K1084; of culture hero and elder brother A525.1; with dragon *B11.11ff.; in dream real F1068.2.2; of the gods and giants *A162.1, F531.6.15.1; between husband and lover T243; of lions and bulls J1022; of men transformed to animals D615.4; on old woman's hand X941.2; between one-legged, twelve-legged birds H619.5; with sea-monster G308.1; of revenant with living person E461. — Animal f. as suitor contest H331.15; charm gives victory in f. D1400.1.10; criminal may f. against odds rather than be judicially executed P513; divination from animal f.

D1812.5.0.8; devil is overcome by man in f. G303.9.6.1.1; devil and his son f. over division of earth G303.11.2.1; disenchantment by overcoming enchanted person in f. D716; dwarfs f. with each other F451.6.4; fairies ordered to f. each other F381.12; fairies return woman after f. over her F329.2; faithful servant remains at home to f. for exiled hero P361.2; foolish f. with sun J1968.1; giant's animals help him in f. F531.6.16.2; holes in hills from f. between gods A964.1; lover kills his lady's relatives in f. T95.1; magic causes enemies to f. among selves *D2091.4; men return home just as needed in f. N699.1; numskull thinks extinguishing of lights at church presages f. J1823.3; quarrel and f. over details of air-castles J2060.1; raven and dove f. over man's soul E756.3; refusal to f. relatives P205; revenants f. each other E467; sham f. to frighten away guests J1563.7; transformation to animals to f. D659.2; trickster attempts to bring about f. between friends K1084.3; trickster bribes guards to start f. K341.10; trickster causes owner and another to f. over goods K348; twelve years' f. as suitor test H328.6; unwitting f. of brothers with each other N733.1; warrior's deceptive f. in "single" combat K2319.2; weak overcomes strong in f. L310ff.; wisdom of deliberation in f. J572.
Fights as valor tests H1561.1.
Fighter. — Devil as f. G303.9.6ff.; lie: remarkable f. X972; magic sleep of dragon-f. D1975.
Fighters. — Constant replacement of f. E155.1.1.
Fighting animals seen in otherworld F171.4; with berserks F610.3.4.1; in fairyland tabu F210.1; in the shade best J1453; with spirits as fear test H1423; stars F961.2.6; on stumps of legs after they have been cut off at knee S162.1; though tired vs. losing for rest J356; with witch G275.9. — Animals f. B266, (for their master) B571.3; continuous f. in battle F1084.0.3; "don't watch two people f." J21.50; friends not f. each other H1558.8; house-spirits f. each other F482.7; hero f. army alone F614.10; hero f. in otherworld F176; hero who wanted to sleep before f. killed K959.2.5; hero uses f. animals to contest with demons B524.1.11; king's attention attracted by f. when it cannot be otherwise gained J1675.1.1; magic object acquired by acting as umpire for f. heirs *D832; maiden queen prefers f. to marriage T311.4; mountains' shape from f. each other A964.2; punishment: f. all who pass through forest Q598; spirit f. person F402.1.12; symbolism: not f. alone Z161; tabus concerning f. C835ff.; no time for minor f. when life is in danger J371; woman induces men's f. over her K1086.
Figure. — Exhibiting own nude f. T55.6; hand of vampire severed by cutting off hand of drawn f. E251.1.2; numskull knocks the f. of Jesus from the ass J1823.1.4.
Figures. — Automatic f. of harp D1620.2.5; instrument's ornamental f. climb down and run about as harper plays D1627.1; lovers converse in f. of speech T42.2; sham f. of wife, paramour attacked in bed K525.1.1.
Filial duty rewarded Q65.

Fill. — Tabu to eat one's f. C205.

Filled. — Barrel f. miraculously with penitent's tears F1051.1; compelling the f. to eat (stuffing geese) H583.4.4; devil's sack f. with dissolute songs G303.24.1.5; house f. by growing snail F983.1.

Filling oneself up before the feast J2178; impossible objects as task H1023.2.2ff.; a sack full of lies (task) H1045; twelve bed-ticks with feathers (task) H1129.2; yard with manure (task) H1129.1.

Filth. — Dupe induced to eat f. K1044; entrance to dwarf home leads through f. F451.4.1.7; why flies live amid f. A2433.5.2; victim suspended in basket over f. and thrown in Q474.

Financier P430ff.

Finch. — Creation of f. A1926; man transformed to f. D151.2; wedding of f. B282.3.6, B282.5.

Find, see also Found. — Inability to f. object one is carrying J2025; man admitted into heaven but must not f. fault *F13; way to otherworld hard to f. F150.1; what is most difficult to f.? (truth) H659.19.

Finder. — Lost ass, saddle and bridle offered as reward to the f. J2085.1.

Finders. — Treasure f. must not take all of money N553.3.

Finding certain secret forbidden C820ff.; extraordinary object as suitor test H355; princess (suitor test) H322. — Animal f. stolen goods B543.2; king (prince) accidentally f. maiden marries her N711; king marries girl f. lost object N713; love through f. ornament T11.4.6; sham wise man hides horse and is rewarded for f. it K1956.2.

Fine for failing to solve riddle H541.2.1. — Ass envies horse in f. trappings J212.1; dress so f. that it goes in nutshell F821.2; judge tired of bickering pays f. J1179.9; man pays f. for enemy W11.5.7.1; tasks as f. H928.1; wounded king exacts f. from would-be slayers Q211.8.1.

Fines for rape T471.0.1. — King spies to levy f. K2246.1.1; payment of f. P531.

Finery. — Woman in f. in church thinks people are standing to see her J953.8.

Finest. — Quest for the f. of (chains) H1303, (linen) H1306.

Finger cut because of absorption in the charms of beloved *T26.1; -drying contest won by deception K95; transformed to axe handle D457.9. — Blood springs from murderer's f. when he touches victim D1318.5.1; cannibal cuts captive's f. to test fatness G82.1; cannibal gives girl's f. to her sister G86.1; child's f.-ends cut off S161.1.1; conception from eating f. bones T511.6.2; cut-off f. proves wife's chastity K1512.1; feats of strong man's little f. F614.2.3; golden f. as sign of opening forbidden chamber C911; ground dries up when first woman cuts her little f. A856.2; holes in stones caused by piercing by saint's f. A972.3; image with pointing f. F855.1; identification by ring springing off f. H94.7; life token: ring presses f. E761.7.1; magic f. D996.1; magic knowledge from sucking f. of knowledge D1811.1.1; ogre sucks victim's f. and drinks all his blood G332.1; recognition by missing f. H57.2; river from man's

f. F715.1.3; stealing ring from f. (task) H1151.4; test of wife's obedience: f. in hole H473.1; waking from magic sleep by cutting off f. D1978.1.; witch's f. marks stone G221.3.1.

Fingers as false tokens of wife's unfaithfulness K2112.1.1; raised in sign-languages H607; of saint give light or fire F552.1.2. — Adam creates five devils by wetting five f. with dew and shaking them behind him G303.1.5; animals from severed f. of woman *A1724.1; backward-pointing f. F441.4.4; biting f. to see if one is dreaming F1041.13; child nourished by sucking its own f. T611.1; deceptive contest in pulling f. K74; demons' f. cut off as proof of killing them H105.5; escape from wives by making substitute f. K521.4.6; fire from warrior's f. F683.1.1; ghostly f. leave mark E542.1ff.; god's marvelous f. A123.5.2; hands with unusual number of f. F552.1.1; jinns' four f. F499.3.1; ladder of f. F848.2; mutilation: cutting off f. S161.1; person with unusual f. F515.1; sound of wild hunt avoided by sticking f. in ears E501.17.5.8; stretching f. to make ladder D485; tempted man burns off his f. T333.2; ten f. answer to wife's riddle H582.3; troll lights f. G304.2.1.1; unusual f. F552.1.

Fingernail. — Devils' caps from man's f. parings G303.25.5.1; drug hidden in f. K873.4; magic sight by looking at polished f. D1821.3.7.2; man created from f. A1263.2; murder by poisoned f. S111.9; severed f. identifies corpse H57.2.2; troll's daughter after being cooked in kettle recognized by golden f. H79.1.

Fingernails become gold D475.1.21; become jewels D475.4.6; grow after death E182; of slain cyclops H105.5.2. — Bride test: bread-making (dough under f.) H383.1.1; extraordinary f. F552.1.3; fear test: cutting devil's f. H1422; fire carried from heaven in f. A1415.1.1; origin of f. A1311.3; trimming f. tabu C726; unusual f. F515.2.

Fingerprints. — Marks on certain fish from (St. Peter's f.) A2217.3, (devil's f.) A2217.3.2.

Finished. — Dead cannot rest until certain work is f. E415; disenchantment when superhuman task is f. D791.1.2; numskull stays till he has f. J1814; structure to be f. when king's daughter marries H1292.18.

Finishing. — Reincarnation to enable f. work E606.2.

Finland. — Origin of cockroach in F. A2061.1.

Finns as magicians D1711.10.1. — Cupbearer abducted from F. P50.4.

Fir Bolg, origin of A1657.2.

Fir fer P557.4.4.

Fir-tree. — Dissatisfied f. finds its own needles best A2723.1; marriage custom: going round f. T135.10.

Fire, see also **Afire, Fiery;** alarm scares off fairies F381.8; announced metaphorically makes headway J1269.12; becomes woman, runs away D439.6; bell rung foolishly, disregarded when needed J2199.1.1; -breathing spirit F401.7; brings cold in otherworld F169.7.1; burns man who doesn't understand it J834; burns up tree while builder brings another

H1129.5; crackles as wizard passes G229.8; drill invented A1414.1.1; drills malfunction D2089.10; forces ghost away E439.5; giants F531.1.10; from heaven F962.2, (kills) F797, F981.4, (destroys pagan objects) V356.2; issues from cold hearth when man approaches H175.4; keeps lover awake H1484.1; from lake to burn forest M477.1; lake in otherworld F162.6.1; lights self D1601.7; noises misunderstood J1812.4.1; in otherworld F165.7; as one of sun's faces A733.3; from peacock's tail burns enemy army K916.1; -producing troll G304.2.1; as punishment Q552.13; -spewing giantess G125; set to distract attention K341.23; -ship K2364; -spirits F497; stolen by swallowing K382; transformed to gold D475.1.5; unable to consume special wood F812.8; from warrior's fingers F683.1.1; and water mixed to make sacrifice J1952. — Angel from f. A52.1.2, A52.1.5; angel of f. A493.0.1; after world f., life recreated from tree A1006.9; Agaria not afraid of f. A1689.2; animal breathes f. *B742; animal preserves f. for abandoned children in a clam shell S352.1; animal sets f. to neglected church B596; animal scorches self while putting out f. A2218.1.1; animal grateful for rescue from f. B364.2; animal who steals f. scorched: cause of his color A2218.3; arrows of f. F831.2; ball of f. for ghost's head E422.1.1.2; bath of f. F872.5.1; beggar escapes from f. N177; behavior of f. as omen D1812.5.0.3; bird set on f. D2061.2.1.1; bird with tail of f. B15.7.14; birds fly into tower of f. B172.10.1; birds pitch selves into man's f. B531.5; birds set f. to besieged city K2351.1; black tribe because woman put on f. A1614.8; bone-dust becomes f. D457.12.1; book written with f. F883.1.2; building f. in otherworld H619.4; castle of f. F771.1.11; chains of f. F863.2; changeling thrown on f. and thus banished F321.1.4.3; charcoal burner drives fairies off with f. F389.1; chariots of f. A136.3.1, F861.4.4; chimera breathes f. B14.1; Christ creates f. in hell A671.0.2.1; city of f. F763; columns of f. in front of angry warrior F1041.16.6.3; conception from f. T535; creation interrupted since God must go to a f. A2286.1; creation of monkeys: old woman thrown into f. A1861.2; crossing river of f. H1542.1; crown of f. F828.2; curse: f. lit under stepmother M431.6; daughter of f. and frog mate A1221.5; deity's child becomes f. A199.3; demons flee f. F405.12; devil as ball of f. G303.3.4.2.1; devil holds f. in hands G303.4.8.2.1; devil and sinful priest disappear amid blaze of f. in the river G303.17.2.4; devil drives carriage drawn by horses whose nostrils shoot f. G303.7.3.2; devil saves heretic from f. G303.22.13; devoured children come out of f. F913.2; disenchantment by lighting f. D784; disenchantment by throwing into f. D712.2.1; dog is flame of f. by night B182.1.5; doors of f. F782.5; dupe burned trying to put out house f. K812.1; dwarf wants to warm self at f. F451.5.7.1; dwarf's friend's house spared in f. F451.5.1.21; dwarfs warm heath by underground f. F451.5.1.15; elves set country on f. C934.3; enraged man spits f. F1041.16.1; escape by throwing captor's clothes on the f. K634.1; extraordinary behavior of. f. F964; eyes flash f. F541.1.1; fairy breathes f. F239.3; fairies set f. to buildings F369.1; father accidentally falls in f. and dies N339.8.1; fingers of saint give light or f. F552.1.2; flesh becomes f. D457.17.2, D457.17.7; flood put out world f. A1019.4; fly steals f. from spider: may eat everywhere A2229.4; fool whose house is burning puts wood on the f. J2162.2; following witch's f. into her power G451; fox produces f. by striking tail to ground D2158.1.1; glow worm thought to be a f. J1761.3; god of f. A493, (and god of rain contest) A975.2.1; god becomes f. D285.0.1; god among seven sheaths of f. A137.17; goddess of f. A493.1; goddess with body of f. A124.3; helpful animals quench executing f. *B526.1; holy man passes through f. unharmed V222.8; horse in wild hunt breathes f. *E501.4.2.4; hospitable f. of his father is sought (bean merchant) H581.2; husband sets f. to house and ousts hidden paramour K1554; illusory f. stops men D2031.11; imitation of jumping into f. unscathed: fool burns J2411.6; jumping over f. H1199.10; ladder of f. F848.4; lake of f. in otherworld F162.6.1; land of f. F702; light f. but do not light it (task) H1067; lightning from f. A1141.7; magic drug gives immunity from f. and iron D1344.2.1; magic extinguishing of f. D2158.2; magic f. *D1271; magic f. moccasins D1566.1.2; magic horse goes through f. B184.1.12; magic journey in f. cloud D2121.7.1; magic object (controls f.) D1566ff., (protects against f.) D1382, (provides f.) D1481.2; magic power by jumping into f. D1733; magic stream quenches f. D1382.8; man brings f. at devil's instigation, burns Q582.2; man transformed to f. D285; man with f. moccasins G345; miraculous rain extinguishes f. used at stake *D1391.1; moon as grinder brings f. from sun A741.3; mother throws children into f. S12.2.2; mountain of f. F753; mountains and valleys formed by f. A969.3; ogre chased away by f. G581; ogre made to believe hero has withstood f. K1733; "only light the f." J2516.3.4; ordeal by f. H221; origin of f. A1414; origin of f. worship A1546.6; origin of illness from f. A1337.8; otherworld f. burns out repeatedly F171.6.5; otherworld people unacquainted with f. F167.8; oven heats without f. D1601.6; passing through f. as chastity ordeal H412.4; penance: hanging for a thousand years head downward over a f. of chaff Q522.6; person in magic sleep surrounded by protecting f. *D1967; pillar of f. F774.2.1, (identifies saint) V222.0.1.2; prisoner whirled away in blaze of f. R122.1; prophecy: death by f. M341.2.7; pursuit by f. R271; quest to upper world for f. H1264; recovering object in large f. H1132.2; riddle about animal living in f. H842.2; river of f. as barrier to otherworld *F142; rivers of f. in hell A671.2.2.3; robin steals f., has breast scorched A2218.5; rock produces f. when struck with steel A975.2; saint unharmed by f. D1841.3.2; salamander subsists on f. B768.2; Satan created from hell f. G303.1.3.5; "sea is on f." J1191.1.1, J1293.1.1; setting f. to house to escape undesired lover T320.6; setting sun mistaken for f. J1806; sham magician belches f. K1963.4; shortsighted use of f. J2162; shortsightedness about f. J2183.6; silver in chain increases in f. D1671; soul of f. E701.4; spear of f. F834.1.1; spirits

ascend by f. F407.1.1; starting f. near cobra's abode H1156.1; stepmother falls into f. from fright N384.3; stones of f. F809.6; suitor
contest: riding through f. H331.1.5; sun bathes in stream of f. A722.5.1;
sun from f. A712.1; sun as f. rekindled every morning A712; sun from
f. flung into sky A714.3; sun god's wife pours f. over earth A1031.4.1;
sun thrown on f. A1068; sun, moon and stars nourished on f. A700.7;
tabu: lighting f. at certain time C751.1; tabu to throw f. into river
C851.2; tabu f., weapon and dog together C887; tabu to urinate on f.
C99.1.1; "tank of water caught f." J1531.1.1; task: building a f. H1129.5;
theft of f. *A1415; thief detected by building straw f. J1143; thieves set
f. to village K336.1; threat to throw on f. causes changeling to cry out
and betray his nature F321.1.1.6; throne of f. F785.3; touching f. in
otherworld tabu C542.2; transformation to steal f. D657.3; tree of f.
F811.1.4; tribe born from f. A1268.1; troll stretches neck so long that f.
comes from lips G304.2.1.2; two beams of f. shoot from devil's eyes
G303.4.1.2.3; unextinguishable f. at end of earth A871.0.2; universe
created from f. world A622; valley of f. F756.1; victim pushed into f.
K925; vow not to flee from f. M155.3; water becomes f. D478.3; water
resembling f. F710.1; wall of f. F744, (about otherworld isle) F148.1;
weighing f. H1145.1; who shall put out f.? J2532; why animals lack f.
A2436; wild hunt heralded by f. E501.13.7; wild huntsmen surrounded
by f. E501.7.6.4; wild huntsmen exhale f. E501.7.6.1; witch as ball of
f. G212.5; wolf makes f. as mock sunrise K1886.3; woman asked for f.,
abducted K762; woman confesses murder: unharmed by execution f.
V21.2; world f. A1030ff.; worship of f. V1.6.3.

Fires burnt in streets to ward off witches G272.4; of hell A671.2.4ff.;
hissing mistaken for muffins cooking J1812.4. — Dead persons build f.
E578; ghosts gather wood for hell f. E755.2.4; hell f. kindled according
to sins E755.2.4.1; king hung between two f. Q414.5; magic control of f.
*D2158ff.; stars as f. in ghosts' hearths A761.4; tabu to neglect sacred f.
C67; twilight reflects f. of hell A1179.1.1; vision of f. of hell V511.2.1;
woman must relight magic f. as punishment Q492.

Firearms, magic D1096.

Firebrand, ghost as E421.3.2. — Stone becomes f. D452.1.7.

Fire-breathing animal *B742; spirit F401.7.

Firefly. — Cruel woman reborn as f. E692.5; helpful f. B482.1; man
becomes f. D184.1.1.

Fireflies as lantern-carrying mosquitoes J1759.3. — Bats keep f. B788;
creation of f. A2094; lies about f. X1287; speech of f. A2426.3.6.

Fire-maiden imprisoned R9.4.

Firemen, drunken X821.

Fireplace. — Curse by stones in f. M418.1; jackal comes to f. for food,
burned K1032.1; moving f. instead of putting out fire J2104; paramour
hidden in f. K1521.1.

Fire-steel, magic *D1175.2.

Fire-tongs, automatic D1601.24.

Firewood continually swept away from swimming man H1129.5.1; of elephant tusks F811.22. — Collecting f. to last lifetime H1095.1; cutting f. from rocks H1116.1; ghosts seek f. to roast man E257; inexhaustible f. D1652.10.1; magic f. D1298; saint's f. miraculously replaced V224.1.

Fireworks, fear of J2627.

Firmament prevents water of heaven from engulfing earth A810.2.1. — Creation of f. A701.0.1; heavenly lights from f. A790.1; windows in f. shed light A1171.2.

First of animals, fruits belong to priest P426.1.1; at combat gets choice of weapons P557.4.1; creature to be greeted will be transformed D526; man to arrive after king's death to be heir P17.1; to become angry must submit to punishment K172; man and woman A1280; man's good luck foolishly imitated by second J2415; objects picked up bring fortune N222; people have everything A1346.2.2; to say "Good morning" shall have disputed property K176. — Bed-partner to receive payment from f. man she meets in morning T456; why cat eats f. A2545.2; child unwittingly promised: "f. thing you meet" S241; contest in seeing sunrise f. K52; criminal accidentally detected: "that is the f." N611; dead arise when one plays organ for f. time in church E419.5; decision left to f. person to arrive M92; devil to have man if he gets him at f. grasp K235.3; districts named from f. person met in each N125.4; divination from f. person (thing) met D1812.5.0.7; why dog eats f. A2545.3; emergence or descent of f. man to earth A1230ff.; fasting the f. month J2135.1; fool experiments to see how f. man killed himself J2374; hateful or lovely child to be born f.? T548.1; hero returns and marries f. love T102; irrevocable judgment causes judge to suffer f. M11; injunction: to cohabit with f. woman met after battle C664.0.1; injunction: to marry f. woman met C664; king vows to sacrifice f. thing he meets (ass beheaded) J1169.4; long span of life for f. men A1323; man must be killed with f. blow C742.1; origin of f. parents A1271; originator of death f. sufferer K1681; payment to be made at harvest of f. crop (acorns) K221; present for the journey: what you f. see L221.1; prince prefers f. love to princess he later marries J414.2; princess to marry f. man who asks for her T62; prophecy on f. participant of feast D1812.5.0.7.1; prophet's f. disciple J1169.8; sun born of f. couple A715; tabu: arriving home f. when dog accompanies C756.1; tabu: wife eating f. animal caught in trap C221.4.1; threat to marry daughters to f. comers N455.12; vow to marry f. person performing act M138; wager: who can call three tree names f. N51; waters created on f. day of creation A910.1; who shall go f.? train leaves J2183.2; who shall speak f.? J2511; witch powerless when person speaks f. G273.2; would be f. in all things, even knavery J1269.3.

First-born cannot see ghosts E421.1.1.0.1; son given to Church V451. — Satan slays f. Egyptian G303.20.9.

Firstlings. — Tabu to eat f. C229.4.

Fish bears men-children after swallowing man's rinsings B631.3; brings lost object from bottom of sea B548.2; bursts with pride J955.1.1; carries man across water B551.1; carrying man shakes him off when struck M205.1.1.1; catching with nets A1527; caught with another's cries (lie) X1156.1; to climb trees if river burns J1904.4.1; come to hear saint preach B251.2.7.1; cleaned by girl becomes man D370.1; with coat of wool B737; in deluge deride God: are flattened with blow *A2231.9; disappear from sea F931.2; driven into tiger's mouth X1114.2; eat other fish: guilty must swim deep A2238.3; enticed into trap K714.8; follows sound of music B767.1; -god A132.13; grants hero wish to impregnate princess B375.1.1; grateful for being transferred from tank to river B375.1.2; guards cow B576.3.1; hero snaring a being tabu C566.1; jumps into boat of disheartened fisherman N625; lured by kindness and killed K815.14.1; magically summoned D2074.1.2; paramour B612; in parson's sleeve J1604; perform races to welcome saint B251.2.2; in pot appears to be many J1813.5; pricks and defeats monster L315.8; -producing tree F811.5.3; promises to spare man in coming flood B527.1; recovers lost urn from sea B548.2.5; refused saint changed to stone Q552.16.1.1; rescues ship B541.5; returned to water: grateful *B375.1; as sacrifice V12.4.10; struck by coconut: hence flat tail A2213.5.2; swallows man to rescue him B541.1.1; thought to be chewed sugarcane J1761.4; trained to answer call B771.4; transformed (to man) D370ff., (to object) D426; from waterless field D2106.1.1.1; wedding B283; as wooer B625; worship V1.8.11.
— Ambergris made from bitumen eaten by f. F826.2; asking the large f. (boy has been given small one) J1341.2; ass falls into water and catches f. in his ear N626; automatic metal f. D1620.2.6; boy born from f. T549.3; boy swallowed by f. escapes when it is cut open K565.1; brahmin's "polluted" f. K344.1.1; why certain f. have bowed backs A2356.2.4; catching f. in boots while wading X1112; catching huge f. without nets or tackle (task) H1154.4; why f. are caught in nets A2465.1; charm prevents f. being caught D1449.4; child half man, half f. T551.5; child promised to devil in exchange for a good catch of f. S227; city's inhabitants transformed to f. D692; origin of color of f. A2411.4; conception from eating f. T511.5.1; coyote calls the largest f. D2074.1.2.1; crane outwits, eats f. J657.3; crane tricks f. into being carried, eats them K815.14; creation of f. A2100—A2139; curse: no f. in river or sea M476.1; curse renders river barren of f. D2085.1; cutting up f. as bride test H383.5; devastating f. carries off daily victim B16.4; devil as f. G303.3.3.5; dividing three f. among two men J1241.3; in dividing f., dupe gets bones K171.6; dividing f. by scripture quoting J1242.2; dragon as modified f. B11.2.1.3; drinking up river to get all f. K231.11; earth originates from f. brought from bottom of sea A811.1; earth rests on bull who rests on f. A844.5; eater of magic f. to spit up treasure M312.3.1; eating small f. now, larger ones later J703.2; extraordinary f. F986; enmity between white f. and pike A2494.15.1; earth

supported by f. A844.3; evil spirit exorcised by burning f. D2176.3.1; fight between eagle and f. B264.2; fisherman fails to make f. dance to his flute J1909.1; food of f. A2435.6ff.; foolish bargain: good f. for worthless shell J2081.2; fox invites f. to live on land J758.3; friendship of deer and f. A2493.5; ghost of f. E523; giant f. B872ff., (lie) X1301; gifts from f. C847.1; god of f. and reptiles A445, A446; God "upward man, downward f." A131.1; goddess scatters pubic hairs on f.: why he has so many bones A2211.15; goose dives for star, thinking it a f. J1791.8; great f. killed by Bhimsen, cut into sixteen pieces A972.7; helpful f. *B470ff.; ice forms while f. leaps F935.2; inexhaustible f. D1652.1.10; killing certain f. tabu C841.9; king observes f. to learn wisdom J52.2; laughing f. reveals unjust judgment *D1318.2.1; leaves turn into f. D1470.2.1.1; life token: blood of f. calls out E761.1.4; little f. in the net kept rather than wait for uncertainty of greater catch J321.2; lost ring found in f. *N211.1; magic catches f. D1444.1; magic dead f. *D1281; magic f. *B175ff., (when eaten brings man to kingship) D1561.1.1.2; magic from f. having eaten magician D1721.2; magic object in f. D849.5; magic object locates f. D1327; magic song received from f. B505.3; magic transportation by skin of f. D1520.5.1; magic wooden f. attracts live f. to fisherman's net D1444.1.2; man catches f. in beard F634.1; man in f. form eaten, reborn D1889.7; man swallowed by f. and later rescued alive (lie) X1723.1.2; man transformed to f. D170ff.; mankind descended from f. A1224.6; markings on f. A2213.2, A2217.3, A2412.4; markings on flying f. A2412.4.5; marks on f. from devil's fingerprints A2217.3.2; marks on certain f. from St. Peter's fingerprints *A2217.3.1; marriage to f. B603, (in human form) B654; marriage to person in f. form B644; master persuaded to buy big f. since small ones creep out of all parts of his body J2334; meat becomes f. D476.3.4; mountains from hacked-up f. drawn from bottom of primeval water A961.2; mythical f. B60ff.; nest in tree for f. J1904.4; oracular f. D925.2; origin of custom of catching f. by day as well as by night A1457.2; origin of f. drug A2834; parable on big f. eating little J133.6; pig becomes f. D412.3.2; pig-fairy transformed to f. D412.3.1; poisoning f. causes storm C41.4; pond supplies both fresh and cooked f. X1546.1; prophetic f. B144; punishment: being eaten by f. Q415.9; punishment: small catch of f. for child-murderers Q553.5; putting the f. aside for Easter in one big pool J2124; recognition by hair in f. H75.3; reincarnation as child within f. E605.7.1; reincarnation as f. E617; reincarnation: man to f. to man E610.1.2; rescue from deluge by f. A1028; riddle: f. was my father, man was my mother H791; saint calls f. from lake D2105.5; saint fills waters with f. D2106.1.1; saint's bachall catches f. D1444.1.1; separable soul in f. E715.2; servant eats f., tells master they're spoiled K344.1.2; silver f. B102.4.1, (with gold fins) B731.12; shores flooded with f. from sea F986.5; soul in form of f. E735; speaking f. B211.5; stranger presented with first f. A1528; stream containing black f. bursts forth F715.3.2; strong man destroys f. and nets F614.5;

swine eating certain f. H1199.7; tabu: giving away gifts received from f. C847.1; tabu to eat f. C221.1.3; tabu to eat f. caught with improper fishhook C221.4.2; tailless f. as devil's hog G303.25.15.1; today's f. catch traded for tomorrow's J321.1.1; transformation to f. (by catching in fish-trap) D533, (to be caught) D646.1; treasure-f. B107; trickster throws f. off the wagon K371.1; trickster's f. burn up J2173.7; trolls steal f. at Christmas F455.6.3.1; unique f. bait Z312.4; ugly f. borrows handsome one's skin K1918.1; victim pounded up with poisoned f. K838; water won't boil until f. returned to holy well V134.3; water-spirit one-eyed f. F420.1.3.2.1; water-spirit gives mortal f. F420.5.1.7.5; why f. attack anything they find A2524.4; why f. come in seasonally A2484.1; why f. face each other in copulation A2496.4; why f. is stupid A2537.1; wisdom from f. B162; wise f. *B124; woman reborn as f. E694.4; woman refuses to look at male f. F647.4.1.

Fish's enemies A2494.15; reasonings about man J2214.5. — Escape from sea on f. back B541.1; origin of f. flat body A2305.1; origin of f. scales A2315; sun and moon from f. belly A713.1; true bride lives in f. belly K1911.2.2.11.

Fishes with men's bodies, razor snouts F711.6. — Angel of f. A445.0.1; beasts and f. exchange places U136.2; bird catches f. by imitating their friend K756.3; coin-producing pumpkin received from f. A1433.2.1; council of f. decide to get rid of men B233.1; creation of particular f. A2110ff.; directing f. to stop at his house J1881.2.3; eaten f. restored by saint D1652.1.10.1; election of king of f. B236.2; how f. got into wine jug J2281; gold-producing gourd from f. A1432.2.1; king descends sea to study f. P15.6; king of f. *B243ff., (eats subjects) K815.17; kingdom of f. B223; little f. escape from the net L331; magic f. talk so that ogre thinks hero has many brothers with him D1613.1; magic meal of f. D1032.1; mermaids like f. in water, like men on land B81.0.1; parent of all f. B60.1; parliament of f. B233; pike helps Christ: made king of f. A2223.4; plenty of f. as reward Q53.2.1; rain of f. J1151.1.3; sea throws out f. at world's end A1063.1; trickster tells lies to f. and causes them to fight K1084.1.

Fishbait. — Human eyes as f. S165.6; unique f. Z312.4.

Fish-beast B70ff.

Fishbone holds back river water D1549.3.5. — Fairies cause f. to choke king F363.1.

Fish-eagle, oracular B154.3.

Fished. — Blind women f. up from a well F1065; island f. up by hero A955.8; men f. for by piercer-of-souls G322.

Fisherman dragged by seal F1088.3.2; fails to make fish dance to his flute J1909.1; fooled by sham-dead trout K522.4.1; as foster father P271.2; of the gods A165.9; as hero L113.1.3; and hunter exchange catches for variety: soon return to original food U136; rears unknown prince H41.5.1; rescues abandoned child R131.4; and his wife *B375.1,

C773.1. — Enmity between f. (and dweller on the river U141); farmer as f. goes hungry in drought J345.2; giant f. G322.1; hospitality of f. to incognito king rewarded K1812.4; magic reward for rescuing f. Q53.2; mermaid caught by f. B81.13.11.1; merman caught by f. B82.6; mighty f. F634; strong man as f.: destroys fish and nets F614.5; tail f. K1021.

Fishermen console themselves J866.1. — Gods as f. A147; jokes on f. X253.

Fishhook made without proper incantations C221.4.2. — Fish recovers lost f. from sea B548.2.3; giant puts elephant on f. F531.3.12.1; infallible f. D1653.2; magic f. D1209.5, *D1257; man becomes f. D258; origin of f. A1457.1; task: recovering lost f. H1132.1.5; trickster gets caught in f. J2136.2.

Fishhooks. — Using stone f. tabu C895.

Fishing in the flax-field J1821; luck lost C933.2; skill as suitor test H326.4; tabu to men on mission C833.9; under sea F931.6. — Accidental success in f. N620ff.; alleged magic f. rod K119.1.1; bear f. through ice with tail A2216.1, K1021; cat f. for master K341.11.1; cheater discovered by f. in the street J1149.2; devil gives luck with f. G303.10.7; extraordinary f. F986; fat man f. from own window X151.2; giant's f. F531.3.12; god of f. A455; lies about f. X1150; origin of f. A1457; owner's attention distracted by man f. in street K341.11; saint's blessing aids f. V229.17; sham prowess in f. K1968; tabu: f. at certain place C182.1; theft from giant by f. through chimney K316.1.

Fish-maiden, marriage to B654.

Fish-men B80ff.

Fishnet. — Creator distributes f. A1440.1; silver f. in otherworld F169.4.

Fishpool. — Saint's curative f. D1242.1.3.

Fishskin, magic *D1025.2.

Fishtail transformed to shark D447.4.

Fishwives. — Talkativeness of Parisian f. X253.1.

Fissure. — Sun at night enters f. between sky and earth A722.7.1.

Fist full of fleas H1129.10. — Person only "f. high" F535.2.7.

Fists. — Devil's thumb the size of two f. G303.4.3.2; gathering wind in f. H1136.2; hero fights with f. alone J246.2.

Fits become epidemic J1511.4. — Witch causes f. G263.4.2.

Fitted. — Punishment f. to crime Q580ff.; reward f. to deed Q101.

Fitting. — Hollow stone f. anyone F809.2; monster f. men to his bed G313; object f. only one thing Z320; recognition by exact f. of clothes H36.

Five devils created by Adam create other devils in same manner G303.1.5; great roads of Ireland discovered at king's birth A994; heavens A651.1.3; as magic number D1273.1.2.1. — Devil has f. claws G303.4.4.1; first f. living creatures from crab A1211.8; formulistic number: f. Z71.3; giant with f. heads F531.1.2.2.3; goddess breaks self into f. parts: hence river's five branches A934.11.3; magic arrow makes f. wounds D1092.0.1; magic weakness for f. days each year D1837.1.1; marriage to f. women.

each with separate duties T145.1; marvelous runner can run round the earth in f. minutes F681.5; universe created in f. periods A601.1; what crows do when they are f. years old (riddle) H865.

Five-cent piece in churn releases curse M429.6.

Fivefold as formulistic number Z71.3.0.1.

Five hundred years' journey to heaven F76.1; years travel across universe A658.2. — Dwarf king Hibich comes to surface every f. years F451.6.12; one wrong and f. good deeds J1605.

Five hundred forty rooms in Bilskilmir F781.2.1.

Flag. — Color of f. on ship as message of good or bad news Z140.1; wind blowing on f. causes prisoner's execution N394.1.

Flags. — Pieces taken from f. serve to identify H103.

Flageolet, magic *D1224.1.

Flagstone. — Child born on f. T581.7; prayer at saint's f. V52.7; saint's f. follows him D1641.2.1.

Flail witness to threshing in heaven H84.3. — Strong man uses stable-roof as f. F614.7.

Flailed. — Dead f. by demons E755.2.6.

Flame of fire to punish Irish A1031.1; freezes Z1623.3; illuminates sacred person's cradle V200.1; issuing from mouth as sign of royalty H41.4; as miraculous index *F1061; settles on charitable person's forehead V411.9. — Bonga as f. F234.3.2; deity departs in f. column A192.2.4; face of angry warrior lights up with f. F1041.16.6.4; hound f. of fire B19.4.4; life bound up with f. *E765.1; man as king's stepping-stone across f.-filled trench P116; oracular f. D1311.5; riddle: the father not yet born, the son already at the top of the house (f. and smoke) H763; tongue becomes f. D457.14.2; tree half green and half in f. in otherworld garden F162.1.2.4.

Flames around God's throne A152.2; issue from corpse's mouth E421.3.7. — Mouth emits f. F544.0.3; rock in f. at hero's death F960.2.3.

Flaming shield unquenchable D1672.1. — Ogre with f. mouth G363.1; otter carries f. wood in mouth B193.

Flapping. — Hills from f. of primeval bird A961.1; wind caused by f. wings A1125.

Flashing eyes F541.1ff. — God with f. eyes A123.3.2; lightning from f. sword A1141.2.

Flask, see also **Bottle;** imparts magic strength to drinker D1335.7. — Looking into f. forbidden C323; trickster drinks from another's f. K499.9.

Flasks. — Non-buoyant f. float F1047.1.

Flat. — Hills f. where gods slept or cooked A972.5.5; man kills ox with f. of hand F628.1.2; origin of animal's f. body A2305ff.; person with f. body F525.4; why animal has f. tail A2378.7; why helldiver has f. stern A2356.2.10.

Flattening. — Strong man f. hill F626.1.

Flatterer's retort to girl J1356.

Flatterers. — Harm of association with f. J455.

Flattering foreman tricked by his master K1637; lies vs. unflattering truths J267.

Flattery causes raven to sing and drop cheese K334.1; of the great J814; punished Q268; unavailing against king of humble lineage J915. — Escape by f. K572; monk avoids f. V461.6.

Flavor. — Dishes of the same f. J81; special f. of forest wood F812.6.

Flax in well leads to adventures N777.3. — Clothing army from one hank of f. H1022.2; fairy boat of f.-stem F242.2.3; key in f. reveals bride's laziness H382.1; magic f. D965.13; making dress from wasted f. as bride test H381.1; making shirt from single f.-seed H1022.4.1; origin of f. A2684.1; recognition by overheard conversation with f. H13.2.6; respite from death gained by tales of the preparation of f. K555.1.1; riddles about f. H885; robber's beard compared to f. K434.1; swimming in the f. field J1821.

Flayed animal resuscitated E171. — Corpse f. by ghosts E255; magic bull to be f. B184.2.3.1; magic mouse to be f. B183.1.1; servant rides through streets on f. ass J1075.1.

Flayer, disguised K1941; skillful F664, (lie) X983.

Flaying alive as punishment Q457ff. — Cutting image into man's back by f. S166.6; disenchantment by f. D721.1; murder by f. S114ff.; punishment for f. live calf Q211.6.1.

Flea and fever exchange night-lodgings J612.1; makes princess speak F954.4.1. — Creation of f. A2032ff.; devil given f. instead of soul K219.7; helpful f. B483.2; louse and f. wish to marry Z31.2; louse invites f. J2137.1; man becomes f. D185.2; picking the louse and the f. J2415.2; reincarnation as f. E616.3; using f. powder K1955.4.

Flea's bite alarms king B521.3.3; wedding B285.5. — Cause of f. movement A2441.3.2; why f. face is red A2330.5.

Fleas. — Assembling many-colored f. H1129.10.1; crayfish from devil's f. shaken off in water A2171.1.1; fist-full of f. H1129.10; fox rids himself of f. K921; god plagues devil with f. A63.4.1; lies about f. X1285.

Fleece. — Quest for golden f. H1332.1; ram with golden f. B101.3, R175.1.

Fleeces. — Witch blowing away f. G283.1.2.5.

Fleeing, see also **Flight;** pancake Z33.1. — Sweetheart mistaken for enemy by f. man N318.1; tame dog prefers food basin to f. hare J487; vow against f. fire, weapon M155.3; west wind exhausted from f. deity A1127.2.

Fleet. — Borrowed f. scares king into giving daughter K1771.9; deceptive emergence of f. K2369.2.1; giant f. of foot F531.1.3.5; hero f. of foot L141.3.

Fleetness, magic D1936.

Flesh of animal A2381; of certain animal alleged to be only cure for disease K961; of certain person alleged cure for disease K961.2; -eating spirits G312.3; magically does not regrow D2062.3; regrows E784; reveals guilt D1318.7ff.; struck from ravisher's ear F304.4.1; transformed to object D457.17. — Boy born with one side f. and one iron T551.4; buying gallows f. or living f. forbidden C781.1; cannibal returning home smells human f. *G84; charm sung over f. chewed by wizard has magic power D1273.0.3; child born as formless lump of f. T551.1.1; dwarfs originate from maggots in f. of giant F451.1.1; eating f. of certain animal forbidden C221.1; effects of wild hunt remedied by eating part of f. thrown down by it E501.19.5; giants wear skins with f. still on F531.4.7.1.1; girl serves her father with piece of her own f. K492; why f. of animal is good A2511; healing by replacing f. F950.9; hero feeds f. to helpful eagle *B322.1; human f. eaten unwittingly *G61; husband nourishes starving wife with his own f. and blood T215.3; magic f. (of animal) *D1017, (of human) D1008; marvelous sensitiveness: meat is dog's f. F647.5.1; old woman feasts on human f. G11.6.3; one pound of f. offered: tongue demanded K255.4; people who prefer raw f. F561.1; pound of f. contract J1161.2; queen delivered of piece of f.; abandoned, it turns into boy, girl T569.1; resuscitation by laying covered f. on pyre E134; taste of human f. induces cannibalism G36; tearing off f. with hot pincers Q469.9.1; trickster's burnt f. becomes gum on trees A2731.1; transformation by eating f. D551.3; why crows eat human f. A2435.4.7; why tigers eat human f. A2435.3.9.3; wild hunt throws human f. on persons who see it E501.18.2; women, driven mad, devour their infants' f. N325.2.

Flies, see after **Fly.**

Flight, see also **Fleeing, Flying;** of bird with man to safety B542.1; of brothers from home to avoid being sacrificed S272.1; of children from father who turns cannibal G31; of devil (Satan) when cock is made to crow G303.16.19.4; of dwarfs to caves for protection F451.6.14; of dwarfs through air F451.3.3.6; of god in bird plumage A171.2; of image through air D1626; on magic horse B552; of maiden to escape marriage T311.1; of roast ducks (magic) D2191; of witch through air. G242. — Attempted f. to heaven punished L421; fairy aids mortal in f. F349.1; fools frightened at the f. of a quail J2614.2; hero's f. to maiden's room K1346; heroine's three-fold f. from ball R221; looking back during f. tabu C331.3; magic arrow f. D1526.1; magic ball f. D1526.2; magic f. D670; method and position of bird's f. A2442ff.; omens from f. of birds D1812.5.0.2; obstacle f. *D672, (Atalanta type) *R231; parson put to f. during his sermon X411; pretended f. draws victim K929.4; reversed obstacle f. D673; shammed f. deceives enemies K2378.3; transformation f. D671.

Flights R220ff.; extraordinary F1021ff.

Flinching. — Test of valor: not f. under a blow H1561.3.

Flint, magic *D1175.2; origin of A1414.5.

Flippers. — Boy with seal f. F515.4.

Flitting (moving) away from brownie impossible F482.3.1.1. — Ghost f. between two graves E419.9.

Floating island A179.2, F388.2; islands of the gods A955.12; rock F804. — Anchor f. on water F1047; children in casket f. down river H157; illusion palace is f. K1889.6; man f. in river too lazy to drink W111.1.5; monkey instead of girl in f. basket K1625; non-buoyant flasks f. F1047.1; object f. in air F1083.0.1; prince finds princess f. on water in basket: marries her N711.5; quest for princess caused by sight of one of her hairs f. on river *H1213.1; spirit f. in air F411.2.

Flock of geese transformed to stone D423.1.1. — Banners appear like f. of birds K1872.5; giant f. of birds B878.1; lie: thick f. of birds X1119.1; shearing a f. of sheep in one day H1106; treasure animal introduced into family's f. K2131.5; wolf loses interest in the sermon when he sees a f. of sheep U125.

Flocks. — Enigma: f. are rock H594.3; fairies kill f. F366.3; god of f. A441.1.2; prophecy: all f. will perish M359.6; stupid monk recovers stolen f. L141.1.

Flogging to death S122; debtor's corpse Q491.2; for eating kid on Friday Q223.9.2; as punishment Q458ff.; suspects brings confession J1141.1.10. — Father f. child S11.6; parents f. daughters P237; saint f. woman who tempts him T331.6.

Flood *A1010ff.; from breaking tabu D984.3; caused by breaking forth of springs A941.6; of mud injures corn Q552.14.2; prophesied M359.8; as punishment Q552.19.6; scatters carpenters everywhere A1445.2.1. — Animal characteristics obtained during f. *A2291; animals from transformations after f. A1711; birds cling to sky in f.: cause of tail feathers A2211.7; bodies of water remnant of f. A910.4; church spared in f. because of prayers D2143.2.1; dragon causes f. B11.7.1.1; fish promises to spare man in coming f. B527.1; giants in f. F531.0.3, F531.2.1.3, F531.6.12.8.2; human sacrifice stops f. S267; husband in hanging tub to ecape coming f. K1522; magic f. D915.6, D2151.8; magic hat brings f. D1542.1.3; magic stones keep f. in check D1388.2; reeds bend before f. J832; rescue from f. as reward Q150.1; riddle about girl's coming and f. H583.10; serpent causes f. B91.6; son dies before father after f. A1335.7; sun from kernels thrown into f. water A718.3; Virgin saves her image from f. V284; watersprite transformed to f. D283.3.

Flooded. — Sending letter by f. river J1881.1.7.

Flooding. — Magic song drives back f. D1549.8; saint's bachall drives back f. river D1549.3.1.

Floor. — Innkeeper deceived into going under f., robbed K343.0.1; lovers communicate through f. T41.2; person magically sticks to f. D2171.1.3; prison f. with spikes in it R41.3.3; red-hot iron f. protects city F767.2; task: sweep the f. and do not sweep it H1066; waterskin dragged across sky's f. A1142.8.

Floor's. — Riddle: where is f. root? H883.

Floors in dwarf home covered with pine twigs F451.4.3.5. — Silver f. in otherworld F165.3.3.

Flounder. — Why f. is flat-bellied A2231.9, A2354.1.

Flounder's — Origin of f. flat body A2126, A2305.1.2; why f. mouth is crooked A2231.1.2, A2252.4, A2341.1.

Flour pot broken before sold J2061.1.3; sprinkled on girl at betrothal T61.4.3. — Bringing back f. scattered by wind (task) H1136.1; feeding stolen money in f. to animal K366.0.1; lover sifting f. shown to wife K1214.1; man dies after eating bread from f. used for abscess plaster N383.2; pepper mixed into enemy's f. K2351.6.1.1; reincarnation of stomach into f. vat E649.2; sack of f. descends on peasant in punishment Q296.1; wolf puts f. on his paw to disguise himself K1839.1; why Zuñi girls rub f. on their faces A1687.1.

Flow of blood magically stopped D2161.2.2; of cow's milk increased by licking saint's garment D2182; of molten metal at world's end A1069. — Direction of river's f. reversed D2151.2.1.

Flowing. — River ceases f. F932.6; river f. around the world A872; unneeded water stops f. F930.5.

Flower becomes girl at night D621.2.2; blooms when touched D2195.1; bouquet brings brothers' recognition H16.3; entices beautiful woman T56.4; fresh as long as seen only by owner D877.2; friendship oath P311.2; from grave E631.1, (bears letters) E631.0.2f.; on head transforms D596.1; magically produced D2178.9; spirits F447; transformed to person D431.1. — Bird brings foreign f. F982.4; birth from f. T543.2; blindness cured by f. F952.3.2; bread transformed to f. D454.2.1; conception from f. (smelling) T532.1.1.1, (eating) T511.4; daughter promised to monster as bride to secure f. she has asked for S228; disenchantment by f. D771.11, (by breaking stalk) D711.4, (by throwing f.) D712.3.3; fairies care for f. bed F339.2; fairies' revenge for stealing f. F361.2.2; fox brings f. in mouth B584.1; life token: f. fades *E761.3; magic f. *D975ff., (opens dwarf home) F451.4.3.7; magic f. pot bears plants with gold letters on leaves D1469.1; man (woman) transformed to f. D212; marriage to f. T117.6; picking only one f. as sex test H1578.1.6; prince buys f. (enchanted girl) from her mother T52.1; prince plucks from grave of vampire a. f. which later becomes a girl E251.2.2; quest for marvelous f. H1333.5; recognition from conversation with f. woman H13.4; resuscitation by plucking f. incarnation E29.4; soul as f. E745.4; soul in f. E711.2.2; transformation by eating f. D551.2.4; transformation by touching with f. D565.8; treasure buried under f. N511.1.10; which is best f.? (cotton) H659.23; woman transformed to f. recognized H63.1.

Flowers appear as innocent approaches H216.1; become golden D475.1.18; bloom in winter F971.5; cause magic sleep D1364.3; drop on washing hands D2193; on ears protect against fairies F384.4; fall from lips D1454.2.1; fall from saint's mouth V222.11; grow from saints in graves V229.2.7; magically preserved D2167.3; as sacrifice V12.8; scent from magic laughter D1773.1; spring up when saint strikes ground F971.6; from tears D1454.4.3; thrown to indicate princess's choice H316.2; transformed to other object D451.4; as token H87; from under the feet of Virgin Mary A2621.1; yield wine F979.9. — Blood becomes f. D457.1.3; boy of f. comes to life D435.1.3; conception from f. hidden in breast T532.3.1; devil avoids cockscomb f. G303.16.14.5; eating f. to cover theft K417.1; extraordinary f. F814; girl gathering f. swallowed by earth and taken to the lower world F92.2.1; girl summons fairy lover by plucking f. F301.1.1.2; goddess (god) of f. A434; instruments of torture transformed to lotus f. D454.16; language of f. Z175.1; lie: remarkable f. X1480; making withered f. green H1023.3.2; obtaining f. as suitor test H335.4; origin of f. A2650ff.; plucking fairy f. tabu F378.5; bridegroom alone plucking f. from bride's grave H31.12.1; quest for bouquet of all f. H1377.2; sewing shirt from f. H1021.9.1; snake reincarnated as f. E691.1; tabu: touching (plucking) f. *C515; test of sex of girl masking as man: choosing f. H1578.1.3; trail of f. R135.0.7; transformation by plucking f. in enchanted garden D515; ugly women complain of falling f. K1984.4; why some f. have no scent A2795.1; women transformed into f. A2611.0.4.1.

Fluid, see also **Liquid.** — Magic f. *D1242; person with pink f. in place of blood F554.1; river of extraordinary f. F715.2ff.

Fluids. — Extraordinary container for f. F866.7.

Flute makes more noise than quarrelsome wife J1541.2; player a hero L113.10; player thinks song meant for the prince is sung to him J953.3. — Bride attracted by f. T56.1.1; dolls vivify as f. plays D435.1.2; dupe wishing to play f. puts tongue in split bamboo K1111.0.1.1; fisherman fails to make fish dance to his f. F1909.1; magic f. *D1223.1; recognition through f. playing H35.1.2; reward for f. playing Q95.1; snake mistaken for f. J1761.6; tabu: playing f. C844; transformation by playing f. D523.1.1.

Flutes announce gods' approach A199.7.

Fluttering of birds after sunset C885.1.

Fly buzzes when cleric returns B251.2.4; cannot light on fast horse B184.1.1.1; dying in meat tub is happy that he has eaten to satisfaction J861.3; helps suitor pass test B587.2; jeers at king's elephant J211.2.1; laughs at dog's death A2479.8; steals fire from spider: may eat everywhere A2229.4; turns into girl's nipple J1833.1.1; warns saint against devil in liquor B483.0.1; as witch's familiar G225.1; worries heretic to death Q415.8; and wren, fox live with cleric B256.10. — Aiming at f. has fatal results N333; why f. is bald A2317.2; bald man aims at f. J2102.3; boastful f.-killer: "seven at a blow" K1951.1; chain tale: f. frightens snake Z43.4; chain tale: old lady swallows a f. Z49.14; contest: coin first attracting f. K92.1; contest in lifelike painting: f. on saint's nose H504.1.1; creation of f. A2031; devil as f. G303.3.3.4.4; enmity between spider and f. A2494.14.1; fairy as f. F234.1.16.1; fairy transforms self to f., allows self to be swallowed by woman and is reborn as fairy F392; how f. got his eyes A2332.1.2; girl to marry man on whom f. lights B152.2; ghost as f. E423.7; giantess as f. F531.1.8.5; grateful f. warns lion B371.2; helpful f. B483.1; how birds began to f. A2442.9; killing the f. on the judge's nose J1193.1; why f. lives amid filth A2239.2, A2433.5.2; magic ability to f. D2135.0.3; man transformed to f. D185.1; marksman shoots left eye of f. at two miles F661.5.3; prince awakened by f. and saved B521.3.3.1; princess lets trickster's f. charm escape K251.3; saint never drives f. from face W10.1; soul in f. E715.3.2; soul as f. E734.7; spider invites f. to rest on her "white curtain" K815.2; spirit as f. going into bottle F401.3.4; tale about f. forgetting her name Z25; thief calls self "F." K359.2.1; transformation to f. to aid weapon selection *D659.14; wedding of f. B285.4; why f. has no voice A2239.2, A2422.5; why f. is hated A2522.7, A2583.1; why f. lives on dung heap A2432.9; witch in form of f. G211.5.1.

Fly's buzz A2239.2, A2426.3.3, B251.2.4; movement A2441.3.3.

Flies on the ark A2031.2; build bridge (lie) X1294.1; on Christ's body rewarded A2221.2.1; try to drink water from elephant's ears J971. — Causing f. to collect around girl's litter K2129.3; charm expels f. D1443.1; charm to dispel f. brings dissatisfaction Q557.8; covering with honey and exposing to f. Q464; cow strikes at f. while boy eats B579.2; don't drive away the f. J215.1; why f. may eat anywhere A2545.1; hero f. with birds' feathers B540.1; king of f. B246.2; standing whole day in July in tower naked exposed to sun and f. K1212; why f. fly around ox's eyes A2479.9; why f. lack tail A2378.2.8; why stinging f. sit on eyes of cattle A2494.14.3; wishing to destroy all f. J2079.2.

Fly-catchers, deities as A132.6.4.

Fly-whisk of life and death E64.1.1.3; magic *D1287.

Flying carts F861.2.1; contest won by deception K25; dragon B11.4.1; Dutchman E511; fish B62; head as ogre G361.2; horse *B41.2, B542.2, D657.2, (wooden) R215.3; island F738; mountain F755.3; squirrel's body made larger A2213.3, A2301.5; tower F772.2.6. — Artificial f. horse D1626.1; bird characteristics from f. contests A2254; devil f. like bird G303.7.9; devil f. away with sentry box G303.9.9.13; dragon f. to nest with human being B11.6.8; dragon f. away with lion B11.6.8.1; escape by f. through air D2165.1; fairy f. off with woman K786; giant f. over water F531.6.17.2.1; ghost's f. head attacks slayer E261.1.1; god f. A171.3; goddess f. in bird's plumage A136.1.8; hero f. away from death K551.24; magic object gives power of f. *D1531; man learns f. F1021.3; power of f. from eating children's hearts D2135.1; resuscitation by bird f. over dead E79.1.1; swan outlasts crow in f. L394; wings cut from f. mountains A1185.

Flying-fish, origin of A2136.

Flyting M401.

Foal, see also **Colt;** born of Loki and stallion T465.2. — Knight protects

f. from storm Q51.1; mare with f. left behind finds road home B151.1.1.1; new f. heavy to carry, peasant doesn't want horse J2212.8; witch drowns f. G265.2.

Foam on beer as life token E761.6.4. — Bringing ocean f. in cloth H1049.1; god discovers the devil in a piece of solid f. G303.1.2.3; origin of f. on waters A1117.

Focus (what he does with his four coins) H585.1.

Foe, see **Enemy.**

Foetus exchanged from one woman to another T577. — Child born from miscarried f. T549.4; plants from f. A2611.0.2.

Fog produced by magic D2143.3. — Demons cause f. D1361.1.0.4; lies about f. X1651; ogre turns into f. G522.1; origin of f. A1134; soul as f. E744.1.

Fold. — Bloodthirsty animal by trickery admitted to f. K828ff.; devil in f. of knight's cloak G303.8.9.1.

Folded. — Tent-house f. and swallowed F923.

Folding. — Magic f. mule D491.1.2; self-f. object D1642.

Followed. — Countess f. around by dwarf F451.5.8.1; fairies f. by hogs F241.3; friend f. into world of dead M253; lawyer's corpse f. by devil G303.25.8; monster shot and f. into lower world F102.1; sound of drum f. into ghost town F102.2; thief f. home J1392.1; wild hunt f. by empty shoe E501.10.1.

Following the devil G303.10ff.; magic object D1427; where you lead J1515; witch's fire into her power G451. — Adventure from f. animal to lower world N773; child f. bird loses its mother N313; disenchantment by f. enchanted woman through lake to underwater castle D759.5; fool f. nose on journey, climbs tree J2461.6; wise man f. fool against his better judgment put to death J1714.1.

Folly, see also **Foolishness;** of father's giving all property to children before his death P236.1; of marrying twice T251.0.1.

Fomorian ogre G100.1.

Fomorians. — Names of F. Z100.1; origin of F. A1659.1; yearly tribute to F. S262.2.1.

Font. — Not to peep at sacred f. C51.1.7.

Food, see also **Eating;** alone keeps off hunger J712ff.; of animal A2435ff.; becomes gold D475.1.16; changed to dust D476.2.1; demanded, supplied must be eaten C288; denied until hands clean: impossible task K278; of devils G303.25.14; disappears because of wastefulness Q585.4; -dropping trees F811.5; given away by saint restored V411.6; given to object J1856; of the gods A153; -goddess A494; which the husband detests and the wife keeps serving him T255.5; for journey to otherworld E433.3; leaves saint's clothing unspoiled F1091; left on magic stone brings good luck thereafter D1561.1.6; left for transformed person D694; magically disappears Q552.3.4; magically dwindles D2089.7.1; magically preserved D2167.1; magically stolen D2087.6; as marriage present H335.5; must be given everyone on journey C675; mysteriously poisoned N332.6; not offered to fairy F361.1.2; placed out for cobold F481.0.1.3; placed out for returning souls of dead *E541.1; produced by prayer D1766.1.8; refused saint becomes putrid Q552.16; supply fails as punishment C934; tabu broken, blackmail follows K443.13; tabus during pregnancy C152.3; tabus following childbirth C154.1; thrown on floor in anger F1041.1.6.10; transformed D476, (to muck) D472.1; vision tempts fasters D2031.16. — Abundant f. in otherworld F166.11; acquisition of f. supply for human race A1420ff.; adulteress detected by f. K1550.1.2; adventures when wife takes f. to husband N788; all nature composed of f. in vision D1731.2.2; angels supply mortal with f. V232.3; animal bribed with f. *B325.1; animal grateful for f. B391; animal persuaded to be tied by promise of f. K713.1.3; animals eat extraordinary f. F989.22; animals grateful for being given appropriate f. B392.1; animals provide f. for men B531; animals from transformed men according to favorite f. A1715.4; animal's f. affects him unusually X1203; animal husband provides animal f. B600.2; animals refrain from spoiling consecrated f. B259.4.1; animals unsuccessfully try to exchange f. U147; ascetic faster increases his sufferings by placing f. and drink before himself V462.2.1; attention drawn by helpful animal's theft of f. from wedding table H151.2; blades in f. kill ogre G519.4; boy behind the tree tells woman about the bad f. he gets K1971.3; bride test: procuring f. quickest H375.3; burning f. test H1511.2; chieftainess preparing f. tabu C564.8; child exposed with f. supply S334.1; child hides f. from starving parents S20.2; children exchanged for f. E234; children refused f. leave home R228; clothes thrown into the cooking f. J1561.1; companion sent away so as to steal common f. supply K343.3; conception from eating f. T511.7; consolation for misfortune found in f. J861; cooked f. grows F1005; creator of f. items A1420.3; cuckoo borrows f. from other birds A2241.4; curse: lack of f. M443.1; curse: not to taste f. from own table M435; customs connected with f. P634.0.1; dead beg f. from living E541.5; dead grateful for f. E341.2; deception into disastrous attempt to procure f. K1020ff.; deceptive eating contest: inexhaustible f. K81.3; demon of gluttony coaxed from man's throat with bits of f. F406.4; demon of gluttony devours f. in man's throat F402.1.7; demons bribed with f. G582.1; demons eat much f. G302.9.7; devils eat huge amounts of f. G303.3.0.2; dogs by river try to get f. in river by drinking the river dry J1791.3.2; dogflesh: "f. you've never eaten" J2469.5.1; dupe persuaded to steal f.: cannot escape K1022; dupe's f. eaten and then blame fastened on him K401.1; dwarfs particular as to f. F451.3.7; dwarfs steal f. F451.5.2.2.2; earth as f. for first men A1420.6; "eat spiritual f., not material" J1511.16; eating f. offered to dogs as penance Q523.3; eating f. without untying container H506.7; extraordinary f. F851; eyes exchanged for f. M225; failure to put out f. for fairy F361.14; fairy grateful for f. F332.0.1; fairy music causes loss of f. F262.5; fairies borrow f. from mortals F391.2; fairies' f. F243; farmer as f. chooser L144.2; father's counsel: let cheap fish be your daily f. H588.2; fingernail conceals basin

of f. F515.2.1; fisher and hunter exchange catches for variety but soon
return to original f. U136; forethought in provision for f. J710ff.; forgetting name of f., thinking it in sand J1924; fox spoils f. rather than divide
with ape W152.1; ghost killing person for f. E253; ghost steals f.
E593.5; girl from elfland must eat earthly f. in order to remain C661;
god blamed for f. scarcity J2215.4.1; god prepares f. for mortal A185.7;
guest made to pay for f. K251.2; habitual f. continued when harmful
U139.1; helpful animal demands f. B322; horse taught to live without
f. J1914; house without f. or drink J2483; human f. fed vampire E251.2.3;
hungry ghosts haunt houses seeking f. E281.1; illness feigned to get
better f. K2091.1; injurious f. with sweet taste K1889.4; inexhaustible f.
*D1652.1ff.; jealous courtiers accuse jackal of stealing lion's f. K2141;
kindness unwise when it imperils one's f. supply J715; lie: remarkable f.
preferences X1031.6; liking for f. and drink J1343; living on small
amount of f. as suitor test H351; living without f. for year F1033; lover
refuses f. T24.6; magic basket supplies f. D1472.1.19; magic bird produces unlimited f. B103.0.2; magic f. *D1030ff., (furnishes treasure)
D1465ff.; magic weakness from f. D1837.5; maid behind statue of Virgin
advises the mistress to give servants better f. K1971.3.1; man created
from f. A1266; man had rather be burned alive than to share f. with a
guest W152.2; monotony of one f. compared to marriage J81.0.1; mortals refuse to eat fairy f. F361.5; mother refuses children f. S12.6;
mountain spirits eat raw f. T460.2.14; murder by over-hot f. S112.5;
mutual agreement to divide f. K231.1.2; no work, no f. W111.3.6; offering
f. for woman's favors K1353.1; ogre used as f. G519.3; one man's f. is
another man's poison U140ff.; origin of f. from body of slain f.-goddess
A1420.1; paradise lost because of forbidden f. A1331.1.1; peasant produces f. for all A1655.1; person transformed to animal refuses human
f. D686.1; poisoned f. sent to enemy camp K2369.11.1; poisoned f.
test H1515; pseudo-magic power to produce f. K1036; pseudo-magic f.-
producing object sold K112; punishment: f. fills with maggots Q501.2.2;
quest to otherworld for samples of magic animals' f. H1251; repartee
about f. J1340; saint causes two youths to be fed best f. V73.3; saint
multiplies f. D2106.1.5; saint renders poisoned f. harmless D1840.1.2.1;
saint's f. miraculously replaced V224.2; salt sprinkled on fairy f.
renders it harmless F384.1.2; salt, water as only f. H588.21; sham death
to get f. K1867; sham miracle: cooked f. turns raw K1975.3; shower of
f. F962.6; shortsighted fool loses his f. J2173; social rank determined
according to portion taken from cauldron of f. H1574.0.1; songs about
improvement in f. J1341.11; sons-in-law driven away by reducing f.
P265.1; spirit takes f. from cupboard F473.6.3; starved lover chooses f.
over lady K1218.1.3.1; stealing f. from dancing children K341.17;
stingy f. to visitor repayed J1511.13; stingy man's wife prays for husband's illness, better f. W152.16; strong man serves ogre as punishment for stealing f. F613.4; supplying f. to ungrateful stepmother
rewarded Q65.1; tabu: eating f. of certain person C240ff.; tabu to

carry f. at night C751.8; tame dog prefers f. basin to fleeing hare J487; task: making many kinds of f. from one small bird H1022.6; task: preparing the f. "Oh my" H1185; testing strange f. on animal J21.4.2; thumbling carried up chimney by steam of f. F535.1.1.2; to each his appropriate f. J81.2; touching f. of another caste tabu C551.1; transformation to be put in f.-bag D657.1; transformation to receive f. D655; trickster discovers adultery: f. goes to husband instead of paramour K1571; trickster dupes jealous wife, steals f. T257.10; trickster eats f. while dupe is under water K16.2; trickster hides in f. and eats it K371; trickster pollutes f. in order to be given all K344.1; trickster works spell over f., eats it K353; troll's f. F455.4.2, G304.2.2; twelve kinds of f. (cumulative tale) Z22.2; unsuccessful imitation of magic production of f. J2411.3; unwelcome guest tells about the hidden f. J1344; vampire brought to life by being fed human f. and drink E251.2.3; voice warns against poisoned f. D1317.4.1; vow never to refuse f. to any man M158; wasting f. tabu C851.1; wholesome f. for the day of hanging J2174.2; why animals sources of f. A1422.0.1; why f. is cooked A1518; wild huntsman pacified with f. E501.17.6.2; young ass avoids f. eaten by animals before being slaughtered J12.

Foods in otherworld F183. — Ignorance of certain f. J1732.

Fool digs holes at road's edge J95; disguise K1818.3; disguised as king, killed N338.2; fasts on roof, falls off J565.1; given intelligent wife T125.1; given the truth on his back J551.2; as hero Z253; laughs at the absurdities he sees about him U15; not to be punished P523.2.1; passes as wise man by remaining silent N685; as prophet M301.9.1; rescues and wins girl R169.10.1; told to get brain pot; marry clever girl J163.2.1; wears crown K1810.1.1; wins beautiful woman L161.2; amongst wise men pours milk J1149.12. — Bigger f. in midday heat J1552.1.1.1; courtier called f. by pope refuses to correct those who may call pope a f. J1289.3; gift of the f. J1272; husband answers behind the statue when wife wants to know how to f. him K1971.1; if his son were only a f. he would let him study to be a priest X426; king and f. look identical F577.3; lucky f. N680.1; man plays f. as protection J822; only a simple f. J1393; "whose f. are you?" J1369.4; wives wager as to who can best f. her husband K1545.

Fool's brothers substitute goat for body of man he has killed K661.1. — Answer f. questions next day J571.5.

Fools *J1700—J2799, P192; frightening each other J2632; learn to be peaceable J24. — Association of wise men with f. J1714; easier to number wise men than f. J1443; poets and f. allied P427.7.2.1.1; quest for the greatest of f. H1312; same company of f. J1265.3; those most respected are the biggest f. J171.2.4; wisdom from f. J156.

Foolish association of young and old J445ff.; bargains *J2080ff.; but handsome son M93; married couples J1713; person becomes clever J1116. — Christ looks for stick to beat those who ask f. questions X435.3;

hero in disguise of f. knight, then of black knight, rescues lady R169.1; magic object acquired through f. bargain D837; magic object makes person f. D1353; officiousness or f. questions rebuked J1300ff.; princess brought to laughter by f. actions of hero H341.3; successful f. son L115; tasks imposed because of f. boast H914, H915, H916; three f. wishes J2071; types of f. imitation J2410ff.; when with fools, act f. J1714.3; wise and f. J (entire chapter).

Foolishly. — Same wishes used wisely and f. J2073; testimony discredited by inducing witness to talk f. J1151.1.

Foolishness brings man death Q6.1; of making washerman minister J677; of noisemaking when enemies overhear J581; of premature coming out from hiding J582; of surrendering weapons J642. — Wisdom from continual reminder of f. in past J167.

Foot, see also **Feet;** cut off as punishment Q451.2.3. — Biting the f. K543; conception from hand or f. T517.1; cutting off giant's f. G512.6; escape from deluge on f. A1026; father's counsel: find treasure within a f. of the ground H588.7; frost-bitten f. (cumulative tale) Z42; giant with one f. 531.1.3.3; giant's f. holds back river F531.3.1.2.1; grave equals five times length of any person's f. D482.5.1; hanging by one f. Q413.8.1; why hyena has short left hind f. A2284.6; magic f. D995; magic power of seeing Death at head or f. of bed D1825.3.1; magic sight by treading on another's f. *D1821.1; man beats his f. for slipping J1867.1; man who has given all in charity has f. amputated: restored miraculously V411.3; man can stand all day on one f. F682; ogress' f. makes oven blaze G345.1; one f. in Ireland, one in Scotland: sod of both carried K2319.1; person with one f. F517.1.1.1; saint strikes earth with f.: fountain flows forth A941.5.2; sexton behind statue tells old maid praying for a husband to raise her f. to her neck K1971.9; sight of wild hunt causes one to stick axe or knife in f. E501.18.9; stones punished for injuring holy person's f. A975.1.1; task: coming neither on horse nor on f. H1053; vows taken by placing f. on post M119.4; witch prevents putting f. on floor G269.20; wolf too near to horse's f. K1121.

Footbridge. — Razor-sharp sword as f. (lie) X1817.1.

Footless man outruns swift horse (lie) X1796.1; people in otherworld F167.7.

Footprint. — Detection by f. J1146; devil's f. A972.2.2; earth, water or blood in f. E761.1.3.1; indention on rock from angel's f. A972.2.1; magic f. *D1294; transformation by stepping in f. D578.

Footprints of the gods A901; of holy man still visible A972.1.3. — Devil's f. without toes G303.4.5.3.2; dew in f. reveals trail R268; ghost leaves no f. E421.2.1; giant's large f. F531.2.1.2, F531.2.4; lover carried by mistress: no f. K1549.3.

Footrace between giant and mortal F531.5.11.2; contest H1594. — Woman bears twins after f. T581.8.

Footsteps in manure show dead man walked H264. — Ghost's f. heard E402.1.2; waters follow f. D1547.2.

Footstool before divine throne A152.6. — Earth as God's f. A133.2.2; self-righteous tailor in heaven throws God's f. at old woman thief on earth F1037.1, L435.3; tortoise as God's f. A139.2.

Footwashing as reconciliation sign P673. — Water from f. protects against witch G272.13.

Footwear, magic D1065.

Forbidden, see also **Tabu;** chamber *C611; expression C498; to think J1511.8; tree (fruit) *C621. — Animals eat deity's f. fruit: punished A2234.2, A2371.3.1; creation of animals as punishment for beating f. drum *A1731; funeral rites f. V62.1; laughter f. A1372.7; one f. thing C600—C649; paradise lost because of f. fruit A1331.1; practicing one's religion f. S466; shouting from f. place H1199.3; tide f. to rise (Canute) L414; wife f. to ride on the dog immediately does so and is bitten T254.2; wife opens f. chest: killed T254.4.

Force. — Adaptability to overpowering f. J830ff.; animals overcome man's adversary by f. B524.1; marriage by f. T192; recognition by f. of nature H175.

Forced labor causes subjects to drive away ruler P15.8; peace valueless U220ff.; prophecies unfavorable M340.2. — Hero (heroine) f. to change places with impostor K1934; man f. to eat dead father's heart goes mad G91.1; mother not loving children of f. marriage P230.2; person f. by magic pistol to run behind the ball D1526.3; wild hunt f. to depart E501.17.8.

Forcing princess to say, "That is a lie" *H342.1; wife tabu C164. — Husband f. wife cursed T288.1.

Ford. — Forbidden f. C617.1; saint creates f. across river F932.9; washers at f. as disaster omen D1812.5.1.1.6.

Fords, combats at H1561.2.3.

Forecaster. — Mandrake as magic f. D1331.13.1.

Forehanded servant J1614.

Forehead. — Devil with eye in middle of f. G303.4.1.2.1; flame settles on charitable person's f. V411.9; giant with golden hair on f. F531.1.6.5; Good Luck lives in man's f. N113.2; gold star on f. F545.2.1; horse's f. as golden chair F874.2; lump on f. identifies fool F192.7; magic horns grow on person's f. *D992.1; magic mark on f. renders invisible D1361.43; man dies because he has killed a man with the sign of the Cross on his f. V86.1.3; marks on f. royalty sign H71.1; moon shines on God's f. A123.10; person with one eye in center of f. *F512.1.1; putrescence from f. F1041.18; remarkable f. F545.2; vagina in f. F547.5.6; why rail has red f. A2330.8; why sheep may keep wool which grows on his f. A2322.5; troll's life in his brother's f. E714.3.1.

Foreheads. — Women's breasts on f. A1313.4.1.

Foreign. — Abandonment alone on f. coast S114.1; all f. elements expelled

20*

from country P711.6; aversion to burial in f. soil P711.8; disguise as f. ambassador K1839.7; hero buried unknown in f. country V69.2; task: recovering money owed by a f. king H1182.1; theft signal given in f. language K358; tribute of youths regularly sent to f. king S262.2; visit to f. country as suitor task H336.1; words in a f. language thought to be insults J1802.

Foreigner may not act as legal security P524.2; may not bring law suit P523.1. — Questions of f. answered: "I don't understand" J1802.1; son marries f., mother kills self P231.7.

Foreigners. — Heads of f. exchanged with devils' A1610.1.1; social status of f. P191.

Foreknowledge of hour of death D1812.0.1. — Fairies' f. of mortal's coming F256.1; saints have f. of coming of guests D1812.0.2.

Foreseen. — All aspects of a plan must be f. J755.

Foresight: call undertaker with doctor J2516.9. — Death through lack of f. J2137ff.; magic f. D1825.7.

Forest burns as magician opens eyes D2158.1.4; devil the one which fell in the forest when driven from heaven G303.8.13.2; magically springs up between enemies D2163.6.1; magically cleared D1641.4; as refuge of eloping lovers R312.1; from twig F979.8. — Abandoned queen entertains in f.: recognized H155; abandonment in f. S143, (to avoid fulfillment of prophecy) M371.0.1, (as punishment) Q438; army appears like f. K1872.1; birth of child in f. T581.1; changeling calculates his age by the age of the f. F321.1.1.5; deity lives in f. A151.7; deity of particular f. A419.1; dwarfs live in a f. F451.4.2.3; dwarfs protect the f. F451.5.1.17; fairies live in f. F216; felling a f. in one night H1095; felling the whole f. K1741.1; fetish clears f. D1601.22; enemies defeated by setting f. afire K2364.1; feigning sleep in f. with hero H1556.5; forbidden f. C612; goddess of wild f. plants A431.1.2; ground swallows f. F947; hair transformed to f. D457.4.2; imprisonment for hunting in king's f. Q433.10; lion leads lost king from f. *B563.1; magic f. *D941; making garden quickly in unplanted f. H1103.1; serpent demon guards treasure f. G354.1.1; strong man son of f. spirit F611.1.2.1; tabu: hunting in certain part of f. C614.1.0.2; tasks performed by helpful f. spirits H973; wife, child abandoned in f. S441; witch lives in f. G236; woman abducted in f. K1337; woman lured into f., captured K788; woman overcomes enemies singly in f. K778.1.

Forests. — God of f. A435; magic f. and trees D940ff.; giants in wild f. F531.6.2.7; why salt disappeared from f. A1196.

Forester, helpful N856; rescues abandoned child R131.8.5; sent to hell J225.7; as wild huntsman E501.1.4.

Forest-spirits, see **Wood-spirits.**

Foretelling. — Dead f. future E545.17.

Forethought J600—J799; in defenses against others J670ff.; in prevention of others' plans J620ff.; in provision for life J700—J749. — Air-castle shattered by lack of f. J2061.

Forever: a day and a night K2314, Z61.2. — Prosperity f. or for a day? L291.

Forewarned. — Stealing horse when owner f. H1151.2.1.

Forge. — Goldsmith's magic f. D2178.7; salvaging anvil from burning f. H1574.3.1.

Forged credentials win girl K1917.6. — Magic object f. by smith to order D853; sun, moon, and stars f. by smith A700.5.

Forgery. — Credit based on f. K455.8; theft by f. K362.7.

Forget-me-not, origin of A2657.

Forgetfulness of actor speaking in his own person J2041ff.; of fool J2671ff. — Curse of f. *D2004.1; magic f. *D1365ff., *D2000ff., (for breaking tabu) C945, (as punishment) Q551.11; medicines of f. and of remembering D1365.8.1.

Forgetting Charon's fee E489.3; leashes of hounds as bad omen D1812.5.1.21; name he went on trip to find out J2241.1; sweetheart causes loss of invulnerability D1847.1. — Fool f. master's message punished J2044; man f. to count self, dies E791; misfortunes from f. to say "If God wills" N385.1; soul f. everything at birth E705.

Forgiven. — Monk who has left his order f. and miraculously reinstated V475.2; mother guilty of incest with son f. by Pope (Virgin Mary) T412.1; vanquished ruler f. by victor J829.3.

Forgiveness brings about conversion V331.10.1; of father vs. mother H588.19; as religious virtue V441; the reward of successful quest H1244; of sin for acts of charity Q171.1. — Confession brings f. of sin V21; dead return to give f. E365.1; incognito king asks victor's f. K1812.5; punishment for finding fault with God's f. of sin Q312.3; sincere confession miraculously obliterated as sign of f. V21.1; suitor test: to earn f. H348; swelling bone as f. sign F991.2.1.

Forgotten fiancée D2003, (plea recalls lover) T56.3, (reawakens husband's memory) D2006.1ff.; name confused with lost treasure J1805.3; traditions J1445; wind J755.1. — Devils instead of angels visit woman who has f. God in her prosperity Q559.1; fairies help f. child J2415.4; father has f. to strike mother J122; much-repeated instructions f. by fool J2671.2.

Fork. — Man received f. in eye for breaking tabu C943.1.

Forked glen F144.1. — Why animal has f. tail A2378.5; soul f. from body by Satan E722.2.4.

Form of dragon B11.2ff.; of culture hero A526; of familiar spirit F403.2.2; of fettered monster A1072; of soul as it leaves body at death E722.1; of vampire E251.4; of witch G210ff.; of wood-spirit F441.4. — Dead wife returns in f. of bird E322.4; fairy in f. of an animal F234.1; fairy offers man change of f. and feature for aid in battle F343.11; jinn can take any human f. G307.2.1; man assuming lover's f., sleeps with princess

K1915.2; marriage to animal in human f. *B650ff.; marriage to person in animal f. *B640ff.; promise made merely as a matter of f. not binding M206; reincarnation in f. determined at death E602; transformation to husband's (lover's) f. to seduce woman D658.2.

Forms exchanged D45ff.; in which devil appears G303.3ff.

Former. — Animal habit a reminiscence of f. experience A2275ff.; identity tested by demanding that person say again what he said on f. occasion H15.1; maiden prince's wife in f. life N741.5; reincarnation: f. lives remembered *E601; "why f. days better?" J311.2.

Formless gods A120.4. — Child born a f. lump T551.1.1.

Formula for creating universe A611.0.1; for girl fleeing: behind me night, etc. R255; -tale saves girl from devil K555.2.1. — Disenchantment by magic f. D789.6; invisibility by reciting f. backwards D1985.2; magic f. *D1273, (exorcises witch) G271.3; marriage f.: "you are mine and I am yours" T135.1; pseudo-magic f. for gold K111.4; secret f. for opening treasure mountain overheard from robbers N455.3.

Formulas *Z0—Z99; for fairy travel T282.2; for selling one's soul to devil M211.5.

Formulistic numbers Z71ff.

Fornication. — No place secret enough for f. T331.4; sight of holy garment restrains man from f. V131.1.

Forsaken merman C713. — Madness from regret for having f. wife F1041.8.9; woman f. by husband dies in lover's arms T88; woman arousing love to be f. C686.

Fort. — Location of f. determined by magic D1816.3; magic f. D1136; magic object found in f. D849.1; magic thread makes f. fall D1400.1.1.18; tabu to erect f. on holy ground C93.7.

Forts. — Origin of stone f. A1435.2; seven f. of river, iron, mud, cow-dung, brick, stone, wood F789.1; tree amidst seven f. F811.23; tree inside seven series of f. H1333.5.0.2.

Forthputting woman T55.

Fortifications. — Magic renders f. useless D1414.0.1; treasure placed in old f. by supernatural beings N511.3.2.

Fortified. — Saint's curse: dwellings cannot be f. Q556.5.

Fortnight. — Lamp lighted every f. A1599.14.

Fortress built on Sunday destroyed by tempest Q552.14.1; demolished by thunder Q552.1.0.1.1; magically revolves D1381.23; in otherworld F163.5; ravaged after saint refused admittance Q595.1. — Magic head causes f. to crumble D1400.1.20.1; magic wheel prevents entrance to f. D1389.4; prophecy: destruction of f. M356.1.4; transformation to gain access to enemy camp (f.) D651.2.

Fortuna N111.

Fortunate youngest son L11. — Blue f. in love matters T3.1; proud animal less f. than humble *L450ff.

Fortune comes to deserving and undeserving N102; to go direction cat jumps K2.1; and Intellect, Knowledge, Health dispute which is greatest J461.1.2; learned from serpent B161.2; personified Z134; -telling dream induced by sleeping in extraordinary place D1812.3.3.2. — Advice from f.-teller *D1814.1; amasser of largest f. to be king P11.4.2; deserted daughter's good f. discovered by accident N732.2; dwelling of F. on lofty mountain F132.2; fairy seeks f. among mortals F393.3; good gifts of f. *N200ff.; hero makes f. through gambling N1.1; jokes on f.-tellers X461; just king brings good f. upon people P12.6; loss of f. for breaking tabu C930ff.; madness from f. loss F1041.8.11; overweening pride in good f. tabu C770.1; priest uses f. dishonestly made to erect monuments to himself W157.1; profligate wastes entire f. before beginning his own adventures W131.1; quest to F. to seek f. H1281; quest to god for f. H1263; reversal of f. L (entire chapter); salt in saltless land sold for f. N411.4; shoes (shirt) of f. N135.3; tabu to offend goddess of f. C50.1; ways of f. N100—N299; wife retrieves f. lost by husband J1545.6.

Fortunes. — Inequalities of men's f. A1599.8; noblemen being ruined by long lawsuit decide wisely to join their families in marriage and save their f. J552.2.

Forty of man's sons to die at once M341.0.2; sons born same day T586.1.5; -nine gates of wisdom J182.1. — Formulistic number: f. Z71.12; penance: standing in water for f. days Q541.2.

Foster brother rescues another from ogre G551.4.1; brother steals bride K1371.1.2; mother summoned D2074.2.4.1; relatives P270ff. — Children prefer f. mother T675.1; cock as f. father N842.1; cowherd as f. father N856.2; cruel f. relatives S30; curse by f. mother M411.1.2; dog buried instead of f. son K525.6.1; fairy f. father F311.2; fairy f. mother F311.3; false boasting of having killed f. brother K1766.1; forester as f. father N856.1; helpful animal f. brother B311.1; human f. child with animal qualities B635; impostor pushes f. brother into water K1931.1.1; kind f. parents chosen rather than cruel parents J391; king and f. son jump into sea F1041.16.7; king's f. son damaged by bee sting J1179.14; magic object from f. parents *D815.7; peasant as f. father N854.1; punishment: taking snakes as f. children Q594; smith as f. father N855.1; treacherous f. son K2214.3.1; treacherous f. brother K2211.2; Virgin Mary as f. mother V271; wise giant as f. father of hero N812.1.

Fostering. — Mortal f. fairy child M242.1.

Found, see also **Find.** — Devil f. by God G303.1.2ff.; disenchantment by being f. D783; lost object f. by throwing spade at ghost D1816.2.1; magic object f. D840ff.; origin of fire—f. in person's own body A1414.1.2; stolen person f. by animal B543.

Foundation sacrifice S261. — Omen at laying building's f. D1812.5.2.8.

Foundations. — God lays earth's f. A141.4.

Founders, religious V210ff.

Foundling helper N861; hero L111.2. — Man made to believe f. is daughter's child K1923.2.

Fountain Hvergelmis filled by deer A661.1.0.4; as lovers' rendezvous T35.1; produced (by sign of cross) *D1766.6.1, (by prayer) D1766.1.1, (by drop of water) D1567.7. — Cleansing f. in heaven A661.0.4; cool and boiling f. in otherworld garden F162.1.2.2; false bride takes true bride's place at f. K1911.1.3; hero finds maiden at f. N715.1; location of f. revealed in dream K1816.1; magic f. *D925ff., (in otherworld) F162.8; magic object produces f. D1567ff.; many-colored f. where saint strikes earth A941.5.2; quest for the f. of youth H1321.3; reincarnation as f. E635; soul in salmon appears in f. E713.1; sweet and bitter f. in otherworld garden F162.1.2.1; tabu: drinking from certain f. C261; task: bringing water from distant f. more quickly than a witch H1109.1; tears become f. D457.18.1.

Fountains as chastity index H411.11.2.

Four ages of the world A1101; -armed people F516.2.2; calves to one cow at birth T586.4.1; cats carry coffin F982.2; children at a birth T586.1.1; choices J210.1; demons in ring H973.2; earth-nails A841.4; earthly paradises F111.0.1; -eyed jaguar B15.4.1.3; -eyed tiger B14.4.1.2; fires in hell A671.2.4.13; -footed bishop J2283; -footed man F517.1.2.1; -headed animal B15.1.2.3; -headed person F511.0.2.3; heavens A651.1.2; -horned ox B15.3.1.3.1; as magic number D1273.1.2; mountains support sky A665.3.1; persons survive flood A1029.2; rivers of Paradise *F162.2.1; rivers rise in paradise waterworld A871.2; sky-columns A665.2.1; suns mark world's end A1052.3; world-columns A841; world systems A651.0.2. — Adam's body made of f. things A1260.1.3; Adam's name from f. stars A1281.6.1; angel with f. wings V231.3; castle carried through air by f. eagles F771.2.1.2; castle suspended on f. chains F771.2.1.1; club takes f. thousand men to carry it F835.2.2; colors corresponding to the f. world quarters Z140.2; demon allowed on earth f. times a year A106.2.1.2; devil disappears in carriage drawn by f. black horses G303.17.2.9; dividing f. coins among three persons J1241.2; earth with f. quarters A871; earth scattered in a circuit or in f. directions on primeval water A814.6; eye with f. pupils F541.3.3; formulistic number: f. Z71.2; four stars from f. quarters of heavens A1281.6.1; god with f. faces A123.2.1.2; golden wagon drawn by f. golden elephants F861.1.2; habitable hill raised on f. pillars F721.2.1; island supported on f. feet F736.1; keeping f. dogs in herd (task) H1112.1; literal numskull cuts peas into f. parts J2461.1.4; magic f.-leaf clover *D965.7; magic plantain causes f. tails to grow D1375.4.1.1; man made of earth from f. places A1241.5; man made of f. elements A1260.1.1; moon weighs pound, for it has f. quarters H691.1.1; persons (animals) with f. eyes F512.2.1; physician willing to believe in f. persons of Trinity J817.2; tunnel of crystal f. miles long F721.1.1; what f. things are hardest to hold (riddle) H659.2; what goes on f. legs in the morning, two at midday, and three in the evening H761; what he does with the f. coins he earns H585.1; woman has f. children: sun, moon, fire, water A700.3.

Fourfold. — Formulistic number: f. Z71.2.0.1.

Fourteen as formulistic number Z71.16.10; lucky daughters N231.

Fourth horse must carry all J761.2. — Suitor contest: riding to f. story of tower H331.1.2; sun created on f. day of creation A719.3; unpromising f. son succeeds L111.10.

Fowl makes another animal believe that he has had his leg cut off J2413.4.1, (neck) J2413.4.2; transformed to object D423. — Chain tale: conflict between f. and thistle Z41.3; enmity of f. and (dog) A2494.4.12, (cockroach) A2494.13.3, (falcon) A2494.13.12; giant's skull so large f. can pass through eye-hole F531.2.3.1; king and peasant: the plucked f. H561.6.1; self-cooking f. D1601.25.1; universe from cosmic f. A647; what is the best f. (riddle) H659.4; wise carving of the f. H601.

Fowls eat gold, silver F989.22.1. — Division of the fat and lean f J1241.4; enmity of owls and f. A2494.13.4.1; god of domestic f. A441.2; ghosts visible to f. E421.1.6; why f. never shut doors at night A2433.4.6.

Fowler asks ransom for goose, loses both J514.6. — Tortoise outwits f., keeps ruby K439.7.1.

Fox as alchemist B121.2; as animals' king B240.8; asking favor set on by dogs J871.1; as beast of ill-omen B147.1.2.1; brings flower in mouth B584.1; burns tree in which eagle has nest L315.3; claims that certain statues are of his ancestors J954.2; in coffer thought to be devil J1785.6; confesses to cock then eats him K2027; as culture hero A522.1.4; deceives lion into entering pit K714.9.1; deceptively sleeps with tiger's wife K1354.2.3; determines road to be taken B151.1.3; destroys boasting bird's nest L462; disguised as scholar K1822.2; distracts goldsmith's attention, steals K341.25; drinks tiger's milk K362.5.1; eating cake gets caught in pot K1022.6; elected mediator to appease angry lion B239.1; executed for thefts B275.1.2; fools crocodile into letting him go K543.1; forgets fables against lion J811.6; frightened in game with titmouse K869.1; holds conversation with his members J2351.1; and crane invite each other J1565.1; eats his fellow-lodger: accuses another animal and demands damages K443.7; with eight-forked tail B15.7.4; fasts as penance B253.3; feigns to be playing with sheep *K2061.2; feigning illness admitted to hen-roost and kills the hens K828.2; finally converses with lion whom he had feared at first U131.1; about to be hanged asks to be allowed to see geese J864.2; in human form betrays identity H48.1; insults caged lion W121.2.2; invites fish to live on land J758.3; jeers at fox-trap J655.2; language B215.3; leads ass to lion's den but is himself eaten *K1632; with lion protector goes hunting alone and is killed J684.1; loses fear of lion J1075.2; masks as dove, loses murder thoughts J512.10; as messenger B291.3.1; and noisy but empty barrel J262.1; outwits wolf, gets lion to kill him K961.1.1; and panther contest in beauty J242.3;

persuaded to talk and release cock from his mouth K561.1; persuades animals to start with the smallest in eating one another K1024; persuades bear to lie in hay, sets fire to it K1075; persuades bird to show him how she acts in a storm K827.1; persuades cock to come down and talk to him K815.1; persuades wolf to eat his own entrails (brains) K1025f.; persuades wolf to lie on the shock in order to be painted K1013.2; prefers to bear weight of his tail rather than give part of it to ape J341.1; pretends to be guarding sky K1251.1.1; pretends work, really sleeps K499.10; produces fire by striking tail to ground D2158.1.1; is promised chickens: driven off by dogs G235.1; had rather meet one hen than fifty women J488; refuses to mediate between lion and lioness J811.2; rescues man from sea B541.2; rids himself of fleas K921; rings the bell K1114; saves man from turtle J1172.4; shams death, catches crows K827.4; sees all tracks going into lion's den but none coming out J644.1; in sheepskin gains admission to the fold and kills sheep K828.1; as shepherd K934; sings formula for trick exchanges Z47.1; and sour grapes J871; spoils his food rather than divide with ape W152.1; stumbles over violin J864.1; in swollen river claims to be swimming to distant town J873; threatens to catch bird, given her young K1788; transformed to person D313.1; transformed to snake D411.8; tries to drown jug, gets drowned J2131.5.7; understands human speech B212.1; weeps B736.4. — Abduction by f. R13.1.11; animals confess sins to one another: f. and wolf forgive each other, punish ass U11.1.1; bear builds house of wood, f. of ice J741.1; birds fight over wounded f., who escapes J581.5; cock singing for f., dog audience kills fox K579.8; color of f. A2411.1.3.1; creation of f. A1832; devastating f. B16.2.1; devil as f. G303.3.3.2.2; does not know whether it is a f. or a hare, but the girl is downstairs J2671.1; dog language understood by f. B215.2.1; enmity between f. and (dog) A2494.4.5, (baboon) A2494.9.1, (chickens) A2494.9.2; fly, wren and f. live with cleric B256.10; flying f. B49.3; friendship of f. and titmouse A2493.10; how f. got his eyes A2332.1.4, A2245; fleeing f. loses an eye in the briars J2182; ghost of f. E522.1; ghost as f. E423.2.3; how f. got white breast A2411.1.3.1.1; grateful f. fetches f. liver as remedy B514.1; gray f. J1457; guarding chickens from f. J2125; helpful f. *B435.1; hungry f. waits in vain for horse's scrotum to fall off J2066.1; jackal rides on f. B557.13; jealous f. betrays wolf to peasant and then appropriates wolf's cave and food W181.4; luring off girl's f. husband K341.29; magic f. heart D1015.1.5; magic hair of f. D1023.2; man transformed to f. D113.3; marriage to f. B601.14; (in human form) *B651.1; monkey cheats f. of bananas K171.9; nine-tailed f. B15.7.7.1; partridge helps f. obtain curds K341.26; peasant betrays f. by pointing K2315; prophetic f. B144; reincarnation as f. E612.4; revenant as f. E423.2.3; sacred f. B811.6; saint's cowl protects f. D1447.2.1; saint's performing f. killed, replaced V224.4; seller of f. skins mixes otter skins with them and thinks to cheat the buyer J2083.3; sheep dupes f. into running to hunter K1178;

singing f. B214.1.6; soul as f. E731.10; speaking f. B211.2.5; tail of f. *A2378.3.4, A2378.6.1, *A2378.8.1f.; tailless f. tries in vain to induce foxes to cut off tails J758.1; tame f. helps dogs J683.3; the third time f. meets lion she has no fear J1075.2; thorn bush blamed by f. for wounding him J656.1; three teachings of the f. *K604; tooth becomes f. D447.6; troll as f. G304.1.1.1; two sheep kill a f. who has licked up the blood they have spilled in a fight J624.1; ungrateful f. hits rescuer W154.5.1; unsatisfied f. W128.2; wedding of f. and hyena B281.1; why f. is sly A2525.3; wisdom from f. B163.1; witch in form of f. G211.2.3.

Fox's boasting overawes lion cubs K1715.14; desire for needles, anchors J1391.8; double dealings with wolf, tiger K2043; elongated shadow makes him proud J953.13; enemies A2494.9; excuse for farmyard visit J1391.5; heart becomes rattle D457.15.1; plan detected by crickets K2061.10; tail drops and frightens animals K2323.1; thieving nature will show itself U129.1. — Bear helps f. mother get berries K461.1; coyote wears f. rattle, caught in brush and injured J2136.1; hair from f. tail opens all doors D1562.2; why f. legs are black A2371.4.2.

Foxes crawl into whale's house, killed K728; crowd into house and are suffocated N339.3; desert their allies, the hares, when they foresee defeat by the eagles J682.1; as giant's lice F531.4.11.2; gnawing on giant's head F531.5.4.2; will meet at furriers J1424; persuade man to plant cooked food K496. — Buying f. "as they run" K196.1; cat lures f. with music K815.15; fire tied to f. tails destroys enemy K2351.1.1; tiger to help f. divide their young K579.5.2; why f. do not live on a certain island A2434.2.2.

Foxglove. — Fairies dance on f. F261.3.2.

Fragile. — Chopping down large tree with f. instrument (task) H1115.

Fragments of gibbet as cure D1500.1.26. — Moon made from shining f. A742; resuscitation from body f. E35.

Fragmentation. — Multiplication of man by f. A1296.

Fragrance, see also **Perfume.** — Clouds with f. F967.2; flower sending f. far H1333.5.0.1; person's remarkable f. F687; pleasant f. in otherworld F169.9; resuscitation by f. E64.8.1; saint's house filled with f. V222.4.

Fragrances. — Evil smells become sweet f. D479.7.

Fragrant. — Air f. at Nativity V211.1.1; air magically made f. D1599.2; magic dog f. B182.1.6.

Franciscan claims cordon will save him from hell J1261.8.

Francolin eats man's grain: man may kill him A2238.2; markings A2232.6, A2412.2.2.

Fraternity initiate dies of fright N384.4.

Fraternizing of giants and men at Christmas F531.5.1.2.

Fratricide S73.1, (punished) Q211.9. — Extraordinary phenomena at f. F960.6; spring dry after f. *D927.5.

Frau Holle *F475.1.

Freak. — Thumbling sold as f. F535.1.1.9.

Frederic Barbarossa *D1960.2, F451.5.1.8; the Great drives dwarfs across Black Sea F451.9.1.13.

Free. — Choice: f. poverty or enslaved wealth J211; differentiation between "f." and "unfree" A1691; dragon fight to f. (lion) B11.11.6, (man) B11.11.5, (princess) B11.11.4; dwarfs f. mortals from enchantment F451.3.3.4; lion sent to kill man so as to f. him from possibility of sinning and sojourn in purgatory J225.2; penance: planting garden and offering f. hospitality to all Q523.5; test of god: when its image is bound it can f. itself H45.3; woman f. from trouble, worry H1195; woman masks as lawyer (judge) to f. her husband K1825.3; woman sacrifices her honor to f. her husband (brother) from prison *T455.2.

Freed. — Captive knight f. for having kept word Q54.2; captives' love rewarded: f. and enriched Q56.2; condemned woman may be f. by marrying a rogue P512; deer in net f. by animals B545.1; hero f. from wedge by magic cranberry D1564.5; husband f. from death by prayers V52.10; one is f. if he can set a task the devil is unable to perform G303.16.19.3; person f. from prison by magic object D1395; slaves f. P178.

Freedom as reward Q121. — Abridgement of f. as punishment Q430ff.; philosopher chooses poverty with f. J211.1; preserving cock's f. J1892; wealth sacrificed for f. J347.

Freemason in league with devil G303.10.6; as wild huntsman E501.1.5.

Freemasons punished Q388. — Jokes on f. X551.

Freezing, see also **Frozen.** — Heavenly fire f. F962.2.4; lies about f. X1623; Mars prevents moon from f. earth A759.7; river f. at saint's command D2151.2.4; river never f. F141.1.3, F715.5; so hot animals f. to death X1633.1; water f. to form mountains A969.5.

Freischütz *D1653.1, D1923.

Frenzied. — Saint cures f. animal V221.4.0.1.

Fresh water in sea F711.4, (origin of) A925.4.

Friar accused of rape, castrated K2111.3; adds missing nose to unborn child K1363.2; awakens girl, follows mother's orders K1354.3.1; disguises as soldier, steals K1839.5; Rush as mischief maker F470.0.1; seduces woman, claims he is administering sacrament K1354.2.2; strangled for attempted seduction Q424.3. — Disappointed lover becomes f. T93.2.1; girl disguised as f. gets into priest's bed K1315.6.3; happy f. becomes unhappier as he receives over more and more money J1085.1; lover disguised as monk or f. meets sweetheart K1826.1.1; miserly f. stays in ditch rather than aid rescuers W153.5; nun tells f. to castrate himself J1919.5.2. sinning f. pardoned after confession V21.4; transformation to f. to instruct D659.6.

Friars exploit false relic K1976.1; unaware of time passing D2011.2. — Devil vexing f. caused to repent by singing "Te sanctum dominum" G303.24.3.

Friday as auspicious day N127.4. — Fasting on "Golden F." V73.5;

fountain gives water on Wednesday and F. F716.1; transformation to werwolf on F. D622.1; why sun shines on F. A1177.

Friend in kitchen learns of friend's distress, helps him N455.8; rescues hero R169.5. — Child sacrificed to provide blood for cure of f. S268; choice of f. over mistress J496; confessor as soul-f. V20.1.2; corpse makes coffin space for f. E477; defeated enemy becomes f. R74.1; deity f. to one mortal A185.6; fight with father's f. as valor test H1561.2.2; giant becomes victor's f. G510.3; hero fights with f. of father and then reveals himself N731.2.1; husband has f. woo wife H492.2; least loved f. proves truest H1558.1.1; lover's f. steals bride K1371.1.3; man eats f. G74; one man prays either to keep f. from death or for both to die E165.1; supper won by trick: the mutual f. K455.1; task: bringing best f., worst enemy H1065; treacherous f. K2297; unfaithful f. P251.1.

Friends P310; identical in appearance F577.1; in life and death M253; offer to die for each other P315; refuse to fight each other H1558.8; who seduce man's wife called dogs in human shape H592.4; in stealing contest H305.2; tested H1558. — Causing f. wife to leave husband K1394; combat of disguised f. P314; dead f. come for dying soul E722.2.9; dupe lured away from f. K725; enemy horses captured by lion join forces and become f. J891; fool f. with birds and beasts P192.5; why God has few f. J1261.1.2; husband asks f. to share his disguised wife K1843.2.3; judicial combat interrupted by f. of loser H218.1; knight saved from devil by f. G303.16.19.8; loyal f. refuse to fight comrade W34.2; magician's f. give magic D1721.0.2; person buried with f. about him V61.3.0.2; priest has no f. until he becomes bishop, then they flock to him U62; resuscitation by f. E127; return from dead to protect f. E379.3; ruler persecutes f., kind to enemies W154.16; scarcity of real f. J401; sun and moon as f. A736.6; trickster attempts to bring f. to fight K1084.3; trickster makes two f. each suspicious of the other's intentions *K2131ff.; two f. exchange forms D45.3; unwitting combat between sons of f. N767; visiting f. take everything from house of dying man W151.2; wolf tries to make f. with lion J411.5; vow not to see f. until quest completed M151.9.

Friendly animals B300—B599; night spirit F475; return from the dead E300—E399. — Emperor f. to everyone W21; giant f. to man F531.5.1; hostile dogs made f. by having them fight common enemy, the wolf J145; land where all creatures f. F111.5; stealing from ogre to help f. king G610.2.

Friendship *P310ff.; between the animals A2493ff.; covenanted A1599.12; pretended to obtain access to girl K2016; of prince and commoner P32. — Avoid enemies' revenge either by making peace and f. or by killing them all J647.1; covenant of f. M246; former f. between domestic and wild animals A2493.0.1; hypocrite pretends f. but attacks K2010ff.; man pretends f. but attacks king to avenge violation of his wife K2010.1; marriage destroys f. T201; singing f. song to enemy K606.0.3; tests of f. H1558; trolls' f. with men F455.6.1; woman destroys men's f. K2131.3.

Fright, see also **Fear;** tests H1400—H1449. — Barrenness as result of f. F1041.17.1; cowardly f. *J2600—J2649; death from f. N384; dying of f. J955.4; forgetfulness from f. D2004.7; pool girl outwits prince in f.-contest J1525; queen dies of f. after prophecy M392.

Frightened soul cannot re-enter body E721.1.2.5; wife shows marks of affection for husband T284. — Boastful coward f. by conspirators K1951.4; cripples at shrine f. and run away without crutches V113.1; devil cheated by being f. K212; devil disappears when f. G303.16.19.17; devil f. by the shrewish wife T251.1.1; fearless hero f. by being awakened with cold water H1441; ghost f. by own reflection K1715.1.2; husband f. by paramour in hog pen K1542; judge f. into decision J1195; lawyer f. into giving when beggar tells him of all the lawyers in hell X312; magic lost by being f. D1741.5; man abed with his wife is f. away by an intruder who steals his clothes K1272; man in tree so f. of lion he drops sword, kills it N331.2.1; ogre (large animal) f. K1710ff.; owner f. from goods by thief *K335ff.; robber f. away by man who scolds his ass N612.1; robbers f. away by numskull's talking to himself N612; treasure-finders f. away N556; wild hunt f. away by scolding F501.17.8.1.

Frightening enemy by transformation D651.2; thing at bridge to land of dead E481.2.1.1. — Chain tale: animal f. another Z43.4; deception by f. *K2320ff.; deity f. child H1401; dwarfs f. mortals F451.5.2.10; escape by f. captors K547; ghost f. people into stream E272.3; ghosts f. people E293; husband's trick f. off wife's lovers K1569.6; plants and animals magically caused to shriek, f. enemy D2091.12; resuscitation by f. dead E25; tale-teller f. listener Z13.1; theft of money from fairies by f. them away from it F351.2.

Frightful meal S183, (as punishment) Q478. — Continuous prayer sustains man through f. vigil V52.2; old robber frees his three sons by relating f. adventures R153.3.3; trolls f. F455.2.6; youngest son alone endures f. experiences in vigil for dead father H1462.1.

Frog abuses bullock J952.5; as beauty-doctor unable to cure his own ugliness J1062.1; carries person B557.14; as child's nurse B535.0.6; eats plowshare (lie) X1342.3; eats rat, baker, horse F911.3.4; escapes crow by telling him to sharpen bill K561.1.2; as host to woman B530.1; language B215.4; leaps after elephant's reflection J1791.5.3; with magic knowledge B126.1; in moon A751.3; outlives tortoise, fish L395; persists in living in puddle on road J652.1; pierces metals, marbles F989.23; recovers keys from sea B548.2.2.1; recovers Sacred Host B548.5; removed from queen's nose N641.2; rescues man from snake kingdom B547.4; returned to spring: grateful B375.2; rises into person's throat, croaks every spring B784.0.1; sits in leaky vessel's hole H1023.2.1.2; swelling up as big as ox J955.1; transformed to person D395; transformed to object D428.1; wants to be shod J512.12; -woman disenchanted by sight of water D789.3.1; -woman betrays self by croaking J1908.3; works in fields for benefactor B292.9.1. — Animal languages learned from f. B165.2; ant pinching f. causes accident chain N381.1; cheese brings f. from person's mouth B784.2.3; color of f. A2411.5.2; croak of f. A2426.4.1; earth supported by f. A844.4; enmity between f. and snake A2494.16.1; fairy in form of f. F234.1.6; friendship between f. and cricket A2493.20; giant f. B876.1; girl swallows f. spawn B784.1.4; god of fate as f. A463.0.1; great f. eaten by one larger and this in turn by crow X1342.1.1; habitation of f. A2433.6.6; helpful f. *B493; why f. has hunchback A2356.2.1; jumping f. contest K17.4; magic f. B177.2; man in moon a f. which has jumped into person's face and remains there A751.3.1; man transformed to f. D195; mankind from mating of f. and fire-daughter A1221.5; marriage to f. B604.5; marriage to person in f. form B645.1.2; mythical f. B98; origin of f. A2162; rat and f. tie paws together to cross marsh J681.1; reincarnation as f. E615.1; revenant as f. E423.4; singing f. B214.1.7; snake as f. king's mount J352.2; snake promises to do no harm to f. K815.6; snake wants to eat f. friend J426.2; soul in form of f. E736.1; why f. cannot speak A2422.7; speaking f. B211.7.1; how f. lost tail A2231.4, A2242, A2378.2.3; toad receives water from f. K231.8; transformation into f. Q551.3.2.3; why f. croaks in wet weather A2426.4.1.2; why f. is spotty A2412.5.2.1; why f. toothless A2239.8, A2345.7.2; woman bears f. T554.8.

Frog's cries misunderstood J1811.2; view of cattle J1772.13; wedding B284.1. — Death from f. bite F1041.1.11.4; fear of f. drowning J1909.7; why f. eyes bulge out A2332.4.3; why f. skin rough A2311.8.

Frogs cast themselves into oven, eat bread F989.24; caught in frozen ice X1130.3; croak at prince's command H71.10.3; decide not to jump into the well J752.1; demand a live king J643.1; to eat insects, snakes to eat frogs J2102.8; fear defeated bull J613.2; fear increase of sun's power which will dry up all their puddles J613.1; reprove ass for lamenting when he falls into morass J2211.1; want to collect honey J512.15; were ducks stolen from Eden A2426.4.1.1. — Animals from f. sent as Egypt's plague A1734; army of f. D2091.2.1; community of f. B226.2; dance of f. B293.2; fools shoot at f. all night to keep their croaking from disturbing prince J2105; king of f. B245.1; lies about f. X1342; magic plague of f. drawn down on foe D2091.2; money thrown to f. J1851.1; placing f. in a tree (task) H1024.2; war between toads and f. B263.1.

Frost-giants F531.1.9; -god A289.1; and hare contest in enduring cold H1541.1; produced by magic D2143.5. — Magic stone protects against f. D1382.12; old woman in control of f. D2143.5.1; origin of f. A1135.3; wind overcomes f. in contest in enduring cold H1541.2.

Frown as "black look" H588.14, J2489.7.

Frozen, see also **Freezing.** — Eating way out of f. animal X1723.3.1; everything f. when man wears cap straight D2144.1.2; hero drives log into f. ground F611.3.2.1; man f. to saddle X1606.2.1.

Fructifier. — God as f. of mankind A189.15.

Fruit affected by judge's judgment H251.3.10; with any desired taste D1665.3; broken too soon, hero punished D1962.6.1; causes sexual desire D1355.14; as chastity index H434; decays on tree E761.3.2; falls if oath false H252.3; flies from hungry man's reach Q501.2.1; juice turns to blood D474.8; by magic D2105.7; of magic tree exhilarating D1359.3.3; magically grows in winter *D2145.2.2; -picking time of sexual promiscuity T485; pierced with pins as love charm D1355.3.3; produced out of season at saint's request F971.5.1; transformed to animal D441.2; transformed to person D431.4; transformed to other object D451.3; tree grows from deer shot with fruit pits X1130.2; from tree tabu C762.4. — Animals eat deity's forbidden f. A2234.2; birth from f. T543.3; conception from eating a f. T511.1; conception from f. thrown against breast T532.3; covering mango grove with f. overnight H1103.3; creation of man from f. A1253; disenchantment from f. by plucking it D711.6; disenchantment by opening f. *D721.5; diving for reflected f. J1791.11; eater of f. to become king M312.3.2; eating rind first: too full for f. J2178.1; extraordinary f. F810ff.; forbidden f. *C621; fruitless tree bears f. F971.4; girl lives in f. *F562.4; god of f. A433.4; the great f. X1411; inexhaustible f. D1652.1.7; knocking off single f. from tree H1199.18; magic f. *D981ff., (gives supernatural knowledge) D1310.10; magic tree continually in f. D1668; man as f. of blooming animal horns A1263.6; man transformed to f. D211; miraculous blossoming and bearing of f. F971; murder by throwing hot f. into mouth K951.1.3; paradise lost because of forbidden f. A1331.1; prophylactic f. D1500.2.7; quest for extraordinary f. H1333.3; red f. thrown at rail's head: hence red lump on head A2215.4; sickness from drying, shriveling f. plant D2064.8; soul as f. E745.5; strong hero engendered by eating of f. F611.1.8; sun from f. kernels A718.3; tabu to eat certain f. C225; task: bringing f. in winter H1023.3; task: getting f. from top of tall tree without cutting tree H1038; task: turning f. into gold H1023.15; touching f. tabu C621.2; transformation by eating f. D551.1; tree bearing f. three times yearly F811.18; tree bears f., flower, and leaf simultaneously F811.16; tree blooms and grows ripe f. nightly F811.13; tree with extraordinary f. F811.7; tree from otherworld f. F162.3.0.1; tree in perpetual f. F162.3.3; trickster feigns death and eats ripe f. from the tree K1866; trickster in tree advises that tree and f. belong to him K1971.11; trying to get f. from fruitless tree J1944, J2066.3.1; vine bears 926 varieties of f. F815.7.1; wanderers in shade of plane tree blame it for not bearing f. W154.7; why some trees have no f. A2791.7; why big trees have small f. A2771.9; witches shake f. off trees G265.10.1; woman bears f. which can transform self to girl T555.1; wounds healed by eating f. of magic tree D1503.11.

Fruits that laugh or cry D1619.3. — Extraordinary f. *F813ff.; ghosts with f. in hair K335.1.12; jinns share f. of earth F499.3.2; magic f. and vegetables D980ff.; only one man can pluck tree's f. H31.12; origin of f.

A2687ff.; sea bears f. F931.9.2.2; sour f. made sweet by saint F979.1;
tree bearing all f. F811.7.1; tree bearing several f. F811.7.1.1; throwing
f. on bridal couple A1555.1.1; tree allows only two f. to be taken
F979.16; tribes from f. of trees A1610.4; woman cooks the magic f.
D866.1; worthless f. sold K147.

Fruitful island F733; tree chosen J241. — Athena chooses olive tree
because it is f. J241.1; magic song makes barren land f. D1563.1.2;
prophecy: granddaughters f. M301.17.1; sign of the cross makes barren
land f. D1563.1.3.

Fruitfulness. — Nature's f. as proof of kingly right H1574.2.

Fruitless tree bears fruit F971.4. — Nature f. after false judgment H243;
nature f. after hero's death F960.2.1; trees made f. D2082.0.1; trying to
get fruit from f. tree J1944.

Fruitlessness. — Formulas signifying f. Z63.

Frying. — Insect f. human blood A2435.5.2; man-eater f. victims G312.4.

Frying-pan, magic D1472.1.12.1.

Fuel sticks to stingy man's hand Q551.2.8. — Carrying f. as task H1129.11;
corpses used as f. S139.2.2.5; fire from extraordinary f. F964.3; grass
as f. for burning ogre G512.3.3; inexhaustible f. D1652.10; saint's
unusual f. V229.9.

Fugitive returns so family may collect reward T215.5; slave takes refuge
in mill house N255.4; slave takes wrong road and is caught N382;
transforms self to stone D671.0.1; woman burdened with child saved
while childless woman is killed N185. — Animal blessed (cursed) for
helping (betraying) holy f. A2221.5, A2231.7.1; empire prophesied for
f. M314.4; ground hides f. F942.1.1; lovers as pursuer and f. K1517.1;
magic hair stretches after f. D1436; magic object compels f. to betray
himself D1612.2ff.; magic object helps f. *D1393ff.; magic objects betray f. *D1612.1ff.; officer accidentally finds f. N618; plant blessed
(cursed) for helping (betraying) holy f. A2711.3, A2721.4; reward for
protecting f. Q46; river pursues f. F932.1; ruler marries f. noblewoman
T121.4; saint hides f. underground K2319.8; saint's spittle protects f.
from attack D1381.2; spider-web over hole saves f. B523.1; sun sets
early to hide f. F961.1.10.

Fugitives have way revealed by magic D1813.4. — Captives and f.
R (entire chapter); clouds protect f. F967.1.

Fulfillment of bargain or promise M202; of warning in dream D1810.8.3.1.
— Fairies give f. of wishes F341; ghost laid at f. of vow E451.3; vain
attempts to escape f. of prophecy M370ff.

Full moon and thirtieth of the month (girl's enigmatic message) H582.1.1;
pot sign that city is filled with fakirs J1293.4. — Fairy returns vessel
ever f. F335.1.

Fuller and collier cannot live together J143.

Fulmar, marriage to B602.2.

Fumes. — Devil chased by f. G303.16.14.2.

Fumigations, transformation by D575.

Funeral for the ineligible husband J1191.3; procession of the hen (cumulative tale) Z32.1; rites *V60ff. — Angels attend saint's f. V241.1;
animal f. B257; at child's f. real father sings, cuckold weeps U119.1.1;
birds take part in saint's f. B251.2.1.2; dead man demands proper f.
E235.2.1; dead without proper f. rites cannot rest E412.3; doctor orders
patient's f. X372.5; dupe tricked into jumping on f. pyre K891.4; evil
mother has fine f., good father poor J225.8; faithless widow betrothed
anew at husband's f. T231.1; foresight of f. procession D1825.7.1; ghost
light indicates f. route E530.1.7; king must not attend f. P13.8; king
on retiring orders f. obsequies given him P16.1.1; man too lazy to turn
around to see f. W111.5.11; man at his lady's f. jests with priest on
unequal returns from women J1264.8; neighbors insist on fool's f.
although he is alive and well J2311.5; origin of f. customs A1547; precautions at f. against revenant E431; resuscitation through ashes thrown
on f. pyre E132; return home to one's own f. N681.0.1; riddle about
father at f. H583.4.5; thieves' mock f. for stolen chickens K375; wager
ends only on f. pyre J2511.1; wife throws herself on husband's f. pyre
T211.2; will spend f. money now J1261.5.

Funerals. — Few f. make bad year for priests X427.

Fungus, birth from T543.4.

Fur made of beards of conquered kings P672.1. — Cloak from f. of all
animals F821.1.3.2; dress of raw f. F821.1.3; ghosts seen through f. coat
sleeve C311.1.1.1; wild huntsman with black f. cap and white staff
E501.8.6.

Furnace falls in on disobedient wife T254.5; transformed to garden
D469.5. — Child born in f. T561.2; fiery f. does not harm saint
D1841.3.2.1; god of the f. A493.2; man leaping into f. unharmed
H1573.1.4; unsuccessful attempt to make gold man in f. J2411.1.2.

Furnished. — Money f. by inexhaustible purse D1451ff.; supplies f. by
cobolds F481.2.

Furnishings, extraordinary F770ff.

Furniture in otherworld F166. — Falling f. threatens bridal couple
T175.1; ghost moves f. E599.6; gold f. in otherworld F166.0.1; magic f.
*D1150ff.; tricksters change f., blame it on demons K1838.1.

Furrows burn witch G273.5.1; from giant's step F531.1.3.4.

Fury personified Z123.

Furies A486.

Fuschia belongs to devil: hence ball and red petals A2743.1.

Futility of distant travel J1076; of trying to hide an obvious deed J1082;
of trying to teach the stupid J1064; of weather prophecies M398. —
Pupil returns from dead to warn master of f. of his studies E368.

Future creator goes to make afterworld A78; husband (wife) met during
magic sleep D1976.2; revealed (in dream) *D1812.3.3ff., (by knowledge
tooth) D1810.3.1. — Avoiding power of f. enemy J645; care against f.

tyranny J643; don't injure yourself to insure your family's f. J322; dream (prophecy) of f. greatness causes banishment L425; in planning f., profit by the past J752; intermediate f. world *A693; king for year provides for f. J711.3; means of learning the f. M302, (magic) D1812.3; ordaining the f. M (entire chapter); present values preferred to f. J320ff.; prophecy: death through f. husband M341.2.12; provision for the f. J701; tasks assigned to learn f. M302.5; vision of f. V516.

Gabriel (angel) addressed in throwing contest K18.1.2; drives Satan and other devils from heaven to earth G303.8.1.2; made from snow A52.1.3. — Seduction by posing as G. K1315.1.1.

Gadfly. — Io transformed to cow with g. ceaselessly pursuing Q501.6; transformation to g. to enter giant's stomach and kill him K952.2.

Gaelic titles given to devil G303.2.4.

Gaels invade Ireland F211.0.2.1.

Gai bulga F832.1.1; invention of A1459.1.4.

Gain. — Feeding with loss or g. H583.9; choices: little g., big loss *J340ff.; choices: small inconvenience, large g. J350ff.

Gains and losses J330—J369. — Disappearance of ill-gotten g. Q552.18.

Gait of animal A2441ff. — Raven tries to imitate dove: punished with awkward g. A2232.10.

Gaiters, magic D1065.6.

Galatea D435.1.1, F423.1.

Gall. — Giant's g. (restores sight) D1505.19, (resuscitates) E117.

Gall-bladder of animal, magic *D1015.2. —Stag vomits his g. A2211.13.

Gall-stone the worst of stones H659.3.1.

Gallows ghost E274; rope breaks when innocent hanged H215.2. — Buying g. flesh or living flesh forbidden C781.1; devil at g. repudiates his bargain with robber M212.2; executioner must show the hero how to use the g. (hanged) K715; lover rescues lady from g. R161.4; oxen bear dead usurer to g. to be buried N277; red cap for the g. J2174.1; return from dead to punish theft of liver from man on g. E235.4.4; saint sustains man on g. V221.6; son on g. bites his mother's nose off Q586; staying under g. at night as fear test H1415; Virgin Mary supports robber on g. V254.1.1.

Galoshes. — Fortune's g. N135.3; devil visible to one who walks in minister's holy g. G303.6.2.4.

Gam (mythical bird) rescues hero from shipwreck R138.2; throws sand in a stream and makes lake B31.2. — Cup of eggshell of g. F866.5; giant as g. F531.1.8.6.

Gambler reformed by love T10.1.1. — Clever g. J1115.1; dead priest returns to save g. E341.5; devil to help g. in exchange for one task yearly M214; giant g. as ogre G101; magic object helps g. win D1407ff.; saint gives liberally to g. J225.6; skillful g. always wins *F679.7; soul of g. won by saint's dice E756.4.1; wretched life of otherworld g. F171.8.

21*

Gamblers *N1; beat incognito prince K1812.2.2. — If you want to gamble then gamble with experienced g. H588.5.

Gambling, see also **Wager, Winning;** cannibal G11.13. — Bankrupt father sells his daughters to pay g. debt S221.1; despised boy wins g. game L177; god of g. A482; hangman's noose gives luck in g. D1407.2; hero g. with ruler of afterworld E489.6; punishment for g. Q381; quest assigned as payment for g. loss H1219.1; tasks to pay g. loss H942; wagers and g. *N0—N99; youth sells himself to an ogre in settlement of a g. debt S221.2.

Game with ancestor's bones P203; between gods A163.1; rolling down hill in snowball X1130.1; -tales Z19.1. — Abandoned child joins parents in g.: recognition follows H151.9; accidental discharge of gun kills much g. X1124.3; accidental fatal ending of g. or joke N334; animals play g. B298ff.; antelope eats g. while leopard away K345.4; ball g. in lower world E494; bride contest a g. H375; claim that dog-head captured g. J1214.1; coming neither with nor without g. H1056; despised boy wins gambling g. L177; devil plays disc g. G303.9.9.9; dog sight of which renders g. helpless B182.1.3; falling in love while playing g. T34.2; why g. is easy to hunt A2551; fatal deceptive g. K850ff.; helping losing player in g. C882, C746; hoarded g. released A1421; human beings as g. in fairy hunt F368; isolated child kills increasingly larger g. T617.1; killed g. revives and flies away E161; king in disguise sees child's g. which represents lawsuit J123; lies about plentiful g. X1119; magic object locates g. D1327; magic object stolen in card g. D861.6; magic wishing-pipe supplies g. D1472.2.3; man from g. animal's blood A1263.1.2; origin of ball g. A1495.1; origin of customs: division of g. A1525; owner enticed to chase g. while goods are stolen K341.5; playing g. with ferocious beast H1537; playing g. with reassembled dead man H1433; plentiful g. as reward Q141.2; poor g. proves rich L216; princess won at g. of chance R111.1.10; pursuers play fatal g. K619.3; pursuit of g. leads to upper world F59.2; runner catches g. on the run F681.6; seduction while teaching a g. K1315.7.2; soul won from devil in card g. E756.2; suitor test: to defeat bride in g. H332.1.2; tabu to look at g. before it dies C311.1.7; why g. animals are elusive A2552; wild hunt asked for g., gives dead child E501.18.1.3.1; winning first g., then playing for higher stakes K2378.1.

Games. — Dead persons play g. E577; fairies attend g. F267; funeral g. V65.5; hero stupid at g. L141.3; mountain-men play g. F460.3.2; origin of g. A1535.2, (of skill) A1468; religious g. A1549.3; ruler jealous of happiness prohibits g. W181.7.

Game-board, golden F899.2.1; magic D1209.7, D1407.3.

Gander. — Dwarfs accept as gift goose but not g. F451.3.6.4; man becomes g. D161.2.1.

Gang nach dem Eisenhammer K1612.

Ganges. — Bathing in G. V96.1, (no cure for liar) U235.1; ghost's skull thrown into G. E459.7; Mother G. Z118.3; soul of G. is sandalwood, frog, cow J1511.2.1; vow to bathe in G. M183.2.

Ganymede carried off by eagle R13.3.2.

Garbage. — Lie: extraordinary g. X1031.7.

Garbling. — Cat g. message from man to tiger A2281.1.1.

Garden becomes wilderness F975; in fairyland F219.2; fills with flowers as innocent approaches H216.1; of the gods A151.2; of Hesperides *F111; under water F725.7; wall that cannot be overleapt D1675. — Barber's and jackal's common g. K171.8; blighted g. magically restored D2195.1; contrasting qualities found in otherworld g. *F162.1.2; entering a g. by swimming down a stream that flows into it K2377; extraordinary g. F818; fairest thing in the g. J1472; furnace becomes g. D469.5; girl sleeps in g. to meet lover T36; goat eats in g. and is caught J2136.3; hero finds maiden in (magic) g. N711.3; holy man restores bloom of g. V222.12; magic g. *D961; magic object from g. D849.4.1; maiden found in magic g. N741.5; making g. in three days H1103.1.1; making g. bloom in winter as suitor test H352; moon steals from a g. A753.3.2; negro so black that he makes whole g. somber F573; planting beautiful g. H1199.1; poor soil transformed miraculously into g. D2157.5; pursuing the rabbit who harmed the g. J2103.2; robbers spade up saint's g. V222.16; sexual promise dependent on g. blooming in winter M261.1; stealing from ingenuously guarded g. H1151.10.1; summer and winter g. D1664; sweet and bitter fountain in otherworld g. F162.1.2.1; task: making g. quickly in unplanted forest H1103.1; turtle induced to rob in man's g. K1022.5; unsuccessful magic production of g. J2411.7; water for thieves in king's g. H1471.1; witch haunting king's g. H1191.2.

Garden of Eden. — Frogs were ducks stolen from G. A2426.4.1.1; souls pass through G. E755.1.3.

Garden of the Hesperides. — Magic apple from G. D981.1.1.

Gardener disguise K1816.1; made king by minister decides against him M13.3; who plants vegetable tends it best J1033; rescues abandoned child R131.8.2. — Flower bouquet tied in certain way by g. H16.3; king tests obedience of g. H1557.6; man disguised as g. enters convent and seduces nuns K1323; son of g. to marry princess H317.3; strong man as g. F614.3; treacherous g. K2257.

Gargantuan feats F531.3ff.

Garland thrown to chosen suitor H316.4. — Ring in g. as identification H94.9; snake becomes g. D425.1.3.

Garlands as token H87; unfading D1652.7. — Marriage by exchange of g. T135.5.

Garlic juice dangerous to poisonous animals B776.0.1; protects against evil D1385.2.8; stalk as knighthood arms for servant J955.3. — Christ's body rubbed with g. A1662.1; extraordinary perception of g. F647.1.1; magic g. D983.4; transformation by eating g. D551.2.6; wedding of g. to onion B286.1.

Garment appears and disappears in reply to command D2188.1.1; fits only true king H36.2; hidden in thigh F1034.3.3; produced by prayer D1766.1.3. — Conception after touching g. T532.5.1; flow of cow's milk increased by licking saint's g. D2182; good thing fool did not have g. on or he would have shot himself J2235; identification by g. H111; magic g. *D1052, (prevents burning) D1382.10, (protects from drowning) D1388.0.4; quest for g. of spider's web H1355.1; red g. to show anger of king Z141.1; sign of cross prevents g. from burning V86.1.2; supernatural wife's g. stolen R227.3; tabu: giving back g. to supernatural wife C31.10; tabu: stealing g. from a rock C91.1.

Garments, see also **Clothes;** of mountain down H1054.4. — Magic shears clip g. from air D1601.12.1; magician makes people lift g. to avoid wetting in imaginary river D2031.1; monster borrows wedding g. one by one and wins girl K1918; old rags preferred to new g. L217; upper g. must be removed above chiefs P94; waterwomen powerless without g. F420.4.6.1; woman's g. cut off: does not know herself J2012.2.

Garter. — Giant slings stone with g. F531.3.2.2; magic g. *D1063.

Garuda-bird B56; attracted by bath of blood carries woman off N335.2.

Gascons. — Don't play tricks on G. J652.4.2.

Gate, see also **Door;** of captured town widened for overlord's spear P555.3; around hell A671.5; entrance to lower world F91; of heaven A661.0.1, E754.2.3; opens, closes to let saint through D1552.6; swallows threatening axes F1009.2; to upper world F59.3. — Cave's entrance as g. to hell A671.0.3; embracing at village g. tabu C194.1; enduring insults to enter city g. H1553.3; extraordinary g. F776; hay wagon and the g. J1411; horse's head nailed over g. F874.1; king demands open g. to vassal's castle P50.0.1.1; perilous falling g. *F776.2; standing neither inside nor outside of g. H1052; temple g. magically opens, shuts D1557.4; tomb g. magically enlarged D482.5.2; vision of g. of hell V511.2.2; wicket g. tabu C614.2; wraith slams g. E723.7.4.

Gates. — Cynic and big g. in little town J1442.6; forty-nine g. of wisdom J182.1; strong man carries off city g. F631.2.

Gathering all stones from brook or field (task) H1124. — Ghost g. wood for hell fires E755.2.4; girl g. flowers swallowed by earth and taken to lower world F92.2.1.

Gay. — Fairies' g. clothing F236.6; literal numskull g. at a fire J2461.1.2.

Gazelle as animals' king B240.6; becomes person D314.1.4; helpful B443.4. — Eagle catches newly born g. B754.7.2.

Geasa. — Demons coerced by g. of druids G583.

Geese, see after **Goose.**

Geist im glas K717.

Gem. — Seduction by alleged retrieving of lost g. K1315.2.2.

Gems, see also **Jewels;** shower from magic anvil D1469.3. — Castle paved with gold and g. F771.1.1.1; dwarf home has chandelier of crystals and

g. F451.4.3.4; eater of fruit will drop g. as he laughs M312.3.2; magic g. sent ruler as wisdom test H501.1; quest for marvelous g. H1348.

Genealogy of summer and winter A1154. — Chiefs' g. tabu C564.6.

General gives kings victory credit W11.8. — Dissension aroused in army by casting suspicion on g. K1088; lowly soldier humbles g. L175.1; what is most g. (riddle) H659.10.

Generalization. — Absurd g. from a particular incident J2214.

Generation. — Blessing to descend from g. to g. M321.1; planting for next g. J701.1; spontaneous g.: child found on deserted island A1234.3.

Generations. — Animal g. compared to men's B841.2.1; man lives nine g. F571.8.

Generosity W11; as amend for stinginess Q589.4; rewarded *Q42. — Man lets himself be sold as slave so as to practice g. W11.4; tests of g. H1552.

Generous. — Vow to serve most g. king M167.

Genesis. Captive released because of ability to recite beginning of G. V151.1.

Genie, see also **Jinn;** called by writing his name on papers and burning them *D2074.2.4; in form of smoke G369.2; sleeps with eyes open G634. — Helpful g. N813; magic object received from g. D812.5; magic object summons g. *D1421.1ff.

Genitals, see also **Member, Penis, Vagina;** cut off through ignorance J1919.5. — Birth from contact of severed male g. with ground T541.9; curse: wolf to carry off man's g. M442.2; enemy's g. prove slaying H105.7; feigning loss of g. to dupe husband K1586; horse's g. (provide treasure) D1469.5, (used in combat) F998; husband feigns loss of g. to test wife H467.1; magic g. *D998; man created from hero's g. A1263.6; misplaced g. A1313.3; mutilated g. S176; oath by placing hand on g. M119.7; origin and nature of animal's g. A2365; placing hand on g. as truth test H252.1; remarkable g. F547; tabu: eating animal's g. C221.3.1; tempted man mutilates g. T333.4; toothed g. F547.1; touching of g. as marriage pact T135.2; women not to eat g. of animals *C229.2.

Genoese compared to beaten donkeys J1021.2. — Why G. children strong J1279.4.

Genoveva K2112.

Gentleman unable to eat excrement, loses bargain K198. — Devil as g. (well-dressed) G303.3.1.2, (invites to feast) G303.25.17.1.

Gentlemen. — Devils as g. G303.3.1.17; devil as three g. G303.3.1.11; thieves disguised as g. K311.9.

Gentlewoman P60.

Genuflexion. — Clerics' continual g. V462.4.1.

Geography, lies about X1500.

Germans, origin of A1611.5.3.

Gestrikland people as magicians D1711.10.2.

Ghee. — Alleged g. deceptively exchanged K144; does g. protect the saucer? J2062.2; soul as g. E745.6.

Ghormuhas B15.7.5.

Ghost conceals herself with dwarfs F451.5.4.1; converses with man running from him J1495.1; frightened by own reflection K1715.1.2; of giant F531.6.14; kills man interfering with him E232.3; of murdered child E225; puts bride in tree, takes her place K1911.1.7; -seer's power from coffin hole D1821.3.5.1; transfers boil to a post D2161.4.2.1; of unknown child passes over parents H175.5; warns of wild hunt's approach E501.6. — Devil chases g. into chapel R325.1; disguise as g. K1833; fool is told that his son has given up the g. J2482; hunter's g. as nightmare F471.1.4; knowledge of g. language D1815.1; lost object found by throwing spade at g. D1816.2.1; magic object received from g. D812.4; man playing g. killed N384.10; mother's g. tries to tear daughter to pieces E222.1; owl (g. of nun) in wild hunt E501.4.5; return from dead to punish indignities to corpse or g. E235, running from g. J1495; sound of drum followed into g. town F102.2; tabu: finding name of g. C824; tabu: masking as g. in graveyard C94.5; tiger made to think goat is g. K547.12; wagon refuses to move because g. is sitting in it *D1317.10.

Ghost's strength waxes and wanes with height of fire *D1836.1.

Ghosts, see also **Souls;** carry off other ghost E446.4; deceived, cannot return to grave E141; with fruits in hair frighten thieves K335.1.12; of objects E530ff.; and other revenants *E200—E599; prevent men from raising treasure N576; seen through sleeve of fur coat C311.1.1; of sun's children cause eclipse A734.4. — Animal g. *E520ff.; animal languages learned from g. B217.3; army of g. F403.2.3.7; copper as defense against g. and magic D1385.5.1; disease caused by g. A1337.0.2; fairy reveals treasure of g. F244.3; fearless traffic with g. H1430ff.; gift of tongues received from g. D1815.0.1; invisible g. E421.1; saint's bachall keeps off g. D1385.8; silver bullet as protection against g. D1385.4; stars as fires in hearths of g. A761.4; sleeping on path of g. tabu C735.2.6; tabu: eating in land of g. C211.2.1; tabu: looking at g. C311.1.1; tabu to laugh at g. C462; things thought to be g. J1782; tree guarded by g. H1151.10; wandering soul detained by g. E721.4; why g. remain on earth A666.2.

Ghoulish charm *D1278, (exorcises witch) G271.8; objects E538; wager won N78.

Ghouls G20ff.

Giant *F531ff., *G100—G199; animal (lie) *X1201ff.; animals *B870ff.; assigns task H939.4; birds *B31.1; breaks from tower prison R211.1; can be killed only with own club Z312.2; carpet F783.1; changes to normal size D55.2.3; as clerk to God of Destiny N111.5; as culture hero A523; cursed: neither heaven nor earth to receive him M445; dog F628.1.5; drinks up ocean A928; eats men on New Year's G15.1; falls through drawbridge K924; in foot-race with mortal H1594.2; gives reward for advice Q111.5; god A133; as gods' orderly A133.3; guards huge otherworld oxen K1784.2; guards otherworld F150.2.1; guards quest path H1236.4; as helper *N812; herdsman G152; heroes Z261; immortal so long as he touches land of his birth D1854; impales self on javelin K897.2.1; killed by rafter cut half through K959.3.1; kills with magic water D1402.24.1; with limbs, organs only on left side F525.5; in love with giantess F531.6.8.1; lured by cheese on crab K827.5; mermaid B81.9.4, (cast ashore) B81.13.13; in moon A751.9.3; ogre guards tree D950.0.1.1; ox ancestor of all animals A1791; responsible for stones A977.1; reveals life span to dwarf who attacks him N484; robber with club G316; shot into upper world by means of magic bow *F65; with sixty daughters and their big wedding X1071; steals magic armor D838.7; swallows man F911.5; thought to be a hill J1769.1; tree F811.14; tricked into becoming mouse K722. — Abduction by g. R11.3; animals from different parts of body of slain g. *A1716.1; appearance of g. F531.1ff.; beheading g. to escape prison R211.8; black cat as servant of g. B292.6; cannibal g. G11.2; capturing deer from herd watched by g. H1154.2; creator's g. servant (makes valley and mountain) A857.2, (puts trees on earth) A857.3; creation from vapor-produced primeval g. A621.1; customs of g. ogres G130ff.; curse by berserk g. M411.10; dwarfs originate from maggots in flesh of g. F451.1.1; escape from g. bird's nest R253; fairy as g. animal F234.1.0.1; fat g. wants to eat self J2119.5; feats of g. F531.3ff.; fight with g. as valor test H1561.6; foot-race between g. and mortal H1594.2; ghost as g. E422.3.2; god as son of a g. A112.4; god transformed to g. with three heads and six arms D42.1; goddess as daughter of g. A112.4.2; hero fights fairyland g. F176.1; hero leaves home with g. equipment F613.2; lakes made by g. A920.1.10; little girl drives out g. L311.4; little man defeats g. in race L312; magic from g. D1727; magic object (acquired by tricking g.) D833, (from g.) *D812.11, (stolen from g.) *D838.6, (summons g.) D1421.4f.; magic serpent heart kills g. D1402.3.1; magician, g. contest over dog's tail D1719.1.3; mountain from buried g. A969.1; mountains from bones of killed g. A961.5; mountains and hills from stones thrown by g. at church A963.4; oversalting food of g. so that he must go outside for water K337; physical characteristics of g. ogres G120ff.; possessions of g. F531.4ff., (ogre) G110ff.; prince pleads with g. not to eat him K567.1; pygmy turns into a g. D55.1.3; rescue by g. R164; rescue of maiden from g. R111.1.4; servant g. gets liquor A1427.0.4; size of g. F531.2ff.; stealing sword from g. H1151.14; strong hero suckled by g. F611.2.5; strong man (kills g.) F628.2.3, (overcomes g.) F639.4, (son of person and g.) F611.1.7; suitor test: lifting strong princess's g. weapon H345.1; sunlight turns g. to stone F531.6.12.2; theft from g. by fishing through chimney K316.1; transformation into g. D28, D55.1.2; ten g. sisters P252.6.1; treasure from defeated g. N538.2; trees pulled up by g. F621.2; universe from body of slain g. A642; wind caused by flapping of ears of a g. A1125.1; witch's g. sons G206; wrestling with g. warrior H1166.1.

Giant's daughter loves hero T91.1; help secured by feeding him N812.0.1; soul in mole E714.9; tongue proves slaying H105.2.1. — Bringing back g. two heads H1174.1; cup can be crushed only on g. forehead F866.8; earth from g. body A831.2; flood from g. blood A1012.3.1; magic object in g. cave D845.1; man builds boat and sails about in g. belly F911.5.1; mankind begotten by g. two feet A1221.1; mountains from stones dropped from g. clothes A963.1; princess rescued from g. cave R111.2.3; resuscitation by g. gall E117; sea formed from g. spittle D483; skillful marksman shoots meat from g. hands F661.1.

Giants as builders F531.6.6; dance F531.6.17.1; enticed over precipice K891.5.1; as magicians F531.6.5ff.; in otherworld F167.3; uphold castle F771.2.3; cast stones: hence hills A963.5; dissuaded from eating nephews K601.2; and dwarfs F451.10; go through small plant hole X1743.1; guarding fairy princess F300.1; with names of sinister symbolism Z100.1; return if tabu broken C963.4; steal magic object D861.9. — Age of g. F531.6.4ff.; automatic g. fight D1620.3.1; castle guarded by g. F771.5.2; chasms mark leaps of g. A972.5.2; defeated g. imprisoned in lower world Q433.2; demons as g. perishing in the flood G302.1.1; dwarfs came after g. had almost died out F451.1.3; fairies as g. F232.6; fairies guard g. treasure F244.6; fight of the gods and g. *A162.1, (at end of world) A1082.1; heads of g. cut off one by one as they enter house K912; homes of g. F531.6.3; incendiary covering of g. cave set afire K812.1.1; indentions on rocks caused by g. A972.6; journey to land of g. F122; knockers as ghosts of g. F456.1.1.2; luring Thor into power of g. H1173; men at first as large as g. A1301; mutual relations of g. F531.6.8; one eye of three g. stolen G612; origin of g. F531.6.1; quest for berries from tree guarded by g. H1333.3.3; relations of g. with men F531.5ff.; silver bullet protects against g. D1385.4; stones as transformed g. A974.2; thunder made by g. in sky A1142.9; winds as children of g. A1123.

Giantess F531; abducts bridegroom R10.4.1; aids quest H1233.4.2; curses him who hears her M411.9; frightened of statue in cave entrance K1726; gives magic object D812.8.1; as helper N812.2; killed with own gift sword K818.2; throws her breasts over her shoulders *F531.1.5.1. — Beautiful g. F531.1.0.1.1; cloak of g. makes man grow D537.2.1; dwarfs kill g. F451.10.2.1; god becomes g. D12.1; god as lover of g. A164.6, T111.4; god as son of g. A112.4.1; giant in love with g. F531.6.8.1; groom prisoner in room of g. R41.4; head of g. cut off as she looks out K912.1; hero's son by g. scorns father P233.3.1; man-eating g. transformed to stone D429.2.2.1; punishment of g. pure illusion D2031.0.5.

Giantesses. — God as son of nine g. A112.5.

Gibbet. — Fragments of g. as cure D1500.1.26.

Gift to animal or object J1851ff.; of fool to queen (children) J1272; to magic lance C835.2.1; of property silences criticism U21.2; as sign of submission P531.1; wood must be split W111.5.1 — Bride's g. to husband T55.4.1; captor deceived into receiving g. K611.3; clothing g. wards off spirit F405.11; donkey g. to ruler J2415.1.1; dwarfs accept as g. goose but not gander F451.3.6.4; fairy g. worthless when tabu broken F348.0.1; fire as g. from god A144.4; girl doesn't dare receive g. from man T456.1; heaven entered by demanding back the charity g. K2371.1.2; helpful animals as g. B312.1; husband gets paramour's g. to wife K1581.12; lover's g. regained K1357, K1581; magic object a g. *D810ff.; man chosen as best g. by primeval women A1276; man finds treasure he refused as g. N224; modest choice: parting g. L222; power of prophecy a g. D1812.1; stolen ornament presented to owner as g. N347.4; tabu to open g. box prematurely C321.2; trickster chooses his g. J1282.

Gifts, see also **Presents;** from angels V232.7; from dwarfs F451.5.1ff.; from fairies *F340ff.; fall from heaven F962.0.1; as reward Q114; at wedding T136.4. — Animal gives man g. B584; choice among several g. L212; dwarf takes back g. he gave F451.5.2.12; dwarfs curse g. they are forced to give F451.5.2.13; dwarfs demand g. F451.5.2.14; emperor thinks day lost when he gives no g. W11.2.2; enemies reconciled by mutual g. K2373; fairy g. to half-mortal child F305.1; fairy g. stopped in revenge F361.2.4; fairies bestow supernatural g. at birth of child F312.1; fairies give three g. F341.1; fairy offers g. to man to be her paramour F302.3.2; forgetting own share of g. J2048; ghosts bestow g. on living E373; giants' g. to men F531.5.6; giants' magic g. return to original form in hands of men F531.5.6.1; gifts as reward for g. Q114.2; good g. of fortune *N200ff.; grateful objects give helper g. D1658.3.3; helpers' g. aid quest H1239.3; host greets guest with g. P324; hypocrite refuses g. but stretches out hands K2057; king has own g. stolen back P14.12; king won't eat till g. given W11.2.2; man beats people bearing him g. W152.20; man demands ever larger g. W154.26; seven g. of God Z71.5.6.8; tabus connected with fairy g. F348; tabu: giving away g. received from animal C847ff.; wife shames adulterous husband into g. K1271.3.1; wisdom lost by accepting g. J186.

Gigantic, see also **Giant;** cup F866.2; cauldron F881.1.1; flower F814.1; grapes F813.2.2; leaves F811.2.3; nut F813.3.2; possessions of giant F531.4ff.; shield F839.2.1; spirit F401.8; sword F833.8; vessels F881; vine F815.7.2; wood-spirit F441.5.2, (with one eye in center of forehead) *F441.4.1.

Gilded images substituted for solid gold K476.4.1. — Deceptive sale of g. ware K123.

Gingerbread house F771.1.10, (lures child) G412; man Z33.1.

Giraffe keeps house with other animals J512.7.1.

Girded. — Bond woman g. with rope P171.2.

Girdle of climbing vine F829.2. — Conception from putting on another's

g. T532.5; dupe allowed to guard king's g. (snake) K1023.1.1; identification by g. H116; magic g. *D1057.1, (clairvoyant) D1323.17, (prevents disease) D1500.2.6; ogre released in return for magic g. M242.3; woman's g. as source of sin T336.1.

Girdles of sinners in hell alternately hot and cold Q562.1.

Girl, see also **Maid, Maiden;** abducted by fairy F324; beautified by burning D1865.2.1; bewitched so no man faithful to her M438.3; as bird visits lover D641.1.1; brings bad luck to everyone N265.1; cruel to mother slain Q281.1.2; curses to revenge father M411.11; drives giant F531.5.10.1; drowned in well as river's origin A934.10; eats only kola nuts and tobacco F561.5; escapes in male disguise K521.4.1.1; fed boys' flesh to hasten growth G72.3; gathering flowers swallowed up by earth and taken to lower world F92.2.1; goes to fairyland and marries fairy F301.3; as helper N831; killed during day, revived at night E155.4; kills man sleeping with her K872.1; in man's clothes K1837, (wins rich woman's love) K1322.1; magically made hideous D1871; masks as doctor to find departed lover K1825.1.4; in menial disguise at lover's court K1816.0.2; mistaken for stone J1763.2; offers to sacrifice herself to save parents S262.4; reincarnated as river for god to lie in its bed A934.11.1; removes dog from lion's claws B848.2; saved by lion from ravishment B549.1; in service of witch G204; sleeping naked goddess or mortal? H47; sees vision of mother in hell, reforms V511.2.3; sold for new church bell V115.2; transformed to (comb) D263.3, (man) G263.3.2; tricked into man's room (or power) K1330ff.; visits fairy lover F301.7; with tree carried to moon A751.8.5; as wooer T55. — Clever g. J1111, (cheats robber) K434, (refrains from eating figs which would bring on magic sleep) J585.1, (asked riddles by king) H561.1; cranes carry away g. B522.4.1; devil abducts g. G303.9.5.1; devil advises young g. not to go to a castle G303.9.7.1; devil tempts g. G303.9.4.7; devil takes place of g. in man's embrace G303.9.9.16; disenchantment of g. by carrying her on back D732.1; disenchantment of g. only by lover D791.2.1; disguise as g. to avoid execution K514; dream shows where stolen g. hidden D1810.8.2.1; dwarfs adopt g. as sister F451.5.1.2; fairy a small pretty g. F232.4.1; flower by day, g. by night D621.2.2; foolish marriage of old man and young g. J445.2; lazy g. does not know where the spring is W111.5.2; little g. cursed M414.4; little g. drives out giant L311.4; magic sickness because g. has thrown away her consecrated wafer *D2064.1; monkey instead of g. in basket K1625; panther devours g. in tree: chain tale Z39.7; poor g. masks as doctor and is made court physician K1825.1.2; prophecy: wealthy marriage for poor g. M312.1.1; queen passes off g.-child as boy K1923.6; quest for g. (about whom parrots speak) H1214.1, (seen in dream) H1381.3.1.2.2; sham magician exposed by clever g. K1963.1; sham physician makes g. grow up K1955.5; single combat for g. H217.2; suitor finds g. immature: father protests she is already a mother J1279.3; tabus for g. going to her husband C161; tabu: g. going forth at puberty C131; tabu: letting sun shine on g. before she is thirty years old *C756.2; thief disguised as g. K311.16; transformation: g. to falcon D152.4; treacherous slave-g. K2251.1; vow to kill self and child if g. born M184; will-o-the-wisp is g. cursed for gathering plants on Sunday A2817.2. ⸗

Girl's long hair as ladder into tower F848.1; sham threat to evade husband K1771.6; spirit controls wind D2142.0.5. — Tasks assigned because of g. own foolish boast H915.

Girls dancing in heaven A661.4; eat their sister G73; going into wood for nuts N771.2. — Country of little g. F709.2; living g. transformed into plants A2617.1; melons analogous to g. ready for marriage H611.1; seven g. appear as seven parrots D658.3.3; swinging seventy g. H506.5; thirty g. fall in love with same man T27.1; three g. task: go and return together, but after different periods J2033.

Giver. — Directions followed literally to sorrow of g. J2516; magic object voluntarily restored to g. D878.

Giving away forbidden C783; all earnings to poor as penance Q542; half better than lending all J1552.4; thief what he wants K362.10. — Coward g. purse to thief W121.6; planned g. hare to thief anyway J1395; tabu: g. away (idol) C51.8, (gifts received from animal) C847.

Glaciers, revenants banished to E437.1.

Glance. — Beam breaks at giant's g. F531.3.14; bewitching by means of g. *D2071; impregnation through g. T515; man's g. kills F592.

Glass, see also **Crystal, Goblet;** boat for fairy F242.2.1; book F883.1.1; bridge *F842.1.1; car F242.1.4; coffin *F852.1; house F771.1.6.2; island in otherworld F162.0.1.1; ladder to upper world F52.1; mountain *F751; ship F841.1.14; shoes *F823.2; staircase F848.5; tower F772.2.4; tree F811.1.6; to wound and detect wife's lover K1565. — Breakage of g. by threes D1273.1.1.2; breaking g. during wedding T135.15; breaking heavy g. bottle over a loaf of rye bread as test of strength H1562.3; broken g. on witch's back G219.9; castle with g. wall F771.1.6.1; city of g. in heaven A661.1.2; climbing g. mountain D753.4; descent into ocean in g. box F1022.1; ghostly crash of breaking g. E402.1.6; identification by ring dropped in g. of wine H94.4; island of g. F731.5; magic g. *D1171.6.2; magic sight by looking into g. of water D1821.3.7.1; pillars of silver and g. in otherworld *F169.1; quest for G. Princess H1381.3.2; quest for g. of all waters H1377.1; rock becomes g. D452.1.5; sea of g. in otherworld *F162.4; ship of g. in otherworld *F169.3; test: guessing nature of devil's wine g. H523.6; worthless g. sold as diamond K142, K451.4; wounding by trapping with g. S181.

Glasses, see also **Spectacles.** — Filling g. with water that has neither fallen from heaven nor sprung from the earth H1073.

Glassware. — Basket of g. is to be sold (air-castle) J2061.1.1; king breaks g. to prevent others from doing so J2522.

Gleaming, see also **Bright, Glowing, Luminous, Shining;** spear F834.3. — Fairies in g. clothes F236.1.5; giant with large g. eyes F531.1.1.2.

Glen of witchcraft F756.4. — Perilous g. F756.5.2, (on way to otherworld) F151.1.2.

Glens, see also **Valleys.** — Fiery g. in hell A671.2.4.5.

Glittering well F718.9. — Breast broad and made of g. metal F546.1.

Gloom. — No g. in otherworld F172.1.

Glory compared to four things Z71.2.7; sacrificed for virtue J347. — Hand of g. D1162.2.1; men unable to endure God's g. A182.0.1; prophecy of g. for a people M325; robber with "hand of g." killed K437.2.

Glove and the lion L431.1. — Giant carries man in his g. F531.5.1.1; identification by g. H114; magic g. *D1066; man mistakes giant's g. for house F531.5.2; touch of g. causes sleep D1364.29; transformation by striking wolf-skin g. D566.1.

Gloves drip blood (life token) E761.1.7.1; make spear infallible D1653.1.2.1; thrown after ship cause disease D1500.4.5. — Murder by boiling victim's g. D2061.2.2.5.1.

Glowing, see also **Bright, Fiery, Gleaming, Luminous, Shining;** animals *B19.4; beds of dead E487; ghosts E421.3ff.; wheel mistaken for devil J1781.3. — Devil has g. (thumb) G303.4.3.1, (eyes) G303.4.1.2.2.

Glowworm thinks he shines like stars J953.12; thought to be a fire J1761.3. — Trying to swallow g. sparks J1849.2.

Glue. — Flight so high that sun melts g. on artificial wings F1021.2.1; swallows warn other birds against roosting in tree with g. J652.2.

Glued. — Death g. to chair Z111.2.2; lecherous king g. with feathers K1218.1.8.

Gluttony, see also **Greed;** W125. — Demon of g. *F496, (coaxed from throat by food) F406.4, (devours food in throat) F402.1.7.

Gnat as snakebite antidote D1515.4.4; as witch's soul G225.1. — Buzz of g. A2236.1, A2426.3.2; creation of g. A2033; devil in form of g. G303.3.3.4.1; man becomes g. D185.3; why g. has no tongue A2236.1, A2344.2.1.

Gnats apologize for lighting on bull's horn J953.10; created by devil to worry God A2033.0.1; having overcome lion are in turn killed by spider L478; in hell A671.2.7; think they have thrown horse down J953.6. — Devil pesters God with g. A63.4.1; lies about g. X1295.

Gnawed bone as weapon F839.1.

Gnawing. — Animals g. on moon A755.4.3; ant g. bow-strings of enemy D651.4; dragon g. tree roots B11.6.9; mice g. through metal B747.3; rodent g. away ladder to heaven A666.2.

Gnomes as mine-spirits F456.

Goading. — Demons g. man G302.9.9; devil g. oxen with pulled-up tree G303.9.2.1.

Goal. — Keeping g. in hurling match for corpses H1436.

Goaling match between fairies and mortals H1593.

Goat appears to be two when aimed at D2031.15; carries one hundred cartloads of grease (lie) X1244.1; as child's nurse B535.0.3; eats while camel talks K334.2; eats in garden and is caught (long beard, little sense) J2136.3; feeds other animals from its body B535.1; gives coins instead of milk B103.3.1; with gold, silver horn B15.3.2.2; Heidrun B19.7; pretends to be chewing rock and frightens wolf K1723; as sacrifice V12.4.5; singing threat bought off K1767; swallows gold, voids it for master K366.5; thief catches tiger instead J1758.1; transformed to person D334; in Valhalla gives mead A661.1.0.2; who wouldn't go home (cumulative tale) Z39.1; who wouldn't leave hazel bush Z39.1.1. — Antelope becomes g. D411.4.2; how g. got his beard A2322.4; big g. bears three kids yearly B196; bride escapes from foolish husband and leaves g. as substitute in bed K1223.1; bull refuses to fight g. J371.1; creation of g. A1885; demon mistaken for g. to be stolen J1769.3; devil as g. G303.3.3.1.6; devil has g. feet G303.4.5.4; devil writes faults of man on g. skin G303.24.1.2; devil's mother rides a g. G303.11.3.1; dwarfs with g. feet F451.2.2.3; eaten g. bleats from eater's stomach D1619.2.2; eating entire g. without leaving scrap H1141.4; enmity of g. and (bear) A2494.8.1, (leopard) A2494.2.3; fairy in form of g. F234.1.2; fattest g. taken away from demon H1423.3; flower-covered g. escapes jackal K521.8; fool thinks g. mimicking him J1835; fool's brothers substitute g. for the body of man he has killed and thus save him K661.1; friendship between g. and (hog) A2493.22, (leopard) A2493.8, A2493.35; ghost as g. E423.1.9; giant g. B871.1.4, (lie) X1244.3; god with g. feet A131.5; helpful g. B413; hidden g. discovered by his horn protruding above ground J582.1; how g. got horns A2326.1.5; husband transformed to g. must witness wife's adultery K1531; why g. lives with men A2433.3.8; lion makes lame g. lieutenant J421.2; lying g. (cumulative tale) K1151, (punished by being half-shorn) Q488.1; magic g. B184.5, (entrails) D1015.3.2, (tail) D1029.2.2; man transformed to g. D114.4, D134; marvelous sensitiveness: woman smells like a g. F647.5; ogress as g. G351.4; one wild g. steps over another on a cliff J133.1; Pan part g. and part man *F442; parson sings like a g. X436; penniless wooer: "House of my father with 150 lights and g. pen" K1917.4; Peter, acting as God, must run everywhere after a g. L423; prophetic g. B141.1; pseudo-magic g. sold K135.1; quest for marvelous g. H1331.5; reincarnation as g. E611.4; selling a g. and bringing it back along with the money H1152.1; bad smell of g. A2416.1; speaking g. B211.1.2, (saves girl) D674; speaking loin of g. meat D1610.7; tailor always associated with g. X222; how g. lost tail A2216.2, A2378.2.2; telling sex of unborn g. H1576.1; test of resourcefulness: carrying wolf, g., and cabbage across stream H506.3; tiger made to think g. is ghost K547.12; treasure-giving g. B103.0.5; why g. lives with man A2513.4; wise division of g. H601.1; witch as g. G211.1.5; witch rides on g. G241.1.2; witch as she-g. kills men G262.3.1; witch's rosary consists of g. dung G243.2.1; wolf sold as a g. K132; wolf tries to entice

g. down from high place K2061.4; woman bears g. T554.6; Zodiac grows
up, the Kid becomes the G. J2212.6.

Goat's liver heals blindness D1505.14.1; milk inexhaustible D1652.3.2;
tongue pierced, witch sick G252.2. — Herd's spirit in last g. tail D859.6;
man carried on g. horns B557.1; man with g. head B24.2; origin of g.
beard A2322.4; origin of g. mane A2322.4.1; pig attempts to imitate g.
tricks J2415.6; spinning wool still on g. back H1024.8; treasure from g.
entrails B119.2; trembling g. shaking frightens off tiger K547.7; why g.
has shaggy legs A2371.2.8; why g. penis as it is A2365.2.0.1.

Goats driven into well to cool off J1959.1; follow fairies F241.4; heads
mistaken for human J1762.9; heat oven (lie) X1244.2. — "Collect g.
under tree": carcasses piled up J2465.10; fairy leaves g. as price for
girl F343.8; lies about g. X1244; pigs become g. D412.3.4; troll lets two
g. pass, waiting for biggest K553.2; two stubborn g. meet each other
on a bridge and neither will step aside W167.1; troll drives two g.
G304.3.2.2; watching g.: kills them when they wander K1451.

"Goat-heads" from curse of Ham A1614.1.2.

Goatherd hero G462.1, L113.1.5; rescues abandoned child R131.3.2.

Goatskin. — As many stars as hairs in g. H702.2.1.

Go-between. — Innocent confessor duped into being g. for adulteress
and lover K1584.

Goblet, see also **Glass;** thrown indicates the princess's choice H316.3. —
Drunkard stung by g. would have drunk out of glass J1324; magic g.
*D1171.6.2, (breaks spells) D1396.1, (cannot be filled) D1652.5.1, (heals
wounds) D1503.8, (indicates falsehood by breaking, truth by reassembling) D1316.6; sun's night journey in golden g. A722.1.

Goblin *F470ff. — Devil as g. horse G303.3.3.5.4; ruler disguises as g.
K1812.6.

God, see also **Creator, Deity, Lord;** *V201; battles (hound of hell)
A1082.2.2, (Leviathan) A1082.4; becomes (crab) D175.1, (eel) D173.1; is
best H648.1; bores hole in hell: hence hot weather A1137; to be brought
from heaven H1262; in calf form D133.4.1; in cat form D142.2; changes
curse to blessing M425; cheats birds of tamarind K499.6; cheats devil
at mowing K42.2.1; compared to toolmaker J1262.6; conquers Satan at
world's end A1082.5; consults angels A42.1.1; created all miracles
F900.2; creates magic objects D803.1; cursed M414.1; of dead needs
men subjects A1335.11; and devil fly together over primeval water
A810.1; and devil torment each other A63.4.1; disguised as menial
K1816.0.1; dislikes offerings beyond one's ability V10.2; of the earth
J1441; enamored of mortal T91.3.3; is everywhere: fool thinks in
elephant J2499.5; as falcon has tail cut off A2216.6; finds that his
statue sells at low price L417; of fire and god of rain contest A975.2.1;
as giantess's lover T111.4; gives Jesus' staff to saint V227.1; grants man
twenty years' more life K551.22.2; in guise of mortal D42; as helper

N817.0.1; issue of brother-sister marriage P3; as magician D1711.6; makes birds, devil reptiles A1903; as mare seduces stallion D658.3.2; as matchmaker T53.4; names animals on first sabbath A2571.0.3; as an object A139.8ff.; is oldest H659.1.1; orders angel assign tasks H927.2; plagues devil with fleas A2032.4; promises never again to destroy world by water A1113; in the puddle J1262.2; punishes (David for his pride) L415, (man for killing ants) J96, (man by killing his child) A1335.15, (many for one sinner) J225.0.2; recognized by supernatural powers H45.1; reincarnated as (cat) E611.5.1, (dwarf) E651, (monster) E652; releases condemned soul E754.1.5; reposed on leaf J2495.5; to reveal self to legitimate K445.1; revenges murder after thirty years Q211.0.1; sends Adam to earth A1285.1.1; sends cold to prevent stones from growing A975.1; sends death when tired of man A1335.9.1; sends stinging bees to punish men A2012.3; sends woman to poison man A1335.12; of space upholds sky A665.1; speaks in vision V510.1; stabilizes the sky A665.0.1; is strongest H631.2; as surety, the abbot pays J1559.2; swallows his wife and incorporates her into his own being F911.1.1; teaches people to work A1403; throws diver's feet after him: hence his feet reach backward A2215.6; took power of speech from animals B210.3; transformed to (animal) *D101, (boar) D114.3.2.1, (dove) D154.1.0.1, (giant) D42.1, (hawk) D152.1.1, (giantess) D12.1, (shower of gold) D235.1; transforms nature every seven years A1103; as vampire E251.4.4; visits earth F32; in wolf form D113.1.2. — Ability to see angel of G. D1825.3.4.1; absurd reasoning about G. J2215ff.; advice from G. D1814.3; always say "if it pleases G." J151.4; angels and G. V248; animal characteristics (result of contest between G. and devil) A2286.2, (punishment for discourteous answer to G.) A2231.1; animal reincarnated as g. E657; animal transformed to g. D43.1; animals created through opposition of devil to G. A1750ff.; animals praise G. at Christ's Nativity B211.0.1; annual resuscitation of a g. E155.2; bargain with G. M201.0.1; cannibalistic g. G11.0.1; child nourished by sucking thumb of a g. T611.1.1.; condemned soul released by G. E754.1.5; contract between hungry g. and untouchable M242.2; conversation between G. and Adam's corpse E545.22; created beings rebel against G. A106.3; creation of animals by G. A1701; culture hero as g. A510.1; dead man praises G. E576; death by kiss from G. Q147.3; death preferred above G. and justice J486; death respite for steps towards G. K551.14; deceiving G. K2371; demon takes on form of g. to deceive faithful F402.1.4.1; devil advises youth to enjoy himself and not to think of G. G303.9.7.2; devil originates from g. G303.1.1ff.; devil is thrust into hell by G. G303.8.3.1; direct communication with g. fatal to all except special devotees C52.1; disguised g. chosen as husband T111.1.1; disrespectful answer to G. brings death A1335.6.1; eaten g. V30.1; fasting against G. P623.0.1; first parents children of g. A1271.3; flaying alive as punishment for contesting with a g. Q457.1; forgetting G. leads to wealth J556.2; gambling with a g. N3.1; generosity to g. in disguise rewarded Q42.3; ghost laid by calling on G. E443.5; hard to think of G. when occupied: proved by milk test J94; hearing voice of G. as reward Q144; heathen beats his g. because of misfortune V381; helpful animal sent by g. B319.1; hospitality to disguised g. rewarded Q45.1; how G. distributed professions A1650.3.2; husband as G. behind tree forces his wife to confess adultery *K1971.5; "I don't want G. to help so much!" J1279.2; inhospitality to g. punished Q292.1; ingeniously worded boon asked of G. K2371.3; invisibility conferred by a g. D1983.1; is shepherd known to G? H1292.17; king shown he is less powerful than G. L418; levity toward name of G. J1261.1; loathly husband g. in disguise D733.3. magic knowledge from G. D1810.9; magic object received from g. D811; magic power from g. (goddess) D1726; man behind statue (tree) speaks and pretends to be G. K1971; man so constantly enriched by G. that he cannot give all his goods to the poor U71; man honored above G.: the dead hen J2215.3; man originates from g. who comes to earth A1215; man put in moon for cursing G. A751.1.2; man sets self up as g. L420.0.1; man willing to sacrifice child to G. S263.2.3; men hide so G. will not see sin J1738.8; marriage to g. in bull form *B641.3; marriage of a mortal and a g. T111.1; misfortune from forgetting to say "if G. wills" N385.1; mortal woman seduced by a g. K1301; mountains from primeval journeys of a g. A962.3; omniscience of a g. D1810.0.1; only man without sin can see G. V510.2; origin of feasts in honor of certain g. A1541.2; peasants want a living G. J2495.4; people taught by G. to work C53.1; person carried to upper world by a g. F63; persecution by a g. N250.3; plants from transformed parts of body of g. A2611.0.4; power of prophecy from g. D1812.1.2; power of self-transformation received from a g. D630.2; quest for the anger of G. H1376.3.1; quest to G. for fortune H1263; recognition of man acceptable to G. H192.1; reincarnation: g. reborn as man E605.2; reincarnation: man becomes g. E605.3; resuscitation by a g. E121.1; riddle on goodness not found by G. H853; riddle: what does G. do H797; rivers where g. drags his staff A934.4; Satan asks G. for man G303.9.8.6; Satan prays to G. G303.9.8.8; seduction by posing as a g. *K1315.1; son of G. sees king; their repartee J1675.8; sons of G. and daughters of men F531.6.1.1; servant of G. beaten J2215.2; soul taken away by G. E722.2.10; spring where g. throws his staff or spear A941.3.2; stars rebel against G. A769.2; steadfastness of love for G. tested H1573.5; sun worships G. by night A722.11; sword with G. engraved F833.10; tabu: disbelief in G. C61.1; tabu: uttering name of g. C431; test of a g.: when its image is bound it frees itself H45.3; thief disguised as g. K311.15; thief as family g., bound K439.8; thinking of G. protects against devil G303.16.2.1.1; three spiritual gifts of G. Z71.1.12; thunder from G. beating his weapon A1142.5.1; transformation by g. D683.5; underworld people from children which Eve hid from G. *F251.4; unsuccessful imitation of g.

J2411.1.2; who is greater than G.? H674; why G. lets sinner die in peace, holy man be slain J225.0.1.1; wisdom from G. J164, (as old man) J151.3; witch's charm: without G. and Holy Mary G224.1; women refuse to show G. the way A1372.8.

God's birth A112ff.; curse M411.4.1; mercy vs. man's shortsightedness J2052; name (engraved on sun) A733.2, (nullifies fairy power) F382.3, (used to lay ghost) E451.4.1; omniscience J1617; promise not to destroy world by water A1011.3; spear of fire F834.1.1; spirit aids strong man F610.9; tears become peas A2612.3; urine (makes chilly fiery) D562.2.1, (used to make pig) A1871.0.1; wastefulness J2215.1; word the sweetest sound H635.2. — Charm containing G. name D1273.0.5; clouds as G. shield A1133.4; conception from G. bow T532.9; demon in G. form F402.1.4.1; devil leaves at mention of G. name G303.16.8; devil's animals and G. *A1751, A2286.2.1; dividing after G. fashion U61; earth rests on G. arm A849.2; eclipse in G. proximity F961.0.2; girl protects self from devil with G. name G303.9.4.7.1; greeting in G. name P682.1; heavens chanting G. praise F961.0.4; hero as g. son A512.3; how much cloth would it take to make G. coat J1291.3.1; lightning as G. messenger A1141.5; man marries g. daughter T111.1.2; mountains made with G. hand A962.2; mythical animals surround G. throne B7.2; not leaving G. court for king's J1269.13; numskulls surprised to hear of G. son J1738.3; one dueler fights with G. help: the other with his brother's J1217.1; shepherd in G. service H1199.12.1; soul leaves body after G. kiss E722.2.12; sun, moon's daily tour under G. orders A726.1; tailor occupies G. throne for a day P441.1; thunder as sound of G. gun A1142.5; trees blossom on G. arrival F971.8; wolf as G. dog A1833.3.

Gods A100—A499; built houses, fashioned tools A1402; captured R8; cause disease A1337.0.1; as culture heroes A520.1; in disguise visit mortals *K1811; exchange forms D45.2; furnish substitute for child sacrifice S263.2.1; help those who help themselves J1034; in human guise A1101.1.3; humble man's pride L473; prophesy about hero M301.16; in relation to mortals *A180ff.; teach people all they know A1404; teach how to seek food A1420.2; transform selves D698; tricked into help in escaping one's fate K2371.2. — Battle of fairies and g. F277; battle of the g. at end of world A1081; degraded g. become angels A52.0.2; demi-g. A500—A599; dwarfs make weapons for g. F451.10.4; fairies as g. F251.1.2; bridge of the g. A986; child sacrificed to gain favor of g. S263.2; end of the g. A1085; fairies as descendants of early race of g. F251.1; flood caused by g. A1015; indentions on rocks from imprint of g. A972.1; heathen g. less powerful than Christian V331.1.3; keeping on good terms with hostile g. J821; magic invisibility of g. D1981.1; making of g. A104ff.; man made from spittle of the g. A1211.3.1; man created by cooperation of the g. A1218; man pursued by hatred of the g. M411.4; milky way as the sperma of the g. A778.6; "not-g." A189.0.1; oaths before g. as test of truth H253; pagan g. become devils G303.1.3.4; personal offenses against g. punished *Q221; punishment for denying pagan g. Q225.2; rainbow from g. emptying their drinking cups A791.6; sacrifice to appease g. S263; sacrifice to g. so ship can continue S263.4.1; sun, moon as divine bodies of g. A718.2; swearing by clan g. M119.2; tabu: eating food of g. C241; tabu: offending the g. *C50ff.; task assigned the g. H902; three g. none may escape Z71.1.10; unacceptable g. as earth's first inhabitants A1205; unnecessary choice of g. J462.1.

Goddess aids quest H1233.5.1; aids task H975.1; arouses heroes' jealousy K1093; assigns task to suitor H335.0.5; breaks self into five parts: origin of river's five branches A934.11.3; cursed M414.2; divides time between upper and lower worlds A316; of earth A400.1; not to eat on earth C212; as fairy F251.1.1; Fortuna N111; gives birth to islands A955.9; as helper N817.0.2; killed for infidelity with mortal Q246.1; in moon A751.8.3, (beating tapa) A751.8.6; not to see mortal husband naked C313.1.1; mounted on drake with snakes A137.9; prevents suicide V10.1; repeatedly transforms self D610.1; standing on head supports earth A842.1; scatters pubic hairs on fish A2211.15; with thousand faces blowing her noses J1261.10; of world of the dead A310.1. — Brown hair sign child descended from g. Z146.1; disguise as g. K1828.2; fainting at sight of g. F1041.1.6.1; hair on ground summons g. D2074.2.2.1; is sleeping naked girl g.? H45.5; land born from g. A954; lifting of throne of g. D1654.17; love of g. for mortal T91.3.2f.; magic knowledge from g. D1810.10; magic object received from g. D811.1; magic power from g. D1726; man not to look at nude g. C312.1.1; man thrown into jail by g. R110.1; mortal's attempt to defile g. punished Q246; origin of feasts in honor of certain g. A1541.2; plants from tread of g. A2621.2; resuscitation by g. E121.1.2; respect to statue, dress of g. C51.1.13; sea creatures as ancestors of g. A111.3.2; sun, moon born of g. impregnated by wind A715.2; tabu: taking food dedicated to g. C51.2.2.1; tasks performed by aid of g. H975.1; transformation by g. D683.5; vow to be servant of g. M177.2.

Goddess's father (as cannibal) G11.0.1.2, (forbidding her marriage) A106.1.1. — Ogre defeated with g. help G537.1; questioning g. veracity punished Q221.7; test of g. favor: throwing away jewels H1577.1.

Goddesses come to earth, produce drought A189.10. — Twin g. A116.2.

Godfather P296.1. — Child promised to devil for acting as g. S224; cohabitation of g. and godmother punished Q242.1; dwarf as g. *F451.5.1.1; mountain-man as g. F460.4.7; playing g. K372; supernatural g. *N811.

Godiva clothed in own hair F555.3.1, H1054.2; riding nude through town not to be looked at C312.1.2.

Godmother P296.2. — Fairy g. F311.1; magic object received from g. D815.3.

Godparent. — Fairies seek human g. F372.2.

Godparents P296. — Dwarfs have mortal g. F451.5.6.
Goggles. — Green g. on cow fed sawdust X1235.3.
Going to certain place compulsory C666. — Task: g. and returning together but at different times J2033.
Goitre cure by striking J2412.8.
Gold in the Bible H261; causes man to become miser G303.9.8.5; demanded of saint disappears Q552.18.1; doors in otherworld F165.1.1; -digging ants B756; -dropping cow B103.1.2, D871.1.1; from fishes' gourd A1432.2.1; furniture, objects in otherworld F166.0.1; hair F555.1, (as sign of royalty) H71.2; hidden in bricks N518; hoard found by cow N534.2; kingdom F707.1; lump appears in Arabia at Christ's birth N529.1; magically produced D2102; magically stolen D2087.5; mast F841.2.1; moon, sun, star F793.1; ox horn H1151.7.1; pale because it is in great danger J1442.3; pieces in (the honey-pot) J1176.3, (the money-scales) N478; robbed from treasury by disguising as corpse K419.7; as sacrifice V12.5; seeds pave city F761.5.1; ship F841.1.10; and silver combed from hair D1454.1.1; sold for trifle J2093.6; staff resuscitates E64.1.1.1; star on forehead F545.2.1; statue of animal F855.3; stolen from witch G279.2.1; in stool as royalty sign H71.11; thrown on shore by siren B53.3; tint as royalty sign H71.6.2; turns to ashes from child's urine J2325.1; turns humble servant into arrogant J1085.2; transformed to animal D442.3; under tongue restores speech *D1507.8; used in medicine D1500.1.31. — Acquisition of g. A1432.2; alleged g.-dropping bear K1252.1; alleged g.-dropping horse sold K111.1; alleged return from dead with g. J2411.5; animal with g. horn B15.3.2; ascetic sees scorpions as g. D1825.8; ass with droppings of g. *B103.1.1; automatic doll spins g. D1620.0.1.1; automatic hen and chickens of g. D1620.2.2; avaricious woman and her g. consumed by fire Q272.4; beetle demands return of g. from God: must hum A2231.11; bird with g. head, silver wings B15.7.3; bow of g., silver, and copper F836.1; bride purchased for her weight in g. T52.3; castles of g. F163.1.4; castle paved with g. and gems F771.1.1.1; city of g. F761.1, (in heaven) A661.1.2; deer of g. and jewels possessing life D1620.2.3; dog vomits g. and silver B103.4.3; dogs of g. and silver F855.3.2; doors of g. in otherworld dwelling F165.1.1; dragon develops from small worm placed on g. B11.1.3.1.1; dress of g., silver, etc. F821.1.5, F821.3; dwarf turns g. into lead F451.3.3.2; dwarf king turns mill which produces g. F451.5.1.5.1; dwarf's g. castle F451.4.3.6; dwarfs possess g. F451.7.1; dwarfs turn peas into g. pieces F451.3.3.1; early pupil finds g. N633; fairies give coals that turn to g. *F342.1; fairies with g. crowns on heads G236.4; first parents originate from g. which is from body of first man A1271.4; fool thinks g. is being destroyed when snails crawl over it J1816; fish with ingot of g. inside it B107.1; "for g." C495.2.2; fortress of g. in otherworld F163.5.1; fowls eat g. F989.22.1; gifts of g. and silver not to be accepted from fairies F348.4; goat swallows g., voids it for master K366.5; god

transformed to shower of g. D235.1; grass covered with g. F817.4; grass turns into g. D451.5.6; guessing nature of devil's g. cup H523.3; hair, skin turn g. color D57.3; hair turns to g. as punishment in forbidden chamber C912; hairless palms from handling g. J1289.16; hidden g. revealed; trickster promises to make it into ornaments K283; house of g. and crystal in otherworld *F163.3.1; island covered with g. F731.1; island with rampart of g. and palisade of silver F731.3; king orders all g. brought to him P14.4; large price offered for g. reveals contraband K447; life bought for g. M234.3; magic flower pot bears plants with g. letters on leaves D1469.1; magic g. *D1252.3, (restores speech) D1507.8; magic stone turns everything to g. D1466.1; magic transportation by g. uniform D1520.7; mermaid gives g. from sea bottom B81.13.4; moon's reflection as g. in water J1791.3.3; mother love dearer than g. H662; mountain of g. F752.1; mule carrying corn escapes while one carrying g. is robbed L453; 999 g. pieces J1473.1; nugget of supposed g. (lead) given to help build church: money then borrowed K476.2.1; objects transformed to g. *D475.1ff.; owner of g. decided by combat H217.3; peacocks of g. F855.3.1; person with g. body F521.3.3; pool paved with g. F717.1; prayer for shower of g. V57.2; quest for g. flower H1333.5.0.3; quest for g. from grave H1392.1; quest for mountain of g. H1359.4; quest for g. mouth-harp H1335.1; raised treasure turns into charcoal but if one takes it along it will turn back into g. N558; recognition through g. found in eagle's nest H91.1; recognition by g. under skin H61.4; reincarnation as g. E645.1; resuscitation by g. E64.15; reward: as much g. as sticks to hair K199.1; rich men's g. sent below by gods L482.1.1; sack of g. retains at will any hand thrust in it D1318.14; saint exchanges coat with beggar: g. sleeves miraculously appear V411.2; saint's bachall discovers g. *D1314.3; serpent with g. under him B106; serpent's life in its g. crown E714.2; ship with g. nails F841.1.7; shipwrecked given g. for death V64.1; snake becomes g. D425.12.1, (in answer to dream) N182; spinning g. (task) H1021.8; spring in otherworld produces g. F166.2; successful suitor must have g. teeth H312.2; supernatural son can produce g. D2102.4; supposed chest of g. induces children to care for aged father P236.2; taking g. in mouth prophesies marriage H41.6; tears of g. D1454.4.1; test of innocence: apple and g. offered H256; test of unknown father: g. on street H485; three quarts of g. as suitor test H312.8; towers of steel, silver, and g. F772.2.2; transformation: putrescence to g. D475.1.12; trickster asks goldsmith what he would pay for lump of g. of certain size (goldsmith cheated) K261; trickster watchman exchanges g. for worthless bag K126; tree does not flourish because g. is hidden under it H1292.2; turning fruit into g. (task) H1023.15; unlucky man given a loaf filled with g. exchanges it for another loaf N351; valley filled with g. at command D2102.2; washer of g. rescues child R131.8.7; whales disgorge g. B583.1; wishing to be turned to g. J2079.1; woodsman and g. axe Q3.1.

Golden age A1101.1, C939.4, M324; animals B102ff.; apple *F813.1.1, (as prize in beauty contest) H1596.1; bed F787.2, F846.2; boat with copper rudder F841.1.8; body as royalty sign H71.2.1; bridge F842.1.4, (to otherworld) F152.1.3; calf H1331.3.3; castle F771.1.1, (in otherworld) F163.1.2; cave F757.1.1; chairs F786.1; clothes F821.1.1; cock in earth-tree A878.3.6; cock warns against attack B143.1.5; cock warns of danger D1317.15; comb F827.5; coffin F852.2; cot D846.1; cup F866.3, (as fairy gift) F343.14; door to troll's castle G304.3.1.1; dove F855.3.3; finger as sign of opening forbidden chamber C911; fish B102.4; flowers F814.4; fruits F813.0.2; game-board F899.2.1; hair F555.1.1; horseshoe F862.1; key F886.1; mansions of gods A151.4.3; moustache F545.1.1.2; nut F813.3.1; oar F841.2.4; pomegranates F813.8.1; reel F867.1; saddle F868.1; shoes F823.1; son can produce gold D2102.4; spinning-wheel F876; stone F805; swing F895; table F784.1; teeth F544.3.1; temple F773.2; tongue F544.2.1; tower F772.2.3; tree F811.1.1; vessel disenchants D771.5; wagon F861.1f.; wood for knife H1359.1. — Animals with g. members B101ff.; bird with g. (feathers) B102.1, (head) B101.1; disenchantment by throwing g. objects D789.5; disenchantment by drinking from g. vessel D771.5; devil's three g. hairs G303.4.1.8.2; disguised hero's g. hair discovered by spying princess H151.13; dragon with g. feathers B11.2.2.1; dwarfs make new g. hair for woman F451.5.1.3; fairies' g. bird F359.2; giant with g. hair on forehead F531.1.6.5; goose that laid the g. egg D876; horse's forehead as g. chair F874.2; magic transportation by g. apple D1520.4; making the beard g. *K1013.1; man becomes g. object D235; Midas' g. touch D565.1; pillar covered with g. flowers H1322.1; quest for animal with g. chain H1332.4; quest for g. (bird) H1331.1.3, (fleece) H1332.1; quest for vulture's egg figured with g. letters H1332.2; recognition by g. hair H75.4; recognition of twins by g. chain under their skin H61.1; return from dead to punish theft of g. arm from grave E235.4.1; saint's image lets g. shoe (ring) fall as sign of favor to suppliant D1622.3; Satan enters G. Calf G303.18.4; Solomon's g. throne F785.1; souls as g. apples E745.5.1; stealing g. apples (task) H1151.1; stealing troll's g. horse (task) H1151.9; sun a g. bowl with peacock on rim A724.2; shooting g. apples into besieged city K2365.2; transformed g. pumpkin J1531.1; tree with g. (fruit) D1461.0.1, (leaves) F811.2.1.2, (top) F162.3.6; troll's daughter after being cooked in kettle recognized by g. fingernail H79.1; value of a g. plow (throne, crown, palace)? (riddle) H713.

Goldfinch, color of A2411.2.1.12; wedding of B282.6.

Goldfish, reincarnation as E617.2.

Goldsmith changes person's voice F556.2; gives money to one addressing him as friend L363; as lover P447.7; robs treasury, makes gold into corpse K419.7; sells thinly plated gold: cheated in return J1511.20; unlucky N256.1. — Beggar asks g. for gold plate J1338; fox distracts attention of g., steals K341.25; magic forge of g. D2178.7; origin of g. work A1447.3; treacherous g. K224.3.

Golem D1635.

Gond are omnivorous A1689.3.

Gong, magic D1213.1, (stolen) D838.11.

Good and bad in all books J174; and bad culture heroes *A525; and bad fairies battle F277.0.3; and bad acts tallied by gods A189.8; "day— a woodchopper" (deaf men converse) X111.10; enter otherworld without fear E750.2.1; gifts of fortune *M200ff.; inclinations enter body at puberty W2; luck personified N113; omens D1812.5.2ff.; shepherd shears his sheep but does not skin them J530.1; spirits F403. — Angels seen over heads of the g. D1825.3.2; animals furnish g. omens A2536, B147.3.1; association of the g. and the evil J450ff.; casket with G. Luck in it given to men by Zeus N113.1.1; conflict of g. and evil creators A50ff.; dragon as power of g. B11.8; fairies make g. wishes for new-born child F312.1.1; father in the vineyard doing g. and bad H583.2; goddess of g. luck (Lakshami) A482.2; hedgehog draws self up at sight of g. man A2479.4; "let king do what seems g." J814.5; magic results from g. deeds D1799.6; magic reward for g. deeds D855.5; man mar-rying often: always looking for g. wife T251.0.3; man who asks for g. weather given a box full of hornets J2327; magic journey during which one must not think g. or evil D2121.6; magic ring brings g. luck D1561.1.2; nothing happens except for one's g. J21.52.8; one wrong and five hundred g. deeds J1605; opposition of g. and evil gods A106; person who never said "g. morning" cannot rest in grave E411.6; right hand for g. *D996.0.1.1; that is g. (cumulative tale) Z51.1; tree of knowledge of g. and evil F162.3.5; why certain animals g. B792; why some women are g.-looking A1372.6; you are an adulteress and a thief and I am as g. as you are J2666.1.

Goods. — Dead returns to restore stolen g. E352; false offer to return g. in place of payment K231.6; man so constantly enriched by God that he cannot give all his g. to the poor U71; thief trusted to guard g. K346.

Good-for-nothing. — Disguised husband shows wife he is not g. K1813.1.2.

Goodness found on earth by man but not by God H853; of God A102.14; preferred to (beauty) J244, (wealth) J247.

Goose best fowl since it makes cabbage sweet and bed soft H659.4.1; boasts superiority to mushroom: both served at same meal L419.1; brings master princess B582.1.1.1; dives for star, thinking it a fish J1791.8; egg becomes hen's D479.4; envious of peacock W195.1; that laid golden egg D876; mates with crow B671; as messenger B291.1.5; mistaken for a tailor J1762.1; transformed to object D423.1; transformed to person D364; without a leg (deception) K402.1. — Bad women from transformed hog and g. A1371.3; barnacle g. B712; bear becomes g. D411.10; bewitched g. eggs G265.8.4.2; brahmin ungrateful to g. rescuer W154.12.2; captured g. warns tortoise B143.1.6; color of g. A2411.2.6.3; deceptive land purchase: boundary fixed by flight of g. K185.3; devil as g. G303.3.3.8; disguise as g.-girl K1816.5; dwarfs accept as gift g. but not gander F451.3.6.4; ghost of g. E524.1; golden g. B102.1.3; helpful g. B469.3; lover's gift regained (g. as gift) K1581.7; magic adhesion to g. D2171.3.1; man transformed to g. D161.2; marriage to g. B602.6; origin of crest of g. A2321.1; reincarnation as g. E613.10; rubies as ransom for g. J514.6; why g. quacks A2426.2.9; revenant as g. E423.3.7; speaking g. B211.3.3; spirits with g. feet *F401.3.5; troll as g. G304.1.1.3; witch as g. G211.3.3; witch uses g. wings as oars G241.4.1.

Geese tell of beauty of their mistress and bring about recognition H151.12. — Boat drawn by g. B558.1; cackling g. spread alarm B521.3.2; dwarfs chatter like g. F451.3.13.2.1; flock of g. transformed to stone D423.1.1; fox about to be hanged asks to be allowed to see g. J864.2; king of g. B242.2.9; lean g. substituted for fat K476.6; lies about g. X1258; hawk flies away with g. on a line (lie) X1267.1; man carried through air by g. (lie) X1258.1; nine or ten g. (absurd counting) J2032.

Goosebridge. — "Go to G.": counsel proved wise by experience J21.16.

Gorge. — Leviathan's g. spreads disease B16.4.1.

Gorgon F526.3. — Blood of G. becomes horse D447.3.2; quest for head of G. H1332.3.

Gorilla transformed to eagle D411.9. — Man tracking g. sees animal's strength and refrains J561.1; origin of body hair of g. A2322.6; python becomes g. D418.1.1; small boy overcomes g. L311.5; why g. has large teeth A2345.9; why g. lives in forest A2433.2.1.2.

Goring to death by elephant Q416.3.1.

Gospel-book of saint buried with him V136.1; causes sight-shifting D1331.4.1; keeps cattle from straying D1446.2; hangs unsupported from shoulders F1011.1.1; restores speech D1507.2.

Gossip punished Q393.2. — Tongue cut out as punishment for g. Q451.4.2; woman tests enduring power of g. by having a servant ride through streets on a flayed ass J1075.1.

Gossipers. — King refuses to exile g. J215.1.2.

Gotham, Wise Men of J1700ff.

Gourd. — Birth from g. T543.5; boat from g. F841.1.12; escape from deluge in g. A1021.0.3; gold from fishes' g. A1432.2.1; magic g. *D965.2; magic produces golden g. seed D1463.3; man transformed to g. D221; marriage to g. T117.7; queen bears g. T555.2; rice-grains magically produced by g. D973.1.1; soul in g. E711.2.1; suitor task: cutting open magic g. H335.2; tabu: opening g. where starwife kept C31.1.5.

Gourds with seven rooms F813.5.1. — Origin of g. A2686.7; refuge from flood in g. A1029.4.

Government *P500—P599; of demons F402.2; among dwarfs F451.4.5ff.; of fairies F252. — Origin of g. A1582; repartee based on church g. J1265ff.

Governor, clever J1115.10.1.

Governors. — Enigma on dismissing old g. for new H599.5.

Gown. — Man forgets magic g., killed N339.6.

Gowther kills his wet-nurses T614.

Grace before meat X434.2; said in host's name by neglected guest J1561.7.
— Asking g. causes fairy banquet to disappear F382.6; prisoners refuse
individual g. R72; saying g. to show food improved J1341.12; vow to
ask nobody for g. M165; vow to die rather than accept g. M161.4.

Graces, three A468.

Gradual disenchantment D701; resuscitation E156; transformation D681;
weakening of testimony J1151.3.

Grafting of feathers to bald head D2161.3.4.1; of hide to man's head
E785.1.1.

Grail, see **Holy Grail.**

Grain as damages for injury to cat B271.2; to grow without beards
(short-sighted wish) J2072.2; imprisoned R9.2; shot down with guns J2196;
sown in unplowed field K1428; theft disguised by replacing husks
K419.6; turns to gold D475.1.6.1; will be cut when farmer attends to
it himself J1031. — Abandoned children find way back by clue of g.
R135; ant keeps g. harvest dry J711.5; apples become g. D451.3.1; bird
carries a g. of sand from a mountain each century (eternity) H701.1;
building granary full of g. overnight H1104.5; chain tale: biting g.
in half Z49.8; chain tale: parched g. sticks in post Z41.6.1; cobold
furnishes inexhaustible g. F481.2.1; conception from eating g. T511.8.4;
contest: bringing g. from closed bamboo K69.1; consecrated g. as remedy
D1500.1.10.4; country without g. F708.2; crow thinks harvesters are stealing his g. J953.7; cure by burning g. where man has died D2161.4.8;
deceptive bargain: as much g. as will go in rope K174.1;
deceptive g. division: corn and chaff K171.2; extraordinary g. F815.2;
fool kills himself in despair because a sparrow has taken one g. from
his field J2518.1; disenchantment by burying victim and sowing g.
over him D719.1; eaten g. and cock as damages K251.1; father makes
many out of few by sowing g. H583.2.2; fool seeks the ears of g.
in the direction of the cloud toward which he has sowed them J1922.2.1;
improvident mouse eats g. stored for famine J711.2; inexhaustible g.
D1652.1.3; magic strength-giving rice-g. D1335.1.1; making ale from
single g. H1022.6.1; numskulls sow cooked g. J1932.1; origin of red g.
of cedar A2731.3, A2755.1; origin of shapes of g. A2793.6; plucking ear
of g. forbidden C512; preparing large quantity of g. (task) H1122; rushes
become g. D451.2.1.1; seven g. sisters A433.2; showers of g. called down
D2105.6; slain father returns as cuckoo and tells where to sow g.
A2275.6; stealing ogre's g. H1151.25; storing g. against famine J711.4;
strong man's labor contract: all g. he can carry F613.2; supplying
superhuman amount of g. H1122.1; threshing g.: granary roof used as
threshing flail K1422; trail of g. R135.0.2; transformation: (apples to g.)
D451.3.1, (g. to gold) D475.1.6.1, (rushes to g.) D451.2.1.1; trickster
demands half of g. supply K446.1; using g. to clean child tabu C851.1.2;

wages: successive harvests from one g. Z21.1.1; why g. grows only at top
of stalk A2793.5; why owl eats no g. A2435.4.9.1; witch aids winnowing
of g. G283.1.2.4; wood becomes g. D476.1.3; wraith binds g. E723.7.6.

Grains munched to keep awake H1483. — As many stars in the heavens
as g. of sand H702.1; characteristics of g. A2793; deceptive wage: two
g. and land to plant them K256.2; devil gives Eve two g. of corn
G303.9.4.1; magic g. D973; magic speed by eating magic g. D2122.1;
man knows how many g. in measure F645.2; sorting a large number
of g. in one night (task) H1091.

Grain-bin. — Filling g. through bottom hole H1023.2.3.

Grain-measure runs away from husband: chain tale Z39.8.

Gram (parched grain). — Chain tale: g. sticks in post Z41.6.1.

Granary now haunted because of devil's defeat G303.15.2. — Building g.
overnight H1104.5.

Grandchildren. — Cruel g. S20; devil's g. G303.11.2.2; grandfather kills
g. S42; grandmother causes g. to be whipped K2175; prince in disguise
to kill g. K1812.14.

Granddaughters. — King prophesies g. fruitful M301.17.1.

Grandeur. — Choice: plainness with safety or g. with danger J212.

Grandfather P291; as creator A1.2; kills grandchildren S42. — Boy
kills g. S25.1; earth is deep for my g. went into it (died) years ago and
has not yet returned H681.2.1; hero slays his g. A525.2; quest for lost g.
H1385.7.1; smith as king's g. P447.1.

Grandfathers. — God dwells with g. A111.3.1.

Grandmother P292; causes grandchildren to be whipped K2175; to be
sacrificed in famine K944, K231.1.1. — Abandoned child cared for
by g. S351.1; attempt to seduce one's g. T423; creator's g. A31; cruel g.
S41; devil's g. G303.11.4; hawk loses g.: still hovers and seeks her
A2275.5.2; help from g. N825.3.3, (ogre's) G530.4; hero's g. A512.1;
I killed my g. because she refused to cook a hare (cumulative tale)
Z49.1; man betrayed into killing his g. K940.2; orphan hero lives with g.
L111.4.1; thief disguised as g. K311.8.5; washing the g. in boiling water
K1462; wolf poses as g. and kills child K2011.

Grandparents, cruel S40ff.

Grandson, cruel S25. — Prophecy: king's g. with dethrone him M311.1;
prophecy: murder by g. M343.2.

Grapes in lifelike painting contest H504.1.3. — Extraordinary g. F813.2;
fox and sour g. J871; magic g. *D981.8; speaking g. D1610.10.1.

Grass not bent by swift runner F681.12; does not grow (on murderer's
grave) E631.2, (where innocent hanged) H215.3, (in certain spot since
extraordinary event has happened there) F974; fuel for burning ogre
G512.3.3; from grave protects against witches G272.18; grows anew
nightly F979.18; from hair of slain person A2611.6.1; huts replace caves
A1435.3; pleasant couch for poor U65.1; transformed to other object
D451.5; transformed to soldiers D431.5.1. — Birds destroy g. B33.1.2;

camel's tail turns to g. R231.2; dead find no rest since g. is pulled on
grave E419.3; dead (fairies) walk on g. without bending it E489.9,
F255.5, F973.2; extraordinary g. F817; fairy rings on g. F261.1; god
of g. A433.5; knots in g. mark underworld path F95.4; magic g. *D965.12,
(furnishes treasure) D1463.6, (holds person fast) D1411.3; man becomes
g. D223; man can hear g. grow F641.1; man with g. growing from him
F529.3; man made from g. A1256.1; moustache becomes. D457.10;
men ate g. A1101.2.2; mowing g.: meadow torn up K1423; origin of g.
A2683; pretending to return stolen g. K323; reincarnation as g. E631.2.1;
St. Peter creates g. as medicine for snake-bite A2623; sham miracle:
may the g. grow up K1975; speaking g. gives advice D1312.3; transformation to buffalo so as to eat g. D655.1; transformation: g. to beard
D451.5.4; visit to lower world through hole made by lifting clumps of
g. F92.1; walking on blades of g. without bending them F973.2.

Grasshopper thought to be the devil J1785.1. — Ant and lazy g. J711.1,
A2233.4; why g. is born blind A2233.4, A2332.6.3; creation of g. A2064;
enmity between g. and starling A2494.13.11.1; friendship between g.
and dungbeetle A2493.21; shooting g. kills friend J1833.1; soul as g.
E734.8; why g. hides in day A2491.5; wedding of g. B285.3.

Grasshoppers. — Lies about g. X1288; sheep transformed to g. D412.7;
war of monkeys and g. B263.6.

Grateful animals B350—B399, (and ungrateful man) W154.8; boys help
hero win girl T66.2; dead *E341ff.; dragon saves hero B11.6.1.2; fairies
F330ff.; objects *D1658ff. — Helper g. for being bought from slavery
N801; magic object received from g. person D817; magic sight as gift
of g. animals D1821.11.

Gratitude W27. — Conversion out of g. V331.6; dragon helps hero out
of g. B11.6.1; joining captor from g. R71; mortal wins fairies' g. by
joining in their sport *F331; tests of g. H1565.

Grave which causes women to laugh C181.7; equals five times length of
any person's foot D482.5.1; fills with sand when dug for sinner Q552.17;
opened to let corpse spit out host V39.7; removes itself D1641.8; rises
with tide D2151.1.2.3; sinks so that grave-robbers cannot get out
Q552.2.2 transformed to animal D442.2.2. — Angels appear above
girl's g. V243.1; blood-brethren watch at g. P312.3; burial in old g.
to deceive angel J2212.2; cleric as g. robber K335.0.8; crawling to g.
on knees Q523.1.1; dead find no rest (since someone daily knocks at g.)
E419.2, (when grass is pulled on g.) E419.3; death feigned to meet
paramour: meetings in the g. K1538; deceived ghosts unable to return
to g. E141; devil sings on g. G303.9.8.3; dew from saint's g. as cure
D1500.1.18.1; earth from saint's g. expels demons D1385.1; escape from
g. R212; faithful animal at master's g. dies of hunger B301.1; food on g.
tabu C247; ghost family visits g. E324.2; ghost haunts g. E334.2; ghost
laid by (blessing g.) E443.1, (piercing g. with stake) E442; ghost shakes

off earth when he rises from g. E410.2; ghost takes bones from g. E593.4; hand from g. gives salvation E373.3; identity of g. revealed by magic king in dream (advises take treasure from his g.) N531.4; light haunts g. E530.1.3; limb broken for stepping on g. C946.1; living, dead fight in g. E461.2; lovers buried in same g. T86; magic g. *D1299.2, (compels person to laugh) D1419.1.1; magic identification of g. D1819.5; magic object from g. D842, (of slain helpful animal) D842.3, (of mother) D842.1; magic reward for g. quest D855.3; man in despair digging own g. finds treasure N545; mistress springs into lover's g. T86.3; nails driven into g. to lay ghost E442.2; numskull lies in an old g. to see the Day of Judgment J2311.6; path from g. to lower world F95.1; plants from g. A2611.0.1; plucking flowers from bride's g. H31.12.1; power of prophecy induced by crawling backward around g. D1812.2.1; priest made sick of his bargain: three words at the g. K262; prince plucks from g. of vampire a flower which later becomes a girl E251.2.2; refuge in g. leads to adventure N778; reincarnation in plant (tree) growing from g. *E631ff.; return from dead (to punish disturber of g.) E235.6, (to punish theft from g.) E235.4, (to demand clothing stolen from g.) *E236.1; rich man falls into sacrificial g. K1603; robbing of g. punished Q212.2; saint moves over in g. for pious man Q147.1; sham revenant takes refuge from robbers in an open g. J2311.3; sinner's g. cursed, rolls M411.14.1; sinners cannot rest in g. *E411ff.; sons meet at father's g. after learning trade M271; soul cannot go far from g. E722.3.1; spending night by g. (fear test) H1416; stars drop on g. F961.2.9; stepson cursed to g. D5.1.1; three-night watch over g. to guard man from devil H1463; tobacco from g. of virgin A2611.2.1; treasure is found when three-legged cat shrieks over a g. N542.2; trolls live in g. F455.1.1; walking around g. raises ghost E386.4; wild huntsman released from wandering by mould from Christ's g. *E501.17.7.1; wild huntsman's dogs cannot pass over g. E501.15.6.4; woman, rival lovers all buried in one g. T86.1.

Graves of giants F531.6.13. — Ghost flits between two g. E419.9; treasure buried in g. N511.1.1.

Gravedigger finds purse on corpse J21.48.

Gravedigging, origin of A1541.1.1.

Gravel rises from lake bottom F934.1.

Grave-mound. — Burial in g. V61.8; king goes himself into g. P16.3.2; quest for armor from g. H1392.

Grave-offerings. — Dead eat g. E541.3; trickster eats g. K1867.2.

Graveyard, see also **Cemetery.** — Angels rise from g. V242.1; casting in g. after sunset tabu C752.1.5; crossing g. without alighting tabu C883; death from fright in g. N384.2; jinns frequent g. F499.3.3; other dead drive sinner from g. E411.0.5; physician hides eyes as he passes g. P424.1; suitors one by one encircled into g. K1218.3; voices of dead heard from g. E401; waiting in the g. for the thief J2214.3.1.

Gravitation, lies about X1741. — Magic control of g. D2149.4; magic object reverses g. D1547.

Gravity. — Cup or contents has greatest g.? J2391; specific g. of river F715.10.

Gray and black hairs: enemies reconciled J83; hair cured by pulling it out so that person is bald J2112f.; hair symbol of departed usefulness Z155. — Devil a little g. old man G303.3.1.5; dwarfs have g. beards F451.2.3.2; dwarfs referred to as g. F451.2.7.3; fairies in g. clothes F236.1.4; fairies ride dapple-g. horses F241.1.1.2; fairy has g. beard F233.10; hair turns g. from terror F1041.9; horse used by mortal under fairy spell changes to g. cat F234.4.1; magic well makes person's hair g. D1341.0.1; magician claims he can make dogs g. K1677; man suddenly acquires long g. beard on scaffold at execution F1044; old g. fox not so good as young red one J1457; revenant g. E422.2.3; saint restores g. hair to black V229.10.3; why men's hair becomes g. A1315.1, J1461; wicked man reforms when his child finds g. hair in his head J761.1.

Grazing cow on roof J1904.1; of shooting star on earth A788.2.

Grease. — Disenchantment by rubbing with magic g. D771.2; ice transformed to g. D476.1.9.

Greased. — Holding shaven and g. tail of bull as chastity ordeal H412.2.

Greasing huge griddle by skating with bacon X1031.4.1; the judge's palms (woman puts butter on his hands) J2475.

Great, see also **Big, Large;** head as ogre G361.2. — Giants have g. age F531.6.4.1; humility of the g. J910ff.; lie: the g. animal *X1201; policy in dealing with the g. J810ff.

Great Bear. — Heavenly chariot takes couple to G. A761.2; Pleiades stars transferred from G. A773.7.

Greater. — Judge awards decision to the g. bribe J1192.1; lowly tries in vain to be g. than he is J955; murderer's penance complete when he kills a g. murderer and prevents a crime Q545; present to go to g. fool (returned to giver) J156.3.

Greatest liar to get his supper free K455.7. — Heroes seek which is g. H1395; quest for the g. of fools H1312; riddle: what is g.? H659.7.

Greatness. — Animal helps man to wealth and g. *B580ff.; dream (prophecy) of future g. F317, L425, M310.1, M311, M312, M371.1.

Grebe, helpful B469.1.

Greece as otherworld F130.1.

Greed, see also **Gluttony;** W151ff. — Animal characteristics as punishment for g. *A2238ff.; punishment for g. Q552.3.5; trickster's g. while hunting causes him to be deserted J2751.

Greedily. — "Don't eat too g." J2541.

Greediness. — Bride test: g. H385; guests accused of g. P334.1; spider transformed for g.: now occupies dark corners A2261.2.

Greedy disciple ignores warning, condemned as thief N347.7; dreamer J1473; god A139.15; gods impoverish rich men L482.1; host J1562ff.;

man magically blinded J514.3; priest reincarnated as insect Q551.5.1.3.
— Barbers g. P446.2; "don't be g. in trade" J21.26; one should not be
too g. J514; ruby shatters for g. lapidary D1641.14.1.

Greeks. — Origin of G. A1611.5.1; Trojans warned not to attack G.
J652.4.1; wisdom from the G. J192.3.

Green beard F545.1.1.1; chapel (cave in green mound) F773.1; city
F762.1; -eyed giantess F531.1.1.6; fairy F233.1; giant F531.1.7.1; goggles
on cow fed sawdust X1235.3; horse B731.2; knight F527.2; as magic
color D1293.2; as otherworld color F178.2; pigeon cheated A2275.4.1;
plants sold as matured K147.1; revenant E422.2.2; she-goat B731.1; as
symbolic color Z145.1. — Brownie dressed in g. F482.2.1; devil dressed
in g. G303.5.2; dwarf clad in g. F451.2.7.2; fairy in g. clothes F236.1.6;
fairies dance on g. F261.3.6; magic object received from g.-clad huntsman D823.1; man transformed to g. knight D57.1; person with g. face
F511.1.4; place of saint's martyrdom perpetually g. V229.2.5; quest to
animals' la**r**d for g. stone H1289.1.1; secret remedies learned from g.-
clad woman N455.5; serpents play with precious g. stone B11.6.2.2;
swallow avoids g. trees for nest A2431.3.5.1; tree half g. and half in
flame in otherworld garden F162.1.2.4; trees with g. birds hanging by
claws F811.9.

Greenest. — Riddle: what is g.? H646.

Greeting before dawn bad omen D1812.5.1.7.1; "come and share it"
taken literally J2499.6; customs P682.1. — First to give g. shall have the
disputed property K176; numskulls quarrel over a g. J1712; riddle on
never g. anyone H588.12; transformation through g. D526.

Greetings. — Dying hero sends g. to friends P310.3; fool's talking taken
as unfavorable g. J2671.2.1; give separate g. to different ages J152.5;
literal following of instructions about g. J2461.2.

Gregory on the stone Q541.3.

Grey, see **Gray.**

Greyhound. — Birds lift g. F982.1.1; fairy as g. F234.1.9.2.

Greyhounds drag mill out of water (lie) X1215.12. — Fairies' horses
size of g. F241.1.8.1.

Griddle. — Cooking g. cakes as bride test H383.1.2; rubbing nose on g.
as punishment Q499.8; tabu to eat g. cakes C229.3.

Grief, see also **Sorrow;** dispelled by magic bell D1359.3.1.3; at queen's
death P27. — Animal pines away with g. B773.2; black as symbol of g.
Z143.1; boy sickens from g. P231.1; excessive g. at spouse's death T211.9;
extraordinary reactions to g. F1041.21; madness for g. F1041.8.2; magic
bird's song dispels g. B172.2; Pleiades girls who died of g. A773.3;
pulling out hair g. sign P678; prophecy of g. fulfilled by death M340.1;
transformation through excessive g. D516.

Grieving to death over fate of children after one's death J2063.1; mortal
taken to heaven, identifies son F12.2. — Man dies from g. over mother's
death F1041.1.3.8.

Griffin B42; aids quest H1233.4.3; disdains to go on ark: drowned, hence extinct A2232.4; as guardian of treasure N575. — Hostile g. B17.2.2; transportation to fairyland on back of g. B542.21.

Griffins in hell A671.2.10.

Grinder. — Cobold furnishes g. with inexhaustible grain F481.2.1; moon as g. brings fire from sun A741.3.

Grinding. — Giants g. F531.5.10.2; man in disguise g. corn K521.4.1.3; man g. rocks into powder F639.11; mill not g. stolen wheat D1318.15; murder by g. in mill S116.1; punishment: g. up in a mill Q469.3; youths g. in mill of underworldlings F106.

Grindstone. — Magic g. *D1262; origin of g. A1446.5.3; picture of g. mistaken for cheese J2685; sun as g. full of fire A714.5; woman gives birth to g. T569.2.

Grindstones kill enemies N696.2.

Griselda H461.

Grizzly bears. — Why g. have three stripes on inside of stomach A2367.2.1; why g. are pugnacious A2524.1.

Groaning dead E547.1. — Dwarf g. while carrying an ear of corn F451.3.9.1; listening to g. of violated women tabu C885.2.

Groat. — Never wager more than a g. J21.8.

Groom, see also **Bridegroom.** — Treacherous stable-g. K2256.

Grooming unruly mare H1155.1.1.

Ground, see also **Earth, Land;** dries up when first woman cuts self, bleeds on it A856.2; elevates itself for saint V229.13; trembles or rumbles when ghost rises from grave E410.1. — Birth from g. T545; city girl asks whether turnips grow in the g. or on trees J1731.1; clever girl comes sitting on animal but with feet reaching the g. H1053.2; contest: jumping into the g. K17.1; deceptive crop division: above the g., below the g. K171.1; devil tries to wall in too large a piece of g. in a night and fails G303.13.3; dragon lives under the g. B11.3.5; dupe caught in crack in g. K1111.2; dwarfs have homes above the g. F451.4.2; dwarfs live under the g. F451.4.1ff.; earth made from broken g. A824; father's counsel: find treasure within a foot of the g. H588.7; flowers spring up when saint strikes the g. F971.6; fox produces fire by striking tail to g. D2158.1.1; girl seduced from beneath g. K1344.1; ghost travels under g. E591; house neither on g. nor in sky H1077; life token: staff stuck in g. E761.2; magic found on g. D849.8; magic object dug from g. D848; magic song causes plowed g. to become unplowed D1565.3; magician's feet must touch g. D1719.10.1; mankind emerges from g. A1234; saint's bachall cleaves g. D1564.3; strong man drives anvil into g. F614.1; pitcher magically sticks to g. D2171.4.1; tabu: touching g. C520ff., (on return from fairyland) F378.1; tails in g. K404.1; transformation by touching g. D565.0.1; temple rises where g. bursts open A992.3; treasure found by sprinkling g. with blood of white cock D2101.1; treasure in g. N511; vehicle travels above and below g. *D1533.2ff.; wild hunt in air

·very close to g. E501.14.1.1; wild hunt throws person to g. E501.18.5; youth will not eat from g. C219.1.

Grouse. — Markings on tail-feathers of ruffled g. A2412.2.1.

Grove. — Covering g. with fruit overnight H1103.3; death excluded from sacred g. Z111.4.

Groves. — Cutting sacred g. forbidden C51.2.2; sacred g. V114.

Growing crop overnight H1103.2.2; mountain F755.4; oil seed on stony ground H1049.2; and ungrowing grass F817.1; rocks F802. — Beard g. through table F545.1.3; garments g. with wearer F821.9; giant g. because of another giant F531.6.8.8; god sends cold to prevent stones' g. A975.1; island g. foot yearly F734; man can hear grass g. F641.1; plant g. to sky F54.2; sham physician controls girl's "g.-up" K1955.5; tree blooming and g. ripe fruit nightly F811.13; tree g. miraculously fast F811.19.

Growth of culture hero A511.4; of members for breaking tabu C946.3; controlled by magic object D1376. — Changeling has abnormal features or g. F321.1.2.1; extraordinary g. of animal F983ff.; girl fed boys' flesh to hasten g. G72.3; gods' food gives supernatural g. A153.2.1; magic quick g. of crops *D2157.2; man's g. controlled by cloak D537.2.1; man's g. and maturity A1360ff.; miraculous g. of tree D2157.4, F811.19; nurture and g. of children *T610ff.; supernatural g. T615.

Growths. — Magic object causes (or removes) temporary g. D1375; temporary bodily g. from magic D2062.5.

Grub's urine waters tree F979.14.

Gruel runs out drinking hole in pot J2176.2.

Grumbling tabu C881.1.

Guarantee. — Cloth g. against being eaten H119.1.

Guard. — Animal as g. B576; black as g. against Evil Eye D2071.1.4; don't set hungry g. over food J215.1.1; escape by blinding g. *K621; escape by deceiving g. K620ff.; escape by putting captor off g. *K611; extraordinary g. for castle F771.5; fidelity of g. tested H1556.0.2; nobody can move cannon, so g. quits J1849.4; theft by giving g. narcotics K332.1; thief as g. for goods K346; transformation to lion in order to be palace g. D659.4.1; victim killed when off g. K839.1.

Guards. — Bribed g. let prisoner escape R211.9; man caught by g.: guard substitutes with his sweetheart K1317.4; putting g. to sleep, then stealing K331.2.1.2; suitor outwits one hundred g. T46.1; thief frightens away corpse g. K335.0.7; trickster bribes g. to start a fight K341.10; wolf proposes abolition of dog g. for sheep K2061.1.1.

Guarded maiden first seen by hero in church T381.1. — Bridge to otherworld g. by animals *F152.0.1; door of habitable hill g. by monster F721.2.2; entrance to other world g. by monsters F150.2; gate of heaven g. by clap of thunder and mysterious sword A661.0.1.1; girl carefully g. from suitors T50.1; magic spring g. *D927.2; magic tree g. by serpent *D950.0.1; quest over path g. by dangerous animals H1236.2; treasure

g. by spirit in hornet form F403.2.3.1; wonderful birds g. by monster G375.

Guardian angel V238; beast overcome by mirrors K335.1.7; sleeps while lovers visit D1965; spirit of land F494.1; of spirit-land F140.1; of treasure *N570ff. — Animal g. of ogress' soul E710.1; bird as g. of primordial fire A1414.6; calabash as g. of girl D1380.2.1; dog as g. of treasure B292.8; fairy g. relaxes, man killed F311.2.1; false g. betrays lovers K2093; magic knowledge from g. spirits D1810.12; means of hood-winking the g. or owner *K330ff.; offending g. spirits C44; old woman as g. of gods' islands A955.12; soul as g. spirit E748; stones as town's g. F809.8; tree as girl's g. D1380.2.2; theft by presenting false order to g. K362.

Guardians of imprisoned virgin put to sleep while man enters to her D1965. — Beast g. of the four quarters A417.1; golden deer entices away girl's g. K341.7.3; invisible g. N810.1.

Guarding the door (lifted off and carried away) K1413; as task H1199.17; those having pact with devil M219.3. — Dragon g. (bridge to otherworld) B11.6.6, (holy land) B11.6.4, (hermit's food) B11.6.5, (sandalwood tree) B11.6.10; ghost g. treasure E291.2; giants g. fairy princess F300.1; gorilla and chimpanzee punished for not g. possessions at creation A2322.6.

Guavas. — Divine friends eating g. A1129.2.

Guelph-Ghibelline feud starts over dog N387.1.

Guessing correctly wins princess for ogre G463; dwarf suitor's name drives him off F451.5.15.3; dwarf's name rewarded with money *F451.5.15.1; name of supernatural creature gives power over him *C432.1; of secret transaction brings magic recovery of speech D2025.3. — Dwarf makes return of child dependent upon g. of riddle F451.5.15.2; tests in g. H510ff.

Guest kills host, asked to restore life J1955.1; made to pay for food K251.2; stays too long, gets black bread J21.9.1. —Acquisition of g.-houses A1435.1; eating after g. tabu C236; host offers to send his g. a cask of wine which he has praised M206.1; host robs g. K385; hosts refrain from telling g. of death in household P323; priest's g. and eaten chickens *K2137; relation of host and g. P320ff.; supper won by disguising as invited g. K455.2; suspicious g. forces host to be killed in his stead K1611.2; tabu: failure to sleep with g. unaccompanied by husband C119.2; unwelcome g. tells about the hidden food J1344; various foods given each g. J81.2; wife abuses husband in presence of g. T252.7; woman advises husband to kill g. she covets T481.7.

Guests and hosts P320ff.; strike man who tries to interfere in their quarrel J1072.1. — Angel forewarns of g. coming V246.3; foreknowledge of g. coming D1812.0.2ff.; greedy g. impoverish host W151.2.2; man kills all g., hoping some day to kill rival S110.2; miserly wife exposed to g. by her husband W153.3; peasant cutting wood as g. arrive P411.2;

practical retorts: hosts and g. J1560ff.; thieving g. at inn K365.2; treatment of difficult g. J1563ff.

Guesting, origin of A1534.

Guide. — Angel as g. V232.5; deity as g. for mortal A185.10; demon g. to otherworld F159.4; fairy as g. F234.2.7.

Guiding beast N774. — Boat g. self D1523.2.5; child in womb g. mother T575.1.6.

Guilt detected by heartbeat J1142.2.1. — Escape by discussing g. K573.1; magic object reveals g. *D1318ff.; tests of g. or innocence *H210—H239; twelve-legged bird symbolizes g. H619.5.

Guilty confronted become insensate F1041.1.3.10.1; person deceived into confession J1141.1; protests innocence J1141.9. — Brother about to drink blood of seemingly g. sister P253.1; fool believes not g. plea J2045; innocent made to appear g. K2150ff.; lawyer makes g. client doubt own guilt X319.1; magic object picks out g. man D1318.0.1; ship refuses to move with g. man aboard D1318.10.1; who is g. of accident? Z49.11.

Guinea eats man's grain: man may kill him A2238.2. — Cackling of g. A2426.2.13; color of g. A2219.1, A2411.2.6.6; helpful g. B469.6; why g. has red feet A2375.2.10.

Guise. — Deity's messenger can assume any g. A165.2.0.1; hero assumes ugly g. A527.3.1.1.

Guises. — Deity in frightful g. H1401.

Guitar. — Magic g. *D1234; resuscitation by playing g. E55.5.

Gull as bird of ill-omen B147.2.2.2; transformed to person D354.2. — Color of g. A2411.2.5.4; creation of g. A1945; giant g. B872.2; man becomes g. D154.4; nest of g. A2431.3.4.

Gullet seen through mouth F544.0.1.1.

Gullible fools *J2300—J2349.

Gum. — Indians chew spruce g. A1681.1; leaky vessel repaired with g. H1023.2.1.1; origin of g. in myrrh tree A2755.3.2; trickster's burnt flesh becomes g. on trees A2731.1.

Gun bewitched G265.8.3.1; mistaken for clarinet J1772.10; as tobacco pipe K1057. — Accidental discharge of g. kills much game X1124.3; blade of grass transformed to g. D451.5.3; devil's g. G303.25.16.1; lie: remarkable g. X1121; magic g. *D2096.1; man shoots devil with silver g. G303.25.7; numskull looks through g. barrel J2131.4.1; silver in g. releases curse M429.7; stolen g. works only for master D1651.11; thunder as sound of God's g. A1142.5; witch causes g. explosion G269.16.

Guns rendered ineffective by witch D2086.2. — Grain shot down with g. J2196; peoples choose bows and arrows or g. and horses A1614.4.3.

Gunfire. — Sneeze mistaken for g. J1809.1.

Gunpowder. —Captor's g. removed, ashes substituted K633.

Guru. — Man from loincloth of g. A1211.7.

Gust. — Dragon-king transformed to g. of wind D429.2.1; measuring g. of wind H1145.2.

Gustatory. — Extraordinary g. sense F647.1.1.

Gut covering in sky A1122.4.

Guts, web of F847.

Gutting of dead man S139.2.2.2.

Gyges' ring D1361.17.

Gypsy. — Disguise as g. K1817.5; treacherous g. K2261.1; why g. may steal: helpful at crucifixion A1674.1.

Gypsies. — Origin of g. A1611.2; why g. have no churches X1863.

Habit, power of U130ff.

Habits of witches G240ff. — Absurd disregard or ignorance of animal's h. *J1900ff.; characteristic h. of various peoples A1680ff.; causes of animal h. A2400—A2499; dragon's h. B11.4ff.; evil person's h. punished Q320ff.; fanciful h. of animals B750ff.; hero with disgusting h. L114.5; hero (heroine) of unpromising h. L114; house dog blames master for teaching him lazy h. J142.1; slave recognized by his h. H38.3; thieves' nocturnal h. J1394ff.

Habitable caves and mounds in otherworld F164; hill F721.2.

Habitat of animal A2434ff.; of dragon B11.3ff.; of witches G230ff. — Present h. of animals result of ancient quarrel A2282.

Habitations, acquisition of A1435.

Hades, see **Hell.**

Hag guards girl from suitors T50.1.3; runs race, loser to be beheaded M221.1. — Fairy in form of h. F234.2.1; fighting with h. tabu C835.4.1; goddess of war as h. A125.1; king tricked into sleeping with h. K1235; love charm on cheeks of h. D1355.13.1.

Hags guard quest path H1236.3.

Haidas. — Why the H. surpass in certain industries A1673.1.

Hail as bad omen D1812.5.1.15; leaves twelve chief rivers in Ireland A934.6; as one of sun's faces A733.3; produced by magic D2143.4; as punishment Q552.14.5. — Angel created from h. A52.1.5; magic h. *D902.3, (on lake causes treasure to spring from it) D1469.4; origin of h. A1135.4.

Hailstone among worst of stones H659.3.1. — Birth from h. T546.2.

Hailstones. — Extraordinary h. F962.5; triangular h. F794.2.

Hair becomes gold D475.1.10; burned to summon fairies F398; burned, victim dies D2061.2.2.4.1; combed with iron S187.2; of dead combed V68.2; of drowned woman speaks E545.20.1; of dwarfs F451.2.4ff.; from fox's tail opens all doors D1562.2; gives clairvoyance D1323.11; gray before the beard (it is twenty years older) H771; on ground summons goddess D2074.2.2.1; growing on tongue F544.2.3; like raven as suitor test H312.5; plaits cut off to escape lover T327.7; -restorer injures patient K1013.5; rises on end F1041.2; rolled in wax as witch-ball G262.4; rope transfers milk D2083.3.2; tied to basket causes dupe's death

K1021.1.1; transformed to (another object) D457.4, (plants) A2611.6, (animal) D447.1; turns to gold as punishment in forbidden chamber C912; turns gray from terror F1041.7. — Animal with h. of iron pins B15.7.10.2; animals from transformed h. A1724.2; ascetic carries woman in h. F1034.2; ascetic's h. garment V462.5.1; bathing h. in buffalo milk D1337.1.3.1; boiling lover's h. fetches him D1355.35; brownie with red h. F482.1.1; burning cut h. to prevent witchcraft D2176.5; cannibal without h. G11.11.2; child born carrying handful of h. T552.4; child finds gray h. in wicked father's head J761.1; color of h. changes D492.3; combing h. of fairies (task) H1192; coming neither naked nor clad (clothed in own h.) H1054.2; corn grows in man's h. F1099.4; creature with single red h. H1331.7; culture hero's pubic h. thought to be bear h. J1772.4; cure by putting h. in tree hole D2161.4.18; cutting h. to escape captor K538; cutting h. as insult P672.2; cutting h. as punishment Q488; daughter pulls out father's magic life-containing h. K976; demon with red h. G342; devil buys a woman's h. G303.25.13; devil's h. G303.4.1.8; disenchantment by burning magic h. D771.1; disenchantment made permanent by holding to a h. D793.1; disguise by cutting off h. K1821.10; dwarf washes, combs and braids h. for sleeping maids F451.5.1.13; dwarfs make new golden h. for woman F451.5.1.3; dupe's h. tied: attacked K1021.1; escape by returning for h. ribbon K551.4.8; fairy borrows comb from Christian maid to comb h. of changeling bride F322.1.1; fairy-mortal baby's long h. F305.3; fairies comb children's h. F313; fairies tied together by h. F239.1; fairies' long h. F232.4; fairies' yellow h. F233.5; flying nets of h. in battle F1084.0.2; girl fastened by h. to rafter S182; girl's long h. as ladder into tower F848.1; ghost laid by burning h. E446.2.1; ghost turns h. white E542.4; giant with golden h. on forehead F531.1.6.5; giant with long h. F531.1.6.3.1; giant without h. F531.1.6.3.2; giant's h. grown into earth F531.1.6.9; giant's strength in h. F531.1.6.13; giant slings stones with his h. ribbon F531.3.2.2; giant's h. grows into rock G122; giants with shaggy h. on their bodies F531.1.6.3; goddess of the h. A499.2; gods fasten world-columns with mother's h. A841.0.1; grass from h. of slain person A2611.6.1; gray h. cured by pulling it out so that the person is bald J2112; guessing which sister's h. is golden H511.2; healing with h. of dog that bit one D2161.4.10.3; heavenly being's h. as sky-rope F51.1.5; hen put in witch's h. to scratch while maid escapes G276.1; hero's golden h. discovered H151.13; hero's three heads of h. A526.4; house-spirit without h. F480.5; husband cuts off h. of wife's substitute in bed K1512; husband tests wife by sleeping on her h. H476; husband tied to bed by h. K713.1.7; identification by h. H75; Jesus' dark h. V211.2.1.2.1; large red h. as suitor test H312.8; long h. prized by Irish P632.5; love through sight of h. of unknown princess *T11.4.1; magic h. *D991, (of animal) D1023ff., (ball) D991.3, (ornaments) D1072, (produces soldiers) D1475.5, (summons helper) D1421.0.3, (wishing) D1470.1.36; magic sleep by combing h. D1962.3.1;

magic strength resides in h. *D1831; magic weapon cuts h. D1564.7; man absorbing h. into head F1041.10; man covered with h. like animal F521.1; man transformed to h. D292; men are first covered with h. A1281.2; mermaid has wooly h. B81.9.1; mermaid's h. reaches her waist B81.9.1; mortal wins fairies' gratitude by letting them cut his h. and shave him F331.2; mountain of women with fair h. F131.1.1; mouse causes thief's h. to fall out Q557.4; why nit lives at edge of h. A2236.6; nude woman clothed in own h. F555.3.1; origin of gorilla's and chimpanzee's body h. A2322.6; origin of h. A1315, A2322ff.; why no h. on ox's lips A2221.5.1; pearls from h. as sign of royalty H71.3; partial transformation: person with animal h. D682.2; prince feels h. on bedding F647.9.1; pubic h. believed to be lying, pulled out J1842.1; pubic h. mistaken for calf's tail J1772.4.1; pubic h. remarkable F547.6; pulling out h. in grief P678; remarkable h. F555ff.; reward: as much gold as sticks to h.: hair tarred K199.1; rope made of person's h. F843.1; saint binds devil with her h. D1831.1; saint causes gray h. to turn black V229.10.3; seven souls released from hell for every h. of saint's chasuble Q174.1.1.1; not to shave or cut h. until a certain time M121; shield cutting h. F839.2.2; sleeping enemies' h. tied to an object prevents pursuit *K635; sleeping maiden's h. tied to tree K635.1; snakes will not cross h. rope B765.18.2; soul in h. E714.12; splitting a h. with a blunt knife (task) H1023.14; straightening a curly h. (task) H1023.4; strength of witches in h. G221.1; summoning by burning h. D2074.2.2; tabu: cutting h. C722; tearing h. from grief F1041.21.6; thief ties owner's h. while he escapes with goods K338; tiger made to believe porcupine bristle is his enemy's h. K1711.1; transformation by braiding h. D577; Virgin Mary's golden h. V250.2; washing h. on sabbath tabu C631.3; water-spirit controlled by long h. F420.5.2.2.1; water-spirit with long h. F420.1.4.10; wearing h. "not too long or too short" J1161.8; weaving a silk shirt from h. H1021.6; wife binds giant's h.: he is slain G530.1.1; wild huntsman with long h. E501.7.7; witch's h. on horse becomes iron G265.3.1; witch's long h. G219.4; woman with animal h. F521.1.1; woman drying h. scares ghost E432.3; woman not to bind h. till enemy is conquered M122; woman sells h. to feed husband T215.8; woman's scented h. attracts deer: husband jealous T257.5.1; woman tells wife to increase her husband's love by cutting a h. from his beard K1085.

Hairs become jewels D475.4.7. — As many stars as h. (on goat) H702.2.1, (in the head) H702.2; counting h. in pig's back (task) H1118; goddess scatters pubic h. on fish A2211.15; gold (silver) h. as sign of royalty H71.2; gray and black h.: enemies reconciled J83; how many h. are in the head (riddle) H703; origin of pubic h. A1315.5; pulling h. from bewitched animal's tail G271.4.9; putting h. under arm H599.4; quest for man caused by bird dropping his h. H1213.1.1; quest for princess caused by sight of one of her h. dropped by bird H1213.1; quest for three h. from devil's beard H1273.2; sinners in heaven numbered by h. in saint's chasuble M364.3.1; young wife pulls out his gray h., old wife his black J2112.1.

Hair-ball for bewitching D2070.1.

Haircut as war preparation P552.5.

Hairdressing, magic sleep by D1962.3.

Hairpin, magic *D1072.2.

Hairy anchorite D733.1; ascetics attacked instead of monkeys J2484; star F961.2.2, (at Nativity) V211.1.2.1. — Bear learns how to catch crabs with his h. claws J102; child born h. T551.13; child born with h. mane T585.5.1; devil as h. man G303.3.1.21; disguise as h. man K1821.4.1; fairies' h. bodies F232.5; wood-spirits h. F441.4.5.

Halcyon builds nest on sea-cliff N255.3.

Half done K372; -friend H1558.1; of kingdom as reward Q112; of offspring like fairy, half like mortal F305.2.1; payment for half-milk, half-water J1551.9; price for half a shave J1522.1. — Army of h.-animals, half men B20.1; boy cut in two: each h. becomes a boy T589.2; Fortuna h. white, h. black N111.2.3; giving up h. property: slave cut in two J2469.3.1; ghost with h. a head, carries h. body E261.1.3; god h. mortal, h. immortal A122; lying goat punished by being h. shorn Q488.1; mermaid h.-beautiful, h.-monstrous B81.9.3; money collected by h.-chick K481; only h. a child born to queen eating half a mango T550.6; parson preaches so that h. the congregation weeps and h. laughs X416; person with h. a body F525; resuscitation of wife by husband giving up h. his remaining life *E165; selling his h. of house J2213.6; spirit has h. a head F401.4.1; thief dressed h. white, h. black K311.0.1; tree h. green and h. in flame in otherworld garden F162.1.2.4; vow to get stubborn girl h.-married only M149.6; youth sees h. of two quadrupeds H583.1.1.

Half-wit abandoned S327.3; as prophet M301.9; successful L121.1.

Halibut, color of A2411.4.1.

Hall of glass F165.3.1. — Beard projected over beams of great h. F545.1.2; fairy h. F223; seating arrangements in royal h. A1539.1; smith as lord of hospitality h. P447.3; tree in king's h. F811.4.3.

Hallowed. — Rich man dragged from h. grave E411.0.5.1.

Hallowe'en. — Dead speak on H. E545.6; devil appears on H. G303.6.1.7; fairy appears to mortal each H. F393.2; fairy army among mortals on H. F255.4; fairy cattle graze on H. F241.2.4; fairy steals on H. F365.0.1; fairies emerge on H. F211.1.1.1; festival of H. V70.5; ghost kills on H. E268; ghosts walk on H. E587.2; going abroad tabu on H. C632; names of those to die heard on H. D1827.1.1; origin of H. A1541.3; roads appear on H. F1099.2; speech magically recovered on H. D2025.5; terrifying experience undergone on H. H1423.2; treasure found on H. N541.3; wonders on H. F900.1.1.

Halter. — Transformation to horse by putting on h. D535.

Halting. — Location determined by h. of an animal *B155; tabu: h. or unloading horse C884.1.

Ham (proper name). — Creatures from curse of H. A1614.1; Fomorians descended from H. A1659.1.1.

Ham as prize for husband who rules his wife T252.4. — Rock substituted for h. K476.1.1; stolen and restolen h. K306.1.

Hamelin. — Pied Piper of H. D1427.1.

Hamlet cutting hooks for father's revenge H591.3. — Enigmatic statements of H. H599.2.

Hammer in coffinmaker's shop makes noise to announce a death D1322.1.1; of thunder god A157.7; worship V1.9.3. — Compressible h. D631.3.5; creator with h. and chisel in hands A18.5; dispute of h. and anvil J461.6; first poetry composed in imitation of tones of h. on anvil A1464.1.1; giant h. F612.3.2; giant thinks blow of h. on head is a nut falling F531.5.4; god with h. A137.1; magic h. D1095, *D1209.4; Thor to give his h. in return for Freyja as wife K235.2.

Hammers. — Persons whose heads are stone h. F511.0.3.

Hammock, magic *D1154.3.

Hampers. — Measuring the tower by piling up h. J2133.6.1.

Hamstringing S162.2, (as punishment) Q451.2.0.3.

Hand cut off for breaking tabu C948.6; of glory *D1162.2.1, K437; from grave gives salvation E373.3; from heaven writes on wall F1036; -less people, F167.6, F515.0.1; of sinner sticks out of grave E411.0.1; of slain enemy nailed to castle S139.2.2.1.5; stuck for beating idol Q222.5.6; of vampire severed by cutting off hand of drawn figure E251.1.2; wagered N2.3.2; withers (as punishment) Q559.5.2, (because of broken oath) M101.4. — Bird in h. foolishly given away in hope of greater gain J321.1; cat's paw cut off: woman's h. missing D702.1.1; conception from h. T517.1; corpse's h. as remedy D1500.1.6.1; corpse's h. used as charm by robber K437.2; curse: person's h. to drop off M431.4.1; cutoff h. transformed to plant D457.9.1; cutting off h. for ring R231.1; dead man stretches h. from tomb to honor saint V222.7; devil cuts off h. of woman and suffocates her S113.2.1; dupe puts h. into cleft of tree *K1111; dwarf promises money and property to mortal father for h. of daughter F451.5.18.1; fool cannot tell right h. in dark J1735; ghost as h. E422.1.11.4; ghostly fingers leave mark on man's h. E542.1.1; god makes man's h. rigid A185.2.2; god with one h. A128.4; greedy person gets h. stuck in jar W151.9; hawk carries man's h. F982.3; hog's forefoot cut off; woman's h. missing D702.1.2; identification by magic h. H145; lotus transformed to human h. D451.4.1; lucky right h. N113.2.1; magic h. *D996; magic healing by h. D1503.9, D2161.4.16.1; magic object clings to h. of guilty person H251.3.8; magic restoration of severed h. D2161.3.2; magic sight by looking in hollow of h. D1821.3.9; man kills ox (cow) with flat of h. F628.1.2ff.; why mole has h. like man A2375.2.6;

mountains made with the h. A962.5; mountains made with God's h. A962.2; oath taken on saint's h. M116; paper in h. which none but king can remove D1654.11; person swearing oath places h. in mouth of image H251.1; price "handful of coppers": h. claimed too J1511.17; pygmy stands on man's h. F535.2.6; recognition by hole burned in h. when woman removes glove H56.1; robber with "h. of glory" killed K437; sack holds person who puts h. into it D1318.14, D1413.9; saint's h. made bright by Lord's touch V222.1.2; saint's h. illumines darkness D1478.1; severed h. as identification H106.1; sham-dead person tested by hot lead poured on h. H248.1; silver h. used as if flesh F1002; softest h. placed between head and pillow H652.1; soul (life) in left h. H714.7; substituted h. E782.1.1; tell-tale h.-mark H58; treasure discovered by h. of unborn child N533.3; victim lured into holding out h.: it is cut off K825.4; Virgin restores saint's severed h. V256.3; waiting for man's h. to fall off J2066.9; witch in form of cat has h. cut off *G252; witch steals child with h. through chimney G261.1; what do I hold in my h. (question to numskull) J2712.

Hands in cleft log as punishment Q469.13; cut off as punishment Q451.0.1; restored E782.1; wagered N2.3.2.1; washed before prayer V58.4. — Boy borrows python's h. and feet: hence python lacks them A2241.8; cold h. and feet for the dead man J2311.7; curse: fire to burn h. and feet M431.3; deceptive contest in squeezing h. K73; flowers drop on washing h. D2193; fool hanging by h. claps them, falls J2133.13; friends clasp h. in death P319.5; giants' magic gifts return to original form in h. of men F531.5.6.1; holy man restores cut-off h. V229.10.2; husband's h. tied, woman drowns K1652; invisible h. (aid task) H986, (serve) E482; magic from clapping h. D1799.2; magic restoration of severed h. D2161.3.2; maiden sends to her lecherous lover h. which he has admired T327.1; man originally without h. and feet A1225.2; mason's h. cut off after building finished S161.0.1; men with tails on h. F515.3; merman lays h. on side of canoe B82.7; mutilation: cutting off h. S161; ogre's h. cut off, hung above gate G512.1.2.1; origin of h. and feet A1311; person unusual as to his h. F515ff.; Pilate appears periodically and washes his h. E411.8; remarkable h. F552ff. revenant with ice-cold h. E422.1.3; robbers' h. cut off K912.0.2; recognition by missing h. H57.4; skillful marksman shoots meat from giant's h. F661.1; soldier with both h. gone fights with teeth P461.1; sons wipe h. on lame brother S12.7; sparks from man's h. F683.1; severed h. as suitor tribute H333.2; strong man kills animals with own h. F628.1, F628.2.5; successful suitor must have whitest h. H312.4; tokens on h. identify god H45.4; tribe all use left h. F515.5; unseen h. lave feet F171.7; unseen h. serve hero H1239.2; warming h. across the river J1945; witch with enormous h. G217; wood-spirit without h. F441.4.2.

Handaxe, magic D1524.12.

Handicrafts. — Aptness in h. as suitor test H326.1; god of h. A451.3.

Handiwork. — Strong man's h. causes quest H1213.2; test of skill in h. H504.

Handkerchief as chastity index H431.2; concealed in nut F813.3.4; left to incriminate woman K2112.5.1; in room condemns innocent wife N348; transformed to other object D454.3.2.1; as token H86.4. — Disenchantment by placing h. between horns D777; extraordinary h. F822; identification by h. H113; love through finding h. T11.4.5; magic h. *D1069.1, (healing) D1500.1.35; princess throws h. high in tree: asks hero to get it H933.1; quest for best-worked h. H1306.1; resuscitation by h. E64.21.

Handle. — God with h. through eyelid A128.2.2; gold, silver knife h. F838.2; tree cut down with axe for which it furnished h. U162.

Handles. — The cup with two and three h. J2665.1.

Handmaid. — Beaten h. reveals secret blemish N465.0.1.

Handprint. — Ineradicable h. proves innocence H215.4.

Handsel. — Bringing h., forgetting purchase J2461.5.

Handsome exterior no indication of soul U119.3; but foolish son M93; man F575.2, (made hideous) D1872.1, (substitutes for ugly bridegroom) K1915.3. — Jealous king massacres h. captives T257.6; father with h. son and hideous daughter J244.1; quest for bride as h. as the hero H1301.1.1; ugly man becomes h. D52.2.

Handspreading. — Feast of "bedding and h." T162.

Hanged, see also **Hung;** man thirsty: demands water E422.0.1; man warns youth E366.2. — Bedridden oldster h. instead of guilty young man J2233.1.1; captured women h. S139.3; deception into allowing oneself to be h. K715; gallows breaks when innocent h. H215.2; god of the h. A310.3; grass won't grow where innocent h. H215.3; if you h. me, you will be in trouble J2185.1; innocent boy h. for cattle theft N347.3; innocently h. person saved by saint R165.2; island sinks into sea after innocent man h. H252.5; lightning strikes where man being h. R341.1; man h. by hair S182.1; slave h. P175.1; tabu to take down corpse of h. man C541.5.

Hanging in game or jest accidentally proves fatal N334.2; sentence remitted Q577; for stealing from church Q411.11.2; on a sunbeam *F1011.2; test H1533; by tongue Q451.4.9; up by feet as punishment Q462.2. — Advice on h. yourself "by the stone which I point out" J21.15; at h. witnesses bigger thieves than culprit U119.1.2; cat h. on wall pretends to be dead K2061.9; deceptive game: h. each other K852; devil cheated by pretended h. K215; devils' feast for woman h. herself G303.25.17.3; dogs with eyes h. out over mouth in wild hunt E501.4.1.4; foolish demands before h. J2174; horse h. self D2061.2.8; lower lip h. down to neck F544.1.1; man finds treasure as h. self N545.1; man h. himself under devil's instruction G303.9.4.2.1; men h. down in chain until top man spits on hands J2133.5; men h. selves to punish sickle J1865.1; murder by h. S113.1ff.; obedient husband h. wife J2523.1;

ogre deceived into h. self G524.1; old man with h. eyelids F571.1;
penance: h. for a thousand years head downward over a fire of chaff
Q522.6; plea for immediate h. so can get back to work J2174.4; prophecies concerning h. M341.1ff.; punishment: h. Q413; thief advises dupe
on h. up slaughtered meat K343.2; thief distracts attention by apparently
h. himself K341.3; tower h. in air F163.7.1; tree h. from sky A652.2;
trees with green birds h. by claws F811.9; usurer charges for rope cut
to save him from h. W154.1.1; wife h. self at husband's death T211.3.2;
wife h. self on tree: friends ask for shoot J1442.11; wisdom acquired
by h. in a tree J162.

Hangman. — Compliments from the h. J1398.

Hangman's noose cures scrofula D1502.2.3.1; noose gives luck in gambling D1407.2. — Bewitched h. rope G265.8.4.1.

Hank. — Task: making many shirts from one h. of flax H1022.2.

Hans my hedgehog C758.1; im Glück J2081.1. — Ring of H. Garvel
G303.9.7.3.

Happiness from eating magic pig D1359.3; during last year of life as
reward Q145.0.1. — Crow searches for h. J136; deaf and dumb man
can see soul taken to h. or punishment D1821.7; distance from h. to
misfortune (riddle) H685; god of h. A467; land of h. *F111; money
does not always bring h. J1085; otherworld land of h. F173; quest for
h. H1376.6; rich man poor in h. J347.4; ruler jealous of h. prohibits
games W181.7; work brings h. J21.50.

Happy couple: wife blind, husband deaf T202; otherworld where dead
are healed *E481.4.1. — Apparently h. man lets another see misery of
his existence U115; apparently h. woman discloses lover's skeleton
U115.1; men too h.: life becomes difficult L482; men too h.: hence pain
A1346.2.3; soldier dies h. at enemy's rout P461.2.

Harbinger. — King's face as h. of evil N119.3.

Hard. — Cliffs become h. A968.1; punishment for h.-heartedness Q291;
way to otherworld h. to find F150.1; why stones became h. A975.

Hardened clay is hard to mold J21.52.3. — Primeval earth h. A856ff.

Harder. — What is h. than stone? (riddle) H673.

Hardest. — What is the h. H637ff.; what four things are h. to hold?
H659.2; what is the h. to skin? H659.15.

Hardheadedness. — Animal punished for h. A2239.8.

Hardness of heart D444.1, W155ff. — Coming neither in softness nor
in h. H1054.4; faithless widow's h. repels new suitor T231.4.

Hardship. — Enduring h. as a test H1502.

Hardships. — Heathcock prefers home with h. to travel in foreign lands
J215.3; heroine endures h. with menial husband L113.1.0.1.

Hardy. — Why certain tree h. A2788; why plum tree so h. A2711.6.

Hare, see also **Rabbit;** as ambassador of the moon K1716; and bride in
pot escape tiger K521.11; becomes person D315.5; carries honey-covered

lion, lures animals K767; changes sex B754.1.2; deceptively strangles wolf, fox K713.3; demands equal rights for all animals J975; escapes lion in brushwood K521.10; eats stuck lion K714.9; flatters other animals, bites off their ears K1018; gets cat to gallop, escapes K562.2; with horns B15.3.4.1; and man contest in watching for leaf to fall; man wins, may eat hare A2256.1; with many friends H1558.4; makes horns of wax and poses as horned animal K1991; instructs his sons to use their eyes to advantage J61; in lion's skin gets meat from lioness K362.5; as messenger B291.3.2; outwits pursuing bear, kills her K929.13; and pig in race H625; promises to dance, escapes captors K571.1; pursued in wild hunt E501.5.5.1; raises animal army for hero B524.6; rejoices when sparrow is carried off by hawk J885.1; rides on elephant B557.11.3; runs away at creation: almost loses tail A2215.2; at third remove J1551.6; as sacrifice V12.4.7; sleeps with open eyes as defense A2461.1; told to go home J1881.2, K131.1; and tortoise race: sleeping hare K11.3; transformed to another animal D411.3; transformed to person D315.5; tricks civet into being eaten by lion K813.2; waits in vain for event J2066.8. — Alleged speaking h. K131.1.1; animals' ears like elephant's until h. bites them off A2216.7; ass thought to be h. J1754; attack on the h. J2612; cat acts as judge between sparrow and h. K815.7; charm to catch h. and monkey D1444.2; chasing h. into every trap in a high tree H1024.3; contest in enduring cold: frost and the h. H1541.1; creation of h. A1856; why h. is deceptive A2525.1; demon in form of h. F401.3.6; devil in form of a h. G303.3.3.2.3; dog chasing h., bringing it to master K135.1.2; dwarf rides on a h. F451.6.2.1; enmity between cat and h. A2281, A2494.1.3; why h. has deep-set eyes A2239.1, A2332.4.1; fairy as h. F234.1.12; fox or h.? J2671.1; friendship between h. and parrot A2493.13; giant h. B871.2.8; why h. shakes head A2474.2; helpful h. B437.4; why h. has short pair of legs A2371.2.11; lion leaves sleeping h. to follow the shepherd J321.3; why h. lives in bush A2282, A2433.3.3; man in the moon a h. A751.2; man transformed to h. D117.2; marriage to h. B601.13; moon is h. covered with silver A759.4; more timid than h. J881.1; obstacle race between deer and h. K11.9; plowing contest won by deception: h. exchanged for horse K41.1; reincarnation as h. E612.3; revenant as h. E423.2.2; skillful barber shaves running h. F665.1; soul in form of h. E731.5; why h. has short tail A2378.4.1; speaking h. B211.2.6; tame dog prefers food basin to fleeing h. J487; too cold for h. to build house in winter: must go without A2233.2.1; troll as h. G304.1.1.2; why h. is gray in summer A2411.1.4.4.1; why h. never drinks from rivers or streams A2435.3.12.1; why h. skips about A2479.2; witch in form of h. G211.2.7; witch transforms self to h. so as to suck cows D655.2.

Hare's food A2435.3.12; legs doubled up in punishment K581.2.1; magic stomach D1015.5.1. — Cause of h. hopping gait A2441.1.11; why h. ears are black *A2325.2; why h. lip is split *A2342.1; why h. nose is closed during sowing season *A2335.2.4; quest for h. milk H1361.5; Santals eat h. entrails A1422.1.1; why ants do not live on h. back A2584.2.

Hares fearing death outrun pursuing dogs U242. — Dog alternately bites and caresses h. K2031; foxes desert h. when they foresee defeat by the eagle J682.1; king of h. B241.2.6; man lays bag by fencehole and all h. run into it X1114; two h. run into each other and are caught X1114.1; troll has h. in stable G304.3.2.4; why h. have cotton tails: deity rubs cotton on A2378.9.3; why men eat h. A1422.1.

Harem ladies recognize impostor king K1934.1. — Messenger to girl-captive in h. K1323.1.

Harlot, see **Prostitute.**

Harmful effects of meeting wild hunt E501.18ff. — Animal h. to holy person cursed A2231.7; avoiding things which are h. by nature J656; refusal to believe that friend h. P317.1.

Harming tree tabu C519.1. — Fairies h. men after enticing them F302.3.4.

Harmless. — Animal usually h. has horns B15.3.4; why animal is h. A2531ff.; magic object renders weapon h. *D1414ff.; magic writing on sword renders it h. D1414.2; salt sprinkled on fairy food renders it h. F384.1.2.

Harmony. — Philosopher instructs king on domestic h. J816.1.1; seek h. at home J1289.9.

Harness. — Plowing the field: horse and h. destroyed K1411; stretching, shrinking h. pulls wagon uphill X1785.1; trading only horse for h. J2085.1.1.

Harnessed. — Man h. and led to dance by witch G269.3; ogres h. to plow G675; wolf eats horses, is h. X1216.1.

Harp comes at owner's call D1649.2.1; music lullaby for snakes D1962.5; playing lures princess into forest K788.1. — Automatic figures on h. D1620.2.5; bride defeated in h. contest H332.1.3; fairy h. F245.1; heroine found in h. L111.2.5; hiding in h. K515.2; magic h. *D1231, (kills) D1402.22, (restores speech) D1507.7, (swine summoned out of) D1449.3; mouth-h. left by bed (token) H142; origin of h.: A1461.2.1; quest for living h. H1335; recognition through h. playing H35.1.1; sound of h. J1626; tick full of h. strings H1129.7; witch plays jew's h. K606.1.4.

Harps. — Playing nine mouth-h. at once F679.9.

Harper P427.10; as love messenger T55.9; puts mother asleep, lover visits maiden K1349.4. — Disguise as h. K1817.3; fairy h. F262.3.1, (enclosed in yew tree) F386.1.1; god as h. A465.2.0.1.

Harpies B52. — Man's food always seized by h. M435.

Harpooning contest won by deception K33. — Spirit h. sleepers F402.1.11.3.

Harrow. — Bluff: h. said to be hero's comb K1718.4; contours of land from hero driving h. A951.3; literal fool carries h. in his hand J2461.1.6; ogre induced to sit on reversed h. K1117.

Harrowing of hell V211.7.1. — Treasure to be found by man plowing with cock and h. with hen N543.2.

Hart eating earth-tree A878.3.2. — Prophetic h. B142.3.

Hartebeest. — Man transformed to h. D114.1.3; mantis transformed to h. D415.1.1.

Haruspices D1812.5.0.5.

Harvest-festival V70.4. — Farmer sleeps through h. time Q585.3; prayer for good h. V57.1; sacrifice at h. A1545.4; tabu to feast at beginning of h. C237; trolls help with h. F455.6.8.1; weeds spoil h. of rich men L482.2; why monkey has first fruits of h. A2433.3.19.1.

Harvested. — Spendthrift's uncut field already h. H586.4; why wheat must be planted one year, h. next A2793.2.1.

Harvesters. — Crow thinks h. are stealing his grain J953.7.

Harvesting contest K42; early for half crop J1932.6.

Hasty killing or condemnation *N340ff. — Avoid h. judgment J571; if you're too h. you won't arrive L148.1; over-h. toad X1862; thumbling born as result of h. wish of parents T553; too h. action forbidden C758.

Hat over eyes if ears cut off J2721. — Alleged bill-paying h. sold K111.2; boy with h. of butter X1153; burial service read into h. to prevent dead walking E431.1; captive throws his h. to lions who fight over it while he escapes K671; churchyard mould in h. prevents witchery D1385.11; devil in green clothing with h. G303.5.2.1; enemies shooting at decoy h. K631.3; fairy's sugar-loaf h. F236.3.3; giant carries man on h. brim F531.5.1.1.3; ghost scorches man's h. E542.4; holding down the h. K1252; magic h. *D1067.1; magic transportation by h. D1520.11; priest mistaken for h. J1763.1; revenant with h. of birch E422.4.1; symbolic interpretation of points on a bishop's h. H608.1; thumbling carried on h. brim F535.1.1.14.

Hats. — Fairies with belts and h. F236.3; removing h. tabu in otherworld C716; why husband and wife shall not exchange h. A1571.1.

Hatched. — Basilisk h. from cock's egg B12.1; birds h. from broken eggs repaired by skillful tailor have red line around necks F662.1.1; cobold h. from cock's egg, boar's testicle F481.0.1.1; helpful bird h. by hero B317.

Hatchel. — Man transformed to h. D257.

Hatchet. — Fairies return lost h. head F343.18; killing tiger by throwing h. into mouth K951.1.1.1.

Hatching. — Absurd ignorance concerning h. of eggs *J1902; numskull tries h. out calf from cheese J1902.2; other birds h. cuckoo's eggs A2229.5, A2431.2.1.1; task: h. boiled eggs H1023.1.

Hated. — Flight from h. husband R227.2; why animal is h. A2583.

Hateful or lovely child to be born first T548.1.1.

Hatred magically induced D1931; released among mankind A1388.1. — Husband's love becomes h. D1908.1; man pursued by h. of the gods M411.4; origin of h. A1388.

Hatter P454.

Haughtiness, punishment for Q552.19.5.

Haughty mistress makes extravagant demands of lover L431.1; punished Q4.

Hauling canoe over dead man's body causes resuscitation E607.3; enormous quantity in short time H1109.2.

Haunt. — Animal's characteristic h. A2433ff.; capture by waiting in enemy's h. K782.

Haunts of giants F531.6.2. — Devil's present h. G303.8ff.

Haunted, see also **Ghosts.** — Buildings h. by ghosts E280ff.; castle h. by demons F771.4.5; faithless lover h. by dead sweetheart E211; house h. to run owners out and leave it for servants to enjoy K336.1; husband h. by dead wife on second marriage E221.1; king's garden h. by witch H1191.2; place of great accident or misfortune h. by ghost E275; places h. by the devil G303.15ff.; staying in h. house as fear test H1411; "when Caleb comes" to h. house J1495.2; witch causes h. houses G269.5.

Hawk attacks hero's enemies B524.1.9; carries off queen's necklace, drops it by girl N698; carries man's hand F982.3; as culture hero A522.2.3; in earth-tree A878.3.4; flies away with geese on a line X1267.1; frightened at snipe's bill J2616; hard to hold by beak H659.2.1; lighting on man points out criminal B152.3; as messenger B291.1.10; persuades doves to elect him their king K815.8; as sky palace architect J2060.3; swims (lie) X1267.2; transformed to person D352.1; transformed to salmon D413.1. — Birds flee from cuckoo, who they believe will later become h. J645.1; buzzard hatched by h. ejected for fouling nest Q432.1; child with head of h. T551.3.2; creation of h. A1937; enmity between h. and hen A2494.13.10.3; flight of h. A2442.2.5; golden h. B102.1.1; why h. has forked tail A2216.5, A2378.5.2; why h. hovers over camp-fire: seeks grandmother A2275.5.2, A2471.3; helpful h. B455.4; how he would act if he were a h. J1391.4; literal fool strangles the h. J2461.1.6; man transformed to h. D152.1; reincarnation as h. E613.3; soul as h. seen in dream E732.9.

Hawks. — Food of h. A2435.4.6, A2435.6.6; why h. put heads of mice, etc. on pile of stones A2452.3; what h. are looking for A2471.7.

Hawthorn protects against witches G272.3; protects travelers D1385.23. — Fairies dance under h. trees F261.3.1.1; magic h. D950.13.

Hay fills empty lake with water D1549.3.6; transformed to horse D441.9.1; wagon and the gate J1411. — Bear on h. wagon thought to be the preacher J1762.2; coachman makes horses run by binding bundle of h. to shaft J1671; fairies dance in h. F261.3.5; fool sticks needle in h. wagon J2129.4; "painting" on the h.-cock K1013.2; selling h. which is not his K282.1; wisp of h. transformed (to bridge) D451.5.7, (to horse) D441.9.1.

Haymakers. — Fairies give h. dinner F343.17.

Hayrick. — Man and bear in h. B855.

Haystack asked to wipe dirty shoe Z41.7.1. — Drunkards war on h.
X818; man throws carriage, horses, driver on h. F624.3.1.
Hazel rod kills snake D1402.10.2; — Ash becomes h. D451.1.1; goat who
wouldn't leave h. bush Z39.1.1; magic h. D950.1.
Hazelcock's body made smaller *A2302.2.
Hazelnuts. — Magic h. D985.3; quest for the h. of ay, ay, ay H1377.3.
Head buried one place, body another V61.4; of corpse thrown on water
to prevent return E431.9.1; cut off (to cure snakebite) X372.2, (and
hung on tree) Q421.1.1, (and successfully replaced) E783.1, (by unseen
sword in forest) F812.5; of decapitated person replaced backwards E12.2;
falls off for lying to saint Q551.8.5; of giant F531.1.2ff.; is king of the
body J1289.19; of murdered child becomes sun A1277.3; of murdered
man displayed before his own house S139.2.1; retains life after being cut
off *E783; separated from body to prevent return E431.7.2.1; shattered
for breaking tabu C948.8; of slain man must not be moved C541.2; split
as punishment Q451.13; taken off, other punishments not necessary
J1293.2; transferred from one man to another *D711.1.1; used as ball
S139.2.2.4.1; wagered N2.3.1; of beheaded witch mends if rubbed with
salt G223. — Abbess puts priest's trousers on her h. K1273; amputated
h. asks for drink E541.4.1; animal frightened by his own reflected h.
K1715.1.1; animal with h. of bone B15.1.3; animal with one h., two
bodies, six legs B15.7.11; animal unusual as to his h. B15.1; why some
animals continually shake h. A2474; apple shot from man's h. F661.3;
bad women because of h. exchanged with devil A1371.1; beautification
by decapitation and replacement of h. *D1865.1; beast with human h.
and shape of smith's bellows B92: beheaded man's h. laid at feet to
prevent return E431.7; beheaded simpleton's h. replaced backwards
(thus learns fear of death) J27; bird with golden h. B101.1; bird flies
on h. of dupe's child K946; birth from person's h. T541.4; blindness
cured by striking h. on tree F952.4; bringing enemy's h. as task H335.4.1;
calf's h. transformed to death's h. D457.3; calf's h. in murderer's hand
turns to corpse's h. Q551.3.3; chaste woman has conqueror cut off her
h. T325.1; cuckold's knife cannot carve boar's h. H425.1; curse: h. to
split in seven M431.9; cut-off h. prophesies D1311.8.2; cutting off h.
at girl's desire H333.1; deity with animal's h. A131.3ff.; demon with
pointed h. G342; devil in dragon's h. on a shield G303.8.10; devil's
h. G303.4.1ff.; disenchantment by decapitation and replacement of h.
D711.1; dog with human h. E423.1.1.2.2; dwarf has small body and large
h. F451.2.1.3; fairies with gold crowns on h. F236.4; false dragon-h.
proof H105.1.1; fate written on h. M302.2.1; fountain where saint's h.
cut off D925.1.2; getting calf's h. out of pot J2113; ghost carries h.
under arm E422.1.1.4; ghost as h. E422.1.11.2; ghost's h. downward unless summoned by king E389.1; ghost's flying h. attacks slayer E261.1.1;
gigantic h. F531.1.2.0.1; giant thinks hammer-blow on h. is nut falling
F531.5.4; god with cat's h. A131.3.1; god monstrous as to h. A123.4ff.;

goddess standing on h. supports earth A842.1; hero cuts off h. so won't
be tempted by virgins T333.5; hero with deformed h. L112.3.1; hero's
breath returns h. to headless horseman D1518.3; how many hairs are in
the h.? H703; hanging for a thousand years h. downward over a fire
of chaff Q522.6; having h. dressed before hanging J2174.3; horse's h.
for extraordinary use F874; horse's magic h. D1380.3.1; human h. as
weapon F839.4; indentions on rocks from h. of infant hero A972.5.1;
"keep h. dry" J21.29; killing with enemy's h. D1402.23; lizard loses
lawsuit: must bob his h. A2255.2; lover's h. put before adulteress at
meals Q478.1.4; magic animal h. *D1011ff.; magic h. *D992, (of saint
heals diseases) D1500.1.7.1.1; magic power of seeing Death at h. or
foot of bed D1825.3.1; magic stone in animal's h. B722; man with
bird's h. B55; man carries his h. under his arm F511.0.4; man cuts off
own h. and eats it (lie) X1726.1; man with dog's h. B25.1; man without
confessor like body without h. V20.1.1; man with deformed h. slays barbers K974; man so small he can put his h. through a mote in a sunbeam F535.2.4; man wagers he can run with his h. off J322.1; man's lip
makes hood over h. F544.1.2; mole struck on h. as he steals fire: hence
flat head A2213.5.1; monster's h. proves slaying H105.4; monster's returning h. G635.1; murder by crushing h. S116.4; murder by driving nail
through h. S115.2.1; murdered man's h. causes calamity D1549.7;
"never show your h. again": pot on head J2489.13; new race from
stones (seeds) thrown over h. after deluge A1245.1, A1254.1; numskull
gets h. caught J2131.5ff.; nut hits cock in h.: he thinks world is
coming to an end (cumulative tale) Z43.3; oath taken on boy's h.
H252.4; ogre monstrous as to h. G361ff.; ogre's h. cut off, hung above
gate G512.1.2.1; old woman supports earth on her h. A842.2; oracular
artificial h. *D1311.7.1; origin of animal's h. A2320ff.; otherworld h.
emits stream F162.5.2; person consisting only of h. F501; person given
animal h. D682.1; person unusual as to his h. F511ff.; person with
(more than one h.) F511.0.2, (one eye in back of h.) F512.1.3;
(wings on h.) F522.1; pestilence in form of h. F493.0.3.1; pieces of
shattered god's h. are hills A962.8; price set on one's h. M208; prophecy:
death by horse's h. M341.2.5; proud milkmaid tosses her h. and spills
milk J2061.2; punishment for splitting h. and eating man's brains
Q211.7; pursuit by rolling h. R261.1; "put it on my h." woman smothered
J2465.7; putting h. under saint's cloak reveals reward in heaven
D1329.1; question: did the man ever have a h. J2381; quest for Gorgon's
h. H1332.3; reincarnation of h. as hill E649.1; resuscitation with misplaced h. *E34; revenant with half a h. E261.1.3; river flows from
man's h. F715.1.4; ruler reproaches son for bringing enemy's h. W11.5.6;
saint's severed h. speaks V229.22; scythe cuts man's h. off J2422; self-
rolling h. D1641.7.1; self-returning h. *D1602.12, (of dragon) *B11.5.5;
separable soul in hydra's h. E715.6; serpent with jewel in h. B101.7;
seven tongues in a h. (riddle) H793; seven-headed witch defeated by

throwing egg at each h. G275.4; severed h. bites earth F1096.3; severed
h. cannot be moved from helmet D1654.14; severed h. gives away thief
J1149.8; severed h. of impious man in well causes water to become bitter
part of each day F933.4; severed h. moves from place to place D1641.7;
severed h. proves killing H106.2; severed h. regrows E783.2; sight of wild
hunt causes swelling of h. E501.18.8; slain enemy's h. must not enter
village C845.1; snake and turtle exchange h. for fangs A2247.2; soul in h.
E714.3; severed h. reddens and whitens E783.3; speaking h. *D1610.5;
spirit in form of horrible h. F401.5.1; spirit with half h. F401.4.1; singing
h. D1615.7; standing on h. G269.26; as many stars in heaven as hairs in h.
H702.2; stingy dead woman raises her h. W152.3; striking off donkey's h.
to punish it J2113.1; substituted h. as execution proof K512.2.3.1; thief
has his companion cut off his h. so that he may escape detection K407.1;
touching chief's h. tabu C564.7; transformation by placing something on
h. D596; transformation by sticking magic pin into h. D582; treasure from
girl's h. D1454.8; visit to lower world h. first F109.1; walking on h. in
otherworld F167.4; water falling on h. death omen J2311.1.3; weapon in
h. causes sickness D2064.7; why babies have soft spots in h. A2875;
why bird's h. is large A2320.5; why crab has no h. A2320.4; why
mudhen's h. red A2320.3.1; why palm-rat has swollen h. A2320.7; why
weaver bird's h. is small A2320.1.1; wife brings paramour husband's h.
K2213.3.2.1; witch extraordinary as to h. G215.

Heads brandished to intimidate foe S139.2.2.1.6; placed on stakes for
failure in performance of task H901.1, Q421.1; of slain advise hero
E545.21; of slain enemies displayed P555.2.1.1; of slain piled up after
battle P555.2.1; of thieves in casks cut off K312; of various people
A1663. — Bridal couple's h. knocked together as they look in mirror
T135.13; bringing animal h. H1154.0.1; child born with two h. T551.2;
cult of h. V1.10.2; dead h. necessary to drinking C281; dwarfs with
red h. and red caps F451.2.7.1; extraordinary h. act as living F1001;
fatal game: putting h. in notches K865; fish with silver and gold h.
B101.6; foreigners' h. exchanged with devils' A1610.1.1; giant's two h.
H1174.1; goat's h. mistaken for human J1762.9; god with many h.
A123.4.1; helpful vital h. N819.3; hero's dogs (horse) prevent dragon's
h. from rejoining body B11.11.2; human h. in ogre's house smile, weep
G461.1; indignities to h. of slain enemies S139.2.2.1; journey to Land
of Men of H. only F129.1; monster with human h. on horns G361.1.1.1;
mother cuts off h. of well to cure sick H583.4.3; origin of bald h.
A1315.2; people in otherworld stand on their h. and pound yams with
their h. F167.4; saint's bachall brings down mountain on h. of enemies
D1549.4; severed h. of monster become birds E613.0.5; spirits without h.
(or with h. under arms) F401.4; three h. of hair F555.5.1; trees with
fruits like human h. F811.8; trees from lovers' graves resemble their
h. E631.0.1.1; tree in hell made of living h. of the dead A671.2.3; troll

with many h. *G304.1.3; wild huntsmen with h. on backward E501.7.3;
women adorning h. immoral below K2051.4.

Headache cure: removing eyes K1011.1; from dwarfs' cursing M424. —
Bride pleads h.: groom retaliates with same plea later K2052.3; magic
object cures h. D1502.1.

Headaches cured by Virgin Mary D2161.5.2.6.

Headdress. — Magic h. bears person aloft D1532.8.

Headdresses. — Live h. F827.1.

Headless animals *B15.1.1; body retains life E783.6; dog B15.1.1.1,
E423.1.1.2.1, (ghostly) E521.2.2, E521.5.0.1; giant F531.1.2.1; horseman's
head returned D1518.3; king, tailless tiger friends J876; ogre G361.3;
person *F511.0.1; revenant *E422.1.1. — Devil in coach drawn by h.
horses G303.7.3.3; fairy as h. woman F234.2.3; ghost as h. horse
E423.1.3.3; magic identity of h. body D1819.3; witch in form of h.
horse G211.1.1.1.

Headman. — Bonga made village h. F347.1.

Headwear, magic D1067ff.

Healed with his own medicine J1513. — Death respite until prisoner h.
K551.15; dragon dips wounds in holy well, is h. B11.12.1.2; happy
otherworld where dead are h. *E481.4.1; diseases h. by magic object
D1500.1; saint miraculously h. V221.0.2; wounded soldiers h. by druid
P427.5.1.

Healer. — Animal as h. B511; queen promises self to h. H346.1; woman
fake h. marries then murders king K959.2.4.

Healer's payment: satisfaction at recovery K233.6. — Herbs grow from
h. grave E631.3.

Healing, see also **Cure;** by animals B510ff.; by dwarfs F451.5.1.10; by
fairies F344; pigskin B184.3.2.3; as reward Q161; sick as task H1199.2.
— Accidental h. N640ff.; angel of h. A454.0.1; curse against wound's
h. M431.5; every sick man practices h. H659.6.1; fairy grateful to mortal
for h. F334; foolish imitation of h. J2412; giant has wound-h. balm
F531.6.5.3; god of h. A454; husband attracted by wife's power of h.
H151.8; life bought with promise of h. M234.4; magic h. grass
D1500.1.4.1; magic h. power *D2161ff.; miraculous h. from passionate
love T25; miraculous h. by saints *V221ff.; magic h. apples H1151.20;
magic h. water H1151.21; man blinded in h. attempt N395; miraculous
h. by Virgin V256; princess given to man for h. her H346; pseudo-
magic h. objects sold K115; quest for h. (apple) H1333.3.1.5, (draught)
H1324.2, (lantern) H1324.1, (water) H1321.2; saint h. enemy V441.1;
sun's h. power A738.3.

Health disputes with Fortune, Intellect, Knowledge which is greatest
J461.1.2; the most beloved H647.2; as most precious choice J232; as
reward for drink Q145.1.1; test H1582. — Fast improves h. V73.2;
magic object gives h. D1342ff.; transformation in h. D53; well-preserved
brother gives h. secret H596.1.1.

24*

Healthful. — Lies about h. atmosphere X1663.1.

Heard. — Dwarfs emigrate invisible but h. F451.9.6; soul striving to be h. E759.1.

Hearers aided by magic music D1359.3.1.1.

Hearing, see also **Overhearing;** bird cry good omen D1812.5.2.5; thunder on setting forth a good omen D1812.5.2.3. — Animal's h. A2428; contest in h. *K86; dead h. saint's bell E545.14; dragon h. child's cry B11.12.6; girl's heart breaks on h. lover kiss another F1041.1.1.2; headless persons without h. F511.0.1.2; insanity from h. strange sound D2065.2.1; magic h. D1827.1ff.; magic object affects h. D1332; not h. questions one doesn't wish to answer X441.1; person of remarkable h. F641ff.; magic object restores h. D1506; magic power of h. D1922; marvelous sensitiveness: fracture from h. man chopping wood F647.8.1; tabu: h. or listening C885.

Heart cremated to lay ghost E441.3; cut free, moves about in chest F1096.1; of dragon B11.2.9; of enemy eaten produces magic strength D1335.1.2; and liver of murderer torn out Q469.6; of man is deepest H643.1; might not stand winning mistress J2572; removed by magic D2062.1; successfully replaced E786; of unborn child renders person invisible D1361.8. — Adulteress caused unwittingly to eat lover's h. Q478.1; animal dies of broken h. F981.6; animal h. transformed D457.15; conception from eating woman's h. T511.6.1; compassionate executioner: substituted h. K512.2; death from broken h. F1041.1.1; disease to be cured by h. of monkey K961.1; disenchantment by eating enchanter's h. D763.1; doctor cures h. palpitation: stops breathing X372.1; eaten h. gives one the owner's qualities *E714.4.1; fairy replaces man's h. with h. of straw F281; giant with stone h. F531.1.6.10.1; girl's h. magically removed and fed to man draws her to him D1905.1; hardness of h. W155ff.; hound killed by tearing out its h. B17.1.2.2; impossible to burn witch's h. G275.3.2; iron bands around h. to keep it from breaking F875; key to house concealed in man's h. F1034.5.1; lamb (ass) without a h. K402, K402.3; magic bird h. *D1015.1.1, (eaten) D859.4.1; magic h. of animal *D1015.1ff.; magic human h. D997.1; magic object in whale's h. D849.5.1; man forced to eat dead father's h. goes mad G91.1; man vomits h. as punishment Q552.21; martyr with sign of cross on his h. V86.2; miser's h. found in his strong-box W153.1; monkey's h. left at home K544; monster's h. torn out F628.1.0.1; murder by hot iron through h. S112.2.1; murder by tearing out h. S139.6; parent's h. is hardest H637.1; person lives on after having h. cut free F1096.1; procuring dead husband's h. F81.1.1; pulling animal's h. out through log K952.3; remarkable h. F559.7; soul (life) in h. E714.4; spirit in h. F408.2; tabu to eat animal's h. C221.3.5; witch eats person's h. G262.2; with his whole h.: devil carries off judge M215; woman dies of broken h. after rivals kill each other T86.1.

Heart's ashes cast into river F932.7.1.

Hearts. — Ogre eats men's h. G312.6; person forced to eat relatives' h. S183.1; person of remarkable sight can see through h. of trees F642.3.1; eating of human h. as cure for insomnia D2161.4.13; power of flying from eating children's h. D2135.1.

Heartbeat. — Guilt detected by h. J1142.2.1.

Hearth abode of unpromising hero (heroine) L131; cleaned by angel D1683, V232.9; -god A411.4; extraordinary h. F893; familiar on magician's h. G225.0.5.1; fire issues from h. as man approaches H175.4; magic h. D1147; needle under h. causes death D2061.2.2.8.1; origin of domestic h. A1455.1; tabu to eat from cooking h. C219.4; water-spirits' h. of human skulls F420.2.5.

Hearths. — Stars as fires in ghosts' h. A761.4.

Hearthstones. — Bridal couple touch h. T137.2.1.

Heartlessness, see **Hardness of heart.**

Heartsease. — Why h. has red stripes A2772.3.

Heartsickness, magic D2064.0.2.

Heat and fury spread pestilence F493.4; prevents church theft D1389.2.1; produced by magic D2144.3; of saint's anger starts fire F1041.16.4; from stove without fire J1976; test H1511. — Alternate h., cold in hell A671.3.2; body with marvelous h. F686; burrowing swine h. ground B19.4.1; conception from h. of fire T535.1; contest in enduring h. H1542; contest of h. and cold D2144.2; excessive h. of otherworld beings F167.16; extraordinary body h. F593.1; god bores hole in hell to h. earth A141.3; goddess from earth's h. A119.2; holding in the h. J1942; magic cake protects from h. D1382.3; magic control of cold and h. D2144; magic h. melts enemies D2091.10; man created from h. A1262.1; person melts away from h. F1041.4; punishments by h. in hell Q566; returning from hell with h. F101.8; sun's h. dries out earth A733.5; sun's great h. A720.2; variations in sun's seasonal h. A739.4.

Heated. — Room h. by crowded corpses F686.2; souls of drowned in h. kettles in hell *E755.2.1.

Heath. — Dwarfs warm h. by underground fire F451.5.1.15.

Heathcock prefers home with hardships to travel in foreign lands J215.3. — Wedding of h. B282.15; witch as h. G211.4.3.

Heathen beats his god because of misfortune V381; city F767.1; to desert spot where saint lost tooth M364.5; king sets test for saint H527; prophesy coming of saint M364.7.2; swallowed by earth H1573.1.1. — Baptism of h. V332; conversion to Christianity because h. gods less powerful V331.1.3; covenant between h. and Israelites M201.0.2; devils dwell in h. idols G303.8.14; ground swallows h. idols F948.1; mother sells her child to h. sailors S328; punishment for taking h. wives Q243.4.

Heaven, see also **Otherworld, Paradise;** *A661; assured by burial in certain ground E754.3; connected to earth by navel string A625.2.1; and earth from egg A641.1; and earth touch each other A657.2; entered by a trick K2371.1; as God's throne A133.2.2; mother and earth father A625.1.

— Admission to h. as reward Q172; angels of death cannot bring soul to h. E754.2.2.1; animals understand language of h. B212.0.1; arrow shot to h. returns bloody F1066; banishment from h. for breaking tabu C955; bolt from h. kills animal F981.4; burning pillar reaching h. F774.2; chairs in h. H619.1; chariot from h. takes couple to sky A761.2; choice between life or h. V311.3; Christ's ascent to h. V211.9; creation of h. A610.2; cynic discusses h. J1442.8; dead and living go together to gate of h. E754.2.3; dead try to carry kettle from hell to h. A1433.0.1; deity ruler of lowest h. A307; demigods descend from h. A513.1; devil misportrays h. G303.9.7.4; devil teaches way to h. G303.9.4.6.1; devil's expulsion from h. G303.8ff.; distance from earth to h. H682.1; drinking as road to h. J1314; drunk woman thinks she's in h. X816; drunken man made to believe that he has been to h. and hell J2322; everyone buried in saint's soil to go to h. M364.11; eyes which can see h. D1820.3; fairy teaches way to h. F251.9; fairies depart to h. F388.1; fairies not good enough for h. F251.11; fairies in h. F215.1.1; fire carried from h. A1415.1.1; fire from h. F962.2, (as punishment) Q552.13; footstool thrown from h. F1037.1; gate as high as h. and huge as a mountain F776.1; gifts fallen from h. F962.0.1; ghost lives midway between h. and earth E481.5; giant with upper lip reaching h. F531.1.4.1; girls dancing in h. A661.4; giving money for those in h. J2326.1; god ascends to h. A171.0.2; god of h. A211; going to h. by holding divine elephant's tail J2133.5.2; hand from h. F1036; Hebrew as language of h. A1482.1; hero ascending to h. A566.2; heron wants no h. without snails U125.1; holy object falls from h. F962.12; how the Jews were drawn from h. X611; husband pursues fairy to h. F300.2; journey to h. *F11; journey to upper world by keeping thoughts continually on h. *F64; knight won't go to h. unless dogs there U134; land thrown down from h. A953; light as souls in h. A1412.2; lost soul given sight of h. E752.6; magic object assures going to h. D1588; magic object falls from h. D811.2; man admitted into h. but must not find fault *F13; man admitted to neither h. nor hell (becomes snipe) A1942.1, *Q565.1; man ejected from h. for folly of marrying twice T251.0.1; miser wants to enter h. with clothes on: gold sewn in W153.15; nine days' fall from h. to earth A658.1; nine nights' riding from h. to hell A658.1.1; object thrown from h. F1037; ocean the son of Earth and H. A921; peace in h. is sweetest H633.2; power of seeing whether dead go to h. or hell B161.4; priest may eat communion supper in h. J1261.2.3; promise of h. entices victim into box K714.2.1; provisions provided by messenger from h. D2105.2; quest for crown from h. H1261; rejoicing at arrival of rich man in h. E758; renouncing h. because companions not there V326; resurrected boys choose to return to h. E755.0.1; rewards in h. Q172.0.2; road to h. *F57; saint promises return from h. V229.2.13; saved soul goes to h. E754.2ff.; self-righteous tailor in h. expelled L435.3; sinner wanders between h. and earth E411.0.4; soul bound for hell given sight of h. E752.6; soul cannot enter h. till body buried E750.0.1; soul leaves body to visit h. E721.7; souls carried to h. by doves E754.2.1; souls in h. *E755.1; storms in sixth h. A1130.2; thief tells pursuer that thief has gone to h. by way of a tree K341.9; threshing in h. H84.3; tree to h. A652.1; Two Sorrows of H. D1856.1.1; unchristened cannot enter h. E412.2.1; vision of chairs in h. V515.1.1; visions of h. V511.1; voice from h. testifies for accused H216.2; voices from h. F966; waters of h. prevented from engulfing earth A810.2.1; wife in h. by day, with husband by night E322.3; wife undertakes man's penances: also to go to h. for him? M292; wisdom from fool: h. refused J156.4.

Heavens A700—A799; break up at end of world A150ff. — Animals in h. B7; deity departs for h. A192.2.1; fairy music like that in h. F262.4; flood from deity stamping on h. A1015.3; highest world has twenty h. A651.1.0.1; magic arrow shakes h. D1549.1; man's voice shakes h. F688.1; seven h. A651.1.4; singing h. D1615.9; how many stars in the h.? H702ff.; stars as decoration for h. A763.2.

"Heaven key," origin of A2622, A2652.

Heavenly Academy F177; body as magic object D1291; books F883.1.6; help in battle D2163.2.1; hierarchy E755.1.1; lights A790ff.; maiden's magic power D1726.1; maidens not jealous T257.0.1; messenger brings food D2105.2; music caused by column under Lord's chair A661.0.2.1; voices proclaim hero's birth M311.0.4. — Ability to see h. beings D1825.3.4; artificial h. bodies F793; extraordinary behavior of h. bodies F961; looking at h. body tabu C315.2ff.; magic control of h. bodies D2149.6; magic object controls h. bodies D1546; riddles of h. distance H682ff.; skies reveal h. company F969.1; soul in form of h. body E741; worship of h. bodies V1.4.

Heavier. — Devil becomes h. G303.3.5.3.

Heaviest. — What is the h.? H645.

Heavy animal B870.1. — Giantess so h. boat sinks F531.2.13; object magically becomes h. D1687, *D2035; oath so h. it dries up stream M115.1.1; remarkably h. club F835.2.1; riddle: how h. is the earth? H691.2; sword so h. that hero must take drink of strength before swinging it F833.1.

Hebrew as language (of angels) V249.2.1, (of heaven) A1482.1. — Host wants to learn H. even at risk of forgetting his own language J344.2.

Hebrews. — Wisdom from H. J192.4.

Hebrides as otherworld F134.1.

Hecate as leader of wild hunt E501.1.8.3.

Hedge to catch sheep's wool J2060.2; to keep in moonlight J1796.1; protects person in magic sleep D1967.1. — Besieger scatters beads in protecting h. K2367; druid's h. prevents attack D1381.1; father puts h. around field H583.2.3; jumping over h. as suitor test H331.1.3.1; magic h. D945.

Hedgehog builds castle B191.5; and crab jump from boat after turtle

J2133.11; forces snake to suck out poison from raja B511.1.3; jumps into tiger's mouth L315.13. — Hans my H. C758.1; helpful h. B449.1; man-h. B29.8; marriage to person in h. form B641.5; revenant as h. E423.2.4; weaver prefers master with one h. J229.8.1; why h. draws himself up A2479.4; witch as h. G211.2.9.

Hedgehog's cry A2426.1.4; skin reward for good deed A2220.1, A2311.4.

Heeding not the past J311; persuasive person or thing forbidden *C810ff.

Heel. — Achilles' h. Z311; boring hole in h. as punishment Q451.2.0.2; cutting off h.-bone S162.4; girl hacks off her h. to get shoe on J2131.3.1.

Heels. — Devil has no h. G303.4.5.7; giant with h. in front F531.1.3.2.

He-goat, see also **Goat.** — Devil speaks with voice of h. G303.4.7; man transformed to h. D134.1; why h. has shaggy legs A2371.2.8.

He-goats. — Devil drives six h. G303.7.7.

Heidrun A661.1.0.2, B19.7.

Heifer as sacrifice V12.4.4.1.1.

Heifers impregnated by supernatural bull T539.4.

Height. — Bat rescues man from h. B542.1.2; curse given from a h. M413.1; ghost's strength waxes and wanes with h. of fire *D1836.1; insanity of princess dependent on h. of fire D2065.4; magic staves scale precipitous h. D1539.3.

Heightening. — Magic h. of mountain D2152.4.

Heimkehrsage N681.

Heir, see also **Inheritance;** to king finding bow, arrow D1812.5.2.9; of Linne J21.15, J1853.1.1. — Bargain with devil for h. M219.1; deceptive report of birth of h. K1847.1.1; first man to arrive after king's death to be h. P17.1; false h. K1923; impostor poses as h. K1938; marriage for a night to insure h. T156.1; miser appoints self his own h. W153.8; pretending to be corpse's h. K451.5; prophecy: birth of h. M369.7.2; tasks to determine king's h. H921.1; test to determine h. H1581; young h. too frank in celebrating his father's death J2358.

Heirs. — Magic object acquired by acting as umpire for fighting h. *D832; murderer punished: male h. die Q211.9.1; quarreling h. destroy entire property J2129.2.

Held, see also **Holding.** — Molten coin h. in devil's mouth G303.4.8.2; mountain h. up by strong man F623; person h. fast by magic object D1411, D1413ff.; ship h. back by strong man F637.

Hell, see also **Lower World, Underworld;** *A671ff.; -hounds accompany soul to lower world E752.5; as a monastery V118.0.1. — Account of punishments prepared in h. brings about repentance J172; artificial paradise and h. to punish and reward F705; beggar frightens lawyer into giving by telling him of all the lawyers in h. X312; broad path to h. F95.2; Christ's descent to h. V211.7; contacts on journey to h. tabu C542.1; creation of h. A610.2; dead try to carry kettle from h. to heaven A1433.0.1; death on beholding h. F1041.1.8; demons plaguing souls in h. E752.1.2.1; descent to h. *F81; descent into h. to learn future M302.3; description of h. dissuades from suicide J628; devil abducts fiddler for h. G303.9.5.8; devil banished to h. A106.2.1; devil dies when he is fastened in door of h. by his beard G303.17.3.2; devil in h. G303.8.3; devil paints h. in glowing terms G303.9.7.4; devil retreats into h. amid thunder and lightning G303.17.2.5; devil's chair in h. made from thrown-away nail pairings G303.25.5; dragons live in h. B11.3.6; dream of all parsons in h. X438; drunken man made to believe that he has been to heaven and h. J2322; dwarf conducts shepherd to h. to collect debt from nobleman F451.5.1.14; eating in h. forbidden C211.2.2; fairies not bad enough for h. F251.11; fiddler in h. breaks strings, must return to earth for repair K606.1.3; god bores hole in h. to heat earth A141.3; hot weather from hole bored in h. A1137; husband chooses to go to h. rather than join shrewish wife in heaven T251.1.2.1; icy h. E481.7, E755.2.5; Jews drawn from heaven by clothes auction in h. X611; journeying to h. for receipt from judge J1289.11; lawyers punished in h. P422.1; looking into the pots in h. forbidden *C325; magic learned in h. D1721.1.1; man admitted to neither heaven nor h. A1942.1, *Q565; man in cold consoles himself thinking of rich men in h. J883.2; man in h. bargains about shrewish wife T251.1.2.2; masses release souls from h. V42; why no millers in h. X213; nine nights' riding from heaven to h. A658.1.1; parents descend to h. instead of sons P241; person from h. stresses religion's importance E367.1; power of seeing whether dead go to heaven or h. B161.4; punishments in h. *Q560ff.; quest to h. H1270ff., (for magic objects) D859.2; relieving souls in h. forbidden C741; release from h. as reward Q174; respite from h. Q560.2; saint's bachall overcomes beast in h. D1400.1.12.1; Satan created from h. fire G303.1.3.5; Satan punished in h. G303.17.3.5; smith punished in h. P447.4; soul leaves body to visit h. E721.7; souls in h. *E755.2ff.; spirit in h. must bathe people endlessly Q501.9; tailor punished in h. P441.3; threat to build a church in h. K1781; three things lead to h. Z71.1.4; twilight reflects fires of h. A1179.1.1; usurer punished in h. Q273.1; visions of h. V511.2; why no weavers in h. X251.1; witches punished in h. G275.11; woman satirists punished in h. M402.1.1.

Hells. — Series of h. E755.2.8.

Helldiver. — Why h. has flat stern A2356.2.10.

Hellebore, origin of A2662.

Helmet left for woman to quarrel with J552.4; shrieks D1610.24.2. — Bowl mistaken for h. J1772.5; child born wearing h. T552.5.1; magic h. D838.8, *D1101.4, (prevents baldness) D1389.8, (unpierceable) D1381.10.3; severed head cannot be moved from h. D1654.14.

Help in performing tasks H970ff.; in suitor tests F601.2; in wooing T66. — Animals h. man in contest K2; call for h. repeated as song J2417.1; child promised to devil for h. on road with broken wagon S225; devil's h. to man with robberies M212; devil called on for h. but man excuses himself C12.1; dwarfs seek human h. F451.5.23; girl makes toilet and calls h. K551.5; luring victim by feigning need of h. K833; magic h. from falling D2166; man called for h. by animal B383; master's h. in theft J2136.5.6.1; person being robbed calls h. K432; plant blessed for h. at Jesus' birth A2711.1; refusal to accept h. until stories told P331; refusing h. to woman tabu C686.1; revealing animal's h. tabu C427; spirits' h. to mortal F403.2; spying on secret h. of angels forbidden C51.4.2; stealing from ogre a h. to friendly king G610.2; wise and foolish wish: h. in whatever one is doing J2073.1.1.

Helped. — Elder brother h. by youngest L31; man h. by animal to wealth and greatness *B580ff.; mother h. by monster child T550.1; mortal h. with labor by fairy F346; pretty sister h. by ugly L145.1; suitor h. with tasks by bride H335.0.1.

Helper in hiding treasure killed N595; steals object of quest K2036; summoned by calling his name D2074.2.4.3. — Angel as h. in battle V232; devil as h. *G303.22ff., (of robber refuses to let women's ornaments be stolen) M212.1; eating animal h. forbidden C221.2.1; foster father as h. P271.5; foster mother as h. P272.2; giant becomes victor's h. G510.3; looking at old woman h. as she eats forbidden C312.2.2; magic h. brings girl to hero's bed K1336; magic object summons h. D1421ff.; mother's brother as h. P293.2; ogre's relative as h. G530ff.; spirit in bottle as h. F403.2.2.4; sympathetic h. robbed K345; trickster poses as h. and eats woman's stored provisions K1983; wild man released from captivity as h. of hero G671; witch as h. G284.

Helpers *N800—N899; on quest H1233. — Deceptive eating (drinking) contest: relative h. K81.2, K82.2; demon's h. G302.8; race won by deception: relative h. *K11.1; succession of h. on quest H1235.

Helpful animal aids fugitives R243; animals B300—B349, K2; animals lost in wager N2.4; deeds of brownie F482.5.4; dwarfs F451.5.1; mountain-men F460.4.2ff.; underground spirit F450.1. — Attention drawn by h. animal's theft of food from wedding table: recognition follows H151.2; grains sorted by h. ants H1091.1; kinds of h. animals B400—B499; magic object found on grave of slain h. animal D842.3; magic strength from h. animal D1834; rescue from ogre by h. animals G552; services of h. animals B500—B599; stolen magic object stolen back by h. cat and dog *D882.1.1; tasks performed by h. forest spirits H973; transformation to act as h. animal D659.4; transformation by h. animals D684; treasure found in slain h. animal B100.1; witch overcome by h. dogs of hero G275.2.

Helpfulness. — Animal characteristics reward for h. A2223.

Helping. — Brothers h. each other P251.5.1; god as human h. men E605.2; gods h. those who help themselves J1034; mortals h. fairies F394; thieves not h. each other J2136.5.8; trolls h. men F455.6.8.

Helpless. — Why children are h. for so long A1361; magic object renders person h. *D1410ff.; person or thing rendered h. D2072ff.; thief rendered h. by magic *K422.

Helplessness. — Victim enticed into voluntary captivity or h. K710ff.

Hemp. — Fairies turn h. into horses F241.1.7; magic h.-seed *D971.2; origin of h. A2684.2; swallow and h.-seed J621.1.

Hen, see also **Chicken;** complains that man eats her, but she eats ant U21.1; hitched to wagon B558.3; lays egg, mouse breaks it, etc. Z39.5; put in witch's hair to scratch while maid escapes G276.1. — Automatic h. and chickens of gold D1620.2.2; capon and h. J1269.6; cat offers to act as doctor for cock and h. K2061.7; cock and h. build pyre B599.1; cumulative tale (master to kill h.) Z32.4, (death of the little h.) Z32.2; dwarf with body like tailless h. F451.2.1.2; enemies of h. A2494.13.10, A2494.5.1, A2494.13.10.1; fox feigning illness admitted to h.-roost and kills hens K828.2; fox had rather meet one h. than fifty women J488; friendship of h. (and sparrow) A2493.34.1, (and duck) A2493.34; funeral procession of h. (cumulative tale) Z32.1; man honored above God: the dead h. J2215.3; long nose used as h. roost F543.1.2; numskull tries to wash black h. white J1909.6; overfed h. stops laying J1901.1; prayer over underdone h. J1342; prophetic h. B143.0.5; revenant as h. E423.3.6; soul in form of h. E732.3; swallow advises h. against hatching out serpent's eggs J622.1.1; treasure to be found by man who plows with cock and harrows with h. N543.2; wedding of cock and h. B282.21; why h. does not know how to steal A2455.4; why h. has no teeth A2345.8; why h. scratches in ground A2477.2; witch in form of h. G211.3.1.

Hens in mourning J1886. — Roast h. fly, heads to sky, tails to ground (lie) X1208.2.

Heptads P541.1.

Herald for chief's troop tabu C564.2.

Heralding. — Animal punished for not h. dawn A2236.5.

Herb, see also **Plant;** bath produces love D1355.17. — Magic h. *D965, (renders invisible) D1361.11, (saves girl from devil) G303.12.5.6; man made from h. A1256; quest for extraordinary h. H1333.2.3.

Herbs in ears as protection D1385.2.1; grow from healer's grave E631.3; as perfume F817.3. — Charm renders medicinal h. efficacious D1577.1; dwarfs know h. F451.3.12.1; magic food from h. D1030.3; magic h. D978; power in words, h., and stones J1581.2; snake heals mutilated maiden with magic h. B511.1.2; tabu to eat forbidden h. C224.2.

Hercules B11.11; fights with Death and rescues Alcestis R185; spins for his beloved K1214. — Bow and arrow of H. D1400.1.4.5; pillars of H. A984.

Herd which came from heaven B19.6; of cattle put into magic cup D491.1.1; of cattle transformed to wolves D412.2.1. — Buffalo h. aids trickster's theft K335.0.13; capturing deer from h. watched by giant (task) H1154.2; keeping four dogs in a h. (task) H1112.1; magic circle keeps h. enclosed D1446.5; magic compensates for loss of h. D859.6;

recognition of own cow in h. of twenty thousand H163; redheaded, white-starred h. C316.1.

Herds of sea monsters G308.3. — Fairies have h. of deer F241.5; herdsman threatens invasion with enormous h. K1784; Huldra tending h. F460.2.11; mountain-men drive off man's h. F460.4.4.6; why certain animals go in h. A2492; witches drive h. of deer G249.1.

Herding rabbits (task) H1112; wild animals B845. — Giant with tree for h.-stick G152.1; household spirit h. sheep F488.1; mountain-men as h.-girls' lovers F460.4.1.1.

Herdsboy. — Devil makes h. a priest M216.2.

Herdsman disguises as abbot and answers questions H561.2; to learn art of love T4.1; neglects his she-goats in favor of wild-goats J345.1; rears abandoned child S351.2; rescues abandoned child R131.3; slaughters animals entrusted to him K346.2; threatens invasion with enormous herds K1784. — Animal as h. B576.3; ascetic becomes h. V462.11; disguise as h. K1816.6; fairy as h. F271.6; giant h. G152, F531.6.17.5; poem taught to h. E377.1; remarkable h. F679.1; treacherous h. K2255; woodpecker from devil's h. transformed A1957.1.

Herdsmen give quest directions H1232.1. — Wild hunt powerless against h. E501.17.1.1.

Here as center of the earth H681.3.2.

Heresy punished Q225.1.

Heretic becomes tongue-tied Q551.7.1.1; loses debate with Christian V351.1; worried to death by fly Q415.8. — Devil saves h. from fire G303.22.13; wise man beats h. in debate K3.4.

Heretics V320ff.; repulsed by saint's sword D1400.1.4.1.1. — Demons burn h. at stake Q414.0.8.1.

Heritage, see Inheritance.

Herla as wild huntsman E501.1.7.1.

Hermaphrodite F547.2.

Hermaphroditic creator A12.

Hermes distributes wit L301.

Hermit, see also Anchorite; P426.2; asks for and receives princess's hand V316.1; curses, men die M411.8.2; explains anger a sin J153.2; fasting to death for fame E754.4; as helper N843; kills his own father, supposing him to be the devil K943; leaving his cell to become robber falls and breaks his neck Q226.1; having rebuked youth falls himself when exposed to the same sin U231; rescues abandoned child R131.10; unsuccessfully tempted by prostitute T331; wins argument with unbeliever V351.2. — Angel ceases to appear to self-righteous h. Q553.2; angel takes h. with him and does many seemingly unjust things J225.0.1; boys rescued from beasts by h. R169.2; chain tale: h. must get cat, cow, etc. Z49.12; devil as h. G303.3.1.8.1; devils leave h. who turns other cheek when struck G303.16.15; disappointed lover turns h. T93.2; dragon guards food of h. B11.6.5; "holy" h. surprised in amorous intrigue K2064; hut of h. at border of otherworld F147.2; hyena leads h. from wilderness B380.1; magic power of h. *D1713; man becomes h. (after wife's death) T211.5, (when he realizes selfishness of his beloved's love) V472.1; nurse disguised as h. K1837.3; reward for austerities of h. Q34; saint as h. V226; self-righteous h. must do penance L435.1; three sins of the h. J485; woman disguised as h. R131.10.1.

Hero and Leander T83.

Hero A500—A599; abducted by loving witch R10.4; accidentally uses poisoned bath N332.1.1; assigns bride to another T141.3; born simultaneously with Christ T589.7.2; born by splitting mother's womb T584.7; buried as unknown in foreign country V69.2; catches hurled spear, kills serpent N654; contests with demons, using fighting animals B524.1.11; cursed to restlessness M455.1; eloping with king's fiancée treacherously slain K929.8; fights with fists alone J246.2; flies off on bird feathers B540.1; as giant's goatherd G462.1; goes north to fight trolls H945.2; granted wish to impregnate princess B375.1.1; as helper N838; kept from battle lest he be slain M341.2.18.1; killed fighting uncle P293.3; killed by ogre's medicines G347; kills hostile hound B17.1.2.2.1; kills ogress, wins her daughter G512.0.3; kills trouble-making strong men G512.0.1; kills witch G275.8; learns name only at first adventure J1730.1, T617.2; leaves bedmate treasure keys for son T645.4; licked by deer mother B635.3.1; locked up while father murdered R54; makes sun and moon from tree A717; as monster L112.1; not to swim in lake C615.2; overcomes devastating animal G510.4; overcomes giant lion B16.2.3; overcomes giant wolf B16.2.4; overcomes otherworld ruler F176; with rakshasi blood defeats rakshasa G369.1.2; rebuked by father P233.2; refuses to slay charioteers, women, or physicians W11.5.12; rescued by friend R169.5; rescued by his lady R161.0.1; rescues children from giant G551.3.1; requested to exhibit figure T55.6.1; returning from quest sent upon another T1241.1; searches for queen leaving message H1229.2; seeks his equal H1381.5; spared for his beauty F1088.1; spits twice at wife in recognition H186; substitutes false bride for father, then kills father K1094.1; takes fairy's wife F302.4.3; undertakes quest for vengeance H1228; unharmed by coiling serpent F1088.2; wins demon contest, disenchanted D785.1. — Abandoned daughter's son becomes h. S371; curse: h. not to stand sight of blood M438.2; destined h. N552.1, Z254; disagreeable tasks set h. H931.2; dragon saves h., rescues him from prison B11.6.1.2; eagle carries h. to safety D659.4.3; fairy rescues h. from battle F302.9; falsely accused h. sent on dangerous mission K2102; fly helps h. select weapons D659.14; gods prophesy about h. M301.16; gravel rises as h. enters lake F934.1; historic or romantic h. as leader of wild hunt E501.1.7; hospitality keeps h. away too long, wife abducted N391.0.1; lie: h. responsible for topography X958; lowly h. marries princess L101; magic animal used by h. in contest B195; magic helps h. win princess D1426.0.1; magic

wind transports h. D1524.9; mare brings h. back from land of no return
F129.5.1; not laughing until h. arrives M151.7; primeval h. moves islands
into their present position A955.3.2.1; prophecy: h. will be invincible
M312.9; prophecy: h. to die early if wins fame M365.1; princess married
to lowly h. Q485.1; rat digs passage to girl's chamber for h. B582.2.2;
semi-divine h. granted free access to men's wives A591; shepherd as h.
P412.1; star indicates location of newborn h. D1314.13; supernatural
wives carry off h. F174; topographical features caused by experiences
of primitive h. A901; transformation to protect h. D651.5; trees bear
first buds to commemorate reign of primitive h. A2771.5; unpromising
h. L100—L199, (as rescuer) R169.10, (last to try task) H991; ungrateful
h. kills helpful animal B336; woman angers h., begs mercy for deer
W133.2; wounded h. sheltered in peasant's house P411.3.

Hero's body taken to fairyland F323; career prophecy for baby M311.0.1;
coming prophesied M394; corpse eaten in ritual G13.1; cross-eyes miraculously straightened F959.2; wife rescued R169.5.1. — Calamities at h.
birth T583.2; crows announce h. coming to otherworld B143.0.8.1;
disguised h. golden hair discovered H151.13; dwarf forced to do h. demands F451.3.2.1.1; dying h. request M257.1; earthquake at h. return
F960.9; extraordinary occurrences at h. death F960.2; extraordinary
phenomena at h. birth F960.1.2; giant shaves h. head, befouls it
F531.5.12; hills from h striking earth A962.7; hills are loads from h.
shoulders A962.10; lakes commemorate event in h. life A920.1.4; light
around h. head F969.3.2; magic use of h. name D1766.7.2; man created
from h. genitals A1263.6; milk drunk from h. skull gives strength M316;
no sunrise at h. death F965.2.1; prophecy: h. birth at certain time
M311.0.2; star signifies h. birth E741.1.1.2.

Heroes *Z200—Z299; dislike to kill sleeping people K959.2.2; seek
greatest H1395. — Biblical h. as wise men J191.2; landing of returning
h. prophesied M369.6; prophecies concerning fate of h. in battle M356.1.2;
tabus of h. C566ff.; transformation to test h. D645.

Herodias as leader of wild hunt E501.1.8.1.

Heroine addresses groom as "tiger's son" H151.15. — Foundling h. L111.2;
lowly h. marries prince (king) L162; menial h. *L113; orphan h. L111.4.2;
tree bends only to h. D1648.1.1; unpromising h. L100—L199.

Heroism W33.

Heron as messenger B291.1.7; wants snails in heaven U125.1. — Ape
pretends to louse h., but plucks out his feathers K874.1; color of h.
A2218, A2411.2.5.2; falcon and h. eaten by wild boar recovered alive
from his belly X1723.2; friendship between turtle and h. A2493.12;
helpful h. B463.2; reincarnation as h. E613.9; ungrateful ape plucks
feathers of rescuing h. W154.5.1.3; why h. has no nest A2431.2.2.

Heron's. — Crab cuts h. neck J631; hearing h. cry good omen
D1812.5.2.5.2.

Herring as king of fishes B243.1.1.

Herring's bad odor A2416.7; eyes A2332.1.3, A2332.5.8.

Hesitation spoils lovers' rendezvous T35.4.-— Disastrous h. J2183.

Hesperides. — Magic apple from garden of the H. D981.1.1.

Hewing way into house as obedience test H1557.5; way from prison R211.5.

Hibernating animals A2481. — Stork is man while h. in Egypt B775.

Hibichenstein associated with dwarfs F451.3.8.1, F451.4.4.1, F451.6.12.

Hidden fruit accidentally poisoned N332.7; paramour taken to own wife K1216; person sees robbers' treasure K439.10; soul (life) E712; wolf gives himself away by talking J2351.2. — Abandoned wife h. under a tub S445; bride h. in fairyland F322.4; children h. to avoid their execution (death) K515.1; children h. from murderous mother R153.2.1; culture hero h. A511.2.3; devil h. in corpse G303.8.15; dream shows where stolen girl h. D1810.8.2.1; eavesdropping wife h. in bushes killed unwittingly by husband N322.2; eyes h. as doctor passes graveyard P424.1; first husband kept h. A1279.1; fugitive magically h. by tree R311.1; genitals h. in body F547.3.5; girl h. by her hair spread on ground F555.3.1.1; hero h. and ogre deceived by his wife (daughter) G532; magic object tells where it is h. D1612.4; magic storm protects h. children D1393.3; magic wand locates h. treasure *D1314.2; monkeys from children h. by Eve A1861.1; paramour successfully h. from husband K1521; quest for h. princess H1381.3.7; rescuer h. by girl R182; return from dead to reveal h. treasure E371; riddle solved with aid of h. informant H573.1; robbers frightened from goods by h. man K335.1.6; sham wise man rewarded for finding horse he has h. K1956.2; sign over h. treasure "Here it is" changed to "Here it is not" J2091.1; suitor test: finding object h. by princess H322.1; sun h. at night A722.6; treasure to be found by hand that has h. it N543.1; treasure h. under the water N513; underworld people from children h. from God by Eve *F251.4; wisdom of h. old man saves kingdom J151.1; woman h. from lover R53.2.

Hide. — Air-castle: to sell h. of sleeping deer J2061.3; alleged oracular horse-h. K114.1.1; deceptive land purchase: ox-h. measure K185.1; devil writes down names of men on h. in church G303.24.1.3; future learned by sitting on h. D1812.3.1; ground opens and swallows h. F948.2; hero sewed up in animal h. carried by bird K1861.1; proud h. humbled J1476; rhinoceros exchanges his red h. for hippopotamus's black A2247.3; servant must keep horns and h. of slain cattle P622.

Hides. — Buffalo and cow exchange h.: hence bad fitting h. A2247.1; cows killed for their h. when large price reported K941.1; fresh h. spread on grass (girl slips up and is deflowered) K1339.1, (enemy slips and falls) K2352.1.

Hide-and-seek as bride contest H375.1. — Deceptive h. game K869.2.

Hiding in bag in order to be carried K1892.1; behind hero to trick enemy F601.4.1; in food in order to eat it K371; from ghosts E434.1,

E434.2; iron tabu C899.1; meat in clothing J1562.3; place speaks and betrays hider D1612.3. — Animals h. boy in belly to protect him B529.1; animal h. sun, causes eclipse A737.6; capture by h. (in foot baskets) K758, (in hollow tree) K763, (under screen) K752; chaste wife deceives suitors by h. them one at a time K1218.1; confederate h. fugitive K649.1; cuckold husband h. K1514.4.2; deception by h. weapons K818.4; devil gets into ark by h. in shadow of Noah's wife G303.23.1; devil h. in people's clothes G303.6.2.12; disenchantment by h. skin (covering) D721.2; dumbness as punishment for h. children Q451.3.1; entrance into woman's (man's) room by h. in chest K1342; escape by h. K515; foolishness of premature coming out of h. J582; god h. from sun A179.8; husband h. to kill paramour K1561.1; knockers h. miners' tools F456.1.2.1.2; king h. in ditch during battle P12.5.1; man in h.-box bought by girl's father K1342.1.1; marooned man h. himself in ogre's clothes outwits him K1616.2; men h. to conceal sins J1738.8; men h. from world-fire renew race A1038; moon h. her star children A764.1.2; nun hidden by abbess from pursuing knight betrays her own h. place to him V465.1.2.1; parts of body as h. place F1034.3ff.; prince first sees heroine as she comes forth from her h. box N712; revealing h. place to evil spirits J2367; secrets of animals accidentally overheard from tree h. place N451.1; spirit captured by h. stick and leg-wrappers F405.13; spirit h. articles F473.2.2; suitor test: h. from princess H321; sun h. A734; thumbling h. in small place F535.1.1.10; woman h. in wood stick D1393.1.1.

Hideous, see also **Ugly;** food at devils' feast G303.25.14.1; giant F531.1.0.2; husband of first parents A1279.1; man married to beautiful woman T268; person magically makes self seem beautiful D2031.4; youth becomes beautiful D682.4.2. — Devil in h. form G303.3.0.1; fairy in h. form F234.2.2; father with handsome son and h. daughter J244.1; magic herbs render h. D1337.2.2; magic object makes beautiful or h. *D1337ff.; man becomes h. D52.1; man grateful not h. as toad W27.1; trolls h. F455.2.2.

Hideousness. — Magic h. *D1870ff.

Hierarchy of gods A161; of heavens E755.1.1; of worlds A651.

High-born recognize equal rank J814.3; wages bring expensive living J342. — Building too h. a tower forbidden *C771.1; extraordinary effect of h. flight F1021.2ff.; gate as h. as heavens and huge as a mountain F776.1; horse jumps over h. wall F989.1; origin of h. sea waves A925.1; poor man wants h. office: made cook L427; short magistrate wears h. helmet X142.4; tree with coiling leaves three thousand miles h. F811.2.3.1; well shoots up h. F718.11; wolf tries to entice goat down from h. place K2061.4.

Highest ranking man in land to be sacrificed for good crops S263.1. — Deceptive wager: whose horse will jump h. K264.1; what is h. (riddle) H642.

Highway. — Do not leave h. (counsel proved wise by experience) J21.5; everything on h. belongs to public J1511.14.

Highwayman, see also **Robber, Thief.** — Boasting coward shown up by wife who masks as h. and robs him K1837.1.

Hildebrand, old K1556.

Hill, see also **Mountain;** lets fugitives pass D1552.8. — Captivity in hollow h. R45; carrying load up h. to roll it down J2165; changeling left on h. and thus banished F321.1.4.4; fairies' room in h. F221.3; giant builds h. home F531.6.6.2; giant thought to be a h. J1769.1; habitable h. F721.2; hero abandoned on high h. K1931.7; hero still alive in hollow h. A571.1; home of the gods inside of h. A151.1.1; illusory animal shapes on h-tops K1886.6; money left on h. to repay helpful mountain-men F460.4.2.2; otherworld under h. F141.0.2; reincarnation of head as h. E649.1; stove runs over h. D1641.3; strong man flattens h. F626.1; wild hunt appears by h. or mountain E501.12.5; wild hunt goes several times around a h. E501.14.4.

Hills from flapping of primeval bird A961.1; because sky asked earth to wrinkle up its feet A969.4. — Abode of dead in h. E481.3.1; helpful spirit warriors dwell in rocks and h. F450.1.1; king's seat on h. P14.10; mountains and h. from hero's angry striking of earth A962.7; primeval sea rolls back, leaves h. bare A816.3; trolls (fairies) live in range of h. F214; weeping h. F801.1; why it rains in h. A1131.0.2.

Hillside animal: two legs short X1381.

Himself. — Cursing h. M411.0.1; unable to hit man h., enemy kills foster brother P273.3; wooing emissary wins love for h. T51.1.

Hind, see also **Deer;** flees before the hounds U121.2. — Adventures from pursuing enchanted h. N774; horns of h. as snakebite antidote D1515.4.3; seeking h. seen in the woods ten years before (maiden) H586.2.1.

Hindmost. — Devil takes the h. G303.19.2.

Hindu drinks from Mohammedan's vessel V383.2.

Hindus. — Origin of H. A1611.6; why English more powerful than H. A1689.11.1.

Hinduism. — Absurdity of trying to convert king to H. J1536.2.

Hints. — Recognition from h. dropped by heroine as menial H151.5.

Hippogriff B42.1.

Hippopotamus. — Color of h. A2247.3, A2411.1.6.2; creation of h. A1872; giant h. B871.2.4; helpful h. B443.6; singing h. B214.1.11.

Hired men sing about bad food J1341.11. — Devil h. out as laborer G303.9.3.

Hireling deceives man J1114.1.

History. — Bird summarizes h. B122.6; recognition by telling life h. H11.1; temper lost from reading h. W185.3.

Hitched. — Horses h. both before and behind the wagon in otherworld F171.6.4.

Hitchhiker. — Ghost as vanishing h. E332.3.3.1.

Hitching-ring. — Strangers entertained by family to whose h. they happen to tie their horses P328.

Hitter. — Lie: remarkable h. X945.

Hive. See **Bee-hive.**

Hoarded game released A1421; gold stolen by spying K322; plants released A1423.0.1; seeds A1425.0.1.

Hobgoblin *F470ff.

Hobson's choice J201.

Hoe. — Bluff: plow as hero's h. K1718.5; magic h. *D1204; reincarnation of feet into h. E649.3; reincarnation of back into h. handle E649.3.1; self-digging h. D1601.16.1.

Hog, see also **Pig;** belongs to whichever place he goes of his own accord J1179.2; with broken leg keeps pea supply secret W151.6; goes to bath but wallows in the mud U123; with giant rib B871.1.2.1.1; good dead but not living H841.2; locked in church all week by mistake X415; refuses food from excommunicated men B259.3; rib as fairy gift F343.16.1; as sacrifice V12.4.3.1; with silver bristles H355.2; taken to roof to graze J1904.1; tired of his daily food W128.1; in Valhalla gives meat A661.1.0.3. — Bad women from transformed h. and goose A1371.3; creation of h. A1871, (incomplete since God has to go to a fire: cause of hog's round snout) A2286.1.1; devil rides on h., drives another G303.7.6; dog and h. dispute over their children P243.1; why h. has evil spirit A2287.1, A2523.1; why h. has good flesh A2221.1, A2381.1; fish as devil's h. G303.25.15.1; foolish bargain: horse for cow, cow for h., etc. J2081.1; friendship between goat and h. A2493.22; ghost of h. E521.5; giant h. B871.2.1; why h. grunts A2426.1.3; helpful h. B414, (wild) B443.5; why h. lives in sty A2433.3.6; man-h. B29.3; mountain-man in shape of h. F460.1.1.1; h. loses pancake in mud: still seeks it A2275.5.1; planting a h. in order to grow pigs J1932.4; revenant as woman riding h. E425.1.5; why h. roots in ground A2275.5.1, A2477.1; why h. has short snout A2287.1, A2335.4.1; soul as h. E731.12; speaking h. B211.1.4; why h. has "toes" on back of fore leg A2287.1.1, A2371.2; treasure-h. B101.2; trickster's sale involving tall h. K196.2; witch as h. G211.1.6.

Hog's forefoot cut off; woman's hand missing D702.1.2.

Hogs follow fairies F241.3; to be killed yearly C684.2; made to sleep in trees J1904.3; as mortgage collateral K231.5.2; in otherworld F167.11.2; root up gold for saint B562.1.1. — Children play at killing h. N334.1; compulsion to kill one of certain h. yearly C684.2; concert by h. J1675.5; eating dwarfs smack like h. F451.3.13.1; why h. inspect one another: seek pancake A2275.5.1, A2471.2; island made to appear to be h. back K1886.7.1; Jesus drives evil spirits into h. A2287.1ff.; lies about h. X1233; mice and h. let loose put elephant cavalry to flight K2351.3.

Holding what four things hardest? H659.2; wild huntsman's dogs E501.15.6.1. — Chastity ordeal: h. shaven and greased tail of bull H412.2; disenchantment by h. D721.4, (enchanted person during successive transformations) D757; disenchantment made permanent by h. to a hair D793.1; magically h. on to sleigh D1413.3; trees created for h. earth together A857.3; turtle h. with jaws till it thunders B761; wild hunt avoided by h. (bread) E501.17.5.6, (plant) E501.17.5.7.

Hole in ground entrance to hell F92.5; in stone from warrior's weapon A972.5.6; to snake kingdom F92.7; from which treasure removed N563; of winds: stopper destroyed A1122.1. — Animal eludes bird watchman and escapes from h. R214; bride put in tree h. K1911.1.7; boring h. in boat to let water out J2119.4; childbearing queen puts head in h., fails to see issue K2115.0.1; cure by putting hair in tree h. D2161.4.18; coffin carried through h. in wall to prevent return of dead E431.4; communication of lovers through h. in wall T41.1; contest: jumping into ground (h. already dug and covered with boughs) K17.1; contest in pushing h. in tree K61; counting out pay: h. in the hat and hat over a pit K275; deceptive drinking contest: h. for water K82.1; deceptive eating contest: h. in bag *K81.1; drinking h. in pot lets gruel run out J2176.2; dupe lured into h. K737.1; escape by digging h. K615; female overpowered when caught in h. in hedge K1384; to find h. fool turns can about and lets oil run out J2127; fool digs h. in which to throw earth from excavation J1934; fool stops h. with money J1851.3.1; god bores h. in hell A141.3; hero pretends he pushed h. in wall: hole really bored before K1733.1; lioness caught in wall h. K771.1; magic by creeping through h. *D1795; magic water-h. D928; monster comes out of h. in evening G346.0.1; numskull sticks his head into h. of millstone J2131.5.4; ogre persuaded to go into h.: buried alive G512.4; people come up h. from underworld A682; porridge in the ice-h. J1938; rainbow lives in h. A791.8.1; recognition by h. burned in hand when woman removes glove H56.1; snake preserved in ark to stop h. with tail A2145.2; test of wife's obedience: finger in h. H473.1; theft through h. in house wall K315.2; visit to lower world through h. made by lifting clumps of grass F92.1.

Holes bored in enemies' boats prevent pursuit K636; in hills from gods' fights A964.1; in stones caused by piercing by saint's finger A972.3; trap those departing from straight path J95. — Absurd disregard of nature of h. X1761; cannibal sent for water with vessel full of h. K605; mats over h. as pitfall K735.1; people in otherworld pour water into tub full of h. *F171.6.2; stars are men peering through h. in sky A761.5; wind comes through h. in sky A1122.4; why certain leaves have h. in them A2763.

Holger Dansk asleep in mountain *D1960.2.

Holiday to last "until log burns out" K197. — Camel mistaken for religious h. J1738.7; witch's h. G247.1.

Holidays the year round J2231. — Knockers observe Jewish h. F456.1.2.3.3.

Holiness, see also **Holy;** of saint tames animal B771.2. — Saint's h. tested H257.

Hollow mountain *F131, F759.2; object used to cheat K499.2; tree as residence for hero F811.10.1; in tree shelters relics F979.7. — Boy in h. tree frightens woodchopper X1854.1; entrance to woman's room in h. artificial animal K1341; fairies have h. backs F232.1; fairyland under h. knoll *F211; king escapes through h. tree R311.2; lost wind found in h. tree: has been banished and is needed by men A1122.3; man in h. tree defends self from beasts X1854; otherworld in h. mountain *F131; treasure found in h. of tree N528.

Hollows. — Origin of h. A983.

Holly. — Riddle about h. H852.

Holmgang H1561.2.1; for bride H217.2; to decide gold's owner H217.3.

Holofernes K872.

Holy man (converses with dead) E545.7, (doesn't want sinner buried atop him) E545.9 (embraces man calling him ugly) J921, (emits light) F574.3, (finds lost object) D1810.0.3.2, (as helper) N848.0.1, (on quest) H1233.3; man's (diet during Lent) V73.6.3, (fall evil omen) D1812.5.14, (hair enormously long) F555.3.2, (touch disenchants) D782.1; men keep devils under control G515; object falls from heaven F962.12; person's birth painless T584.0.3; persons save one from the devil G303.16.11; spring restores sight D1505.5.4. — Animal characteristics: punishment for working on h. day A2231.3; animal curse for refusing to carry h. fugitive across stream A2231.7.2; animal leads cleric to h. place B563.4; bright star indicates birth of h. person F961.2.1; chastity tests of h. men H426; condemned soul saved by h. person E754.1.4; cure by h. man D2161.5.1; demon cannot hurt h. person G303.16.2.5; devil visible to one who walks in minister's h. shoes G303.6.2.4; diseases cured at h. man's birth D2161.6.3; disguise as h. man K1827; dragon makes bridge across stream for h. man B549.2; dwarfs emigrate because mortals desecrate h. day F451.9.1.11; extraordinary nature phenomena at birth (death) of h. person F960.1ff.; footprints of h. man still visible A972.1.3; four things prevent h. life Z71.2.6; learning art of love so as to become h. T4.1; heaven entered by slipping in along with h. person K2371.1.5; miraculous spring bursts forth for h. person F933.1; origin of plant from h. person's staff A2624; plants originate from experience of h. person A2620ff.; prince disguised as h. man R24.1; punishment for desecration of h. places (images) *Q222; punishment for opposition to h. person Q227; refugee entertained in h. place P322.3; repartee between h. man, king on religion J1289.10; resuscitation by h. man E121.5; reward for attendance on h. man Q38; reward for protecting h. fugitive *Q46.1; seduction by posing as h. man K1315.6; sham h. man K1961.1.5; sun darkened by death of h. person F965.2; tabu to look at h. objects C311.2; tree bows down to h. person D1648.1.2; do not trust the over-h. J21.18; uncharitableness to h. person punished Q286.1; wisdom from h. man J153.

Holy Family. — Leopards guide H. to Egypt B563.5.

Holy Ghost. — Nun claims her child is by H. J1264.6.

Holy Grail D1171.6. — Prophecy: hero to achieve H. M361.1; resuscitation by H. E64.5.1; vow to find H. M183.3.

Holy of holies. — Stream from under H. A941.7.3.

Holy land, see also **Jerusalem;** V317.1; not ravaged by deluge A1005.3. — Dragon guards H. B11.6.4; pilgrimage to H. V531.

Holy water V132; breaks fairy spell F382.2; destroys veil over well D1562.6; exorcises witch G271.2.2; gives magic knowledge D1810.6; as magic object *D1242.1.2; and mass prevent demons alighting on grave D1385.15. — Conception from drinking h. T512.3.1; devil chased by h. G303.16.7; man enabled to read baptismal service by washing in h. D1819.4.1; ordeal by h. H222.2; plenty of h. J2513; resuscitation by h. E80.4; saint's h. makes fairy vanish F379.4.

Homage. — King avenges lack of h. P12.12; tabu: refusing h. to saint's bell C94.8.

Home, see also **Abode, Dwelling;** of brownies F482.3; of dwarfs F451.4ff.; of Fortuna in otherworld N111.1.1; of giants F531.6.3; of the gods A151. — Ass is not at h. J1552.1.1; animal told to go h. J1881.2; better things at h. K1952.2; child unwittingly promised: "what you have at h." S242; choice: staying at h. with loving wife or going to tavern and having an unfaithful wife J229.1; curse for leaving h. Q556.3; disenchantment by sight of old h. D789.3; escape from h. R213; ghost asks to be taken h. E545.18; ghost vanishes when taken h. E599.8; ghost's bones brought h. from foreign soil E459.2; goat who would not go h. (cumulative tale) Z39.1; heathcock prefers h. with hardships to travel in foreign lands J215.3; husband (lover) arrives h. just as wife (mistress) is to marry another *N681; husband (wife) of supernatural being longs for old h. and visits relatives T294; magic flower opens dwarf h. F451.4.3.7; man marries fairy and takes her to his h. F302.2; new h. no escape from bad luck N250.2; prophecy of future greatness fulfilled when hero returns h. unknown N682; why rams live at h. A2433.3.7; resuscitation by returning corpse h. E138; sight of old h. reawakens memory and brings about return from otherworld *D2006.2; sleeping at one's own h. tabu C735.2.10; staying too long at h. forbidden *C761.2; strong hero sent from h. F612ff.; thief followed h. J1392.1; unpromising son leaves h. L133; unusual sight on road h. bad omen D1812.5.1.22; water-goddess's underwater h. F420.7.1; wife of supernatural husband must not see old h. C713.2.

Homes of fairies F220. — Fairies revenge for destroying h. F361.12; flood survivors' h. A1029.6.

Homecoming giant heard far away F531.3.8.3. — Adulteress kills h. husband K1510.1.

Homeland sinks beneath waves F944.2. — King helps take h. back N836.3; promise to bury father in his h. M258.3.

Homesickness. — Magic h. D2036.

Homocentaurus born after bestiality T465.3.

Homosexuality T463; punished Q253.2.

Hone. — Magic h. D1188.

Honest miller incomprehensible to baker X212. — Recognizing h. merchant J1661.1.9.

Honestly. — Luck only with h. earned money N143.

Honesty rewarded Q68.2; tests H1555. — Cynical retorts concerning h. J1370ff.; intemperance in h. J556; merchants try h. for a year and find that it pays J23; partnership of H. and Fraud: Fraud loses K1635; pretended h. to mulct victim K2054.

Honey collected, lightened tree springs back, kills K1112.1; as excrement of bees A2385.3; flows up high mountain (lie) X1547.2.1; from royal bee-hive H1332.7. — Air-castle: jar of h. to be sold J2061.1; attempts to take h. from jug X431.1; bees feed woman h. F561.6; bees leave h. on infant's lips B147.3.1.2; bees sting h.-thieves Q597.3; conception from eating h. T511.7.1; "don't require h. from strange country" J21.40; man in pit consoled by a drop of h. J861.1; covering with h. and exposing to flies Q464; drones dispute possession of h. J581.4; drop of h. causes chain of accidents N381; error was in the h. (bribed judge) J1192.2; frogs want to collect h. J512.15; getting h. from the wasp-nest K1023; giving away comb, eating h. K476.7; gold pieces in the h.-pot J1176.3; magic h. *D1037; magic healing h. D1500.1.29; man falls into jar of h. and is drowned N339.1; man hunting h. encounters lost maiden N785.1; milk and h. flow in land F701.1; new h. protection against ghosts E439.10; origin of h. A2813; palace surrounded by rivers of wine, rosewater, and h. F771.7; peasant leaves h. tree standing J241.2; riddle: always eat bread with h. H588.11; rainbow of h. F162.7; riddle about bees, h., and lion's carcass H804; river of h. F715.2.4, F771.2.4.1; river is transformed h. A934.11.4; rivers of h. in otherworld *F162.2.3; saint suckles with h. T611.5.1; sea of h. F711.2.5; shower of h. F962.6.3; water becomes h. D478.5; what is sweeter than h. (riddle) H671; wayward son tells mother h. is sweet J2497; wine becomes h. D477.0.1.2.

Honey-bees, see also **Bees.** — Creation of h. A2012.0.1.

Honeycomb. — Man wants roasted h. J1731.2.

Honeysuckle king of trees D965.0.1.

Honor W45; to be foster father to king's son P271.4. — Angels sing in h. of saint V234.1; envoys debate which due greatest h. W161.1; feasts to h. certain god A1541.2; man killed defending sweetheart's h. T326.2; mother-son incest to test his h. T412.3; mountains fight for h. F1006.1; quest to recover one's h. H1223.1; stranger thinks humiliating donkey ride an h. Q473.5.1; wit interprets unfavorable decision of court as doing him great h. J835; woman deceived into sacrificing h. K1353; woman sacrifices life for son's h. W28.2; worldly h. like shadow J152.6.

Honors. — High h. as reward Q113.0.1.

Honoring. — Angels h. mortal V241, h. saint V234.1; lion's precept on h. the woods J22.2.

Hood holds wine F866.7.1; renders invulnerable D1344.8.1. — Disguise with h. over face K1815.0.1; gigantic h. of serpent king B244.1.3; land purchase: as much as saint's h. covers K185.4.1; lawyer's h. and robe stolen K362.9; lip makes h. over head F544.1.2; magic h. *D1067.3, (enables person to pass under water) D1525.1; not naked but with h. on J2499.2.

Hoods. — Icy h. worn in hell Q567.1.

Hoodwinking dancers K826. — Means of h. guardian or owner *K330ff.

Hoof. — Ass's charter in his h. J1608; ghost horse's h. -beats E402.2.3; recognition through branding with h.-marks H55.1; springs originate from horse's h.-prints A941.1; why ass does not have cloven h. A2376.1.1.

Hoofs of devil's horses strike fire G303.7.3.5. — Animals' h. A2376; clods thrown up by horses' h. look like birds K1872.5.1; devil's abode is between h. of swine G303.8.7; devil detected by his h. G303.4.5.3.1; dragon's cloven h. B11.2.4.2; ghostly horse enters house and puts h. on breast of sleeper E281.2; horses' h. drop from heat F988.2; person with h. F517.1.6; thunder from h. of god's horses A1142.6.

Hooks, see also **Fishhook.** — Cutting h. to revenge father H591.3; self-suspension on h. under armpits Q541.4.

Hooked nose F543.1.3.

Hoop snake X1321.3.1. — Penance: carrying iron h. on head until it falls off Q521.3; pursuit of rolling h. leads to quest H1226.1.

Hoopoe's creation A1952; wedding B282.18. — Origin of h. crest A2321.2; shepherd transformed to h. still calls sheep (explanation of h. cries) *A2261.1.

Hooting. — Owl's h. (bad omen) D1812.5.1.27.1, (explained) A2427.3, (misunderstood by lost simpleton) J1811.1.

Hop-o-my thumb *F535.1.

Hope is most general H659.10.1. — Creditor has had his reward in h. of payment K231.7.

Hopping of animals explained A2441.1.0.1; of hare A2441.1.11; of raven A2441.2.1.

Horizon. — Sky-window at h. F56.3.

Horn, see also **Drinking-horn;** blows down wall D1562.3; fills with blood (life token) E761.1.2; of Roncevalles R187; will tell the tale on goat J1082.1. — Alleged resuscitating h. K113.7; animal with h. pointing to sky H312.8; creature with h. mounting to heaven H1331.7; elf-knight produces love-longing by blowing h. F301.2.1; gnats apologize for lighting on bull's h. J953.10; ghost summoned by h. E384.3; hidden man blows h., lovers flee K1271.1.4.2; magic h. (musical) *D1222, (stolen) D861.7.1, (has power over animals) D1440.1; man covered with h. F558; magic animal h. *D1011.1; merry-h. and angry-h. B501.1.1; old

king eats from h. F571.5; quest for lost h. H1386.1; respite from death
until victim has blown on h. K551.3; stealing gold h. of three-horned
ox H1151.7.1; three blasts on h. before sunrise to rescue prisoner from
mound R112.1; wild huntsman blows h. E501.15.1.

Horns call out when girl tries to escape D1612.1.1; of dragon B11.2.5;
on forehead *F545.2.2; grow on cuckold *H425.2; for summoning
buffalo B501.1. — Animal h. bloom and bear man as fruit A1263.5;
animal unusual as to his h. B15.3ff.; camel asks for h.: punishment, short
ears A2232.1; cattle shed h. in grief B301.6.1; child with h. T551.3.4.2;
conception from drinking elixir from goat's h. T512.1; cow with silver
h. B101.8, H355.1; creator with two h. on head A18.2; curiosity satisfied:
riding the ox's h. J2375; devil has h. G303.4.1.6; disenchantment by
placing handkerchief between h. D777; earth rests on h. of bull A844.5;
fairy h. heard by mortals F262.8; fawn, in spite of his fine h., runs from
the dog U127; growth of ox h. F983.4; hare (jackal) makes h. of wax
K1991; hind with golden h. B106.1; magic h. (grow on person's forehead)
*D992.1; magic object causes h. to grow on person *D1375.1ff.; magic
object removes h. from person D1375.2ff.; magic object returned in
payment for removal of magic h. D895; man carried on goat's h.
B557.1; man with h. B233; man pulls out devil's h. G303.9.6.1.1; monster
with human heads on h. G361.1.1.1; mounds from h. cast by cattle
A967.1; origin and nature of animals' h. A2326ff.; originally cock had
h. A2326.2.3; person with h. F511.3; servant must keep h. and hide of his
cattle that are slain P622; stag's h. borrowed from dog A2241.1; stag
scorns his legs but is proud of his h. L461; stealing two h. of a savage
bull (task)H1151.7; taming the bull by cutting off his h. J2107; why dog
has no h. A2326.2.2; witch with h. G215.2; witch's h. discovered by
lousing her *G253; wolf tied to cow's h. K1022.2.

Hornbill borrows tomtit's bill A2241.9; king of birds B242.1.3. — Man
transformed to h. D153.3; why h. speaks through his nose A2423.1.5.

Horned god A131.6; snake B91.3; water monster B68. — Devil's cows
one-h.: God makes them two-h. A2286.2.3; how h. viper got horns
A2326.1.6; origin of h. serpent A2145.0.1.

Hornet. — Creation of h. A2013; remedy for h. sting D1517.1; soul
in h. E715.3.3; spirit in h. form guards treasure F403.2.3.1.

Hornets sting opposing army B524.2.1. — Army of h. B268.8.1; bridegroom
driven from bridal chamber by h. T171; bull's eye becomes h. D457.11.1;
helpful h. B481.5; man who asks for good weather given a box of h.
J2327; ornaments of h. F827.3; thieves directed to nest of h. K421.2.

Hornless cow B15.3.0.1. — Milk from the h. cow J1512.1; why some
animals are h. A2326.2ff.

Horny. — Animal with h. skin B15.7.10.1; first man covered with h.
substance A1281.1.

Horoscope taken by means of stars M302.4. — Choosing bride by h.
T54.

Horrible sights in hell A671.2. — Revenant as h. female figure E425.1.6; spirits appear h. F401.5.

Horrifying. — Rescued person h. rescuers R188.

Horripilation F1041.2.

Horror. — Death from h. F1041.1.12.

Horrors. — Climax of h. (cumulative tale) Z46.

Horse, see also **Colt, Donkey, Mare, Mule, Stallion;** accidentally poisoned instead of master N332.2; bewitched G265.6.3; in blood up to knees E761.1.9; born of egg B19.3; catches thief K427.1; with crimson mane, green legs B731.2.1; dies after owner refuses large sum for him J21.26; drawn across ice, skin rubbed off J2129.7; enchanted so that he stands still D2072.0.2.1; executed for crime B275.1.1; exchanged by rider for food M225.1; fair forbidden C619.3; finds unknown person B151.1.1.0.3; -god A132.3.1; -goddess A132.3.2; with golden mane B19.5; hangs self D2061.2.8; helper on quest H1233.6.1; indicates election of emperor H171.3; jumps over high wall F989.1; -keeper rescues abandoned child R131.8.1; kicks up jewel B562.1.2; kicks murderer to death B591.2; kills another, owner forewarned J1141.1.12; kills dog with kick J2413.5; kills master's enemies B524.1.7; kneels before stolen sacrament V35.1.1; lies down when grain falls from load B159.2; lives from time of Adam A1881.0.1; made to appear as tree-trunk D2031.7; magically becomes immovable D1654.12; meat becomes mutton D476.3.3; as messenger B291.2.1; -nail stumps bewitch G224.13.1; painted different colors by thief K419.5; paramour B611.3; permits only certain rider H172.1; pulling ghost in cart goes mad E272.1; pushes sleep-thorn from master's head B511.3; pulled out of earth by magic D1399.1; recognizes false rider, throws him H62.2; recognizes transformed kol H62.2; refuses to carry one who speaks falsehood B133.4; replies to man's remarks B210.1; requests wolf to start eating at rear, kicks him to death K553.4; rescues children B540.2; as sacrifice V12.4.9; sewed in buffalo-hides F984.1; stands in blood to his knees (life token) E761.1.9; is the strongest (riddle) H631.1; as suitor B621.7; taught to live without food J1914; trade involving eating its excrement K198; transformed to another animal D412.4; transformed to object D422.1; transformed to stone D422.1.2; transports to fairyland F213.3; tried for crime B272.2.1; unable to draw evil dead man E411.0.3; unable to move enchanted wagon D2072.0.2.1.1; used by mortal under fairy spell changes to gray cat F234.4.1; wading in blood at Armageddon A1080.1; warns hero not to wash in water B521.1.1; weeps B301.4ff., B736.2, (for master's death) B141.2; that went like a ship J2481; in wild hunt breathes fire *E501.4.2.4; wins jumping contest for man B587.1; as witch's companion G225.2; withheld as sacrifice to a saint refuses to move K231.3.4; worship V1.8.2. — Air-castle: old woman thinks about h. she is finally to get from the sale of pail of milk J2061.2.1; alleged gold-dropping h. sold K111.1; alp rides h. sweaty at night F471.1.1.1; angry man kills his own h. by mistake

K942; arrow in leg of sun's h. A732.2.1; artificial flying h. D1626.1; ass envies h. in fine trappings J212.1; ass is jealous of the h. until he learns better L452; automatic statue of h. D1620.2.1; new backbone for h. made from a stick X1721.1; bear riding h. lets paws fall on horse's flanks J2187; bird-h. B41ff.; blacksmith's and h.-trader's dreams J1622; blade of grass transformed to h. D451.5.1; breaking h. as strength test H1562.6; bridling a wild h. (task) H1154.3.1; bull mistaken for h. J1759.4; bundle of wood magically acts as riding-h. D1523.3; cat transformed to h. D412.1.1; capture by tarring h. K741.1; capturing magic h. H1154.8; carrying the plow h. so as not to tramp up the field J2163; cleaning the h. K1443; clever, swift h. of fanciful origin B710.2; color of h. A2411.1.6.1; coming neither on h. nor on foot (task) H1053; creation of ass from proud h. A1882.1; creation of h. A1881; damages claimed for "lost" h. hidden by owner K251.4; deduction: h. drinks ass's milk J1661.1.5; devastating h. B16.1.3; devil in h. race G303.9.9.12; do not cross bridge without dismounting from your h. J21.7; deceptive contest in carrying a h. K72; deceptive sale of h. K134; deceptive wager: whose h. will jump highest K264.1; devil drives h. and wagon G303.7.3ff.; devil as h. G303.3.3.1.3; devil rides h. G303.7.1ff.; devil in the stable wrapped in h.-hide G303.8.12; difficult riding of h. as suitor contest H331.1; discourteous answer: why. h. is always eating A2231.1.1; "don't run h. down hill" J21.24; not to dismount from h. C521; do nothing but attend to the h. J2516.3; dragon becomes h. D419.1.2; dragon as modified h. B11.2.1.7; dragon from transformed h. B11.1.2; dupe believes h. will fly J2349.1; dwarf rides through air on wooden h. F451.6.2.2; entrance to maiden's room on flying h. K1346; escape by asking to die on a h. K551.6; escape on flying h. B542.2; escape from flying wooden h. R215.3; escape from lower world on h. F101.6.2, excuse for not staying on h. J1483.4; why h. has eye-like marks on forelegs A2262.1, A2371.2.7; fairy as h. F234.1.8; why h. has only two eyes A2286.1.2; A2332.2.1; fairy rides on h. F366.22; fairies ride mortal's h. at night F366.2; faithful h. B301.4ff., (to be abandoned) B842.1, (killed through misunderstanding) B331.1.1, (follows dead master to grave) B301.4; farmer kills anyone riding his h. L434; foal so heavy, h. not wanted J2212.8; fool advises buyer that the h. is worth little or his father would not sell it J2088.1; foolish bargain: h. for cow, etc. J2081.1; footless man outruns swift h. (lie) X1796.1; fourth h. must carry all J761.2; fugitive kills pursuer and takes his extraordinary h. to continue flight R233; ghost of h. *E521ff.; ghost rides h. E272.2, E581.2; ghostly h. enters house and puts hoofs on breast of sleeper E281.2; giant h. B871.1.5; giant so large he cannot be carried by a h. F531.2.7; giant who can find only one h. able to carry him F531.2.8; giant with h. head F531.1.2.4; giant ogre as h. G126.2; gnats think they have thrown h. down J953.6; god rides on wind-swift h. A171.1; golden h. B103; gorgon's blood becomes flying h. D447.3.2; great h. X1241.1; green h.

B731.2; guessing nature of devil's h. H523.1; hardhearted h. allows ass to be overburdened until it is crushed W155.1; hay transformed to h. D441.9.1; headless ghost rides h. E422.1.1.3.1; helpful strong h. caught B312.5; helpful h. *B401; hero kills h. to feed ravens B391.3; hostile h. B17.1.4; husband's slaying of h. tames wife T251.2.3; imagined refusal of h. loan tests friendship H1558.6; inciting h. tabu C857; if h. can pull one load he can pull two J2213.4; imprint of h. in rocks A972.4; king leads to victory by leaping h. overboard W32.1; kite tries to neigh like h. J512.2; land bargain: land surrounded by a h. in one day K185.7.1; laughing contest: dead h. winner K87.1; leading dead h. J2047; do not lend out your h. J21.10; loosing knots permits h. to return home D1782.3.2; lover's h. explained to husband: cow has foaled K1549.4; lover's gift regained: h. and wagon as gift K1581.2; magic h. *B184.1, (brings about mortal's death) K985, (hairs compel horse to follow) D1427.3, (made by carpenter) D853.1, (powerless after tabu broken) C942.2; magic power by crawling through ear of magic h. D1733.2; magic spell tames h. D1442.6.1; magic transportation from kick of h. D2121.9; man keeps h. in sleeve F1016.1; man helps h. against stag K192; man secure from devil on h. G303.16.19.1; man transformed to h. *D131ff., H62.0.1; man walks faster than h. F681.9; marriage to person in h. form B641.6; marvelously swift h. F989.17; mill h. when taken to war keeps going in a circle U137; mill gives birth to h. J1531.1.1; mouse transformed to h. D411.6.1; "my h. ten times better than best" J2217.1; mythical h. belonging to water-spirit B19.3.2; nag becomes riding h. D1868.1; Norse man-h. B21.1; numskull to die when his h. breaks wind three times J2311.1; numskull doesn't recognize his own h. J2023; oaths taken over severed pieces of h. M111; one-eyed man as appraiser of h. X122; one-footed h. draws chariot A136.2.2; plowing the field: h. and harness destroyed K1411; plowman to get h. for saying paternoster H1554.3; prince identifies marvelous disguised h. H62.3; prophetic h. B141.2; pursuer's h. stolen K341.4.1.1; quest for marvelous h. H1331.4; quest for wonderful, vicious h. H1363; race of ox and h. A2252.2; rainbow is rain-god's h. A791.7; rakshasa eats h. G369.1.4; recognition by overheard conversation with h. H13.1.1; recognizing a good h. by screwing ears F655.1; refusal to lend h. brings lawsuits J1552.3; reincarnation as h. E611.1; revenant as h. E423.1.3; riding h. kingship test H41.7; riding speckled h. credential test H242.1; riding, taming wild h. H1155.1; riddle about h. and rider H744; riddle: black h. and white h. chasing each other H722.2; runaway h. carries bride to her lover N721; sacred h. B811.1; saint's h. miraculously preserved H1573.3.2; sea h. B71; sea-riding h. transports to fairyland F213.3; seal transformed to h. D411.7.1; sham wise man hides h. and is rewarded for finding it K1956.2; six-legged h. B15.6.3.1.1; skillful smith shoes running h. F663.1; slander: woman as h.-eating thief K2127.2; speaking h. B211.1.3; spirit in form of h. F401.3.1; spring breaks forth where

fairy h. lies down A941.4.2; squirrel transformed to h. D411.1.1; staying
in haunted house where h. carcass drops down chimney (fear test)
H1411.1.1; stealing h. as task H1151.2, (troll's) H1151.9; stingy h.
refuses ass little feed, though he promises much for later time W152.8;
striped h. with purple mane, white feet B731.2.3; strong man lifts h.
F624.1; suitor test: riding strong princess's h. H345.2; sword cleaves h.
in two F628.2.10; where h. got his upper teeth A2241, A2345.1; tabu:
touching h. C537.3; tabu: whipping magic h. C762.3; tame h. exchanged
for vicious bullock K1456; task: capturing magic h. H1154.8; teaching
h. to speak H1024.7.1, K491.2; test of strength: breaking spirited h.
H1562.6; thief guards his pursuer's h. while the latter follows a false
trail K346.1; thief pretends to show how h. can be stolen: rides it off
K341.8; tournament won on borrowed h. K28; trading only h. for harness
J2085.1.1; trained h. as harvester and hunter (lie) X921.3; transformation to h. by putting on bridle D535; tree grows out of h. and gives
rider shade X1130.2.1; trickster pretends to ride home, steals h. K341.8.1;
trickster steals h. from dealer K341.8.2; thief returns h. after using it
K416.1; transformation to flying h. D657.2; transformation of h. by
spurring D566.3; Trojan wooden h. K754.1; truth-speaking h. B133;
two presents to the king: the beet and the h. J2415.1; ungrateful Jew
steals Christian's horse W154.19; wild huntsman has his h. beaten
E501.15.2; wild huntsman waters his h. *E501.15.7; wild huntsman's h.
*E501.4.2ff.; wind serves Solomon as h. and carries him everywhere
F963.1; wisp of hay transformed to h. D441.9.1; witch in form of h.
G211.1.1; witch rides h. G241.3; witch transforms man to h. and rides
him G241.2.1; witch's hair on h. become iron G265.3.1; winning h.
race three times (suitor test) H331.5.3; woman exchanges h. for sack of
bones J2099.1; woman killed by h. got through immoderate request
Q582.6; wraith rides h. E723.7.7; youth trusts self to h. over which he
has no control J657.1.

Horse's head for extraordinary use F874; image vivified D445.1; leg
cut off and replaced *E782.4; magic head protects D1380.3.1; magic
strength from hair combing D1835.2; neighing indicates important spot
B155.4; sex organ provides money D1469.5. — Animal with h. body,
hound's legs B14.2; body and hands human, head and ears h. B21.2;
combat with h. sex organ F998; death respite until wolf reads h. passport K551.19; devil has h. foot G303.4.5.3; escape by reversing h. shoes
K534.1; fairies plait h. mane, tail F366.2.1; fox waits in vain for h.
scrotum to fall off J2066.1; ghormuhas; men's bodies, h. heads, cannibals B15.7.5; ghost h. hoofbeats E402.2.3; ghost as man with h. head
E425.2.2; king asleep in mountain will awake when his h. shoes are
worn down D1960.2.1; king induced to kiss h. rump K1288; magic h.
rider immune D1381.30; man with h. mouth B213; origin of h. arched
neck A2351.6; person with h. (foot) F551.1.2, (ears) F511.2.2, (head)
F511.0.9.1; pins in h. heart release curse M429.2; prophecy: death by h.

head M341.2.5; punishment: tying to h. tail Q473.2; spring from h. urine A941.1.1; springs from h. hoof-prints A941.1; tying cat to h. tail K2383; water that has neither fallen from heaven nor sprung from earth (h. sweat) H1073; weapons from h. bones B338; why h. penis is long A2365.2.1.1; if witch grabs h. tail on bridge, man is safe from her G273.4.1; youth sees one and one-half men and a h. head H583.1.

Horses B802; become sick as punishment Q551.4.1; carry lost riders to safety B563.1.1; descended from heaven B811.1.1; determine road to be taken *B151.1.1; fail for slight to saint Q589.1; as fairy gifts F343.9.1; of the gods A155.2; hoofs drop from heat F988.2; knead dough (lie) X1241.2.3; mutilated to humiliate owner S175; as offspring of the devil G303.10.8; procured for boy at birth T602; refuse to remain with cursed owner B133.4.1; from sea serve man D2156.10; sent into enemy's camp to cause stampede K2351.6; spring at those unentitled to throne H71.10.4; travel between clerics without guidance B151.1.1.0.1. — Abused and pampered h. B316; artificially colored h. B731.2.2; birds frighten enemy's h., who throw riders K2351.5.1; blood-red h. draw devil's coach G303.7.3.5; breeding fine h. from an ass J1909.4; bringing as many h. are there are days in the year (task) H1117; clods from h. hoofs look like birds K1872.5.1; coachman makes the h. run by binding hay to the shaft J1671; curse: h. will die M471.3; dead person drives h. E582; demons race h. F419.1; devil stampedes h. G303.9.9.15; devil disappears in carriage drawn by four black h. G303.17.2.9; drawing asunder by h. Q416; driving h. over ashen yoke tabu C833.4; dwarfs have little h. F451.7.5; enemy h. captured by lion join forces and become friends J891; fairy gives man h., cattle, etc. F343.9; fairy kills mortal's hounds (h.) F369.3; flood caused by loosing fairy h. A1012.2.1; fairies' h. F241.1; farmer who trades h. with the devil is cheated G303.25.12; fire-breathing h. B742.3; frightened h. backed into enemy K2351.5; getting ninety h. H1154.2.1; ghosts visible to h. alone E421.1.2; hero's marvelous h. A524.1.2; immortal h. B19.3.1; infuriated h. kill driver B17.1.4.1; insects eat team of h. X1280.2.1; lies about h. X1241; lightning from heavenly h. striking hoofs A1141.3; magic bridle restrains all h. D1442.1; magic cloth leads owner to lost h. D1314.9; man tied to h., hounds set after Q415.1.2; man works h. to death, complains that borrowed one overeats W154.27; mountain-folk ride through air on h. F460.2.2; murder by trampling of h. S116.6; nine hundred h. draw strong man's chariot F639.12; ogress devours h. G312.7; people choose bows and arrows or guns and h. A1614.4.3; phantom coach and h. E535.1; people in otherworld hitch h. both before and behind the wagon F171.6.4; quest for the finest of h. H1308; race between wooden h. D1719.1.4; relics protect h. V144.2; repartee concerning runaway h. J1483ff.; resourcefulness test: find how old three h. are H506.1; spirit and h. F402.1.14; spirit rides, wears out h. at night F473.4.1; stealing h. from king H1151.13.3; stealing twelve h. out of stall (task) H1151.2; strong man sent for wild h. F615.2.3; tabu: h. eating foreign provender C224.4; tabus concerning h. C884; telling their h. apart J2722; there are ten h.: why then when he is mounted only nine? J2031.2; three h. from dove's egg on last day A1091.1; thunder from hoofs of gods' h. A1142.6; various colored h. of brownie F482.4.1; waves as manes of sea god's h. A1116.1; wild hunt heralded by noise of h. E501.13.3; witch disguised as queen eats h. G264.3.1; witch rides h. at night *G265.3; wolf boasts of having eaten h. J2351.4.

Horses'. — Wild hunt throws h. feet on persons who see it E501.18.3.

Horseback journey to otherworld F159.2. — Death on h. F492; ghost on h. E332.3.1; hero feigns fear of h. K1777; journey to upper world on h. F66; old king cannot get on h. F571.6.

Horseblock. — Cast-forth wife must sit at h. of palace Q482.4.

Horseflesh, see **Horsemeat.**

Horsehairs. — Magic h. (when rubbed) compel horse to follow D1427.3.

Horsehead. — Reincarnation: man as h. E611.1.1; speaking h. *B133.3.

Horseheaded men reborn as money-lenders E605.8.

Horsehide. — Alleged oracular h. K114.1.1.

Horseman. — Automatic statue of h. D1620.1.2; copper h. indicates route *D1313.3; head restored to headless h. D1518.3.

Horsemen taken to be men on cattle J1766.1. — Children transformed into h. D98; impious h. swallowed up by earth Q221.4.3.

Horsemanship. — Parson's poor h. X443.

Horsemeat. — Tabu to eat h. C221.1.1.2, C756.4; penance for eating h. Q499.6; transformation: h. to mutton D476.3.3.

Horse-racing. — Demons' h. F419.1; origin of h. A1535.6.

Horseshoe brings good luck D1561.1.3; protection against witches G272.11. — Devil unable to enter house with h. over the door *G303.16.17; extraordinary h. F862; lost h. nail (cumulative tale) Z45, (brings train of troubles) N258; magic h. *D1286; woman with h. on one foot F551.1.2.1.

Horseshoes. — Countertask: making h. for cavalry from one needle H1022.2.1; fairies' horses have round h. F241; transformation to horse by wearing h. D535.1; witch as horse shod with h. *G211.1.1.2.

Horseshoeing. — Imitation of miraculous h. unsuccessful J2411.2.

Horseskin. — Magic h. D1025.7.

Horsewhips. — Origin of h. A1459.1.5.

Hose. — Magic adhesion to h. D2171.3.4; witch known by h. unbound on one leg G255.

Hospitable fire of his father is sought (bean merchant) H581.2; man impoverished by greedy guests W151.2.2; person saved from death Q151.3.

Hospital. — Harshness frightens h. patients K1955.1.2; recognition at h. H11.1.1.

Hospitality *P320ff.; of a citizen saves city from destruction Q152.1;

enforced on hero keeps him away too long N391.0.1; to incognito king rewarded K1812.4; rewarded Q45, (opposite punished) Q1; as a virtue W12. — Animal characteristics reward for h. A2222; customs of h. A1598; excessive h. causes chieftain to become poor Q42.1.3; execution escaped by invoking laws of h. J1183; fairy grateful for h. F332; fairy kills man refusing his h. F361.17.7; gods disguised as beggars test h. K1811.1; hero dispenses h. A547; inhospitable host punished for h. J1561.2; planting garden and offering free h. to all as penance Q523.5; quest as payment for h. H1219.7; sex h. T281; smith as lord of h. P447.3; test of h. H1564; trickster abuses h. K354; trickster feigns deafness and gets h. from miser K1981.1.

Hospitaller. — Disguise as h. K1825.4.

Host (person) entertains otherworld seeker F151.0.1; and guest P320ff.; imposes tabu C901.1.4; offers to send his guest a cask of the wine he has praised (verba honoris) M206.1; rebukes negligent servant J1573; robs guest K385; wants to learn Hebrew even at risk of forgetting his own language J344.2. — Bungling h. J2425; forgery dupes h. K455.8.2; luxury of h. rebuked J1566; magic object stolen by h. D861.1; suspicious guest forces h. to be killed in his stead K1611.2; treacherous h. K2294; winespilling h. rebuked J1511.5.

Host (sacrament) *V30ff.; put into beehive C55.3. — Devil disappears when given h. G303.16.5.2; devils worship h. G303.24.2; incredulity about h. confounded by miracle V33.1; princess must recover h. stolen by rat H1292.4.1; priest carries h. across stream J1261.2.8; punishment for desecration of h. Q222.1; sacred image appears on h. V39.5.

Host's. — Knight unsuccessfully tempted by h. wife T331.2; tabu to eat before h. house righted C231.4.

Hosts P320ff. — Phantom h. E500ff.; practical retorts: h. and guests J1560ff.; stolen sacred h. put into coffin, fill bag V35.2.

Hostage. — Prince imprisoned as h. P34; son gives mother as h. S21.3.

Hostages P533.1; buried alive S123.0.1; cursed M414.7; escape prevented as reward Q157; sacrificed S265.1. — Covenant confirmed by h. M201.6.

Hostel. — Forbidden h. C619.1.

Hostess who had no spoons J1561.4.1. — Virgin Mary supplies mead for unprepared h. V262.

Hostile animals B17; beasts B17.1; beings in otherworld F360.0.1; brides kill husbands in the bridal bed T173.2; brothers P251.5.3; dogs made friendly by having them fight common enemy, the wolf J145; twins T685.2. — Children abandoned by h. relative S322; giants h. to Christianity F531.5.8.1; keeping on good terms with h. gods J821; unworthy origin ascribed to h. tribes A1610.1.

Hostility. — Animal characteristics as punishment for h. at crucifixion *A2231.2ff.; prevention of h. by inspiring fear in enemy J623.

Hot rain F962.2.5; springs rise where Christ bathed his feet A942.1; weather from God boring hole in hell A1137. — Breasts h. enough to cook on F546.5; chastity ordeal: holding h. iron H412.4.1; devil's money h. G303.21.3; dupe opens mouth, closes eyes: h. stones thrown in K721.1; dupe sits on h. iron K1074; dupe sits on h. stone K1032; fairies punish girl who pours h. water into their spring F361.5; flood from h. liquid A1016.2; fountain h. or cold as desired F716.3; god's throne becomes h. A152.9; lies about h. weather X1630; murder by h. object in mouth K951.1.1; murder by over-h. food S112.5; numskull feeds hens h. water so they will lay boiled eggs J1901.2; ogre killed by throwing h. stones into his throat G512.3.1; ordeal by h. iron H221.2; origin of h. springs A942; punishment: climbing h. rod Q469.2; red-h. floor protects city F767.2; red-h. meal forced on person S183.0.1; remarkably h. spear F834.1; saint invulnerable to red h. iron D1841.3.2.3; second lover burns paramour at window with h. iron K1577; sham-dead person tested by h. lead poured on hand H248.1; stream becomes h. in which saint performs his ascetic devotions F932.3; sun originally so h. all life threatened A727.1; sun's son too h. to hold A736.5.1; voice made rough by swallowing h. iron F556.1.

Hotel. — Lie: great h. X1035.

Hound, see also **Dog;** attack as valor test H1561.7; becomes lap-dog D412.5.2; of every color B731.6; flame of fire B19.4.4; of hell *A673; kills ogre's wife G519.1.1; strikes unique vulnerable spot N335.5. — Devil's h. G303.10.15; dog is h. by night, sheep by day B182.1.4, H1331.9; dog is h. by day, fire by night B182.1.5; fairy kills mortal's h. F369.3; fight between animal and h. pack B264.1; god battles h. of hell A1082.2.2; hostile dog (h.) B17.1.2, (killed by reaching through hollow log in its jaws and tearing out heart) B17.1.2.2; magic animal proof against h. D1841.7; magic boar drowns h. pack B184.3.1.1; magic whelp kills h. B182.1.3.1; pet h. killed, man dies of its blood Q582.4; quest for unknown h. H1383.1; saint's song silences h. D1442.5; savage h. guards door H1423.1; stealing king's h. H1151.13.4; venomous h. B776.3; whelp leaps through h. F916.2.

Hound's blood from magic spear D1404.2. — Animal with horse's body, h. legs B14.2.

Hounds must be followed C681.1; set after man Q415.1.2. — Chief's wolf-h. C564.3; forgetting leashes of h. bad omen D1812.5.1.21; giant's skull holds three h. F531.2.3.2; hell-h. accompany soul to lower world E752.5; hunter manages h. F679.5.1; wild hunt heralded by baying of h. E501.13.4.

Hour of grace used up in disputing J2183.4; has come but not the man M219.2.3. — Foreknowledge of h. of death D1812.0.1; sun changes h. F961.1.7.

Hours. — Bird calls out h. F989.3; canonical h. V48.

House appears overnight to shelter priest V229.21; -building learned from wasps A1445.2.2; burned down (cumulative tale) Z51.1, (with all inside) S112.0.2, (to rid it of insects) J2102.4, (to rid it of rats) J2103.3; burns for no reason F473.2.4; crushed by magic D2099.3; destroyed by magic D2089.6; -door transformed to stone D471.2.1; where false judgment given slips down hill Q559.8; goes wherever owner commands F675.3; has neither eyes nor ears H583.8; of fairy F221; of my father with 150 lights and goat pen K1917.4; that Jack built Z44; to make house-spirit surrender booty F480.3.1; neither on ground nor in sky H1077; the old man was to build (cumulative tale) Z44.1; in otherworld F163.3; of saint filled with fragrance V222.4; seems afire K1889.1; spirit leaves after clothing gift F405.11; spirits F480ff.; transformed to stone D471.2; unlighted taken over by ghosts E593.3; without food or drink J2483. — Animal as guard of h. B576.1; animals keeping h. together; all goes wrong J512.7; bees caught in a sack which is opened in the h. J2131.2.1; blowing the h. in Z81; bodies of victims in front of ogre's h. G691; brownies live in h. F482.3.1; building iron h. overnight H1104.3; burning own h. for access to woman K1349.7; children wander into ogre's h. G401; criminal's h. burned down Q486.1; dead's h. of cloud E481.8.4; departing h. F1063; devil as h. G303.3.4.9; devil haunts h. G303.15.3; devil unable to enter h. with horseshoe over the door *G303.16.17; devil's grandmother keeps h. for him G303.11.4.1; devil's h. is visible on the way to hell G303.8.3.3; dog will not help build h.: must remain out of doors A2233.2; dupe burns h. because trickster reports high price paid for ashes K941.2; egg becomes h. D469.1.1; extraordinary h. *F771ff.; fairies build h. F346.2; fairies occupy peasant's h. F365.3; fairy h. disappears at dawn F221.1; fool roofs his h. on the inside J2171.2.2; fool whose h. is burning puts wood on the fire J2162.2; friendly ghost haunts h. E338.1; ghost laid by destroying haunted h. E451.8; ghostly horse enters h. and puts hoofs on breast of sleeper E281.2; ghosts haunt h. E281; gingerbread h. F771.1.10; if host does not return h. shall belong to the guest P326; husband in the chicken h. K1514.1; husband made to believe that h. has moved during his absence J2316; incombustible h. D1656.2; jinn kills occupants of his h. G307.3; kid perched on h. jeers at wolf J974; magic beautification of h. *D1867; magic h. D1133, (removed) D2136.9; magic object produces h. D1599.4; magic object taken from ogre's h. D838.1; man mistakes giant's glove for h. F531.5.2; means of entering h. or treasury K310ff; monkey pretends that his h. always answers him K1722; moon has h. A753.2; not to leave h. within ten days C755.1; not recognizing own h. converted to mansion J2316.1; objects keep h. together J512.7; ogre attacks intruders in h. in woods G475.1; ogre imprisoned in own h. G514.2; only fault with the h. J2236; peasant's h. P411.1.1; putting h. in order tabu C743; repairing the h. K1415; riddle on h. full of dead H831; robber-proof h. D2072.5; selling half his h. J2213.6; sham wise man does not know where his own h. is K1956.4; small niche in h. brings large price K182.1; snail grows and fills h. entirely F983.1; Socrates builds himself little h. J401.1; staying in haunted h. H1411; stream runs through h. F715.4; strong hero lifts

h. F624.6; sunlight carried into windowless h. in baskets J2123; tabu: being in h. with fire, weapon, dog C887; tabu to eat before host's h. righted C231.4; tabu: sleeping in h. lighted after sunset C735.2.4; too cold for hare to build h. in winter: must go without h. A2233.2.1; trickery to buy h. cheaply K1838; trickster appropriates host's h. K354; trickster pollutes h. so that he is left in possession K355; trumpet blown before h. of one sentenced to death P612; underwater h. F133.2, F725.3.3; victim burned in his own h. K812; victim lured into h. and killed K811; vow not to enter any h. before one's own M182; wild hunt avoided by keeping in h. with windows closed E501.17.5.3; wild huntsman's dog cannot be dislodged from h. it has entered E501.15.6.5.

Houses at border of otherworld F147; in lower world of dead E481.1.2; magically enlarged D488. — Acquisition of guest h. A1435.1; burning h. to sell ashes K941.3; fairies' h. F220; gods built h. A1402; jinns in ruined h. F499.3.3; wild hunt goes through h. when front and back doors are on a line E501.14.6; witch causes haunted h. G269.5.

Household articles act at command D1601.9; gods A411, (speak) A182.1.1. — Acquisition of h. implements A1446.5; animal as h. spirit B593; bewitched h. articles G265.8.1; entire h. dies same night F1099.1; jokers set h. at variance K2134.1; king slain by own h. P16.7; poltergeist malevolent h. spirit F473; magic h. articles answer for fugitive D1611.9; magic olive branch makes woman master in h. D1359.1.1.

Housekeeper. — Boy as h. for buffaloes N832.1; devil's grandmother is his h. G303.11.4.1; mysterious h. B537, N831.1; true bride as mysterious h. K1911.3.5.

Housekeeping. — Cows grateful for hero's h. B396.

Housemaid disguised as minister K1839.10.

House-pillars warn D1317.21. — Magic h. *D1149.3.

Housepost. — Man becomes h. D268.1; speaking h. D1610.30.1.

Housewife frightens away guests J1563.5.

Housework. — Grateful fairies do h. F339.3.1.

Hovel. — Noble person must live in h. Q485.

Hovering. — Angels h. over mortal V238.1; birds h. over battlefield F989.14; hawk loses grandmother: still h. and searching A2275.5.2; soul h. over body E722.2.8.2; spirits h. over battle F418.

Howe as home of (dwarf) E451.4.1.9, (troll) F455.1.1.

Howling of animal at night explained A2427. — Divination from dog h. D1812.5.0.9; dogs' h. as bad omen D1812.5.1.12.1; eaten magic dog h. from eater's belly D1619.2.1.

Huckauf *F472.

Huge, see also **Enormous, Gigantic, Large.** — Breaking h. rock to pieces (task) H1116; devil bound with h. chain G303.8.4.1; gate h. as mountain F776.1.

Hugh of Lincoln V361.

Hulls. — Man compelled to live on peas comforted by seeing a man once rich eating h. J883.1.

Hum. — Beetle demands return of gold from God: must h. A2231.11.

Human and animal offspring from marriage to animal B633; beings devoured, see **Cannibalism**; beings descended from seals B631.2; -dragon marriage B11.12.3.1; flesh eaten unwittingly *G60ff.; head used for divination D1311.8; helpers N820ff.; offspring from marriage to animal *B631; sacrifice S260.1; son of animal parents T566; sons of animal companions are friends P311.3. — Animal with h. eyes B15.4.4; animal in h. form recognized H48; animal substituted for h. sacrifice A1545.2; animals with h. emotions B773; animals in otherworld pass in and out of church and become h. beings *F171.5; animals or objects treated as h. J1850—J1899; animal uses h. speech B211ff.; animals with h. traits B200—B299; conception from eating parts of h. being T511.6; deity appearing before h. A189.6; deity in h. form A125; demons assume h. forms (to deceive) F402.1.4, (to revenge) D651.1.2; devil given animal instead of h. K219.6; devil's horse has h. feet G303.7.1.2.1; devil in h. form G303.3.1ff.; devils as h. beings voracious G303.3.0.2; dragon flies to nest with h. being B11.6.8; druids perform h. sacrifice P427.1.1; dwarfs seek h. help F451.5.23; dwarfs and h. beings F451.5ff.; eating of h. hearts as cure for insomnia D2161.4.13; fairies and h. children F310ff.; fettered monster in h. form A1072.1; first h. pair as creators A2.2; ghost haunts in h. shape E279.1; ghosts eat h. beings E541.2; giants marry h. beings F531.5.7; gods borne by h. woman A112.9; incarnation of a god: puts on h. form to help men E605.2; lotus transformed to h. hand D451.4.1; magic h. bodily members *D990ff.; mankind from h.-animal mating A1221.6; marriage to animal in h. form *B650ff.; offer to make pups born of woman in shape of hound h. D601; origin of h. sacrifice A1545.5; overheard h. conversation N455; partial transformation: animal with h. mind D682.3; parts of h. body furnish treasure D1454ff.; person substitutes for h. sacrifice K1853.2; pestilence in h. form F493.0.3; pisāca eats h. flesh G312.1; primeval h. pair A1270ff.; reincarnation in another h. form E605; relation of planets to h. life A787; revenant in h. form E425; spirit in h. form F401.6; star descends as h. being A762; sun as h. being A736; trees with fruits like h. heads F811.8; troll in h. form F455.2.5; why tigers eat h. flesh A2435.3.9.3; wild hunt throws h. flesh on persons who see it E501.18.2.

Humanity. — Objects attempt to destroy h. A1009.2.

Humble disguise K521.4.3, K1815; man asks aid of incognito king K1812.1.1; man miraculously saved from drowning Q151.5; rewarded Q4. — Incognito king helped by h. man K1812.1; king of h. lineage cannot be flattered J915; parents make selves h. before their son M312.2; proud ruler becomes h. L410ff.; transformation to h. man D24; wise man h. in death J912.

Humiliated lover J1251.1, K1214.1.1. — Princess h. for loathly marriage S322.1.4.

Humiliating owner by mutilating horses S175; penances Q523ff.; punishments Q470ff. — Deception into h. position *K1200—K1299.

Humiliation curse M438. — Seal of h. L11.1.

Humility J900—J999; rewarded Q66; as suitor test H313. — Devil spares abbot because of h. Q61.2; lightning strikes monk who despises h. Q552.1.1; magic depends on h. D1749.2; seven daughters of H. Z71.5.6.13.

Humming. — Ceaseless h. as punishment Q501.8; fools frightened at h. of bees J2614.1.

Hummingbird can see fowler's net but eagle is caught L333. — Industrious h. rewarded Q5.2.

Humor X (entire chapter); of discomfiture X0—X99; based on drunkenness X800—X899; of lies and exaggeration X900—X1899; of physical disability X100—X199; dealing with professions X300—X499; concerning races or nations X600—X699; concerning sex X700—X799; concerning social classes X200—X599; dealing with tradesmen X200—X299.

Humors. — Four h. Z71.2.3.

Hump. — Why animal has h. on back A2356.2.1, A2356.2.6, A2356.2.9; fairies remove hunchback's h. F344.1; giant with h. F531.1.6.11.

Humps. — Magic object causes h. to appear on back D1375.5.

Hunchback cured F953.1, (by fairies) F344.1; dwarf F451.2.1.4; healed as reward Q161.3; leads blind man N886.1; springs into fire, dies J1812.4.1. — Princess elopes with h. T91.6.4.3; three h. brothers drowned K2323; witch causes h. G269.11.1.

Hundred-handed giants F515.0.2.1; -headed serpent B15.1.2.10.2; league stride D2122.2; rajahs in love with one woman T27.3. — Alms to be returned h-fold J1262.5; city with h. palaces, gardens F761.1.1; cow makes a h.-fold return K366.1.1; eating h. onions J2095; monster with h. hands, h. palms on each, h. nails on each palm B15.7.15; prophecy: girl shall have h. lovers M345.1; surely saw h. wolves W211.2.

Hundreds. — Carrying h. of sheep across stream one at a time H1111; dwarfs come into the land by h. F451.3.14.1; person h. of years old F571.7.

Hundred-thousand. — Monkey becomes h. feet high D411.5.5.

Hung, see also **Hanged.** — Clothes h. on sunbeam *F1011.1; king h. between two fires K2213.15, Q414.5; stars h. in heavens as decoration A763.2; wolf h. by man B275.1.3.1.

Hungary. — Battle between lice of Strassburg and of H. X651.

Hunger cure J1606; in hell A689.3. — Faithful animal at master's grave dies of h. B301.1; food alone keeps off h. J712; magic object causes constant h. D1373ff.; magic object produces immunity from h. D1349.1; mice die of h. J1269.10; origin of h. A1345; starving colt fierce from h. J2214.10; tightening belt to counteract h. F1076; wager on whose h.

greater: man or beast? N73; wolf prefers liberty and h. to dog's servitude with plenty L451.

Hungry ghost reborn as jackal E694.1; ghosts haunt house seeking food E281.1; man eats fish intestines next morning J1606.1; old woman shakes, causes earthquakes A843; parson and porridge-pot X431. — Changeling always h. F321.1.2.2; coming neither h. nor satisfied (task) H1063; contract between h. god and untouchable M242.2; don't set h. guard over food J215.1.1; dwarf children are h. F451.3.5.3; fruit flies from h. man's reach Q501.2.1; mother drives away h. and compels the filled to eat H583.4.4; retorts from h. persons J1340ff.

Hunt for extraordinary animal F989.15. — Convening h. tabu C751.3; devil carries off h.-loving priest M219.2.4; king (prince) lost on h. has adventures N771; man on h. falls into ogre's (witch's) power G405; otherworld journey as h. F4; parents to abandon children on h. S345; skill in h. as suitor test H326.3; treacherous murder during h. K917; wild h. (see **Wild Huntsman** for analysis of this item) *E501ff.; wonderful h. (lie) X1110.

Hunter P414; beats dog which has grown old in his service W154.4; discovers girl being reared in cave N724; kills devil G303.16.19.20; mistakes louse for game J1759.2; reduced to ashes by power of heroine's chastity *D2061.2.5; rescues abandoned child R131.1; throws away what he catches and what he does not catch he carries with him (lice) H583.3; wants to be shown lion tracks, not lion himself W121.1. — Child born with weapon and game animal to be h. N121.1.2; devil as a h. in green G303.5.2.2; fairies give h. a dog F343.2; fisher and h. exchange catches for variety: soon return to original food U136; hero as mighty h. A526.2; lie: remarkable h. X1100; magic object from h. D823; one bird escapes as h. bends his bow: other remains and is shot J641.1; prophecy: success as h. M326, M369.10; skillful h. F679.5.

Hunter's ghost as nightmare F471.14; mass J2474; prey stolen D2087.2.

Hunters. — Beast seeks saint's help against h. B251.4.1.1; goddess protects animals from h. A189.12; jokes about h. X584, X1100; magic birds lure h. B172.6; Pleiades from h. marooned in sky A773.5; prophecy: h. will encounter boar M397; stag escapes h. to be eaten by lion N255.1; transformation to lure h. D659.10; women h. E501.3.10, F565, F565.4.

Hunting as animal's occupation A2452ff.; contest H1592, (won by deception) K30ff.; cry must be followed C681.1; fairy animal F241.0.1; a madness of kings P12.1; pig tabu C841.4; tabu in certain season C755.6; tabu on shortest day C636; of wild boar explained A1422.3; woman beaten, corpse's ankles tied E442.1. — Accidental success in h. N620ff.; devil destroys h. party with terrible wind G303.20.2; devil in disguise h. souls E752.1.1; devil dressed in h. clothes G303.5.5; devil gives luck in h. G303.10.7; devil h. lost souls G303.7.1.3; earl imprisoned for h. in king's forest Q433.10; enemies caused to lose sight while h. D2062.2.4; fairies h. human beings F368; ghost h. lost article E415.1; giant carries prodigious h. prey F531.3.13.1; giant's h. F531.3.12; god of h. A452; infallible h.-dog B121.1.1; intercourse at h. season forbidden C119.1.3; lame man h. from wheel chair X143.1; magic h. collar *D1068.1; Milky Way a h. party A778.1; origin of h. A1458, (customs) A1520ff.; otherworld reached by h. F159.1; prince h. enters on quest H1222; sham prowess in h. K1968; tabu: h. in certain forest C614.1.0.2; trickster's greed while h. causes him to be deserted J2751; women not to participate in h. activities C181.2; wild huntsman wanders for h. on Sunday *E501.3.6.

Huntsmen. — Wild h. *E501.

Huntswoman. — Wild h. wanders for daughter's murder E501.3.10.

Hurling. — Playing in h.-match for corpses H1436; rock h. down hill slays enemy K914.2.

Hurting. — People magically continue h. themselves D2184.

Husband, see also **Bridegroom**; abandons wife to become ascetic V462.0.3; accepts children born buring long absence J2342.2; afraid of wife's paramour J2626.1; answers behind statue when wife wants to know how to fool him K1971.1; arrives home just as wife is to marry another *N681; assigns task to king stealing his wife H931.1.1; attracted by wife's power of healing: recognition follows H151.8; behind statue of saint advises wife to spin and weave K1971.4; becomes cannibal from eating wife's breast G36.1; concealed in wife's ear F1034.1; as cuckold K1500ff.; deceives wife with substituted bedmate K1844; digs up alleged treasure: wife taken K1388.1; discredited by absurd truth J1151.1.2; disguised as wife's relative K1839.13; disguised as woman answers wife's riddle with ten fingers H582.3; disguises as woman to spy on wife K1836.1; eats wife G77; eats wife's share of food W125.5; fondles second wife in presence of first as punishment for adultery Q484; forgiven for murdering wife: afterwards builds monastery Q171.1.1; follows witch G249.6; free from jealousy required M137.1; as God behind the tree forces his wife to confess adultery *K1971.5; ignored or discouraged by ghost wife E385.1; killed for having married against father's wishes K959.2.1; kills returning adulteress Q411.0.1; learns of wife's unfaithfulness by ring H94.0.1; loses willingness to die for mate H1556.4.5; magically forgets wife D2003.1; more merciful than blood relations P213; outwits adulteress and paramour *K1550ff.; persecutes wife S410ff.; poses as wife's brother K1919.1; pursues fairy wife to heaven F300.2; recognized by tears at sight of bird H14.1; refuses to believe wife unfaithful J2342; refuses to murder his wife for high honors (wife not so faithful) H492.1; rescues wife R151, (from burning to death) N658; resuscitated by cutting off wife's nose E165.2; has his strong servant substitute in bed with strong wife K1844.1; in seclusion during wife's pregnancy T583.10.1; shames wife's lover over kisses K1218.10; substitutes leaky vessel so that his wife and paramour are drowned Q466.1; tied to bed, wife's lover kills him K713.1.7; transformed to mouse to rescue wife R115.1; tricks poet into slaying wife's lover K863.1; unwittingly instrumental in wife's adultery K1544; and wife *P210ff., (burn their mouths) J1478, (each receive money to bury the other) K482.1, (poison each other) K1613.2; to wife: "let him have what he wants" K1354.2.1. — Adulteress lures h. to his death K778.5; animal h. C36ff., (killed, wife throws self into pyre) B691, (provides animal food) B600.2; animal wins h. for mistress B582.1.2; adulteress outwits h. K1510ff.; adulteress pretends to faint when h. strikes her with rose K2051.2; beast-h. not to stay too long at home C713.3.1; to be beaten by deceiver of h. J1182.1; bride not to eat on journey to h. C232.1; burial of living h. or wife with dead spouse S123.2; cannibal h. *G81; continent h. and auda- cious water T315.2.1; crab shape of h. destroyed D719.2; cruel h. *S62; dangers to h. in bridal chamber T172; dead h. protests wife's second husband E221.3; dead wife asks h. go to spirit world E322.2.1; dead wife lives with h. until his death E322.6; dead wife haunts h. on second marriage *E221.1; departing h. assigns his wife tasks *H922; devil gives suspicious h. ring G303.9.7.3; devil-h. eats corpses G20.1; devil follows wife's curse, takes h. C12.5.7; disguised h. visits his wife K1813; not to eat food of transformed h. C243; eavesdropping wife hidden in bushes killed unwittingly by h. N322.2; fairy avenges herself on inconstant h. F302.3.3.1; fairy wife deserts mortal h. for repulsive lover F302.2.1; faithful h. T210.2; false bride fails when h. tests her K1911.3.3; false h. duped into entering jar J1172.3.1; fault- finding h. nonplussed J1545.3; first h. hideous, is hidden A1279.1; fox-h. lured off K341.29; future h. foretold M369.2.1; future h. met during magic sleep D1976.2; future h. revealed in dream D1812.3.3.9; which was most generous, h., robber, or lover? H1552.1; guest un- accompanied by h. slept with C119.2; heartbreak when former h. found alive F1041.1.3.7; henpecked h. returns home after hearing rooster crow J1811.4.1; heroine endures hardships with menial h. L113.1.0.1; impoverished h. begs from expelled wife L432.3; im- poverished h. in wife's service recognized H152.2; imprisoned h. freed through wife's prayers V52.10; injured h. will not kill naked man P641; jealous h. T257, (kills innocent wife) N348; king rewards h. of woman spurning him Q87.1.2; kissing supernatural h. forbidden C121; lazy h. W111.4; leave of absence for obedient h. J2523; loathly h. god in disguise D733.3; loss of wife (h.) for breaking tabu C932; magic belt protects against h. D1387.3; magic hairs summon h. D1425.2; magic forgetting of wife when h. removes shirt she has given him D2004.6; man with unfaithful wife comforted when he sees jealous h. who carefully guards wife cuckolded J882.2; offending supernatural h. forbidden *C32ff.; olive branch insures fidelity of h. D1355.8; only h. of certain queen can rule P29.1; origin of code of conduct between h. and wife A1571; peace bought for h. M236; poor suitor makes good h. L143.2; predestined h. T22.3; prediction by bird

that girl will have dead h. M353; prophecy: death through future
h. M341.2.12; property disposal rouses sham-dead h. J2511.1.1; quest
for vanished h. H1385.4; resuscitation of wife by h. giving up half his
remaining life *E165; retorts between h. and wife J1540ff.; not to
reveal secret of supernatural h. *C421ff.; rose sheds petals when h.
thinks of wife H1556.4.6; second h. ordered to return wife to first in
pregnant condition J1173.1; seduction by masking as woman's h.
*K1311; of seven wives each has h. one day T145.1.2; sham threat to
evade h. K1771.6; stupid h. J1702; sun and moon as h. and wife
A736.1.4.2; supernatural h. resumes true shape C32.1.2; supernatural
h. takes wife to heaven F2.1; tabus for girl going to her h. C161;
thief feigns pursuit by drunken h. K314; tiger-h. disenchanted D789.9;
transformation to cure inconstant h. D662; transformed h. C32.1.1;
twofold death of fairy's mortal h. C435.1.1.1; unexpected meeting of
h. and wife N741; unfaithful h. loses magic wife C31.12; unrestricted
intercourse between h. and wife A1352.1; when death comes wife points
to h. K2065.1; whiskerless h. mistaken for lover in bed J1485.1; wife
assigns h. tasks H934.1; wife betraying h. to father K2213.7; wife confesses for h. V29.5; wife flees h. R227; wife gives h. money to buy self
genitals J1919.8; wife persuades h. he has cut off her nose J2315.2; wife
reforms wayward h. J1112.1; wife rescuing h. from supernatural H923.1;
wife tempts h. as another woman H1556.4.2.1; wife behind tree advises
h. K1971.4.1, K1971.6.1; wife deceives h. with substituted bedmate
K1843; wife in disguise wooed by her faithless h. K1814; wife persuades
h. (to have a good tooth pulled) J2324, (that he is dead) J2311.0.1,
(that house has moved during his absence) J2316, (that she has returned
immediately) J2315, (that yarn has changed to tow) J2325; wish for h.
realized (animal) C26, (exalted) *N201, (supernatural) C15; witch transforms h. into dog G263.1.4; woman deceived into sacrificing honor when
ruler promises to release her h. K1353; woman devours her h. G11.6.4;
woman dies of shame at seeing naked h. F1041.1.13.2; woman with more
than one h. T146; woman as scorpion to punish h. E693.3; woman seeks
lost h., entertains all travelers H152.1.1; woman subservient to h.
A1571.2; woman substitutes for h. in combat K3.3; woman suckling h.
R81.1.

Husband's hands tied, wife drowns K1652; love turns to hatred D1908.1;
magic gift returns to him N212.1; return simulated, wife abducted
K755.1. — Animals warn wife of h. danger B521.4; dead h. friendly
return *E321; death from hearing of h. death F1041.1.2.2; faithless h.
intrigue exposed K1271.3; forgotten fiancée reawakens h. memory
D2006.1ff.; lost h. bones found among cannibals G691.4; lover sees
mistress in h. father's house T35.5; magic sword protects woman from
fairy lover in h. absence D1386.1; procuring dead h. heart F81.1.1;
quest assigned by wife through appeal to h. love for her H1212.2; sham
death to escape h. plot K522.3; transformation to h. form to seduce
woman *D658.2; woman battles demons for h. soul E756.5.

Husbands. — All h. have perished on bridal night *T172.0.1; characteristics of wives and h. *T250ff.; gullible h. *J2301; hero chooses h. C566.4; hostile brides kill h. in the bridal bed T173.2; six short, fat h. married to fat, tall wives X151.1; tests for true h. H422; wager: h. able to do what wives tell them N13; wagers on h. N10ff.; woman with two h. is to be killed J1171.3.

Husking. — Bear h. millet B571.4.

Husks. — Replacing h. disguises grain theft K419.6.

Hussars. — Dwarfs mistaken for h. F451.6.2.3.

Hut becomes mansion D1867.1; for invalid to prevent noxious odor P661; transformed to palace D478.8. — Hermit's h. at border of otherworld F147.2; hero lives in h. L134; peasant's h. contrast to castle P411.1.1; stick becomes spirit h. D451.6.2; stone transformed to h. D452.1.1; wall of snow around h. in answer to prayer D2143.6.2.

Huts. — Grass h. as dwellings A1435.3; spirit h. V112.1.

Hvergelmir A661.1.0.4.

Hyades, origin of A775.

Hybrid animals A2382, B11—B14.

Hydra B15.1.2.8.1. — Poison of h. corrodes the skin F1041.5; separable soul in head of h. E715.6.

Hydrax. — Why h. has no tail A2235, A2378.2.5.

Hyena changes sex yearly B754.1.1; leads hermit from wilderness B380.1; poses as father, kills child K2011.1.3; with 365 different colors B731.14; turns into man D313.4. — Color of h. A2411.1.7.1; creation of h. A1834.3; devil as h. G303.3.3.2.9; helpful h. B435.6; man transformed to h. D113.5; mean person reborn as h. E692.2; reincarnation as h. E612.9; wedding of fox and h. B281.1; why h. stayed in burrow A2282, A2433.3.4; why h. has short left hind foot A2284.6, A2375.2.5.

Hyena's enemies A2494.3ff.; walk A2441.1.4.

Hyenas. — Army of h. B268.13.

Hymenoptera, creation of A2010ff.

Hymn drives away devils G303.16.2.4; prevents starvation D2105.1.1. — Devil sings h., becomes angel G303.8.1.2.1; magic h. *D1275.3, (assures heaven for person singing it) D1588.3, (effects prison escape) D1395.7, (protects) D1380.14.1, (protects against demons and vices) D1385.16, (protects against poison) D1383.4.1, (protects against poverty, death and dishonor) D1389.9, (protects from fire) D1382.7.1; magic results from singing h. D1766.9; origin of h. A1464.2; reward for writing h. Q35; saint writes h. to free self from wife T253.3; sight miraculously restored while poet writes h. F952.0.1.

Hymns V83. — Dwarfs dislike singing of h. F451.5.9.2; seas sing h. F931.12.

Hypnotic. — Magic sleep by h. suggestion D1962.4; snake's h. stare B765.14.

Hypnotised. — Person h. into believing himself transformed K1262.

Hypocrisy in confession: false shame over trivial sin V26; punished

Q267; of wife showing what she has done for her husband, but not what she has done for herself T263. — Detection of h. K2060ff.; doctor glad that all h. will have an end J171.2.3.

Hypocrite acclaimed as saint U116. — Blind tiger recognizes h. F655.2.

Hypocrites *K2000—K2099.

"I can't hear you" X441.1; "don't understand" J1802.1.

Ibexes. — Fairies own i. F241.5.1.

Ibis. — Riddle about i. H842.3.

Ibycus, Cranes of N271.3.

Icarus's wings melt F1021.2.1.

Ice bridge F842.1.2; controlled by magic D2144.5; flakes magically made small D491.4; forms while fish leaps from pool F935.2; transformed to grease D476.1.9. — Bear builds house of wood, fox of i. J741.1; bear persuaded to fish with tail through i. K1021; dupe forced on to thin i. drowns himself K893; flood from i. melting A1016.3; magic beads break i. jam D1549.11; magic i. D904; magic transportation on i. sheet D2125.2; man cuts i. with own head (lie) X1858; man falls through i. with his horse and wanders about on river bottom X1737.1.1; mermaid can pass through i. B81.8; mountain of i. F759.5; palace of i. F771.1.7; porridge in the i. hole J1938; pursuers tricked onto thin i. K893.1; rabbits freeze feet fast to i. at night X1115.1; revenant with i.-cold hands E422.1.3; sea of i. in otherworld F162.4.1; sea-scum becomes i. D469.4; sea turns to i. to permit flight D675; treasure found if one goes with one-night old colt onto one-night old i. N542.1; universe created from i. A623.

Ichneumon. — Helpful i. B433.3.

Ichor. — Gods have i., not blood A139.9.2.

Ichthyophages (people who live on fish) F561.2.

Icicles as firewood F962.9. — Dancers upon whom i. hang F572; saint's breath makes i. burn D1566.1.4.2.

Icy hell E481.7, E755.2.5.

Identical persons F239.2, H1381.3.5. — Adopted child i. with real one T678; culprit exposed to situation i. to one in which he sinned H1573.7.1; fairy women i. F239.2; friends i. in appearance F577.1; magic object to be chosen from among i. worthless objects K859.5; quest for woman i. with another H1381.3.5; recognition of transformed person among i. companions H161.

Identically. — Choosing princess from others i. clad H324; man does not know himself from another i. clad J2012.5; warriors i. equipped Z210.0.1.

Identification by cloth or clothing H110ff.; by a hair H75; by matching parts of divided token H100ff.; by ornaments H90ff. — Magic i. of headless body D1819.3.

Identifying rice in sack H522.3. — Ghost i. self E451.4.1; recognition by i. of property H19.1; trip to otherworld for i. dead F12.2.

Identity established, execution evaded N686; tests *H0—H199. — Boys scolded to conceal i. K649.3; death result of mistaken i. N338; disclosing own i. forbidden C436; fairy dry in rain reveals i. F259.3; lover's gift regained: accidental discovery of i. K1581.4; magic knowledge of stranger's i. D1810.0.13; objects with mistaken i. J1770ff.; revealing i. of certain person forbidden C422; talking bed reveals king's i. N617; uncertainty about own i. *J2010ff.

Idiocy. — Pretending i. as protection J822.1.

Idiot thinks he's been dead twelve years J2311.11.

Idiot's magic power D1716.1.

Idle sons-in-law driven away by reducing food P265.1. — Devil writes down all i. words spoken in church G303.24.1.6.

Idleness begets woe J21.50. — Fool sleeps so as to avoid i. J2243.

Idol, see also **Image;** drinks milk D1633.1; opens to hide fugitive R325.2. — Alleged i. promises pay for book K1971.13; heathen beats i. because of misfortune V381; magic i. as chastity test H411.9.1; magic from stone i. D1726.2; marriage of girl to i. T117.4; naked i. considered poor J2216; punishment for beating i. Q222.5.6; saint's bachall defaces i. V356.3; Satan builds i. G303.9.1.14; speaking i. D1610.21.2; storm overturns i. F962.0.2; tabu: giving away i. C51.8.

Idols found on faces after saint's arrival V347. — Christian hero overthrows heathen i. V356; devils dwell in i. G303.8.14; ground swallows heathen i. F948.1; origin of i. A1544; worship of i. V1.11.

Idolators. — Branches turn to avoid i. F979.20; devil makes i. of believers G303.9.4.5.1.

Idolatry punished Q237; tabu C62. — Demons teach i. G302.9.8; love as inducement to i. T6; magic spring detects i. H251.3.9.1.

Ignorance. — Absurd i. J1730—J1749, (of animals' nature or habits) *J1900ff.; boy reared in i. of world T617; child confined to keep him in i. of life J147; feigned i. of person's identity K1792; ingratitude from i. W154.23; men not chosen for their i., else he should have reached heaven J911.1; ogre deceived by feigned i. of hero G526; repartee based on clerical i. J1263.1; seduction through i. of intercourse K1363; wise man acknowledges his i. J911.

Ignorant surpasses learned man L143. — Devils are i. of thoughts of men G303.13.1; only husband i. of wife's infidelity J2342.5; sheep and i. shearer J229.2.

Ignoring the unpleasant J1086.

Iguana persuades jackal to let him go K551.2.1. — Man becomes i. D197.1; oil sold to i. J1852.1.2; reincarnation as i. E614.5; why i. lives in stream A2433.6.4.

Ill-gotten. — Devil in each stone of church built with i. wealth G303.8.4.2; eagle carries off i. gain Q557.3.

Ill-mannered. — Dwarfs are i. F451.3.13.

Ill-omen. — Beast of i. B147.1.2ff.; bird of i. B147.2.1ff.

Illegible. — Curse makes books i. D2089.5.

Illegitimacy discovered by urinalysis F956.2. — Adulteress on deathbed reveals children's i. T238; boy twitted with i. seeks unknown (father) H1381.2.2.1.1, (mother) H1381.2.2.2.1; child not guilty of i. P526.2.

Illegitimate, see also **Bastard;** child exposed S312; children *T640ff.; son preferred to legitimate P233.4. — Father of i. child must walk in front of cross J1515.1; king must resign if begets i. son P16.2.1; lots cast to determine father of i. child N126.2; man as God behind the tree forces the girl to admit having an i. child K1971.5.1; murdered i. children as nightmares F471.1.3; Pleiades seven i. children A773.4.

Illicit sexual relations *T400—T499.

Illiterate pretends to be weeping over book K1795.

Illness, see also **Disease, Sickness;** from fear W121.8; feigned (to call physician paramour) K1514.11, (to cause child sacrifice) S268.1, (to bring about capture) K757, (causes death) Q591.1, (destroys magic) *D866.2, (to escape) K523, K1227.5, (by fox to enter hen-roost) K828.2, (to impose quest) H1212; (to go to mistress) K1569.3, (to learn secret) K2091, (to take life of helpful animal) *B335.2, (to seduce) K1326, K1339.3, K1393, (to surprise wife with paramour) K1553.1, (to test wife) H467.1, (by thief) K325 K411.1; (to woo hero) T55.5; from grief F1041.21. — Dream warns of i. D1810.8.3.1.1; extraordinary i. F1041.9; intercourse during i. tabu C119.1.1; origin of i. A1337.8; prayer that overbearing knight's i. be increased W185.2; quest assigned because of feigned i. H1212; water-spirits cause i. F420.5.2.12; witch causes i. G263.4.0.1.

Illogical use of numbers J2213.

Illuminating. — Self-i. stones in heaven A661.0.7.

Illusion dissipated by cross D2031.0.3. — Adultery presented as i. to husband K1518.1; deception by disguise or i. *K1800—K1899; extraordinary valley gives i. of earthly paradise F756.2.1; magic i. *D2031ff., (prevents raising treasure) N564, (as protection) D2031.6ff.; saint's i. deceives army D2163.7; unwitting murder because of insane i. N325; wizard gives i. man has been away twenty (forty) years D2012.2.

Illusions *K1870ff.; caused by magic object D1368ff.

Illusory, see also **Imaginary;** enemies K1883; light K1888. — Captor persuaded into i. punishment *K580ff.

Image, see also **Idol;** of animal vivified D445; of boy made of flowers comes to life D435.1.3; of child as substitute for one T677; of deceased comes alive E53.2; detects false oath H251.3.5; of God of Love sent to fetch bride T56.2; of horse will be vivified for only one person D445.1.1; in mirror mistaken for picture J1795; pierced with pins as love charm D1355.3.2; takes 1,000 men to carry it F855.4; transformed to person D435; of Virgin tries in vain to keep nun from leaving convent V265.1; of Virgin miraculously heals V256.2; of Virgin works miracles V268.5. — Ass who carried divine i. thinks people bow before him J953.4;

basilisk killed by seeing own i. B12.3; Christ's i. has broken his arm J1823.1.2; exorcism by injuring witch's i. G271.4.2; extraordinary i. F855ff.; god as an i. A139.8.6; hidden man behind i. gives unwelcome answer to supplicant: i. is blamed K1971.8; living person acts as i. of saint K1842; magic i. of animal relieves from plague D1586.1; man created in creator's i. A1212; man made from clay i. and vivified A1241.3; man worships devil's i. in order to secure advancement V55; mankind from vivified wooden i. A1252.1; murder by abuse of i. D2061.2.2.3; oracular i. *D1311.7; person cured by repairing i. that has the same deformity D2161.4.4; reincarnation of man to stone i. E648.2; recognition through i. H22; sacred i. miraculously appears on stolen sacrament V35.1.2; soul as i. E743.2; speaking i. D1610.21; sacred i. appears on host V39.5; sacred i. cannot be removed D1654.8.1; seeking wife to resemble i. T51.3.1; symbolism of church and i. H619.2; tabu: unseemly acts while carrying divine i. C56; tabu to throw away holy i. C94.6; temple about to be taken over by pagans saved by appearance of i. of the Virgin V344; test of god: when its i. is bound it frees itself H45; thief successfully claims that stolen i. has been given him by the saint himself K405.3; transformation to wooden i. C961.3.1; wooden i. frightens invaders K2346; wooden i. substituted for stolen child F451.5.2.3.1; wrestling match between fever, stone i. K12.4; youth gazing at own i. drowned N339.10.

Images *V120ff.; act as if alive *D1620ff. — Demons in stone i. exorcised D2176.3.3.1; gilded i. substituted for solid gold K476.4.1; misunderstanding concerning i. of Christ J1823.1; oracular i. occupied by spirits or priests who give the answers K1972; origin of religious i. A1544; spittle i. enable escape K525.10.

Imaginary, see also **Illusory;** debt and payment J1551. — King pays for i. weapon K499.7; lies about i. animals X1370; magician makes people lift garments to avoid wetting in i. river D2031.1.

Imagination. — Active i. W211; magic journey through power of i. D2121.3.

Imbolg. — Festival of I. V70.6.

Imitating witch with ointment in eye G242.8. — Dupe i. trickster's thefts is caught K1026; magic results from i. desired action D1782.1; tabu: i. god C51.5.

Imitation of animals cry to distract owner's attention from his goods K341.7; of cockcrow deceives devil G303.16.19.4.1; and the real pig J2232. — Animal characteristics from i. of other animal or object A2272ff.; cure by i. F957; fatal i. of how first man killed himself J2374; first poetry composed in i. of tones of hammer on anvil A1464.1.1; foolish i. *J2400—J2449; origin of death from unsuccessful i. of bad creator *A1335.2.

Immaculate Conception V312.

Immature. — Suitor finds girl i.; father protests she's already a mother J1279.3, U117.

Immediate death for breaking tabu C921.

Immediately. — Task: hatching eggs i. H1023.1.2.

Immersing. — Disenchantment by i. in water D766.1; transformation by i. D591.

Immersion. — Ascetic i. V462.8.

Immigrants repopulate Ireland A1006.6.

Immoderate request punished *A2232ff., Q3, *Q338.

Immolation S125; as punishment Q455ff.

Immortal animals B843; bird B37; fairies F259.1.4; giant F531.6.4.3; as helper N819.1; horse B184.1.8; serpent B91.7; sky A702.9. — God half i. A122; middle head of hydra i. B15.1.2.8.1; sight of mermaid bathing makes man i. B81.13.3; twin gods: one mortal, other i. A116.1.

Immortals, Land of F116.

Immortality D1850ff. — Belief in i. V311; druids teach doctrine of i. V311.0.1; fairies as sprites who have been given i. F251.5; fairies' food gives i. F243.5; magic drink gives i. to gods A154.1; magic food give i. to gods A153.2; magic object gives i. D1346ff.; quest for i. H1376.7; quest for plant of i. H1333.2.1; reincarnation origin as message of i. E600.1; request for i. punished by transformation into tree Q338.1; serpent given i. A1335.5; Solomon refuses water of i. for himself J369.1; tabu broken, i. lost C937.1; tabu to disbelieve in i. C61.2.

Immovability. — Magic i. of saints D1654.0.1.

Immovable fountain jet F716.4; object *D1654ff. — Animal rendered i. D2072.0.2ff.

Immunity from disaster as reward Q150ff.; to poison by eating poisons F959.6.2; from pestilence through kissing relic J762.1; from punishment for sin as reward Q171; from violent death as reward Q154. — Magic drug give i. from fire and iron D1344.2.1; magic i. (from fatigue) D1924, (from hunger and thirst) D1349.1; magic peach gives i. from age D1338.3.2, D1349.2.1; prophecy: i. from certain types of death M367.

Immunities of saints V228.

Immutable god A102.3.

Imp as witch's familiar G225.8.

Impalement as punishment Q461.

Impaling children on cleaning pretense K1461.3; enemies' heads S139.2.2.1. — Giant i. self on javelin K897.2.1.

Impatience W196.

Impenetrable breastplate D1381.10.1.

Imperfect god A102.18. — Recognition through i. disguise H151.6.2.

Impersonated. — Captive i. by rescuer R121.2; fugitive i. by magic object *D1611ff.

Impersonation. — Objects stolen by magic i. K359.5.

Impiety punished *A2231ff., *Q220ff.

Impious man's head embitters well F933.4. — Devil exhibits benovolence to i. people G303.22.5; devil plagues i. people Q220.1; devil in wagon drawn by two black horses carries off i. people G303.7.3.1; lake bursts forth to drown i. people A920.1.8.

Implement, see also **Tools.** — Animal characteristics from transformation of i. A2262ff.; chopping down tree with blunt i. (task) H1115; mountain-men leave broken i. for man to mend F460.4.3.

Implements bewitched G265.8.3. — Acquisition of household i. A1446.5; extraordinary i. F887; magic i. *D1170ff.

Important man quarrels with commoner J1141.8; and unimportant work J370ff. — Wealth is most i. J707.

Importunate lover (put asleep in street) Q473.4, (made ridiculous) K1213ff.

Impossible for cuckold's knife to carve boar's head H425.1; demand rebuked J1512ff.; for devil to eat in an inn G303.4.8.4; for devil to enter house with horseshoe over door *G303.16.17; for devil to take one who has read Pater Noster G303.16.2.1; for devil's unfinished work to be completed by human hands G303.14; for ogre to cross stream G638; for ogre to endure daylight G632; to please everyone J1041; quests H1371; to rid oneself of cobold F481.3; task assigned by plaintiff H919.4; tasks *H1010—H1049; tasks drive off fairies F381.11. — Castle revolving at night so that entrance is i. to find F771.2.6.2; comfort in the contemplation of i. pleasure J864; construction from i. amount of material (task) H1022; construction from i. kind of material (task) H1021; courage makes i. possible U243; devil cheated by imposing an i. task K211; death sentence escaped by propounding riddle i. for king (judge) to solve *H542; ghost laid by i. task E454; guests make i. demands J1563.2; land in which i. things happen *X1503; ogre sets i. tasks G465; punishment: performing i. task Q512; resuscitation i. after certain length of time E162; woman who asked for news from home gets i. answers J2349.4

Impostor acting as God in tree burned K1971.12; of low origin recognized by habitual speech H38.2ff.; punished *Q262, (by boiling in tar) Q414.1.1, (by burning) Q414.0.6. — Kingdom lost to i. P15.3; seduction by i. K1315; youngest daughter suspects i. L62.

Impostor's. — Girl takes i. place in marriage bed K1611.3.

Impostors. — Country of i. F709.3; marital i. K1910ff.; treacherous i. K1930ff.

Impostures K1900—K1999.

Impotence humiliates lover K1233; induced by magic T591.

Impotent husband gets substitute for virility test K1848.1. — Devil is made i. by confession G303.16.9; woman rids self of i. husband T271.1.

Impounded water *A1111.

Impoverished, see also **Poor;** fairy seeks fortune F393.3; husband begs from wife's new husband L432; husband recognized H152.2; lover falsely accused of theft K401.3; man given high post N227; nobleman offers wife to ruler W11.7.1; overrich i. by gods L482.1.

Impregnated. — Brother said to have i. sister K2121.1; girl i. by god driven from home S12.5.1; goddess i. by wind A715.2; sneering princess i. by magic L431.3.

Impregnation, see also **Conception;** of princess by hero B375.1.1; of woman by shooting stars A788.3. — Child born of artificial i. exposed S312.4; miraculous i. T510ff.; unusual i. of animals B754.6.1.

Imprisoned, see also **Prison, Prisoner;** woman refuses to eat newborn child L71. — Animals help i. master B544.1; brother unjustly i. P251.5.5; children i. in grain pot S337; fairy i. in tree F386.1; ghost i. E459.4; gods i. A173.2; man i. by ogre G422; ogre i. in his own house G514.2, (cave) G514.2.1; proud king i. L416.1; rescuing i. princess as suitor test H322.2; souls of dead i. in tree E755.4.1; virgin i. to protect virginity *T381.

Imprisonment R0—R99; by magic D1417, D2177; of person under holy protection Q227.1.1. — Care against future i. J648; dream of future greatness causes i. L425; magic i. in cleft tree Q435; punishment: i. Q433ff., (in white-hot iron house) Q414.2.

Improvement. — King's i. of kingdom for sons J701.2; man never does work so well there is no room for i. J1073.1; servant's absurd i. of master's statements J2464.

Improvident mouse eats grain stored for famine J711.2.

Impudence punished Q326.

Inability to count J2030ff.; to dislodge dog of wild huntsman from house it has entered E501.15.6.5; to find object one is carrying J2025; to find own members *J2020ff.; of flesh of stolen animal to be cooked D1318.7.1.1; of horse to draw evil dead man E411.0.3; to move D5.1; of soul to go far from grave E722.3.1; of wild huntsman's dogs to pass over a grave E501.15.6.4.

Inaccessible city F767.

Inanimate objects (act as if living) F990ff., (blamed for theft) K419.9. — Devil in form of i. objects G303.3.4.

Inappropriate action from misunderstanding J1820ff.; entertainment repaid J1565.

Inauguration. — King's i. espousal to goddess P11.6.

Incandescent objects *D1645ff.

Incantation for testing guilt H245.1. — Adulteress covers husband's eyes during i. K1516.4; dream from i. D1812.3.3.3; magic sight overcome by i. D1822.1; storm raised by i. D2141.0.7; repeating i. continuously H1508.1; resuscitation by i. E73; sham recovery of goods by i. K1956.1.1; snake killed by own i. K1613.5; woman warns lover of husband by parody i. K1546.

Incantations. — Fishhook made without proper i. C221.4.2; husband sings i. about adultery K1556.1.

Incarnated. — Culture hero i. through birth from virgin A511.1.3; resuscitation by destroying i. object E29.4.

Incarnation of god: puts on human form to help man A184. — Newborn baby's tatoo tells of former i. T563.4.

Incense relieves from plague D1586.3; as sacrifice V12.10. — Ant collects i. for Christ A2221.4; magic i. *D1295, (summons genie) D1421.1.7.

Incest *T410ff.; accidentally averted N681.3; of devil's son and his mother G303.11.1.1; punished Q242; tabu C114; unwittingly committed *N365. — Allusive expression for gods' i. A1599.16; banishment to punish i. Q431.8.1; brother-sister i. A164.1, A1331.2, A1337.0.7, A2006, G37, M365.3, Q520.3, T415, T471.1; burning as punishment for i. Q414.0.3; child of i. exposed S312.1; children of i. sterile Q553.3.2; creation of animals as punishment for i. A1733; dog tells of i. B134.1.1; father-daughter i. M344.1, Q242.2, T411, *V132.1; flood as punishment for i. A1018.2; girl becomes cannibal because of brother-sister i. G37; holy water prevents a man from committing i. with his daughter *V132.1; insects from brother-sister i. A2006; magic lost through i. D1741.6; monstrous births from brother-sister i. A1337.0.7; mother falsely accuses son of i. with her K2111.5; mother lets daughter commit i. P232.2; mother dies of fright when she learns that she was about to commit i. with her son N383.3; mother-i. prophecy M344; new race from i. after world calamity A1006.2; paradise lost because of brother-sister i. A1331.2; prophecy: daughter shall commit murder and i. M345; riddle betrays i. H582.2.1; standing on pillar as penance for i. Q541.3.

Incestuous brother burned to charcoal D1865.2.1; first parents A1273.1; marriage arranged by trick K1377; youth reincarnated as root E692.6. —Girl flees i. brother R224; god from i. union A112.1; goddess of music from i. union A112.1.1.1.; tribe's i. origin sanctions intermarriage T131.5.1.

Inciting. — Fairy i. mortals to war F369.4.1; vision i. saint V513.1.

Inclinations. — Origin of evil i. A1384.

Inclosure during calamity preserves best types A1005.2.

Inclusa K1523.

Incognito, see also **Disguise;** king (given hospitality by enemy) K1812.14.1, (joins robbers) K1812.2, (helped by humble man) K1812.1; mistress T476, (overhears lover, leaves him) J2364; prince beaten J18; prophet as matchmaker T53.1; queen accused of killing child K2116.1.4.

Incombustible objects D1656ff.

Inconstant, see **Unfaithful.**

Incontinence of clergy J1264ff., V465.1; punished Q240ff. — Burning as punishment for i. Q414.0.3; discovery of abbot's (abbess's) i. brings permission to monks (nuns) to do likewise K1274; priest catches bishop in i. J1211.1.1; tabu: i. while treasure is being raised N553.1.

Inconvenience disregarded when booty is in sight J352. — Choices: small i., large gain J350ff.; man refuses cure which brings greater i. J343.

Incorrigible liar X909.1.

Incorruptible. — Dead body i. E182.

Increasing-decreasing paradox task H1075. — Carrying ever-i. burden up mountain H1114.2; miraculous i. of food D1652.1.0.1.

Incubus F471.2.

Incurable. — Curing i. ulcer H1199.2.2; lying is i. U235.

Incurables. — Mountebank cures i. F958.

Indecent. — Princess brought to laughter by i. show made in quarrel with old woman at well H341.3.1; wife in i. posture told to lock up shop J1545.5.

Indecision W123.

Indelible blood D1654.3.

Indentions on oak-leaves A2761.1; on plants from biting A2721.2.2, A2732, A2751.3.1; on rocks from prints left by man (beast) A972; in stem of reed A2751.3.1.

Indenture. — Identification by i. H102.

Index. — Chastity i. H430ff.; flame as miraculous i. *F1061; life i. *E760ff.; quest for life i. H1353.

India as otherworld F130.1. — Origin of tribes of I. A1611.4; women wear veils in I. A1599.3.

Indian says belongings safe, no white man near J1373. — American I. tribes A1611.1; ghost as I. E425.2.4; naked I. not cold: "me all face" J1309.1.

Indians chew spruce gum A1681.1; rescue children R131.20; sprang from legs of first man A1614.7. — Escape by overawing I. K547.2; hanging innocent oldster to appease I. J2233.1.1; woman alone makes I. think men are home K548.1.

Indication of desired place by magic object *D1314ff.; of road by magic object D1313ff.; of what is burning by color of flame F1061.2.

Indications of chastity H400ff.

Indifference bred by security U270ff.; of the miserable U150ff.

Indignity to corpse E235, E341.1.1, Q491.

Indispensible. — Banished minister found i. and recalled P111; deer, oppossum, and snake each render i. aid to man J461.4; smith honored by king as i. P447.5.

Indolent, see **Lazy.**

Indra carried by cock B552.3; controls fairies F252.1.2; sends down buffalo B184.2.3.3; separates the winds A1142.7. — Fairies come from I. kingdom F282.3; fairies dance before I. F261.3.7.

Indra's palace on Milky Way A151.6.1; tank F964.5, H1359.3.

Indus. — Plunge into I. tests valor H1561.10.

Industrial processes magically interrupted D2084. — Dwarfs emigrate because of i. development F451.9.1.4.

Industrious. — Lazy boy and i. girl matched T125; obedient and i. nun V461.1.

Industry rewarded Q5; test H1569.1; as tribal characteristic A1673. — Bride test: i. H382; reward for i. Q86; value of i. J1010ff.

Inedible substances transformed into edible D476.1. — Dwarfs given i. food F451.3.7.3; edible substance changed to i. D476.2.

Ineffable name of God A138, (magic) D804.

Inept child surpasses others L141.4.

Inequalities of fortunes among men A1599.8; of life U0—U99. — Origin of i. among men A1618.

Inexhaustible object *D1652ff.; purse furnishes money D1451ff.; treasure D2100.1. — Alleged i. bottle sold K117; deceptive eating contest: i. food K81.3; fairy gift of i. meat F348.5.1.1; house-spirit furnishes i. supply of food F481.2.2.

Inexorable fate N101.

Infallible article D1653ff. — Skillful tracker i. F677.1.

Infant, see also **Baby, Child;** allowed in river, drowns J2175.4; to be drowned spared by slaves K512.0.1; exposed to avoid fulfillment of prophecy M371; fed by bees B531.1; Jesus V211.1.8; marriages T143; picks out his unknown father H481; of slain mother cares for itself T612. — Father kills i. S11.4.4; girl child fed on i. boys' flesh to make her grow faster G77; indentions on rocks from head of i. hero A972.5.1.

Infants. — Baptism of i. V81.4; women, driven mad, devour their i. N325.2.

Infectious. — Priest's fear of i. disease repayed J1551.10.

Inference. — Wisdom (knowledge) acquired from i. *J30ff.

Inferno, see **Hell.**

Infertile, see **Barren.**

Infidel defies God to strike him with lightning Q552.1.8. — Monk seduces girl, kills her, and becomes i. V465.1.1.1.

Infidelity, see also **Adultery.** — Crown exposes i. of husbands H422.1; dog (bird) betrays woman's i. *B134.1, B131.3; girl disguised as man accused of i. K2113.1; goddess killed for i. Q246.1; husband refuses to believe wife's i. J2342; man falsely accused of i. K2114; object as token of i. discovered T247; satyr reveals woman's i B24.1; spirit reveals wife's i. F403.2.3.5; supernatural person reveals i. F345.2.

Infirm. — Magic power of the i. D1716.

Inflaming. — Women i. warrior's wounds K2014.

Inflated giant floats through air F531.6.17.2.

Information from dream D1810.8.2; about sought robbers reward for rescue Q53.2. — Angel gives soul i. E759.2; magic object gives supernatural i. *D1310ff.; oracular image refuses i. except to hero D1651.6.

Ingenuity. — Lie: remarkable i. X1012.

Ingratitude *W154ff.; punished *Q281. — Dwarfs emigrate because of mortals' i. F451.9.1.12.

Inhabitant of upper world visits earth F30ff.

27*

Inhabitants of extraordinary castle F771.4ff.; of otherworld F167. — City's i. transformed to fish D692; gods as earth's first i. A1205.

Inhabited. — Castle i. by ogres F771.4.1; island in otherworld garden i. half by dead and half by living F162.1.2.5.

Inheritance. — Blood-test for i. H486.1; cat as sole i. N411.1.1; children substituted to gain i. K1847.1; king's son returns for i. division N699.2; modest i. best L223; oath broken: i. of earth lost M101.5; orphan deprived of his i. S322.0.1; sickle as only i. N411.2.1; thankless children think that chest of stones contains their i. P236.2.

Inherited. — Animals' characteristics i. X1202; friendship i. P310.4.1; magic object i. D816; magic power i. D1737; numskull destroys i. property J2461.1.8; trickster's ability i. by his daughter J1111.2; witch's power i. G224.9.

Inhospitable. — Father's deception of i. daughter J1561.5.

Inhospitality W158; punished Q1.1, Q292; repaid J1561; reproved enigmatically H594.

Initials recall forgotten wife D2006.1.9.

Initiation into witchcraft G286. — Mock i. for dupe K1286.

Injunctions of helpful animal disobeyed B341.

Injured husband will not kill naked man P641. — Numskull i. J2131.

Injuring yourself to insure your family's future J322. — Persons duped into i. each other K1080ff.; Satan i. man G303.20.8.

Injurious food with delusive sweet taste K1889.4.

Injury by deception K2382. — Accidental self-i. N397; curse: bodily i. M431; dead return to repair i. E345; death or bodily i. by magic *D2060ff.; fairy causes i. F362.4; fitting bodily i. as punishment Q583; marvelous sensitiveness: i. from rose leaves falling F647.3; pursuer deceived into self-i. K533.1.

Injuries. — Unintentional i. bring unfortunate consequences N385.

Injustice deadliest of monarch's sins P12.2; punished Q296. — Apparent i. chosen over greater wrong J225; justice and i. U10; small i. permitted rather than to cause troubles of state J221.

Ink transformed to light beams D454.14. — Saint throws i. bottle at devil D2176.3.3.3.

Inkwell. — Pouring water into i. proves that slave girl belonged to author J1176.1.

Inn at border of otherworld F147.4. — Day's journey from earth to heaven since there is no i. to stop at on the way H682.1.2; devil builds an i. for man G303.9.1.10; devil never eats in i. G303.4.8.4; guest at i. put in mistress's bed K1396; guests at i. thieves K365.2; magic object stolen by host at i. D861.1; princess (queen) compelled to keep an i. *Q481; recognition at i. where all must tell their life histories H11.1.1; "sleep not at i." J21.41.1; trickster reports lost money: searchers leave him in possession of i. K341.1; woman outwits landlord of i. K1837.5.

Inns. — Tabu: invading i. C856.2.

Innkeeper sells substitutes for wine, meat K476.3.1; sold hay by trickster K282.1. — Stingy i. cured of serving weak beer J1341.7; treacherous i. K2241.

Innkeeper's. — Devil woos i. daughter G303.12.1.

Innkeepers. — Thieving i. guilty of arson J1149.9.

Innocence. — Bird reveals suspect's i. B131.7; blood indicates guilt or i. *D1318.5; dry branches on grave blossom as proof of i. E631.0.5.1; irrevocable sentence carried out even when i. is proved M12; the guilty protests his i. and thus detected J1141.9; one-legged bird symbol of i. H619.5; primeval human pair live in i. A1270.1; tests of guilt or i. *H210—H239; test of i.: apple and gold offered H256.

Innocent girl sells her "love" and later receives it back K1362; made to appear guilty K2150ff.; man accidentally suspected of crime N347; man executed because he fits noose J2233.1; man hanged, island sinks into sea H252.5; person condemned for theft K401.2.3; person saved from hanging by saint R165.2; queen burned at stake Q414.0.7; woman accused of murder K2116; woman falsely incriminated K2112. — Blood of i. maiden as cure for leprosy D1502.4.2.1; dead father proves son i. E327.3; don't draw sword against the i. J21.2.3; each drop of i. blood turns to burning candle D1318.5.3; extraordinary phenomena at cruelty to i. F960.7; flame where i. murdered F1061.4; premature darkness at execution of i. F965.1.1; repeated attempts to seduce i. maiden T320.1; springs from i. king's blood A941.5.8; three i. children Z71.1.5; tree from i. man's blood E631.0.5; Virgin Mary defends i. accused V252.

Innocents. — Slaughter of i. to avoid fulfillment of prophecy M375.

Inquiry, see **Questioning.**

Inquisitive fools J2370—J2399.

Inquisitiveness punished *Q342.

Insane hero L116; man accidentally cured by blow on head N642; man burns heretic in his bed: restored to his senses as reward V321. — Adulteress pretends husband i. K1548; creditor falsely reported i. when he demands money K242; driving i. by keeping awake S191; fairies dance with youth till he goes i. F302.3.4.2; faithless wife drives husband i. T230.2; man falsely reported i. K1265; sight of dead woman spinning drives people i. E561.1; sight of wild hunt renders person i. *E501.18.6; tabu to violate i. woman C118.1; unwitting murder because of i. illusion N325.

Insanity for breaking tabu C949.1; as curse M452; causes death C928; from love T24.3; magically cured D2161.3.8. — Fairies cause i. F302.3.4.2, F362.2; magic i. *D2065ff.; magic object causes i. *D1367ff.; witch causes i. G263.7.

Insatiable. — Devil as i. queen G303.3.1.12.5; girl frightened by love becomes i. K2052.2.

Inscription accidentally seen saves hero R217; on forehead F545.2.3; of holy name aids resuscitation E174; on home of riddle solver: "I have no care" H562; of name on article as ownership token H88; rots, devil claims debtor K231.12.1; on walls for condensed education J168. — Reading i. unique ability H31.11; treasure indicated by stone with i.: "Dig here" N535.

Inscriptions. — Equivocal i. at parting of three roads telling what will happen if each is chosen N122.0.1; origin of ogam i. A1484.1; proud i. sole remains of powerful king L413.

Inscrutable ways of providence J225.0.3.

Insect asks to be put in loosely-woven basket K581.6; army B268.8; as creator A13.3; grateful for being turned over B364.3; helps select magic object D859.5; inside jewel J1661.1.6; in murdered person simulates snoring K661.3; points out deity by settling where he is H162.1; swallowed by man comes out alive E32.1; transformed to another animal D415; transformed to object D424; transformed to person D380ff.; as witch's familiar G225.1; wedding B285. — Devil as i. G303.3.3.4; fairy as i. F234.1.16; marriage to person in i. form B643; origin of color of i. A2411.3; hair transformed to i. D447.1.2; man transformed to i. D180ff.; marriage to i. in human form B653; reincarnation as i. E616; separable soul in i. E715.3; soul in form of i. E734: witch as i. G211.5.

Insect's enemies A2494.14.

Insects teach wisdom J137; worry large animal to death L315.6. — Cause of walk of i. A2441.3ff.; creation of i. A2000—A2099; creator sent down i. to plant plants A2601; cutting down tree without scratching for stinging i. H1184; devastating i. B16.6; expensive means of being rid of i. J2102ff.; food of i. A2435.5ff.; giant i. B873ff.; haunts of i. A2433.5; helpful i. B482ff.; king of i. B246; kingdom of i. B224; language of i. B215.6; lies about i. X1280; markings on i. A2412.3; saint destroys disastrous i. D2156.6; sham dead tested by stinging i. H248.2; sounds of i. A2426.3; speaking i. B211.4.

Insensate. — Guilty confronted, become i. F1041.1.3.10.1.

Insensible. — Bath rendering one i. F872.6.

Inside. — City i. a tree F765; fish with larger fish i. X1154.1.1; fool roofs house on i. Z171.2.2; journey i. the earth F114; serpent i. man's body G328.1.

Inside out. — Garments i. exorcise will-o'-the-wisp F491.3.1.

Insignia. — Kingly i. worn only in battle P13.3.1; magic i. D1299.1; origin of family i. A1578; test of valor worthy for kingship: taking possession of royal i. H1561.5.

Insolence W187.

Insomnia. — Angel of i. A472.0.1; eating of human hearts as cure for i. D2161.4.13.

Inspection test for suitors H311.

Inspiration. — Divine i. for writing sacred books D1811.2.1; prevention of hostility by i. of fear in enemy J623.

Instinct. — Bridegroom learns power of i. from ducklings J64.

Instructing, see also **Teaching.** — Fairies i. mortals F345; man wins wife by i. her how to answer her mother's riddles H551.1; seduction by i. in marital duties K1315.7.1; vision i. saint V513.1.

Instructions for magic D806; of mother followed literally by daughter when she marries J555.1. — Disastrously following i. J2460.1; literal following of i. about actions J2461.1; numskull talks about his secret i. and thus allows himself to be cheated J2355; smith receives i. from underground spirit F450.1.2.

Instrument for unlawful work sticks to user Q551.2.5. — Ghost plays musical i. E554; giant plays musical i. F531.6.17.4; man condemned to lose his eye is allowed to choose the i. P511.2; musical i. causes magic sleep D1364.25; reincarnation as musical i. *E632ff.; resuscitation by withdrawal of wounding i. E21; prophecy: death by particular i. M341.2; waking from magic sleep by removal of enchanting i. D1978.3.

Instruments of torture transformed to lotus flowers D454.16. — Fairies' musical i. F245; magic musical i. *D1210ff.; self-playing musical i. D1601.18ff.

Insult repeated as harmless remark K1775; worse than wound W185.6. — Daughter overlooks i. of father proffering new husband K2052.4.3; man called rogue by noble man makes joke of i. J817.1; pulling a man's beard as i. P672; scalding punishment for i Q469.10.3.

Insults in pseudo-magic letter K115.1.2. — Dumb princess brought to speak by i. of shepherd H343.1; enduring i. to enter city gate H1553.3; "show me how to bear i." J1284.1; seeds rattling mistaken for i. J1812.1; words in foreign language thought to be i. J1802.

Insulted. — Dwarf is i. when scolded F451.3.6.1.

Integrity rewarded Q68. — Devil appears to persons ready to abandon their i. G303.6.2.5.

Intellect doesn't reach to heels; small men preferred J493; and Fortune, Knowledge, Health dispute which is greatest J461.1.2. — Human i. unable to conceive God A182.0.2.

Intelligence personified Z128.1; of various people A1667. — Luck or i. more powerful? N141; tasks performed through cleverness or i. H960ff.

Intelligent ship *D1310.3. — Alliances with the i. J685; dwarfs are i. F451.3.12; fool given i. wife T125.1.

Intercession of queen P21.1; of the dead for mortal E576.1. — Friend's i. saves man from execution P319.3; woman's i. for her accusers W11.5.9.1.

Intercourse, see **Sexual intercourse.**

Interest. — Giants repay loan with large i. F531.5.5; owner's i. distracted to steal goods K341; what is sweetest? one's own i. H633.4; woman enamored of unknown knight loses i. when she finds he is her husband T236.

Interested. — Beware of following i. adviser J758; executioner kept i. until rescue comes K555.

Interesting. — The valuable neglected for the i. J345.

Interior. — Devil in i. of earth G303.8.5; thieves disguised as i. decorators K311.7.

Intermediate future world *A693.

Intermittent river D915.4.

Internal markings of animals A2367.2; parts of plant A2755ff. — Magic i. organs (human) D997, (animal) D1015.

Interpretation of riddling remarks by girl at end of journey H586ff. — Misfortune from mistaken i. of prophecy N398.

Interpretations, symbolic H600ff.

Interpreter. — God uses i. to address women A182.3.0.4.

Interpreters. — Wasps as language i. K137.1.

Interrupted calculation J2035; cooking G475.1. — Industrial processes magically i. D2084; judicial combat i. by friends of loser H218.1; man i. each time he tries to eat something X12; mass i. by devil with pretended battle G303.9.9.2; trickster's i. feast revenged J1564.1.

Interrupting story reveals guilt J1177.0.1.

Intervention of gods in battle A172; of queen for condemned courtiers P21. — Husband's i. prevents wife's seduction H492.2.2.

Intestines, see also **Gut;** wagered N2.3.5. — Eating fish i. next morning J1606.1; exposed F1096.2; horse twists i. out of himself K1444; murder by twisting out i. S139.1; person lives on with i. exposed F1096.2.

Intimidating. — Brandished heads i. foe S139.2.2.1.6; sham warrior's boasting i. soldiers K1951.3.

Intoning. — Parson i. instructions to sexton as a part of mass X441.

Intoxicated, see also **Drunk;** father impregnates girl T411.2. — Animals become i. B299.3; creator i. A32.3.2.

Intoxicating drink's first use A1427.0.3; nurse to keep lovers' rendezvous T35.3. — Secret learned by i. dupe K1165.

Intoxication avoided by hole in cup K82.1.2; from magic food D1359.4. — Capture by i. K776; fatal i. K871; god of i. A481; resisting i. as suitor test H328.1.

Intruder. — Adulteress makes husband watch for i., meets lover K1514.10; owner burns i. in house K812.4.

Intruders. — Ghosts punish i. into ghost town E241; ogre attacks i. G475ff.

Invalid. — Hut for i. to prevent noxious odor P661.

Invasion as punishment Q429.2. — False report of impending i.: trickster paid to buy it off K1784.1; otherworld journey as i. F3; prophecies concerning i. M369.5.

Invasions. — Hero defends Ireland against i. A536.1.

Inventer of death machine uses it K1681.1. — Lie: great i. X1011.

Inventions. — Patriarchs because of long life made i. A1440.3.

Invested. — Blind man's stolen money i. by thief K1667.1.2.

Investigation. — "Don't do anything without i." J21.48.

Inviolable curse M415. — Guest's life i. P324.3.

Invisibility cap admits to woman's room K1349.10; of creator A11.1; of demons G302.4.2; of island F742. — Charm gives i. D1561.2.4; dragon's power of magic i. B11.5.2; escape from battle by magic i. K531; fairies lose i. F235.8; fairies seen by mortals lose i. F255.3; magic i. *D1980ff.; magic mist of i. *D902.1; seduction by wearing i. coat K1314; theft by coat of i. K324; theft by magic i. K359.1.

Invisible arrow F831.1; creator A11; devil G303.4.8.13; god A102.9; dwarfs at christening feast made to speak by brewing beer in egg-shell F451.5.17.1; echo A497.1; ghosts E421.1; guardians N810.1; hands aid task H986; man eats bread, owners quarrel K1883.6; objects D1655ff.; witches steal G266.1. — Devil appears i. among dancers G303.6.2.1; dupe persuaded that he is i. J2337; dwarfs made i by magic caps F451.3.3.8; dwarfs emigrate i. but heard F451.9.6; exorcising i. man D2176.6; fairy car i. F242.1.1; fairy horse i. F241.1.5; fairies i. F235.1; fairies' cattle become i. F241.2.2; flight on i. horse B184.1.6.1; ghost i. during day E452.2; giants can make selves i. F531.6.5.1; huldra i. F460.1.7; magic i. pig B184.3.2.1; magic object renders i. *D1361ff.; magic power to see i. creatures D1825.3; making an i. knot with an egg H1021.5; monster husband i. T118.1; trolls i. F455.5.1; why spirits are i. A2862; wild huntsmen i. *E501.9; witch i. G210.0.1.

Invitation to buy taken as offer of gift K247. — Accepting an i. tabu C744; deaf peasant and wedding i. X111.4; deceptive i. to feast J1577; man refuses fairy i., killed F361.17.7; symbolic i. to liberality H595.1.

Invitations. — Stingy man cancels i. W152.9.

Invited. — Fairy takes revenge for not being i. to feast F361.1.1; traveler i. into devil's wagon G303.7.1.2.2; until singer is i. to feast beer will not stop foaming C682.

Inviting. — Ogress i. boys to her house G414; penance: i. brahmin to dinner Q527.

Invoice. — Thieves' i. of stolen goods J2214.3.3.

Invoking deity A183.1. — Invulnerability by i. saint D1846.5.1.

Invulnerability reward for piety Q162; of witches G229.4. — Drug of i. T325.1; magic i. *D1840ff.; magic object gives i. *D1344ff.

Invulnerable berserk F610.3.1. — Dragon i. B11.12.1; escape by reporting oneself i. and overawing captor K541; magic i. horse B184.1.11.

Io transformed to cow with gadfly ceaselessly pursuing Q501.6.

Ireland as otherworld F130.3; repopulated by flood escapees A1006.5; — Ark sails to I. A1021.0.1; coming to I. tabu in peacetime C755.3; first convert to Christianity in I. A1546.3.1; first judgment in I. A1580.1.1; first woman in I. dies of grief F1041.1.2.2.2; five great roads of I. A994; "flame of fire" plague to destroy I M356.2; hero defends I. against invasions A536.1; nine wonders of I. Z71.6.3; no snakes in I. M318; one foot in I, one in Scotland K2319.1; origin of women in I. A1611.5.4.1; otherworld king in I. F184.1; preservation of life in I. during flood

A1005.1; stay in I. in return for magic shirt M226; three-fourths of men in I. die one night Z76.1; three worst things in I. Z71.1.15; vision of flames covering I. V515.1.3; why there are no snakes in I. A2434.2.3.

Irish saint as Virgin Mary V250.1; Solomon J1170.2; souls judged by St. Patrick E751.3. — Hero invents, teaches I. language A541.1; origin of I. language A1616.2; snakes will not cross I. earth B765.18.3; tribute slaves must not know I. P172; world-fire to punish I. A1031.1.

Iron axe becomes silver D475.3.4; in bamboo in deceptive contest K44.1; bands around heart to keep it from breaking F875; birds in hell A671.2.11; blessed by saint incapable of wounding D1674; boat F841.1.13; chains sever neck in contest H1562.7; created to punish cedar's pride A978.2; -eating tribe F561.8; first used for food A1432.1.1; forehead F545.2.4; -headed person F511.0.3.1; locks, doors around otherworld F148.5; magically disappears D2089.1; man F521.3.2; nail in witch's forehead G272.14; pillars steady the earth A841.3; powerful against fairies F384.3; tools become earth D479.2; tree F811.1.9; -winged locusts eat wheat crop B16.6.3. — Animal with hair of i. pins B15.7.10.2; animal with i. snout B15.5.2; arrow discovers i. pit D1314.1.6; bacon becomes i. D476.3.2; basket of things becomes i. D479.5; bath of molten i F872.5; bird with i. beak B15.7.13.1; boy born with one side flesh and one i. T551.4; boy forged from i. T544.2; breaking i. with wooden axe H1116.2; building i. house overnight H1104.3; captive hews through i. prison R211.5; chastity ordeal: holding hot i. H412.4.1; coffin with i. band E431.20; confinement in i. house to avoid prophecy fulfillment M372.1; contest in eating i. K63.1; crushing i. wall with fists F611.3.2.3; destruction of i. castle H1562.12; devil strikes man dead with i. bar G303.20.3; dwarf cave closed by i. doors F451.4.3.1; enemy lured into i. house, roasted K811.4; fairy's i. arms F231.1.1; garden warbler hears smith beat i.: learns his song A2272.1.3; ghost rides i. chest E581.5; ghost unlaid until hidden i. found E415.1.1; giant with i. nails F531.1.6.1.1; giant can be killed only with own i. club Z312.2; giant's i. weapons F531.4.5.1; hiding i. tabu C899.1; magic i. D1252.1.1; magic i. eaten D1721.5; magic i. measure D1470.1.47; magic drug gives immunity from fire and i. D1344.2.1; magic i. chain *D1251; magic i. glove gives strength D1335.3; magic i. rod causes waters to divide and close D1551.2; man proof against i., stone, and wood D1841.1; man with one side of i. F525.1.1; mice alleged to eat i. J1531.2; murder with hot i. S112.2, (in mouth) K951.1.1; oath on the i. K1115; ogre killed with own i. bar G519.2; ogre terrified by i. man K1756; ordeal by hot i. H221.2; origin of i. A1432.1; "painting" with a red hot i. K1013.3; penance: carrying i. hoop on head until it falls off Q521.3; penance: i. band forged round man's waist Q522.5; person vomits i. F1041.20; promise to be fulfilled when i. shoes wear out *M202.1; pulling i. bars through hole as strength test H1562.11; quest for magic i. rod H1342; remarkable thrower of i. F636.1; saint invulnerable to red hot i. D1841.3.2.3; shooting through i. with arrow H1562.13; smith forges i. man, who helps him D1620.1.3; spear driven through i. plates F625.1; strong hero struck by smith from i. F611.1.12; strong man: breaker of i. F625; sun's i. weapons A739.9; throwing i. ball as suitor test H331.16.1; time measured by worn i. shoes *H1583.1; touching with i. forbidden C531; trustee claims that mice have eaten i. scales J1531.2; one twin eats other, body becomes i. T587.2.1; voice made rough by swallowing hot i. F556.1; vomiting i. F1041.20; wandering till i. shoes are worn out *Q502.2; why tortoise may be killed with i. spear A2231.7.3; witch with i. members G219.1; witch with i. teeth G214.2; witch's hair on horse becomes i. G265.3.1; working i. under sun tabu C842.1.

Irrational men as reincarnated animals E656.1.

Irreplaceable magic object D1661. — Wife saves father as only i. male P211.1.

Irresistible. — Hero's i. beauty spot A526.3; who are i.? meat, drink H659.20.

Irreverent young people punished by outraged old man Q283.

Irrevocable judgments M10ff.; king's promise M203. — Decree of gods i. A196.2.

Isaac. — Devils fear St. I. G303.25.2; sacrifice of I. S263.2.1.

Ishtar unveiled F85.

Island becomes canoe at will D632.1, D1524.4; created by magic D2153.1.1; of the dead *E481.2.0.1; inhabited by one woman F112.0.1.1; made to appear hog's back K1886.7.1; magically transported D2136.6; mistaken for dog J1771.5; in otherworld garden inhabited half by dead and half by living F162.1.2.5; of Promise F111.2.1; sinks for man's offense to saint Q552.2.3.2.3; sinks into sea F944.3; sinks into sea after innocent man hanged H252.5; split apart C984.8; to be towed by ships to new location J2287. — Abandonment on i. *S145; bird steals i. B172.11; captivity on i. R43; dragon lives in isolated i. B11.3.8; drunk man goes to the king and wants to buy an i. X812; escape from deluge on i. A1025; fairyland on i. F213; fairies battle for i. F277.0.2; fairies go to floating i. F388.2; flying i. F738; giant extends across whole i. F531.2.1.4; glass i. in otherworld F162.0.1.1; god's dominion over floating i. A179.2; gods' home on i. A151.3.2; hero still alive on i. A571.2; home of Fortuna on i. (in otherworld) N111.1.2; impostor abandons hero on i. K1931.6; lake bursts forth where i. is plowed out A920.1.9; looking on i. tabu C315.5; magic i. *D936, (moves at owner's wish) D1643.3; magic object found on an i. D849.3; magic object from otherworld i. D813.3; man on I. of Fair Women overcome by loving women F112.1; man (woman) transformed to i. D284; monastery on otherworld i. V118.1; no sun on druid i. F961.1.6; otherworld on i. *F134; quest to submerged i. H1287.1; refuge on an i. R316.1; saints bargain over i. ownership K185.13; stone becomes i. D452.1.8; storm appears to be i. D2031.17; storm breaks i. F962.1; tabu to land on gods' i. C93.8; tabu to point boat toward gods' i. C51.9;

treasures buried on i. N511.1.12; wandering i. F737; whale thought to be i. J1761.1; women tabu on i. C619.4.

Island's ownership determined by saint's staff D1524.1.2.1, K185.13.

Islands of birds F167.1.2.1; of the blest *A692; in sea of fire in hell A671.2.4.2. — Devil builds two i. in a lake G303.9.1.9; extraordinary i. *F730ff.; journey to otherworld i. F129.4; origin of i. A955; series of otherworld i. F134.0.1.

Isle of Man as otherworld F134.1. — Banishment to desert i. Q431.2.2; journey to I. of Laughter F111.1; journey to otherworld i. F129.4.

Israel. — Covenant between I. and God M201.0.1.1; creation on condition I. accept Tora A74.1; god as protector of I. A184.1; no snakes in I. M318.1; Satan fights I. G303.9.6.1.2.

Israel's — Paths open in sea for I. tribes F931.9.3.

Israelites feed on quail swarms F989.16.1. — Covenant between heathen and I. M201.0.2.

Italians. — Origin of I. A1611.5.2.

Itch. — Magic i. D2063.4; ointment producing i. X34; origin of i. A1319.10, A1337.5.

Itself, see also **Automatic, Self.** — Object sent to go by i. J1881.1; treasure opens i. N552.

Ivory bed F787.3. — Magic wishing i. tusk D1470.1.37.

Ixion lashed to wheel Q501.5.

Jabbering of magpie outside ark over drowned world A2542.1.1.

Jack and the Beanstalk F54.2; the Giant-killer G500—G599; o' Lantern A2817, F491. — House that J. built (cumulative tale) Z44.

Jackal as beast of ill-omen B147.1.2.4; boasting, falls, eaten by alligator L476; caught in bullock's carcass J2136.6.1; cheats other animals of elephant K171.0.3; comes to fireplace for food, burned K1032.1; demands camel's tongue K255.4; in elephant's carcass K565.2; escapes by asking for drink K551.17.2; escapes crocodile by false plea K551.23; escapes farmer by calling self king K547.4; escapes tiger's house K563.1; feigns holiness to seize rats K815.16; forces all animals to praise him W116.8; gets buffalo, tiger to kill each other: feeds on meat K1084.1.1; imprisoned in elephant's dead body K1022.1.1; inside carcass pretends his voice is God's K1973; as judge J1172.3.1; as judge comes late J1531.1.1; and king discuss husbands ruled by wives T252.2.2.1; leads lost men B563.4.1.2; as leopard cubs' nurse K2061.11; and leopard tie tails together J681.1.1; made king, howls at night, killed J512.13; makes horns of wax and poses as horned animal K1991; and man engage in flattery J814.3; ordered to take meat to lion's family takes it to his own K361.1; persuades deer to steal, informs on him K2037; persuades hyena to jump A2284.6; put head in anus of sham-dead camel K1036.1.1; realizes partridge too clever J423.1; refuses payment for being carried K233.5; released: grateful B375.10; rides on fox B557.13; as sham saint K1961.1.5.1; swallowed to drink water in elephant's belly K952.1.1; swung by tail, fears man J17.1; tooth as madness cure D1508.3; as trickster

J1117.1; tries to pose as peacock J953.14; tries to roar like lion J2413.8.
— Why j. has black back A2218.2, A2356.3.2; camel and j. exchange
food J512.11; clever j. covers up own inabilities J873.1; creation of j.
A1834.2; elephant lets j. into stomach F929.1; enemies of j. A2494.5,
A2494.5.1ff.; envious j. makes lion suspicious of bull K2131.2; friendships of j. A2493.11, (and elephant) M246.1.1, (and lion) A2493.30.1,
(and tiger) A2493.11.3; helpful j. B435.2; hungry ghost reborn as j.
E694.1; iguana persuades j. to let him go K551.2.1; jealous courtiers
accuse j. of stealing lion's food K2141; king j. captured J951.5; lazy j.
punished Q5.1; making j. laugh H1194.2; man becomes j. D113.4;
marriage to j. B601.11; origin of j. B710.1; ox claims dogs chasing j.
K1725.1; painted j. an outcast J951.4.1; prophetic j. B142.2; quick
thinking saves j. J1662.1; reincarnation as j. E612.10; riddle about
deaths of elephant, snake, and j. H803; struggles with j. free captive
buried alive R212.1.2; tailless j. persuades others to cut off tails J758.1.2;
wager: will j. howl or ass bray first? N92; why j. cries at night A2427.1;
why j. has bare tail A2317.12.2; why j. has burnt tip on tail K581.5;
why j. has short tail A2378.4.5; why j. may go everywhere A2434.1.5.

Jackal's head caught in blue dye pot: made king J2131.5.6; vanity punished
Q331.21. — Barber's and j. common garden K171.8; crow tied to j. tail
J2132.3.1.

Jackals enter pit to escape storm, killed K811.2; as judges P421.1; jump
into well J1791.3.4. — Enemies buried alive, exposed to j. S123.6;
houses to keep howling j. warm J1873.4; king of j. B241.2.9; marriage of
j. and turtles F414.3; tiger settles argument for j. K555.3; why j. make
noise at night A2479.3; why j. do not go in herds A2492.1.

Jackdaw, see **Daw.**

Jacob as man in the moon A751.10.2. — Riddle: who has had, here below,
two names? (J.-Israel) H817.

Jacob's face on God's throne A152.8; sons throw hero into pit K1931.4.

Jaguar. — Ant-eater deceives j. K1721.2; color of j. A2411.1.1.2; creation
of j. A1817; food of j. A2435.3.16; four-eyed j. B15.4.1.3; hero offspring of j. A511.1.8.2; heroes born from human wife of j. A511.1.4.3;
human offspring of j. B631.7; man becomes j. D112.6; marriage to j.
B601.15; speaking j. B211.2.2.2: strong man kills j. F628.1.1.3; two-
headed j. B15.1.2.1.3.

Jaguars. — Tiger has family of j. B672.

Jailed, see **Imprisoned.**

Jailor. — Competition in friendship: prisoner and j. P315.1; tokens sent
to j. as warrant of king's authority H82.1.

Jar of honey is to be sold (air-castle) J2061.1. — Child born in j. T561;
coins concealed in j. J1655.3; deity animates j. beneath tree A199.1;
escape from deluge in j. A1029.3; false husband duped into j. on
woman's head J1172.3.1; getting melon out of j. resourcefulness test
H506.8; greedy one gets stuck in j. W151.9; literal numskull drags j. on

string J2461.1.1; magic j. D1171.7.1; night kept in j. A1174.3.1; putting a large squash whole into a narrow-necked j. H1023.11; striking at reflection in j. J1791.7.1; tiger hides guests in j. K649.1.2; wolf puts head through j. handle K1022.7.

Jars. — Breaking j. to make weeping seem natural J1142.4.1.2; man dreams of j. of wealth N531.5.

Jasmine. — Quest for j. flower H1333.5.4.

Javelin. — Fairies drive iron j. through man's door F361.17.8; giant impaling self on j. K897.2.1; hurling j. as challenge P556.2; magic j. D1085.

Jaws. — Leaving j. at home to prevent quarrels F513.3; small animal grateful for release from j. of large one B371.

Jawbone cut from slain opponent P555.2.12. — Ass's magic j. D1402.3.4, D1472.1.24.2; water from j. D925.1.3.

Jay borrows cuckoo's skin A2241.6; in peacock's skin unmasked J951.2. — Color of j. A2411.2.1.8; creation of j. A1921; why j. is quiet at noon A2236.7.

Jealous co-wife kills woman's children S322.3; father kills daughter's suitors S11.4.1; father sends son to upper world on stretching tree *S11.2; husband T257, (kills bird to which wife falsely says she has been listening) Q587, (kills innocent wife) N348; king banishes son S322.1.5.1; mother casts daughter forth S322.2; and overhasty man kills his rescuing twin brother N342.3; queen dupes child-bearing one K2115.0.1; wife T257, (of god) A164.7, (makes merchant turn out queen) S463, (tells sister to look below: pushes her over cliff) K832.1; women mutilate attractive one S160.2; woman reborn as chilly E692.4. — Ass j. of horse, but sees horse later working in a mill L452.1; god j. of mortal A189.4; husband j. of wife who goes to confession is punished by the priest T257.4; ogre's wife j. G674; raven j. of partridge's way of flying W181.5; seduction by making woman j. K1368; sun's love for girl makes moon j. A736.7; tasks (quests) assigned at suggestion of j. (rivals) H911, (brothers) H912; vow never to be j. of one's wife M137.

Jealousy W181; punished Q301. — Death from j. F1041.1.9; first human killed out of j. A1297; fratricide through j. S73.1.2; friendship despite j. H1558.10; god's j. A194.3; goddess arouses heroes' j. K1093; husband free from j. required M137.1; origin of j. A1375.

Jeering at saint punished Q559.5.

Jennet. — Man transformed to j. D132.

Jephthah's vow S241.

Jericho. — Walls of J. overthrown by magic D2093.

Jerusalem, see also **Holy Land**; suspended in air F1083.0.1.3. — Pilgrimage to J. V535; prophecy: death in J. M341.3.1; signs before destruction of J. M369.5.1.

Jester comments on bid for queen's favors U66.1.1; disguises as prince K1839.4; punished G303.6.1.3, Q387; wins prince's pardon by clever remark J1181.3. — Clever j. J1124; sham execution fatal to j. N384.7.

Jesting punished Q387, (by appearance of devil) G303.6.1.3, G303.6.2.3.

Jesus, see **Christ.**

Jew claims he has burned up priest's counterfeit money J1511.10; refuses to be rescued from pit on Saturday J1613. — Devil carries J. to hell G303.9.5.7; devil as J. G303.3.1.15; discussion between priest and J. carried on by symbol H607.1; punishment of J. for apostacy Q232.2; ungrateful J. steals Christian's horse W154.19; Virgin Mary converts a J. V266; wandering J. Q502.1; washing J. as devil's task G303.16.19.3.3.

Jew's harp. — Witch plays j. K606.1.4.

Jews P715.1; bribe woman to steal host for them: miraculous manifestations V35.1; eating with heathen tabu C246.1; keep aloof from others A1689.13; protesting against marriage of Jewess and Christian are struck dumb V343; repaying devil with persons M211.4. — Christian traditions concerning J. *V360ff.; jokes concerning J. X610ff.; knockers as ghosts of J. F456.1.1.1, F456.1.2.3.2; pity for the poor J. J2383; seven whistlers are souls of J. who crucified Christ A1715.3; why J. don't worship idols A1544.0.1; why J. read, write from right to left: king's ugly name A1689.6; why J. smell bad: rubbed Christ's body with garlic A1662.1; why J. do not eat pork A1681.2.

Jewel found on donkey's neck N534.8; hidden in thigh F1034.3.4; present brings false accusation of theft K2104; responds to owner's voice D1651.13; for summoning animal's help B501.3; transformed to person D432.3. — Animal discovers j. B562.1.0.1; child born wearing j. T552.7; dragon with j. in head B11.2.14; fairyland quest for j. H1286.1; giant's enormous j. F531.4.6; hero will marry girl possessing certain j. H361; horse kicks up j. B562.1.2; identification by j. H93; insect inside j. J1661.1.6; luminous j. in animal's head B722.3; magic j. *D1071, (carried off by bird) D865, (heals wounds) D1503.6; (transports) D1520.29; mountain formed of a j. F752.3; playing marbles with j. H151.1.1; parrot recovers j. from sea B548.6; rabbi returns j. found with bought ass W37.3; serpent with j. in head B101.7; sham wise man sees j. hidden, gets reward K1956.2.1; sisters throw unique j. into lake: killed and thrown after it Q582.1; snake becomes j. D425.1.2; soul in j. E711.3; stone becomes j. D452.1.4; throwing away j. J2093.3; what is finest j.? H659.24; whispering announcement of finding lost j. K2095.1; woman gives j. for salad J2093.2; woman sells favors to obtain a j. T455.1; wearing unauthorized sacred j. forbidden C51.2.1.

Jewels, see also **Precious Stones;** aid in search for treasure D1314.8; float at new moon N513.6; of the gods A156.1; from hair D1454.1.2; magically shower from sky D2101.2; in otherworld streams F162.2.10; as reward Q111.7; as sacrifice V12.2; sold for trifle J2093.6; from tears D1454.4.2. — Animals with j. as ornaments F826.1; animals with members of j. B101ff.; beauty of j. admired, virtues neglected J264; birth with j. royalty sign H71.7.1; children as mother's j. T265; city of j. F761.4; clever ways of concealing j. J1655; deer of gold and j. possessing life D1620.2.3; dissatisfied with gold, looking for j. J514.5; diving for alleged j. K1051.1; dwarfs possess j. F451.7.1; extraordinary j. F826ff.; father leaves sons three j. J462.3.1; "four j. of Tuatha Dé Danann" F244.1; fruits containing j. F813.0.1; girl's ghost lends j. E363.5.1; god's temple of j. A151.4.1; husband coveting wife's j. pretends he is giving them to deity K361.6; island's stones are j. F731.4; kite steals j. and thus saves condemned man B522.2; lover's gift regained: j. as gift K1581.6; man dissatisfied with gold looks for j., loses all J514.5; millstone preferred to j. J245.1; objects transformed to j. D475.4; palace of j. F771.1.5; power of excreting j. D1561.2.1; quest for castle of j. H1343; rain of j. F962.8.2; seduction by scattering j. K1332.1; serpent steals j., person accused N352.3; temple of j. F163.2.1.1, F773.3; trail of j. R135.0.3; treasure and j. in otherworld F166.1; tree with leaves of j. F811.2.2; underground palace of j. F721.5.1; wagon of j. F861.3; walls of j. in otherworld F165.3.2.

Jewel-box thrown away to test goddess's favor H1577.1.

Jewelry magically disappears D1641.14. — Magic ashes produce j. D1469.10; stealing j. from sleeping king and queen K331.7.

Jewess makes parents believe that she is to give birth to the Messiah but bears a girl J2336; must entreat Virgin to bear child T580.1.

Jewish automaton will not work on Saturday V71.1. — Origin of J. worship A1546.4; sixty thousand J. souls in heaven E755.1.4.

Jinn, see also **Genie;** G307; escapes bottle, kills captor N339.17; falls into boiling oil G512.3.4.

Jinns F499.3.

Joan, Pope K1961.2.1.

Job hears of successive misfortunes N252.

Jobs. — Men exchange j.: each thinks the other's is easier K1687.

Jockey. — Naked man imitating j. riding himself G269.21.3.

Jogi. — Disguise as j. K1827.2.

Jogi's. — Magic thread from j. garment D1400.1.18.

John the Baptist as first martyr V463.2; or John the Evangelist greater? J466.2. — Feast of J. A1002.1, V70.3.1.

John-crow. — Why j. has bald head A2317.11.

John Damascene V256.3.

John the Divine F451.5.9.4.

John the Evangelist J466.2.

John Henry: remarkable rock driller X991.

Joined. — God with two j. bodies A123.1.2; riddle: what are the two fixed, the two moving, and the two j.? H851; two persons with bodies j. F523.

Joining. — Mortal wins gratitude by j. in fairies' sport *F331; theft of money from fairies by j. unperceived in their game of money-throwing F351.1.

Joint creators A37; rescuers quarrel R111.7; rule of brothers P17.5. — Three j. depositors may have their money back when all demand it J1161.1.

Jointless bodies of bone F559.1; person F529.7.1.

Joke. — Accidental fatal ending of j. N334; man called rogue by nobleman makes j. of insult J817.1.

Jokes, see also **Humor;** X (entire chapter).

Joker playing dead killed N384.11.

Jokers set household at variance K2134.1.

Joking. — Preventing sisters-in-law from j. H1199.17.2.

Jonah as sacrifice S264.1; swallowed by whale F911.4, (riddle) H821. — Fish shows hell to J. F109.2.

Joseph and his Brethren N733.3; threatens to leave heaven when man who has always prayed to him is refused admittance V254.6; and Potiphar's wife K2111; places cup in sack of his brethren H151.4. — Brothers throw J. into pit K1931.4; crown of thorns given J. V211.1.6; dream (prophecy) of future greatness causes banishment of J. L425; origin of thorn tree from J. of Arimathea's staff A2624.1.

Joshua makes sun stand still D2146.1.1; as man in the moon A751.10.1.

Jotunheimar. — Giants in J. F531.6.2.0.1.

Journey to Avalon *F111; beyond seven seas Z71.5.2; to Land of Men of Heads only F129.1; to lower world *F80ff.; to otherworld *F0—F199; on Sabbath tabu C631.1; of soul to world of dead on reindeer E750.3; started too soon: evening star taken for morning J1772.7; to terrestrial otherworlds F110ff.; to underground animal kingdom *F127; to upper world F10—F79. — Animal accompanies man on j. B579.1; animals direct man on j. B563; animals go on j. *B296; branches as j. token H84.1; bridal j. to husband's home T137.6; day's j. from earth to heaven since Christ went to heaven in one day H682.1.1; dead tells of j. E374; deity accompanies mortal on j. A185.10; disenchantment by naked virgin undergoing frightful j. at midnight D759.3; "don't go alone on j." J21.36; eating on j. forbidden C232; fasting for prosperous j. V73.4; food compulsion on j. C675; hero directed on j. by princess J155.1; large boot-supply for j. H1231; magic aging by contact with earth after otherworld j. D1896; magic air j. from biting an ear D2135.2; magic j. D2121ff.; magic object protects from discomfort or accident on j. D1384ff.; modest request: present from the j. L221; numskulls go on j. J1711; objects go on j. F1025; prayer for j. to land of dead V52.9; rainbow spirit helps on j. F439.1.2; remaining on j. too long forbidden C761.1; riddling remarks of traveling companions interpreted by girl at end of j. H586ff.; soul goes on j. E721ff.; sledges turned in the direction of the j. J2333; start your j. early in the day: counsel proved wise by experience J21.19; tabu to rest on j. C731; turning back after beginning a j. forbidden C833.3; unborn child directs mother's j. T575.1.6.1; worn-out shoes as proof of long j. *H241.

Journeys. — Mountains from primeval j. of (a god) A962.3, (first man) A962.6; prophecies connected with j. M358; tabus for j. C833ff.; tabus connected with otherworld j. *C710ff.

Journeyman. — Devil helps j. win wager with master G303.22.8.

Jousting. — Knight j. with all comers P52.

Jove. — Saturn swallows stone instead of J. G11.0.1.1.

Joy. — Cure from excessive j. K1889.2; death from excessive j. F1041.1.5; fairy music causes j. F262.3.6; god's j. A194.4; magic object causes j. D1359.3; only j. felt in otherworld F165.6; quest for king's j. H1378.2.

Joys. — Good that all j. are mixed with sorrow J171.2.2.

Joyfully. — Woman saves herself from soldiers by receiving them j. rather than fearfully K2361.

Judaism. — Conversion to J. V336; power of J. tested H1573.4.1.

Judas Iscariot appears in sea E489.7; spills salt at Last Supper N131.3.1. — Tree on which J. hanged himself cursed A2721.5.

Judge *P421; frightened into decision J1195; of the gods A169.1; lenient to own son J1197; must yield bench after false judgment Q265.3; orders bride to consummate marriage T166; pays fine himself, tired of bickering J1179.9; put out of countenance J1212; reduces penalty, accused his son U21.5; saves one ear for other litigant J1289.8; sends fool back for rest of bribe money J2662; wants to know how the theft was committed J2372. — Animal as j. B274; bribed j. J1192ff., (punished) Q265.1; cat acts as j. between sparrow and hare K815.7; cynic as j. of wine J1442.5; deaf litigants and deaf j. misunderstand one another X111.14; death sentence escaped by propounding riddle j. cannot solve *H542.; druid as j. P427.6; drunk calls j. very wise J1289.12; fool as clever j. P192.2; God as j. of men A187.1; irrevocable judgment causes j. to suffer first M11; jackal as j. comes late J1531.1.1; king as j. P19.4.1; poet as j. P427.7.7; repartee with j. *J1280ff.; repartee on getting receipt from j. in hell J1289.11; ruler unable to intimidate j. rewards him Q54.1; saint made j. of doom Q173; skin of unjust j. stretched over a footstool J167; upright j. refuses bribe W35.2; why man picked as bull-fight j. W35.1; with his whole heart: devil carries off j. M215; woman masks as j. and frees her husband K1825.3; youngest j. gives decision first P516.

Judge's bad-luck boots N136; humility, modesty J904; judgment affects fruit H251.3.10; temper leads to unjust death sentence W185.5. — Greasing j. palms J2475; killing fly on j. nose J1193.1; rascals pull of j. breeches and leave him exposed K1285.

Judges in the lower world A675; in upper world A669.1. — Seven thousand killed for stoning j. N340.2; why city with so many j. not destroyed? X332.

Judged. — Escape by debating which must be j. K622.1; judge not lest you be j. J571.6.

Judgment of Paris H1596.1; by testing love J1171. — Avoid hasty j. J571; child in mother's womb reveals unjust j. T575.1.1.3; death for unjust j. Q552.0.1; dream warns of error in j. D1813.1.2; false j. of distance in mountain area J2214.12; first j. in Ireland A1580.1.1; heroes seek j. as to which is greatest H1395; higher the office, heavier God's j. P16.1.3; house where false j. given slips down hill Q559.8; Last J. V313; laughing fish reveals unjust j. *D1318.2.1; magic object renders j. D1326; nature fruitless after false j. H243; stone bursts as sign of unjust j. *D1318.1.1; vision of j. V512; wise man follows fool against his better j. J1714.1; woman who has passed j. on girl who has a bastard is punished L435.2.

Judgments and decrees *M0—M99. — Clever or wise j. J1170ff.; image renders j. *D1621; irrevocable j. M10ff.; wise j. settle village quarrels J1170.1.

Judgment Day, see **Doomsday.**

Judicial combat H218. — Clever j. decisions J1170ff.

Judith and Holofernes K872.

Jug. — Child born in a j. T561; crow drops pebbles into water j. so as to be able to drink J101; disenchantment by weeping j. of tears J753.2; hero pitches giant j. F636.5; mending a broken j. (task) H1023.9; small j. of wine filled, large, not J1317; snake in j. bites would-be thief N332.3.2; test of curiosity: mouse in j. *C324, H1554.1; turning broken j. wrong side out H1023.9.1; woman duped into putting head in j. K714.5.

Jugs. — Carrying many water j. in one day as suitor test H331.10.

Juggler P483; promises to fly, escapes K1967. — Disguise as j. to enter enemy camp K2357.13; marvelous j. F698; transformation into j. D29.2.

Juice. — Fruit j. turns to blood D474.8; magic fruit j. D981.0.1; nuts yield purple j. F813.3.3; rejuvenation by j. of plant D1338.2.1.

July. — King's beard worth months J., August, and September H712.1.

Jump. — Disastrous j. to retrieve object J2146; magic horse makes prodigious j. B184.1.10; man boasts of his j. in Rhodes J1477; prodigious j. F1071, (tests strength) H1562.4.

Jumper. — Lie: remarkable j. X966; marvelous j. F684.

Jumping across river in one bound H1149.10; back from midair X1741.2; into the breeches J2161.1; contest won by deception K17; as chastity ordeal H412.7; over fire H1199.10; horse over palace H331.1.2.1; image D1639.6; over pit proves man's sex H1578.1.4.2; into the river after their comrade J1832; into river with treasure N513.1. — Animal characteristics from j. contest A2253ff.; dupe tricked into j. to his death K891; escape from ship by j. into sea R216.1; game killed by j. on it N622; horse j. over high wall F989.1; horse wins j. contest for man B587.1; magic power by j. into fire D1733.1; ogre j. on one's back *F472, G311; one animal j. through body of another F916; precocious hero j. across river F611.3.2.4; rejuvenation by j. over cliff D1889.11;

28*

resuscitation by j. over E13; strong man j. across river F614.11; suitor
contest: j. river on horseback H331.1.6; transformation by j. over D561;
unsuccessful imitation of j. into fire unharmed J2411.6.

Jungle. — Centaur rescues man from j. B547.3; exposure in j. for
refusing father's wishes S322.1.2.1; man from j. as cannibal G11.14;
prince in love with girl exposed in j. T91.6.3.1; rat servants cut down
j. B292.9.3; separation in j. N316; why man fears j. A1382.1; why
squirrel stays hidden in j. A2433.3.9.1; why tiger lives in j. A2433.3.21.

Jupiter. — Origin of J. (planet) A782.

Jury. — Animal j. B276.

Jus primae noctis A1556.4, T161.

Just king brings good fortune to people P12.6.

Justice W35; and injustice U10ff.; of God A102.16; lacking in one-price
city J21.52.1. — Animals ring bell and demand j. B271.3; Death preferred
above God and J. J486; god of j. A464; god consults j. on his left A42.2;
goddess of j. A464.1; origin of j. A1580.1; reign of peace and j.
A1101.1.1.

Jutlanders. — Bees mistaken for J. J1762.5.

Kabonterken F485.

Kali. — Vow always to serve K. M177.2.

Kamar offers liquor to gods A1689.5.

Kangaroo. — Why k. has short front legs A2371.2.10.

Kangaroo-rat. — Why k. has white band around his body A2412.1.4; why
tail of k. is not bushy A2317.12.1.

Karumba kills hero G347.

Kava. — Enormous k. F816.2; origin of k. plant A2686.3.1; why k. plant
is gray A2751.4.6.

Keen. — Chariots, stones, weapons join in k. F994.2; horse joins in k.
at hero's death B301.4.3.

Keeping first thing touched: ladder up to wealth K285; four dogs in
herd (task) H1112.1; it if girl, sending it if boy T645.2; up a certain
work all night (task) H1128. — Host as pledge for k. one's word V39.6;
journey to upper world by k. thoughts continually on heaven *F64;
mouse, bird and sausage k. house together J512.7; power of k. up all
day what one starts D2172.2; wife k. half of money for shrine W152.17;
wild huntsman punished for not k. fast day E501.3.5.

Kept. — Soul k. in object E711.

Kernel tries to escape death J1875.1.

Kernels. — Sun from fruit k. A718.3.

Kettenmärchen Z20ff.

Kettle borrowed from fairies and not returned F353; heating in hell for
certain person Q561.2. — Alleged self-cooking k. sold K112.1; devil cooks
folk in k. G303.25.4; as dwarfs emigrate each deposits coin into k. for
mortals F451.9.4; first money from k. A1433.0.1; giant's huge k. F531.4.9;
great k. X1031.1.1; hiding in k. K515.4; magic k. *D1171.3, (turns stones

to food) D1472.1.11.1; mosquitoes flying off with k. X1286.1.4; pot calls k. black J1063; refuge under k. R336; treasure buried in k. N511.18; treasure found in k. N525; wife refuses to take cover off k. T255.6.

Kettles. — Souls of drowned in heated k. in hell *E755.2.1.

Key in flax reveals bride's laziness H382.1; found in fish N211.1.2; to house concealed in man's heart F1034.5.1. — Bloody k. as sign of disobedience C913; disenchantment by finding k. D791.4; disenchantment by taking k. from serpent's mouth at midnight D759.1; duck recovers k. from sea B548.2.2.2; eighth k. awaits prince's rule C611.1.1; extraordinary k. F782.4; fish recovers k. from sea B548.2.2; golden k. F886.1; magic k. *D1176; penance: being locked in cellar and k. thrown into water Q544; question (on quest), where is the lost k.? H1292.6; task: recovering lost k. from sea H1132.1.2; thief copies k. by making wax impression K317; thief detected by psalter and k. H251.3.2; transformation: k. becomes bloody D474.1; troll in form of k. G304.1.2.2; wife to husband: "You have k." J1545.5.

Keys as protection against revenants E434.6. — Druid's "k. of wisdom" D1810.0.8.1; frog recovers k. from sea B548.2.2.1; hero leaves bedmate treasure k. for son T645.4; looking for k. to abbey J703.1; old and new k. (proverb) Z62.1; tricky animal secures treasury k. K341.18.

Keyhole. — Magic sight by looking through k. D1821.3.6; thumbling enters k. F535.1.1.11.1.

Keyholes. — Beautiful woman found in bed with man after he has plugged k. to keep elves out F304.3; witches go through k. G249.7.

Khijur. — Why k. leaves are long and narrow A2741.5.

Kick. — Magic transportation from k. of horse D2121.9.

Kicked. — Dragon k. in vulnerable spot B11.12.1.1; lecherous monk k. down stairs T322.1; man k. so hard he flies through air F1021.4; skeptic k. by sacrificed animal V346; wolf k. in mouth by ass who begs wolf to pull thorn out of foot before eating him *K566; wolf (lion) approaches too near the horse: k. in face K1121; youth made lame: had k. his mother J225.1.

Kicker. — Lie: remarkable k. X967.

Kicking. — Ass foolishly k. against pricks J833; man k. down mountain F626.2; punishment: k. to death by horses Q416.1; return from dead to punish k. of skull E235.5; strong man k. through door F639.5; witch k. helper into pit G269.1.1.

Kid perched on house jeers at wolf J974; puts tigress's cub in his place: she eats it K1611.5. — Man transformed to k. D134.3; well-trained k. does not open to wolf J144; Zodiac grows up: K. becomes Goat J2212.6.

Kidnapped woman escapes by asking for drink K551.17.1. — Miser k. W153.12; mortals k. by dwarfs F451.5.2.4; water-spirit returns k. man F420.5.2.2.1.

Kidnapping. — Echo k. men F443.1; fairies k. boy F325.1; missing girl saves man condemned for k. hero N692.1.

Killed game revives and flies away E161; man restored, invulnerable D1846.6; man can return to life E167. — Animal k. by magic object D1445; animals k. by strong man with own hands F628.1; husbands k. by brides in the bridal bed T173.2; child sold to be k. S210.2; creditor k. or driven away K235; faithful servant k. on quest P361.1.2; fairy k. by mortal F389.4; first human k. by his brothers A1297; ghost k. and thus finally laid E446; giant k. by strong man F628.2.3; goose that laid the golden egg k. D876; helpful animal k. (through misunderstanding) B331ff., (by hero's enemy) B335; king k. when old P16.3; love rival k. T92.10; magic animal k. B192; magic shows where person k. D1314.0.1; maiden enticed and k. by elf-knight F301.5; male children k. by Amazons F565.1.2; man not fated to die cannot be k. N146; man k. defending sweetheart's honor T326.2; man k. by snake in revenge B765.20; man must be k. with first blow C742.1; man plotting murder k. by Jesus (angel) J225.4; men k. by look of beautiful princess F574.1.3; ogre k. G512ff.; people k. by devil G303.20ff.; person unwittingly k. N320ff.; Red Riding Hood k. by wolf K2011; sham-dead k. by intended victim K311.1.1; slave k. P175; swallower k. from within F912; teller k. in own story Z13.2; victim lured by kind words and k. K815; witch k. G275.8.

Killer. — Lie: remarkable k. X955; prophecy: your k. will grow up in Braja M306.4; prophecy on your child's k. M306.5; prophecy: son to be k.; parents make him butcher M306.2; witch as k. G262.3.

Killers. — Would-be k. killed K1626.

Killing, see also **Slaying;** all earlier suitors H335.4.3; certain animals forbidden C841; children in cure attempt J2175.6; by deception K800; with Evil Eye D2071.2; ferocious beast (task) H335.3, H1161; giant's baby F531.5.14; if it is a girl T645.2.1; king tabu C563.6; by magic object D1402ff.; sacred beings forbidden C92; trees test H1522. — Abandoned children return, k. parents S366; accidental k. at sea bad omen D812.5.1.23; accidental k. or death M330ff.; advice on k. attacker J21.52.6; attempts at k. hero fail *H1510ff.; brother unwittingly k. brother N733.2; chain tale: animals k. each other provide meat Z43.6; cumulative tale: master refrains from k. hen, other animals Z32.4; deception into k. own family or animals K940ff.; devil tries to incite man into k. his wife G303.9.4.3; disenchantment by k. D712.9; dragon's breath k. man B11.2.11.2; dupe tricked into k. own children K1464; eighteen sisters k. one another P252.7; evil spirit cast out by k. E728.1.1; fairy k. man in revenge F361.17.7; fairies k. each other F259.1.1; faithless wife k. family K2213.3.1; father k. child S11.3; ghost k. man E247; ghost k. man in haunted house E281.0.1; girl k. man who threatens her virtue T320.2; god punishes man by k. his child A1335.15; hasty k. or condemnation *N340ff.; hero k. those who scorn him L156; husband k. unwelcome suitor K1551.1; husband k. wife's paramour K1561.1; husband and wife k. selves to avoid separation T211.3; innocent woman

accused of k. her new-born children K2116.1.1; lover k. rival brother
T92.5; moon k. sun's children A736.1.4.1.1; mother k. child S12.2;
promise not to kill on "any day": night k. K929.3; scorned lover k. successful T75.2; scorned woman prevented from k. man T72.3; shaving head
compared to k. thousands H599.4; sister k. sister P252.1.1; stone
from sky k. all but one couple A1009.3; strong hero sent from home for
k. playmates F612.2; strong man k. lions F615.2.2; tabus for man-k.
tiger, lion C549.1; witch k. person G269.10.1.

Killings. — Chain of k.: from bulbul to boy Z49.13.

Kiln. — Children abandoned in potter's k. S152.

Kin, see also **Relatives.** — Enormity of k. murder Q211.0.2; if I were
not your next of k. E229.1.

Kind foster parents chosen rather than cruel parents J391; and unkind
*Q2; words lure fish K815.14.1. — Choices between k. stranger and
unkind relatives J390ff.; girl persuades father to marry k. widow S31.5;
magic object renders k. D1354; peasant has k. words for daws but
kills them K2090.1; suitor chooses k. girl H384.0.1; victim lured by k.
words killed K815.

Kindling. — Magic k. of fire D1506.1, D2158.1; saint k. lamp without
fire D2158.1.5.1.

Kindness W10ff.; rewarded Q40ff.; unwise when it imperils one's food
supply J715; wins over enemies J26, L350.1. — Bride test: k. H384;
devil repays k. G303.22.1; disenchantment by obedience and k. D731;
loving k. of God A102.13; objects repay k. D1658.1.

Kine. — Fat and lean k. in (dream) D1812.3.3.5.1, (otherworld) F171.1.

King and abbot H561.2; absent hunting, angel holds mass V49.2; accepts
criticism as patience test H1553.2; acquires wisdom after long sleep
F564.3.3; accidentally finds maiden and marries her N711; advised to
marry maid rather than widow J482; allows self to be killed to insure
nation's triumph P711.9; asks for new trick H1182.2; assigns quest
H1210.2; has amours with great men's wives so as to learn secrets from
them J155.2; of animals *B240ff.; Arthur vows to watch at frightful
place all night M156; asleep in mountain *D1960.2; assigns tasks to his
unknown son H921; in the bath: years of experience in a moment
D2012.1, L411; brought to sense of duty by philosopher J816.1.1; blows
nose after giving to beggar: ruby appears V411.7; goes blind from
overweeping F1041.3; breaks own tabu C901.4.1; breaks promise to care
for a family M205.4; buried in deflected river's bed V67.3.1; buried in
his war car V61.5; buys spendthrift's bed J1081.1; and clever youth
H561.4; called baker's son since he has given the poet only loaves of
bread J816.2; causes own men to be burned, killed K947; changes clothes
with thief who steals his horse K346.1.1; cheats wounded chieftain in
land grant K185.7.3; chooses personal troubles to help realm J221.2;
chosen by test *H1574.3; covets subject's wife T91.6.2.0.1; cursed M414.5;

deceived about heir's birth K1847.1.1; defeated in repartee by boy H507.1.0.2; deflowering all twelve year old girls T161.0.1; demands subjects put milk in his cup J1391.7; of demons F402.2.1; descends sea to learn wisdom from fish J52.2; dies in tunnel to underground world J2137.7; in disguise K1812, (to learn subjects' secrets) N467; does not want daughter to marry T50.2; in dream advises take treasure from his grave N531.4; eaten, revived daily E155.6; exchanges riddles with rabbi H548.1; finding golden bow, arrow, lucky D1812.5.2.9; finds his children in floating casket H157; of fishes *B375.1, (eats subjects) K815.17, (prophesies hero's birth) B144.1; and fool look identical F577.3; forbidden to look at his son C319.1; forces follower onto throne: follower killed K1845.2; and foster son jump into sea F1041.16.7; of giants G156; given sleeping potion, beheaded by wife K873.1; of the gods A161.2; to have head pounded by strange queen M369.9; as helper N836; honors poet, critic J811.3; humble J912; imprisons all living creatures R9.6; improves kingdom for sons J701.2; of land under water F252.1.0.1; grows lean from fear of death U241; Lear judgment M21; lights first fire C751.1.1; loses ring while trying to learn art of stealing K341.8.4; lost on hunt has adventures N771; in love with lowly girl T91.6.2; made to change places with wronged subjects Q7; as magician D1711.7; makes peacock machine F675.1; may not marry anyone previously wed T131.7; and minister *H561.5; mourns vanished bride F1041.9.1.2; must cut off son's head to marry fairy H313.2; must summon ghost E389.1; neglected in exile, courted when regains throne U83; observes retaliation among animals and becomes just J52; orders own execution; believes will be king in next birth J1189.3; of otherworld F167.12; overhears girl's boast as to what she should do as queen N455.4; overlooks wife's unfaithfulness rather than to cause troubles of state J221.1; pardons thieves for confession J1198.1; participates in battle after he sees who is winning K2369.2.2; persuaded his desired ocean of milk is curdled J811.5; possessing one marvelous object sends hero on quest for another like it H1218; prefers poverty, primitive culture to civilization J245.2; pretends going in peace, really to battle K1774; as prophet M301.17; propounds riddles H540.3; prefers educated men as company J146.1; no priest's son J1827; punishes by killing one man in every house Q411.8; questions six doctors J171.2; refuses to exile gossipers J215.1.2; refuses fine tomb J912.2; refuses quarrel with bird J411.9.1; rejects crown and its cares J347.2; rescues abandoned child R131.11.2; restrained from hasty judgment J571.5; returns to rescue native country R191; saved in spite of self V523; searches for mate to marvelous object H1218; seeks prime minister who left him H1385.12; seeks bride only because counselors insist T64; seeks one richer than himself H1311.1; selected by cricket H162.2; selected by elephant's bowing to him H171.1; sends messenger to dead father H1252.4; sets sons task to determine heir

H921.1; for seven years Z71.5.4; and the cheap slippers J829.1; snake B765.22; speaking before druids tabu C402.1; speaks before people C402.2; strangles falcon when it kills eagle Q424.1; sulks until quest is accomplished H1212.3; takes off crown, licks spittle in penance Q523.9; takes subject's wife T481.5; tests gardener's obedience, plays thief H1557.6; told to seek harmony at home J1289.9; transformed to menial D24.1; transformed to parrot frees captured parrots R115; given three wheels to control his anger J571.2; traveling alone tabu C563.1; of trees A2777.2; tricked into sleeping with hag K1235; of underground kingdom F721.3.1; unwittingly killed N362; unwittingly shot by own order K1612.2; to be victorious as long as he rides muzzled gelding N125.3; weds common girl T121.8; weighs princess in chastity test H455; won't eat till gifts given W11.2.2; as wild huntsman E501.1.1; wooes through his daughter T51.2; of world of dead E481.9; for a year provides for future J711.3. — Absurdity of turning k. into brahmin J1293.3; animal parliament elects k. B236; why certain animal is k. A2547; animals dance for k. B293.0.1; animals make jackal k. J2131.5.6; army faces enemy rather than anger of their k. J216.1; banished youth becomes k. L111.1.1; bargain with k. of mice M244.1; bath in blood of k. as (cure for mange) D1502.5.1, (remedy) D1500.1.7.3.4; bird indicates election of k. H171.2; bird k. transforms quails to save them D666.1; borrowed fleet scares k. into giving daughter K1771.9; brahmin teaches k. J179.1; candle of k. lights itself H41.3; cannibalistic k. G11.7; "cease being a k. if too busy to hear me" J1284.2; clever answers to k. H561.4, H583; clever dealing with a k. J1675; contact with things belonging to a k. forbidden C501; conquering k. tricked, sleeps with princess's maid K1223.5; crow fat remedies k. F959.3.5; crown suspended over k. F828.1; cruel k. lured by execution invitation, killed K811.3; cruel k. slays brother, brother's son S11.3.5; death sentence escaped by pro-pounding riddle k. cannot solve *H542; deduction: k. is a bastard J1661.1.2; devil k. G302.2.2; disguised k. (recognized by habitual speech) H38.1, (rewards rescuer from robbers) Q53.1, (taught courtesy by peasant) P15.1.1; disobeying the k. forbidden C64; dog made k. B292.10; don't give k. ruby cup J21.49; dragon-k. B11.12.5, (transformed to gust of wind) D429.2.1; dream warns k. of error D1813.1.2; druid's spells kill Christian k. D1402.13; drunk man goes to the k. and wants to buy an island X812; dwarf k. F451.4.5.1, (comes to surface every 500 years) F451.6.12, (lives in mill) F451.4.2.5, (prevents father from shooting son) F451.5.1.16, (has silver miner's torch) F451.7.4, (wears costly crown) F451.2.7.7; dwarf serves k. sleeping in mountain F451.5.1.8; dwarfs emigrate when their k. dies F451.9.1.15; eagle regains throne for k. B589.1; eater of magic bird-heart will become k. M312.3; eater of fruit to become k. M312.3.2; enigmatic conversation of k. and peasant H585; execution substitute thinks he will become k. of heaven K841.1; exiled k.

teaches ruler wisdom J55; fairy k. F252.1, (captive) F361.7, (with yellow hair) F233.5.1, (punishes ravisher of his daughter) F304.1; feigned ignorance not to reveal k. K1792.1; fiery sword between hostile k. and queen D2196; first of three sons to kiss his mother (earth) will be k. J1652; foolish k. J1705.4; foreign k. wages war to enforce demand for princess in marriage T104; Fortune's wheel turned by dead k. in mountain N111.3.1; freeing k. from magic doll H1196; frogs demand a live k. J643.1; garment fits only true k. H36.2; giants' k. F531.6.8.5.1; god gives k. advice A182.3.4.1; god as k. A137.10; god refuses k. a son on account of his many wars Q553.3.1; good luck leaves palace night k. is to die N113.3; no great knights because no great k. U211; harem ladies recognize impostor k. K1934.1; hawk persuades doves to elect him their k. K815.8; headless k. and tailless tiger as friends J876; heathen k. tests saint H527; husband assigns tasks to k. stealing his wife H931.1.1; imaginary clothes for k. K445; incognito slave becomes k. Q42.4; inhuman decisions of k. M2; jackal calls self k., escapes farmer K547.4; jackal made k., howls, killed J512.13; lake where blind k. plucks rushes A920.1.12; lamp prevents k. murdering queen D1381.29; letting k. starve S123.4; letting k. hear something that neither he nor his subjects have ever heard (task) H1182; lesson learned from example of k. in exile J55; greatest liar made k. of Schlaraffenland X905.2; line of kingship taken from k. defying saint Q494.1; lion as k. makes ass his lieutenant J421.1; lover masks as k. K1371.4.1; lowly boy becomes k. L165; lowly heroine marries k. L162; lowly successful hero invites k. and humbles him L175; loyalty to k. rewarded Q72.1; magic object received from dragon k. D812.7; magic poem causes k. to waste away D1402.15; man breaking oath to woman can't be k. M205.3; man fated to become k. does so despite breaking lucky tooth N101.4; man strikes k. saving his life N656; man before whom riderless car stops chosen k. H171.4; man buried alive with k. escapes from the tomb R212.1; munificent k. W11.2; oath concerning k. in act of marrying M192; old k. F571.5; one-eyed k. has rocks counted J1675.4; otherworld k. F184; oxen stop for k. H171.4.1; paper in hand which none but k. can remove D1654.11; parable on k. not leaving castle J97; parents murder all sons except one speaking of k. S311.1; peacock proves to be a bad k. J242.4; peasant surprised k. not larger J1742.4; pike helps Christ: made k. of fishes A2223.4; plagues during reign of wicked k. Q552.10.1; plot to make k. criminal: succession to be forfeit K1166; poor man happier than k. J1085.3; prophecy: child to become k. M311.4; praying before the K. of Kings J1269.7; two presents to the k.: the beet and the horse J2415.1; prophecy: man will become k. M314; prophecy: son of certain name to become k. M395; proud k. humbled L410.1; proud k. displaced by angel L411; queen aids lover to dispossess k. K2213.8; quest to avenge k. H1228.1; quest to k. for military aid H1224; quest for lost k. H1385.10;

quest for bride for k. *H1381.3.1; rainbow is transformed k.: lesser rainbow, his wife A791.5; red garment to show anger of k. Z141.1; repartee between k. and philosopher on destroying city J1289.10; riddle: how much is the k. worth? H711; riddle of k. and courtiers H731; riddle of k. surrounded by his nobles H825; robber helps k. N884.1; saint kills k. of cats F981.7; saint reforms vicious k. D2163.5.2; saint saves almsgiving k. from hell V229.15; Satan as k. G303.3.1.25; seat in which only fated k. can sit H41.9; seduction by posing as k. K1315.14; serpent-k. assigns tasks H939.4.1; sex hospitality to k. T281.2; sham dead k. jumps up, kills slave K911.4; shipwrecked men kill k. in revenge K913.1; silent man asks k. what can he say to fool J1714.5; silver k. F521.3.4.1, (with silver attendants) F576; slaying k. under holy protection Q227.1; sleeping k. abducted by fairies N661; sleeping k. in mountain as guardian of treasure N573; son frees father by bringing riddle the k. cannot solve R154.2.1; son of k. and son of smith exchanged K1921.1; son telling k. truth banished J551.6; stealing from a k. H1151.13; stealing from ogre to help a friendly k. G610.2; he who steals much called k. U11.2; stingy k. who will not hire soldiers defeated W152.6; stone roars under k. H171.5; stone screams under k. H71.10.6; sun as k. of earth and sky A731; symbolic wounding of k. Z182; tabu for k. to sleep after sunrise C735.2.3; tabu: people speaking before k. speaks C402.1.1; tabu: quarreling in house (presence) of k. C873; tact in reproving k. J816; to test favorite k. says that he is going to retire from the world J1634; treacherous k. K2246.1; thunder report of birth of k. F960.1.1.1; trickster goes around k., gets reward for encircling kingdom J1289.14; unjust k. compared to donkey H592.5; vanquished k. gives hero daughter T68.4; Virgin Mary supplies mead for unprepared hostess of the k. U262; vow to live, die with k. M161.3; vow not to eat until knowing if k. alive M151.6; vow to serve most generous k. M167; waves' roaring danger omen to k. D1812.5.1.24; what is strongest? k. H631.9; wild animal performs for k. B771.5; woman in disguise made k. K1837.8; woman drinks poison that son may be k. W28.1; woman, fake healer, marries k., kills him for kingdom K959.2.4; wounded k. fines would-be slayers Q211.8.1; youth in court for calling k. fool J1162.4.

King's capriciousness compared to ass in stream J1675.3; crown in well F166.4.1; curse M411.17; death prophesied M341.1.2.1; demands on winter guests P337; descendants indicated by stone D1311.16.1; downfall prophesied M342.1; enigmatic order to minister H587; example makes merchant wealthy N415; face ill-omened N119.3; magic power of sight D1820.2; preventives against assassination J634; promise irrevocable M203; race determined by magic stone *D931.0.2.1; son to die from thirst M341.2.2.6; son persuaded to woo father's bride, killed K1094; sons called kings P30.1; third son sacred V205.1; unique ability to occupy certain seat H41.9; vision of whelps, foster sons V515.2.1.1.

— Asking for k. daughter tabu C196; bird cut out from k. stomach J1842.3; courtier shields k. love affair J1211.3; crosswise spears test obedience of k. subjects H1557.5; demigod son of k. sister A511.1.3.1; demons carry off k. soul F402.1.5.1; disenchantment by maiden sitting at head of enchanted k. bed D759.7; druid attempts to shake k. faith H1573.1.3; dupe guards k. "litter" K1056; eagle seeks k. bride D647.2; exposed infant reared at strange k. court S354; fairy k. crown stolen F355; girl to be k. bride cloistered T381.0.1; hero takes refuge at k. court R331; holding k. sword makes one his inferior K1292; impostor poses as dead k. son K1952.4.1; Irish roads discovered at k. birth A994; magic knowledge of k. dream D1819.7; milk of two k. children protects hero in dragon fight D1385.14; mule as descendant of k. warhorse J954.1; outcast wife's castle like k. H153; philosopher spits in k. beard J1566.1; prophecy: k. grandson will dethrone him M311.1; quest for k. joy and woe H1378.2; rats gnaw k. saddle girths, cause defeat L316; retrieving k. falcon H1154.7.1; servant rescues k. children R169.4.2; slaying k. son to prevent father's death H1162.2; smith as k. grandfather P447.1; springs from innocent k. blood A941.5.8; stealing k. horse as he rides it H1151.2.2; stealing tray from k. bedside H1151.3.1; swearing on k. hand M116.0.1; taking k. place by changing dresses K1810.1.3; thief lies by k. bed, steals jewelry K331.7; thunder at k. birth F960.1.1.1; tokens sent to jailor as warrant of k. authority H82.1; vow not to fight k. relatives M166.5; tournament to avenge k. death P561.2; water for thieves in k. garden H1471.1.

Kings P10ff.; exchange forms and kingdoms for a year D45.1. — Betting contest between two k. N1.3; calumniators try to make friendly k. fight K1084.4; four k. try to save falcon N836.3; fur made from beards of conquered k. P672.1; guessing contest between k. H515; names of future k. foretold M369.4; origin of k. A1653.1; sacrifice so descendants may be k. W215.3; tabus of k. C563.

King Arthur's. — Indentions on rocks from K. dog A972.5.3; prophecy: end of Round Table for K. knights M356.5; symbolism of K. Round Table Z162.

King Hiram sends Solomon riddles H540.3.1.

King of Kings. — Fighting for K. J1164.

King Lear M21.

King-salmon. — Markings on k. A2412.4.2; why k. is thick around root of tail A2378.9.1.

Kingdom of demons G302.2.1; lost to impostor P15.3; as reward Q112.0.1; where seven rivers meet F715.8; well by day burns by night H1292.20. — Animal k. *B220ff.; extraordinary k. F707; half k. as wager N2.5.2; half of k. as reward Q112; origin of k. A1583; prophecy of downfall of k. M342; pygmy k. F535.6; tricky queen gets k. for her son K2213.11;

underground k. F721.3, (of animals) *F127; vow to destroy k. by
austerities M193; whole k. as wager N2.5; wisdom of hidden old man
saves k. J151.1.

Kingfisher. — Creation of k. A1951; marriage to k. B602.8; why k. lives
in the air A2433.4.5.

Kingfisher's. — Origin of k. crest A2321.5, (beak) A2343.1.1; why k.
beak is long A2343.1.5.

Kingly duty rewarded Q67. — Nature's fruitfulness proves k. right
H1574.2; unknown prince shows his k. qualities in dealing with his
playmates H41.5.

Kingship line taken away as punishment Q494.1; renounced to become
ascetic V462.0.1; restored as reward for charity V434. — Achieving k.
by bringing silk H1355.4; fratricide to gain k. S73.1.1; magic bird-heart
brings man to k. D1561.1.1; magic fish (when eaten) brings man to k.
D1561.1.1.2; parricide to obtain k. S22.1; test of valor worthy for k.:
taking possession of royal insignia H1561.5

Kiss of forgetfulness D2004.2. — Betrayal by a k. K2021; death from
joy of k. F1041.1.5.4; death by k. from God Q147.3; deserted wife asks
for one last k. and chokes departing husband K951.0.1; disenchantment
by k. D735; disguised wife makes husband buy k. K1814.4; dwarf stays
away from house after maid tries to catch and k. him F451.5.19.1;
escape by asking a last k. K551.10; fairy's k. fatal F302.3.4.1; fairy wins
k. in game K786; fatal k. from dead E217; girl refusing lover final k.
provokes rival to admit selling kisses K1275.1; god's k. causes painless
death A185.6.1.1; heart breaks when girl hears lover k. another
F1041.1.1.2; leper cured by saint's k. V221.3.1; lover given rump to k.
*K1225; resuscitation by k. E65; soul leaves body after God's k.
E722.2.12; spirit's k. fatal F402.1.11.4; transformation by k. D565.5;
waking from magic sleep by k. D1978.5; witch's k. disfigures G264.2;
witches k. devil's tail G243.1.1.

Kissed. — Dreaming of being k. by fairy J2345; living person k. by
ghost E471; ox k. by patriarch on the lips A2221.5.1; pig k. by literal
numskull J2461.2.1.

Kissing leper as curse M438.1; leper as punishment Q499.1.1; lover shamed
by wife's husband K1218.10; the mother first J1652. — Adulteress prohibits k.: mouth loyal to husband K1595; brother first k. saint will be
king P11.0.1; clever decisions concerning k. and rape J1174; cure by k.
saint's letter V221.7; fairy k. man F302.3.4.1; father k. son while
planning death S11.4.2; god k. mortal A185.6.1; magic results from k.
*D1794; man dies from woman's k. T81.4; newborn child k. dying mother
T585.6; ordeal by k. serpents H224.1; only k. in bed tests fidelity
H1556.4.1; pig's licking mistaken for k. by sleeping man X31.2; princess
k. ugly poet Q88.2; stealing money while k. it K378; tabu: k. C120ff.;
vow against k. until father revenged M152.1.

Kitchen. — God of k. A411.2; great k. X1031.1; magic k. *D1141.1; queen is placed in k. and abused by butcher Q482.2.

Kite (bird) devours meat it is entrusted with J2124.1; as king of chickens J643.2; steals jewels and thus saves condemned man B522.2; tries to carry off so many partridges that he drops them all J514.1; tries to neigh like horse J512.2.— Creation of k. A1938; enmity between jackal and k. A2494.5.2; enmity of k. and crow A2494.13.2; helpful k. B455.5; lawsuit between owl, k. B270.1; man becomes k. D152.6; martens recover magic ring from k. B548.1.1; rhyme for summoning k. B501.2; wedding of eagle and k. B282.2.1; wind god as k. A139.8.4.

Kites, crows quarrel over wounded fox J581.5. — King of k. B242.2.3.

Kitten. — Deer steps on k. Z49.6.

Klabautermann F485.

Knapsack. — Devil cannot endure cross made by straps of k. G303.16.3.2; devil pounded in k. until he releases man K213.

Kneaded. — Serpent k. into dough H1407.

Knee. — Birth from k. T541.16; colored k. F548.1; person with black k. F548.1; sea as k.-deep H681.4.2; woman so old her chin reaches her k. F571.3.1.

Knees. — Afraid of his k. J2617; devil's k. backwards G303.4.5.6; indentions on rocks from k. of hero's enemy A972.5.4; giant with k. backwards F531.1.3.2; penance: crawling on k. Q521.1.1; person with k. backwards F517.1.5; witch's k. are beads G229.4.4.

Kneecaps. — Origin of k. A1312.1.

Kneeling. — Clothes of knight k. in mud before host as it passes miraculously kept clean V34.4; horse k. before stolen sacrament V35.1.1.

Knife accidentally kills girl N331.1.1; in bed as protection against witches G272.3; as childbirth precaution T582.4; drips blood (life token) E761.1.7.2; in ground exorcises spirit F491.3.2; leaps into hand of God's man H192.1; as tongue deceives ogre G572.2. — Alleged resuscitating k. sold K113.6; attempt to kill by throwing k. K2388; blade of grass transformed to k. D451.5.2; bleeding k. F991.1.1; bloody k. F1066.1, (left in innocent person's bed brings accusation of murder) K2155.1.1; breathing drives enemy on to k. D2061.2.9; cannibal sharpens k. to kill captive G83; child born with k. T552.5.3; child born carrying k. and calabash T552.3; compassionate executioner: k. with animal blood substituted K512.1.1; criminal detected by having child hand k. to him H211; cuckold's k. cannot carve boar's head H425.1; dupe persuaded to throw away his k. K1141; extraordinary k. F838; fairy k. stolen F361.2.4; fools try to use buffalo tongue as a k. J1971; giant killed with magic k. G512.1.1; golden wood for k. handle H1359.1; leaf becomes k. D451.8.2; life token: k. stuck in tree rusts (becomes bloody) E761.4.1; magic journey by throwing k. into whirlwind *D2121.8; magic k. *D1083, (carving)

*D1173; man will not lift k. to cut the rope about to hang him W111.1.2; obstinate wife: cutting with k. or scissors T255.1; ogre killed with k. G512.1; ogress with k. tail G510.5; penance: killing oneself with wooden k. Q522.2; precious k. as gift to helper Q114.1; recognition by k. H132; sheath and k. as analogy for mother and unborn child T579.1; sight of wild hunt causes one to stick axe or k. in foot E501.18.9; trickster gives a woman a k. to cut him a slice of white bread K344.1; whetting the k. K1418; wife's k. frightens off lovers K1569.6; witch with k.-like tail G219.8.2.

Knives on bridge to otherworld F152.1.6.1; as protection against revenants E434.7. — Bridge to otherworld covered with k. F152.1.6.1; deceptive game: throwing away k. K857; ladder of k. H225.1; oranges grow on tree-limb k. F811.7.2.2; snake killed by k. in animal he is swallowing K897.1; sound of clashing k. frightens tiger K2345.1; wounding by trapping with sharp k. S181.

Knife-holder. — Why catfish carry marks of k. A2261.3.1.

Knife-maker robbed by purse-cutting knife K341.8.3.

Knight *P50ff.; captured in pitfall K735.3; covers foal from storm Q51.1; dismisses devil in name of cross G303.16.3.5; disregards servant's insult J411.9; falsely accused of sedition K2126; feigns murder to escape city K579.6; jousts with all comers P52; pleads for fighting blasphemer J1164; ravishing nun captured Q244.2; saved from devil by friends G303.16.19.8; ungrateful for rescue W154.12.1; unsuccessfully tempted by host's wife T331.2; wants dogs in heaven U134; weds peasant girl T121.1. — Clothes of k. who kneels in mud before host as it passes miraculously kept clean V34.4; devil as a distinguished-looking k. G303.3.1.3; devil serves k. faithfully G303.22.10; devils appear to k. to try to call him from doing penance G303.9.4.5; fairy smith gives k. magic sword F343.3; hero in disguise of foolish k. rescues lady R169.1; king doubles reward to k. W11.12.1; lover disguised as other k. K1810.3; lover masks as k. K1371.4.1; madness from k. forsaking wife F1041.8.9; nearsighted k. mistakes own servant for enemy X124; nun hidden by abbess from pursuing k. betrays own hiding place to him V465.1.2.1; queen flees disguised as k. K1812.8.1; spendthrift k. Q42.1; sultan's daughter in love with captured k. T91.6.4.1; treacherous red k. K2265; uncharitable k. drives bargain even in giving alms: devoured by serpents V422; unknown k. R222; wronged k. conquers, pardons enemy W11.5.3; young k. substitutes for old K3.2.

Knight's. — Devil in fold of k. cloak G303.8.9.1; devil steals k. cloak G303.9.9.3.

Knights drink from huge nine-gallon cup F531.4.3; in wild hunt E501.2.1. — No great k. now because no great king U211.

Knighthood as reward Q113. — Garlic stalk as k. arms for servant J955.3.

Knitting. — Dead husband helps wife's k. E321.2.1; dead person k. E563; devil k. G303.9.8.1.

Knocked. — Bridal couple's heads k. together T135.13; dwarf carries his k.-off leg on his shoulder F451.6.13.

Knockers F456.1.

Knocking off single fruit from tree H1199.18. — Dead find no rest since someone is daily k. at grave E419.2; ghost k. E402.1.5.

Knoll. — Brownies live in k. F482.3.2; fairies loyal to mortal who owns their k. F336; fairyland under hollow k. *F211.

Knot. — Disenchantment by untying enchanting k. D765.2; magic k. *D1282.1; making an invisible k. with an egg (task) H1021.5; making a k. of spilled brandy (task) H1021.4.

Knots in grass mark underworld path F95.4; to be untied at childbirth T582.3. — Magic from loosing k. D1782.3; origin of k. in wood A2738, A2755.4; string with thirteen k. G271.10; transformation: handkerchief with three k. to (articles) D454.3.2.1, (animals) D454.3.2.2; why the saja tree has k. A2755.4.1; wind raised by loosing certain k. D2142.1.2.

Know. — Choice: do what you k. or learn to do something J483; devils do not k. or understand thoughts of men G303.13.1; Europeans k. more than natives A1667.1; how does priest k. about hell? J2221; "I don't k." thought to be a person's name J2496; I k. not how J1431; person does not k. himself J2012; all questions to be answered, "I don't k." C495.1; wise boy says, "I don't k." instead of "I know" J21.52.7.

Knowing. — Clever king k. everything in advance P12.7.

Knowledge, see also **Wisdom;** of animal languages B216; Fortune, Intellect, Health dispute which is greatest J461.1.2. — Acquisition and possession of k. J0—J199; cheating through legal k. K453; cripple healed by distributing k. H1292.4.3; eating magic salmon gives k. M315; hero's k.-giving member A527.2; learned man gave k. away H1292.2.1; magic charm gives k. D1310.6; magic sight from thumb of k. D1821.2; magic k. *D1810ff.; magic k. from touching "k. tooth" with thumb D1810.3; man with magic k. wins quest H1239.4; practical vs. theoretical k. J251; quest assigned because of hero's k. of animal languages H1214; recognition through common k. H10ff.; sacrifice for k. V17.5; saints have miraculous k. V223; salmon of k. F162.5.3, B124.1.1; sham wise man pretends k.: really overheard conversation K1956.7; supernatural k. from eating magic fish B162.1; tree of k. J165, (forbidden) *C621.1, (in otherworld) F162.3.5.

Kola. — Girls eat only k. nuts and tobacco F561.5.

Krishna plays cards with wives A164.3.1.

Kyffhäuser (king asleep in the mountain) *D1960.2, F451.5.1.8.

Kynanthropy D141.0.1.

Labor, see also **Childbirth;** contest won by deception K40ff.; — Beginning of division of l. A1472; fairy helps mortal with l. F346; food at first comes without effort: plan changed so that man must l. A1420.4, L482.5; ghosts forced to l. E558; intemperance in undertaking l. J557; king works so subjects cannot complain of enforced l. P15.7; man must l. for a living (at first everything too easy) A1346.2; race of ox and horse: ox must l. A2252.2; results of l. lost in a moment of procrastination J1071; strong man makes l. contract E613ff.; tribal characteristics: l. A1671.

Labors. — Strong man's l. F614ff.

Laboratory. — Substitute specimen for l. test K1858.

Laborer. Animal as farm l. B292.9.

Laborer's. — Stealing l. pajamas H1151.22.

Laborers P410ff. — Fairies as l. F271.

Laboring. — Object l. automatically *D1601ff.; statue l. for owner D1620.1.6; tabu: l. of bearded man C565.1.

Labyrinth F781.1. — Clue to find way out of l. R121.5.

Lac. — Earth made of l. A821.

Lace. — Murder with poisoned l. S111.2.

Lacing bedcovering to shoe J2161.3.

Lack, see also **Without;** of proper education regretted J142. — Absurd l. of logic J2200ff.; animal's l. of hearing A2428.1; why certain animals l. legs A2371.3; why animals l. tail A2378.2; why animals l. tongue *A2344.2ff.; why certain birds l. nests A2235.1, A2431.2; why countries l. certain animals A2434.2; countries with one conspicuous l. F708; why dogs l. restraint A2526.1; why emus l. wings A2377.1; saint's bones for l. of worship remove themselves from church V143; witches l. bread and salt G229.3.

Lacquer. — Seven coats of l. on chopsticks H1199.16.

Ladder to heaven A666; as symbol of upward progress Z139.7; to upper world F52. — Extraordinary l. F848ff.; forbidden l. C611.3; girl's long hair as l. into tower F848.1; lover reaches mistress's room by l. K1348; making l. which whole army cannot set up (task) H1147; stretching fingers to make l. D485; walking on l. of knives H225.1.

Ladders. — Knockers harm miners' l. F456.1.2.1.4; thief says that he is seller of l. J1391.2.

Ladle. — Gigantic l. F881.1.2.

Lady, see also **Woman.** — Chain tale: old l. swallows a fly Z49.14; hero in disguise of foolish knight, then of black knight, rescues l. R169.1; knight's duty to perform as l. bids P52.1; loathly l. D732; magic object received from l. in dream D812.8; magic sword received from L. of Lake D813.1.1; noble l. P60ff.; pardon given if hero produces the l. about whom he has boasted M55; revenant as l. in white E425.1.1.

Lady's. — Crime mitigated if committed at l. request P517.

Ladies in wild hunt E501.2.2. — Devils as l. G303.3.1.17.

Lady-slipper. — Origin of l. A2658.

Laid. — Curse l. on child by fairy F316; treasure l. in lake by serpent B103.5.1; walking ghost l. *E440ff.

Lake becomes bloody D474.2; deeper than the bottomless J2217.2; drunk dry D1641.12.1; entrance to lower world F93.2; magically transported D2136.4; of milk by tree of life A878.2; -monster G308; removes itself D1641.12; -serpent B91.5.2. — Animal dives into l., disappears F989.13; bathing in l. restores blindness F952.7; big l. under the earth A659.2; bringing a l. to king (task) H1023.25; creator emerges from l. A25.1; curse on l. M477; devil builds two islands in a l. G303.9.1.9; disenchantment by following enchanted woman through l. to underwater castle D759.5; diving into l. which makes person old K1072; dragon guards l. B11.7.2; dragon lives in l. B11.3.1.1; drying up l. in one night H1097.1; emptying l. with pail in one day H1143.1; extraordinary l. F713; fairyland at bottom of l. H1286.0.1; fairies' cattle under a l. F241.2.3; forbidden l. C615.1; giant lives under l. F531.6.2.2.2; hero battles under l. F691.0.1; huldra l. F460.2.5; lovers first see each other on shores of l. N715; magic healing l. D1500.1.18.4; magic l. sent against enemy D2091.7; magic light illuminates l. bottom D1478.2; magic spell dries up l. D1542.3.4; magic tree at bottom of l. D950.0.2; magic cauldron received from l. spirit D813.1.2; magic l. D921; magic sword returned to l. whence it was received D878.1; magic sword received from Lady of L. D813.1.1; mankind emerges from l. A1232.2; mermaid lives under l. B81.13.12; monster turning over causes l. to overflow F713.3; rajah sacrifices entire family to purify l. S263.3.3; saint makes l. of milk V229.16; serpent king resides in l. B244.1.2; serpents' palace on l. bottom F127.1.1; sun emerges from l. A719.1; tabu: telling children about l. monster C423.6; tabus concerning fairyland l. F378.2; threat to pull the l. together with a rope K1744; unsuccessful magic production of l. J2411.7; village under l. F725.5.1; water withdrawn from l. C939.1.

Lakes in otherworld F162.6. — Bottomless l. F713.2; extraordinary occurrences concerning l. F934; magic control of l. D2151.7; magic stone makes rivers and l. D1486.1; origin of l. A920.1.

Lake-horse paramour B611.3.2.

Lakshmi A482.2.

Lamb chooses her foster mother, the she-goat J391.1; prefers to be sacrificed in temple rather than to be eaten by a wolf J216.2; without a heart K402; symbolizes Christ Z177. — Daw tries to carry off l. like eagle J2413.3; devastating supernatural l. B16.1.6.1; devil cannot change into a l. G303.3.6.3; dwarf lets l. escape waiting for ram K553.2.1; escaped l. delivers himself to shepherd rather than to slaughter J217.1; golden l. promised to goddess (common l. sacrificed) K231.3.2; king seizes poor man's l. U35.1.1; man disguised as l. K1823.3; man transformed to l. D135.1; only l. punished of all animals U11.1.1.1; reven-

ant as l. E423.1.6; sheep licking her l. is envied by wolf J1909.5; using
l. to get lawyer's audience J1653; vegetable l. B95ff.; wolf persuades l.
to bring him drink K815.11; wolf unjustly accuses l. and eats him
U31.

Lambs. — Fairies cause ewes to have two l. F339.3.2.

Lambskin disguise as hairy man K1821.4.1.

Lame boy (girl) as helper N822; child as hero L112.8; god A128.5; man
given hardworking wife T125.1. — Blind girl marries l. man T125.2;
blind, l., and deaf as witnesses in court X141; blind man carries l. man
N886; blind man carrying l. man treasure guardians N577; curse: horse
will be l. M471.3.1; magic power of the l. D1716.2; mother abusing l.
son S12.7; thief makes l. excuse J1391; youth made l.: has kicked his
mother J225.1; why l. make good soldiers J1494.

Lameness magically cured D2161.3.7. — Animal feigns l. K1818.5; humor
of l. X143; trickster pretends l. and is taken on woman's back: violates
her K1382.

Lamentations for the dead A1547.3; for heavenly bodies F961.0.3. —
Animal's l. for person lost when animal was transformed A2275.1.

Lamia B29.1; eats children G262.0.1.

Laming horse for sale K134.8; as punishment Q451.2. — Fairies l.
miller F361.17.1; knockers l. miners F456.1.2.1.5; payment for l. man
K251.6; witch l. G263.4.3.

Lamp gives vision of Most High D1323.19; lighted over murderer's body
E185.1; lit at least every fortnight A1599.14; unlighted, ghosts take over
house E593.3. — Cover face: no need to put out l. W111.2.9; disenchantment by breaking l. D789.2; entrance into woman's room in l. stand
K1342.0.2; lighting l. with king's moustache P672.4; lighting empty l.
by magic D1933; magic l. *D1162.1, (summons genie) D1421.1.5; miser
running back to put out burning l. W153.11.2; oil l. blown out: had
thought that it outshone stars L475; suitor brings own l. J1575.1.

Lamps burn with urine F964.3.1; converse overheard N454.2. — Giants
with l. under coats F531.4.7.2; saint's breath kindles l. D1566.1.4.

Lampblack. — Magic l. D931.1.3.

Lamplighter, treacherous K2259.2.

Lampoon. — Fear of druidic l. P427.4.1.

Lancaster rose A2656.2.

Lance cast through leaf F661.8.1; foretells owner's defeat D1311.17.3;
imbedded in earth cannot be moved D1654.4.3; for witch killing
G229.4.1. — Bleeding l. flows into silver cup F991.1; demon occupies
l. F408.1; extraordinary l. F832; gae bulga (barbed l. which cannot be
withdrawn) F832.1.1; ghost points l. at murderer E231.2; gift to magic
l. necessary C835.2.1; magic l. D1086, (flaming) D1645.8.3, (kills)
D1402.7.3; skillful marksman casts l. through ring F661.8; stretching l.
D482.3.

Lances. — Eyes impervious to l. F541.10.

Lanced. — Cheek l. rather than reveal fig in mouth W111.5.8.

Land, see also **Country, Earth;** of Cimmerians F129.3; of Cokaygne *X1503; of the dead E481; grants M207; made magically fertile D2157.1; measured by amount in view H1584.1; of happiness *F111; of Immortals F116; of Lotus Eaters *F111.3; of Men of Heads Only F129.1; of moon *F16; of Mossynoikoi F129.2; of plenty F701; of Promise F111.2, F979.10; of the Saints V511.4; that has seen the sun only once (riddle) H822; sinks and lake appears as punishment Q552.2.1; -spirits F494; made magically sterile *D2081; of the sun *F17; of Thunders F117; of the Unborn F115; under Water F252.1.0.2; of Women F112; of youth D1338.7. — Building bridge over l. and sea (task) H1131.1; China first l. in world A802; clearing l.: axe broken K1421; curse on l. M474; deceptive l. purchase K185; dwarfs came into the l. by the hundreds F451.3.14.1; eel becomes dry l. D426.1.2; fairies clear l. F271.5; giant immortal so long as he touches l. of his birth D1854; head of divinity as protection of l. D1380.3; leaving l. unoccupied tabu C868; lies about l. features X1510; magic l. features D930ff.; magic l. and water ship D1533.1.1; magic song makes barren l. fruitful D1563.1.2; mortal goes to l. of dwarfs F451.5.4; much l. as reward Q111.8; penniless wooer; patch of l. K1917.1; plowing enormous amount of l. in one day (task) H1103.2; riddle about l. that has seen sun once only H822.1; roots hold l. firm A857.3.1; supplying water in l. where it is lacking (task) H1138; trespasser's defense: standing on his own l. J1161.3.

Landing on gods' island tabu C93.8; on island tabu C755.7; of returning heroes prophesied M369.6. — God's l. place A151.12; voyager l. on sea-beast's back B556.

Landlord. — Woman in disguise outwits tricky l. K1837.5.

Landlord's — Dead supplies l. money E373.4.

Landlords have biggest bellies J1289.17.

Landmarks. — Man who removes l. cannot rest in grave E416; remover of l. punished Q275; removing l. forbidden C846.

Landowner. — Devil punishes l. G303.9.3.1.1.

Landscape of otherworld F162. — Illusions in l. K1886.

Language of heaven A667, A1482.1, B212.0.1; learned by swallowing characters D1735.2; misunderstandings J2496.2. — Angels' l. V249.2; animals, men spoke same l. B210.3; answers in foreign l. C495.2.2; change of l. for breaking tabu *C966; first animals knew human l. B212.0.2; Hebrew as l. of heaven A1482.1; hero invents, teaches Irish l. A541.1; Irish l. A1616.2; king brought to sense of duty by feigned knowledge of bird l. J816.1; learning foreign l. quickly F695.3.1; magic knowledge of animals' l. D1815.2*; origin of l. A1482; poets' difficult l. P427.7.2.1; saints' l. abilities V223.5; sign l. H607; trickster teaches dupe strange l. K1068; use of strange l. to show education W116.7; witness who cannot speak l. of accusation discredited J1152.

Languages. — Animal l. B215ff., (knowledge of) *B216, (learned) *B217;

cold before theft of fire impedes speech: explanation of difficulty of certain l. A1616.1; dupe scalding self to learn l. K1046; magic knowledge of strange l. *D1815; magic object teaches animal l. D1301; murder discovered through knowledge of bird l. N271.4; origin of particular l. A1616; understanding animal l. leads to treasure N547.

Lantern. — Aesop with the l. J1303; cat carrying l. K264.2; ghost carries l. E599.7; Jack o' L. A2817, F491; magic l. heals wounds D1503.5; magic wishing l. D1470.1.17; quest for healing l. H1324.1; quest for magic l. H1341; witch power from swinging red l. G224.6.

Lanterns. — Dwarfs have little l. F451.7.3; "hang out l." J2516.5.

Lap. — Baby placed in bathing queen's l. T589.6.1.1; ball thrown into l. to test sex of girl masking as man H1578.1.4; eagle lays eggs in l. of Zeus L315.7; sleeping with head in wife's l. T299.1.

Lapdog dies when mistress dies B301.7. — Fairy as l. F234.1.9.1; first l. in Ireland H1831.2; hound becomes l. D412.5.2; split l. becomes two rocks A977.5.4.

Lapdogs B182.1.0.1.

Lapis lazuli cart F861.3.1.

Lapland. — Origin of gnats in L. A2033.1.

Lapwing. — Why l. flies in curves A2442.2.3.

Lard made from bark D476.1.4. — Man transformed to l. D271.1; obtaining wild boar's l. H1154.11.

Larder. — Inexhaustible l. D1652.18.

Large, see also **Big, Great;** animal frightened by bluffing smaller K1715.12; loaves need large oven X434.1. — Why animal's mouth is l. A2341.2; beggar with small bag surpasses the one with the l. L251; choices: small inconveniences, l. gain J350ff.; devil as a l. strong man G303.3.1.1; dwarf has small body and l. head F451.2.1.3; exceptionally l. or small men F530ff.; extraordinarily l. fruit F813.0.3; fairies with unusually l. ears F232.3; ghost as l. man E422.3.2; giant with l. (beard) F531.1.6.4, (gleaming eyes) F531.1.1.2; giants l. or small at will F531.6.5.2; lie: remarkably l. person X922; men at first as l. as giants A1301; remarkably l. mouth F544.0.1; remarkably l. nose F543.2; putting a l. squash into a narrow-necked jar H1023.11; small trespasses punished: l. crimes condoned U11.

Larger. — Animal becomes l. A2301ff., D2038; devil becomes l. and l. G303.3.5.1; hero professes to be able to perform much l. task than that assigned K1741; making the earth l. A853; objects become l. D480ff.; person becomes magically l. D55.1; robber promised l. sum at office: cheated K439.7; surprise that king is not l. J1742.4.

Lark causes elephant to fall over precipice L315.5. — Creation of l. A1911; helpful l. B451.1; smallness of offense no excuse when hunter prepares to kill l. U32; wedding of l. B282.3ff.

Larks. — King of l. B242.2.12.

Larvae. — Manking descended from l. A1224.2.

Lash confers invulnerability D1846.4.1.

Lasso. — Priest caught in l. by rival lover K1218.1.6.

Lassoed buzzards rescue man from hole B547.2.1.

Last belongs to devil G303.19.1. — Borrower to get the corn at same place as l. year J1381; devil disappears on l. day G303.17.1.2; devil is to have l. one who leaves "black school" S241.2; evil woman in glass case as l. commodity K216.1; Judas spills salt at L. Supper N131.3.1; knight divides his l. penny Q42.1; payment to be made when l. leaf falls K222; unpromising hero l. to try task H991.

Late bird alone succeeds at bird convocation L147.1. — Animal who arrives l. performs tasks for man B571.2; animal l. at distribution of qualities: hence his characteristics A2235; lover made l. at rendezvous by incessant talker *T35.0.1; too l. for same advice J1363; witch returns home l. G249.4.

Latin. — Boy pretends to speak only L. J1511.11; injuring dupe as he is taught L. K1068.2; prearranged L. answers J1741.3; priests (shoolmasters) ignorant of L. J1741; sham priest repeats few words of L. K1961.1.2; speaking L. so birds won't understand J1894.

Latrine too small for dining room table J2236.

Laugh. — Dwarfs' l. F451.6.6; enigmatical l. reveals secret (knowledge) N456, (prophecy) M304; magic object compels person's l. D1419.1; prophecy from enigmatical l. M304; suitor test: causing princess's l. H341ff.; task: causing person's l. H1194.

Laughing animal B214.3; ass J1169.5; and crying at the same time *F1041.11; fish reveals unjust judgment *D1318.2.1; at ghosts tabu C462; jackal H1194.2; mountain F755.1.1; skull advises hero E366.1; statue reveals crime D1639.4; tabu C460ff.; at thief who gets nothing J1392.4. — Avoiding punishment by getting king l. J823; bean split from l. F662.3, (causes black stripe) A2741.1; bearded man l. tabu C461; deceptive l. contest K87; devil l. when men weep G303.4.8.8; fruits l. or crying D1619.3; magic results from l. *D1773; magic l. object D1617; man l. at blind made blind Q583.1; numskull l. at his child's death J2461.3; patient l. at foolish diagnosis of sham physician breaks his abscess and gets well N641; person never l. F591; philosopher l. at world's sin U15.1; preaching leaves half congregation l., half crying X416; spurned favorite makes rajah l.-stock K1678; thief imagines people are l. at him, confesses N275.4; vow against l. until hero arrives M151.7; women l. (at grave) C181.7, (explained) A1372.2.

Laughter from chagrin F1041.11.1; forbidden A1372.7; produces rain D2143.1.11; thought to be spirits J1784.1. — God of l. A489.4; inordinate l. brings misfortune N399.2; journey to Isle of L. F111.1; magic compels l. D1419.1; man whose l. brings rain H1194.1; origin of l. A1399.1; sick fairy cured by l. D813.2; sister is mourning last year's l. H583.5; wife's l. checks husband J1545.7.

Laundress. — House of l. of clothes for church spared in great fire V137;

stingy dead woman lifts her head to correct exorbitant account of l. W152.3.

Laurel causes forgetfulness D1365.1.3; and olive tree scorn thornbush as umpire in their dispute J411.7. — Magic l. (plant) *D965.9, (tree) D950.17; magic wishing-l. D1470.1.3; man (woman) transformed to l. D215.1; why l. tree is bitter A2771.8.2.

Lava flow as punishment Q552.24. — Ogresses caught in l. flood G514.6.

Laving, see **Washing.**

Law courts *P510ff.; against rape A1556.1; student forgets speech J2046. — Animals at l. B270ff.; cheating through l. K453; cleverness in l. court J1130—J1199; culture hero establishes l. and order A530ff.; god rewards enacting good l. Q176; magic object helps win in l. court D1406ff.; marriage for a night to evade l. T156; natural l. suspended D2137.

Laws P522; given directly by deity A1580.2; on property division within family A1585. — Absurd disregard of natural l. J1930ff.; dwarfs are subject to l. of nature F451.3.5; king's l. must be kept until his death: sends back bones M14; making of l. P541; natural l. inoperative at end of world A1091; origin of l. A1580ff.; vow to abide by l. M185.

Lawbreaker. — Ungrateful l. seduces magistrate's wife W154.15.

Lawbreakers. — Dogs track down l. B578.

Lawlessness. — Banishment for l. Q431.2.3.

Lawsuit against animals B272.1. — Animal characteristics result of l. A2255ff.; noblemen being ruined by long l. join their families in marriage to save fortunes J552.2; riddle as solution to l. H542.1; wisdom of child decides l. J123.

Lawsuits of animals B270ff.; involving lending horse J1552.3. — Bishop fond of l. J552.2.1.

Lawyer P422; outwitted into settling debt K1623. — Devil follows corpse when a l. is buried G303.25.8; the doubly-feed l. K441.2; woman masks as l. and frees her husband K1825.2.

Lawyer's dog steals meat (double damages as fee) K488; mad client (Pathelin) *K1655. — Thief steals l. hood and robe K362.9; using lamb to get l. attention J1653.

Lawyers. — Jokes on l. X310ff.

Lay. — Division between religious and l. activities A1472.1.

Laying see also **Laid.** — How birds began l. eggs A2486.4; woman l. eggs F569.1.

Layman ignorant of medicine J1734; made to believe he is a monk J2314. — Priest disguises as l. K1824.

Laymen. — Peasant as priest preaches on the troubles of l. K1961.1.1ff.

Laziness *W111ff.; punished *Q321, Q5. — Key in flax reveals bride's l. H382.1; monk falsely accused of l. K2129.1; origin of l. A1377.

Lazy boy asks god to delay plowing season J713.1; boy and industrious girl matched T125; hero L114.1; husband W111.4; pupil reforms by watching home builder J67.1; servant W111.2ff.; wife W111.3, (taken naked in bundle of straw to a wedding) Q495.1; woman resumes her work when she sees little bird peck hole in stone J1011. — Ant and l. cricket J711.1; ass buyer returns ass which has associated with l. companions J451.1; creation of monkey from l. man A1861.3; God throws sand on l. shepherds (origin of insects) A2005; house dog blames master for teaching him l. habits J142.1; mother wishes l. daughter may marry devil C12.4.1; shoving, killing l. child J2465.3.1; tabu: bearded man being l. C565.2; why shoemakers are l. P453.1; witches punish l. spinning women G282.

Lead is heaviest (riddle) H645.1. — Bath of molten l. F872.5; dwarf turns gold into l. F451.3.3.2; murder by hot l. poured into ear S112.3; punishment: boiling l. Q414.1; reward for the bag of l. K476.2.2; saint unhurt by melted l. D1841.2.2; sham-dead person tested by hot l. poured on hand H248.1.

Leader of the Wild Hunt E501.1ff. — Coming of religious l. prophesied M363; foolish imitation of l. J2417; man transformed to beast becomes l. of herd B241.3; warriors battle l. as valor test H1561.8; you be l. and I will follow J1515.

Leader's — Shooting off l. tail X1124.1.

Leaders in single combat for victory H217.1.

Leadership test H1567.

Leading. — Animals l. men B563ff.; drunk men l. one another home X814.

Leaf falls on altar F962.12.5; sent down stream as a warning to one below H135; serves as boat D1524.8.1; thrown at animal's rump: hence tails A2215.1; transformed to another object D451.8; transformed to person D431.3. — Bringing plantain l. without tearing it H1041; crossing river on l.: God reposed on one J2495.5; deceptive wage: rice on l. K256.1; disenchantment from l. by breaking it from tree D711.5; hare and man contest in watching for l. to fall A2256.1; impregnation by l. of lettuce T532.1.3; last l. never falls from oak: devil cheated K222; living on food piled on l. H351.1; magic l. *D955, (bears person aloft) D1532.9; origin of l.-dress A1453.4; recognition by l. H135.1; resuscitation by l. E64.18; transformation by eating l. D551.5; why hare skips about like a l. A2479.2; why rat's tail looks like folded l. A2378.9.5; witch flies on l. G242.3.

Leaves become gold plates D475.1.19; fall from tree as life token E761.7.3; of life and death E64.1.1.2; magically enlarged D489.1; of plant A2760ff.; transformed to animal D441.5; of tree open and close to give saint passage F979.2. — Beauty contestants covered with l. K98.1; blister on back from lying in rose l. F647.9; conception from eating l. T511.2.0.2; counting l. daily falling off tree H1118.2; dead l. changed to gold D475.1.3; devils put to flight by cross made of l. G303.16.3.3; doing penance till green l. grow on a dry branch Q521.1; fairies dance on undisturbed l. F261.2.1; flower with "ave" on l. E631.0.2.1; injury from rose l. falling F647.3; magic flower pot bears plants with gold letters on l. D1469.1. magic l. turn white bird black D1337.2.1; prophecy on l. blown by winds M301.21; remedy: covering with dry l. K1010.1; resuscitation by l. E105; riddle: how many l. are on the tree? H705; riddle: tree with l. white on one side and black on the other H721.2; riddle: tree with twelve branches, each with thirty l., black and white H721.1; shame for nakedness appears to first women (l. for clothes) A1383.1; sky rests on top of trees: hence flat l. A2741.3; touching l. forbidden C511; tree with extraordinary l. F811.2; tree sheds l. in sympathy F979.15; why all trees have l. A2760.1; why certain l. have holes in them A2763; why certain l. are hollow A2764; why l. hang head downward A2768; why khijur l. are long and narrow: split by arrow A2741.5; waiting in vain for l. to fall J2066.8; wild huntsman repays with l. that turn to gold *E501.15.4.

Leak. — Helpful animal stops l. in Noah's Ark *B527.2; seduction by l. in roof over woman's bed K1339.8; tiger frightened of l. J2633.

Leaky. — Carrying water in l. vessel (task) H1023.2.1; embarkation in l. vessel as punishment Q466; filling l. vessels with water from a bottomless jar as punishment Q512.1; pumping out a l. ship (task) H1023.5.

Lean dogs envy arena-dog his fatness but later see their error L455. — Division of fat and l. fowls J1241.4; fat and l. kine in otherworld F171.1; king grows l. from fear of death U241.

Leander drowned as he swims to Hero T83.

Leap. — Cliff from lovers' l. A968.2; enormous l. F1071.2.1; horse's tremendous l. F989.1.1.

Leaps. — Chasms mark l. of giants A972.5.2.

Leaping a camping place tabu C876; to death with woman in arms Q411.0.1.3; over stone yearly compulsion C684.3. — Cat l. through man like arrow of fire, burns him to ashes B16.1.1.2; corpse l. up in emotion at saint's passing nearby E597; soul l. from body E722.2.5.

Lear, king M21.

Learned man giving away knowledge reincarnated as tree H1292.2.1; person worth two unlearned J252; professions P420ff.; words misunderstood by uneducated J1803. — Animal characteristic l. from another animal A2271; animal language l. B217ff.; ignorant surpasses l. man L143; man gains entrance to l. girl's presence K1321.1.3; means of resuscitation l. E181; remedy l. from overhearing animal meeting *B513; valuable secrets l. *N440—N499.

Learning art of love T4; the Bavarian language X652; fear H1440ff.; to pray V51; quickly to read F695.3; to read by magic D1819.4; as suitor test H327; or wit more important? N141.1. — Choice: doing what you know or l. something J483; god of l. A465.3; saint helps with l. V223.4; test of l. H502; wisdom before l. J1217.2.

Leash. — Dogs on l. in wild hunt E501.4.1.9; life token: dogs pulling on l. E761.7.5.

Leashes. — Forgetting hounds' l. bad omen D1812.5.1.21.

Least loved friend only true H1558.1.1. — Contest: who will eat l.? H81.4.

Leather. — Stirrup l. breaking bad omen D1815.5.1.28.

Leave. — "Have we l. to go?" K475.2.

Leaven tabu for cooking C888.

Leaves, see after **Leaf.**

Leavetaking. — Buffaloes fail to come at god's l. A2231.12; trees fail to come at god's l., punished A2721.7.

Leaving purchase, remembering extra token J2461.5. — Bridegroom l. bride, impelled by magic T177; cat l. house when report is made of death of one of his companions *B342; fairy l. when named F381.1; excuse for returning home after l. wife J1545.3.3; guests l. after shabby hospitality P334; manner of soul's l. body E722.2ff.; punishment for l. holy orders Q226; tabu: women l. hero's land C566.3; Virgin miraculously prevents nun from l. convent V265.

Lecherous, see also **Lustful;** brother T415.1; father T411.1; king glued with feathers K1218.18; prince in disguise to kill grandchildren K1812.14. — Tiger tears l. teacher Q243.6.

Lechery. — Man saved from l. through prayer V52.1.

Led. — Lost king l. from forest by lion *B563.1; man harnessed and l. to dance by witch G269.3; person l. astray by spirit F402.1.1.

Leech. — Girl reborn as l. to avenge murder E693.1; indestructibility of l. B745; origin of l. A2182.2; reincarnation as l. E618.1; why l. is blind A2332.6.8; why l. feeds on human blood A2435.6.3.

Leeches. — Don't pluck off well-fed l. J215.1.3.

Leek in beer poison protection D1383.5. — Magic l. *D983.3; rush becomes l. D451.2.1.

Leeks. — Test of wife's obedience: not to eat l. H473.3; to eat a hundred l. J2095.

Left, see also **Leaving.** — Body l. or entered by soul E720ff.; chaste woman to surrender when rocks have l. the coast M261; earthly bride l. for service of Virgin T376.1; implement l. by mountain-men F460.4.3; man l. by fairy mistress when he breaks tabu F302.6; money l. on hill to repay helpful mountain-men F460.4.2.2; truth deserts city because there is no place l. for her Z121.1; witch's body l. by soul *G229.1.

Left (adjective) eye only vulnerable spot Z311.1; eye renders fairies visible F235.8.2; -handed tribe F515.5; hand's power for evil *D996.0.2.1; -sided giant F525.5. — Amazons cut off l. breast of daughters so that they can handle bow F565.1.1; familiar spirit acquired by carrying egg under l. arm-pit F403.2.1.1; ointment cures l. cheek, not right D1663.2; skillful marksman shoots l. eye (of fly at two miles) F661.5.3, (of serpent) F661.5.1; soul (life) in l. hand E714.7; tabu: turning l. side of chariot toward certain town C643.

Leg, see also **Foot.** — Bringing l. to fit dragon's claw H322.3; broken l. saves man from fatal fight N178.1; child born with one l. T551.12;

clever girl comes with one l. on animal's back, one on ground H1053.3; coyote persuaded to break l.: therefore has thin right l. A2284.5; dwarf carries his knocked-off l. on his shoulder F451.6.13; fairy breaks servant's l. F361.17.4; fairy horse with one l. F241.1.3.1; giant with one l. F531.1.3.3.1; fowl makes another animal believe that he has had his l. cut off J2413.4.1; ghost laid when l. is buried E441.1; giant's l. stops ship at sea F531.3.1.2; god with one l. A128.3.1; goose without a. l. K402.1; horse's l. cut off and replaced *E782.4; -less deity supported on animal A128.3; marvelous runners keeps l. tied up F681.1; mountain stretches l. out to meet beloved A965.1; numskull ties rope to l. as cow grazes on the roof J2132.2; ogre with sharpened l. G341.1; ogress can extend l. or arm any distance G365.2; ox's l. as person F988.1; pumpkin tied to another's l. J2013.3; return from dead to punish theft of l. from grave E235.4.2; sawing l. off J2131.3.3; severed l. regrows E782.4.2; substituted l. E782.4.1; trained deer drinks wine until he breaks his l. but thereafter abstains J133.3; trickster receives power of sharpening l. without harm if he will use it but four times J2424; village of people with one l. F768.3; witch known by hose unbound on one l. G255; wooden l. overawes Indians K547.2.

Leg's length from earth to heaven H682.1.8.

Legs cut off as punishment Q451.2.4. — Animal with two short l. for living on hillside X1381; animal with one head, two bodies, six l. B15.7.11; animal with body of horse, l. of hound B14.2; animal with six l. F451.4.3.9; why animals lift their l. A2473; animals with unusual l. or feet B15.6; armless people have l. growing from their shoulders F516.1.1; breaking l. for prowess in dancing K1013.6; cat devours man's l. B161.1.3; corpse's l. cause murder accusation K2152.2; daddy-long-legs' long l. A2371.2.12; devil will not carry usurers to hell but will drag them by the l. X513; devil's l. G303.4.5ff.; disenchantment by passing between l. D798; earth supported on birds' l. A844.10; ghost with thin l. E422.1.6.2; god with many l. A123.6; Indians and whites from l. of first man A1614.7; loss of eating contest: because of weak l. J2228; magic animal l. D1012.1; magic drink deprives of l. D1410.6; magic sight by looking under one's l. D1821.3.3; man lets l. burn in fire rather than move them W111.1.1; men with two faces, three l., and seven arms F526.5; miser breaks l. trying to retrieve single grain J2146.1; mutilation: cutting off l. *S162; numskulls cannot find their own l. J2021; ogre terrified by woman's l. K1755; origin and nature of animal's l. A2371ff.; person unusual as to his l. F517; putting l. together proves sex H1578.1.4.1; remarkable l. F548; riddle: four l. in the morning, two at midday, and three in the evening H761; riddle: two l., three l., four l. H742; riddle about two l. better than three H761.1; snake with l. B765.23; stag scorns his l. but is proud of his horns L461; witch burns child's l. for wood, heals them D2161.3.3.1.

Leg-wrappers. — Copper l. capture spirit F405.13.

Legal. — Animals in l. relations B270ff.

Legend. — Riddles based on l. H810ff.

Legerdemain. — Deception by l. K1871.

Legible. — Decalogue l. on both sides F883.1.3.

Legitimacy of children tested by dipping them in river H222.1. — Child's missing toe proves l. T318; children not l. T640ff.; wrestling to test son's l. H218.2.

Legitimate. — God reveals self to those of l. birth K445.1; not of l. birth J1803.1.

Leinster. — Broad-headed spears in L. A1459.1.2.

Leisure. — Why women have no l. A1372.8.

Lemon indicates head, foot of couch H506.6; thrown to indicate princess's choice H316.1. — Conception from eating l. T511.1.5.

Lemons, three D211.1.

Lemur looks where forbidden: has big eyes A2234.3; marriage to B601.6.

Lender discredited J21.38.

Lenders. — Practical retorts: borrowers and l. J1550ff.

Lending. — Animal characteristics: l. and refusing to receive back A2243; chain tale: l. and repaying Z41.5; counsel on not l. your horse J21.10; dwarfs l. to mortals F451.5.1.11; ghost l. jewels E363.5.1; promise on l. wife M267; tabu: l. C784; trolls' l. F455.6.2.

Length. — Grave equals five times l. of any person's foot D482.5.1.

Lengthened days in spring A1155. — Day magically l. D2146.1.1; night magically l. D2146.2.2; summer magically l. D2145.2.1.

Lenore (dead lover returns) E215.

Lent V73.6; to be short since winter was J1743.2. — Meat disguised as butter during L. K498.

Lents. — Three l. Z71.1.6.

Lentil in the soup J2469.1. — Monkey and lost l. J344.1.

Lentils. — Chain tale: l. get into sack Z41.9.

Leopard ashamed of lizard bite J411.10; in human form B651.11; leaves victim claiming to hold up sky K547.14; mistaken for calf J1758.4; with nine tails B15.7.7; persuaded to enter bag, see trick K711.2; poses as brother, kills child K2011.1.4; released: grateful B375.7; as suitor B621.5; transformed to person D312.3; traps lion in cave K730.3; tied in bag in water floats to shore, finds mate N228. — Abduction by l. R13.1.9; antelope sends l. for fire, eats game K345.4; why l. cannot capture animal who passes him on right side A2463.1; dog becomes l. D412.5.5; color of l. A2411.1.1.1; enemies of l. A2494.2ff.; friendship of l. and (goat) A2493.8, (cat) A2493.35; (night-jar) A2493.8, (squirrel) A2493.7; helpful l. B431.1; jackal as l. cubs' nurse K2061.11; jackal, l. tie tails together J681.1.1; why l. lives where he does A2433.3.18; why l. cats live in cold, damp, shady places A2433.3.12; lizard defeats l. L315.11; lizard frightens l. away K1715.5; magic l. gall causes death D1402.3.2; man transformed to l. D112.4; marriage to l. B601.4; ox-demon transformed to l. D412.2.4; sham-dead l. betrays self K607.3.3; spots on l. A2412.1.2; strong man kills l. F628.1.1.2;

strong man throws l. F624.1.3; tortoise cheats l. of meat K476.1.2; trickster tells l. he is too dirty to eat K553.6; transformation: handkerchief with three knots to golden l. etc. D454.3.2.2; why l. walks alone A2433.2.3.1; why l. is strong A2528.1; cause of walk of l. A2441.1.9.

Leopard's food A2435.3.17; haunt A2433.3.1.2. — Stone falls, knocks l. teeth out K1015.2.

Leopards as God's messengers A165.2.1.1.5; guide Holy Family to Egypt B563.5. — Children spotted like l. after bestiality T465.4.

Leper P162; controls winds D2142.0.4; as helper N864; hero L112.7.1; intercepts letter and takes paramour's place with princess K1317.2; laid in queen's bed K2112.2; as villain K2276. — Christ disguised as l. V211.2.1.1; curse: man to kiss l. M438.1; disguise as l. K1818.1, (to spy) K2357.11; kissing l. as punishment Q499.1.1; risking life to carry l., Christ in disguise Q25.1; seduction by posing as l. K1315.11; spring flows where l. pulls out rushes A941.5.3; transformation into l. *D27; wisdom from dream: the l. with the cup of water J157.1; woman consorts with l. T232.1; woman disguised as l. seduces, binds enemies K778.2.

Lepers are sacred V293.

Lepidoptera. — Creation of l. A2040ff.

Leprechauns F451.0.1; from Ham's curse A1614.1.1.

Leprosy from breaking tabu C941.1; cured except on thumb Z311.3; as curse M431.7; as punishment Q551.6.0.1; as punishment for desecration church Q222.5.3. — Ashes cause l. D1500.4.6; devil of l. A478.5; escape by shamming l. K523.2; magic object cures l. *D1502.4ff.; mistress accuses wife of l. K2110.1.1; origin of l. A1337.6; saint cures l. V221.3; Satan smites man with l. G303.9.4.0.2; sunlight ray causes l. D1500.4.4.

Leprous. — Wife alone remains with l. husband T215.7.1.

Lesson. — Son learns l. from mother's sufferings P236.7.

Letter believed despite contrary evidence J2528; of Christ V211.10; delivered to wrong man, substitute lover K1317.2.2; falsified for false elopement T92.4.2; from man in hell Q564; of salvation given from grave E373.3; shot into sky F883.2.1; from soul in purgatory E755.3.1; written on human skin F883.2. — Alleged healing l. sold *K115.1; alleged l. from king dupes victim K825.4; angel leaves l. of instructions V246.0.1; bird as l. carrier B291.1.0.1; carrying l. in person: no one else can read it J2242.1; cobra writes l. on prince's tongue B165.1.3; cure by kissing saint's l. V221.7; dead wife's l. to husband E322.7; extraordinary writings (book, l.) F883; forged l. obtains credit L455.8.1; holy man's l. stops devastation D2163.5.2.1; husband discovers love l. to wife K1557.1; husband's l. altered into execution order K2117.1; innocent man compelled to write treasonable l. K2156; intercepted love l. leads to substitute lover K1317.9; king's l. must be explained on pain of death H587.0.1; love l. hidden in apple K1872.3; magic l. protects against attack D1381.24; man desirous of traveling sent six miles to deliver a l. J1076.1; page throws l. in fire, thereby proving his guilt H262; rabbit sold as l.-carrier *K131.1; reading l. written by Christ protects against attack D1381.24.1; sending l. by flooded river J1881.1.7; sham teacher pretends to read document brought him as a l. K1958; substituted l. *K1851; Uriah l.: man carries written order for his own execution K978; Uriah l. changed *K511.

Letters in book have become small; were big in school J1746.1, J2258; in clouds interpreted as call to ministry ("P.C." in clouds as "preach Christ" or "plow corn") X459.1.1. — Adam's name from initial l. of four stars A1281.6.1; clouds form l. F795.1; flower from grave bears l. E531.0.2; inscription of golden l. on bird B7.3; magic flower pot bears plants with gold l. on leaves D1469.1; magic object from exchanging l. D836; quest for vulture's egg figured with golden l. H1332.2; symbolic meaning of l. H602; taking l. to dead H1252.2..

Lettuce. — Impregnation by leaf of l. T532.1.3; nun eating unblessed l. eats a demon G303.16.2.3.4.

Level. — Student hands back l. bushel and keeps surplus K223.

Leveling. — Magic l. of mountain D2152.1.

Leviathan B61; casts up gorge which spreads disease B16.4.1; keeps sea warm A1119.2; surrounds globe A876.1. — Angels battle l. A1082.7; cataclysm from l. striking earth with tail B16.4.1.1; creation of l. A2135.2; earth rests on l. A844.11; god battles l. A1082.4; god plays with l. A179.9.

Levitation D2135.0.1.

Levites as religious order V453. — Institution of L. as reward Q113.4.1.

Levity about biblical passages J1262.4. — Repartee based on l. toward sacred persons and things J1261ff.

Lewd. — Banishment for l. conduct Q431.5.3.

Lia Fáil H171.5.

Liar brings about fight between dupes K1084; cannot be healed U235.1; discredits own confession J1155.1; escapes from devil H1318; praises apes' beauty and receives reward J815.1. — Attempt to lie out of having called another a l. J1456; give and prove me a l. J1333; greatest l. to get his supper free K455.7; greatest l. made king of Schlaraffenland X905.2.

Liars. — River drowns l. D1318.17.

Libations V12.9.

Liberal girl rewarded with riches Q101.1. — Ruler l., gives more than treasurer writes W11.12.

Liberality as amend for stinginess Q589.4. — Cause l. to be depicted J1576; invitation to continued l. H595.1.

Liberating woman captive in elephant's ear H1151.18.

Liberty. — Wild animal finds his l. better than tame animal's ease L451; wolf prefers l. and hunger to dog's servitude and plenty L451.

Lice, see after **Louse.**

Licked. — First man from maid having l. semen-stained cloth A1211.7; river valley l. out by giant beast A951.1.

Licking brew gives serpent power G224.7; husband's body K1085.1. — Animals l. Christ-child B251.10; boar l. holy man's wounds B256.6.3; conception from l. spittle T512.5; cow l. saint's feet B251.2.6.2; deer l. saint's tomb daily B251.2.6; lion l. sick man J413.1; magic cure by l. D2161.4.17; magic results from l. *D1775; pig heals wounds by l. B511.2.2; water-monsters l. saint's feet B251.2.6.1; wolves l. saint's shoes B251.2.3.

Lid. — Murder by slamming down l. of chest S121; eye with remarkably heavy l. F541.7.

Lie, see also **Liar, Lying;** becomes truth as punishment Q591. — Forcing princess to say, "That is a l." *H342.1; telling skillful l. as test H509.5.

Lies precipitate fight K1084. — Filling a sack full of l. *H1045; flattering l. vs. unflattering truths J267; humor of l. and exaggeration *X900—X1899; hungry apprentice attracts master's attention by telling l. on him J1341.5; shoemaker drinks more than his portion of "drink of l." X242.

Lieutenant. — Lion as king makes ass his l. J421.1.

Life beheads simpleton J27; as ever-decreasing paradox answer H1075; index *E760ff., H1353; kept in special part of body E714; -lights in lower world E765.1.3; -long penance for brother-sister marriage Q520.3; the most beloved (riddle) H647.1; personified as old woman Z113; preferred to death and vengeance J327; prolonged D1855ff.; restored to dead E0—E199; saved by accident N650ff.; spans M341.1.6.1; spared as reward Q151; token *E761ff.; wagered N2.2. — After world-fire, l. recreated from tree A1006.9; animal saves person's l. *B520ff.; how ants can secure longer l. H1292.11; bargains to spare l. M234; belief in future l. V311; bodily member sacrificed to save l. J351; cooked animal comes to l. E168; daily l. of the gods A150ff.; darkness comes in day-time in order to save l. of maiden about to be executed F965.1; dead awaken after three days to new l. and great wisdom E489.1; dead tree comes to l. *E2; deer of gold and jewels possessing l. D1620.2.3; dying man refuses to believe in l. to come V311.2; fairy grateful to mortal for saving his l. F337; forethought in provision for l. J700ff.; fountain miraculously supports l. D1472.1.1; girl demands suitor's l. H333; giving l. for friend P316; guessing with l. as wager H512; hidden l. E712; lake of milk by tree of l. A878.2; law: l. for a life P522.1; long l. by cutting off finger-ends S161.1.1; long l. as reward Q145.1; long l. of first man A1323; man learns the fear of Death by meeting L. J27; married l. *T200—T299; marriage promised as l. saver M268; marvelous things needed to save girl's l. H355.0.1; miraculously long l. as reward Q145; nature of l. U (entire chapter); no time for minor fights when l. is in danger J371; oath taken on person's l. M119.8; ordering of human l. *A1300ff.; patriarchs because of long l. made inventions A1440.3; person comes to l. E1; picture comes to l. D435.2.1; preservation of l. during world calamity A1005; prophecy of long l. M321; quest for apple of l. H1333.3.1.2; quest for water of l. H1321.1; recognition by telling l. history H11.1; resuscitation of wife by husband giving up half his remaining l. *E165; return to l.: see **Resuscitation;** short l. of first man A1325; soldier prefers l. to death with revenge J327; staff of l. and death E64.1.1; tree of l. *E90ff.; unusual manner of l. F560ff.; vampire brought to l. E251.2; wands of l. and death D1663.1; water of l. *E80ff., F162.6.2; water-spirit claims a l. every seven years F420.5.2.1.6; well indicates l. span D1663.5; why animal has long l. A2578; witch offers man his l. if he will marry her G266.

Life's inequalities U0—U99.

Lives. — Giants playing with men's l. F531.3.15.

Lifelike. — Contest in l. painting H504.1.

Lifted. — Sun falls, l. back to sky A721.5; woman can be l. only by lover D1651.13.

Lifter. — Fairy as mighty l. F253.1.1.1; mighty l. F624ff.; remarkable l. X941.

Lifting cat (serpent that embraces the earth) H1149.2; mountain H1149.9; power of widow prepared for suttee H479.1; stone as test of strength H1562.2; strong princess's giant weapon as suitor test H345.1; sword tests strength H1562.2.1. — Cannibal hard l. G92; five men for l. club F835.2.1; magic object l. heavy object D1547.3; miraculous l. into air, dashing to death Q551.10; strong man l. stone F624.2; tree l. person up F979.4; visit to lower world through hole made by l. clumps of grass F92.1.

Light appears at holy man's death F960.2.4; carried into windowless house in baskets J2123; extinguished and woman stolen R31; from hand-of-glory renders person helpless D1410.2; indicates hidden treasure N532; keeps evil from corpse E752.10.2; moving toward cemetery sign of death D1322.2; put out by spear F834.2; seen from tree lodging place at night leads to adventures N776. — Why certain animals avoid l. A2491; angels shed l. on saint's tomb V241.2.1; beams of l. tie sun to earth A733.4; burning l. scares off ghosts E439.7; chariot of l. E754.5; clothes of l. F821.7; cock's elixir makes people l. B739.1; column of l. descends on chosen man V222.1.3; combat between god of l. and dragon of ocean A162.2; crime inevitably comes to l. *N270ff.; dazzling l. marks saint's birth V222.0.1.3; devil gives smith l.: smith known as jack-o'-lantern A2817.1; devil appears in intense l. G303.6.3.4; extinguishing l. to hide paramour K1516.3; extraordinary l. at royal birth F960.1.6; fingers of saint give l. or fire F552.1.2; ghost l. follows ghost E530.1.1; ghost l. reveals murderer E231.3; god of l. A107; hand-of-glory renders l. invisible D1361.7; hero's l.: appears around head of hero aroused to extraordinary feats of valor F969.3.2; holy man emits l. F574.3; illusory l. K1888; ink becomes l. beams D454.14; "letting in the l." J1738.6; life bound up with l. *E765.1; life token: l. goes out E761.7.4; magic l. *D1162; magic object provides l. D1478; man's body emits l. D1645.10;

mankind from peace and quiet fructified by l. A1221.2; marvelous l.
F969.3, (accompanying saint) V222.1; moon dragged up to l. earth when
sun sinks A735.1; mother shows l. of world to one who has not yet seen
it (assists at birth) H583.4.1; mountain-men cannot enter house till l. is
quenched F460.2.3; origin of l. A1412; quest for l.-giving child H1396;
quest for sword of l. H1337; soul as l. *E742ff.; soul as point of l.
E722.1.3; spirit of l. F499.1.1; sun gives l. to stars A769.5; theft of l.
*A1411; tree planted on moon to diminish its l. A751.6.1; trying to
catch l. in a mouse-trap J1961.1; vast l. at Nativity V211.1.31; white
sheep-skin used as source of l. J1961; why some nights are l. A1174.2.

Lights tabu on Sabbath C631.4. — Blue l. follow witches G229.7; exhibi-
tion of l. at saint's birth F960.1.3; fairy l. seen in low places F217.1;
ghost-like l. E530.1; ghostly l. frighten treasure seekers N576.2; heavenly
l. A790ff.; mountain of seven l. F759.8; numskull thinks the extinguishing
of l. at the church presages a fight J1823.3; spirit puts out l. F473.2.3;
wish: no l. except in own home J2076.1.

Lightbeam renders witch powerless G273.1.1.

Lighted. — Lamp l. every fortnight A1599.14; sacred fire from which
all others l. V1.6.3.1.1.

Lighting the cat's tail J2101.1; empty lamp by magic D1933; the road
K1412. — Disenchantment by l. fire D784; magic lamp indicates falsehood by l. D1316.2; test of king (pope): candle l. itself H41.3; troll l.
fingers G304.2.1.1; Will o' the Wisp l. people to their homes F491.2;
woman's face l. up the dark F574.1.

Lightning, see also **Thunder;** effective against serpent B765.17; flashes
from hero's armpits A526.9; kills ogre G512.10; made from the old
moon J2271.2.1; in magic box kills army D1400.1.23.2; strikes excommunicated person who enters church V84.1; strikes monk who despises
humility Q552.1.1; strikes where innocent man is being hanged R341.1;
slays devils A162.3.2; as torches of invisible dancer A1141.7.1; weapon of
the gods A285.1. — Angel of l. A285.0.1; devil retreats into hell amid
thunder and l. G303.17.2.5; disastrous l. as punishment C984.5; eyes
flash l. F541.1.2; extraordinary l. F968; giants fear l. F531.6.11.1; giants
killed by l. F531.6.12.4; god of l. A285; god clothes self with l. A179.7;
god with l. as sword A137.14.4; impregnation by l. T528; man becomes
l. D281.2; origin of l. A1141; osprey produces l. B172.8; prophecy: death
by l. M341.2.11; resuscitation by striking with l. E29.7; sister's face as
l. R321.1; trolls killed by l. F455.8.2; why bija tree often struck by l.
A2791.12; why elder tree is never struck by l. A2711.2.1; why l. spares
the nut-tree A2791.2; witch produces l. D2149.1.1.

Like. — Quest for woman exactly l. another H1381.3.5.

Likeness of Christ criticized V124. — Devil's l. kills beholder Q338.2;
seduction by displaying obscene l. K1385; transformation to l. of another
*D40ff., D592.

Likes. — Follow your master's l. U42.

Liking. — Devil's l. for negligence in men G303.25.3.

Lily as chastity index H432.2; from grave E631.1.1; issues from devotee buried in unconsecrated ground V255.1. — Bee rests on water l. which closes over it at night and kills it J2137.3; soul as l. E745.4.1; stretching l. plant D482.2.

Lilies. — Lie: remarkable l. X1481.

Limb. — Animal dupe cuts off l. A2284.1, J2413.4; disenchantment by cutting off animal's l. D712.1.1; murderer torn l. from limb Q469.12; numskull cuts off tree l. on which he sits J2133.4; severed l. prevents detection K407.

Limbs affected by breaking tabu C946; cut off as punishment Q451.2.0.1; of dead fettered to prevent return E431.5; of dead voluntarily reassemble and revive E31; successfully replaced E782. — Animals with unusual l. or members B15ff.; bodies from which l. cut impaled Q461.2; child with extraordinary l. T551ff.; creaking l. (of tree) J1872; escape by catching hold of tree l. K685, R219.1; extraordinary animal l. F988; fairy's l. F231; magic appearance of human l. D61; magic cure of broken l. D2161.3.3; numskull injures his l. J2131.3; ogre revives after l. are severed G635; severed l. as identification H106; severed l. replaced by Virgin Mary D2161.5.2.4; swelling of l. C941.2; why all l. dependent on body A1391.1; witch breaks person's l. G269.12.

Lime sold as gold K121; supply for church miraculously renewed D1652.16, V224.5; used in building church as cure D1500.1.35. — Magic l. *D931.1.4, (healing) D1500.1.2.4; magic l. tree *D950.7; throwing into l. pit as punishment Q465.4; why the l. tree is cursed A2721.6.

Limitations. — Deity's l. A196; peculiar l. of fairies F255.

Limited amount of magic in world D1719.11; number of wives for king P18.2; number of wishes granted *D1761.0.2. — Heaven stay l. F11.3; invulnerability for l. time D1845.

Limitless wishes granted D1761.0.1.

Limping soldier told every step a virtue P711.2.

Linden. — Transformation to l. tree D215.4.

Line. — Birds hatched from broken eggs repaired by skillful tailor have red l. around necks F662.1.1; crossing l. to commit adultery K1588; magic l. D1272.1; hunting wolves with rod and l. X1124.4; stepping outside l. tabu C614.1.0.3.

Lineage. — Son-to-be will destroy l. M342.2.

Linen. — Fairies bleach l. F271.4.1; making sails for a ship from one bundle of l. H1022.3; making shirt from piece of l. three inches square H1022.4; quest for the finest of l. H1306.

Lingering. — Soul l. in body E722.2.8.1.

Lintel. — Death from striking head against door l. N339.13.

Lion approaches too near to horse (kicked in face) *K1121f.; bear, and wolf resuscitate master B515; blows life into cubs three days after birth B751.4; buried in cave with gold letters V61.9; calls insult worse than

wound W185.6; carries off child R13.1.2; carries person B557.5; cubs
awed by fox's boasting K1715.14; comforted for his fear of the cock
J881.2; cub killed by bull gives lioness no right to complain U36;
despite his strength is in man's power A1421.1.1; disguised as monk
K1822.1; divides the booty J811.1.1; divides slain bullock Q3.2; as
domestic servant B292.2.3; follows man who saved him B301.8; freed
from net by mouse B363.1; frightened away by stabbing from cage
K1715.11; kills wolf at fox's instigation K961.1.1; kills wolf who has
killed mistress's sheep B591.1; as king makes ass his lieutenant J421.1;
as king of animals *B240.4; leads lost king from forest *B563.1; leaves
sleeping hare to follow the shepherd J321.3; licks sick man J413.1; lies
down at saint's feet B251.2.11; with magic wisdom B121.6; protects
saint's body B773.3; rescued from net by rat eats rat W154.3.1; ridden
by drunkard J1758.5; sent to kill a man (frees him from possibility of
sinning and sojourn in purgatory) J225.2; spares mouse: mouse later
releases lion from net B371.1; and the statue J1454; suitor B621.2,
(allows teeth to be pulled and claws to be cut) J642.1; thankful rescued
by snake B374.1; thinks man is devil J1786.5; thinks man astride him
monster J1786.7; transformed to person D312.1; and wild boar make
peace rather than slay each other for benefit of vulture J218.1; worship
V1.8.9. — Androcles and the l. B381; animals confess sins to l. U11.1.1.1;
arranging for l. to eat adulterous mate K813.1; ass follows after l. and
is punished J952.2; ass insults dying l. W121.2.1; ass punished for
stealing mouthful of grass: l. and wolf forgiven for eating sheep U11.1;
automatic statue of l. D1620.2.4; bringing in fierce l. alive H1154.12;
camel killed by l. in game K869.3; deceived l. stuck in cave entrance:
eaten by hare K714.9; deity rides l. A136.1.7; devil as l. G303.3.3.2.5; dog
follows l. but flees at lion's roar J952.3; dogs tear up l. skin but fear
living l. W121.2.4; dragon fight to free l. B11.11.6; dragon flies away
with l. B11.6.8.1; enemies of l. (dog) A2494.4.7, (leopard) A2494.2.2,
(monkey) A2494.7.1, (wolf) A2494.7.2; enemy horses captured by l. join
forces and become friends J891; envious jackal makes l. suspicious of
bull K2131.2; fox finally converses with l. whom he had feared at
first U131.1; fox deceives l. into entering pit K714.9.1; fox insults caged
l. W121.2.2; fox with l. protector goes hunting alone and is killed J684.1;
fox as mediator to appease l. B239.1; fox refuses to mediate between l.
and lioness J811.2; fox's fables against l. forgotten J811.6; fox's fear of
l. wears off J1075.2; friendship between l. and (jackal) A2493.30.1,
(monkey) A2493.14.2, (tiger) A2493.30; giant l. B871.2.5, (overcome by
hero) B16.2.3; girl saved by l. from ravishment B549.1; glove and the
l. L431.1; gnats having overcome l. are in turn killed by spider L478;
gold-producing l. B103.0.6; grateful fly warns l. B371.2; hare shows l. his
reflection K1715.1; hairs of l., when burnt, get owner out of difficulties
D1390.1; helpful l. B431.2; honey-covered l. lures animals K767; killing
devastating l. H1161.6; killing l. guarding girl H335.3.2; leopard traps

l. in cave K730.3; lovers transformed into l. and lioness for desecrating temple Q551.3.1; magic l. dismembers perjurer H251.1.1; man in tree so frightened of l. he drops sword, kills it N331.2.1; man-killing l. must not touch certain animals C549.1; man with head of l. B27; man, l., and bear in pit J685.1; man resuscitates a l. which devours him J563; man transformed to l. D112.1; marriage to l. in human form B651.3; oath of truth before magic l. H254; only one, but a l. J281.1; oracular brazen l. D1311.7.2; owner frightened from goods by trickster's l. K335.0.6; precepts of the l. to his sons J22ff.; prophetic l. B142.4; reincarnation as l. E612.1; saint kills l. with slipper D2156.11; sick l. K961; singing l. B214.1.5; shepherd shuts up the l. in the yard with the livestock J2172.2; soul as l. E731.11; speaking l. B211.2.2; stag escapes from hunters to be eaten by l. N255.1; stone l. becomes man D435.1.5; suitor task: saddling, mounting a l. M145.1; why l. stays away from settlement A2433.3.16; strong man kills l. with own hands F628.1.1; the third time fox meets l. she has no fear J1075.2; transformation to l. in order to guard palace D659.4.1; treasure from stone l. D1469.13; war between l. and other animals B263.8; why l. does not attack dog A2464.1; why l. is brave A2524.5; wolf tries to make friends with l. J411.5; yoking together l. and wild boar H1149.1.

Lion's blood venomous B776.5.2; dance B293.4; daughter marries mouse, tramples him to death B363.1; human offspring B631.8; roar causes havoc at 300 miles B741; share J811.1; strong teeth B747.1; tail as broom H1151.11. — Animal lured into l. den K714.6; ass in l. skin unmasked when he raises his voice J951.1; children rescue mother from l. den R154.0.1; creation of cat: sneezed from l. nostrils A1811.2; fox sees all tracks going into l. den but none coming out J644.1; girl removes dog from l. claws B848.2; imprisonment in l. den R45.2; jealous courtiers accuse the jackal of stealing the l. food K2141; magic hair of l. tail D1023.3; quest for l. milk H1361; riddle about bees, honey, l. carcass H804; stone l. eyes become bloody D474.9; thorn removed from l. paw B381; wolves, wild pigs condemned to death in l. court B275.1.3.2.

Lions despise what asses admire U149.1; do not harm falsely accused adulteress B522.3; do not mate with their fellows but prefer leopards *B754.3; fall from furnace instead of golden men (unsuccessful imitation) J2411.1.2; fear cock's crow J2614.3; as God's messengers A165.2.1.1.6; in hell A671.2.12; as king's pets P14.22; placed in city to prevent entrance B847; tamed by Moses' rod B771.2.3; on way to otherworld F144.1. — Being fed to l. Q415.4; captive throws his hat to l. who fight over it while he escapes K671; fight of l. and bulls J1022; hungry l. do not harm saint B771.2.1; king of l. B241.2.1; land of l. B221.3; magic rod tames l. D1442.4.1; man saved from l. as reward Q151.11; presumptuous wolf among l. J952.1; quest to land of l. H1289.1.1; seeds cast on l. and tigers render them helpless D1410.1; strong man sent to kill l. F615.2.2.

Lioness bears man child B631.4; helps recover magic D882.1.2; pursuing hare puts head in hole, stuck K771.1. — Fox refuses to mediate between lion and l. J811.2; friendship between cow and l. A2493.30.2; magic milk of l. D1500.1.33.1.2; penance: l. foregoes meat Q535.2; transformation of lovers to lion and l. for desecrating temple Q551.3.1.

Lip. — Cure for leprosy by drinking from opposite l. of horn from that which caused it D1783.2; giant covers eye with l. F531.1.1.1.1; giant with upper l. reaching heaven and lower, earth F531.1.4.1; moon splits hare's l.: hence hare-lip A2216.3, A2234.4.

Lips cut in laughing contest K87.1; of giant F531.1.4; sewed together as punishment for slander Q451.12. — Honey on infant's l. B147.3.1.2; magic l. *D992.2, (animal) D1011.5; mutilation: l. cut off S166.5; origin and nature of animal's l. A2342; remarkable l. F544.1; revenant with cold l. E422.1.4; roses fall from l. *D1454.2.1; troll stretches neck so long that fire comes from l. G304.2.1.2.

Liquid, see also **Fluid.** — Disenchantment by l. D766; life token: troubled l. E761.6ff.; magic l. *D1242.

Liquids. — Animal "drinks apart" mixed l. B781.

Liquor, see also **Wine;** for betrothal T61.4.1; blessed by saint causes magic sleep D1364.7.1. — Animals discover l., get drunk B299.3; ghost drinks l. E556.1; gods discover l. A154.3; kamas offer l. to gods A1689.5; magic dog vomits any l. required of him B182.1.1; much l. from single grain F815.2.1; parson takes a drink of l. during the sermon X445.1; queen pours l. for champions P29.3.

Liquors. — Acquisition of spirituous l. A1427.

Lisping sisters K1984.1.

Listening tabus C885. — Six dwarfs l. to singing by confirmed children F451.5.21.

Literal following of instructions by one daughter, liberal by other J555.1; fool *J2450—J2499; obedience J2460ff., (to oath) K2312; payment of debt (not real) K236; pleading: letter of law has been met J1161. — Trickery: l. bargain K196.

Literary contest won by deception H507.6. — Origin of l. arts A1464.

Literature known to poets C568.1.

Litter. — Dupe guards "king's l." K1056.

Little, see also **Small;** bird as large bird's mate J1293.1; child drives out giant L311.4; Christmas V72.1; fish in the net kept rather than wait for uncertainty of greater catch J321.2; fishes escape from the net L331; girl bribes prince to marry her T55.4; men preferred to big J493; old men help perform task H971.2; people from the sky F205. — Death of l. hen (cumulative tale) Z32.2; devil a l. gray old man G303.3.1.5; dwarf follows countess around like l. dog F451.5.8.1; dwarfs have l. horses F451.7.5; fool advises buyer that horse is worth l. or his father would not sell it J2088.1; girl who ate so l. K1984.2; help from l. man N821; husband to wife's lover: "keep a l. for me" K1218.10; identification of man by his l. toe H79.2; Socrates builds himself l. house J401.1.

Live (adjective) bird earrings *F827.1; head-dresses F827.2; man thought to be returning corpse K2151.1. — Eyes of l. coals F541.1.3; steaks cut from l. cow who heals herself by magic D2161.2.1; tabu to eat l. animals C221.5.

Liver removed for breaking tabu C948.4. — Cow with tallow l. B15.7.9, H1331.3.2; divination by condition of animal's l. D1812.5.0.5; dragon's l. of thunder H1332.6; heart and l. of murderer torn out Q469.6; human l. as medicine D1248; inexhaustible l. D1652.19; magic bird l. D859.4.2; magic l. D997.3; magic l. of animal D1015.4; magic potion mixed with brains (l., etc.) of deceitful person as remedy for snakebite D1515.4.6; origin of l. A1319.5; return from dead to punish theft of l. from man on gallows E235.4.4; soul (life) in the l. E714.5; victim eats swallower's l. F912.3; why adder's tail tastes like l. A2378.9.4; witch takes man's l. G262.5; woman has l. stolen by bird (cumulative tale) Z41.1.

Livestock. — Killing ogre's l. G614; magic object furnishes l. D1477; question (propounded on quest): why do the l. die? H1292.3; shortsightedness in caring for l. J2172.

Living corpse *E422; man in dead man's shroud E463; mountain F755ff.; person acts as image of saint K1842; person in service of a dead man E596; torn to pieces by dead E267. All l. things from Jesus' spattered blood A1724.3; ass good l. but not dead (riddle) H841.1; cow good l. and dead (riddle) H841.3; culture hero still l. A570ff.; dead husband l. with his wife E321.2; dead and l. go together to gate of heaven E754.2.3; dead try to carry off l. E266; enchanted princess l. with dwarfs F451.5.4.3; fight of revenant with l. person E461; ghosts bestow gifts on l. E373; ghost laid when l. man speaks to it E451.4; god of the l. and the dead in the otherworld A108; gods and men formerly l. together A189.9; hog good dead but not l. (riddle) H841.2; inanimate objects act as if l. F990ff.; island in otherworld garden inhabited half by dead and half by l. F162.1.2.5; king imprisons all l. creatures R9.6; men l. by gods' breath A1394; ogres l. in trees G637; peasants want a l. God J2495.4; people l. in tree nests F811.10; people l. under sea F725.5; people weary of l. A1335.9; quest for the l. harp H1335; revenant overawed by l. person E462; sacrifice for l. 300 years V17.6; stars as l. beings A761.6; two dead men struggle over l. man E467.1; why l. cannot go to land of dead E489.8; why there are more l. than dead (riddle) H773; wolf not good l. or dead (riddle) H841.4.

Lizard defeats leopard L315.11; frightens leopard away K1715.5; got tail from snake A2247, A2378.1.3; in human form D712.9.1; jumps into person's mouth B784.1.7; offspring of the devil G303.10.10; as ogre G354.3; paramour B613.3; transformed to person D397; tries to make himself as long as the snake J512.9; wins contest with toad: why lizard changes skin A2250.2. — Boy reborn as l. E694.3; why l. bobs head up and down A2255.2, A2211.9, A2474.1; burning down house to drive out l. J2516.6; chain tale: l. and eagle involved Z49.10; contest lost by toad, won by l. A1319.12.1; creation of l. A2148; divination by house-l. B147.3.0.1; dragon as modified l. B11.2.1.2; enmity between chameleon and l. A2494.16.2; enmity of bird and l.: latter muddies water A2494.16.4; why giant l. is blind A2332.6.2; how l. got red head A2211.8, A2320.3; helpful l. B491.2; leopard ashamed of l. bite J411.10; man becomes l. D197; man's hand modeled on that of l. A1311.1; marriage to l. B604.4; mountains from accident to primeval l. A961.3; reincarnation as l. E614.2; sun, moon born of l. A715.6; thread sold to l.: treasure reward J1852.1.1; treacherous l. K2295.4; wooden l. kills evil spirits F839.7.

Lizard's language B215.5.1; lungs inflated H522.1.3. — Crushing l. eggs tabu C544.1; toad exchanges daughter for l. K476.5.

Lizards hero's parents A511.1.8.3. — Child born holding l. T552.2.1; god of l. A446.1; king of l. B244.3; why l. change skins A2311.9.

Llama, multicolored B731.3.

Llewellyn and his dog B331.2.

Load. — Ant carries l. as heavy as himself A2251.1; carrying l. up hill to roll it down J2165; compressible l. D631.3.4; contest in flying with l. K25.2; if the horse can pull one l. he can pull two J2213.4; huge l. carried by saint D1691.1; strong man carries giant l. F631ff.; victim killed while l. is being removed K837.

Loads. — Hills are l. from hero's shoulders A962.10.

Loaded. — Magic gun is always l. D1652.4; man in otherworld l. down with wood F171.6.1.

Loading ferocious camels H1154.3.5.

Loadstone draws ship to it *F806.1.

Loaf of bread locates drowned man D1314.6; bursts in oven because sign of cross not made V86.6. — Child divides last l. with fairy (witch) Q42.1.1; great l. of bread (cake) X1811.1; test of strength: breaking heavy glass bottle over a l. of rye bread H1562.3; unlucky man given l. filled with gold exchanges it for another N351.

Loaves and fishes D2106.1. — Large l. need a large oven X434.1; lies about l. of bread X1811; saint restores eaten l. D1652.1.10.1.

Loan. — Fairy grateful for l. F335; giants repay l. with large interest F531.5.5.

Loans refused J1552ff., (by usurer) P435.2.

Loathly bridegroom D733, (carried on back in basket by wife) T216; deed proves Christian virtue H1573.1.2; lady *D732; man father of supernatural boy L112.1.1. — Adulteress chooses l. paramour T232.2.

Loathsome. — Person forced to eat l. animal S183.2; princess's l. disguise to avoid demon-lover T327.6.

Lobster. — Helpful l. B495.2; origin of l. A2171.3; why l. is flat A2305.1.3; why l. is shallow: cattle stepped on it A2213.2.4.

Lobsters mistaken for Norwegians J1762.7. — Stealing l. from shark guardians K341.16.

Local deluges A1011; gods A410ff.; moon J2271.1; winter D2145.1.1.

Location determined by halting of an animal *B155; of fort determined by reading in book D1816.3; of fountain revealed in dream D1816.1; of lost person by magic object D1315; of otherworld F130ff.; of stone determines king's race D931.0.2.1; of sought object learned by eavesdropping N455.9. — Angel reveals l. of object D812.10.0.1, V232.6; extraordinary l. of castle F771.3ff.; extraordinary l. of tree F811.4; magic discovery of desired l. D1816ff.

Lochinvar steals bride K1371.1.

Lock magically opens for saint D1557.1. — Entrance into wine cellar by removing l. D317.2; extraordinary l. F782.4; magic l. *D1164; sun will l. moon in deep ditch A1066.

Locks in house to be shot during childbirth T582.2; marvelously open R121.6.2, D2088; spring open for troll G304.2.3.1. — All l. opened on Christmas Eve D2088.0.1; "keep everyone's l. in your hand" J2489.2; seduction access by removing l. K1349.5; thief burns off l. K317.1; take people by the l. H588.16.

Locked doors open for ghost E599.11. — Fairy enters l. city D2088.1; filling l. pen K1427; husband l. out by adulteress K1511; securing dishes l. in vault H1199.15; tiger l. into house K737.2; witch escapes from l. room G288; wolf almost l. in the stable by the shepherd J2172.2.1.

Locking. — Adulteress l. up husband K1514.6; faithful servant l. up master R53.4; husband's comment to wife on l. up shop J1545.5; jealous husband l. up wife T257.9.

Locksmith. — Prophet not a l. J1289.1.

Locust carries person B557.9; with strong teeth B747.2. — Enmity of starling and l. A2494.13.11.2; magic l.-egg cures D1502.7.1.

Locusts. — Army of l. B268.8.2; helpful l. B486.1; iron-winged l. eat wheat crop B16.6.3; origin of l. A2062; why l. hide in day A2491.5; why l. live in certain towns A2434.3.1.

Lodes. — Knockers show miners richest l. F456.1.2.2.1.

Lodge-Boy and Thrown-Away as joint adventurers Z210.1.

Lodging of bird's feathers built in one night H1104.1. — Troublemaker in night-l. K2138.

Lofty. — Otherworld on l. mountain *F132.

Log-birth slander K2115.2.2; transformed to bear D441.3.2. — Animal seizes hollow l.: heart pulled through it K952.3; escape from descending l. by digging hole K615; fool tries to make l. obey commands J1828; forgetting by stepping over l. D2004.5.1; frogs given l. as king J643.1; ghost becomes l. during day E553; great snake mistaken for l. X1321.1.2; hands in cleft l. as punishment Q469.13; hero drives l. into frozen ground F611.3.2.1; holiday until l. burns out: log soaked K197; magic l. of wood D1401.8; magic hollow-l. boat D1121.1; man in hollow l. fires rifle, scares off Indians K547.3; man transformed to l. D216; meddler gets himself caught in the cleft of a l. K1111; thread made to appear as a large l. carried by a cock D2031.2; wolf thought to be a l. of wood J1761.5.

Logs. — Marking l. by pinching out piece X952; why tortoise lives in l. in stream A2433.6.1.1.

Logger. — Lie: remarkable l. X987, X1081.

Logic. — Absurd lack of l. J2200—J2259.

Logical. — Lies: l. absurdities X1700.

Logician's argument over ghee, saucer J2062.2.

Loin. — First man from maid having licked l. cloth A1211.7; magic l. cloth transforms self D697.1; rainbow as l. cloth F829.1; speaking l. of goat meat D1610.7; wearing of l. cloths A1683.5.

Loins. — Origin and nature of animal's l. A2364.

Loki. — Foal born of L. and mythical stallion T465.2; fetter for L. F864.2; serpent above L. continually drops venom in his face Q501.3; son of L. transformed to wolf Q551.3.2.1.

Lonely creator A73. — Devil met by night in l. spot G303.22.12.

Lonesomeness. — Creation because of creator's l. A832.

Long armed people F516.3; -bearded dwarf F451.2.3.1; day (fifty o'clock) J2466.3; distance sexual intercourse K1391; ears F542.1; hair F555.3, (prized by Irish) P632.5; -legged people F517.0.2; nose F543.1; pregnancy T574; teeth F544.3.5; term of service imposed on suitor H317; span of life for first men A1323; tongue F544.2.2. — Why animal has l. tail A2378.3; animals with l. life B841; cannibal has l. tooth and nail G88; child born with l. hair T551.13.1; devil has a l. nose G303.4.1.4.1; doing thing too l. forbidden C761; fairies have breasts l. enough to throw over their shoulders *F232.2; fairies in l. robes F236.2; giant with l. beard F531.1.6.4; hair robe "not too l., not too short" J1161.8; hero prefers fame to l. life L212.3; how l. to live? frog wins L395; lizard tries to make himself as l. as snake J512.9; magic object makes nose l. D1376.1ff.; man suddenly acquires l. gray beard on scaffold at execution F1044; miraculously l. life as reward Q145; prophecy of l. life M321; sausage for the l. winter K362.1; strong hero's l. nursing F611.2.3; way short yet l. J21.5.3; why animal has l. life A2578; wife of merman not to stay too l. at home C713.3; wild huntsman with l. hair E501.7.7; witch with l. teeth G214.1; worn-out shoes as proof of l. journey *H241.

Longest. — Riddle: what is l. H644.

Longevity of saints V229.2.12. — God of l. A474.2; heroes' l. A564; magic l. D1857; magic object gives l. D1345ff.

Longing in fairyland to visit home F374; of human child of sky-mother to visit father on earth D2006.2.1. — Death from l. F1041.1.4; fairy dies of l. F259.1.3; inordinate l. F1041.15; magic l. D2037; magic object causes l. D1374.

Longings. — Tasks assigned because of l. of pregnant woman *H936.

Look. — Fairy's l. burns mortal F363.4; "have a black l." H588.14, J2489.7;

dupe induced to l. about: seized and killed K832; why animals always l. down A2471.9; why mortal cannot l. at sun A733.2.

Looked. — Hero feigns fear when l. at too much K1777.

Looking in magic object reveals witch G259.1; at saint's corpse punished Q227.2. — Advice on l. about in strange place J21.34.1; why dog is always l. A2471.6; magic sight by l. in certain place D1821.3ff.; magic strength acquired by l. at necklace D1835.1; rejuvenation by l. into mirror D1889.2; separation of persons by l. for water N311; tabu: l. *C300—C399, (around while raising treasure) N553.4, (at supernatural husband) *C32.1, (at supernatural wife) C31.1; transformation by violation of l. tabu D513.

Looking Glass, see **Mirror.**

Looks. — Man's l. depend on wife's obedience T254.3.

Loom of woman's breasts, vagina F856.1. — Countertask: making a l. from shavings H1021.6.1; countertask: making spindle and l. from one piece of wood H1022.3; making l. from a rod H1022.2.2.

Loon. — Why l. has big beak A2343.1.3; color of l. A2411.2.6.1; why l. holds legs backward A2371.2.9; ugly voice of l. A2423.1.3.

Loop. — Cure by passing patient under l. D2161.4.5.

Loophole. — Leave l. for escape J762.

Loosing ferocious animals against attackers B17.1.1. — Magic results from l. knots D1782.3; wind raised by l. certain knots D2142.1.2.

Loquaciousness. — Man rebuked for l. speaks after thirty-seven days W225.1.

Lord, see also **Creator, God;** above, lord below K1525; above will provide for child of illicit union K1271.5; has departed J1823.1.3; has risen J1399.1. — Cowardly to leave battle while l. alive W34.3; devil carries away l. on his back G303.9.5.2; rich l. who robs poor widow of her cow chokes on first mouthful Q552.6; sheep helpful to the L.: get wool A2221.10; to have good servants a l. must be good U212; treacherous l. K2247.

Lord's — Man escapes devils by reading L. blessing G303.16.2.3.1; three faiths: L. and his two children's J1262.9; woman shows that the L. Prayer is the best V51.3.

Loris. — Why l. never look at sun A2231.13.

Loser in bride-race must die H331.5.0.1. — Judicial combat interrupted by friends of l. H218.1.

Losing luck as punishment N134.1.3. — Gambler l. everything N9.1; help to l. player in game C746; tabu: l. consecrated wafer *C55.

Loss of all evil, corruption as reward Q150.2; of goods by thief *K420ff.; of invulnerability D1847; of magic object D860ff.; of magic object's power through overuse D877; of magic power D1740; of magic power of stolen flageolet D1651.7.3; of magic sight D1822; of miraculous powers after son born V229.20.1; of property as punishment Q595; of skill D2099.1; of speech as punishment *Q451.3.

— Accidental l. of property M350ff.; choices: little gain, big l. *J340ff.; choice: l. of beauty or speech J213; feeding with l. or gain (slaughtered hen or milk) H583.9; riddle propounded on pain of l. of (property) H541.2, (official position) H541.3; ringing of church bell causes l. of devil's power G303.16.12; tasks to pay gambling l. H942; weight of bodily member chosen rather than its l. J341.

Losses. — Gains and l. J330—J369.

Lost object discovered by magic D1816.2; object (found by holy man) D1810.0.3.2, object (found by throwing spade at ghost) D1816.2.1, object (returns to its owner) N211; parson asks devil's help, dies C12.5.4; person in ogre's power G406; soul in raven feathers E752.4; souls E752; wind found in tree A1122.3. — Absurd searches for the l. J1920ff.; angel reveals l. object V232.6; animal leads l. man B563.4.1; animal retrieves l. object B548; chimpanzee leads l. hunter home B563.1.2; deaf persons: search for the l. animal X111.1; death message l. K978.2; deer l. through premature celebration J2173.4; disenchantment by being found when l. D783; fairies grateful for returning l. child F339.3; fool gets l. playing blind J2387; forgotten name confused with l. treasure J1805.3; ghost returns to hunt l. article E415.1; horses carry l. riders to safety B563.1.1; king marries girl who finds l. object N713; love l. by magic D1908; luck in hunting l. for breaking tabu C933; magic causes person to be l. D1418; magic power to see l. things D1825.4.3; magic powers l. *D1741ff.; magic object locates l. person D1315; magician recovers l. object with the devil's help G303.22.2; mortals keep l. fairy child F329.4.1; person reported l. joins search for self N692; power of prophecy l. D1812.6; quest for l. magic mirror H1346; quest for l. persons H1385; quest to lower world for l. words H1276; recovering l. objects H1132; rescue of abandoned or l. persons R130ff.; vow not to eat until l. son found M151.8; warrior having l. a city claims that he did not wish to sell it for a higher price J875.

Lot on altar chalice indicates guilt H233.1. — Kings chosen by l. P11.1.1; oath concerning l. drawing M187; one's fated l. as paradox answer H1075; sacrificial victim chosen by l. S262.3.

Lot's wife, having had father and mother, is not dead like other mortals (riddle) H815; wife transformed to pillar of salt for breaking tabu C961.1.

Lots cast to determine fate N126. — Casting l. for queen's gown J2060.4; casting l. as truth test H245; incantation over l. H245.1.

Lotus causes forgetfulness D1365.1.1; disappears at plucking attempt D1641.15; flower as chastity index H432.3; flower flourishes in water J97; flowers on cherry tree F811.7.2.3; leaf full of rice as deceptive wage K256.1; leaf raft in primeval sea A813.2; on Vishnu's navel A123.9, H1289.4.1, T541.11; transformed to human hand D451.4.1. — Birth from l. T543.2.1; earth from l. seed placed on water A814.8; elephant becomes l. D421.3.1; golden l. F814.4.1; instruments of torture transformed to l. flowers D454.16; magic l.-flower *D975.1; magic l. plant *D965.6; magic stick kills l. guardians D1402.10.1; quest for l. flower H1333.5.1; reincarnation as l. E631.1.3; soul as l. E745.4.1; stealing golden l. H1151.1.1; voyage to Land of L. Eaters *F111.3; woman becomes l. D212.3.

Lotuses shower at hero's birth F960.1.2.1.1.

Loudest mourners not greatest sorrowers J261.

Louse on eyelash mistaken for game J1759.2; fattened *F983.2; and flea wish to marry (cumulative tale) Z31.2; neither man nor jinn nor beast nor bird (riddle) H862. — Altar casts away host with l. baked in it V31.4; conception from eating l. T511.5.3; cormorant's tongue pulled out by putting l. on it K825.1; creation of l. A2051; cumulative tale: l. eats crow Z33.4.1; flea bites man and jumps away, but bed is searched and l. killed J2137.1; friendship between l. and crow A2493.23, M246.1.2; giant l. B873.1; magic l. answers for fugitive D1611.13; as obstinate wife sinks she makes a sign of cracking l. T255.3; picking the l. and the flea J2415.2; pricking l. to release curse M429.5; why l. has mark on back A2412.3.1.

Lice banned by magic D2176.2; become gems D475.4.2; as cleanliness test H1585; made smaller A2302.6. — Battle between l. of Strassburg and of Hungary X651; cleanest girl to be eaten: one pretends to have l. K619.1.1; earth transformed to l. D442.2.1; foxes as giant's l. F531.4.11.2; hunter throws away what he catches (l.) and what he does not catch he carries with him H583.3; lies about l. X1296; philosopher nourishing large population of l. J1452; seat covered with l. skins F894.

Lousing as task set by ogre *G466. — Daughter reveals secret while l. mother N466; deception by pretended l. K874; escape by pretended l. *K611.1; goddess discovered by l. A475.1.1.1; magic sleep by l. *D1962.2; tabu: l. supernatural wife C31.7; theft by putting owner to sleep by l. K331.2.1.1; transformation by l. D583; witch's horn discovered by l. her *G253.

Lousy. — Witch makes person l. G263.8.

Love *T0—T99; among giants, other supernatural beings F531.6.15.2; between foster sister and brother P274.1; charm put in princess's food K1831.2.1; detected by quickening pulse J1142.2; falsely pledged for wooer's benefit K2094; image grants man wife D1595.1; induced by magic *D1900ff.; letter hidden in apple K1872.3; like salt H592.1; like wind in hot sun H592.1.1; -longing produced by elf F301.2.1; lost by magic D1908; -mad queen kills husband K2213.2.1; -making in otherworld F181; -producing magic objects *D1355ff.; purified by magic D1900.0.1; rewarded Q56; -sickness T24.1, (cured by bath of beloved's blood) T82, (produced by magic) D1355.0.1, D2064.0.1; -songs A1554; -spot D1355.13; wagered N2.7; -working stone B722.1. — Adulterous l. changed into chaste T372; all women fall in l. with man at sight N202.1; angel kills man because of too much l. for his child J225.5;

animal helps person to success in l. *B582; boy falls in l. with first woman he sees after mother T371.1; bride to suitor giving greatest l. token H315.2; brothers' great l. for sister P253.10; brotherly l. and patience both dead J1633; castle warmed by l. F771.13; choice between l., wisdom J231.2; clerical vows after disappointment in l. V472; conversion through l. V331.5; courtier shields king's l. affair J1211.3; disguised husband wins faithless wife's l. K1813.1; dwarfs in l. with supernatural beings F451.10.3; dwarf's magic l. seduces girl K1672; fairy abducts those with whom in l. F302.3.1.4; false message of l. causes trouble K2132; father unwittingly in l. with daughter N365.2.1; fiancée falls in l. with another man, elopes T157; fidelity in l. tested H1556.4; first man falls in l. with fairy A1275.9; giant in l. with giantess F531.6.8.1; girl masked as man wins princess's l. K1322; girl to be perfect in l. but die of it M365.2; girl frightened by l. becomes insatiable K2052.2; gods, goddesses in l. with men A188; god of l. A475; hero may win lady's l. but die early M366; injunction: to forsake woman who arouses l. C686; innocent girl sells her l. and later receives it back K1362; insanity from l. T24.3; judgment by testing l. J1171; magic object acquired by gaining l. of owner D856; making princess fall in l. H315.1; man in l. with own sister learns her identity N681.3.2; man unwittingly in l. with mother N365.1.1; mother l. P231.3, (dearer than gold) H662, (in animal) F989.8; mountain in l. stretches leg out to meet beloved A965.1; peasant preaches about bishop's l. J1211.1; prince to fall in l. with witch's daughter M436; prince prefers first l. to princess he later marries J414.2; prophecies concerning l. M369.2; queen in l. with own brother K2213.3.4; quest assigned by wife through appeal to husband's l. for her H1212.2; relative pleasure of l. taught by parable J99.1; return from dead to ask back l. tokens E311; sham magician promises to induce l. K1963.2; stepmother in l. with stepson P282.3; suitor with only l. to offer wins L393; tabu: boasting of l.-conquest C453; test of mother's and father's l. for children H491; tragic l. T80ff.; two men in l. with one girl strike bargain M296; what is most pleasant? l. H659.13.1; woman in picture arouses l. H1381.3.1.2.1; woman tricked into giving poison to her husband: thinks it a l.-philtre K945; youth in court for kissing prince's daughter pleads his l. for her J1174.1.

Loved. — Least l. friend truest H1558.1.1.

Lovely. — Hateful or l. child to be born first? T548.1.1.

Lover, see also **Paramour, Suitor;** allowed to sleep with bride few nights after marriage to another T161.1; arrives home just as mistress is to marry another *N681; asks girl to kill her father S56.1; with ass's head G269.22; away too long, returns, finds fiancée married N391; as bird visits mistress D641.1; commits suicide on finding beloved dead N343.4; dies beside dying sweetheart F1041.1.2.1; disguised in enemy's clothes K1810.1.2; disguised as fool K1818.3.2; disguised as monk K1826.1.1; has head cut off at girl's desire H333.1; identified by scratches H58.2;

identifies mistress by chalk marks H58.1; imposes tabu C901.1.3; kills fool for disclosing adultery J2365; kills self believing his mistress dead (Pyramus and Thisbe) N343; made ridiculous K1213ff.; masks as doctor to reach his sweetheart K1825.1.1; only one can lift woman D1651.13; put off till girl bathes and dresses K1227.1; refuses to take back unfaithful paramour Q241.2; rescues his lady R161; slow to follow advantage J2166; stays awake by washing eyes H1484.1; taken to fairyland F302.3.4.4.; transported to girl in fortress by spirit F414.1; unloads wood on door to keep husband out K1514.9; wins gamble as girl distracts opponent K92.3. — Adulteress has l. killed K2231.1; arrogant mistress repaid in kind by her l. L431; avoiding wife's l. by going home slowly J2523.2; brothers persecute sister's l. P253.7; clandestine l. identified by paint marks left on his skin by his mistress H58; clandestine l. recognized by tokens H81; chaste woman promises herself to her l. when rocks leave coast *M261; color formula for girl's l. Z65.1.1; conqueror must be called "l." W11.5.11.1; cure by seeing lost l. F950.8; curse on wife's l. M414.14; dead girl frightens father and l. J2621; dead l. haunts sweetheart E214; dead l. sets tasks E212; death feigned to meet l. K1862; demon l. F471.2.0.1; devil in guise of girl's l. G303.12.5.7; disenchantment of girl only by her l. D791.2.1; disenchantment from tree form by embrace of l. D735.3; drawing l. out of wall with single thread rope H412.6; dwarf l. of mortal girl F451.5.18; escape from undesired l. *T320ff.; fairy l. F301, (abducts wife) F301.6; fairy avenges herself on inconstant l. F302.3.3.1; foolish l. ignorant of mistress's flaws J1737; which was most generous, husband, robber, or l.? H1552.1; generosity enables impoverished l. to entertain his lady W11.7; ghost of tragic l. E334.2.3; girl falsely accused of murdering l. K2116.1.3; girl goes to fairy l. F301.7; girl has monster as l. T118; girl has unworthy l. T232; girl masks as doctor to find departed l. K1825.1.4; god as giantess's l. A164.6; goldsmith as l. P447.7; heart breaks when girl hears l. kiss another F1041.2; humiliated l. in repartee J125.1.1; husband and l. fight for wife T243; husband tricks poet into slaying wife's l. K863.1; importunate l. put asleep in street Q473.4; impoverished l. falsely accused of theft K401.3; lamia devours her l. G262.0.1.1; magic object draws l. to woman D1425; magic object protects from unwelcome l. *D1386ff.; magic view of future l. D1825.1.2; maiden sent to rendezvous to capture l. K787; man kills wife's l. Q411.0.1.2; marriage tokens identifying l. H82.2; menial disguise of l. of princess K1816.0.3; mistress expecting l. accidentally changes places with maidservant N391.1; one l. disguised and carried out of house by other K1517.1.1; princess's clandestine l. punished Q256; prostitute's favorite l. T450.4; quest for vanished l. H1385.5; repulsed l. kills woman's child S322.5; riddle of murdered l. H805; ring springs asunder when faithlessness of l. is learned *D1318.9.1; sandhill surrounds l. F969.6; scorned l. poses as rich man and cheats his scornful mistress L431.2; seduction by bearing false order from l.

K1354.4; spells to recall dead l. E218; tests for true l. H421; transformation combat between l. and maid D615.3; transformation to escape l. D652.3; treacherous l. K2232, (rival) K2221; wife tricks husband into freeing l. K2213.10; witch causes maiden to hate l. G263.6; woman punished for preferring mortal l. Q255; wraith stays in room where l. died E723.5.

Lover's fidelity tested in bed H1556.4.1; joke frightens mistress to death N384.9; magic sleep at rendezvous D1972; place in bed usurped by another *K1317ff.; spur catches in sheet, prevents escape N386.1; wound breaks while he is in bed with mistress N386; — Apparently happy woman discloses l. skeleton U115.1; dead l. friendly return E310ff.; dead l. malevolent return *E210ff.; dream reveals l. death D1813.1.5; flood from l. tears A1012.1.2; girl in disguise at l. court K1816.0.2; son killed at l. instigation S303; transformation to l. form to seduce woman *D658.2.

Lovers abducted by pirates R12.3; buried apart found in one grave E419.6; fleeing slavery recaptured R352; give each other up when they learn that they are brother and sister T415.4; identical in appearance F577.4; involved in adultery K1500ff.; are man's son not his wife's and wife's daughter not her husband's T491; meet in their dreams T11.3.1; not destined to meet in life, faithful after death M369.2.2; as pursuer and fugitive K1517.1; ransomed from prison R121.7; reared as brother and sister learn to their joy that they are not related T415.3; on stile bewitched G269.23; visit while guardian sleeps D1965; vow to marry only each other M149.1. — Accidental meeting of l. N710ff.; accidental reunion of l. N737; accidental separation of l. N318; baffled l. *K1210ff.; dead l. become stones together E642.1; parts of dragon identification between l. H105.6; false guardian betrays fleeing l. K2093; forest as refuge of eloping l. R312.1; forgotten fiancée reawakens husband's memory by detaining l. through magic D2006.1.1; humiliated l. *K1210ff.; mermaids tear mortal l. to pieces B81.2.2; mountain-men as herding-girls' l. F460.4.1.1; origin of rainbow: souls of l. A791.9; predestined l. T22, (born simultaneously) T22.4; prophecy: girl shall have a hundred l. M345.1; stars as transformed l. A761.3; sun and moon as l. A736.3; three l. mourning dead girl T29.14; tokens between l. H82.3; tops of trees from graves of l. show shapes of their heads E631.0.1.1; treacherous l. K2230ff.; twining branches grow from graves of l. E631.0.1; Virgin Mary as protectress of illicit l. *T401; witch transforms her l. into animals G263.1.0.1; woman entertains two l. on alternate nights T72.4.

Lovers' assignation by symbolic messages Z175.2; tragedy re-enacted E337.3. — Bird carries off veil, causes l. separation N352.1; cliff from l. leap A968.2; message falsified to bring about l. death K1087.1; news of l. death breaks heart F1041.1.1.4; smoke from l. funerals mingles E643.1.

Loving. — Curse: not l. same woman long M455.2; foster children l. foster father P271.6; man on Island of Fair Women overcome by l. women *F112.1; mother not l. children of forced marriage P230.2; polygamist l. all wives T145.6.

Loving-cup at betrothal T61.4.2.

Lower lip hangs down to neck F544.1.1. — Consorting with l. class punished Q243.5; giant with l. lip reaching earth F531.1.4.1.

Lower world, see also **Hell, Underworld;** *F80—F109. — Adventure from following animal to l. N773; captivity in l. R47; descent to l. F81; eating in l. forbidden C211.8; emergence of tribe from l. A1631; expressing surprise in l. forbidden C413; goddess divides time between upper and l. A316; impostors abandon hero in l. *K1931.2; journey to l. *F80ff.; land of dead in l. *E481.1; life-lights in l. E765.1.3; nature of l. A670ff.; parents rescue son from l. on rope R153.1.1; princess(es) rescued from l. R111.2.1; quest to l. H1270ff.; series of l. A651.2; tear from upper world of mortals falls on departed in l. E361.1.

Lowlands. — Dwarfs undermine l. for homes F451.4.1.6.

Lowly animal tries to move among his superiors J952; hero L100, (marries princess) L161; heroine marries prince (king) L162; person in love with royalty T91.6.1; tries in vain to be greater than he is J955. — God brings low the proud and exalts the l. H797.1; great refuse to associate with l. J411; presumption of the l. *J950ff.; princess declares her love for l. hero T55.1; queen rewards l. man's love Q56.3; self-deception of the l. J953.

Loyal. — Fairies l. to mortal who owns their knoll F336.

Loyalty, see also **Fidelity,** W34; rewarded Q72. — When debt is due trickster offers creditor his l. K231.5.1.

Luchrupain, see **Leprechauns.**

Lucifer, see also **Devil;** appointed chief for demons A1187; causes fall of man A63.5; as serpent D191.1. — Mouse created by L. A1751.1; saints battle L. at world's end A1082.6.

Luck in gambling N6; in hunting lost for breaking tabu C933; lost by leaving fairy wife F302.5.3; only with honest money N143; personified N112. — Bad l. put into a sack N112.1; casket with Good L. in it given to men by Zeus N113.1.1; devil gives l. with fishing and hunting G303.10.7; escape by prophesying ill l. K573; fishing l. lost C933.2; food left on magic stone brings good l. thereafter D1561.1.6; goddess of good l. A482.2; knockers bring ill l. F456.1.2.1.1; magic object brings good l. D1561ff., (to gambler) D1407; magic brings bad l. D1409.1; nature of l. and fate N100ff.; one not to wish hunter good l. C493.1; princess brings ill l. to bridegroom K443.12; quest for l. H1376.9; speaking of good l. forbidden C424; spilling oil good l. J2214.7; spirit of ill l. A482.1.1; sudden love gives bad l. T10.3; ways of l. and fate N100—N299; why spider brings good l. A2536.3; youngest son always has good l. L11.

Lucky accidents *N400—N699; bargain *N421; person N203. — Foolish imitation of l. man J2415; yellow l. color Z148.

Lucretia seduced by threat K1397.

Lugaid. — Seven sons all named L. T586.1.2.2.

Luggage. — Man carries extraordinary l. F1016.

Lulling to sleep by "sleepy" stories (songs) D1962.4.1.

Lumber. — Squaring l. on stone H1199.13; witch breaks up l. pound G283.1.2.6; wraith selects coffin l. E723.7.5.

Luminous, see also **Bright, Gleaming, Glowing;** face as sign of royalty H71.6.1; ghosts *E421.3; god A124ff.; jewel in animal's head B722.3; person F574ff.; spirits F401.2; witch-boat G222.2; witches G222. — Cat's l. eye *B721; following l. tree in the desert K1886.1.1; hero l. F574.3.3; men originally self-l. A1281.4; men with l. arms F574.2; saint's l. tooth F544.3.2.1; self-l. objects *D1645ff.; wild huntsmen l. *E501.7.6.

Lump on forehead identifies fool P192.7.

Lumps. — Little l. of sugar are sweeter but servant takes large ones J1341.8.

Lunatics. — Jokes on l. X541.

Lunch with Christ J1261.3. — Farmer's hot l.: mustard sandwich W152.12.2.

Lungs cut out for breaking tabu C948.5. — Guessing origin of animal l. H522.1.3.

Lured. — Fairy l. away from house by treasure which he claims F381.5; hunters l. by magic birds B172.6; victim l. by (gingerbread house) G412, (ogre in animal form) G403, (ogre's disguised voice) G413.

Luring hunters by transformation D659.10. — Devil as woman l. man G303.3.1.12; murder by l. to feast, then suffocating S113.2.3; music l. to otherworld F175.

Lust personified Z127.2. — Repression of l. T317, (by magic object) *D1356, (by observation of dying people for year) J62.

Lustful, see also **Lecherous;** stepmother T418. — Conception through l. glance T515.1.

Lute. — Listening to l. tabu C885.3; magic l. D1232; recognition by unique manner of playing l. H35.1; playing l. at funerals A1547.2.

Luxury of dwarfs' underground palace F451.4.1.3; of host rebuked J1566. — Abbot's l. and cardinal's J1263.4.1; repartee concerning clerical l. J1263.4.

Lye. — Milk becomes l. D476.2.3.2.

Lying (telling falsehood), see also **Liar, Lies;** goat K1151, (punished by being half-shorn) Q488.1; incurable U235; punished *Q263. — Contest in l. X905; lawyer who tries to practice without l. fails X314; origin of l. A1343; ruler wants l. confessor J1263.6; tabu broken by l. K1076.

Lying (reclining) on ancestors' bones tabu C541.4. — Capture by l. in wait for enemy K782; girl summons fairy lover by l. under tree *F301.1.1.3; Thumbling l. by sleeping man is blown to window by man's breath F535.1.1.3; trickster blackmails princess after l. with her K443.6.2.

Lynx. — Enmity of l. and rabbit A2494.6.1; face of l. mashed in A2213.2.1; how l. got his squint A2211.1, A2330.2; man transformed to l. D112.3; wedding of l. B281.4; why l. has short, blunt nose A2335.2.2.

Lyra. — Origin of L. A776.

Lyre. — Ass tries in vain to play l. J512.4; man transformed to ass plays the l. *D693; magic l. D1231.1, (charms stones into their place in building) D1565.2; origin of l. (from tortoise) A1461.2.

Mac Con, man suckled by dog T611.10.

Mace-bearer attacked, throws away mace J1166.2.

Machinery. — Ghost causes m. to run unattended E299.1; lie: remarkable m. X1025.

Machines of war P552.4.

Mackerel's creation A2121.

Mad elephant F628.1.6, H1155.4; fisherman as hero L113.1.3; patients cured in pit J1434. — Bite of wild huntsman's dogs drives other dogs m. E501.15.6.3; devil drives cow m. G303.7.8; lawyer's m. client *K1655; remedy for m. dog bite D1515.5; sham m. man H599.2; usurer prays rich sons will go m. P435.1; woman who drives those who see her m. F581.

Mädchen ohne Hände Q451.1.

Made. — Objects m. by magic *D2178ff., (boat) *D1121.0.1, (bridge) *D1258.1, (fort) D1136.1, (iron chain) D1251.1, (water-hole) D928.1.

Madman disguise K1818.3, (tests bride) H384.1.2; may not bring law suit P523.2. — Clever m. J1116.1; disguise as m. to enter girl's room K1349.1.2; escape from m. K611.21; princess unwittingly promised to m. S241.3; saint subdues m. V221.4; woman gives m. food, falsely accused K2112.5.2.

Madman's contract void P525.1.

Madmen P192. — Jokes on m. X540.

Madness cured (by coition) F950.4, (by magic object's recovery) D880.0.1; feigned to escape unwelcome marriage K523.0.1; from fright N384.0.1; from grief F1041.8.2; from loss of fortune F1041.8.11; from loss of magic D860.0.2; from love T24.3; miraculously cured F959.1; as punishment Q555; from seeing beautiful woman *F1041.8.1; from strange sight F1041.8; from spirit leaving body E721.3.1. — Cannibalism brings m. G91; escape by shamming m. K523.1; feigned m. catches thieves F439.9; feigned m. unmasked by threatening man's child J1149.1; jackal-tooth as cure for m. D1508.3; meeting ghost causes m. E265.2; nudity as sign of m. Z181.1.

Madonna, see also **Virgin Mary.** — Pagan sybil draws picture of M. and Child in sand V341; reward for offering food to M. Q32.

Maelstrom. — Prayer saves mariners from m. V52.6.

Magellanic. — Origin of M. Clouds A778.0.1.

Maggots multiply inside girl B784.1.6; squirm from god's mouth A123.2.2.1. — Creation of m. A2053; dwarfs originate from m. in flesh of giant F451.1.1; punishment: m. fill food Q501.2.2; sun from transformed m. A718.4; saint changes m. into jewels V222.15.

Magi. — Youngest of M. becomes senior D1897.

Magic D (entire chapter); aids to witches' flight G242.6; animal supplies treasure B100.2; animals B100—B199; boat to fairyland F213.1; change of color D57; change of size D55; contains life essence E765.3.5; cup tests truth H251.3.13; drink gives immortality to gods A154.1; enables hero to drink sea dry H1142.2.1; fluid takes away magic powers D1410.3; folding mule D491.1.2; food gives immortality to gods A153.2; flight D670ff.; flower opens dwarf home F451.4.3.7; holds mortals in otherworld F182; herb protects from witch G272.2; illusion prevents raising treasure N564; manifestation required as proof in test of saint-liness H1573.2.1; manifestation as omen D1812.5.0.13; manifestation at execution proves innocence H215; manifestations as punishments Q551; object (aids task) H987, (guards treasure) N581, (lost, person dies) E765.3.0.1, (reveals witch) G259.1, (sinks into earth) F948.3; objects *D800—D1699, (characteristics of) D1600—D1699, (as decoy for pursuer) D672.1, (functions of) D1300—D1599, (kinds of) D900—D1299, (in otherworld) F166.4, (ownership of) D800—D899, (powerful against fairies) F384, (received from animal) B505; perils threaten bridal couple T175; phantom army F585.2; power from animal *B500ff.; pig heals wound its skin touches B511.2.1; power lost by breaking tabu C947; powers and manifestations D1700—D2199; prevention of childbirth T572.1; pro-tection (against pestilence) F493.3.3, (against revenants) *E434ff.; remedies for barrenness or impotence T591.1; rescue of prisoner from mound R112; as saintliness test H1573.2.1; shirt as reward Q53.2; spells control witch G272.15; stick chosen over money L222.3; tree F979.16. — Animals made by m. exchanged for real K139.1; ascent to sky by sticking to m. feather *F61.2.1; ascent to upper world by m. F68; atten-tion drawn by m. objects: recognition follows H151.1; barrenness or impotence induced by m. T591; birth obtained through m. or prayer T548; bridegroom driven from bridal chamber by m. T171; building m. castle (task) H1133.1; capturing m. pig carrying scissors, comb, and razors between its ears (task) H1154.1; chastity test by m. objects or ordeals H410ff.; childbirth assisted by m. T584.0.1; children given for being taught m. S233; compressible m. animals D491.1; conception from contact with m. object T532.1; contest (in m.) D1719.1, (won by m.) K1; copper as defence against ghosts and m. D1385.5.1; coughing up m. object K331.4; daughter pulls out father's m. life-containing hair K976; deception into m. bag which closes on prisoner K711.1; deceptive ex-change: useless given for m. object K140.1; destructive m. object tried out on something inanimate K525.8; destructive m. powers D2050—D2099; devil cheated by religious or m. means K218; devil's m. power turned on himself K214; disenchantment (by m. contest) D785, (by use of m. object) D771; dwarf's m. love seduces girl K1672; dwarfs steal m. objects F451.5.2.2.1; employment of m. powers D1760ff.; escape from lower world by m. F101.4; escape by playing m. music K606.1.1; fairy defeated by druid's m. F389.5; fairy gives m. cloak F343.5.1; fairy mother gives son m. powers F305.1.1; fairy offers mortal m. objects F343.0.1; fairy smith gives knight m. sword F343.3; fairies made visible through use of m. object F235.4; fairyland quest for m. object H1286.2; familiar spirit brings news with m. speed F403.2.3.4; fool loses m. objects by talking about them J2355.1; foolish imitation of m. J2411; ghost laid when tells m. secrets E451.1.1; giant killed with m. knife G512.1.1; giants' m. gifts return to original form in hands of men F531.5.6.1; god made by m. A119.1; god has m. vision only from his throne A199.2; herd of cattle put into m. cup D491.1.1; husband's m. gift returns to him N212.1; identification by m. hand H145; journey to otherworld for m. object H1254; lasting m. qualities D1800—D1949; life bound up with m. object E765.3.0.1; lover caught on m. basin *K1217; magic object teaches m. D1302; maiden in m. (garden) N711.3, (castle) N711.2; manifestations of m. power D1800—D2199; miraculous or m. rewards *Q140ff.; ogre tied so he may learn m. K713.1.5; owner of m. object chosen king P11.3; possession of m. powers D1710—D1799; pursuit of m. arrow H1226.2; pursuit revealed by m. D1813.2; quest for m. objects or animals H1320ff.; quest to other world for samples of m. animals' food H1251; quest as payment for m. object H1219.1.1; reading m. book H31.7.2; recognition by unique ability to perform m. act H31.7; resuscitation by m. *E50ff., (object) E64, (root) E104.1; rocks leave coast by m. *M261; river issues from m. nut F715.1.1; source of witch's m. G224; stealing during alleged m. spell K341.22; stolen objects powerful in m. D838.1; suitor task: cutting open m. gourd H335.2; sympathetic m. for exorcism G271.4; tabu: eating m. catch before mother C231.3.1; tabu imposed by m. C901.3; tests of m. power H1576; temporary m. characteristics D1950—D2049; test of truth by m. object H251ff.; thief rendered helpless by m. *K422; treasure discovered by m. object *N533; unfaithful husband loses m. wife C31.12; unique ability to perform m. H31.7; unpromising m. object chosen *L215; using m. power too often forbidden *C762.1; using m. tabu after sunset C752.1.6; weaving m. cloth H383.2.2; woman must relight m. fires as punishment Q492.

Magically conceived children M146.3. — Corpse is m. killed and laid E446.1; cows m. multiply Q141; cutting down huge tree which m. regrows H1115.1; journey to otherworld by clinging m. to an object *F155; stolen object m. returns to owner K423.

Magician *D1711; able to cast mountains upon enemies D2152.2; assigned three places at table confesses to carrying two persons in his body J1141.2; becomes paddybird D169.2; as beggar frees prisoners D2031.4.3:

carries mistress with him (in his body) *F1034.2, (in glass coffin) *D2185; who causes plague punished Q392; claims he can make dogs grey K1677; controls winds D2142.0.1; fights as dragon D199.2.1; as foster father P271.1; in generosity contest H1552.1.1; and giant contest over dog's tail D1719.1.3; of the gods A165.8; as helper N845; helps exposed woman S45.3; loses contest with saint V351.3; makes people lift garments to avoid wetting in imaginary river D2031.1; rebukes usury D1810.0.2.1; recovers lost object with devil's help G303.22.2; sells self to devil, coffin bursts E411.9; shoots arrow of each finger D2091.14; teacher D1810.4; transforms self to seduce queen D2031.4.2. — Abduction by m. R39.1; advice from m. *D1814.1; agar-tree a transformed m. A2731.4; animal as m. B191; child sold to m. S212; contest with m. won by deception K5; druid as m. D1711.4; dwarf as m. F451.3.3ff.; hero as m. A527.3; imitation of m. unsuccessful J2411.4; magic knowledge of m. D1810.0.2; magic power from m. *D1721; princess rescued from m. R111.1.7; pupil surpasses m. L142.2; resuscitation by m. E121.7; seduction by posing as m. K1315.3; seventh daughter to be m. N121.4; sham m. K1963ff., (causes simpleton's death) N384.6, (has paramour fall in trap) D1574.1, (identifies enemies as dishonest) K1956.10; sick crew accused as m. K2129.2; test of gratitude: m. makes pupil believe himself superior H1565.1; theft by posing as m. K353; transformation by m. D683; trickster as sham m. makes adulteress produce hidden food for her husband K1571.1; wolf from man transformed by m. A1833.2.

Magician's familiar animal G225.7.1; gifts D812.13. — Anchorite immune to m. powers V228.2; conception by m. power T513.1.1; false bride fails m. test K1911.3.3.2; familiar in m. cellar G225.0.5; magic from fish fed on m. flesh D1721.2; magic power when m. feet on ground D1719.10.1.

Magicians. — Family of m. D1711.11; giants as m. F531.6.5; transformation contest between m. D615.1.

Magistrate. — Deduction: m. is a bastard J1661.1.2.1.

Magistrates. — Jokes on X330ff.

Magnetic mountain F754; stone F806.

Magnificent. — King seeks one more m. than himself H1311.1.

Magpie is hybrid of dove and raven: not baptized during flood A2382.1; leads other magpies into master's net K2032; refuses to get into ark, sits around outside jabbering, is unlucky A2542.1.1; as suitor B623.3. — Color of m. A2411.2.1.10; creation of m. A1922; why m. is cursed A2542.1; dove and m. exchange eggs (dove's seven for magpie's two: why dove has two eggs) A2247.4; feathers of m. A2247, A2313.2; helpful m. B451.6; prophetic m. B143.0.2; soul in form of m. E732.4; how m. got long tail A2236.4, A2378.3.1; why m. is bald A2317.6; why m. has no tongue A2236.4, A2344.2.6; why m. has long neck A2351.4.2.

Magpie's wedding B282.14. — Punishment for slitting m. tongue Q285.1.1.1; why m. tail is like chisel A2378.7.2.

Mahadeo turns wood chips into insects A2002.1. — Animals created while M. quarrels with wife A1758.

Mahogany ship F841.1.3.

Mahrtenehe, die gestörte C31ff.

Maic Milid A1611.5.4.2, invade Ireland F211.0.2.1.

Maid behind statue of Virgin advises mistress to give servants better food K1971.3.1; cuts off breast to heal man's serpent wound D1515.4.1; given to lover's companion as bed-partner T484; impersonates wife K1843.4; rebukes pilgrim for eating too much J1346; substitutes for princess in conquering king's bed K1223.5; substituted in mistress's bed H1556.4.3, N391.1. — Bride has m. sleep in husband's bed to conceal pregnancy *K1843.1; clever m. J1111.6; devil dances with a m. till she dies G303.10.4.1; devil impersonates woman's m. at toilette Q331.2.1.1; hen put in witch's hair to scratch while m. escapes G276.1; king advised to marry m. rather than widow J482; making love to m. fidelity test H1556.4.2; mistress's m. saves paramour K675.1; mistress sends m. out for man T271.1.1; ogre's m. as helper G530.6; old m. promises devil her first born S223.3; priest's fifty-year old m.: one 20, one 30 J2212.1.1; queen and m. conceive from eating same food T511.0.1; recognition of m. as substitute bride H38.2.3; tasks set m. by elfin knight before she can marry him F301.4; transformation combat between lover and m. D615.3; treacherous m.-servant K2252; wife dismisses m., husband's mistress J1112.2; woman jealous of a fair m. in her house T257.1.

Maid's confederate comes out of woman's room K2112.2.3. — Man takes m. place in mistress's bed K1347; old m. plea: "Anybody, Lord" J1811.1.1.

Maids. — Faithless men-servants corrupt m. in household P365.1; jokes on old m. X750ff.; reincarnation of old m. as birds E613.0.3; wife's m. disguised as saints K1827.1.

Maiden abducted R10.1, (by monster) *R11.1, (by pirates) R12.1, (by transformed hero) R16.1; at bridge to hell A672.2; in castle gives quest directions H1232.3; daughter of giantess and prince F531.5.7.1.3; queen offers hand as reward Q53.3; queen sets hero tasks H933.2; sent to rendezvous to capture lover K787. — Allegorical game of witch, devil, m., church Z178; burial alive of m. to keep her from rival S123.5; cat transformed to m. runs after mouse J1908.2; darkness comes in daytime in order to save life of m. about to be executed F965.1; disenchantment by m. sitting at head of enchanted king's bed D759.7; falsely accused m. dies of sorrow F1041.1.3.1; giant rescues m. R164.1; gull a transformed ravished m. A1945.2; magic from celestial m. D1726.1; magic from m. walking naked in public *D1796; magic object received from m. D825; magic object from m.-spirit D812.15; magic object from otherworld m. D813.3; man hunting honey encounters lost m. N785.1; snake heals mutilated m. B511.1.2;

well rises for m. F933.1.3.1; winner of m. queen becomes king H1574.3.2;
witch causes m. to hate lover G263.6.

Maiden's — Animal tamed by m. beauty B771.1.

Maidens slain in revenge Q411.12; take mortal to heaven F63.1. —
Disenchantment by m. walking with lighted candles in procession D759.6;
four m. as earth-supports A841.2; holy m. invulnerable to glowing embers
D1841.3.2.4.

Maidservant, see Maid.

Maimed victims at ogre's house G691.3. — Broken oaths cause of m.
people M101.2; dupe's animals m. K1440ff.; king must resign if m.
P16.2; ogre m. *G510ff.

Maiming, see also Mutilation; animal exorcises witch G271; by deception
K800; by magic D2062. — Magic object m. D1403; witch m. animals
G265.5.

Maina. — Friendship between parrot and m. A2493.26.

Maine. — Seven sons all named M. T586.1.2.1.

Maize. — Man becomes m. D214.2.

Majority. — Ruler should follow advice of m. J21.35.

Make-believe eating, make-believe work J1511.1.

Make-up. — Woman vowing not to use m. rewarded V39.5; women as
painters in m. art H659.16.

Male children killed (by Amazons) F565.1.2, (for fear that they will overcome parent) M375.1; Cinderella L101; from deity's body by his mere
thinking A1211.0.1; and female creators A12.1; and female waters
A918; rabbit bears young B754.4; sungod while ascending, female while
setting A227.1; transformed in womb to female T577.1; witch G207. —
Adam names m. animals, Eve, female A2571.0.2; adulteress pretends
shame before m. statue K2051.1; beef neither m. nor female H1074;
cloud on m. mountain bows to female mountain A969.2; ghost in m.
dress E422.4.5; god presides over all m. spirits A161.4; origin of m. sex
organs A1313.1; princess not to see m. person C313.0.1; tabu: m. presence in girl's puberty-hut C132; women blush in presence of m. statue
(fish) F647.4.

Males. — All new-born m. slaughtered S302.1.

Malediction. — Execution escaped by threats of m. J1189.2.

Maledictions. — Old woman's m. inform abandoned hero of his parentage
and future S375.

Malevolent dwarf F451.5.2ff.; fairies F360ff.; mountain-men F460.4.4ff.;
return from the dead E200—E299. — Tabu: uttering name of m.
creature C433.

Malice. — Baffling m. with ready answers J1251.

Malicious wife reports her husband as famous doctor H916.1.1.

Mallet. — Saint's m. cures D1500.1.14.

Mammal transformed to person D310—D349. — Domestic m. transformed
(to another animal) D412, (to object) D422, (to person) D330ff.; man

transformed to wild m. D110ff.; soul in form of m. E731ff.; wild m. transformed (to another animal) D411, (to object) D421.

Mammals magically called D2074.1.1. — Creation of m. A1800—A1899; cries of m. A2426.1; food of m. A2435.3ff.; gait or walk of m. A2441.1; haunts of various animals: m. A2433.3; lies about m. X1210; markings of m. *A2412.1ff.; origin of color of m. A2411.1.

Man, see also **Person;** acts as statue of saint in order to enter convent K1842.1; admitted into heaven but must not find fault *F13; as animal's servant, supplies their food J2214.5; calls wife "my swallow": she becomes swallow D511.1; -cat B29.4; controls rising, setting of sun A725; by day, animal by night D621.1.1; in every house killed to punish king Q411.8; excels woman A1376; -goat B24.2; with horse's mouth B21.3; honored above God: the dead hen J2215.3; -killing flower H1333.5.0.4; lacking money better than money lacking a man J482.2.1; lion, and bear in pit J685.1; looks at copulating snakes: transformed to woman D513.1; made to appear to pursuers as woman carrying babe D2031.6.1; made to believe that he is someone else J2013; in moon A751, (lets himself down) X1851; in otherworld loaded down with wood F171.6.1; not to be present at childbirth C151; poses as bride for beggar K1911.4; proof against weapons D1841.5.1; reincarnated as god E605.3; rescues his wife from fairyland F322.2; scorned by his beloved T75; magically becomes smaller D55.2; magically stretches himself D55.1; transformed (to animal) D100—D199, (to ass plays lyre) *D693, (to cannibal) D91, (to different man) D10—D99, (to beast leads herd) B241.3, (to green knight) D57.1, (to insect) D180ff., (to person of different social class) D20ff., (to woman) D12, (to woman has children) D695; and tiger in contest: winner to live in town A2250.1.1; undertakes disastrously to do his wife's work J2431; unharmed in den of animals B848; as weapon F628.2.7; will not do woman's bidding W214. — Animals created to serve m. A1705; animal by day, m. by night D621.1; automatic statue of m. D1620.1; creation of ant: avaricious m. transformed A2011.2; devil developed from m G303.1.3.1; devil fights with m. G303.9.6.1; devil helps ugly m. win wife G303.22.7; devil in place of dead m. in shroud G303.18.2; disguise as m. to escape lover K1236; disguise of m. in woman's dress *K1836; dragon from transformed m. lying on his treasures B11.1.3; enmity between tiger and m. A2494.10.1; fairy entices m. into fairyland F302.3.1; falling in love with m. disguised as woman T28; friendship between m. and dog A2493.4; giant obtains treasure from m. F531.6.7.2; giant's skull holds a m. seated F531.2.3; giant swallows m. F911.5; girl masked as m. wins princess's love K1322; girl transformed into m. G263.3.2; god reborn as m. E605.2; god as part m., part fish A131.1; hare and m. contest in watching for leaf to fall off tree A2256.1; headless m. lives four years E783.7; killing certain m. as task H1162; lie: the large m. X920; madness from seeing beautiful m. F1041.8.1.1; magic changes in m. D50ff.; magic change of size in m.

D55; magic object received from old m. D822; marriage to beast by day and m. by night *B640.1; mermaid swallows m. B81.10; mistress sends out for m. T271.1.1; Norse m.-horses "fingalkn" B21.1; old m. contented till forbidden to leave city H1557.3; old m. nods "yes" J1521.2; old m. of the sea G311; one m. for worship, two for cultivation, three for journey Z64.1; precept of lion to his sons: beware of m. J22.1; pregnant m. T578; punishment: m. reborn as girl Q551.5.1.1; punishment: m. to do woman's work Q482.6; reincarnation of m. as (animal) E610.1, (nature spirit) E653, (objects) E648, E671; revenant as m. E425.2; serpent swallows m. F911.7; sun is m. during day B722.13; sun as m. who left earth A711; sun and moon as m. and woman A736.1; transformation: m. to baby at will D55.2.5; transformed m. as hostile dog B17.1.2.3; transformation of m. to animal as punishment Q584.2; treacherous dark m. K2260.1; tree by day, m. by night D621.2; why animals serve m. A2513; wild m. as king of animals B240.3; wisdom from old m. J151ff.; witch transforms m. to object G263.2; woman not to look at m. C313; woman reborn as m. E605.1.1; woman transformed to m. D11; woman dies at seeing naked m. F1041.1.13.2; woman disguises as m. to enter enemy camp K2357.6.

Man's Fall A63.5, A1420.5, A2236ff., A2631.1.1, A2721.8. — Dead m. tooth as cure for toothache D1502.2.1; disguise of woman in m. clothes *K1837; soul leaves m. body and enters animal's E725.1; universe from parts of m. body A614.1.

Men deceived into killing each other K929.7; as God's advisers A41; previously menstruated A1355.3; swallow men F911.1. — Adulteress feigns disdain of m. K2051.3; animal learns through experience to fear m. J17; animals that live with m. A2433.2.4; are there more m. or women? H708; beast-m. in lower world B20.2; council of fishes decide to get rid of m. B233.1; first m. without beards A1597.1; giants and m. F531.5ff.; why goat lives with m. A2433.3.8; god lived among m. A151.9; journey to Land of M. of Heads Only F129.1; land of m. F113; land where women live separate from m. F566.2; soldiers of fairy king are trees by day, m. by night F252.3.1; stars are m. peering through holes in sky A761.5; strong man kills m. F628.2.5; tabus on m. C182ff.; trolls and m. F455.6; village of m. only F566.1; Virgin tests m. with hot iron H221.2.1; why m. become old A2861; wise m. J191; young sparrows have learned to avoid m. J13.

Man-eating ants B16.6.1; birds B33; cattle B16.1.5; giantess D429.2.2.1; god A123.2.2.1, A135; humans, see **Cannibals;** mice B16.2.8; monster B16.0.3; sea-monster B16.5.1.2; sow H1155.3; tree F811.24, H1163; woman G11.6.

Mandrake. — Magic charm uproots m. D1599.5; magic m. *D965.1; origin of m. A2611.5, A2664.

Mandrakes. — Elephants have sexual desire only after eating m. B754.2.

Mane. — Bells on horse's m. P651.2; child born with hairy m. T585.5.1;

dog-headed man with horse's m. B25.1.1; eel with fiery m. B15.7.12; horse with golden m. B19.5; origin of goat's m. A2322.4.1; origin of hair and m. A2322ff.

Manes. — Fairies plait horses' m. F366.2.1; sea waves are m. of sea horses A1116.1.

Mange. — Magic object cures m. D1502.5.

Manger. — Dog in the m. W156.

Mangling. — Murder by m. with axe S139.4.

Mango. — Conception from m. T511.1.3; covering m. tree grove with fruit overnight H1103.3; half child born to queen eating half m. T550.6; hero gets into m. seed D55.2.6; magic m. returns to tree D868.1; man becomes m. D211.4, D215.8; rajah to marry when cut m. blooms M261.1.1; white m. tree F811.3.2.

Mangoes. — Dying woman requests m.: priests claim them J1511.18.

Maniac's. — Casting of image of Buddha delayed until m. mite is thrown into the furnace V125.

Manifestation. — Magic m. as omen D1812.5.0.13.

Manifestations of magic power D1800—D2199.

Manioc. — Acquisition of m. A1423.4; origin of m. A2685.5; transformation by eating m. D551.2.7.

Maniplies. — Cow swallows book: cause of m. in stomach A2219.2.

Mankind. — Witches at emergence of m. F203.2.

Mankind's journeyings A1630ff.

Manna D1031.0.1; does not fall on Sabbath D1676.1, V71.2; tastes bitter to gentiles D1665.4. — Shower of m. F962.6.2.

Manner. — Recognition by unique m. of performing an act H35; tabu: doing thing in certain m. C854; unusual m. of life F560ff.

Mannikin. — Magic sack furnishes m. who cudgels owner's enemies D1401.2; soul as m. E747.

Mansion. — Hat becomes m. D1867.1.

Mansions. — Golden m. of gods A151.4.3.

Mantis transformed to another animal D415.1. — Origin of m. A2093; vulva hair becomes m. F547.5.9.

Mantle, see also **Cloak;** ever new D1652.12; will not fit unchaste woman H411.7. — Beautiful m. F821.4; drunken officer's stolen m. J1211.2.1; escape under invisibility m. K532; escape, only m. injured K525.5; magic m. *D1053, (changes color) D682.4.1; night from deity wrapping self in dark m. A1174.4; recognition from gold wrapped in m. H91.2; servant by using master's m. deceives his master's lady K1317.1; sleeping under same m. transforms D592; saint's m. determines land grant K185.4.2; weaving m. from single sheep's wool H1022.4.2.

Mantles. — Custom of wearing m. A1683.3.

Manufactured object transformed D454, (to animal) D444, (to person) D436. — Man transformed to m. object D250ff.

Manure, see also **Dung, Excrement.** — Why beetles live in m. A2433.5.4;

cleaning m.-filled barn H1102.2; clearing out m. K1424; devil's money m. G303.21.2; filling the yard with m. (task) H1129.1; footsteps in m. show dead man walked H264; murdered person's corpse put in m. heap S139.2.2.8; nest made of m. not for nightingale U144; sensitivity to food raised in m. F647.5.2; witch power from standing on m. pile G224.6.

Manuscript. — Law involving ownership of m. P526.1; penitent's m. of sins V29.6; resuscitation by m. E64.7.1.

Many admit theft: real thief concealed K415.1; children at a birth T586.1; -eyed antelope B15.4.1.1; -headed animal *B15.1.2; -horned animal B15.3.1. — Animals with m. legs B15.6.3; father makes m. out of few (sows grain) H583.2.2; finding how m. people are in dark, closed room as test of resourcefulness H506.2; hare with m. friends H1558.4; invulnerability bestowed by m.-headed monster D1846.2; people with m. (arms) F516.2, (eyes) F512.2, (feet) F517.1.2, (hands) F515.0.2; person with m. (ears) F511.2.3, (teeth) F513.1.2; same reward promised to m. K2034; strong man kills m. men at once F628.2.1.

Marauder pretends beggary K2369.1.

Marble cup becomes crystal D475.5. — Acquisition of m. A1439.1; fortress of m. in otherworld F163.5.4; man transformed to m. column D231.2.

Marbles. — Devil plays m. in church G303.9.9.19; playing m. with jewel H151.1.1.

March. — Tabu: going to certain place in M. C755.4.

Marching. — Swine m. like soldiers B290.1.

Marcolf and Solomon H561.3, H1595.1.

Mare, see also **Horse;** brings hero back from land of no return F129.5.1; with foal left behind finds road home B151.1.1.1; not to pull corpse C181.11; from water world disappears when scolded C918. — Adulteress transformed to m. and stirruped Q493.1; contest in lifelike painting: m. and curtain H504.1.2; dancing m. rescues persecuted boy in belly K551.3.6.2; fairies milk mortal's m. F366.1.1; god as m. seduces stallion D658.3.1.2; grooming unruly m. H1155.1.1; helpful m. cools boiling bath for master B526.2; man-eating m. B16.1.3.1; outstripping wild m. F681.6.1; paramour unties m. K1514.14; revenant as m. E423.1.3.2; seduction on promise to transform woman into m. K1315.3.2; strong man son of man and m. F611.1.6; which m. colt's mother? real one swims to it J1171.4; white m. thought to be church J1761.2.

Mare's egg J1772.1. — Crows reveal m. killing B131.1; guessing sex of m. offspring H528.1.

Mares. — Riddle about catching m., walking sticks H586.8.

Marienkind C611, K2116.1, Q451.3.

Marine counterpart to land F133.1; lamb B95.2.

Mariners saved by prayer V52.6.

Marital, see also **Marriage;** experiences of the devil G303.12ff.; impostors K1910ff. — Refusal of m. relations punished Q257.

Mark of Cain (as curse on murderer) Q556.2; of mother's hand on moon
A751.5.3; of tiger's paw on moon A751.5.4; of wandering soul seen on
body E721.0.1. — Ghostly fingers leave m. on man's hand E542.1.1;
holy water removes m. made by devil V132.2.1; indelible m. D1654.3.1;
magic m. on forehead renders invisible D1361.43.

Marks from ghost's strike E542.1.4.2; of royalty H7. — Animal pressed:
hence facial or bodily m. A2213.2; battle m. in rock F1084.0.4; dead
returns to replace boundary m. he has removed E345.1; lucky m. on
body N135.4; recognition by bodily m. or physical attributes H50ff.;
why women have m. on belly A1310.4.

Market. — Numskull buys water at m. J2478; princess must sell goods
on m. as punishment Q483; queen exposed in m. place Q483.1; witches
steal m. goods G266.1.

Marking coveted object with name: claiming it later K448; the place
J1922; way in unfamiliar country J765. — Appearance of animal from
m. or painting A2217ff.; devil m. person he touches G303.4.8.10; groom
m. bride's forehead at wedding T135.4; marked culprit m. everyone else,
escapes detection K415.

Markings on bark of plant A2751.3. — Origin of animal m. A2221.3,
*A2412ff.

Marko (king asleep in mountain) *D1960.2.

Marksman. — Fairy's skill as m. F273.1; lie: great m. X1120; skillful
m. F661ff.

Marksmanship. — Lie: remarkable m. X1122.

Marmot. — Man transformed to m. D117.4; why m. has short tail
A2378.4.3.

Marooned man reaches home and outwits marooner K1616; person in
ogre's power G406. — Pleiades are hunters m. in sky A773.5.

Marooning as punishment Q467.5.

Marplot at creation A60ff. — Food at first comes without effort: m.
changes plan so that man must labor A1346.2, A1420.4.

Marriage, see also **Wedding;** *T100—T199; to avoid shame at undress
J2521.3; of beautiful woman and hideous man T268; of child of demon
king to mortal F402.2.3; of clerics V465.1.1.2; compared to drowning
J1442.12; customs T130ff.; destroys friendship T201; of earth and sky
A702.5; with equal or with unequal J414; with fairy *F300ff.; forbidden outside the parish X751; -god A475.0.2; of the gods A164; into
house full of wild animals J347.5; of kings P18; of lowly hero to
princess L161; of lowly heroine to prince (king) L162; of man to girl
who guesses his riddles H552; of mountain-girl to mortal man F460.4.1;
of person to animal *B600—B699; to person in animal form *B640ff.;
of poor boy, rich girl L161.1; of prince, princess prophesied M331;
promise induces fight between foster brothers P273.2.1; promised to
save life M268; prophecy for newborn princesses H41.6; of queen P28;
ring protects from devil D1385.3; tests H300—H499; tokens identifying

lover H82.2. — Angel warns against forcing girl into m. V231.5; brother-sister m. T415.5; consummation of m. J1306, N681.3.1, T160ff.;
continence in m. T315; covenant confirmed by m. M201.5; dead man
seeks m. E353; dead wife haunts husband on second m. E221.1; death
feigned to escape unwelcome m. K522.0.1; death to come same year as m.
E765.4.4; disenchantment depends on m. D791.2.2.1; death prophecies
connected with m. M341.1.1.1ff.; dream of m. with another's wife
T11.3.2; elopement to prevent undesired m. R225.2; erecting m. hall
overnight H1104.4; eyes burst for urging saint's m. Q551.8.4; faithfulness in m. T210ff.; faithlessness in m. T230ff.; father will die at
daughter's m. E766.4.1; foolish m. of old man, young girl J445.2; friendship covenant concerning m. of children M246.2; ghostly m. E495; how
m. was consummated J1306; human-dragon m. B11.12.3.1; humiliating
m. as punishment Q499.7; ignorance of m. relations J1744; infant's
m. to twelve-year-old to avoid death prophecy M341.0.3; Jews protesting
against m. of Jewess and Christian are struck dumb V343; joke on Jewish m. ceremony X613; king must have m. P13.4; life long penance for
brother-sister m. Q520.3; love kept up despite m. to another T88.1;
mankind from human-animal m. A1224.0.1; marathon m. F1073; monkey
saved from trap by feigning m. K579.4; mother tries to prevent
daughter's m. P232.1; murder for m. against family's wishes K959.2.1;
origin of customs of courtship and m. A1550ff.; origin of m. A1555;
prince's m. to common woman prophesied M359.2; princess humiliated for
loathly m. S322.1.4; promise to dying father on m. M258.2; prophecies
concerning m. M369.2; races from offspring of animal m. A1610.3;
sacrificing self for m. T24.8; seasons produced by m. of North and South
A1153; seduction upon false promise of m. K1315.8; tabu: m. with certain person C162; tabu connected with m. C160ff.; treasure to be found
by man after his m. to the daughter of the original owner N543.3;
trickster exacts promise of m. as price of silence after having seen a
princess naked *K443.6; trickster falsely announces m. celebration and
distracts owner's attention K341.12; unusual m. T110ff.; unwitting m.
to cannibal *G81; vow concerning m. M134ff.; wealthy m. foretold for
poor boy M312.1; woman promises m. for earrings K233.8; woman
refuses second m. (if husband is good she will fear to lose him, if bad
she will repent) J482.1.

Marriages. — Relationship riddles arising from unusual m. of relatives
H795; riddle about no sons after three m. H585.2.

Married life *T200—T299. — Devil m. to widow who maltreats him
G303.12.2; foolish m. couples J1713; girl in fairyland m. to fairy F301.3;
maiden m. to merman B82.1; man disguised as woman m. by another man
K1321.3; man m. to spirit of willow tree F441.2.3.1.1; mermaid m. to
man *B81.2; moon m. to woman A753.1.4; moon m. to sky-god's son
A753.1.4.1; mortal man m. to fairy woman F302ff.; numskull believes
that he is m. to a man J2323; parents made to believe that they are

dead and are m. to each other again J2311.8; sun and moon m. A736.1.4; tailor m. to princess betrays trade by calling for needle and thread H38.2.1; witches m. to fairies G287; wolf punished by being m. K583.

Marrow. — Bath of m. F872.4; corpses' m. used in sorcery D1278.2; obtaining wild pig's m. H1154.11; wounds healed by m. bath F959.3.3.

Marry. — Counsel to m. new wife every week (not to see your wife too much) H588.3; disenchantment by promise to m. D741ff.; father casts daughter forth when she will not m. him S322.1.2; giants m. human beings F531.5.7; how girl thus far avoided by suitors can m. H1292.5; husband (lover) arrives home just as wife (mistress) is to m. another *N681; king advised to m. maid rather than widow J482; moon wants to m. his sister the sun A751.5.2.1; magic plant bears fruit to indicate that heroine is ready to m. D1310.4.2; mother wishes lazy daughter may m. devil C12.4.1; not to m. a girl from abroad J21.4; prince agrees to m. a servant girl if she will help him on a quest H1239.1; punishment for refusal to m. after girl is pregnant Q245; quest undertaken before hero will m. H1227; tasks set maid by elfin knight before she can m. him F301.4; trickster concealed in sacred tree advises that he is to m. princess K1971.10; vow not to m. till iron shoes wear out M136; why brothers and sisters do not m. A1552.1; youth lamed by man whose daughter he refuses to m. Q451.2.1.

Marrying first woman met C664; person to die same year E765.4.4. — Advice against m. more than one woman J21.32; condemned woman may be freed by m. a rogue P512; demons m. among selves G302.7.2; devil m. G302.12.5; fairy punished for m. mortal F386.2; first man m. a fairy A1275.9; girl m. man on whom fly lights B152.2; girl complains about m. stranger J2463.2; girl m. lover who thought her dead K1839.2; king does not want daughter m. T50.2; man m. fairy F302.3.1.3; man m. often: always looking for good wife T251.0.3; man m. tree maiden F441.2.3.1; mortal m. otherworld king F167.12.1; oath concerning m. king M192; parson with bad eyes m. wrong couples X413; returning home after m. fairy tabu C644; sun m. woman A736.7.1; tabu: m. until hero chooses husband C566.4; witch m. man G264.4.

Mars lies on moon A759.7.

Marshall P50.2. — Treacherous m. K2245.

Marshsnipe's enmity with raven A2494.13.6.

Marsyas flayed Q457.1.

Marten. — Color of m. A2411.2.1.17; enmity between m. and squirrel A2494.12.6; man transformed to m. D124.3; origin of m. A1824; wedding of m. B281.5.

Martens recover magic ring from kite B548.1.1.

Martin, St. — Jesus appears to M. V411.8; nun refuses to see M. T362.1.

Martyr with Sign of Cross on his heart V86.2. — "Live confessor better than dead m." J1261.9.

Martyrdom to preserve virginity T326.3. — Colors symbolizing m.

Z141.2ff.; place of saint's m. perpetually green V229.2.5; religious m. V463.

Martyrology. — Reciting m. prevents body's decomposition V52.14.

Marvel as sign of royalty H71.10. — King questions six doctors: what must you most m. at on earth? J171.2.4ff.; respite given to witness m. K551.28; sign of cross enables relating of m. D1766.6.3; tabu: expressing astonishment at m. C491; transformation by expressing astonishment at m. D512.

Marvels *F (entire chapter); seen in dreams D1731.2. — Recognition by ability to perform m. H151.1.3; seventeen m. at Christ's birth V211.0.3; tabu: asking about m. which one sees C411.

Marvelous creatures *F200—F699; manifestations at death of witch G278.1; objects as prince's marriage price T55.4; occurrences F900—F1099; otherworld journeys F0—F199; places and things F700—F899. — King's quest for m. object H1218; quest for m. objects or animals H1320ff.; quest for m. thing seen in dream H1229.3; quest for m. water H1321; quest for most m. thing: needed to save life H355.0.1; tabu: revealing the m. C423; wager on second m. object N72.

Mary, see also **Virgin Mary;** "of the Gael" V250.1. — Girl named M. has virginity spared by knight who has bought her T321.2.

Mary's — Origin of M. "bed straw" (thymus serpyllum) A2654.

Maries. — Three M. Z71.1.7.

Mashed. — How wildcat got his m. face A2330.1.

Mask disguise for disfigured warrior K521.2.3; mistaken for face J1793. — Abduction with m. rendering invisible R23; magic m. D1067.4, (renders invisible) D1361.32.

Masks' origin A1465.6.

Masking as ghost in graveyard forbidden C94.5. — Capture by m. as another K755; girl m. as man wins princess's love K1322; lowly m. as great J951; ogre's secret overheard by m. as bird G661.2; peasant boy m. as prince betrays self by answers H38.2.2; seduction by m. as woman's husband *K1311; test of sex of girl m. as man H1578.1; Thor m. as woman kills giant K235.2; women learn witchcraft by m. as men G286.1; wound m. another wound K1872.4.

Mason P455. — Why m.-wasp looks for fireplace A2471.8.

Masons mutilated to prevent duplication S161.0.1.

Mass V40ff.; of the dead *E492. — Chaplain searches the prayer-book for hunter's m. J2474; color symbolism in m. vestments Z140.3; dead man asks for m. E443.2.1.1; death respite until m. said K551.1.2; devil is cheated of his reward when priest dismisses m. early G303.16.16; devil interrupts m. by pretended battle G303.9.9.2; disenchantment by m. of Pope D781; ghosts punish intruders into m. of ghosts *E242; holy man has his own m. (hangs coat on sunbeam) V43; holy water and m. prevent demons alighting on grave D1385.15; knockers' midnight m. in mines F456.1.2.3.1; magic articles made during m. D1766.5.2; magic produced by saying m. D1766.5; parson and sexton at m. X441; penance: holding midnight m. until someone will make responses Q521.6; priest may use his own mother's m. money J1261.6; priest who never reads m. J1263.1.3; priest's rushing through m. J1263.1.3.1; punishment for neglect of m. Q223.7; snakes have m. B253.1; stay at church till m. is finished (delay saves youth from death) J21.17; symbolism of m. Z176; treacherous priests prolong m. to let enemy destroy city K2354; Virgin's private m. for lady unable to attend V255.2; well floods until m. said F933.7.

Masses used along with magic for cursing D1766.5.1; work miracles V41. — Charity rewarded above prayer or hearing of m. V410.1; ghost laid by saying m. E433.2.1; ghost of priest failing to say m. E415.3; seven m. to free soul from hell Z71.5.6.6; sons break promise to have m. for father M256.1.

Massacre. — Punishment for wholesale m. Q211.11.

Massacring prisoner R51.4. — Jealous king m. handsome captives T257.6.

Mast. — Climbing the m. (bluff) K1762; gold (silver) m. F841.2.1; human sacrifice carried on m. S264.1.1; riding up m. as suitor contest H331.1.3; witch sits atop m. D2142.0.1.2.

Masts transformed to serpents D444.11.

Master, see also **Servant;** asked to help in theft J2136.5.6.1; as magician tricks servant K1963.3; rescues disciple R167; and servant *P360ff.; takes serving man's place in woman's bed K1317.1.1; tests disciple by river plunge H1561.10; thief *K301ff. — Animal cares for wounded m. B536; animal recognizes returned m. H173.1, H173.3; animals help imprisoned m. B544.1; ass tries to caress his m. like the dog J2413.1; boat transforms self at will of m. D632; choice between bad m., bad official, or bad neighbor J229.5; contentment with evil m. for fear of worse successor J229.8; contest in lying: m. brought to say "You lie" X905.1; cumulative tale: m. goes to kill animals Z32.4; dog wants most powerful m.: stays with man A2513.1.1; faithful horse follows dead m. to grave B301.4; fool releases bear while m. is away J2191; horse's devotion to m. B301.4ff; magic object from m. D829.1; man blames m. for not correcting him in youth J142.2; only m. able to bend bow D1651.1; pupil returns from dead to warn m. of futility of his studies E368; pupil surpasses m. L142; servant boasts where the m. cannot hear K1776; servant plans to deceive his m. by refusing to eat J2064; servant repays stingy m. J1561.4; servant saves m. from death H187; skillful smith calls self m. of all masters F663.0.1; Solomon as m. of magicians D1711.1.1; stag found by m. when overlooked by servants J1032; strong hero overawes m. F615.3; transformation contest between m. and pupil D615.2; tree as m. of ceremonies F979.22; trickster sends m. running after the paramour K1573; which is servant, which m.? J1141.1.6; why a woman is m. of her husband A1557.

Master's. — Boat obeys m. will D1523.2.4; faithful animal at m. grave dies of hunger B301.1; follow your m. likes and dislikes U42; helpful cat borrows measure for his m. money K1954.1; pupils think dog's tail their m. J2015.

Masters. — Cobolds furnish supplies to their m. F481.2; hard-hearted m. punished Q291.2.

Masterful. — Magic object makes woman m. D1359.1.

Mastery. — Husband in armor establishes m. of house T251.2.2.

Masturbation. — Mankind from m. of creator A1216.1; universe from m. of creator A615.1.

Mat. — Man transformed to m. D265; sleeping m. on head J1819.3.

Mats over holes as pitfall K735.1. — Eating off new m. forbidden C219.3.

Match. — Creation m. between god, goddess A85; cursing m. M401; magic m. D1175; three on a m. D1273.1.1.1; tobacco, pipe, and m. debate usefulness to smoker J461.3.

Matches. — Striking all m. to try them J1849.3.

Matching. — Identification by m. (parts of divided token) H100ff., (weapon wound) H101.1; quest for m. ornament H1317.

Matchmaker T53; passes off fool as eligible K1372.2. — Bee as m. B582.2.4; swan as m. B582.2.3.

Mate. — Animal grateful for rescue of its m. B365.1; creation of first man's (woman's) m. A1275; willingness to die for m. disappears at death H1556.4.5.

Mated. — Lovers m. before birth T22.1.

Material of bridge to otherworld F152.1; rewards Q110ff. — Construction from impossible amount of m. (task) H1022; construction from impossible kind of m. (task) H1021; extraordinary m. of (bridge) F842.1, (castle) F771.1, (dress) F821.1, (ship) F841.1, (trees) F811.1ff.; transformation: m. of object changed D470ff.

Materialization. — Creation as m. of creator's thinking A612.

Maternity test: producing baby within year H494.

Mating. — Animals from m. of sun and moon A1771; creation of animals from unusual primeval m. A1770; lions not m. with their fellows, prefer leopards B754.3; mankind from unusual primeval m. A1221.

Matins. — Cardinal's decision on monks sounding m. J1179.13.

Matriarchy T148; among gods A164.4.

Matricide punished Q21.1.2.

Matron of Ephesus K2213.1. — Fortune personified as m. Z134.1.

Mattress. — Ear used as m. F542.2.

Maturity. — Man's growth and m. A1360ff.; changeling plays on a pipe and thus betrays his m. F321.1.1.2; vegetables reach m. miraculously quickly F815.1.

Maundy Thursday. — Eating flesh on M. tabu C235.

Maxims for law court J1131.

May Day V70.1.1. — Golden plow (throne, crown, palace) is worth a rain in M. H713.1; month of M. is greenest H646.1; tabu for Monday after M. Day C751.4.

Mayor. — The ass as m. J1882.2.

Mead. — Bog becomes flowery m. D479.1; life spared in return for poetic m. M234.1; rivers of m. in otherworld F162.2.4; stealing m. of poetry H1151.16; Virgin Mary supplies m. for unprepared hostess of the king V262; water becomes m. D478.6.

Meadow. — Tabu: staying too long in otherworld m. C761.4.2.

Meadow-lark. — Enmity between coyote and m. A2494.12.4.

Meal. — Accidental meeting of seeker of exiled prince with prince at m. N745; cannibal's gigantic m. G94; commemorative religious m. A1549.1; feeding army from one measure of m. H1022.5; feeding pigs wet m. J2465.1; fool tries to dry up spilt wine with m. J2176.1; frightful m. S183, (as leadership test) H1567.1, (as punishment) Q478; how much m. is in sack J2062.1; magic m. of fishes D1032.1; mill-ground m. blood color E761.1.12; rider takes the m.-sack on his shoulder to relieve the ass of his burden J1874.1; widow's m. J355.1.

Meals. — Children search for stolen m. J124; origin of time for m. A1511.

Mean person reborn as hyena E692.2.

Meander-pursuit (fugitive's doublings cause a river's windings) A931.

Meanings. — Symbolic m. H600ff., (of numbers) H602, (of playing cards) H603.

Measure. — Feeding an army from one m. of meal H1022.5; helpful cat borrows m. for his master's money K1954.1; if you don't believe it, go m. it yourself (center of earth) H681.3.1, (water in sea) H696.1.2, (width of heaven) H682.2.1; inexhaustible m. D1652.5.3; magic iron m. D1470.1.47, L222.4; riddles of m. H696.

Measures. — Origin of weights and m. A1471.2; putting empty m. into pot J2461.1.4.2; use of false m. punished Q274.3.

Measured. — Sky m. by bird A702.6.

Measurement. — Magic m. *D1273.4, (protects against devil) D1385.17, (protects against sudden death) D1389.10.

Measuring fairy gifts tabu F348.6; ocean (task) H1144; sick as means of cure F950.3; time by worn iron shoes *H1583.1; wild boar H1154.3.3.1; the world A1186; worm rescues from a height B542.1.3. — Attempts at m. sky's height, sea's depth L414.1; difficult m. tasks H1145.

Meat changed to toad as punishment for ungrateful son D444.2; disguised as butter during Lent K498; distributed according to rank P632.2; fed to cabbages J1856.1; irresistible H659.20; transformed D476.3, (to roses) D457.5.1 — Bird's red eye cooks m. F989.2; chain tale: animals killing each other in man's field, provide m. Z43.6; children eat m. of luck-bringing animal, becomes fortunate N251.6; cooked m. changed to raw D476.2.2; conception from eating m. T511.7.3; diamond in m. carried to eagle's nest N527.1; dog drops m. for reflection J1791.4; dog waits to be hit with m. J2066.6; "eat m." J21.29; eaten m. of bear lover causes unborn son to have bear characteristics *B635.1.1; eating m. forbidden C221; fairy gift of inexhaustible m. F348.5.1.1; fairies eat m. F243.3; grace before m. X434.2; guessing nature of devil's roast m. H523.4; hungry student cleverly obtains m. J1341.10; why Indians cache their m. A1526; lioness foregoes m. as penance Q535.2; magic m. *D1032; man made from m.-ball A1266.1; man transformed to m. D271; marvelous sensitiveness (m. is dog's flesh) F647.5.1, (m. tastes of corpse) F647.1; message of chastity: uncooked m. left behind T386; modest choice: bones preferred to m. L222.2; mouse dying in m. tub is happy that he has eaten to satisfaction J861.3; murder by slipping coins into m. K929.5; origin of tribes from m. they choose A1616.4.1; people pelt each other with whale m. J2195; quest for best m. H1305.1; secret m.-eating betrayed by greasy mouth N478.1; sending m. home by bird: bird eats it J2124.1; sick queen under red satin mistaken for m. N335.2.1; skillful marksman shoots m. from giant's hands F661.1; stolen m. and the weighed cat J1611; stolen m. handed about K475.1; tabu to eat m. with milk C229.5; tender m. of cocks kept from intercourse B754.5; thief advises that slaughtered m. be hung up over night K343.2; transformed animal refuses to touch m. of that animal D686; transformation: stolen m. to roses D457.5.1; trickster steals m.: blind men accuse each other and fight K1081.2; wolf scorns salt m. in vain expectation of other booty J2066.4; woman has m. stolen by bird (cumulative tale) Z41.1.

Mecca. — Mosque magically turns toward M. D2136.2.1; pilgrimage to M. V532.

Medallion. — Recognition by m. H94.8.

Meddling punished *Q340ff. — Animal characteristics: punishment for m. A2237; queen m. in state affairs P25.

Mediator. — Fox as m. B239.1, (between lion and lioness) J811.2.

Medical books A1487.2.

Medicinal properties of trees A2783. — Charm renders m. herbs efficacious D1577.1.

Medicine, see also **Drug;** changes voice F556.3; against quarreling T256.2; shown by animal *B512; used to abduct woman K1364. — Blowing m. disenchants D778.2; disenchantment by m. D771.6; dwarfs give m. F451.5.1.10; evil spirit exorcised by burning m. D2176.3.1.1; fatal overdose of m. J2115; gold in m. D1500.1.31; healed with his own m. J1513; layman's ignorance of m. J1734; magic m. *D1240ff., (causes loss of memory) D1365.8, (charm) *D1241, (fluid) *D1242ff., (pill) *D1243, (powder) *D1246, (salve) *D1244; magic speed by eating magic m. D2122.1; St. Peter's grass as m. for snake-bite A2623; sham physician refuses to take his own m. K1955.7.

Medicines kill hero G347. — Conception from eating m. T511.8.2; origin

32*

of m. A1438; resuscitation by m. *E100ff.; trickster eats m. that physic him J2134.2.

Medicine-man. — Supernatural m. as helper N819.4.

Medicus F956.2.

Meditation as clerical virtue V461.5. — Magic power obtained by m. D1732.

Medusa. — Origin of Pegasus from neck of slain M. E783.2.1.

Meek. — Who are really m.? Cows, daughters H659.21.

Meeting certain persons (animals) as omen D1812.5.1.7, D1812.5.2.2; ghost causes sickness (madness) E265; old woman with water good omen D1812.5.2.2.1; to take place only after death M396. — Accidental m. with person involved in overcoming curse N718; giants m. larger giants F531.6.8.7; hero misses m. man he seeks N187; lovers' m. *T30ff.; men m. in narrow passage; rude retorts J1369.3; sham illness to escape m. K523.0.2; tabu to hold m. in certain place C853.1; women m. when bathing P611.

Meetings of the dead E490ff.; of witches in which church services are burlesqued G243. — Accidental m. N700—N799; devil appears at m. of witches G303.6.2.2.

Melody. — Leaves of tree make m. for saints F979.3; magic m. D1275.2.

Melon in murderer's hand turns to murdered man's head Q551.3.3.1. — Bringing m. 12 cubits long H1047; getting m. out of jar as resourcefulness test H506.8; great m. (lie) X1411.1; thanks for being hit by nut, not m. J2571; tribes emerge from m. A1236.2.

Melons. — Origin of m. A2687.2; ripe m. symbolic of marriageeable girls H611.1; vegetable lamb born from m. (as from eggs) B95.1.

Melting. — Bull m. away after evil spirit has issued from him F981.2; flood from ice m. A1016.3; heat m. enemies D2091.10; magic m. of ice D2144.5.2; magically m. snow D2143.6.4; magic poem causes man's m. D1402.15.1; person m. away from heat F1041.4; sword m. from battle heat F1084.0.1; stars m. chariots F961.2.6; sun m. glue on artificial wings F1021.2.1; witch's body m. stone G229.6.

Melusine *C31.1.2.

Member, see also **Genitals, Penis.** — Bodily m. sacrificed to save life J351; disenchantment with missing m. D702.1; loss of one m. after fairy abduction F329.3; missing bodily m. E419.7; recognition by missing m. H57; resuscitation with missing m. *E33; trickster with painted m. K1398.

Members. — Belly and the m. A1391, J461.1; bodily m. as advisers D1312.1; bodily m. wagered in gambling N2.3; disenchantment by cutting off and reversing bodily m. D712.1; magic bodily m. (animal) *D1010ff., (human) D990ff.; inability to find own m. J2020ff.; resuscitation by arrangement of m. *E30ff.; vital bodily m. E780ff.; witch with iron m. G219.1.

Memory test H1595. — Lost m. recovered in battle N645; magic object causes m. *D1366; magic m. D1910ff.; magic reawakening of m. D2006ff.; remarkable m. F692.

Mended. — Head of beheaded witch m. by rubbing with salt G223; object miraculously m. F1098.

Mendicant. See **Beggar.**

Menial hero L113.1. — Attention attracted by hints dropped by heroine as m. H151.5; disguise as m. *K1816; god serves as m. on earth *A181; heroine in m. disguise discovered in her beautiful clothes H151.6; punishment: noble person must do m. service *Q482; thief disguised as m. K311.12.

Menstrual period of 12 years claimed K1227.10.1. — Alleging m. pain to escape lover K1227.10; disease caused by m. blood A1337.0.4; ignorance at first m. period J1745.2; magic m. blood D1003.1; moon's waning caused by m. period A755.7.

Menstruation of men F569.2. — Couvade during wife's m. T583.1.0.2; origin of m. A1355; tabu connected with m. C140ff.

Mental. — Origin of m. and moral characteristics A1370ff.; dwarfs make promises with m. reservations F451.5.10.8; sun's m. powers A738.2.

Mentality. — Lie: remarkable m. X1010.

Mention. — Devil leaves at m. of God's name G303.16.8; love from mere m. or description T11.1.

Mentioning, see also **Speaking;** origin of supernatural wife forbidden C31.2; tabus *C400—C499. — Oath against m. secret M188.

Mentula loquens D1610.6.2.

Mercenary soldier (princess's lover) L161.3, (unsuitable as husband) T65.2 .

Merchant P431; as helper N851; rescues abandoned child R131.7. — Clever m. J1115.7; daughter of m. intimate with slave T91.5.1.1; devil as m. G303.3.1.19; disguise as m. to enter enemy's camp K2357.10; fortune from trifling sum sent abroad with m. N412; king in disguise of m. K1812.14.1; monk outwits m. depriving him of fowl J1638; paramour disguised as cloth m. K1517.9; prince in disguise as m. K1812.14; rich m. poor in happiness J347.4; seduction by posing as m. K1315.12; swindling m. suffocated Q274.2; thief disguised as m. K311.14; treacherous m. K2249.4; wife makes m. turn out queen S463.

Merchants try honesty for a year and find that it pays J23.

Merciful. — Christians have a m. God J1263.3; husband (wife) more m. than blood relations P212, P213.

Mercy. — God consults m. on his right A42.2; god of m. A483; olive branch laid on altar of M. as sacrifice V15.

Merit. — Officers praised in reverse from their real m. (trouble for them and their master) K2136.

Mermaid *B81ff.; rescues hero from shipwreck R138.1; rescues heroine who has been thrown overboard R137. — Child promised to m. S214;

giant son of king and m. F531.6.1.4; sight of m. bad omen D1812.5.1.9; siren in m. form B53.0.1; strong hero suckled by m. F611.2.2.

Mermaid's magic power D1719.7. — Possession of m. belt gives power over her D1410.4.

Mermaids give stones to fairies D2066.1.

Merman *B82ff.; forsaken by human wife C713; transformed to horse D131.1.

Message after a week J2192.1; of chastity: uncooked meat left behind T386; from Christ V211.10; of death fatal to sender *K1612; falsified to bring about lovers' death K1087.1; rewarded Q91.4. — Arrow as man's m. shows lion how terrible man himself must be J32; captive sends out secret m. R82; carrying m. to king's father in otherworld H1252.4; carrying his own m. J2242; consoling m. from the dead E361.2; death m. softened by equivocations K2313; false m. of love causes trouble K2132; false m. from otherworld causes man to go on pyre K929.12; falsified m. *K1851; foolish messenger muddles m. J2671.4; girl sends sign m. to prince H611.2; mealtimes from m. from God A1511.1; messenger without the m. J2192; miscarried m. of immortality as reincarnation origin E600.1; misunderstood m. causes messenger to be killed or accused N341; queen's m. on stone H1229.2; spirit delivers false m. F402.1.9; symbolic m. Z174; tabu: failing to heed m. of god C63.

Messenger of Death imprisoned R6; of the gods A165.2; to harem poses as singer K1323.1; sent away as only battle survivor N693; without the message J2192. — Animal as m. *B291ff.; animal sold as m. K131; bluff: trickster as deity's m. K1715.9; court m. P14.15.2; deity's m. can assume any guise A165.2.0.1; devil as m. to adulterers G303.9.4.5.2; earl throws water at m. F1041.16.11; fairy as m. F234.2.6; faithless widow ready to marry m. who brings news of husband's death T231.3; foolish m. muddles message J2671.4; identifying tokens sent with m. H82; king disguised as own m. K1812.15; lightning as God's m. A1141.5; no thanks to the m. J1358; origin of death: wrong m. goes to God A1335.1.1; pestilence brought to man by m. from Creator A1337.0.1.1; pretending to be m. from enemy's relative K477.3; proof that m. comes from certain person H242; provisions provided by m. from heaven D2105.2; rainbow spirit as m. F439.1.3; river as m. F932.5; why snipe m. for warriors A2261.6.

Messengers announce successive misfortunes N252. — Animals compete as m. to call father of newborn child H483; animals mistaken for m. J1762.0.1; death's m. J1051, Z111.6; discourtesy to Gods' m. punished Q221.1.1; enemy's m. mutilated Q451.1.6; four m. sent with four winds Z71.2.8; undesired suitor's m. imprisoned Q433.11.

Messiah. — Jewess makes parents believe that she is to give birth to the M. J2336.

Messiah's coming prophesied M363.2. — Tabus concerning time of M. advent C428, C897.3.

Messianic men beautiful F575.2.2. — Diseases cured in M. era D2161.6.2.

Metal tower F772.2; as defense against spirits D1385.5. — Animals of precious m. B101; breast broad and made of glittering m. F546.1; fairy chariot of precious m. F242.1.3; fence of m. or crystal in otherworld F169.5; flow of molten m. at end of world A1069; magic m. *D1252ff.; magic multiplication of m. D2106.1.3; men of m. F521.3; ogre killed by throwing hot m. into his throat G512.3.1; origin of m. ornaments A1465.3.3; origin of m.-working A1447; otherworld fortress of m. F163.5.1; punishment for burying m. E419.11; recognition through precious m. H91; tree with m. leaves F811.2.1.

Metals. — Acquisition of m. A1432; city of precious m. and stones F761; god of m. A492; mankind originates from m. A1247.

Metamorphosis, see also **Transformation;** brought about by baptism V813.

Metaphors literally interpreted J2470ff., J2489.

Metaphorical riddles H720ff. — Fire announced in m. language J1269.12.

Meteor. — Cannibal m. G11.8; god as m. A137.16; reincarnation as m. E646.

Meteors. — Origin of m. A788.

Mewing. — Cat's m. aids thieves K341.7.2; monster m. G346.1; witch causes person's m. G269.21.2.

Mice. See after **Mouse.**

Michael creates cat to destroy mouse A1751.1; and Gabriel drive Satan from heaven G303.8.1.2. — Angel M. created from fire A52.1.2; archangel M. as porter of heaven A661.0.1.3.

Michelangelo. — Presumptuous man's comment on M. J957.

Midas with ass's ears *F511.2.2, (secret discovered by barber) N465; with golden touch D565.1.

Midday. — Bigger fool in m. heat J1552.1.1.1; four legs in morning, two at m., three in evening (riddle) H761; ghosts walk at m. E587.1.

Middle. — Castle at m. point of earth F771.3.4; each of two wants to sleep in the m. J221.3.1; one eye in m. of forehead *F512.1.1, *F531.1.1.1, G303.4.1.2.1; wager: turning somersault in m. of square N56.

Midgard Serpent surrounds the earth *A876. — Thor battles M. serpent at end of world A1082.3.

Midge. — Skillful surgeon removes speck from eye of m. F668.2.

Midnight. — Between m. and cockcrow best time for unearthing treasure N555.1; burial at m. E431.19; cows kneel at m. on Christmas Eve B251.1.2.3; devil appears at m. G303.6.1.1; disenchantment at m. D791.1.8; disenchantment by naked virgin undergoing frightful journey at m. D759.3; disenchantment by taking key from serpent's mouth at m. D759.1; in dwarf land sunrise is at m. F451.4.6; flower found only at m. F814.3; ghost laid at m. E459.5; ghosts seen by those born at m. E421.1.1.1; ghosts walk at m. E587.5; mermaid appears at m. B81.3.1, B81.12.1; penance: holding m. mass until someone will make responses

Q521.6; stone moves at m. D1641.2.4; treasure reveals itself only on Christmas at m. N541.1; tree blossoms at m. F971.5.2.1; tree maidens bathe at m. F441.2.1.4; wild hunt appears at m. E501.11.1.1.

Midocean. — Tree in m. F811.4.1.

Midsummer V70.3.

Midsummer's Eve. — Sleeping with wife on M. tabu C751.2.

Midway. — Ghost lives m. between heaven and earth E481.5.

Midwife substitutes child for king's stillborn K1923.5. — Brownie rides for m. F482.5.4.1; devil is employed as a m. G303.9.3.2; fairies take human m. to attend fairy woman *F372.1; fool seeks a m. J2661.2; husband acts as m. when no woman is available T584.0.2; lover masks as pregnant woman to meet m. K1514.16; riddle about mother as m. H583.4.5; wolf offers to act as m. for sow K2061.6; woman assists tigress as m. B387.

Mightiest. — What is m.? Rain H631.6.

Migration of animals A2482ff. — Unusual m. of birds at Doomsday A1002.4, A1091.4.

Mild. — Priest who gives m. penances succeeds where others fail L361.

Mildness triumphs over violence L350ff.

Miles. — Carpet sixty m. square F783.1; man can hear ant leave nest fifty m. away F641.2; skillful marksman shoots left eye of fly at two m. F661.5.3; tree with coiling leaves three thousand m. high F811.2.3.1; tunnel of crystal four m. long F721.1.1.

Milesians foster Tuatha Dé Danann's children P273.4; invade Ireland F211.0.2.1.

Milestone. — Fairies assemble at m. F217.2.

Military affairs P550ff.; strategy K2350ff. — Absurdity of giving bishop m. mission J1536.1; quest to king for m. aid H1224.

Milk agitates at death E761.6.6; bath as poison antidote D1515.3; becomes bloody E761.1.10; bought on credit poured into one container K231.6.1; of "cow of plenty" tabu C241.1; dropping from woman's breast reveals her hiding R351.1; drunk from hero's skull gives strength M316; from finger F552.1.5; of the gods A154.4; goes long distance into child's mouth H495.2; gushes from cows in deity's presence H45.2; and honey flow in land F701.1; from the hornless cow J1512.1; as magic drink *D1043; magically appears in woman for orphan T611.6; in man's breast F546.6; overheated to break cat's taste for it K499.4; poured on tree roots D1658.1.5.2; -producing bird B36; sack transformed D454.5; from saint's cows forms lake F989.9; of special cow drunk by man to make wife fruitful T591.1.2; stays in overturned pail D2171.8; in stream as signal H135.2; suddenly appears in woman's dry breast T592; tasting of wine, honey F1094; transformed to blood D457.2; transformed into other substance D476.2.3; transformed to stone D471.4.1; turns dark E761.4.5; of two king's children protects hero in dragon fight D1385.14. — Air castle: pail of m. to be sold J2061.2; animal gives treasure as

m. B103.3; bath in magic m. rejuvenates D1338.4; bath of m. F872.1; bathing hair in buffalo m. makes it unusually long D1337.1.3.1; blow recalls mother's m. Z61.4; bird gives m. B735; boiling m. thought to be overflowing J1813.2; blood turns to m. D457.1.2; brewing ale from m. H1021.10; brotherhood through partaking of m. from same woman P313; carrying m. without spilling makes man forget God J94; charm makes cows give plenty of m. D1449.1; communication by pouring m. into stream K1549.5; cow gives marvelous m. through saint's virtue B597; cow's m. flows by itself B155.2.2; cows made to give bloody m. D2083.2; cow with inexhaustible m. D1652.3.1; cup full of m. symbolic offering to unwanted saint H607.4; cure by bathing in m. *D2161.4.14.1; cure by m. of Virgin Mary D2161.5.2.3; curse: cow will give red m. M471.1; disenchantment by bathing in m. D766.4; disenchantment from bird when queen milks own m. into bird's beak D759.2; disenchantment by drinking m. of queen who has borne two boys D764.1; doe furnishes man m. B292.3; does magically give m. D2156.1; dragon fed m. to keep him pacified B11.12.4.1; dragon likes m. B11.12.4; drinking m. tabu C271; dropping m. pregnancy sign T579.8.3.; dwarfs bewitch cows to give no m. *F451.3.3.5; eating thick m. forbidden C229.1; fairies m. cows F271.1; fairies m. mortal's cows dry F366.1; faithful woman must milk cow for saint's m. V229.2.3; flow of cow's m. increased by licking saint's garment D2182; flowers float on river of m. F814.6; fool takes wife's m., starves baby J2214.4; fountain gives m. on Sunday F716.1; god in sea of m. A151.8; horse fed with worms' m. B710.2.1; how banyan got its m. A2791.3; idol drinks m. D1633.1; infant bathed in m. T601; jester takes cow tells king people have m. U67; king demands m. from all hornless cows: given poison from wooden K839.4; king persuaded ocean of m. has curdled J811.5; lake of m. D921.3.1, (by tree of life) A878.2, (from saint's virtue) A920.1.13; lie about cow's rich m. X1235.2; life token: m. becomes red E761.6.2; living only on fairy cow m. F241.2.5; location of settlement at place a cow stops and where m. flows by itself B155.2.2; magic bag sucks m. from cows D1605.2; magic cow gives red m. *B182.1; magic cow gives extraordinary m. B184.2.1.1ff.; magic m. of animal *D1018; magic cure by bathing in m. D2161.4.14.1; magic healing m. D1500.1.33.1; magic m. produces immunity from hunger and thirst D1349.1.3; magic m. heals wounds D1503.7.1; man recognizes m. of stolen cows F647.5.3; martyrs' wounds emit m. V229.2.6; men fond of m. previously calves J2214.6; Milky Way as m. from breast of a woman A778.5; miraculous increase of cow's m. D2156.2; numskull puts the m. back into goat J1903.2; ocean of m. J2349.3; old woman gives m. F598; plant characteristics from Virgin Mary's m. A2731.2.1.1; plant from mother's m. A2615.2; pond of m. F713.4; pouring water instead of m. into large container K231.6.1.1; prayers believed to stop m. boiling over J1813.2.1; quest for lion's m. H1361; rain of m. J1151.1.3; recognition of son by gushing up of m. in mother's breasts H175.1; rejuvenation by burning and throwing bones into tub of m. D1886.1; resuscitation by bathing in m. E80.1.1; resuscitation by magic m. E102.1; rock becomes m. D476.1.7; river of m. F715.2.3; rivers of oil, m., wine, and honey in otherworld F162.2.6; saint makes lake of m. V229.16; sea of m. F711.2.1; snake eats bread and m. with child B765.6; snake sucks woman's m. A2435.6.2.1, B765.4.1; spring augments mothers' m. D927.3; strength from drinking mother's m. F611.2.0.1; strong man sent to m. lions: brings lions back with him F615.2.1; tabu to eat m. with meat C229.5; test of mother by weighing m. J1142.1; water turns to m. D478.1; watered m. sold K287; well of m. D925.0.2; wife offers starving husband m. from her breasts T215.2; wise men and fool pour m. into tank J1149.12; witch curdles m. D2083.2.2; witch snared by setting out m. G274.1; woman created from sour m. A1275.5.

Milk-bottle. — Child feeds snake from its m. B391.1.

Milk-cup. — Thistle serves as m. for Virgin Mary A2711.4.2.

Milked. — Cow comes to be m. for infant saint B251.2.10.1; cow grateful for being m. B294; cows m. dry by vampire E251.3.2; cows m. at night by snake B765.4; magic bull can be m. B184.2.3.2.

Milker. — Skillful m. F678.

Milking into mouth directly J2173.8; unruly cow H1155.2. — Absurd ignorance about m. animals J1905; husband m. cow blindfolded K1516.5; task: m. a bull H1024.1; transformation to aid m. buffaloes D659.13; unusual m. animal B531.2.

Milkmaid. — Forgotten fiancée reawakens husband's memory by serving as m. and talking to calf *D2006.1.2; proud m. tosses her head (air castle) J2061.2.

Milky Way. — God's palace on M. A151.6.1; origin of M. A778; water monster becomes M. D429.1.

Mill gives birth to horse J1531.1.1; made to turn backwards D2089.4; -mouse told field mouse is dead F405.7.1; slaying scene, grinds red wheat Z141.2.2; as symbol of saint Z185. — Ass jealous of horse but sees horse later working in a m. L452.1; automatic m. D1601.21; crushing in rice m. as punishment Q414.3.1; devil as builder of m. G303.9.1.3; dwarf king (lives in a m.) F451.4.2.5, (turns m. which produces gold) F451.5.1.5.1; earth swallows m. which refused saint's grain Q552.2.3.2.1; fright at m. noise J2615.1; fugitive slave takes refuge in m. house, where he must work harder than ever N255.4; gigantic m. in otherworld F163.4; greyhounds drag m. out of water (lie) X1215.12; grinding up in a m. as punishment Q469.3; magic m. *D1263; murder by grinding in m. S116.1; spirits keep m. from working F416.1; self-grinding salt-m. *D1601.21.1; strong man drags m. F631.1; strong man sent to devil's m. F615.1; wild hunt appears at old m. E501.12.10; youths grind in m. of underworldlings F106.

Mill's clatter thought to be pursuers J1789.3.

Miller P443; of hell A677.2; rescues abandoned child R131.2; rescues princess R131.2.1; refuses to sell house to king P411.1; his son, and the ass try to please everyone J1041.2. — Double-cheating m. K486; fairies lame m. F361.17.1.

Miller's tale (Chaucer) K1225, K1522, K1577.

Millers. — Jokes about m. X210ff.

Millet. — Bear husks m. B571.4; why m. is red on top A2793.8.

Milliner P452.

Milling. — Origin of m. A1442.

Millipede. — Fight between snake and m. B264.4.

Millstone among best of stones H659.3.1; dropped on guilty person Q412; hung around neck Q469.4; kills giantess F451.10.2.1; preferred to jewels J245.1. — Baby drags m. F611.3.2.2; dwarfs suspend large m on a thin thread F451.5.4.2; magic m. D1262.1; magic m. guards treasure N581.1; man transformed to m. D231.1; numskull sticks his head into the hole of a m. J2131.5.4; self-grinding m. D1601.20; stealing m. J2461.1.7; strong man lifts m. F624.2.1; strong man attacked with m. puts it on as collar F615.3.1; task: sewing together a broken m. H1023.7.

Millstones said to be pearls of the hero's mother K1718.2. — Waters dissolve m. F930.7.

Mill-wheel. — Giant with m. as shield F531.4.1.

Mimicking. — Fool thinks goat m. him J1835.

Minaret. — Bathroom in the m. J2237; scorned lover plunges from m. top T75.6.

Mind. — Discontented ass longs for death but changes m. when he sees skins of dead asses at fair J217.2; partial transformation: animal with human m. D682.3; power of m. over body U240ff.; strength of m. wins contest H1562.14.

Minding. — Reward for m. own business H1554.2.

Mine ghosts E336; spirits F456. — "All of these are m." K1917; difference between "m." and "thine" J179.1; ghost haunts m. E275.1; rich m. discovered N596; voice warns of danger in m. V542; whistling in m. tabu C480.1.1; wraith before m. disaster E723.8.1.

Mines found where balls fall N533.5.

Miner. — Imprisoned m. kept alive by masses performed by his wife V41.1.

Miner's. — Dwarf king has silver m. torch bright as the sun F451.7.4.

Miners. — Devil compels two m. to follow him G303.9.5.3; ghosts annoy m. E336.2; knockers aid m. F456.1.2.2; knockers hide m. tools F456.1.2.1.2; knockers' malicious action against m. F456.1.2.1; knockers as spirits of dead m. F456.1.1.3.

Mineral. — Birth from m. T544; dwarf cave has ceiling of m. white as snow F451.4.3.3; man made from m. substance A1240ff.; man transformed to a m. form D230ff.; reincarnation as m. E645; transformation: m. form to person D432.

Minerals. — Origin of m. A978.

Mining. — Origin of m. A1448.

Minister aids woman escape devil G303.12.5.4; in generosity contest H1552.2; makes gardener king: king decides against him in law case M13.3; taught obeisance to king J80.2; tells king to do what seems good J814.5. — Choir imitates apologizing m. J2498.1; clever m. J1115.10.2; falsely accused m. reinstates himself by his cleverness K2101; ghost laid by m. E443.2.4; housemaid disguised as m. K1839.10; king asks m. for new trick H1182.2; king propounds riddles and questions to his clever m. *H561.5; king's enigmatic order to m. H587; prime m. leaves king in anger H1385.12; royal m. rescues abandoned queen R169.7; treacherous m. K2248; washerman failure as m. U129.3; woman in disguise made m. K1837.8.1.

Minister's daughter to marry first arriving bachelor T62.2; son recovers prince's lost wife R131.11.5. — Clever m. daughter J1111.5; devil visible to one who walks in m. holy shoes G303.6.2.4; treacherous m. son K2248.1.

Ministers. — Royal m. P110ff.

Minivet. — Why tail of m. is red A2378.8.5.

Mink as culture hero A522.1.5. — Burnt smell of m. A2416.2; cat sold as m. skin K261.1; color of m. A2411.1.2.5; enmity between raven and m. A2494.13.7, A2494.12.5.

Minotaur B23.1.

Minstrel repays cobbler for stealing songs J1632. — Clever m. gets new robe J1115.5.1; fairy m. F262.3; fairy m. asks admission to heaven as reward Q172.0.1; fairy m. learns mortals' heroic deeds F393.1; lover masks as m. K1371.4.2; prince disguised as m. R24.2.

Miracle attests fact that man does not need to confess V29.3; manifested to nonbelievers *V340ff.; must wait till one man is sacrificed K1785; to permit confession V23; saves saint from unjust censure V229.2.11; wrought for animal B255. — Conversion to Christianity through m. V331.1; corpse exclaims over m. E545.10; escape from undesired lover by m. T321; foolish imitation of m. J2411; masses work m. V41; seduction on threat of performing m. K1315.6.2; sham m.: may the grass grow up K1975; tabu to use m. for trifling purpose C96.

Miracles F900; performed under Virgin's protection V268; at shrine V113.0.1. — Saint asked to perform m. as test H257; saint performs m. while yet unborn T579.5; sham m. K1970ff.; sham relics perform m. V142.1.

Miraculous birth *T540ff.; blindness as punishment Q451.7.0.2; conception T510ff.; manifestation (acclaims saint) *V222, (at birth of holy person) *F960.1, (at confession) V24, (during act of charity) V412, (to scoffers of the Cross) V86.4; power of prayer *V52; powers of relics V144; punishments Q550ff.; rescue R122; rescue of children R131.0.2; reward Q140ff., (for charities) V411; working of the host V34. — Flame as m. index *F1061; holy person loses m. powers after son born

V229.20.1; incredulity as to sacredness of host confounded by m. appearance V33.1; imitation of m. horse-shoeing unsuccessful J2411.2; Jews bribe woman to steal host for them: m. manifestation V35.1; magic object confers m. powers D1561ff.; recognition by m. sight of seer H184; tasks requiring m. speed H1090ff.

Miraculously. — Host m. given when it is refused a man by the priest V32; sacred image m. appears on stolen sacrament V35.1.2.

Mirage K1886.1.

Miriam's. — Miracles cease at M. death F900.3.1.

Mirror begrimed by snail J451.4; held up to show whom he loves T91.6.1.1; -reflection makes dupe think he is captive K1883.7; transformed to mountain D454.12. — Breaking m. as evil omen D1812.5.1.3; bridal couple look in m., heads knocked together T135.13; clairvoyant m. *D1323.1; devil appears when woman looks at herself in m. after sunset G303.6.1.4; dragon attacks own image in m. K1052; girl borrows m. from fairy F324.1; image in m. mistaken for picture J1795; life token: m. becomes black E761.4.3; love through sight in magic m. T11.7; magic m. *D1163, (as chastity index) H411.15, (kills enemy soldiers) D1400.1.13, (quest for lost) H1346; magic wishing m. D1470.1.38; numskull steals m. J2461.1.7.1; peacock admires self in m. W116.4; standing before m. with eyes shut to see how one looks in his sleep J1936; sword as m. F833.3.1; taking m. to bed to see if he sleeps with mouth open J1936.1; transformation by looking in m. D579; treasure found by clairvoyant m. N533.2.

Mirrors. — Guardian beast overcome by m. K335.1.7; sun and moon metal m. in sky A714.4.

Misappropriation of goods K254, K361, punished M368.

Miscarriage. — Charm prevents m. D1501.1; child born from m. T549.4.

Mischief maker, see also **Trickster.** — Friar Rush as m. maker F470.0.1.

Misconstruction. — Literal m. of order to get revenge J2516.0.1.

Misdeed. — Man unable to persuade wife to confess m. to priest succeeds when he makes her drunk U181.

Misdeeds. — Parents' m. innocently betrayed by children J125.

Misdirected kiss K1225. — Accidental death through m. weapon N337; pursuer m. by animal R243.1; pursuer m. by tree to help fugitive D1393.4.

Misdirecting. — Confederate m. pursuer K646.

Miser breaks legs to retrieve single grain J2146.1; enticed by "money tree" report K341.28; goes to mass before committing usury K2097; induced to enter bag, caught K711.2.1; picks up everything H614.1; tricks thieves into digging field K2316; tries to eat money, chokes to death Q272.3. — Bad choice between poor man and m. J229.6; devil marries old maid who proves to be m. G303.12.3; gold causes man to become m. G303.9.8.5; spirit transports m. to treasure F414.2; thief robs blind m. K2096.2; trickster feigns deafness and gets hospitality from m. K1981.1.

Miser's treasure stolen (advised to imagine his treasure still there) J1061.4.

Miserliness *W153.

Misfortune with oneself to blame the hardest U160ff. — Cloud symbol of m. Z156; consolation in m. J850—J899; distance from happiness to m. (riddle) H685; escape from one m. into worse N255; faithfulness of married couple in m. T215; ghost haunts place of great m. E275; man pursued by m. N251; prophecy of general m. M340.3; prophecy of great m. M340.6.

Misfortunes. — Equanimity despite m. W25.1; poor man consoles self by thinking of m. of rich J883.

Misgovernment. — Ruler diverts attention from m. by beginning war K2381.

Misguiding. — Devil m. people G303.9.9.6.

Misinforming. — Man m. competitors on quest H1239.4.

Misleading. — Devil m. travelers G303.9.9.7; ghost m. traveler E272.5.

Mismanagement of king's treasury a mortal offense P13.2.

Misplaced genitalia A1313.3. — Resuscitation with m. head *E34.

Misreported remarks K1775, message A1335.1, K1851.

Misrepresentation. — Unique weapon obtained by m. K362.0.1.

Misshapen child from brother-sister incest T550.3.

Missile thrown among enemy causes them to fight one another K1982.1. — Disenchantment by striking with a m. D712.3.1; magic m. *D1093; suitor contest: aiming with m. H331.7; weapon (m.) miraculously removed F959.3.4.

Missing. — Disenchantment with m. member *D702.1; druid finds m. person D1816.5; person with m. member cannot rest in grave E419.9; quest for m. ring H1386.2; recognition by m. hair H75.6; resuscitation with m. member *E33.

Mission. — Falsely accused hero sent on dangerous m. K2102; tabus for men on m. C833.9.

Missionary. — Disguise as m. K1826.4.

Mist as barrier to otherworld F141.2; on mirror as life token E761.4.3. Deity arises from m. A115.3; egg transformed to m. D469.1; extraordinary m. F962.10; fairy m. mistaken for enemy smoke K2369.9; fairies's magic m. F278.2; giant disappears in m. F531.6.12.1.1; land of m. F704; magic m. D902.1, (aids fugitive) R236.1, (battle defense) D2163.4, (causes person to become lost) D1418.1, (of invisibility) D1361.1, K532.1, (protects against attack) D1381.22, (separates person from his companions) D1361.1.1; man shoots into wreath of m. and brings down fairy *F302.4; origin of m. A1134; saints create concealing m. V229.8; soul as m. E744.1; transportation from heaven in m. F61.3; trying to swim in m. J1821.1; universe created from m. A623.

Mists which lead astray K1886.2.

Mistake. — Servant refused payment because of single m. K231.9.

Mistakes. — Account-book of m. J1371.

Mistaken identity J1485; hasty killing or condemnation N340ff. — Animal or person m. for something else J1760; giant's glove m. for house F531.5.2; objects with m. identity J1770ff.; one thing m. for another J1750—J1809.

Mistletoe prevents barrenness D1501.1.1. — Magic m. *D965.4; prophecy: death by m. *M341.2.1.

Mistreated orphan hero L111.4.4. — Devil promises to help m. apprentice G303.22.12.

Mistreatment by poltergeist F473.3; of prisoners R51.

Mistress aids task H974.1; deceives lover with a substitute *K1223; disguised as wife K1843.1.1; identified by chalk marks H58.1; who saves lover H592.3; summoned by wish D2074.2.3.1. — Arrogant m. repaid in kind by her lover L431; bower for fairy's m. D2185.1; choice of friend over m. J496; disguise as m. enables murder D40.2.1; fairy m. F302ff., (insists man leave wife) F302.5.4, (strikes human lover) F361.17.9, (surrenders man to mortal wife) F302.5.1; foolish lover sees no flaws in m. J1737; former m. as sons' foster mother P272.3; incognito m. T476, (overhears lover, leaves him) J2364; lover arrives home just as m. is to marry another *N681; maid behind statue of Virgin advises m. to give servants better food K1971.3.1; magician carries m. with him in his body *F1034.2; moon mutilates earth m. S160.5; otherworld m. helps hero H335.0.1.1; priest gives up parish and immediately loses fickle m. J705.1; quest for vanished m. H1385.3; Rakshasa's m. decapitated G369.1.7; servant repays stingy m. J1561.4; sham illness to escape m. K523.0.1.1; sister as robber's m. K2212.0.2; taking friend's m. K2297.2; treacherous m. K2231; wife has been m. of servant, knight, fool, and priest J1545.2; wife dismisses maid, husband's m. J1112.2; wife sends disguised m. to husband K1843.1.1; wife substitutes for m. K1223.3; wife takes place of m. in husband's bed K1843.2; wife transformed to m. D659.7; winning m. hard on heart J2572.

Mistress's descendant to serve handmaid's M369.2.5; nose cut off for faithlessness Q451.5.1.1. — Exposing m. person to public Q476; thief steals m. ornaments K346.6.

Misunderstanding. — Animal m. remark flees victim K547.5; criminal confesses because of m. of a dialect N275.2; helpful animal killed through m. B331ff.; task assigned from m. H946.

Misunderstandings due to language difference J2496.2. — Absurd m. J1750—J1849.

Misunderstood message causes messenger to be killed (accused) N341; wife banished by husband S411.1; words lead to comic results X111.7. — Criminal confesses because of m. animal cries N275.1; physical phenomena m. J1810ff.

Mite. — Casting of image of Buddha delayed until maniac's m. is thrown into furnace V125.

Mithian. — Village founded where m. bellows B155.2.1.

Mitten transformed to dog D444.10.2.

Mixed. — All joys m. with sorrow J171.2.2; blood of contractors m. to seal bargain M201.1.1; society, like a dish, must be m. J81.1.

Moaning ghost E402.1.1.2; waves F931.4.2.

Moccasins. — Magic m. *D1065.4; man with fire m. G345; ogre's own m. burned K1615.

Mock, see also **Sham;** battle to scare enemy K2368.2; sunrise K1886.3.

Mockers. — Wild hunt harmful to m. E501.18.1.1.

Mocking punished Q288. — Birds m. ascetic B787; ghost punishes person for m. him E235.1; tabu: m. animal C94.3.

Models. — Tribes from clay m. A1610.6.

Moderate request rewarded; immoderate punished *Q3.

Modest choice best L210ff.; woman forced to disrobe, outwits robber K551.4.3. — Absurdly m. wish J2076.

Modesty brings reward L200—L299; of God A102.15; personified Z139.6. —Bride's false m.: wears clothes to bed K2052.1; false m. *W136; king's m. P12.14; parable on M. having no address J91; Zeus gives man m., but it leaves when love enters T1.

Modus Liebinc J1532.1.

Mogli flower. — Why the m. is cursed A2721.6.

Mohammed goes to the mountain J831; lures doves to ears, claims God sends them K1962.1.

Mohammedan. — Riddle: what is the best religion, Christian or M. H659.5.

Moistest. — What is m.? H659.8.

Mole pretends that he sees, smells, and hears J958; struck on head while stealing fire: hence flat head A2213.5.1; as trickster killed in his own tunnel K1642. — Why m. is blind A2332.6.5, A2239.8, A2378.1.4; why m. burrows underground A2491.3; burying the m. as punishment K581.3; creation of m. A1893; why m. has hand like man A2375.2.6; giant's soul in m. E714.9; helpful m. B449.2; why m. lives underground A2433.3.20; where m. got tail A2332.6.5, A2378.1.4.

Mole's. — Why m. "hands" are turned backward A2375.2.7.

Moles. — Golden wagon drawn by m. F861.1.1.

Molten. — Devil holds m. coin in mouth G303.4.8.2; flow of m. metal at world's end A1069.

Moly (magic plant) *D965.5.

Moments thought years D2012. — Years seem m. to creator D2011.3; years seem m. while man listens to song of bird D2011.1.

Monarch, see **King.**

Monastery site magically indicated D1314.4.0.1. — Accepting blow from m. superior H1553.4; anchor catching in submarine m. N786; bell from underwater m. F725.6; burning m. for monks' incontinence Q414.0.3.1; quest to submarine m. H1287; saint's m. to be persecuted M364.1; submarine m. F133.3; thief as monk robs m. K311.4; Virgin becomes m. abbot K1837.7; witch lives in m. G235; woman disguised as monk enters m. P425.3.3.

Monasteries V118.

Monday after May Day tabu C751.4; unlucky day N128.2. — Judgment day on M. E751.7.

Money, see also **Treasure;** borrowed from fairies F358; from broken statue J1853.1.1; cannot be kept from where it is destined to go N212; given by dwarfs F451.5.1.5; does not always bring happiness J1085; of the hardhearted transformed to scorpions D444.1; hidden where object jumps E539.1f.; hung on tree stolen K331.6; left on hill to repay helpful mountain-men F460.4.2.2; loss as punishment Q595.4; from offertory as cure *D1500.1.10.3; received from ghosts as reward for bravery E373.1; in the stick J1161.4; spent for vanity W116.2; tempts anchorite V475.5; tests friendship H1558.7; tested by throwing it into stream to see if it will swim J1931; thrown to frogs J1851.1.1; tied on corpse thrown overboard from ship in order to secure burial V64; to be taken from chest only twice C762.5; transformed to ashes D475.2.3; transformed to pewter D475.2.4; turns to counterfeit C939.2; vanishes after saint ransoms prince K236.3.1; will grow if buried J2348. — Accidental acquisition of m. N630ff.; "Agnus dei" as a prayer for m. J1741.2; alchemist steals m., claims he made it K1966.1; animal earns m. for master B579.7; animal handles m. B294.2; blind men duped into fighting: m. to be divided K1081.1; borrowing m. from fairy F342.2; carrying off huge quantity of m. (task) H1127; Chapperbands coin false m. A1689.8; child proves his innocence by choosing apple rather than m. H256; child sold for m. S221ff.; children envious of m. given by deceased father to bishop V415; city without provisions but with much m. starves J712.1; coin left in m. scales betrays secret wealth N478; dead dog transformed to m. D422.2.1; dead husband protests wife's spending his m. E221.4; dead returns to repay m. debt E351; dead supplies tribe with m. E373.4; deposit m. secured by false order to banker's wife K362.6; devil's m. G303.21ff.; devils carry away stones of church built with ill-gotten m. Q274.1; "don't travel without m." J21.39; dwarf promises m. to mortal father for hand of daughter F451.5.18.1; eavesdropping sexton duped into giving supplial m. K464; escape by throwing m. for guards to fight over K626.1; fairies give mortal m. F342; feeding stolen m. in flour to animal K366.0.1; fool stops hole with m. J1851.3.1; fools send m. by rabbit J1881.2.2; ghost demands stolen m. E236.5; ghost rebukes those withholding church's m. E415.2; ghost seeks return of stolen m. E236.8; ghosts laid by giving beggars m. E451.5.1; half m. paid for half-milk, half-water J1551.9; heller thrown into others' m. K446; helpful cat borrows measure for his master's m. K1954.1; horse-headed men become m.-lenders E605.8; inexhaustible purse furnishes m. D1451ff.; judge's ruse to obtain m. from rich J1192.1.2; king caught trying to steal man's m. M205.4; king fleeing without m. L410.2; labor contract: as much m. as my companion (strong man) can carry F613.2.1; luck only with honestly earned m. N143; man divides m. into three (four) parts H585.1, W11.3; man eats up m. before dying W151.7; man lacking m. better than money lacking a man J482.2.1; miser enticed by "m. tree" report K341.28; miser trying to eat m. chokes to death Q272.3; numskull gives away old water bag in which m. is hid J2093.1; numskull puts m. into exchange so as to participate in business J2428; object transformed to m. D475.2; origin of m. A1433; payment with the clink of the m. J1172.2; penniless wooer: m. in hand K1917.2; planting m. in hole J2489.12; possession of m. brings luck N135.2; pseudo-magic m.-dropping ass K249.3; putting m. in sheep's anus J1851.4; quest for m. in hell H1275; recovering m. owed by a foreign king (task) H1182.1; return from dead to demand m. stolen from corpse E236.5; ruler settles quarrel between loser, finder of m. W11.6; secret wealth betrayed by m. left in borrowed m.-scales N478; selling a sheep and bringing it back along with the m. H1152.1; sending back by venal judge for rest of the m. J2662; shower of silver (m.) F962.8.1; sons given equal amounts of m. H501.3; speaking of lost m. tabu C401.3.1; spirits give m. to mortal F403.1; star drops from heaven: is m. F962.3; stealing m. while kissing it K378; stick with m. in it breaks and betrays thief H251.3.4; stingy man forced to share his m. when he lies and says he has none W152.4; tabu: giving certain m. away C783.1; tabu: misuse of m. in alms box C51.1.4; taking m. instead of revenge J229.11; thief hides in m. bag K307.1; tree gives m. to good brother D1663.6; transformation: water to m. D475.2.2; theft of m. from fairies F351; trickster reports lost m.: searchers leave him in possession of premises K341.1; unknown prince reared by fisher spends m. for princely tastes H41.5.1; unlucky man given a loaf filled with m. exchanges it N351; Virgin Mary returns borrowed m. and reveals cheat V252.1; vow never to touch m. M172.1; wife keeps half of m. for shrine W152.17.

Money-lender. — Stones turn to gold for charitable m. V411.4.

Money-stick. — Robber's m. K437.4.

Mongoose with golden hair, silver ears B101.9; leads to witch's house G402.2. — Creation of m. A1857; enmity of m. and snake A2494.12.2; helpful m. B433.4; reincarnation as m. E612.7; woman slays m. which has saved her child B331.2.1.

Mongooses. — King of m. B241.2.14.

Monk, see also **Cleric, Priest;** appropriates girl's dowry K361.4; who did not ask for the position made abbot Q61.1; avoids flattery V461.6; becomes husband at night K1915.1; confesses intention to rob monastery V21.3; who dies without his cowl cannot rest in grave E411.7; discouraged by large amount of work to be done persuaded to undertake but a small amount each day J557.1; escapes sin by living alone J495;

fails to escape work J215.4; falsely accuses novice of laziness K2129.1; forces devil to sing hymn G303.8.1.2.1; goes into desert to avoid women T334.1; learns about temptation U231.1; leaves monastery after seeing devil: sees scores in world U230.0.1; who has left his order (forgiven and miraculously reinstated) V475.2, (punished) V475.1; loses temper at cup W185.4; loses temper at overturned cup H1553.5; neglecting to prostrate self punished Q223.13.1; obedient only as long as work is agreeable W126.1; outwits merchant depriving him of fowl J1638; under pressure from abbot forgives the crucifix which has fallen and hurt him U221; resists woman he formerly loved T331.8; says that he is a stallion J1361; seduces girl afloat in box K1367; tells parable of modesty J91; unsuccessfully tempted in nunnery T331.1. — Angel shows m. value of work, prayer H605; devil blamed by m. who takes what does not belong to him G303.25.10; devil comes out of man when m. recognizes the devil's voice in man G303.16.19.7; devil as old woman seduces m. G303.3.1.12.4; devils cause m. to perspire and stay away from church service V5.3; dissatisfied m. admonished W128.5; doves show m. treasure B562.1.3; feigned ignorance to keep hero as m. K1792.2; disappointed lover becomes m. T93.2; first m. A1546.3.2; hospitality to m. rewarded Q45.3.1; incognito princess travels as m. K1812.8.2; incontinent m. V465.1.1; layman made to believe that he is a m. J2314; lion disguised as m. K1822.1; lover disguised as m. or friar meets sweetheart K1826.1.1; paramour disguised as m. K1517.6; peasant exchanges places with m. U119.2; penance: adulteress masks as m. and lives chastely in monastery Q537.1; reward to almsgiving m. Q44.1; self-righteous m. rebuked by abbot L435.1.1; stupid m. recovers stolen flocks L141.1; thief becomes m. to rob monastery K311.4; truthful m. refuses to cheat even for his order V461.2; Virgin Mary has dissolute m. buried in consecrated ground (his only mass is that of the Virgin) V255; Virgin Mary reproves m. who sleeps at altar V5.1; Virgin pardons overworked m. for neglecting prayers V276.2; vow to become m. if execution escaped M183.4; woman kicks lecherous m. down stairs T322.1; woman has husband made m. while he is drunk K1536; devil disguised as m. K1961.3.

Monk's enemies quarrel and thus save him J581.3; cordon saving him from hell J1261.8; curse M411.15; lust conquered by cruelty T317.6; prayers weave garment for Virgin V276.1.

Monks P426.3; sacrifice themselves S263.5.2; sharing with poor receive supplies Q141.1; shrive selves clean under threat of complete exposure of their sins by brother possessed of fiend V29.2. — Animal m. B252.1; bishop wishes all m. were castrated X457.1; cardinal's decision on m. sounding matins J1179.13; chastity tests of m. H426; twenty-four nuns for twelve m. J1264.9; two m. renew their appetites (locked up for a day) J1606.

Monks' bread given to poor inexhaustible V412.2; revenge on millers X214. — Monastery burned for m. incontinence Q414.0.3.1.

Monkey as animals' king B240.12; attracts attention of mowers until young birds can fly away from the harvest field K644; borrows deer's tail A2241.11; buys liquor B294.2.2; causes girl to cry: eats her food K461.2; cheats fox of bananas K171.9; cuts throat in imitating cobbler J2413.4.3; cut in two becomes two D1652.9; in danger on bridge of crocodiles pretends that king has ordered them counted K579.2; destroys nest of bird who has made sport of him Q295; as domestic servant B292.2.1; dresses in dead mistress's gown K1839.3; gives tiger sore-producing ointment K1043.1; gives wrong answer to princess H343.2; a god A132.2; instead of girl in floating basket K1625; jumps into water after a butterfly J2133.10; jumps over a ravine with his sword girded on and falls to his death J2133.2; jumps through body of tiger F916.1; killed by girls pretending to wash it K831.2; -like people F529.8; and lost lentil J344.1; lures tiger into tree, sets it afire K812.3; mistaken for nobleman J1762.6; paramour B611.6; plays chess B298.1; released: grateful B375.5; safe in tree insults gorilla *W121.2.6; saved from trap by feigning marriage K579.4; shows husband how to rule T252.2.2; sneezes in king's presence: killed J2413.6; terrified by tiger attacking his shadow J1790.3; tricked into drowning self K891.3; transformed to other animal D411.5ff.; transformed to person D318.1. — Abduction by m. R13.1.7; buying m. instead of cow J2081.4; charm to catch hare and m. D1444.2; color of m. A2411.1.5.1; crocodile opens mouth, m. escapes K561.3; disease to be cured by heart of m. K961.1; enmity of m. and (leopard) A2494.2.7, (lion) A2494.7.1; escape in m. skin K521.1.3; fakir returns to m. friends W34.4; friendships of m. A2493.14; ghost as man-m. E423.2.9; hair transformed to m. D447.1.1; helpful m. B441.1; how m. got its tail A2378.1.8; man given members by m. A1225.2.1; man transformed to m. D118.2; man tries to kill m. rescuer W154.5.1.2; marriage to m. B601.7; marriage to person in m. form B641.7; patient laughs at m., cures self N641.1; pay for teaching m. to talk K491.1; person plans to marry m. B601.7.1; pet m. in sheet frightens owner K1682.1; prince married to m. fairy F302.11; rebirth as m. prophesied M354.1; reincarnation as m. E612.12; speaking m. B211.2.10; transformation into m. Q551.3.2.4; transformation: handkerchief to golden m. D454.3.2.2; wedding of m. B281.10; why m. lives in tree A2433.3.19; why m. has first fruits of harvest A2433.3.19.1; woman bears m. T554.4.

Monkey's money stolen B294.2.1. — Cause of m. walk A2441.1.1; snake's brain as only cure for m. disease K961.2.1; thorn removed from m. tail B381.2; why m. buttocks red A2362.1; why m. face black A2330.3; why m. tail is short A2378.4.6.

Monkeys attack by throwing coconuts B762; carry off tortoise's salt K343.4; construct bridge across the ocean B846; copy men B786; plan to found city but desist J648.1. — Birhors eat m. A1422.2; devils in form of m. G303.3.3.2.7; king of m. B241.2.2; kingdom of m. B221.1; man carried off by m. steals magic cups K311.6.2; man descended from m.

A1224.5; men as m. without tails A1224.5.1; merchant traps robbing m. J1115.7.1; promise to return m. to their human form T68.5; war of m. and grasshoppers B263.6; why m. do not fall from trees A2576.

Monogamy among animals A2497.

Monopoly. — Fee from two persons for the same m. K441.3.

Monotony of one favorite food: compared to marriage J81.0.1.

Monsoon's origin A1129.2.

Monster born because of hasty wish of parents *C758.1; disguises and wins girl K1918; guards door of habitable hill F721.2.2; as hero L112.1; killed from within K952; with life in neck E714.8; turning over causes lake overflow F713.3; ungrateful for rescue W154.2. — Abduction by m. R11; all-swallowing m. F911.6; bride's m.-father T172.3; daughter promised to m. as bride to secure flower (bird) she has asked for S228; devastating m. G346; devil puts convert's body on sea m. M219.2.6; disenchantment of m. when prince promises to marry the monster's mother D741; earthquakes (from movements of subterranean m.) A1145.1; (from sea m.) A1145.2; earth rocks at m. fight F969.4.2; eclipse caused by m. devouring sun or moon A737.1; fairy becomes ape-headed m. D49.3; fettered m. A1070ff.; four-headed m. B15.1.2.3.1; giant sea m. B877.1ff.; girl married to (enamored of) m. T118; god reincarnated as m. E652; grateful m. helpful to hero N812.5; hero conquers sea m. A531.4; hero as sacrifice to m., kills him K1853.2.1; hero shoots m. and follows it into lower world F102.1; insects from body of slain m. *A2001; invulnerability bestowed by many-headed m. D1846.2; killing m. as suitor test H1174; magic adhesion to m. *D2171.2; magic object received from m. D826; magic object vomited by m. D826.1; magic power of m. child D1717.1; periodic sacrifices to m. S262; person transformed to m. D494; plague as m. F493.0.1.1; sea m. G308; severed heads of m. become birds E613.0.5; skull transformed to water m. D447.2; snake from blood of slain m. A2145.1; strong man slays m. F628.1.0.1; tabu: finding age of m. C821; tabu to tell children about lake m. C423.6; transformation to m. D47; watch for devastating m. H1471; water m. becomes Milky Way D429.1; water m. dragged to house by horse K1022.2.1; youngest daughter to marry m. L54.1.

Monster's arm token of dog's innocence H105.3; blood makes tree poisonous D1563.2.2; returning head G635.1. — Dying m. request and promise M257; fettered m. chains renewed A1074.7; magic from reversing m. orders D1783.4.

Monsters *G301; kill each other off A1087. — Battle of gods and m at end of world A1082; cannibal m. G11.16; culture hero overcomes m. *A531; entrance to otherworld guarded by m. F150.2; killing m. as suitor task H335.3.7; magic spring guarded by demons (m.) D927.2; path between m. G333; saint's bachall keeps off m. D1385.8; stepbrothers kill m. P283.1; saint overcomes m. V229.4; valley full of m. F756.5.1; youths, maidens yearly tribute to m. S262.2.1.

Monsters' birth at world's end A1070.1. — Flood from m. conflict A1015.1.1.

Monstrous births *T550ff., (from incest) A1337.0.7, (as punishment for girl's pride) Q552.5; child exposed S325.0.1; creatures in otherworld F167.11; gods A123; offspring from animal marriage B634; persons F510ff. — Cannibal with m. features G11.11; curse: m. birth M437; god m. as to body A123.1ff.; ogres with m. features G360ff.; woman deserts husband for m. lover T232.

Mont Saint Michel built by devil G303.9.1.11.

Month of May is greenest (riddle) H646.1. — Fasting the first m. J2135.1; full moon and thirtieth of m. (enigma) H582.1.1; tree bears fruit each m. F811.18.1; woman bears child every m. T586.5.1.

Months. — Determination of m. A1160ff.; twelve m. as youths seated about fire Z122.3.

Monuments. — Origin of erection of m. to mark boundaries A1599.2; priest uses fortune dishonestly made to erect m. to himself W157.1.

Moon A740—A759; blessed for beautiful light L351.2; bloody at Crucifixion V211.2.3.2; -boat A757; brings murder to light N271.1.1; answers questions D1311.6.1; captured R9.1.2; as creator A19.1; curses son A736.9; as deity A121.1; doesn't shine during deluge A1010.1; eats wife's corpse G27; at end of world A1053; on forehead royalty sign H71.1.1; falls into sea, causes flood A1016.6; from fish's belly A713.1; forged by smith A700.5; -god A240ff., (threatens to withhold rain) A182.3.6; as god's child A700.8; as gods' home A151.6.2; keeps star children in hiding A764.1.2; kills sun's children A736.1.4.1.1; as land of dead E481.8.2; from light A712.1; magically provides D1470.1.49; mutilates earth mistress S160.5; as next world A695; nourished on fire A700.7; as omen D1812.5.1.5; punishes for tabu breach C905.2; purchased A700.6; as real traveller H726; shines on God's forehead A123.10; splits hare's lip with hatchet A2216.3; steals food from gods A153.3.1; steals tree of life E90.1; tied to sun, when sun sinks, moon dragged up A735.1; transformed to person D439.5.1. — Absurd theories concerning the m. J2271; animals think m. shines for them J953.15; animals from mating of sun and m. A1771; banished devil appears on earth only on day of dark m. A106.2.1.1; barking to dog in m. K1735; bride like m. Z62.2; castle east of sun and west of m. F771.3.2; chest of murdered child becomes m. A1277.3; deity departs for m. A192.2.1.1; directions on quest given by m. H1232; color of sun, m., and stars F821.1.5; drinking the m. J1791.1; eating the m. (task) H1035; escape to m. R321.2; extraordinary behavior of m. F961.3; feast of the new m. V70.7; falling stars as pieces of m. A788.1; full m. and thirtieth of the month (enigma) H582.1.1; ghosts walk at full m. E587.6; gold m. F793.1; half-m. indicates treasure N532.1; handkerchief color of sun, m., and stars F822.1; hare as ambassador of the m. K1716; how much the m. weighs (riddle) H691.1; jewel-box in tank floats at new m. N513.6;

local m. J2271.1; looking at m. when shooting game forbidden C315.2.1; magic objects received from sun, m., and stars D814; making m. shine in north H1023.16; man in the m. A751; man put in m. for cursing Q235.1; marriage of mortal and m. T111.2.2; moonmakers make new m. F675.2; new m. with old moon in her arms a sign of storm D1812.5.1.5.1; origin of eclipse of m. A737.0.1; original m. becomes the sun, sun the moon A736.8; prophecy: man will make m. stand still M312.8; pursuit of sun by m. A736; quest to m. for answers to questions H1283; rescuing the m. J1791.2; stars as pieces of the m. A764; sun and m. (from cave) A713, (kept in pots) A721.0.1, (as man and woman) A736.1, (placed for eyes in sky) A714.1, (placed in top of tree) A714.2, (as uncle and nephew who ascended to sky) A711.1; sun, m., and stars (bring forth first parents) A1271.1, (are highest) H642.1; sun-god couples with m. A220.0.2; sun as offspring of m. A715.5; sun will lock m. in ditch A1066; tabu to offend m. C75.1; thunder from crashing of stones in m. A1142.5.1.1; tide inquires whether m. is up J1292; tower reaches m. F772.1.2; treasure nearest to surface at full m. N555.2; vision of m. entering husband's mouth V515.1.2; visit to land of m. *F16.

Moon's. — Diving for m. reflection in water J1791.3.3; marvelous sensitiveness: ulcer from m. rays F647.7; stars as drops of m. blood A764.2; stars as m. children A764.3; stars are m. spittle A764.4.

Moons. — Sovereigns compared to new, full m. H599.3.

Moonbeam. — Robber persuaded to climb down the m. *K1054.

Moonbeams. — Partridge subsists on m. B768.1.

Moonlight. — Brownies sew by m. F482.5.2; conception from m. T521.1; crabs eaten on m. walks K772.1; dwarfs play in the m. F451.6.3.5; hedge to keep in m. J1796.1; why sunlight stronger than m. A733.1.

Moorish girl substituted for mistress K1317.8. — Virgin Mary destroys M. army V268.3.

Moors free great painter Q88.1. — Friends ransom selves from M. P319.1.

Moose mistaken for mouse J1759.1. — Body of m. made larger A2301.1; creation of m. A1876; man becomes m. D114.1.7; why m. eat willows A2435.3.6.

Morass. — Frogs reprove ass for lamenting when he falls into m. J2211.1.

More. — Greedy man keeps demanding m. J514.3.

Morning. — Bed-partner to receive payment from first man she meets in m. T456; fairies leave at m. star's rise F383.4.2; four legs in the m., two at midday, and three in evening (riddle) H761; god of m. star A251; origin of birds' m. songs A2425.2; origin of m. star A781.1; quest to m. star for answers to questions H1282; sun eats all children except m. star A764.1.2.

Morning-glory. — Origin of wild m. A2665.

Mortal, see also **Human, Man, Person;** abandons world for fairyland

*F373; as ally of gods A189.1ff.; characteristics of fairies F254; in deity guise D43; man marries or lives with fairy woman F302ff.; marries star-girl A762.2; rules fairyland F252.1.0.1; as servant in fairyland F376; son of giant F531.5.7.1; as umpire of quarrel between gods A187.2; visited by angel V235; woman seduced by a god K1301. — Angel carries m. V232.2; angel and m. struggle V230.3; angel punishes m. V245; child of demon king marries m. F402.2.3; divinity becomes m. A192.4; fairy becomes m. F259.1.2, (for husband) F302.6.2.2; fairy causes m. husband's death C435.1.1.1; fairy lover entices m. girl F301.2; fairy mistress surrenders man to his m. wife F302.5.1; god in guise of m. D42; god half m. A122; horse used by m. under fairy spell changes to gray cat F234.4.1; magic spear always inflicts m. wounds D1402.7.2.1; marriage of m. and supernatural being *T111ff.; salt renders fairy m. F384.1.1; transformation by offspring of fairy and m. D683.7.1; twin gods: one m., other immortal A116.1; Virgin Mary substitutes for a m. K1841; wedding of m. and fairy F303; why m. cannot look at sun A733.2.

Mortal's attempt to defile goddess punished Q246. — Tasks test m. prowess before gods H927.1.

Mortals become gods A117; as captives in fairyland *F375; help fairies F394; unable to cross river F141.1.2; unable to endure God's glory A182.0.1. — Demigods fight as allies of m. A536; dwarfs direct m. to treasure F451.5.1.9; dwarfs serve m. F451.5.1.7; fairy living among m. F393.0.1; fairies and m. F300—F399; fairies borrow from m. F391; fairies call out to m. F276; fairies heal m. F344; gods in relation to m. *A180ff.; gods (saints) in disguise visit m. K1811; hero assists m. A581.1; tear from upper world of m. falls on departed in lower world E361.1.

Mortality of fairies *F259.1.

Mortar transformed to tigress D444.8. — Carrying heavy m. as punishment J2044; found m. taken to king reveals peasant girl's wisdom H561.1.2; ogre carrying m. and pestle G676; tigress becomes m. D421.4.1.

Mortgage. — Hogs as m. collateral K231.5.2.

Moses L111.2.1; as prophet M301.7.1; rescued by princess R131.11.1. — Cure by M. D2161.5.4; God's radiance upon face of M. A124.4; God speaks to M. A182.3.0.1; what kind of man was M.? He was a day laborer X435.1; wisdom gates open to M. J182.1.

Moses's staff (tree that became flesh) H823, (has drunk water for its sustenance and eaten after death) H824. — Lions tamed by M. rod B771.2.3; miracles cease at M. death F900.3.1.

Moslem. — Moving away from M. land to escape Allah J1823.4.

Mosque magically turns towards Mecca D2136.2.1.

Mosques V112.2.

Mosquito advises hero B569.3. — Bringing quantity of m. bones H1022.9; serpent transformed to m. D418.1.3.

Mosquito's buzz A2426.3.5.

Mosquitoes prick king, show they are stronger L392.1. — Bumblebees crossbreeding with m. X1280.1.1; deity's wife creates m. to drive husband from jungle A2034.1; fireflies as lantern-carrying m. J1759.3; gods' m. A155.4; lies about m. X1286; numskulls try to kill m. with bows and arrows J2131.0.1; origin of m. A2034; why certain district free of m. A2584.1.

Moss grows overnight F971.1.3. — Dwarfs grown over with m. F451.2.0.2; face covered with m. F545.4; origin of m. rose A2656.1; resuscitation by smelling of m. E72; why rocks at river are covered with m. A976; sieve filled with m. so as to carry water H1023.2.0.1.

Mossynoikoi. — Voyage to Land of M. F129.2.

Mote. — Man can put head through m. in sunbeam F535.2.4.

Moth. — Fairy as m. F234.1.16.2.

Moths. — Souls feed on night m. E752.7.1.

Mother ape burns bear L315.4; and daughter P232, (rivals in love) T92.6; who devours her children when they grow up (riddle) H734; dies from joy at son's return F1041.1.5.3; does for another what the latter cannot do for her (enigma) H583.4; does not love children of forced marriage P230.2; falsely accuses son of incest K2111.5; guilty of incest with son whose honor she is testing T412.3; of the gods A111.1; will die when daughter is wooed E765.4.2; guards girl T50.1.1; -incest prophecy M344; kills husband for daughter's murder P211.2; -love in animal F989.8; -love dearer than gold (riddle) H662; of men A1282; prefers son P230.1; as procuress for son T452.1; recognizes child's flesh when served G61.2; rescues son R153.4; resuscitated by breaking nuts on head E181.1.1; of saint admitted to heaven Q172.8; sends son to find unknown father H1216; shown what would have been evil fates of her dead children N121.2; and son *P231; -son incest T412; -son marriage of the gods A164.1.1; sought in upper world F15.1; test H495; of Time F118, H1285, Z122.2; treats changeling well, own child returned F321.1.4.8; tricked by forcing child's cry D2034; of unbaptized child cannot rest in grave E412.2.2; of world bears three sons A1282.1. — Abandoned child cared for by m. secretly S351; Adam and Eve, having neither father nor m., are dead H813; adopted child reproaches foster m., returned to real one T672; accidental meeting of m. and daughter N736; accidental meeting of m. and son N735; animal m. of man helps him B631.1; backbone of ogre's m. broken G512.7; bird prevents m. from killing babe B524.4; boy unwittingly commits incest with his m. N365.1; chaste m. of wife J482.3; child does not recognize m. in new skin A1335.4; child mystically recognizes m. H175.2; child seeks unknown m. H1381.2.2.2; children rescue m. from lion's den R154.0.1; colt's real m. will swim to it J1171.4; creative m. source of everything A3; cruel m. *S12; dead m. appears and makes disobedient child eat fatal serpent Q593; dead son tells m. death inevitable E361.3; devil's m. G303.11.3; devils carry off girl who abuses her m. Q281.1.1; disenchantment of

monster when prince promises to marry monster's m. D741; earth as
virgin m. of Adam A1234.1; Elias, having had father and m. is not
dead H814; fairy foster m. F311.3; fairy m. bestows magic powers
on son F305.1.1; father hides children from murderous m. R153.2.1;
foolish m. does not understand how babies cry J1911.2; formerly I was
daughter, now I am m. H807; foster m. summoned D2074.2.4.1; girl
hidden in skin of her dead m. R318; goddess as m. of Pacific Ocean
A109.2; grandmother as foster m. P292.1; gullible m. J2303; help
from ogre's m. G530.3; hero licked by deer m. B635.3.1; infant picks
out unknown m. H482; jealous m. casts daughter forth S322.2; journey
to hell to retrieve soul of m. F81.4; killing m. by overfeeding J2465.3.2;
kissing the m. (earth) J1652; in large family father unwilling but m.
willing to sell children H491.1; lazy m. given shoes of cotton W111.5.1;
Lot's wife, having had father and m., is not dead like other mortals
H815; magic object received from m. D815.1; magic power from m.
D1737.1; magic object from foster m. D815.7.1; master's m. killed by
wood on head K1466; moon's m. A745.2; mortal m. ignores changeling
F321.1.4.7; moon stays with his m. under earth during day A753.3.3;
naïve remark of child: "You forgot to strike m." J122; origin of relation
of m. and children A1575; prophecy: either youth or m. will die M341.5;
prophecy: m. will be killed by children M343.0.2; rescue by captor's m.
*R162; river flows from corpse of hero's m. A511.1.1.1; St. Peter's m.
dropped from heaven because of hard-heartedness Q291.1; seduction
by bearing false order from m. K1354.3; son buries aged m. alive S21.1;
son chastizes father for scorning m. P233.9; son must not see m. in
intercourse C114.1; son warns animal m. B631.0.1; stolen m. returns
from fairy land each Sunday to minister to her children *F322.3;
strong man son of bear who has stolen his m. F611.1.1; succession by m.
right P17.6; tabu: eating magic catch before m. C231.3.1; task for virgin
wife to accomplish: have by departing husband a son whose real m.
she is H1187; tasks assigned by jealous m. H913.1; test of m. by weighing
milk J1142.1; to every son belongs his m. P526.2; transformed m. called
by her child D792; transformed m. suckles child D688; transformed m.
as helper N819.2.1; trickster leads m. into sham murder K522.7; trickster
secures man's help against m. K2384; vision of m. in hell leads to good
life V511.2.3; will-o-the-wisp is girl cursed by her m. A2817.2; woman
pretends to be m. of future king K1923.4; youth made lame: had kicked
his m. J225.1.

Mother's bosom is softest H652.2; breast is sweetest H633.3; brothers
P293.1; curse on son causes eclipse A737.2; eyes are brightest H651.2;
weeping for thief made plausible J1142.4.1. — Child betrays m. adultery
J125.2.1; dead m. friendly return *E323ff.; dead m. malevolent return
E222; disregarding m. warning J1054; false bride makes child demand m.
clothes K1911.1.8.1; girl avoids eating m. flesh G61.1.1; magic object
found on m. grave D842.1; man dies over m. death F1041.1.3.8; mark

of m. hand on moon's shoulder A751.5.3; plant from m. milk A2615.2; recognition of son by gushing up of milk in m. breasts H175.1; retrieving m. soul F81.4; son on gallows bites his m. nose off Q586; son returns on day of m. marriage N681.4; tabu: listening to m. counsel C815; tasks assigned because of m. foolish boasting H914; unborn son's soul issues from m. mouth E726.2; using m. corpse to get presents K2321.1.

Mothers exchange children S216, K1921.2; of saints give curing milk D1500.1.33.1.1. — Birth from nine m. T541.12; child with several m. T589.9; city of married m. X1563; six imprisoned m. eat own children, seventh refuses Z215.

Mother Earth *401. — First humans from womb of M. A1234.1.1; marriage of M. and ogre T126.1; sun, moon from breasts of M. A715.4.

Mother-in-law *P262; casts woman's children forth S322.6; humiliated as cure for daughter-in-law's malady K1945.1.1; seduces son-in-law T417.1; tabu C171. — Cruel m. S51; devil frightened by threatening to bring m. K2325; man unwittingly lies with m. N365.4; treacherous m. K2218.1.

Motionless. — Hero has lain m. since birth F583.

Motley. — Dwarfs clad in m. F451.2.7.10; wife orders m. wear for husband J1112.1.1.

Mould put on table for the dead E433.1; thrown on corpse to prevent return E431.3. — Magic churchyard m. *D1278.1; wild huntsman released from wandering by m. from Christ's grave *E501.17.7.1.

Mound, see also **Grave-mound.** — Captivity in m. R45; fairy m. destroyed R121.8; magic rescue of prisoner from m. R112; man becomes m. D287; task: removing m. in one night H1101; witch lives in fairy m. G233.

Mounds from horns cast by cattle A967.1. — Burial m. fairy dwellings F211.0.1; habitable caves and m. in otherworld F164; origin of m. A967; pagans flee into fairy m. P426.0.1; sitting on sepulchral m. tabu in autumn C755.5.

Mount Meru. — Moon travels around M. A759.4.

Mount Sinai. — Tora given on M. F960.10.

Mountain, see also **Hill;** at borders of otherworld F145; at center of earth A875.1.1; of cheese (lie) X1528.1; -climber's rope cut, murdered K963.1; of fair-haired women F131.1.1; god A499; of grain to be eaten through on way to Schlaraffenland X1503.4; in human shape prophesies M301.15; in labor brings forth mouse U114; moved by prayer D1641.2.2, D2136.3.1; pass to otherworld F151.2; reaches to sky F55; -sheep A2326.3.5; -spirits *F460ff.; where sun goes through A722.7; supports sky A665.3; of Venus F131.1. — Abandonment on m. S147; abode of dead in m. *E481.3; bird carries a grain of sand from a m. each century H701.1; brush becomes m. D454.7; carrying m. on head H1146; climbing glass m. D753.4, H1114; cloak becomes m. D454.3.4.1; covering m. with killed birds H1109.3; creator's giant servant makes valley and m. A857.2; culture hero asleep in m. *A571; deity of particular m. A418;

demon looks like m. F531.2.11; dragon's home at top of m. B11.3.2;
dwarf moves mortal's castle from one m. to another F451.5.1.12; dwarfs
seen on a m. F451.4.2.6; dwarf serves king sleeping in m. F451.5.1.8; eating
m. of bread (task) H1141.1; entrance to lower world through m. F92.4;
escape from deluge on m. A1022; false judgment of distance of m.
J2214.12.1; gate as huge as m. F776.1; giant bestrides m. F531.3.5.1;
girl having been stolen by m.-folk must be baptised anew V81.1; glass
m. from mirror D454.12; god speaks from m. A182.3.0.5; holy m. free
from plague D2162.4; home of gods on high m. *A151.1; house inside
m. F771.3.5.1; illusory m. K1886.7; king asleep in m. *D1960.2; lifting
m., placing it on shoulders H1149.9; magic leveling of m. D2152.1; magic
m. *D932; man becomes m. D291; man kicks down m. F626.2; mankind emerges from m. A1234.2; marriage of m. and cockle-shell T126.2;
Mohammed goes to the m. J831; mortal transformed to god on m. top
A117.4; Old Man of the M. K1889.3; otherworld in hollow m. *F131;
otherworld on lofty m. *F132; quest for m. of gold H1359.4; remaining
on m. as punishment C983; removing m. in one night (task) H1101; rescue
of princess from m. R111.2.2; rock transformed to m. D452.1.2; saint
causes m. to melt D2149.2; saint's bachall (brings down m. on heads
of enemies) D1549.4, (leads stream through m.) D1549.3.2; slamming
door on exit from m. otherworld *F91.1; stream bursts from side of m.
A934.9; strong man throws m. F624.2.0.1.1; strong man holds up m.
F623; submarine castle on a m. F725.3.1; suitor contest: riding up glass
m. H331.1.1; tails fall off m. spirits when they are baptized V81.2;
touching sacred m. tabu C526; stones of m. for church D1552.7; transformation to m. ridge C961.4; treasure buried on top of m. N511.1.11;
trolls' riches inside m. F455.4.1.1; upper world (heaven) as a m. A662;
weighing m. as task H1149.8; wild hunt appears by m. E501.12.5; witch
dwells on glass m. G232; wrestler boasts he can carry m. K1741.4.

Mountains, see also **Hills;** fall together at end of world A1062; magically transported D2136.3; open and close *D1552ff.; in otherworld
F162.9; push water westward A914; seem to be fighting D2031.14. —
Clouds in sky to shade m. A1133.2; creation of m. A960ff.; dwarfs
live in hills, m. F451.4.1.11; extraordinary m. *F750ff.; extraordinary
activity of m. F1006; failure to bless m. gives mountain-men power
F460.4.6; flood from m. made of flat earth A1016.5; giant hurls
m. F531.3.2.4; giants live in m. F531.6.2.1; giants sit on m. and
wash feet in stream below F531.3.9; god's voice shatters m.
A139.5.1; icy m. in hell A671.3.2; lies about m. X1520; magician
casts m. upon enemies D2152.2; man born from m. A1245.5;
piling up m. to reach heaven forbidden C771.2; why porcupine lives in
high places in m. A2433.3.11; ship becomes m. D454.10.1; Sion appointed
chief of m. A1187; strong man pulls down m. F626; valleys created by
stamping down m. F756.2.2; why dinner time comes soon in m. J2276.1;
wings cut from flying m. A1185.

Mountaineer. — King disguised as m. K1812.16.

Mountebank cures incurables F958.

Mounting tower takes year F772.1.1. — Mutilated master m. prone horse B301.4.5.

Mourners. — Loudest m. not greatest sorrowers J261.

Mournful. — Sea's m. sound A925.5.

Mourning customs P681; dead ass: cumulative tale Z32.5; dead lover T85; tabus C898. — Bride's constancy tested by seven years' m. over supposed dead lover H387.1; failure to observe m. punished Q223.12; fairy music causes m. F262.3.5; forgetfulness by m. D2004.8; heavenly bodies m. Adam F961.0.3.1; hens in m. J1886; king m. on wife's grave P27.2; loud noise of m. F1051.2; magic object causes m. D1359.2; objects m. saint's death V229.19; pigeon cheated out of chick: always m. A2275.4.1; professional m. V65.4; sister is m. last year's laughter H583.5; stepmother m. stepson's death P282.2; sun smears face in m., hence eclipse A737.8; swallows put on m. at crucifixion: have never taken it off A2221.2.4.1; three lovers m. dead girl T92.14; what shall be his m.? J1301.

Mouse as beast of ill-omen B147.1.2.3; bird, and sausage keep house together J512.7; bursts open when crossing a stream (cumulative tale) Z41.4.1; and cat's association over when danger ends J426.1; causes thief's hair to fall out Q557.4; created by Lucifer, cat by Michael to destroy mouse A1751.1; destroying elephant H1161.3.1; dying in meat tub is happy that he has eaten to satisfaction J861.3; in jug (test of curiosity) H1554.1; gathers rice for man: may eat a little of his rice daily A2223.3; on lion's mane J411.8; regains its tail (cumulative tale) Z41.4; stronger than wall, wind, mountain L392; teaches her child to fear quiet cats but not noisy cocks J132; torments bull who cannot catch him L315.2; trampled to death by his lion bride B363.1; transformed to (cat) D411.6.2, (person) D315.2, (another animal) D411.6. — Cat transformed to maiden runs after m. J1908.2; chain tale: fat m. cannot get into hole Z49.2.1; creation of m. A1853; devil as a m. G303.3.3.2.4; dying person's soul as m. B766.1.1; elephant poisoned by m. L315.5.1; enmity between m. (and cat) A2494.1.1, (and dog) A2494.4.3, (and owl) A2494.13.4; enticing cat and fortune with m. K2.1; how m. got his eyes A2332.1.1; friendship between m. and butterfly A2493.28; friendship of cat and m. A2493.9; ghost as m. E423.2.11; giant tricked into becoming m. K722; gold, silver m. H151.1.2; helpful m. B437.2; husband transformed to m. to rescue wife R115.1; improvident m. eats grain stored for famine J711.2; lawsuit between owl and m. B270.2; lion spares m.: m. grateful B371.1; magic m. B183.1; magic m.-skin bears person aloft D1532.1.1; man transformed to m. D117.1; marriage to m. B601.3.1; mill-m. told field-m. dead F405.7.1; moose mistaken for m. J1759.1; mountain in labor brings forth m. U114; singing m. B214.1.9; speaking m. B211.2.8; soul in form of m. E731.3; swallowing m. without vomiting

H1567.1.1; tabu to eat m. C221.1.1.7; thumbling hides in m. hole F535.1.1.10.2; town m. and country m. J211.2; transformation to m. C962.1; wedding of m. and (cockroach) B281.2.2, (frog) B284.1.1, (weasel) B281.2.1; why m. does not defend self against cat A2462.3; why m. crushed in crossing road: elephant's curse A2239.9; witch in form of m. G211.2.5.

Mouse's body made smaller A2302.1; food A2435.3.7; magic skin *D1025.3; nose pulled out long A2213.4.3; prayer granted D1766.1.6; tail causes person to cough up magic object K331.4, K431. — Chain tale: m. acquisitions Z39.9; why elephant hurts self in grass: m. curse A2239.10.

Mice army saves kingdom from invasion K632.1; consecrate bishop (lie) X1226.1; cursed M414.8.1; dying of hunger since priest receives only forty florins a year J1269.10; escape into their holes where weasels cannot follow them L332; engendered after flood from rottenness: no mice on ark A1853.1.1; gnaw enemies' bowstrings and prevent pursuit K632; gnaw through metal B747.3; gnawing garments bad omen D1812.5.1.12.4; hitched to wagon B558.5; and hogs let loose put elephant cavalry to flight K2351.3; overcome camel L315.10; win war with woodcutters L318. — Army of m. B268.6; bargain with king of m. M244.1; cat hangs on wall pretending to be dead but m. detect plan K2061.9; cat makes truce with m. then eats them K815.13; clock ticking thought to be gnawing of m. J1789.2; why m. eat grease and salmon A2435.3.7.1; exterminating m. infesting city H1109.4; giant man-eating m. B16.2.8; giant m. B871.2.7; how m. can rid themselves of cats H1292.10; iron-eating m. J1531.2; king of m. B241.2.5; land of m. B221.5; lies about m. X1226; troll has team of m. G304.3.2.1; weasel paints self to deceive m. J951.4.

Mouse-trap, trying to catch light in J1961.1.

Moustache becomes grass D457.10; pulled out as punishment Q497.1. — Being swung by m. without crying H328.2; god with white m. A137.18; golden m. F545.1.1.2; lighting lamp with king's m. P672.4; transformation by m. D537.3.

Mouth bleeding as death omen J2311.1.2; crooked from ghost's strike E542.1.3; expanded for breaking tabu C948.1; full: cheeks cut open to find abscess J1842.2; -less people F513.0.3. — Adulteress's m. loyal to husband K1595; animal captor persuaded to talk and release victim from m. K561.1; animal impregnated through m. B754.6.1.1; why animals move m. A2476; birth from m. T541.4.1; boy throws ball into hostile dog's m. N623.2; burning wood in m. tests sham dead H248.4; child born without m. T551.6; coin placed in m. of dead to prevent return E431.11; consecrated bread kept in m. (and fed to toad produces love) D1355.10.1, (in order to be witch) G281; curse: toads from m. M431.2; death respite until m. washed K551.4.6; devil holds molten coin in m. G303.4.8.2; disenchantment by taking key from serpent's m. at midnight D759.1;

dupe opens m.; hot stones thrown in K721.1; dupe's m. smeared with butter brings accusation of theft K401.1; earthquake spirit's long m. F438.2; fish with coin in m. B105.4.1; flame issuing from m. as sign of royalty H41.4; flames issue from corpse's m. E421.3.7; flounder's crooked m. A2231.1.2, A2252.4; ghost's blow makes m. crooked E265.1.3; god's unusual m. A123.2.2ff.; headless person with m. on breast F511.0.1.1; husband proves intrigue by secretly blacking paramour's m. K1504; lily issues from buried devotee's m. V255.1; man with horse's m. B21.3; "a measured m." as health secret H596.1.1; mirror in bed to see if sleeping with m. open J1936.1; moon enters husband's m., star enters wife's V515.1.2; murder by throwing hot stones in m. K951.1; ogre monstrous as to m. G363; opening m. makes door open D1782.1.1; origin and nature of animal's m. A2341ff.; peasant opens his m. at dinner for his wife J2473; penance: carrying water in m. from a distance and watering dry staff until it blooms Q521.1.2; person swearing oath places hand in m. of image H251.1; person unusual as to his m. F513; remarkable m. F544; river flows from man's m. F715.1.5; saint silent by holding stone in m. V73.6.2; silver and gold run from cod's m. B103.4.1.1; sinner in hell falls into devil's m. Q569.3; skillful marksman shoots pipe from man's m. F661.2; snake crawls into sleeper's m. B765.5; snake creeps into man's m. and heals him B511.1.1; sore m. as punishment C941.3.1; stolen fig in m. leads to cheek lancing W111.5.8, J1842.2; spear pins animal's m. shut N623.1; stopping up m. to keep wisdom in J1977; thundergod's long m. A284.3.1; transformation by placing pill in m. D551.6.1; treasure falls from m. *D1454.2; unborn soul issues from mother's m. E726.2; what princess puts in m. prophesies marriage H41.6; why animal's m. is closed A2341.3; witch recognized by seeing wasp enter m. while asleep *G251.1; wood-spirit without m. F441.4.2; yawning person cannot close m. D2072.0.5.2.

Mouths. — Animal with many m. B15.2ff.; cannibal with seven m. G11.17; contest in making m. water H509.2; flowers grow from m. of saints in graves V229.2.7; husband and wife burn their m. J1478.

Mouth-harp left by bed H142. — Magic m. D1225.1; quest for gold m. H1335.1.

Move. — Enchanted person cannot m. D5.1; ghost light indicates impending m. E530.1.4; giants by night m. buildings built by men in day F531.6.6.1; horse withheld as sacrifice to a saint refuses to m. K231.3.4; ship refuses to m. with guilty man aboard D1318.10.1; wagon refuses to m. because ghost is sitting in it *D1317.10.

Moved. — Castle m. from one mountain to another by dwarf F451.5.1.12; dead move when cemetery is m. E419.4; murdered body cannot be m. Q559.3; objects magically m. D2136ff.; stone cannot be m. by perjurer H251.2.1.

Movement of leaves A2762. — Auguries from animal m. D1812.5.0.8.1; wild hunt disappears with m. of tree tops E501.16.2.

Movements. — Animal's habitual bodily m. A2470ff.; earthquakes from m. of subterranean monster A1145.1.

Moving mountain F755.6. — Devil prevents m. of little stone by sitting on it G303.9.9.1; futile m. to avoid death M382; poor man's m.: putting out fire, whistling for dog W226; soul of sleeper prevented from returning by m. the sleeper's body E721.1.2.2; tabu: m. dead cat or dog C537.3; two fixed, two m., etc. (riddle) H851.

Mower. — Swift m. F681.11.

Mowers sing about bad food J1341.11. — Monkey attracts attention of m. until young birds can fly away from the harvest field K644.

Mowing contest with household spirit F488.2; contest won by trickery K42.2; grass: the meadow torn up K1423.

Much. — Gift seems too m.: sign of death W11.13.

Muck. — Food transformed to m. D472.1.

Mucus turns to gold D475.1.13. — Birth from m. from the nose T541.8.3; sky-rope of m. F51.1.7.

Mud flood injures corn Q552.14.2; sold as butter K144.3. — Adulteress falls in m. at lover's door K1523; animal grateful for rescue from m. B364.5; bread made from m. D476.1.1; bringing much m. without buffaloes H1129.1.1; cakes of m. gilded K122; dead walk on m. without sinking E489.9; earth made by m. shaken off boar A822; lawyer thrown back into m. when rescuers learn that he is a lawyer X317; lies about m. X1655; man caused to sink into m. D2092; man in m. too lazy to take hand extended to help him up W111.5.5; numskulls carrying each other through m. J2163.1; priest walks in m. J82; seduction access through fall in m. K1349.6; sinking into m. in duel F943; why pigs in m. lift their legs A2479.5; woman hidden in m. cabin R53.1; world is transformed m. parrot A822.1.

Muddy. — Death respite until m. victim dries self K551.12; lizard makes water m., hence enmity with bird A2494.16.4; magpie tells why sow was m. J2211.2.

Mudhen's red head A2320.3.1.

Mudpuppy poisonous B776.3.2.

Muffins. — Fire's hissing mistaken for m. cooking J1812.4.

Muirlan removes itself D1641.5. — Magic m. D1256; speaking m. D1610.23.

Mulatto child's birth explained by adulteress J2338.

Mulberry. — Origin of m. tree A2681.9; transformation to m. tree D215.6.

Mule, see also **Ass, Donkey;** as descendant of king's warhorse J954.1; paralyzed by witch D2072.0.2.4. — Access to mistress by riding rival's m. K1349.3; adulteress kicked to death by m. as punishment Q416.1.1; Dante beats m. driver J981.1; going wherever his m. wants to J1483.2; helpful m. B403; magic folding m. D491.1.2; man chooses to remain transformed to m. rather than to live with his shrewish wife T251.1.3; man transformed to m. D132.2; overloaded m. J1302; selling old m. back to owner K134.3; speaking m. B211.1.3.2; why m. is sterile A2561.1; thumbling drives m. F535.1.1.1.1; three brothers take turns using m. J1914.2; witch as m. G211.1.2.

Mule's bite causes death B766.4; double ancestry L465.

Mules. — Adulterers tricked into riding thirsty m.: drowned K1567; lies about m. X1242; spirit rides, wears out m. at night F473.4.1.

Mullet. — Creation of m. A2112.

Multicolored fires F882.2; llama B731.3. — Fairy's m. dress F236.1.7; fairies m. F233.7.

Multipede. — Origin of m. A2182.5.

Multiple births T586; disguise K1834. — Nimrod's m. throne F785.2.

Multiplication of objects D1652, D2106ff.; of man by fragmentation A1296. — Asking for too great magic m. of coins forbidden C773.1.1; magic m. of cows Q141; magic m. of objects by saints D2106.1; wife's m. of secret J2353.

Multiplying. — Coin m. self D2100.2; magic object m. objects D1599.3; magic ring m. wealth D1456.2.1.

Mummified dog resuscitates E53.1.

Münchhausen tales X900.

Munching grains to keep awake H1483.

Munia. — Why m. wears his crop on back of neck A2351.7.

Murder *S110ff.; avenged in like manner Q581.1; causes dwarf to lose his soul F451.5.9.6; of child to avoid fulfillment of prophecy M371.1; feigned to effect escape K579.6; of homecoming husband by adulteress K1510.1; made known in dream D1810.8.2.3; opportunity presented to assassin H1556.3; will out N271; of pregnant woman to avoid prophecy fulfillment M376.2; punished *Q211; by slaves P176; by sympathetic magic D2061.2.2. — Animal avenges m. B591; bird reveals m. B131.1; blood smeared on innocent person brings accusation of m. K2155.1; child in mother's womb reveals m. T575.1.1.1; daughter's betrothal as m. compensation T69.3.1; dog clears master of m. B134.5; dog betrays m. B134.2; earth from m. of first brother and sister A831.4; earthquake at m. F960.2.5.1; external soul avenges m. E710.2; flame indicates m. site F1061.4; friendship feigned to avenge m. K2010.2; ghostly m. sounds E337.1.1. grass will not grow where m. committed F974.1; horse stops where m. has occurred B151.1.1.0.2; innocent person accused of m. K2116; last moment prevention of m. by burning N657; light where m. is committed D1318.11.1; magic detection of m. D1817.0.3; magic m. D2061; nobleman unpunished for m. E34; origin of m. A1336; origin of penalty for m. A1581.1; prince, princess join in spouse-m. pact S63; prophecy: daughter shall commit m. and incest M345; quest as punishment for m. H1219.2; resuscitation after m. E185; return from dead to reveal m. *E231; speaking blood reveals m. D1318.5.4; speaking bones of murdered person reveal m. E632.1; speaking earth reveals m. D1318.16;

speaking flesh reveals m. D1318.7.0.1; sun refuses to shine where m. is done F961.1.1; trickster's sham m. by mother K522.7; truth-telling dog killed to hide m. B339.1; various kinds of treacherous m. K950ff.; voluntary exile as punishment for m. Q431.1; walling up as punishment for m. of children Q455.1; wild huntswoman wanders for daughter's m. E501.3.10; woman confesses m.: unharmed by execution fire V21.2.

Murdered girl, reincarnated as bird, resumes original form E696.1; person cannot rest in grave E413; person recognized by fingernail H57.2.2; person's request and promise M257.2. — Abandoned or m. children *S300ff.; animal reincarnation of m. child B313.2; animals in wild hunt reincarnation of m. persons E501.4.0.1; bones of m. person tabu C541.3; carrying m. man's blood as ordeal H227; earth from body of m. child A831.5; ghost of m. child E225; ghost of m. person haunts grave E334.2.1; infant eats m. father's corpse G25; insect in m. person simulates snoring K661.3; magic properties of m. man's head D1549.7; object substituted for m. person K525.3; person unwittingly m. N320ff.; reincarnation of m. child as bird *E613.0.1; riddle of the m. lover H805; son of first couple m. by tiger A1277.3; stepfather m. P281.2; tongue as proof that man has been m. H105.2; vulture's chicks will not eat m. hero B159.4.

Murderer cannot rest in grave E411.1; or captor otherwise beguiled *K600ff.; detected by actions of murdered man's dog J1145.1; does penance Q520.1; -emperor abducted by devil R11.2.1.1; escapes on sky rope R323.1; forced to eat victim's flesh, dies G62; makes outcry to accuse innocent K2116.4; refused payment for killing, killed K231.10; tricked into false accusation J1141.12. — Ball of fire haunts m. E530.1.2; Christianized Jewish priest as m. V364; corpse bleeds when m. touches it D1318.5.2; corpse of murdered man sticks to m. Q551.2.4; dead mother curses m. -son E222.3; demand m. restore victim's life J1955; escape by questioning would-be m. on guilt K573.1; faithful servant kills master's m. P361.1.1; ghost causes m. to confess E231.5; ghost reveals m. E231.1ff.; ghost slays own m. E232.1; horse kicks m. to death B591.2; mother m. uses her corpse K2321.1; murdered man's body leads to exposure of m. Q559.3; queen marries fiancé's m. P22; ruler pardons his would-be m. W11.5.2; saint offers m. refuge R325.3; son as pledge for father m. P233.1; test of friendship: substitute as m. H1558.2; victim's son aids m. W15.1; woman shelters m. of her son out of charity W15.

Murderer's children become dwarfs F451.1.2; short hair H75.7; wraith confesses E723.4.2. — God kills m. son Q589.3; grass does not grow on m. grave E631.2; melon in m. hand turns to murdered man's head Q551.3.3.1; punishment: calf's head in m. hand turns to corpse's head Q551.3.3.

Murderers. — Hardhearted person refuses reprieve to m. W155.4.

Murderess forced to leap from cliff Q417.1. — Devil appears to m. who prays over pit where she has thrown the bodies of her babies G303.6.2.7; paramour shuns m. K2213.3.2.2.

Murdering. — Brownie m. travelers for blood F363.2; king m. man after killing his sons M2.1; mother kills husband for m. daughter P211.2; young queen m. old husband K2213.12.

Murderous bird H1161.1; bride T173; witch G262. — Dogs flee from m. master J2211.3; father hides children from m. mother R153.2.1; girl marries m. husband S62.1.

Murmuring against deity tabu C66.

Murrain upon cattle as punishment Q552.3.7.

Muses, nine A465.0.1.

Mush scattered on heroine's body as test H1503.

Mushroom. — Goose boasts superiority to m.: both served at same meal L419.1; great m. X1424; origin of m. A2613.1, A2686.1; "whoever eats this m. is my wife" N365.3.2.

Mushrooms shrink in water J1813.1. — Why m. are slimy A2794.1.

Music attracts bride T56.1; of bird's wing enchants saint D2011.1.1; of heaven A661.0.2; of the spheres A659.1; tabu on sabbath C631.6; teacher charges double for those who have taken music before X351. — Abduction by sleep-giving m. R22.2; acquisition of m. A1461; animal tied to learn m. K713.1.6; animals attracted by m. B767; ascetic avoids m. V462.6; bitches enchanted by fairy m. B182.1.7; boar makes m. for saint B256.6.2; cat lures foxes with m. K815.15; dead make m. on their ribs E548; devil's m. G303.25.16.1; disenchantment by m. D786; dupe persuaded to play m. for wedding party K844; dwarfs emigrate because they dislike peasants' dancing and loud m. F451.9.1.9; dwarfs have m. F451.6.3.3; escape by playing m. K606.1ff.; ethereal m. E402.4; fairies make m. F262; fairy m. evil omen D1812.5.1.13; fairy m. prevents elephant grazing F369.8; fish follow sound of m. B767.1; ghost summoned by m. E384; god of m. A465.2; goddess of m. A112.1.1.1; harp m. makes merman restore stolen bride B82.1.2; heavenly m. caused by columns under Lord's chair A661.0.2.1; hero escapes tiger by playing m. K551.3; magic m. *D1275.1, (lures to otherworld) F175; man pretending to enjoy m. told when to applaud W116.6; merman teaches m. B82.4; recognition by m. H12; respite from death while captor plays m. K551.3.2; resuscitation by m. E55; saint leaves religious order for m. V475.4; sleep-bringing m. in otherworld F156.1; soul leaps from body on hearing heavenly m. E722.2.5; sound of plates and spoons is best m. J1343.1; three strains of m. Z71.1.3; wild hunt heralded by m. E501.13.2; women transformed to bitches enchanted by m. B297.2.1.

Music-box continues playing when it is touched contrary to tabu *C915.1.1; plays by itself at death E761.7.11.

Musical animals B297; fountain F162.8.3, F716.5; pillar F774.3; rock F803. — Ghost plays m. instrument E402.1.3, E554; giant plays m. instrument F531.6.17.4; magic m. branch *D1615.2; magic m. instruments *D1210ff.; magic pipe (m.) *D1224; man becomes m. instrument D254;

34*

reincarnation as m. instrument *E632ff.; test of m. ability H503; three magical m. strains *D1275.1.1; tree with m. branches F811.6.

Musician P428; playing for devil's dances G303.25.17.2; in wolf-trap B848.1. — Disguise as m. to (enter enemy's camp) K2357.1, (escape) K521.4.2; dwarf m. F451.3.3.1; imprisoned m. defends himself J814.1; skillful m. F679.9.

Musicians. — Thieves disguised as m. K311.11.

Musk. — Origin of m. A2812.

Muskox. — Bow shoots m. F836.4; man becomes m. D114.1.5.

Muskrat. — Beaver and m. exchange tails A2247.6; dwelling of m. A2432.5; how m. got long, thin tail A2378.3.2; why m. lives in water A2433.3.10.

Mussel. — Color of m. A2411.5.4; dog mistakes m. for an egg J1772.2; reincarnation of ears into m. shell E649.4.

Musselman. — Contest between Yogi and M. V351.5.

Mustard sandwich as farmer's hot lunch W152.12.2; smeared on bridal couple T135.12. — Counting seeds in m. package H1118.1; peasants in city inn order whole portion of m. J1742.3; thieves deceived into stealing m. J1517.1.

Mustard-seed trail R267. — Magic m. *D971.1, (causes man to turn to ashes) D1402.16; suitor test involving mountain of m. H1091.3.

Mustelidae, creation of A1820ff.

Mute water-maidens F420.1.2.2.

Mutilated god A128; man chased into forest S143.3. — Child m. to avoid prophecy fulfillment M375.4; children m. by father S11.1; false bride's m. feet K1911.3.3.1; girl wants to marry m. lover T99.2; primordial animal m. to produce present form A1727; prisoners m. R51.3; wife carries m. husband on her back so that he may beg T215.1; woman deserts husband for m. lover T232.

Mutilating. — Animal m. self to express sympathy B299.5.1.

Mutilation S160ff.; of children's bodies for identification H56.2; of girls punished Q411.5; as punishment C948, Q451ff.; to repel lover T327; substituted for death K512.2.4. — Beheading punishes m. Q421.0.5; cruel m. punished Q285.3; disguise by m. so as to escape K521.2.2; fairy causes m. F362.4; girl demands suitor's m. H333; magic m. of sexual organs D2062.4; self-m. to remove temptation T333.

Mutinous clerics expelled Q226.2.

Mutton. — Horse meat becomes m. D476.3.3.

Mutually. — Senseless debate of the m. useful J461ff.

Muzzle, see also **Mouth.** — Origin and nature of animal's m. A2335.4; why wolf's m. is black A2335.4.5.

Myna. — Creation of m. A1928.

Myrrh. — Ant collects m. for Christ A2221.4; origin of gum in m. tree A2755.3.2.

Myrtle, magic *D965.10.

Myself K602.

Mysteries. — Revealing sacred m. tabu C423.5.

Mysterious animal punishes penitent Q554.5; death as punishment Q558, (remitted) Q574; ghostlike noises heard E402; housekeeper N831.1; poisoning of food N332.6; punishments in other world F171.6; stranger performs task H976; visitation as punishment Q554ff.; voice announces death of Pan F442.1; voice announces prohibition C601. — Knowledge from m. woman J155.7.

Mystically. — Child m. recognizes mother H175.2.

Mythical animals *B0—B99; beasts B19; being asks for girl to marry T50.3. — Soul in form of a m. animal E738; witch as m. animal G211.9.

Mythological motifs A (entire chapter).

Naboth's vineyard will not be sold to king P411.1.

Nag becomes riding horse D1868.1.

Naga (serpent demon) B91.1; -king B244.2.

Nagas' dance B293.5.

Nagging wife T253; will never make a husband virtuous T253.2.

Naglfar ship F531.6.7.1.2, F841.1.5.

Nail, see also **Fingernail.** — Cannibal has long tooth and n. G88; extraordinary n. F844; devil's chair in hell made from thrown-away n. parings G303.25.5; girl has "wolf's n." T611.10.1; iron n. in witch's head G272.14; murder by driving n. through head S115.2.1; throwing away n. trimmings tabu C726.1; train of troubles from lost horseshoe n. N258; vessel full of n.-scrapings H1129.8.

Nails for Crucifixion made by smith's wife V211.2.3.0.2; driven into grave to lay ghost E442.2; on witch's back G219.9. — Carpenter blames the n. J1891.2; earth from worm scratched by creator's n. A828; fiery n. in hell A671.2.4.10; four earth n. A841.4; ghost with peculiar n. E422.1.8; giant with n. like claws F531.1.6.1; giant's n. grown into earth F531.1.6.9; horse-n. used to bewitch G224.13.1; long n. of beings born in hell A671.6; magic n. D1252.1.2; transformation by sticking n. in feet D582.1; ship with gold n. F841.1.7; witch has long n. G219.3; woman fed human n. G11.6.2.

Nailing horse's head over gate F874.1; to pillar as punishment Q462.1; wolf's tail to tree X1132.1.

Naked, see also **Nude;** ghost asks for shirt E412.3.2; idol considered poor J2216; leper P162.1; man imitates jockey riding himself G269.21.3; person made to believe that he is clothed J2312ff.; servant used to incriminate innocent woman K2112.4; soldier becomes general N684; tribe F568; woman pursued and cut in two by rider E501.5.1.1. — Aphrodisiac given n. woman in stream K1395; brother who conforms to n. people's customs honored J815.2; coming neither n. nor clad (task) H1054; country of the n. F709.1; dandy tailored by devil, n. G303.9.9.11; dead not to be buried n. V68.4.1; disenchantment by n. virgin undergoing frightful journey at midnight D759.3; endurance

test: scalding mush scattered on heroine's n. body H1503; fairies n.
F238; girl dies at being seen n. F1041.1.13.1; girl has had relations with
priest (not n. but with a hood on) J2499.2; girl shows herself n. in
return for youth's dancing hogs *K1358; Godiva rides n. through
streets to obtain freedom for citizens M235; guilty woman to go n.:
accused undresses J1141.1.8; humiliated lover shows women n. to
friends K1218.4.1; injured husband will not kill a n. man P641; king
boasts of wife, shows her off n. T295; land of n. people F129.7; lazy
wife taken n. in bundle of straw to a wedding Q495.1; looking at supernatural wife n. forbidden C31.1.3; loser of shooting wager to go n.
into thorns for bird N55.1; magic from maiden walking n. in public
*D1796; man at first n. A1281.3; men shamed for their cowardice by woman
standing n. before them J87; paramour exposes adulteress n. K1213.1;
penance: creeping n. through thorns Q522.3; rebuke for going with a n.
head in public J2521.2; revenant as n. woman E425.1.2; seducer led n.
through streets Q473; sleeping n. on cold floor H1504; sleeping n. girl:
goddess or mortal? H45.5; standing n. in winter river H328.4; trickster
exacts promise of marriage as price of silence after having seen a
princess n. *K443.6; weakness from seeing n. woman C942.3; woman
dies at seeing n. man F1041.1.13.2; women n. in beauty contest H1596.3.

Nakedness for life as punishment for nudity Q589.2. — Origin of shame
for n. A1383.

Name on article as ownership token H88; does not alter condition U119.5;
tabu *C430ff.; of victorious youngest son L10.1. — Accidental calling
on God's n. held to outweigh a life of wickedness V91; Adam's n. from
initials of four stars A1281.6.1; bonga girl surrenders man to his mortal
wife if he will n. first daughter after her F302.5.1.1; calling sacrificial
animal by son's n. K527.5; charm containing God's n. D1273.0.5;
criminal's n. accidentally spoken out N611.1.1; dead's n. not on heavenly
roll E586.4; deceptive bargain based on an unusual n. K193; devil becomes powerless when called by n. G303.16.19.9; devil leaves at mention
of God's n. G303.16.8; devil produces animals only in God's n. A1756;
disguise by changing n. K1831.0.1; do not walk half a mile with a man
without asking his n. J21.11; dwarf promises mortal much money if he
will guess his n. *F451.5.15.1; dwarf suitor desists when unwilling maiden
guesses his n. F451.5.15.3; earl's n. preferred to king's P50.1.1; escape by
using equivocal n. K602; fairies disappear when some n. of the Christian
Church is used F382; fly asks what is her n. Z25; genie called by writing
his n. on papers and burning them *D2074.2.4; ghost tells murderer's n.
E231.1; ghost laid by using God's n. E443.5; ghosts summoned by n.
E386.3; girl with the ugly n. K1984.3; god gives n. to child A182.2;
god's ineffable n. A138; guest under false n. P322.2; helper summoned
by calling n. D1420.4; hero learns n. at first adventure T617.2; high-
sounding n. frightens off enemy chief K1951.5; "I don't know" as a n.
J2496; ignorance of own n. J1730.1; ineffable n. creates magic D804;

king of Jews' ugly n. A1689.6; knight dismisses devil in n. of cross
G303.16.3.5; luck changing after change of n. N131.4; magic results
produced in n. of deity D1766.7.1; magic from uttering n. D1766.7; man
burns temple so that his n. will be remembered J2162.1; marking
object with n. to claim it later K448; not recognizing own n.: accustomed
to nickname J2016; ogre sings own n. G652; own n. inscribed on stolen
object J1162.3; person accidentally met knows other's n. N762; person
summoned by saying his n. D2074.2.4ff.; prophecy: son of certain n.
to become king M395; prophecy: death at hands of man bearing a
certain n. M341.2.15; rat changes n., wins bride K1371.3; secret n. overheard by eavesdropper *N475; senses regained by hearing n. F959.1.1;
service under false n. K1831; tabu: asking n. of supernatural husband
C32.2.1; tabu: desecration of God's n. C51.3.1; tabu: finding n. of
ghost C824; theft by assuming equivocal n. K359.2; transformation by
breaking n. tabu D511; trip to find n. wife already knows J2241.1;
unusual n. K193, S243; voice from grave answers to pet n. E324.1.

Names applied to devil G303.2ff.; of dogs literally interpreted J2493;
for dwarfs F451.8ff.; of future kings foretold M369.4; of giants have
sinister significance Z100.1; given the soul E700.1. — All things receive
n. A1191; animals with queer n. (henny-penny) Z53; how animals
received their n. A2571; devil writes down n. of men on a hide in
church G303.24.1.3f.; dogs' n. give warning K649.5; extraordinary n.
X1506; friends exchange n. P311.0.1; gods have many n. A139.1; guessing
n. in magic writing H517; Jacob-Israel had two n. (riddle) H817; lands
with extraordinary n. F703; mortal completes fairies' song by adding
the n. of the days of the week F331.3; murder revealed by unusual n.
of boys N271.2; origin of personal n. A1577; princess calls her suitors
ugly n. T76; servant deceives by unusual n. K1399.2; symbolic meaning
of n. H602.3; symbolic n. Z183; trolls may not utter holy n. F455.7.3;
wager involving learned and common n. of trees N51.1.

Named. — Districts n. from first person met in each N125.4; fairy leaves
when he is n. F381.1; king's son n. for king's foster father P271.7;
seven sons all n. the same T586.1.2.2; son n. for mother T148.1.

Nameless. — Adam at first n. A1281.6; hero at first n. Z252.

Namesake. — Bonga's n. first daughter F302.5.1.1; eating animal n. forbidden C221.2.

Naming of children T596; events which have not yet happened H1011;
the stars A765. — Angel n. child V241.4.1; disenchantment by n. D772.

Nandia provides warrior's equipment D2107.1.

Naphtha. — Riddles about n. H886.

Napkin. — Miraculous image of Christ impressed on n. V121; sickness
cured by n. of Veronica F950.1.

Narcissus T11.5.1. — Origin of n. A2665.1.

Narcotic. — Capture by giving n. K776; escape by giving n. to guards

K625; fatal deception by giving n. K873; girl foiled by hero's refusal to take n. K625.1; origin of n. plants A2691ff.

Narcotics. — Theft by giving guard n. K332.1.

Narrow road to heaven F57.1. — Broad and n. road in otherworld F171.2; rude retorts of men meeting in n. passage J1369.3; task: putting a large squash whole into a n.-necked jar H1023.11.

Narwhale's origin A2135.1.

Nasal. — Origin and nature of animals' n. organ A2335.

Nation of thieves K304.

Nations P710ff. — Humor concerning n. X600—X699; number of n. A1601; wise n. J192.

Nativity of Christ V211.1. — All locks opened on N. night D2088.0.1; angels sing at N. V234.2; animals rejoice at N. B251.1; animals speak at N. B211.0.1; children speak in wombs at N. T575.1.5; devil exorcised at N. G303.16.19.10; fetters loosed at N. D1395.8; magic fruit blooms at N. D2145.2.2.1; treasure found at N. N529.1, N541.4; wells break forth at N. A941.5.0.2; whale cast ashore at N. B874.3.2.

Natural child, see **Illegitimate;** is easiest (riddle) H659.14.1; law suspended D2137; laws inoperative at end of world A1091; phenomena accompanying the devil's appearance G303.6.3ff.; son refusing kingship P17.9.1; son succeeds to throne P17.9; underground treasure N511.2. — Absurd disregard of n. laws J1930ff.; establishment of n. order A1100ff.

Nature fruitful during good king's reign Q153; fruitless after false judgment H243; gods A405; transformed every seven years A1103; will show itself U120ff. — Absurd attempt to change animal n. J1908; absurd disregard or ignorance of animal's n. *J1900ff.; animal should not try to change his n. J512; dwarfs are subject to laws of n. F451.3.5; extraordinary n. phenomena F960ff.; fruitfulness of n. proves kingly right H1574.2; recognition by "force of n." H175; reincarnation of man as n. spirit E653; tasks contrary to laws of n. H1020ff.; why powers of n. work on Sabbath A1102.

Naught. — Nix-N.-Nothing S243.

Navel of the earth A875.1. — Child helps mother in severing n. string T584.8; heaven, earth connected by n. string A625.2.1; intercourse by n. A1352.3; long n. F559.2; lotus grows from god's n. A123.9; witch sucks blood from child's n. G262.1.3.

Navigable streams shoot from well F718.11.

Navigators. — Bird conducts n. B563.7.

Nearsighted knight mistakes own servant for enemy X124; man persuaded he can see J2341.

Necessity is strongest (riddle) H631.7; of work J702. — Wisdom (knowledge) taught by n. J100ff.

Neck hard as ivory F559.5.1. — Bird's n. broken, witch dies G252.3; birds hatched from broken eggs repaired by skillful tailor have red line around n. F662.1.1; burial alive up to n. Q456.1; chain around n.

tests truth H251.3.6; child born with chain around n. H71.7; fowl makes another animal believe that he has had his n. cut off J2413.4.2; ghost leaves mark on n. E542.1.2; giant with one eye in n. F531.1.1.1.1; horse breaks n. J21.24; where horse got arched n. A2351.6; lower lip hangs down to n. F544.1.1; man whose n. fits rope to be executed P14.18; millstone hung around n. Q469.4; monster with life in n. E714.8; origin and nature of animal's n. A2351ff.; red thread on n. of person who has been decapitated and resuscitated *E12.1; sea as n.-deep H681.4.2; sexton behind statue tells old maid praying for a husband to raise her foot to her n. K1971.9; snake disenchanted by being allowed to wrap itself three times around person's n. D759.8; transformation to swans by taking chains off n. D536.1; troll stretches n. so long that fire comes from lips G304.2.1.2; why man's n. its present size A1319.13.

Necks. — Contestants tug iron rings, sever n. H1562.7.

Necklace bursts after emotion F1041.6.1; dropped by crow in snake's hole K401.2.2; of human eyes F827.4, S165.5; transformed D454.8.1; of unsuccessful suitors' heads S110.3.1. — Bride's n. to match mother's H355.5; dead anchorite to accept n. M151.5.1; fairy n. stolen F357; gathering ruby n. from sea H1023.21; girl gives suitor n. to pay bride-price T52.6; hawk carries off queen's n. N698; identification by n. H92; magic n. *D1073; magic strength acquired by looking at n. *D1835.1; man becomes n. D263.2; pig swallows n. F989.22.3; princess's n. in hell F102.3; resuscitation by removing n. E155.3; soul in n. E711.4; speaking n. D1610.27.1; stealing Freya's n. H1151.15; stolen n. does not have same scent as defendant uses J1179.7; transportation by n. D1520.34; tree to heaven from goddess's n. A652.1.1.

Necromancy. — Ghost summoned for n. E387.3.

Necrophilism T466.

Nectar in poison H592.3; -yielding cow B19.2. — "Poison in n." H592.2; riddle involving ruby, n., faithless creature H587.1.

Need. — "Friend is known in n." J401.0.1; magic ownership to be used only in extreme n. D805; parson has no n. to preach X452; philosopher in n. J1289.4; spring breaks forth at primitive hero's n. A941.4.2.

Needle falls into the sea: sought the next summer J1921; in garment as sign H119.2; goes on warpath F1025.2.1; kills an elk (slips into his stomach) L391; put in food causes eater to say "Oh my!" H1185; under hearth causes death D2061.2.2.8.1; that pierces anvil F663.2; and thread as symbol of sex J86, Z186; transformed to another object D454.4; as thumbling's sword F535.1.1.12. — Abbot cannot find his n. J1651; blinding by n. in eyes S165.3; chain tale: pulling n. out of seamstress's hand Z41.8; fool sticks n. in haywagon J2129.4; lie: roofs on n. X1743.3; magic n. *D1181, (from heaven) D811.2.1; man so small he can go through eye of n. F535.2.2; man transformed to n. D253; sewing many garments simultaneously with one n. F662.0.1.1; sexton puts n. in sacramental bread (parson sticks his hand) X411.2; shooting n. from long distance F661.5.5; soul as n. E745.2; squirrel steals dog's n.: enmity between them A2281.2; in storm on ice, numskull sticks n. into ice to keep from blowing away J1965; tailor married to princess betrays trade by calling for n. and thread H38.2.1; thief throws n. containing stolen cloth K341.13.1; swallowed n. emerges through relative's skin X1739.1; threading n. by convent guest H509.1; transformation by magic n. D582.2.

Needles and anchors as fox's excuse J1391.8. — Making n. as devil's task G303.16.19.3.2; origin of tree's n. A2767; piercing with n. as punishment Q469.9.2; skillful marksman throws n. F661.7; sowing n. (like seed) J1932.5.

Needlework. — Fairies' n. F271.8; recognition by unique n. H35.3.

Negating. — Curse given n. good wish M416.

Negative penances Q535ff.

Neglect not what four or five say J21.35.1. — Fairy takes revenge for n. to offer food (drink) F361.1.2; ghost of wife dead from n. E221.5; penance: seven years' service for seven days' n. of religious duty Q523.7; punishment for n. of services to gods (God) Q223ff.; tabu: n. of service to deity C57ff.; untrained colt result of master's n. J143.

Neglected surpasses favorite child L146; wife T271; wife given trifle boasts of it W117.1. — Dead mother returns to care for n. baby *E323.1.2; king n. in exile, courted on throne U83; what one has is n. in search for other things J344.

Neglecting religious exercise V5. — Animal n. its young B751.5; gorilla's large teeth as punishment for n. possessions A2345.9; tabu: n. sexual relations in marriage C163.

Negligent. — Devil likes n. men G303.25.3; host rebukes n. servant J1573.

Negro so black that he makes whole garden somber F573; cannibal G11.4; takes refuge under princess's throne R314; tries in vain to be washed white J511.1. — Treacherous N. K2261; white man made to believe that he is a N. J2013.1; white person transformed to N. D31; why the N. works A1671.1.

Negroes as curse on Ham for laughing at Noah's nakedness A1614.1; made from leftover scraps at creation A1614.5.

Neigh. — Kite tries to n. like a horse J512.2.

Neighbor. — Choice between bad master, bad official, or bad n. J229.5; magic object stolen by n. D861.2.

Neighbors. — Precept of the lion to his sons: keep peace with the n. J22.3; wisdom from n. J179.3.

Neighing of stallion in Assyria impregnates mares in Egypt B741.2. — Wild hunt heralded by n. of horses E501.13.3.2; witch causes person's n. G269.21.2.

Nemesis. — Villain n. Q581.

Neophyte impervious to piercing by saint F1041.0.1.

Nephew P297. — Accidental meeting of n. and uncle N738; cruel n.

S74; murder by n. prophesied M343.3; sun and moon as uncle and n. A711.1; treacherous n. K2217.1; uncle poisons n. S71.1.

Nephew's. — Uncle sleeps with n. beloved H1556.4.4.

Nephews. — Giants dissuaded from eating n. K601.2; king lured to kill n. K948.

Nephites. — Three N. Q45.1.1; three N. granted immortality D1856.2.

Nereid F423.1.

Nessus-shirt burns wearer up D1402.5.

Nest built in tree for fish J1904.4; in penitent's hair Q541.5. — Animal destroys bird's n. in revenge B275.4; abandonment near bird n. S147.1.1; birds forced from n. by mother J65; bird n. of salt J171.5; burning wasp n. J2102.5; why crow cannot enter sparrow's n. A2431.3.6.1; why crow's n. is not tightly built A2431.3.6.2; dove rebuilds her n. in the place where she lost former brood J16; eagle carries giant to its n. F531.6.17.3; eagle's n. as refuge R322; escape from n. of giant bird R253; fools see bee's n. reflected in water: try to carry off well J1791.9; fox burns tree in which eagle has his n. E315.3; fox destroys boasting bird's n. L462; hero prevents destruction of n. B365.2; magic bird n. *D1292; man can hear ant leave n. fifty miles away F641.2; man kills n. of ants J96; prince grows up in eagle's n. B535.0.5; punishment for breaking bird's n. Q285.1.2; recognition through gold found in eagle's n. H91.1; train of troubles for destroying bird's n. N261.1; treasure carried by bird to n. N527; trickster pollutes n. and brood of bird K932.

Nests. — Birds' n. A2431ff.; tree in which people live in n. F811.10.

Net. — Animal grateful for rescue from n. B363; animal rescues from n. B545; birds fly away with n. K581.4.1, K687; dead place n. across river to prevent living man from returning to earth F93.1.1; dove helps deity draw wife into n. B582.2.5; doves in n. console selves J869.1; giant's n. hems in forest F531.4.12; girl comes (drawn by horse on n.) H1053.4, (wrapped in n.) H1054.1; hero captured by n. A511.2.1.1; lion freed from n. by mouse B363.1; lion rescued from n. by rat: eats rat W154.3.1; little fish in n. kept rather than wait for uncertainty of greater catch J321.2; little fishes escape from the n. L331; magic n. *D1196; magpie leads other magpies into master's n. K2032; origin of fishing n. A1457.3; owl warns other birds from limed n. B521.3.5; rat gnaws n. B545.2; traveler says he must look after his n. to see if it has taken fish (enigma) H586.2.2; unraveling a n. in a short time (task) H1094.1.

Nets. — Catching huge fish without n. or tackle (task) H1154.4; catching fish with n. A1527; flying n. of battle hair F1084.0.2; strong man destroys fish and n. F614.5.

Nettle. — Milk added to saint's n. pottage K499.2.2; person compared to ungrateful n. W154.22.

Nettles in bag make man cry out H1185.1; on moon A751.6. — Butter made from n. D476.1.5; reincarnation to n. E648.1; thistles and n. are the devil's vegetables G303.10.13.

Never *Z61. — Ghost laid by n.-ending task E454; giant ogre n. crosses water G131; literal fool: something n. experienced J2469.5; person who n. laughs F591; sham threat: something he has n. done before K1771.3.

New creation shouted away A636; race from single pair (or several) after world calamity A1006.1; star for each birth E741.1.1.1; sun after world catastrophe A719.2. — Clothes remain ever n. F821.11; emperor's n. clothes *K445; father's counsel: marry a n. wife every week H588.3; fool in n. clothes does not know himself J2012.4; old chosen rather than the n. L214; person transforms self, is swallowed and reborn in n. form *E607.2.

News. — Alleged n. of absent lover used to seduce K1349.2; clever ways of breaking bad n. to a king J1675.2; familiar spirit brings n. with magic speed F403.2.3.4; magic object tells n. D1310.4; merchants as spreaders of n. P431.1; promise of dying man to bring n. of other world M252; quest for n. of ancestor H1252.1.1; telling only very good n. J2516.3.5; woman who asked for n. from home J2349.4.

New Year's. — Cow disappears N. night D2087.3.1; dwarfs emigrate N. Eve of 1800 to return N. Eve of 1900 F451.9.3; giant eats men on N. Day G15.1.

Newborn babe reveals secret N468; baby's protest saves life S341.1. — Fairy predicts n. child's greatness F317; fairies make good wishes for n. child F312.1.1; innocent woman accused of killing her n. children K2116.1.1; murder of n. children punished Q418.2; woman eats n. child G72.2; woman refuses to eat own n. child L71.

Next. — If I were not your n. of kin E229.1; planting for the n. generation J701.1.

Niche. — Small n. in house brings large price K182.1.

Nicholas, St., brings Christmas gifts N816; drives off fairies F382.5; saves girl from slavery R165.1; steals bread which is later restored V412.1.

Nick, Old *G303ff.

Nickname. — Not recognizing own name: accustomed to n. J2016.

Niece P298. — Aunt kills n. S72.1; intercourse between man and n. tabu C114.2; uncle slanders n. to appropriate patrimony K361.5.

Night controlled by magic D2146.2; as gods' period A189.17; spent in tree F1045; -spirits *F470ff. — Ability to see by n. F642.4; animals in n.-quarters K1161; castle revolving at n. so that entrance cannot be found F771.2.6.2; children by day and by n. J1273; coming neither by day nor by n. H1057; day husband: n. husband T482; day as son of n. and dawn A1171.4; dead man visits wife every n. E321.2.2; devil comes and works with man who continues to work after n. G303.22.9; devil destroys by n. what is built by day G303.14.1; devil takes the place of woman who went to spend n. with priest G303.25.11; devil promises to help mistreated apprentice if youth will meet him by n. in lonely spot G303.22.12; devil tries to wall in too large a piece of ground in a n. and fails G303.13.3; dwarfs heard at n. F451.3.4.0.1; fairies ride mortal's horses at n. *F366.2; fairies visible only at n. F235.2.1; fear test: spending n. (in church) H1412, (under gallows) H1415, (by grave) H1416; felled tree raises itself again at n. *D1602.2; fool locked in dark room made to believe that it is continuous n. J2332; giants by n. move buildings built by men in day F531.6.6.1; going out at n. alone tabu C755.8; illusory n. K1889.5; intercourse at n. tabu C119.1.6; magic power at n. D1719.9.1; magic stolen at n. D838.13; man attacked on Christmas n. by dancing ghosts E261.3; man protected from the devil by holding three-year old child through the n. G303.16.19.6; marriage to beast by day and man by n. *B640.1; marriage to man alive only at n. T113; marriage for a n. to evade law T156; marriage to tree by day, man by n. T117.5.1; numskull plants seed in daytime and takes it out at n. J2224; object borrowed for one day, one n. retained K232.2; ointment makes n. seem day D1368.11; one sun-god for n., another for day A227.2; origin of n. A1174; person dead by day, alive at n. E155.4; pigeons cover sun, lengthen n. H982.1; prepare for n. camp while it is still day J21.20; princess speaking all n. H343.0.1; riddle of day and n. H722ff.; rivers cease flowing in dead of n. F932.6.3; saint banishes n. for a year *D2146.2.5; size of object transformed at n. D621.4; slaying king by n. P13.6; soldiers of fairy king are trees by day, men by n. F252.3.1; sun caught by man, thus causes n. A728.3; sun shining at n. A1052.2, F961.1.5; sun's n. journey A722; tabu to carry food at n. E751.8; tabu: feasting by n. at beginning of harvest C237; thieves' n. habits J1394ff.; things thought at n. to be other frightful object J1789; thinking it is still n.: mat on head J1819.3; transformation to snakes at n. in order to sleep D659.1; trolls go about at n. F455.3.6; vow to kill wild boar alone at n. M155.1; waxing of strength at n. D1836.3; why animal howls at n. A2427; wife in heaven by day, with husband by n. E322.3; wild hunt appears at n. E501.11.1; witch rides person all n. G269.3.2; witch scatters tools at n. G265.1; woman alive by day, dead at n. E155.4.1; work of day magically overthrown at n. *D2192.

Night's steeds A1172.3.

Nights. — Tabu: staying two n. in one place C761.4.1; why more days than n. (riddle) H772.

Nightcap. — Disguised man wears wife's n. K521.4.1.4.

Nightfall. — Witch's familiar comes at n. G225.0.6.

Nightingale borrows blindworm's eye A2241.5; cannot live in manure nest U144; hears boy call oxen: learns her song A2272.1.1. — Creation of n. A1912.2; helpful n. B451.2; jealous husband kills n. which his wife gets up to hear T257.5; man transformed to n. D151.3; wedding of n. B282.3.1.

Night-jar. — Friendship of leopard-cat and n. A2493.7.

Nightly resuscitation of same man E155.3. — Ghost visits earth n.

E585.3.1; island with n. noise of drums F745; slain warriors revive n. E155.1; tree blooms and grows ripe fruit n. F811.13.

Nightmare F471.1.

Nightmares. — Curse: to be plagued by n. F431.10.

Night-spirits *F470ff.

Night-swallow. — How n. got voice A2421.1.

Nimrod's multiple throne F785.2. — Hill as unfinished tower built like N. tower A963.8

Nine children at a birth T586.1.3; days' fall from heaven to earth A658.1; -headed dragon B11.2.3.4; -headed giant F531.1.2.2.5; heavens A651.1.6; -horned sheep B15.3.1.2; hundred ninety-nine gold pieces J1473.1; as magic number D1273.1.3.1; magic waves D911.1.1; nights' riding from heaven to hell A658.1.1; ranks of heaven A651.1.6.1; -tailed fox B15.7.7.1; -tailed leopard B15.7.7; thousand nine hundred ninety-nine as magic number D1273.1.7.2; worlds A651.0.1; worlds tremble at rebirth F960.1.5. — Are there n. or ten geese? J2032; birth from n. mothers T541.12; boar with n. tusks in each jaw B15.7.8; cauldron warmed by breath of n. maidens F686.1; child born with n. faces, arms, feet T551.10; descendants of n. robbers never to exceed n. M461; devil's n. daughters G303.11.5.1; formulistic number: n. (99, 999, 99,999, etc.) Z71.6; ghost will vanish if walked around n. times E439.8; giant occupies space of thrice n. men F531.2.9; god as son of n. giantesses A112.5; hydra: n.-headed monster B15.1.2.8.1; knights drink from a n.-gallon cup F531.4.3; pygmies n. inches tall F535.2.1; man can breathe n. days under water F691; resuscitation by n.-day dance E63.2; ten for the price of n. J2083.4; witch's n. rows of teeth G214.3.

Ninth. — Leaving capital n. night tabu C751.6.

Ninety. — Getting n. pigs and horses H1154.2.1.

Ninety-nine wise men J1149.12. — Devil has n. heads G303.4.1.1.1; formulistic number: 99,999 Z71.6.

Nine-hundred horses draw strong man's chariot F639.12. — Disenchantment after n. years D791.1.5.

Niobe boasts of her children C452.

Nipple from brother's caress J1833.1.1.

Nipples. — Black n. reveal virginity loss T494; thorns around n. F546.4.

Nisser (brownies) F482; in form of cows D133.1.1.

Nit lives at edge of hair A2236.6, A2433.5.1.

Nix-Naught-Nothing S243.

Nkundak's. — Origin of n. (crest) A2223.2, A2321.6, (feathers) A2313.4, (voice) A2421.5.

"No" C495.2.2.1. — Answering only "Yes" and "N." J1255; princess must answer all questions by "N." K1331; witness always to answer "N." J1141.13.

Noah saves a giant on the ark F531.5.9. — Dove returns to ark in obedience to N. A2221.7; raven does not return to N. A2234.1ff.

Noah's curse admits devil to ark C12.5.1; secret betrayed by his wife K2213.4.2. — Father of N. sons J2713; helpful animal stops leak in N. Ark *B527.2; devil gets into ark by hiding in shadow of N. wife G303.23.1; persons excluded from N. ark build another A1021.0.1.

Nobility of character of kings P12.9. — Animal granted patent of n. A2546; prohibition on intercourse with girls of n. C110.1; royalty and n. *P0—P99; tokens of n. left with exposed child S334.

Noble lady P60ff.; in love with lowly T91.6; person must do menial service as punishment *Q482; poets refuse to associate with lowly born J411.3.1. — Disguised n. recognized by habitual speech H38.1; special food of n. girl tabu C246.2; tests for n. blood H1574.1.

Nobles ruin peasant's crops U35.2. — Riddle: the king is surrounded by his n. H825.

Nobleman P50; after death must serve as menial Q482.3; marries, abandons poor girl T72.2; rescues lady R111.5; unpunished for murder U34; as wild huntsman E501.1.2. — Conflict between peasant and n. decided so that each must answer riddles H561.1.1; deaf man and proud n. X111.6; dwarf conducts shepherd to hell to collect debt from n. F451.5.1.14; impoverished n. offers wife to ruler W11.7.1; perseverance wins place for n. Q81.1; seduction by posing as n. K1315.5; sham n. K1952.

Nobleman's. — Troubled n. request not to be refused P95.

Noblemen who quarreled over a device J552.1. — Origin of n. A1656.

Noblewoman weds shepherd T121.2.

Nocturnal, see also **Night.** — Deceptive n. noises K1887.2; thieves' n. habits J1394ff.; vow against n. assault M163.

Nod. — Son obeys aged father's n. J1521.2.

Nodding. — Dwarfs appear n. F451.2.0.4.

Nodes. — Why bamboo has n. A2756.

Noise heard before death D1827.1.3; in house as ghost J1782.3. — Capture by causing animal to make n. K756.2.1; catching a n. (task) H1023.12; devil goes through stove with great n. G303.17.2.3; flute makes more n. J1541.2; foolishness of n.-making when enemies overhear J581; giants' shouts are storms or great n. F531.3.8; great n. from bass-viol (lie) X1866; husband deceived by paramour's n. K1549.7; island with nightly n. of drums F745; making n. tabu on way to otherworld C715.2; marvelous sensitiveness: fainting from n. of wooden pestle and mortar F647.8; wild hunt disappears with loud n. E501.16.1; wild hunt heralded by n. E501.13.1.

Noises. — Deceptive nocturnal n. K1887.2; mysterious ghostlike n. E402; poltergeist makes n. F473.5.

Noisy things often empty J262. — Mouse teaches her child to fear quiet cats but not n. cocks J132; ogre kills n. children G478.

"Noman" *K602.

Non-believers. — Miracle manifested to n. *V340ff.

None. — "Let n. in" J2516.6; riddles with "n." as answer H881.
Nonsense. — Cumulative n. tales Z20.1.
Noodle. — Strong hero born from n. F611.1.11.1.
Noonday. — Fairies visible only at n. F235.2.2.
Noose changed, ogre's daughter killed K1611.4; used by suicide as protection from accident D1384.2. — Capture in n. K743; hangman's n. cures scrofula D1502.2.3.1; hangman's n. gives luck in gambling D1407.2; ogre caught in n. and killed G514.3.
Norns prophesy at childbirth M301.12.
Norse custom of vow taking M119.3.
North as abode of evil spirits G633; forbidden direction C614.1.1; wind tempers fury of south wind A1127.1.1. — God of N. Star A253; hero goes n. to trolls H945.2; hell located to the n. A671.0.1; land of dead in n. E481.6.1; making sun, moon shine in n. H1023.16; origin of N. Star A774; saint's body laid n. and south E411.0.8; sky supported by N. Star A702.3.
Northern. — Origin of the N. Lights A795.
Northwest. — Giants live in n. F531.6.2.4; otherworld in n. F136.3.
Norwegians. — Lobsters mistaken for N. J1762.7.
Nose cut off (to get it out of the light) J2119.1, (as punishment) Q451.5ff., (for breaking tabu) C948.2, (to fulfill wish) J2072.6, (for not paying tax) P536.1; -flute A1461.7; made from clay from previous man A1316.1.1; mutilated S172; wagered N2.3.4. — Animal unusual as to his n. B15.5; why animals move n. A2476ff.; birth from mucus from the n. T541.8.3; child born through n. T541.8.3.1; contest in life-like painting: fly on saint's n. H504.1.1; corpse bites off woman's n. E259.1; cut-off n. K1512; devil's n. G303.4.1.4; "follow your n.": fool climbs tree J2461.6; fool and visitor's large n. J2512; giant with peculiar n. F531.1.6.6; huldra's long n. F460.1.6; husband believes he has cut off wife's n. J2315.2; improving the wife's face by cutting off her n. J2119.1.1; killing fly on judge's n. J1193.1; law: n. for a nose P522.1.1; magic object makes n. long (restores it) D1376.1ff.; man too lazy to wipe n.: loses bride W111.1.4; nature of animal's n. A2335.2ff.; ogre monstrous as to n. G362; person unusual as to his n. F514; remarkable n. F543; resuscitation by powder in n. E108.1; rubbing n. on hot griddle as punishment Q499.8; ruby appears as charitable king is blowing n. V411.7; sharp instrument as n. deceives ogre G572.2; son on gallows bites his mother's (father's) n. off Q586; treasure from n. D1454.9; why tapir has long n. A2335.3.2; wife's n. cut off, husband resuscitated E165.2.
Noses. — Convention of all with long n. X133; distribution of n. A1316.1; ears, fingers and n. of demons cut off as proof of killing them H105.5; noseless man persuades others to cut off n. J758.1.1; numskulls count selves by sticking their n. in the sand J2031.1; robbers' n. cut off K912.0.1; scavenger eats human n. G63; thousand-faced goddess blowing her n. J1261.10.

Nosebleed. — Amulet cures n. D1504.2; devil dies of n. G303.17.3.1.

Noseless man persuades others to cut off noses J758.1.1; ogre G362.1; pygmies F535.4.3; person F514.1.

Nose-ring. — Shooting jewels from n. F661.10; spear shot through n. F661.3.1.

Nostril. — Devil has only one n. G303.4.1.4.2; upper lip curls over n. F544.1.1.

Nostrils. — Creation of cat: sneezed from lion's n. A1811.2; devil drives carriage drawn by horses whose n. shoot fire G303.7.3.2; devil without n. G303.4.1.4.2; greedy one stuffs food in n. W151.10; remarkable n. F543.4.

Notary collects invented debts K441.2.1. — Ignorant n. incompetent J1749.2.

Notches in elder twigs reveal witch G257.6. — Cutting n. in table reveals witch G257.3; game of putting heads in n. K865.

Noteriety. — Burning the temple to attain n. J2162.1.

Nothing. — Boy who worked for n. at all demands it J2496.1; Christ, not having married, knew n. about suffering T251.0.2; first man created from n. A1275.7; getting n. H1045.1; lazy man spoiling materials, makes n. W111.5.9; lazy wife's defence: has done n. W111.3.4; Nix-Naught-N. S243; poor husband has n. to give guest P336.2; to get "n." and show it K1218.1.8.

Notice. — Death feigned in order to leave without n. K1864; transformation to escape n. D642.5.

Nourished. — Men n. by animals B530ff.; starving wife n. with husband's flesh and blood T215.3; sun, moon and stars n. on fire A700.7.

Nourishing. — Transformation for n. animal D518; wood of sixty trees n. three hundred men apiece F812.2.

Nucleus. — Creator sends crow to scout for earth n. A812.3.

Nude, see also **Naked;** woman clothed in own hair F555.3.1. — Certain peoples go n. A1683.4; small-pox deity rides n. on ass A137.8.

Nudes' sex unknown since no clothes on J1745.1.

Nudity a sign of anger Z181. — Hair protection against n. F555.3.4; magic power of n. D1796.1; princess brought to laughter by n. of old woman in quarrel at well H341.3.1.

Number of animals' eyes A2332.2ff. — Extraordinary n. of children in family T586.2; feet with unusual n. of toes F551.2; hands with unusual n. of fingers F552.1.1; test of resourcefulness: finding n. of people in dark, closed room H506.2; thirteen as unlucky n. N135.1.

Numbers. — Chains based on n. Z21; formulistic n. Z71ff.; illogical use of n. J2213; in n. there is strength J1279.4; lies about n. X1710; magic n. *D1273.1; riddles of n. H700ff.; symbolic meaning of n. H602ff.

Numskull, see also **Fool;** bribed to keep silent in elephant sale N613; injured J2131; talks to himself and frightens robbers away N612.

Numskull's outcry overawes tiger N691.1.

Numskulls go a-travelling J1711; quarrel over a greeting J1712.

Nun aids capture of ravisher Q244.2; asked why she did not call for help when raped says it was during the silent period J1264.4; claims her child is by the Holy Ghost J1264.6; eating unblessed lettuce eats a demon G303.16.2.3.4; falsely accused of adultery K2112; forgets to hail Mary and goes into the world to sin V254.5; leaving convent wounded by Jesus's image V122.1; refuses to look at man T362; sees Jesus after prayer D1766.1.2; tells friar to castrate self J1919.5.2; turned to stone Q551.3.4.3; who saw the world K1841.1. — Disappointed sweetheart becomes n. T93.2.1; image bars way of n. trying to escape convent to join lover V122; incontinent n. *V465.1.2; long-suffering n. rewarded Q87.3; maiden banished because she wants to become a n. Q431.3; obedient and industrious n. worthiest in the convent V461.1; owl (ghost of n.) in wild hunt E501.4.5; prophecy: unborn child to be n. M364.7.4; tabu for n. to ring church bell C94.7; Virgin appears to n. V277.1; Virgin miraculously prevents n. from deserting convent V265; woman continent in two marriages becomes n. T315.3; youth says he is associating with a pious person (n. as mistress) J1264.5.

Nun's illegitimate child T640.1. — Maggots in n. sores become jewels V222.15; pregnant n. virginity restored T313.1.1; wager on n. chastity N15.2.

Nuns fondled infant Christ V211.1.8.2; seduced by men in disguise K1321.4. — Abbess has 24 n. for 12 monks (12 n. left for guests) J1264.9; devil brings about seduction of n. Q220.1.1; devil seduces impious n. G303.3.1.12.1; priest impregnates five n. J1264.7.

Nunnery, see **Convent.**

Nuptial tabu C117.

Nurse begs alms to feed child R131.0.1; exchanges children so favorite will be wealthy K1923.1; rescues child R169.1.3. — Absent-minded n. puts child down well J2175.3; animal n. *B535; divine n. T605; fairy n. as helper N815.1; fairies take human n. to attend fairy child F372; faithful n. exposes own baby instead of tyrant's P361.4; identification by n. H183; prince stolen while n. dances K341.17.1; repentant n. disguises as hermit K1837.3; sham n. kills enemy's children K931; wolf waits in vain for n. to throw away child J2066.5.

Nurse's eye covered to conceal lover K1516.2; false plea admitted: child demanded J1162.1.

Nurses. — Diabolical child kills his wet-n. T614.

Nursing of Christ by saint V211.1.8.1; of hero A511.2.2; mothers' milk augmented by spring D927.3. — Baby saint not n. on fast days V229.2.3.1; strong hero's long n. F611.2.3; why bears have no breasts for n. A2353.3.

Nurture and growth of children *T610ff.

Nut clarifies waters F930.8; falls and wakes man about to be bitten by snake N652; hits cock in head: he thinks world is coming to an end X43.3; transformed to another object D451.7; transformed to person

D431.11. — Antelope transformed to n. D421.2.1; ape throws away n. because of its bitter rind J369.2; boy follows n. into lower world F102.4; creation of man from n. A1253.2; deceptive n. and olive division: inside and outside K171.3; earth from n. in devil's mouth A835; extraordinary n. F813.3; fairy's share of feast a n. F263.1; giant thinks hammer blow on head is n. falling F531.5.4; magic n. *D985ff.; magic n. tree D950.16; man becomes n. D222; ungrateful wanderer pulls n. tree to pieces to get the nuts W154.6; why lightning spares n. tree A2791.2.

Nuts held by curly hair F555.9. — Devil in woods to gather n. on Christmas Eve G303.8.13.3; fairies eat n. F243.2; girl eats only kola n. and tobacco F561.5; girl summons fairy lover by pulling n. F301.1.1.4; girls looking for n. have adventures N771.2; god blamed for small n. J2215.6; men from long n., women from short ones A1253.2.2; men wait in vain for n. to fall from tree J2066.3; picking all n. from tall tree as task H1121; pulling n. forbidden C517; resuscitation by breaking n. on head E181.1.1; sexton hears thieves in cemetery cracking n. X424; test of sex of girl masking as man: n. and apples offered H1578.1.5.

Nutshell. — Dress so fine that it goes in n. F821.2; wagon of n. F861.4.2.

Nutshells. — Boat made of n. F841.1.4.

Nymph of Luck and Ill-Luck N141.3; wives make hero sleep with fingers in mouth K521.4.6. — Magic object received from river-n. D813.1.

Nymphs of Paradise F499.2. — Man sees celestial n. F642.5.

Oak smell maddens swine B783. — Bashful suitor woos o. T69.4; fairies dance under o. tree F261.3.1.2; fettering to o. Q434.2; last leaf never falls from o. K222; magic o. tree *D950.2; numskulls try to get pears from an o. J1944.1; origin of o. A2681.2; sacred o. V1.7.1.1; why o. leaves are indented A2761.1.1.

Oaks. — Talking to o. to warn sons K649.6.

Oar. — Ferryman puts o. into king's hand and he must remain ferryman P413.1.1; golden o. F841.2.4; magic o. *D1124; silver o. F841.2.3.

Oars and masts transformed to serpents D444.11. — Boat with many o. mistaken for animal J1772.14; goose wings as witch's o. G241.4.1.

Oarsman. — Lie: remarkable o. X971.

Oasis. — Unexpected encounter in o. N761.

Oath to break oaths J1458; on boiling oil as chastity test H412.4.2; that devil may whet scythe C12.3; of friendship between cat and rat A2493.9.1; on the iron K1115; literally obeyed K2312; taken on boy's head: boy dies if false H252.4; taken before image H251.3.5. — Animal makes religious o. B251.7; attitudes of animals toward o. B279.2; escape by equivocal o. K550.1; false and profane swearing of o. forbidden C94.2; fruit falls if o. false H252.3; faithless wife's o. to be faithful J2301.1; impostor forces o. of secrecy *K1933; magic o. *D1273.5; magic o. stops killer D1400.1.11.1; unjust o. countered by another J1521.4; wife's equivocal o. K1513.

Oaths and vows *M100—M199; before gods as test of truth H253; drive ogres away G571. — Goddess of o. A484.1.

Oatmeal. — Miller disturbs fairies' o. F361.17.1.

Oats transformed to wheat D451.2.3.

Obedience W31; to bride as suitor test H313. — Animal blessed for o. to deity A2221.6; bride test: o. *H386; disenchantment by o. and kindness D731; intemperance in o. J555; literal o. J2460ff.; test of wife's o. *H473ff.; tests of o. *H1557.

Obedient husband: the leave of absence J2523; and industrious nun the worthiest in the convent V461.1; woman's pestle magically suspended J2411.9. — Boat o. to master's will D1523.2.4; magic object o. to master alone *D1651ff.; wager on the most o. wife *N12.

Obeisance to devil at witch's sabbath G243.1; to king taught J80.2.

Object-birth slander K2115.2; bleeds F991; magically attaches itself to a person D2171.1; magically made hideous D1873; sent to go by itself J1881.1; sinks into earth F948; thought to be animal J1771; transformed to animal D440ff.; transformed to another object D450—D499; transformed to person D430ff.; of wild hunt's pursuit E501.5ff. — Animal characteristics from transformation of o. A2262; animal or o. indicates election of ruler H171; animal retrieves lost o. B548; animal thought to be o. J1761ff.; animal transformed to o. D420ff.; child born bearing an o. T552; disenchantment by use of magic o. D771; earth from o. thrown on primeval water A814; escape by use of substituted o. *K525ff.; fairy in form of o. F234.3; fairies made visible through use of magic o. F235.4; food given to o. J1856; forbidden o. C620; gift or sale to o. J1850ff.; inability to find o. one is carrying J2025; life dependent on external o. *E765ff.; looking at certain o. forbidden C315; magic o. received from animal B505; magician recovers lost o. with the devil's help G303.22.2; man made from o. A1240—A1269; man transformed to o. *D200—D299; marriage of person and o. T117; moon from o. thrown into sky A741; object transformed to o. D450—D499; one o. thought to be another J1772; partaking of one particular o. forbidden C620ff.; person enamored of an o. T461; pestilence in form of o. F493.0.3; quest for lost o. H1386; reincarnation in o. *E630ff.; resuscitation by magic o. E64; size of o. changed at will D631.3; soul as o. E745ff.; soul kept in o. E711; soul of o. E701ff.; suitor test: finding o. hidden by princess H322.1; sun from o. thrown into sky A714; test of truth by magic o. H251ff.; transformation to o. for breaking tabu C961; transformation by magic o. D685; transformation: pig to o. D422.3; treasure discovered by magic o. *N533; troll in form of o. G304.1.2; witch in form of o. G212.

Objects attacked under illusion that they are men K1883.2; effect change of luck N135; go journeying together F1025; with mistaken identity J1770ff.; as part of wild hunt E501.10ff.; thought to be devils, ghosts J1780ff.; of worship V1ff. — Absurd sympathy for animals or o.

J1870ff.; animals or o. treated as human J1850—J1899; attention drawn by magic o.: recognition follows H151.1; capture by hiding in disguised o. K753; chastity test by magic o. H410ff.; devil in form of inanimate o. G303.3.4; fool loses magic o. by talking about them J2355.1; furniture and o. in otherworld F166; ghosts of o. E530ff.; heavenly bodies from o. thrown into sky *A700.1; invisible o. D1982; magic o. D800—D1699, (acquisition) D810ff., (characteristics) D1600—D1699, (function) D1300—D1599, (kinds) D900—D1299, (loss of) D860ff., (in otherworld) F166.4, (ownership) D800—D899; mountain with marvelous o. at top F759.1; princess defeated in repartee by means of o. accidentally picked up H507.1.0.1; quest to devil for o. H1273; recognition by overheard conversation with o. H13.2; recovering lost o. from the sea (task) H1132; religious edifices and o. *V100—V199; stars from o. thrown into sky A763; tasks contrary to nature of o. H1023; vital o. E770ff.

Obligation. — Return from dead to repay o. E340ff.

Obliterated. — Sin o. by saying of "Aves" *V254.1; sincere confession miraculously o. as sign of forgiveness V21.1.

Oblong. — How the earth became o. A851.

Obscene language tabu C496; pseudo-magic letters K115.1.3; tricks played on simpleton wishing to marry K1218.9. — Giantess in o. skirt F531.4.7.1.2; man seduced by woman's o. trick K1386.

Observation of dying people for a year takes man's thoughts from lust J62. — Deductions from o. J1661.1; imitation of diagnosis by o.: ass's flesh J2412.4; tasks performed by close o. *H962; wisdom (knowledge) acquired from o. *J50ff.

Observer insists on sharing love intrigue K1271.1.4.2.

Obstacle flight *D672, (Atalanta type) *R231, (reversed) D673; race between deer and hare K11.9.

Obstacles. — Magic object removes o. D1562ff.; remove o. from path J753.

Obstinate wife *T255ff.

Obvious. — Futility of trying to hide an o. deed J1082.

Occasion. — Identity tested by demanding that person say again what he said on former o. H15.1; tabu: looking at supernatural wife on certain o. *C31.1.2.

Occasions. — Prayer on special o. V57.3.

Occult. — Contours of land from o. hero harrowing A951.3; studying o. tabu C825.

Occupation. — Hero (heroine) of unpromising o. L113.

Occupational tricks on new employees J2347.

Ocean, see also **Sea;** from creator's sweat A923; of milk J2349.3; the son of Earth and Heaven A921; under this world A816.2. — Catching o. foam in cloth H1049.1; devil piles sand in o. so that vessels may run aground G303.9.9.5; ditch is really o. F1071.2; drunk wagers he can drink o. dry J1161.9; extraordinary descent into o. F1022; giant wades o. F531.3.1; riddle of o. and rivers H734; task: measuring o. H1144; witch in bed gets o. water G259.5.

Octopus grows inside girl B784.1.4; holds sky against earth A665.5; transformed to stone D426.2. — Demigod conquers great o. A531.4.1; demon-o. G308.9; enmity of o. and rat A2494.16.7; helpful o. B477; mythical o. B63; rat defecates upon rescuing o. K952.1.2, (origin of tubercles on head) A2211.14; thieving o. K366.8.

Odd number strokes in beating the devil G303.16.19.19; numbers (formulistic) Z71.0.1.

Odes. — Marriage o. T136.3.2.

Odin *A128.2; battles Fenris Wolf at end of world A1082.2; as falcon D152.4.1; as magician D1711.6.1. —Going to bed with O. H1199.11.

Odor, see also **Smell**; reveals witch G259.2; of wine cask J34. — Animals ask for goddess's perfume: punishment, bad o. A2232.5; devil has a sulphurous o. G303.4.8.1, G303.6.3.4; foul o. in hell A689.2; marvelous sensitiveness: woman has o. of goat's milk F647.5; person's remarkable o. F687; sea's unpleasant o. A925.3, A1119.3; sweet o. in heaven A661.0.8; why herrings have bad o. A2416.7.

Odors. — Soul sustained on pleasant o. E708.

Odysseus, see also **Ulysses**; bends his bow H31.2; and Polyphemus K521.1, K602, K603, K1011; recognized by his dog H173; returns in humble disguise K1815.1; and Sirens J672.1.

Oedipus exposed and reared at strange king's court S354; fulfills prophecies (parricide) M343, (mother-incest) M344; solves riddle of Sphinx *H541.1.1.

Offending the gods C50ff., (punished) *Q221; spirits tabu C40ff.; supernatural husband forbidden *C32ff. — Christianity o. dwarfs F451.9.1.6.

Offense to skull *C13. — Magic knowledge of o. to deity K1810.0.12; smallness of o. no excuse when hunter prepares to kill lark U32.

Offensive. — Curses because of o. answer to saint M411.8.3.

Offering. — Base money in the o. J1582; merman demands cattle as o. B82.2; sexton's own wife brings her o. K1541; punishment for failure to give o. to gods Q223.14; theft of cup from fairies o. mortal drink F352.1.

Offerings to holy wells V134.2. — Tabu: eating from o. to gods C57.1.3; trickster shams death and eats grave o. K1867.2.

Offertory. — Money from o. as cure D1500.1.10.3.

Office. — Robber promised larger sum at o. D439.7; Virgin designates favorite for election for o. V261; Virgin restores o. to ignorant man V261.1.

Offices. — Animals perform o. of church B253; largest burdens laid on smallest asses, best o. to most ignorant men U12.

Officer accidentally finds fugitive N618. — Common man transformed to grand o. D22.1; rescuer disguised as o. saves prisoner K649.2.

Officer's. — Drunken o. stolen mantle J1211.2.1.

Officers praised in reverse from their real merit K2136. — Treacherous o. and tradesmen K2240ff.

Official. — Choice between bad master, bad o., or bad neighbor J229.5; clever o. J1115.10; riddle propounded on pain of loss of o. position H541.3; symbolic interpretation of o. robes H608; theft by disguising as palace o. K311.10.

Officials. — Presumptuous o. disregarded J982.

Officiousness rebuked J1300ff.

Offspring, see also **Children, Descendants;** of fairy and mortal F305; of first parents A1277; of human and animal intercourse B636; of living and dead person E474.1; of marriage to animal *B630ff.; of water-spirit and mortal F420.6.1.6. — Charm for begetting o. K115.1.4; first parents devour o. A1277.1; horses as o. of the devil G303.10.8; lizards are o. of the devil G303.10.10; man as o. of creator A1216; monstrous o. from animal marriage B634; quality of o. preferred to quantity J281; sun as o. of moon A715.5; universe as o. of creator A615.

Often. — Tabu: doing thing too o. C762.

Ogam inscription on shield misreported K511.2. — Origin of o. inscriptions A1484.1; recognition by o. carving H35.4.1; till o. and pillar be blent Z61.1.

Ogre, see also **Giant;** allows self to be tied to learn magic K713.1.5; appeased by being called uncle Q41.1; assumes form of widow's husband K1919.2; bribes boy not to cut tree N699.5; defeated G500—G599; disguised as holy man K1827.0.1; frightened into rolling self in mat K711.3; frightened at rustling K2345; as helper *N812; helps tortoise who catches him K1111.3; keeps girl in drum R49.3; overawed K1710ff.; poses as mother, kills child K2011.1.1; produces water for caravan N812.6; released in return for magic girdle M242.3; sees beautiful woman reflected in water and attempts to drink lake dry J1791.6.2; suitor persuaded to bury woman's murdered lover K912.3; tars hero's boat, thinking to injure him J2171.1.2; tempts fugitive with ring R231.1; vulnerable only if face turned away Z315. — Abduction by o. R11; adventure from following o. to cave N773.1; ants' nest thrown on o. K621.1; bringing an o. to court (task) H1172; calling on o. forbidden C20ff.; centipede kills o. B524.1.10; child sold (promised) to o. *S211; flight on a tree, which o. tries to cut down *R251; giant o. can be killed only with own club Z312.2; giant o. guards tree D950.0.1.1; girl promised by parents to o. S240.1; grateful o. resuscitates benefactor G513.1; madness from seeing o. F1041.8.3; magic adhesion to o. *D2171.2; magic fish talk so that o. thinks hero has many brothers with him D1613.1; magic tree guarded by giant o. D950.0.1.1; man becomes o. D94; ornament compels woman to follow o. D1427.2; prophecy of o.-child so pregnant woman will be killed K2115.3; rescue from o. G550ff., R111.1.1; secret of killing o. N476.3; sex exchanged with o. D593;

sham doctor kills o. K824.1; skillful marksman shoots both eyes of o. F661.5.4; strong man serves o. as punishment for stealing food F613.4; sultan's daughter as bribe to o. S222.4; sun, moon born from an o. A715.3; tasks assigned o. H932; treacherous mother marries o. and plots against son S12.1; troll as o. *G304ff.; youth sells himself to an o. in settlement of a gambling debt S221.2.

Ogre's beard caught fast K1111.1; exchange of sex D10.1; life in feather in pocket E715.1.3.1; magic invisibility D1981.4; separable soul in many objects E718; son guards treasure N571.1; soul in spot below ear E714.10. — Falling into o. power G400—G499; magic object taken from o. house D838.2; man married to o. daughter T115; noose changed, o. daughter killed K1611.4; stealing o. grain H1151.25; substituted string causes o. death K1611.1.

Ogres G (entire chapter); duped into fighting each other K1082; live with men A1101.1.3; overawed by stray objects N691. — Castle guarded by o. F771.5.2; castle inhabited by o. F771.4.1; country ridded of o. A1416; giant o. G100—G199; invulnerable o. D1840.3; men transformed to o. D47.2.

Ogress bathes in pool, beautified G264.0.1; with breasts thrown over her shoulder *G123; captured and reformed R9.3; demands eyes of six raja wives K961.2.2; disguised as queen H919.6; frightened of child with moustache K547.10; in frightening guises H1401.2; puts bride in tree, takes her place K1911.1.7; reincarnated as bramble bush E631.4; transformed to man D11.1; turns child into cannibal G34; whets teeth to kill captive G83.1; -wife orders rajah expel other wives S413.1. — Cannibal o. G86.1; children devoured by o. F913.2; dagger indicates o. dead or alive E761.7.15; escape from o. by substituting pig K525.7; princess becomes o. D47.3; separable soul of o. E710.1; slander: woman an o. K2124; stealing drum of o. H1151.24; tongue of o. becomes surfboard D457.14.1; transformation to escape o. D642.6; winning daughter of o. for bride H305.

Oil, see also **Ointment;** becomes jewels D475.4.9; bursts from ground as saint made bishop V222.5; poured in dog's ear brings rain D1542.1.6; from relics has curative powers V211.0.1.1; sold to iguana J1852.1.2; on tree prevents pursuit K619.2; well driller drills for fifty years W37.1. — Bath of boiling o. F872.2; boiling to death in pitch or o. Q414.1, S112.1; burning o. thrown on ogre G572.1; discovery of edible o. O1429.1; discovery of o. A1426.1; escape from boiling o. R215.2; hot o. poured on guinea fowl's feet A2375.2.10; jar of o. broken before sold J2061.1.4; jinn falls into boiling o. G512.3.4; magic object provides o. D1482; magic o. D1242.4; magic o.-spouting fountain D925.0.1; man becomes o. D242; murder by burning in o. K955.2; oath on boiling o. H412.4.2; ordeal by burning o. H221.3; origin of o. press A1446.5.6; pressing out large quantity of o. F639.7; quest for magic pig's o. H1332.5.1; quest for o. to anoint dying H1265; rivers of o., milk, wine and honey

in otherworld F162.2.6; saint unhurt by boiling o. D1841.2.2; saint
uninjured by boiling o. D1841.2.2.1; selling old o. wells for post holes
X1761.1; shower of o. F962.6.4; spilling o. good luck J2214.7; thieves
hidden in o. casks K312; underground o. pools discovered N597; water
becomes o. D478.7; well of o. runs into river F932.4; where is o. in
sesame flower? J1291.4; why palm o. is red A2877.

Ointment, see also **Oil;** in eye to imitate witch G242.8; makes night
seem day D1368.1.1. — Fairies made visible through use of o. F235.4.1;
invulnerability by being burned and anointed with magic o. D1846.1;
itch-producing o. X34; magic o. *D1244; pepper given as o. for burns
K1014; transformation by rubbing with o. D594.

Oisin's poor diet in Patrick's house J1511.13.

Ojibwa. — Origin of the O. A1611.1.1.

Old, see also **Age;** age personified Z114; age must be planned for J761;
chosen rather than new L214; devil dies when he is fastened in hell's
door by his beard G303.17.3.2; god slain by young A192.1.1; king
attacked P16.3.1; maid marries devil G303.12.5.1; man (burns self with
gunpowder, then hot water) N255.6, (as creator) A15.3, (contented till
forbidden to leave city) H1557.3, (and Death) C11, (desires human flesh)
G95, (as godfather to underground folk) F372.2.1, (helper) N825.2,
(in love with young woman) J1221, (married to young, unfaithful wife)
T237, (of the sea) G311, (from sky as creator) A21.2; Nick *G303ff.;
ox yoked with young ox J441.1; people killed in famine S110.1; person
commits suicide when strength fails P674; person helps perform task
H971; person helper on quest H1233.1; shoes patched with new J2129.5;
sweetheart chosen in preference to new J491; teacher wants to marry
young girl T91.4.1.1; warrior longs for more adventure H1221.1; wine
chosen (must honor old age) J1313; woman (beautiful as in youth)
F575.1.2, (has control over frost) D2143.5.1, (doesn't want to die for
daughter) H1556.4.5.1, (gives chickens to devils) G303.25.6, (as guardian
of gods' islands) A955.12, (helper) *N825.3, (intercepts letter and takes
girl's place in man's bed) K1317.2.1, (has lived for ages) D1857.1, (in
ogre's house) G530.5, (and her pig: cumulative story) Z41ff., (as prophet)
M301.2, (ruler of dead in lower world) E481.1.1, (by spring as helper)
N825.3.2, (substituted for bride) K1911.1.5, (substitutes for wife in bed)
K1843.3, (suckling babies to prove child hers) H495.3, (and tiger flee
each other) K2323.3; woman's (curse) M411.5, (maledictions inform
abandoned hero of his parentage and future) S375, (pleas tabu) C745.1.
— Abduction by o. woman R39.2; angel in form of o. man V231.6;
association of young and o. J440ff.; bedridden o. man hanged, guilty
youth spared J2233.1.1; conception in o. age T538; creation of monkeys
from o. woman thrown into fire A1861.2; deity disguised as o. person
K1811.2; defeating certain o. woman (task) H1149.3; demon as o. woman
G302.3.3; devil a little, gray, o. man G303.3.1.5; devil marries o. maid
who proves to be a termagant and miser G303.12.3; disguise as o. man

K1821.8; disguise as o. man to enter enemy's camp K2357.3; diving into lake makes person o. K1072; dwarfs have o. faces F451.2.5.1; escape in o. woman's skin K521.1.4; extremely o. person F571; foolish youth in love with ugly o. mistress J445.1; Fortune as o. woman N114; in o. age spirits become gods A117.3; jokes on o. maids X750ff.; king killed when o. P16.3; king seizes o. woman's cow U35.1; king too o. goes himself into grave P16.3.2; magic object makes person o. *D1341ff.; magic object received from o. (man) D822, (woman) D821; new bags for o. K266; not to go where o. man has young wife J21.3; ogre so o. that his eyelids must be propped up G631; owl advises o. man of gods' visit B569.1; princess brought to laughter by indecent show made in quarrel with o. woman at well H341.3.1; prophecies from o. man who writes in a book M301.4; revenant as o. man E425.2.1; resourcefulness test: finding how o. three horses are H506.11; Satan as o. man G303.3.1.24; selling three o. women (task) H1153; sexton behind crucifix tells o. maid she will have no husband K1971.8.1; supplies from toe of o. woman D1470.2.4; tasks performed with help of o. woman H971; thief disguised as o. woman K311.16.1; three hundred year o. man has had intercourse only every two years T317.0.1; transformation to o. man to escape recognition D1891; transformation: prince to o. man D93; treacherous o. woman K2293; what becomes of the o. moon J2271.2; where the devil can't reach, he sends an o. woman G303.10.5; why men become o. A2861; wild hunt appears at o. (battlefield) E501.12.6.1, (mill) E501.12.10; wine very o. but small serving J1316; wisdom from o. man J151ff.; women o. from their birth T615.2.

Older, see also **Age, Elder.** — "Ass of twenty o. than man of seventy" J1352.2; enigmatic counsels of o. brother H596.1.1; inquirer always sent to o. person *F571.2; transformation to o. person *D56.1.

Oldest son responsible for others' welfare P233.5; warrior preferred as suitor T92.13. — What is o. (riddle) H659.1.

Olive branch (insures fidelity of husband) D1355.8, (laid on altar as sacrifice) V15, (makes woman master in household) D1359.1.1, (symbol of peace) Z157. — Athena chooses o. tree because of its fruitfulness J241.1; deceptive nut and o. division: inside and outside K171.3; laurel and o. tree scorn thornbush as umpire J411.7; magic o. tree D950.9; why o. is bitter A2771.8.1.

Ollamhs sacred V291.

Olympus A151.1.

Omen, see also **Divination.** — Animals of good o. A2536; ghost as death o. E574; ghost light as death o. E530.1.6; magic spear gives o. of victory D1311.17.1; mermaid appears as o. of catastrophe B81.13.7; priest makes the o. come true J1624; stars as o. D1291.2.1; wild hunt as o. E501.20ff.; wraith as calamity o. E723.8.

Omens in love affairs T3. — Beasts furnish o. B147.1ff.; fool believing in o. refuses to prepare for death J2285.1; foolish interpretation of o.

J2285; future learned through o. *D1812.5ff.; house where o. work by contraries X1505.1.

Omnipotent god A102.4.

Omnipresent god A102.5.

Omniscience of a god A102.1, D1810.0.1; not possessed by fairies F254.2.
— God's o. J1617; magic seat gives o. D1310.1.

Once. — Door to fairyland opens o. a year F211.1.1; fairies can set down an object o. but cannot raise it again F255.2; magic effective when struck o. D806.1; strong man kills many men at o. F628.2.1.

One, see also **Unique;** bull, one cow survive plague F989.6; day from happiness to misfortune H685.1; day and one night taken as forever K2314; -eyed (see heading following this); -footed animal B15.6.0.1; forbidden thing C600—C649; -horned (cows) A2286.2.3, (ox) B15.3.0.2; hundred brothers seek 100 sisters as wives T69.1; hundred one as magic number D1273.1.7.1; killed none and yet killed twelve H802; lie a year X901; -legged horse F241.1.3.1; man disappears each night S262.0.1; -sided man F525.1; wish granted D1761.0.2.2; wrong and five hundred good deeds J1605. — Bluff: only o. tiger, you promised ten K1715.2; calf of o. color the property of the devil G303.10.9; can drink only o. kind of wine at a time J1511.15; cat's o. trick J1662; chaste woman can blow out candle with o. puff and relight it with another H413.1; devil builds road for farmer in o. day G303.9.2.2; devils have only o. leg G303.4.5.1; disenchantment by only o. person D791.2; dwarfs must return to spirit world by o. o'clock a.m. F451.3.2.2; fairies visible to o. person alone F235.3; formulistic numbers: a number plus o. Z71.0.2; fox had rather meet o. hen than fifty woman J488; ghost visible to o. person alone E421.1.1; giant with o. (hand, foot) F531.1.6.12, (arm) F631.1.6.7, (foot) F531.1.3.3, (leg) F531.1.3.3.1; if the horse can pull o. load he can pull two J2213.4; invulnerability for o. day D1845.1; image of horse will be vivified only for o. person D445.1.1; island inhabited by only o. species F743; making the beard golden: such a o. *K1013.1; making many kinds of food from o. small bird (task) H1022.6; making many shirts from o. hank of flax (task) H1022.2; man can stand still all day on o. foot F682; man to have wishes if he can repeat them in o. breath D1761.0.2.1; more than o. swallow to make a summer J731.1; objects on o. side of palisade in otherworld garden black, on other white F162.1.2.3; only o., but a lion J281.1; only o. oath binding M115; only o. person can help secure magic object D827; only o. person possesses power to heal certain wound D2161.4.10.0.1; only o. present to be asked for at home of spirit son-in-law C714.1; person with o. leg F517.0.1; person using only o. leg, hand, eye F682.0.1; pledge to say but o. phrase M175; pretended exchange of confidence as to the o. thing that can kill K975.1; riddle about turning o. into two (split peas) H583.4.6; suitor test: to get imprisoned princess in o. year's time H322.2; tabu: putting house in order for o. man C743; three women have among them but o. (eye)

*F512.1.2, (tooth) F513.1.1; treasure found by going with o.-night old colt onto o.-night old ice N542.1; two for the price of o. J2083.2; two giants with o. axe G151; weaver prefers master with o. hedgehog J229.8; witch known by hose unbound on o. leg G255; woman with horseshoe on o. foot F551.1.2.1; youth sees o. and one-half men and a horse's head H583.1.

One-eyed child T551.11; demon G369.7; giant F531.1.1.1, G511.1; god *A128.2, (transforms islands) A955.5; king J1675.4; man as appraiser of horse X122; monster, the Antichrist A1075; one-footed, one-handed men F525.3; parson X413; person *F512.1; pig B15.4.5; sow in wild hunt E501.4.3.1; villain K2273; witch G213.1. — Deduction: the o. camel J1661.1.1; king will not permit a o. man in his presence P14.2; why o. soldiers good J1494; why women o. A1316.3.2.

One hundred. — Crow refuses to marry o. year old titmouse B282.22.1; eating o. carcasses H331.17; getting o. oxen H1154.2.1; valley of o. giants G105; person wandering for o. and fifty years F1032.1.

One-third for the price of one-fourth J2083.1.

One thousand men to string bow F836.3.1.

Oneself. — Counting wrong by not counting o. J2031; curse by o. M411.0.1; quest for bride for o. H1381.3.1.2.

Onion. — Hot o. to the eye as cure J2412.1; origin of o. growing A1441.5; wedding of o. and garlic B286.1.

Onions. — To eat a hundred o. J2095; transformation by eating o. D551.2.5.

Only, see also **Once, One, Unique.** — Cat's o. trick J1662; otherworld dwellings open o. at certain times F165.2.

Onyx offered in innocence test H256.1. — City of o. F761.3.

Opaque. — Ability to see through o. objects F642.3.

Open Sesame D1552.2, N455.3. — Genie sleeps with eyes o. G634; king demands o. gate to vassals' castle P50.0.1.1; man claims to sleep with o. eyes and beguiles ogre K331.1; mouth o. for forty days F544.0.4; sleeping with eye, ear o. F564.4; temple rises where ground bursts o. A992.3.

Opened. — Dwarf home o. by magic flower F451.4.3.7; locks o. by magic D2088.

Opening bottle tabu C625; box forbidden C321ff.; gift prematurely tabu C321.2; mouth makes door open wider D1782.1.1. — Disenchantment by o. fruit D721.5; door to fairyland o. once a year F211.1.1; earth o. at command F942.3; earth o. for fugitive R327; ghosts summoned by o. sacred book E383; ground o. swallows up person F942.1; hair from fox's tail o. all doors D1562.2; idol o. to grant refuge R325.2; images o. eyes D1632; kingship for o. palace door P11.4.1; magic escape o. in house D2165.4; magic object miraculously o. and closing *D1550ff.; otherworld dwellings o. only at certain times F165.2; tabu: o. gourd where starwife kept C31.1.5; treasure o. itself N552; tree leaves o. to give saint passage F979.2; visit to lower world through o. rocks

*F92.3; well-trained kid not o. for wolf J144; wife o. forbidden chest, killed T254.4; witches o. doors, windows G249.8.

Operation. — Caesarean o. a custom T584.3; doctor performs useless o. X372.4.

Operations. — Lies about surgical o. X1721.

Opium produces reincarnation qualities A2733; substituted for tobacco in pipe K873.3. — Origin of o. A2691.4.

Opium-smoker lost on journey J2027.

Opossum. — Deer, o., and snake each render indispensable aid to man J461.4; marriage to person in o. form B641.8; why o. has bare tail A2317.12; why o. has large mouth A2341.2.1; why o. plays dead when caught A2466.1.

Opponent. — Boasting scares o. from contest K1766; vow not to be killed by single o. M162.

Opponents agree not to fight, remain undefeated M237.1; humble selves, become friends J917. — Creator's o. A50—A69.

Opposite of present A633, A855. — Girl must do o. of commands H580.1; land where all is o. from the usual X1505; power over monster obtained by reversing orders: hero does exact o. of the command D1783.4; witch's charm o. of Christian *G224.1.

Opposites. — Dream interpreted by o. D1812.3.3.10.

Opposition of dead to return of living from land of the dead F105 (cf. F93.1.1); of good and evil gods A106. — Animals created through o. of devil to God A1750ff.; man's miraculous death for o. to dogma of Immaculate Conception V312.2; punishment for o. to holy person Q227.

Oppression. — Famine as punishment for o. Q552.3.2; magic stone protects church from o. D1389.1.

Optimist becomes pessimist when money stolen U68.

Oracle, see also **Divination;** D1712; tells whether eunuch to be father J1271; that the first of three sons to kiss his mother will be king J1652. — Ambiguous o. M305; fatal deception: changed message from o. *K981.

Oracles from holy well V134.1.

Oracular animal *B150ff.; fish D925.2; images occupied by spirits or priests who give the answers K1972; object used for divination *D1311ff. — Pseudo-magic o. object sold K114.

Orange thrown indicates the princess's choice H316.1. — Birth from o. T543.3.1; conception from eating o. T511.1.4; magic o. *D981.3; transformation to o. D211.1.

Oranges grow on tree-limb knives F811.7.2.2.

Oratory. — Submarine o. V118.2.1.

Orchard. — Fairies dance in o. F261.3.3; magic chain renders o. barren D1563.2.1; tearing up the o. K1416.

Orchestra of ghosts E499.2.

Ordaining the future M (entire chapter). — God o. ceremonies A176.
Ordeal substantiates unjust claim J1521.4. — "Bear the o. in peace"
K1354.2.2; chastity tested by o. H412ff.; substitute in o. K528; thief
betrays self in o. J1141.16; trial by o. subverted by carrying magic
object D1394.1.
Ordeals *H220ff.
Order, see also **Command;** for spirit's help left on card D2074.2.4.4. —
Culture hero establishes law and o. A530ff.; death o. evaded K510ff.;
God reduces elements to o. A175; establishment of natural o. A1100ff.;
islands by o. of deity A955.0.1; king's enigmatic o. to minister H587;
literal misconstruction of o. to get revenge J2516.0.1; marriage by royal
o. T122; seduction by bearing false o. from husband or father K1354;
theft by presenting false o. to guardian K362.
Orders. — Dwarfs give o. to mortals F451.5.20; punishment for leaving
holy o. Q226; religious o. *V450—V499; sun, moon under God's direct
o. A726.1.
Ordering of human life A1300—A1399.
Orderly. — Battle between God's o. and plague A1626; giant as gods' o.
A133.3.
Ordination. — Forced o. of ignorant priest U41.
Oreads F450ff., F460ff.
Organ. — Bird rewarded for moving woman's o. to its present position
A2229.6; combat with horse's sex o. F998; dead arise when one plays o.
for first time in church E419.5; ghost plays o. E554.1; horse's o. provides
treasure D1469.5; monk recognized by o. H79.7; origin of o. A1461.3;
wants the o. to come and play for her J1888; woman lends female o. to
boy D11.2.
Organs, see also **Genitals;** exchanged with animal E789.1. — Child with
all o. displaced T551.14; cutting off sex o. in madness Q555.4; enemy's
sex o. prove slaying H105.7; magic animal sex o. D1029.4; magic
mutilation of sex o. D2062.4; man's o. replaced with animal's X1721.2;
remarkable physical o. F540ff.; remarkable sex o. F547ff.; removable o.
F557; sex o. mutilated S176; skillful surgeon removes and replaces
vital o. F668.1.
Orient. — Dwarfs emigrate to the O. F451.9.2.2.
Origin. — Hero (heroine) of unpromising o. L111; prohibition against
mention of o. of person or thing *C440ff.; sword of magic o. *D1081.1;
test: guessing o. of certain skin H522.1.
Origins A (entire chapter).
Original creator followed by transformers A72. — Giants' magic gifts
return to o. form in hands of men F531.5.6.1; person returns to o. form
when tabu is broken C963ff.; quest for o. of picture H1213.1.2; reflection
in water thought to be the o. of the thing reflected J1791; treasure to be
found by man who marries o. owner's daughter N543.3.
Orion's origin A772.

Ornament as chastity index H433; transformed to other object D454.8.
— Fairy's o. snatched F354; magic o. provides treasure D1456ff.; man becomes o. D263; quest for matching o. H1317; stolen o. presented to owner as gift N347.4.

Ornaments bride wore in former birth H1371.4; buried with hero V67.1.
— Animal with jeweled o. F826.1; clouds as sky's o. A1133.2; devil as helper of robber refuses to let woman's o. be stolen M212.1; extraordinary o. F827ff.; identification by o. H90ff.; magic o. *D1070ff.; origin of metal o. A1465.3; recognition by o. under skin H61; serpent's bite produces o. and clothes B103.6.1; thief steals mistress's o. K346.6; trickster promises to turn gold into o. K283; trickster tries on o., steals them K351.3.

Ornamental. — Choice between useful and o. J240ff.

Ornamented. — Sky o. with clouds A1133.2.

Orphan deprived of inheritance S322.0.1; gets wife because swollen creek prevents other marriage N699.4; hero L111.4; inquires about parents T621. — Bird must bring o. to king H901.0.2; marriage of dragon and o. T118.2; milk magically appears in woman for o. T611.6.

Orphans. — Inhospitality to o. punished Q292.2; kindness to o. repaid by dead parents Q47.

Orpheus journeys to land of dead to bring back wife F81.1.

Orthoptera. — Origin of o. A2060ff.

Osprey. — Magic o. produces lightning B172.8; man becomes o. D152.5.

Ostrich. — How o. lost beautiful feathers A2252.3, A2402.2; kite fails to secure o. at wedding B282.2.1.

Other. — Devils leave hermit who turns o. cheek when struck G303.16.15; sinful person spoken of as "the o." C433.1.

Others. — Consolation by thought of o. worse placed J880ff.; fortuneteller shows o. how to get rich but remains poor himself X461.1.

Otherworld journeys *F0—F199; mistress helps hero H335.0.1.1. — Answers found in o. to riddles propounded on way H544; arrow shot to o. F638.4; birds in o. sing religious songs B251.3.1; birds show way to o. B151.2.0.2; flower from o. F979.10; food appears, disappears in o. D1982.4; hero sees guarded maiden in o. T381.1.1; home of Fortuna in o. N111.1.1; huge oxen on o. island K1784.2; immediate return to o. because of broken tabu C952; journey to o. foretold M358.2; journey to o. with magic speed D2122.0.1; magic aging by contact with earth after o. journey D1896; magic knowledge from queen of o. D1810.1; magic object from o. D813.3; magic received from o. D859.2.1; magic sight of earthly object from o. D1825.2.1; malevolent beings in o. F360.0.1; person carried off to o. for breaking tabu C954; person must remain in o. because of broken tabu C953; quests to the o. H1250—H1299; rejuvenation by going to o. and having digestive tract removed D1889.5; sight of old home reawakens memory and brings about return from o. *D2006.2; slamming door on exit from mountain o. *F91.1;

tabu: staying too long in o. meadow C761.4.2; tabu to touch fire in o. C542.2; tabus connected with o. journeys *C710ff.; telling adventure in o. tabu C757.2; transformation to go to o. D641.4; visions of the o. V511.

Otter becomes person D327.1; carries flaming wood in mouth B193; persuaded to rob K1022.5.1; retrieves magic object B548.3. — Blood of o. venomous B776.5.4; color of o. A2411.1.2.3; creation of sea o. A1821.1; dog becomes o. D412.5.3; foolish seller of fox skins mixes o. skins with them J2083.3; helpful o. B443.1; man transformed to o. D127.2; reincarnation as o. E612.14; water-spirit as o. F420.1.3.12.

Otters recover magic ring B548.1.2; supply man with fish, wood B292.7.

Outcast builds castle like king's, is recognized H153. — Prophecy of luck for o. child M312.7.

Outcry. — Murderer makes o. to accuse innocent R2116.4; robbers frightened from goods by man's o. K335.1.3.

Outcries. — Abducted woman's o. drowned by thieves wailing K419.8.

Outdoors. — Chief going o. tabu C564.9.

Outhouse. — Paramour trapped in o. K1574.2.

Outlaws. — Fairies o. in hiding F251.14.

Outlets. — Riddle: dam up o. H588.9.

Outside. — Ghost haunts o. E279.1; marriage o. the group T131.5.

Outstripping. — Marvelous runner o. March wind F681.2.

Outweighing. — Magic jewel o. many heavy objects in the scale D1682.

Outwitted. — Adulteress and paramour o. by (husband) *K1550ff., (trickster) K1570ff.; husband o. by adulteress K1510ff.; husband o. by wife J1545; wife o. by husband J1541.

Outwitting. — Suitor test: o. princess *H342.

Oven door jumps into room E539.1; heats without fire D1601.6. — Captivity in o. R49.2; cure by putting children into o. D2161.4.11; dwarf has o. F451.7.2; father throws son in o. H165; ghost drives priest into o. E264; Jewish child thrown into o. by father for baking eucharist preserved by Virgin Mary V363; large loaves need a large o. X434.1; murder by roasting in o. S112.6; ogre burned in his own o. G512.3.2; ogress makes o. blaze with foot G345.1; wife not to go into o. while husband is away H473.2; woman in moon's o. seen on clear night A751.8.4.

Overawed. — Captor o. with help of magic object D1613; master o. by strong hero F615.3; ogre o. *G570ff., K1710ff.; revenant o. by living person E462.

Overawing. — Escape by o. captor *K540ff.; son o. father P236.6.

Overbearing husband loses fortune J1545.6; wife T252.

Overboard. — King brings victory by leaping horse o. W32.1; passenger brings ship bad luck: cast o. N134.1.5; person thrown o. (and abandoned) S142, (by faithless wife and paramour) K2213.2, (by impostors) *K1931.1.

(to placate storm) S264.1; throwing shipboard rivals o. when food gone K527.4.

Overcome. — Contest in enduring cold: frost o. by wind H1541.2; devil o. by man G303.9.6.1.1; fairy's curse partially o. by another fairy's amendment F316.1; magic sight o. by incantation D1822.1; man on Island of Fair Women o. by loving women F112.1; man's adversary o. by animal B524; person o. by magic object D1400ff.; robber o. K437; strong o. by weak in conflict L310ff.; vampire's power o. E251.1; witch o. or escaped *G270ff.

Overcoming robbers as suitor task H335.4.2. — Amazon o. enemies in forest K778.1; cannibal disenchanted by o. it G33.1; disenchantment by o. enchanted person in fight (contest) D716; enduring and o. curses M420ff.; hero o. devastating animal G510.4; lowly hero o. rivals L156.1; suitor test: o. princess in strength *H345; youngest animal o. adversary L72.

Overdose. — Fatal o. of medicine J2115.

Overdressed. — Spilling dirty water on o. youths X32.

Overeaten. — Girl claims having o. on bird thigh K1984.2.1; madness from having o. F1041.8.5.

Overestimating. — Enemy o. opponents retreats K2368.

Overflowing river D2151.2.2, F932.8; well F718.6, *F933.6.1.

Overhasty man kills his rescuing twin brother N342.3.

Overheard secret tabu C420.3; wish realized N699.6. — False accusation o. causes hasty killing N342.4; magic power from o. talk D1739.1; ogre's secret o. G661ff.; recognition by o. conversation with animals or objects H13ff.; remedy learned from o. animal meeting *B513; secrets o. N450ff.; sham wise man utilizes o. conversation K1956.7; tasks performed by means of secrets o. from tree *H963.

Overhearing. — Deception by o. prearranged conversation J1517.

Overheating. — Devil dies of nosebleed resulting from o. G303.17.3.1.

Overleapt. — Garden wall that cannot be o. D1675.

Overlooking. — Beggar o. money N351.2.

Overlord. — Death for slaying o. Q411.4.1; riddle about o. H853.

Overnight. — Food baked o. tabu C152.3.1.

Overpopulation. — Death from world's o. A1335.8; diseases to combat o. P721; flood from o. A1019.3.

Overpowered. — Bird o. by stepping on his shadow D2072.0.4; female o. when caught in tree cleft K1384.

Oversalting food of giant so that he must go outside for water K337.

Oversight of the thievish tailor X221.

Overtaking. — Only one person o. hero Z313.1.

Overthrown. — "He who throws himself against wave is o." J21.52.9; walls o. by magic D2093; work of day magically o. at night *D2192.

Overuse. — Magic object loses power by o. D877.

Overwary. — Game animals magically made o. D2085.

Overweening ambition punished *L420ff.; conceit punished Q330ff.; pride forbidden *C770ff.

Overworked. — Virgin pardons o. monk for neglecting prayers V276.2.

Overzealous. — Emperor rebukes o. servant J554.

Owl advises old man of gods' visit B569.1; advises where to plant crops B569.2; is baker's daughter punished for stinginess to Jesus A1958.0.1; as bird of ill-omen B147.2.2.4; birds' king B242.1.8; ends elephant and ape's dispute J461.8; (ghost of nun) in wild hunt E501.4.5; invites cricket to share his nectar K815.5; likes own children best T681; made bird king over peacock J515; proud of son's feet T681.1; reveals deity's secret: power of speech removed A2239.3.1; saves man from cliff B521.5; saves man from drowning B527.3; as suitor B623.2; thinks hoot's echoes praise J953.16; warns other birds from limed net B521.3.5. — When one learns age of o. he kills it K1985; why o. avoids daylight A2491.2; why o. is blind by day A2233.3, A2332.6.6; color of o. A2411.2.4.2; creation of o. A1958; devil as o. G303.3.3.3.6; disenchantment as o. hoots D791.1.8; enmity between o. (and crow) A2494.13.1, (and mouse) A2494.13.4; fools attack o. J1736.2; friendship of o. (and bat) A2493.2, (and prairie-dog) A2493.1; helpful o. B461.2; lawsuit between o. and kite B270.1; lawsuit between o. and mouse B270.2; lazy o. punished Q5.2; man transformed to o. D153.2; why o. lives where he does A2229.3, A2433.4.1; priest throws chalice at o. J1261.2.7; prophetic o. B143.0.3; reincarnation as o. E613.2; revenant as o. E423.3.5; truth-telling o. B131.0.1; wedding of o. B282.4; weeping man turned to o.: still bewails A2261.5; where o. got his eyes A2332.1.5; why o. hoots at night A2427.3; why o. shakes head A2474.3; wise o. B122.0.3; witch as o. G211.4.4.

Owl's food A2435.4.9; hoot misunderstood by lost simpleton J1811.1; hooting bad omen D1812.5.1.27.1; wings borrowed from rat (or other animal) A2241.2. — Crow accepts o. hospitality, then kills him K2026; origin of o. cries A2426.2.17.

Owls and crows dispute over day, night vision B299.2.1. — Crow learns secret of o., defeats them K2042; enmity of o. and fowls A2494.13.4.1; god of o. A433.2.1; vampire with eyes of o. E251.4.3; war between crows and o. B263.3.

Own. — Adopted child deserted when o. child born T674; falling in love with one's o. reflection T11.5.1; king in disguise as one of o. men K1812.19; one's o. kind preferred to strangers J416; person eats o. flesh G51.

Owner assists thief J1392; disguised as monk enters own captured castle K2357.0.2; of magic object chosen king P11.3; resolves to sell swearing ram B211.1.1.1.1. — Lost object returns to his o. N211; magic birds die when o. is killed B192.0.1; magic harp plays only for o. D1651.7.1; magic object acquired by gaining love of o. D856; magic ring permits o. to learn person's secret thoughts D1316.4; means of hoodwinking the guardian or

o. *K330ff.; object stops or dies when o. dies E766; ring to be cut in two: real o. laments J1171.11; stolen property sold to its o. K258; thief accuses o. of having stolen property K401.5; trickster reports treasure's o. dead: gets it K482.2; well rises only for sheep's rightful o. H251.3.9.2; witch punishes o. by killing animals G265.4.0.1.

Owner's. — Foolish thief asks o. help J2136.5.6; magic object comes at o. call D1649.2.

Ownership of magic objects D800—D899. — Divided o. of cow J1905.3; imagined o. derived from dream J1551.7; name on article as o. token H88; skillful companions create woman: whose is the o. *H621.

Ox bought, buyer also claims wood load J1511.17; curses man M411.19.2; demon F401.3.2, (as magician) B191.2, (transformed to pig) D412.2.2, (transformed to tiger) D412.2.3; and donkey not to plow together C886; with gold and silver in horns B101.8.1; -hide (carried by strong man) F631.5, (saves persons) K515.3; with golden horns B15.3.2.3; head divided according to scripture J1242.1; horns' growth F983.4; to jackal, "dogs are chasing you" K1725.1; lent fairies must not be worked after sunset F391.1.1; likes loving strokes of man: flea fears them U142; with magic wisdom B121.5; as mayor J1882.2; rib as fairy gift F343.16; as sacrifice V12.4.4; transformed to another animal D412.2ff. — Ass who has worked with o. thinks himself his equal J952.4; at the blessing of the grave the parson's o. breaks loose X421; boy lives on o. F562.1; bringing home ten instead of one o. K1741.2.1; complaint about stolen o. J1213.1; cry of giant o. impregnates all fish B741.1; deceptive bargain: o. for five pennies K182; deceptive land purchase: o.-hide measure K185.1; devil as an o. G303.3.3.1.4; why o. is draft animal A2252.2, A2513.5; dragon eats o. each meal B11.6.7; enmity of o. and antelope A2494.12.3; eating o. forbidden C221.1.1.1; exchanging wife with o. J2081.3; in preparation for slaughter feet of o. are cut off the evening before J2168; fool kills himself in despair because o. has been killed J2518.2; four-horned o. B15.3.1.3.1; frog tries in vain to be as big as o. J955.1; giant o. B871.1.1.1, (ancestor of all animals) A1791; giant o.-rib B871.1.1.1.1; gold horn of three-horned o. H1151.7.1; great o. X1237; guests call each other o., ass: given appropriate food J1563.4; why o. has no hair on his lips A2342.2; helpful o. B411.2, (wild) B443.7; how o. got horns A2326.1.4; killing o. as task H1161.2.1; lakes from digging of primeval o. A920.1.2; land grant: as far as o. can be heard K185.14; magic o. B184.2.4; man kills o. with flat of hand F628.1.2; man transformed to o. D133.3; monkey transformed to o. D411.5.4; monster o. killed B16.1.5.1; old o. yoked with young one J441.1; one-horned o. B15.3.0.2; oracular o. B154.1; origin of o.-goad A1446.3; origin of race colors from eating of o. A1614.4.1.1; parson rides o. into church X414; race of o. and horse: o. must labor A2252.2; reincarnation as o. E611.2.2; runaway o. leads to Adam and Eve's burial place N774.3.1; speaking o. B211.1.5.1; strong man carries o. F631.4; strong man lifts o. F624.1; three-horned o. B15.3.1.3; thief punishes the escaped o. J1861; treacherous o.-herd K2255.2; why o. is draft animal A2515.1; why o. serves man A2513.5.

Ox's leg as person F988.1; tail in another's mouth K404.2. — Cause of o. walk A2441.1.8; curiosity satisfied: riding the o. horns J2375; escape by reversing o. shoes K534.1; why flies fly around o. eye A2479.9.

Oxen bear dead usurer to gallows to be buried N277; decide not to kill butchers, since inexpert killers might replace them J215.2; protect child B535.0.10; stoop for king H171.4.1. — Devil drives several teams of o. G303.7.5; devil pulls up tree to goad his o. G303.9.2.1; eating three hundred fat o. (task) H1141.2; fool cuts off tails of o. so that they will look like fine steeds J1919.4; getting one hundred o. H1154.2.1; giant guards huge hornless o. in otherworld K1784.2; magic object furnishes o. D1477; nightingale hears boy call o.: learns her song A2272.1.1; nisser have o. F482.4.2; origin of custom of yoking o. A1441.2; saint carried by wild o. B557.2; wild o. plow for man B292.4.1; warriors hidden on o. driven into enemy's camp K2357.15; why not milk idle o.? J1905.4.

Oyster. — Dividing discovered o. K452.1; why o. lives in salt water A2433.6.2.

Oysters. — More small o. to hundred J2213.8.

"P. C." in clouds X459.1.1.

Pacific Ocean's goddess mother A109.2.

Pacified, see **Peaceable.**

Packhorse becomes palfrey D412.4.1.

Package. — Night (darkness) in p. A1174.1.

Packet. — Magic p. D1283.

Pact. — Flying Dutchman sails because of p. with devil E511.1.2; Virgin frees man from p. with devil V264.1.

Pads. — Why rabbits have soft p. on feet A2375.2.4.

Paddle. — Magic p. D1124.1; marvelous p. F841.2.7.

Paddles broken in enemies' boat K636.1.

Paddy as life token E761.7.13. — Exorbitant price for lending p. K255.2; man becomes p.-bird D169.2; man becomes p. sheaf D218.1.

Paddies. — Rice p. controlled by toad D2149.5.

Pagan gods become devils G303.1.3.4; loses dispute with Christian V352.1; otherworld F160.0.3; punished for conversion to Christianity Q232.1. — Punishment for denying p. gods Q225.2; saint's kindness converts p. priest L350.2.

Pagans flee clerics P426.0.1.

Page P50.3; dreams of being king J955.2.1; hides under woman's bed K2112.2.2. — Appointment to p. as reward Q113.2; lovers' meeting: hero as p. in service of heroine T31.

Paid, see **Paying.**

Pail. — Milk stays in overturned p. D2171.8; proud milkmaid tosses her head and spills p. of milk J2061.2.

Pain because men too happy A1346.2.3; preferred to poverty J229.14;

stopped by prayer D1766.1.4; of souls in hell ebbs and flows Q562. — Animal grateful for relief from p. B380ff.; bird indifferent to p. (cumulative tale) Z49.3; magic girdle protects from p. D1389.16; magic relieves p. D1514; man beheads rescuer for leaving him so long in p. W154.17; pulling out the eye so that the p. will cease J2412.2; reward for enduring p. Q84; saint transfers sick man's p. to himself D1500.3.1.1.

Pains of childbirth magically eased D2161.1.3; as punishment Q553.3.6; repeated in person of the man T583.1.1. — Girl promises unborn child to devil if he will suffer p. S223.1; origin of p. A1351.1.

Paine's. — Ghost flits between Thomas P, graves E419.9.

Painless. — Birth of holy person p. T584.0.3.

Paint. — Dead rubbed with red p. V68.5; husband threatens to scrape p. off wife's cheeks Q331.2.1.3; keeping p. on bride's feet J2489.11; man in the moon from p. A751.5.

Painted jackal an outcast J951.4.1. — Doves see p. cups of water and dash into them J1792.1; life story p. on wall H11.1.2; weasel p. to deceive mice J951.4.

Painter can paint from description of a dream F674. — Devil pulls p. from chair P482.1; great p. freed by Moors Q88.1; house-p. P457; image of Virgin saves p. from falling D1639.2.

Painters. — Who are best p.? Women H659.16.

Painting on the haycock K1013.2; the house red (house set on fire) K1412; with a red hot iron K1013.3; on wife's stomach as chastity index H439.1.1. — Appearance of animal from p. A2217ff.; contest in lifelike p. H504.1; creator p. clothes on clay models of men A1453.6; disguise by p. (body) K1821.2, (so as to escape) K521.3; girl p. face because pregnant T579.8.2; lie: realistic p. X1788; thief p. horse different colors K419.5.

Paintings. — Erotic p. reform continent husband T315.2.2.1.

Pair, see also **Couple, Twin(s);** of culture heroes A515. — Capturing p. of every wild animal H1154.9; first human p. from drops of wine A1211.6; primeval human p. A1270ff.

Pairs of animals in ark *A1021.1. — Everything created in p. A610.1.

Pajamas. — Stealing laborer's p. H1151.22.

Palace, see also **Castle;** appears to be floating: actually glass K1889.6; filled with tongues, hands, etc. of sinners Q561.4; of 8760 stones (riddle) H721.4; haunted by Satan G303.15.4.2; in heaven for pious king Q172.4; model brings about recognition of lost brother H16.1; with seven gates F776.3; shakes from man on roof F639.8; turns to gold D475.1.15; underneath tank F725.3.4. — Animal lured into p. by trickster K811.0.1; animals build p. for man B572.1; building p. and city as task H1133.5; building p. of gold H1133.4; child exposed at p. gate S335; constructing p. overnight F675.4; diamond reveals underground p. D1551.7.1; dwarfs live in luxurious underground p. F451.4.1.3; extraordinary p. *F771ff.; fairies' underground p. F222.1; fool thankful that God has built a p. without columns J2565; Good Luck leaves p. night king is to die N113.3;

guarding p. at night H1199.17.1; hawk as sky p. architect J2060.3; hut transformed to p. D479.8; jumping horse over p. H331.1.2.1; magic diamond reveals underground p. D1557.3; magic p. *D1132; mosquitoes with p. in mouth X1286.1.6; mountain-spirits help build p. F460.4.2.1; nut transformed to p. D451.7.1; one hundred doors in p. F165.1.0.1; princess as price for sparing p. T52.7; queen kept in p. of forty doors R41.5.1; serpents' subterranean p. F127.1.1; submarine p. F725.3; sunken p. magically raised D2136.2.2; theft by disguising as p. official K311.10; thieves abduct p. bride K315.3; transformation to lion in order to guard p. D659.4.1; tree branch becomes p. D451.1.0.1; underground p. full of jewels F721.5.1.

Palaces. — Devil as builder of p. G303.9.1.5; gods' p. A151.4.

Palanquin. — Magic p. D1154.3.2; tabu to use p. in temple C93.5.1.

Pale moon as evil omen D1812.5.1.5.2; sun restored by using egg, yellow grass A721.4. — Dwarfs p. F451.2.0.6; why moon is p. A759.3.

Palestine. — Punishment for leaving P. Q232.2.1; world calamity will begin in P. A1007.

Palfrey. — Imagined refusal of p. tests friendship H1558.6; packhorse becomes p. D412.4.1.

Palisade around otherworld F148.3. — Island with rampart of gold and p. of silver F731.3; objects on one side of p. in otherworld garden black, on other white F162.1.2.3.

Palladium D1380.0.1.1.

Palm blooms at Nativity D2145.2.2.1; tree grows on serpent B765.26; trees on moon A751.9.1. — Coat fits in p. of hand F821.2.1; counting p. trees within view of palace H1118.3; drinking p.-drink tabu C272.3; dwarf makes p. wine F451.3.4.9; lake filled with p. wine A920.1.16; like Christ on P. Sunday J1265.1; magic p. tree D950.19; origin of p. tree A2681.12; parents fed, clothed from one p. tree A1420.5; prophecy by reading p. M303; scurf becomes p. tree D457.6; stars on p. of hand royalty sign H71.1.1.; why p. oil is red A2877; why p. is tall A2778.2; why sap comes from top of p. A2791.8.

Palms as reward Q193. — Greasing the judge's p. J2475; origin of p. A2681.5; hairless p. from handling gold J1289.16.

Palm rat pretends deafness, cheats bargain K231.15. — Enmity of dog and p. A2494.4.13; why p. has swollen head A2320.7.

Palmer disguise K1817.2; as helper N846.1; rescues abandoned child R131.13.

Palmetto gives flying power D1531.10.

Palmyra residents (as magicians) D1711.10.5, (have narrow eyes) A1666.2.

Palsy cured by saint V221.1.

Pan *F442. — Mysterious voice announces death of P. F442.1.

Pancake. — Fleeing p. (cumulative tale) Z33.1; hog loses p. in mud: still seeks it A2275.5.1.

Pancakes growing on lime-tree (lie) X1472.1; made of snow D476.1.6.

Pandora not to look into box *C321; sent as temptress F34.

Pangs of childbirth, see **Pains of childbirth.**

Panther devours girl in tree: chain tale Z39.7. — Enmity between p., antelope, and tortoise A2494.12.1; fox and p. contest in beauty J242.3; giant p. B871.2.3; helpful p. B431.4; sweet smell of p. protects him from other beasts B732.

Panthers. — Lies about p. X1213.

Pants. — Stealing p. by pretending to dirty them K344.3.

Pap, see also **Breast.** — Severed p. regrows when woman bears child E788.

Paps. — Saint's two p.: one milk, one honey T611.5.1.

Paper in hand which none but king can remove D1654.11. — As many stars in the heavens as points on p. H702.3; boy with hat of butter, clothes of p. X1854; fairy gifts turn to p. when shown F348.9.1; spirit tears p. off rooms F473.6.1.

Papers. — Genie called by writing his name on p. and burning them *D2074.2.4.

Papiha. — Creation of p. A1997.

Parable. — Pleading in court by p. J1163; wisdom (knowledge) taught by p. J80ff.

Paradise, see also **Heaven;** lost because of one sin *A1331. — Animal characteristics from carrying devil into p. A2236.2; artificial p. and hell F705; bird from p. B39.1; blindfolded emperor seeks p. J2326.3; Christian p. A694; crops' extraordinary growth in p. F815.3; dawn the reflection of roses of p. A1179.2.1; earthly p. on mountain F132.1; false p. K1889.3; fig from p. F813.7.2; four rivers of p. *F162.2.1; four rivers rising in p., water world A871.2; hero taken to p. alive D1856.1; how many exits from p.? H682.3; journey to earthly p. *F111; journey to upper-world p. *F11; nymphs of p. F499.2; plain that is earthly p. F756.2; quest for location of p. H1257; quest to p. for anointing oil H1265; serpent as deceiver in p. B176.1.1; stream of p. from roots of world-tree A878.1; student from p. (Paris) J2326; supernatural lapse of time in p. F377.1; tree blossoms as God arrives in p. F971.9.

Paradises, eight A661.2.

Paradoxical quests H1378; tasks H1050—H1089.

Parakeet. — Helpful p. B469.9.1.

Parakeets. — Land of p. B222.3.

Paralysis for breaking tabu C941.5; from spirit's blow E265.1.1. — Death from p. for breaking tabu C929.2.1; magic p. D1419.2; *D2072ff., (of foe) D2091.9, (as punishment) Q551.7, (as punishment remitted) *Q573.

Paralyzed. — All body p. except tongue saying "Ave" V254.3.1; man fleeing saint p. Q583.3.

Paramour, see also **Lover;** beats husband K1514.4.1; bites off mistress's nose S172.1; carried off in chest, accused of being robber K675.1; hidden in chest frightens off robbers K335.1.6.1; quarreling with mistress about escape caught by her husband J581.2; leaves token with girl to give their son *T645; successfully hidden from husband K1521; threatens to kill hiding husband K1514.4.1. — Adulteress and p. (fettered) Q434.1, (plot against her stepson) S31.1; animal p. B610ff.; death is wife's p. J2349.2; fairy offers gifts to man to be her p. F302.3.2; hidden p. buys freedom from discoverer *K443.1; husband afraid of cornered p. J2626.1; husband frightened by p. in hog pen K1542; husband outwits adulteress and p. *K1550ff.; husband substitutes leaky vessel so that his wife and p. are drowned Q466.1; king may have any woman for p. P19.2; man returning home thinks newborn son sleeping with his wife is p.: restrains himself J21.2; magician's mistress carries p. in her body *F1034.2; mother and p. plan son's death S12.1.1; prospective p. imposes tests H939.2; taking money from wife's p. J229.11; tasks assigned by wife and p. H916.3; terrorizing the p. K1213; theft by wife's p. K365.3; thief steals from wife's p. K341.14; treacherous wife plots with p. K2213.3; trickster outwits adulteress and p. K1570ff.; unknown (clandestine) p. *T475; wife's p. tied to horse's tail and conducted through streets Q473.2.1; woman substitutes figures of p., self in bed: husband attacks them K525.1.1.

Paramours. — Vengeful p. send syphilitic man to substitute in woman's bed K1317.3.

Parapet. — Breaking egg on castle p. H1149.6.

Parasol goddess A499.7.

Parchment. — Devil shows priest long p. roll of sins of congregation G303.24.1.1; identification by fitting together p. pieces H102.1.

Pardon given if hero produces lady about whom he has boasted M55; in return for confession J1198. — Confession brings p. V21; delay in p. allows deserved execution N394; jester wins p. from prince J1181.3.

Pardons. — Seller of p. robbed by man whom he has pardoned beforehand K1684.

Pardoner's tale K1685.

Pardoning of criminal comes too late P515. — King p. person addressing courtier as king P15.1.2; ruler p. his enemies W11.5.1.

Parent rescues child R153; seeks relief from abandoned child H154; will die on same day as daughter E765.4.3.1. — Animal nurses fight real p. for children B535.2; child seeks unknown p. H1381.2.2; curse by p. M411.1; deer foster p. resuscitated E138.1; helpful animal reincarnation of p. *B313.1; like p., like child U121; task assigned by jealous p. H913; unnatural children eat p. G71.

Parent's heart is hardest H637.1. — Fairy p. gift D630.3.

Parents affiance children without their knovledge T69.2; become servants to secure wedding funds T132.2; and children *P230ff.; exchange children K1921; expose son to tiger H105.5.4; of the gods A111; go to hell instead of sons P241; will humble themselves before their son M312.2; killed by abandoned children S366; learn to wean children A1566; meet daughter they tried to drown N732.3; pray to have a child T548.1. — Abandoned child joins p. in game: recognition follows H151.9; bride's p. help suitor H335.0.1.2; children punished for offenses of p. Q402;

children rescue p. R154; cruel p. *S10ff.; daughter unwittingly turns p. out N367; daughters flogged by p. P237; dead child's friendly return to p. E324; eating p. at their deaths G23; fate of p. revealed in dream J157.2; foster p. P270; ghost of unknown child passes over p. H175.5; kind foster p. chosen rather than cruel p. J391; kindness to orphans repaid by dead p. Q47; land where p. marry children as babies X1503.1; marriage against will of p. T131.1.3; married man not to eat in country of his p. C215; noodles push p. over a rock as a favor to them J2119.3; offspring of first p. A1277; origin of first p. A1271; punishment for murder of p. Q211.12; prophecy: death at hands of p. M343.5; quest for unknown p. H1381.1; recognition when p. come to son (priest, pope) to be confessed H151.3; son returning home after long absence unwittingly killed by p. N321; swearing by one's p. M119.8.1; unnatural p. eat children G72.

Parentage, see also **Paternity;** of culture hero A512. — Brothers deem p. unworthy, pose as princes K1952.3; repartee concerning p. of children J1270ff.

Pari. — Love between P. and mortal T93.5.

Parings. — Devil's chair in hell made from thrown-away nail p. G303.25.5.

Paris exposed M371; judges beauty contest H1596.1; returns to father's court N731.1. — Talkativeness of P. fishwives X253.1.

Parish. — Marriage forbidden outside p. X751; priest gives up p. and loses his fickle mistress J705.1.

Parishioner steals alms J1262.5.

Park. — Ghost haunts p. E279.4.

Parka. — Daughter born with p. T552.8.

Parliament of animals B230ff.; of devils G303.25.19; of giants F531.6.8.5.2; of women F565.3.

Parody of church ceremony at witch's sabbath G243.2; sermon *K1961.1.2.1. — Woman warns lover of husband by p. incantation K1546.

Parricide S22; because of love rivalry T92.9.1; prophecy M343, (slaughter or exposure of child to prevent fulfillment of) M371.2, M375.2, (unwittingly fulfilled) N323; punished Q211.1. — Magic spring detects p. H251.3.9.1; wild huntsman wanders because of p. *E501.3.3.

Parrot advises queen playing chess B565; and cat cheat each other at dinner J1565.3; as messenger B291.1.6; prefers cold freedom to luxury in palace L451.4; recovers jewel from sea B548.6; scouts enemy camp B122.8; sold as speaking foreign language K137.2; and sparrow argue right to inherit property left by man B271.1; suggests task H919.3; transacts business of trader B294.5; transformed to person D357; unable to tell husband details as to wife's infidelity J1154.1; warns of sex test H1578.1.6. — Clever p. J1118.1; color of p. A2411.2.6.11; creation of p. A1994; enmity of p. and starling A2494.13.11.3; faithful p. killed by mistake B331.3; friendship between p. (and hare) A2493.13, (and maina) A2493.26; helpful p. B469.9; hungry p. set to guard figs J215.1.1; king transformed to p. frees captured parrots R115; why p. lives in tree A2433.4.4; man transformed to p. D157; marriage to p. B602.7; ogre with life in p. speaks from inside parrot E715.1.3.2; prophesying p. B122.0.4; raja enters body of dead p. K1175; reincarnation as p. E613.12; why p. says A2426.2.11; separable soul in p. E715.1.3; seventy tales of a p. prevent wife's adultery K1591; speaking p. B211.3.4; why tail of West African grey p. is red A2378.8.2; thief disguised as p. K311.6.3; warning p. B143.1.3; why p. helps man A2493.36; wife demands p. who has accused her B335.4; witch's soul in p. G251.1.1; world is transformed mud p. A822.1.

Parrot's cry frightens off robber K1796. — Why p. beak is black A2343.2.1.

Parrots carry couple across the sea B551.2.1; sham death, are released K522.4; speak of beautiful girl H1214.1. — Image of p. vivified D445.2; king of p. B242.2.8; land of p. B222.4; seven girls as seven p. D658.3.3; why p. fly high A2442.1.2.

Parsley. — Dog P. in the soup J2462.1; effects of wild hunt remedied by asking the huntsmen for p. E501.19.3.

Parson P426.1; deceived into marrying his intended bride to her real lover K1371.1.1; and sexton at mass X441; tricked into giving up room: afraid of snake K2335. — Card-playing p. N5; deaf p. praises youth's foolish answers X111.12; ghost as p. E425.2.3; lost p. asks devil's help, dies C12.5.4; sham p. K1961.1ff.

Parson's share and sexton's J1269.1.

Parsons. — Jokes on p. *X410ff.

Part. — Animal gives p. of body as talisman for summoning its aid *B501; birth from unusual p. of person's body T541; coming with p. of body clothed (neither naked nor clad) H1054.3; effects of wild hunt remedied by eating p. of flesh thrown down by it E501.19.5; man created from p. of body A1263; soul kept in special p. of body E714.

Parts of human body furnish treasure D1454; of slain animals as token of slaying H105. — Animals from different p. of body of slain giant A1716.1; cannibals cut off p. of children's bodies G86; eating certain p. of animals forbidden C221.3; gods born from various p. of creator's body A112.3; quest for marvelous p. of animals H1332; treasure-producing p. of animals *B110ff.

Partaking in booty of wild hunt E501.19.4. — Not p. of one forbidden object C620ff.; tabu: p. of certain feast C286.

Partial disenchantment D702ff.; overcoming of fairy's curse F316.1; transformation D682ff. — Buyer refuses more than p. payment K233.7.

Participants in wild hunt E501.2ff.

Particular. — Dwarfs p. as to foods F451.3.7; magic object received through p. intermediaries *D827; origin of p. stars A770ff.

Partner misappropriates common goods K364. — Hero made business p. of rich man Q111.1; sham sickness so p. must work K495; treacherous p. K2296.

Partner's — Smoke prevents p. eating K336.2.

Partners. — Jackal and tiger as business p. A2493.11.3; rabbit and elephant p. as traders B294.6.

Partnership valid after forty years' absence P319.4. — Deceptive p. between man and ogre K170.1; sham physician and the devil in p. K1955.6.

Partridge distracts girls, fox eats their curds K341.26; entices woman from food, jackal eats it K341.5.2; subsists on moonbeams B768.1; too clever for jackal J423.1. — Color of p. *A2411.2.6.8; why p. has pretty feet *A2375.2.1; friendship between p., monkey and elephant A2493.14.5; friendship between jackal and p. A2493.11.4; reincarnation as p. E613.8.1; revenant as p. E423.3.3; striking at p. on another's head J1833.1.2; treacherous p. K2295.1; how p. got voice *A2421.4; witch as p. G211.4.2.

Partridge's — Crow tries to imitate p. walk J512.6.

Partridges. — Kite tries to carry off so many p. that he drops them all J514.1.

Parturition, see also **Childbirth,** *T584. — Unusual p. of animal B754.7.

Pass. — Fairy unable to p. crossroads F383.1; ghosts cannot p. crossroads E434.4; mountain p. magically closes D1552.3; mountain p. to otherworld F151.2; wild huntsman's dogs cannot p. over grave E501.15.6.4.

Passage of time U260ff. — Dwarfs live in underground p. F451.4.1.4; fairies excavate p. F271.2; leaves of tree open and close to give saint p. F979.2; thief enters treasury through secret p. K315; underground p. magically opens D1555; underground p. to paramour's house K1523.

Passages. — Underground p. F721.1.

Passenger. — Ungrateful river p. kills carrier from within K952.1.

Passengers within winged serpent as boat F911.3.2. — Man sacrifices self to save other p. W28.3.

Passer-by — Woman mistakes p. for lover K1317.7.

Passeriform. — Creation of p. A1910ff.; man transformed to p. D151ff.

Passing through hound-guarded door H1423.1; under magic rod as chastity ordeal H412.1. — Physician p. graveyard hides eyes P424.1.

Passion. — Fool as actor in P. Play J2041.1, J2495.3; king overcomes p. for beautiful captives P12.9; moon's p. A753.3.4; queen's illicit p. for diseased man T481.2; sun's p. A738.2.2.

Passions. — Sword vanquishes five evil p. D1389.14.

Passionate. — Devil has p. look in eyes G303.4.1.2.5.

Passover V75.1. — Magic power at P. D1719.9.2; miracles at P. F900.1.2; origin of P. A1541.5.

Password. — Recognition by p. H18.

Past. — Bringing p. time to present H1026.2; consolation by thinking of the p. J866; in planning future, profit by p. J752; present preferred to p. J310ff.; rue not a thing that is p. J21.12; wisdom from continual reminder of foolishness in the p. J167.

Paste turns to gold D475.1.11.

Pastry. — Magic p. D1031ff.; woman cannot find p. which is sticking to her posterior J2025.2.

Pastries. — Thief distracts owner, steals p. K341.15.

Pasturing black sheep until they become white Q521.4; cow which runs all day H1112.2; unusual p. as task H1199.12.

Patches on fairies' coats F236.5.1. — Brown p. on soil where marvelous cow lay A989.1.

Patent. — Animal granted p. of nobility A2546; dog loses his p. right and seeks it: why dogs look at one another under the tail A2275.5.5; place to live given as p. right to dog A2433.1.3.

Paternal aunt as aid P294.1.

Paternity, see also **Parentage.** — Brother duped into killing each other over p. slander K1092; dying mother tells children p. J1279.1; man doubts children's p.: kills them S11.3.1; test of p. H486ff.

Paternoster, see also **Prayer.** — Cheaters examined apart: first made to repeat P. J1141.3; devil unable to take one who has read the P. G303.16.2.1; levity regarding P. J1262.4.1; plowman to get horse for saying P. H1554.3; saint's P. outweighs ox V52.13.

Path, see also **Way;** to heaven *F57; to lower world F95; between monsters G333; to sun on sun's rays (eyelashes) F154; to world of dead F95.0.1. — Father makes evil greater by closing p. H583.2.1; Milky Way as p. (of a bird of passage) A778.7, (of souls) *A778.2.1; remove obstacles from p. J753; quest over p. guarded by hags H1236.3; perilous p. (to hell) *F95.3, (to otherworld) *F151.1, (for soul to world of dead) E750.2, (traversed on quest) H1236; straight p. not always shortest J2119.2.

Paths open in sea for Israel's tribes F931.9.3.

Pathelin (lawyer's mad client) *K1655.

Patience *W26; rewarded Q64. — Brotherly love and p. both dead J1633; children teach p. J124; lack of p. W196; test of p. *H1553; why weavers have p. P445.2.

Patient. — Doctor gives advice after p. dies J756.1; man p. in misfortune finally elected ruler N251.1; quieting p. by killing J2489.5.

Patients frightened from hospital by harshness K1955.1.2. — Repartee concerning doctors and p. J1430ff.

Patriarchs because of long life made the inventions A1440.3.

Patrick (Saint) curses Welsh F251.13; judges Irish souls E751.3. — Angel speaks to P. from bush A182.3.0.1.1; people to live "till coming of P." M300.1, M363.1.2; poor man's hospitality to P. rewarded Q45.1.2; vision of flames as faith brought by P. V515.1.3.

Patrick's — Oisin's poor diet in P. house repayed J1511.13.

Patriotism P711.

Patron. — Serpent as p. of wealth B108.1.

Pattern. — Taking a p. (picture) of conduct J2471; task: making a rope of sand (countertask: first showing the p.) H1021.1.1.

Paunch fat removed as stomach cure F959.4.

Pauper, see **Penniless.**

Paved. — Castle p. with gold and gems F771.1.1.1; city p. with precious seeds F761.5; great road p. in short time H1108; pool p. with gold F717.1.

Pavement. — Extraordinary p. F865; feet magically fixed to p. D2171.7; treasure found while digging p. N534.7.

Pavilion as lovers' rendezvous T35.2.

Pavilions produced by magic D2178.3.

Paw. — Cat with missing p. G252.0.1; cat's p. cut off: woman's hand missing D702.1.1; wolf puts flour on his p. to disguise himself K1839.1.

Paws. — Bear riding horse lets p. fall on horse's flanks J2187; dog's claws as grains under p. A2376.2; dupe puts p. into cleft of tree *K1111; indentions on rock from p. of King Arthur's dog A972.5.3; rat and frog tie p. together to cross marsh J681.1.

Pawn. — Wife's foolish p. J2086.

Pawned. — Stolen cow successively p. K408; stolen pot p. with the real owner K405.2.

Pawning. — Thief finally confesses when p. stolen goods N276.

Pay. — Calamity follows failure of king to p. soldiers C831; counting out p. (hole in hat) K275; helper on quest demands p. H1235.1; monk refuses p. V473.

Paying dwarfs makes them cease help to mortals F451.5.10.9. — Buying things in common, each p. full price J2037; custom of p. soldiers A1596.1; dwarfs buying peas and p. more than they are worth F451.5.10.5; dwarfs p. for being ferried across water F451.5.10.6; suitor p. for bride H318; wife p. paramour T232.5.

Payment with the clink of the money J1172.2; precluded by terms of the bargain K220ff.; with "something or other" J2489.10. — Bed-partner to receive p. from first man she meets in the morning T456; crane pulls bone from wolf's throat: wolf refuses p. W154.3; deception in p. of debt K200—K249; imaginary debt and p. J1551; too large a p. J1559.3; literal p. of debt K236; magic object returned in p. for removal of magic horns D895; quest as p. for gambling loss H1219.1; spiritual p. for misfortune J893.

Pea. — Chain tale: bird's p. stuck Z41.6; sack of earth in giant's hand resembles p. F531.2.15; princess on the p. H41.1; removing p. from ear J1115.2.2.

Peas become pearls D475.4.4; strewn on stairs so that person will slip K1071; transformed to stones D451.9.1. — Cannibal crunching human bone says noise is only eating of p. G87; Christ changes stones to p. D452.1.6.1; dwarfs buy p. from mortals and pay more than they are worth F451.5.10.5; dwarfs turn p. into gold pieces F451.3.3.1; fairy leaves when mortal strews p. in his path F381.2; fool thinks p. will burn walkers' feet J2214.1; God's tears become p. A2612.3; hog won't tell where p. are W151.6; literal numskull cuts p. into four parts J2461.1.4; man compelled to live on p. takes comfort when he sees man once rich eating the hulls J883.1; origin of p. A2612.3, A2686.2; riddle about splitting p. H583.4.6; why p. do not soften in boiling A2721.3.1; sorting a large amount of p. in one night H1091; sweeping, winnowing p. as devil's task G303.16.19.3.1; test of sex of girl masking as man: p. spread on floor H1578.1.1.

Peace among the animals J1421; between sheep and wolves K191; bought for husband M236; in heaven is sweetest (riddle) H633.2; more important than truth in marriage T203; reward for good law Q176. — Angel of p. A467.1; avoid enemies' revenge either by making p. and friendship or by killling them all J647.1; bishop struck for breaking the p. J1823.2; druid as p. emissary P427.2; enemies make p. rather than slay each other *J218; forced p. valueless U220ff.; god establishes p. between mortals A185.15; magic branch of p.: warfare ceases when it is shaken D1351.2; making p. tabu C642; mankind from P. and Quiet fructified by Light A1221.2; olive branch symbol of p. Z157; origin of p. ceremonies A1533; otherworld land of p. F173.2; precept of the lion to his sons: keep p. with the neighbors J22.3; prophecy: eternal p. in an early death or long troublesome life M365; reign of p. and justice A1101.1.1; seven year's p. Z71.5.3; sham p. discussion to get reinforcements K2369.7; strengthening self during p. J674.2; tabu: coming to Ireland in p. time C755.3; two groups of animals make p. treaty B260.1; vow to ask nobody for p. M165; wisdom from fool: make p. before rather than after the war J156.1.

Peaceable. — Why elephant is p. A2531.3; fools learn to be p. J24; magic object makes person p. D1351f.; why grizzly bear is p. A2531.2; wild huntsman made p. E501.17.6ff.

Peacefulness W43.

Peacemaker killed in feigned quarrel K929.6 — Dolphin and whale scorn crab as p. J411.6.

Peach branch exorcises devil D2176.6. — Conception from eating p. T511.1.6; magic p. *D981.2, (tree) D950.3; man becomes p. D211.6.

Peaches. — Putting p. back on tree H1023.18; thank God they weren't p. J2563.

Peacock admires self in mirror W116.4; as bird of ill-omen B147.2.2.7; birds' king B242.1.7; and crane in beauty contest J242.5; dissatisfied with her voice W128.4; on golden bowl of sun A724.2; on king's steeple as dowry C655.1; preens too long, loses kingship J515; proves to be bad king J242.4; shows rivers way to valley A934.12; spies on adulterous wife K1591.1; pregnant without intercourse B754.6. — Birds envious of p. point out ugly voice, legs W195.1; color of p. A2411.2.6.7; constructing automatic p. H326.1.1; creation of p. A1996; golden p. B102.1.2; horse with p. tail H1331.4.2; how p. got its tail A2378.1.9; jackal tries to pose as p. J953.14; king makes wooden p. machine F675.1; making p. of silk H1021.11; man carried by p. B552.2; man transformed to p. D166.2; person carried by p. B557.12; quest for golden p. H1331.1.3.2; reincarnation as p. E613.11; star from girl and p. mating A760.2; thrush's hospitality to p. rewarded by being given motley coat of feathers A2222.1; tortoise dances with p. J684.3; warning p. B143.1.2; why p. is vain A2527.2; why p. has ugly (feet) A2232.7, A2236.2.2, A2375.2.1, *A2375.2.2, (voice) A2236.2.2, A2423.1.2; wedding of turkey and p. B282.1.

Peacock's feathers ruffled in presence of poison B131.5. — Fire from p. tail burns enemy army K916.1; jay in p. skin unmasked J951.2; origin of p. feathers A2245, A2313.3, A2411.2.6.7.

Peacocks of gold F855.3.1. — Four p. to sit on four pinnacles of palace H1154.7.3; king of p. B242.2.5; land of p. B222.2.

Peanut — Man becomes p. D222.1; reincarnation as p. plant E631.5.2.

Pear. — Enchanted p. tree K1518; great p. X1411.4; magic p. *D981.6, (tree) *D950.5; man transformed to p. tree D215.2; quest for marvelous p. H1333.3.2; silver p. F813.4; transformation by eating p. D551.1.3.

Pears. — Numskulls try to get p. from an oak tree J1944.1; stealing p. from guarded garden H1151.10.1.

Pearl-dropping cow B103.1.2.1; found in fish N529.2; kingdom F707.4. — Centipede plays with p. B109.2; conception from swallowing p. T511.8.6; dragon's p. stolen B11.6.2.3; magic p. draws storm away D1541.2.2; mountain formed of a p. F752.3.1; pavement of p. F865.1; servant takes p. to wife instead of merchant N351.1; transportation by magic p. D1520.29.1.

Pearls from hair as sign of royalty H71.3; from magic tortoise shell D1469.14; shed for tears H31.7.1. — Animals live on p. F989.22.4; cock prefers single corn to peck of p. J1061.1; death respite until king reaps p. K551.21; deer with p. around neck B105.2; fairy's tears F239.6; impossible to eat p. J1191.5.1; island of p. F731.6; magic p. cure disease D1500.1.9.2; millstones as p. of the hero's mother K1718.2; origin of p. A2827; peas become p. D475.4.4; quest for unpierced p. H1348.2; recognizing p. by their smell F655.1; refusing p. for worthless stones J2093.3.1; saint refuses p. as alms V462.2.2.1; shooting p. from wife's nose-ring F661.10; spider catches p. B109.1; stealing p. from king H1151.13.5; swans live on p. B768.3; tortoise gives p. B103.1.6.

Peasant *P411; always busy producing food A1655.1; ashamed of being thrown off by ass J411.4; asks to be knighted J955.3.1; betrays fox by pointing K2315; boy masking as prince betrays self by his answers H38.2.2; exchanges place with monk U119.2; girl married to king longs for old food U135.3.1; girl betrays her hiding place to nobleman W136.1; girl outwits prince L151; as helper N854; hero L113.4; leaves honey tree standing J241.2; opens his mouth J2473; preaches about bishop's amour J1211.1; as priest preaches on the troubles of laymen K1961.1.1; rescues abandoned child R131.6. — Clever p. J1115.6; clever p. daughter J1111.4; clever p. girl asked riddles by king H561.1; devil as a p. G303.3.1.10; disguise as p. K1816.9; disguised king punished by p. P15.1f.; dying p. summons bishop who dies D1715.2; king disguised as p. flees battle

K1812.10; king and p. vie in riddling questions and answers H561.6; knight weds p. girl T121.1; mountain-folk steal from p. F460.4.4.5; mountain-men chain captive p. F460.4.4.2; prince substitutes p. girl for father's bride K1911.1.9; son ashamed of p. father who brings him money W165; stupid p. J1705.1; treacherous p. K2258; wife banished for p. origin S412.1; wounded hero restored by p. R169.14.

Peasant's enigmatic conversation with king H585; share is the chicken J1562.2. — Spirits tangle up p. cows F402.1.3; trolls' horses water at p. well F241.1.2.1.

Peasants in city inn order whole portion of mustard J1742.3; fed white bread demand the rye bread to which they are accustomed U135; as foster parents for king's son P270.1; give quest directions H1232.1; persecuted by one-eyed, dog-headed savages B25.1.2; want a living God J2495.4. — Wise men disguised as p. debate J31.1.

Peasants' — Dwarfs emigrate because they dislike p. dancing and loud music F451.9.1.9.

Peasantry. — Origin of p. A1655.

Peau d'âne K1815.

Pebble, see also **Stone;** for each sin J2466.1; put in box for each mass heard V46. — Abandoned children find way back by p. clue R135ff.; magic p. D931.2, (prevents burning) D1382.1, (splits wood) D1564.1; swallowed p. grows into snake B784.1.2.

Pebbles. — Animal attacks by throwing p. B762.1; crow drops p. into the water jug so as to be able to drink J101; quails become p. D423.2.

Peccary. — Man transformed to p. D114.3.1; origin of p. 1871.2; why p. has spots A2412.1.6.

Peck. — Deceptive bargain: p. of grain for each stack K181.

Pecking. — Bird eaten by king escapes by p. on his stomach F915.1; bird p. hole in sky F56.2.

Peddler causes delay in starting, not dog J1475. — Defeated king as p. L410.4; disguise as p. K1817.4.1, (to enter woman's room) K1349.1.3.

Peddler's. — Child born with claws from p. curse T551.9.

Pedestal supports island F736.2. — Otherworld door in p. F156.2.

Pedestrian. — Ghost chases p. E272.4.

Peeling. — Thrifty p. of apple as bride test H381.2.1.

Peeping at sacred font forbidden C51.1.7; Tom C312.1.2, C943.

Peewit. — Voice of p. A2421.7.

Pegasus B41.1; from neck of slain Medusa E783.2.1.

Pegs driven into backs of baboons become tails A2262.2. — Sitting on p. to make anus F529.2.1.

Pegged. — Bonga p. to ground F386.3; ogress p. to boulder G514.5.1.

Pelican as birds' king B242.1.4; kills young and revives them with own blood B751.2. — Rejuvenation by song of p. D1889.3.

Pelt. — Woman draws a p. to her instead of her husband K1281.

Pelts. — Ear tips become p. D457.19.

Pen. — Birds drop quill for man's p. B159.1; creator distributes p. A1440.1; filling locked p. K1427; fish recovers p. from sea B548.2.4; recovering p. from sea (task) H1132.1.4; saint confines self in p. V262.8.1.

Penalty. — Judge reducing p. when accused his son U21.5; origin of p. for murder A1581.1; riddle propounded with p. for failure H541.

Penalties. — Origin of special p. A1581.

Penance magically concluded by confession V27; for sin A1549.4. — Admission to heaven as reward for p. Q172.3; condemned soul saved by p. E754.1.3; devils appear to knight to try to call him from doing p. G303.9.4.5; failure to do p. punished Q223.8; fox fasts as p. B253.3; ghost laid when p. is done E451.2; husband duped into doing p. while rascal enjoys the wife K1514.2; imagined p. for imagined sin J1551.2; literal p.: boy outwits pope J1161.5; origin of p. for sins A2835; otherworld journey as p. F5; priest's p. saves soul from devil K218.6; return from dead to do p. E411.0.2.1; robber gives priest double his p. and then takes his horse J1635; self-righteous hermit must do p. L435.1; true p. effective J557.1.1.

Penances Q520ff. — Priest who gives mild p. succeeds where others fail L361; wife undertakes man's p. for him: also to go to heaven for him? M292.

Peninsula's — origin A956.

Penis, see also **Genitals, Member.** — Dwarf splits wood with p. F451.3.4.10; extraordinary p. F547.3; man threatens to cleave bear's skull with p. K1755.1; nature of animal's p. A2365.2; sham-dead tiger betrayed by live p. K607.3.1; why animal's p. is large A2365.2.1.

Penitent worries over little sins, belittles big U11.1.1.2.

Penitent's manuscript of sins V29.6. — Barrel filled miraculously with p. tears F1051.1.

Penniless, see also **Poor;** bridegroom pretends to wealth K1917; hero L123. — Man robbed and p. entertained by wealthy widow and enriched N225.

Penny from bad man, two from good J1672; baked in the wafer J1582.1. — Anger bargain: may God give you a p. K172.1; blessing not worth a p. J1261.4; buying p-worth of wit J163.1; pretence of taking trip to return p. debt K2054.1.

Pennies. — Deceptive bargain: an ox for five p. K182.

Pension. — Double p. falsely received K441.1.

Pent cuckoo flies over the hedge J1904.2.

Pentecost's origin A1541.6.

People, see also **Human beings, Men, Persons;** created by magic D2178.5; to whom devil appears G303.6.2. — City of extraordinary p. F768; city of petrified p. F768.1; fairies carry p. away to fairyland *F320ff.; trees in which p. live in nests F811.10; ways in which the devil kills p. G303.20ff.; wild huntsman makes p. carry him on their backs *E501.15.3.

Peoples, see also **Nations, Races, Tribes.** — Characteristics of various p.

(in industry and warfare) A1670ff., (in personal appearance) A1660ff.; distribution and differentiation of p.: general A1600ff.; treacherous p. K2299.2.

Pepper eaten instead of cooking it J1813.6; given as ointment for burns K1014; plant from body of slain person A2611.4; as remedy K1014; as sham doctor's remedy K1955.2.1. — Dirt becomes p. D452.4.1; dupe persuaded to put too much p. in food K1045; red p. for the slow ass: man tries it on himself X11; spitting p. into opponent's face K11.7; theft by blinding with p. K333.5; witch killed by putting p. inside skin G229.11.

Peppers. — Horse with p. sent against enemy K2351.6.1.

Peppercorn. — Conception from eating a p. T511.3.1.

Peppercorns. — Armies like seeds and p. J1625.

Perception. — Extraordinary powers of p. F640ff.

Perch. — Color of p. A2218, A2411.4.2; magic birds keep falling off p. D1649.1.2.

Percival must ask meaning of strange sights he sees *C651.

Percute hic (inscription on stone) N535.

Perfect god A102.7.

Perfume, see also **Fragrance.** — Garments emitting p. F821.10; girl lives on p. F647.12; herbs as p. F817.3; magic p. *D1245, (produces immunity from hunger and thirst) D1349.1.2; recognition by p. H44.

Perfumed mountain F759.4.

Peri. — Raja refuses to marry a p. F302.3.0.2.

Peris in sky-world F215.2.

Peril. — Animals grateful for rescue from p. of death B360ff.; sword which will break in only one p. Z314.

Perils of the soul *E750ff. — Magic p. threaten bridal couple *T175.

Perilous bed F846.1; falling gate *F776.2; path (to hell) *F95.3, (to otherworld) *F151.1, (for soul to world of dead) E750.2, (traversed on quest) H1236; river as barrier to otherworld F141.1.1; river in otherworld F162.2.11; seat H31.4; trap bridge *F842.2.1.

Periodic habits of animals A2480ff.; resuscitation *E155; sacrifices to a monster S262; transformation D620ff.; weakness D1837.1. — Origin of p. sowing A1441.4.1.

Periodically. — Dead person visits earth p. E585; wild hunt appears p. E501.11.3.

Perjurer cannot rest in grave E411.3; dismembered by magic lion H251.1.1; stricken dead Q558.2. — Magic paralyzes p. D1419.2.1.

Perjurers. — Devil and his servants live where p. dwell G303.8.6.

Perjury punished *Q263. — Tree tests p. H251.3.1.

Permanent. — Command would become p. J1521.3; disenchantment made p. D793.

Permission to pull lion suitor's teeth J642.1. — Chaste woman refers lover to her husband for p. K1231; demon given p. to be on earth four times a year A106.2.1.2; discovery of abbot's incontinence brings p. to monks to do likewise K1274; entering castle without p. angers king P14.11; execution escaped by use of special p. granted the condemned *J1181; fraudulent p. sold K157; tabu: entering assembly without p. C864.1; tabu: stranger to play with someone without asking p. C892.

Perpetual summer in otherworld F161.1. — Tree in p. fruit F162.3.3.

Persecuted queen meanly clothed and set where all are commanded to spit on her Q471.1; wife *S410ff. — Brother faithful to p. sister P253.2.1; dead mother returns to aid p. children *E323.2; quest for p. woman H1381.3.6.

Persecution by bad luck N250.2; of wife punished Q421.0.8.

Persecutions. — Cruel p. *S400—S499.

Perseus fights dragon B11.10; seeks Gorgon's head H1332.3.

Perseverance rewarded Q81.

Person, see also **Human being, Man;** comes to life E1; changes size at will D631.1; disenchanted D700ff.; mistaken for object J1763; mistaken for something else J1760ff.; swallowed without killing F911; thought to be animal J1765; transformed to object D200—D299. — Animal as guard of p. B576.1; animal thought to be p. J1762ff.; animal transformed to p. D300ff.; certain p. to find treasure N543; deity takes form of particular p. K1811.4; escape by substituting another p. in place of the intended victim *K527; extraordinary nature phenomena at birth of holy p. F960.1; fairy in form of p. F234.2; fairies visible to one p. alone F235.3; invisibility conferred on a p. D1983; living p. becomes God A104.1; lucky p. N203; magic cure by certain p. D2161.5; magic object rescues p. *D1390ff.; man in moon is p. thrown or sent there as punishment A751.1; marriage to p. in animal form *B640ff.; moon as a p. A753; not to look at certain p. or thing C310ff.; object transformed to p. D430ff.; prophecy: death by certain p. M341.2.9; remarkable p. F500—F599; spirit leads p. astray F402.1.1; swallowed p. alive in animal X1723.1; tabu imposed by p. C999.1.1; transformed p. sleeps before girl's door, at foot of bed, in bed K1361.1; vulnerability only by one p. Z313; witch rides on p. G241.2; wound healed only by p. who gave it, D2161.4.10.2.

Persons, see also **Men, People;** with extraordinary powers F600—F699; magically stick together D2171.5. — Clever p. *J1100—J1129; curses on p. M430ff.; magic objects effect changes in p. D1300—D1379; sacred p. *V200—V299; wild hunt harmful to certain p. E501.18.1.

Personal appearance of wild huntsman E501.7ff.; offenses against gods punished *Q221. — Foolish disregard of p. danger J2130ff.; unfavorable traits of character: p. W110ff.; vows concerning p. appearance M120ff.

Personification of (death) Z111, (luck and fate) N110, (time) Z122, (truth) Z121, (wind) Z115; prophesies M301.8.

Personifications Z110. — Giants as p. F531.6.1.5.

Perspiration, see also **Sweat,** in winter from emotion F1041.12. — Boy drinks p. F561.7; transformation by eating rice mixed with p. D551.6.2.

Perspire. — Devils cause monk to p. and stay away from church service V5.3.

Persuaded. — Ogre p. to go into hole and buried alive G512.4; woman p. by trick *K1350ff.

Persuading persons to intercourse A1352.2. — Wife only one p. husband P216.

Persuasive person or thing not to be heeded *C810ff.

Perversions, sexual T460ff.

Pessimist. — Optimist becomes p. when money stolen U68.

Pests. — Ridding country of p. Q512.3; why white ants are p. A2522.3.

Pestilence, see also **Plague;** F493ff.; brought to man A1337.0.1.1;magically sent D2094. — Fast to prevent p. V73.1; goddess of p. A478.1; locality sanctified against p. *D2162.3; magic p. D2064.0.3; priest keeps in container relic which when kissed renders people immune from p. J762.1; spirit of p. F493; saint's shrine suppresses p. V221.0.1.3; wild hunt as omen of p. E501.20.1.2.

Pestle to frighten away guests J1563.5.1.—Fainting from noise of wooden p. and mortar F647.8; fencer's opponent picks up p. J676; magic p. D1254.3, (draws storm away) D1541.2; obedient woman's p. magically suspended J2411.9; origin of p. A1446.5.2; sky struck by p. A625.2.2.

Pet. — King's wives jealous of p. animal T257.1.1; man transformed to animal kept as p. by heroine T33; snake wants to act like p. J512.14; transformation to child or p. to be adopted *D646.2; visible sun is p. of real sun A722.12.

Pets. — Lions as king's p. P14.22.

Petals. — Flower sheds p. when husband thinks of wife H1556.4.6.

Peter (Saint) acts as God for a day: tires of bargain L423; addressed in throwing contest K18.1.2; called fool for enduring poverty J1263.4.2; creates grass as medicine for snake-bite A2623; drives devil out of a man G303.16.11.1; lets key of heaven fall: origin of "Heaven Key" (primrose) A2622; as porter of heaven A661.0.1.2; receives the blows twice K1132; reminded of his denial of Christ admits soldiers to heaven J1616; rules air, rain A287.2. — Angel helps P. escape prison V232.8.

Peter's contest with Simon Magus V351.3.1; fingerprints on fish A2217.3.1; mother dropped from heaven because of hard-heartedness Q291.1; wife meets him with a broomhandle T251.3. — Heaven entered by trick: sitting on P. chair K2371.1.4.

Peter Ox J1882.2.

Petition. — One-word p. J1618.

Petrification as curse M458; by glance D581; on hearing woman's voice D529.1; by magic *D231; by magic formula D573.2; of suitors D581.1.

Petrified. — Approachers p. by magic bird B172.1; city of p. people F768.1; gravity p. in p. forest X1741.3; passersby p. by river F715.7; wood p. by lake F934.3.

Petulance W127.

Pewter. — Money transformed to p. D475.2.4.

Phaëton drives sun's chariot A724.1.1.

Phalanx P552.3.

Phantom army attacked K1883.1; hosts E500ff.; house disappears at dawn F771.6; sailors E510ff. — Sight of p. ship a bad omen D1812.5.1.10.

Phantoms F585ff.

Pharaoh as magician D1711.7.1.

Pharaoh's drowned army origin of (animals) A1715.1, (birds) A1901, A1944.1, (mermaids) B81.1.

Phases. — Causes of moon's p. A755.

Pheasant. — Color of p. A2411.2.6.9; friendship between ant and p. A2493.29; helpful p. B469.10. — Why cheeks of p. are red A2330.6.

Phenomenon. — Enigmatic p. explained H614.

Phenomena at appearance of wild hunt E501.13ff.; at disappearance of wild hunt E501.16ff. — Natural p. accompanying the devil's appearance G303.6.3ff.; natural p. associated with gods A139.11; physical p. misunderstood J1810ff.

Philandering god A188.1; man's wife has affair K1510.2.

Philanthropist will give his spurs if someone will drive his horse for him W11.1.

Philemon and Baucis entertain Zeus Q1.1.

Philistines. — Riddle about P. H831.

Philosopher, see also **Sage;** P485; advises on life J152.3ff.; brings king to sense of duty by feigned conversation of birds J816.1; chooses poverty with freedom J211.1; conquers evil fate M137; forgets Charon's fee E489.3; instructs king on domestic harmony J816.1.1; keeps silent J1074.1.1; laughs at world's sins, vanities U15.1; loses all wealth, thankful to be out of business J2569; spits in king's beard J1566.1; teaches son to beg from stone statue H1553.1; tells king to seek harmony at home J1289.9. — Cynical p. lives in tub J152.1; holy man tells p. wisdom before learning J1217.2; needy p. asks king for money J1289.4; wealthy girl marries penniless p. T121.5.

Philosopher's sham threat to break head K1771.5; stone from cocoanut D451.3.2. — Drunk p. foolish wager J1161.9.

Philosophical watchman J2377.

Philosophy. — Suitor task: to study p. H335.0.2.1.

Philosophies. — Aristotle drinks both red and white wine to show that all p. are good J462.2.

Philtre. — Magic love-p. D1355.2; mutual love through accidental drinking of love p. *T21.

Phoenix B32; creator's companion A36.

Phorcides F512.1.2, K333.2.

Phrase. — Using only one p. C495, J2516.3.3.

Phylactery. — Magic p. D1282.1.2.

Physical characteristics of culture hero (demigod) A526; characteristics of giant ogres G120ff.; circumstances of devil's disappearance G303.17.2; features of underworld F80.1; phenomena misunderstood J1810ff.; requirements for suitors H312. — Devil's p. characteristics G303.4ff.; extraordinary p. reactions of persons F1041ff.; fanciful p. qualities of animal B720—B749; humor of p. disability X100—X199; magic cure of p. defect *D2161.3; magic object works p. change D1330ff.; recognition by p. attributes H50ff.; remarkable p. organs F540ff.

Physician, see also **Doctor;** *P424; cures by imitation F957; dupes patient, entertains mistress K1516.1.1; of the gods A144; removes animal from patient's stomach B784.2.4; tells who inflicted wound F956.4; willing to believe in four persons J817.2. — Animal p. B299.6; clever p. J1115.2; double dealing p. K2041; druid as p. P427.5; fairy p. F274, (abducted to heal mortals) R33, (has healing powers) F344.2; illness feigned to call p. paramour K1514.11; no p. at all J1432; poor girl masks as a doctor and is made court p. K1825.1.2; sham p. *K1955; skillful p. F668.0.1; treacherous p. K2292.

Physicians. — Hero refuses to slay p. W11.5.12; origin of p. A1594.1.

Physics. — Eating p. by mistake J2134.2.1.

Pice. — Riddle involving p. H587.1.

Pick. — Dripping water as ghost with p. J1782.2.1; man transformed to p.-handle D266.

Picked. — First objects p. up bring fortune N222; guilty man p. out by magic object D1318.0.1; transformation to be p. up D646; unknown father p. out by infant H481.

Picking all nuts from tall tree (task) H1121; things up only when master gives the signal J2516.2; up everything in path indicates miser H614.1. — Magic statue of archer put into action by p. up precious object from ground D1620.1.5.1.

Pickpockets strike man so he takes hand off purse K357.

Pickpocketing while confederate in pillory K341.24.

Picture as chastity index H439.1; comes to life D435.2.1; falls from sky F962.12.3; magically made hideous D1873.1; mistaken for original J1792; burns black (life token) E761.4.2; of a voice H1013. — Eye with p. in the pupil F541.2; ghost-like p. E532; hero ransoms saint's p. N848.1; hoodwink: "cuckold can't see this p." J1492; image in mirror mistaken for p. J1795; imagining other half of p. J1551.11; king seeks bride like p. H1381.3.1.1.1.; love through sight of p. T11.2; magic p. *D1266.2. (causes bed-wetting) D1379.4; marvelous p. falls from sky in storm F962.13.3; pagan sybil draws p. of Madonna and Child in sand V341; recognition through p. H21; stone turns red when saint's p. removed V229.23; taking a p. of conduct J2471; tiger-p. comes to life, kills M341.2.10.2; Virgin Mary's p. (appears to devotee) V263, (saves priest) K218.5; vow to starve until original of p. found M151.2.1; wizard shows p. of thief D1817.0.1.4; woman in p. arouses man's love H1381.3.1.2.1.

Pictures of creator A18; of gods A137ff. — Bridegroom chosen from p. T131.1.2.2; match arranged by p. T51.3.

Pie deceptively goes to clerks K362.8. — Cat eats p. instead of mouse J2103.1.1.

Pieces taken from flags serve to identify H103. — Fixing the two p. of a broken sword together (task) H1923.8; magic needle makes everything fall to p. D1562.4; murder by slicing person into p. S139.7; stars as p. of the moon A764.

Piecemeal mutilation as punishment Q451.11. — Creator creates earth p. A837. — Murder by p. destruction of separable soul K956.1.

Pied Piper of Hamelin D1427.1.

Piercer-of-souls G322.

Piercing magic object D1404. — Frog p. metals F989.23; ghost laid by p. grave with stake S442; murder by p. with pins, needles S115.3.

Piety, see also **Pious;** renders magic ineffective D1745.2; rewarded Q20ff. — Magic power from p. D1736; paramour pretends p. by attending matins after visiting mistress K2059.3; pretended p. K2058; wager over mortal's p. G303.9.8.7.

Pif Paf Poltrie Z31.1.

Pig, see also **Hog, Sow, Swine;** attempts to imitate goat's tricks J2415.6; big as mountain H1149.8; boiling only after true stories H251.3.11; born with man's head after bestiality T465.5; cooked when true story is told D1316.10; dedicated to St. Anthony tramples would-be slayer Q228; and dog's plowing contest K41.2; -fairy transformed to fish D412.3.1; as healer B511.2; impersonates plague, owner flees K335.0.2.1; licks sleeping man who thinks it is a kiss X31.2; as magician's familiar G225.7.1; in pit as unknown animal J1736.3; as sacrifice V12.4.3; as suitor B621.6; swallows necklace F989.22.3; theft exposed by child's curiosity K433; transformed to object D422.3; transformed to person D336.1; with venomous bristles B776.4.1. — Beggar's ghost laid by p. E451.6; cart as back legs for crippled p. X1202.1; eating magic p. prevents disease D1500.2.5; escape from ogress by substituting p. K525.7; fattening the p. J1903.3; god's urine used to make p. A1871.0.1; greedy p. looks up into tree, killed J514.4; happiness from eating magic p. D1359.3.2; hare and p. in race H625; how p. is domesticated A2513.3; hunting p. tabu C841.4; husband wishes wife into p. J2075.4; inexhaustible p. D1652.1.9.1; industrious p. rewarded Q5.1; imitation and real p. J2232; killing giant p. as suitor task H335.3.5; killing golden p. H1161.4; literal numskull kisses a p. J2461.2.1; magic p. B184.3.2ff., (burned to prevent resuscitation) B192.1, (carrying scissors, comb, and razors between its ears) H1154.1, (dead) D1281.1, (invisible) B184.3.2.1, (heals wound its skin touches) B511.2.1; monster cat born of a p. B16.1.1.1; oil of magic p. H1332.5.1; old woman and her p. Z41; one-eyed p. B15.4.5; ox-demon transformed to p. D412.2.2; quest for marvelous p. H1331.2; thief disguised as p. K311.6.5; venomous p. B776.4; stingy parson and slaughtered p. K343.2.1; woman meets a p. (cumulative tale) Z33.3; wedding of p. B281.6.

Pig's blood disenchants D766.2.1; bones become pig D447.7; flesh magic
*D1032.4; food A2435.3.14. — Counting hairs in p. back (task) H1118;
devil has p. foot G303.4.5.5; divination from p. liver D1311.10.2; goddess
with p. head A131.3.2; goddess with p. teeth A131.8; obtaining wild p.
marrow H1154.11; sham all-knowing p. head K1956.10.

Pigs become other animals D412.3ff.; bewitched G265.6.1.1; cursed
M414.8.2; cut from sow's body: raised T584.4; paralyzed by witch
D2072.0.2.5. — Acorns alleged to protect p. K119.2; curse: p. to be lean
M471.2; deceptive division of p.: curly and straight tails K171.4; demigod
keeps wild p. B845.1; devil payed when p. walk, not run, home K226;
feeding p. wet meal J2465.1; getting ninety p. H1154.2.1; making p.
dance (task) H1186; miser killing his own p. W153.9; planting hog in order to grow p. J1932.4; resuscitation of dismembered p. E32.3; roast p.
run around ready for eating X1208.1; St Anthony's p. B256.2; slain p.
revive nightly *E155.5; slaughter of wild p. in vengeance J1866.1; sow
saves p. from wolf coming to baptize them K1121.2; spirit owns herd of
p. F241.3.1; why the p. shriek J1733; trickster shears sheep, dupe p.
K171.5; why p. in mud lift their legs A2473.2, A2479.5; why p. are plentiful A2582.1; why wild p. ravage rice-fields A2545.5; wolves, wild p.
condemned to death for killing sheep B275.1.3.2; woman bears three p.
T554.9.

Pigskin. — Magic p. *D1025.1; quest for magic p. H1332.5; stealing p.
from a king H1151.13.1.

Pigsty abode for unpromising hero (heroine) L132. — In duel with long
poles the ogre is forced into the p. K785; suitor locked in p. K1218.2.

Pigeon god A132.6.5; hastily kills his mate for stealing wheat N346; as
messenger B291.1.12. — Creation of p. A1947; creation of sea p. A1947.1;
crow befriends p. to steal from his household K359.4; green p. cheated out
of chick: mourns A2275.4.1; helpful p. B457.2; how was p. killed?
J2133.14.1; jay in p. skin unmasked J951.2; man becomes p. D154.2;
marriage to p. B602.3; reincarnation as p. E613.6.1; tabu to eat p.
C221.1.2.2.

Pigeon's entrails fetch lover D1355.3.4; wedding B282.3.4, B282.20. —
Heroine with p. head L112.11.

Pigeons cover sun with wings to aid hero H982.1. — Breaking p. egg on
castle parapet H1149.6; king of p. B242.2.4; land of p. B222.1; racing p.
tabu C865.1.

Pike helps Christ: made king of fishes A2223.4. — Creation of p. A2111;
enmity between white fish and p. A2494.15.1; devil cannot change into
p. G303.3.6.1; friendship between p. and crawfish A2493.33; helpful p.
B475; man becomes p. D179.2; woman tricks lover with p. head K1222.

Pilate appears periodically at Mt. Pilatus and washes his hands E411.8.
— Bittern from P. transformed A1965.1; Christ's coat of mercy protects P.
D1381.4.1.

Pilav. — Father's counsel: let p. be your daily food H588.2.

Pilgrim rebuked for eating too much J1346. — Devil in form of p. G303.3.1.9; disguise as p. to enter enemy's camp (castle) K2357.2; first p. A1546.3.2; pious p. dies unknown in father's house K1815.1.1; woman disguised as p. questions lover K1837.2.

Pilgrimage with hands and loins weighted with iron as penance Q522.4; as penance Q526. — Girl vows not to marry until p. K1227.7; reward for p. Q28; stubbornness loses woman chance for p. W167.2.

Pilgrimages V530. — Religious p. V85.

Pill transformed to white rabbit D444.3. — Alleged oracular p. sold K114.3; disenchantment by removal of enchanting p. from mouth D765.1.1; magic p. *D1243; transformation by placing p. in mouth D551.6.1.

Pills. — Magic p. bring twin sons D1347.3.1; snake gives away magic p. J621.1.1; throwing away p.: sores result J2075.3.

Pillar of fire *F964.0.1, (guides person to church) D1314.10, (from heaven to earth) F962.2.2, (rises over woman pregnant with saint) V222.0.1.1; -stone as weapon F614.2.1; supporting sky A665.2. — Captivity in p. R41.6; castle stands on a p. F771.2.5; demon as fiery p. G302.3.1; fiery p. sign of Christ's visit V211.2.1; god flies in p. of floating clouds A171.3; quest for silver p. H1322.1; rice in hands joined around p. J2119.6; river issues from p. F715.1.2; soul hidden in p. E712.5; standing on p. as penance for incest Q541.3; till ogam and p. be blent Z61.1; transformation to p. of salt for breaking tabu C961.1.

Pillars of dead chief's bones A151.4.4; of Hercules at Gibraltar set up by Hercules A984; magically dance D1599.1; of silver and glass in otherworld *F169.1; of smoke, light lead to heaven E754.6; supporting sky A665.2.0.1. — Castle on golden p. F771.2.5.1; extraordinary p. F774ff.; gold p. in otherworld F169.1.2; habitable hill raised on four p. F721.2.1; sky extended by p. A665.2.1.3; twelve iron p. steady the earth A841.3.

Pillory. — Man stands in p.; confederate picks pockets K341.24.

Pillow causes magic sleep D1364.11. — Horse's skull as p. F874.2.1; magic p. *D1154.5; one feather makes hard p. J2213.9; stone becomes p. D452.1.9; treasure hidden in p. under dead man's head N522.

Pillows as chastity test H411.10.

Pilot. — Saint's staff as sea p. D1313.5.1.

Pin pricks which do not bleed reveal witch G259.3. — Disenchantment by removal of enchanting p. D765.1.2; lost p. found in fish N211.1.1; magic p. *D1182; pricking with p. to keep awake H1484; swallowed p. emerges through relative's skin X1739.1.

Pins in horse's heart release curse M429.2; stuck in soles of dead man's feet to prevent return E431.12. — Murder by feeding with bread full of p. K951.2; murder by piercing with p. S115.3; object pierced with p. as love charm D1355.3.2, D1355.3.3; witch sticks victim with p. G269.17.

Pincers. — Tearing off flesh with p. Q469.9.1.

Pincher. — Remarkable p. X952.

Pinching. — Fairies p. as revenge F361.17.3; shell-fish p. trickster J2136.4; witches p. victim G269.19.

Pine bender G314; and thornbush dispute as to their usefulness J242.2. — Discontented p. tree: cause of p. needles A2723.1, A2767.1; fairy's back like p. cones F232.1.2; floors in dwarf home covered with p. twigs F451.4.3.5.

Pining. — Animal p. away with grief B773.2; fairy child p. away F329.4.2.

Pink. — Person with p. fluid in place of blood F554.1.

Pious, see also **Piety;** child able to carry water in sieve H1023.2.0.2; die on birthday F1099.7; woman rescues child R131.18. — Angels as souls of p. A52.0.4; animal characteristics reward for p. act *A2221; animals leave wicked, go to p. master B292.0.2; devil prevented from revenge by p. priest G303.16.11.2; living with ordinary vs. p. man J417; oath uttered by p. against temptation M110.3; souls of p. advise creator A45; souls of p. as angels E754.7; tree supports p. family F979.19; youth associating with a p. person (nun as mistress) J1264.5.

Pipal protection against witch D1385.2.4. — Why p. leaves tremble A2762.3.

Pipe. — Changeling plays on a p. and thus betrays his maturity F321.1.1.2; dead man smokes p. E555; devil's p. G303.25.16.1; gun as tobacco p. K1057; magic p. (musical) *D1224, (causes magic sleep) D1364.25.3; opium substituted for tobacco in p. K873.3; recognition by tobacco p. H147; skillful marksman shoots p. from man's mouth F661.2; tobacco, p., and match debate usefulness to smoker J461.3; wind raised by blowing into tobacco p. D2142.1.6.1.

Pipes. — Fairy tobacco p. F246.

Piper. — Ghost as p. E425.2.5.

Piracy. — Brothers help each other in p. P251.5.1.

Pirate excommunicated V84.3.

Pirates. — Abduction by p. R12; escape from p. R211.4; man patiently undergoes cruelty of p. N251.1; partner abducted by p. P319.4.

Pisāca drink blood and eat human flesh G312.1.

Pistol. — Magic p. *D1096.2.

Pit entrance to (lower world) F92, (otherworld) F158; placed under bed K735.4.1. — Abandonment in p. *S146; animals grateful for rescue from p. B361; blind leading blind falls into p. J2133.9; burning p. will close only for rider F1061.3; devil appears to girl who prays over p. where she has thrown the bodies of her babies G303.6.2.7; dupe tricked in race into falling into a p. K1171; dupe takes prisoner's place in p. K842.2; escape from snake p. R211.7; fox climbs from p. on wolf's back K652; jackals enter p. to escape storm, killed K811.2; jumping over p. chastity test H412.7.2; jumping over p. proves sex H1578.1.4.2; man, lion, and bear in p. J685.1; mankind emerges from p. A1232.31; moon buried in p. A754.1; moon falls into p. A754.1.1; pig in p. as unknown J1736.3; riding across p. as suitor contest H331.1.4; sun shut up in p. A721.0.2; throwing into p. as punishment Q465; traitor thrown into p. Q417.2; traveler saves monkey, snake, tiger, and jeweler from p. W154.8; warriors hidden in battlefield p. K2369.2; witch kicks helper into p. G269.1.1.

Pitch becomes cold water D478.14; shower as punishment Q475.2; smeared on threshold to trap fleeing girl J1146.1. — Boiling to death in p. S112.1; saint unhurt by boiling p. D1841.2.2.

Pitcher magically sticks to ground D2171.4.1. — Identification by ring dropped in p. of wine H94.3; magic p. *D1171.4; water drowns girl filling p. D1432.1.

Pitchfork. — Devil with p. G303.4.8.7.

Pitchforks wrench souls in hell E755.2.1.1.

Pitfall. — Capture in p. K735; deceiver arranges p. but is himself caught K1601; husband catches the paramour in a p. K1562; mats over holes as p. K735.1; origin of p. A1458.1; victim escapes p. K1601.1.

Pittance. — Man dismissed after years of service with a p. W154.1.

Pity. — Calf's p. for draft-ox ill-placed L456.

Pitying. — God p. mortal A185.16.

Pixies F200.1; in dancing contest F302.3.4.2.1.

Placard. — Importunate lover wears humiliating p. K1218.6.

Placating ghosts by sacrifices E433; ruler with soft words J811.4.

Place of bad omen D1812.5.1.30; and conditions of childbirth T581; of giving curse M413. — Absurd ignorance concerning p. for animal to be kept J1904; animal council assigns p. and work to all B238; compulsion to go to certain p. C666; devil helps man p. cart wheel when it becomes unfastened G303.22.4; devil in p. of dead man in shroud G303.18.2; devil takes p. of woman who went to spend night with a priest G303.25.11; fear test: staying in frightful p. H1410ff.; forbidden p. C610ff., (for bathing) C721.2, (for drinking) C260ff., (for eating) C210ff., (for sleeping) C735.2; forgetfulness caused by p. D2004.9; fortune-telling dream induced by sleeping in extraordinary p. D1812.3.3.2; husband takes p. of paramour K1569.4; magic discovery of desired p. D1816ff.; magic object causes things to seek their proper p. D1565ff.; magic object indicates desired p. *D1314ff.; marking the p. J1922; Nero has reserved p. in hell for lawyers X316; origin of p.-name A1617; princess rescued from p. of captivity R111.2; prophecy: death in particular p. M341.3; sea rises and changes p. F931.1; tabu: being in certain p. at sunrise C751.7.1; tabu: staying too long in certain p. C761.4; thief persuades owner to take his p., robs him K341.9.1; transformation to reach difficult p. D641.

Places changed in bed with ogre's children *K1611; and conditions of captivity R40ff.; haunted by the devil G303.15ff. — Avoiding p. which have been fatal to others J644; congregating p. of fairies F217; curses on p. M411.8.2; extraordinary p. F700ff.; origin of particular p. A980ff.; quest for unknown objects or p. H1382; saints in several p. at once V225.

Placenta covering as escape disguise K522.1.1. — Child born from p. T549.4.1; motifs associated with p. T588; origin of p. A1313.5; plant from transformed human p. A2611.0.3.

Placidas pursued by misfortune N251.

Plague, see also **Pestilence;** as bad omen D1812.5.1.19; banished by burying girl alive S266; for breaking tabu C941.4; ceases after pestilence spirit destroyed F493.3.1; from Jews' poisoning wells V362; magically invoked D2061.1.5; as punishment Q552.10; strikes down boasting usurer Q558.3; talk frightens away guests J1563.8. — Battle between God's orderly and p. A162.6; bull, cow survive p. F989.6; cannibalism during p. G78; end of p. as reward Q146; enemy tricked into fleeing p. K2368.3; "flame of fire" p. to destroy Ireland M356.2; holy mountain free from p. D2162.4; magic incense protects against p. D1389.15; magic p. of frogs drawn down on foe D2091.2; magic object relieves from p. D1586; proclamation of dogma of Immaculate Conception stops p. V312.1; pseudo-magic letter against p. K115.1.3; punishment of magician who causes p. Q392; recognition by p. H94.8; spirit of p. F493; woman stricken by p. dies in lover's arms T88.

Plagues. — Animals from frogs sent as one of Egypt's p. A1734; ten p. Z71.16.2.1.

Plain at borders of otherworld F144; that is earthly paradise F756.2; people put on vain display W116.3; sinks to become lake bottom F944.4. — Crossing p. after sunset tabu C752.1.2; hero crosses impassible p. in path of magic object D1562.5; magic p. *D937, (to which one sticks) D1413.19; otherworld as p. F160.1; quest to P. of Wonders H1288; sea appears like flowery p. D2151.1.4; strong man clears p. F614.9.

Plains of heaven A663. — Burning p. in hell A671.2.4.4; extraordinary valleys and p. F756; god clears p. A181.1; heroes clear p. A537.

Plainness. — Choice between p. with safety or grandeur with danger J212; magic needle transforms a room from p. to beauty D1337.1.7.

Plaintiff assigns impossible task H919.4. — Animal as p. B271; judgment as rebuke to unjust p. J1172.

Plaiting — Fairies p. horse's manes F366.2.1.

Plaits. — Hair p. cut off to escape lover T327.7.

Plan. — All aspects of a p. must be foreseen J755.

Plans. — Absurd p. J2060ff.; forethought in prevention of others' p. J620ff.; modest business p. best L250ff.; swindler's p. foiled J1521.

Plane-tree blamed for not bearing fruit W154.7; tests perjury H251.3.1.

Planet. — Sun, moon pursued by dark p. in black chariot A735.2.

Planets A780ff.

Plank test H1534.

Planks. — Skillful tailor sews together scattered p. in capsizing boat F662.2.

Planning for greater office J703. — Father p. child's death S11.4; in p. future, profit by the past J752; servant p. to possess his master's goods P365.2; woman p. to eat her children G72.1.

Plant from blood of slain person E631.0.3; grows to sky F54.2; from scrapings of princesses' bodies H522.2; shrieks when uprooted F992; transformed into animal D441.4; transformed to other object D451.2;

transformed to person D431.6; wife T117.10. — Animal languages learned from eating p. B217.2; birth from p. T543; cockscomb p. used to kill sun A1156; conception from eating p. T511.2; creator sent down insects to p. plants A2601; deceptive land purchase: to raise certain p. K185.11; disenchantment by eating p. D764.6; guessing nature of p. H522.2; girl persuaded to sit on certain p.: seduced K1315.2.1; grateful p. D1658.2.3; guessing unknown p. (test) H522ff.; hand becomes p. D457.9.1; heavens created after p. world A700.4; magic p. *D965ff., (furnishes treasure) D1463ff., (bears fruit to indicate that heroine is ready to marry) D1310.4.2, (heals broken bone) D1518.4.1, (heals wounds) D1503.10; man made from p. A1255; one p. transformed into another A2616; origin of p. names A2781; owl advises where to p. crops B569.2; quest for extraordinary p. H1333.2; quest for p. of immortality H1333.2.1; recognition by overheard conversation with p. H13.2.3; reincarnation as p. E631.5; reincarnation in p. growing from grave *E631ff.; sickness from drying, shriveling p. D2064.8; soul in p. E711.2; touching p. forbidden C510ff.; vampire p. E251.5; wild hunt avoided by holding certain p. E501.17.5.7; why leaves of p. are flat A2741.3, A2761.3; woman gives birth to p. T555.

Plants as gods' bodies D210.1; grow after sky lifted A625.2.5; magically shriek D2091.12; and trees miraculously unbent F973. — Creator p. tree on moon A751.6.1; creator sent down insects to plant p. A2601; devil plows and p. for farmer in one day G303.9.2.3; extraordinary behavior of trees and p. F970ff.; extraordinary p. F815; God p. fields A432.0.1; goddess of forest p. A431.1.2; hoarded p. released A1423.0.1; lies about p. X1400; magic flower pot bears p. with gold letters on leaves D1469.1; magic gardens and p. D960ff.; magic object makes p. grow D1487; origin of trees and p. A2600—A2699; procuring food p. as bride contest H375.3; quest for extraordinary p. H1333; strong man as gardener destroys p. F614.3; sun's power over p. A738.4; tabu to eat certain p. C226; why leaves of p. are flat A2741.3, A2761.3; why p. no longer reach sky A2775.0.1.

Plantain. — Bringing p. leaf without tearing it H1041; magic p. *D965.11; man becomes p. stalk D213.6; why p. bears but one stalk A2722.1, A2771.2.

Plantains. — Green p. sold as matured K147.1.

Planted — Why wheat must be p. one year, harvested next A2793.2.1.

Planting animal's tail to produce more animals J1932.4.1; beautiful garden H1199.1; cooked food K496; the earth A2602; for the next generation J701.1; a hog in order to grow pigs J1932.4. — Origin of p. A1441.4; snow taken away by p. certain root D2143.6.1.

Plate. — Guessing nature of devil's p. H523.7; magic p. *D1172.1; stolen church p. E236.7; turning the p. around J1562.1.

Plates. — Dogs with eyes like p. B15.4.3; leaves become gold p. D475.1.19.

Plated. — Deceptive sale of p. ware K123.

Platform. — Magic p. *D1157.

Platter. — Stealing silver p. K362.3.1.

Play. Why great man joins in children's p. J25; prince will not join p. of common children J411.3; sun's p. with moon A722.9; unknown prince chosen chief of children in p. *P35.

Players. — Card p. scared by ghost E293.2.

Playful fairies F399.4; ghost E599.10.

Playing cards with devil in church (fear test) H1421; flute forbidden C844; game with reassembled dead man (fear test) H1433; at marriage tabu C167.1; poison K439.4. — Animal with men in its belly p. cards F911.3.3; captive escapes by p. further and further from watchman K622; changeling p. on a pipe betrays his maturity F321.1.1.2; dead persons p. games E577; devil p. fiddle at wedding G303.9.8.2; dwarfs p. in moonlight F451.6.3.5; dupe p. for wedding K844; fox feigns to be p. with sheep K2061.2; giants p. with men's lives F531.3.15; mortal wins fairies' gratitude by p. for their dance F331.4; mountain-men p. games F460.3.2; recognition by unique manner of p. lute H35.1; resuscitation by p. music E551ff.; recognition by unique manner of p. lute H35.1; serpents p. with precious green stone B11.6.2.2; symbolic interpretation of p. cards H603; tabu: stranger p. without asking permission C892.

Playmates. — Strong man kills p. F612.2; unknown prince shows his kingly qualities in dealing with his p. H41.5.

Plea by admitting accusation and discomfiting accuser J1162. — Escape by false p. *K550ff.

Pleas. — Tabu: heeding p. of old woman for food and warmth C745.

Pleading. — Clever p. J1160ff.; princess skillful in p. J1111.1.1.

Pleasant women A1372.7. — What is most p.? Love H659.13.1.

Pleasing. — Animal's p. voice A2423.2; impossibility of p. everyone J1041.

Pleasure. — Bringing greatest p. giver H1065; comfort in the contemplation of impossible p. J864; otherworld land of p. F173.1; relative p. of sexes in love J99.1, T2.

Pledge with enemy P557.2. — Drinking blood as covenant p. T312.1; host as p. to keep one's word V39.6; mother of illegitimate child given as p. for his crime T640.2; parting lovers p. not to marry for seven years T61.2; son as p. for father murderer P233.1; tabu to give arms in p. C835.2.6.

Pledged, see also **Promised.** — Love falsely p. K2094; maid p. to celibacy is given beard T321.1; princess secretly p. to many K2034.1; Virgin Mary substitutes for woman whom husband has p. to the devil K1841.3.

Pleiades. — Origin of the P. A773.

Plentiful. — Why certain animals are p. A2582.1; wild hunt as omen of p. year E501.20.2.

Plenty. — Horn of p. D1470.2.3; land of p. F701; in time of p. provide for want J711; wolf prefers liberty and hunger to dog's servitude and p. L451.

Plot. — Man knowing of murder p. against his friend disguises and is killed in his place P316.1; faithless wife and paramour p. against husband's life K2213.3; sham stupidity to overhear p. K1818.3.3; treacherous mother and ogre p. against her son S12.1; triangle p. and its solutions T92.1.

Plotting. — Angel kills man p. murder J225.4.

Plover. — Creation of p. A1941.

Plow without horse or wheels (lie) X1855. — Bluff: p. as hero's hoe K1718.5; cow and bullock yoked to p. A1689.1; creator distributes p. A1440.1; cutting at p.: fool cuts bullock's legs J2465.8; elephant draws p. to mark empire's boundaries B599.3; extraordinary p. F887.1; furnishing p. animals determines crop share J1179.11; golden p. D1620.2.7, F858; magic p. D1209.3; ogre harnessed to p. G675; saint yokes wild animals to his p. B558.6; stags p. for man *B292.4; strong man lifts p. F624.4; tiger injured by p. K547.9; tilling with gold p. D1620.2.7.

Plow's — Heating p. colter to release curse M429.4.

Plowboy. — Fairies' revenge on p. F361.17.3.

Plowed. — Fairy unable to cross p. ground F383.3; island p. out by goddess A955.4; lake bursts forth where island is p. out A920.1.9; land purchase: as much as can be p. in a certain time K185.8; magic song causes p. ground to become unplowed D1565.3; men formerly p. with cattle as their masters A1101.2.1.

Plowing in certain place forbidden C522; contest K41; enormous amount of land in one day (task) H1103.2; the field K1411; field of vipers (task) H1188; above tree: numskull hauls plow into tree J2465.12; with donkey and ox tabu C886; by magic servants D1719.8.; swiftly F681.10; as test for bishop H1573.2.3. — Boy shows foolishness of p. up crop J92; brother is running back and forth (p.) H583.3.1; contours of land caused by p. of goddess A951; devil p. and planting for farmer G303.9.2.3; dog p. for man B292.4.3; extraordinary p. F1099.6; god implored to delay p. season J713.1; letters in clouds seen by man p. corn X459.1.1; origin of p. A1441.1; rain produced by p. D2143.1.5; stags p. for saint B256.9; tiger p. for man B292.4.2; treasure to be found by man p. with cock and harrowing with hen N543.2; wild oxen p. for man B292.4.1.

Plowman god A432.0.2; promised horse for saying paternoster H1554.3.

Plowshare frightens tiger K547.11.

Plucked. — Bird's feathers p. out by another bird K2382.1; flower p. from grave becomes a girl E251.2.2; king and peasant: the p. fowl H561.6.1.

Plucking fairy flowers tabu F378.5; flowers forbidden *C515; fruits as unique ability H31.12. — Conception from p. flower T532.1.1; disenchantment from flower by p. it D711.4.1; disenchantment from fruit by p. it D711.6; girl summons fairy lover by p. flowers F301.1.1.2; raven p. out men's eyes B17.2.3.1; transformation by p. flowers in enchanted garden D515.

Plum. — Magic p. D981.7; why the p. tree so hardy A2711.6.

Plumage. Goddess in bird's p. A136.1.8.

Plumed serpent B91.2.

Plunging into stream suitor test H353.

Pluto's. — Ability to see P. messengers D1825.3.4.2.

Plutus in bad company J451.3.

Plymouth. — Devil and Drake carry waters of English Channel from Dartmoor to P. G303.9.2.4.

Poaching. — Attempt to chastise devil for p. C12.5.6.

Pocket. — Elephant put in p. to show friends X941.3; giant carries man in his p. F531.5.1.1; magic p. *D1064; thumbling carried in p. F535.1.1.13; tortoise escapes from p. with hole K563.2.

Poem for poem: all for all J1581.1. — Beggar rewarded for p. P163; dead poet teaches p. E377.1; ghost laid when p. cited E451.10; king rewards p. Q91.3; kingdom as reward for p. Q112.0.1.2; magic p. *D1275.4, (causes king to waste away) D1402.15, (causes man to melt) D1402.15.1, (kills animals) D1445.4, (makes land sterile) D1563.2.3, (raises blotches on face) D1403.1, (causes man to die) D1402.15.2; quest for unknown lines of p. H1382.2.1; unrequited love expressed in p. T75.3.

Poems, see also **Poetry;** as presents to king J2415.1.2. — Magic p. protect D1380.14.

Poet P427.7; calls king baker's son J816.2; cursed M414.6; leaps to death with woman in arms Q411.0.1.3; may not act as legal security P524.1; as prophet M301.18; puts others out of countenance J1224; rescues child R131.19; as satirist P427.4; silent until fourteen L124.1.1; sings after death E371.3; uses confounding words J1684. — Blind p. unintentionally kills friend N337.1; contest in making p. ridiculous H509.4.1.1; dead p. teaches poem E377.3.1; disguise as p. K1817.3.1; dwarf p. F451.3.3.1; dwarf p. swims in human drinking-horn X142.2; female p. traced through poetry H12.1; future p. chants in womb T575.1.4; hero as p. A527.4; husband tricks p. into slaying wife's lover K863.1; king honors p. and critic J811.3; magic knowledge of p. D1810.0.11; princess kisses ugly p. Q88.2; sight restored while p. writes hymn F952.0.1; turning away from p. tabu C872; ugly child becomes great p. L112.9; waters react to words of p. F996.

Poet's curse M411.18; slayer eaten by wolves Q415.7.1; story brings reparation for destruction J1675.6.

Poets carry on obscure discussion H607.2; interpret dreams D1812.3.3.0.2; lose ability as punishment Q559.6; as sacred persons V291. — King must procure whatever p. ask P19.3; noble-born p. refuse to associate with lowly-born J411.3.1; seven orders of p. Z71.5.6.7; tabus of p. C568.

Poetic ability (tested) H509.4, (uncovers missing female poet) H12.1; mead M234.1.

Poetry, see also **Poems;** personified Z117. — Acquisition of p. A1464.1; first p. composed in imitation of tones of hammer on anvil A1464.1.1; god of p. A465.1; "spirit of p." as hideous youth beautified D682.4.2; stealing mead of p. H1151.16.

Poignard. — Magic p. *D1083.1.

Point. — Castle at middle p. of earth F771.3.4; god dwells at particular p. on earth A151.10; justice depends on the p. of view U21.

Points. — As many stars in heavens as p. on paper H702.3; quest over path bristling with sharp p. H1236.1; symbolic interpretation of p. on a bishop's hat H608.1.

Pointed leg F548.0.1. — Deity p. out by insect settling where he is H162.1; demon with p. head G342; direction p. out by lazy man with his foot W111.5.3; magic object p. out by bird D849.2; road p. out by magic object D1313ff.; treasure p. out by supernatural creature (fairy, etc.) N538; unchaste woman p. out by magic object H411.

Pointing at door causes fall D2069.1.1; forbidden C843. — Animal with horn p. to sky B15.3.5; death by p. D2061.2.3; image with p. finger F855.1; peasant betrays fox by p. K2315; where is tail p.? (toward rear) J1305.

Poison damsel F582; flows out of ale vessel F1092; of hydra corrodes the skin F1041.5; in nectar H592.2; magically separated from drink D2168.1; pool F717.2; transformed to stone D471.7. — Animal warns against p. *B521.1; bath in milk of white, hornless cows as antidote for p. D1515.3; doctor who can cure can also p. P424.2; drinking p. prepared for victim Q582.8; eating lover's heart with p. Q478.1.1; elephant eats p. man intended for self N627; god of p. A499,6; husband shows his wife p. to avoid: she takes it and died T254.1; immunity to p. by eating poison F959.6.2; lover at tomb takes p.: beloved revives, shares fate T37.1; magic antidote for p. *D1515ff.; magic detection of p. D1817.0.2; magic object detects p. *D1317.0.1; magic object protects from p. *D1383ff.; magic ring warns of p. *D1317.5.1; magic used against p. D2168; man proof against p. D1841.8; marvelous cure for p. F959.6; nectar in p. H592.3; one man's food is another man's p. U140ff.; ordeal by p. H223; peacock's feathers ruffled in presence of p. B131.5; poisoner poisoned with his own p. K1613; prophecy: death by p. M341.2.8; resuscitation by removal of p. E21ff.; rivers of p. in hell A671.2.2.1; saint invulnerable to p. D1840.1.2, H1573.3.1; serpent feeds other serpents p. A2219.3; sign of cross protects against p. D1766.6.4; sleeping potion substituted for p. K512.4, K1856, K2111.1; snake created to suck p. from earth A2145.3; substitute bridegroom to save husband from p. maiden K1844.2; transformation: p. to stone D471.7; vessel of poisoned ale inverted: only p. flows out F1092; why water snake has no p. A2532.1.1; woman tricked into giving p. to her husband K945.

Poisoned arrows F831.3; cakes intended for husband eaten by thieves N659.1; clothing test H1516; food (drink) fed to animal instead of to intended victim K527.1; food sent to enemy camp K2369.11; weapons P553.1; woman revives T37.0.1. — Attempt to kill hero by feeding him p. food H1515; boar with p. bristles K898; centipede's p. sting A1335.13; cup said to be p. by friend P317.1; enemy tricked into thinking self p., retreats K2351.6.1.1; enemies invited to feast, p. K811.1.2; falcon saves master from p. water B143.1.4; greedy animal eats p. fruit W125.1; hus-

band believes he is p. and lies down for dead J2311.2; murder by
leaving p. wine K929.1; murder by throwing p. bread into mouth K951.3;
queen sells p. cheese K1817.4.1.1.1; resuscitation by removal of p. apple
*E21.1; robbers fed p. food K439.6; saint makes p. food harmless
D1840.1.2.1; sword with p. edge F833.6; thief leaves food untouched when
owner pretends to be p. by it K439.4; victim pounded up with p. fish
K838; woman sells p. curds to man A1335.12.

Poisoner. — Double-dealing p. K2041.1.

Poisoning fish causes storm C41.4; by magic D2061.1.3. — Accidental p.
N332; adulteress p. husband T232.3; disappointed lover attempts p. girl
T93.4; disguise as physician for p. K1825.1.6; husband p. wife to avoid
her being ravished T471.3; murder by p. S111ff.; plague from Jews' p.
wells V362; punishment by p. Q418; queen falsely accused of p. husband
K2116.1.2; saint immune to p. V228.1; sister p. brother K2212.0.1; uncle
p. nephew S71.1; wife p. husband for paramour K2213.3.2; woman p.
rival K2221.1.

Poisonous, see also **Venomous;** eyebrow causes death to beholder F555.7;
toad sits on food of undutiful children Q557.1; water cures man N646.
— Birds with p. spells on wings B33.1.4; monster's blood makes tree and
surroundings p. D1563.2.2; origin of p. plants A2692; person with p.
teeth F513.1.4; rebel god authors all p. things A63.7.

Poker. — Long nose used as p. F543.1.1; reversing p. protects from witch
G272.9.

Pole for coffin-rests appears at door at death E767.1; through horse's body
pulls fairy chariot F241.1.6. — How did the cow get on the p.? J2382.

Poles. — In duel with long p. ogre is forced into pigsty K785.

Policeman. — Don't make friends with p. J21.46; trickster dupes jewels
from p. and his wife K714.1.1.

Policy in dealing with the great J810ff. — Truth the best p. J751.1.

Polished. — Magic sight by looking at p. object D1821.3.7.

Polishing. — Origin of p. stone A1465.4; resuscitation by p. sword E142.

Polite rescuers J2516.3.2; travelers miss train J2183.2.

Politeness rewarded Q41.

Political visions V515.2.

Polluted. — Brahmin decides that dog has p. clothes by walking under
them J2184; Brahmins p. fish K344.1.1; house p. so that trickster is left in
possession K355; nest and brood of bird p. K932; water-spirits revenge
for p. water F420.5.2.6.6; well p. by (battle blood) D1563.2.2.1, (ogre)
G585.

Poltergeister *F470ff.

Polyandry T146; among gods A164.5.

Polychromatic dogs B731.6.0.1.

Polycrates *N211.1.

Polygamy T145; of the gods A164.3. — Advice against p. J21.32; parents'
code towards children of p. A1576.

Polygonum persicaria (heartsease) has red stripes A2772.3.

Polyphemus F512.1.1.

Pomegranate and apple tree dispute as to which is worth most J466.1. — Demon imprisoned in p. D2177.2; eating p. without letting seed fall H326.2; eating p. seed forbidden C225.1; extraordinary p. F813.8; magic p. D981.12; soul in p. E711.2.4; transformation to p. D211.2.

Pond, see also **Pool;** always clear for deity's bath F713.5; of milk B531.2.1. —Bailing out a p. (task) H1113; bringing a p. to king (task) H1023.25; digging a p. quickly (task) H1105; enigmatic statement: the tank (p.) does not belong to you H594.2; extraordinary p. F713; killing eels with snakes in p. J2114; large p. emptying into smaller ones (parable on spending) H614.2; lies about p. X1546; magic control of p. D2151.5; magic p. D921, (causes disease) D1500.4.3; ogre persuaded to drink p. dry bursts G522; otherworld at bottom of p. F133.4; "soak me in the p." K553.5; victim persuaded to look into p.: pushed in K832.1.1; wild hunt goes thrice around p. E501.14.3; world at bottom of p. F725.8.

Ponds. — Giant's eyes like p. F531.1.1.2.2; origin of fish p. A1457.6.

Pontius Pilate. See Pilate.

Pool fills with sand in answer to prayer D1766.1.5. — Attire for certain p. C61.15.5; blind wives fall into p., bear children there T581.2.2; bottomless p. F713.2; extraordinary p. F717; ice forms while fish leaps from p. F935.2; looking in p. to see if it is raining J2716.1; man looking at birds pulled into p. K832.6; transformation to p. of water D283.1; woman becomes p. of water A920.1.11.

Poor, see also **Impoverished, Poverty;** boy finds treasure in deserted city N534.5; boy marries rich girl L161.1; boy said by helpful cat to be dispossessed prince K1952.1; boy's boast of building palace comes true N234; bride pretends to wealth K1911.5; girl chosen rather than the rich L213; girl masks as doctor and is made court physician K1825.1.2; man consoles self by thinking of misfortunes of rich J883; man surpasses rich L143; man happier than king J1085.3; man banishes bad luck, becomes rich N250.4; man deceives rich, causes his death K890.1; man imitates rich J2416; man presented rich robe jailed as thief N347.5; man rejects wealth J1085.4; man wants high office: made cook L427; people given alms, recognized H152.1; person's great effort to entertain guests P336; prince overcomes king L311.3; son-in-law preferred to rich J247.1; suitor served good supper J1561.3.1.—Bad choice between p. and miserly man J229.6; daughter punished by marriage to p. man T69.5; difference between a p. man and a rich (riches) H875; excessive hospitality makes chieftain p. Q42.1.3; fortunes of rich and p. man N181; grass pleasant couch for p. U65.1; judge favors p. defendent J1192.1.2; king seizes p. man's lamb U35.1.1; man so p. all he does to move is put out fire W226; marriage between rich and p. T121; naked idol considered p. J2216; nobleman marries, abandons p. girl T72.2; prophecy: rich man's son to marry p. girl M359.7; prophecy of future greatness for p. youth M312;

prophecy of wealthy marriage for p. girl M312.1.1; rich girl in love with p. boy T91.5.1; rich man made p. to punish pride L412; rich and p. in love T91.5; Satan at feast where p. are absent G303.15.4.3; sun as caretaker of the p. A739.8; water-spirits help p. F420.5.1.2; when p. man eats H659.17; why the p., being in the majority, do not kill off the rich J2371.4.

Poorest. — Quest for bride richest and p. H1311.2.

Poorly dressed woman chosen as wife L213.1.

Pope V294, (Boniface VIII) K2282.1, (Clement V) K2282.1, (Joan) K1961.2.1; calls persistent courtier a fool J1289.3; disguised as caulker K1816.2; guilty of simony V466.1; overawes captor, escapes K546, reconciles estranged couple N741.3; selected by chair moving towards him H171.6; tests women's disobedience: not to look into box H1557.4. — Audience secured with the p. by rudeness D477.1; bells sounds to designate p. D1311.12.1; bird indicates election of p. H171.2; disenchantment by prayer of p. D781; magic knowledge of the p. D1810.0.9; man magically made to believe himself bishop, archbishop, and p. D2031.5; mother guilty of incest with son forgiven by p. T412.1; pretender as p. K1961.2; priests stamp on stone to prove truth of p. A972.1.2; seduction to engender a p. K1315.1.2.1; recognition when parents come to son as p. to be confessed H151.3; test of p.: his candle lights itself H41.3; uncharitable p. wanders after death V425; wine gives courage to face p. J1318; woman in disguise becomes p. K1961.2.1.

Pope's decision on priest's wife J1179.10. — Devil flees at p. blessing G303.16.2.3.2; magic wind blows open church door for p. body Q147.2; rich man shakes ducats into p. lap J1263.2.2; wind aids p. burial F963.3.

Poplar cursed for serving as cross A2721.2.1.2; leaves tremble A2762.2.

Poplars from weeping maidens transformed by god A2681.3.

Poppy characteristics from reincarnations A2733; seeds poured into ghost's mouth E439.4.

Popularizing. — Dream advises against p. science J157.3.

Population P720. — Differences in p. sizes A1621; over-p. A1019.3, A1335.8, P721.

Porcupine as controller of cold D2144.1.1; crawls inside buffalo and kills him K952.1; duped into leaving food K335.0.4.2; pricks rabbit host P332. — Beaver and p. trick each other K896.1; broom, transformed into p., drives away would-be ravisher B524.5; creation of p. A1858; enmity of p. and snail A2494.12.10; why p. lives underground A2433.3.22; why p. has only four claws A2376.3; why p. lives in high places in mountains A2433.3.11; wrestling between p. and deer K12.5.

Porcupine's dwelling A2432.4; skin A2311.5.

Porcupines absent from Cape Breton Island A2434.2.1.

Pork. — Tabu to eat p. C221.1.1.5; why Jews do not eat p. A1681.2; women not to eat p. C181.8.

Porpoise helper on quest H1233.6.3. — Man transformed to p. D127.6.

Porridge eaten in different rooms J2167; in the ice hole J1938. — Complaint of p. pot J1875.2; fool spits in the hot p. J2421; hot p. in the ogre's throat K1033; hungry parson and p.-pot X431; magic p.-pot keeps cooking *C916.3; substituted p. K471; speaking p. D1610.31.1.

Portent, see Omen.

Porter rescues abandoned child R131.9. — Disguise as p. K1816.7; (to enter girl's room) K1349.1.1; lost soul to serve as p. in hell for seven years E755.2.3; Saint Peter as p. of heaven A661.0.1.2; treacherous p. K2244.

Porter's revenge for three wise counsels J1511.6.

Porters. — Man robbed by p. who carry his treasure J2092.

Portia masks as lawyer K1825.2.

Portrait, see also Picture; of the Virgin appears to devotee V263.

Portraits exude oil V128.2. — Devils dwell in p. G303.8.14.

Portrayal. — Punishment for foul p. of Jesus Q222.3.

Posing *K2000ff. — Escape by p. as member of murderer's family or tribe K601; hare (jackal) with horns of wax p. as horned animal K1991; seduction by p. *K1310ff.; theft by p. as doctor K352; trickster p. as helper eats women's stored provisions K1983.

Position. — Deception into humiliating p. *K1200—K1299; fortune-telling dream induced by sleeping in extraordinary p. D1812.3.3.2; high p. as reward Q113.3; loss of social p. Q494; riddle propounded on pain of loss of official p. H541.3; tabu: sleeping in certain p. during certain time C735.1.0.1; tests of social p. H1574; shape and p. of animals' eyes A2332.4ff.; wife gets would-be seducer's p. for husband K443.2.1.

Possessed. — Devil cast out of p. man D2176.3.4; people p. by trolls F455.6.10.

Possession of magic powers D1710ff.; by spirit of dead person gives second sight D1821.8; of wisdom J180ff.; of woman disputed by skillful creators *H621. — Acquisition and p. of wisdom (knowledge) J0—J199; demoniacal p. K2385; exiled wife's dearest p. J1545.4; fairy gift not to leave p. of mortal's family F348.3; lovers flee, leave hidden man in p. K1271.1.4.2; madness from demonic p. D2065.1; monk's most valuable p., virtue T331.9; test of valor worthy for kingship: taking p. of royal insignia H1561.5.

Possessions, see also Belongings; of brownies F482.4; buried with the dead E433.2; of dwarfs F451.7ff.; of fairies F240ff.; of giant ogre G110ff.; not to be counted C776. — Allies and p. of the devil G303.10ff.; gigantic p. of giant F531.4ff.; great p. bring great risks U81; guessing nature of devil's p. H523ff.; lie: remarkable p. X1020; not to touch p. of god C51; present p. preferred to future possibilities J321; soul leaves p. on road to resting place E750.4; troll's p. G304.3ff.

Post falls when owners lose estate E766.3; hole murder K959.6; wears down from top D1688. — Earth supported on p. A843; ghost transfers boil to a p. D2161.4.2.1; insects from devil's p.-hole A2004; origin of sacred p. A992.1; vows taken by placing foot on certain p. M119.4.

Posterior. — Why man's p. large A1319.4.

Posthumous child exposed S312.3. — Hero a p. child A511.1.6, T682.

Postponing death *D1855, T211.1; demanding of promised boon M204; payment to gather reinforcements K2369.4; wedding by hiding girl R53.3. — Constant p. tests suitor H317.4; penance: always p. sentence Q520.4.

Pot breaks (life token) E761.5.1; of Basil T85.3; cannot be lifted D1654.16; calls kettle black J1063; of flour broken before sold J2061.1.3; has a child and dies J1531.3; on head after command not to show head J2489.13; jumps, indicates hidden money E539.2; too heavy with ghosts to lift E499.3; transformed D454.6; -tilter G331. — Alleged soup-making p. sold K112.2.1; animals help repair p. B579.4; bluff: huge cauldron called hero's kitchen p. K1718.3; boiling p. seen as threat, broken J1813.10; boiling p. thought to be self-cooking J1813.4; breaking p. with sword to show new sight J2469.5.2; child born in p. T561.4; cock under p. crows for guilt H235; damages for broken p.: pay for elephant K251.5; dividing eggs in p. J1241.5; dwarf falls into porridge p. X142.1; escape from deluge in p. A1029.3; filled milk p. shows city full of fakirs J1293.4; filling p. with dew H1129.4; getting the calf's head out of the p. J2113; great cabbage and great p. to put it in X1423.1; hare in p. escapes tiger K521.11; magic flower p. bears plants with gold letters on leaves D1469.1; magic p. *D1171.1, (with demons who beat owner's enemy) D1401.4; man transformed to p. D252; numskull licks out p. and gets it caught on his head J2131.5.2; only one man can lift p. H31.4; poisoned p. J2311.2; reckoning in the p. J2466.2; spring made to flow into p. D2151.6.2; stolen p. pawned with real owner K405.2; tabued p. broken: town appears C917.1; thief uses p. in hole as feeler K315.2; three-legged p. sent to walk home J1881.1.3; universe created from clay p. A617.1; wife bangs p. on husband's head while guest is present T252.7; woman thinks boiling p. is complaining J1875.2.

Pots symbolic of sons' inheritances J99.2. — Ass in potter's shop breaks p. J973; banishment for breaking water p. Q431.16; earthen and brazen p. in river J425.1; eating from fine p. forbidden C219.1; filling p. with subterranean outlets H1023.2.5; looking into the p. in hell forbidden *C325; man smells p. boiling far away F652.2; old woman's maledictions because of broken p. inform abandoned hero of his parentage and future S375; sun and moon kept in p. when they do not shine A721.0.1.

Potatoes as "eggs of the earth" J1772.1.2. — Lies about p. X1435; lazy man digs three p. in one day W111.5.12; plowing p. out of ground J2465.13; why p. are hard A2793.4; witch steals p. D2087.8.

Potion, see also **Drink, Medicine.** — Magic p. *D1242.2, (heals wounds) D1503.13, (remedies impotence) T591.1.1; sleeping p. *D1364.7, (given suitors) H347.

Potiphar's wife K2111.

Potlatch. — Origin of p. A1535.1.

Potsherd. — Transformation: handkerchief with three knots to clod, p., and charcoal D454.3.2.1.

Pottage. — Conception from eating p. T511.8.3; milk surreptitiously added to saint's p. K499.2.2.

Potter as creator A15.4.1. — Disguise as p. K1816.4; king formerly p. retains earthenware J913; treacherous p. K2249.1, K2259.3.

Potter's. — Ass in p. shop J973.

Pottery. — Goddess of p. A451.4; origin of p. A1451; piling up p. by breaking pots into fragments J2465.2.

Pottle of brains like clever girl J163.2.1.

Pouch transformed to ptarmigen D444.9.

Pouka-herb speaks D1610.3.3.

Poultry. — Fairy p. F241.8.

Pound. — Literal pleading frees man from p. of flesh contract J1161.2; moon weighs p., for it has four quarters H691.1.1; people in otherworld stand on heads and p. yams with their heads F167.4.1; witch breaks up lumber p. G283.1.2.6.

Pounded, see also **Beaten.** — Devil p. in knapsack until he releases man K213; king to have head p. M369.9; victim p. up with poisoned fish K838.

Poured. — Water p. into tub full of holes in otherworld *F171.6.2.

Pourer. — Remarkable p. of water F636.3.

Pouring water instead of milk: each member cheats K231.6.1.1; water on fire as witch protection G272.8. — Fire p. on earth A1031.4.1; ghost summoned by p. blood of sacrifices into trench E382; rain produced by p. water *D2143.1.1.

Poverty, see also **Poor;** to be no bar to marriage of friends' children M246.2; personified Z133; as saintly virtue V461.8. — Angel of p. A473.0.1; blackmail about p. K443.10; choice between free p. or enslaved wealth J211; former p. chosen over new riches L217.1; magic prevents p. D1389.9; outcast wife and son live in p. S442; pain preferred to p. J229.14; prophecy: p. from birth M359.5; seven causes of p. Z71.5.6.1; saints called fools for enduring p. J1263.4.2; wealth and p. U60ff.

Powder. — Captor's p. removed, gun doesn't work K633; magic p. *D1246, (transforms) D572.6; resuscitation by magic p. E108; sham physician using the flea p. K1955.4.

Powders. — Transformation by smelling p. D564.3.

Powdered skull as remedy D1500.1.7.1.

Power of habit U130ff.; of mind over body U240ff.; of dwarf in his belt F451.3.1; to which sacrifice is made V11; of self-transformation received from (a god) D630.2, (wood-spirit) D630.1; in words, herbs, and stones J1581.2. — Aspiring to too much p. forbidden C773; avoidance of others' p. J640ff.; changeling shows supernatural p. to work and thus betrays maturity F321.1.1.4; devil's magic p. turned on himself K214; not to disclose source of magic p. C423.1; failure to bless mountain gives mountain-men p. F460.4.6; fairy comes into man's p. when he steals her wings

*F302.4.2; falling into ogre's p. G400—G499; fatal deception into trickster's p. K810ff.; girl tricked into man's p. K1330ff.; hero's p. to transform girl to carnation brings about recognition H151.7; how devil's p. may be escaped or avoided G303.16ff.; husband attracted by wife's p. of healing: recognition follows H151.8; magic journey through p. of imagination D2121.3; magic object gives p. (over animals) D1440ff., (of flying) *D1531ff., (over other persons) D1400—D1439; magic object loses p. by overuse D877; magic p. (from animal) *B500ff., (of prophecy) *D1812ff., (lost by breaking tabu) C947; magic results from p. of thought *D1777; magic smoke carries p. of saint D1572; man given p. of wishing *D1720.1; man obtains p. over fairy mistress F302.4; miraculous p. of prayer *V52; silence under punishment breaks p. of enchantment *D1741.3; tests of p. to survive *H1510ff.; not to use magic p. too often *C762.1; vampire's p. overcome E251.1f; why one people superior in p. to another A1689.11; wild hunt's p. evaded E501.17.4ff.; wisdom of concession to p. J811ff.; witch sells p. to control winds D2142.0.1.1; witch's hair has p. to bind or to transform G221.1.1.

Powers of dragon B11.5ff.; of nature as God's messengers A165.2.4. — Abnormally born child has unusual p. T550.2; extraordinary p. (of deduction) H505, (of perception) F640ff.; extraordinary physical p. of fairies F253; fairy mother bestows magic p. upon half-mortal son F305.1.1; falsely claiming the p. of a god forbidden C51.6; fluid takes away magic p. D1410.3; kingly p. P19.4; magic object confers miraculous p. D1561ff.; magic p. *D1700—D2199; persons with extraordinary p. *F600—F699; special p. of (chaste women) D413, (troll) G304.2.3; unpromising hero given great p. L103.

Powerful man as helper N835. — Angels p. V230.2; king show he is less p. than God L418; magic objects p. against fairies F384; prophecy: son to be more p. than father M312.2.1.

Powerless. — Demons p. over souls commended to God before sleep E754.1.1.1; dwarf rendered p. F451.3.2; fairy rendered p. F383; magic horse becomes p. because of broken tabu C942.2; ogre p. to cross stream G638; ogres p. after cockcrow G636; wild hunt p. E501.17ff.; witch rendered p. G273ff.

Practical and impractical defenses J671. — Clever p. retorts *J1500—J1649.

Prairie-dog. — Enmity between crow and p. A2494.13.5; friendship of p. and owl A2493.1.

Praised. — Object grateful for being p. D1658.1.1ff.

Praising. — Animals p. B251ff.; husband p. suitor causes wife's love T13.

Pranks played by (devil) G303.9.9ff., (dwarfs) F451.5.2.7.

Prattlers. — Why women are p. A1372.1.

Prawn. — Chain tale: man bitten by p. Z49.6.3.

Prawns. — Creation of p. A2132.

Prayer, see also **Paternoster**; *V50ff.; -contest to prove which religion better V351.4; creates house D1133.1.1; either to keep friend from death or for both to die E165.1; over the underdone hen J1342; by the soul E757. — Adam's p. that he father mankind A1285.1.1; Agnus Dei as a p. for money J1741.2; angel answers mortal's p. V243; angel shows value of work with p. H605; animal tamed by saint's p. B771.2.2; barrenness removed by p. D1925.3; beautification by p. D1864; birth obtained through p. T548; boon granted after p. R123; charity rewarded above p. or hearing of masses V410.1; child as reward for p. Q192; claim that a trap is a p. house K730.1.1; conception by p. T526; condemned soul saved by p. E754.1.1; deity answers p. and aids task H975.0.1; devil's power over one avoided by p. G303.16.2; disenchantment by p. of pope D781; efficacy of p. V316; flood caused by p. A1017.2; food supplied by p. D1030.1.1; ghost laid by p. E443.2; holy man's p. reforms rich man J153.1; magic house made by p. D1133.1.1; magic results produced by p. *D1766.1; mountain moved by p. D2136.3.1; neglect of p. punished Q223.1; one saved from the devil by p. to Virgin G303.16.2.2; pain stopped by p. D1766.1.4; provisions in answer to p. D2105.1; repression of lust through p. T317.2; respite from death granted until p. is finished *K551.1; resuscitation by p. E63; river answers desert travelers' p. D2151.2.5.1; rivers from saint's p. during drought A934.5; saint changes boat's course in answer to p. T321.6; saint's p. causes wolf to bring back child B256.8; saint's p. wins battle D2163.5ff.; sea calmed by p. D2151.1.3; storm produced by p. D2141.0.7.1; summoning by p. D2074.2.5; sun turned from one hour to another through the p. of Moses alone F961.1.7; vampire's power overcome by endurance and p. E251.1.1.

Prayers for cruel tyrant J215.2.1. — Adulteress pretends going to say p. K1514.12; animal tamed by saint's p. B771.2.2; ceremonies and p. used at unearthing of treasure N554; church spared in flood because of p. D2143.2.1; control of weather by saint's p. D2140.1; dead grateful for p. E341.3; devil appears among youths who jest while they say their evening p. G303.6.2.3; loud reproofs during p. J2254; magic spells mixed with Christian p. *D1273.0.2; monk's p. weave garment for Virgin V276.1; origin of p. A1546.0.2; resuscitation by holy man's p. E121.5.2; reward for saying p. Q33; seven p. of saint Z71.5.6.10; sinner saved through p. of confessor V52.9; wife's p. save usurer J155.5.

Prayerbook. — Ghost cannot pass cross or p. E434.8.

Praying with arms forming cross V86.5; before the King of Kings J1269.7; over corpse saves soul from devil K218.7; ship sink since prayers are never answered J1467.1. — Animals p. B251.4; cat is really p. when it purrs A1811.3; escape from p. captor K562.1; long p. as test H1508; man murdered while p. K918; Satan p. to God G303.9.8.8; Satan stops p. G303.9.4.5.3; sexton behind statue tells old maid p. for a husband to raise her foot to her neck K1971.9; unnecessary choice between p. or reading J465.

Preach. — Footprints still visible where holy man stood to p. A972.1.3;

numskull tries to p. while the priest is preaching J2131.1.1; parson has no need to p. X452; return from dead to p. repentance E367.

Preacher. — Bear on haywagon thought to be p. J1762.2; saint's follower miraculously becomes p. F660.21.

Preaching, see also **Sermon.** — Fish come to hear saint p. B251.2.7.1; repression of lust through p. T317.3; saint p. three days F1086; time flies as saint is p. D2011.1.2.

Prearranged answers fail J1741.3; conversation brings comic results C495.2, J1741.3, X111.9.

Precedence shown by shield's position P632.4.1. — Strangers to be given p. over man at home P631.

Preceptor, see **Teacher.**

Precepts, see also **Counsels;** of the lion to his sons J22ff. — Reward for fulfilling p. Q20.2.

Precious properties of the gods A156. — City of p. metals F761; magic statue of archer put into action by picking up p. object from ground D1620.1.5.1; recognition through p. metal H91; sacrament too p. to be bought J1261.2.4.

Precious stones, see also **Jewels;** in heaven produce music A661.0.2.2; in otherworld F162.0.1.2. — City of p. F761; doors of p. F782.2; fourteen daughters find p. N231; pillars of p. F774.1; snakes play with p. B765.12.

Precipice. — Disrobing woman pushes robber off p. K551.4.3; dupe induced to jump over p. K891.4.5; fools make a boat go over a p. J2129.1; hero is pushed over a p. H1535; lark causes elephant to fall over p. L315.5; wife throws husband down p. K1514.8.

Precipitation, see also **Rain;** produced by magic D2143ff. — Extraordinary p. F962ff.; lies about p. X1650.

Precocious hero A527.1, (leaves cradle for war) T585.7, (as mighty slayer) F628.0.1; infant T585; speech T615.1; strength F611.3.2.

Precociousness T615.

Predestined husband T22.3; lovers T22; rescuer R169.8; slayer D1812.4.1; wife T22.2.

Predicted. — Birth of child p. by fairy *F315; saint's birth p. V222.0.1; sex of unborn child p. by sham physician K1955.3.

Predicting. — Dead p. death E545.2; dead p. war E545.16.1; dwarf p. F451.3.3.7; fairy p. death F361.17.9; fairy p. newborn child's greatness F317; sea ghost p. death E271.2.

Pre-existing world of gods above A631.

Prefect dies of fish bone in throat N339.12.

Preferring one's own children T681; one's own kind to strangers J416; ugly to pretty sister L145.

Pregnancy, see also **Impregnation;** T570ff. — Bride has maid sleep in husband's bed to conceal p. *K1843.1; girl punished for p. Q254; origin of medical treatment during p. A1562; pseudomagic potion for p. K115.3; premarital p. among sisters H507.4; tabus during p. C152ff.

Pregnant abbess secretly delivered of her child by Virgin Mary T401.1; nun's virginity restored T313.1.1; wife left in friend's charge H1558.9; woman abandoned S414; woman crushed beneath chariot S116.2; woman dreams of unborn child's fate D1812.3.3.8; woman ordered to kill child S324; woman vitiates snake's power D1837.4; woman's longings assign quest H1212.4. — Adulteress's p. belly pierced Q451.14; cruelty to p. woman S185; deduction: camel ridden by p. woman J1661.1.1.1; dog indicates p. woman B152.1; king with seven wives, seven mares, all p. seven years Z71.5.7; lover masks as p. woman to meet midwife K1514.16; man made to believe that he is p. J2321; Mother Earth p. with Adam A401.1; numskull praises his daughter as being p. J2427; paramour disguised as p. woman K1517.7; peacock p. from eating male's semen B754.6; punishment for refusal to marry after girl is p. Q245; seducer disguised as p. woman K1321.1.1; prophecy of ogre-child so p. woman will be killed K2115.3; snake p. seven years B765.25; stars descend to earth, make woman p. A788.3; tasks assigned because of longings of p. woman *H936.

Premature aging as punishment Q551.12; darkness F965. — Deer lost through p. celebration J2173.4; failure to resuscitate because of p. disturbance of members to be left in cask for nine days E37.1; foolishness of p. coming out of hiding J582; sitting on stone to prevent p. birth T572.1.1.

Prematurely dead man sent back to earth E121.1.3. — Child speaks p. T585.2.2; god born p. A112.7.4.

Prenatal influences T576, (of magic object) D1352.

Prepared. — Punishments being p. in hell Q561; royal children p. for life's hazards J702.2.

Preparing the food "Oh my" H1185; of food taught by gods A1420.2; large quantity of grain as task H1122.

Prescription. — Fool eats paper with p. on it J2469.2; imitation of the p. J2412.3; sham physician hands out p. K1955.9.1.

Prescriptions. — Drawing p. by lot K1955.9.

Presence of cursed person brings disaster to land M491. — Flame indicates p. of beautiful woman F1061.1; marvelous sensitiveness: women blush in the p. of male statue F647.4; not to be in p. of god *C52.

Present evil preferred to change for worse J215; or retaining fee J1559.1; starts quarrel for its possession K1083; values chosen J300—J329. — Absent person seems to be p. K1881; bringing past to p. H1026.2; coming neither with nor without a p. H1056; devil's p. haunts G303.8ff.; devotee of Virgin Mary given p. by her V281; food as marriage p. H335.5; green figs as p. to king thrown in fool's face J2563; modest request: p. from the journey L221; one p. from spirit son-in-law C714.1; why former days better than p.? J311.2; wisdom from fool: the p. returned J156.3; Zeus refuses wedding p. from snake J411.2.

Presents, see also **Gifts.** — Ceremonial p. produced by magic D2178.6; dividing the winnings: p. from man's own wife M241.2; parting p. L222,

T136.4.2; sun and moon divine hero's wedding p. A759.2; two p. to the king: beet and horse J2415.1; wedding p. T136.4.2.

Presentiment. — Future revealed by p. D1812.4.

Preservation of life during world calamity A1005. — Magic p. D2167ff.

Preserved. — Fig magically p. F813.7.1; best types of men, animals p. in inclosure during calamity A1005.2; snake p. in ark to stop hole with tail A2145.2.

Presiding. — Fairy p. at child's birth F312.

Pressed. — Mountains p. together by God A962.4.

Pressing. — Man's feat at p. out oil F639.7.

Presumption of the lowly *J950ff.

Presumptuous man's comment on Michelangelo J957; officials disregarded J982.

Pretence K2000ff.; of adulteress to unusual sensitiveness K2051; of penniless bridegroom to wealth K1917; of sham physician to diagnose entirely from urinalysis K1955.2; of sham teacher K1958. — Absurd p. allowed puts pretender out of countenance J1214; adulteress refuses to admit husband under p. that he is a stranger K1511.1; captured animal's p. to help captor bring more desirable victim K553.1; maid vexes suitor by p. T77; thief leaves food untouched because of owner's p. to being poisoned by it K439.4.

Pretended, see also **Feigned;** abduction R10.2; virtue K2050ff. — Devil interrupts mass by p. battle G303.9.9.2; girl escapes from robber through p. combing of her hair K551.5; punishment: death p. becomes real Q591.1; sham cure by p. extracting of object from patient's body K1871.2.

Pretender as pope K1961.2.

Pretending. — Blind man p. he can see X128; cat hangs on wall p. to be dead K2061.9; consolation by p. that one does not want the thing he cannot have J870ff.; enemy induced to give up siege by p. to have plenty of food K2365.1; escape by p. to dance and thus be untied K571; hypocrite p. friendship attacks K2010ff.; man behind statue p. to be God K1971; repentant thief p. to have found stolen cow upbraids owner for not guarding her better K416; temporary advantage by p. to yield in a combat K2378.

Pretty feet F551.3; white hands F552.3. — Better send ugly woman to devil than p. one J229.4; fairies' p. room F221.3; ugly preferred to p. sister L145.

Prevented. — Animal p. from straying by magic object D1446; attack p. by druid's hedge D1381.1; child p. from being stolen from cradle by sign of cross V86.1.1; children magically p. from nursing T611.4; devil p. from revenge by pious priest G303.16.11.2; disease p. by magic object D1500.2ff.; escape p. by magic circle D1417.1; father p. from shooting his son by dwarf king F451.5.1.16; man p. from committing incest with his daughter by holy water *V132.1; moving of little stone p. by devil sitting on it G303.9.9.1; nun miraculously p. by Virgin from deserting convent V265; person p. from rising from chair by ring D1413.2; soul of sleeper p. from returning to his body E721.1.2; woman who has p. birth of children casts no shadow Q552.9.

Preventing burial of corpse E273.1. — Banishment till rose grows from table for p. childbirth Q431.4; dead p. living man from returning to earth F93.1.1; murderer's penance complete when he kills a greater murderer, p. a crime Q545.

Prevention of childbirth T572; of marriage by excessive demands H301; of hostility by inspiring fear in enemy J623; of witchcraft by burning cut hair D2176.50. — Forethought in p. of others' plans J620ff.

Preying. — Animals p. on one another teach of death J52.1; vulture p. on fettered monster A1074.4.

Price of consecration (ova or oves) J1263.2.1; depends on where object for sale U84; set on one's head M208. — Bride-p. T52; city where everything sold at one p. J21.52.1; every woman has her p. U66.1; exorbitant p. demanded, received K255; fairy leaves goats as girl's purchase p. F343.8; half p. for half a shave J1522.1; land where everything sold for same p. X1503.3; large p. for curing ogre G682; large p. for corpses: wives killed K941.1.1; town of one p. F769.1.

Prices. — Escape by reporting high p. elsewhere K576; reduced p. but false weights K286; trickster's false report of high p. causes dupe to destroy his property K941.

Pricks. — Ass foolish to kick against the p. J833.

Pricking feet exposes thief posing as corpse J1149.7; with pin to keep awake H1484. — Sham dead tested by p. H248.3.

Pride, see also **Proud;** brought low *L400—L499; punished Q331. — Dead brother reproves sister's p. E226.1; dove's p. in her large brood linked with fear for their loss U81.1; false p. W165; iron created to punish cedar's p. A978.2; magic destroys p. D1359.6; monstrous births as punishment for girl's p. Q552.5; overweening p. forbidden *C770ff.; owl's p. in son's feet T681.1; rich man made poor to punish p. L412; teacher dies of p. over success of pupil P341.

Priest, see also **Cleric, Monk;** P426.1; buys worthless glass as diamond K451.4; carries host across stream J1261.2.8; catches bishop in incontinence J1211.1.1; catches thief at dying man's house J1261.2.6; caught in lasso by rival lover K1218.1.6; chases devil away G303.16.14.1; claims lent only counterfeit money to Jew J1511.10; commends the poor miller X212.1; dies from being duped F1041.1.3.4; dies fleeing girl's corpse N384.8; disguised as layman K1824; disguises as devil to haunt house K1838; drags heavy sack, symbol of sin H606; draws sow instead of woman K1281.1; exorcises witch G271.2.4; exorcising demon taken for demon, killed J1786.4; frightens away guests, tells of plague J1563.8; has no friends until he becomes bishop U63; as helper N846.2; who gives mild penances succeeds where others fail L361; joins devils after death because he let woman die without confessional Q223.4.1; keeps in con-

tainer relic which when kissed renders people immune from pestilence
J762.1; with large hat mistaken for hat J1763.1; makes the omen come
true J1624; multiplying his talents: impregnates nuns J1264.7; must give
up his charge or his mistress J705.1; punished for refusal to bury dead
unless paid in advance Q286.2; refuses to lend but donates grain J1552.4;
saves own promised soul from devil M216.1; seduces man's wife J652.3;
sells distracting donkey J357; separates girl from devil G303.16.14.1.1;
shows absurdity of being forbidden female servant J1539.1; shows host
through window, told to imagine payment J1551.10; shows power of excommunication over host V84.2; of snakes B252.3; stamps on stone to
prove truth of pope A972.1.2; as surety K455.5; throws chalice at owl
J1261.2.7; trapped as lover in chest, enacts Lazarus K1218.1.4; trapped in
window, humiliated K1243; told that he is unfit offers to exchange
places with bishop J1265.2; uses fortune dishonestly made to erect monuments to himself W157.1; walks in the mud J82; will sell self only for
large sum J1263.2.3. — Appointment of p. as reward Q113.4; bishop
forced to ordain ignorant p. U41; boy disguises as woman to embarrass
incontinent p. K1836.2; at child's funeral real father, p., sings U119.1.1;
Christianized Jew becomes p., murders V364; church door magically opens
for innocent p. H216.3; devil carries off hunt-loving p. M219.2.4; devil
bargains to help man become p. M216; devil is cheated of his reward
when p. dismisses mass early G303.16.16; devil cheated when his victim
becomes a p. K218.3; devil in form of p. G303.3.1.8; devil prevented
from revenge by pious p. G303.16.11.2; devil shows p. long parchment roll of sins of congregation G303.24.1.1; devil and sinful p. disappear amid blaze of fire in the river G303.17.2.4; devil takes the place
of woman who went to spend night with a p. G303.25.11; devils disappear
when p. blesses bread G303.16.2.3.3; discourtesy toward p. tabu C94.1.3;
discussion between p. and Jew carried on by symbols H607.1; disguise
as p. K1826.5; father calls p. son a thief H581.4; fig tree is chief p. of trees
A2777.1.; frightening off parasite p. K2338; ghost drives p. into oven E264;
ghost laid by p. E443.2.4; ghost of p. failing to say masses E415.3; ghost
steals book from p. E593.2; ghost steals collar of p. E593.1; ghosts attack
bishop who has suspended p. for singing for all Christian souls E243;
god as p. A137.13; greedy p. reincarnated as feeding insect Q551.5.1.3;
host taken away from sinful p. V31.1; ignorant p. forces rolls of cloth
instead of sacrament down dying man's throat J1738.1; incontinent p.
V465.1.1; numskull tries to preach while p. is preaching J2131.1.1; recognition when parents come to son as p. to be confessed H151.3;
renegade p. punished by death Q222.1.1; resuscitation by p. E121.5;
ruler in disguise to frighten uxorious p. K1812.6; scolding p. merely
trying to get even for all scolding he must undergo J1269.4; seduction
by p. during confession K1339.6; sham p. K1961.1ff.; sharing wife with
p. J1919.6; suspected p. detected by husbands J1141.11; thief frightens p.,
confederate steals from him K335.0.5.2; treacherous p. K2284; trickster

tells p. chicken owner a heretic K455.4.1; unquiet dead sinner taken to p. for absolution E411.0.2.

Priest's concubine cannot rest in grave *E411.2.1; curse M411.14; dead wife found alive J1179.11; fifty-year-old maid: two young ones J2212.1.1; guest and eaten chickens *K2137; penance saves him from devil K218.6; words repeated by fool J2498.2. — Abbot escapes in p. disguise K521.6; disregarding p. warning J1055; girl disguised as friar gets into p. bed K1315.6.3; king no p. son J1827.

Priests claim they are entitled to dying woman's last wish: get burned J1511.18; compete in rushing through mass J1263.1.3.1; drinking only one wine at a time J1511.15; ignorant of Latin J1741; outwitted in dream interpretation J1527; substitute gilded images for gold K476.4.1. — Bad year for p.: few funerals X427; devils created from sinful p. G303.1.6; druids as p. P427.1.2; ghost as p. E425.2.3; how many p. one should have in one place J1291.3; why ignorant p. are favored J1263.1.1; magic invisibility of p. D1981.5; negligent p. buried under bags filled with words omitted from service V5.2; oracular images occupied by p. who give the answers K1972; origin of p. A1654.1; tabus of p. C573; treacherous p. prolong mass to let enemy destroy city K2354.

Priesthood — Origin of p. A1654; removal from p. as punishment Q494.2; selling soul to obtain p. M216.1.

Primary elements of universe A654.

Primata. — Creation of p. A1860ff.

Primeval chaos *A605; human pair A1270ff.; water A810ff.

Primitive. — King prefers p. to civilized culture J245.2; topographical features caused by experiences of p. hero (demigod, deity) A901.

Primrose. — Origin of p. A2622, A2653.

Prince abducted by giantess F531.5.7.1.3; accidentally finds maiden and marries her N711; adopts exposed child S354.3; agrees to marry a servant girl if she will help him on a quest H1239.1; avoids misfortune prophecy M391.1.1; awakened by fly, saved from enemy B521.3.3.1; born with gold bow H71.7.2; can feel hair on bedding F647.9.1; chooses dangerous road H1561.9; chooses exile with honor J347.3; disguised as holy man abducts princess R24.1; disguised as madman tests bride H384.1.2; disguises as another prince K1812.3; donates all, including tooth W11.9; of democratic tastes chosen J412.1; escapes home to see world R213.1; to give up life in exchange for learning a secret M232; grows up in eagle's nest B535.0.5; a-hunting enters on quest H1222; identifies disguised horse H62.3; to learn trade as suitor task H335.0.2.2; lost on hunt has adventures N771; in love with lowly girl T91.6.2; and low caste man exchange appearances D22.2; who never laughs F591.1; married to monkey F302.11; must rule five years before receiving all keys C611.1.1; offered as prize T67; overrules king's decisions J123.1; plans to kill wicked father S22.2; penalizes cursing, although he himself curses W133.1; pleads with giant not to eat him K567.1; plucks from grave of

vampire a flower which later becomes a girl E251.2.2; refuses to play
with common children J411.3; regains eyesight: steals other's eyes
E781.1.1; reincarnated as common man E605.5; rescues abandoned child
R131.11.3; as riddle-solver H561.9; steals magic from bathing fairy
D838.10; stolen while nurse dances K341.17.1; substitutes peasant girl
for father's bride K1911.1.9; sulks until quest is accomplished H1212.3;
transformed to old man D93; will want me back: hero spared K512.0.2.
— Angels help boy p. slay uncle V232.1.1; bishop and p. J1289.2; blinded
p. regains sight F952.0.2; common man reincarnated as p. E605.6; day-
light renders fairy p. mortal F383.4.1; disenchantment of monster when p.
promises to marry the monster's mother D741; disguised p. seduces queen
K1814.1; fairies charm p. into deathlike sleep F302.3.4.5; father brings
daughter P. Sobur H946.1, J1805.2.1; flute-player thinks song meant for
the p. is sung to him J953.3; friendship between p. and common man
P311.8; girl sends sign message to p. H611.2; have you seen my p.?
H1292.13; how p. can be cured H1292.4; incognito p. beaten by gamblers
K1812.2.2; incognito p. beaten, realizes folly J18; king's family from
fairy p. A1653.2; little girl bribes p. to marry her T55.4; lowly heroine
marries p. L162; magic spindle brings back p. for heroine D1425.1; man
who unwittingly kills p. is exiled N324; peasant boy masking as p. betrays self by his answers H38.2.2; plant droops when p. in trouble
D1310.4.3; poor boy said by helpful cat to be dispossessed p. K1952.1;
poor p. overcomes king L311.3; quarreling p. and princess vow to
maltreat each other if married M149.4; quest for lost p. H1385.10; repartee between king and p. accused of rape J1289.6; search for p. named
Sabr H946.1, J1805.2.1; sham p. K1952; slander: p. is bastard K2128;
sluggish p. reformed by falling in love T10.1; snake cannot kill p. until
princess bears sons J1173.1.1; taming wild p. grown up among animals
K1399.1; treacherous p. K2246; unknown p. shows his kingly qualities
in dealing with his playmates H41.5; wax p. comes to life D435.1.4; why
p. plays with children J1661.1.7; young p. sent to his uncle P293.4.

Prince's lost wife rescued R131.11.5; marriage to common woman prophesied M359.2; motto on charity V410.2; pulse beats violently as beloved passes H175.3; spouse-murder pact with princess S63. — Human
sacrifice to prolong p. life S268.1.1; princess from p. body A1275.1.1;
protecting p. slumber by shooting frogs all night J2105; secret of p.
father learned by eavesdropper N455.7; servant entrusted with crown p.
care P362; youth in court for kissing p. daughter pleads his love for her
J1174.1.

Princes *P30ff.; asked what they most desire: answers determine who
shall rule P17.3; banished for lewd conduct Q431.5.3; tested for throne
H1574.3.0.1. — Seven p. seek seven princesses T69.1.2.

Princess abducted *R10.1, (through underground passage) R25.1; becomes
ogress D47.3; brings ill luck to bridegroom K443.12; builds tower of
skulls of unsuccessful suitors *S110.3; calls suitors ugly names T76; can

not marry anyone weighing more than she T69.2.2; catches robber K434.2; compelled to keep an inn *Q481; cured by seeing lover F950.8; declares her love for lowly hero T55.1; declares love in sign language H607.3; discovers hero's disguised hair H151.13; disenchanted by seven year old boys D759.10; in disguise aids impoverished man N227; disguised as man accused of adultery with queen K2113; elects husband T55.8; escapes captor by cutting hair K538; falls in love with lowly boy T91.6.4; feigns sickness to woo hero T55.5; follows jeweled mouse, recognized H151.1.2; gives self away to save people T455.7; hangs up weapons of dead lover as continual reminder T85.2; hides in straw R313; humiliated because of loathly marriage S322.1.4; in love with knight T91.6.4.1.1; loves man disguised as woman T28; lured into forest K788.1; married to wounded prince, both left in jungle T89.1.1; marries clever thief Q91.1; to marry first man who asks for her T62; must never see male person C313.0.1; must sell goods on market as punishment Q483; offered as prize *T68f.; on the pea H41.1; price for sparing palace T52.7; from prince's body A1275.1.1; punished by displaying self Q473.6; rescues abandoned child R131.11.1; sacrificed to dragon H335.3.1; secretly pledged to many K2034.1; serves as menial Q482.1; sets hero tasks H933; sick because toad has swallowed her consecrated wafer *V34.2; skillful in argument J1111.1; so lovely everyone loves her T15.1; in tank makes serpent release water F914.1; threatens to kill amorous king T322.2; transforming self to woo T55.11; tricked into engagement K1372.1; has unrestricted choice of husband T131.0.1; will marry whoever gives her all she wishes H313.1; wins wrestling match with suitor by revealing her breast H331.6.1.1. — Abandoned p. raised by herdsmen S351.2.1; abducted p. gives birth R35; abducted p. wishes self with rejected suitor, is N425; altered letter of execution gives p. to hero *K1355; animals help hero win p. B582.2; brothers having extraordinary skill rescue p. R166; calumniated p. corpse of fails to rot H251.3.14; captive p. causes giant's death G527; cast-out p. prospers N145; choosing p. from others identically clad H324; clandestine visit of p. to hero betrayed by token H81.2; crane recognizes p. H188; decapitated p. resuscitated by hero E149.2; demon seduces bathing p. F402.1.15.1; disguised p. recognized by bull H162.3; dragon fight to free p. B11.11.4; dumb p. is brought to speech by tale ending with a question to be solved F954.2.1; enchanted p. lives with dwarfs F451.5.4.3; enchanted p. in castle F771.4.7; fairy p. with golden hair F232.4.2; fairies' gifts to p. F340.1; flea makes p. speak F954.4.1; fruit with p. inside H1333.3.0.2; gardener's son to marry p. H317.3; goose brings sleeping p. B582.1.1.1; grateful dead man helps hero win p. *T66.1; hero directed on journey by p. J155.1; hero substitutes for p. sacrificed to monster K1853.2.1; hero wins p. by magic D1426.0.1; illness spirit enters body of p. F493.0.1.2; incognito p. K1812.8; insanity of p. dependent on height of fire *D2065.4; impostors steal rescued p. K1935; light weight p. F584.1; look of beautiful p. kills F574.1.3; love through

sight of hair of unknown p. T11.4.1; lowly hero marries p. L161; making
p. fall in love H315.1; man slandered as having deflowered p. K2121;
menial disguise of lover of p. K1816.0.3; merman demands p. B82.1.1;
mighty blower slows down racing p. F622.1; newcomers forced to sleep
with p. P616; not to look at p. on public appearance C312.2.1; ogre
guesses correctly and gets p. G463; overly choosy p. marries idiot J2183.5;
Pleiades a p. and six suitors A773.1; prince prefers first love to p. he
later marries J414.2; prophecy: p. will marry bastard M369.2.1.2; prophecy: p. to marry prince M331; prophecy: p. will wed physician, fisherman, prince all in one M306.3; quest for faraway p. H1301.1.2; quest for
Glass P. H1381.3.2; quest for hidden p. H1381.3.7; quest for p. caused
by sight of one of her hairs (dropped by a bird) H1213.1, (stolen) H1385.1,
(transformed into skein of silk) H1381.3.4; race with p. for her hand
H331.5.1; recognition of disguised p. by bee lighting on her H162; rescue
of captive p. *R111; reward for finding abducted p. Q112.0.1.3; robbers
show p. how to treat husband J178; sad-faced p. F591.2; silent p. F569.3.1;
sleeping p. not watched long enough D759.9; sleeping by p. three nights
without looking at her or disturbing her H1472; sneering p. impregnated
by magic L431.3; tailor married to p. betrays trade by calling for needle
and thread H38.2.1; tigers abduct p. to be their ward's wife R13.1.4.2.1;
token taken from sleeping p. H81.1.1; transformed p. as dragon
B11.1.3.0.1; treacherous p. K2246.0.1; trickster concealed in sacred tree
advises that he is to marry the p. K1971.10; trickster exacts promise of
marriage as price of silence after having seen a p. naked *K443.6; tricky
animal secures treasury keys from p. K341.18; trickster blackmails p.
after lying with her K443.6.2; weighing p. against flower H455; whirlwind carries p. away R17.1; question on quest (where is the lost p.?)
H1292.7, (how can p. be cured?) H1292.4.1; winner of most skillful p.
to be king P11.2.3.

Princess's necklace left in hell F102.3; secret sickness from breaking tabu
*C940.1; speech sweeter than sugar H633.5. — Grateful dead man kills
p. monster husband T172.2.1; guessing p. birthmarks *H525; identification by p. garment H118; impostor claims to be father of p. child K1936;
listening to p. counsel tabu C815.1; man disguised as woman carried into
p. room K1343.2; negro takes refuge under p. throne R314; phenomena at
p. birth F960.1.6.

Princesses *P40ff. — Marriage prophecy for newborn p. H41.6; ogress
keeps p. in cave G334.1; plant from scrapings of bodies of p. H522.2;
seven p. compete for hero H375.1; seven p. sought by seven princes
T69.1.2; seventy p. in love with hero T27.2; suitor tests for p. H300ff.;
tabus of p. C567.

Printer P459.1.

Prints. — Indentions on rocks from p. left by man (beast) A972.

Prior pardons sinning friar V21.4.

Prioress's Tale V254.7; V361.

Prison, see also **Captives, Imprisoned;** door opened by prayer D1766.1.7. — Captivity in p. R41ff.; god speaks to saint in p. A182.3.0.2; long p. term leads to marrying princess H317.3; lovers meet in heroine's father's p. T32.1; magic object frees person from p. D1395; man in cold consoles himself thinking of rich man in hell or p. J883.2; means of rescue from p. *R121; saint opens p. door with prayer D1766.1.7; victim tricked into p. and kept there K714.1; wife swims to husband in p. T215.6; witches vanish from p. G249.9; woman sacrifices her honor to free her husband (brother) from p. *T455.2.

Prisoner assigns quest H1219.5; recognized by smile H79.4; to be released after he uses up charmed shoes M202.1.1. — Bishop exchanges places with p. W16; competition in friendship between p. and jailor P315.1; escaping p. falls onto tiger's back N392.1; escaping p. forced to accept hospitality, aided P322.1; king on hunt taken p. N771.1; prayers of family comfort p. V53; rescuer disguised as officer gains custody of p. K649.2; tasks assigned p. so that he may escape punishment H924.

Prisoner's miraculous release F960.5. — Wind blowing flag causes p. execution N394.1.

Prisoners choose between emasculation and blinding J229.12; promise not to escape secretly, ask leave K475.2; released as celebration of king's success P14.1; sacrificed to goddess S260.1.3; starved in corpse-filled pit Q465.2; use up hour of grace in dispute J2183.4; of war hanged S113.1.2. — Magician as beggar frees p. D2031.4.3; mistreatment of p. R51; ogre keeps human p. G334; ogre tricked into carrying his p. home in bag on his own back G561.

Privacy of God not to be betrayed C51.4.1.

Private parts, see **Genitals.**

Privation as curse M448.

Prize — Arrow accidentally makes p. shot N621.1; golden apple as p. in beauty contest H1596.1; ham as p. for husband who rules his wife T252.4; impostors claim p. earned by hero K1932; largest part of a p. to go to the guilty man J1141.1.1; prince offered as p. T67ff.; princess offered as p. *T68; suitor contest: p. to one whose staff blooms H331.3.

Problem. — Easy p. made hard J2700—J2749; solution to p. in dream D1810.8.4; unsolved p. as ending of tale H620ff.

Problems. — Ghost answers person's p. E557.1.

Proboscis. — Origin and nature of animal's p. A2335.3.

Procession of the dead E491. — Disenchantment by maidens walking with lighted candles in p. D759.6; funeral p. of the hen (cumulative tale) Z32.1; ghosts punish intruders into p. of ghosts *E242.

Processions. — Bad omen for two bridal p. to meet D1812.5.1.8.

Proclamation of dogma of Immaculate Conception stops plague V312.1. — Angel's p. V249.1; ceremony of the p. of a Buddha V88.

Procrastination, see also **Laziness,** — Result of labor lost in moment of p. J1071.

Procrustes makes men fit his bed G313.

Procurator. — Devil follows corpse of a p. G303.25.8.1; serpent as p. of rats B221.2.1.

Procuress. — Mother as p. for son T452.1; tables turned on p. by chaste wife K1683.

Procuring. — Hospitality repaid by magic p. of provisions Q45.6.

Prodigal as favorite of fortune N172; son returns P233.8.

Prodigious jump F1071; weeping F1051. — Giant eats p. amount F531.3.4ff.; giant steps p. distance F531.3.5.

Prodigy, see also **Marvel;** as evil omen D1812.5.1.1; as punishment Q552.

Prodigy's rude retort to sarcastic oldster J1369.2.

Production. — Fifth of land's p. belongs to king P13.9.2; unsuccessful imitation of magic p. of food J2411.3.

Profane calling up of spirit forbidden *C10ff.; swearing of oath forbidden C94.2.

Profaning sacred day forbidden *C58; shrine forbidden C51.1.

Professional fool P192.1. — Disguise as p. man K1825; origin of different social and p. classes A1650ff.; transformation into p. man D25.

Professions. — Assignment of p. by Creator A1440.1; clever p. J1115; god of p. A450ff.; how God distributed p. A1650.3.2; humor dealing with p. X300—X499; learned p. P420ff.; trades and p. P400—P499.

Professor examines by signs H607.2.1. — Student enjoys wife of p. K1594.

Proficiency rewarded Q88.

Profit from past in planning future J752.

Profits. — Deceptive division of p. K171; losing chance for future p. J1493.

Profitable association of (great and lowly) J412, (of young and old) F441.

Profligacy *W131ff.

Prognostications from weather *D900.0.1.

Prognosticator — Saint as p. V223.6.

Progress in school J1487. — Ladder as symbol of p. Z139.7.

Progressive purchase of woman's favors K1361.2; type of foolish bargain J2081.

Progressively lucky bargains N421.1.

Prohibitions. — Unique p. *C600ff.

Prolific grain F815.6. — Inexhaustibly p. plant F815.6.1.

Prometheus chained to mountain Q501.4.

Promiscuity. — Fruit-picking time of sexual p. T485.

Promise to return from death E374.1. — Breaking p. to fairy tabu C46.1; disenchantment by p. to marry D742; dwarfs exact p. from mortals F451.5.13; dwarfs p. to emigrate if captured dwarfs are released F451.9.1.5; god's p. not to destroy world by water A1011.3; Land of P. inhabitants F211.0.2; punishment for breaking p. Q266; singer repaid with p. of reward J1551.3; voyage to Land of P. F111.2.

Promises. — Bargains and p. *M200—M299; dwarfs make p. with mental reservations F451.5.10.8; god makes p. A182.3.4; quest to fulfill p. H1229.1.

Promised. — Children sold or p. S210—S259; city falsely p. to enemy K2366; daughter p. to animal suitor *B620.1; that which was p. him J1615; to divide what he has been p. (blows) K187; youth p. to ogre visits ogre's home G461.

Promising. — Devil p. to help mistreated apprentice if youth will meet him by night in lonely spot G303.22.12; disenchantment of monster after prince p. to marry the monster's mother D741; dwarf p. money for girl F451.5.18.1; man p. more to church than he can provide Q266.1; wife p. to die with husband T211.2.2.

Pronouns. — Tale avoiding all p. Z15.

Proof. — Disenchantment as p. of truth: prodigy convinces judge that witness is speaking truth D797; dragon-tongue p. H105.1; dry branches on innocent man's grave blossom as p. of innocence E631.0.5.1; false p. of storm K1894; garment p. against all but man's own sword D1381.3.1; priest stamps on stones as p. A972.1.2; tale-bearer killed for lack of p. S461; worn-out shoes as p. of long journey *H241.

Prop. — Earth supported by p. A849.3.

Props. — Clouds as p. of the sky A702.7; hero removes world p. A1058.

Proper names for dwarfs F451.8.2. — Dead without p. funeral rites cannot rest in grave E412.3; ghost returns to demand p. burial E235.2; lack of p. education regretted J142.

Property acquired by prayer V52.12; claim based on lie X905.3; disposal rouses sham dead J2511.1.1. — Accidental loss of p. N350ff.; all-red, all-black, or all-white calf the p. of the devil G303.10.9; all p. as wager N2.5; corpse who has left good p. not entirely dead H586.5; dividing p.: man keeps house, gives wife road J1541.4; dupe's p. destroyed K1400—K1499; dwarf promises money and p. for hand of girl F451.5.18.1; fire from heaven destroys p. Q552.13.2; fitting destruction of p. as punishment Q585; folly of father's giving all p. to children before his death P236.1; gift of p. silences criticism U21.2; half of p. as reward Q112.0.2; laws on p. division within family A1585; loss or destruction of p. as punishment Q595; magic used against p. D2080ff.; man offers all his p. to daughter's rescuer R111.0.1; misdeed concerning p. punished Q270ff.; mortal confiscates p. of dwarfs F451.5.10.7; original fire p. of one person A1415.0.2; punishment for misappropriation of p. M368; quarreling heirs destroy the entire p. J2129.2; return from dead to demand stolen p. E236; riddle propounded on pain of loss of p. H541.2; Satan causes p. destroying storm G303.9.4.0.1; thunder destroys p. as punishment Q552.1.0.1; transformation to destroy enemy's p. D651.3; vow not to pass into other's p. M186; witch abuses p. *G265ff.; younger brother's clever p. division J242.8.

Prophecy of future greatness (causes banishment) L425, (fulfilled when hero returns home) N682; of ogre-child so pregnant woman will be

killed K2115.3; personified Z139.8. — Animals distribute body according
to p. F989.10; crow tries to make p. like raven J951.3; escape by false
p. K575; gift of p. from fairyland sojourn F329.1; god of p. A471; goddess
of p. A471.1; love through p. that prince shall marry the fairest T12;
magic object gives power of p. D1305.1; magic power of p. *D1812ff.;
marriage p. for newborn princesses H41.6; misfortune from mistaken
interpretation of p. N398; parricide p. unwittingly fulfilled N323; power
of p. induced D1812.2; speaking tree gives p. D1311.4.2; suicide from
evil p. F1041.1.11.3.

Prophecies *M300—M399. — Identical p. for fated lovers T22.4.

Prophesying. — Dead p. Christ's coming E367.3; devil p. in enchanted
castle H1411.3; fairy p. future greatness of (newborn) child F317; fairy
p. lover's fate F302.7; mermaid p. B81.7.1; man's spirit p. own death
E489.4.

Prophet aids quest H1233.3.3; gives prophetic gift M300.3; as helper
N847; locates lost child D1825.4.3.1. — Abandoned person in woods
comforted by p. and birds S465; animal as p. *B140ff.; asking p. for signs
tabu C415; Christ as p. V211.0.4; god as p. A178; incognito p. as matchmaker T53.1; false p. K1962; magic power from p. D1722.1; prophecy:
unborn child to be p. M311.6; resuscitation by p. E121.5.3; water saves
p. from drowning F930.3.

Prophet's curse M411.8; humility J903. — Judge agrees to be p. first
disciple J1169.8; madness on hearing p. voice F1041.8.8.

Prophets M301. — Water-spirits as p. F420.4.10.

Prophylactic. — Magic p. fruit D1500.2.7.

Proposal tests wife H467.2. — Reductio ad absurdum of p. *J1290ff.

Prosperity forever or for a day? L291. — Fairies control p. F366.4; god
promises mortal p. A182.3.4.2; goddess of p. A473.1.1; possession of
relic brings p. V141; prophecy of p. for a people M325; sacrifice to secure
p. S263.3.1; sister honors brother only in p. W175.1; wren helps restore
p. to world A1348.1.

Prosperous. — Men too p.: life becomes difficult L482.

Prostitute, see also **Concubine, Courtesan;** claims to be victim's daughter,
robs him K347.1; frightens lover, calls "Thief!" K1213.2; paid with
counterfeit K1581.11; poses as noble woman K1315.5.1; with venereal
disease sent to king Q244.3; weeps at leaving lover his coat W151.1; will
always deceive lover U129.2. — Clever p. J1115.8; devil causes girl to
become p. T451; father kills daughter lest she become p. T314; go to p.
early in the morning H588.17; man robbed by p.: swallows her pearls
K306.3; wife born to be p. T450.1; wisdom from p. J155.8; woman
slandered as p. K2112.

Prostitutes pursued in wild hunt E501.5.1.2. — Disguised p. take wife to
"convent" K1592; jokes concerning p. X520ff.; women call each other
p. J1351.

Prostitution *T450ff.; punished Q243.1.

Prostrating. — Neglect of p. self punished Q223.13.1; stones p. selves D1648.3.

Prostration. — Prolonged religious p. causes death V383.1.

Protean beggar D611; sale D612.

Protected son has bad luck, unprotected son makes fortune N171. — Child p. all night against demon G442.2; forest p. by dwarfs F451.5.1.17.

Protecting hedge surrounds sleeper K1967.1. — Deity p. mortal A185.2; ghost p. friends E379.3; ghost p. the living E363.2; helpful snake p. man from attack B524.3; person in magic sleep surrounded by p. fire *D1967; reward for p. fugitive Q46; spirit p. each animal species F419.3.

Protection against (Nightmare, Alp) F471.1.2, (pestilence-spirit) F493.3, (witches) G272ff.; during ghost-laying E443.0.2; of sinners by confession V20.1. — Beast invokes saint's p. B251.4.1; church bell rung as p. against storm D2141.1.1; dwarfs flee to caves for p. F451.6.14; extraordinary p. for animal F984; goddess of p. A489.1; giants, heroes for dwarfs' p. F451.10.1; magic illusion as p. D2031.6ff.; magic object as p. *D1380ff., (against wild animals) D1447; magic p. against revenants *E434ff.; mortals under fairies' p. F396; panther's sweet smell as p. from other beasts B732; punishment for slaying king under holy p. Q227.1; sacrifice as p. against disease S276; seduction by offering unneeded p. K1315.9; Sign of Cross as p. from injury V86.1; transformation for hero's p. D651.6; warrior disgraced by slaying of those under his p. P557.5.

Protector. — God as p. of Israel A184; fox with lion p. goes hunting alone and is killed J684.1; supernatural bird as p. of children B524.4.

Protectress. — Virgin Mary as p. of illicit lovers *T401.

Protruding eye F541.5.

Proud, see also **Pride**; animal less fortunate than humble *L450ff.; hide humbled J1476. — Creation of ass from p. horse A1882.1; God brings low the p. and exalts the lowly (riddle) H797.1; lowly hero overcomes p. rivals L156.1; men are too p.: snakes created L482.3; why snakes are p. A2523.2.

Proving, see **Proof.**

Proverbs Z64.

Proverbial wisdom (counsels) J171ff.

Providence. — Escape by intervention of P. R341; ways of P. inscrutable J225.0.3.

Provider. — Magic object as p. D1470ff.

Providing. — Man in tree p. for child of illicit lovers K1271.5; waiting for God's p.: starving J2215.4.

Provision saving tabu C785. — Forethought in p. for life J700—J749; ghosts punish failure of p. for their wants E245; king for year makes p. for future J711.3.

Provisions for the swimming match (bluff) K1761; magically furnished D2105; received from magic object D1470.2ff. — City without p. but with much money starves J712.1; fairy-wife furnishes p. F343.7; hospitality repaid by magic procuring of p. Q45.6; trickster poses as helper and eats woman's stored p. K1983.

Provost's purse stolen K311.9.

Prowess. — Recognition by extraordinary p. H32; sham p. *K1950ff.; tests of p. H900—H1399; vow to perform act of p. M155.

Proxy wedding T135.3.

Prudence J500—J599; in demands J530ff. — Extreme p. W215.

Prudery. — Extreme p. J2521.

Pruning. — Father doing good and bad when p. vines H583.2.

Psalms. — Seven penitential p. Z71.5.6.9.

Psalter. — Thief detected by p. and key H251.3.2.

Psyche. — Venus jealous of P. and Cupid's love W181.6.

Ptarmigan. — Man becomes p. D166.4; pouch transformed to p. D444.9; why p. lives in country A2250.1, A2433.4.3.

Puberty. — Good inclinations enter body at p. W2; why a lad at p. is energetic A1365; tabu connected with p. C130ff.

Pubic hair mistaken for calf's tail J1772.4.1; thought to tell lies, pulled out J1842.1. — Goddess scatters p. on fish A2211.15; magic p. D991.2; origin of p. A1315.5; remarkable p. F547.6.

Public. — Everything on highway belongs to p. J1511.14; king shows self in p. only once a year P14.21; knight feigns murder of p. enemy K579.6; magic from maiden walking naked in p. *D1796.

Publicity. — Love of p. W161.

Publishing. — Advice against p. sin J21.52.4.

Pudding. — Devil descends chimney, spoils p. C12.5.5.

Puddle. — Devil disappears in p. G303.17.2.6; God in the p. J1262.2.

Puddles. — Dark p. in hell A689.1; ghost leaves water p. E544.1.3; sinners in hell sit in dark p. Q569.1.

Puff. — Chaste woman can blow out candle with one p. and relight it with another H413.1.

Puffing. — Bird p. itself up, dies J955.1.2.

Pug-nosed ogre G362.2.

Pugilist. — Mighty p. F616.

Pugnacious. — Why animal is p. A2524ff.

Pugnacity. — Intemperate p. J552.

Pulled. — Bedclothes p. off by spirits F470.1; dead find no rest since grass is p. on grave E419.3; giant's arm p. off G512.6.1; girl p. about by hair S182.2; man looking at birds p. into pool K832.6; mountains p. down by strong man F626; shortsighted wish: all p. on to follow J2072.3; tree to goad oxen p. up by devil G303.9.2.1.

Puller. — Lie: strong p. X953.

Pulling iron bars as strength test H1562.11; nuts forbidden C517. — Deceptive contest in p. fingers K74; girl summons fairy lover by p. nuts F301.1.1.4; life token: dogs p. on leash E761.7.5; magic by p. through a hole *D1795; magic object p. person into it D1412ff.; test of strength: p. up tree by roots H1562.1.

Pulpit sawed almost through by sham parson K1961.1.3. — Hiding from ghosts in p. E434.2.

Pulpits *V117.

Pulse beats violently as loved one passes H175.3. — Cattle formerly ate p. A1101.2.2; detailed diagnosis by feeling p. F956.1; feeling p.: doctor severs arteries instead K1017; let them eat p. J2227.1; love detected by quickening p.J1142.2.

Pumice. — Man becomes p. D244; sea of p. F711.2.3.

Pumping out a leaky ship as task H1023.5.

Pumpkin thought to be an ass's egg J1772.1; tied to another's leg J2013.3; transformed to carriage D451.3.3. — Boiling p. thought to be talking J1813.3; carriage from p. F861.4.3; dog becomes p. D422.2.2; escape in p. shell K521.5; god blamed for large p. fruit J2215.6; lie: large p. X1411.2; magic p. D981.11, (furnishes treasure) D1463.2.1, (yields year's supply of rice) D1472.2.6; man thinks he is dead, p. falls on him J2311.1.3.1; origin of p. A2687.4; silver coins from p. A1433.21; transformed golden p. J1531.1; woman bears p. T555.1.1.

Punctual surpassed by tardy L147.

Punctured. — Persons with p. bodies F529.1.

Pundits. — Foolish p. J1705.3; silly p. as two-footed cattle J1717.

Punish. — Decision not to p. a jealous husband: he already suffers enough T261.1; dwarfs p. F451.5.2.6; ghosts p. failure to provide for their wants E245; iron created to p. cedar's pride A978.2; return from dead to p. indignities to corpse or ghost E235; rich man made poor to p. pride L412; trickster makes woman believe that her husband is coming to p. her adultery *K1572; witches p. lazy spinning women G282.

Punished. — Animal or object absurdly p. J1860ff.; animal p. B275; broken promise p. by animal M205.1; cheaters p. by trickster as sham doctor K1825.1.3; children p. for fathers' sins P242; confession without giving up sin p. V25.2; disguised king p. by peasant P15.1; deeds p. Q200—Q399; fairy p. F386; incredulity as to sacredness of host p. V33; inhospitable misdeed p. by king in anger on Easter day J571.3; monk who has left order p. V475.1; ravisher of his daughter p. by fairy king F304.1; Satan p. in hell G303.17.3.5; scorn of unloved suitor p. T75.1; tailor p. in hell P441.3; usurer p. in hell Q473.1; witches p. in hell G275.11.

Punishing daughter by marrying her to poor man T69.5. — Angel p. mortal V245; fairies punish mortal who needs p. F361.16; ghost p. injury received in life E234ff.; ghost p. molesting person E279.6; god p. man by killing his child A1335.15; god p. many for one sinner J225.0.2; long delay in p. nobleman U34.1; witch p. person G269.10.

Punishment for broken (oaths) M101, (tabu) *C900—C999; for failure to pay tax P536; for profane use of the cross V86.3; and remission Q570ff. — Animal characteristics as p. A2230ff.; any p. except having two wives T251.1.6; automatic p. by fetish-medicine D1601.19; avoid hasty p. J571.4; calamity as p. A1003; city sinks in sea as p. F944.1; clever means of avoiding legal p. J1180ff.; creation of animals as p. A1730ff.; Christ's coat of mercy protects Pilate from p. D1381.4.1; deaf and dumb man can see soul taken to happiness or p. D1821.7; death as p. for scorning deity A1335.6; disease as p. A1337.0.5; disenchantment by three nights' silence under p. D758.1; eclipse as p. by deity A737.9; flood as p. A1018; immunity from p. for sin as reward Q171; kinds of p. *Q400—Q599; losing luck as p. N134.1.3; man must work as p. for theft of fire A1346.1; miraculous p. through animals Q557; moon's phases as p. A755.6; mountains as p. A969.7; origin of death as p. for scorning deity A1335.6; origin of plant as p. A2631ff.; origin of stones: p. for discourtesy A973; plant characteristics as p. A2720ff.; quest assigned as p. for murder H1219.2; rainy weather sent by saint as p. A1131.2; reason for Flying Dutchman's p. E511.1ff.; reincarnation as p. E692; reincarnation as p. for sin E606.1; return from dead to inflict p. E230ff.; saint shares sinner's p. V414; silence under p. breaks power of enchantment *D1741.3; stone's p. for injuring holy person's foot A975.1.1; strong man serves ogre as p. for stealing food F613.4; tasks assigned prisoner so that he may escape p. H924; transformation as p. *D661, Q551.3; vampire brought to life through endurance of p. by her victim E251.2.1; waters created as p. A910.2; wife saves husband from adultery p. K1596; world-fire as p. for Irish A1031.1.

Punishments paid in next reincarnation E601.3. — Chain of p. Q401; account of p. prepared in hell brings about repentance J172; mysterious p. in otherworld F171.6; rewards and p. Q (entire chapter).

Pupil, see also **Student;** returns from dead to warn master of futility of studies E368; surpasses master L142. — Architect kills p. surpassing him V181.2.1; early p. finds the gold N633; eye with picture in the p. F541.2; lazy p. reformed by watching home builder J67.1; magician makes p. believe himself superior so as to test gratitude H1565.1; teacher and p. P340ff.; teacher seduces p. K1399.5; transformation contest between master and p. D615.2; wizard makes p. think himself emperor W154.28.

Pupils all clap their hands when man sneezes and he falls back into the water J2516.3.2. — Eye with several p. F541.3.

Puppet. — Compassionate executioner: substituted p. drowned K512.2.3.

Puppy, see also **Dog.** — Girl transformed to p. D141.1.1; quest for unknown p. H1383.1.

Puppies born of woman D601; tested by gripping hide H1588.1.

Purchases. — Destroying festive p. by mistake J1846.

Purchased, see also **Bought;** cobold F481.0.1.2. — Bride p. T52; helpful animal p. B312.4; hero wakened from magic sleep by wife who has p. place in his bed from false wife *D1978.4; good counsels p. J163.4;

magic object p. D851.1; night p. A1174.3; sun and moon p. A700.6; wisdom p. J163.

Purchaser. — Unwitting p. of stolen ornament jailed as thief N347.4.

Purchasing lover's worthless goods K1581.9. — Custom of p. wives A1555.2; progressive p. of woman's favors K1361.2.

Purgatory. — Deceased husband chooses to remain in p. rather than to return to his shrewish wife T251.1.2; husband duped into believing he is in p. K1514.3; letter from soul in p. E755.3.1; lion sent to kill man frees him from possibility of sinning and sojourn in p. J225.2; masses release souls from p. V42; souls in p. E755.3; visions of p. V511.3.

Purging not needed by heavy drinker J1115.2.1.

Purified. — Love p. by magic D1900.0.1.

Purifying in kettle of boiling oil as preparation for marriage to fairy F303.1. — Saint p. monk V221.5; saint p. poisoned ale V229.6.2; sea bath as p. rite V81.5.

Purity of God A102.11.

Purple as royalty symbol Z147.1; tree F811.3.1. — Casting lots for royal p. J2060.4; nut's p. juice F813.3.3; royal p. P13.3; angry warrior becomes red and p. F1041.16.6.5.

Purpose. — Man's p. greater than God H674.

Purring. — Origin of cat's p. A2236.8.

Purse-cutting knife K341.8.3; found by gravedigger J21.48; lost in bath house J21.33. — "A close p." health secret H596.1.1; bluff in court: the stone in the p. K1765; envy punished: the found p. Q302.1; escape from prison by use of magic p. D1395.3; guessing nature of devil's p. H523.8; magic p. *D1192; man to bring wife a p.-full of sense *J163.2; not the same p. as was lost J1172.1; prophecy: one son p. cutter M306.2; trickster fills found p. with lead K1696.

Pursued animal indicates building site B155.2.4; sweetheart becomes tree D642.3.1. — Attendant p. by dead when shroud bursts E261.2; giant women p. by giants F531.6.8.2; man p. by witches G267; unbaptized children p. by fairies F360.1; woman p. by wild hunter E501.5.1.

Pursuer felled by rock D2153.2; persuaded to sing while captive escapes K606.0.1. — Animal saves man from p. B523; lovers as p. and fugitive K1517.1; magic objects as decoy for p. D672.1; shadow mistaken for p. J1790.1.

Pursuers confused by magic D2031.6.1ff. — Beaver sacrifices scrotum to save life from p. *J351.1; escape by pretending to be one of p. K579.3.1; son appears to p. as spinning wheel D2031.6.2; transformation to elude p. D642.7.

Pursuit by animal C986.1; of bird leads to ogre's house G402; of game leads to upper world F59.2; by giantess F531.5.7.0.3; by hatred of the gods M411.4; of magic arrow leads to adventures H1226.2; by magic object *D1430ff.; of man by ghost E261.4; by misfortune N251; revealed by magic D1813.2; by river F932.1; of rolling cake leads to quest H1226;

by spirit F402.1.10; of sun by moon A735; by wandering skull *E261.1. — Adventures from p. of enchanted animal N774; cumulative p. Z492; intemperance in p. J561; magic object answers for fugitive and delays p. *D1611ff.; magic prevents p. D2165.3; river bursts from well in p. A934.7; shammed p. saves fugitive K649.8.

Pursuits R260ff.

Pus sold as ghee K144.1.

Pushed. — Dupe p. into pond or well K832.1.1; husband p. down mountain by wife K1641.1; man p. in boat out to sea by companion on shore S141.1; mistress p. into crocodile hole by slave bathing her back in river K831.1; victim looks for tree, p. off cliff K832.5; victim p. into fire K925; victim p. into water K926; true bride p. into water by false K1911.2.2.

Pusher-into-hole G321.1. — Lie: remarkable p. X954.

Pushing. — Murder by p. off cliff K929.9; naked woman p. lover in water K1645; witch p. man around on floor G269.18.

Puss in boots B582.1.1, K1952.1, K1954.1, K1917.3, N411.1.1; as name for devil G303.2.1.

Puteus K1511.

Putrefaction of food and drink refused saint Q552.16. — Animal born from p. B713.2; magic p. D2096, (of food as punishment for opposition to holy person remitted) Q575; no p. on island F746.

Putrescence becomes gold D475.1.12; flows from forehead F1041.18.

Pygmalion D435.1.1.

Pygmy turns into a giant D55.1.3.

Pygmies F535; from Ham's curse A1614.1.1. — Hermaphrodite p. F547.2.1; journey to land of p. F123.

Pyramus and Thisbe N343, T41.1.

Pyre. — Animal husband killed, wife throws self into p. B691; chickens build p. B599.1; dead burned on p. V61.2; dupe tricked into jumping on funeral p. K891.4; escape from execution p. by means of wings *R215; extraordinary p. F882.1; false message causes man to jump on p. K929.12; resuscitation by laying flesh on p. E134; resuscitation through ashes thrown on p. E132; selling wood for raja's p. W153.13; wife throws herself on husband's p. T211.2.1; woman cast on husband's p. as punishment Q414.6.

Pyres. — Smoke from p. of brother and sister refuses to mix F1075.

Python becomes gorilla D418.1.1; goddess A499.1. — Marriage to p. in human form B656.1; recovering object from hole of p. H1132.3; why p. lacks hands and feet A2241.8.

Quack doctor hero L113.7.

Quadrupeds. — Animal kingdom: q. **B221ff.; king of q. B241; magic q. B180ff.; war of birds and q. B261; youth sees half of two q. H583.1.1.

Quadruplet heroes T686.

Quail as food for Israelites F989.16.1. — Creation of q. A1946; flesh of

Artemis eaten as q. V30.1.1; fools frightened at flight of q. J2614.2; friendship of squirrel and q. A2493.6; how q. got voice A2421.4.1; reincarnation as q. E613.8; transmutation of the q. J1269.5; why q. has no tail A2378.2.1; wedding of q. B282.17.

Quails caught in net rise up in a body and escape J1024; transformed for safety D666.1; transformed to sticks and pebbles D423.2. — Army of q. B268.5.1; king of q. B242.2.6.

Quaking of earth (by magic) D2148, (as punishment) Q552.2.0.1.

Quality preferred to quantity J280ff.

Qualities. — Contrasting q. found in otherworld garden F162.1.2; eaten heart gives one the owner's q. *E714.4.1; fanciful q. of snakes B765; human foster child with animal q. B635; man to be judged by his own q., not his clothes J1072.

Quantity. — Carrying off huge q. of money as task H1127; quality preferred to q. J280ff.

Quarrel of dead and living E481.0.2; between earth and waters A917; and fight over details of air-castles J2060.1. — Animal characteristics as result of q. A2258; attention of ruler turned to abuses by starting q. with unjust official *K1657; eclipse from q. of sun and moon A737.7; enmity between animals from original q. A2281ff.; habitat of animals result of ancient q. A2282; interference in strong's q. fatal to weak J2143.3; king settling q. tabu C563.4; mortal as umpire of q. between gods A187.2; murder by feigned q. K929.6; numskulls q. over a greeting J1712; present starts q. for its possession K1083; princess brought to laughter by indecent show made in q. with old woman at well H341.3.1; profitable league made with both parties to a q. K253; ruler generously settles q. W11.6; sun-moon q. when sun eats up all their children A736.1.4.1; tabu: settling q. among thralls C560.1; twins q. before birth in mother's womb T575.1.3; why some married people q. A1375.1; wise man before entering a q. considers how it will end J611.

Quarrels among family of deaf X113; introduced among animals A2575. — Origin of q. A1341.3, A1599.10; ruler too lazy to stop q. W111.5.7; wise judgments settle village q. J1170.1.

Quarreling couple were previously tiger and dog T256.0.1; heirs destroy entire property involved J2129.2; prince and princess vow to maltreat each other if married M149.4; sons and bundle of twigs J1021; tabu to men on mission C833.9; tabu in house (presence) of king C873; wife T256. — Gods and demons q. A106.0.1; joint rescuers q. R111.7; murderers q. and reveal crime N271.11; noblemen q. over a device J552.1; origin of q. A1342; paramour who insists in q. with mistress about escape caught by her husband J581.2; soldiers q. over possessing girl T321.4; while thieves q. over booty, owner comes W151.8.

Quarrelsomeness punished Q306.

Quarter. — One door for each world q. F782.1.1.

Quarters. — Colors corresponding to the four world q. Z140.2; determination of world q. *A1182; earth square with four q. *A871; four stars in q. of heavens A1281.6.1; gods of the q. *A417; moon divided into q. A755.4.2; moon weighs a pound for it has four q. H691.1.1.; own q. need it more J1269.11; tabu on entering woman's q. C182.2; winds of the four q. established *A1127.

Quartered thief's body sewed together K414.

Quartering in effigy Q596.1; by horse as punishment for breaking betrothal Q416.0.1.

Queen banished for defeating king in argument S416; banished for remark on man's condition S411.2.1; begets son while king away T481.6; burned at stake: innocent of husband's death K2116.1.2; changes own twins for slave's son K1921.3; chosen to live rather than king P17.2; compelled to keep an inn *Q481; of demons F402.2.2.; dies of fright from evil prophecy N384.5; disguised as peddler K1817.4.1.1; does not care for son unlike her P230.3; driven from palace, garden withers F975.2; expelled for poisoning stepson Q211.4.1; exposed in leather in market place Q483.1; of fairies F252.2; finds, adopts abandoned child S354.1; flogs jewel-thief suspects J1141.1.10; forced to become courtesan L410.7; gives away a sleeve of her dress: miraculously restored V411.1; gives quest directions H1232.2; of the gods A161.3; as helper N837; hesitates over high bid for her favors U66.1.1; hides her child and accuses wolf of eating it S332; instigates tasks H919.6; kept in palace of forty doors R41.5.1; in love with own brother kills husband K2213.3.4; aids lover dispossess king K2213.8; Mab F252.2; and maidservant conceive from eating same food T511.0.1; makes all men copulate with her T492; passes off girl child as boy K1923.6; placed in kitchen and abused by butcher Q482.2; propounds riddles H540.2f.; promises self to healer H346.1; rescued from slavery R111.1.6.1; of Sea sets tasks H933.5; shames cowards for weeping W121.4; stabs self, accuses princess K2103; takes husband's place in battle F565.1.3; transforms self to defeat death god D651.1.3; transformed to menial D24.2; of watersnakes B244.1.1; writes message on stone: hero searches for her H1229.2.—Abandoned q. blinded S438; abandoned q. entertains in forest, is recognized H155; burial service for fairy q. F268.1; courtier in love with q. T91.6.1.1; devil as insatiable q. G303.3.1.12.5; disenchantment from bird when q. milks own milk into bird's beak D759.2; disenchantment by drinking milk of q. who has borne two boys D764.1; fairy visits q., begets son K1844.4; fairies aid q. in childbirth F312.3; giants' q. F531.6.8.5.1; he who wins maiden q. is king H1574.3.2; incognito prince seducing q. K1814.1; incognito q. K1812.8; incognito q. accused of killing child K2116.1.4; innocent q. burned at stake Q414.0.7; jealous q. dupes child-bearing one K2115.0.1; king overhears girl's boast of what she would do if she were q. N455.4; lady answers q. straightforwardly J751.1.1; love-mad q. pushes husband into well K2213.2.1; magic knowledge from q. of otherworld D1810.1; magician's transformations to seduce q. D2031.4.2; maiden q. offers hand as reward Q53.3; maiden q. prefers fighting to marriage T311.4; maiden q. sets hero tasks H933.2; monkey as fairy q. F302.1; otherworld q. F185; parrot advises q. playing chess B565; persecuted q. meanly clothed and set where all are commanded to spit on her Q471.1; pregnant q. chained to king T579.7; prophecy: girl will be q. M314.0.1; prophecy: one more q. will give rajah son M311.0.3.2; quest for fairy q. H1381.3.8; quest for saree for q. H1355.2; royal minister rescues abandoned q. R169.7; servant falsely accused of familiarity with q. K2121.2; shrewish q. reformed by cobbler T251.2.4; sparrows enact tragedy prophecy before dying q. M369.2.1.1; statue left instead of abducted q. K661.4; stealing belt from q. as task H1151.5; tabu to marry q. C162.1; treacherous q. K2213.8ff.; treacherous q. kills brother K2212.0.3; tricky q. gets kingdom for her son K2213.11; vow to marry q. of fairies M146.1; wisdom from dying q. J155.6; witch disguised as q. eats horses G264.3.1.

Queen's illicit passion for diseased man T481.2; quarters searched before king enters J634.2; royal purple J2060.4. — Fairy q. beauty temporarily destroyed by intercourse with mortal F304.2; girl disguised as doctor exposes q. paramour K1825.1.1.1; king abdicates after q. adultery P16.1.2; leper (beggar) laid in q. bed K2112.2; man with unfaithful wife comforted when he sees q. unfaithfulness J882.1; thief lies by q. bed, steals jewelry K331.7; token betrays q. lover H81.3.

Queens P20ff.

Queer, see also **Extraordinary.** — Animals with q. names (cumulative tale) Z53.

Quenched. — Execution fire q. by helpful animals *B526.1; fire q. by magic (object) D1566.2ff., (stream) D1382.8; heavenly fire cannot be q. F962.2.3; mountain-men cannot enter house till light is q. F460.2.3.

Quenching the burning boat J2162.3; world-fire A1035.

Quest, see also **Search;** H1200ff.; for beauty as king's bride T11.1.1; to hell for magic objects D859.2; imposed for breaking tabu C991. — Beast on a q. N774; couple reunited after q. N741.4; curse: undertaking dangerous q. M446; daughter succeeds on q. son failed L152; fool's q. J2346; host sends guests on q. J1563.2; maiden to marry after q. accomplished T151.0.1; object of q. stolen K2036; servant follows on dangerous q. P361.1.2; substitute on q. K1848.3; vow not to marry until q. concluded M151.2; vow not to see friends until q. completed M151.9.

Quests H1200—H1399. — Attendant circumstances of q. H1200—H1249; nature of q. H1250—H1399; suitors assigned q. H336.

Questing beast N774.

Question. — Answer to certain q. (quest) H1388; dumbness cured by q. F954.2; finding answer to certain q. as test H508; manner of telling tale forces hearer to ask particular q. Z13; one compulsory q. *C651; reductio ad absurdum of q. or proposal *J1290ff.; resting until q. answered tabu C735.2.9; tales ending with a q. Z16; voyagers ask landsman first q. P682.2.

Questions asked on way to otherworld H1291; to dead are dangerous E545.5. — Asking q. forbidden C410ff.; children ask too difficult q. J2370.1; Christ looking for stick to beat those who ask foolish q. X435.3; dwarfs give riddles and q. to mortals F451.5.15; fettered monster asks q. of visitor A1074.3; foolish q. rebuked J1300ff.; hero unwilling to answer q. until dressed P644; magic object answers q. D1311ff.; man answers all q. F645.1; not to ask q. about extraordinary things J21.6; princess must answer all q. by "No!" K1331; quest to morning star for answers to q. H1282; reward for asking proper q. Q85; riches the reward of q. solved on quests H1243; single speech answering many q. H501.2; student is helped by the devil when he can answer three q. in rhyme G303.22.3; theological q. answered by propounding simple question in science J1291.2.

Questioned. — Guests fed before being q. P324.2.

Questioning. — Clever youth answers king's q. in riddles H583; tabu: q. supernatural (husband) C32.2, (wife) C31.4.1.

Quibbling answers J1252.

Quick thinking saves jackals J1662.1. — Magic q. growth of crops D2157.2.

Quiescent. — Dead q. during day E452.1.

Quiet. — Magic objects maintain q. so that fugitive may escape D1393.2; mankind from Peace and Q. fructified by Light A1221.2; mouse teaches her child to fear q. cats but not noisy cocks J132.

Quieting patient by killing J2489.5.

Quill. — Birds drop q. for man's pen B159.1.

Quilt. — Magic q. *D1167; washing dirty q. without soap H1023.6.1.

Quiver. — Magic hair draws back q. from which it has been taken D1428.1; magic q. D1092.1.

Quoits. — Devil throws q. on Sunday: stones' origin A977.2.3.

Rabbi feigns death to approach enemy K2357.4; and king exchange riddles H548.1; returns jewel found with bought ass W37.3; tears out eyes to escape temptation T333.3.1. — Resuscitation by r. E121.5.1.

Rabbit, see also **Hare;** burns self under chin when he steals ember A2218.7; as culture hero A522.1.2; eats seed-grain from fields: nose closed during sowing season A2238.1; and elephant partners on trading expedition B294.6; dupes porcupine into leaving food K335.0.4.2; laughs, cause of hare-lip A2211.2; as king of animals B240.2; slays rhinoceros L315.12; sold as letter-carrier *K131; transformed to another animal D411.3; transformed to person D315.5. — Abduction by r. R13.1.8; bird boasts about capturing r. J2173.3; briar-patch punishment for r. K581.2; creation of r. A1856; dead sweetheart as white r. E211.1; enmity of r. (and coyote) A2494.6.2, (and dog) A2494.4.4, (and fisher) A2494.6.3, (and lynx) A2494.6.1; fools send money by r. J1881.2.2; friendship between monkey and r. A2493.14.4; frightened r. puts head in charred tree: hence black ears A2212.1; helpful r. B437.4; male r. bears young:

female drowned in Flood B754.4; man in the moon a r. A751.2; pill transformed to a white r. D444.3; porcupine pricks r. host P332; pursuing the r. who harmed the garden J2103.2; race won by deception: r. as "little son" substitute K11.6; revenant as r. E423.2.2; skillful flayer skins running r. F664.1; soldiers on r. F535.2.8; theft of horses by letting loose a r. so that drivers join in the chase K341.5.1; turnips called bacon, cat called r. J1511.2; why r. continually moves mouth A2476.1; why r. has long ears A2325.1.

Rabbits afraid of waves J1812.2; freeze feet fast to ice at night (lie) X1115.1. — Herding r. (task) H1112; magic production of r. D2178.4.1; why r. have soft pads on feet A2375.2.4; servant sent to bring in cows is found chasing r. J1757.

Rabbit-herd. — Hero as r. P412.3.

Raccoon. — Witch as r. G211.2.8.

Raccoons. — Hunter bags frozen r. X1115.

Race (= speed contest) with fairies N775; as suitor contest H331.5; won by deception K11; between wooden horses D1719.1.4. — Angels run r. before saint V241.3; animal characteristics determined by r. A2252ff.; animal haunt established by r. A2433.1.1; deceptive land purchase: bounds fixed by a r. K185.5; despised boy wins r. L176; demons hold horse r. F419.1; devil in r. with man G303.9.9.12; dupe tricked in r. into falling into a pit K1171; earth darkened because of sun's defeat in r. against coyote D2146.2.4; escape during r. K624; ghost horse wins race E521.1.3; hag runs r., loser to be beheaded M221.1; hero fattened for r. with cannibals K553.0.1; little man defeats giant in r. L312; mighty blower slows down princess with his breath and causes her to lose r. F622.1; Milky Way as r.-track A778.9; running a r. tabu C865; woman bears twins after foot r. T581.5.

Race (= a people) will always have illustrious woman M317. — Continuous winter destroys the r. A1040ff.; culture originated by previous r. of men A1401; curse: couple to wander until they find new seat of r. M455.4; curse: r. to lose sovereignty M462; fairies as descendants of early r. of gods F251.1; first r. perishes when sun rises A1009.1; heroes as fourth r. of men A502; new r. from girl-rat union A1006.4; new r. after world calamity A1006.1; tabu: marrying a queen of certain r. C162.1; transformation to person of different f. D30ff.

Races, see also **Tribes**; P715. — Deity settles disputes between r. M4; humor concerning r. X600—X699; monstrous r. F510.1.

Racehorse. — Old r. in mill laments vanity of youth J14.

Racing. — Abductors r. while captive escapes K624; foot-r. contest H1594; horse-r. A1535.6.

Radiance fills church at saint's death V222.1.1; of saint's face F574.3.1. — God's r. upon Moses' face A124.4.

Raffia cloth's origin A1453.7.

Raft in primeval sea A813. — Flood scattered carpenters on r. every-where A1445.2.1; lotus-leaf r. in primeval sea A813.2.

Rafter as weapon F614.2.2. — Giant killed by half-cut through r. K959.3.1; girl fastened by hair to r. S182.

Rag in king's wardrobe thinks self ribbon J953.18.

Rags. — Accustomed r. preferred to new garments L217; fairy as bundle of r. F234.3.3; treasure found in bundle of r. N526; wearing r. to avoid vainglory J916.

Rage. — Battle r. *F873.0.1; father kills son in battle r. N349.2; sight of naked women calms r. K774.2.

Ragwort. — Witch rides r. G242.1.2.

Rail (bird). — Origin of red lump on head of r. A2215.4, A2321.8; why r. has red forehead A2330.8.

Railroads. — Crooked r. in mountains X1526.1; lies about r. X1815.

Rain of blood F962.4; does not wet fairy F259.3; drops large as hand F962.13; drops' sound J1812.3; enters contest between wind, sun L351.1; invoked to destroy world-fire A1035.1; as ogre in bull form G372; produced by magic D2143.1; of sausages (figs) J1151.1.3; of stones as punishment Q552.14.4; -withholding deer B192.2. — Buddhists become slaves of Taoists because they cannot produce r. V355; conception from falling r. T522; elephants bring r. B791; extraordinary r. F962; giant's snoring as r. F531.3.8.2; king's beard worth a May r. H712.2; lazy boy calls dog from r. to feel paws W111.2.4; leaky roof over woman's bed: in r. she beds with seducer K1339.8; lies about r. X1654; magic fountain causes r. D1541.1.3; magic object controls r. *D1542ff.; magic r. *D902; man proof against wet from r. D1841.4.1; man's laughter brings r. H1194.1; numskulls take out clothing and cover trunks to keep r. out J2129.6; origin of r. A1131; owl's knowledge of r.-fall distribution B569.2; peasant and boy sleep during r. in hay barn W111.2.7; protecting from r. as stork does J2442; regulation of r. A1131.0.1; reward for bringing r. Q93.1; saint controls fall of r. D1841.4.4; skillful fencer keeps sword dry in r. F667.1; wise man and r. of fools J1714.2; sun thrown on fire: period of darkness, r. A1068; witch produces r. G283.3.

Rains withheld to punish king Q553.7. — Gold, silver r. at royal birth F960.1.1.2.

Rain-god A287; blamed for heavy rain J2215.5; causes rainfall D2143.1.0.1; discovers liquor A1427.0.2; drags waterskin along sky A1142.8; threatens withhold r. A182.3.6. — Contest between fire-god and r. A975.2.1; rain from r. A1131.5; sea-god and r. conflict A1015.1.

Rain-god's. — Rainbow as r. horse A791.7.

Rain-goddess A287.1.

Rain-spirit. — Dragon as r. B11.7.

Rainbow bridge to otherworld *F152.1.1; -goddess A288; at hero's death F960.2.2; of honey F162.7; as loincloth F829.1; as an ogre G306. — Cloud in r. form F967.4; conception from r. T521.2; god descends on r.

A171.0.3.1; looking at r. tabu C315.2.3; magic control of r. D2149.7; no r. before Judgment Day A1002.3; origin of the r. A791; pointing at r. forbidden C843.1; prophecy of r. at saint's death M364.6; reincarnation as r. E644; snow makes r. behind runner F681.13; treasure at end of r. N516.

Raining. — How to find if it is r. J2716.

Raised. — Habitable hill r. on four pillars F721.2.1; king r. from dead P19.5; object magically r. in air D2135.0.2.

Raising a buried treasure (task) H1181; fallen elephant power of chaste women H413.4; of the sky A625.2; the sun A727; sunken church bell V115.1.2. — Ghost laid by r. a. cross E443.4; mermaid prevents r. of sunken churchbell B81.13.10; return from dead as punishment for attempted r. of ghost E235.3.

Raja betroths daughter as murder compensation T69.3.1; enters body of dead parrot K1175; magically protected from hurled stones D1400.1.22; to marry when cut mango blooms M261.1.1; offends goddesses A189.10; outwits priests in dream interpretation J1527; to prosper by marriage M369.2.4; refuses to marry peri F302.3.0.2; sacrifices entire family to purify lake S263.3.3; substitutes self for condemned man K842.4; warned in dream stranger is son D1810.8.2.5. — Doctor accidentally saves r. N688.1; infertile r. marries beggar T121.8.1; land where every r. dies H1289.5, P16.8; ogress demands eyes of six r. wives K961.2.2; poison sucked out from bitten r. B511.1.3; recognizing r. by his generosity F655.1; wazir fulfills prophecy, murders r. M370.1.1.

Raja's blindness magically healed D1505.14.1; favorite exposed: makes king laughingstock K1678. — Barber reveals r. secret D2161.4.19.1; hero r. neglected grandson L111.9; ogress-wife turns out r. other wives S413.1; prophecy on r. having son M311.0.3.2; wager: r. daughter to bring servant dinner N12.1.

Rajas. — Hundred r. in love with one woman T27.3.

Rake. — Surrender to r. J2613.

Rakshasa G369.1; devours everyone around her G262.3; dies after bird's neck broken G252.3. — King decides son is r. N349.3; maiden rescued from r. R111.1.11; magic power from r. D1721.1.4.

Rakshasas. — Quest to world of r. H1289.6.

Ram blesses plum tree A2711.6; carries off girl D13.2.1; -god A132.14; with green feet and horns B731.9.1; promises to jump into wolf's belly K553.3. — Devil as r. G303.3.3.1.7; dwarf waits for r. K553.2.1; dividing two sheep and a r. J1241.1; dragon as modified r. B11.2.1.9; entrance to woman's room in golden r. K1341.1; escape on r. with golden fleece R175.1; gold-producing r. B103.0.3; lie: great Darby r. X1243.1; revenant as r. E423.1.7; thief forced to buy wethers from r. K439.5; why r. smells bad A2416.5; speaking r. B211.1.1.1; wolf poses as r. K828.3.

Ram's — Escape under r. belly *K603; god with r. head A131.3.3; Satan entangles r. horns on altar G303.9.9.20.

Rams. — Why r. live at home A2433.3.7.

Rama. — Sun, moon as eyes of R. A714.7.

Rammer. — Killing with r. F628.2.6.

Rampart. — Fiery r. around otherworld F148.1; island with r. of gold and palisade of silver F731.3.

Rancher unrecognizable after he cleans up W115.3.

Ranis suspected of eating child G369.1.4.

Rank betrayed by habitual conversation H38ff.; of the gods in Hades A318. — Customs concerning r. P632; high-born alone recognizes one of equal r. J814.2; tests of social r. H1574.

Ransom disappears when prisoner retained Q552.18.3. — Animal grateful for r. from captivity B366; captor contributes to captive's r. W11.5.8; captured animals arrange own r. B278; friends pool r. money P319.1; magic as captive's r. D859.8; miser held for r. W153.12; no r. if captured without arms P557.1; saint's r. bursts into flames Q552.18.1.1; tasks assigned as r. H924.1; wife sells self for husband's r. R152.2.

Ransomed. — Dead grateful for having corpse r. *E341.1; lovers r. R121.7.

Ransoming. — Fairy r. self F341.2; hero r. saint's picture N848.1; saint r. prince, money vanishes K236.3.1.

Rape T471. — Clever decisions concerning kissing and r. J1174; king who intends r. killed P12.4; law against r. A1556.1; lightning strikes woman accusing saint of r. Q552.1.7; magic sickness prevents r. T321.5; no r. during king's reign C563.3; punishment for attempted r. Q244.1; repartee between king and son accused of r. J1289.6; ruler beheads son for r. M13.1; torn garment proves man innocent of r. J1174.5.

Raped, see also **Ravished.** — River r. F932.10; water-spirit r. by mortal F420.6.1.7; women r. by ogre G477.

Raphael. — Angel R. created from water A52.1.4.

Rapids. — Ogre's ashes cast on stream cause r. to stop G655.

Rapping. — Ghost r. E402.1.5; magic object acquired by r. on tree D859.1.

Rascal, see **Trickster.**

Rat changes name, wins bride K1371.3; cures man B511.4; defecates on octopus's head: origin of tubercles on head A2211.14; defecates upon rescuing octopus K952.1.2; digs passage to girl's chamber for hero B582.2.2.; and frog tie paws together to cross marsh J681.1; gives magic medicine B191.4; gnaws net B545.2; imagines self camel's owner J953.17; leaves serpent behind, though spared to rescue him K1182; paramour B611.7; persuades cat to wash face before eating: escapes K562; released: grateful B375.6; releases deer from snare K642.1; servants cut jungle down, till soil B292.9.3; -skin shoes F823.3; as suitor B621.4; trained to aid gambling N7; transformed to another animal D411.2; transformed to person D315.1. — Association of r. with cat ceases as soon as mutual danger has passed J426; cat chooses r. meat at feast J135.1; cat kills attacking r. B524.1.3; color of r. A2411.1.4.3; creation of r. A1854; dwarf as r. reincarnation F451.1.5.1; enmity of bird and r. A2494.13.9; enmity of octopus and r. A2494.16.7; enmity between cat and r.

A2494.1.4; food of r. A2435.3.10; friendship of cat and r. A2493.9.1; ghost as r. E423.2.8; helpful r. B437.1; huge r. borrows into enemy city K2351.8; lion rescued from net by r.: eats r. W154.3.1; man transformed to r. D117.3; marriage to r. B601.3; owl's wings borrowed from r. A2241.2; palm r. pretends deafness, cheats in bargain K231.15; race from union of girl and r. A1006.4; reincarnation as r. E612.13; speaking r. B211.2.9; where r. got tail A2378.1.2; wedding of r. and cockroach B281.11.1, B285.8; witch as r. G211.2.6.

Rat's. — Why r. snout long A2335.4.6; why r. tail looks like folded leaf A2378.9.5; why r. tail round and hairless A2317.12.3.

Rats cause cats to be killed K2172; devour hard-hearted man Q415.2; gnaw king's saddle girths L316; leave sinking ship B757; playing with fire, house burns W111.1.1.2. — Ability to see unborn r. within mother F642.33; Agaria eat r. A1681.4; enmity of r. and spiders A2494.12.8; house burned to get rid of r. J2103.3; jackal feigns holiness to seize r. K815.16; king of r. B241.2.4; kingdom of r. B221.2; lies about r. X1227; procurator of r. B221.2.1; why r. do not stick their eyes out in the straw J2371.3; why we have r.; one escapes slaughter A1854.1.

Rath. — Druids as r.-builders P427.8; god as r.-builder A179.1; magic r. always seems distant D2031.13; smith as r.-builder P447.2.

Raths marked out with brooch A1435.2.1. — Hero builds r. A538; origin of r. A1435.2.

Rattle. — Coyote wears fox's r.: caught in brush and injured J2136.1; devil disappears amid terrible r. G303.17.2.7; fox's heart becomes r. D457.15.1; magic r. D1212; origin of the use of the r. A1461.4; wild hunt heralded by r. of chains E501.13.1.2.

Rattlesnake. — Capturing squirrel and r. (task) H1154.6; copperhead guides r. to prey B765.13; death from r. bite because of breaking tabu C925; enmity of earthworm and r. A2494.16.6; why r. is dangerous A2523.2.1; why r. harmful: earthworm feeds him chili pepper A2211.11.

Rattlesnakes. — Female r. mate with black snakes B754.3.1.

Raven, see also **Crow;** as bird of good omen B147.2.1.1; as bird of ill omen B147.2.1.1; carries off souls of damned E752.3; with cheese in his mouth K334.1; as creator A13.2.1; as culture hero A522.2.2; does not return to ark: black color as punishment A2234.1.1; and dove fight over man's soul E756.3; drowns young, saves one refusing to help him in old age J267.1; on horns thinks he has led bull J953.10.1; inside whale F911.2.1; jealous of partridge's way of flying W181.5; killed by apes who will not receive his teaching J1064.1; as messenger B291.1.1; plucks out men's eyes B17.2.3.1; rescues man from pit B547.2; singes feet: why its wings clap when it flies A2218.6; steals the robes of Red Willow Men and finds them useless J2194; tries to imitate dove's step J2413.9; tries to imitate dove: punished with awkward feet A2232.10; transformed to water bird D413.2; wants to be as white as a swan W181.3. —Alliance of r. and crow B267.2; why r. is bald A2317.5; why r. is black A2411.2.1.5; burial learned from

watching r. bury its dead A1591.1; why r. claps wings in flying A2218.6,
A2442.2.1; creation of r. A1919; croaking of r. A2426.2.7; crow tries to
prophesy like r. J951.3; devil in form of r. G303.3.3.3.1; dog asks raven
why he sacrifices to Athena, since she hates r. because of his powers of
augury J821.1; why r. lays eggs in March A2251.1, A2486.1; enmity
between r. and (marsh-snipe) A2494.13.6, (mink) A2494.13.7, A2494.12.5;
helpful r. B451.5; killing r. forbidden *C92.1.1; lost soul in r. feathers
E752.4; magpie as hybrid of dove and r. A2382.1; man transformed to r.
D151.5; why r. has nose marked as if it had been broken off A2335.2.3;
prophetic r. B143.0.4; red as blood, white as snow, black as a r. Z65.1;
reincarnation as r. E613.7; revenant as r. E423.3.4; soul as r. E732.8; soul
in r. E715.1.6; speaking r. B211.3.6; tabu to kill r. C92.1.1; why r. hops
A2441.2.1; why r. cannot talk A2422.6; why r. is thief A2455.3; why r.
suffers thirst A2234.1, A2435.4.3; youth shoots r. and takes feather to
raven's sister as token H78.1.

Raven's croaking ill omen D1812.5.1.27; wedding B282.16. — Cowardly
soldier turns back when he hears r. croak W121.3; dove rewarded with
r. sheen by Noah A2221.7; resuscitation by r. blood E113.1.1.

Ravens as attendants of god A165.1.1; carry message to enemies B291.1.1.1;
follow wild huntsman E501.4.4; pursue murderer N271.3.1; show Adam
how to bury dead: are born with white feathers A2223.7. — Abduction
by r. R13.3.1; hero kills horse to feed r. B391.3; giant r. B31.3; why r.
have crooked legs and walk lame A2371.2.3; why young r. have white
feathers A2313.5.

Ravenous demons F402.4; ogres D47.2. — Feeding r. beast to satisfaction
(task) H1123.

Ravine. — Changeling thrown into r. and thus banished F321.1.4.2;
monkey jumps over a r. with his sword girded on J2133.2.

Ravines. — Dwarfs live in r. F451.4.2.2.

Ravished, see also **Raped.** — Fairy r. by mortal F304.4.1; girl saved by
lion from being r. B549.1; gull a transformed r. maiden A1945.2; husband poisons wife to avoid having her r. T471.3; woman enjoys being r.
by enemy T458.

Ravisher unwittingly rapes own sister T471.1. — Chaste maiden vanishes
from r. D1714.1.1; fairy king punishes r. of his daughter F304.1; punishment for r. *Q244; woman kills would-be r. T320.2.1.

Ravisher's grave and body miraculously burnt Q414.0.4.1.

Raw. — Dress of r. fur F821.1.3; people who prefer r. flesh F561.1; sham
miracle: food turns r. K1975.3.

Rays. — Blindness healed by sun's r. F952.2; conception from dragon r.
T521.3; marvelous sensitiveness: ulcer from moon's r. F647.7; path to
sun on sun's r. F154.

Razor drips blood (life token) E761.1.7.2; magic *D1173.1; -sharp sword
as footbridge (lie) X1817.1.

Razors. — Capturing magic pig carrying scissors, comb, and r. between its ears (task) H1154.1; stairway set with r. H1531.2.

Reach. — Magic objects keep out of r. D1606; man with elastic r. F516.4; never try to r. the unattainable J21.14; transformation to r. difficult place D641. •

Reaching. — Burned pillar r. heaven F774.2; magic object obtained by r. in certain cardinal direction D859.3.

Read. — Books in church r. without man's tongue F1055; devil unable to take one who has r. the Paternoster G303.16.2.1; how Jews r. A1689.6; learning to r. by magic D1819.4; man's thoughts r. by fairies F256; teaching ass to r. H1024.4

Reading ability identifies transformed person H62.1.2; inscription unique ability H31.11; magic book H31.7.2; smaller letters than in school J2258. — Divination by r. in book D1816.3; extraordinary r. ability F695; ignorance of r. J1746; man escapes devils by r. Lord's blessing G303.16.2.3.1; origin of r. A1484; rejuvenation by r. in book D1889.1; task: r. Bible: devil unable K211.1; unnecessary choice between praying or r. J465.

Real and apparent values J230—J299; mother preferred to foster mothers T675. — Officers praised in reverse from their r. merit K2136; scarcity of r. friends J401; value depends upon r. use J1061.

Realistic dream F1068; painting H504.1.

Realization. — Man falls dead from sudden r. N383.

Reaping. — Bride as r. contest prize H331.1.7; devil aids farmer in r. contest G303.19.2; prophecy on not r. what thou sowest M306.1; sowing and r. same day F971.7; sowing, r. in one day royalty test H481.8; time for r. A1150.1.

Reared. — Exposed child r. secretly S350.2; human being r. in fairyland F371; hunter discovers girl being r. in cave N724; lovers r. as brother and sister learn to their joy that they are not related T415.3.

Rearing of children taught by hero A1357. — Bad r. causes son to bite parent's nose off Q586; strong man's birth and r. F611ff.

Reason. — Cynic praises power of r. J1442.1.1; magic object restores r. D1508ff.; not to ask for r. of an unusual action C411.1; ruling by r. alone untrustworthy J21.28.

Reassembled. — Fear test: playing game with r. dead man H1433.

Reassembling corpse E422.1.10.1. — Felled tree restored by r. all cut parts E30.1; limbs of dead voluntarily r. E31.

Reassuring. — Dead r. the living E363.4.

Reawakening. — Magic r. of memory D2006ff.

Rebel angels A54 (oppose creation of man) A1217.1; god author of all poisonous things A63.7.

Rebelling. — Created being r. against God A106.3; goddess r. against father A106.1.1; lesser gods r. against chief A162.8; objects r. against owners D1649.6; sons slain in r. against father P17.0.1; stars r. against God A769.2.

Rebirth, see also **Reincarnation.** — Extraordinary occurences at r. F960.1.5; prophecy of r. as monkey M354.1; rejuvenation by r. D1889.7; superior r. as reward Q143.

Reborn. — Culture hero r. A510.2; god r. of human woman A162.5; man r. as girl in punishment Q551.5.1.1; person transforms self, is swallowed and r. in new form *E607.2; rejuvenation by being r.; man in fish form eaten and r. D1889.7; theft of light by being swallowed and r. *A1411.2; woman r. as man E605.1.1.

Rebounding. — Death by r. bow N335.3.

Rebuke for poor, long story J1223. — Judgment as r. to unjust plaintiff J1172.

Rebuked. — Hero r. by father P233.2; miser r. by friend W153.10; officiousness or foolish questions r. J1300ff.

Rebuking absurdities J1536ff. — Father's ghost r. child E327.4; god r. mortal A182.3.2; speaking beans r. wife for misdeed D1619.1.

Reburial. — Angel arranges r. in sanctified ground V244; ghost laid by r. E441.

Recalled. — Banished minister found indispensible and r. P111.

Recalling common experiences brings recognition H15.2; someone else's dream H1042. — Spells for r. dead lover E218.

Recapture of fugitive R350ff.

Receding eye F541.5, (of witch) G213.3.

Receive. — "He that asks shall r." V316.1; transformation to r. food D655.

Received. — Provisions r. from magic tree D1470.2.1; soul r. at birth E726.1.

Receiver of stolen goods J1169.6.

Receivers. — Inflicters rather than r. of wounds chosen J481.

Receptacle. — Contents of forbidden r. are released C915; not to look into certain r. C320ff.

Recipe. — Thankful that the r. is left J2562.

Reciting. — Captive released after r. beginning of Genesis V151.1; invisibility by r. formula backwards D1985.2; magic object recovered by r. magic formula D886.

Recklessly. — Tabu to eat animals r. killed C221.4.3.

Reckoning of the pot (125th day of month) J2466.2.

Recognition H0—H199; by bodily marks H50ff.; of captive's voice brings about rescue from ogre G556; by child (of devil's tail) G303.4.6.1, (of relative's flesh) G61.1; through common knowledge H10ff.; of devil's voice in a man G303.16.19.7; through personal peculiarities H30ff.; by resemblance H20ff.; by tokens H80—H149; of witches G250ff. — Circumstances of r. H150—H199; disenchantment by r. D772.1; remarkable power of r. F654; sham duel to bring about r. K1791; transformation to old man to escape r. D1891.

Recognized. — Magic horse r. by everyone B184.1.9; son must threaten father to be r. P233.7.

Recognizing trolls F455.10. — Man not r. his own reflection in the water J1791.7; mortal not r. fairy who gives him gift F348.5; not r. own house, family J2014; not r. own house converted to mansion J2316.1; not r. own name J2016.

Recompense, see **Payment.**

Reconciliation of separated couple T298. — Estranged couple pay trickster for r. K441.4; footwashing as r. sign P673; serpent having injured man avoids r. J15.

Recover. — Journey to hell to r. devil's contract F81.2; princess must r. consecrated wafer stolen from her first communion H1292.4.1; transformation to r. stolen goods D659.11.

Recovered. — Condemned soul r. E754.1; falcon and heron eaten by wild boar r. alive from his body X1723.2; lost object r. with devil's help G303.22.2; money lost twice: r. third time N183; stolen flocks r. by stupid monk L141.1; stolen cup r. by fairy posing as beggar F361.2.1.

Recovering lost objects as task H1132ff.; money owed by a foreign king H1182.1.

Recovery of fairy mistress F302.6.2; of lover's gift K1581; of magic object D880ff. — Fainting brings r. of speech F954.3; healer's payment: satisfaction at r. K233.6; magic r. of speech D2025.

Recreated. — Earth r. after world-fire A1036.

Recruiting. — Conflicts with r. officers P551.7.

Recruits. — Drunk r. war on haystack X818; secret where r. are being raised P361.7.

Rectum snakes G328.

Red as blood, white as snow *Z65.1; earth from slain child's blood A1277.3; eye F541.6.2; fairy F233.3; knight F527.1.1; as magic color *D1293.1; as otherworld color F178.1; or pale moon as evil omen D1812.5.1.15.2; plant from blood of slain person E631.0.3.1; Riding Hood and wolf K1822, K2011; river F715.9; sea F711.3.2; as symbolic color Z141; teeth as sign of royalty H71.9; thread on neck of person who has been decapitated and resuscitated *E12.1. — Angry warrior becomes r. and purple F1041.16.6.5; bird's r. eye cooks meat F989.2; bottom of R. Sea has seen the sun only once H822; blue, r., yellow horses in fairyland F241.1.1.3; brownie with r. hair F482.1.1; Canaanites' r. eyes A1666.1; one cheek white, other r. F545.3.1; child born blood-r. T551.15; coins thought to be r. beans J1772.3; creature with single r. hair H1331.7; dead rubbed with r. paint V68.4.1; devil dressed in r. G303.5.3; devil has r. beard G303.4.1.3.1; devil's hair blood r. G303.4.1.8.1; dwarfs wear r. coats F451.2.7.5; dwarfs with r. heads and r. caps F451.2.7.1; fairies have r. cows F241.2.1.1; fairies with r. caps F236.3.2; fairies in r. clothes F236.1.1; ghost in r. cap E422.4.6; giantess in r. dress F531.4.7.3; girl born with r. string around neck T552.1; goddess of war in shape of r.

woman A125.1.1; half-r., half-blue man F527.6; king in r., courtiers in different colors (riddle) H731.3; king in r., courtiers in white (riddle) H731.1; magic cow gives r. milk B184.2.1.1.1; magic r. stone D1383.6, magic r. swine B184.3.0.3; magic r. wind D1408.2; man about to be hanged keeps asking for his r. cap. J2174.1; man wears r. cap after his father's death J1462; milk becomes r. (life token) E761.6.2; mountain-men in r. caps F460.1.4.2; pygmies dressed in r. F535.3.2; quest for r. pear H1333.3.2.1; revenant r. E422.2.1; sick queen under r. satin carried off by bird N335.2.1; swallowing r.-hot stones as test H1511.1; tabu: following three r. men C863; why tail of West African grey parrot is r. A2378.8.2; treacherous r. knight K2265; troops of black, white, and r. soldiers F873.1; turning r., white from love T24.5; warning against stepping on r. cloth T299.2.1; why palm oil is r. A2877; why sun is r. A739.5; wild huntsman dressed in r. E501.8.2; witch with r. eyes G213.2.

Red-bird. — Color of r. A2411.2.1.13.

Redcap (Redcomb) murders for blood F363.2.

Reddened. — Man from earth r. with human blood A1241.4.

Reddening weapons tabu C835.2.5. — Severed head r. E783.3.

Redeemers. — True r. recognized by tokens H80.1.

Redeeming. — Three r. kisses D735.2.

Redoubt. — Bees thrown into r. drive out enemies K2351.2.

Reducing. — Teller r. size of lie X904.1.

Reductio ad absurdum of (judgment) *J1191ff., (question or proposal) *J1290ff., (riddle: stallions of Babylon) H572, (task) H952.

Reed as direction finder D1313.5.2; pricks dog urinating on it L391.1; transformed to person D431.7. — Bride reincarnated as r. K1911.3.4; decision rests on ability to go through r. J1141.1.7; fire stolen in hollow r. A1415.1; magic speaking r. betrays secret *D1316.5; man becomes r. D244.

Reeds bend before wind (flood) J832; make ships seem like island K1872.2. — Addressing field of r. J1883.1; devil owns the r. G303.10.12; dwarfs' house of r. F451.4.3.8; mankind from mating of pairs of r. A1221.3; why certain r. are hollow A2757.

Reef is old, ship new J2212.4. — Goddess as coral r. A139.8.2.

Reel. — Extraordinary r. F867.

Re-enacting the accident injuring self J2133.14. — Ghost r. own life E337ff.

Re-entering. — Dead man r. body E1.2.

Reeve's tale K1345.

Reflection in water thought to be the original of the thing reflected *J1791ff. — Falling in love with r. in water T11.5; fugitive discovered by r. in water R351; lover declares self by showing beloved's r. T57.1; soul as r. E743.2; weak animal shows strong his own r. and frightens him K1715.1.

Reflections. — Effect of r. J1791.

Reforged. — Man to be r. chooses present unhappiness J323.

Reform. — Curse removed with victim's r. M423. — Repartee concerning false r. J1400ff.

Reformed. — Harlot r. by sight of holy fringe on garment V131.1; rich man r. by holy man's prayer J153.1; sinner r. after visit to heaven, hell V522.

Reforming. — Parable on r. world J133.5; wife r. husband J1112.1.

Refound. — Maiden disenchanted, deserted, and r. D795.

Refuge. — Captivity as r. R53; cities of r. P518; dogs rescue fleeing master from tree r. *B524.1.2; gods take r. underground A189.13; guest given r. P322; killing animal in r. tabu C841.0.3; man taking r. in woman's house causes her false accusation K2112.3; tabu: violating r. with saint C51.2.5.

Refuges *R310ff.

Refugee entertained in holy place P322.3.

Refusal to believe that a friend has spoken ill of one P317; of crow to marry titmouse, since she is 100 years old B282.22.1; to fight relatives P205; to grant request punished Q287; of great to associate with lowly J411; to return borrowed goods K232; of sham physician to take his own medicine K1955.7; of ship to move with guilty man aboard D1318.10.1; of wagon to move because ghost is sitting in it *D1317.10. — Debtor's r. to pay his debt *K231; friendship without r. P319.7; imagined r. as friendship test H1558.6; only one r. to weep at hero's death Z351; peasant's r. to sell possessions to king P411.1; punishment for r. to (have children) *Q251, (marry after girl is pregnant) Q245; toad's r. to weep over its dead children: dries up when dead A2231.8; transformed animal's r. to touch meat of that animal D686.

Refused. — Host miraculously given when it is r. a man by the priest V32; loans r. J1552ff.; lover abducts maiden r. him R10.1.2.1; owner has r. to accept it K373; reward r. by hero L225; youth lamed by man whose daughter he has r. to marry Q451.2.1; unconsecrated host r. V31.3; wisdom from fool: heaven r. J156.4.

Refusing combat to anyone forbidden C835.1; larger payment than instructed to take J2461.8; a request tabu C871. — Animal curse for r. to carry holy fugitive across stream A2231.7.2; generous person never r. anything W11.15; girl r. her lover final kiss provokes rival to admit selling kisses K1275.1; person never r. a request M223.1; son r. to marry father's choice T131.1.2.4; sun setting and r. to rise; must be coaxed back from underworld A739.6; tabu: r. to elope with woman who desires it C192; tabu: r. a feast C282; vow against r. food to any man M158; wife r. bring warm water, beaten T254.6.1; wife r. to sleep with husband T288.

Regency. — To test a favorite king offers him r. J1634.

Regeneration, see also **Reincarnation.** — Cauldron of r. E607.5.

Regrets. — King sends r. for man he is executing K2098.

Regretted. — Lack of proper education r. J142; parson has never r. silence J1074.1.

Regrowth of flesh E784; of huge tree when cut down H1115.1; of severed head E783.2.

Reigning. — Vow against r. until picture's original found M151.2.1.

Reincarnated person identifies former weapons H19.1.1. — Bride r. as reed K1911.3.4; deity r. A179.5; giants as r. animals F531.6.1.8; girl r. as river so god may lie in its bed A934.11.1; husband r. as cat H1385.4.1.

Reincarnation, see also **Rebirth;** *E600—E699; in form fitted to crime Q584.3; as punishment Q551.5. — Animals in wild hunt r. of murdered person E501.4.0.1; attempts to kill person in r. S401; dwarf as r. F451.1.5; helpful animal r. of (parent) *B313.1, (murdered child) B313.2; newborn child r. of recently deceased person T589.5; punishment: r. as buffalo Q560.1.1.

Reincarnations. — Poppy characteristics from r. A2733.

Reindeer hose protect D1380.26. — Journey of soul to world of dead on r. E750.3; origin of r. A1875.1; food of r. A2435.3.11; why r. has so many qualities A2510.1; where r. got his small teeth A2345.3.

Reinforcements. — Enemy tricked, think r. arrive K2368.4; magic r. D2163.2; postponing payment to gather r. K2369.4.

Reinstatement of true bride *K1911.3.

Rejected suitor wages war T104.1. — Buried body r. by earth E411.0.6.

Rejoicing at arrival of rich man in heaven E758.

Rejuvenating. — Alleged r. object K116; food r. A153.4; man r. self by changing skin A1319.12; quest for r. fruit H1333.3.0.1.

Rejuvenation by animal *B594ff.; by magic object *D1338ff; of other-world people F167.9.1. — Goddess's self-r. when old A191; imitation of magic r. unsuccessful J2411.1; magic r. *D1880ff.

Relation as helper on quest H1233.2. — "Lean upon no r. when in distress" J21.44; nearest blood r. must avenge slaying P525.3.

Relations, see also **Relatives, Sexual intercourse;** by law P260ff. — Business r. of dwarfs and mortals F451.5.10ff.; illicit sexual r. *T400—T499; intimate r. of dead and living E470ff.; multiple births from r. with several men T586.3; refusal of conjugal r. punished Q257; wife more merciful than blood r. P212.

Relationship. — Trickster's claim of r. causes owner to relax vigilance K347.

Relative substitutes in contest K3.1. — Death of r. as punishment Q411.3; fairy r. slain, revenged F361.8; magic object received from r. D815ff.; master discovers that slave he wants to marry is a r. T410.1; not to offend supernatural r. C30ff.; ogre's r. aids hero G530ff.; quest to other world for r. H1252; race won by deception: r. helpers *K11.1; rescue from ogre by r. G551; resuscitation by r. E125ff.; seduction by posing as r. K1315.4; task imposed or r. dies H901.0.1; uttering name of r. tabu C435ff.; woman suckles imprisoned r. through prison wall R81.

Relative's flesh eaten unwittingly *G61. — Dead r. friendly return E320ff.; dead r. malevolent return *E220ff.

Relatives, see also **Kin, Relations;** of the devil G303.11ff.; killed in revenge for wife's wrongdoing S452; steal magic object D861.8. — Animal r. C37; choices between kind strangers and unkind r. J390ff.; cruel r. S0—S99; cruel r.-in-law S50ff.; difficult choice between r. J226; enigmatic counsels of r. H596; ghost protects wife from r. E236.6; lover opposed to sweetheart's r. T95; marriage between r. A1552; ogre overawed by hero's boast about marvelous r. K1718; person forced to eat hearts of r. S183.1; prince drives r. away S110.4; refusal to fight r. P205; relationship riddles arising from unusual marriages of r. H795; tabu connected with husband's or wife's r. C170ff.; token sent with youth to r. H82.6; treacherous r. K2210ff.; treacherous r.-in-law K2218; trickster gets goods for alleged r. in distress J2326.4; wife's r. kill cannibal G551.5.

Release. — Animal grateful to captor for r. B370ff.; animal grateful for r. of relative B365.3; man gives daughter in return for r. T69.3; prisoner's miraculous r. F960.5; woman deceived into sacrificing honor to r. her brother (husband) K1353.

Released. — Dwarfs promise to emigrate if captured dwarfs are r. F451.9.1.5; when ferryman will be r. from his duty H1292.8; prisoners r. in celebrations of victory P14.1; wild huntsman r. from wandering E501.17.7; wild man r. from captivity aids hero G671.

Releasing. — Ogre deceived into r. prisoner G560ff.

Relic. — Cure by r. of Virgin Mary D2161.5.2.2; death feigned to establish reputation of false r. K1865; false miraculous r. K1976; priest keeps in container r. which when kissed renders people immune from pestilence J762.1; sacred r. as magic object *D1296.

Relics of saint cure disease V221.0.1; sacred V140ff. — Resuscitation by sacred r. E64.12; sacred r. protect against attack D1381.20; saint's r. assume Buddha's form D457.16.1; saint's r. control fires D2158.1.3.1; swearing on sacred r. M114.4; tree releases bag of r. D1648.1.2.2; tree shelters r. F979.7.

Relieving beast of burden J1874; souls in hell forbidden C741.

Relighting. — Chaste woman blowing out candle with one puff and r. it with another H413.1; woman r. magic fires as punishment Q492.

Religion *V (entire chapter). — Different r. as marriage obstacle T131.8; king asks holy man for heart of r. J1289.18; person from hell tells of importance of r. E367.1; practicing one's r. forbidden S466; vow to change r. M177; what is best r. (riddle) H659.5.

Religions. — Conflicts between r. *V350ff.

Religious animals *B250ff.; ceremony exorcises witch G271.2; ceremony as magic cure D2161.4.9.1; ceremonials A1549; edifices and objects V100—V199; orders *V450—V499; person suggests tasks H919.2; personages tested H1573.2; rewards Q170ff.; sacrifices *V10ff.; services *V0—V99; sun and moon A738.2.1; tests H1573; vows M183; words or exercises interpreted with absurd literalness J2495. — Child sacrifice as r. rite S260.1.1; coming of r. leader prophesied M363; curse by head of r. order

M411.22; devil cheated by r. or magic means K218; division between r. and lay activities A1472.1; evil spirit exorcised by r. ceremony D2176.3.3; ignorance of r. matters J1738; magic object acquired as reward for r. austerities D855.2; magic results produced by r. ceremony *D1766; no rain falls on r. man D2143.1.0.2; origin of r. ceremonials A1540ff.; origin of r. images A1544; person under r. ban cannot find rest in the grave E412; test of r. learning H502.1; treasure hidden in r. shrine N514; value of r. exercises V4; witch's power from altering r. ceremony G224.5; witches avoid r. ceremonies G285; worldly man puts r. man out of countenance J1217.

Reliquary. — Saint's bones remove self from broken r. V143.1.

Remains, see **Body, Corpse.**

Remaining on journey too long forbidden C761.1. — Person r. in other-world because of broken tabu C953; resuscitation of wife by husband giving up half his r. life *E165.

Remark. — Speculative r. causes ghost's appearance E386.5.

Remarks. — Misreported r. K1775; test: making senseless r. H507.2.

Remarkable, see also **Extraordinary, Marvelous, Marvels;** persons F500—F599; physical organs F540ff.; skill F660ff. — Lie: r. man X910.

Remarriage. — Cynic's comment on r. J1442.12; dead wife's r. to husband E322.8; vow against r. M135.

Remedy for effects of seeing wild hunt E501.19ff.; learned from over-hearing animal meeting *B513. — Animal fetches r. for man B514; blood as r. for barrenness in woman D1347.2; carrying person to the r. instead of opposite J2214.8; magic object as r. D1500.1ff.; magic potion mixed with brains (liver, etc.) of deceitful person as r. for snake-bite D1515.4.6; magic r. learned by magic D1818; quest for marvelous r. H1324; secret r. overheard in conversation of animals (witches) N452; sympathetic helper sent for r. and robbed K345.1.

Remedies for animal in stomach B784.2ff.; worse than the disease J2100ff. — Magic r. for barrenness or impotence T591.1.

Remembering former lives after reincarnation E601. — Man r. all he ever learned D1911; man r. all people he has met F654; medicine of r. D1365.8.1; something for r. always: nose cut off J2072.6.

Reminder. — Unjust judge's skin stretched over a footstool as r. to others to be just J167.

Reminders. — Recognition by r. of what has been said H17.

Remission of punishment Q570ff.

Remorse. — Man cuts out own tongue in r. Q451.4.7.

Removable eyes F541.11; organs F557; vagina F547.5.1.

Removal and replacement of vital organs F668.1. — Dry spring restored by r. of certain stone F933.2; magic object returned in payment for r. of magic horns D895; resuscitation by r. of poisoned apple E21.1; waking from magic sleep by r. of enchanting instrument D1978.3.

Removed. — Birthmark r. at touch of dead man's hand E542.2; dead returns to replace boundary marks he has r. E345.1; girl's heart magically r. and fed to man draws her to him D1905.1; hunchback's hump r. by fairies F344.1; lover's gift regained: the r. article K1581.1; magic weakness never entirely r. D1837.2; obstacles r. by magic object D1562ff.; rejuvenation by going to otherworld and having digestive tract r. D1889.5; temporary growths r. by magic object D1375.

Remover of landmarks cannot rest in grave E416.

Removing mountain (mound) in one night (task) H1101. — Disenchantment by r. cause of enchantment D765.1; disenchantment by r. covering of enchanted person D720ff.; magic forgetting of wife at husband's r. shirt she has given him D2004.6; self-r. object D1641ff.; saint's bones for lack of worship r. themselves from church V143; tabu: r. landmarks C846; transformation by r. chains from neck D536; treasure r. itself N562.

Remuneration, see Payment.

Rendezvous. — Devil comes to r. instead of lover K1317.10; keeping r.: trouble between man and wife K1085.2; lover's magic sleep at r. D1972; lovers' r. T35; maiden sent to r. to capture lover K787; obscene tricks played on lover keeping r. K1218.9.1; sham illness to escape r. K523.0.1.1.

Rending. — Animals r. one another B265; stiff hair r. garments F555.8.1.

Renewal of world after world calamity A1006f., A1038, A1045. — Miraculous r. of saint's objects V224.

Renouncing clerical vows *V475; heaven: companions not there V326. — Heaven as reward for r. life Q172.6.

Rent. — Dragon eats people for r. B11.10.2; king punished for raising old woman's r. Q281.4; stone r. at crucifixion A979.1; tricksters feign father's death, flee with r. K356.

Repaid. — Arrogance r. L430ff.; kindness r. by devil G303.22.1.

Repair. — Animals help r. pot B579.4; dead returns to r. injury E345; living smith must r. wagon belonging to wild hunt E501.15.5.

Repairing the house K1415; the roof (not needed in dry weather, impossible in wet) J2171.2.1. — Mortal r. fairies' utensils F338; person cured by r. image that has same deformity D2161.4.4; water carried in leaky vessel by r. it with clay or gum H1023.2.1.1.

Reparations. — Life bought with promise of r. M234.4.

Repartee J1250—J1499. — Test in r. H507.

Repay. — Giants r. loan with large interest F531.5.5; money left on hill to r. helpful mountain-men F460.4.2.2; numskull throws money to frogs to r. them J1851.1.3; return from dead to r. obligation E340ff.

Repaying deceptive loan J1556. — Chain tale: lending and r. Z41.5; troll r. loan F455.6.2.1.

Repayment with leaves (shavings) that turn to gold *E501.15.4. — Ghost seeks r. of stolen money E236.8.

Repeated impressions penetrate mind J67; reincarnation E670ff.; resus-

citation *E151; transformation *D610ff. — Death for r. adultery
Q411.0.1.4; fool's r. expressions scare off adulterers J2461.2.2.

Repeatedly. — Animal feigns death r. and then entices owner from goods
K341.2.1.

Repeating the ceremony J2498; incantation continuously H1508.1; within
stories Z17. — Fool keeps r. his instructions so as to remember them
J2671.2; identity test: r. what formely said H15.1; sham parson keeps r.
same expression K1961.1.2.

Repelled. — Incestuous sister r. by brother T415.2.

Repentance of devil vexing friars G303.24.3; test H1573.7. — Account of
punishments prepared in hell brings about r. J172; conversion through r.
V331.4; false r. of the sick U236; power of r. V315.1; return from dead
to preach r. E367; reward for r. Q36.

Repentant thief pretends to have found stolen cow K416. — Blood from
r. woman F962.4.2; devil tempts r. sinner G303.9.4.9; Virgin aids r. slayer
V276.3.

Repenting. — Creator r. of certain creations A74.2; son r. of plot to kill
father S22.3.

Repetition. — Magic r. D2172.1.

Replaced. — Bodily members successfully r. *E780ff.; magic object cannot
be r. D1661; polygamy so head wife may be quickly r. T145.8.

Replacement. — Beautification by decapitation and r. of head *D1865.1;
constant r. of fighters E155.1.1; disenchantment by decapitation and r. of
head *D711.1; miraculous r. of objects for saint V224; resuscitation by
r. of soul E38.

Replica. — Building wax r. of castle H1133.6; soul as r. of body E747.1.

Replying. — Animals r. to person's remarks B210.1; usurers not r. when
called on to rise in church X512.

Repopulated. — Ireland r. after flood A1006.5.

Report. — Birds sit on Odin's shoulder and r. what they see and hear
*B122.2; owner frightened from goods by r. of approaching enemy
K335.0.1.

Representative. — Moon as sun's r. at night A756.

Representations. — Pictorial r. of creator A18.

Repression of lust T317.

Reprimanded. — Boaster of victory over a weaker person r. J978.

Reproached. — Person r. for having no relatives P202.

Reproduction of life stops in absence of goddess of fertility A431.1.1.

Reproductive energy from god A175.1.

Reproving. — Dead brother r. sister's pride E226.1; dead wife r. husband's
second wife *E221.2; father r. son in vision P233.10; tact in r. the great
J816.

Reptile, see also **Serpent, Snake;** leaps into unjust bishop's throat
V229.2.11.1; -men as magicians D1711.13; as ogre G354; paramour B613;
transformed to object D425; transformed to other animal D418; as wooer

B622. — Abduction by r. R13.4; cause of movement of r. A2441.4ff.; devil as r. G303.3.3.6; enemies of r. A2494.16; giant r. B875ff.; magic r. B176; marriage to person in r. form B646; marriage to r. B604ff., (in human form) B656; prophetic r. B145; reincarnation as r. E614; soul in form of r. E733; speaking r. B211.6; wise r. B123.

Reptiles transformed to persons D390ff. — Color of r. A2411.5; creation of r. A2140ff.; devastating r. B16.5; God makes birds, devil r. A1903; haunts of r. A2433.6ff.; king of r. B244ff.; kingdom of r. B225; lies about r. X1320; man swallows r. F929.2; man transformed to r. D190ff.; mythical r. B92; war between birds and r. B263.4.

Repulsing. — Animals r. shipwrecked man B772; ruler marries maiden r. his advances Q87.1; transformation as revenge for r. amorous adventures D661.1.

Repulsive. — Disguised husband shows wife he is not r. K1813.1.1; fairy wife deserts mortal husband for r. lover F302.2.1; woman's r. lover T232.4.

Reputation. — Death preferable to loss of r. for hospitality W12.1; overlooking adultery for sake of r. J221.1.1.

Request, see also **Wish;** for immortality punished by transformation into tree Q338.1. — Condemned man's last r. (red cap left in prison) J2174.1; dwarfs r. that cow stable be moved F451.4.4.3; fallen trees upraised at saint's r. D1602.2.1; fruit produced out of season at saint's r. F971.5.1; immoderate r. punished *Q338; moderate r. rewarded, immoderate punished Q3; modest r. best L220ff.; person never refuses a r. M223.1; refusal to grant r. punished Q287; refusing a r. tabu C871; reward for carrying out dead man's r. Q37; troubled nobleman's r. must not be refused P95.

Requests. — Departed deity grants r. to visitors *A575; tabus concerning r. made in otherworld C714; vow that no bards will make r. M164.

Requiem. — Ghost chooses own r. E545.11.

Rescue *R100—R199; of abandoned or lost person R130ff.; alone from shipwreck chosen over drowning with goods J222; of captive R110ff.; from deluge as reward Q150.1; from fairyland F321.3, F322.2, F322.5; by ghost from drowning E379.1; of hero by dragon B11.6.1.2; from ogre G550ff.; by magic object *D1390ff.; of sister from ogre by another sister G551.2; tokens *H83. — Animals grateful for r. from peril of death B360ff.; bat undertakes r. H1562.2.2; dog is to r. the farmer's child from wolf and receive reward K231.1.3; dogs r. fleeing master from tree refuge *B524.1.2; extraordinary companions r. hero F601.4; magic horn summons army for r. D1421.5.1; magic object received from man in return for r. of child D817.1; monster ungrateful for r. W154.2; prince will marry girl who will r. him from embarrassing position T67.3; reward for r. Q53; tasks assigned before man may r. wife from spirit world H923; transformation to r. D643.

Rescued animal threatens rescuer W154.2.1. — Captive r. by animal

*B544; drowning man r. by siren B53.1; girl r. by companions H621.2;
hero captured by man he has formerly r. N763; impostors steal r. princess
K1935; incognito king r. in fighting K1812.19; man attacked by the devil
r. by Virgin Mary V264; man swallowed by fish and later r. alive (lie)
X1723.1.2; moon falls into pit, r. by man A754.1.1; stolen child r. by
animal nurse B543.3; victims r. from swallower's belly F913; woman r.
from mountain men F460.4.4.1.1.

Rescuer disguised as officer gains custody of prisoner K649.2. — Actual r.,
not watchers, gets woman J1179.12; animal r. or retriever *B540ff.;
bungling r. caught by crab J2675; daughter unwittingly promised to dog
r. S247; disguised king rewards r. from robbers Q53.1; enchanted person
attracts attention of r. D794; girl leaves r. for younger lover T92.3; man
kills r. to collect reward W154.12; man rescued from drowning kills r.
W154.9; princess offered as prize to r. T68.1; rescued woman stolen from
r. R111.8.2.

Rescuers *R150ff.; polite J2516.3.2. — Escape by reporting approach of
r. K545.

Rescuers' Sabbath (Jew fallen into pit) J1613.

Rescuing drowning man forbidden C41.1; the moon (reflected in water)
J1791.2. — Animal r. man from dangerous place B547ff.; dog tries to
bite man r. him from well W154.5; fairy r. hero from battle F302.9; god
r. sleeping man A185.2.1; horse r. children B540.2; husband r. wife's
paramour K1544.1; wife r. husband from supernatural H923.1.

Resemblance of children to mother's brothers P293.2.1. — Close r. of un-
related children F1072; recognition by r. H20ff.

Reserved. — Certain objects r. for royalty P93.

Resewoir emptied for crane J758.2.

Resignation of king if he begets natural son P16.2.1; of maimed king compulsory P16.2.

Resin. — Revenant with chip of r. between teeth E422.1.7.

Resisting. — Girl r. devil G303.9.4.7.1; man r. blandishments of leader's
fiancée W34.1.

Resources. — Never use your entire r. J1073.

Resourcefulness test. H506ff.

Respect. — Druid inspires r. P427.0.1; foolish trading to gain r. J2096;
king's champion enforces r. P14.15.

Respice finem J21.1.

Respite granted dragon in fight B11.11.1. — Deceptive r. in payment obtained K238; definite r. from death granted K551.22; year's r. for unwelcome marriage T151.

Responsible. — Oldest son r. for others P233.5.

Rest. — Bluff: You take one, I can manage the r. K1715.8; dead find no r.
because of a sin E411; ghost finds r. when certain thing happens E451;
losing all for a r. J356.

Resting forbidden C730ff.; near lake tabu C615.4; tabu until question answered C735.2.9. — Creator r. on tree or stake A813.3; gods make earth for r. feet on A5.1; snake kills men while creator r. A1335.10.

Restlessness as curse M455; of dead E410ff. — Magic r. in bed D2063.2.

Restored. — Broken weapons magically r. D2163.1; dry spring r. by removal of certain stone F933.2; dumb man's speech r. by saint V221.2; magic object voluntarily r. to giver D878; nose r. by magic object D1376.1ff.; reincarnated person r. to original form E696; severed hand magically r. D2161.3.2; stolen sun r. to sky A721.3; treasure given away by saint r. V411.5; unshriven man r. to life in order to confess V23.1.

Restoring life to murder victim J1955.1. — Brownie r. stolen property F482.5.4.2; dead r. stolen goods E352; deity r. city A185.8; herbs r. sight D1505.1; prayer r. shattered vessel V52.5; son r. mother wished into pig J2075.4.

Restrained. — Animal r. by magic object *D1442ff.; hasty judgment r. when man sees someone sleeping with his wife (newborn son) J21.2; man r. from fornication by sight of holy fringe on garment V131.1.

Restrictions, see also **Tabu;** on burial V62. — Betrothal r. T65; marriage r. T131; sexual r. A1556.

Resurrected boys choose to return to heaven E755.0.1. — False daughter accepted as r. child K1926; Jewish child r. after burning V363.1.

Resurrection, see also **Resuscitation;** of gods A193; at Judgment Day E178; as reward Q151.9; on Sunday E751.6. — Christ's r. V211.8; place of saint's r. prophesied M364.4; reward: burial and r. in one place Q175.

Resurrections. — Two r. E751.0.1.

Resuscitated. — Boy r. by lie H252.4.1; death feigned to learn how soldiers r. K1863; faithless r. wife *K2213.5; intercourse with r. wife tabu C117.1; ogre r. to help hero G513; recognition of r. person by missing member H57.0.1.

Resuscitating. — Companions r. girl: to whom does she belong? H621.1; evil spirit cast out of person by killing and r. E728.1.1; faithful animals r. master B301.5; god r. man A185.12.1; lion, bear, and wolf r. master B515; ogre r. benefactor G513.1; ogre r. princess G335; pseudo-magic r. object sold *K113; pupil r. people demon kills K1955.6.1; reward for r. dead Q93.2; wife's constancy r. husband T212.1; Virgin Mary r. man V251.1.

Resuscitation *E0—E199; by animals B515; of unshriven man in order to confess V23.1. — Beautification by death and r. D1865ff.; fatal game: death and r. K856; false death, r., to exploit relic K1865; failure at r. E186; foolish imitation of r. J2411.1.1; magic pig burned to prevent r. B192.1.

Retainers. — Military rights of r. P551.8.

Retaining fee J1559.1.

Retaliation on cheating goldsmith J1511.20. — Bridegroom's r. to bride pleading headache K2052.3; king observes r. among animals and becomes just J52.

Retiring. — Divinity r. to end of the world A567; kings r. from world P16.1.

Retorts. — Clever r. J1250—J1649.

Retreat in return for cessation of attack M263.

Retreating warriors driven back to battle P551.4. — Good king never r. P12.5; treasure hidden by r. army N511.1.7.

Retrieving attempt fatal to jumper J2146; king's falcon H1154.7.1. — Animal r. lost person or object *B540ff.; seduction by alleged r. of lost gem K1315.2.2; wife r. husband's fortune J1545.6.

Return of dead soon after burial E586; from dead E200—E599, (to inflict punishment) E230ff., (to protest against easy-going priest) V25.1, (to repay obligations) E340ff., (to return and ask back love tokens) E311; of hero A516, Z293; home in humble disguise K1815.1; home to one's own funeral N681.0.1; to master of animal who shams death and is sold K366.1.3.1; from lower world F101; from upper world F10.1. — Culture hero's expected r. *A580ff.; dead lover's r. (malevolent) E210ff., (friendly) E310ff.; dead relative's r. from dead (malevolent) E220ff., (friendly) E320ff.; dwarf makes r. of child dependent upon guessing of riddle F451.5.15.2; dwarfs emigrate New Year's Eve of 1800 to r. New Year's Eve of 1900 F451.9.3; dwarfs must r. to spirit world by 1:00 a.m. F451.3.2.2; dwarfs r. what they borrow F451.5.10.4; expected r. of deity A192.3; friendly r. from the dead E300ff.; immediate r. to otherworld because of broken tabu C952; land of no r. F129.5; lover threatens to await husband's r. K1581.5.2; magic object causes things to r. to their proper place D1565ff.; magic object received from man in r. for rescue of child D817.1; magic r. of stolen object to owner K423; malevolent r. from dead E200—E299; quest to devil in hell for r. of contract H1273.1; refusal to r. borrowed goods K232; sacrifice for r. of abducted person V17.7; saint promises r. from heaven V229.2.13; witch recognized by seeing wandering soul r. G251; wizard compels thief to r. stolen property D1817.0.1.3.1.

Returned. — Adopted child r. to real mother T672; box on ears r. (sent around table) K2376; magic sword r. to lake whence it was received D878.1; present r. to giver (to give it to no one who is not a greater fool) J156.3; purchase money r. to suitor T52.2; rescued princess r. to her betrothed R111.4; stolen kiss to be r. *J1174.2.

Returning exile succeeds L111.1; hero marries first love T102; magic object D868. — Culture hero r. A581; dead place net across river to prevent living man from r. to earth F93.1.1; excuse for r. home after leaving wife J1545.3.3; fairies grateful for r. lost child F339.3; food placed out for r. souls of dead *E541.1; husband r. secretly, spies on wife K1551; landing of r. heroes prophesied M369.2; man given ability of r. to life E167; relics r. to original church V143.2; self-r. head *D1602.12; soul of sleeper prevented from r. to his body E721.1.2; treasure r. after it removes itself N562.1.

Reunion of lovers after many adventures T96; of outcast wife with husband and children S451; of soul with body E726.3. — Accidental r. of families N730ff.; accidental r. of lovers N737, of couple N741.

Reveal. — Man persuaded to r. fatal secret C420.1; return from dead to r. (hidden treasure) E371, (murder) *E231, (whereabouts of stolen goods) E371.1; speaking bones of murdered person r. murder E632.1.

Revealed. — Crime r. by laughing statue D1639.4. guilt r. by magic object *D1318ff.; murder r. (by child in mother's womb) T575.1.1, (by unusual names of boys) N271.2; peasant girl's wisdom r. by found mortar taken to king H561.1.2; substitution of false bride r. by animal *K1911.3.1; truth r. by magic object *D1316ff.

Revealing name of god forbidden C51.3; secrets of supernatural wife forbidden C31.9. — God r. himself to mortals A182; princess wins wrestling match with suitor by r. her breast H331.6.1.1; treasure r. itself only at certain times N541.

Revelation of magic secret permits animal to be killed D1445.1. — Animals observe sacred r. B251.8; clerics fast for r. P623.0.1.1; mountains fight to be spot for r. A964.2.1.

Revelations of a satyr U119.1.

Revelry. — Breaking up r. tabu C874; ghostly r. sounds E337.1.3.

Revenant, see also **Ghost.** — Sham r. goes out to get a breath of air J2311.3; wind stopped by r. D2142.2.1.

Revenants E200—E599.

Revenge given up as reward Q45.4; by interrupting feast J1564.2; for killing animal Q211.6; by literally misconstruing order J2516.0.1. — Animal takes r. on man B299.1; avoiding enemy's r. J647; blinded slave's r. K1465; curse in r. of father's murder M411.11; curse: undertaking dangerous r. M446.1; creation of animals as r. A1732; cutting hooks for father's r. H591.3; death and r. preferred to life J494; devil prevented from r. by pious priest G303.16.11.2; fairy's r. F361; ghost laid when r. accomplished E451.9; importunate lover's r. on women humiliating him K1218.4.1; king slain in r. P16.7; maidens slain in r. Q411.12; philanderer's wife has affair in r. K1510.2; porter's r. for three wise counsels J1511.6; queen kills husband in r. K2213.13, P22.1; queen offers son in r. for first husband P23.4; reincarnation for r. E693; rejected suitors' r. T75.2.1; stealing from ogre for r. G610.1; taking money instead of r. J229.11; transformation as r. for repulsing amorous adventures D661.1; vow not to take r. M168; vow on r. or death M161.2; wife's r. for second wife K2213.16; wife prepares r. but prefers to die with husband T211.2.1.1; will-o'-the-wisp's r. F491.5.

Revenged. — Theft charge r. Q411.13.1.

Reverberating waves F931.4.1.

Reversal of fortune L (entire chapter).

Reverse magic *D1783ff. — Officers praised in r. from their real merit K2136; witch's charm r. of Christian G224.1.

Reversed obstacle flight D673; transformation flight D671.1. — Facial features of goddess r. A282.0.1.1; judgments of church r. by Virgin Mary M91; ogre with feet r. G365.1; sun's night journey with r. face A722.2.

Reversing the poker protects from witch G272.9. — Disenchantment by cutting off and r. bodily members D712.1; disenchantment by r. enchantment D765; escape by r. K534ff.; power over monster (wizard, king) obtained by r. order D1783.4; resuscitation by r. wooden blocks E79.2.

Revival by day of pigs killed by night H1331.2.3; of lady found in tomb apparently dead K426, T37; of ogre after limbs are severed G635. — Disenchantment by burial then r. D719.1.1.

Reviving trees by magic object D1571; unconscious man with hot iron J2119.7. — Apparently dead woman r. before burial N694; witch r. dead G263.5.

Revolt of bad gods against good *A106.1; of evil angels against God A106.2.

Revolting devil banished to hell A106.2.1; murders or mutilations S100ff.

Revolver. — Sausage as r. scares off robber K437.3.

Revolving animal's skin B738; bleeding rock F809.4.1; castle F771.2.6, (in otherworld) F163.1.1; door of tent F782.6; fortress D1381.23.

Reward for accomplishment of task deceptively withheld K231.2; for the bag of lead K476.2.2; given for return of animal B343; of helpful animal B320ff.; for information claimed by sham dead J2511.1.2; of the uncharitable V420ff. — Animal characteristics as r. A2220ff.; debtor tells creditor that he has had r. in the hope of payment K231.7; devil is cheated of his r. when priest dismisses mass early G303.16.16; devil to enter girl and sham physician to collect r. for driving the devil out K1955.6; double r. successfully claimed K441ff.; false claim of r. K442; foolish r. offered J2085; forgiveness the r. of successful quest H1244; fugitive returns so family may collect r. T215.5; half of kingdom as r. Q112; helpful animal as r. B319.2; hero refuses r. L225; impostors claim r. earned by hero K1932; king gives own wife as r. P14.13; magic object acquired as r. D855; man kills rescuer to collect r. W154.12; modesty brings r. L200—L299; money received from ghosts as r. for bravery E373.1; mortal chooses to sleep with fairy as r. for saving her life F304.5; origin of plant as r. A2632; plant characteristics as r. A2710ff.; princess offers r. for princely husband T55.10; riches the r. of questions solved on quests H1243; sacrifice equal to r. J2067; same r. promised to many helpers K2034; singer repaid with promise of r. J1551.3; stranger dies from joy on receiving r. from ruler F1041.1.5.2; thief (abductor) returns and enforces r. for stolen object (princess) K442.1; transformation as r. D663; worship of deity brings r. V526.

Rewards and punishments Q (entire chapter). — Dwarfs object to r. F451.5.10.2; nature of r. Q100—Q199; revenant r. its conqueror E465.

Rewarded. — Charity r. V410ff.; deeds r. *Q10—Q99; faithfulness to Virgin Mary, even if not to Christ, r. V253; gift of horse r. with a beet J2415.1; hero claims ancestors want him r. K362.11; liar r. by apes J815.1;

mortal r. by god A185.11; owner r. for discarding cobold F481.0.1.2.1; poet r. P427.7.8; sham wise man hides horse and is r. for finding it K1956.2; to be r. by his kind J1364.

Rheumatism cure X1787.

Rhine. — Expelled dwarfs plan to dig underground bed for R. F451.5.22; refusal to tell of R. treasure K239; wine washed in R. J1312.2.

Rhinoceros carries off man R13.1.3. — Color of r. A2247.3, A2411.1.6.7; rabbit slays r. L315.12; tortoise jumps on, kills r. N622.1.

Rhyme for summoning kite's aid B501.2. — Man interrupted at eating answers in r. X12.1; student is helped by the devil when he can answer three questions in r. G303.22.3.

Rhymes about cakes wife has stolen K435.1. — Formulistic r. Z80ff.; hidden cuckold reveals presence by r. K1556.

Rib. — Creation of first woman from man's r. A1275.1; ox r. as fairy gift F343.16.

Ribs crushed in embrace F639.9. — Dead men make music on their r. E548; mutilation of r. S173; skeleton has all his r., hence Adam story false J1262.8; substituted r. E782.2; why an uneven number of r. A1312.2.

Ribald. — Devil as r. traveler G303.3.1.3.1.

Ribbon long enough to reach from ear to ear K195. — Escape by returning for hair r. K551.4.8; giant slings stones with his hair r. F531.3.2.2; magic blue r. D1078.1; magic strength from blue r. D1835.4.

Rice in boy's hands joined around pillar, saved J2119.6; magically produced D973.1.1; paddies flooding controlled by toad D2149.5; producing million-fold F815.4; with remarkable scent F815.4.1; scent identifies children H49.1; thrown at weddings T136.2; transformed to gold D475.1.6; wheat and dal dispute superiority J461.5. — Acquisition of r. A1423.2; all r. cooked for one meal J1813.9.1; bag with r. for the road K444.3; cattle formerly ate r. A1101.2.2; cooking r. without fire H506.9; cows in r. field made to disgorge K366.1.4; creator made earth like r. cake A836; death from thorns in r. M341.2.16; deceptive wage: r. on leaf K256.1; disenchantment by consecrated r. D771.9; dog to scent r. J1341.3; god of r.-fields A433.1.1; gold, silver traded for r. J2093.5; hiding in r.-bin K515.5; hoarded r. once more made available A1421.0.1; identifying r. in sack H522.3; magic growth of r. D2157.2.0.1; magic pumpkin yields r. D1472.2.6; magic r. D965.8.1, *D1033.1; magic r.-grains *D973.1; magic r. harvest D1563.1.6; man becomes r.-grain D214.1; mouse gathers r. for man: may eat a little of his rice daily A2223.3; origin of r-beer A1426.2; origin of r. growing A1441.3; quest for magic r. H1333.2.4; sand becomes r. D452.3.1, D476.1.11; singing r.-pot D1615.6; sowing and reaping r. in one day royalty test H41.8; sowing r. seed in others' fields J2129.8; tortoise cursed for going under water while ferrying r.-goddess A2231.7.3; tortoise given hard shell for ferrying r.-goddess A2223.6; trail of r. husks R135.0.2.1; transformation by eating r. mixed with perspiration D551.6.2; transformation by throwing r. D571.1; vow to make husband eat boiled r. M149.4; wages: successive harvests from one r. grain Z21.1.1; why rats eat r.: brought original rice-plant A2435.3.10.1; why r. is abundant A2793.7; why r. has ears only at top A2771.4.1; why wild pigs ravage r.-fields A2545.5.

Rich girl in love with poor boy *T91.5.1; man P150ff.; man caught in church door Q551.2.8.1; man dragged from grave E411.0.5.1; man falls into sacrificial grave K1603; man humble, knows he can't take wealth with him J912.3; man ignores poor sister J411.11; man poor in happiness J347.4; man made poor to punish pride L412; man in rags treated as beggar J1072.2; man seizes poor widow's cow U35; man shakes ducats into pope's lap J1263.2.2; man as wild huntsman E501.1.3; man's ghost rebukes children withholding church money E415.2; man's trial in heaven Q172.2.1; and poor in love T91.5; but stingy couple adopt son T673; woman falsely accuses ascetic K2113.2. — Child adopted by r. man in order to get rid of him K2015; devil carries off r. man Q272.1f.; devil marries r. girl G303.12.5.3; eater of magic bird-heart will become r. M312.3; false repentance of sick r. man U236.1; fortunes of the r. man and the poor man N181; hero made business partner of r. man Q111.1; holy man's prayer reforms r. man J153.1; how the r. man paid his servant (cumulative tale) Z23; lowly ascetic wins r. woman's love K1322.1; man fated to be r. N213; marriage to r. master's widow N251.3; marriage between r. and poor T121; men are too r.: gods punish L482; newly-r. enjoy giving to beggars U130.1; philosopher advises rascals to throw at a r. man J1602; why the poor, being in the majority, don't kill off the r. J2371.4; poor girl chosen rather than r. girl L213; poor man deceives r. K890.1; poor man imitates r. J2416; poor man consoles self by thinking of misfortunes of r. J883; poor man surpasses r. man L143; prophecy: r. man's son to marry poor girl M359.7; quest to hell for return of contract from deceased r. man H1273.1.1; rejoicing at arrival of r. man in heaven E758; robber's defense for stealing from r. J1269.8; St. George teaches the poor man, "who steals somewhat and lies somewhat will be r." J556.1; sermon about r. man X435.5; sham r. man K1954; when r. man eats H659.17; widow makes penniless man r. N225.

Riches the difference between poor man and rich (riddle) H875; reward Q111ff., (of questions solved on quests) H1243. — Trolls' r. F455.4.1.

Richer. — Birds seeking r. lands are nearly all killed J513.1.

Richest. — Quest for bride r. and poorest H1311.2; quest for the r. person H1311; riddle: what is the r.? H636ff.

Rid. — Adulteress getting r. of husband while she entertains lover K1514; attempt to get r. of man by selling him as slave P173.4; expensive means of being r. of insects J2102ff.; getting r. of fairies F381; house set on fire to get r. of cat J2101; impossible to r. oneself of cobold F481.3; quests (tasks) assigned in order to get r. of hero H931, H1211.

Ridden. — Images of animals r. D1631; land bargain: land r. around during a sermon K185.7.2; punishment: being r. as horse Q493.

Ridding city of thieves H1199.8; country of ogres A1416; country of pests Q512.3; person of animal in stomach B784.2ff.

Riddle. — Death sentence escaped by propounding r. H542; dwarf makes return of child dependent upon guessing of r. F451.5.15.2; ogre gives r. on pain of death G681; quest to devil for r. answer H1278; smith reveals r. solution despite king's orders J1161.7; solving sphinx's r. fatal to sphinx *C822; son frees father by bringing r. the king cannot solve R154.2.1; thief dupes owner, gets him to solve r. K418; witch travels in r. G241.4.3.

Riddles H530—H899; as poetry tests H509.4.2. — Asking r. to test patience H1553.6; dwarfs give r. and questions to mortals F451.5.15; girl gets answers to devil's r. G303.12.5.5; husband discovers wife's adultery by r. K1557.

Ride. — Ghost asks traveler for r. E332.3; husband forbids wife to r. on the dog (she immediately does so and is bitten) T254.2; vow to r. the forest all night and slay all comers M157; warrior whose horse is cut in two continues to r. on the half-horse (lie) X1864.

Rider exchanges parts of body for food M225.1; on magic horse immune D1381.30; takes the meal-sack on his shoulder to relieve ass J1874.1. — Dead R. (Lenore) E215; ghost with horseback r. E332.3.1; lie: remarkable r. X1004; magic horse renders r. invulnerable D1846.3; man chosen king before whom car without r. stops H171.4; naked woman pursued and cut in two by r. E501.5.1.1; riddle of horse and r. H744; tree grows out of horse and gives r. shade X1130.2.1.

Ridgepole. — Man becomes r. figure D268.2.

Ridicule. — Exposure to r. when wig snatched off X52.1.

Ridiculing. — Children r. drunken father P236.5; each stutterer thinks others r. him X135.1.

Ridiculous. — Fool sent on r. quest J2346; witch makes person r. G269.21.

Riding contest won by substitution K27; dirty on black-heeled horse tabu C891.1; horse kingship task H41.7; speckled horse credential test H242.1; three times around hill to free captive confined within R112.2; through street on bull as punishment Q473.1. — Alp r. horse sweaty at night F471.1.1.1; dead person r. E581; coyote r. with sun A724.1.0.1; deceptive contest in carrying tree (horse): r. K71, K72; devil r. horse G303.7.1ff.; devil's mother r. a goat G303.11.3.1; dwarf r. F451.6.2; fairy r. behind man on horse F366.2.2; fairy r. man's back F339.1; fairies r. (calves) F366.1.3, (mortal's horses) F366.2; flying contest won by deception: r. on the other K25.1; ghost r. (in cart) E272.1, (horse) E272.2, (on man's back) *E262; giant r. church-roof F531.3.3; gods r. through air A171; man r. on ant F535.2.5; mountain folk r. through air on horses F460.2.2; philosopher as r. horse for woman K1215; race won by deception: r. on the back K11.2; revenant as woman r. hog E425.1.5; spirit r. horses at night F473.4.1; suitor contest: difficult r. H331.1; suitor test: r. strong princess's horse H345.2; trickster r. dupe K1241; trolls r. F455.3.3; unusual animal as r.-horse *B557; witch r. G241ff., (horses at night) *G265.3, (man) G269.3.1.

Riesenspielzeug F531.5.3.

Rifle. — Man fires r. in hollow log, scares off Indians K547.3.

Right hands cut off enemy Q451.1.6; hand's power for good *D996.0.1.1. — Fool cannot tell his r. hand in the dark J1735; why God changed r. hand into left A1311.2; lucky r. hand N113.2.1; magic sight by looking over r. shoulder D1821.3.2; ointment cures left cheek, nor r. D1663.2; prayer into r. hand efficacious V52.15; sword can be moved only by r. person D1654.4.1; "that is r." C495.2.2; throbbing of r. eye a favorable omen D1812.5.2.1.

Righteous save sinful city from destruction M294.

Righteousness tested H1573.6.

Righthandwise circumambulation D1791.1.1. — Carrying book r. insures victory D1381.25; turning r. (brings luck) N131.2, (insures safety) D1384.3.1.

Rime. — Cow from dripping r. of universe's creation B715.

Rind. — Ape throws away nut because of its bitter r. J369.2; eating r. first J2178.1; giant pomegranate r. holds thirteen men F813.8.2.

Ring as baptismal token H82.4; broken as token of broken engagement Z151; can make or break a king P13.3.2; as chastity index H433.1; to be cut in two: real owner laments J1171.1.1; divided by selling it, dividing money J1243; of Fastrada T85.4.1; fits only one person Z321; with inscribed names as tokens H86.3; with life in it E771; made of coffin-hinge as remedy D1500.1.15.2; proves theft H84.4; to put on corpse's finger K362.2; rises to water's surface D2149.4.2; tabu at certain time C635; transformed to another object D454.8.2; transforms D572.2; under dead girl's tongue enchants D765.1.1.1. — Animals recover lost wishing r. B548.1; betrothal by gold r. T61.4.5; bird carries off r. which lover has taken from sleeping mistress's finger N352; burying r. raises tank's water D2151.5.1.1; cutting off hand to get r. R231.1; dead husband sends his r. to his wife E321.1; demons in r. H973.2; devil gives suspicious husband r. G303.9.7.3; discovering r. thief H1199.9.1; disenchantment by r. D771.10; disenchantment by removing r. from under dead girl's tongue D765.1.1.1; dolphins seek King Solomon's r. *A2275.5.4; dress to go through r. H355.6; extraordinary r. F825; fairy gives r. F343.12; fairy music from fairy r. F262.10.2; fairies visible through magic r. F235.6; fish recovers r. from sea *B548.2.1; fit of r. measures time H1583.2; getting r. from python's hole H1132.3.1; ghost leaves r. E544.1.2; gold r. as reward Q111.4; groom's mother gives bride-to-be r. T133.6; hero will marry girl possessing certain r. H361; identification by r. *H94ff.; king loses r. while studying art of stealing K341.8.4; king marries girl finding his lost r. N713.2; life token: r. (presses finger) E761.7.1, (rusts) E761.4.4, (bursts asunder) E761.5.3; lost r. found in fish *N211.1; magic r. *D1076, (carried off by bird) D865.1, (protects from attack) D1381.7, (stolen)

D865.1, (summons genie) D1421.1.6, (works by sun) D1662.1.1; magic
wishing-r. loses power D877.1; man puts marriage r. on the finger of
statue of Venus (Virgin Mary) T376; martens recover magic r. B548.1.1;
mortal gives fairy mistress r. F302.1.2; murderer traced through r.
N271.8; oath taken on r. M112; otters recover magic r. B548.1.2; person
transformed to r. D263.1; quest for missing r. H1386.2; quest for most
beautiful r. H1319.4; quest for magic r. *H1352; recognition by means of
r. enclosed in wound H61.3; recovering lost r. from sea H1132.1.1; resuscitation by r. E64.13; return from dead to demand stolen r. E236.1.1;
saint's image lets golden r. fall as sign of favor to suppliant D1622.3;
sight of mistress's r. causes husband to withhold himself from his wife
T286; skillful marksman casts lance through a r. F661.8; stealing r. from
finger as task H1151.4; touch of r. causes sleep D1364.29; vanishing man
leaves r. D2188.2.1; wearing deceased wife's r. as bride test H363.2;
witch cannot rise if r. lies under her chair G254.1; woman casts r. into
sea boasting L412.1.

Rings exchange places on fingers E761.7.14.— Bringing princess another
princess's r. H933.3; fairy r. on grass F261.1; false set of r. offset genuine
K476.4; father gives son r. symbolizing religions J462.3.1.1; giving away
r. tabu C783.2; gold r. on hands as suitor test H312.4.1.

Ringdove eats man's grain: man may kill him A2238.2. — Why r. brings
good luck A2536.2; nest of r. A2431.3.3.

Ringing bell tabu C756.0.1; of churchbell causes devil to lose his power
G303.16.12; churchbell as fear test H1412.1; of church bell by nun C94.7;
of bells herald wild hunt E501.13.1.4. — Disenchantment by r. bell
D789.10; saints curse by r. bells M411.8.1.

Rioting. — Queen incites husband's r. P23.1.

Rip Van Winkle D1960.1.

Ripe. — Saint causes wheat to become r. prematurely D2157.2.2; tree
blooms and grows r. fruit nightly F811.13.

Ripping. Disenchantment by r. armor D712.8.

Rise. — Chanticleer believes that his crowing makes the sun r. J2272.1;
king vainly forbids tide to r. L414; maids must r. even earlier K1636;
magic song causes tree to r. to sky *D1576.1; sun refuses to r. A739.6;
witch known by inability to r. from chair with four-leaf clover under
it G254; usurers do not r. for special blessing X512.

Rising into air despite gravity X1741.1; and falling sky F791; river F932.1;
smoke as omen D1812.5.0.4. — Concubine's r. from stone impossible
Q551.2.7; counsel on r. earlier J21.23; earth r. from sea A816; fugitive
supernaturally r. into air R324; island r. up in sea (river) F735ff.; man
controls r. of sun A725; man r. too early J1394.2; object r. into air F1083;
ring prevents person from r. from chair D1413.2; sea r. and changing
place F931.1; sun and his brother r. and setting alternately A736.3.3.

Risks. — Great possessions bring great r. U81.

Rite. — Christian child killed to furnish blood for Jewish r. V361.

Rites, see also **Ceremonies.** — Birth r. confer royalty P37; dead man speaks demanding proper funeral r. E235.2.1; dead without proper funeral r. cannot rest in grave E412.3; funeral r. *V60ff.; magic r. for obtaining a child T548.2.

Ritual cannibalism G13.1. — Changing r. tabu C65; devils' wives attempt resuscitation r. K113.0.1; fasting a part of magic r. D1766.8.1; ghost returns to perform in r. E379.5.

Rituals. — Magic from special r. D1799.3.

Rival induces mother to kill children S342. — Burial alive of maiden to keep her from r. S123.5; jealousy of r. wives T257.2ff.; magic object stolen by r. for wife D861.4; man kills all guests, hoping some day to kill r. S110.2; searching for r. to wife's beauty H1301.1.3; successful r. gives lady to friend P319.6; transformation of love r. *D665.1; vow to kill successful r. M149.3; young r. derides old one: oldster's retort J1352.2.

Rivals kills each other over woman T86.1; in love T92ff. — Tasks assigned at suggestion of jealous r. H911; treacherous r. K2220ff.

Rivaling the gods forbidden C65; poets P427.7.10; smiths P447.6.

River, see also **Stream, Water;** as barrier to otherworld F141.1; becomes sea D483.1; bed earth saves soul E754.1.7; carrier throws off passenger to drown S131.1; crossed by magic D1524.5; connecting earth and upper and lower worlds A657; entrance to lower world F93.1; of fire as barrier to otherworld *F142; flows from corpse of hero's mother A511.1.1.1; -god A425; grateful for being given color D1658.1.6; grateful for being praised even when ugly D1658.1.1; in heaven E755.1.2; in hell filled with weapons A672.3; of honey (lie) X1547.2; issuing from cave controlled by race of Amazons D915.5; magically rises against enemy D2091.7.1; never freezes F141.1.3; personified Z118.3; produced by magic *D915.1; rises to drown liars D1318.17; says, "The time has come but not the man" D1311.11.1; -spirit F424; Styx A672, M119.1.1; taken to sky becomes star A761.1; that flows around the world A872; valley licked out by giant beast A951.1; water's heat prevents thieves' crossing D1389.2.2. — Adventures from pursuing object on r. N791; bathing in sacred r. V96.1; besiegers drowned by diverting r. K2369.5; boat sails on dry r. bed X1781.1; bones of dead thrown into r. E607.1.1; bracelet gift from r. goddess N815.0.2.1; bride spinning at bottom of r. K1911.2.2.2; carrying woman across r. without wetting feet H1046; city won by turning r. from course K2369.6; corpse thrown into r. as punishment Q491.8; course of r. deflected for king's burial V67.3.1; crossing r. of fire H1542.1; crossing r. with tree's aid F1071.1; curse on r. M476; curse makes r. barren of fish D2085.1; dead place net across r. to prevent living man from returning to earth F93.1.1; devil and sinful priest disappear amid blaze of fire in r. G303.17.2.4; dogs by r. try to get food in r. by drinking r. dry J1791.3.2; dry r. bed bad omen D1812.5.1.16; epidemic does not cross r. at saint's command D2162.2; exposure astride wood floating down r. S141.3; extraordinary r. *F715ff.; father throws boy into r. S11.3.6; flood from rising r. A1011.2; flowers floating on r. of milk F814.6; fool will not drink from a r. because he cannot drink it all J2525; fox in swollen r. claims to be swimming to distant town J873; giant astride r. F531.3.5.3; giant digs trench for r. course F531.6.6.3; giant drinks up r. F531.3.4.2; giant's foot dams r. F531.3.1.2.1; horse transformed to r. D422.1.1; how much water in r.? H696.1.4; impassable yellow r. surrounds city F767.1; intermittent r. D915.4; island rises up in r. F735.0.1; jumping r. on horseback H331.1.6; jumping into r. after their comrade J1832; legitimacy of children tested by dipping them in r. H222.1; lie: remarkable r. X1547; magic object controls r. D1549.3; magic object received from r.-nymph D813.1; magic r. *D915; magician makes people lift garments to avoid wetting in imaginary r. D2031.1; man leaps over r. F1071.2.1; man lives under r. F725.4; marriage to r. T117.9; measuring r. as task H1149.8; Milky Way as a r. A778.3; numskull waits for r. to run down J1967; object magically lifted from r. bottom D1547.3; oracular r. D1311.11; origin of r. worship A1546.1; pursued animal runs through imaginary r. D2031.3; quest for princess caused by sight of one of her hairs floating on r. H1213.1; reading book causes r. to dry up D1542.3.2; sacrifice to r. V11.2.1; sacrifice to r.-god who has stopped boat S263.4; saint's bachall drives back flooding r. D1549.3.1; soldiers fighting force r. from bed F1084.3; source of r. where earth, sky meet A659.3; spirits put corpse into r. F402.1.8; standing naked in winter r. H328.4; swimming in imaginary r. D2031.1.2; tabu: drinking from certain r. between two darknesses C263; tabu: going with dry feet over certain r. C862; tears become r. D457.18.2; treasure hidden in r. N513.4; ungrateful r. passenger K952.1; warming hands across r. J1945; water shallows so r. can be crossed D1551.0.1; wearing shoes only when crossing r. F1015.2; woman enamored of a r. T461.1; woman sells self for help across r. T455.5.

Rivers of blood in hell A671.2.2; of fire A661.0.1.1.1; in hell A671.2.2ff.; in otherworld F162.2; of wine, rose-water and honey surround palace F771.2.4.1. — Angel of r. A425.0.1; why beaver lives along r. A2433.3.12; countertask: stop all the r. H696.1.1, H1142.3, H1143; creator of r. A930.1; dissatisfied r. complain against sea W128.3; eleven r. spring from well in midst of earth A875.2; extraordinary occurrences connected with r. F932; four r. of Paradise A871.2, *F162.2.1; hero regulates r. A533; magic control of r. D2151.2; magic object makes r. and lakes D1486; origin of r. A930ff.; origin of worship of r. A1546.1; palace surrounded by r. of wine, rosewater, and honey F771.7; riddle of ocean and r. H734; sacrifice to r. and seas S264; serpent king dams r. A1019.2; seven fair r. in Eden Z71.5.6.12; standing in r. as penance Q541.1.1.

Road to heaven *F57; to otherworld F151; from reading magic book D1484.2; runs through house F771.9. — Angels defend r. to heaven V511.1.2; animal determines r. to be taken *B151ff.; animals refuse to help make r. and are punished A2233.1; birds point out r. to hero B563.2; broad and narrow r. in otherworld F171.2; children know local r.; why doesn't stranger? J2212.9; choice of dangerous r. as valor test H1561.9; coming neither on nor off the r. H1051; devil builds r. G303.9.1.7, (for farmer in one day) G303.9.2.2; do not prefer new r. J21.5.1; equivocal inscription telling what will happen if each r. is chosen N122.0.1; escape from robbers by pretending to be going the same r. K579.3; father's counsel: dress up the trunks of trees (cover the r.) H588.6; forbidden r. C614; friendly r. ghosts E332ff.; frog persists in living in puddle on r. J652.1; fugitive slave takes wrong r. and is caught N382; giant and wife build Roman r. F531.6.6.5; haunting ghost deceived so that he cannot find r. to return E432.1; holes in edge of r. J95; lighting the r. (house set on fire) K1412; magic object makes r. D1484; magic object points out r. *D1313ff.; man keeps house; gives wife r. J1541.4; Milky Way a r. A778.2; ogress takes lives along r. G321.2; paving r. in short time H1108; picking wrong r. reveals identity H38.2.5; rice for the r. K444.3; sloth refuses to help make r. A2233.1.4; why snake does not go on the r. A2233.1.2, A2441.4.1; spirit blocks person's r. F402.1.2; squirrel points out r. B563.3; "take side r. rather than main" J21.5.2; wild hunt avoided by keeping on one's r. E501.17.5.1.

Roads appear on Hallowe'en F1099.2; appear at hero's birth F1099.2.1; go over houses X1551.1; marked out by supernatural cows A989.2. — Divination by choice of r. D1812.5.0.17; five great r. of Ireland discovered at king's birth A994; ghosts which haunt r. E272; god of r. A413; lies about mountain r. X1526; magic power at cross-r. *D1786; pilgrimage to r. Christ walked V531.1.

Roar. — Dog following lion flees at his r. J952.3; lion's r. causes havoc at 300 miles B741; river in paradise with terrible r. F162.2.8.

Roaring. — Jackal's attempts at r. like lion J2413.8; magic shield r. when bearer is in danger D1317.13.

Roast cock comes to life and crows E168.1; ducks fly (by magic) D2191. — Ghosts seek firewood to r. man E257; guessing nature of devil's r. meat H523.4.

Roasting. — Ghosts r. girl E251.3.1.1; literal numskull throws water on r. pig J2461.1.3; murder by r. alive S112.6.

Robbed. — Fool's talking causes himself and companions to be r. J2356; girl screams when she is r. but not so loud when she is raped J1174.3; merchant profits by being r. J1115.7.1; rich lord having r. poor widow of her cow chokes on first mouthful Q552.6; thief pretends to have been r. K401.4.

Robber, see also **Highwayman, Thief;** attempting to steal cow at night grabs tiger N392; bridegroom K1916; does penance Q520.2; or dog in church thought to be a ghost J1782.1; frightened off by parrot's cry K1796; helps king N884.1; innocent because he is merely following traditions of his ancestors J1179.4; persuaded to climb down the moon-beam *K1054; -proof house D2072.5.1. — Coward gloats over r. slain by another person W121.2.5; which was most generous, husband, r., or lover? H1552.1; giant r. with club G102; he who steals much called king: he who steals little called r. U11.2; king punishes r. violating safe conduct promise M203.1; man curious as to what a r. is going to do waits to intervene J2378; man scolds his ass and frightens r. away N612.1; meeting with r. band N765; old r. frees his three sons by relating frightful adventures R153.3.3; parable on r. plundering weak J133.6; paramour poses as r. K1517.8; snap of finger kills r. F628.2.8; treacherous r. partner K2296.1; Virgin Mary protects r. calling "Ave" V254.8; Virgin Mary supports r. on gallows V254.1.1; wild man son of woman and r. F611.1.4.

Robber's defense for stealing from rich J1269.8; false plea admitted: counter accusation J1162.2.

Robbers P475; commiserated J1392.2; frightened by dog B576.1.2; frightened from goods so that trickster can steal them K335.1; give hero sword J642.2; kill on new road J21.5.1; leave booty to temple idol K1971.14; mistake man for devil X424.1; share loot with simpleton L141.2; spade up saint's garden V222.16; vow to honor shrine V113.2. — Child abducted by r. R12.2.1; descendants of nine r. never to exceed nine M461; incognito king joins r. K1812.2; indentions on rock from weapons of r. A972.3.1.1; magic swine cause drowning of r. Q428.2; man escapes r. by promising to show treasure K567.2; man takes refuge from r. in an open grave J2311.3; overcoming r. H1162.1; overcoming r. suitor task H335.4.2; person deceives r., gets help K432; princess rescued from r. *R111.1.2; riches for helping against r. Q111.3; servants frighted by ferocious actions of r. K335.0.11; sham wise man accidentally unmasks r. K1956.1; sham wise man declares that r. committed the theft K1956.3; thumbling aids r. F535.1.1.11; wife scares r., says husband home D2031.6.3; wisdom from r. J178.

Robbers' heads cut off one by one as they enter house K912; plans overheard: owner warned N455.2. — Rescue from r. den R116.

Robbery. — Advice against r. of women alone J647.2; overheard boast about hidden money brings about r. N455.1; thief beaten for not giving r. warning J1191.6.

Robberies. — Devil agrees to help man with r. M212; Russians like r. A1674.2.

Robe "not too long or too short" J1161.8; for saint not wet by water F930.1.0.2. — Carrying live coals in r. without harm H221.1.1; clever minstrel gets new r. J1115.5.1; dagger cleaned on inside of r. A1599.7; extraordinary r. F821ff.; lawyer's r. stolen K362.9; magic r. *D1052; murder with poisoned r. S111.6; poor man's rich r. causes his jailing N347.5; resuscitation by magic r. E64.11; not to wear unauthorized sacred r. C51.2.1.

Robes. — Druids' white r. V131.2; fairies in long r. F236.2; raven steals r. of the Red Willow Men and finds them useless J2194; religious r. V131; symbolic interpretation of official r. H608.

Robert the Devil (birth) S223.0.1, (kills his wet-nurses) T614; of Sicily
*L411.

Robin steals fire, has breast scorched A2218.5. — Creation of r. A1914;
why r. has red breast A2221.2.2, A2353.2.

Roc (giant bird) *B31.1.

Rock, see also **Stone;** aflame at hero's death F960.2.3; bridge appears
for fugitives R246.1; changed into milk D476.1.7; of extraordinary
color F807; hurled down hill slays enemy K914.2; made repository of fire
A1414.7.2; produces wine D1472.1.2.2; pursues person D1431.1; refuses
to be moved D1654.1; in sea created by magic D2153.1; substituted for
ham K476.1.1; transformed to another object D452.1. — Adulteress
hurled from high r. escapes injury: she may not be punished again
J1184.1; battle marks in r. F1084.0.4; bear persuaded to slide down r.
wears off tail K1021.3; birth from r. T544.1; bleeding r. F991.5; breaking
huge r. to pieces (task) H1116; breaking off r. unearths mine N596.2;
cutting firewood from r. struck by lightning H1116.1; deer causes r. to
fly asunder D1552.9; dream of r.-casting contest D1731.3; dwarfs' r.-door
F451.4.3.1.1; falling asleep on r. which shoots upwards N314; giant
throws a great r. F531.3.2ff.; giant's hair grows into r. G122; holding
the r. K1251; huge r. columns combat each other, form earth's features
A901.2; magic r. *D931; noodles push parents over a r. as a favor to
them J2119.3; oath so great it splits r. M115.1.1; ogre clothed in r. G371.1;
ogre tied to r. G514.5; offended rolling r. C91.1; penance: staying on r.
in sea Q525.1; rain from striking r. D2143.1.7; refuge on r. in sea R316;
roc drops r. on ship B31.1.2; saint's bachall splits r. D1564.3; speaking r.
D1610.18; spirit-woman in r. G312.2; spring flows where saint smites r.
A941.5.1; stone from wictim's r. kills murderer Q582.3.1; striking certain
r. tabu C546; stroke of staff brings water from r. *D1567.6; strong man
moves enormous r. F624.2.0.2; urine softens r. D562.2.2; why sorrel grows
on certain r. A2771.7.

Rocks that clash together at intervals D1553; of one mountain enter caves
of another mountain F1006.4; falling together suggest intercourse J86;
moved by magic *D2136.1; open and close *D1552ff.; piled up to sky
F55.2. — Chaste woman promises herself to lover when r. leave coast
*M261; clashing r. test H1525; why coney lives among r. A2433.3.5;
extraordinary r. and stones F800ff.; helpful spirit warriors dwell in r.
and hills F450.1.1; origin of fire: children strike r. together A1414.3;
origin of r. A970ff.; saint prevents r. from falling D2149.4.1; saint's curse
splits r. D1792.1; saint's spittle splits r. D1564.2; sharp r. on otherworld path F151.1.6; strong man grinds huge r. F639.11; universe from
pre-existing r. A644; visit to lower world through opening r. *F92.3; water
becomes r. D478.12.

Rocking. — Chain tale: wormwood r. me to sleep Z41.7; chair r. by spirit
F473.2.1; witches r. chairs G249.11.

Rocky mountain F759.7.

Rod with alleged fishing magic K119.1.1; from magic hazel-tree kills snaked immediately D1402.10.2; transformed to serpent D441.7.1; used in saint's birth roots, becomes tree T584.0.5. — Chastity ordeal: passing under magic r. H412.1; divining r. locates hidden treasure D1314.2; doing penance till green leaves grow on dry r. Q521.1; dry r. blossoms F971.1; hunting wolves with r. and line X1124.4; magic r. *D1254.2, (produces love) D1355.16; magic wishing r. D1470.1.25; magic r. swallows other rods D1693; magic r. used for divination *D1311.15; making loom from a r. H1022.2.2; poet's r. P427.7.6; quest for magic iron r. H1342; transformation by touching with r. D565.2.

Rods. — Brass r. bitten, powdered in anger F639.10; silver r. cause magic sleep D1364.26.

Rodent gnaws away ladder to heaven A666.2; transformed to man D315. — Helpful r. B431; man transformed to r. D117.

Rodents. — Creation of r. A1840ff.; expensive extermination of r. J2103.

Rogue married with great pomp and celebration T135.0.1. — Condemned woman may be freed by marrying a r. P512; man called a r. by a nobleman makes a joke of the insult J817.1.

Roll. — Dead's name not on heavenly r. D586.4; devil shows priest long parchment r. of sins of congregation G303.24.1.1.

Rolled. — Stones can be r. up F809.9.

Rolling. — Animal occupation: r. A2457; fatal game: r. down hill on barrel K866; giant r. like wheel F531.6.17.6; god r. back primeval sea A816.3; ogre r. self in mat K711.3; pursuit by r. object R261ff.; pursuit of r. hoop leads to quest H1226.1; pursuit of r. cake leads to quest H1226; snake with tail in mouth r. like wheel B765.1; transformation by r. D561.1.

Roman fails to kill Hannibal P711.5. — Giant and wife build R. road F531.6.6.5.

Romans hate Jesus's poverty V385.

Rome hanging by thread (lie) X1561. — Animal journeys to R. B296.1; crawling to R. on knees as penance Q523.1; his father has been to R. J1274; Scipio saves R. from destruction P711.4.

Romeo and Juliet's self-poisonings T37.1.

Romulus and Remus L111.2.1, B535.

Roncevalles' horn calls aid of waiting soldiers R187.

Roof "has no eaves" H594.1; as refuge R335; spouts run with blood E761.1.11; taken off above sick man who cannot die E722.2.3. — Ass tries to jump on r. like ape J2413.2; captive knocks off prison r. R211.5; castle with silver (golden) r. F771.1.2.1f.; cow taken to r. to graze J1904.1; cure by putting children on r. D2161.4.11; devil in r. of church into which he thrusts voices of loud singers Q554.2; does not need r. when it is fair, cannot put it on when it rains J2171.2.1; fasting fool falls off r. J565.1, fox pretends to be holding up the r. and cannot help the bear K1251.1; lover caught in r. K1211.1; mountain-men throw person over church r.

F460.4.4.3; numskull ties rope to his leg as cow grazes on r. J2132.2; shading r. with carts J1879.1; stone-throw carries away r. F636.4.3; strong man throws trees on r. and breaks it F614.6; strong man's throw of stone carries away timber of r. F639.3; strong man on r. F639.8; stupid woman swims on the r. J1972; thatching r. with feathers H1104.1.2; turf from church r. gives clairvoyance D1323.7; women not to climb on r. C181.4; youth promises to marry old maid if she will sit all night on the r. X753.

Roofs. — Lie: r. on needle X1743.3.

Roofed. — King punished for failing to have monks' huts r. Q553.7.

Roofing over fog X1651.1. — Shortsightedness in r. J2171.2.

Rook. — Color of r. A2411.2.1.7.

Room heating in hell for certain person Q561.3. — Clearing out the r. J2465.5; corpse makes r. in coffin for friend E477; dwarf cave has large square r. with little doors leading to all sides F451.4.3.2; eating r-full of salt H1141.3; entrance into girl's (man's) r. by trick *K1340ff.; fairies' r. in hill F221.3; finding how many people are in dark, closed r. H506.2; ghost haunts r. E281.3; in hell one r. for dead, one for unborn, one for evil spirits A678; lover buys admission to woman's r. T45; magic needle transforms r. from plainness to beauty D1337.1.7; magic object found in underground r. D845; magic r. *D1141; no r. left for the feast J2178; parson tricked into giving up r. K2335; suitor tricked into r.: left alone K1218.13; treasure hidden in secret r. N517.1; washing the r. J2465.6; wild huntsman lives in r. on farm E501.15.8.

Rooms in otherworld dwellings F165.3; prepared in heaven for good man Q172.4.1. — Extraordinary r. *F781ff.; gourds with seven r. F813.5.1; porridge eaten in different r. J2167; seven r. in ascetic's house filled with extraordinary things F771.11.

Roost. — Long nose used as hen r. F543.1.2.

Rooster, see **Cock.**

Root of eternal youth D1338.2.2; transformed to person D431.9. — Why animals r. in ground A2477; conception from eating r. T511.2.0.1; demon lives at tree r. F402.6.1.1; incestuous youth reincarnated as r. E692.6; magic makes r. bitter D479.3; magic r. acquired by trickery D839.1; magic r. reveals truth D1316.12; magic r. snaps bar in two D1562.7; magic storm by pointing tree r. D2141.0.12; snow taken away by planting certain r. D2143.6.1; where is floor's r.? H883; youth asks for branch of tree; promised r. H611.

Roots hold land firm A857.3.1; of world-tree H619.3. — Dragon gnaws tree r. B11.6.9; magic r. *D967; man confined under r. of tree R45.1; numskull to water r. of tree J2126; origin of edible r. A2686.4; spring flows from tree r. F933.1.2; spring from r. of sacred tree shot by arrow A941.7.2; streams from r. of earth-tree A878.1.1; test of strength: pulling up tree by r. H1562.1; three wells under three r. of earth-tree A878.1.2; why banyan's r. hang down A2791.13.

Rooted. — Giant r. to ground, nails and hair grown into earth F531.1.6.9; staying r. to one spot while birds nest in hair Q541.5.

Rooting. — Contours of land from swine's r. A951.2.

Rope bridge to otherworld F152.1.5; cut almost in two so prisoner escapes K647; to lower world *F96; of chaff (sand) X1757; cut and victim dropped *K963; transformed to person D434.2; to upper world F51. — Ants carry silk threads to prisoner, who makes r. and escapes R121.4; bluff: animal shows r. as tail K1715.12; climbing into air on a magic r. D1582; climbing r. of excrement J2133.12; deceptive bargain: as much grain as will go in r. K174.1; drawing lover with single-thread r. H412.6; escape by tying r. to post K638; extraordinary r. F843; gallows r. breaks when innocent hanged H215.2; ghostly r. of suicide E538.2; hero tests r. on which he is to be pulled to upper world K677; magic r. *D1203; magic transportation by r. D1520.31; making a r. (of chaff) H1021.2, (of sand) H1021.1; man drawn up into female apartments on r. K1343; man will not lift knife to cut r. about to hang him W111.1.2; miser refrains from suicide: saves r. W153.7; mountain climber's r. cut K963.1; murderer escapes on sky r. R323.1; numskull catches buffalo by r. and is dragged to death J2132.1; numskull ties the r. to his leg as cow grazes on the roof J2132.2; obtaining bucket of well water without r. H1023.20; ordeal by r.-walking H225; parents rescue son from lower world on r. R153.1.1; ring turns to r. and robber is hanged M212.2; robber tries to pull up confederate on r., caught K434.2; saving by r. succeeds in well, fails from tree J2434; serpent acts as r. to collect wood B579.5; spying parent pulled up chimney on r. K1663; stealing only a small amount (r. with mare on the end of if) K188; threat to haul away the warehouse with r. K1745; threat to pull the lake together with r. K1744; watchman outwitted by having r. stretched across the road while fugitives escape K623.

Roper. — Lie: remarkable r. X1003.

Rosary identifies werwolf H64.2. — Disenchantment by r. D771.7; witch's r. consists of goat dung G243.2.1.

Rose as chastity index H432.1; from grave E631.1.2; grows from table F971.2; sheds petal whenever husband thinks of wife H1556.4.6; transformed to person D431.1.1; -water gives magic beauty D1337.1.8.1; — Adulteress pretends to faint when her husband strikes her with a r. K2051.2; banishment till r. grows from table for preventing childbirth Q431.4; conception from eating a r. T511.4.1; contest between r. and amaranth J242.1; digging r.-tree hole reveals treasure N534.7.1; magic r. *D975.2; man becomes r.-bush D213.2; marvelous sensitiveness (blister on back from lying in r. leaves) F647.9, (injury from r. leaves falling) F647.3; origin of r. A2656; origin of color of r. A2772.1; palace surrounded by rivers of wine, r.-water and honey F771.7; river of r.-water F771.2.4.1; transformation to r. D212.2; white r. the symbol of death Z142.1.

Roses fall from lips D1454.2.1; from lips as sign of royalty H71.4; lose thorns when saint walks on them V222.14. — Bringing r. in winter H1023.3; dawn reflection of r. of paradise A1179.2.1; meat becomes r. D457.5.1.

Rotating. — Circular house r. on cock's claw F771.2.6.1; kingship r. among brothers P17.4.

Rotting. — Calumniated corpse not r. H251.3.14; sea from r. snakes A924.2.

Rough treatment of object injures witch G275.13. — Disenchantment by r. treatment D710ff.; resuscitation by r. treatment *E10ff.; voice made r. by swallowing hot iron F556.1.

Round river: runs in circle X1547.1; well F718.2. — Devil as r. bowl G303.3.4.8; fairies' horses have r. shoes *F241.1.4; going r. and round fire marriage custom T135.10; marvelous runner can run r. earth in five minutes F681.5; why hog has r. snout A2335.4.2.

Rounds (stories which begin over and over again and repeat) Z17.

Round Table. — Finding Holy Grail before returning to R. M183.3; prophecy on end of R. M356.5; symbolism of R. Z162.

Rousing sham-dead with whip J2311.12. — Test of valor: r. servant's anger H1561.4.

Rout. — Soldier dies happy at enemy's r. P461.2.

Route. — Copper horseman indicates r. *D1313.3.

Roving. — Why women are r. A1372.3.

Rowan helps Thor out of river A2711.5; -sticks defeat devil G303.9.9.9, G303.16.4.3; -tree used to lay ghost E442.1; wood protects against witches G272.2.1.

Rower prefers to be stoned by his master rather than remain out in the storm J229.7. — Strong man as r. breaks boat F614.4.

Rowers pull in opposite directions J2164.1.

Rowing boat by magic D1523.2.8; contest won by deception K14. — Escape by r. boat stern foremost K534.4; shortsightedness in r. J2164.

Royal bride conducted by embassy to husband's kingdom T133.2; descendants as reward Q112.0.7; family as sacred V205; marriages with close relatives A1552.2. — Identification by r. garments H111.1; marriage by r. order T122; seating arrangements in r. hall A1539.1; sexual incontinence punished by extinction of r. line Q243.0.1; test of valor worthy for kingship: taking possession of r. insignia H1561.5; wild animal will not attack r. person B771.3.

Royalty, see also **King, Prince, Princess, Queen;** and nobility *P0—P99; unable to endure coarse entertainment U146. — Favor with r. induced by magic D1900.1; lowly person in love with r. T91.6.1; marks of r. H71; origin of r. A1653; phenomena at birth of r. F960.1.1; purple as r. symbol Z147.1; recognition of r. by personal characteristics H41ff.; tokens of r. left with exposed child S334.

Rubbed. — Eye must be r. before it can see F541.4; head of beheaded witch mends if r. with salt G223.

Rubber. — Origin of r. A1439.3.

Rubbing charm provides garments D1473.2. — Blindness cured by r. sand on eyes F952.3; disenchantment by r. D714, (with magic grease) D771.2; magic powers from r. D1734f.; resuscitation by r. bones on ground E29.2.

Rubbings. — Man created from r. of skin A1263.3.

Rubbish magically becomes food, clothing D2105.3.

Rübezahl (mountain and storm spirit) F465.

Ruby appears as charitable king blows nose V411.7; shatters for greedy lapidary D1641.14.1; transformed to person D432.3.1. — Bringing r. in serpent's head H1151.26; cup made of single r. J21.49; picking r. from trayful H1198; riddle involving r., nectar and faithless creature H587.1; speaking r. D1610.27.2; tortoise keeps r. from fowler K439.7.1.

Rubies baked in bread J1655.2; found in whirlpool D1467.2; as ransom for goose J514.6. — Blood transformed to r. D457.1.1; gathering necklace of r. from sea H1023.21; stream of r. flows through building F771.12; village where r. sell cheaply X1564.

Rudder. — Golden boat with copper r. F841.1.8.

Rudderless. — Embarkation in r. boat Q466.0.1; self-guiding r. boat D1523.2.7.1.

Rude retorts J1350ff. — "Never be r. to man of low birth" J21.52.2.

Rudeness to sacred person or thing forbidden C94ff.

Rue from drops of Christ's blood A2611.7; not a thing that is past J21.12; protects against evil D1385.2.2. — Magic r. D965.16.

Rug, see **Carpet.**

Rule must work both ways J1511. — Man created to r. the earth A1201; quest for lost ecclesiastical r. H1386.4; unsuccessful search for man who can r. his wife T252.1.

Rules. — Monk, merchant sticking to the r. J1638; prize for husband who r. his wife T252.4.

Ruler, see also **King;** angered by evil, placated by soft words J811.4; diverts attention from misgovernment by beginning a war K2381; forbids lovers to marry T87; learns lesson from uncharitable king J56.1; persecutes friends, kind to enemies W154.16; refuses spendthrift's hospitality J1566.2, should follow majority's advice J21.35; sent gems as wisdom test H501.1; too lazy to stop quarrels W111.5.7; vies with minister in generosity H1552.2. — Animal or object indicates election of r. H171; bad r., bad subject U210ff.; do not trust a r. who rules by reason alone J21.28; exiled king teaches r. wisdom J55; lady in love with r. T55.3; man patiently undergoing misfortune finally elected r. N251.1; old woman r. of the dead in lower world E481.1.1; poet puts r. out of countenance J1224.2; shepherd's life as preparation for r. P412.1.1; proud r. humbled L410ff.; repartee with r. *J1280ff.; transformation to likeness of r. D41.1;

treacherous r. delivers city to enemy K2364.3; ungrateful r. deposed
Q281.2; woman asks r. how to bear insults J1284.1.

Ruler's absurdity rebuked J1536. — Prophecy: r. death to insure victory
M362; smith sells secret for 100 crowns with r. likeness J1161.7.

Rulers of inferior character C938.

Ruling by reason alone untrustworthy J21.28. — Animals r. celestial
spheres B7.1; man r. all animals A1421.1.1; stepmother r. realm P282.1.

Rum as man's enemy J1319.1. — Salamander in r. drink G303.9.8.4; water
substituted for r. K231.6.2.1.

Rumination of animals A2472.

Rump. — King induced to kiss horse's r. K1288; lover given r. to kiss
*K1225; stick (leaf) thrown at animal's r.: hence tails A2215.1.

Rumpelstilzchen C432.1.

"Runs" within a tale Z14.

Runaway cavalry hero K1951.2; horse carries bride to her lover N721. —
Repartee concerning r. horses J1483ff.

Runes cause frenzy D1367.5. — Dwarfs cut r. F451.3.12.4; magic r.
*D1266.1.

Runner. — Fairy's skill as r. F273.2; marvelous r. F681ff.

Running from ghost J1495. — Brother is r. back and forth (plowing)
H583.3.1; buying foxes "as they're r." K196.1; cripples r. away from
shrine without crutches V113.1; devil cannot cross r. water G303.16.19.13;
fairy unable to cross r. stream F383.2; fawn, in spite of his horns, r. from
the dog U127; magic by r. through a hole *D1795; skillful barber shaves
r. hare F665.1; skillful flayer skins r. rabbit F664.1; skillful smith shoes
r. horse F663.1.

Rupee. — One r. to charity brings back ten Q44.3.

"Rupees make more rupees" J2489.12. — Magic coin fills bell with r.
D1452.5; sham miracle: r. turn to ashes K1975.2.

Ruse, see also **Trick, Trickery.** — Accidental cure by doctor's r. N648;
confession obtained by a r. J1141; detection through r. J1141.11; woman
won by r. K1302.

Rush transformed to leek C462.1, D451.2.1. — Why end of r. is black
A2721.1, A2772.2; Friar R. as mischief maker F470.0.1.

Rushes transformed to grain D451.2.1.1. — Lake where blind king plucks
r. A920.1.12; skillful marksman throws r. into a curtain F661.7.1; spring
flows where leper pulls out r. A941.5.3; uprooted r. reveal spring F933.5.

Rushing. — Priests r. through the mass J1263.1.3.1.

Russian calendar A1689.7.

Russians like thefts and robberies A1674.2; wear red shirts A1683.1.1. —
Why R. wear their shirts outside their breeches A1683.1.

Rustic. — Scholar disguised as r. K1816.0.4.

Rusting. — Life token: r. of object E761.4ff.

Rustling. — Ogre frightened at r. K2345.

Rusty. — Transformation to person of r. color D57.5.

Rye. — Origin of r. A2685.3; peasants fed white bread demand r. U135; sowing r., getting crop next day H1023.17; strong man lifts ton of r. F624.5; test of strength: breaking heavy glass blottle over a loaf of r. bread H1562.3.

Sabbath *V71ff.; -breaker A751.1.1; -keeping cow B259.2. — Breaking the s. forbidden *C631; devil appears to s. breakers G303.6.2.14; failure to observe s. punished Q223.6; fine for s.-breaking J1289.11; god names animals on first s. A2571.0.3; intercourse on s. night only T310.1.1; intercourse on s. tabu C119.1.2; mill refuses to work on the s. D1676; no punishment in hell on s. Q560.2.1; origin of s. A1541.4; ram swears on s. B211.1.1.1.1; removing silver tabu on s. F752.2.1; rescuers' s. J1613; reward for observing s. Q113.4.1; why powers of nature work on s. A1102; witch's s. G243.

Sabbatical fountain F716.1; river *D915.4.1.

Saber with king's name as token H86.1. — Magic s. *D1082; ring transformed to s. D454.8.2.1.

Sack, see also **Bag;** in giant's hand looks like pea F531.2.15. — Bad luck put into a s. N112.1; bees caught in s. which is opened at home J2131.2.1; casting into water in s. Q467.1; charcoal s. magically multiplies D2106.2; deceptive bargain: a s. of corn as reward K174; devil in church fills his s. with dissolute songs G303.24.1.5; dupe persuaded to take prisoner's place in a s. K842; filling s. full of lies (truths) H1045; heaven entered by trick: "wishing s." thrown in K2371.1.3; how much meal is in the s. J2062.1; inexhaustible wheat s. D1472.1.22.2; magic s. C521.1, *D1193; milk s. transformed D454.5f.; origin of insects: released from s. A2003; pious man hangs s. on sunbeam V29.3; priest drags heavy s., symbol of sin H606; recognition by cup in s. (alleged stolen goods) H151.4; soul in s. E711.5; suitor enticed into s., beaten by husband K1218.1.5; witch gets boy into s. K711.4; woman exchanges a horse for a s. of bones J2099.1.

Sacks. — Gold s. traded for rice s. J2093.5; slaves forced to carry earth in s. A1657.2.

Sackcloth. — Fasting in s. Q523.10.

Sacrament, see also **Eucharist, Host** *V30ff. — Administering s. destroys devil's power G303.16.5; disrespect for the s. J1261.2; friar seduces woman, claims administering s. K1354.2.2; ignorant priest forces rolls of cloth instead of s. down dying man's throat J1738.1; sick men die after they hesitate to take s. V39.8; Virgin Mary withdraws s. from a scoffer Q553.1; willing to receive water from leper, therefore must be willing to receive s. from unworthy priest J157.1.

Sacred animal unwittingly killed N361; animals B811, (branded) H55.2; fire V1.6.3.1; groves V114; healing stone D1500.1.2; persons *V200—V299; prostitution T457; relic as magic object D1296; relics protect against attack D1381.20; tree V1.7.1; wells V134. — Why animal is s. A2541ff.; death excluded from s. grove Z111.4; frog recovers s. Host

B548.5; ghosts summoned by opening s. book E383; oath taken on s.
object M114; origin of s. places A992; punishment for harming s. animal
Q228; sexual intercourse forbidden in s. precinct C116; trickster concealed in s. tree advises that he is to marry the princess K1971.10; woman
hidden in s. place R53.2.

Sacrifice of animals to dragon B11.10.0.1; consumed by heavenly fire
F962.2.1; drives devil away G303.16.19.16; equal to the reward J2067;
of human being to dragon *B11.10; made to free moon from sickness
A755.3.1; mixed with sage's blood K1673; of virginity T301. — Camel
induced to offer himself as s. K962; deceptive s. of nuts and dates
K171.3.1; earth reddened with blood of human s. A1241.4; earth by s. of
son and daughter of first couple A831.3; ghosts punish failure to s. to
them E246; man put in moon for disdainful s. A751.1.3; miser reducing
promised s. W153.14; monthly human s. to devastating fox B16.2.1;
mutual agreement to s. family members in famine K231.1.1; neglect to s.
punished Q223.3; refusal to make s. after need is past K231.3; reward
for religious s. Q21; self-s. W28; ship moved by s. D2136.8; smoke from
s. tabu for chief C564.5; substitute s. K1853; sun, moon as circles animated by human s. A714.8; sun from youth offered in s. A718.1; tabu to
kill animals for s. C92.1.0.1; tabu; neglect of s. to deity C57.1; trickster
eats s. offerings K254.2; wild huntsman pacified by s. E501.17.6.1;
woman drowns herself as s. to water-gods T211.1.1.

Sacrifices *S260ff.; at unearthing of treasure N554.1. — Cruel s. S200—
S299; druid performs s. P427.1; funeral s. A1547.1; ghosts killed by s.
E433.4.1; ghosts placated by. s. E433; ghost summoned by pouring blood
of s. into trench E382; magic results produced by s. *D1766.2; origin of
s. A1545; religious s. *V10ff.

Sacrificed. — Animals s. to provide food for dead E433.3; bird allowed to
sing before s. K551.3.7; bodily member s. to save life J351; deity saves
person to be s. S255; lamb prefers to be s. in temple rather than to be
eaten by wolf J216.2; man s. for breaking tabu C929.6; miracle must wait
till one man is s. K1785; moon from chest of s. youth A741.2; princess to
be s. to dragon H335.3.1; wealth of wife s. N531.5.

Sacrificial. — Escape from s. altar R175.1, rich man falls into s. grave
K1603.

Sacrificing animal with son's name K527.5; self to marry beloved T24.8.
— Dupe s. animal, gives it to trickster K158; friend s. life for other P316;
intemperance in s. J558; magic power from s. D1736.1; power of wild
hunt evaded by s. to huntsman's dogs E501.17.4.3; woman s. self to save
beloved T89.2; women s. in temple tabu C181.12.

Sad. — Why animal is s. A2521.

Sad-faced princess F591, H341.

Saddle. — Ass deprived of his s. J1862; balancing s. load with rock
J1874.2; enemies heads hung on conqueror's s. S139.2.2.1.4; extraordinary
s. F868; fortune from informing foreign king of use of s., bridle, and stir-

rups N411.3; lost ass, s., and bridle offered as reward to the finder
J2085.1; magic s. *D1209.2; man freezes to s. (lie) X1606.2.1.

Saddled. — Being s. as punishment Q493; horse must agree to be s. and
bridled to secure man's help K192.

Sadhu as helper N844.1; a thief K2058.1.

Sæhrimnir A661.1.0.3.

Safe provision for life not to be lightly surrendered J705. — Belongings
s., no white man near J1373; champion grants enemies s. convoy W11.5.10;
king carries out s. conduct promise M203.1; soul hidden in s. E712.2.

Safety in shadow of wall N253. — Animal allows himself to be tied to
another for s. K713.1.2; captive sends token of s. H85; charm gives s. on
journey D1384.3; country mouse prefers poverty with s. J211.2; dream
tells of person's s. D1810.8.2.4; plainness with s. or grandeur with danger
J212; umpiring dispute in exchange for s. guarantee M222.

Sage aids quest H1233.3.3; curses city M411.24; sees worm in loaf
. F642.3.2; as villain K2286. — Blood of s. mixed into sacrifice K1672;
quest to distant s. for advice H1393; wisdom (knowledge) from s. J152.

Sages. — Couple live with s. in Great Bear A761.2; youth educated by
seven s. J141.

Sago palm's abundant sap A2791.10. — Why fruit of s. palm looks like an
eye A2791.9; why s. bears fruit from the stem A2771.3.

Sail. — Bronze s. F841.2.5; tin s. F841.2.6.

Sails. — Color of s. on ship as indication of good or bad news Z140.1;
ghost s. over sound on bundle of straw E581.7; making s. for ship from
one bundle of linen H1022.3.

Sailing against contrary conditions D1520.15.1; in leaky boat without
sinking D2121.13. — Demon ship s. against wind F411.3; ghost s. on
straw E581.7; man building boat and s. about in giant's belly F911.5.1;
selling soul for s. through sky M211.6.

Sailor offers saint a candle as large as a mast K231.3.1; prays ship sink,
since gods never answer J1467.1. — Returning s. told fine house and
child God's bounty J1279.2; treacherous s. K2259.4.

Sailors rescue abandoned child R131.14; rescue hero R169.12. — Flying
Dutchman has dead men as s. E511.2.1; ghost hurts s. E271.1; goddess of
s. A456.1; mother sells her child to heathen s. S328; phantom s. E510ff.;
Virgin Mary protects s. V282.

Sailors'. — Ship in storm saved because of s. "Ave Maria" V254.2.

Saint *V220ff., V221ff. (see these numbers for many additions to references
given here); as ball player F697.2; calls fish from lake D2105.5; causes
druids to bless D2076; chooses early death J216.6; controls animals
D2156.2.1ff.; cures blind hyenas B384; and devil (binds devil with hair)
D1831.3, (battles Lucifer at world's end) A1082.6, (dispels pagan devils)
V356.1, (renders pacts with devil ineffective) M218.1; drives chariot over
displeasing person Q227.3; effects magic, miracles (magic beautification)
D1864, (boat's course changed) T321.6, (boy created from blood-clot)

T541.1.1.1, (canal dug with tree roots) D2121.14, (crime magically detected) D1817.2f., (chant kills animal) D1445.3, (crozier falls from heaven) F962.12.1, (death of person delayed) D1855.3, (demons flee stone) F405.10, (closed doors passed through) F694, (door, lock magically opens) D1557.1, (dumbness cured) F954.2.2, (earth scratched, treasures appear) D2157.1.1, (epidemic ended by fasting) D2162.1, (fluid carried in broken container) F866.7.2, (food leaves clothing unspoiled) F1091, (journey with magic speed) D2122.5, (huge load carried) D1691.1, (magic journey over water, bog) D2125.0.2ff., (poison unharmful) H1573.3.1, (magic sleep induced) D1964.5, (song silences hound) D1442.5, (spearhead removed) F959.3.4.1, (stone set afire) D2158.1.2, (fiery sword comes between enemy king and queen) D2196, (magic thirst caused) D2063.3.1.1, (thunderbolt produced) D2149.1, (pagan tree falls through fasting) P623.0.5, (virtue finds lost articles) N211.1.0.1, (miraculous visions) V513, (water produced from tree) D927.1.1, (well produced) D926.1.1; exposes self to temptation for greater reward in heaven T335; flogs tempting woman T331.6; forced to return to monastery walks in backwards K2312.2; gives calf to wolf W10.2; gives liberally to gambler, little to beggar J225.6; goes to heaven each Thursday A182.3.0.3.1, Q172.8.1; leaves order for music V475.4; as matchmaker T53.3; and nature phenomena (cloud evoked) D2147.3, (cold water warmed) D2144.3.1, (fog dispelled) D2143.3.1, (icicles burn) F962.9, (lake dries up) D2151.7.1, (river brings object) F932.5.1, (river frozen in summer) D2151.2.4, (river ford created) F932.10, (sea doesn't encroach upon grave) F931.3, (sea leaves cowl untouched) F930.1.0.1, (sea rises) F931.1.1, (spring where water spilled) F933.1.1, (spring follows) D927.4, (spring, fountain produced) A941.5ff., F932.3, (much water confined in small ditch) D491.3, (waves don't touch) D2151.3.2, (wells caused to fail) D2151.6.1, (winds controlled) D2142.0.2; offered any gift chooses wisdom L212.1; overpowers sea monster B877.1.2; perceives chest D1810.0.3.1; performs miracles while yet unborn H579.5; plucks out eye to avoid marriage T327.3; possessed by gluttony F496.1; prays with woman, learns she is his sister N734.2; prefers to die in exile Q431.0.1; prevents abduction of fairy F389.2; propounds riddles H540.4; proves power of Christianity (horse miraculously preserved) H1573.3.2, (man unharmed by fiery furnace) H1573.1.4, (by transformation) H1573.3.3, (wizard burned) H1573.3.4; as riddle solver H561.10; silent by holding stone in mouth V73.6.2; sleeps with maidens without sin T331.7; suckled by wolf T611.10.2; and symbolism of full milk cup H607.4; threatens to take homicide's place in hell W28.4; wins soul in dice game E756.4.1; in womb renders woman invisible D1361.39; wrests soul from demons E756.4. — Angel reveals relics to s. V140.1; angels singing for s. V234.1; animal deluded by s. B256.0.1; animals aid s. (fly warns against devil) B483.0.1, (hawk carries off hand of displeasing man) F982.3, (hogs root gold) B562.1.1, (lion protects body) B773.3, (oxen carry) B557.2, B256, (tiger carries wood)

B292.11, (whale fights pursuing monster) B523.2; animals from parts of
body of deity or s. A1725; angels entertained unawares (hospitality to
disguised s. rewarded) Q45.1; attempt to give s. poison H1515.2; beast
invokes protection of s. B251.4.1; benevolence of s. (aids man to sleep with
princess) K1915.2, (bestows beauty) D1862.2, (bestows father's goods on
poor) V437, (bestows immortality) D1851.3, (bestows invulnerability)
D1846.5, (charity shown) V433, (feeds two youths) V73.3, (gives credit
for good deeds to another) Q42.8, (has tribute remitted) K2314, (heals
enemy) V441.1, (helps gambler) N6.3, (hides fugitive from king underground) K2319.3, (wins over pagan priest with kind words) L350.2,
(never drives fly from face) W10.1, (murderer offered refuge) R325.3,
(souls asked to be released from hell) Q174.1.1, (sinner's punishment
shared) V414, (child suckled) T611.5, (another's danger assumed) P319.8,
(sick man's pain assumed) D1500.3.3; cow follows s. B159.3; daily visit
to s. C687.1; dead s. (body moves in grave to face north) E411.0.8, (corpse
sits up from open grave) E235.8, (exonerates cleric) E376.1, (in grave
makes room for pious man) Q147.1, (returns from dead to give blessing)
E367.2; (returns from dead to preach of heaven and hell) E367.1; dying
s. leaves wise message J154.1; extraordinary phenomena at anger of s.
F960.4; flower from land of promise appears to s. F979.10; gate lets s.
through D1552.6; God speaks to s. A182.3.0.2, hospitality to s. repaid
Q45.1.3; humility before s. in disguise Q66.1; infant s. rebukes mother
T585.4; ladder symbol of s. Z139.7.1; magic lime tree distills sustenance
for s. D1472.1.3.1; mill symbol of s. Z185; phenomena when remains of s.
moved F960.8; princess marries s. T121.5.1; prophecy: unborn child to
be s. M311.3; punishment for opposition to saint (for jeering) Q559.5,
(beheading for turning back) Q421.2, (transformation for denouncing)
D661.2; sacrifice to s. V11.8; salmon caught out of season for s. F986.2;
sham s. (bear mistaken for s.) J1762.2.1, (hypocrite acclaimed) U116,
(jackal) K1961.1.5.1, (seduction by posing as s.) K1315.6.4, (wife's maids
disguised) K1827.1; shame's effect on s. F1041.23; stone on which s. born
detects perjury H251.2.3; tabu: violating refuge with s. C51.2.5; test of
s. H257; time flies as s. preaches D2011.1.2; marvelous light reveals man
hiding from s. F969.3.1.

Saint's *V220ff., *V221ff.; anger produces extraordinary nature phenomena F960.4; birth (dry rod blossoms) F971.1.1, blood covenant with
animals P312.0.1; body (blood cures) D1500.1.7.3.2, (blood restores
speech) D1507.6, (face radiant) F574.3.1, (breath causes drunkenness,
death) D1500.4.2.1f., (head, tears, produce fountain) D925.1.1f., (hand
lights darkness) D1478.1, (magic from name) D1766.7.3, (shadow cures)
D2161.4.15, (tears effect conception) T512.4, (tooth luminous) F544.3.2.1,
(teeth give off sparks) F544.3.2, (voice heard from distance) F556.4; curse
M411.8, (stops army) D2091.13, (splits rocks) D1792.1; death (rainbow
appears from monastery to heaven) F960.2.2; hymn to free himself from
wife T253.3; land bargain: staff touching island wins K185.13; mother

admitted to heaven Q172.8; motives maligned on entering brothel N347.2; possessions have magic power (bachall defaces idol) V356.3, (bell gives weakness) D1336.5, (bell carried on floating stone) D1524.3.2, (bell heard, never found) K1887.3, (book brings victory) D1381.25, (cloak reveals rewards of heaven) D1329.1, (cure disease) D1500.1.13, (cowl protects fox) D1447.2.1, (holy water makes fairy vanish) F379.4, (magically transported) D2136.5, (Pater Noster outweighs ox) V52.13, (relics recovered) V140.2, (relics transformed) D457.16.1, (staff determines island's ownership) D1524.1.2.1, (sword sacred) D1400.1.4.1.1, (tunic doesn't burn) F964.2; prayer wins battle D2163.5ff.; prophecy on successor D1812.5.0.7.2; vision of three cities in heaven A661.1.2. — Animal eating s. body stricken Q558.11; contest in lifelike painting: fly on s. nose H504.1.1; corpse leaps at s. passing E597; fasting to enforce s. dues P623.0.6; future greatness if s. will followed M310.1.1.1; gospel hung from s. shoulders F1011.1.1; homage to s. bell C94.8; idols found on faces after s. arrival V347; land purchase: as much as s. hood covers K185.4.1; milk from s. cows forms lake F989.9; oath taken on s. hand M116; prayer at s. flagstone V52.7; punishment for looking at s. corpse Q227.2; sham miracle: s. statue raises arm K1972.1; tree grows through s. bell F979.6; thunderbolt prevents intimacy of s. communities F968.2.

St. Andrew A1372.10.

St. Anthony's pigs B256.2, Q228.

St. Cecilia D1840.1.3.

St. Christopher Q25; and the ass J1269.9.

St. Colum K11, V515.1.3.

St. Eligius J2411.2.

St. Eugenia K1837.7.

St. Francis J1261.8.

St. George's precept to poor man J556.1; wolves K1725.

St. Isaac G303.2.5.2, S263.2.1.

St. John the Baptist compared with St. John the Evangelist J466.2. — Feast of S. A1002.1, V70.3.1.

St. John Damascene V256.3.

St. John the Divine F451.5.9.4.

St. John the Evangelist J466.2.

St. John's night. — Dew falling on S. restores sight D1505.5.2.1; fairies emerge on S. F211.1.1.2; fern blossom on S. D965.14; wild hunt appears on S. E501.11.1.3.

St. Loy J2411.2.

St. Martin. — Jesus appears to S. V411.8; nun refuses see S. T362.1.

St. Nicholas brings Christmas gifts N816; saves girl from slavery R165.1; steals bread V412.1.

St. Nicholas' song drives off fairies F382.5.

St. Oswin D1505.12.

St. Patrick. See under **Patrick.**

St. Peter. See under **Peter.**

St. Theodora Q537.1.

St. Thomas' Day E587.2.1.

St. Valentine B232.1.

St. Veronica's napkin F950.1, V121.

Saints *V220ff., *V221ff.; confirm covenant by cutting off thumbs M201.4; exchange bachalls P311.7; have visions of heaven V511.1.1; as prophets M301.5; sacrifice themselves S263.5.1.— Deceiving the s. K2371; devil tempts s. G303.9.4.6; fasting against s. P623.0.4; Irish s. Z71.1.8ff.; land of the s. A661.0.10, V511.4; prophecy: boys to be fathers of s. M312.6; transformation combat between s. D615.5.

Saja. — Burning s. wood tabu C514; why s. bark is white A2751.4.4; why s. tree has knots A2755.4.1; why s. tree has no sap A2755.2.1.

Salad. — Poisoned s. kills faithless wife Q418.1; woman gives a jewel for a s. J2093.2.

Saladin asks to become Christian V331.7.

Salamander enters barefoot person B784.1.8; in rum drink G303.9.8.4; subsists on fire B768.2. — Creation of s. A2148.2; mythical s. B99.1; riddle about s. H842.2.

Salamander's magic blood D1382.13; blood quenches fire D1566.2.7.

Sale to animal (or object) J1850ff.; of worthless articles K110—K149. — Protean s. D612; sacrament for s. J1261.2.1.

Salesman guarantees sow to bear male, then female, then kid X1233.4.1.

Saliva, see also **Spittle.** — Fairies made visible through use of s. F235.4.5; healing power of saint's s. D1500.1.7.2.1; magic circle of s. kills dragon D1402.14.

Salmon appears every seventh year F986.3; caught out of season for saint F986.2; of knowledge B124.1.1, F162.5.3; as oldest and wisest of animals B124.1; transformed to person D376. — Catching s. proof of virginity H411.16; disenchantment by eating s. D764.3; eating magic s. gives knowledge M315; giant s. B874.4; hawk transformed to s. D413.1; helpful s. B474; king of s. B243.2.1; magic s. carries hero over water *B175.1; man transformed to s. D176; origin of flat body of steel-head s. A2305.1.1; origin of s. A2125; reincarnation as s. E617.1; soul hidden in apple in s. E713.1; stones from transformed s. A977.5.2; how s. swims A2444.3; transformation: hawk to s. D413.1; transformation: s. to child D374; why s. has purple belly A2412.4.2.1; why s. has tapering tail A2378.9.1.1.

Salt bullet kills witch D1385.4.1; under chair prevents witch's rising G254.2; exorcises witch G271.3; food without drink as punishment Q501.7.1; given Death's messengers Z111.6.2; of hospitality P321; to keep people clean A1372.10; powerful against fairies F384.1; protects against witches G272.16; in saltless land sold for fortune N411.4; transformed to stone *D471.5. — Acquisition of s. A1429.4; why animals eat everything without s. A2435.2.1; bird nest of s. J2171.5; burning s. love

charm D1355.3.7; dried snow sold for s. X1653.3; dupe persuaded to
over-s. food K1045; dupe rubs s. on wounds K1045.2; dwarfs dislike
bread baked without s. F451.3.7.2; eating roomful of s. as task H1141.3; effects of wild hunt remedied by asking the huntsmen for s. E501.19.2; enigma
on s. as only food H588.21; fool liking s. decides to eat nothing else
J2524; giant turns to s. F531.6.12.3; head of beheaded witch mends if
rubbed with s. G223; lazy ass loaded with s. and then with sponges J1612;
literal host serves bread and s. J2476; load of s. melts in rain (flying
contest) K25.2; love like s. H592.1; magic s. *D1039.2; man becomes s.
D241; man says his s. is stones: it becomes so Q591.2; man on sinking
ship eats s. J861.2; monkeys steal tortoise's s. K343.4; murder by throwing
s. in eyes K957.1; origin of s. springs A942.2; person with animal in
stomach fed s. B784.2.1; reincarnation as s. E642.0.1 why sea is s. A1115;
why sea stinks when it is full of s. J2371.2; self-grinding s.-mill
*D1601.21.1; sleeping on s. gives thirst for a week J1322.2; sowing s. to
produce s. J1932.3; spilling s. brings bad luck N131.3; stone becomes s.
D452.1.3; tabu to eat s. C229.6; thumb cut and s. put on it in order to
remain awake H1481; too much s. in food of giant makes him go outside
for water K337; transformation to pillar of s. for breaking tabu C961.1;
washing s., it melts away J2173.9; why s. disappeared from forests A1196;
witches lack bread and s. G229.3; wolf scorns s. meat in false expectation
of other booty J2066.4.

Salting man's flayed back S114.2; skin prevents witch's reentering
G229.1.1. — Victim enticed into drinking by over-s. food K839.3.

Salty water turns into fresh D478.10. — Mankind from s. stone licked by
cow A1245.4.

Salvatio Romae D1323.4.1.

Salvation *V520ff. — Letter of s. given from grave E373.3; since s. predestined, asceticism useless V462.0.2.

Salve, see also **Ointment.** — Magic s. *D1244; person enchanted by witch's
s. so as to be ridden by witch G241.2.2.

Same. — All children born s. day as prince become his companions P32.1;
buying s. article several times over K258.2; disease cured by s. thing that
caused it D2161.4.10ff.; effects of wild hunt remedied by seeing it a year
later in s. place E501.19.1; prophecies about children born at s. time
M369.8; sowing and reaping s. day F971.7.

Samhain festival V70.5.

Sample. — Injunction: to give s. of food to dog before eating C685.

Sampo F871.

Samson makes water flow from jawbone D925.1.3. — Feast gives S. riddle
clue H565.1; riddle about S. and Philistines H831.

Sanctified — Angel brings about reburial in s. ground V244.

Sanctity of saints V229.2. — Books' s. tested in water H222.4; books' s.
tested in fire H221.1.3; long beard and s. J1463; woman dies when spoiled
of s. T312.1.

Sanctuary. — Escape by taking s. in church R325; punishment for desecrating s. Q411.11.1; treasure hidden in s. N514.1; tabu: unworthy to enter, see s. C51.1.9.

Sand instead of sandalwood for bathing J1511.2.1; mass advances upon city Q552.14.3; permits walking on water D1524.1.4; transformed to rice D452.3.1, D476.1.11. — Binding together s. and string as punishment Q512.2; bird carries a grain of s. from a mountain each century (illustration of eternity) H701.1; blindness cured by rubbing s. F952.3; canoe of s. J2171.1.3.1; city buried in s. F948.5; cooking in hot s. H506.9; demon eats s. F171.8; devil piles s. in ocean so that vessels may run aground G303.9.9.5; earth from s. strewn on primeval water A814.2; eye sockets filled with s. S165.4; food in s. J1924; fortune told by cutting s. D1812.3.2; God throws s. on lazy shepherds (origin of insects) A2005; magic s. *D935.1; making rope of s. H1021.1; man made from s. sprinkled with water A1241.2; marking place in the s. J1922.3; numskulls count selves by sticking their noses in s. J2031.1; ogre teaches smith how to transform s. in his smithy G651; origin of hill: everybody passing by brings s. A963.7; as many stars in heavens as grains of s. H702.1.

Sandal. — Bill of sale on s. F1015.3; prophecy: death from hands of man with one s. M341.2.9.1.

Sandals. — Magic s. *D1065.5; magic from loosing s. D1782.3.1.

Sandalwood brings high price where it is lacking N411.5; tree guarded by dragon B11.6.10. — House of s. F675.3; origin of s. tree A2681.7; praying for raja's death so s. will be sold W153.13; sand substituted for s.; substitute pay J1511.2.1.

Sandhill surrounds lover F969.6.

Sandpiper. — Creation of s. A1944; why s. fights A2524.2.

Sandpipers' — Annoyance of s. chirp J215.1.4.

Santa Claus, see also **St. Nicholas;** as bringer of Christmas gifts N816.

Santals eat hare's entrails A1422.1.1.

Saora wave weapons, shout while dancing A1689.4; women's earrings C181.9.

Sap. — Earth-tree furnishes health-giving and hunger-satisfying s. A878.4; fig tree rewarded with s. of all other trees A2711.7; magic plant-s. D974; origin of blood-colored s. in trees A2721.2.1, A2755.2; sago palm's abundant s. A2791.10; why s. comes from top of palm A2791.8; why the saja tree has no s. A2755.2.1.

Sapling. — Recognition by unique ability to bend s. H31.5.

Sapphire gives magic sight D1331.1.5.1. — House of s. F771.1.5.2; magic s. cures disease D1500.1.9.1; tremendous s. F826.4.

Sapphires. — Book of s. F883.1.5.

Sarai. — Quest for s. flower H1333.5.2.

Sardine. — Man becomes s. D179.3.

Saree. — Hero climbing up girl's s. killed N339.11; quest for s. for queen H1355.2.

Satan, see also **Devil,** *G303ff.; attempts to create another world A63.8; disguised as deer K1823.5; forks soul from body E722.2.4; jealous of Adam A63.5.1. — Demons help S. G302.9.5; devil in serpent form tempts first woman (S. and Eve) A63.6; dialogue between Christ and S. V211.7.2; fall of S. from heaven A106.2.2; father hides son from S. R153.3.6; God conquers S. at world's end A1082.5.

Satans. — Boy who has newer seen a woman: the S. T371.

Satchels. — Falling of s. evil omen D1812.5.1.26.

Satiated. — Coming neither hungry nor s. H1063.

Satin. — Wearing s. tabu C878.1.

Satire M402; causes face ulcers D1402.15.3; as punishment Q499.4. — Magic s. *D1275.4, (as curse) D2175.3, (causes king to waste away) D1402.15, (causes man to melt) D1402.15.1, (kills animals) D1445.4, (makes land sterile) D1563.2.3, (raises blotches on face) D1403.1; man dies as result of magic s. D1402.15.2; origin of s. A1464.3; punishment for s. Q265.2.

Satirist. — Poet as s. P427.4; saint limits s. V229.6.1; woman s. M402.1.

Satisfaction. — Feeding ravenous beast to s. H1123; fool regrets that he has not eaten seventh cake first since that was the one that brought s. J2213.3.

Satisfied. — Refusing to pay for woman's favors: not s. K1353.1.

Saturday. — Jewish automaton will not work on S. V71.1; knockers refrain from work on S. F456.1.2.3.3; souls released from hell every S. Q560.2.2; why sun shines on S. A1177.

Saturn swallows stone instead of Jove G11.0.1.1.

Satyr B24; reveals woman's infidelity B24.1. — Revelations of a s. U119.1; wild man son of woman and s. who overpowers her F611.1.3.

Saucepan. — Man transformed to s. D251.1.

Saucer. — Devil has s. eyes G303.4.1.2.4; does s. protect the ghee? J2062.2.

Sausage mistaken for animal J1771.2; rain J1151.1.3; as revolver scares off robber K437.3. — Fool unacquainted with s. J1732.1; mountain-men make s. of Christans F460.4.4.4; mouse, bird, and s. keep house together J512.7; sale of a s. filled with blood K141; sending back s. skins for refilling W152.14.2; sexton's dog steals s. from parson's pocket X411.1; thumbling in s. F535.1.1.8.

Save it for the beggar C490.1.1. — Animals s. person's life *B520ff.; darkness comes in daytime in order to s. life of maiden about to be executed F965.1; transformation to s. D666.

Saved by mere luck N141; souls E754ff. — Boy doomed to die miraculously s. Q27; condemned soul s. E754.1ff.; heretic s. from fire by devil G303.22.13; kingdom s. by wisdom of hidden old man J151.1; life s. by accident N650ff.; man promises to built church if he is s. at sea M266; man s. from death sentence by animal B522; man s. by enemy W11.5.7; one s. from the devil by prayer to Virgin G303.16.2.2; stolen woman s. from trolls' dance F455.6.6.1.

Saving girl's life with marvelous things H355.0.1; life by guessing troll's name H516; the promised child S250ff.; provision tabu C785; by rope: succeeds in well, fails from tree J2434; from soldiers by receiving them joyfully rather than fearfully K2361. — Children s. parents from hell P241.1; citizen s. country's honor P711.3; extraordinary companion s. hero F601.4.2; fairy grateful for s. family F337; mortal s. fairy's life, sleeps with her F304.5; princess as prize for s. country T68.3; servant s. master H187; son s. kingdom F611.4; woman sacrifices self s. beloved T89.2; wraith s. person's life E723.1.1.

Savings. — Giving s. away: double return for charity J2489.6.

Savior, see **Christ.**

Saw for coffin-making announces death D1322.1; invented by devil A1446.1; in vagina F547.5.8. — Giant with teeth like those of s. F531.1.6.2; ship built with a wooden s. J2171.1.1.

Sawdust. — Quest for s. H1378.1.

Sawed. — Boat for rowing contest already s. through K14; captive soldier s. in two P461.3; legs of table s. so that it collapses K1431; sham parson: the s. pulpit K1961.1.3.

Sawing iron tree H1115.2; leg off by mistake J2131.3.3; in two as punishment Q469.8.

Sawmill. — Lie: remarkable s. operator X1082.1.

Scab. — Magic s. (from skin) *D1009.1.

Scabbard. — Magic s. D1101.5.

Scaffold. — Man suddenly acquires long gray beard on s. at execution F1044.

Scaffolding. — Builders throw away beams from the s. until it all falls down J2171.3.

Scald-crow. — Tabu to kill s. C92.1.5.

Scald-head disguise K1818.2.

Scalding to make dupe strong K1012.2; as punishment Q469.10. — Dupe s. self to learn languages K1046; endurance test: s. mush scatters on heroine's naked body H1503; making the dupe strong by s. K1012.2; murder by s. K955.1; numskull s. children J2175.5.

Scalds. — Charm for s. D1503.3.1.

Scales of dragon B11.2.10; test of witch H234; with wind as beams, heat as pans H1022.9. — Coin left in money s. betrays secret wealth N478; creator distributes s. A1440.1; fortune's s. to weigh man N111.3.2; giant with dragon s. for feet F531.1.3.1; origin of fish's s. A2315; thief's money s. borrowed J1141.6.

Scandal-mongering punished Q314. — Man never listens to s. W23; marriage to avoid s. K1383.

Scapular. — Disenchantment by s. D771.7.

Scar. — Recognition by s. H51.

Scars. — Hands with s. as suitor test H312.4.1; wounds cured by saint leave no s. V221.8.

"Scar-face" as hero L112.6.

Scarcity of real friends J401.

Scarecrow. — Queen used as s. Q482.5.

Scarification. — Conception from s. T537; invisibility by s. D1985.1.

Scaring. — Fairies s. off treasure seeker F244.4; fools s. one another J2632; ghost s. thief E293.1.

Scarlet thread as death omen J2311.1.4.

Scattered. — Bringing back flour s. by wind (task) H1136.1; mountains from s. parts of serpent's body A961.4; skillful marksman shoots eggs s. over table F661.4; skillful tailor sews together s. planks in capsizing boat F662.2; tools s. at night by witch G265.1.

Scattering. — Bride s. presents T136.4.3.

Scavenger carrying wood bad omen D1812.5.1.29; unwittlingly eats human noses G63.

Scavenger's — Royal couple reborn as s. children Q551.5.1.2.

Scene. — Ghosts haunt s. of crime, sin E334.1.

Scent, see also Odor, Perfume; of flowers from magic laughter D1773.1; of rice identifies children H49.1. — Why animals s. from distance A2475; man's body exudes sweet s. F595; rice with remarkable s. F815.4.1; why some flowers have no s. A2795.1.

Scenting. — Animal useful because of s. power A2512.

Scepters. — God's s. A156.3.

Schlaraffenland *X1503.

Scholar disguised as rustic K1816.0.4; given nonexistent egg he has proved to be there J1539.2. — Devil appears to s. G303.6.2.10; fox disguised as s. K1822.2; many books do not make a s. U111.

Scholars. — Jokes on s. X370ff.

School of animals B234. — Progress in s. (at devil and all his works) J1487; seven years s. course Z72.4.

Schooling. — After one day of s. children to cease associating with unlearned J977.

Schoolmaster. — Ogre s. G11.9.

Schoolmasters ignorant of Latin J1741.

Schrätel und Wasserbär K1728.

Science of reincarnation E600.2. — Dream advises against popularizing s. J157.3; theological questions answered by propounding simple question in s. J1291.2.

Sciences. — Origin of s. A1487.

Scientific. — Absurd s. speculations J2371ff.; absurd s. theories J2260—J2299; pseudo-s. methods of detecting J1142.

Scipio saves Rome P711.4.

Scissors drip blood (life token) E761.1.7.2. — Capturing magic pig carrying s., comb, and razors between its ears H1154.1; magic s. *D1183; obstinate wife: cutting with knife or s. T255.1.

Scoffers turned to stone Q551.3.4.1. — Miraculous manifestations to s. of the Cross V86.4.

Scoffing. — Punishment for s. at church teachings *Q225.

Scolded. — Boys s. to conceal their identity K649.3; dwarf is insulted when s. F451.3.6.1; mortals s. by dwarfs F451.5.2.9.

Scolding contest H507.5; drowning child instead of helping him J2175.2; priest says he is merely trying to get even for all the scolding he must undergo J1269.4; punished Q304; supernatural wife forbidden C31.4.2. — Transformation by s. D527; wild hunt frightened away by s. E501.17.8.1.

Scorching. — Animal s. self while putting out fire A2218.1.1; ghost s. hat E542.4; sinners in hell alternately s. with heat, cold Q562.1.

Scorn of unloved suitor punished T75.1. — Caesar's s. of his wife's advice leads to disaster J155.3; illness from shame of s. F1041.9.3; stag's s. of his legs L461.

Scorned hero saves king L154; lover T70ff.; princess sets task H933.4; suitor consoles self J877. — Fairy avenges self on man who has s. her love F302.3.3; wise man's advice s. J2051.

Scorning. — Death for s. deity A1335.6; giantess's son s. father P233.3.1; prince marries, punishes s. girl T72.2.1; son chastizes father for s. mother P233.9; unpromising hero kills those s. him L156.

Scorpio. — Origin of S. A777.

Scorpion bites as punishment: brings poor man fortune N426; in spite of himself, stings the turtle carrying him across the stream U124; scoops out men's eyes B17.2.4.1. — Giant s. B873.2; origin of s. A2092; reincarnation as s. E629.1; woman reborn as s. E693.3.

Scorpions in hell A671.2.9. — Army of snakes, s. B268.7.1; ascetic sees s. as gold D1825.8; money of hard-hearted transformed to s. D444.1; ornaments of s. F827.3.

Scotland. — One foot in Ireland, one in S. K2319.1.

Scotsman mistakes moose for mouse J1759.1.

Scott. — Michael S. extends river's tide G303.9.2.5.

Scourging. — Angel s. mortal V245.1.

Scout. — Creator sends crow to s. for earth nucleus A812.3; vulture as s. after world-fire A1039.1.

Scouts. — Birds as s. B563.6; bird s. sent out from ark A1021.2; parrots as s. B122.8.

Scraping. — Thrifty s. of tray as bride test H381.2.2.

Scrapings. — Plant from s. of princesses' bodies H522.2.

Scraps. — Negroes made from left-over s. at creation A1614.5.

Scratch. — Deceptive agreement not to s. H1184, H263; hen put in witch's hair to s. while maid escapes G276.1; witch begs man to s. her back *G269.1.

Scratches identify clandestine lover H58.2. — Man in the moon from s. A751.5.

Scratch-berries. — Trickster eats s. J2134.1.

Scratched. — Earth from worm s. by creator's nails A828; man in the moon: moon's face s. by hare A751.5.1.

Scratching. — Contest: s. skin off each other K83.2; deceptive s. contest K83; magic s. D2063.4; strong hero asks that chickens stop s. F615.3.1.1; torturing by s. S187; transformation by s. D565.10; witch s. G269.15.

Screams. — Girl's s. louder when robbed than when raped *J1174.3; stone's s. indicate king's successors D1311.16.1.

Screaming at terrible sight forbidden C491.1; woman summons help against robbers K432.1. — Ghost s. E402.1.1.3; monk s. to repel temptress T331.9; stone s. under king's feet H71.10.6; witches s. G249.2.

Screen. — Paramour hidden behind s. K1521.5.

Scribe can't read own writing P425.1; can't write letter with bad leg J2242.1; of the gods A165.6.

Scripture. — Dividing by s. quoting J1242.

Scriptures. — Neglect of s. punished Q223.10; tabu to disbelieve in s. C61.3.

Scrofula cured by magic object D1502.2.3.

Scroll from heaven F962.12.4. — Sacred s. returns to heaven D1641.11; witch as s. G213.3.

Scrotum. — Beaver sacrifices s. to save life *J351.1; hungry fox waits in vain for horse's s. to fall off J2066.1.

Scullion. — King rewards s. for bon-mot Q91.2.

Scum's origin A2847.

Scurf becomes palm tree D457.6.

Scylla F526.2; and Charybdis G333.

Scythe cuts one man's head off: all have theirs cut off J2422. — Going to store with s. K1162; "May the devil whet my s." (devil does) C12.3; on return to body soul crosses on s.-blade as bridge E721.6.

Scythes. — Hero breaks s. F611.3.3.2.

Scythed chariot F861.2.2.

Sea, see also **Ocean**; animal found inland F989.12; animals magically summoned D2074.1.2; bath as rite V81.5; -bird A165.1.3, B463.1; has burned up (lie) X908; is calm for beautiful woman F575.13; -cat 17.2.1.3, B73; -charm D1523.2.7; cow B72; creatures as goddess's ancestors A111.3.2; dragon transformed to serpent D419.1.1; is on fire: protests colt decision J1191.1.1; foolishly accused of cruelty J1891.3; -fowl B267.4; -ghosts E271; of glass in otherworld *F162.4; -god A421; -god and rain-god conflict A1015.1; -horse B611.3.1, B634.1; of ice in otherworld F162.4.1; makes extraordinary noise, throws out fishes at world's end A1063.1; -mammal F531.1.8.8; otter A1821.1; people give the ogre brandy (tar) G525; personified Z118; produced by magic D2151.1.1; -queen (entices lovers) A421.1.1, (sets tasks) H933.5; -rat B17.2.1.1; rolls in overland as punishment C984.4.1; -scum D469.4; -spell Q467.3.1; turns to ice to permit flight D675; of unusual substance F711.2; turtle B177.3; water

made like earth D2031.12; water mixes with fresh at world's end A1063.2.
— Angel of s. rebels A54.1; animal drowning if taken from s. H842.1;
animal rescues man from s. B541; animals helpless in s.-voyage together
J1711.1; bell sunk in s. can be raised only under certain conditions
D1654.10.1; binding waves of the s. H1137; birds fill s. with dirt A1028.2;
boots carrying owner on s. D1524.2.1; building bridge over land and s.
H1131.1; building castle in s. H1133.3; castle built on s. F771.2.4; church
and congregation sink to bottom of s. F941.2.2; city sinks in s. F944;
dashing s. does not touch saint's cowl F930.1.0.1; dipping out the s. with
a spoon H1143; dragon's home in bottom of s. B11.3.1; drinking the s. dry
H1142.2; how many drops in the s.? (riddle) H704; earth rises from s.
A816; earth sinks into s. at end of world A1061; epidemic does not cross
river (s.) at saint's command D2162.2; escape from ship by jumping into
s. R216.1; extraordinary occurrences connected with s. F931; extraordinary s. F711; fish brings lost object from bottom of s. B548.2ff.;
foolish fight with the s. J1968; giant's leg stops ship at s. F531.3.1.2;
giant's spittle transformed to s. D483; giants live under s. F531.6.2.2.1;
gods' home under s. A151.3; hero wades across s. F1057; how deep is. s.?
H681.4; how much water in s.? H696.1; impostors throw hero overboard
into the s. *K1931.1; island rises up in s. F735; king descends to bottom of
s. P15.6; land rises from s. A952; why s. does not get larger when it rains
in it and nothing flows out J2371.1; magic enables one to stay on s.
bottom D1388.0.5; magic formula causes s. to open D1551.9; magic object
controls s. D1545; magic s. *D911; magic song drives back s. D1549.8;
man falls dead when he realizes that he has been riding over frozen
s. N383.1; men living beneath s. A1101.2.4; mermaid gives gold from s.
bottom B81.13.4; moon falls into s. A1016.6; needle falls into s.: sought
next summer J1921; old man of the s. G311; penance: staying on rock in
s. Q525.1; people enabled to walk across s. D1766.1.5; people live under
s. F725.5; person submerged by s. F945; quest for bottom of s. H1371.2;
rain from s. in upper world A1131.3; recovered articles dropped by rescuing animals into the s. D882.2; recovering lost objects from s. H1132.1;
river becomes s. D483.1; rock in s. created by magic D2153.1; sacrifice
to s. V11.2; saint's bachall (causes s. to divide) D1551.5, (permits him to
walk on s.) D1524.1.2; shipwrecked shepherd distrusts s. J11; sinners'
souls under s. water E751.5; strong hero son of woman of s. F611.1.14;
torment in s. as respite from hell Q560.2.3; tree under s. F811.4.2; water
led to s., ends deluge A1028.1; well located under s. F718.1; why s. is
blue A1119.1; why s. is salt A1115; why s. is warm A1119.2.

Sea's unpleasant odor A1119.3. — Attempts at measuring s. depth L414.1.

Seas. — Extraordinary occurrences concerning s. F930ff.; journey beyond
seven s. Z71.5.2; magic control of s. D2151.1; origin of the s. A920ff.;
sacrifice to rivers and s. S264; seven s. encircle world A872.1; three s.
surrounding earth Z71.1.9.

Sea-beast allows voyager to land upon his back B556; causes land disease, kills birds and fish B16.4.1.1.2. — Man sacrifices self to s. S263.5.3, W28.3; speaking s. B211.2.7.

Sea-beasts. — Hostile s. B17.2.1.

Sea-foam. — Birth from s. T546.1; devil created out of s. *G303.1.3.3; goddess born from s. A114.1; man created from s. A1261.1; person becomes s. D283.4.

Seagull. — Ghost as s. E423.3.9; soul in form of s. E723.5.

Seagulls save abandoned child T611.7.

Sea-monster G308; honors saint B251.2.8. — Devastating s. B16.5.1.2; devil puts convert's body on s. M219.2.6; earthquakes from movements of s. A1145.2; giant s. B877.1; tide from breathing of s. A913.2.

Sealand plowed out by goddess A955.4.

Seaserpent B91.5, X1396.1.

Seashore flooded with fish F986.5. — Dwarfs live on high s. F451.4.1.8; future hero found on s. L111.2.2; prophecy: death on s. M341.3.4.

Sea waves, see **Waves.**

Seaweed becomes vegetation A2615.4. — Man becomes s. D225.

Seaweeds. — Magic ring makes s. grow D1487.1.

Seal becomes person D327.2; -god A132.11; in human form B651.8; of humiliation put on rivals' backs L11.1; -man B80.1; transformed to another animal D411.7ff. — Boy with s. flippers F515.4; eating s. meat tabu C221.1.1.3; fisherman dragged through sea by s. escapes F1088.3.2; ghost as s. E423.2.5; god's s. A156.4; helpful s. B435.5; magic s. skin D1025.9; man transformed to s. D127.1, G263.1.2; marriage to s. B601.18; numskulls celebrate their new charter by burning up its s. J2181; reincarnation as s. E612.6; soul in s. E715.4.4; soul in form of s. E732.5; speaking s. B211.2.7.1.

Seal's — Ghost with s. head E425.1.7.

Seals. — Chieftain's vision of s. sucking his breasts V515.2.1; ghosts visible to s. E421.1.5; human beings descended from s. B631.2; origin of s. A1837.

Seam. — Milky Way as a stitched s. in the sky A778.4.

Seamanship. — Acquisition of s. A1459.2.

Seamen. — Hungry s. eat human flesh G70.1.

Seamstress's. — Chain tale: pulling needle out of s. hand Z41.8.

Search, see also **Quest;** for confessor V29.1; for a girl like statue artist has made T11.2.1.1; for prince named Sabr H946.1. — Animal's s. for dead man B546; children left at home s. for brothers and sisters S356; husband will not s. for shrewish wife who has run away from him T251.7; jewels aid in s. for treasure D1314.8; unsuccessful s. for man who can rule his wife T252.1.

Searches. — Absurd s. for the lost J1920ff.

Searching queen's quarters before king enters J634.2. — Children s. for stolen meals J124; dead mother s. for dead child E323.5; not to speak while s. for treasure C401.3; wife s. for lover K2213.3.3.

Season. — Defenses in and out of s. J674; fruit produced out of s. at saint's request F971.5.1; intercourse forbidden at hunting s. C119.1.3; procuring bird out of s. H1024.6; which is coldest s.? J1664.1.

Seasons. — Calculation of the s. A1485; causes of s.: deities move sun A1157; determination of s. A1150ff.; four s. personified Z122.4; god of the s. A496; magic control of s. *D2145ff.; proper s. for crops J713; wild hunt appears at certain s. E501.11.2.

Seasonal. — Variations in sun's s. heat A739.4.

Seasonally. — Why animals crowd together s. A2484; why fish come in s. A2484.1.

Seat covered with lice skins F894; heating in hell for certain person Q561.3; magically sticks to person D2171.1.1; next to king as reward Q112.3; in which only king can sit H31.4; pillars indicate settlement site D1314.11. — Capture in trap s. K735.2; he who fills s. to be king P11.5; king's s. on hills P14.10; king's unique ability to occupy certain s. H41.9; magic s. *D1151; vow not to sit on father's high s. until revenge is had M152.2.

Seats. — Devil moves s. in church G303.9.9.18.

Seating arrangements in royal hall A1539.1.

Second blow resuscitates (first kills) *E11.1; born son successor P17.3.1; sight D1825.1, (from dead) D1821.8; wife orders husband persecute first S413.2; wife saves king K2213.15. — Animals have s. sight B120.0.1; crocodile goes aftes s. child J2173.6; dead return s. day after burial E586.3; dead wife haunts husband on s. marriage E221.1; dead wife returns to reprove husband's s. wife for abusing her stepchildren *E221.2.1; deathbed promise concerning the s. wife M255; foolish attempt of s. man to overhear secrets *N471; husband fondles s. wife in presence of first as punishment for adultery Q484; magic object effective when struck on ground once only: s. blow renders useless D806.1; magic object recovered by using s. magic object D881; no s. punishment for same offense J1184; person's s. nose F514.5; wager on s. marvelous object N72; wife's revenge for s. wife K2213.16.

Seconds. — How many s. in eternity (riddle) H701ff.

Secrecy. — Impostor forces oath of s. *K1933.

Secret of eternal soul deceptively learned K975.2; learned by intoxicating dupe K1165; of vulnerability disclosed by hero's wife K2213.4.1; of strength treacherously discovered *K975. — Alchemist paid for "s." K1966.2; barber cured by revealing s. D2161.4.19.1; bargain to keep s. M295; betrayal of husband's s. by his wife K2213.4; birds tell a s. B122.1.1; curiosity about s. ensnares animal K713.1.4; exposed child brought up in s. S350.2; fairies lose power of invisibility if mortals gain knowledge of their s. F235.8.1; fatal s. revealed C420.1; false accusation of being in s. service K2126.2; finding certain s. forbidden C820ff.; god's abode s. A151.0.2; groom's ruse to hear bride's s. K1844.3; guessing name of devil's s. plant K216.2.1; husband's s. magic object discovered and stolen by wife D861.5; if you can't keep s., you must not expect me to J1482;

illness feigned to learn s. K2091; illness from keeping a s. F1041.9.2; jokes on s. societies X550ff.; keeping princess's s. suitor test H338.1; magic ring permits owner to learn person's s. thoughts D1316.4; magic s. *D1316.5; magic speaking reed (tree) betrays s. *D1316.5; mortal not to betray fairies' s. F348.5.1; numskull talks about his s. instructions and thus allows himself to be cheated J2355; ogre's s. overheard G661; no place s. enough (for fornication) T331.4, (for sin) U232; prince to give up life in exchange for learning a s. M232; princess's s. sickness from breaking tabu *C940.1; revelation of magic s. permits animal to be killed D1445.1; speech magically recovered when third person guesses s. transaction D2025.3; spying on s. help of angels forbidden C51.4.2; tabu to mention s. water spring C429.1; tabu to utter overheard s. C420.3; test of wife's ability to keep s. H472ff.; thief enters treasury through s. passage K315; treasure hidden in s. room N517.1; vow not to eat until s. learned M151.1; wife cannot keep s. T274; wife multiplies the s. J2353; witch divulges s. powers G275.5; woman dies as s. love exposed F1041.1.3.3.

Secrets discussed in animal meeting *B235; forced from monster G510.2; learned by deception C420.1. — Animals tell hero their s. B561; fairy escaped by learning and using his s. F381.4; foolish attempt of second man to overhear s. *N471; ghost laid when tells magic s. E451.1.1; god reveals s. A182.1; king has amours with great men's wives so as to learn s. from them J155.2; man betraying s. cursed M414.11; ogre tells power s. to wife G534; reward for ability to keep s. Q62; not to reveal s. (of god) C51.4, (of supernatural wife) C31.9; tasks performed by means of s. overheard from tree *H963; uttering s. forbidden *C420ff.; valuable s. learned *N440—N499; wife obtains husband's s. J1112.5; wife threatens husband with death if he will not tell s. T252.3.

Secretions. — Birth from s. of the body T541.8.

Security breeds indifference U270ff. — Dog offered as s. for debt B579.6; don't go to satirist for s. M402.2; legal s. P524; stag tries to borrow grain from the sheep with wolf as s. J1383; tabu: giving s. for one excommunicated C95.

Sedan bearers carry master to search for dog: they refused to search J2163.2. — Choosing sweetheart's s. chair suitor test H324.1.

Sedition. — Knight falsely accused of s. K2126.

Seduced. — Creator's wife s. by his son A32.3.1; dead man asks marriage with s. girl E353; girl s. by brother becomes cannibal G37; monk having s. girl kills her and becomes infidel V465.1.1.1; paradise lost because first woman is s. A1331.2.1; virtuous man s. by woman T338; wife s. by husband's friend H492.2.

Seducer led naked through streets Q473.3. — Dead sweetheart haunts s. E211.1; mermaid ruins her daughter's s. B81.13.9; youngest daughter avoids s. L63.

Seducer's. — Deceived fiancé may sleep with s. wife J1174.2.1.

Seducing foster brother's sister P273.2.2; friend's ejected wife K2012. —

Daughters s. father T411.2.1; demon s. princess F402.1.15.1; devil s. nuns G303.3.1.12.1; devil as woman s. man G303.3.1.12.2; disguised prince s. queen K1814.1; friends s. wife likened to dogs H592.4; magician s. queen D2031.4.2; ogre s. girl to devour her G17; ogress s. men G264.3; priest s. man's wife J652.3; repeated attempts at s. innocent maiden T320.1; transformation for s. woman *D658.1ff.; ungrateful lawbreaker s. magistrate's wife W154.15; wife s. husband's servant T481.4; woman as leper s. enemies K778.2; woman's wager on s. anchorite T337.

Seduction *K1300ff.; punished Q243.2. — Child's remark prevents mother's s. J122.1; service in disguise for s. K1831.2.1.

Seductions. — Wife warns against women's s. T299.2.2.

Seductive. — Revenant as s. woman E425.1.3.

Seed. — Earth from lotus s. A814.8; extraordinary s. F815.5; god carries s. of gods A111.3.0.1; growing oil s. on stony ground H1049.2; magic s. *D971ff., (produces golden gourd) D1463.3; mustard-s. trail R267; numskull plants s. in daytime and takes it out at night J2224; origin of s. A1425; sowing s. in others' fields J2129.8; suitor test involving mountain of mustard s. H1091.3; traveler to look for s. he sowed in street H586.2; white field, black s. (riddle) H741.

Seeds rattling mistaken for insults J1812.1. — Armies like s. and peppercorns J1625; "battle s." P551.9; city paved with precious s. F761.5; countertask: sowing cooked s. and harvesting the crop H1023.1.1f.; counting s. in mustard package H1118.1; dwarfs emigrate because mortals put caraway s. into bread F451.9.1.1; eater of fruit s. will drop gems as he laughs M312.3.2; magic bird collects s. B172.3; magic turns s. into insects D1594.1; man created from s. A1254; poppy s. poured into ghost's mouth E439.4; trail of s. R135.0.2.

Seeing, see also **Sight;** ability lost if ears cut off J2721; all earth from upper world F10.2; one's wraith E723.2; tabus C300ff.; trolls F455.5.4; without eyes X1724. — All-s. god A102.2; bad omen: s. unusual sight on road home D1812.5.1.22; contest in s. *K85; giant s. great distance F531.1.1.4; insanity from s. strange sight *D2065.2; madness from s. beautiful woman *F1041.8.1; marvelous cure without s. person F950.7; numskull's attempt at s. abstract quality J2488; only particular persons s. treasure in its true form N543.0.1; suffering from merely s. work done F647.2; tabu: bridal couple s. each other before wedding T134.1; tabu: wife of supernatural husband s. old home C713.2; witches s. in dark G249.10.

Seek. — Gods teach how to s. food A1420.2; magic arrow shot to determine where to s. bride D1314.1.3; transformation to s. person D647.

Seeking. — Animal's s. attitude from ancient loss A2275.5ff.; children left at home s. exposed brothers and sisters S356; dwarf s. to enter church F451.5.9.5; hero just misses man he is s. N186; why animals are continually s. something A2471ff.

Seen. — Deceptive grant: as much land as can be s. K185.12; falling in love with person never s. T11; ghost s. in two places at once E599.9;

jinn s. only by those he wishes G307.2.2; one and one-half men and a horse's head s. by youth H583.1; son next s. to be king M314.2.

Seer D1712; banishes ghost E439.8. — Recognition by miraculous sight of s. H184.

Segregated. — Otherworld inhabitants s. F167.14.

Seizing. — Tree s. person F979.4; witch s. man with snuff G269.2.

Selection of king by elephant's bowing to him H171.1. — Care in s. of creature to carry one J657.

Self, see also **Automatic;** -abnegation rewarded Q61; -boiling kettle D1601.10.3; -chopping axe D1601.14; -cooking vessel D1601.10ff.; -created deity A118; -cutting shears D1601.12; -deception of the lowly J953; -dependence J1030ff.; -digging spade D1601.16; -grinding (mill) D1601.21, (millstone) D1601.20; -growing and self-gathering corn D1601.2; -immolation S125.1; -inflicted wounds to accuse another K2116.3; -luminous object *D1645ff.; -mutilation H160.1; -playing musical instruments D1601.18ff.; -returning (cow) K366.1.3, (dragon's head) *B11.5.5, (magic object) *D1602ff.; -righteous anchorite tempted T332.1; -righteousness punished L435; -ringing bell D1601.18.1; -sacrifice W28; -sewing needle D1601.11; -torture as penance Q522; -tying thread D1601.13. — Accidental s.-injury N397; angel ceases to appear to s.-righteous hermit Q553.2; child born of slain mother cares for s. during infancy T612; deception into s.-injury *K1000—K1199; dupe tricked into killing s. K890ff.; giant's s.-returning head F531.1.2.3; inability to transform s. D502; irrevocable judgment causes s. to suffer first M13; magic s.-moving vehicle D1523ff.; magic s.-propelling vehicle *D1523ff.; magic s.-rejuvenation *D1881; man named "s." K602.1; man stretches s. till he reaches otherworld F59.1; never be rude to s.-made man J21.52.2; ogre deceived into s.-injury *G520ff.; origin of animal characteristics: animal persuaded into s.-injury A2284ff.; person eats s. up G51.1; power of s.-transformation D630ff.; pursuer deceived into s.-injury K533.1; treasure opens s. N552; wife s.-sacrifice A1545.5.1.

Selves. — Persons duped into injuring s. K1080ff.

Selfish quest P332. — Why cock is vain and s. A2527.1.

Selfishness. — Origin of s. A1375.

Sell, see also **Sold.** — In large family father unwilling but mother willing to s. children H491.1; peasant refuses to s. possessions to king P411.1; princess must s. goods on market as punishment Q483.

Seller of fox skins mixes otter skins with them J2083.3. — Buyer and deaf s. X111.11; considerate s. at auction warns prospective buyer J2088.

Selling animal and keeping him (task) H1152; forbidden C782; for four rupees instruction: fool refuses six J2461.7; old mule back to master K134.3; oneself and escaping K252; soul to devil G224.4; what is not his K282; to witch tabu C782.2. — Children s. mother S20.1; dog s. rotten peas B294.3; man s. soul to devil M211; wife s. privilege of sleeping with husband T296; wife s. self to ransom husband R152.2; witch s. power over winds D2142.0.1.1, G283.1.3; woman s. favors for particular purpose *T455ff.; woman s. poisoned curds A1335.12; woman substituting child for her own and s. it *K1922; youth s. himself to an ogre in settlement of a gambling debt S221.2.

Semen bellicosum P551.9; in love philtre D1355.2.3. — Birth from s. thrown on ground T541.10; magic strength in s. D1831.3; mankind from maid having licked s.-stained cloth A1211.7; peacock eats s., impregnated B754.6.

Senate ruler amuses small son J553.2. — Overcurious wife learns of s. deliberations of s. J1546.

Senator. — Old simpleton resolves to become s. J955.4.

Sender. — Message of death fatal to s. K1612.

Sending, see also **Sent;** meat home by bird J2124.1; object by itself J1881; to the older F571.2.

Seneca opens own veins and bleeds to death Q427.

Sense. — King brought to say "what is the s. in that?" H507.2; loss of s. after abduction by fairies F329.3; man to bring wife a purse-full of s. *J163.2.

Senses regained by hearing name F959.1.1. — Druids bereave men of s. D2065.3; fairies cause man to lose s. F361.2.2.

Senseless from grief J1041.21.5; judicial decisions M1. — Spying on holy man renders s. D1410.8.

Seneschal. — Treacherous s. K2243.

Sensitiveness of dwarfs F451.3.6. — Adulteress feigns unusual s. K2051; marvelous s. F647ff.; test of s. H1571.

Sent, see also **Sending.** — Companion s. away so as to steal common food supply K343.3; identifying tokens s. with messenger H82; objects magically s. to certain place D2136.10; objects s. through air D2135.5; strong hero s. from home F612ff.

Sentence. — Animal saves man from death s. B522; death s. escaped by propounding riddle king (judge) cannot solve *H542.

Sentences. — Penance: king must postpone all s. Q520.4.

Sentry. — Devil flies away with s. box G303.9.9.13; officer disarmed by s. J1526.1.

Separable soul *E710ff.

Separate examination of witnesses discredits testimony J1153. — Land where women live s. from men F566.2; line drawn by saint's bachall to s. calves from their mothers D1574; marriage to five women, each with s. duties T145.1.

Separated. — Bridal couple s. on wedding night T165.4; husband and wife kill themselves so as not to be s. T211.3; lions succeed only when bulls are s. J1022; lover searching for lost ring becomes s. from mistress N352; lovers treacherously s. T84; reconciliation of s. couple T298; riddle: what are the two s. by jealousy H851.

Separately. — Serve the water and wine s. J1312.1.

Separation of nations A1600ff.; of sexes in otherworld F112.0.2; of souls for heaven, hell E755.0.2; of sun and moon by creator A736.1.4.3. — Accidental s. N310ff.; girl to die of s. from her love M365.3; loving couple die of s. T212; why s. of a good woman from a bad man is a benefit T287.

September. — King's beard worth months of July, August, and S. H712.1.

Sepulchre. — Girl lives in s. to preserve chastity T328; magic s. *D1299.2; stretching s. D482.5.

Seraphim as creator's advisers A42.1.

Serf made to climb tree, shot as cuckoo K1691.1.

Serfs congratulate master, curse by mistake J1845.

Series, see also **Chain, Cumulative, Succession;** of clever unjust decisions J1173; of creations *A630ff.; of enclosed coffins F852.4; of glass coffins F852.1.1; of helpers on quest *H1235; of husbands try to control adulteress T241; of lucky successes N680.2; of lower worlds A651.2; of quests H1241; of tasks H941; of upper worlds A651.1; of witches with increasing numbers of horns G215.2.1; of world catastrophes A1001. — Man created after s. of unsuccessful experiments A1226; soul hidden in a s. of coverings E713.

Sermon, see also **Preaching.** — Boy applies the s. X435; parody s. K1961.1.2.1; parson put to flight during s. X411; parson refreshes himself during the s. X445ff.; priest's short s.: "You're wicked" J1647; wager: to begin s. with illustration from card-playing N71; witty funeral s. V66; wolf loses interest in the s. when he sees a flock of sheep U125.

Serpent, see also **Reptile, Snake;** above Loki continually drops venom in his face Q501.3; acts as rope to collect wood B579.5; asks victim feed him honey K815.18; brew gives witch power G224.7; bursts asunder F981.1; carried by bird lets poison drop in milk and poisons drinkers N332.3; charmed into helplessness by magic formula D1410.5; as child's nurse B535.0.14; chokes woman's undutiful son Q557.2; cursed M414.8.3; damsel F582.1; -eye F541.1.4; given immortality, renews skin A1335.5; guards treasure N583; -hall F771.5.3; as house-spirit F480.2; having injured man refuses reconciliation J15; with human head B29.2.1; inside man's body G328.1; with jewel in (head) B101.7, (mouth) B103.4.2; king B244.1, (assigns task) H939.4.1, (causes flood) A1019.2, (resides in lake) B244.1.2; kneaded into dough H1407; language B215.5; as magician B191.7; as procurator of rats B221.2.1; produces storm D2141.0.11.1; released: grateful B375.9; releases swallowed-up water supply F914.1; relieved of sand in eyes: grateful B385; as saint's whip B292.12; shows condemned man how to save prince's life B522.1; steals from God's coat a stick for his back A2262.3; steals jewels, person accused of theft N352.3; subsists on dust B768.4; supports earth A842.1; supports sky A665.6; swallows canoe F911.4.1.2; swallows man F911.7; taken for island J1761.1.2; transforms self to staff, picked up, bites enemy K928.1; transformed to person D391; tries to bite a file J522.3; as wooer

B622.1; worship VI.8.6. — Animal languages learned from s. (eaten) *B217.1.1, (not eaten) *B165.1; ants overcome s. L315.14; automatic brazen s. D1620.2.9; bird grateful for being saved from s. B364.4; blue s. B731.11; blowing s. B743; brain becomes s. D447.10; bridal chamber invaded by magic s. T172.2; child born with figure of s. on body T563.3; child born with s. in caul T551.8; childless woman adopts a s. (transformed man) T676.1; corpse transformed to s. D449.2; creation of s. A2145; dead mother appears and makes disobedient child eat fatal s. Q593; devastating (man-eating) sea-monster (s.) B16.5.1.2; devil in s. form tempts first woman A63.6; dragon as modified s. B11.2.1.1; earth rests on tortoise, s., elephant A844.6; fiery s. B19.4.2; giant s. B16.5.1, B875.1; giant as s. F531.1.8.2; God makes s. ugly A2286.0.1; going into bath on return from s. kingdom forbidden C711; gold-producing s. B103.0.4; golden s. B102.6; hair transformed to s. D447.1.3; helpful s. *B491; hero unharmed by coiling s. F1088.2; human sacrifice to water s. S263.3.1; hundred-headed s. B15.1.2.10.2; husband lets s. bite him to save wife T211.1.2; immortal s. B843.1; journey to s. kingdom F127.1; lake dangerous from haunting s. G308.4; Lucifer as s. D191.1; magic s. *B176.1, (head) D1011.0.3, (heart) *D1015.1.3, (statue cures) D1500.1.12.1, (urine) D1027.1; magic tree guarded by s. *D950.0.1; man attempts to kill faithful s. at wife's instigation B335.1; man transformed to s. D191; man warned of s. unwittingly carried in sack N848.12; men lured into s. pit, killed K912.2; marriage to s. in human form B656.2; Midgard S. *A876; mist after s. fight F962.10.1; multi-colored s. B731.10; mythical s. B91; nine-headed s. B15.1.2.8.2; only one s. has sting: fed poison to rest A2219.3; origin of enmity between s. and man A2585.1; origin of death: s. given immortality instead of man A1335.5; origin of horned s. A2145.0.1; penance: wearing s. Q522.8; rat leaves s. behind, though spared to rescue him K1182; revenant as s. E423.5; rod transformed to s. D441.7.1; sacrifice to s. V11.7.1; sea drag-on in s. form to accompany hero D659.4.2; sea dragon transformed to s. D419.1.1; seven-headed s. *B15.1.2.6.1; six-mouthed s. B15.2.1; skillful marksman shoots s. through left eye F661.5.1; soul in form of s. E733.1; strong man kills s. F628.1.3; tail and head of s. quarrel as to usefulness J461.1.1; ten-headed s. B15.1.2.9; thousand-headed s. B15.1.2.10.3; three-headed s. B15.1.2.2.2; twelve-headed s. B15.1.2.10.1; two-headed s. B15.1.2.1.1; venomous s. B776.7; why s. has no ears A2325.8; wax prince animated by s. D435.1.4; winged s. as boat F911.3.2; wisdom from s. B161; wise s. B123.1; wolf defends master's child against s. B524.1.4; worm becomes s. D418.2.1.

Serpent's beautiful wife directs journey J155.1.1; bite produces ornaments, clothes B103.6.1; deaths to predict king, queen's P17.2; jewel covered with spiked helmet K1058.1; life in its gold crown E712.4. — Bringing ruby in s. head H1151.26; cause of s. ugliness A2286.0.1, A2402.1; disen-chantment by eating s. head D764.8; disenchantment by taking key from s. mouth at midnight D759.1; earth from s. head A815.1; earth-quake at s. slaying F969.4.1; man with s. head B29.2.2; magic s. crown *D1011.3.1; mountains from parts of giant s. body A961.4; origin of s. blood and venom A2367.3.1; person with s. head F511.0.9.3; swallowed person tickles s. throat F912.3.1; sword with s. image F833.7; why s. mouth closed A2341.3.1; wise man destroys s. eggs F622.1.

Serpents in hell A671.2.1; in otherworld F167.11.1. — Blood becomes s. D447.3.1.1; bread transformed to s. D444.4; castle on s. F771.2.7; copulation of s. A2496.2; diamond charms s. D1442.11; husband charmed back from land of s. R152.4; king of s. B244.1; kingdom of s. *B225.1; magic in country of s. D838.4; man kills s., toads, dragons with own hands F628.1.3.1; oars, masts transformed to s. D444.11; ordeal by kissing s. H224.1; quest to land of s. H1289.1.1; silence in land of s. H1506; sorcerer's body becomes s. D447.9; uncharitable knight devoured by s. V422; war between s. and storks B263.7; winged s. pull chariot B558.7; world of s. A696.

Servant, see also **Maid;** allowed anything he can take with teeth J1161.10; asks master for arms of knighthood J955.3; becomes arrogant when rich J1085.2; cheats master boasting of eyes in back of head J1511.9; deceives family by assuming unusual names K1399.2; deceives sons falsifying father's will K1628; exposes liar master X907; falsely accused of familiarity with queen K2121.2; girl helps prince if he will make her his chief wife T55.2; girl lies about fairy, leg broken F361.17.4; girl's industry tested H1569.1.1; given garlic as knighthood arms J955.3; of God beaten J2215.2; impersonates dead master, makes false will K1854; to improve on master's statements J2464; in his master's place K1317.1; inadvertently throws master into stream J2133.5.1.1; kills self at master's death F1041.1.3.2; lays skin of dead dog in the bed of his mistress and master K2134; literally takes "year to do errand" J2461.4; passes self off as prince K1952.0.2; plays at being emperor J955.2; poses as master K1969.3; plans to deceive his master by refusing to eat J2064; refused payment because of single mistake K231.9; repays stingy master (mistress) J1561.4; rescues abandoned child R131.5; rescues king's children R169.4.2; saves master from death H187; steals back magic D882.3; substitutes for husband in bed, deceives him K1844.1.1; takes pearl to wife instead of merchant N351.1; tells of few customers, dismissed J551.7. — Animal as s. of saint B256; awkward s. J2665; bringing best friend, worst enemy, best s. etc. H1065; cat as s. of witch G225.3; clever s. J1114; clever maid s. J1111.6; clothing the s. J2491; creators' giant s. puts trees on earth A857.3; creator's giant s. makes valley and mountains A857.2; devil's s. G303.10.16; disinterested party asked to punish s. J571.4.1; dragon fly as snake's s. B765.24; eavesdropping s. realizes own misery N455.11; enemy's s. as helper N857; fairy punishes s. F361.14; faithful s. locking up master R53.4; faithful s. *P361ff.; forehanded s. throws parson's suit of clothes into tub of

for s. of god Q20.1; strong man in s. to ogre as punishment for stealing food F613.4; warriors enter conqueror's s. R74; wild huntsman wanders for disturbing church s. E501.3.8; youth takes s. with (merman) B82.3, (ogre) G452.

Services of grateful objects D1658.3; of helpful animals B500—B599. — Dwarfs hold church s. F451.6.3.6; magic objects perform other s. for owner D1560ff.; penance: performing all s. asked for by anyone Q523.8; punishment for neglect of s. to gods (God) Q223ff.; religious s. *V0— V99; sale of worthless s. K150ff.

Serving by invisible hands E482. — Animal s. only certain man H172; animals s. men A2513, B570ff.; demon s. girl whose chastity is inviolable G303.16.19.5; disenchantment by s. transformed D754; dwarfs s. mortals F451.5.1.7; fairy s. mortal *F346.0.1, F346.2; forgotten fiancée reawakens husband's memory by s. as milkmaid *D2006.1.2; man's descendants s. his brother's P251.5.6; ten s.-women carried in bottle *D55.2.4.

Servitude. — Wolf prefers liberty to dog's s. L451.3.

Sesame. — Open s. D1552.2, N455.3; where is oil in s. flower? J1291.4.

Setting out vineyard in one night H1103. — A step-ladder for s. the table J1573.1; fairies s. down an object once cannot raise it again F255.2; man controls s. of sun A725; saint prevents sun's s. for year A725.1.

Settlement. — Ball indicates place for s. D1314.4; divining rod indicates place for s. D1314.2.1; location of s. at place cow stops and where milk flows by itself B155.2.2; why lion stays away from s. A2433.3.16.

Settlements. — Origin of s. A996.

Settling. — Insect points out diety by s. where he is H162.1.

Seven children at a birth T586.1.2; brothers seek seven sisters as wives T69.1.2; daughters of Humility J901; days silence at world's end A1057; demigods A501.1; devils' wives attempt resuscitation ritual K113.0.1; -fold doors to room F782.3; as formulistic number Z71.5; girls appear as seven parrots D658.3.3; -headed (dragon) B11.2.3.1, (ogre) G361.1.4, (serpent) B15.1.2.6.1, (witch) *G215.1; heavens A651.1.4; Irish saints never died V229.2.12.1; -league boots D1521.1; -legged beast B15.6.3.3; lower worlds A651.2.3; as magic number D1273.1.3; -mouthed cannibal G11.17; princesses sought by seven princes T69.1.2; reincarnations E604.1; rivers meet F715.8; rooms in ascetic's house F771.11; seas encircle world A872.1; seven-years olds save princess D759.10; significances of sign of cross V86.7; Sleepers *D1960.1; stags killed by one shot F679.5.3.1; substances in human body A1260.1.4; suns mark world's end A1052.3; tongues in a head (riddle) H793; walls around otherworld F148.5; week days have passed since the time of Adam H706.1; whistlers are souls of Jews who crucified Christ A1715.3; worlds above and below A651.1.3.1; year old girl has child T579.3; years between feasts Z72.3; years' pregnancy T574.2; years of service imposed on suitor

H317.1; years, seven months, seven days Z72.2; years' service for seven days' neglect of religious duty Q523.7. — Boastful fly-killer: s. at a blow K1951.1; bones in s.-fold cloth D717.1; bridegroom only son of s. children H1381.7; butcher wonders that man who has been buying his meat for s. years can still be alive X231; bride's constancy tested by s. years' mourning over supposed dead lover H387.1; cast-forth wife buried up to waist for s. years and despitefully used Q456.1.1; child born each day for s. days T586.5.2; dead person visits earth every s. years E585.1; disenchantment at end of s. years D791.1.1; evil eye covered with s. veils D2071.0.1; eye with s. pupils F54.3.4; fairy music makes s. years seem one day F262.9; fairy wife for s. years only F302.10; formerly s. (moons) A759.5, (suns) A720.1; gourds with s. rooms A1029.4; guilty of everything connected with the s. senses X331; headless man lives s. years E783.7; hero "son of s. mothers" Z215; hero wins contests with s. demons D785.1; hero's s. pupils in each eye, seven toes on each foot, seven fingers on each hand A526.5; island rises every s. years F735.0.2; island supported on s. feet F736.1.1; laws made in groups of s. P541.1; man lives with fairies s. years F379.3; man requires s. women T145.1.1; men with two faces, three legs, and s. arms F526.5; master of s. liberal arts begs from wagoner X371; mountain of s. lights F759.8; nature transformed every s. years A1103; not to speak during s. days of danger C401.2; palace with s. gates F776.3; parents wooing one of s. daughters T69.2.1; parting lovers pledge not to marry for s. years T61.2; person of remarkable sight finds tracks of swine stolen s. years before his birth F642.2; producing s. pairs of chopsticks in s. plates H1199.16; prophecy: s. days' life for baby M341.1.2.5; rivers formed where s. children place stones A934.2; snake s. years pregnant B765.25; lost soul to serve as porter in hell for s. years E755.2.3; spear thrust through s. iron plates H1149.7; strong hero suckled by s. women F611.2.4; swearing by "S. Things Served" M119.6; train of troubles for s. brothers N261.1; tree inside s. series of forts H1335.5.0.2; water-spirit claims life every s. years F420.5.2.1.6; wild hunt appears every s. years E501.11.3.1; woman's beauty shows through s. veils F574.1.2; youth educated by s. sages J141.

Sevens. — Dwarfs are superstitious about the three s. in 1777 F451.3.15.1, F451.9.1.3.

Sevenfold: formulistic number Z71.5.0.1.

Seventh cake satisfies J2213.3; daughter predestined to be magician N121.4. — Cure by s. son of seventh daughter D2161.5.7; death on s. day of marriage M341.1.1.2; holy day on s. day A1541.4.0.1; punishment comes in s. generation Q404; salmon comes every s. year to certain place F986.3.

Seventeen as formulistic number Z71.16.12; marvels at Christ's birth V211.0.3; -storied heaven A651.1.8.1.

Seventy tales of a parrot prevent a wife's adultery K1591. — Swinging s. girls H506.5.

Seventy-two kinds of wisdom J182.2, (mastered by Adam) D1811.0.1; as formulistic number Z71.14.

Seventy-seven as formulistic number Z71.15. — Devil claims to be 7,777 years old G303.4.8.3.

Seven hundred. — Disenchantment after s. years D791.1.6.

Seven thousand people killed for stoning judges N340.2.

Several, see also **Many.** — Person with s. bodies F524; eye with s. pupils F541.3; wild hunt goes s. times around a hill E501.14.4.

Severed, see also **Cut, Dismembered;** finger as sign of crime H57.2.1; heads of monster become birds E613.0.5; limbs as identification H106; limbs replaced by Virgin Mary D2161.5.2.4. — Magic restoration of s. hand D2161.3.2; oaths taken over s. pieces of horse M111; ogre revives after limbs are s. G635.

Sewed. — Hero s. up in animal hide so as to be carried to height by bird K1861.1; horse s. in buffalo-hides F984.1; man s. in animal's hide carried off by birds K521.1.1; quartered thief's body s. together K414.

Sewing clothes on to boy's skin H1505; contest won by deception K47; each other up (fatal game) K861; magic shirt H383.2.2; a shirt of stone (task) H1021.9; shirts to trees J2465.9; together broken object H1023.7. — Brownies s. by moonlight F482.5.2; disenchantment by s. shirts for enchanted brothers D753.1; dwarf s. F451.3.4.4; empress s. in humility J918; resuscitation by s. body together E35.1; statue of Virgin s. for suppliant D1620.1.4; tailor s. up broken eggs F622.1; unsuccessful imitation of magic s. J2411.8; woman skillful in s. F662.0.1; women punished for not s. Q321.1.

Sex *T (entire chapter); activity tabu for warriors C566.6; hospitality T281; organs, see under **Genitals;** tabu *C100—C199; of unborn child (guessed) H528, (prophesied) M369.7.3; (wagered on) N16.1; of witches G220.0.2. — Animal changes s. periodically B754.1; animal controls s. of offspring F987ff.; curse: change of s. M454; disguise of s. to avoid execution K514; exchange of s. with ogre D593; farmer seeks laborer ignorant of s. K1327; god of double s. A111.3.0.1; humor concerning s. X700—X799; ignorance of s. J1745; killing children of undesired s. S11.4.3; mountain spirits change s. at will F460.2.15; origin of s. differentiations A1313.0.2; origin of s. functions A1350ff.; reincarnation with change of s. E605.1; sham physician predicts the s. of the unborn child K1955.3; simulated change of s. to baffle Evil Eye D2071.1.3; tabu confined to one s. C180ff.; telling s. of unborn goat H1576.1; of ten original men one magically changes s. A1275.3; test to discover person masking as of other s. H1578; transformation to person of different s. *D10ff.; transformation of s. to seduce *D658.3; vows concerning s. M130ff.; yearly transformation of s. D624.3.

Sexes of pygmies distinguished F535.4.1. — Relative pleasures of s. in love J99.1; separation of s. in otherworld F112.0.2; why s. differ A2853.

Sexton behind crucifix tells old maid she will have no husband K1971.8.1. — Cock crows at church and the s. awakes and begins to sing X451; eavesdropping s. duped into giving supplication money K464; parson and s. at mass X441.

Sexton's — Parson's share and the s. J1269.1.

Sextus seduces Lucretia K1397.

Sexual habits of animals B754; intercourse, see following heading; relation of man, demons G302.7.1; relations in dog fashion unearth treasure N551.2; relations with fairy F304; relations with wood-spirit fatal F441.6.3; restrictions A1556; sins punished Q240ff. — Boasting of s. prowess P665; devil's s. relations with mortals G303.12.7; doctor prescribes s. intimacy for widow: daughters follow treatment K2052.4.1; eaten fruit causes s. desire D1355.14; illicit s. relations *T400—T499; magic ox from unusual s. union B184.2.2.1; magic ring gives s. prowess D1335.5.1; neglect of s. relations tabu C163; unusual s. union of animals B754.0.1;

Sexual intercourse, see also **Copulation;** of animals A2496; forbidden *C110ff.; on Friday only T310.1.1; of mountain woman F460.4.1.2; with woman in childbed S185.2. — Bride refuses s. until court orders it T166; bridegroom must be taught s. T166.2; cocks kept from s. have tenderest meat B754.5; conception from (dream of s.) F460.4.1.2.1; (extraordinary s.) T517; death from s. H182; disenchantment by s. D743; husband objects to wife's enjoyment of s. T257.8; imagined s., imagined payment J1551.1; Incubus comes in sleep, has s. F471.2; long-distance s. K1391; luck changed after s. N131.1; needle and thread symbolize s. J86, Z186; origin of s. A1352; peacock pregnant without s. B754.6; refraining from s. as penance Q535.3; seduction through ignorance of s. K1363; suitor test: s. with princess despite sleeping potion H347; tabus concerning s. C119ff.; transformation by s. D565.5.1; trickster advises s. K1354.1.1; urinalysis reveals s. as illness cure J1149.4; wife denies s. to enforce demand T283; witches' s. with devil G243.3.

Shabby hospitality forces guests to leave P334.

Shade. — Clouds in sky to s. mountains A1133.2; fighting in the s. best J1453; tree grows out of horse and gives rider s. X1130.2.1; wanderers in s. of plane tree blame it for not bearing fruit W154.7.

Shades. — Land of s. *E482.

Shading roof from sun J1879.1; self with foot sole F551.5.

Shadow freezes X1623.1; mistaken for substance J1790ff.; on water marks demon's victim G336.1. — Bird overpowered by stepping on his s. D2072.0.4; bird as s. of god A195.3; cure by lying on saint's s. D2161.4.15; demons cast no s. G302.4.4; devil gets into ark by hiding in s. of Noah's wife G303.23.1; devil gets s. instead of man F1038.2; devil takes farmer's s. G303.19.2; elongated s. swells fox's pride J953.13; ghost as s. E421.4; ghosts cast no s. E421.2; God creates the devil from his own s. G303.1.1.1; god hides in cloud's s. A179.8; god whose s. is a

lizard A446.1.1; impregnation by s. T532.8; man steps aside so that only
his s. is caught K525.2; ogre without s. G369.3; person without s. F1038;
person whose s. pierced, dies D2061.2.2.1; safety in s. of wall N253;
soul as s. E743; spell over s. brings death D2061.2.2.2; suit about the
ass's s. J1169.7; undesired lover asked not to step on s. K1277.6; woman
who has prevented birth of children casts no s. Q552.9; worldly honor
like s. J152.6.

Shadows. — Fairies seen as dark s. F235.7.

Shaggy. — Giants with s. hair on their bodies F531.1.6.3.

Shake. — Numskull tries to s. birds from tree like fruit J1909.3; why
some animals continually s. head A2474ff.

Shaken. — Apple-tree grateful for being s. D1658.1.5; heavens s. by
man's voice F688.1; parable on stones s. in jar J98; tree asks to be s.
D1610.2.0.1.

Shaking of staff stuck in ground as life token E761.2.1. — Disenchantment by s. certain tree D789.7; water-spirit s. ship F420.5.2.7.2.

Sham, see also **Bluff, Feigned, Masking, Pretended;** astrologer K1964;
blind man throws suspicion on real blind K2165; churchman K1901ff.;
dead claim reward for information about their death J2511.1.2; dead
deceived into moving K607.3.2; dead man deceived into making gesture
K607.3; dead man killed by his intended victim K311.1.1; dead man
punished J2311.6; death (to avoid debts) K246, (for copulation with
divine maidens) K1325.0.1, (to escape) K522, (to be sold) K366.1.3.1,
(to steal) K341.2, (to wound enemies) K911.1; eating K81.1; fight to
frighten guests J1563.7; illness, see under **Illness,** feigned; mad man
H599.2; magician K1963ff.; miracles K1970ff.; nurse kills enemy's
children K931; parson (priest) K1961.1; physician *K1955; prince
(nobleman) K1952; prowess *K1950ff.; pursuit saves fugitive K649.8;
relics perform miracles V142.1; rich man K1954; sickness, see under
Illness; sleep to kill enemy K911.3; suicide to soften lover's anger
K1232.1; teacher pretends to read document brought as a letter K1958;
warrior K1951; wise man K1956. — Foolish imitation of s. death
J2411.1.1; money received to bury s. dead person K482; property
disposal rouses s. dead J2511.1.1; race won by deception: s. sick trickster
K11.5; robbers frightened from goods by s. dead man K335.1.2.2;
trickster as s. magician makes adulteress produce hidden food for her
husband K1571.1.

Shams. — Deception through s. K1700—K2099.

Shaman sent down by Creator equipped with medicine A1438.1.

Shaman's wife controls weather D2140.2.

Shamanism A1654.

Shame and disgrace for refusing love C929.1; for nakedness A1383.1.
— Adulteress pretends s. before male statue K2051.1; death from s.
F1041.1.13; effect of s. on saint F1041.23; false s. over trivial sin:
little over great V26; illness from s. F1041.9.3; what is greatest? S.
H659.7.2.

Shameful. — Riddle: what is most s.? H659.12.

Shaming. — Wife s. adulterous husband into gifts K1271.3.1; wife escapes king's lust by s. him T320.4.

Shampooing. — Servant injures master while s. him J2665.2.

Shape of bee's body A2300.1; of leaves of plant A2761; and position of animals' eyes A2332.4ff. — Detecting man in demon's s. J1141.1.7; devil changes s. G303.3.5; divine beings assume their own s. in sleep D796; dwarf can take s. he wants F451.3.3.0.1; fairy as s.-shifter F234.0.2; god as s.-shifter A120.1; Isle of S. F129.4.3; origin of island's s. A955.3; origin of s. of animal's back A2356.2ff.

Shapes. — Wandering soul assumes various s. E721.5.

Share. — Lion's s. J811.1; man had rather be burned alive than to s. food with a guest W152.2; parson's s. and the sexton's J1269.1; peasant's s. is the chicken J1562.2.

Shared. — Strokes s. K187.

Sharing invitation taken literally J2499.6; his wounds J1621. — Child s. food with toad B391.2; friends s. good and evil P310.1.

Shark bites off god's head A179.4; as king of fishes B243.1.3; -man ogre G308.5. — Fishtail becomes s. D447.4; giant s. B874.5; helpful s. B471; mythical s. B65; man becomes s. D178; reincarnation as s. E617.3; stealing lobsters from s. guardians K341.16; tabu to eat s. C221.1.3.4.

Sharks. — Creation of s. A2137; hero kills s. F628.1.4.2; kingdom of s. B223.1.

Sharp elbowed women G341, (duped into fighting each other) K1082; instrument shown ogre as nose G572.2; knife F838.1. — Dancing on s. instruments H1531.1; dupe induced to eat s. fruit K1043; dupe sits on s. stones K1116; quest over path bristling with s. points H1236.1; shield s. enough to cut hair F839.2.2; sword extraordinarily bright, s. F833.3.

Sharpened. — Knife s. by cannibal to kill captive G83; murder by feeding s. pieces of wood K951.6; ogre with s. leg G341.1; tools magically s. D2199.2.

Sharpening leg J2424. — Crow s. bill lets frog escape K561.1.2.

Shattered. — Pieces of s. god's head as hills A962.8; saint's breath restores s. vessel D1565.4.

Shave. — Half price for half a s. J1522.1; mortal wins fairies' gratitude by letting them s. him F331.2; vow not to s. or cut hair until a certain time M121.

Shaved. — Cast-off wife's head s. S436; chastity ordeal: holding s. and greased tail of bull H412.2; creditor to wait till debtor is s. K238.1; importunate suitor s. and tarred K1218.1.7; madmen's heads s. P192.6; magic object in return for being s. D817.2; numskull wants to be s. (orders wife to cut off his ears) J2426; ride on donkey's back with s. head Q473.5.1; running hare s. by skillful barber F665.1.

Shaving head as killing thousands H599.4; head as punishment Q488.2;

tabu C722.0.1. — Barber's contest in s. H504.2; bearded woman ghost laid by s. E451.7; disenchantment by s. D718; disguise by s. off beard so as to escape K521.2.1; fatal game: s. necks K858; giant s. hero's head F531.5.12; loud sound of s. J1484; origin of custom of s. A1597.2; squaring accounts by s. the wife J2082.

Shavings transformed to gold D475.1.2. — Countertask: making a loom from s. H1021.6.1; raised treasure turns into s. N558; wild huntsman repays with s. that turn to gold *E501.15.4.

Shawl. — Deceptive land purchase: as much land as a s. will cover K185.4; making large s.-cloth from one cocoon's silk H1022.4.3; prayer s. V58.5.

Shawls. — Thief guards s., steals them K346.4; women spread s. in enemy's path and entangle them K2352.

She-bear. — Strong man son of man and s. F611.1.5.

She-devil. — Man marries s. G303.12.6.1.

She-dragon B11.2.0.1.

She-fox. — Widowed s. rejects suitors who do not resemble her deceased husband T211.6.

She-goat. — Green s. B731.1; man transformed to s. D134.2.

She-goats. — Herdsman neglects his s. in favor of wild-goats J345.1.

Sheaf. — Devil as s. G303.3.4.7.

Sheaves prostrate selves E761.5.6.

Shearer. — Good s. does not skin sheep J531; sheep and ignorant s. J229.2.

Shearing flock of sheep in one day H1106. — Deceptive division of animals for s. K171.5.

Shears. — Magic s. *D1183, (produce love) D1355.15; mountain-man carries s. at side like sword F460.1.3; thief detected by sieve and s. H251.3.3.

Sheath and knife as analogy for mother and unborn child T579.1.

Sheba. — Queen of S. propounds riddles to Solomon H540.2.1.

Shedding of animals periodically A2483.

Sheep becomes dog at night B182.1.4, D621.5, H1331.9; born with human head as a result of bestiality T465.1; -dogs unite to hunt wolf J624.2; duck, and cock in peril on sea together J1711.1; with fiery collar B19.4.3; helpful to Lord: get wool A2221.10; and ignorant shearer J229.2; with inexhaustible wool D1652.14; jealous of dog because he does nothing W181.1; kill a fox who has licked up the blood they spilled in a fight J624.1; kill wolves F989.5.1; killed by the butcher, who they are persuaded will spare them J2137.5; licking her lamb is envied by the wolf J1909.5; magically disappear D2087.3; makes fox run to hunter K1178; protect child B535.0.10; as sacrifice V12.4.6; sleeps if shoe tied to ear B782; as souls redeemed from hell F81.6; thief confesses in church N275.5.1; thief forced to buy ram wethers K439.5; thinks that his weak legs are the reason for loss of eating contest J2228; thrown in well become crimson F933.3; transformed to grasshoppers D412.7; unharmed by beasts F989.5. — Alliance of s. and dog B267.2; black s. thought to be devil J1785.7; black s. turn white F985.1; calf-s. B14.3; carrying hundreds of s. across stream one at a time (task) H1111; cattle and s. of the sun A732.1; creation of s. A1884; deceptive division of s. K171.7.2; deity gives persecuted child s. S464; destructive s. B16.1.6; devil cannot change into a s. G303.3.6.3.1; devil stands in church door and writes down names of his own people on s. skin G303.24.1.4; dividing two s. and a ram J1241.1; divination by shoulder-bone of s. D1311.10.1; diving for s. K1051; dog caresses sick s. (hopes for his death) K2061.3; eagle warns shepherds that wolf is eating s. J715.1; enmity of leopard and s. A2494.2.6; fairy s. F241.7; fairy as s. F234.1.11; fairies threaten s. watcher F361.11; famished wolf asks s. to bring him water K2061.5; first s. in Ireland A1884.0.1; fox feigns to be playing with s. K2061.2; ghosts visible to s. E421.1.4; giant s. B87.1.3; give s. good care but do not let it fatten (task) H1072; good shepherd shears his s. but does not skin them J531; helpful s. B412; hound by day, s. by night D412.5.4; how s. got horns A2326.1.3; hundreds of s. to be carried over stream one at a time (endless tale) Z11; husband says he'll bear a s. J2321.3; inexhaustible s. D1652.1.9.2; island of s. F743.2; why s. has thin legs A2231.7.2, A2371.2.1; lies about s. X1243; magic s. B184.6; magic sight by looking at shoulder-bone of s. D1821.3.8; making s. laugh and dance: mutilation K1445; man boasts he fears saint no more than hornless s.: killed by them Q582.5; man taken to be s. J1765.2; man transformed to s. D135; nine-horned s. B15.3.1.2; numskulls quarrel as to which way the s. shall return J2062.1; pasturing black s. until they become white (penance) Q521.4; peace between s. and wolves K191; why s. is a good runner A2555.1; selling a s. and bringing it back along with the money (task) H1152.1; shearing a flock of s. in one day (task) H1106; why s. do not speak A2231, A2422.2; speaking s. B211.1.1; stolen s. dressed as person K406.1; thief's excuse: bitten by the s. J1391.3.1; three crimes in killing s. with two unborn lambs J1169.9; trickster gets s. for shearing, the dupe pigs K171.5; wager that s. are hogs K451.2; well rises for s. F933.1.3.2; well rises for s. only for rightful owner H251.3.9.2; white s. comes to upper world, black to lower F67; why s. walk with bowed heads: bowed to God A2221.9; witch as s. G211.1.4; wolf locked up with s. J2172.2.2; wolf proposes abolition of dog guards for s. K2061.1.1; wolf sold as a s. K132; wolves' false truce with s. K2010.3; wolves, wild pigs condemned to death for eating s. B275.1.3.2; why s. may keep wool which grows on his forehead A2255.1, A2322.5.

Sheep's head has eaten dumplings J1813.8. — Casting s. eyes at the bride J2462.2; cause of s. walk A2441.1.12; crow sits on s. back, afraid to sit on dog's W121.2.3; hedge to catch s. wool J2060.2; putting money in s. anus J1851.4; thieves claim to be looking at s. teeth J1391.3; test of wife's ability to keep secret: the buried s. head H472.1; tiger in s. clothing stolen by sheep-thief K1621; weaving mantle from one s. wool H1022.4.2; why s. tongue is black A2344.3.1.

Sheepfold. — Ghost laid in s. E437.7.

Sheepskin. — Fox in s. gains admission to the fold and kills sheep K828.1; magic s. *D1025.8; treasure-producing s. B114.1, D1469.11; white s. used as source of light J1961.

Sheet. — Lover escapes behind s. K1521.5.1; milk sack transformed to s. of water D454.5.1; saint stretches protective s. over followers D2163.9; stealing s. from bed on which person is sleeping (task) H1151.3; witch heals child by covering with s. D2161.3.3.1.

Sheets. — Owner and monkey put on s. to frighten K1682.1.

Sheherezade J1185.1.

Sheldrake. — Reincarnation as s. E613.1.1.

Shell transformed to (boat) D452.2.1, (person) D432.2.1. — Blindness cured by s. F952.3.1.1; carrying s. from which ashes fall forms path K321.1; clam s. lures man into sea G308.7; deity arises from s. of darkness A115.6; discourteous answer: tortoise's s. A2231.1.4; fairy lives in s. F225; foolish bargain: good fish for worthless s. J2081.2; ghost sounds conch s. E402.1.3.1; magic cocoanut s. *D985.1; man transformed to s. D233; mankind originates from s. A1246; origin of animal's s. A2312ff.; origin of dents in crab's s. A2312.3; origin of moon from s. A743.1; origin of s. money A1433.3; origin of snail's s. A2312.2; thread tied to ant who pulls it through coils of snail s. H506.4; thumbling hides in s. F535.1.1.10.2; tortoise given hard s. for ferrying goddess A2223.6; transformation when one expresses astonishment at smith drawing water in egg s. D512.1.

Shells. — Origin of s. A2826; sacred s. V1.6.4.2; trickster sacrifices only s. of nuts and inside of dates K171.3.1.

Shellfish. — Devastating s. B16.5.3; dragon as modified s. B11.2.1.4; origin of black scales of s. A2315.1; trickster pinched by s. J2136.4.

Shelter. — Animals grateful for s. B393; animals provide s. B538; curse: lack of s. M443.1; forethought in provision for s. J740.

Sheltering. — Beard s. men from rain F545.1.4; tree s. abandoned girls D1556.2.

Shepherd *P412; who cried "Wolf" too often J2172.1; frightens tiger by threatening report to ass K547.8; -god A453; in God's service H1199.12.1; as helper *N841; as hero L113.1.4; mistaken for ass J1765.1; in palace sickens for country air U135.2; rescues abandoned child R131.3.1; shuts up the lion in the yard with the livestock J2172.2; transformed to bird still calls sheep A2261.1. — Animal as s. for man B292.1; baboon as s. for man B292.1.1; bittern from transformed s. A2261.1, A1965.2; clever s. J1115.9; disguise as s. K1816.6; dog caresses sick sheep but s. knows that he hopes for sheep's death K2061.3; dumb princess brought to speak by s. who insults her H343.1; dwarf conducts s. to hell to collect debt from nobleman F451.5.1.14; escaped lamb delivers himself to s. rather than to slaughter J217.1; fox as s. K934; good s. shears his sheep, does not skin them J531; hungry s. attracts attention J1341.6; is s. known to God? H1292.17; lion leaves sleeping hare to follow the s. J321.3; noble-woman weds s. T121.2; saint's staff as s. D1446.4; shipwrecked s. distrusts the sea J11; wolf almost locked in the stable by the s. J2172.2.1; wolf offers to act as s. *K2061.1.

Shepherd's consecrated staff keeps cow from straying D1446.3. — Origin of s. pipe A1461.6.

Shepherds. — Angel announces Christ's birth to s. V235.1; eagle warns s. that wolf is eating sheep J715.1; God throws sand on lazy s. A2005.

Shepherdess born of egg T542.1.

Sheriff. — Proud s. has only nine farmers in his jurisdiction J2331.1.

Shield in front of otherworld palace F150.3.1; shrieks in battle F995. — Cast of s. annihilates enemy F639.3; child born with s. T552.5.3; clouds as God's s. A1133.4; devil in dragon's head on a s. G303.8.10; engraving s. with unique pattern H1199.4; extraordinary s. F824.2, F839.2; fairy gives invulnerable s. F343.10.3; flaming s. as life token E761.7.9; giant s. F612.3.2; giant's s. F531.4.5.5; giant with millwheel as s. F531.4.1; god's s. A157.4; inscription on s. misinterpreted K511.2; light from s. of cobra A1412.1; magic s. *D1101.1; sword and s. as proxy at wedding T135.3.1; transformation to s. owner's likeness D40.1; turning left side of s. as challenge P556.1.

Shields. — Capture by being pressed between s. R5.2; castles thatched with golden s. F163.1.3; clashing s. in heavens evil omen D1812.5.1.17.2; falling s. as evil omen D1812.5.1.25; god with clouds as s. A137.14.3; precedence shown by position of s. P632.4.1; roaring of s. evil omen D1812.5.1.17.3; roof of s. P552.3.1.

Shift. — Magic s. *D1058.1.

Shifting blame to another J1166; married couples in bed K1318.

Shillings. — Incognito king joins robbers: to take only six s. K1812.2.1.

Shingling the fog X1651.1.

Shining. — Castle of wax, s. like gold F771.1.8; devil has s. teeth G303.4.1.5.1; magic castle s. from afar D1645.3; magic sight by looking at s. object D1821.3.7ff.; moon made from s. fragments A742; origin of s. patches beneath sea A925.7; sun not s. when murder is done F961.1.1; sun s. at night F961.1.5; sun s. for twelve days, nights F961.1.5.1; sword s. as fire, sun F833.4.1; troll bursts in s. sun G304.2.5; well s. at night F718.5.

Shinny. — Deceptive s. match K23; egg as s. ball F878.

Ship, see also **Boat;** becomes small boat D491.7; builder F671; built with a wooden saw J2171.1.1; with devil aboard sinks G303.25.9; of glass in otherworld *F169.3; held back by otherworld women F402.1.13; held back by magic D2072.0.3; of hell A676; magically sunk D2098; moved by sacrifice D2136.8; sails on fog X1651.2; will sink if murderers aboard

N271.10; -spirits F485; in storm saved because of sailors' "Ave Maria" V254.2; summoned by wish D2074.2.3.2; transformed D454.10, (to stone) D471.3; wrapped with feather-beds and canvass and pitched (so as to save it) F1031. — Bells hung at every corner of s. P651; boat expected to grow into s. J2212.7; box transformed to s. D454.1.2; capture by hiding in disguised s. K753.1; capture by taking aboard s. K775.1; color of sails on s. as indication of good or bad news Z140.1; dead body not to be on s. C541.1; demon s. sails against wind F411.3; escape from s. while captors quarrel R216; escape on s. on wheels K611.3; extraordinary s. *F841ff.; fairies stop s. to entice man F302.3.1.2; fire-s. K2364; fish swallows s. F911.4.1; fish rescues s. B541.5; Flying Dutchman's s. E511.2; ghost s. E535.3; giant blows to prevent s. approaching F531.3.1.4; giant's leg stops s. at sea F531.3.1.2; giants' s. Naglfar F531.6.7.1.2; gold, silver shower on king's s. F960.1.1.2; great s. X1061.1; horse that went like a s. J2481; loadstone draws s. to it *F806.1; magic land and water s. D1533.1.1; magic s. *D1123; magic submarine s. D1525; making sails for s. from one bundle of linen H1022.3; making s. of stone H1021.3; man complains of injustice of gods' wrecking s. because of one man's sin U21.3; man magically appears aboard s. D2121.11; money tied on corpse thrown overboard from s. in order to secure burial V64; mountain opens. s. on wheels comes out D1552.4; passenger brings s. bad luck: cast overboard N134.1.5; phantom s. E535.3; pictures that cannot be removed in s. D1654.8; praying that s. sink since prayers never answered J1467.1; pumping out a leaky s. (task) H1023.5; reef is old, s. is new J2212.4; rivals aboard s. thrown overboard when food is gone K527.4; sacrifice to gods holding s. back S263.4.1; sea is salt because of wrecked salt s. A1115.1; seduction by luring woman to look for s. K1339.2.1; seduction by taking aboard s. to inspect wares K1332; sewing together broken s. H1023.7.2; shipman refuses alms: s. turned to stone V421; sick voyagers on s. accused as magicians D1711.12; sight of phantom s. a bad omen D1812.5.1.10; snake becomes s. D425.1.4; strong man carries s. F624.7; strong man holds back s. F637; travelers mistake brushwood at a distance for a s. K1886.4; treasure buried in sunken s. N513.5; vision prevents taking passage on s. which sinks V541; vow to die before surrendering s. M161.4.1; water-spirit holds back s. F420.5.2.7.4; witch raises wind, keeps s. in port G283.1.2.1.

Ship's course left to winds and fate N118.1. — Fairy mistaken for enemy's s. burning K2369.9; magic prevents s. moving D1419.3.

Ships burned to prevent flight R244. — Defending oneself against many s. H1199.8; detonation hurls s. out to sea F1078; devil piles sand in ocean so that s. may run aground G303.9.9.5; fifty s. promised (49 molded out of earth) K236.1; giant fishes for s. G322.1; reeds make s. appear like island K1872.2; sham war threat holds s. back K1771.7.

Shipwreck to avenge self K815.12; as punishment Q552.12. — Animals from transformed survivors of s. A1715.5; bush loses clothes in s.

A2741.4; couple separated in s. reunited N741.2; extraordinary s. F931.5; magic object protects from s. D1388.1f.; mountain-spirit causes s. F460.4.4.7; rescue alone from s. chosen over drowning with goods J222; rescue from s. R138; runes protect against s. D1388.13; separation by s. N317; sham prophecy of s. to leave vacancy K1771.8; Virgin Mary saves from s. V268.4; water-spirit causes s. F420.5.2.7.3; witch causes s. G269.8.

Shipwrecked given piece of gold for death V64.1; man lands on enemy territory N399.1; man repulsed by animals B772; men use false names K1831.1; shepherd distrusts the sea J11. — Bat, diver, and thornbush s. A2275.5.3; disguised s. men kill king K913.1; seaman who defies God s. Q221.4; water-spirits save s. F420.5.1.1.1.

Shirt as chastity index H431.1; made by woman free from trouble, worry H1195. — At betrothal maid makes s. for her lover T61.3; ghost asks to wash s. E412.3.2.1; in return for magic s. hero stays in Ireland M226; luck-bringing s. N135.3; magic forgetting of wife when husband removes s. she has given him D2004.6; magic s. *D1056, (protects against opposition) D1389.7; making s. from piece of linen three inches square (task) H1022.4; making s. from single flax-seed H1022.4.1; man's head is cut off so that the s. sewed together at the neck can be put on him J2161.2; naked ghost asks for s. E412.3.2; Nessus-s. (burns wearer up) D1402.5; sewing magic s. H383.2.2; sewing s. for bridegroom's father H383.2.3; sewing s. from flower petals H1021.9.1; sewing a s. of stone (task) H1021.9; weaving a silk s. from hair (task) H1021.6; weaving s. from piece of thread H1022.2.2; wife lazy: husband has no s. to die in W111.3.5.

Shirts. — Disenchantment by sewing s. for enchanted brothers D753.1; making many s. from one hank of flax (task) H1022.2; Russians wear red s. A1683.1.1; why Russians wear their s. outside their breeches A1683.1; sewing s. to trees J2465.9.

Shock. — Electric s. scares away treasure diggers N561.

Shod. — Coming neither barefoot nor s. (task) H1055; frog wants to be s. J512.12; running horse s. by skillful smith F663.1; transformation to horse by being s. with horseshoes D535.1; witch as horse s. with horseshoes *G211.1.2.

Shoe beating as bride test H386.1; test H36.1. — Asking haystack to clean dirty s. Z41.7.1; bringing lost s. as suitor test H322.4; captive throws his s. at serpent who chokes while he escapes K672; empty s. follows wild hunt E501.10.1; god with thick s. A128.5.1; girl hacks off her heel to get s. on J2131.3.1; lacing bed-clothes to s. J2161.3; magic s. points out road D1313.13; saint's image lets golden s. fall as sign of favor to supplicant D1622.3; shoeless husband threatens wife with s. J1545.3.2.

Shoes, see also **Boot(s), Moccasin(s), Sandal(s), Slipper(s);** as adultery fee J761.3; buried with dead V67.2; carried into the tree J1521.1; dropped to distract owner's attention K341.6; enable hero to climb stone D1532.3.1. — Big s. in front of the barn K1717; cobbler rewarded for giving s. to poor boy Q42.9; dancing to death in red-hot s. (punishment) Q414.4; dead man asks for s. E412.3.3; devil visible to one who walks in minister's holy s. G303.6.2.4; devil's s. empty G303.4.5.1.2; escape by reversing s. K534; extraordinary s. F823; extraordinary occurrences connected with s. *F1015ff.; fairies make s. for shoemaker F346.1; fairies' horses have round s. *F241.1.4; fool makes s. for animals as well as men, since he expects a cold winter J1873.1; fortune's s. N135.3; hurting feet to save s. J2199.4.1; inverted s. indicate banishment Z174.1; king asleep in mountain will awake when his horse's s. are worn down D1960.2.1; lazy mother given s. of cotton: son knows that she will not wear them out W111.5.1; magic s. *D1065.2; man with earth from his own land in his s. says he is on his own land J1161.3; man puts on s. only when he wades river H591.1; old s. patched with new J2129.5; prisoner's release dependent on charmed s. M202.1.1; promise to be fulfilled when iron s. wear out M202.1; recognition by s. H36.1.1; riddle about wearing new s. H588.13; silver s. F823.4; sleeping in s. to avoid insect bites P2102.1; stag with iron s. J2335; stingy wear out their feet to save s. W152.11; tabu: wearing s. at shrine C51.1.15; tanning s. with bark from saint's tree Q551.6.2.1; time measured by worn iron s. *H1583.1; traveling till iron s. are worn out H1125; vow not to marry till iron s. wear out M136; wandering till iron s. are worn out (punishment) Q502.2; wearing enemy's s. on shoulders L416; wearing s. on pilgrimage tabu C99.2; why s. worn only wading river H591.1; wolves lick saint's s. B251.2.3; woman sells favors for new s. T455.3.1; worn-out s. as proof of long journey *H241.

Shoemaker, see also **Cobbler** P453. — Devil as s. G303.3.1.18; fairies make shoes for s. F346.1; repartee between s., ruling lord J1289.7.

Shoemaking. — Origin of s. A1454.

Shooting, see also **Shot;** contest *H1591, (with bride) H332.1.5, (on wager) N55, (won by deception) K31; dead antelope until it will come to fool J1909.2; drives away ogre G584; at enemy's reflection in water J1791.5.1; object breaks spell G271.4.8; star (as angel) V231.2, (as good omen) D1812.5.2.6; (origin of) A788.2, (signifies a birth) E741.1.2, (signifies a death) *E741.1.1; through iron with arrow H1562.13. — Bad luck follows man s. stork N250.1; cowboy s. injured wife J1919.9; disarming by a s. test K631.2; disenchantment by s. D712.7; dwarf king prevents a father from s. his son F451.5.1.16; dwarfs resentful of mortals s. at birds above Hibichenstein F451.4.4.1; enemies s. at hat held outside shelter K631.3; fire beams s. from devil's eyes G303.4.1.2.3; island created by s. arrow A955.2; liar's s. boast involves odd number X905; man s. into wreath of mist brings down fairy *F302.4.1; resuscitation by s. arrow E61; revenant forced away by s. E439.1; suitor contests: s. H331.4; tabu: s. at consecrated wafer C55.2; test of paternity: s. at father's corpse *H486.2; wishing by s. star D1761.1.1.

Shop. — Animal guards s. B576.5; ass in potter's s. J973; creator opens s., distributes crafts and professions from it A1440.1.

Shore, see Seashore.

Short, dangerous vs. long, sure road J266; magistrate wears high helmet X142.4; pregnancy T573; -sighted (judgments) M20ff., (wish) J2072. — Absurd s.-sightedness J2050—J2199; why animal has s. (tail) A2378.4, (tongue) A2344.1; hair robe "not too long and not too s." J1161.8.1; why hog has s. snout A2335.4.1; why lynx has s., blunt nose A2335.2.2; magic object causes members to grow long or s. D1376; murderer cursed with s. life Q556.10.1; taking the s.-cut J2119.2.1; time seems s. to those who play, long for those who wait U261; vegetables which mature in miraculously s. time F815.1; "way s. yet long" J21.5.3.

Shortened. — Arm s. for breaking tabu C946; day magically s. D2146.1.2; life s. by incontinence T317.0.1; night magically s. D2146.2.3.

Shortest. — Hunting tabu on s. day C636; straight path not always s. J2119.2.

Shortness of life U250ff.

Shot, see also **Shooting.** — Devil s. with silver gun G303.25.7; giant s. into upper world by means of magic bow *F54; king unwittingly s. by own order K1612.2; lie: hunter's remarkable s. X1122; lucky s. with arrow (foot and ear of deer) N621; monster s. and followed into lower world F102.1; on rainy day when s. will not go man flogs his s. J1864; stars from arrows s. at sky A763.1; thousand at one s. K1741.2; youth having s. raven takes feather to raven's sister H78.2.

Shots. — Spirit throws back s. fired at it F473.6.5.

Shoulder. — Divination by bone from sheep's s. D1311.10; dwarf carries his knocked-off leg on his s. F451.6.13; giantess throws her breasts over her s. *F531.1.5.1; Hercules tells driver to put his s. to wheel J1034; looking back over left s. tabu C331.1; magic sight by looking over right s. D1821.3.2; man searches for axe which he carries on s. J2025.1; mark on moon's s. A751.5.3; mountain-wife has breasts so long that she throws them over her s. *F460.1.2; rider takes the mealsack on his s. to relieve the ass of his burden J1874.1; witch power from looking over s. G224.6; at communion witches spit out wine over s. G285.1.

Shoulders. — Armless people have legs growing from their s. F516.1.1; arms magically fall from s. D1403.3; bird rests on person's s. B575.2; birth from man's s. T541.13; cross between s. as sign of royalty (nobility) H71.5; fairies have breasts long enough to throw over their s. *F232.2; giant three spans between brows and three yards between s. F531.2.2; hills are loads from hero's s. A962.10; placing mountain on s. H1149.9; snakes issue from dragon's s. B11.2.7.

Shout remains in air three days F688.2.

Shouts. — Giants' s. are storms or great noise F531.3.8; throwing contest: trickster s. K18.1; wild hunt heralded by s. of huntsmen E501.13.5.

Shouted. — New creation s. away A636; two person believe other must be s. at X111.3.

Shouting after bathing leads to adventure N784; from forbidden place H1199.3. — Battle-s. A1341.1; mysterious s. in glen F756.5; resuscitation by s. at dead E26.

Shovel. — Magic s. *D1205.

Shoving lazy child with knives, killing him J2465.3.1.

Shower of stones seems snowfall to giant F531.5.4.1. — Extraordinary s. F962; god transformed to s. of gold D235.1; gold, silver s. at royal birth F960.1.1.2; prayer for s. of gold V57.2.

Showers. — Fiery s. in hell A671.2.4.3; why the sea is salt: heavy rain s. on ashes of wood burnt by primeval fire A1115.3.

Showing fairy gifts tabu F348.9.1. — Executioner s. hero how to use gallows K715; king s. self in public once a year P14.21; wine s. through woman's white throat F647.6; woman's beauty s. through seven veils F574.1.2.

Shreds. — Trail of s. of dress R135.0.4.

Shrew blows nose into snout A2211.5. — Why s. dies on road A2233.1.3, A2468.1; taming the s. T251.2.

Shrew-mouse. — Tabu to kill s. C92.1.3.

Shrewish wife T251. — Marrying s. wife as punishment Q599.2.

Shriek. — Dragon's s. makes land barren *B11.12.2; giant's loud s. G158; magic object compels person to s. D1419.1.

Shrieking plants, animals D2091.12; shield F995; sword D1081.4. — Contest in s. or whistling K84.1; magic compels s. D1419.1; plant s. when uprooted F992; spirits hover in air s. over battle F418; three-legged cat s. over grave permits finding of treasure N542.2.

Shrike as birds' king B242.1.5. — Why the s. is disliked A2522.2.

Shrimp. — Color of s. A2411.5.7; man becomes s. D179.4; marriage to s. B603.1; origin of s. A2171.4.

Shrine bleeds F991.4; of saint supresses pestilence V221.0.13. — Begging cripples hurry away from s. lest they be healed and lose their livelihood X531; cure at s. of Blessed Virgin D2161.5.2.1; profaning s. forbidden C51.1; tabu: leaving corpse at s. C51.1.14; tabu: wearing shoes at s. C51.1.15; treasure hidden in religious s. N514; vow to build s. M183.1.

Shrines V113. — Saint dispels devils from s. V356.1.

Shrinking of magic dog D491.1.3. — Lies about s. X1785.

Shroud alone left in grave E411.0.7. — Dead arises when s. bursts and pursues attendant E261.2; devil in place of dead man in s. G303.18.2; drunk man lying under his bed thinks he is lying in his s. X811; living man in dead man's s. E463.

Shrouds. — Corpses laid by s. E456.

Shrubs grow after sky lifted A625.2.5. — Sundry characteristics of s. A2792.

Shutting sun up in pit A721.0.2. — Fowls never s. doors at night A2433.4.6; husband rebukes wife and paramour for not s. door K1569.2.

Shuttle. — Magic s. *D1185; making a boat from splinters of spindle
and s. (task) H1022.7.

Siamese twins F523.

Sibyll as prophet M301.21.

Sick crew accused as magicians K2129.2; hero overcomes antagonist L311.1;
hung in well to cool off: drown J2412.6; lion K961; man offers deity
more bulls than he owns K231.3.5; men hesitate to take sacrament, die
V39.8. — Attendance on s. rewarded Q57; cauterizing "s." wheel
J2412.7; curse: children to be s. M460.1; cruelty to s. persons punished
Q285.2; deaf man visits the s. X111.9; deduction: bread is made by a
s. woman J1661.1.3; disguise as s. man *K1818; dog caresses s. sheep
K2061.3; dwarfs become s. F451.3.5.2; false repentance of s. U236;
healing s. as task H1199.2; helpful animal cares for s. master B536; lion
licks s. man J413.1; love-compelling man made s. of bargain D1904;
magic sickness from wounding s. person D2064.6; mother is cutting off
heads of well to cure s. H583.4.3; numskull makes himself s. J2134;
punishment: animals become s. Q551.4.1; race won by deception: sham-s.
trickster K11.5; reductio ad absurdum: father is s. from snake-bite in
winter H1023.3.1; river from blood of s. F162.2.13; roof taken off above
s. man who cannot die E722.2.3; sham s. man aroused by beating K1676;
stingy man's wife prays husband become s. W152.16; transformation to
s. man D53.1; well man made to believe that he is s. J2317.

Sickening. — Boy s. at mother's death P231.1; shepherd in palace s.
for country air U135.2; spouse s. at separation T213.

Sickle bought at great cost given back J2514; with life in it E772; put
into water to cure fever J1959.1.1; told to cut by itself J1881.1.6. —
Alleged self-operating s. K119.1.2; magic s. D1206.1.

Sickly. — Changeling is s. F321.1.2.3.

Sickness, see also **Disease, Illness, Plague;** ascribed to quarreling wines
J1891.1; because men too happy A1346.2.3; from love T24.1; from
meeting ghost E265.1; brought on ship causes accusation as magicians
D1711.12; or weakness for breaking tabu *C940ff.; personified Z112. —
Animal's flesh as cure for s. K961; bringing s. to certain tribe H1199.2.1;
devil in God's absence puts s. in Adam's body A1293; feigned s., see under **Illness,** feigned; magic s. *D2064ff., (because of Evil Eye) D2064.4,
(as punishment remitted) Q572, (prevents rape) T321.5, (as punishment)
Q551.6; magic toad under king's bed causes s. *B177.1.1; moon's waning
caused by her s. A755.3; quest for only person curing s. H1319.1; sacrifice frees moon from s. A755.3.1; sham s., see under **Illness,** feigned;
theft by reporting relative's s. K343.1.2; wandering soul cause of s.
E721.3; witch causes s. G263.4; witch pretending s. and kicking helper
into pit G269.1.1; wood-spirits cause s. F441.6.1.

Side made numb by ghost E542.3. — Birth through mother's s. T584.1;
boy born with one s. flesh and one iron T551.4; child born beautiful on
one s., hairy on other T551.4.1; conception through mother's s. T517.2;
culture hero snatched from mother's s. A511.1.1; do not leave my s.

(youth obeys command to absurd lengths) J2516.4; druid ugly on one s., beautiful on other D2031.4.1; fairy has one s. green F233.1.1; lips on s. of face F544.1.3; man with one s. of stone (iron) F525.1.1; man with only one s. F525.1; objects on one s. of palisade of otherworld garden black, on other white F162.1.2.3; stitch in s. from being told about hearing a man chopping wood F647.8.1.1.

Sides. — Tearing out person's s. S187.1.

Siege. — Enemy induced to give up s. K2365; king occupies s. perilous H41.9.

Sieve protection against witches G272.6. — Formula: as many children as holes in a s. Z75; mountains from breaking of God's s. *A971.2; murdered person's ashes put through s. S139.2.2.8; special power of chaste woman: carrying water in s. *H413.3; task: carrying water in s. H1023.2; thief detected by s. and shears H251.3.3; witch travels in s. G241.4.3; witches use s. for a boat G249.3; well like a s. F718.10.

Sighs. — Five s. for our sins Z71.3.1; origin of tears and s. A1344.

Sight, see also **Seeing;** of dead woman spinning drives people insane E561.1; of fairies fatal F363.3; lost by magic D2062.2ff.; of magic twigs gives foreknowledge of day's events D1311.4.0.1.1; of magic wheel causes blindness D1331.2.5; of mermaid bad omen D1812.5.1.9; never seen before: oil pot broken with sword J2469.5.2; of old home reawakens memory and brings about return from otherworld *D2066.2; of phantom ship a bad omen D1812.5.1.10; restored by animal B516; restored by magic D2161.3.1, F952; restored as reward Q161.1; -shifting caused by magic D1331.4ff.; tests H1575; of wild hunt renders person insane *E501.18.6; of woman as source of sin T336. — Animals have second s. B120.0.1; boy loses his s. (no butter on bread) J1561.4.2; cat with remarkable s. B181.1.1; contest between runner swift as thought and one swift as s. F681.3.1; disenchantment by s. of old home D789.3; enemies caused to lose s. of each other K1886.2.1; frog-woman disenchanted by s. of water D789.3.1; herbs restore s. D1505.1; love at first s. T15; love through s. of picture T11.2; loss of s. for breaking tabu C943; insanity from seeing strange s. *D2065.2; magic object restores s. *D1505ff.; magic power of long distance s. D1820.2; magic s. *D1820ff., (of blind man) D1820.1.1; marvelous runner swift as s. F681.4; object gives magic s. D1331.1; person of remarkable s. F642ff.; poor s. of elephant A2332.6.7; princess restoring blind man's s. R161.2; prophecy: death at s. of son H341.1.7.1; recognition by miraculous s. of seer H184; second s. from spirit of dead D1821.8; shooting test won by deception: proof of good s. K31.2; speaking of extraordinary s. forbidden C423.2; tiger's short s. by day, good sight at night A2491.4; unusual s. bad omen D1812.5.1.22.

Sights. — Extraordinary s. in otherworld F171; horrible s. in hell A671.2.

Sign of great plague F493.5; hung out informing brothers whether mother has borne boy or girl T595; language H607; of the Cross V86. — Conversation by s. language mutually misunderstood J1804; devil made to disappear by making s. of the cross G303.16.3.4; disenchantment by s. of cross D788; flame issuing from mouth as s. of royalty H41.4; magic results from s. of the cross *D1766.6; magic s. D1299.1, (assures warriors will not flee from battle) D1359.5; permanent s. of disobedience for breaking tabu *C910ff.; severed finger as s. of crime H57.2.1; stone bursts as s. of unjust judgment *D1318.1.1; touching head s. of accepting bargain P675; unacquainted lovers converse in s. language T42.1; wrong s. put out leads to boys' leaving home N344.1.

Signs before Judgment Day A1002.2; of royalty H71. — Weather s. D1812.5.0.15.

Signal. — Lovers' s. T41.3; mantle used as s. for rendezvous with lady is used by serving-man to deceive her K1317.1; milk in stream as s. H135.2; theft s. given in foreign language K358; wife's pre-arranged s. catches paramour K1569.5.

Signature forged to obtain money K362.7.

Silence in fairyland C405; points to guilt J1141.8; under punishment breaks power of enchantment *D1741.3; wager J2511, (leads to sham death) J2511.1.2; wagerers arrested as thieves J2511.2. — Church bell cannot be raised because s. is broken V115.1.3.1; disenchantment by maintaining s. D758f.; hanging for s. about treasure Q413.7; has never regretted s. but often regretted speech J1074.1; Island of S. F129.4.6; maintaining s. as ascetic practice V462.1; maintaining s. in snake pit H1506; power of wild hunt evaded by s. E501.17.4.4; priest induced to betray secrets of confessional: money then exacted from him for s. K443.8; princess to break s. H343; seven days s. at world's end A1057; trickster exacts promise of marriage as price of s. after having seen a princess naked *K443.6; trickster sells s. after lying with princess K443.6.2; value of s. J1074; wager to s. the washerwomen of Bloys N76; two years' s. imposed on suitor H317.2.

Silent dead E545.0.2; hero L124.2; man asks king what to say to fool J1714.5; person F569.3; wife T272. — Causing s. person to speak H1194.0.1; child s. till seven L124.1; during the s. period (why nun did not call for help) J1264.4; elements s. at Nativity V211.1.5; fool passes as wise man by remaining s. N685; girl who cannot keep s. thereby provokes her rival to admit unchastity K1275; philosopher keeps s. J1074.1.1; quarrelsome wife conquered by s. husband T256.1; saint s. by holding stone in mouth V73.6.2; soldier s. before king as before all stupid persons J1369.5; with a s. person one is alone J817.3.

Silk as battle clothing C878.2.1. — Achieving kingship by bringing s. H1355.4; making large shawl from s. of one cocoon H1022.4.3; making peacock of s. H1021.11; origin of s. A2811; quest for princess transformed into skein of s. H1381.3.4; transformation to skein of s. D264; wearing s. tabu C878.2; weaving a s. shirt from hair (task) H1021.6.

Silkworm's origin A2182.1.

Sill. — Ghost cannot cross new door s. E434.10.

Silver animals B102ff.; apple F813.1.2; boat F841.1.9; bullet (protects against

giants, ghosts, and witches) D1385.4, (injures devil) G303.16.19.14; castle
F771.1.2; chairs F786.1; coffin F852.3; coins from pumpkin A1433.2.1;
-colored fairy F233.2; demanded of saint disappears Q552.18.1; dish becomes wooden D475.3.5; floors in otherworld F165.3.3; in gun releases
curse M429.7; hair F555.2; hairs as sign of royalty H71.2; in chain increases in fire D1671; king and attendants F521.3.4.1; kingdom F707.2;
leaps into magic pitcher D1469.9; magically hides self D1555.3; magically produced D2103; mast F841.2.1; object becomes black (life token)
E761.4.2f.; oar F841.2.3; pear F813.4; pillar H1322.1; seeds pave city
F761.5.2; staff kills E64.1.1.1; statue of animal F855.3; tree F811.1.2;
wall around otherworld F148.2; weapon F830.1. — Animal with s. horn
B15.3.2; animals with s. members B101ff.; bird with gold head, s. wings
B15.7.3, B101.1.1; bow of gold, s., and copper F836.1; castles of s.
F163.1.4; city of s. in heaven A661.1.2; dead usurer fed molten s. by
devil Q273.1.1; dogs of gold and s. F855.3.2; dog vomits gold and s.
B103.4.3; dress of gold, s., color of sun, moon, and stars F821.1.5; dress
of gold, s., and diamond bells F821.3; dwarf king has s. miner's torch
bright as sun F451.7.4; fairies give woman s. spoons F342.1; fish of s.
B102.4.1; floors of s. in otherworld dwelling F165.3.3; fortress of s. in
otherworld F163.5.2; fowls eat s. F989.22.1; gold and s. combed from
hair D1454.1.1; heart breaks at third drink from s. canister F1041.1.1.1;
house of s. F163.3.2; island with rampart of gold and palisade of s.
F731.3; king is worth twenty-nine pieces of s. H711.1; man shoots the
devil with a s. gun G303.25.7; moon is hare covered with s. A759.4;
mountain of s. F752.2; objects transformed to s. D475.3; origin of s.
coins A1433.2; person with s. body F521.3.4; person with s. horns
F511.3.1; pillars of s. and glass in otherworld *F169.1; reincarnation
as s. E645.1; shower of s. F962.8.1; towers of steel, s., and gold F772.2.2;
transformation: objects to s. D475.3; tree with s. branches D1461.0.2;
wall of s. about otherworld F148.2; wattling of s. in otherworld
dwelling F165.3.4.

Silversmith restless until silver mixed with alloy U138.1. — Voice changed
by work of s. F556.2.

Silvery. — Dwarfs have s. white hair F451.2.4.2.

Simian transformed to person D318. — Man transformed to s. D118.

Simile. — Proverbial s. Z62.

Simon Magus a druid P427.0.4. — Contest of St. Peter with S. V351.3.1.

Simony V466.

Simorg B31.5.

Simpleton, see also **Fool, Numskull;** dissuades from suicide J628; fools
robbers into sharing loot L141.2; put to ordeal by holy water H222.2.
— Obscene tricks played on s. wishing to marry K1218.9; owl's hoot
misunderstood by lost s. J1811.1.

Simplicity. — Woman loses magic when s. lost D1749.2.

Simultaneous births T589.7.

Simultaneously. — Father and daughter die s. P234.2; tree bears fruit, flower, leaf s. F811.16.

Sin personified Z127. — Anger is s. J153.2; calamity as punishment for s. A1003; cities of s. F769.2; confession brings forgiveness of s. V21; confession without giving up s. punished V25.2; dead cannot rest because of a s. E411; dream reveals s. to saint D1817.2.1; forgiveness for s. for acts of charity Q171.1; giants cause s. F531.5.15; imagined penance for imagined s. J1551.2; immunity from punishment for s. as reward Q171; magic detection of s. D1817.0.5; magic power of person without s. D1714; monk escapes s. by living alone J495; nature of s. U230ff.; "never publish a man's s." J21.52.4; no carnal s. in otherworld F167.10; only man without s. can see God V510.2; pebble for each s. J2466.1; priest drags heavy sack symbolic of s. H606; penance for s. A1549.4; reincarnation as punishment for s. E606.1; sacrifice after s. V17.2; saying of "Aves" obliterates s. *V254.1; sexual desire as original s. T8; sight or touch of woman as source of s. T336; test of s. H263; wild huntsmen wander because of s. E501.3ff.

Sins determine size of hell fires E755.2.4.1. — All s. since the birth of Christ J1743.1; children punished for fathers' s. P242; confession of s. V20ff.; devil accuses congregation of s. G303.24.1; devil's two books for noting s. G303.24.1.9; eight deadly s. Z71.16.1.1; five sighs for our s. Z71.3.1; fox confesses s. but is immediately ready to steal again K2055; fox and wolf forgive each other's s. but punish ass U11.1.1; hiding s. from God J1738.8; man's s. forgiven when he kills a greater sinner Q545; origin of penance for s. A2835; person obnoxious for his s. unnamed C433.1; saint can reveal hidden s. V223.3; reward for confessing s. Q36.1; Seven Deadly S. Z71.5.6.2; three s. of hermit J485; world fire as punishment for s. A1031.1.

Sincerity. — Suitor's s. tested H314.

Sinful city burnt Q486.1.1. — Devil and s. priest disappear amid blaze of fire in river G303.17.2.4; host taken away from s. priest V31.1.

Singer repaid with promise of reward: words for words J1551.3. — Bad s. thinks he is talented: driven from theatre J953.2.

Singers. — Devil in roof of church into which he thrusts voices of loud s. Q554.2; magic identification of s. D1819.6.

Singing, see also **Song**; animal B214.1; apple D1615.3; blossoms F979.12; bones *E632ff.; at death's approach J2461.1.2.1; like leader: sing his distress call J2417.1; mountain F755.2; raises water from tank D2151.5.1; rice-pot D1615.6; snake brings death K445.2; snowshoes D1615.5; snails rebuked J1885; tabu C481; tree D1615.1; water D1615.4; at wedding T136.3.2; wolf's power over humans Z33.4.2. — Animals s. songs of praise B251.2ff.; automatic s. doll D1620.0.1.2; birds' s. ceases at revelation B251.8.1; bird shows way by s. B151.2.0.3; boy learns s. from spirits F403.2.3.3; camel and ass together captured because of ass's s. J2137.6; choral s. accompanies saint V222.3; contest in s. H503.1; dead s.

E546; death respite while s. K551.3.2.1; deer summoned by s. D2074.1.1.2; devil s. on grave G303.9.8.3; devil vexing friars caused to repent by s. "Te sanctum dominum" G303.24.3; dupe loses booty through s. J2351.3; dupe s. on trickster's body K827.3; dwarfs dislike s. of hymns F451.5.9.2; echo of giantess's s. F531.3.8.4; embryos s. in womb T575.1.5.1; fairies s. F262.1; fool s. in small bathroom J2237; ghost s. E402.1.1.4; huldra s. F460.2.13; humor of bad s. X145; husband s. about adultery K1556.1; magic s. D2173; magic object acquired by s. D858; magic results from s. *D1781; magic s. object *D1615ff.; men rulers s. in their houses T252.5; mermaid's s. causes girl to sleep, drown B81.11; mermaid s. in choir B81.3.2; mermaid s. divinely in church B81.13.6; minstrel's birds s. accompaniment F262.3.2; ogre s. constantly G652; parson's s. reminds woman of goat X436; pet swan saves self by s. death song N651; poet s. after death E371.3; punishment for s. worldly songs Q391; pursuer s. while captive escapes K606.0.1; quest for s. (apple) H1333.3.4, (tree) H1333.1.1, (water) H1321.5; rain produced by s. D2143.1.2; rescue from ogre by means of s. G555; sheep encourage wolf's s. K561.2; six dwarfs listen to s. by confirmed children F451.5.21; stars s. together A767; storm because of bird's s. D2141.0.6; thief hears owner's s., thinks self detected N611.4; waves s. gives information D1310.7; water raised from tank by s. D2151.5.1; wolf s. as dog's guest J581.1.

Singeing. — Animal characteristics from burning or s. *A2218ff.

Single combat (between bird chiefs) B264, (judicial) H218, (to prove valor) H1561.2; person entering house after sunset tabu C752.1.3. — Dogs in s. file in wild hunt E501.4.1.8; invulnerability for s. day D1845.1; pledge to say but a s. phrase brings accusation of crime M175; skillful axe-man cuts down trees with s. stroke F666ff.; tabu: going to assembly in company of s. warrior C864.2; vow not to be killed by s. opponent M162.

Single-handed. — Annihilating army s. (task) H1135.

Sink. — Magic s. hole *D933.

Sinking of bodies of water in primitive abyss A910.3; of church and congregation to bottom of sea F941.2.2; of earth as punishment Q552.2; into earth as curse M448; into earth as punishment C984.7; of ship with devil aboard G303.25.9. — Building s. into earth F941; demons s. in sea D1400.1.23.1; divining rod s. at place where tribe shall settle D1314.2.1; heathen idols s. into earth V356.2.1; island s. in punishment Q552.2.3.2.3; lies about s. X1733; magic object s. if person guilty H251.3.7; magic veil keeps man from s. in water D1388.0.2; man s. (into earth) F942, (into mud) D2092; rats leave s. ship B757; vision prevents taking passage on s. ship V541; witch s. ships G283.1.2.3.

Sinkings. — Extraordinary s. F940ff.

Sinless. — Only s. person may touch dead H1558.12; quest for s. couple's son H1381.4.

Sinner confesses before sinning, pardoned V21.5; reformed by visits to heaven, hell V522; thinking of God saved V525; wanders between earth and heaven E411.0.4. — Angel holds nose when handsome s. passes U119.3; dead man begs s. not be buried atop him E545.9; devil harries repentant s. G303.9.4.9; extraordinary island upon which no s. can die (be buried) F747; hand of s. sticks out of grave E411.0.1; other dead drive s. from graveyard E411.0.5; repentant s. comforted by angel V235.2; unquiet dead s. taken to priest for absolution E411.0.2.

Sinner's grave cursed, rolls M411.14.1; punishment: rain or famine J229.13. — Devil leaves s. body G303.18.0.1; tree from s. grave E631.0.6.

Sinners to be burnt on Doomsday M341.2.7.1; endure hell tortures for one year Q560.3; go to heaven as reward for hymn Q172.5; going to heaven numbered by hairs in saint's chasuble M364.3.1. — Devils tormenting s. in hell E755.2.7; decrying of female s. A1556.3.1; protection of s. by confession V20.1; souls of s. spend seven years under water E751.5.

Sinning. — Eating what is stolen without s. H1151.19; god controls mortals' s. A185.14; lion sent to kill man: frees him from possibility of s. and sojourn in purgatory J225.2.

Sion appointed chief for mountains A1187.

Siren *B53ff.; in mermaid form B53.0.1. — Curse: to be swallowed by a s. M434; woman becomes s. D199.3.

Sirens and Odysseus J672.1.

Sirius as bad omen D1812.5.1.6.1.

Sister Beatrice K1841.1; and brother *P253; -brother incest A1331.2, A1337.0.7, A2006, G37, M365.3, Q520.3, T415; -brother marriage of first parent's children A1552.3; escapes to stars from brother R321.1; faithful to transformed brother P253.2; hidden in thigh F1034.3.1; honors brother only in prosperity W175.1; in-law *P264; is mourning last year's laughter H583.5; rescues brother(s) R158; secures blessing due another K1988.1; as wager N2.6.1. — Abandoned s. rescued by brothers S357; accidental meeting of brother and s. N734; begetting child with s. by earbox J1919.7; blood of brother and s. will not mingle *F1075; brother as deer seeks s. D647.1; brother accused of impregnating s. K2121.1; brother flogs unchaste s to death Q458.2.1; brother and s. arrange marriage of their unborn children M146.4; brothers eat their s. G73.1; cruel brothers forced to beg from abused s. L432.1; dwarfs adopt girl as s. F451.5.1.2; earth from murder of first brother and s A831.4; girls eat their s. G73; husband, wife disguised as brother, s. K1839.14; insects from brother-s. incest A2006; magic object received from s. D815.4; man in love with own s. learns her identity N631.3.2; man unwittingly ravishes his own s. T471.1; moon, sun are s. and brother A736.1.4.2; only youngest brother helps s. L32; quest for lost s H1385.6; rescue of s. from ogre G551; resuscitation by s. E125.2; rich man ignores poor s.

J411.11; riddle: white brother, black s. H722.1; rivers as offspring of Ocean and his s. A938; sacrifice of s. S260.1.2; seven brothers and one s. Z71.5.1; sun s. and moon brother A736.1.1; sun brother and moon s. A736.2; treacherous s. *K2212; treacherous s.-in-law K2212.2; vow to find vanished s. M155.2; woman drugs s., substitutes for her with lover K1317.6.1.

Sister's — Dead brother reproves s. pride E226.1; dead s. return E325; brother qualifies as s. bridegroom H310.2.

Sisters *P252; and brothers do not marry A1552.1; curse child by Thor M437.2; in love with same man T92.8; rescue sisters R157. — Accidental meeting of s. N743; brothers and s. *P250ff.; guessing which of veiled s. has golden hair H511.2; lisping s. K1984.1; man married to several s. T145.1.3; moon ate up her s. A753.1.4.2; queen sets tasks to disenchant s. H933.2; sun and moon as s. A736.4; seven brothers marry seven s. Z71.5.8; three witch s. G201; wit combat among s. for dowry: their pregnancies H507.4.

Sister-in-law tabu C172. — Advances to s. punished Q242.3; brother-in-law seduces s. T425; cruel s. S55; name of s. tabu C435.2.1.

Sisters-in-law assign tasks H934.2. — Chaste sleeping with six s. T355; guarding six s. as task H1199.17.2; tasks set by s. H939.3.

Sisyphus's punishment Q501.1.

Site. — Building s. for church miraculously indicated V111.3; building s. determined by animal B155.1.0.1.

Sitting on eggs (to finish their hatching) J1902.1, (without breaking them) H962.1; on hero saves him K649.1.3; on mounds tabu C755.5; on pillow-covered egg H1568.1; on a sunbeam *F1011.2; in uncomfortable position as penance Q541; up with corpse as test H1461 — Avoiding s. on foot of couch H506.6; brother s. between heaven and earth (in tree) H583.3.2; devil prevents moving of little stone by s. on it G303.9.9.1; dupe s. on hot stone K1032; dupe s. on sharp stones K1116; dupe tricked into s. on hot iron K1074; fairies kill mortals by s. on them F364.1; for six months bride only s. in husband's house T165.7; future learned by s. on hide D1812.3.1; giants s. on mountains to wash feet in stream below F531.3.9; God finds the devil s. under a tree G303.1.2.1; magic power by s. D1733.4; move stool before s. on it J21.34; repression of lust through s. in water T317.1; mermaid s. on knight's bedpost B81.5; thumbling drives wagon by s. in horse's ear F535.1.1.1; vow against s. on father's seat until revenged M152.2.

Siva. — Brahma takes men to S. F12.3.

Six characteristics of demons G302.4.1; children at a birth T586.1.1.1; dwarfs listen to singing by confirmed children F451.5.21; -headed dragon B11.2.3.3; -headed giant F531.1.2.2.4; -headed man F511.0.2.4; -headed ogre G361.1.3; -headed ogre slain G512.8.3; -legged animal F451.4.3.9; -legged horse B15.6.3.1.1; months' respite from unwelcome marriage T151.1. — Animal with one head, two bodies, s. legs B15.7.11; devil drives s. he-goats G303.7.7; devil has s. wings G303.4.2.1; earthborn men with s. arms F516.2.1; formulistic number: s. Z71.4; giant with s. arms F531.1.6.7.2; giants fifty feet tall with footprints s. feet long F531.2.1.2; god with s. faces A173.2.1.4; incognito king joins robbers: to take only s. shillings K1812.2.1; king questions s. doctors J171.2; mountain-man must die s. times F460.2.12; persons (animals) with s. eyes F512.2.1; prophet speaks s. nights a year M301.0.2; universe created in s. days A601.2; what s. things are not worth doing H871.

Sixteen. — Death at s. M341.1.4.1; fish killed by hero, cut into s. pieces A972.7; formulistic number: s. Z71.10.

Sixth toe cut off K512.2.4.1. — Magic created on s. day D803.1; storms in s. heaven A1130.2; when crows are five years old they start their s. year (riddle) H865.

Sixty. — Carpet s. miles square F783.1; formulistic number: s. Z71.13; giant with s. daughters in big wedding X1071; king with s. thousand sons T586.2.2; prophecy: death at s. M341.1.4.5; wood of s. trees nourishing three hundred men apiece F812.2.

Sixteen hundred as formulistic number Z71.16.7.

Sixty thousand Jewish souls in heaven E755.1.4.

Size of animals' eyes A2332.3ff.; changed at will D631; -changing god A120.2; of giant F531.2ff.; of object transformed D480ff.; of revenant E422.3. — Ancient animal squeezed: hence small s. A2213.1; animal's s. increased by stretching A2213.3; battle fury changes warrior's s. F1041.16.6.2; bride test: s. of feet H365; castle of extraordinary s. F771.8; demons' s. changed at will G302.3.0.1; devil's thumb the s. of two fists G303.4.3.2; doubling the s. of the earth A853.1; effects of age and s. absurdly applied J2212; fairies' s. F239.4; magic change of person's s. D55; magic object changes persons's s. D1377; person the s. of a thumb F535.1; trolls the s. of ten or twelve year old child F455.2.1.

Skating avoided over water when spirits are offended C41.3.1.

Skein. — Quest for princess transformed into s. of silk *H1381.3.4

Skeins. — Traveling till two s. of thread are unwound (task) H1125.1.

Skeleton in closet U115; giant G124. — Bone becomes s. D457.12.2; ghost as s. E422.1.11.4; ghost s. reveals murderer E231.2; lover's s. hung in adulteress's room Q478.1.3; origin of human s. A1312.

Skeletons. — Land of s. E485.1.

Skeptic kicked by sacrificial animal V346.

Skis. — Flight on s.: two on one pair R241.

Skiing. — God of s. A459.1; sacrifice for good s. V17.4.1.

Skill as suitor test H326. — Bride test: domestic s. H383; brothers having extraordinary s. rescue princess R166; fairy's remarkable s. F273; loss of s. D2099.1; magic object gives s. D1343; origin of games of s. A1468; remarkable s. F660ff.; son surpasses father in s. L142.3; test of s. H1563, (in handiwork) H504.

Skills. — Lie: extraordinary s. X960.

Skillful companions F601.0.1; companions create woman: to whom does she belong? *H621. — Fairies as s. smiths F271.3; trolls s. as smiths F455.3.1; winner of most s. princess to be king P11.2.3.

Skin changes color because of broken tabu C985; of magic pig heals wounds B184.3.2.3; of murdered person found in enemy's house S114.1; like snow suitor test H312.5. — Animal jumps out of s. so only s. caught K525.4; animal slips out of s. F1088.4; animal with unusual s. B15.7.10; animal's food-producing s. B531.3; animal's s. revolves, while flesh, bones stay still B738; ass in lion's s. unmasked when he raises his voice J951.1; barber kills child; blames thin s. J1166.1; beautification by s. removal D1866.2; bluff: digging canal instead of bringing water in s. K1741.3.1; boats of s. unsuccessful C841.0.1; boy hidden under s. R318.1; burning s. disenchants D793.2; change of animal's and man's s. A1281.2.1; contest: scratching s. off each other K83.2; dead husband's s. worn to seduce wife K1311.0.2; not to destroy animal s. of enchanted person too soon *C757.1; devil blows s. off man who belongs to him and goes into the s. G303.18.3; devil in place of dead man in dead man's s. G303.18.2; devil stands in church door and writes down names of his own people on sheep s. G303.24.1.4; devil writes faults of man on goat s. G303.24.1.2; devil unpeels woman's s. G303.20.5; disenchantment by hiding s. D721.2; disenchantment by removing s. D721; donning s. makes woman fleet D1936.1; escape by dressing in animal (bird) s. *K521.1; feathered s. magically grafted to bald head D2161.3.4.1; giants dressed in s. F531.4.7.1; girl hidden in s. of her dead mother R318; guessing origin of certain s. H522.1; hedgehog's s. reward for good deed A2220.1; impostor dresses in s. of his victim K1941; jay borrows cuckoo's s. A2241.6; jay in peacock's s. unmasked J951.2; magic bag made from s. of crane (transformed woman) D1193.1; magic s. of animal *D1025ff.; magic transportation by animal s. D1520.5; magic unpierceable s. protects against attack D1381.3.2; man created from rubbings of s. A1263.3; man rejuvenated by changing s. A1319.12; mermaid's s. B81.9.5; mutilation: shoulder s. torn off S166.3; mutilation: s. cut from back S166; origin of animal's s. A2311ff.; origin of man's s. A1319.14; origin of s. color A1614.6; pig's s. heals wounds B511.2.1; poison of hydra corrodes the s. F1041.5; punishment: animal s. grows on man's back Q551.2; recognition of ornaments under s. H61; rejuvenation by changing s. D1889.6; riddle: what is the hardest to s. H659.15; serpent renews s. A1335.5; servant lays s. of dead dog in the bed of his mistress and master K2134; sewing clothes into s., tearing them off together H1505; sky changes s. like snake A702.9; soul absent from witch's s. G251.2; substituted s. E785.1; transformation by putting on s. D531; unchaste woman's s. boiling away H411.11.1; unjust judge's s. stretched over a footstool and kept in the presence of judges J167; vital s. E785; why man doesn't change s. A1319.12.1; why men have s. A1310.3; why snakes and lizards change s. A2250.2; witch killed by placing salt or pepper inside s. while it is laid aside G275.8.1; witch out of s. G229.1.1.

Skins. — Origin of death when early people put on new s. A1335.4; saint wears animals' s. V462.5.1.1; seller of fox s. mixes otter s. with them J2083.3; tribe with double s. F558.1; trolls dressed in s. F455.2.4.

Skin-Sore as hero L112.7.

Skinning buffalo alive, turning them loose to grow new skin X983; farmers J2472; a stone (task) H1023.10. — Skillful flayer s. running rabbit F664.1.

Skirt. — Giantess in obscene s. F531.4.7.1.2; woman trips over s., devil laughs Q331.2.3; woman hoists s. to raise thunderstorm D2141.0.10.

Skittles. — Playing s. with demons H1421.1.

Skull of suicide must roll in dust until it has saved a life Q503.1; transformed to water monster D447.2; used as drinking cup Q491.5; with writing on it F559.4.1. — Adulteress drinking from paramour's s. Q478.1.2; deity born from s. A114.3; ghost's s. thrown in Ganges E459.7; giant's s. holds a man seated F531.2.3; helpful speaking s. N819.3.1; horse's s. as pillow F874.2.1; human s. used for divination D1311.8; identification by s. H79.5; king's gigantic s. F511.0.8; laughing s. advises hero E366.1; magic s. D992.4; man makes drinking water from his own s. (lie) X1739.2; man's fate written on his s. M302.2; milk drunk from hero's s. M316; mistress keeps murdered lover's s. in flower-pot T85.3; numskull does not understand about baby's s.: sticks needle through it J1911.1; offended s. *C13; origin of sky from Ymir's s. A701.2; powdered s. as remedy D1500.1.7.1; return from dead to punish kicking of s. E235.5; return from dead to punish theft of s. E235.4.5; speaking s. E261.1.2; swearing on s. M118; trickster puts on buffalo's s. and gets head caught J2131.5.1; wandering s. fulfills prophecy M391.2; wandering s. pursues man *E261.1; whale becomes s. D421.7.1; wild huntsmen carrying s. under arms E501.7.4.

Skulls as sacrifice V12.3. — Bird carries deity's daughter home from land of s. A2223.2; cup of s. F866.4; fear test: eating and drinking from s. H1434; fear test: fetching s. from charnel house H1435; hearth of human s. F420.2.5; house of s. F771.1.9; land of s. *E485; princess builds tower of s. of unsuccessful suitors *S110.3; water-spirits have hearth made of three human s. F420.2.5.

Skunk. — Bad smell of s. A2416.3; color of s. A2411.1.2.4; walk of s. A2441.1.6; why s. is disliked A2522.4.

Skunks. — Why porcupines and s. do not live on Cape Breton Island A2434.2.1.

Sky afire as plague sign F493.5; asked earth to wrinkle up feet: hence hills A969.4; dwellers must not eat on earth C211.3; as helper N818; lowering on people F791.1; -mother's child longs for earth-father D2006.2.1; ornamented with clouds to shade mountains A1133.2; as overshadowing tree A652.4; -basket F51.2; -father and earth-mother

A625; -god A210ff., A736.4, A753.1.4.1, F12.1; -rope *F51; -spirits E752.8, F499.1; -traveling snake B91.4; window F56. — Absurd theories concerning the s. J2273; attempts to measure height of s. L414.1; bottle-fly finds stolen woman in s. B543.1; children escape to s. and become thunder A1142.3; clay dropped from s. forms hill A963.9; creator in s. beneath us A651.2.0.1; creation of the s. A701; creator goes to s. A81; dragon's visit to s. B11.3.3; earth let down from s. on to primeval ocean A817; extraordinary s. and weather phenomena F790ff.; fairyland in s. F215.1; first man descends from s. A1231; four s.-columns A665.2.1; fox pretends to be guarding s. K1251.1.1; giant reaches to the s. F531.2.1.5; heavenly bodies from objects thrown into s. *A700.1; house neither on ground nor in s. H1077; how many stars in s. (counterquestion) H705.3; journey to land without s. F126; land of dead in s. E481.8; leopard releases victim claiming to be holding up s. K547.14; little people from the s. F205; looking down on earth from s. tabu C335; magic song causes tree to rise to s. D1576.1; marriage of earth and s. T126.3; marvelous picture falls from s. in storm F962.12.3; moon from object thrown into s. A741; mountain reaches to s. F55; murderer escapes to s. R323.1; nature of the s. *A702; old man from s. as creator A21.2; origin of s. from Ymir's skull A701.2; rain from container in s. A1131.4; rain from waterskin in s. A1131.4.1; rain produced by spitting blood toward s. D2143.1.4; raising of the s. A625.2; river taken to s. becomes star A761.1; several suns, moons in s. simultaneously F961.0.1; stars from objects thrown into s. A763; stolen sun restored to s. A721.3; sun a fat woman walking across s. A738.1.2; sun and moon as uncle and nephew who ascended to s. A711.1; sun at edge of s. A739.1; sun from object thrown into s. A714; three suns shine in s. F961.1.3.2; tree hanging from s. A652.2; tree stretches to s. *F54.1; tribe climbs down from s. A1631.2; waterskin dragged along s. floor A1142.8; why plants no longer reach s. A2775.0.1; why tortoise looks towards s.: seeks his wife, a star A2351.5; wife carried up tree to s. in bag in husband's teeth J2133.5.1; woman from s.-world marries mortal man T111.2; woman who fell from s. A21.1.

Skies open, reveal heavenly company F969.1.

Skylight. — Woman flown through s. K786.

Slain, see also **Slaying;** warriors revive nightly E155.1. — Animals from body of s. person A1724.1; fairies cannot be s. F259.1.4.1; giant s. by man F531.6.12.6; girl s. to save virginity T321.4; girl's animal lover s. by spying relatives B610.1; god of the s. A310.2; insects from body of s. monster *A2001; magic object found on grave of s. helpful animal D842.3; men s. for girl F1041.1.3.6; parts of s. animals as token of slaying H105; plant from blood of s. person E631.0.3; plants from body of s. person or animal A2611ff.; tabu: stripping dead and s. C877.

Slamming door to otherworld *F91.1, F156.4; drawbridge to otherworld *F152.2. — Ghost s. door E402.1.7.

Slander K2100—K2199; punished Q297. — Quest assigned by s. H1219.6; undoing s. like picking up water J84.

Slandered queen reunited with husband N741.3; wife locked into tower to be burned R41.2.1. — Champion saves s. wife R41.2.1; man absents self from church because he does not like to hear people s. J1269.2; woman s. as adulteress K2112.

Slanderers kill woman, put her near Buddha K2115.2.

Slandering. — Fire consumes woman s. abbot Q552.13.3; uncle s. niece to appropriate patrimony K361.5.

Slap turns man's face around F1041.24. — Public s. accepted by friend H1558.11.

Slapped. — Child s. to stop crying, accidentally killed N333.1.1.

Slapping. — Ghost s. cheating son E234.1.

Slashing. — Spirit s. clothes F473.6.2.

Slaughter of animals by stampede K927; of innocents to avoid fulfillment of prophecy M375; of the ox J2168; from wheel rolling over Europe M341.2.20. — Blood as s. omen D1812.5.1.1.5; escaped lamb delivers himself to shepherd rather than to s. J217.1.

Slaughtering animals to avenge self J1866. — Conservative but absurd s. method kept U139.2.1; ignorance about s. animals J1906; tabu: s. buffalo in temple C93.5.

Slave, see also **Enslaved;** -driver mysteriously stricken dead Q558.7; -driving punished Q285.4; freed as reward for killing enemy Q42.4.1; hero L113.1.7; killed for following owner's order Q211.13; may not bring lawsuit P523.3; not to go near fetish C561; poses as wealthy man's son to gain wife K1917.8; as princess's helper N863; recognized by habits H38.3; shoots arrow into sun's horse A732.2.1; washing mistress's back in stream pushes her into crocodile hole K831.1. — Allowing self to be sold as s. K365.1; animals with human child as s. B292.0.1; clever s. J1114.0.1; clever s. girl J1111.6.1; deceptive sale of another as s. K252.1; disguise as s. K1816.13; dividing property: cuts s. in two J2469.3.1; former s. sickens for accustomed food U135.3; man rewarded for freeing s. Q42.4; master discovers that s. girl he wants to marry is a near relative T410.1; man lets himself be sold as s. so as to practice generosity W11.4; merchant's daughter intimate with s. T91.5.1.1; princess living in s. quarters Q485.1; princess in love with ex-king as s. T91.6.4.2; revenge of blinded s. K1465; sham dead king kills s. K911.4; treacherous s. K2251.

Slaves P170ff.; freed as reward Q121.1; killed by hanging S113.1.1; ordered married are brother, sister N734.1; spare infant they are ordered to drown K512.0.1. — Buddhists become s. of Taoists because they cannot produce rain V355; magic object furnishes s. D1476; origin of s. A1657; paramours dress selves as s., thinking to humiliate mistress K1234; robbers sold as s. K437.5; two 15-year old s. ordered: fool brings one 30 years old J2212.1.

Slaver. — Snake from devil's s. A2145.4.

Slavery. — Child sold into s. S210.1; criminal's wife and children sold into s. Q437.1; escape from s. R211.4; father unwittingly buys daughter who has been sold into s. N732.1; helper grateful for being bought from s. N801; incognito king sold into s. K1812.11; king sells self and family into s. M203.3; lovers fleeing s. R352; origin of s. A1473; person sold into s. R61; princess ransomed from s. R111.1.6; queen rescued from s. R111.1.6.1; saint saves girl from s. R165.1; sale into s. as punishment Q437; wife sells self into s. to ransom husband R151.1.1; woman escaping from s. kills would-be ravisher T320.2.1.

Slayer returns from dead to kill wicked person E232. — Daughter marries husband's s. to save father P234.1; faithless widow marries husband's s. T231.5; ghost's flying head attacks s. E261.1.1; hero as mighty s. F628.0.1; king's s. marries widow, gets kingdom P17.11; strong man as mighty s. F628ff.; Virgin aids repentant s. V276.3.

Slaying, see also **Killing;** to prevent being slain J675; as task H1150ff.; of person unwittingly done N320ff. — Fairy takes revenge for s. F361.8; ghost s. enemies E232ff.; husband's s. horse tames wife T251.2.3; prophecy: first side s. in battle to be defeated M356.1.3; two soldiers s. each other think they are s. common enemy K1883.3.

Sled thongs cut to prevent pursuit K637.

Sledge. — Bringing moon in s. J2271.4; coming neither on horse nor on foot (on s.) H1053.4; dwarf borrows s. F451.5.10.3.1; table thrown out of s. to go home by itself J1881.1.4; tree-trunks laid crosswise of the s. J1964.

Sledges turned in the direction of the journey (at night turned around by joker) J2333.

Sleep-bringing music F156.1, K606.1.2; charm D1364.22; denied to ogre G585; feigned to kill enemy K911.3; forbidden until quest accomplished H1247; is sweetest (riddle) H633.1; thorn D1364.2; walker thought to be ghost J1782.7; — Beggar buys right to s. near the girl K1361; children not left alone to s. A1579.1; cynic helps robber so both get s. J1392.3; death as punishment for feigning s. Q558.10; death thought s. E175; devil writes names of those who s. in church G303.24.1.7; deception by pretending s. K1868; demons powerless over souls commended to God before s. E754.1.1.1; devil works during God's s. at creation A63.1; disenchantment by proper person waking from magic s. *D762; divine beings assume their own shape in s. D796; endless s. given Endymion M433; fairy music brings s. F262.3.4, (to wounded) F262.6; fairies charm prince into deathlike s. F302.3.4.5; feigning s. in bed with hero H1556.5; goddess of s. A472.1; fairy takes lover back to fairyland in magic s. F302.3.4.4; guardian magically made to s. while girl goes to lover D1965; hero lies by princess in magic s. and begets child T475.2; horse pushes s. thorn from master's head B511.3; hospitality: wife to s. with guest C119.2; indebted merchant enjoys untroubled s. J1081.1; injunction: s. where night overtakes you C683: liquor blessed by saint causes magic s. D1364.7.1; long s., long waking F564.3.1; magic bird's song brings s. B172.2.1; magic birds cause s. by shaking wings B172.9; magic cure during s. D2161.4.12; magic power lost in s. D1741.1; magic s. D1364ff., *D1960ff., (causes lover to miss rendezvous) T35.0.2, (takes lover to fairyland) F302.3.4.4; man disguised as woman beguiles hostile chief and kills him in drunken s. *K1321.3.1; man stands before mirror with his eyes shut to see how he looks in his s. J1936; man walking in s. taken for ghost J1782.7; mermaid's singing causes girl to s., drown B81.11; murder in s. K959.2; origin of s. A1399.2.1; otherworld woman appears to mortal in s. F393.4; owner put to s. and goods stolen K331.2; preciousness of untroubled s. J1081; protecting prince's s. by shooting at frogs all night J2105; riddle involving s. H573.2; riddle solved by listening to talk in s. H573.3; saint takes little s. V462.5.2.1; seduction by feigned s. K1325.1; siren's song causes s. B53.4; soul wanders from body in s. E721.1; talking in s. betrays weaver H38.2.4; transformation during s. D696; transformation to snakes at night in order to s. D659.1; unusual s. habits F564.

Sleeper answers for the dead man J2618; not to be awakened since soul is absent E721.1.1. — Contest in seeing sunrise first: s. wins K52.2; ghost disturbs s. E279.2; ghost pulls blanket off s. E544.2; ghostly horse enters house and puts hoofs on breast of s. E281.2; mighty s. D1960.1.1; soul of s. leaves body as bee E721.1.2.4.

Sleepers. — Magic object does not awaken s. D1575f.; seven s. D1960.1; spirit harpoons s. F402.1.11.3.

Sleepers' hair tied to prevent pursuit K635.

Sleeping army *E502; beauty D1960.3, (found in magic castle) N711.2; with fairy a boon for lifesaving F304.5; ghost E568; with head in wife's lap T299.1; king in mountain as guardian of treasure N573; maiden's hair tied to tree K635.1; naked on cold floor H1504; naked girl: goddess or mortal? H45.5; outside prohibited by mosquitoes A2034.1.1; person grazed by arrow, awakes F661.9; place kept dry by magic D1542.4; potion given newcomers sleeping with princess P616; potion substituted for poison K512.4, K1856, N332.4, T37.0.1, T93.4; on salt J1322.2; potion D1364.7, (given to man who is to pass the night with a girl) K675; on totem-tree bed tabu C848; trickster's feast stolen J2173.1; watchman N396; with wife tabu on Midsummer's Eve C751.2. — Adulteress meets lover while husband s. K1514.17; adventures from s. beneath tree N776.3; advice on s. before suicide J21.2.2; advice against s. in strange circumstances J21.41; chaste s. together T350ff.; children s. in village dormitory T688; consorting with princess without s. H347; devil cheated on s. bargain K216.3; dupe tricked into s., killed K834.1;

dwarf washes, combs and braids hair for s. maids F451.5.1.13; fool s.
to avoid idleness J2243; fortune-telling dream induced by s. in extraordinary place K1812.3.3.2; genie s. with eyes open G634; ghost s.
with living E472; girl kills man s. with her K872.1; girl sees man s. by
wayside N723; girl s. in garden to meet lover discovered next morning
T36; god rescues s. man A185.2.1; goods stolen while owner is s.
*K331ff.; hero lies by s. girl and leaves identification token with her
H81.1; heroes dislike killing s. people K959.2.2; hero s. during first of
battle K2378.5; husband tests wife by s. on her hair H476; intercourse
with s. girl T475.2.1; king given s. potion K873.1; lengthy s. F564ff.;
man assuming lover's form s. with princess K1915.2; man can hear one
s. F641.3; paramour unwittingly drinks s. potion K675.1; people s. in
same room frighten each other H1194.1; person never s. F564; saint s.
with maidens without sinning T331.7; sun s. at woman's house J2272.3;
tabu: s. C735, (in saint's bed) C93.1; test: s. by princess three nights
without looking at her or disturbing her H1472; transformation to likeness of another by s. with arms about him under the same mantle D592;
warrior accused of killing s. adversary K2116.5; wrong man s. with
king's daughter K1612.1.

Sleepless dragon B11.4.3; god A102.8; person of diabolical origin F564.1;
son of waterspirit and mortal F420.6.1.7; watcher magically put to sleep
D1961.

Sleeplessness from breaking tabu C995; secret discovered N465.1.

Sleeve. — Fish in the s. J1604; queen gives away a s. of her dress:
miraculously restored V411.1; ghosts seen through s. of fur coat
G311.1.1.1.

Sleeveless. — Cutting off arms for s. sweater J2131.3.1.1.

Sleigh, see also **Sledge;** as swift as thought D1521.3; makes person magically hold on D1413.3. — Animals try in vain to repair s. B831; devil
invites girls into s. G303.7.1.2.3; magic s. *D1115; standing between
summer and winter (between wagon and s.) H1058.

Sleipnir (eight-legged horse of Odin) A136.1.2.1.

Slept. — Hills flat where gods s. A972.5.5.

Slicing. — Murder by s. person into pieces S139.7.

Slide. — Bear persuaded to s. down rock K1021.3.

Slighted. — Fairy takes revenge for being s. F361.1.

Slime. — Sea of s. F711.2.4.

Sling-stick becomes boat D454.9.2; -stones' origin A1459.1.3. — Lucky
cast from s. N623.4; magic s. *D1087.

Slinging. — Disenchantment by s. against something D712.2; giant s. stone
with his garters F531.3.2.2; resuscitation by s. E27.

Slipper test H36.1. — Love through sight of s. of unknown princess
T11.4.2; saint kills lion with s. D2156.11.

Slippers, see also **Shoes.** — King and the cheap s. J829.1; magic s. *D1065.7;

murder with poisoned s. S111.7; resuscitation by removal of poisoned s. E21.4; unavailing attempt to get rid of s. N211.2.

Slippery. — Cannibals enticed to climb s. barricade fall K895; dupe tricked on to s. road lined with knives K897; why animal is s. A2306.

Slipping on floor to imitate leader J2417.2; slipping into heaven along with holy person K2371.1.5.

Slope. — Return from lower world up steep s. F101.1.

Slopes. — Lies about steep s. X1523.

Sloth, see also **Laziness;** personified Z139.1; refuses to help make road: may not look on sun A2233.1.4.

Slovenliness W115ff.

Slow. — Extraordinarily s. person F596; red pepper for the s. ass: man tries it on himself X11; second son heir due to s. message P17.3.1.

Slowing down racer with mighty breath F622.1. — Hero's confederate s. down princess with his breath H331.5.1.1.1.

Slowly. — Walking home s.: wife's lover gone J2523.2.

Slowness surpasses haste L148.

Sluggish prince reformed by falling in love T10.1.

Slumber, see **Sleep.**

Sly. — Why fox is s. A2525.3.

Small, see also **Little;** fruit from big trees A2771.9; hero overcomes large fighter L311; jug of wine filled J1317; men preferred to big J493; trespasses punished: large crimes condoned U11. — Why animal has s. waist A2355.1; beggar with s. bag surpasses the one with the large L251; big piece of cake with my curse or a s. piece with my blessing J229.3; choices: s. inconveniences, large gains J350ff.; devil (troll) makes self s. D55.2.2; dwarfs are s. F451.2.1.1; dwarf has s. body and large head F451.2.1.3; easy escape of the s. *L330ff.; exceptionally large or s. men F530ff.; giants large or s. at will F531.6.5.2; help from s. man N821; humor of s. stature X142; man so s. he can go through eye of needle F535.2.2; monk discouraged by large amount of work to be done persuaded to undertake but a s. amount each day J557.1; ogre made to believe s. hero is large K1711; princess brought to laughter by s. animals H341.2; remarkable s. men F535; revenant as s. man E422.3.1; spirit as s. black man F403.2.2.6; stealing only a s. amount K188; very s. hero L112.2; wine very s. to be so old J1316.

Smaller the evil the better J229.10. — Animal's body made s. A2302ff.; devil becomes s. G303.3.5.2; making the earth s. A852; person becomes magically s. D55.2.

Smallest woman the best bride J1442.13. — Beginning with the s. K1024; quest for the s. of dogs H1307.

Smallpox deity rides nude on ass A137.8. — God of s. A478.2; origin of s. A1337.7.

Smeared. — Blood s. on innocent person brings accusation of murder K2155.1; fat s. on broom in preparation for witch's flight G242.1.1.

Smearing. — Sun s. face in mourning A737.8.

Smell, see also **Odor.** — Animal characteristics: color and s. A2410ff.; aromatic s. of saint's body V222.4.1; conception by s. of cooked dragon heart T532.1.4; headless person cannot s. or hear F511.0.1.2; marvelous sense of s. F652; origin and nature of animal's s. A2416ff.; panther's sweet s. protects him from other beasts B732; peculiar s. of body A1662; recognition by s. of jewels H93.0.1; woman brought up on goat's milk has s. of goat F647.5.

Smells. — Evil s. transformed to sweet D479.7; man soon learns to stand the s. of the tannery U133; ogre carries the sham-dead man (he s. already) K522.2.

Smelling out theft J2355.2. — Cannibal s. human flesh makes exclamation *G84; clever deductions by s. J1661.2; conception from s. (flower) T532.1.1.1, (bone dust) T532.1.4.1; foul s. coat to repel lover T323.2; resuscitation by s. of moss E72; rejuvenation by s. apple D1889.4; transformation by s. D564.

Smelting. — Origin of s. A1447.4.

Smile of child as foundation sacrifice wins freedom S261.1; saves infant's life S350.1. — Bat makes sun s. A1046.1; detection of guilt by s. J1149.5; enigmatical s. reveals secret knowledge N456; recognition by s. H79.4.

Smiling vines F815.7.3. — Ascetic never s. V462.7.

Smith, see also **Blacksmith;** *P447; disturbs fairies at night F361.17.2; exorcises sick child G271.9; forges iron man who helps him D1620.1.3; of the gods *A142; of hell A677.1; hero L113.6; with lantern wanders between heaven and hell known as jack-o'-lantern A2817.1; excessively jealous of wife T257.9; as prophet M301.19; rescues abandoned child R131.8.4; swallowed by monster F913.1. — Disguise as s. K1816.12; fairy s. gives knight magic sword F343.3; fettered monster's weakened chains renewed by stroke of a s. A1074.8; giant as s. *F531.6.10.1; heavenly s. is hammering on the moon A744; helpful s. N855; lie: remarkable s. X982; living s. must repair wagon belonging to wild hunt E501.15.5; magic object forged by s. to order D853; monk becomes s. P426.3.1; ogre teaches s. how to transform sand in his smithy G651; presumptuous s. chants the Divine Comedy J981; skillful s. F663ff.; son of king and son of s. exchanged K1921.1; strong hero struck by s. from iron F611.1.12; sun, moon and stars forged by s. A700.5; supernatural s. under lake *D921.3; tailor and s. as love rivals F92.12.1; transformation when one expresses astonishment at s. drawing water in an egg-shell D512.1; underground spirits instruct a s. F450.1.2; youths tutored by Vulcan, s. of hell F107.

Smith's wife made nails for Crucifixion V211.2.3.0.2. — Beast with human head shape of s. bellows B96.

Smiths. — Dwarfs as s. *F451.3.4.2; fairies as skillful s. F271.3; magic hymn protects against s. D1385.16.2; princess as s. P31.1; king cursed by dwarf s. P15.4; trolls skillful as s. F455.3.1.

Smith-work. — Goddess of s. A451.1.1.

Smithy. — Ghosts blow s. into air E279.7; salvaging anvil from burning s. H1574.3.1.

Smock. — Magic wishing-s. D1470.1.10.

Smoke ladder to upper world F52.2; from funeral pyres of brother and sister refuses to mix F1075; from lovers' funerals mingles in sky E643.1; rises from saint F1041.23; rising shows good health H1582.2; from sacrifice tabu for chief C564.5; test H1511.3; transformed to bridge D469.2. — Ascent to upper world in s. F61.3.1; breath in the cold thought to be tobacco s. J1801; choking with s. as punishment Q469.5; clouds come from s. J2277.1; clouds as s. rising A1133.3; devil detected, goes up chimney in s. G303.17.2.1; diagnosis based on s. F956.3; divination from rising s. D1812.5.0.4.1; dwarfs dislike tobacco s. F451.3.6.3; fairies protect selves with s. F399.2; father not yet born, son already at the top of the house (flame and s.) H763; filling house with s. to prevent partner's eating K336.2; genie in form of s. G369.2; house filled with s. so that owner gives trickster lodging K336; magic s. carries power of saint D1572; magic sword causes fire and s. D1566.1.3; magic transportation on s. D2121.7.3; man transformed to s. D285.1; Milky Way as s. A778.8; origin of s. A2816; raven caught in s.-hole: hence is black A2218.1; recognition of good health by s. rising from chimney H1582.2; rising s. as omen D1812.5.0.4; rising s. shows sacrifice accepted V19.1; reincarnation as s. E643; soul as s. E743.1; wolf overeats in the s.-house K1022.1.

Smoker. — Substitute s. K528.1; tobacco, pipe, and match debate usefulness to s. J461.3.

Smokers' punishment in hell Q569.5.

Smoking test H1511.4. — Dead man s. pipe E555; loss of strength by s. C942.1; person lives by s. tobacco F561.4; repartee on donkeys not s. J1289.20; why men like tobacco but spit when s. A2854.

Smooth. — Voice made s. F556.1.1.

Smothering old woman in grain J2465.7. — Death by s. for breaking tabu *C922; numskull s. children J2175.5.

Snail grows and fills house entirely F983.1; kills lion (lie) X1345.1; transformed to person D398. — Color of s. A2411.5.3; enmity of porcupine and s. A2494.12.16; magic s. body cures D1502.8.2; man becomes s. D198; mirror begrimed by s. J451.4; origin of s. A2181; stag defeated by s. vomits his gall-bladder A2211.13; test of resourcefulness: putting thread through coils of s. shell H506.4; thumbling hides in s. shell F535.1.1.10.2.

Snail's — Origin of s. shell A2312.2; origin of s. voice A2423.1.6.

Snails. — Fool thinks gold is being destroyed when s. crawl over it J1816; lies about s. X1345; enmity of cattle and s. A2494.12.3.1; heron wants no s. in heaven U125.1; singing s. rebuked J1885.

Snake, see also **Reptile, Serpent;** accidentally poisons hidden fruit N332.7;

adopts abused bride K1911.3.6; avoids object B765.18ff.; -body, woman's head B29.2.3; cannot die until he gives away treasure E765.4.6; can't kill prince until princess bears as many sons as snake J1173.1.1; carries devil into paradise: loses feet A2236.2.1; carries into fire man who has banned snakes Q597.1; coils self about faggots bundle H1023.19; complains to Zeus that people step on him J623.1; as creator A13.4.1; as creator of rivers and lakes A930.1.1; does not die before sunset B752.2; disenchanted by being allowed to wrap itself three times around person's neck D759.8; disregards warnings to improve his manners: eaten by crab J1053; as follower of the devil G303.10.3; as frog's mount J352.2; gives gold daily B103.0.4.1; gives man antidote for poison B514.3; -god A132.1; grateful to man feeding her young B391.1.2; grateful for milk B391.1.3; gives away magic pills J621.1.1; grows in person's stomach B784.1.2; hard to hold by tail H659.2.1; as healer B511.1; heals mutilated maiden with magic herbs B511.1.2; helps girl after winding self around her Q82.1; as house-spirit B593.1; inside woman comes out for cock B784.2.1.1; keeps house with other animals J512.7.1; killed by knives in animal he is swallowing K897.1; killed by own incantation K1613.5; kingdom under the sea B225.1.1; kills self B752.3; kills ungrateful tamer W154.10; magically enlarged D487.1; as messenger B291.4.2; mistaken for flute J1761.6; mistaken for whip J1761.6.1; in mouth as murder punishment Q418.2; around neck chastity test H412.5; as ogre G354.1; paramour B613.1; in person enticed out by milk B784.2.1.0; preys on mankind A1335.10; promises to do no harm to frog K815.6; protects man B524.3; refuses to help choose road: may not use road A2233.1.2; reincarnated as flowers E691.1; rendered powerless by pregnant woman D1837.4; rids himself of wasps J2102.2; at roots of earth-tree A878.3.1; spits out lump of gold B103.4.2.1; strikes person opposing saint Q557.6; shoots river rapids B748; sucks poison from bite D2161.4.10.2.2; sucks poisonous dew from grass B765.3; sucks woman's milk B765.4.1; swallows young to protect them B751.1; takes fugitives across river R245.2; transformed to object D425.1; transformed to other animal D418.1; transformed to person D391; in troll child's dough F455.10.1; turns to gold in answer to dream N182; and turtle exchange head for fangs A2247.2; vomits jewels B103.4.2.2; wanted by stepmother for daughter J2415.7; wants to act like pet J512.14; wants to eat frog friend J426.2; and weasel stop fighting in order to catch mouse W151.4; -woman as paramour B613.1.1; -woman's magic ashes D1469.10.1. — Abduction by s. R13.4.1; animals from mating of s. and person A1772; bad breath, forked tongue reveal disguised s. king K1822.3; bedstead warns of danger of s. D1317.11; big tree thought to be s. J1771.1; bird kills s. attacking master's family B524.1.6; blindness cured by killing s. K2161.4.10.5; child born with s. around neck T552.2; child feeds s. from its milk-bottle B391.1; child tears s. to pieces F628.1.3.2; crab saves hero from s. B524.1.12, B549.5; creation of s. A2145; crow's revenge on s. K401.2.2; cure for s. bite F959.5; death of s. encircling world A1082.3.1;

deer, opossum, and s. each render indispensable aid to man J461.4; deity's s. children A132.1.1; devil in form of s. G303.3.3.15; dog becomes s. D412.5.7; double s., male and female B726; earthworm thought to be s. J1755; enmity between frog and s. A2494.16.1; enmity of mongoose and s. A2494.12.2; escape from s. pit R211.7; fairy in form of s. F234.1.7; fettered monster as s. A1072.3; fight between s. and millipede B264.4; food of s. A2435.6.2; fox transformed to s. D411.8; friendship between s. and crow A2493.25; frog rescues man from s. kingdom B547.4; why s. does not go on the road A2233.1.2, A2441.4.1; head of killed s. bites king N332.3.1; hedgehog forces s. to suck out poison B511.1.3; helpful bird kills s. attacking master's wife and child B524.1.6; helpful s. protects man from attack B524.3; how to cure s. of blindness? H1292.4.2; why s. has no legs *A2371.3.1; how s. got small head A2213.1, A2320.1; lightning as fiery s. A1141.1; lion thankful rescued by s. B374.1; lizard tries to make himself as long as s. J512.9; magic dust kills s. D1402.27; magic object from redeemed s. D817.1.2; magic pills reduce s. to ashes D1402.25.1; magic rod kills s. D1402.10.2; magic s. compresses, expands B176.1.2; magic s. liver D1500.2.8; magic s.-oil causes illusions D1368.1; magic s. tail D1029.2.3; man cannot die: s. will not bite him N101.3; man fears s.-like rope J11.1; man with s.-like feet F551.1.1; man transformed to s. D191; marriage to five-headed s. B646.1.1; marriage to person in s. form B646.1; marriage to s. B604.1; mistaking own toe for s. J1838; murder by feeding poisonous s. S111.8; murder by wrapping s. around man K953.3; person swallows s. semen B784.1.3; poisonous s. bite test H1517; prophetic s. B145.2; punishment: s. sucks woman's breasts Q452; rainbow as s. A791.2; reductio ad absurdum: father is sick from s.-bite in winter H1023.3.1; reincarnation as s. E614.1; rescue of woman from s.-husband R111.1.5; resuscitation by s. E122.2; resuscitation when s. licks his bite E17.1; riddle about deaths of elephant, s., and jackal H803; revenant as s. E423.5; rod from magic hazel-tree kills s. immediately D1402.10.2; why s. sheds skin A2483.1; singing s. B214.1.10; soul in s. E715.5; spirit as s. F401.3.8; speaking s. B211.6.1; sun-god bitten by s. leaves earth for heaven A222; thrifty man saves even s. W216.1; transformation by eating s. eggs D551.6.3; transformation: handkerchief to s. etc. D454.3.2.2; treasure found in s. hole N511.4; treasure-guarding s. around princess's chamber H335.3.4; underworld s. kingdom F92.7; water s. carries boy across river B551.4; where s. got his fangs A2247.2, A2345.5; whoever hears singing s. must die K445.2; why water s. has no poison A2532.1.1; witch as s. G211.8.1; witch transforms self into s. when she bathes G245.1; woman bears s.-child T554.7; woman promises unborn child to s. S222.2; Zeus refuses wedding present from s. J411.2.

Snake's blood venomous B776.5.3; brain as only cure for monkey's disease K961.2.1; habitat A2433.6.8; human offspring B631.9; qualities B765ff.; strike causes swelling X1205.1; venom poisons tree D1563.2.2.2.

Snakes attend goddess A137.9; banned by magic D2176.1; brought to eat frogs, eat family J2102.8; controlled by saint D2156.5; created to humble proud man L482.3; expelled from human body D2156.5.2; have mass B253.1; issue from dragon's shoulders B11.2.7; put to sleep by music D1962.5. — All s. but one placated by music Z355; army of s. B268.7, D2091.2.1; bonga house filled with s., tigers and lions F221.2; why s. are venomous A2532.1; bridal chamber filled with coiled s. T172.1; culture hero banishes s. *A531.2; fanciful qualities of s. B765; four royal families of s. B244.1.4; god girdled with s. A123.10; goddess's bed of s. A155.6; imaginary s. X1396; king of s. B244.1; lies about s. X1321; man looks at copulating s.: transformed to woman D513.1; Muria eat s. A1681.3; no s. in Ireland A2434.2.3, M318; ornaments of s. F827.3; priest of s. B252.3; prison filled with s. R41.3; punishment: taking s. as foster children Q594; quest to land of s. H1289.1.2; rattlesnakes mate with black s. B754.3.1; reptile-men's power over s. D1711.13; rectum s. G328; saint banishes s. V229.3; saint breaks s. in bare hands D1840.1.1; saint turns s. to stone V229.24; sea from rotting s. A924.2; suckling s. eyeballs T611.11; throwing into pit of s. as punishment Q465.1; transformation to s. at night in order to sleep D659.1; why s. change skin A2250.2, A2311.9; why s. are proud A2523.2; witch gives birth to s. G243.3.1.

Snakebite punishment for breaking tabu C992. — Blindness from s. D2062.2.5; charms as antidote for s. D1515.1.1; frog's bite mistaken for s. F1041.1.11.4; head cut off as s. cure X372.2; prophecy: death from s. M341.2.21; St. Peter's grass as medicine for s. A2623.

Snap of finger kills robber F628.2.8.

Snapping door traps victims K736.

Snare, see also **Trap.** — Birds in s. fly out one by one Z11.2; first man catches woman in his s. A1275.10; frog causes deer to dance into s. K730.2; resuscitation by catching in s. E23; sun caught in s. A728; witch caught in s. G274ff.

Snares. — Sun tied to earth by s. of light A733.4; vision of earth in devil's s. V513.2.

Snaring. — Tabu: s. a being C566.1.

Sneering princess impregnated by magic L431.3.

Sneeze mistaken for gunfire J1809.1.

Sneezer wished long life A1537.1.

Sneezing of ghost in form of bear E552; of lion creates cat A1811.2. — Bear frightened by s. K2345.2; magic object causes continued s. D1372; monkey s. in king's presence J2413.6; omens from s. D1812.5.0.1; origin of s. A1319.9; treasure from s. D1454.9.

Sniff. — Why dogs s. each other A2232.8, A2471.1.1.

Snipe. — Hawk frightened at bill of s. J2616; man becomes s. D154.3; origin of s. A1942; where s. got his long beak A2343.1.2; why s. messenger for warriors A2261.6.

Snoring misunderstood J1812.5. — Ghost s. E402.1.1.5; giant's s. as thunder F531.3.8.1; insect in murdered person simulates s. K661.3; numskull thinks bishop's s. is death rattle J1833.

Snout. — Animal unusual as to s. B15.5; origin and nature of animal's s. A2335.4ff.; person with cat's s. F514.3; troll with s. F455.2.7; why rat's s. long A2335.4.6.

Snow always melts on certain hill F759.3; is devil's grandmother bleaching *G303.11.4.2; -child J1532.1; on house death omen D1812.5.1.18; magically burns D2143.6.4; makes rainbow behind runner F681.13; melts above dwarfs' dwelling F451.4.1.10; produced by magic D2143.6.3; tastes of wine F962.11.1; transformed to dogs D449.4. — Angel created from s. A52.1.3; angels melt s. around saintly babe V238.2; drying s. on the stove J2121; drying s. to make salt J1947; earth created from s. under divine throne A835.1; fairy dances in s.: no tracks left F261.2; lies about s. X1653; lover left standing in s. while his mistress is with another K1212; magic control of s. D2143.6; magic journey in s. whirl D2121.7.2; magic s. D903; man who sold dried s. for salt X1653.3; order for six loads of s. K1661; origin of s. A1135.2; pancakes made of s. D476.1.6; person not wet by s. D1841.4.2; red as blood, white as s. Z65.1; riddle: bird without feathers flies on tree without leaves (s. falls on bare tree) H764; sacrifice for s. V17.4.1; saint controls s. fall D1841.4.4; soul in s. E711.11; tribute paid in enchanted s. K236.3; wall of s. around hut in answer to prayer D2143.6.2; witch produces s. G283.3.

Snowball. — Game: rolling down hill in s. X1130.1; only s. can kill dwarf F451.3.2.4.

Snowbirds. — Why s. are everywhere A2434.1.3.

Snowbunting. — Transformation into s. D151.2.1.

Snowdrop. — Origin of s. A2661.

Snowshoes. — Escape by reversing s. K534.2; magic s. *D1065.3.

Snowstorm. — Child born in s. T581.5.

Snuff. — Cannibals persuaded to take s.: killed K827.2; taking s. with devil G303.9.9.8; witch asks for s. so that she may seize man G269.2.

Soaking. — Death respite for s. to make juicy K553.5.

Soap. — Magic s. *D1195, (gives clairvoyance) *D1323.6, (makes fairies visible) F235.4.2; washing dirty quilt without s. H1023.6.1.

Soapstone. — Man transformed into s. G263.2.1.1.

Sobbing, see **Weeping.**

Sobriety from magic food D1359.4.

Social etiquette A1537. — Beginning of s. relationships A1470ff.; culture hero establishes s. system A546; humor of s. classes X200—X599; loss of s. position as punishment Q494; lovers meet at s. gathering T34; origin of different s. classes A1650ff.; origin of s. ceremonials A1530ff.; transformation to person of different s. class D20ff.; unfavorable s. traits W150f.

Society *P (entire chapter); like a dish, must be mixed J81.1. — Tests of position in s. H1574.

Societies. — Jokes on secret s. X550ff.; why birds don't live in s. A2492.2.

Sock. — Giant carries man in s. F531.5.1.1.1.

Socrates builds himself a little house J401.1; and Xanthippe: "after thunder rain" T251.4.

Sod. — Magic s. *D934.1, (indicates falsehood by turning grassy surface downward, truth by turning it upward) D1316.7, (serves as boat) D1524.7; ordeal by creeping under s. H228.

Sodomist makes sport of confession V29.4. — Wife substitutes for s. husband K1843.2.4.

Sodomy forbidden C113; punished Q253.

Sofa. — Magic s. *D1154.2.

Soft answer turneth away wrath J817; words placate ruler J811.4.

Softening breadcrusts J1341.1.

Softer. — What is s. than swan down H672.

Softest. — What is s. (riddle) H652ff.

Softness. — Coming neither in s. nor in hardness H1054.4.

Sohrab and Rustem N731.2.

Soil dropped to form mountains A963.3. — Carrying s. to cover stony ground H1129.3; lies about s. X1530; magic control of s. and crops D2157; magic s. *D935; magic object controls condition of s. *D1563ff.; patches on s. where cow lay A989.1; poor s. transformed overnight into garden D2157.5; why s. is poor A2871.

Sold, see also **Selling.** — Brothers die at sight of brother they s. N384.13; child s. to fairies F321.0.1; children s. S210ff., S240ff.; city where everything s. at one price J21.52.1; criminal's wife and children s. into slavery Q437.1; girl s. for new church bell V115.2; goods s. to animals J1852ff.; goods s. to object J1853ff.; land where all things s. for same price X1503.3; magic s. object returns to owner D1602.17; person s. into slavery R61; relatives s. to otherworld H1252.3; wife s. unwittingly by husband T292.

Soldier P461; asks enemy to stab him in chest J216.4, W45.1; as helper N852; prefers life to death with revenge J327. — Death imprisoned by s. Z111.1.1; disguise as s. K1825.5; don't make friends with s. J21.46; dwarfs attack s. F451.5.2.11; cowardly s. turns back when he hears raven's croak W121.3; friar disguised as s. steals K1839.5; king disguised as s. killed K1821.7; literal s. breaks woman's oil pot J2469.5.2; lowly s. invites general, humbles him L175.1; magic s.-producing cow B184.2.1.2; mercenary s. unsuitable as husband T65.2; mercenary s. princess's lover L161.3; seduction by masking as s. K1315.13; sleeping s. mistaken for statue J1763.3; treacherous s. suggests task H919.5; woman disguised as s. K1837.6.

Soldier's bargain with death K555.2.2; ghost haunts battlefield E334.5; retort to officer J1526.

Soldiers P551; abduct girl R10.1.1; of enchanted army tabu C549.2; of fairy king are trees by day and men by night F252.3.1; of magic army constantly revived E155.1.2; in wild hunt E501.2.6. — Animal s. B268; custom of paying s. A1596.1; fighting s. force river from bed F1084.3; grass transformed to s. D431.5.1; king not to fail to pay s. C831; magic mirror kills s. D1400.1.13; magic object furnishes s. *D1475ff.; sham warrior intimidates s. with his boasting K1951.3; stingy king will not hire s.: defeated W152.6; troops of black, white, and red s. F873.1; two s. slay each other thinking that they are slaying a common enemy K1883.3; why lame, one-eyed are good s. J1494; woman saves herself from s. by receiving them joyfully rather than fearfully K2361; women throw ashes in eyes of attacking s. so that they are defeated K2356.

Sole. — Ghost demands soul; given shoe s. E459.1; girl stipulates to be s. wife T131.6; giving devil s. for soul K219.5; origin of s. A2126.1.

Soles. — Foot s. covered with hair F517.1.8; pins stuck in s. of dead men's feet to prevent return E431.12; shading self with foot s. F551.5; thief undetected cuts s. off boots F676.2; unique weapon: spits through s. of feet Z312.1; yellowing feet s. death omen J2311.1.5.

Solomon K1921.1; able to detect truth J1140.1; follows angel's warning J158.1; and Marcolf H561.3; as master of magicians D1711.1.1; in memory test H1595.1; offered any gift chooses wisdom L212.2; refuses water of immortality for himself when he cannot have it for his possessions also J369.1; requests wisdom J231.1; as riddle solver H540.3.1; H561.3.1; as wise man J191.1. — Irish S. J1170.2; magic knowledge of S. D1810.10; queen of Sheba propounds riddles to S. H540.2.1; wind serves S. as horse and carries him everywhere F963.1; wisdom gates open to S. J182.1.

Solomon's golden throne F785.1; judgment: the divided child J1171.1; magic ring D1335.5.2; three thousand parables J80.1. — Dolphins seek King S. ring A2275.5.4.

Solomon Grundy born on Monday Z21.1.3.

Solstices. — Deities push sun back and forth at s. A1157.

Solution to problem discovered in dream D1810.8.4.

Solve. — Death sentence escaped by propounding riddle king (judge) cannot s. *H542.

Solvers of riddles H561ff.

Solving. — Means of s. riddles H561ff.

Soma. — Quest to bring S. to wedding H1285.1.

Somersault. — Transformation by s. D561.2; wager: turning s. in public square N56.

Something or other as payment J2489.10. — Searching for food called "S." J1805.4.

Son avenging father's death H1228.2; to be brave, wise but not remain M365.2; as creator A19.1; called daughter to save him from enemy K649.4; drinks poison he intended for father K1613.4; endures embrace: disenchants animal father D735.4.2; of first couple murdered by tiger

A1277.3; insists on following father's trade P401; killed, mistaken for someone else N338.3; kills father who returns to life as cuckoo A2275.6; killed at lover's instigation S303; of the king and of the smith exchanged K1921.1; must not see mother's intercourse C114.1; of the sun A225; on gallows bites his mother's (father's) nose off Q586; named for mother T148.1; next seen to be king M314.2; refuses to marry father's choice T131.1.2.4; rescues father R154.2; rescues mother R154.1; returning home after long absence unwittingly killed by parents N321; returns on day of mother's marriage N681.4; seeks unknown father H1381.2.2.1; slays father in self-defence J675.1; substitutes false bride for father, then kills father K1094.1; succeeds father as king P17.0.2; surpasses father in skill L142.3; warns animal mother B631.0.1. — Abandoned s. exposed to tiger H105.5.4; accidental meeting of mother and s. N735; boon: to have a s. Q115.3; bridegroom only s. among seven children H1381.7; choice between adopted or long-missing s. J226.1; choice between long-lived blind or short-lived healthy s. J226.2; choice between foolish s., wise daughters J226.3; clever man pretends to be s. of God J1675.8; creator's s. A32.1; cruel foster s. S37; cruel s. *S21; dead mother makes s. strong E323.7; dead s. tells mother death inevitable E361.3; defeated enemy's s. changes allegiance R74.2; devil's s. G303.11.2; devil's s. is with his mother at night in the father's place G303.11.1.1; dead mother called up from grave to give her s. charms E323.3; disenchantment of monster when his mother acknowledges him as s. D741.1; divination which s. to be born first D1812.5.0.17; dog buried instead of foster s. K525.6.1; dream warns raja stranger is s. D1810.8.2.5; dwarf king prevents a father from shooting his s. F451.5.1.16; dwarfs steal s., leave image in his place F451.5.2.3.1; earth from body of s. of deity A831.1; fairy s. pale, dark, ugly F233.4; faithful s. guarding father falsely accused N342.1.1; father demands s. break all relations with beloved T131.1.2.3; father feels s. in danger D1813.0.3; father and s. *P233; father kills s. S11.3.3; father orders unrecognized s. thrown into sea N338.3.1; father and s. as love rivals T92.9; first s. died before father A1335.7; fool didn't know that his s. had a ghost to give up J2482; foster s. P275; ghost slaps cheating s. E234.1; God refuses king a s. on account of his many wars Q553.3.1; help from ogre's s. G530.2; hero fights s. without recognizing him A515.5; hero is served at table by his unknown s.: recognition of his wife follows H151.11; hero s. of half-mortal father A511.1.5; human s. of sun A736.10; hungry s. outwits father, gets cherries J1341.9; judge lenient to own s. J1197; king decides oldest s. is rakshasa N349.3; king assigns tasks to his unknown s. H921; king no priest's s. J1827; king's s. persuaded to woo father's bride: killed K1094; king's third s. sacred V205.1; king unknowingly adopts own s. N731.1.1; man gives bangles for s.: takes them back, son dies M101.3.2; man mourns drowned s. in bed F1041.9.1.1; mermaid has s. by human father B81.2.1; miller, his s., and the ass trying to please everyone J1041.2; mortal adopted s. of god A189.11; mortal s. of giant F531.5.7.1; mother and s. *P231; mother-s. marriage A164.1.1; mother dies from joy on greeting long-absent s. F1041.1.5.3; mother kills s. thinking him a wild beast N325.3; mother sends s. to find unknown father H1216; murderer's s. dies as revenge Q589.3; paramour leaves token with girl to give their s. *T645; parents kill own s. for slaying foster son P270.3; parents rescue s. R153.1; poisoner's own s. takes stepbrother's drink K1613.3; prodigal s. favored over faithful N172.1; prophecy: death at sight of s. M341.1.7.1; prophecy: parents will humble themselves before their s. M312.2; prophecy: s.-to-be will destroy lineage M342.2; prophecy: s. will tie father to horse's leg, strike him M312.0.5; prophecy: s. to be more powerful than father M312.2.1; quest for unknown s. H1381.6; quest for vanished s. H1385.3.1; recognition of s. by gushing up of milk in mother's breasts H175.1; recognition when parents come to s. to be confessed H151.3; resuscitation by s. E125.1; sacrifice of one s. to get another J2067.1; philosopher consoles woman for loss of s. J152.4; senate ruler amuses s. J553.2; sinless couple's s. H1381.4; sister's s. P253.0.1; slaying king's s. to prevent father's death H1162.2; strong man s. of unusual parents F611.1ff.; father who wanted s. exposes (murders) daughter S322.1.1; stupid s. eavesdrops, learns magic N455.10; sun is s. too hot to hold A736.5.1; tabu imposed on s. by father C901.1.1; theft by disguise as owner's s. K311.8; treacherous s. leads revolt against father K2214.3; unexpected meeting of father and s. N731; ungrateful s. punished by having a son equally ungrateful Q588; ungrateful s. reproved by naive action of his own son: preparing for old age J121; victim's s. aids murderer W15.1; victorious youngest s. *L10ff.; vigil for dead father: youngest s. alone endures frightful experiences H1462.1; vow concerning birth of s. to chief's wife M184.1; vow not to eat until lost s. found M151.8; wild man s. of woman and robber F611.1.4; woman drinks poison so s. may be king W28.1; woman unwittingly poisons her s. N332.5; youngest s. refuses to shoot at father's corpse H486.2.

Son's acts of charity save his father's soul V413; voice answers mother from grave E324.1. — Calling animal by s. name, sacrificing it K527.5; dead father clears s. name E327.3; death from hearing of s. death *F1041.1.2.2.4; foreknowledge of s. unhappiness D1812.0.4; friendship despite s. jealousy H1558.10; mother orders s. death S12.3; queen offers s. death to revenge first husband P23.4; sword bursts in s. hand when he is about to kill his father *D1317.6.1; unborn s. soul issues from mother's mouth E726.2; woman murders s. wives Q211.4.2; wrestling to test s. legitimacy H218.2.

Sons break promise to have masses for father M256.1; falsifying father's will, deceived K1628; as helpers N832.2; meet at father's grave after learning trade M271; rescue father R154.2.3; surrender witch G275.6; tested for skills H500.1; tested for wisdom by equal amounts of money H501.3; united make living, separated fail J1021.1. — Creator's two s.

A7.1; faithful servant sacrifices s. to save life of king P361.3; father rescues s. R153.3; fathers dream of bloody s., murder omen D1812.5.1.13; father describes s. in uncomplimentary riddle H581.4; first-born and tenth s. given to church V451; forty of man's s. to die at once M341.0.2; gods as s. of supreme god A112.6; king propounds questions to his s. to determine successor H508.1; king sends s. on fatal quests K948; king's vision of s. changed into animals V515.2.3; king sends man's s. to death, murders man M2.1; king sets s. task to determine heir H921.1; magic pills bring twin s. D1347.3.1; man falls dead when all s. reared in sin killed Q582.9; mother of world bears three s. A1282.1; mountains as s. of gods A962.9; no s. left to rule after father: slain in rebelling against him P17.0.1; obedience of s. tested by offering them apple H1557.1; persecuted s. of co-wife S471; pots symbolic of inheritances of four s. J99.2; recognition from overheard conversation of s. H13.3; riddle about no s. after three marriages H585.2; riddle about four wells as father and three s. H588.8; snake can't kill prince until princess bears s. J1173.1.1; stupid s. learn trades, father killed J2499.7; thiefs' s. frightened by punishment threats K335.1.11; tiger, spirit, and man s. of same mother T554.1; two s. granted: one wise and ugly, other fool and handsome M93; unwitting combat between s. of friends N767; wife incites s. to war on father K2213.9; witch has giant s. G206.

Son-in-law P265; given choice, eats all meal W125.3; seduces mother-in-law T417. — Blind s. X124.2; cruel s. S56; lazy s. W111.5.6; one present from spirit s. C714.1; poor not rich s. chosen J247.1; prophecy: murder by s. M343.1; thief disguised as s. K311.8.2.

Sons-in-law treated as unwelcome guests J1563.6.

Song, see also **Singing;** increases cow's milk D2182.2; as protection on journey D1384.5; causes magic sleep D1364.23; duel H503.1; learned in dream *D1731.1; protects against poison D1383.4; protects from fire D1382.7; warns lover of husband K1546.1. — Beer brewed by means of magic s. D1045.0.1; bird's s. consoles man B292.5; birds captured by imitating their s. K756.1; bird shows way by s. B151.2.0.3; bribed boy sings the wrong s. *K1631; child's s. reveals murder N271.6.1; church sinks: s. heard from underground F941.2.1; confederate's s. delays pursuers so that fugitive escapes K643; disenchantment by s. D786.1; dog sings s. B214.1.4; escape by singing s. K606; flute-player thinks s. meant for prince is sung to him J953.3; funeral s. V65.4.1; goat singing threatening s. K1767; holy s. drives off fairies F382.5; love-producing s. D1355.1.1.; magic bird's s. B172.2ff.; magic s. *D1275, (causes paralysis) D2072.6, (as curse) D2175.3, (received from fish) B505.3; mortal wins fairies' gratitude by joining in their s. and completing it F331.3; one compulsory s. before beer can be brewed C671; origin of particular s. A1464.2.1; paramour encouraged by s. K1546.2; recognition by s. H12; resuscitation by s. E55.1; respite from death gained by long drawn-out s. K555.2; riddle: what is the sweetest s. H634; saint's s. silences hound D1442.5; siren's s. causes sleep B53.4; thrush steals woodcock's s. A2245.1; transformation through s. D523; unrequited love expressed in s. T75.3; water chants s. F930.6; years seem moments while man listens to s. of bird D2011.1.

Songs about bad food, its improvement J1341.11; of the angels V234. — Boat guided by magic s. D1523.2.6; creator gives men s. A1503; devil in church fills his sack with dissolute s. G303.24.1.5; love-s. A1554; lulling to sleep by "sleepy" s. D1962.4.1; magic power from s. D1733.6; magic strength from s. D1835.5; origin of religious s. A1543; two animals learn s. together: one successfully, the other unsuccessfully A2283.

Soon. — Dead person returns s. after burial E586; giant comes to bake too s. and spills dough F531.3.7; not to do thing too s. C757; not to look at supernatural wife too s. C31.1.1; not to open bag too s. C322.2; spirit must speak as s. as addressed F404.1.

Soot. — Magic s. *D931.1.1, (opens mountain) D1552.10; naked lover as devil in s. barrel K1555.2.

Soothsayer D1712. — Animal acts as s. *B154.

Soothsaying learned from god D1726.0.1. — Power of s. from serpents' licking ears B161.1.

Soporific given contest opponent K51.1. — Abduction by giving s. R22.

Sorcerer and books in mountain F721.2.3; loses magic with teeth D1741.8.

Sorcerer's army of magic animals B268.4; body becomes serpents D447.9; magic objects D801.1.

Sorcerers can see ghosts E421.1.1.2; use corpse marrow D1278.2.

Sorceress marries man every day, transforms him in evening T113.1; swallowed by transformed husband D1749.1. — Girl exchanges form with s. D45.4; quest to confines of hell for blood of s. H1277; toes of s. become dogs D447.5; transformation by s. D683.2.

Sorcery. — Acquisition of s. A1459.3; god of s. A499.4; magic circle averts s. D1385.7.

Sore on body prohibits sexual intercourse C110.1; eyes from breaking tabu C943.3; -producing ointment K1043.1.

Sores from breaking tabu C941.3. — Woman raises s. to preserve chastity T327.5.

Sorghum's origin A2684.2.1.

Sorrel. — Why s. grows on certain rock every winter A2771.7.

Sorrow, see also **Grief;** is not eternal C498.1; of captivity in otherworld F165.6.1. — Directions followed literally to the s. of giver J2516; feast for those who have not known s. N135.3.1; going to bed for s. F1041.9.1; heart breaks from s. F1041.1.1.3; inexorable fate: no day without s. N101.1; magic musical horn (bell) relieves hearers of s. D1359.3.1.1; object expresses s. F994; quest for person who has not known s. H1394; woman dies of s. for brother P253.9.

Sorrows. — "Two S. of Heaven" D1856.1.1.

Sorrowers. — Loudest mourners not greatest s. J261.

Sorry. — If you take it you will be s.; if you don't you will also be s. J171.1.

Sorting a large amount of grains in one night H1091.

Soul *E700—E799; absent from witch's skin G251.2; leaves body to point out treasure N538.1; of witch leaves the body *G229.1; wanders and demands that a temple be built for him E419.1. — Ability to see the s. F642.7; animals help man overcome monster with external s. B571.1; container for s. can be split only by man's own sword D1651.10; deaf and dumb man can see s. taken to happiness or punishment D1821.7; debate of body and s. E727.1; deity provides man with s. A185.12; devil appears to claim s. offered to devil by farmer in jest G303.6.1.3; devil cheated of his promised s. K210ff.; devil gets another s. instead of one bargained for K217; dwarf loses s. after murder F451.5.9.6; demons as s. of giants G302.1.1; devil cannot touch man's s. G303.25.18; escape by alleged possession of external s. K544; external s. *E710ff.; familiar spirit equivalent to man's s. F403.2.2.3; four places cleanse the s. Z71.2.4; ghost demands s.; given shoe sole E459.1; god removes mortal's s. A185.12.2; handsome exterior no indication of s. U119.3; hidden s. E712; journey to hell to retrieve s. F81.4; magic ability to see s. D1825.3.3; magic armature protects s. D1389.11; magic sight of s. leaving body D1825.3.3.2; man sells s. to devil M211; murder by destroying s. K956; ogre killed by burning external s. G512.5; person with more than one s. E707; prophecy: child to have external s. M354; resuscitation of man with s. in necklace E155.3; resuscitation by replacement of s. E38; resuscitation by returning s. to body E38.1; secret of location of external s. learned by deception K975.2; seeing s. in living man (repartee) J1262.7; separable s. of witch G251.1.1; witch recognized by seeing wandering s. return G251; witch's s. crushed to forehead G275.4.1.

Souls. — Bridge tests s. H210.1; demons have s. without bodies G302.4.3; devil hunts lost s. G303.7.1.3; fairies as s. of departed *F251.2; food placed out for returning s. of dead *E541.1; four categories of s. at Judgment Z71.2.5; light as s. of dead A1412.2; limited number of s. necessitates reincarnation E603; magic sight of s. after death D1825.3.3.1; masses release s. from hell (purgatory) V42; mountain spirits as s. of dead F460.0.1; not to relieve s. in hell C741; sheep as s. redeemed F81.6.

Sound of drum followed into ghost town F102.2; of ghostly object E402.3; of harp J1626; of magic wheel causes deafness D1332.1.2; of wild hunt avoided by sticking fingers in ears E501.17.5.8. — Divination from s. D1812.5.0.11; ghost sails over s. E581.7; hair emits s. F555.11; insanity from hearing strange s. D2065.2.1; riddle: what is the sweetest s. H635ff.; sea's mournful s. A925.5; thunder as s. of God's gun A1142.5.

Sounds heard before death D1827.1.2; of invisible animal ghost E402.2. — Ghostly s. of re-enacted actions E337.1ff.; illusory s. K1887; lies: animals responding to s. X1206; sunken bell s. *F993; vocal s. of ghost E402.1.1ff.

Soup of dog's head cures madness D1508.4. — Alleged s.-making stone (pot) sold K112.2; black beans, white s. J1291.1; bones in s. mistaken for peas J1772.6; dog Parsley in s. J2462.1; lentil in s. J2469.1; stingy woman will not give s. to man until she spills it W152.5.

Sour fruits made sweet by saint F979.1. — Fathers have eaten s. grapes, children's teeth on edge U18; fox and the s. grapes J871; tamarind fruit s. A2791.5; woman created from s. milk and cream A1275.5.

South forbidden direction C614.1.2; wind is moistest H659.8. — Land of dead in s. E481.6.3; north wind tempers fury of s. wind A1127.1.1; saint's body moves to lie s. E411.0.8.

Southern. — Origin of the S. Cross A771.1.

Sovereigns compared to new, full moons H599.3.

Sovereignty for hour as reward Q112.2; personified Z116. — Curse: race to lose s. M462.

Sow, see also **Pig**; kicks wolf into stream, saves pigs K1121.2; in wild hunt E501.4.3. — Cat brings suspicion between eagle and s. K2131.1; devastating s. B16.1.4.2; feeding man-eating s. H1155.3; ferocious s. G353; ghost of s. E521.5.1; giant devastating s. B16.1.4.2; house-spirit in form of a s. F480.1; priest draws s. instead of woman K1281.1; salesman guarantees s. to bear male, then female, then kid X1233.4.1; why s. was muddy J2211.2; wife's former incarnation as s. E601.1; wolf offers to act as midwife for s. K2061.6.

Sows'. — Piglings cut from s. bodies T584.4.

Sowed. — Cooked grain s. by numskulls J1932.1; hempseed s. to acquire magic sight D1331.1.1; slain father returns as cuckoo, tells where grain to be s. A2275.6; traveler says he is going to the city to see what has become of the seed he s. in the street H586.2.

Sowing cheese to bring forth a cow J1932.2; dragon's teeth (task) H1024.5; grain in unplowed field K1428; impossible amount of land overnight H1103.2.1; needles (like seed) J1932.5; and reaping same day F971.7; reaping, winnowing in one day royalty test H41.8; and not reaping M306.1; rice seed in others' fields J2129.8; rye, getting crop next day H1023.17; salt to produce salt J1932.3; seed, then burning land J2460.1. — Countertask: s. cooked seeds and harvesting the crop H1023.1.1; devil s. stones A975.1; disenchantment by burying victim and s. grain over him D719.1; father is making many out of few (s. grain) H583.2.2; origin of s. A1441.4; sacrifice at s. time A1545.4; time for s. A1150.1.

Sown. — Plants grow without being s. F979.17.

Space. — God of s. upholds sky A665.1; tests of s. H1584.

Spade. — Lost object found by throwing s. at ghost D1816.2.1; magic s. *D1205.1; man buried in earth goes for s. and digs self out X1731.2.1.

Spádísar prophesy victory M301.13.

Spain as land of dead E481.0.2; as otherworld F130.2.

Span. — Determination of s. of life A1320ff.; extraordinary bridge s. F842.2.3; giant reveals life s. to dwarf N484.

Spans. — Giant with three s. between brows F531.2.2.

Spangles. — Sun, moon as s. from creator's forehead A714.6.

Spared. — House of woman who launders clothes for church s. in great
fire V137; man he is about to devour s. by animal B525; mother who
is suckling children s. by angel of death V233.1; Old Age, Cold, Poverty,
and Hunger s. by culture hero A531.1.

Sparing. — Reward for s. life when in animal form Q55; vow not to
deceive man s. one's life M168.1.

Spark detonation hurls ships to sea F1078.

Sparks come from man's feet F683. — Devils created from s. produced
by Satan's striking two stones together G303.1.4.2; when devil combs
witches, s. fly G222.1; teeth giving off s. F544.3.2.

Sparrow carries burning straw to fire desecrated church Q222.5.5;
dissatisfied with pond wants to go to sea W128.6; family enact her fate
to dying queen M369.2.1.1; intervenes in elephant quarrel J2143.1;
taught to sing by lark A2271.2; where are you going? Z39.4.2. — Cat
as judge between s. and hare K815.7; chain tale: wormwood rocking s.
Z41.7; color of s. A2411.2.1.11; creation of s. A1927; crow crowds s.
from nest J684.2; fairy as s. F234.1.15.3; fool kills himself in despair because a s. has taken one grain from his field J2518.1; friendship of hen
and s. A2493.34.1; helpful s. B451.7; man becomes s. D151.8; why s. is
disliked A2522.1; old wife provokes s. to speak, drop new wife K929.10;
parrot and s. argue right to inherit property left by man B271.1; separable soul in crop of s. E715.1.2; speaking s. B211.3.7.

Sparrow's nest A2431.3.7; wedding B282.3.3, B282.10. — Crow appropriates s. nest J684.2, K354.1; train of troubles for s. vengeance N261;
why crow cannot enter s. nest A2431.3.6.1.

Sparrows of Cirencester (set fire to a besieged city) K2351.1. — Aphrodite's
team of s. (doves) A136.2.1, A155.3; king of s. B242.2.7; young s. have
learned to avoid men J13.

Spayed. — Ghosts cannot approach s. bitch E439.6.

Speak. — Animal persuaded to s. and release victim K561.1; causing
silent person to s. H1194.0.1; why cormorant cannot s. A2344.2.5,
A2422.8; dwarfs appear nodding and anxious to s. F451.2.0.4; mother
trains old maid to s. properly X756; penance: not to s. Q535.1;
princess made to s. desired words when hero threatens to report (falsely)
her amorous conduct K1271.1.2; refusal to s. from grief F1041.21.3.1;
spirit must s. as soon as addressed F404.1; suitor test: bringing dumb
princess to s. H343; teaching animal to s. H1024.7; think thrice before
you s. J2516.1.

Speaker. — Bungling s. J2666; deception into listening to s. K477.2.

Speaking bedlegs overheard N454.1; and bleeding trees (reincarnated
persons) E631.0.4; animals B210ff.; bird tells where treasure is buried
N537; blood reveals murder D1318.5.4; bones of murdered person reveal
murder E632.1; corpses J2311.9; earth reveals murder D1318.16; flesh
reveals murder D1318.7.0.1; forest F812.4; grass D1312.3; he-goat saves

girl D674; horse-head *B133.3; image of saint V126; lamp prevents murder D1381.29; mountain F755.1; river F932.12; sea F931.11; severed head E783.5; skull E261.1.2; spittle reveals truth D1316.3; stars A769.4, F961.2.4; statue D1620.1.7; tabu *C400—C499; tabu in fairyland C715.1; trees A1101.1.2, D1311.4.2; wraith E723.7.1. — Animals, men s. same language B210.3; animals s. at Christmas B251.1.2; ashes of dead dog s. E521.2.1; child s. at birth T585.2; child s. in mother's womb T575.1ff.; cooked human flesh s. out G64; culture hero s. before birth A511.1.2; dead s. E417, E545; deaf and dumb s. F954, F1041.22; devil s. with voice of a he-goat G303.4.7; ghost laid by living man's s. to it E451.4; disenchantment by s. D762.1, D789.6.1; disfiguration for s. falsely H244; flowers fall from s. saint's mouth V222.11; girl possessed by ghost s. unknown dialect E725.2; god s. to mortals A182ff.; gods s. A182.1.1; helpful s. skull N819.3.1; magic results from s. *D1774; magic s. objects *D1610ff.; magic s. reed (tree) betrays secret *D1316.5; man at grave pretends to be dead s. K1974; men refuse to kill s. beasts B210.3; person s. with pestilence dies F493.2.1; pestilence-spirits s. together F493.2.2; quest for s. bird H1331.1.4; reproving each other for s. at prayers J2254; severed head of saint s. V229.2.2; three persons s. at birth Z71.1.13; victim s. from swallower's body F915; wife's s. privates tell of adultery K1569.7.

Spear becomes tree D454.9.1.1; bends on hero's chest F615.4; can be wielded by only one person D1651.1.1; carried crosswise into house as obedience test H1557.5; -casting contest H1591.1; changes size D631.3.8; driven through iron F625.1; in ground pointed toward ferocious animal protects D1381.17; killing king cast into cataract P16.5; made to appear reed D2031.11; pierces person's shadow D2061.2.2.1; shot through nose-ring F661.3.1; stuck in ground ends deluge A1028.1. — Automatic s. D1601.4.2; drawing s. thrust through iron plates H1149.7; enduring s. blow as test H328.3; extraordinary s. F834; fairy gives magic s. F343.10.2; feat on s. point H1149.5; flaming s. cooled in blood D1645.8.1.1; gate of captured town widened for overlord's s. P555.3; giant's enorm- ous s. F531.4.5.6; gift on unknown helper's s.-shaft Q114.1; god's s. A157.3; hero catches s. hurled at him, kills snake N654; identification by s. H125.2; lips used as s. F544.1.4; lucky cast of s. N623.1; luring man by securing his s. K1399.4; magic s. *D1084, (dries up spring) D2143.2.2, (slays ogre) G512.8.3, (point harmless, shaft inflicts mortal blow) D1402.7.2.3; murder by thrusting s. into mouth K951.1.2; own s. kills murderer Q582.3; performing on s. points F698.2; prophecy: king to be slain by certain s. M341.2.17; quest for magic s. H1345; recognition by unique ability to swing s. H31.3; skillful axe-man makes s.-shafts with three chippings F666.1; spell causes s. to pursue and slay man D1438.1; spring breaks forth where magic s. strikes ground A941.3.1, spring where god throws his s. A941.3.2; stealing king's s. H1151.13.2; strong man's s. -cast F628.4; suitor contest: riding up s. H331.1.3; tabu to slay

woman with s. C835.2.4; why tortoise may be killed with iron s.
A2231.7.3; woman wins s. contest F610.0.1.1; wound healed by same
s. that caused it D2161.4.10.1.

Spears cannot penetrate magic garment D1381.3.3. — Broad-headed s.
in Leinster A1459.1.2; god with s. as torches A137.14.2; jumping hedges
of s. H331.1.6.1; origin of obsidian-tipped s. A1459.1.2.1.

Spear-head miraculously removed from wound F959.3.4.1; not to touch
stone C835.2.2; tabu between teeth C835.2.3. — Charm causes s. to return
D1428.2; magic s. *D1084.1, D1564.4.1.

Specimen. — Substitute s. for laboratory test K1858.

Speck. — Skillful surgeon removes s. from midge's eye F668.2.

Speckled. — Devil s. G303.4.8.9; journey in s. garment on s. steed C833.8;
riding s. horse credential test H242.1.

Spectacles. — Clergy in no need of s. J1263.5; ignorance of reading s.
J1748; magic pair of s. D1299.5.

Spectral ghosts E421.

Spectre as evil omen D1812.5.1.17. — Strong man slays s. F628.3; transformation: man to demon (s.) D95.

Speculations. — Absurd scientific s. J2371ff.

Speech, see also **Speaking.** — Animal understands human s. B212; apology
for not answering challenge (has never regretted silence but often regretted s.) J1074.1; choice: loss of beauty or s. J213; dumb man recovers s.
in order to confess V23.2; evil s. punished Q393; husband's dangers bring
wife to s. T272.1; law student forgets s. J2046; loss of s. as punishment
*Q451.3; magic object restores s. *D1507ff.; magic recovery of s. D2025;
precocious s. T615.1; princess's s. sweeter than sugar H633.5; respite
from death gained by long drawn out s. K555.1; saint deprives enemy
of s. Q572.5; saint restores dumb man's s. V221.2; single s. answers
many questions H501.2; why dog lost s. A2422.1; why God took power
of s. from animals B210.3; why owl's s. removed A2239.3.1.

Speeches. — Abusive s. drive ogres away G571.

Speechless vigil in church as test H1451. — Fly punished by failing to
answer question: is s. A2239.2.

Speed. — Giant's prodigious s. G157; journey with magic s. *D2122ff.;
lies concerning s. X1796; spirit travels with s. F411.0.1; sun's s. depends
on hour, season A728.4; tasks requiring miraculous s. H1090ff.; usefulness better than s. J243.

Spell chanted over person's shadow brings death D2061.2.2.2. — Druids
boil s. P427.9; holy water breaks fairy s. F382.2; magic object breaks s.
D1396; magic results of reversing a s. D1783.1; magic spear protects
against s. D1389.5; magic s. *D1273ff., (causes insanity) D1367.3, (causes
birds to roost) D1442.6.2, (causes fortress to revolve, preventing entrance) D1381.23; stealing while owner under alleged magic s. K341.22;
tabu to eat food from s. C220.1; transformation by s. D573; trickster
works magic s. over food, eats it K353.

Spells to recall dead lover E218. — Birds with poisonous s. on wings B33.1.4; drawing witch's blood annuls her s. D1741.2.1; druid's s. kill enemies D1402.13.1; druid's s. to drive away saint V229.6.4; magic s. control witch G272.15.

Spending money for lover's worthless goods K1581.9. — Parable on s. without return H614.2; rude retort on s. to become known J1369.1; subject s. more than he earns chastised J1566.2.

Spendthrift hero L114.2; knight divides his last penny Q42.1; loses friends when poor H1558.7; wife T275.

Spendthrift's sarcastic advice to thrifty J1363; uncut field already harvested H586.4. — King buys s. bed J1081.1.

Sperm. — Conception from drinking s. T512.6; Milky Way as the s. of the gods A778.6.

Spewing. — Ghost kills by s. water from mouth E268.

Sphere. — Magic clairvoyant s. D1323.4; magic s. D1264, (burns up country) D1408.1.

Spheres. — Music of the s. A659.1.

Sphinx *B51. — Riddle of S. *H761.

Spiced wine becomes bitter D477.0.1.3.

Spices. — Origin of s. A2814.

Spider bite cured by Virgin Mary D2161.5.2.5; as creator A13.3.1; as culture hero A522.7; dropping on front lucky D1812.5.2.11; hands box to ant and refuses to take it back: hence ants carry huge loads A2243.1; has no blood B724; invites wasp (fly) to rest on her "white curtain" K815.2; performs penance B253.4; on person's back ill omen D1821.5.1.12.3; spins web across sky F989.21; in stingy woman's house grows thin W152.7; thinks that it has held back the wind J953.9; transformed to man D381; -web garment H1355.1; -web sky-rope F51.1.1; as witch's familiar G225.1. — Color of s. A2221.2.3, A2411.3.2; cowardly s. W121.5; why s. is cursed A2231.5, A2542.2; devastating s. B16.6.4; devil as a s. G303.3.3.17; dog becomes s. D412.5.6; enmity of s. and (crab) A2494.16.5, (wasp) A2494.14.2, (fly) A2494.14.1, (cat) A2494.1.7; fly steals fire from s.: may eat everywhere A2229.4; ghost as s. E423.8; giant s. B873.3; gnats having overcome lion are in turn killed by s. L478; haunts of s. *A2433.5.3; helpful s. B489.1; magic s. catches pearls B109.1; man so small he dances in s. web F535.2.3; man transformed to s. D181; why s. has markings on back A2356.3.4; mythical s. B93; origin of s. A2091; soul in form of s. E734.3; -web over hole saves fugitive B523.1; why s. has thread in back of body A2231.6, A2356.2.8; why s. has small waist A2355.1.1; why s. brings good luck A2536.3; why s. lives under stones A2433.5.3.1.

Spider's body made larger A2301.2. — Boar in s. web F989.18; bed of s. webs F787.1; earth made by cups placed on s. web A823; escape from lower world by s. thread F101.7.

Spiders. — Abandoned souls feed on s. E752.7.1; enmity of rats and s.

A2494.12.8; islands from webs woven by primeval s. A955.7; wishing to destroy all s. J2079.2.

Spike magically appears D1285.1, (causes death) D2061.2.6. — Magic s. *D1285.

Spikes. — Prison floor with s. in it R41.3.3.

Spiked-cask punishment Q462. — Serpent's jewel covered by s. helmet K1058.1.

Spilled. — Animal has color s. on him: cause of his color *A2219.1; fool tires to dry up s. wine with meal J2176.1; dough s. by giant who comes to bake too soon F531.3.7; making a knot of s. brandy H1021.4.

Spilling dirty water on overdressed youths X32.

Spinach. — Conception from eating s. T511.3.2.

Spindle in well leads to adventures N777.4. — Magic s. *D1186; making a boat from splinters of s. and shuttle (task) H1022.7; making s. and loom from one piece of wood (countertask) H1022.3; old woman with s. in the moon A751.8.1; prophecy: death through s. wound M341.2.13.

Spine test H1531. — Fairy physician can heal anyone whose s. is not severed F344.2; soul fastened to s. E714.13.

Spines. — Dragon combats attack with showers of fiery s. B11.11.3.

Spinner P451.

Spinning as bride test H383.2.1; fairies lured away F381.8; forbidden C832; gold (task) H1021.8; on holy days tabu C631.2; impossible amount in one night (task) H1092; wool still on goat's back H1024.8. — Automatic gold-s. doll D1620.0.1.1; bewitched person s. on bedpost G269.25; bride s. at bottom of river K1911.2.2.2; dead person s. E561; devil s. G303.9.8.1; dwarfs s. F451.3.4.6, F455.3.4; dwarfs help human s. F451.5.1.19; fairies s. F271.4.3; goddess of s. A451.3.1; golden s. equipment H1359.2; Hercules s. for his beloved K1214; hidden husband advises wife on s. K1971.4; magic s. D2183; magic s. rod D1399.1; origin of s. A1453.1; sight of dead woman s. drives people insane E561.1; sight of deformed witches causes man to release his wife from s. duty J51; three witches deformed from much s. *G201.1; wife too lazy for s. W111.3.5; witch s. G244; witches punish lazy s. women G282.

Spinning-wheel continues spinning after tabu broken C916.4; sent home by itself J1881.15. — Golden s. F876; phantom s. E534; son appears to pursuers as s. D2031.6.2; test of sex of girl masking as man: s. brought H1578.1.2.

Spires. — Penance until s. of Benares rebuilt Q521.7.

Spirit causes deluge A1015.2; changes to animal D493; causes flood A1015.2; gives power of exorcising D1721.1.3; host fighting as evil omen D1812.5.1.17.1; huts V112.1; as prophet M301.11; reincarnated as man E605.2.1; takes any form D49.2; takes man's shape D42.2; -woman devours men, cattle G312.2; woman sleeps whole year F564.3.5. — Animals s.-sighted B733; bull melts away after evil s. has issued from him F981.2; dead wife asks husband to accompany her to s. world

E322.2.1; evil s. cast out of person E728.1; evil s. exorcised *D2176.3; female s. of tree F441.2.3; god's s. dwells among mortals A151.11; half-s., half-man A506; magic ring protects from s. D1385.3.1; man behind statue (tree) speaks and pretends to be s. K1971; man carried by s. or devil on magic journey D2121.5; man reincarnated as s. E605.4; mortal as s. D44; order for help of s. left on card D2074.2.4.4; power of self-transformation received from wood-s. D630.1; profanely calling up s. forbidden *C10ff.; soul as black or white s. over coffin E722.1.1; storm from calling on evil s. D2141.0.1; witch's familiar s. G225.

Spirit's curse M411.7.

Spirits become gods A104.4; of disease F493.1; frightened off by threatening to eat them K1715.4.1; guard otherworld F150.2.2; live with men A1101.1.3. — Animal wards off s. B785; avoidance of evil s. at childbirth T582.1; cannibalistic s. G11.10; evil s. conjured away in name of deity *D1766.7.1.1; fighting with s. as fear test D1423; Jesus drives evil s. into hogs: hence short snouts A2287.1.1ff.; journey to world of s. F121; magic control of s. D2198; magic object protects from evil s. *D1385ff.; metal as defence against s. D1385.5; mountain-s. *F460ff.; north as abode of evil s. G633; offending s. of water, mountain, etc. forbidden C40ff.; oracular images occupied by s. who give the answers K1972; sacred s. V202; sacrifice to appease s. S263; stealing from s. forbidden C91; tasks performed by (captive s. of the dead) H972.1, (helpful forest s.) H973; things thought to be s. J1784; thunder-s. A284.3; transformation by evil s. D683.6; uttering secrets heard from s. forbidden C423.4; why s. are invisible A2862.

Spiritual exaltation from eating human flesh *G13; recompense for temporal misfortune J893. — "Eat s. food, not material" J1511.16; marvel that those who speak of s. matters are usually the most depraved J171.2.5; three s. gifts of God Z71.1.12.

Spit. — Adultery detected by s. marks J1142.3; monsoon from divine s. A1129.2; recovering cooking-s. H1132.1.6.

Spits. — Unique weapon: s. through feet soles Z312.1.

Spite. — "In s. of devil" C12.5.8; king saved in s. of himself V523.

Spitter. — Remarkable s. F635, X934.

Spitting in face as punishment Q471ff.; on head of slain enemy S139.2.2.1.3; of men while smoking: Adam spat A2854; of all parties into vessel to seal bargain M201.3; on old castaway brooms gives one to devil G303.16.19.2. — Animal s. treasure B103.4ff.; captor s. out smaller animal K683; enraged man s. fire F1041.16.1; Evil Eye averted by s. D2071.1.1; fool s. in hot porridge in imitation of smith J2421; forgetfulness by s. D2004.4; hero s. twice at wife in recognition H186; high-s. the test of a chief H41.2; magic results from s. *D1776; ordeal by s. on fire H211.5; origin of s. A1399.3; philosopher s. in king's beard J1566.1; power of prophecy lost by s. D1812.6.1; protection from witch by s. G272.5; rain produced by s. blood toward sky D2143.1.4; top man of human chain s. on his hands J2133.5; trickster s. in wine given it K355.1; witches s. out communion wine over shoulder G285.1; universe created by s. A618.2.

Spittle, see also **Saliva;** changes to blood D474.7; images enable escape K525.10; transformed to person D437.5. — Birth from s. T541.8.2; blood in s. tests subjection H252.2; conception from licking s. T512.5; devil originates from God's s. G303.1.1.2; earth from creator's s. A814.10.1; healing s. of Virgin V256.1; healing s. during pregnancy T579.4; lesser gods from great god's s. A114.1.1.2; licking s. from ground in penance Q523.9; magic s. *D1001, (animal) D1029.5, (kills) D1402.14.1; man created from s. of holy person A1263.4; man becomes s. D295; plant from s. A2613; stars are moon's s. A764.4; stolen wife makes trail of speaking s. for husband R135.0.1.

Splinter. — Accidental death from flying s. of bone N335.4; child born of s. T541.2.1.1.

Splinters. — Making a boat from s. of spindle and shuttle (task) H1022.7.

Split dog put together again X1215.11; lapdog becomes two rocks A977.5.4. — First man s. in two to form mate A1275.2; why hare's lip is s. *A2342.1; things s. by magic object D1564ff.

Splitting a hair with a blunt knife H1023.14; wood with penis F451.3.4.10; wood as suitor contest H331.12. — Earth s. when tabu broken F944.4; hero s. mother's womb T584.7; man s. into two parts F525.2; punishment for s. head and eating man's brains Q211.7; suitor contest: s. antlers H331.8.

Spoil. — Hero divides s. for animals B392.

Spoils. — Giant cheated in division of s. of chase K171.0.1.

Spoiled fish eaten by servant K344.1.2. — Owner persuaded that he has s. goods K344.

Spoiling the rice-field with dung K344.2. — Animals refrain from s. consecrated food B259.4.1.

Sponge in dead mouth causes illusory breathing K1885.1. — Men with s. feet F517.1.3.

Spontaneous creation of universe A620ff.; generation of mankind A1234.3.

Spoon. — Dipping out the sea with a s. (task) H1143; guessing nature of devil's s. H523.5; magic s. D1177.

Spoons. — Fairies give woman silver s. F342.1; hostess says that she has no s. J1561.4.1.

Sport. — King demands s. from guests P337; king wants men engaging in s. P14.8; mortal wins gratitude by joining in fairies' s. *F331; parts of corpse used in s. S139.2.2.4; vow against man ignorant of s. M171.

Sporting. — Fairies s. with mortal F399.4.1.

Spot. — Dream of marking s. with his excrements X31; invulnerability except in one s. Z311; fairies made visible by stepping on certain s. F235.5; grass refuses to grow in certain s. F974; love-s. D1355.13;

murderers kill all at certain s. S110.5; ogre's soul in pale s. E714.10; yellow, green, blue, purple s. on cheek F545.3.2.

Spots on leopard A2412.1.2.

Spotted. — Children s. like leopards after bestiality T465.4; devil s. G303.4.8.9.

Spouse, see also **Husband, Wife;** murder pact S63. — Cruel s. S60ff.; curse by s. M411.20; future s. foretold M369.2.1; future s. met during magic sleep *D1976.2; loss of s. for breaking tabu C932; tasks imposed by s. H916.

Spouse's. — Dead s. malevolent return *E221; uttering s. name forbidden C435.

Spout. — Filling bottle with s. downward H1023.2.2.

Spouts. — Roof s. run with blood E761.1.11.

Spreading goddess's cloth on spot: water flows A941.5.6. — Girl's hair s. out on ground F555.3.1.1.

Spriggins F456.1.

Spring as refuge R317; is most beautiful H641.1; with water lighter than wood F716.2. — Causing dry s. to flow again (task) H1193; entrance to lower world through s. F92; from wooden s. iron bucket makes stones from which water flows (riddle) H765; ghosts haunt s. E278; god of s. A496.1; gods live in s. A151.3.1; goddess's sacred s. C51.1.11; goddess of splendor of s. A430.1.1; gold-producing s. in otherworld F166.2; lazy girl does not know where the s. is W111.5.2; magic s. *D927, (curing) D1500.1.1.2, (detects perjury) H251.3.9; numskull tries to dig up a s. J1933; ogress tricked into boiling s. G519.1.4; old woman by s. as helper N825.3.2; origin of a particular s. A941.0.1; quest for biggest river's s. H1315; question (propounded on quest): why has s. gone dry H1292.1; saint drives demon from s. D2176.3.3.2; secret water s. C429.1; spear dries up s. D2143.2.2; transformation to s. D283.2; treasure hidden in s. N513.3.

Springs. — Extraordinary occurrences connected with s. F933; flood from s. breaking forth A1011.1; god of s. A427; hot s. arise where Christ bathed his feet A942.1; lies about hot s. X1543; magic control of s. D2151.6; magic s. fertilize or sterilize earth D1563.0.1; origin of s. A941.

Springing. — Identification by ring s. off finger H94.7; murder by s. bent tree S135; ring s. asunder (as life token) E761.5.3, (when faithlessness of lover is learned) *D1318.9.1.

Sprinkling salt on fairy food renders it harmless F384.1.2. — Healing by s. water F950.9; treasure found by s. ground with blood of white cock D2101.1.

Sprites. — Fairies as s. who have been given immortality F251.5.

Sprouting. — Dream of s. tree indicates hero's birth M312.0.4.1.

Spruce. — Indians chew s. gum A1681.1.

Spun. — Riddle: who first s. and when (Eve) H811; cotton already s. A1346.2.1.

Spur. — Lover's s. catches in sheet when he tries to escape N386.1.

Spurs. — Philanthropist will give his s. if someone will drive his horse for him W11.1.

Spurge-laurel as the devil's bush G303.10.11.

Spurned ruler rewards maiden Q87.1.1; woman's attempts at revenge K2111.

Spurring. — Horse transformed by s. D566.3.

Spy. — Bee as God's s. overhears devil's secrets A33.3.1.

Spies listen to defendants J1149.10; report falsely on enemies' weakness K2363.

Spying on animal husband C36.2; on holy cloak renders senseless D1410.8; on magic object D830.1; on secret help of angels forbidden C51.4.2; on secret hoard K322. — Blindness as punishment for s. Q451.7.0.2.5; death for s. on uncanny persons Q411.14; disguise for s. K1835, K2357.0.1; disguised husband s. on wife K1813.2; fairies take revenge on person s. on them F361.3; husband s. on adulteress K1551; king disguised for s. K1812.17; king s. to levy fines K2246.1.1; miserly husband s. on wife to see that she does not eat too much burned in the chimney W153.2; sham dead woman s. on husband killed N384.12; transformation for s. D641.2.1.

Square. — Dwarf cave has large s. room with little doors leading to all sides F451.4.3.2; earth s. with four quarters *A871.

Squaring lumber on stone H1199.13.

Squash. — Putting a large s. whole into a narrow-necked jar (task) H1023.11.

Squatting god A137.6.

Squeal. — Wild boar given permission to s. before wolf eats him K551.3.4.

Squeezer. — Remarkable s. X951.

Squeezing to death as punishment Q429.4. — Animal characteristics from s. or stretching ancient animal A2213ff.; contest in s. water from a stone (cheese or egg used) K62; deceptive contest in s. hands K73; milk transferred from another's cow by s. axe-handle D2083.3.1; murder by s. K953.

Squid. — God of s. A445.1.

Squint. — How lynx got his s. A2330.2; son with s. breaks bottle X121.1.

Squinting as punishment D2062.2.3.

Squirrel becomes person D315.4; in human form B651.10; points out road B563.3; released: grateful B375.4; transformed to a horse D411.1.1; tries to dip out lake with tail J133.5. — Why s. barks when attacked A2462.1.; capturing a s. (task) H1154.6; chattering s. in earth-tree A878.3.3; climbing match won by deception: s. as child K15.1; color of s. A2411.1.4.1; cry of s. A2426.1.2; devil as s. G303.3.3.11; enmity between s. and (dog) A2281.2, A2494.4.1, (marten) A2494.12.6; friendship of s.

and (quail) A2493.6, (leopard-cat) A2493.7; ghost as s. E423.2.12; helpful s. B437.3; why s. lives in tree A2433.3.9; all nuts to be picked from tall tree (done by grateful s.) H1121; one woman to catch s.: other to get cooking pot J2661.3; origin of flea: from s. A2032.3; stripes of s. A2413.3; wedding of s. B281.8; why s. stays hidden in jungle A2433.3.9.1; where s. got tail A2241.7, A2242, A2378.1.5.

Squirrel's body made smaller A2213.1, A2302.3; food A2435.3.13; markings and immunity from falling as reward A2221.8. — Origin of s. call: queries viper A2426.1.2.1.

Stabbing. — Dancer s. spectator K916; murder by s. S115ff.; queen s. self to accuse princess K2103; sham death for s. brother K911.2; by s. bag of blood trickster makes dupe think that he is bleeding *K1875; ogre deceived into s. himself G524.

Stabilizing. — God s. the sky A665.0.1.

Stable. — Abandonment in s. S153; child born in s. T581.4; cleaning Augean s. in one night (task) H1102; devil in the s. wrapped in horsehide G303.8.12; disguise as s.-boy K1816.8; farmer prefers s. smells to flowers U133.1; dwarf home is underground, beneath cow s. F451.4.1.5; dwarfs request that cow s. be moved F451.4.4.3; great s. X1037; hero is s.-boy L113.1.2; man in s. mistakes animals for ghosts J1782.4; prisoners as s. boys escape during race K475.2; strong man uses s.-roof as flail F614.7; thief finds tiger in s. *N392; treacherous s.-groom K2256; wolf almost locked in the s. by the shepherd J2172.2.1.

Stables. — Forbidden s. C611.2; king banishes mother to s. S21.4.

Stack. — Deceptive bargain: a peck of grain for each s. K181; mountain-man has s. of butter before his door F460.2.4.

Stacking wood from felled forest in one day H1095.2.

Staff of life and death: silver stick kills, golden one restores to life E64.1.1.1; stuck in ground as life token E761.2. — Angel transports saint's s. V232.2.0.2; blooming s. as chastity index H432.4; bottom and top of s. (riddle) H882; creator puts out world-fire with s. A1035.2; ferule to fit s. H1344; god gives Jesus's s. to saint V227.1; magic s. *D1254ff., (blossoms) D1673, (gives supernatural information) D1310.5; moss grows on s. overnight F971.1.3; only one ferule fits certain s. Z322; origin of plant from s. of holy person A2624; riddles about Moses's s. H823, H824; rivers where god drags his s. A934.4; saint's s. pierces man's foot F1041.0.1, V331.1.4; saint's s. as sea pilot D1313.5.1; saint's s. transformed to spear, wins land grant K185.13; serpent transforms self to s., picked up, bites enemy K928.1; spring where god throws his s. A941.3.2; suitor contest: prize to one whose s. blooms H331.3; wild huntman with black fur cap and white s. E501.8.6.

Stag, see also **Deer;** becomes wind D421.5.1; defeated by snail vomits his gall-bladder A2211.13; found by master when overlooked by servants J1032; -god A132.4; with golden antlers, silver feet B101.4.1; killed by lion into whose den the fox puts him K813; escapes from hunters to be eaten by lion N255.1; scorns his legs but is proud of his horns L461; with iron shoes J2335; with stripe of every color B731.7.1; weeps B736.5. — How s. got antlers *A2241.1, A2326.1.1, A2326.3.2; fairy in form of s. F234.1.4; helpful s. B443.1; hidden s. discovered when he begins to eat grapevine too soon J582.2; invulnerable s. D1840.2.2; speaking s. B211.2.1; visitors of sick s. eat up all his provisions so that he starves W151.2.1; witch as s. G211.2.4.1.

Stags live one thousand years B841.4; plow for man *B292.4; plow for saint B256.9. — Seven s. killed by one shot F679.5.3.1; yoking s. H1154.3.6.

Stagnant. — Enigma on s. water H599.1.

Stair to lower world *F94.

Stairs up giant's body G154; of glass F848.5; to which person sticks D1413.4; set with razors to trap hero H1531.2. — Adulteress caused to fall down s. from which steps have been removed Q469.1; earth at foot of s. to swallow up man M341.2.25; magic s. *D1144; man buried beneath s. V61.3.0.3; man pulled down s. by wives T145.5; penance: living under s. as mendicant Q523.4; robbers make s. slippery K897.3.

Stake miraculously bent F1093; through body overcomes spirit F405.9; turns corpse to worm H47. — Disenchantment by driving s. D712.10; fettered monster vainly loosens his s. A1074.6; ghost is laid by piercing grave with s. E442; giant rescues woman from burning at s. R164.2; innocent queen burned at s. K2116.1.2, Q414.0.7; rescue at s. R175ff.; son rescues mother from burning at s. R154.1.1; speech magically recovered on execution s. D2025.1; Virgin Mary saves criminal from fire at s. V252.2.

Stakes thrust through slain warriors S139.2.2.7. — Extraordinary s. at gambling N2; heads placed on s. for failure in performance of task H901.1, Q421.1; throwing away fence s. J2516.8; unjust umpire keeps s. K452.2.

Stalk as sky-rope F51.1.3. — Disenchantment from flower by breaking s. D711.4; magic s. D977; plantain disobeys mother: hence bears but one s. A2722.1.

Stalks. — Man from sugar cane s. A1255.1.

Stall. — Stealing twelve horses out of s. (task) H1151.2.

Stallion. — Devil as a white s. G303.3.3.5.3; foal born of Loki and mythical s. T465.2; god as mare seduces s. D658.3.2; monk says that he is s. J1361; neighing of s. in Assyria impregnates mares in Egypt B741.2, H572.

Stampede slaughters animals K927.

Stampeding enemy's horses K2351.6. — Devil s. horses G303.9.9.15; ghost s. cattle E234.2.

Stamping. — Flood from deity s. on heavens A1015.3; priests s. on stone to prove pope true A972.1.2; wild hunt heralded by s. of horses E501.13.3.1.

Stanched. — Blood s. by magic object D1504ff.

Stand. — Magic staff thrown causes wild animals to s. still D1442.4.

Standard. — Extraordinary s. F899.1.

Standing in uncomfortable position (punishment) Q541. — Bewitched person s. on head G269.26; charm chanted s. on one foot with one eye shut, etc. D1273.0.4; child s. at birth T585.8; devil s. in church door writes down names of his own people on sheep skin G303.24.1.4; fairies made visible by s. on another's foot F235.5.1; magic sight by s. (alone) D1821.10, (on certain stone) *D1821.5; man s. all day on one foot F682; people in otherworld s. on their heads F167.4; person buried s. V61.3.0.2; pygmy s. on man's hand F535.2.6; saint s. for seven years without sleep V462.5.2.2; water s. still before prince H71.10.2.

Stanza. — Baby's protesting s. saves life S341.1; supplying missing s. as test H509.4.1.

Star drops from heaven: is money F962.2; on breast F546.3; on forehead as sign of royalty H71.1; -gazer falls into well J2133.8; -girl A762.2; -god A250ff.; indicates location of newborn hero D1314.13; as magic object D1291.2; shines through day at Nativity V211.1.2; signifies hero's birth E741.1.1.2; takes mortal maiden as wife A762.1; transformed to person D439.5.2. — Conception from s. T525; evening s. mistaken for morning s. J1772.7; fairies live in s.-world F215; god descends as shooting s. A171.0.3.2; gold s. F793.1, (on forehead) F545.2.1; goose dives for s., thinking it a fish J1791.8; hero marries s. in girl form T111.2.1; man becomes s. D293; morning s. leads to heaven F63.4; quest to morning s. for answers to questions H1282; remarkable s.-gazer F642.1; shooting s. (as angel) V231.2, (as good omen) D1812.5.2.6, (signifies a birth) E741.1.2, (signifies that someone is dying) E741.1.1; sky supported by north s. A702.3; sky's most distant s. as moon's mother A745.2; soul in form of s. E741.1; tortoise looks towards sky: seeks his wife, a s. A2351.5; transformation into falling s. Q551.3.5.1; vision of s. entering wife's mouth V515.1.2; visit to s.-world F15; wish for s.-husband realized C15.1; wish for s. wife C15.1.1.

Stars A760—A789; answer questions D1311.6.1; as cannibals G11.8.1; as deities A121; fall down at end of world A1051.1; forged by smith A700.5; made from the old moon J2271.2.2; nourished on fire A700.7; as omens D1812.5.1.6; on palm royalty sign H71.1.1. — Absurd theories about s. J2275; Adam's name from initials of four s. A1281.6.1; black s. seen over heads of the bad D1825.3.2; counting s. tabu C897.1; directions on quest given by sun, moon, wind, and s. H1232; dress of gold, silver, color of sun, moon, and s. F821.1.5; end of world when s. in one constellation overtake those in another A1051.2; extraordinary behavior of s. F961.2; fugitives rise in the air and become s. R321; handkerchief color of sun, moon, and s. F822.1; heavenly horses strike hoofs on s. A1141.3; horoscope taken by means of s. M302.4; magic objects received from sun, moon, and s. D814; man deriding faith in s. becomes astrologer N186; rain shed by s. A1131.6; riddle: how many s. are in the heavens H702ff.; sun to eat up s. at world's end A1066; sun, moon, and s. (are highest) H642.1, (bring forth first parents) A1271.1; wishing by s. D1761.1.

Starling. — Color of s. A2411.2.1.16; soul in s. E715.1.5.

Starling's enemies A2494.13.11. — Why s. beak is split A2343.3.1.

Started. — Magic gift: power to continue all day what one has s. D2172.2.

Starting. — "Not s. from here" directions J1648.

Starvation prevented by hymn D2105.1.1. — Murder by s. S132; prostitution to avoid s. T450.3; suicide from s. fright F1041.1.11.1.

Starved. — Lover imprisoned, s. K1218.1.3.1; prisoners s. R51.1; prisoners s. in corpse-filled pit Q465.2.

Starving king in mountain chamber S123.4; parents come to abandoned daughter for food S362; while waiting for God to provide J2215.4; woman eats newborn child G72.2; woman to death for her treasure K2116.2.2. — Bird carries food from deserted child to s. parents S361; child hides food from s. parents S20.2; fat abbot cured by s. K1955.1.1; fool s. self at table, later steals food J2541; lazy man s. to death rather than open mouth W111.5.8.1; lovers s. selves to death T87; numskull s. himself J2135; vow on s. until picture's original found M151.2.1; wife offers s. husband milk from her breasts T215.2; woman sells hair for s. husband T215.8.

Statement. — Clever interpretation of judge's s. J1193; ghost summoned to make s. E387.1.1.

Statements. — Enigmatic s. H580ff.

Statue in cave entrance frightens giantess K1726; comes to life *D435.1.1; inscription gives suitor tasks H335.0.4; left instead of abducted queen K661.4; mistaken for living orignal J1794; mourned and buried in order to account for murdered person K661.2; transformed to drinking vessels D454.15. — Dog becomes s. D422.2.3; fool sells goods to s. J1853.1; God finds that his s. sells at low price L417; gold (silver) s. of animal F855.3; lion and the s. J1454; love through sight of s. T11.2.1; magic s. *D1268, (betrays a thief by indirection) K428; maid behind s. of Virgin advises mistress to give servants better food K1971.3.1; man acts as s. of saint in order to enter convent K1842.1; man behind s. speaks and pretends to be God K1971; marriage to s. T117.11; money from broken s. J1853.1.1; not to steal from holy s. C51.2.4; offended s. carries host off to otherworld *C13; sham miracle: s. raises arm K1972.1; sleeping soldier mistaken for s. J1763.3; tabu: disrespect to goddess's s. C51.1.13; talking s. when destroyed, cannot be replaced for thirty thousand years D1661.1; woman blushes in presence of male s. F647.4, K2051.1; young man betrothed to s. T376; youth makes s. of girl and seeks a girl like the statue T11.2.1.1.

Statues animated by water or wind F855.2. — Origin of calf s. A1546.0.3.

Stature. — Humor of small s. X142.

Staves. — Magic s. D1539.3.

Staying too long in certain place tabu C761.4ff.; too long in otherworld forbidden C712. — Choice: s. at home with loving wife or going to tavern and having unfaithful wife J229.1; fear test: s. in frightful place H1410ff.

Stead. — Foster brother killed in man's s. P273.3.

Steadfastness of love for God tested H1573.5.

Steadying the earth A857.

Steak cut from hero's body G269.9. — Contest: pulling on s. with teeth K64.

Steaks cut from live cow who heals herself by magic D2161.2.1.

Steal, see also **Robbery, Stolen, Theft, Thief.** — Animals sent to s. fire but are lazy and fail A2436; devil helps person to s. G303.22.6; fox confesses sins but is immediately ready to s. again K2055; transformation to s. D657ff.; why Gypsy may s. A1674.1.

Stealing as animal's occupation A2455; from blind beggar's stick K333.4; fairy necklace F357; from fairies F350; with help of trained animal K366; ghosts E593; as greatest villainy H659.7.4; from ogre G610ff.; only a small amount (rope with a mare on the end of it) K188; from sacred booty tabu C51.1.2.1; servants caught by arising early J21.23; as a task H1151; as tribal characteristic A1674; a wife Q252.1. — Beasts s. fruit B16.0.1; bird s. island B172.11; brahmin s. to feed guests W11.4.1; bride s. K1371; child-s. demon G442; devil appears to s. person G303.6.2.15; devil s. Thunder's instruments A162.3.1; dwarfs emigrate because mortals object to their s. F451.9.1.8; dwarfs s. from human beings F451.5.2.2; fairies s. F365, (child from cradle) F321, (man's wife and carrying her off to fairyland) F322; fairies' revenge for s. F361.2; false bride s. true bride's garments K1911.1.8; father kills son for s. S11.3.3.1; fear test: s. clothes from ghosts H1431; giant s. from giant F531.6.8.3.2; giant s. from man F531.6.7.2.1; helper s. object of quest K2036; hanging for s. from church Q411.11.2; impostors s. rescued princess K1935; horse s. tabu C884.2; magic object acquired by s. D838; man put into moon for s. A751.1.4; moon s. food A153.3.1; moon s. from a garden A753.3.2; mountain-folk s. from peasant F460.4.4.5; one s. much called king, little called robber U11.2; parishioner s. alms J1262.5; rabbit s. ember A2218.7; robber's defence for s. from the rich J1269.8; seduction (or wooing) by s. clothes of bathing girl K1335; serpent s. jewels N352.3; servant excuses s.: must support family J1636; strong man serves ogre as punishment for s. food F613.4; tabu: s. (from altar) C51.1.2, (from god or saint) C51.2, (from spirits) C91, (god's wife) C51.2.3; task: s. H1150ff.; trolls s. F455.6.3; witches s. G266.

Stealth. — Wife banished for eating by s. S411.4.

Steam. — Earth from s. made by fire thrown into primeval water A814.5; thumbling carried up chimney by s. of food F535.1.1.2.

Steamship thought to be the devil J1781.1.

Steed, see also **Horse.** — Devil as black s. G303.3.3.5.2; speckled s. tabu C833.8; warrior gives s. to his enemy W11.5.9.

Steeds of night and day A1172.3. — Dwarfs have s. and wagons F451.7.6; fool cuts off tails of oxen so that they will look like fine s. J1919.4.

Steel castle (house) F771.1.4; protects against will-o'-the-wisp F491.3.3; on rock produces fire A975.2. — Casting s. releases troll's treasure F455.6.4.2; dragon must give up treasure when s. is thrown on him B11.6.2.1; lie: remarkable s. worker X1083; merman attacked by putting s. in the water B82.5; magic s. *D1252.1; ship of brass within, s. without F841.1.6; towers of s., silver and gold F772.2.2.

Steep. — Return from lower world up s. slope F101.1.

Steeple. — Cat crawls to s. and tries to fly J2133.3; devil destroys church s. G303.24.4; owl will not betray curate: therefore may live in s. A2229.3; witch marks church s. G241.3.3.

Steer, see also **Bull;** swung round by horns F628.1.2.2. — Helpful s. B411.6; man transformed to s. D133.5.

Stella Maris V282.

Stems. — As many leaves on tree as s. (riddle) H705.1.

Stench. — Devil disappears amid a terrible s. G303.17.2.8; ghost leaves s. behind E588.

Step. — Giant's s. leaves furrows F531.1.3.4; one s. from earth to heaven (riddle) H682.1.9.

Steps to submarine world F725.1. — Death respite for six s. toward God K551.14; giant god goes with three s. through the world A133.2.1; giant s. prodigious distance F531.3.5; grass becomes stone s. D451.5.5.

Stepbrother P283. — Boy accidentally drinks poison intended for s. N332.4. — Cruel s. S33; murder of s. S73.1.0.1; poison for s. drunk by own son K1613.3; treacherous s. K2211.3.

Stepchild. — Transformation of s. D665.2.

Stepchildren. — Banishment of s. demanded S322.4.1; dead wife returns to reprove husband's second wife for abusing her s. *E221.2.1; hen's s. starve: lesson to man J134.1.

Stepdaughter heroine L55. — Cow refuses to help s. B335.7.

Stepfather P281. — Cruel s. S32; lustful s. T418.1.

Stepmother P282; cursed by fire lit under her M431.6; falls into fire from fright N384.3; falsely accuses faithful son N342.1.1; hides heroine from suitor T47; orders stepdaughter killed S322.4.2; wants rich snake for daughter J2415.7. — Cruel s. *S31, (enchants stepdaughter on eve of wedding) T154; curse by s. M411.1.1; death passes by man who fed his s. Q151.2; drowning punishes flight with s. Q552.19.4; evil s. casts boy forth S322.4; hypocritical s. K2056; lustful s. T418; quest for witch s. H1397.1; sparrows enact prophecy of cruel s. M369.2.1.1; supplying food to ungrateful s. rewarded Q65.1; task assigned by s. H913.1.3; witch s. *G205.

Stepping into fairy ring F235.5.2; outside line forbidden C614.1.0.3; stones as sight test H1575.1. — Bird overpowered by s. on his shadow D2072.0.4; conception from s. on an animal T532.2; fairies made visible by s. on certain spot F235.5; islands as deity's s.-stones A955.1;

man as king's s.-stone across fire P116; resuscitation by s. (over) E13, (on corpse) E13.1; tabu: princess s. in water C562; tabu: s. on sacred bread C55.1; transformation by s. in footprint D578; warning against s. on red cloth T299.2.1; one wild goat s. over another J133.1.

Steprelatives P280ff. — Cruel s. S30ff.

Stepsister P284. — Cruel s. S34.

Stepsisters cause flies to collect around girl K2129.3. — Treacherous s. K2112.1.

Stepson cursed to stick in grave mound D5.1.1. — Adulteress and paramour plot against her s. S31.1; queen poisons s. Q211.4.1; stepmother mourns death of s. P282.2; woman spurned by s., attempts to poison him K2111.1.

Stepsons. — Stepmother incites s. to murder S322.4.3.

Sterile, see also **Barren;** land as punishment C934.2; woman's magic power D1716.3. — Why certain animals are s. A2561; druid's curse makes land s. M411.6.1; land made magically s. *D2081; magic medicine makes s. land fertile D1347.3; magic poem (satire) makes land s. D1563.2.3; magic swine make land s. B16.4.

Sterility from breaking tabu C949.3; curse on enemy's wife M431.8; of land as punishment Q552.3.1.1; magically cured D2161.3.10; as punishment Q553.3; among women A1358. — Goddess of s. A431.1.4.

Sterilized. — Earth s. by magic springs D1563.0.1.

Sterilizing. — Son tries s. father S21.5.

Stew. — Canons compared to s. J81.3.

Steward. — Ignorant s. straightens his master's accounts L144.1; treacherous s. K2242.

Stewing. — Resuscitation by s. E15.3.

Stick, see also **Staff, Wand;** with money in it breaks and betrays thief H251.3.4; burns in water F964.4; at corpse's side to chase away scavengers J1442.4.1; for scratching back becomes cobra A1335.14; thrown at animal's rump: hence tail A2215.1; transformed to other object D451.6; under table: imitation diagnosis J2412.4.1. — Alleged rejuvenating s. K116.2; bull's tail becomes s., exterminates army D1400.1.21; coming neither on horse nor on foot (on a s. horse) H1053.5; devil carries a thorn s. G303.4.8.5; flight by vaulting on s. R252; fool puts but one s. of wood in stove J1963; giant with tree for herding-s. G152.1; guilty man's s. will grow J1141.1.4; life in s. E711.6; magic power in s. D1718.1; magic s. D1254, (beats person) D1401.1, (chosen instead of money) L222.3, (transforms) D572.1, (of wood) D956; man becomes s. D217; money stolen from blind beggar's s. K333.4; money in the s. J1161.4; new backbone for horse made from s. X1721.1; serpent steals from God's coat a s. for his back A2262.3; sky black because raised by dirty s. A702.8; sweeping with s. instead of broom J1822; taking a s. from the body (task) H1021.7; tortoise speaks and loses his hold on the s. J2357; transformation by smelling s. D564.1; treasure left in s. N521; wild huntsman's dog when seized becomes s. E501.15.6.7; witch exorcised by burning s. G271.1; word for "s." confused with "stone" A1333.1; woman charms s., hides in it D1393.1.1.

Sticks transformed to animals D441.7. — Fiery s. in hell A671.2.4.8; magic pair of s. D1254.1.1; origin of fire: rubbing s. A1414.1; quails become s. D423.2; quarreling sons and the bundle of s. J1021; resourcefulness test: find relationship among s. H506.10.

Sticking to magic object D1413ff.; object into tracks exorcises witch G271.4.6. — Advice on s. fast: fool seizes ass J2489.9; ascent to sky by s. to magic feather *F61.2.1; captive s. out bone instead of finger G82.1.1; greedy person's hand s. in jar W151.9; hand of sinner s. out of grave E411.0.1; magic knife s. in tree causes wine to flow D1472.2.11; ogre jumping on one's back and s. there magically G311; pitcher magically s. to ground D2171.4.1; princess brought to laughter by people s. together H341.1; staff s. in ground as life token E761.2.

Sticky. — Transformation by eating s. rice D551.6.2.1.

Stifle. — Strong bride tries to s. husband in bed T173.1.

Stile. — Lovers on s. bewitched G269.23.

Still. — Extraordinary s. F891.

Stillborn. — Curse: child s. M441.1; live child substituted for king's s. K1923.5; plants from body of s. child A2611.0.2.

Stilled. — Storm magically s. *D2141.1.

Stilts. — Art of walking on s. A1491.

Sting, see also **Stung.** — Bees pray for s.; punishment, first s. suicidal A2232.2; centipede's poisoned s. A1335.13; cure for insect s. D1517; only one serpent has s. A2219.3; origin and nature of insect's s. A2346ff.

Stinger. — Snake has s. B765.16.

Stinginess *W152ff.; punished Q276. — Amends for s. Q589.4; guests accuse family of s. K2129.4; woodpecker punished for s. A2239.4.

Stinging insects test sham-dead H248.2. — Bees s. opposing army B524.2.1; dupe induced to eat s. fruit K1043; god sends s. bees to punish men A2012.3; resuscitation by s. E16; task: cutting down tree without scratching for s. insects H1184; thorns not s. at night J1819.1.

Stingy almsgiving repaid J1581; innkeeper cured of serving weak beer J1341.7; woman's cloth stolen by tailor K341.13. — Beggar tells s. to go beg J1334; rebuke to the s. J1522ff.; rich but s. couple adopt son T673; servant repays s. master (mistress) J1561.4; woodpecker transformed from s. woman A2261.4.

Stink, see also **Smell.** — Fool has himself buried because of his s. J2193; scientific query: why does the sea s. when it is full of salt J2371.2.

Stirring. — Fool frightened by s. of (animal) J2614, (wind) J2622.

Stirrup leather breaking bad omen D1825.1.28.

Stirrups. — Fortune from informing foreign king of use of saddle, bridle, and s. N411.3; tiny person on horse with long s. X142.3.

Stitch in side from being told about hearing a man chopping wood F647.8.1.1.

Stock, see **Livestock.**

Stocking. — Devil must wait for man to tie his s. before the man comes into his possession K551.4.2.

Stockings. — Magic s. *D1062.

Stolen, see also **Robbed, Steal, Theft, Thief;** bedcover J2672; chickens turn to stone D471.8.1; child rescued by animal nurse B543.3; meat and the weighed cat J1611; mother returns from fairyland each Sunday to minister to her children *F322.3; objects powerful in magic D838.1; property sold to its owner K258; ring proves theft H84.4; sacrament V35; sun restored to sky A721.3; woman rescued from lower world R111.2.1.1. — Animal characteristics: s. from another animal A2245; animal finds s. person B543; animal finds s. goods B543.2; animals s. from saint miraculously replaced V224.3; beast brings back s. child D2156.3; brownie restores s. property F482.5.4.2; child of deity s. F31.1; children s. by witch *G261; complaint about the s. kiss J1174.2; crops s. by magic *D2087.1; dead returns to restore s. goods E352; dog's horns s. by deer A2326.2.2; dragon's pearl s. B11.6.2.3; dream shows where s. girl is hidden D1810.8.2.1; fairy girl returns s. goods for man F302.3.1.1; father rescues son s. by animals R153.3.2; fairy's wings s. bring her into man's power *F302.4.2; fire s. from spider by fly A2229.4; flesh of s. animal cannot be cooked D1318.7.1.1; ghost demands s. money E236.5; ghost reveals whereabouts of s. goods E371.1; girl having been s. by mountain-folk must be baptized anew V81.1; husband rescues s. wife R151.1; king has own gifts s. back P14.12; knight's cloak s. by devil G303.9.9.3; magic object s. back D882ff.; man refuses to eat fifth descendant of s. cow F647.10; magic object raises alarm when s. D1612.5ff.; magic object s. D861; mill will not grind s. wheat D1318.15; moon s. A755.4.2; night s., kept in jar A1174.3.1; priest's collar s. by ghost E593.1; purchaser of s. ornament jailed as thief N347.4; quest for s. princess H1385.1; receiver of s. goods J1169.6; recognition by cup in sack: alleged s. goods H151.4; rescued person s. R111.8; return from dead to demand s. property E236; saint's bell when s. miraculously returned D1602.8; sign of cross prevents child from being s. from cradle V86.1.1; strong man son of bear who has s. his mother F611.1.1; stupid monk recovers s. flocks L141.1; things s. by magic object working for master D1605; transformation to recover s. goods D659.11; wizard locates s. property D1817.0.1.2; wolf returns sheep s. from saint B256.11; woman has meat (liver) s. by bird Z41.1.

Stomach, see also **Belly;** borrowed by animal E787; huge from overeating F559.6.1; removed at man's wish J2072.4. — Animal lives in person's s. B784; child's s. split to cure him of wandering J1842.4; eyedrops prescribed for s. ache X372.3; eye treated for the s. ache J1603; giantess tearing woman's s. F531.1.8.5; magic animal s. D1015.5; magic water cures s. trouble D1502.11; murder by cutting up s. S139.5; needle in elk's s. L391; painting on wife's s. chastity index H439.1.1; paunch fat as s. cure F959.4; person with eyes in s. F512.3; person with mouth in s. F513.0.1; reincarnation of s. into flour vat E649.2; ridding person of animal in s. B784.2ff.; tormenting beast in man's s. B16.0.2; transformation to enter s. D641.3; victim pecks on swallower's s. F915.1; when sad, man lets one lip fall to s. F544.1.2; wood-spirits' teeth on s. F441.4.6.

Stone, see also **Rock;** barrier to otherworld F149.1; becomes silver D475.3.3; beheaded, believed to be enemy K1883.4; bleeds three days before church is plundered D1317.12.1; boat (ship) F841.1.1; breaks: life token E761.5.5; breaks in unchaste presence H411.1.1; canoe D1524.3.1; in church sheds blood in prophecy Q222.0.1; -cast quells burning house F679.6; catches fire F964.3.4; changes color as omen D1812.5.0.14; cross indicates treasure W535.1; of destiny roars out under king *H171.5; emerges from primeval water A816.1; falling from sky kills all but one couple A1009.3; fated to kill, powdered up M377.1; under fertile woman gives milk; under barren, blood H1572.1; fish-hooks tabu C895; giants G371; -headed giant F531.1.2.5; with hole protection against witches G272.13; necklace protects from attack D1381.6; produced by magic D931.0.1; to be protected C665; rolls after saint prays D1654.1.1.1; screams under king's feet H71.10.6; substituted for newly-born babies K2115.2.1; transformed to animal D442.1; transformed to person *D432.1; of truth H251.2; turns red when saint's picture removed V229.23; -spirit F495; transformed to another object D452.1; thrown into greedy dupe's mouth K1035; from victim's rock kills murderer Q582.3.1; as witness against farmer J1141.1.3.1; -woman as creator A1.3. — Adulteress turns man to s. K1535.1; alleged healing s. sold K115.2; angel passes over blessed s. V242.3; ascetic sleeps on s. V462.5.2; bat lifts s. H1562.2.2; boaster throws back flung s. H1562.5; blood drops from s. to indicate girl's innocence D1318.5.5; bluff in court: s. in purse K1765; breaking s. in anger F1041.16.3.2; castle inhabitants turned to s. F771.4.6; child born carrying s. T552.6; cloak given to s. to keep it warm J1873.2; conception from swallowing s. T511.8.1; contest in squeezing water from s. K62; corpse buried under s. so that sun will not shine on him again E431.10; cynic and the bastard s.-thrower J1442.7; deity of s. A498; devil builds bridge minus one s. G303.14.2; devil as s. G303.3.4.6; devil in a s. G303.8.11; devil in each s. of church built with ill-gotten wealth G303.8.4.2; devil prevents moving of little s. by sitting on it G303.9.9.1; devil takes s. away C12.5.2; devil turns object to s. A977.4; disenchantment by throwing s. D712.3.2; dragon becomes s. D429.2.2; dry spring restored by removal of certain s. F933.2; duck becomes precious s. D423.3; dwarfs turn to s. at sunrise F451.3.2.1; earth from s. thrown on primeval water A814.1; earth founded on s. A849.1; eel becomes s. D426.1.1; elephant becomes s. D421.3.2; evil spirits imprisoned in s. D2177.3; fairy music from s. F262.10.1; fairies made visible through use of magic s. on eyes F235.4.3;

fairyland entrance under s. F211.2; flock of geese transformed to s. D423.1.1; food concealed from saint changed to s. Q552.16.1; food left on magic s. brings good luck thereafter D1561.1.6; fool kills chickens by throwing them off balcony against s. J2173.5; fugitive transforms self to s. D671.0.1; ghost laid under s. E437.4; giant with s. heart F531.1.6.10.1; giant's s. boat F531.4.8; giant's s. club F531.4.5.4; giantess becomes s. D429.2.2.1; girl mistaken for s J1763.2; God creates the devil by striking a s. with his whip G303.1.1.4; God finds devil under s. G303.1.2.2; god with s. head A123.4.2; handling heavy s. as unique ability H31.9; horse becomes s. D422.1.2; injunction: protect certain s. from molestation C665; is more of s. above or below ground? H527; lazy woman sees how little bird pecks hole in s. J1011; magic sight by standing on certain s. *D1821.5; magic staff draws water from s. D1549.5; magic s. *D931, (transforms) D572.5; making ship of s. (task) H1021.3; man proof against iron, s., and wood D1841.1; man dies for throwing s. at Virgin's image Q558.5; man lifts large s. F624.2; man sinks into s. F943.1; man with one side of s. F525.1; man transformed to s. *D231; man's bones made of s. A1260.1.5; oath taken on holy s. M114.2; object transformed to s. D471; octopus becomes s. D426.2; oracular s. D1311.16; ordeal by s. from bucket H233; origin of polishing s. A1465.4; persons whose heads are s.-hammers F511.0.3; punishment: carrying corpse of murdered man until s. as long as murdered man is found Q511.1; quest for magic s. H1351; recognition by overheard conversation with s. H13.2.2; reincarnation as s. E642; remarkable s.-thrower F636.4; resuscitation by magic s. E64.17; riddle: what is harder than s. H673; river crossed by means of magic s. D1524.6; rose grows from s. F971.2; sacred s. assists childbirth T584.0.6; sacrifice to s. V11.3; saint sets fire to s. D2158.1.2; saint steps on s., demons flee F405.10; saint's bachall cuts s. D1564.3; salt turns to s. as punishment Q591.2; serpents play with precious green s. B11.6.2.2; sewing a shirt of s. (task) H1021.9; Sisyphus must keep rolling great s. up hill Q501.1; sitting on s. to prevent premature birth T572.1.1; skinning a s. (task) H1023.10; snake becomes s. D425.1.1; soul in s. E711.7; strong man plunges sword into s. F628.4.1; strong man's throw of s. carries away timber of roof F639.3; sunlight turns giant to s. *F531.6.12.2; swearing on a s. M119.5; talking s. as Doomsday sign A1002.2.3, A1091.3; test of strength: lifting s. H1562.2; throwing contest: bird substituted for s. K18.3; throwing s. at own reflection J1791.5.2; transformation: s. to salt C456.3; transformation by striking with s. D566.2; transformation to s. (for breaking tabu) C961.2, (as punishment) Q551.3.4; test of strength: heavy s. flung at boaster H1562.5; treasure hidden in s. N523; treasure under s. N511.6; trolls turn to s. F455.8.1; troublesome bonga (fairy) pegged to ground and placed under s. F386.3; unborn son's soul as s. E726.2; unerring s. missile D1653.1.6; warrior deceived into attacking substituted s. K1845.1; witch melts s. G229.6; witch transforms to s.

G263.2.1; word for "s." confused with stick A1333.1; worship of s. idols V1.11.2; yearly leap over s. C684.3.

Stone's. — Sea a s. throw deep (riddle) H681.4.1.

Stones become jewels D475.4.1; burn enemies' feet D2091.10.1; cast in ocean keep dry D1841.4.3.2; for church miraculously supplied V111.2; erected where enemy falls P557.3; fall on churchyard desecrators Q222.5.1; falling from tree kill enemies N696.2; join in keen F994.2; to keep cow from blowing away J2119.8; kill ogre G512.8.2; magically fly through air D2135.3; from mermaids, fairies, elves, devil D2066.1; move for king's passage H71.10.5; prostrate selves E761.5.5.1; rained upon raja hurled back D1400.1.22; reproducing J1896.1; say "Amen" after saint preaches V229.2.10; in throat to lay ghost E441.2; transformed to gold coins D475.2.1; turn to gold for charitable money-lender V411.4; watered to make them grow J1932.7. — Angels from s. stuck against each other A52.0.8; boy throwing s. killed by them Q582.7; city of precious metals and s. F761; children said to come from s. T589.6.6; corpse buried under s. E431.10.1; curse makes s. useless D2089.2; dead live in s. E481.3.2; dead lovers are now two s. lying together E642.1; devils are created by sparks produced by Satan's striking two s. together G303.1.4.2; devils carry away s. of church built with ill-gotten money Q274.1; digging up certain s. tabu C523.1; doors of precious s. F782.2; dupe eating s. K1043.2; dwarfs live in s. F451.4.1.12; extraordinary rocks and s. F800ff.; fairy protects self with s. F278.1; fiery s. in hell A671.2.4.9; from wooden spring iron bucket makes s. from which water flows (riddle) H765; gathering all s. from brook or field (task) H1124; god of s. A499.3; heat test: swallowing red-hot s. H1511.1; hills from s. cast by giants A963.5; hot s. thrown in dupe's mouth K721.1; invulnerability from hurled s. D1841.5.1.1; island's s. are jewels F731.4; islands from s. cast by giantess A955.6; magic lyre charms s. into their places in building D1565.2; magic protective s. from holy well D1382.1.0.1; man created from s. A1245; mountains from s. dropped A963; murder by throwing hot s. in the mouth *K951.1; number of s. indicate battle survivors P554; origin of groups of s. A977; origin of s. A970ff.; palace consisting of 8760 s.: twelve trees, thirty branches (riddle) H721.4; parable on s. shaken in jar J98; penance: carrying bag of s. (one for each murder) on back until it falls off Q521.2; peas transformed to s. D451.9.1; pillars of precious s. F774.1; rain of s. as punishment Q552.14.4; rivers formed where certain s. are placed A934.2; sacred s. V1.6.4.1; self-illuminating precious s. in heaven A661.0.7; shower of s. seems snowfall to giant F531.5.4.1; stepping s. as sight test H1575.1; strength in words, in herbs, and in s. J1581.2, T251.5; swindlers given s. for money K1675; take away all the s. and I will weigh earth H691.2.1; throwing s. to express love H316.5; thunder from crashing of s. in moon A1142.5.1.1; trick exchange: s. for bread K149.1; twelve s. unite in one D491.6, F1009.4; war prisoners shut up between s. Q433.13;

what are best and worst s.? H659.3; when pleading fails man brings thief down from tree with s. J1088; wolf cut open and filled with s. as punishment Q426.

Stoned. — Ogre s. to death G512.2; owner of evil eye s. D2071.0.1.1; rower prefers to be s. by his master rather than remain out in the storm J229.7.

Stoning to death (as punishment) Q422, (for breaking tabu) C929.4. — Seven thousand killed for s. judges N340.2.

Stony. — Carrying soil to cover s. ground H1129.3; growing oil seed on s. ground H1049.2.

Stool. — Gold in s. royalty sign H71.11; magic s. D1620.3.2; move s. before sitting on it J21.34; woman becomes golden s. D235.2.

Stooped. — Dwarfs walk s. F451.2.0.3.

Stopped. — Boat s. by magic D2072.0.3; boiling blood s. E761.1.5.1; emergence of tribe from lower world s. A1631.1; pouring of inexhaustible pitcher s. only at owner's command D1651.4; ship at sea s. by giant's leg F531.3.1.2; wind s. by magic D2142.2.

Stopping. — Attempt at s. dog's mouth with food K2062; countertask: s. all the rivers H1142.3; forgotten fiancée attracts attention by magically s. wedding carriage of new bride D2006.1.5; tabu: s. enroute while carrying image of a god C56.2.

Store produced by magic D1149.1. — Going to s. with scythe K1162.

Stored. — Trickster poses as helper and eats women's s. provisions K1983.

Stork as child's nurse B535.0.7.1; killed along with cranes J451.2; is man while hibernating in Egypt B775. — Bad luck follows man who shoots s. *N250.1; children brought by the s. T589.6.1; color of s. A2411.2.5.3; courtship of s. and crane B282.23; creation of s. A1966; friendship between monkey and s. A2493.14.3; helpful s. B463.4; why s. is holy A2541.2; king sees how male s. kills his unfaithful wife and follows its example T252.2.1; why s. must hunt for living A2452.2; man transformed to s. D155.1; bill and legs of a s. to make him look more like a real bird J1919.1; protecting as s. does J2442; tabu to kill s. C92.1.4; why s. has (black back) A2411.2.5.3.1, (long neck) A2351.4.1; Zeus gives frogs s. as king J643.1.

Storks become men in Egypt in the winter D624.1. — War between serpents and s. B263.7.

Storm appears to be island D2031.17; as barrier to otherworld F141.2.1; from broken tabu C984.2; calmed by wizard D2141.0.8.1; frees marooned tortoise N662; of gigantic hailstones F962.5.1; overturns idol F962.0.2; produced by magic *D2141; as punishment Q552.14, (for profaning temple) Q222.4; at royal birth F960.1.1.3. — Animal allows himself to be tied so as to avoid being carried off by s. K713.1.1; church bell rung as protection against s. D2141.1.1; confession of sins of a pilgrim calms a great s. at sea V24.1; death from magic s. F1041.1.7; devil fetches soul in s. M219.2.1; electric s. breaks island F962.1; false proof of s.: cloak dipped in water K1894; father saves self in s. S141.2; Flying Dutchman sails because he defied the s. E511.1.3; fox persuades bird to show him how she acts in a s. K827.1; human sacrifice to s. spirit S264.1.1; laying ghost causes s. E443.0.1; magic object raises s. D1541.1; magic s. *D905, (produced by animal) D2141.0.11; man scorns the s.: killed by it L471; man thrown overboard to placate s. S264.1; man transformed to s. D281; marvelous picture falls from sky in s. F962.12.3; new moon with old moon in her arm as sign of s. D1812.5.1.5.1; poisoning fish causes s. C41.4; prophecy: death by s. M341.2.2; Rübezahl as s. spirit F465; Satan causes property-destroying s. G303.9.4.0.1; thief escapes in magic s. K532.2; wild hunt (disappears during s.) E501.16.5, (heralded by s.) E501.13.6.

Storms on land (runaway horse) J1483.3; magically drawn down on foe D2091.5; when wind-spirit awakes A1128.2. — Ghost causes s. E292; giants' shouts are s. or great noise F531.3.8; herb protects from s. at sea D1388.1.2; lies about s. X1610; magic object controls s. *D1541ff.; origin of s. in sixth heaven A1130.2; phantom condemned to wander through s. E512; saint controls s. D2140.1.1.

Stormy. — Origin of s. sky A1147; wild hunt appears on s. nights E501.11.1.4.

Story, see also **Tale;** to king brings reparation J1675.6; restrains king's hasty judgment J571.5; told to discover thief J1177.1. — Cast-forth wife must sit at horse-block of palace and tell s. to each newcomer Q482.4; execution escaped by s.-telling J1185; fool believes realistic s.: inappropriate action J1849.1; free keep in inn exchanged for good s. M231; king makes everyone tell him s. P14.14; leaving during s. reveals guilt J1177.0.1; life s. in ten hours Z24.1.1; magic s. D1266.3, (protects) D1380.13; quest for unknown s. H1382.2; rebuke for poor, long-winded s. J1223; recognition through s.-telling H11; robbery as s. of theft told K341.20; tabu: chief being in ale-house when there is no s.-telling C564.1; telling s. to allay woman's desires K2111.0.1.

Stories creep out of man's belly C672.1. — Lulling to sleep by "sleepy" s. D1962.4.1; pig boils only after true s. H251.3.11; putting out of countenance by telling evil s. J1211; refusal to accept help until s. told P331; telling true s. H252.0.1.

Stove runs over hill D1641.3. — Candle put in the s. to dry J2122; devil goes through s. with great noise G303.17.2.3; drying snow on the s. J2121; fool puts but one stick of wood in the s. because several others have burned up J1963; grateful s. D1658.2.1; heat from s. with no fire J1976; magic s. *D1161; numskull ties yarn about s. to keep heat from escaping J1942; recognition by overheard conversation with s. H13.2.7.

Straight. — Forest of s. and tall trees F812.1; those departing from s. path fall in holes J95; why wolf has s. back A2356.2.2.

Straightened. — Master's accounts s. by ignorant steward L144.1.

Straightening curly hair (task) H1023.4; dog's tail H1023.4.1.

Straightforwardly. — Lady answering queen s. J751.1.1.

Straining stream after bathing C721.3.

Strange. — Animals of s. and varied coloring B731.0.1; aversion to burial in "s. clay" V61.11; don't fall asleep in s. place J21.41; don't require honey from s. country J21.40; in s. place look about you J21.34.1; insanity from seeing s. sight *D2065.2.

Stranger accidentally chosen king because picked up by sacred elephant N683; not interested in you J1087; presented with first fish A1528; playing without permission tabu C892; should not sleep J21.41.2. — Adulteress refuses to admit husband under pretence that he is s. K1511.1; children know local road; why doesn't s.? J2212.9; marrying a s. J2463.2; mysterious s. performs task H976; rescue by s. R169.15; rewarded s. dies from joy F1041.1.5.2.

Stranger's. — Brass statue at city gates blows on trumpet at s. approach *D1317.9.1; magic knowledge of s. identity D1810.0.13.

Strangers to be given precedence over man at home P631; umpire beauty contest H1596.2. — Choices: kind s., unkind relatives J390ff.; entertaining s. tabu C745; man seeks s. for hospitality W12.2; no food for s. until one of them wrestles W213; not to speak to s. C492; sacrifice of s. S265; tabus of s. C576.

Strangled. — Animal s. by victim which he tries to eat K1643.

Strangling hawk inside his shirt J2461.1.5. — Demons s. children G302.9.4; fairies s. child J2415.4; miser s. self after he dreams of spending money W153.6; murder by s. S113; murderer s. companion in bed K951.0.2; punishment: s. Q424; suicide by s. A1599.9.

Strangulation. — Adventures from s. attempt N776.2; hare deceives wolf, fox into s. K713.3.

Strap. — Recovering s. from sea (task) H1132.1.3.

Straps. — Devil unable to endure cross made by s. of knapsack G303.16.3.2.

Strassburg. — Battle between lice of S. and of Hungary X651.

Strategy aids hero L311.2; to escape undesired lover T323. — Animals overcome man's adversary by s. *B524.2; fairies' s. F278; military s. K2350ff.; murder by s. K910ff.

Straw becomes animal D442.1; becomes gold D475.1.20; immobilizes witch G273.7.2; on shoulder to identify self J2012.6; transformed to snake D441.9. — Abandoned child wrapped in s. S336; bean, s., and coal go journeying F1025.1; bridge of s. F842.1.5; burning animal in s. to release curse M429.3; covering house with s.: mother suffocates K1462.2; covering mistress instead of roof with s. J2489.8; dead person sails over sound on bundle of s. E581.7; fairy replaces man's heart with heart of s. F281; ghost sails on s. E581.7; magic s. *D1276; magic from swallowing s. D1735.1; old maid with bundle of s. in bed X752; origin of s. A2685.2; princess hides in s. R313; reincarnation as grass s. E631.2.1; soul as s. E745.3; talkative animals given twice threshed s. as punishment J2362; wife covered with s. J1805.1.1; witch in form of blade of s. G212.1; witch's horse transformed from s. G241.3.1.

Straws protection against witches G272.12.

Straying. — Horse s. tabu C884.2; magic object prevents animal from s. D1446.

Stream, see also **Brook, River, Water;** becomes hot in which saint performs his ascetic devotions F932.3; carries message to prisoner R121.9; changed to egg D476.1.8; as deity's wife A425.1.1; devil's trap, kills drinker G303.16.2.3.5; magically appears D2151.2.5; of paradise from roots of world-tree A878.1; runs through house F715.4. — Aphrodisiac given naked woman in s. K1395; not to bathe in clear s. C721.2.1; burial on far side of s. E442.2; carrying hundreds of sheep across a s. one at a time (task) H1111; communication by milk in s. K1549.5; crossing weed-filled s. H1197; devil as s. G303.3.4.11; do not cross a swollen s. until it has run down J21.21; entering a garden by swimming down a s. K2377; fairies ferried across s. F213.2; fairies live in trees by s. F216.1; fairy unable to cross running s. F383.2; flowing s. forms arc over other-world isle F162.2.9; fresh water s. in sea F711.4.1; ghost frightens people into s. E2; giants carry a church across a s. F531.3.6; hair transformed to s. D457.4.1; why iguana lives in s. A2433.6.4; jackal covers up inability to cross s. J873.1; leaf sent down s. as warning to one below H135; long tongue cut out and used to bridge s. F544.2.2.1; magic book conjured away by throwing it on s. D2176.4; magic s. quenches fire D1382.8; man carried and dropped in mid-s. K1268; man helping another across s. drops him *W155.2; milk in s. as signal H135.2; money tested by throwing it into s. to see if it will swim J1931; numskull bales out the s. with nutshell J1967; oath so heavy it dries up s. M115.1.1; ogre's ashes cast on s. cause rapids to stop G655; plunging into s. suitor test H353; prison with s. of water in it R41.3.2; prophecy: drowning in particular s. M341.3.3; reward for carrying Christ across a s. Q25; saint's bachall leads s. through mountain (or up-hill) D1549.3.2; separation by being on different banks of s. N315; servant accidentally throws master into s. J2133.5.1.1; sun cools off in s. A722.5.2; test of resourcefulness: carrying wolf, goat, and cabbage across s. H506.3; transformation: s. becomes bloody D474.2; trickster carries girl across s., leaves old woman K1339.7; turning low s. to fill high s. H1138.1; witch powerless to cross s. *G273.4.

Streams of battle blood F1084.1; of blood magically drawn down on foe D2091.3; from roots of earth-tree A878.1.1; of sugar, milk and molasses dry up in punishment Q552.3.5; of wisdom flow from magic well D1300.3.1. — Four s. from four corners of earth A871.1; magic medicine causes s. to dry up D1542.3.1; navigable s. from well F718.11; origin of s. *A930ff.

Street. — Fishing in the s. J1149.2, K341.11; test of unknown father: gold on s. H485.

Streets. — Fires burnt in s. to ward off witches G272.4; god of s. A413; punishment: disgraceful journey through s. Q473.

Strength, see also **Strong;** from anger F1041.16.3ff.; preferred to cleverness J246; in unity J1020ff.; of witches G221.3; in words, in herbs, and in stones J1581.2, T251.5. — Appetite of twelve men given with the gift of twelve men's s. M416.1; contest in s. won by deception K70ff.; devil performs deeds of unusual s. *G303.9.2; dwarf-hero of superhuman s. F610.2; fairies' extraordinary s. F253.1.1; fanciful marvelous s. of animal B740ff.; giant's s. in hair F531.1.6.13; god of s. A489.2; hero's precocious s. F611.3.2; king chosen for s. P11.4; lion's great s. A1421.1.1; loss of s. from broken tabu C942; loss of magic s. by smoking C942.1; magic cup prevents s. loss D1389.3; magic object restores s. D1519.1; magic s. *D1830ff.; in numbers there is s. J1279.4; object gives magic s. *D1335ff.; old person commits suicide when s. fails P674; saint's s.: breaks wall V229.14; secret of s. treacherously discovered *K975; strong hero acquires his s. F611.3; strong hero suckled by mermaid given s. of twelve men F611.2.2; suitor test: overcoming princess in s. *H345; sword so heavy that hero must take drink of s. before swinging it F833.1; test of s. H1562; tiger challenged to s. contest K547.9; trial of suitors' s. H331.14; troll's food gives s. G304.2.2.1, F455.4.2.1; witch has extraordinary bodily s. G221.3.

Strengthening. — Defenses by s. one's own weakest spots J672.

Stretching the beam J1964.1; cliff D482.4; mountain F55.1; tree *D482.1, K1113, (refuge for fugitive) R311.4. — Animal characteristics from squeezing or s. ancient animal A2213ff.; animal's size increased by s. A2213.3; lies about s. X1785; magic hair s. after fugitive D1435; magically s. self to overcome opponent in battle D55.1.1.1; magically s. self to sink tent pole D55.1.1.2; man magically s. self (overcomes cliff) D55.1.1, (reaches otherworld) F59.1; mountain in love s. out leg A965.1; troll s. neck so long that fire comes from lips G304.2.1.2; woman enticed to upper world on a s. tree K1339.2.

Strewing. — Fairy driven away by s. peas in his path F381.2; ghost detected by s. ashes *E436.1.

Stride. — Giant's mighty s. F531.3.5; hundred-league s. D2122.2.

Strife. — Supernatural beings associated with s. F400.1.

Strike, see also **Struck.** — Naïve remark of child: you forgot to s. mother J122; not to s. (monster twice) *C742, (supernatural wife) C31.8; people and things that s. one another in otherworld F171.3.

Striker. — Lie: remarkable s. X945.

Striking inquirer to death in re-enacting event J2133.14.1; at reflection in jar J1791.7.1; self blows D2184.1. — Blind men s. each other as they try to kill pigs X125; blindness cured by s. F952.3.1, F952.4; devils are created by sparks produced by Satan's s. two stones together G303.1.4.2; disenchantment by s. D712.3; fairy mistress s. human lover F361.17.9; death by s. head against door lintel N339.13; disenchantment by s.

D712.3; flowers spring up on saint's s. ground F971.6; fox produces fire by s. tail to ground D2158.1.1; girl s. man who tries to kiss her T322; God creates the devil by s. a stone with his whip G303.1.1.4; hills from hero's s. earth A962.7; man s. king saves his life N656; ogre killed by s. G512.8; quack goitre cure: s. J2412.8; transformation by s. D566.

String with thirteen knots in child's mouth G271.10. — Disenchantment by removing neck s. D723.2.1; girl born with red s. around neck T552.1; life token: zither s. breaks E761.5.2; literal numskull drags jar (bacon) on s. J2461.1.1; magic ball of s. to which one sticks D1413.18; magic s. *D1184.2; prince born with silver s. H71.7.2; substituted s. kills ogre K1611.1; transformation by binding with s. around neck D585; unknown paramour discovered by s. clue T475.1.

Strings leading blind men to water removed K1081.3.

Strip. — Maid eloping with pretended lover is forced by him to s. T72.1.

Stripes. — Child of three fathers born with three s. T563.1; origin of animal's s. A2413ff.; why grizzly bears have three s. on inside of stomach A2367.2.1.

Stripping. — Tabu: s. dead and slain C877.

Strokes shared K187. — Odd number s. in beating devil G303.16.19.19.

Stroked. — Magic object works by being s. D1662.

Stroking. — Beautification by s. D1863; magic strength by s. D1835.3.

Strong, see also **Strength;** bride tries to stifle husband in bed T173.1; man as magician D1711.8; women *F565.2. — Association of s. and weak J420ff.; alliances with the s. J684; dead mother makes son s. E323.7; devil as a large, s. man G303.3.1.1; diving to become s. K1051.3; dwarfs are s. F451.3.8; husband has his s. servant substitute in bed with s. wife K1844.1; lie: remarkably s. man X940; making dupe s. K1012; making self s. in peace time J674.2; quest for s. adversary H1225; quest for s. man H1213.2; remarkably s. (hands) F552.2, (man) F610ff.; rights of the s. *U30ff.; subordination of weak to s. J421; suitor test (lifting s. princess's giant weapon) H345.1, (riding s. princess's horse) H345.2; sword only for s. hero D1654.4.1.1; trolls s. F455.2.2; trouble-making s. men G512.0.1; weak fear company of s. J425; why animal is s. A2528; wooing s. and beautiful bride T58.

Stronger and strongest Z42. — Child s. than mother at birth T585.1.1; mouse s. than wall, wind, mountain L392.

Strongest man to punish thieves K335.1.11. — Quest for s. H1316; what is s. (riddle) H631ff.

Stronghold in otherworld F163.6. — Fairy duped, loses s. K232.2.1; fairy s. F222.2; fairy s. as riddle answer H768; king's s. on island P14.17.

Struck, see also **Strike.** — Animal characteristics from being s. A2213.5; magic object s. on ground D806.1; man s. dead with iron bar by devil G303.20.3; strong hero s. by smith from iron F611.1.12.

Structure, see also **Building;** to be finished when king's daughter marries H1292.18. — Not to build too large a s. C771.

Structures. — Giants as builders of great s. F531.6.6.

Stubborn couple J2511. — Vow to get s. girl half-married only M149.6.

Stubbornness *W167ff.

Stucco ears after clipping J1184.2.

Stuck, see **Sticking.**

Student, see also **Pupil;** competes with master P342; enjoys professor's wife K1594; from paradise J2326; is helped by devil when he can answer three questions in rhyme G303.22.3; resuscitates whole family E181.2; returns from dead to warn master of futility of his studies E368. — Devil as s. G303.3.1.14; hungry s. talks to cat, gets served J1341.10.

Study. — Magic learned by s. D1721.6; thief observes night s. J1394.1.

Studying magic arts D1738; occult books tabu C825; philosophy as suitor task H335.0.2.1.

Stumble reveals drinking horn N223; reveals treasure N534.1.

Stumbling over bloody corpse brings accusation of murder N342.2. — Forgetting by s. *D2004.5; man s. on bathing maiden N716.1.

Stump. — Lie about pulling s. X1237.1.1; lie: remarkable extrication from tree s. X1133.1; magic s. supplies drink D1472.1.28; treasure buried under s. N511.1.13.

Stumps. — Fighting on s. of legs after they have been cut off at knee S162.1.

Stung, see also **Sting;** by the goblet J1324. — Numskull s. J2131.2.

Stupid classes J1705; devil *G303.13ff.; fear clever J423; hero L121; house-spirit F488; husband J1702; monk recovers the stolen flocks L141.1; ogre *G501; person surpasses clever L141; sons learn trades, kill off father J2499.7; wife J1701; youngest son becomes clever L21. — Futility of trying to teach s. J1064; moon as sun's s. brother A736.3.2; quest for three persons as s. as his wife H1312.1; riddle: three s. things H871.1; soldier silent before king as before all s. persons J1369.5; why animal is s. A2537.

Stupidity, see also **Fools.** — Child cast out because of his s. S327; man pretends s. before plotters K1818.3.3; seduction by feigned s. K1327.

Stuttering. — Humor of s. X135.

Sty. — Why hog lives in s. A2433.3.6.

Styx A672. — Oath by S. M119.1.1.

Subaqueous monastery V118.2.

Subdivisions. — Origin of tribal s. A1640ff.

Subdued. — Wild animals s. by saint's bachall D1442.3.

Subject. — Origin of s. tribes A1657.

Subjects driving away ruler P15.8. — Men die so god of dead may have s. A1335.11.

Subjection. — Blood in spittle tests s. H252.2.

Submarine home of the gods under the sea A151.3; otherworld *F133; world F725ff. — Deity's s. home A192.2.3; magic s. ship (boat) D1525; quest to s. monastery H1287.

Submerged. — Person gradually s. by sea F945.

Submission as clerical virtue V461.4. — Disenchantment by s. D730ff.

Subordination of weak to strong J421.

Subservient. — Riddle on making people s. H588.16; women s. to men A1372.9.

Subsiding. — Primeval water s. in specified time A810.2.

Substance. — Shadow mistaken for s. J1790ff.

Substitute for candle repaid with substitute for money J1551.5; in contest *K3ff.; for the corpse J1959.2; man killed in friend's place P316; used to save promised child S252.1. — Animal adopted as child s. T676; chaste wife deceives gallant with a s. in bed K1223.4; compassionate execution: s. child K512.2.2; death postponed if s. can be found *D1855.2; devil a s. for (dead man) G303.18.2, (new-born child) T684, (woman who went to spend night with a priest) G303.25.11; fairy steals child from cradle and leaves fairy s. *F321.1; fool's brothers s. a goat for the body of the man he has killed K661.1; ghost as s. for bride E363.1.1; gods furnish s. for child sacrifice S263.2.1; image of child as child s. T677; king as s. for condemned man J1189.3; mistress deceives lover with a s. *K1223; recognition of maidservant s. bride by her habitual conversation H38.2.3; test of friendship: s. as murderer H1558.2; husband as s. for wife receives punishment for her adultery T261.1; old woman as s. for girl in man's bed K1317.2.1; wife as s. for (husband's mistress) T318, (princess jailed with husband) K1814.2, (servant discovers husband's adultery) K1585.

Substituted arrows *K1617; bride *K1911ff.; bridegroom K1915; caps cause ogre to kill his own children *K1611; children K1920ff.; eyes *E781.1; letter *K1851; limbs E782.0.1; weapons win combat K97.2. — Animal s. for child served at meal K512.2.1; animals s. for newborn children K2115; compassionate executioner: s. puppet drowned K512.2.3; calumniated wife: s. letter K2117; escape by use of s. object *K525ff.; girl s. for boy to avoid slaughter by father K514.1; leaky vessel s. by husband so that his wife and paramour are drowned Q466.1; maid s. for mistress in assignation bed H1556.4.3; wooden log s. in cradle for unbaptized child by devil G303.9.9.4; worthless object s. for valuable K331.3.

Substitution of false bride revealed by animal *K1911.3.1; of horses causes angry man to kill his own K942; of low-caste boy for promised child H38.2.5; of self for another condemned to die K528.2; of transformed wife for husband's mistress D659.7. — Cheating by s. of worthless articles K476; deception by s. *K1840ff.; deception into fatal s. K840ff.; riding contest won by s. K27; robber cheated by s. K437.1; seduction by disguise or s. *K1310ff.

Substitutions for penances Q520.0.1.

Subterfuge. — Task evaded by s. H950ff.

Subterranean, see also **Submarine;** castle *F721.5; paradise F111.4; world F721ff. — Captivity in s. palace R41.1.1; earthquake from movements of s. monster A1145.1.

Subverted. — Trial by ordeal s. by carrying magic object D1394.1.

Success in battle wins bride H331.2.1; of returned exile L111.1; in replacing eyes *E781ff.; of unpromising hero (heroine) L160ff.; of youngest brother on quest H1242. — Accidental s. in hunting and fishing N620ff.; animal helps person to s. in love *B582; magic medicine brings s. D1561.1.4; unusual s. in love T27.

Succession, see also **Chain, Cumulative, Series;** of creations and cataclysms A632; of helpers on quest H1235; to the throne M314.2, P17, (lost in gambling) N2.5.1. — Bungling fool has s. of accidents J2661; plot to make king criminal, forfeit s. K1166.

Successive disguises K1834. — Disenchantment by holding enchanted person during s. transformations D757; escape by s. disguises K533; five children at birth for four s. years T586.1.4; god in s. animal forms A132.0.1ff.

Successor. — Do not leave kind deed to your s. J1284; dying king names s. P17.3; king propounds questions to his sons to determine s. H508.1.

Succubus F471.2.1.

Sucker. — Why s. has small bones in body A2367.1.1.

Sucking heals wounds F950.6; monster G332. — Ghost s. people's breath E251.3.4; punishment: snake s. woman's breasts Q452; resuscitation by s. out poison E21.5; serpent s. man's breath B16.5.1.2.1; snake s. milk from woman A2435.6.2.1; snake s. poison from (own bite) B765.8, (bitten raja) B511.1.3; vampire s. blood E251.33; witch s. blood G262.1; witch transforming self to hare, s. cows D655.2.

Suckled. — Child s. by transformed mother D688; imprisoned relative s. by woman through prison wall *R81; man s. by siren B53.2.

Suckling of children *T611. — Adoption by s. T671; angel of death spares mother who is s. children V233.1; baby goes to mother for s. H495.1; dead mother returns for s. child *E323.1.1; strong hero's s. F611.2; woman s. all babies at son's circumcision H495.3.

Sudden love gives bad luck T10.3.

Suddenly. — Man s. acquires long gray beard on scaffold at execution F1044; tabu: coming s. on supernatural creatures C52.2.

Sued. — Father-in-law s. for not dying as predicted W151.5.

Suffering healed by time U262. — Choice: s. in youth or old age J214; dwarfs s. abuses by mortals F451.5.11; girl promises unborn child to devil for s. the birth pangs S223.1; long-s. god A139.12; marvelous sensitiveness: s. from merely seeing work done F647.2.

Sufferings. — Ascetic faster increases his s. by placing food and drink before himself V462.2.1; mother's s. impress undutiful son P236.7.

Suffocation as punishment Q425. — Murder by s. P16.3.1.1, S113.2ff.

Sugar transformed to ashes D476.2.4; turns to earth as punishment Q591.2.1. — Fish thought to be chewed s. cane J1761.4; let them eat s. J2227.1; ogress attracted by s. cane scent G677.

Suggestion. — Assignment of tasks in response to s. H910ff.; birth by s. J2338; magic sleep by hypnotic s. D1962.4.

Suicidal. — Wisdom taught by s. example J173.

Suicide in belief loved one dead N343; cannot rest in grave E411.1.1; to carry out own promise M203.2; from fright of evil prophecy F1041.1.11.3; from fright of starving F1041.1.11.1; ghost E266.1; of lover who believes his mistress dead N343; over hasty condemnation N340.1; to make wife widow J2106; of man falsely accused N347.6; to prevent brother-sister marriage T415.7; punished Q211.5; by strangling A1599.9; to save virginity T326. — Adulterous wife convicted, commits s. T249.1; architect commits s. when surpassed by pupil W181.2.2; brahmin induced to s. J1181.0.1; burial of s. to prevent walking E431.16ff.; curse of s. M451.1; devil gains two souls through s. K217; devil persuades man to commit s. G303.9.4.2; disappointed lover a s. T93.3; dissuasion from s. J628; dupe tricked into s. K890ff.; earth from body of divine s. A831.7; faithful animal plans s. when it thinks master dead B301.3; father commits s. believing that son is dead N344; future s. weeps in mother's womb T575.1.2; ghost haunts s. spot E334.4; ghostly rope of s. E538.2; girl s. rather than marry unwanted suitor T311.2.1; god of s. A310.4; goddess prevents s. V10.1; husband s. when wife dies T211.3.1; king commits s. P16.3.0.1; lover deceived by false s. agreement K1232; man s. in grief for wife T211.9.2; miser doesn't commit s.: saves rope W153.7; mother commits s. over son's marrying foreigner P231.7; nagging wife drives husband to prepare for s. T253.1; noose used by s. as protection from accident D1384.2; old person commits s. when strength fails P674; outcast wife commits s. when she sees relatives' heads S452; poor host commits s. when unable to entertain P336.1; queen commits s. P26; sacrificial s. S263.5; scorned lover's s. T81.2.1; sham s. to soften lover K1232.1; skull of s. must roll in dust until it has saved a life Q503.1; sleeping before s. J21.2.2; snake s. B752.3; wife commits s. at husband's death P214.1; wife threatens s. to get own way T252.6; wife's s. at husband's death T211.2; wild huntsman wanders because of s. *E501.3.2; witch commits s. G279.1; would-be s. cured by drinking poison N646; would-be s. finds treasure N545.2.

Suicides. — Ghost causes s. E266.2.

Suitor, see also **Lover;** asked to kill child by his first wife S303.1; bathing in boiling water without cooling it H1023.24; brings own lamp, outwits girl's mother J1575.1; finds girl immature: father protests she has children J1279.3; with only love to offer wins L393; sent from one relation to the other for consent to the wedding Z31.1; task: make fairies dance H1177.1; test involving mountain of seed H1091.3; test: threats to his person H1406; tests *H310—H359. — Abduction by rejected s. R18; abducted princess successfully wishes self with rejected s. N425; animal s. B620ff.; bashful s. woos oak T69.4; chief performs s. task, rival steals bride K1371.6; devil as s. assigned building task H1131.2; dwarf a s. of mortal girl F451.5.18; dwarf s. desists when unwilling maiden guesses his name F451.5.15.3; extraordinary companions help hero in s. tests F601.2; fly helps s. pass test B587.2; girl behind tree advises unwilling s. K1971.6; girl promises herself to animal s. S215.1; house-spirit as s. F482.8; husband kills unwelcome s. H1551.1; husband praises s., woman falls in love T13; impudent s. threatened with hanging Q413.5.1; killing monster as s. test H1174; lion s. allows his teeth to be pulled and his claws cut J642.1; magic sleep induced by disappointed s. D1964.2; ogre s. buries woman's murdered lover K912.3; poor s. served good supper prepared for rich one J1561.3.1; princess rescued from s. R111.1.9; scorn of unloved s. punished T75.1; scorned s. consoles self J877; shrewd s. blackmails usurer K443.11; spurned s. rewards girl offered by her mother Q87.13; strong girl mutilates s. Q451.0.3; ugly picture makes girl refuse s. T11.2.0.1; undesired s. killed Q411.2; unsuccessful s. pretends friendship with husband, kills him K2022; woman kills impudent s. Q414.0.12.1.

Suitor's. — Scorned s. testimony on adulteress disbelieved J1151.4; undesired s. messengers imprisoned Q433.11.

Suitors ill-treated T75.0.1; receive enigmatic answers H593. — Commonplace expressions scare off wife's s. J2461.2.2; entrapped s. K1218.1; father kills daughter's s. S11.4.1; girl promised to three s. kills self T92.0.1; girl remains virgin after s. killed T311.3; girl's demon s. F402.1.15; girls keep up appearances to deceive s. K1984; gods attempt to settle dispute among s. N817.1; killing all other s. as suitor task H335.4.3; necklace of unsuccessful s. heads S110.3.1; princess builds tower of skulls of unsuccessful s. *S110.3; widowed she-fox rejects s. who do not resemble her deceased husband T211.6.

Sukasaptati K1591.

Sulking. — King's s. chamber P14.6; prince s. until quest accomplished H1212.3.

Sulphur in the censer J1582.2. — Devil's odor of s. G303.4.8.1, G303.6.3.4.

Sultan as beggar tests friends H1558.7.1; of flies B246.2; frees prisoner recognized by smile H79.4; tries to avoid adversity J2488.2.

Sultan's daughter as bribe to ogre S222.4; daughter in love with captured knight T91.6.4.1.

Summer and winter garden D1664; produced by magic D2145.2. — First day of s. V70.1; genealogy of s. A1154; hedging in cuckoo to keep s. year round J1904.2.1; more than one swallow to make s. J731.1; perpetual s. in otherworld F161.1; standing between s. and winter H1058; tie horse between s. and winter H583.7; winter becomes s. at saint's funeral F960.2.6.

Summers. — Year with two s. X1602.

Summit. — Magic transportation to highest s. D2135.4.

Summoned dead prophesies M301.14. — Animals s. by magic object
D1441; ghost s. E380ff.; god s. by weeping A189.2; helper s. by magic
object D1421ff.; kite teaches rhyme by which he may be s. for help
B501.2; person s. by thinking of him D2074.2.1.

Summoning the devil *G303.6.1.2; fairy lover F301.1; souls punished
E380.1. — Animal gives part of body as talisman for s. its aid *B501;
means of s. spirits F404.

Sun A710—A739; answers questions D1311.6.3; is brightest H651.1;
brings all to light N271.1; brothers each work one month, play other
eleven A739.3; captured R9.1; caught in snare A728; cooks for saint
D2149.3; is creature that is of all countries, that is loved by all the
world, and that has no equal (riddle) H762; cursed by man for burning
L351.2; cursed by moon A736.9; darkened at Crucifixion V211.2.3.3;
darkened at death of holy person F965.2; as deity A121.2; devoured by
monster at end of world A1052.1; does not shine during deluge A1010.1;
eats all own children except morning star A764.1.2; at edge of sky A739.1;
at end of world A1052; falls, causes world-fire A1031.4; father A221;
forged by smith A700.5; gives light to stars A769.5; -god A220ff., (as
creator) A1; as god's child A700.8; as gods' home A151.6.2; -god banished rain, wind A287.0.1; -Eod's wife pours fire over earth A1031.4;
as helper N818.1; as hero's father A512.4; kills brother sun with cockscomb plant A1156; to lock up moon, eat stars at world's end A1066;
made to stand still D2146.1.1; makes magic ring work D1662.1.1; as
magic object *D1291.1; as magician D1711.3; moon, and stars bring
forth first parents A1271.1; moon, and stars are highest H642.1;
nourished on fire A700.7; purchased A700.6; -ray D1291.1.1; as real
traveler H726; refuses to shine when murder is done F961.1.1; revives
self after death E4; sends heat to cook saint's meat V222.13; sets at
noon to hide fugitive R236.2; shines only two hours at hero's death
F960.2.6.1; shining at night Doomsday sign A1052.2; smears dung on
moon's face A751.5.2: steals tree of life E90.1; is swiftest H632.3; takes
mortal to heaven F63.3; thrown on fire A1068; turns fiery face upward:
hence cold A1135.1.1; in underworld A681; has woman wife T111.2.3.
— Absurd theories concerning the s. J2272; animals from mating of s.
and moon A177; bargain: if the s. reverses its course K194; bat makes
s. smile, ends eclipse A1046.1; bird running before the s. B7.3; blindness
healed by rays of s. F952.2; bottom of the Red Sea has seen the s. only
once (riddle) H822; bridegroom like s. Z62.2; castle east of s. and west
of moon F771.3.2; cattle of the s. A155.1; cloud magically made to cover
s. D2147.1; contest in seeing sunrise first: s. on the trees K52.1; cows
of the s. B19.6.1; coyote rides with s. A724.1.0.1; contest of wind and
s. L351; corpse buried under stone so that s. will not shine on him
again E431.10; creator with s. and moon in hands A18.6; deities push s.
back and forth at solstices A1157; devils carry away the s. when they
fall from heaven G303.8.2; directions on quest given by s., moon, wind,
and stars H1232; dress of gold, silver, color of s., moon, and stars F821.1.5;

druid causes s. to stand still D2146.1.1.1; extraordinary behavior of s. F961.1; first men perish when s. first rises A1009.1; foolish fight with s. J1968.1; frogs fear increase of power of s. which will dry up all their puddles J613.1; god hides from s. A179.8; gold moon, s., star F793.1; handkerchief color of s., moon, and stars F822.1; hat which turns the s. D1546.1.1; head of murdered child becomes s. A1277.3; how much does s. earn for his daily work (riddle) H715; jackal carries s. in bag on back: burns his back black A2218.2; looking at s. tabu C315.2.2; love like wind in hot s. H592.1.1; magic object controls s. *D1546.1; magic objects received from s., moon, and stars D814; making s. shine in north H1023.16; man's desire for s. A1017.1; moon deceives s. A753.3.1; moon as grinder to bring fire from s. A741.3; not to let s. shine on girl before she is thirty years old *C756.2; original moon becomes s., sun, moon A736.8; path to s. on sun's rays F154; pigeons cover s. to aid hero H982.1; prophecy: man will make s. stand still M312.8; quest for place s. rises H1371.1.1; quest to place where s. sets H1284.1; quest to s. for answer to questions H1284; riddle of the course of the s. H725; riddle about s. shining only once in land H822.1; selling ability to influence s. K154; sloth may not look on s. A2233.1.4; stars as children of the s. eaten by their father A764.1.1; setting s. mistaken for fire J1806; tabu to face s. while urinating C99.1; tribes from choices s. offers people A1610.5; troll bursts when s. shines on him G304.2.5; tying s. with stone chain H1023.23; visit to land of the s. *F17; war with the s. A739.2; why loris never looks at s. A2231.13; why s. sets early in autumn A1156; why worm avoids s. A2433.6.9.

Sun's children most brilliant stars A764.3; disposition A738.2. — God's palace with doors for s. journey A151.4.2; moon as s. younger brother A745.3; man's beauty eclipses s. F574.1.4; variations in s. seasonal heat A739.4.

Sunbeam as support *F1011ff. — Catching a s. H1023.22; clothes hung on s. *F1011.1; magic journey on s. D2121.10; man so small he can put his head through mote in s. F535.2.4.

Sunday, see also **Sabbath;** christening of Thursday births brings nightmares F471.1.5. — Devil throws quoits on S. A977.2.3; fortress built on S. destroyed Q552.14.1; fountain gives milk on S. F716.1; man in moon burns brush as punishment for doing so on S. A751.1.1; mill refuses to work on S. D1676; respite in hell on S. Q560.2.1.1; resurrection to take place on S. E751.6; stolen mother returns from fairyland each S. to minister to her children *F322.3; tabu: journeying on S. C631.1; well full on S. F718.7; wild huntsman wanders for hunting on S. *E501.3.6; not to work on S. C631; will-o'-the-wisp is girl cursed for gathering plants on S. A2817.2.

Sundays. — Souls leave hell on S. E755.2.0.1.

Sundial covered to protect it J1943.1. — Examining the s. by candle-light J1943.

Sunfish. — Markings on s. A2217.3, A2412.4.1.

Sunk, see also **Sink.** — King's coffin s. into river P16.9; ship magically s. D2098; sword that is to kill one is weighted and s. so as to avoid prophecy M377.

Sunken bell sounds *F993; church bell cannot be raised V115.1.3; palace magically raised D2136.2.2. — Captivity in s. valley R42; disenchantment of s. castle, town D789.8; mermaid prevents raising of s. church bell B81.13.10; raising s. church bell C401.4; treasure buried in s. ship N513.5.

Sunlight carried into windowless house in baskets J2123; fatal to fairies F383.4.3; ray causes leprosy D1500.4.4; turns giant or troll to stone *F531.6.12.2. — Conception from s. *T521; cynic tells king to get out of his s. J1442.1; not to be exposed to s. C842; transformation by s. D567; why s. stronger than moonlight A733.1.

Sunrise direction tabu C614.1.5; to help sick man F961.1.2.1; tabu C751.7ff. — Cock crows at s. A2489.1.1; contest in seeing s. first K52; dwarfs turn to stone at s. F451.3.2.1; in dwarf land s. is at midnight F451.4.6; mock s. K1886.3; no s. at hero's death F965.2.1; origin of colors at s. A797; prayers at s. V58.1; tabus on action after s. C752.2ff.; tabu for king to sleep after s. C735.2.3; tabu on sleeping at s. C735.1.1; trolls turn to stone at s. F455.8.1.

Sunset direction tabu C614.1.5. — Delayed s. F961.1.5.3.1; devil appears when woman looks at herself in mirror after s. G303.6.1.4; early s. hides fugitive F961.1.10; no s. F961.1.5.3; one must not whistle after s. else the devil will go along with one G303.16.18; origin of colors at s. A797; ox lent by fairies must not be worked after s. F391.1.1; prayers at s. V58.1; sun reappears after s. F961.1.5.2; sun's children take human form at s. A736.5.2; tabu: doing thing after s. C752.1ff.; tabu: sleeping after s. in lighted house C735.2.4; trees disappear at s. F811.11.

Sunshine. — Bird wants s., worm clouds U148.1; father's counsel: walk not in s. from your house to your shop H588.1; regulation of s. A1172.1.

Sunwise circuit for good luck D1791.1.

Superhuman race's magic D1719.3, D1728; tasks H1130ff. — Curse mitigated by s. task M428; devil in s. form G303.3.2ff.; disenchantment when s. task is finished D791.1.2; supplying s. amount of grain H1122.1; wild man of s. strength F610.1.

Superior troops distributed throughout army P552.2. — King is s. to all P12.10; why one people s. in power to another A1689.11.

Superiors. — Lowly animal tries to move among his s. J952.

Superlative. — Many times the s. J2217; riddles of the s. H630ff.

Superman. — Magic knowledge of s. D1810.0.7.

Supernatural adversary in gambling N3; being becomes goat D134.4; bird prevents mother killing babe B524.4; birth of culture hero A511; creature aids quest H1233.4; creatures propound riddles *H540.1; creatures tabu after sunrise C752.2.1; creatures change size at will D631.4; growth T615; helpers *N810ff.; lapse of time in fairyland F377;

lover performs girl's work T91.3; lover's food tabu C243.1; manifestations at death (of pious person) Q147, (of wicked person) Q550.1; origin of hero Z216; person seen in dreams gives advice K2035; person reveals infidelity F345.2; person causes sun to stand still D2146.1.1.2; powers identify God H45.1; substitute for pious warrior K3.2.1; voice points out criminal N278; wife leaves husbands stealing from her R227.3; wife bestows beauty D1862.1; woman promises to return if she bears boy M272.
— Abandoned child reared by s. beings S353; affront to s. spirit punished Q552.14.0.1; bargains and promises between mortals and s. beings M242; changeling shows s. power to work and thus betrays maturity F321.1.1.4; child of s. birth exposed S313; dismembered s. woman C312.2.3; drop from magic cauldron gives s. information D1310.2; fairies bestow s. gifts at birth of a child F312.1; hero's s. helpers A528; husband (wife) of s. being longs for old home and visits relatives T294; love of mortal and s. person T91.3; magic object causes both s. sight and blindness D1331.3; magic object gives s. information *D1310ff.; magic object gives s. wisdom *D1300ff.; magic object received from s. being D812; magic wisdom received from s. being D1811.2; man created by s. creature A1291; marriage of mortal and s. being T111; mother reveals son's s. father P231.5; not to offend s. relative C30ff.; observing s. helper tabu C311.1.5; people eating child become s. G55; princess rescued from s. being R111.1.10; recognition by s. manifestation H192; rejuvenation by s. person D1882; resuscitation by s. person S121; not to see s. C311; reward for s. help Q93; tabu: coming suddenly on s. creatures C52.2; tabu connected with s. beings C0—C99; tabu to name s. wife C435.1.1; tests for husband s. wife H310.1; task performed with help of s. wife H974; three s. ogre helpers N812.7; treasure placed in ground by s. beings N511.3; not to utter name of s. creature *C432; wife rescuing husband from s. H923.1; wish for s. husband realized C15.

Supernaturals flee at mock sunrise K1886.3.3; tricked into daylight exposure K839.6.

Supernaturally born boy L112.1.1; impregnated woman bears dragon T554.11.

Supervised. — Planets s. by angels A780.1; stars s. by angels A769.3.

Supper won by trick: the mutual friend K455.1. — Undesired lover kept overlong at s. K1227.9.

Suppliant. — Image blamed by s. for misfortune V123; image indicates favor to s. D1622ff.; hidden man behind image gives unwelcome answer to s.: image blamed K1971.8; statue of Virgin sews for s. D1620.1.4.

Supplication. — Feet seized in s. P676.

Supply. — Spirit drinks water s. dry G346.4; water-spirit controls water s. F420.4.9.

Supplies received from magic box D1470.2.2. — Cobolds furnish s. to their masters F481.2.

Supplying food by magic *D1030.1; objects through prayer V52.4; stones for church V111.2; superhuman amount of grain H1122.1; water in land where it is lacking (task) H1138.

Support of the earth A840ff.; of the sky A665. — Bird thinks that the sky will fall if he does not s. it J2273.1; castle (house) with extraordinary s. F771.2ff.; island with extraordinary s. F736; sunbeam as s. *F1011ff.

Supporting. — Old cobra s. earth A1412.1; precocious boy s. mother, self by wits T615.4.

Suppression of prophecy M300.4.

Supreme god A101.

Surely. — As you s. will J1481.

Surety. — First s. A1586; God as s.: the abbot pays J1559.2; priest as s. K455.5.

Sureties. — Hero slain during absence of his s. K929.8.

Surf. — Origin of s. A925.6; rejuvenation by riding s. D1889.8.

Surfboard. — Ogress's tongue becomes s. D457.14.1.

Surge. — Tidal s. marks death place A913.1.

Surgeon. — Skillful s. F668.

Surgical. — Useless s. operation J1842.

Surly. — Dumbness for s. speech Q583.2.

Surpassing. — Unpromising s. the promising L140ff.

Surprise capture R4. — Not to express s. in lower world of dead C413; woman veils self as expression of s. P671.

Surprised. — Wife s. in adultery feigns death K1549.2.

Surrender to the rake J2613. — Capture of castle by pretending to s. and entering K777.

Surrendering R75. — Foolishness of s. weapons J642; fairy mistress s. man to his mortal wife F302.5.1; vow to die before s. ship M161.4.1.

Surreptitiously. — Butter s. added to broth K499.2.1.

Surrounded. — Deceptive land purchase: as much land as can be s. in a certain time K185.7; palace s. by rivers of wine, rosewater, and honey F771.7; person in magic sleep s. by protecting fire *D1967; wild huntsmen s. by fire E501.7.6.4.

Survive. — Tests of power to s. *H1510ff.

Survivor. — Lone woman s. of doomed city A1006.7; messenger sent away only s. of battle N693; unique s. Z356.

Survivors of flood A1029.6.

Susanna and the elders J1153.1, K2112.

Suspected. — Impostor acting as God in tree s. and tree burned K1971.12; innocent man accidentally s. of crime N347.

Suspended. — Building castle s. between heaven and earth (task) H1036; castle s. on four chains F771.2.1.1; crown s. over king's head F828.1; god's function s. during his absence A173.1; large millstone s. on thread over head F451.5.4.2; pestle magically s. J2411.9; sinners in hell s. Q569.4; woman s. by breasts Q451.9.1.

Suspension between heaven and earth as punishment Q552.23. — Magic s. of weight D1691; self s. on iron hooks under armpits Q541.4.

Suspicion. — Dissension aroused in army by casting s. on general K1088; escape from s. of crime K661; killing or condemnation on s. *N340ff.; sham blind man throws s. on real blind K2165.

Suspicious. — Devil advises s. husband G303.9.7.3; trickster makes two friends each s. of the other's intentions *K2131ff.; youngest daughter s. of impostor L62.

Sustenance. — Prisoner's s. from outside prison R84.

Suttee P16.4.1. — Lifting power of widow ready for s. H479.1; origin of s. A1545.5.1.

Swallow advises hen against hatching out serpent's eggs J622.1.1; and the hemp-seeds J621.1; as messenger B291.1.11. — Association of swan, s. J429.1; why s. brings good luck A2536.1; color of s. A2218, A2219.1, A2411.2.1.4; creation of s. A1917; why s. does not like green trees for nest A2431.3.5.1; why s. has black feathers and only two feathers A2378.8.6; why s. has forked tail A2214.1, A2378.5.1; magic skin of s. *D1025.4; man calls his wife "my s.": she becomes s. D511.1; man transformed to s. D151.1; more than one s. to make a summer J731.1; reincarnation as s. E613.4; why s. is thief A2455.2; why s. has no tongue A2344.2.3.

Swallow's lost voice A2422.9; nest A2221.2.4, A2431.3.5. — Annoyance of s. chirp J215.1.4; meaning of s. song A2426.2.12.

Swallows put on mourning at crucifixion: have never taken it off A2221.2.4.1; warn other birds against roosting in tree with glue J652.2. — Contest in beauty between s. and crows J242.6; why s. migrate A2482.1.

Swallowed person becomes bald F921; person reborn E607.2.1. — Boy s. by fish, escapes K565.1; culture hero s. and recovered from animal A535; curse: to be s. by a siren M434; children s. at birth to avoid prophecy fulfillment M376.3; children s. by earth R142; death by being s. C929.5; fairy transforms self to fly, allows self to be s. by woman and reborn as fairy F392; frog spawn s. by girl B784.1.4; heathen s. by earth H1573.1.1; man to be s. up by earth at foot of stairs M341.2.25; man never knowing want s. up by earth L424; man s. by fish and later rescued alive (lie) X1723.1.2; overweeningly proud man s. up C770.1; person s. up by earth F942.1, (and taken to lower world) F92.2; person transforms self, is s. and reborn in new form *E607.2; pregnant wife s. to prevent birth of son M376; princess sick because toad has s. her consecrated wafer *V34.2; sun s. and spit out A721.2; temple s. by earth F941.2.3; tent-house folded and s. as means of carrying it F923; theft of light by being s. and reborn *A1411.2.

Swallower. — Victim kills s. from within F912; victim rescued from belly of s. F913.

Swallowing hot coals because husband unfaithful T818; prostitute's pearls to avenge theft K306.3; stolen goods to escape detection K417. —

49*

Animal s. another to save him K649.1.1; animals s. thumbling F535.1.1.7; conception from s. a stone T511.8.1; cow s. book: cause of maniplies in stomach A2219.2; curse: ground s. children M448.1; darkness from awk s. sun A721.2.1; deceptive s. contest K82.4; dragon s. arrow intended for hero B529.2; fish bears men-children after s. man's rinsings B631.3; fish s. man to rescue him B541.1.1; fire stolen by s. K382; giant s. men F531.3.11; heat test: s. red-hot stones H1511.1; husband s. sorceress D1479.1; magic gate s. axes D1381.31; magic powers from s. D1735; man s. magic servants D1719.8; mermaid s. man B81.10; person s. animal eggs from brook B784.1.1; person s. pebble, snake grows in stomach B784.1.2; person s. snake semen B784.1.2; rakshasa in deer's head s. men G369.1.6; rod s. other rods D1693; Satan s. victim G303.20.7; star s. others F961.2.7; voice made rough by s. hot iron F556.1; wager on s. egg in one gulp N75.

Swallowings. — Earth s. as punishment Q552.2.3; extraordinary s. *F910ff.

Swamp spirit F494.1.1. — Punishment: drowning in s. Q467.3.

Swan birds' king B242.1.9; blamed when crow drops filth J429.2; as crow's wife absurd J1293.1.1; as chastity test H411.17; maiden *D361.1, (finds her hidden wings and resumes her form) D361.1.1; maidens as guardians of treasure N572.2; as matchmaker B582.2.3; song B752.1; transformed to person D361. — Angel whiter than a s. (riddle) H663; association of s., swallow J429.1; color of s. A2411.2.6.2; crow demands young s. in payment K255.3; fairy as s. F234.1.15.1; god rides s. A136.1.4.1; helpful s. B469.2; killing s. tabu C841.5; magic adhesion to s. D2171.3.2; man transformed to s. D161.1; marriage to s. maiden *B652.1; origin of s. A1981; pet s. saves self by singing death song N651; prophetic s. B143.0.1; revenant as s. E423.3.2; sacred s. B811.5; slow s. lasts longer than speedy crow L394; soul as s. E732.7.

Swans do not suffer harsh weather after conversion to Christianity V331.9; harnessed to chariot B558.2; live on pearls B768.3. — Boat drawn by s. B558.1; divine s. on inaccessible island F134.4; king of s. B242.2.10; transformation to s. by taking chains off neck D536.1.

Swarm. — Charm calls down s. of bees D1441.2.

Swarms. — Extraordinary s. of birds F989.16.

Swastika A137.3.1.1.

Swaying. — Transportation by stretching and s. tree D1520.1.1.

Swearer. — False s. not allowed to approach altar M101.1.

Swearing, see also **Oaths, Vows.** — Person s. oath places hand in mouth of image H251.1; wolf s. by God B251.7.1.

Sweat, see also **Perspiration;** used in medicine D1500.1.36. — God born from another god's s. A114.1.1.1; goddess born from s. of rock washed by sea A114.1.1; horse's s. as water that has neither fallen from heaven nor sprung from earth H1073; man created from s. A1262; man from

s. of creator A1211.2; man to earn bread by s. of his brow A1346; ocean from creator's s. A923; origin of s. A1319.8.

Sweating as punishment for theft Q212.3. — Man s. blood F1041.10; resuscitation by s. E15.2; till front is s. J2499.1.

Sweaty. — Alp rides horse s. at night F471.1.1.1.

Swedes as magicians D1711.10.2.

Sweeping as bride test H383.3; peas as devil's task G303.16.19.3.1; with stick instead of broom J1822. — Old woman s. strikes sky, raises it A625.2.3; tiger s. temple for saint B256.7.

Sweet and bitter fountain in otherworld garden F162.1.2.1; potato's origin A1423.1, A2686.4.1. — Blood of certain animal said to be s. K961.0.1; fruits always s. F813.0.4; honey is s. J2497; man's body exudes s. scent F595; sea flows s. water F931.9.2.1; sour fruits made s. by saint F979.1; when s. fails, try bitter J1088.

Sweets turn into bugs D449.1. — Magic s. D1038.

Sweeter. — What is s. than honey (riddle) H671.

Sweetest. — What creature has s. blood: gnat's tongue torn out A2236.1; what is s. (riddle) H633ff.

Sweetheart, see also **Mistress;** kills self when lover dies N343.4. — Dead lover haunts faithless s. E214; dead man warns youth against visiting s. E366.2; dead s. haunts faithless lover E211; forcing attentions on friend's s. K2297.1; invulnerability lost if man forgets s. D1847.1; lover dies beside s. F1041.1.2.1; man thinks s. an enemy, flees N318.1; old s. chosen in preference to new J491; pursued s. becomes tree D642.3.1; tasks imposed by s. H916; wraith of s. stays in room where lover died E723.5.

Sweetmeats. — Preacher's wife gives s. away J1262.5.1.

Swelling from grief F1041.21.2; of limbs from breaking tabu C941.2. — Animal venom causes s. X1205; sight of wild hunt causes s. of head E501.18.8.

Swift. — Devil carries man through the air as s. as wind (thought) G303.9.5.4; devil is s. G303.4.8.6; giant s. despite size F531.1.3.5; king and jester flee: the king's s. horse J1483.1; magic journey as s. as thought *D2122.3; why certain animals are s. A2555.

Swifter. — Eye s. than bird, wing, or lightning H661; horse s. than the rain K134.2.

Swiftest horse on earth B184.1.1.3. — Riddle: what is the s. H632ff.

Swiftness. — Breaking legs to overcome s. K1013.6.

Swill. — Entrance to dwarf home under s. hole F451.4.1.7.

Swim. — Fish eat other fish: guilty must s. deep A2238.3; learn to s. before going into the water J2226.

Swimmer. — Marvelous s. F695; remarkable s. X964.

Swimming with birds tabu C858; in the flax-field J1821; in imaginary river D2031.1.2; in lake tabu C615.2. — Animal's method of s. A2444ff.; attempt at s. in mist J1821.1; beheaded man s. F1041.14; bluff: provisions for the s. match K1761; dwarf s. in human's drinking-horn X142.2; entering a garden by s. down a stream that flows into it K2377; fatal s. race: spirits drowned K869.4; firewood continually swept away from s. man H1129.5.1; giant s. across rivers as others cling to him F531.3.13.2; magic prevents s. fatigue D1384.4.1; strong man s. as he carries companions F631.3; stupid woman s. on roof J1972; wife s. to imprisoned husband T215.6.

Swindler punished *Q274; takes money for parents in heaven J2326.1.
Swindler's plans foiled J1521.
Swindlers given stones for money K1675.
Swine, see also **Hog, Pig, Sow;** bridegroom disenchanted D733.2; eating certain fish H1199.7; -god A132.7; kick trees for fruit F989.7; maddened by oak forest smell B783; magically kept from fattening D2089.3.1; march like soldiers B290.1; shaking tree bole H1199.6; transformed to (another animal) D412.3, (person) D336; worship V1.8.4. — Burrowing s. heat ground B19.4.1; clerics expelled in shapes of s. Q226.2; devastating s. B16.1.4; devil in form of s. G303.3.3.4; devil's abode is between hoofs of s. G303.8.7; eaters of s. not to enter Venus's temple J1447; fairy as s. F234.13; fat from s. never farrowed H1025; magic harp summons s. D1449.3; magic s. B184.3, (cause robbers' drowning) Q428.2, (blight corn and milk) B16.4.3, (make land sterile) B16.4.4; man reincarnated as s. *E611.3; man transformed to s. D114.3, *D136, (will regain human form) M313; marriage to s. B601.8; red or green s. B731.8; revenant as s. E423.1.5; sitting among s. so as to learn Bavarian language X652; person of remarkable sight finds tracks of s. stolen seven years before his birth F642.2; vow taken on holy s. M114.3; venomous s. B776.4.
Swine's. — Contours of land from s. rooting A951.2; elephants fear s. grunting J2614.3; why s. belly is bare A2317.1.
Swineherd P412.2; finds paradise F111.0.2; as hero L113.1.1; rescues abandoned child R131.3.4. — Chieftain recognized by s. H173.1; disguise as s. K1816.6; transformation into s. D24.3; treacherous s. K2255.1.
Swineherds. — Magician and queen as s. D2031.4.2.
Swing. — Dupe takes fugitive's place in s. K845; golden s. F895; magic s. D1154.3.1; pursuer duped into supposed s. K845; recognition by unique ability to s. spear H31.3.
Swinging by moustache H328.2; ogre G327; seventy girls H506.5; steer by horns F628.1.2.2. — Deceiver in s. contest killed *K1618; Evil Eye averted by s. cat over child's cradle D2071.1.2; fatal s. game K855.
Swollen creek causes orphan's marriage N699.4.
Swooning, see also **Fainting;** from cowardice W121.8.1; from grief

F1041.21.7; for love T24.2. — Magic power by s. D1733.5; rescuers s. on seeing rescued R188; wife s. at husband's death T211.9.1.1.

Sword causes death whenever drawn D1402.7.1.2, D1653.1.1.1; causes magic sleep D1364.27; as chastity index H435.1; bridge to otherworld F152.1.6; can be moved only by right person D1654.4.1; of fire from heaven Q552.13.0.2; hidden by old man N511.1.0.2; hidden under water N513.2; inlay melts in battle F1084.0.1; large or small at will D631.3.3; leaves no trace of blow behind it D1666; left for posthumous son to kill father's murderer T645.1; made magically helpless D2072.0.1; magically changes to wood when executioner is to decapitate innocent person H215.1; magically dulled D2086.1; of chastity T351; of Damocles F833.2; that is to kill one is weighted and sunk so as to avoid the prophecy M377; pierces rock F997; as reward Q114.3; received from dead father E373.2; resuscitates princess E149.2; rusts E761.4.7; and shield as proxy at wedding T135.3.1; splinters arrow with each strike F667.2; spoken to as human F997.1; sticks to magic hand D1413.12; as tongue deceives ogre G572.2; too heavy to lift against friend H1558.8.1; tested F611.3.3; transformed to wood D473.1; threat overcomes witch G275.15.1; which will break in only one peril Z314. — Captor deceived into giving up s. K611.3; choice of two s. sheaths H511.1.1; conqueror's s. between teeth signifies defeat P551.1; curse: s. to fail in danger M441.1; deceptive s. game K867.1; deceptive s. loan J1556.1; demon occupies s. F408.1; devil kills man with fiery s. G303.20.1; disenchantment by s. D771.8; don't draw s. against the innocent J21.2.3; extraordinary s. F833; execution s. turned to wood D2086.1.1; extraordinary s. sinks into earth F948.4; fairy gives magic s. F343.10.1; fairy smith gives knight magic s. F343.3; felling wood with s. F1041.16.3; fiery s. between hostile king, queen D2196; fixing the two pieces of a broken s. (task) H1023.8; garment proof against all but man's own s. D1381.3.1; getting s. to lift cheese J2173.2; ghost summoned for s. E387.2.1; giant s. of culture hero A523.1; god makes s. drop from hand A185.2.3; god's s. A157.5; groom's s. marks bride's forehead T135.4; hero's s. falls, cuts enemy F1087; hills from hero's striking earth with s. A962.7; holding king's s. makes one his inferior K1292; identification by s. H125.1; incandescent s. D1645.4; lifting s. tests strength H1562.2.1; lightning from flashing s. A1141.2; lightning as God's s. A137.14.4; lost s. found in fish N211.1.4; magic sight by looking at polished s.-blade D1821.3.7.4; magic song dulls s. D1414.4; magic s. *D1081, (gives warning) D1317.6, (received in dream) D812.12.1; magic wand breaks enemy's s. D1414.1; magic writings on s. render it harmless D1414.2; man kept alive by consecrated s. E163; man passes s. to captive, killed K818.1; man plunges s. into stone F628.4.1; marriage of girl to a s. T117.2; monkey jumps over a ravine with his s. girded on J2133.2; monster fettered with s. just out of reach A1074.1; mountain-man carries shears at side like s. F460.1.3;

needle as thumbling's s. F535.1.1.12; oath taken on s. M113.1; ogre killed
with s G512.1; person lives after s. cutting F1096; quest for person who
can withdraw s. H1313; quest for s. of light H1337; quest for Thunder
S. H1337.1; recognition by unique ability to dislodge s. from stone or
tree H31.1; robbers give hero s.: used to kill them J642.2; rock beaten
by s. provides water D1549.5.1; resuscitation by polishing s. E142; sign
of cross endows s. with magic D1766.6.2; skillful fencer keeps s. dry in
rain F667.1; soul in s. E711.10; spring from striking earth with s.
A941.3; stealing s. from giant H1151.14; strong man's mighty blow with
s. F628.4; substituted s. of wife's paramour T247.1; testing s. by
cutting steer in two F611.3.31; unseen s. decapitates in forest F812.5;
unsheathing s. thrice before attack J21.2.1.

Swords sheathed in scabbards as thrown in air F661.7.2. — Lengthening
s. by twirling them F679.2; precautionary drawing of s. J2255; wild
hunt heralded by clash of s. E501.13.1.3.

Swordfish. — Man becomes s. D179.5.

Sword-thrusts. — Magic fly-whisk stops s. D1381.13.

Swordsmanship. — Mountain-spirit teaches hero s. F460.4.2.3.

Sworn brethren P311; brothers as culture heroes A515.1.2.

Syballine books bought at great price J166.1.

Sybil draws picture of Madonna and Child in sand V341.

Symbol. — Magic s. D1299.1.

Symbolic interpretations H600ff.

Symbolism *Z100—Z199; of worship A1546.0.1.

Sympathetic animals B303; helper robbed K345; magic *D1782.

Sympathy. — Absurd s. for animals or objects J1870ff. — Animal
mutilates self to express s. B299.5.1; extraordinary s. with animals F648;
leaves shed in s. F979.15; river drying up in s. F932.6.2.

Symplegades D1553.

Synagogues V112.3.

Syphalitic. — Vengeful paramours send s. man to substitute in woman's
bed K1317.3.

Tabernacle. — Devil disappears after T. erected G303.17.1.3; dust of T.
H411.18.

Table always set in otherworld dwellings F165.4; thrown out of the sledge:
to go home by itself J1881.1.4. — Beard grows through t. F545.1.3;
browbeaten husband from under the t. T251.6; compressible t. D491.2.2;
cutting t. reveals witch G257.3; dead children "invited to eat at God's t."
E754.2.4; extraordinary t. F784; fool leaves when placed between two
fools at t. J1715; magic t. *D1153; mould put on t. for the dead E433.1;
rose grows from t. F971.2; scratching contest with devil: man's wife
shows scratches in her oak t. K83.1.1; stepladder for setting the t. J1573.1;
trickster saws legs of t. so that it collapses K1431.

Tables in otherworld F166.10.

Tablecloth. — Escape from prison by use of magic t. D1395.2; magic t *D1153.1.

Tablets of trees from lovers' graves unite E631.0.1.2. — Theft of t. of fate A1417.

Tabu, see also **Restrictions;** C (entire chapter); against whistling after sunset G303.16.18; fear of threatening animals while treasure is being raised N553.5; imposed as punishment Q430.1; looking around while raising treasure N553.4; spitting on castaway broom G303.16.19.2. — Blackmail about breach of food t. K443.13; boy breaks t., fairies kidnap him F325.1; death postponed by keeping t. D1855.4; disenchantment by breaking t. D789.4; dupe tricked into breaking t. by lying K1076; earth splits, plain sinks when t. broken F944.4; fairy gift worthless when t. broken F348.0.1; fairy mistress leaves man when he breaks t. F302.6; fighting in fairyland t. F210.1; flood from breaking t. A1018.1; girl summons fairy lover by breaking t. *F301.1.1; lake from violating t. A920.1.8.1; magic mango withdrawn for broken t. D868.1; magic sleep from breaking t. D1962.6; mother forces child to break eating t. S12.2.3; rival prevailed on to break t. K2220.0.1; transformation by breaking t. D510ff.

Tabus connected with fairy gifts F348; connected with trip to fairyland F378; in effect while treasure is being unearthed N553. — Death from violating t. fated N101.2; demons coerced by druid t. G583; origin of eating t. A1517; origin of t. A1587.

Taciturn man W225.

Tact in reproving the great J816.

Tadpoles. — Mankind descended from t. A1224.1.

Tail in ground betrays calf's killing K1686; and head of serpent quarrel as to usefulness J461.1.1; buried (thatched) and dupe attacked K1021.1; of dragon B11.2.8. — Animal puts t. in man's hands, caught X1133.3.1; animal tied to another's t., killed J2132.5; bear bites the seemingly dead horse's t. K̃ ̃47; bear fishes through ice with t. *A2216.1; bear persuaded to slide down rock wears off t. K1021.3; beaver borrows muskrat's t. and never gives it back A2241.10; bird with t. of fire B15.7.14; bush-rat bites off tortoise's t.: hence tortoise's short t. A2216.4; calf's (fox's) t. from earth to heaven H682.1.7; camel's t. cut off, turns to grass R231.2; chastity ordeal: holding shaven and greased t. of bull H412.2; crow's beak and t. alternately stick on tarred bridge Z39.3; devil's t. G303.4.6; why dogs look at one another under the t. A2275.5.5; dog's t. mistaken for master's J2015; dog's t. mistaken for gun J1772.12; dog's t. wagging raises wind D2142.1.1; dragon encircles city with t. B11.2.8.1; fairy's long t. F232.8; fish struck by coconut: hence flat t. A2213.5.2; fox with eight-forked t. B15.7.4; fox prefers weight of his t. rather than give part of it to ape J341.1; fox produces fire by striking t. to ground D2158.1.1; fox's t. drops and frightens animals K2323.1; fox's t. pulled out long A2213.4.2; giantess with t. F531.1.6.14; god with t. A123.11; hair from fox's t. opens all doors D1562.2; hawk's t. cut in two by sword as he is being transformed A2216.5; herd's spirit in last goat's t. D859.6; huldra with cow's t. F460.1.5; hot tin under horse's t. K1181; if witch grabs horse's t. on bridge, man is safe from her G273.4.1; lighting the cat's t. J2101.1; little child recognizes devil by his t. G303.4.6.1; lion's t. as broom H1151.11; lizard's t. imitated from snake's A2272.2; magic animal t. D1029.2; magic object causes t. to grow D1375.4; magpie tells man he is to die next day: no tongue and long t. A2236.4; man escapes from bee's nest on bear's t. X1133.4; man has head and t. of cat B29.4.1.1; as many hairs in the head as in ass's t. H703.1; miller ties cow's t. to himself J2132.3; monkey borrows deer's t. A2241.11; mouse regains its t. Z41.4; mouse's t. in mouth of sleeping thief causes him to cough up swallowed magic ring K431; nailed wolf's t. X1132.1; ogress with knife t. G510.5; origin and nature of animal's t. *A2378ff.; person formerly animal retains t. H64.3; planting animal's t. to produce young J1932.4.1; pulling hairs from bewitched animal's t. G271.4.9; pursuers hanging on to animal's t. shaken off R231.2.1; punishment: tying to horse's t. Q473.2; pursuer pulls out t. of fugitive's horse R265; resuscitation by animal's t. E64.16; shooting off leader's t. (lie) X1124.1; snake hard to hold by t. H659.2.1; snake preserved in ark: to stop hole with t. A2145.2; squirrel borrows coney's t. A2241.7; straightening dog's t. H1023.4.1; swallow thrown on his t.: cause of split t. A2214.1; task: stealing elephant's t. H1151.6; thief escapes by leaving animal's severed t. and claiming that the animal has escaped and left his t. K404; thief maintains that bird had no t. K402.2; tiger explains t. as boil K2011.2; toad trades his t. for mole's eyes A2247.5; why jackal's t. bare A2317.12.2; why rat's t. round and hairless A2317.12.3; where is t. pointing? toward rear J1305; witches kiss devil's t. G243.1.1; woman created from dog's t. A1224.3.

Tails fall off mountain spirits when they are baptized V81.2; tied together for protection *J681.1. — Beaver and muskrat exchange t. A2247.6; deceptive division of pigs: curly and straight t. K171.4; devil pulls off goats' t.: hence they lack t. A2216.2; drawing by horses' t. as punishment Q416.2.1; fool cuts off t. of oxen so that they will look like fine steeds J1919.4; God changes t. of devil's cows A2286.2.4; leopard with nine t. R15.7.7; men with t. on hands F515.3; men as monkeys without t. A1224.5.1; why men have not long t. A1319.2; pegs driven into backs of baboons become t. A2262.2; persons with t. F518; tailless animal tries in vain to induce foxes to cut off t. J758.1; thief steals animals and sticks severed t. into the ground K404.1; witch with t. G219.8.

Tailless fish G303.25.15.1; fox J758.1; jackal J758.1.2. — Dwarf with body like t. hen F451.2.1.2.

Tailor *P441; hero L113.9; married to princess betrays trade by calling for needle and thread H38.2.1; rests head on royal robe J1289.19; and smith as love rivals T92.12.1; throws stingy woman's cloth out window K341.13; work in fairyland F376.1. — Clever t. J1115.4; crab mistaken for t. J1762.1.2; devil as t. to dandy G303.9.9.11; devil can't learn to be t. P441.2; goose mistaken for t. J1762.1; self-righteous t. in heaven expelled L435.3; skillful t. F662ff.; trickster dupes t., steals goods K351.1.

Tailor's dream J1401.

Tailors. — Jokes about t. *X220ff.

Taking of vows and oaths M110ff. — Transformation by t. off clothes D537; devil t. hindmost G303.19; disenchantment by t. off bridle *D722; dwarf t. back gifts F451.5.2.12; ghost t. things from people E593; wife t. away only what she brought S446.

Tale, see also **Story;** of the cradle K1345. — Bearer of t. unjustly killed S461; dragon deceived into listening to t.: hero cuts off his head K835; dumb princess is brought to speech by t. ending with question to be solved F954.2.1; formula-t. saves girl from devil K555.2.1; telling t. punished A2726; unsolved problem: enigmatic ending of t. H620ff.; weddings as end of t. T135.8.

Tales. — Exaggerated t. about escapes K657; seventy t. of a parrot prevent wife's adultery K1591; not to tell t. except at certain time of year (or day) C755.2.

Talents. — Priest multiplying his t. J1264.7.

Talionis. — Lex t. P522.1.

Talisman found in bird's stomach N527.2. — Animal gives part of body as t. for summoning its aid *B501; compulsion: taking back t. which opened treasure mountain C652; ghost laid by t. E444; magic power by rubbing t. D1734.1.

Talk. — Escape by persuading captor to t. K561; fox persuades cock to come down and t. to him K815.1; ghost summoned to t. to E387.1; testimony discredited by inducing witness to t. foolishly J1151.1; why trees do not t. A2791.1; unlucky encounter causes treasure-seekers to t. and thus lose treasure N553.2.

Talkative animals incense master J2362; fools *J2350—J2369; thief caught J2136.5.2; wife discredited J1151.1.1; wife's tongue paralysed D2072.0.53.

Talkativeness W141; of Parisian fishwives X253.1.

Talker keeps person from eating J1564. — Lover late at rendezvous: detained by incessant t. *T35.0.1.

Talking animals B210ff.; bed N617; with dead wife E322.9; dragon B11.4.5; flowers F814.2; formerly was by animals and birds, men dumb A1101.2.3; to oaks to warn sons K649.6; to oneself misinterpreted J2671.2.1; private parts betray unchastity H451; in sleep betrays weaver H38.2.4; in sleep gives away riddle's answer H573.3; stone as Doomsday sign A1002.2.3, A1091.3. — Animal betrays himself to his enemies by t. J2351; crocodile betrays self by t. K607.2.1; fool loses magic objects by

t. about them J2355.1; forgotten fiancée reawakens husband's memory by serving as milkmaid and t. to calf *D2006.1.2; numskull's t. to himself frightens robbers away N612; pay for teaching t. monkey K491.1; punishment for t. too much Q393.1.1; resuscitation by t. E67.

Tall trees A2778, F812.1. — Extremely t. giant F531.2.1; giantess twice as t. as man F531.2.1.6; lie: remarkably t. person X921; lower world people t. F108.1; remarkably t. men F533.

Tallow. — Cow with t. liver B15.7.9.

Talos (man of bronze) F521.3.1.

Tamarind. — God cheats birds of t. fruit K499.6; why t. fruit is sour A2791.5; why t. leaves are small A2769.1; why t. bark is black A2751.4.3.

Tame doves close wild ones in trap and thus help common enemies J683.2; dog prefers food basin to fleeing hare J487; elephant not accepted by others B261.1.1.

Taming animal by (holiness of saint) B771.2, (maiden's beauty) B771.1, (magic object) *D1442ff.; horse F618.1; the shrew N12, T251.2; wild animals B771ff., H1155; wild prince K1399.1.

Tangle. — Spirits t. up peasant's cows F402.1.3.

Tank has no water despite rains F935.1. — Beheading in water t. K558.2; beggar to stand in t. all night K231.14; enigma: t. doesn't belong to you H594.2; Indra's t. F964.5, H1359.3; magic control of t. D2151.5; magic diamond opens t. passage D1551.7; magic t. *D921.4, (causes disease) D1500.4.3.1; no water will remain in t. D1542.3.5; palace at bottom of t. F771.3.7; palace underneath t. F725.3.4; sacrifice to t. S264.2; water raised from t. by singing D2151.5.1; waters in t. rise up, engulf boy F420.5.2.2.2.

Tanks. — Human blood makes leaky t. hold water S261.0.1.

Tankard magically sticks to lips D2171.1.2. — Magic t. *D1171.6.1.

Tannery. — Man soon learns to stand t. smells U133.

Tanning shoes with bark from saint's tree Q551.6.2.1.

Tantalus's punishment Q501.2.

Taoists. — Buddhists become slaves of T. because they cannot produce rain V355.

Tapa. — Clouds as t. beaten out by woman in moon A705.1.2; goddess in moon beating t. A751.8.6, A1142.5.1.1.

Taper. — Soul as t. E742.1.

Tapir paramour B611.8. — Creation of t. A1889.1; why t. has long nose A2335.3.2.

Tapping. — Beautification by t. D1863; knockers' t. tests F456.1.2.2.3.

Taprobane at end of world A871.0.1.

Tar and feathers as punishment Q475; slake remains after devil killed G303.16.19.20. — Capture by t. baby K741; covering with t. as punishment Q473.5.1; covering the whole wagon with t. K1425; man sends naked wife on all fours in t. and feathers K31.1, K216.2; man in t., feathers frightens off robbers K335.1.8; ogre captured by t. decoy

G514.7; origin of t. in heart of trees A2734.2, A2755.3; punishment: boiling in t. Q414.1; sea people give the ogre t. G525; woman in t. and feathers does not know herself J2012.3; ogre daubs t. on the hero's boat J2171.1.2.

Tara feast A1535.4; festival V70.5.

Tardiness. — Plant punished for t. A2725.

Tardy surpasses punctual L147.

Target. — Impaled head used as t. S139.2.2.1.2.

Tarnkappe renders invisible D1361.15.

Taro. — Origin of t. A1423.1, A2686.4.2; prolific t. F815.6.1; why t. leaves are hollow A2764.1.

Tarring importunate suitor K1218.1.7. — Capture by t. horse K741.1; man in the moon: t. of the moon A751.4.

Task. — Chief performs suitor t., rival steals bride K1371.6; curse mitigated by superhuman t. M428; devil cheated by imposing impossible t. K211; devil to help gambler in exchange for one t. yearly M214; devil to release man for performing seemingly impossible t. K216; disenchantment when superhuman t. is finished D791.1.2; dwarfs help in performing t. F451.5.1.20; false bride finishes true bride's t. and supplants her K1911.1.4; ghost laid by never-ending t. E454; hero professes to be able to perform much larger t. than that assigned K1741; husband busied with t., paramour escapes K1521.6; lousing as t. set by ogre *G466; magic prevention of performance of t. D2072.5; one is freed if he can set a t. the devil cannot perform G303.16.19.3; punishment: performing impossible t. Q512; reward for accomplishment of t. deceptively withheld K231.2; stealing from ogre as t. G610.3; substitute for t. K1848; tabu: eating before t. is finished C231.2; true husband of woman determined by assigning superhuman t. J1176.5.

Tasks *H900—H1199; assigned to learn future M302.5; assigned suitors *H335ff.; performed by use of magic objects D1581; set maid by elfin knight before she can marry him F301.4. — Animals perform t. for man *B571ff.; bride test: performance of t. *H373; dead lover sets t. E212; disenchantment by accomplishment of t. D753; extraordinary companions perform hero's t. F601.1; impossible t. drive off fairies F381.11; ogre sets impossible t. G465; royal children learn all t. J702.2.

Taste of human flesh leads to cannibalism G36. — Food has t. of any dainty desired D1665; injurious food with sweet t. K1889.4; meat takes on t. desired D476.3.1; well with t. of oil, wine, honey F718.4.

Tastes. — Unknown prince's princely t. H41.5.1.

Tasted. — Every fruit t. by fool before he gives it to his master J2245; man who only t. wine W123.1.

Tattoo on newly born baby tells of former incarnation T563.4; on penis F547.3.4. — Catfish transformed from woman carries her t. A2261.3; moon spots are t. marks A751.5.5; origin of animal markings: deities t. all creatures A2412.0.1; recognition by t. H55.3.

Tattooer in otherworld F167.15.

Tattooing on way to otherworld F151.1.5. — God of t. A465.5.1; origin of t. A1465.1, A1595.

Taught, see also **Teach.** — Animal languages t. by magic object *D1301; arts and crafts t. by culture hero A541; bridegroom must be t. intercourse T166.2; dance-loving maid t. by devil to dance G303.10.4.3; people t. by God to work claim to be self-taught C53.1; swordsmanship t. by mountain-spirit F460.4.2.3.

Taunted. — Dispossessed prince t. P36; heroine t. with her unknown past S412; illegitimate child t. by playmates T646.

Tavern. — Choice: staying at home with loving wife or going to t. and having unfaithful wife J229.1; clerk who enters t. arrested with others for murder N347.1.

Tax. — Banishment for assaulting t. collectors Q431.10; captive released on promise to pay t. R74.3; saint to bring about remission of t. M364.2; triple t. N635; weaver evades doorway t. J1289.13.

Taxes. — Hares carry t. to court B291.3.2.1; usurper imposes burdensome t. P12.3.

Taxation P531.

Tea. — Savory t.: peasant puts in many ingredients J1813.7; serving boiled t. leaves J1732.3.

Teach, see also **Taught.** — Cat omitted to t. tiger all he knew A2581; fairies t. bagpipe-playing F262.2; gods t. how to seek food A1420.2; gods t. people all they know A1404; return from dead to t. living E377; spirits t. boy how to sing F403.2.3.3.

Teacher instructs pupil in love, cuckolded K1692; and pupil P340ff.; seduces pupil K1399.5. — Alleged idol to pay t. for book K1971.13; angel as saint's t. V246.2; escape by posing as tiger's t. K601.1; father calls t. son a beggar H581.4; magician t. D1810.4; old t. wants to marry young girl T91.4.1.1; princess to embrace t. on wedding day M261.2; seduction by posing as t. K1315.7; sham t. K1958.

Teachers. — Jokes on t. X350ff.

Teaching, see also **Instructing;** chickens to talk J1882.1. — Deity t. mortal A185.3; dwarfs t. mortals F451.5.1.18; escape by t. song to watchman K606.0.2; god t. people to work A1403; hero t. women to rear children A1357; respite given for t. animal to speak K551.11.

Teachings. — Punishment for scoffing at church t. *Q225; three t. of the fox (bird) *K604.

Team. — Aphrodite's t. of sparrows (doves) A136.2.1; troll has a t. of mice G304.3.2.1.

Teams. — Devil drives several t. of oxen G303.7.5.

Tear from upper world of mortals falls on departed in lower world *E361.1. — Sinner's t. marks bring about pardon V21.6; waking from magic sleep by letting t. fall on sleeper D1978.2.

Tears become jewels D475.4.5; of blood F541.9, (as evil omen) D1812.5.1.1.1, (from grief) D1041.21, (sign of royalty) H71.8; bring recognition H14.1; change to blood D474.6; falling give away presence H151.14; of gold D1454.4.1; of living save soul E754.1.8; transformed to other object D457.18. — Animal sheds t. B736ff.; barrel filled miraculously with penitent's t. F1051.1; bird sheds t. B736; bird's t. restore sight D1505.5.1; birth from t. T541.3; blindness cured by t. F952.1; bodies of water from t. A911; conception from drinking saint's t. T512.4; creation from creator's t. A613; disenchantment by t. D766.3; disenchantment by weeping jug of t. D753.2; fairy's t. pearls F239.6; flood from t. A1012.1ff.; flowers from t. D1454.4.3; fountain from saint's t. D925.1.1; isle of t. F129.4.1; jewels from t. D1454.4.2; lakes originate from t. A920.1.5; magic t. *D1004; origin of t. and sighs A1344; pearls shed for t. H31.7.1; plant characteristics from t. A2731.2; plants from t. A2612ff.; quest for t. shed into the sea H1371.3; rain from t. A1131.1; resuscitation by t. E58; river from t. F162.2.12; river of t. F715.2.5; saint's t. of blood V229.2.6.1; springs originate from t. A941.2.

Tearing boat apart with hands F639.6; down huge wall H1116.3; garments grief sign P678.1; hair, clothes from grief F1041.21.6; opponent to bits F1041.16.3.3; up the orchard (vineyard) K1416; out person's sides S187.1. — Birds t. ogre to pieces G512.9.2; bringing thorn leaves without t. them H1046.2; child t. snake to pieces F628.1.3.2; hound killed by t. out its heart B17.1.2.2; mermaids t. mortal lovers to pieces B81.2.2.

Teased. — Fairies' revenge for being t. F361.10.

Teasing. — Brownies t. F482.5.3; dwarfs dislike t. F451.3.6.2, F451.9.1.7; dwarfs t. people F451.5.14.

Teats. — Dog rescues cow's t. from fire: origin of his black muzzle A2229.1; origin and nature of animal's t. A2363; saint cuts off cow's t. to feed children T611.5.2.

Tedious penances Q521ff.; punishments Q500ff.; tasks H1110ff.

Teeth, see after **Tooth.**

Tegillus. — Riddle about T. H842.2.

Telegraph. — Articles sent by t. J1935.

Telepathy with animals F648. — Magic t. D1785.

Telescope. — Magic clairvoyant t. D1323.15.

Tell shoots apple from son's head F661.3; -tale hand-mark H58; -tale magic objects D1612ff.

Telling adventure too soon tabu C757.2; of fairy gifts tabu F348.7; only very good news J2516.3.5; true stories as test H252.0.1.

Telltown. — Origin of games at T. A1535.3.

Temaie Festival V70.5.

Temper. — Bad t. punished Q313; monk loses t. at overturned cup H1553.5; violence of t. W185.

Temperate and intemperate zeal J550ff.

Temperature. — Extraordinary body t. F593; fountain of any desired t. F162.8.1, F716.3; saint regulates waters' t. D2151.0.1.

Tempering. — North wind t. fury of south wind A1127.1.1.

Tempermental goddess A139.13.

Tempest-box raises storm D1541.1.5.

Temple about to be taken over by pagans saved by appearance of a sign of the cross (image of the Virgin) V344; cedars bear fruit F811.7.2.1; as God's home A151.10.1; in otherworld F163.2.1; rises where ground bursts open A992.3; swallowed by earth F941.2.3. — Animal sacrificed at edification of t. V12.4.0.1; burning the t. to attain notoriety J2162.1; earth swallows t. vessels F948.1.1; god builds t. in heaven A141.2; god's t. of jewels A151.4.1; imprisoned princess rescued from t. R111.2.4; lamb prefers to be sacrificed in t. than to be eaten by wolf J216.2; lovers meet at t. N711.4.1; magic from t. demons D812.5.1; man hiding in t. gets robbers' booty K1971.14; punishment for profaning t. Q222.4; soul of dead in a t. E755.4.2; soul wanders and demands that a t. be built for him E419.1; tabus in connection with t. C93.5; treasure in t. N514.2.

Temples *V112. — Applying hot iron to man's t. J2119.7; nature laments t. destruction F960.3.2; why Brahma has no t. A162.4.

Temporary advantage gained by pretending to yield in combat K2378; magic characteristics D1950—D2049. — Magic object effects t. change in person D1360ff.

Temptation. — Anchorites under t. *T330ff.; monk learns about t. U231.1; monk wants ever-present t. V462.12; oath uttered by pious against t. M110.3; penance: resisting t. Q537; plea by showing t. to crime J1165; punishment for yielding to t. Q233.

Temptations. — Test of fidelity through submitting hero to t. H1556.2.

Tempted. — Clergyman t. by devil G303.9.4.4; man unsuccessfully t. by woman T331; mother t. by incognito son to see whether all women are wicked T412.2.

Tempter. — Devil as t. G303.9.4ff.

Tempting. — Demons t. men G302.9.2; devil in serpent form t. first woman (Satan and Eve) A63.6; wife t. husband H1556.4.2.1.

Temptress sent by deity F34.

Ten as formulistic number Z71.16.2; heavens A651.1.7; as magic number D1273.1.4; measures of magic in world D1719.11.1; for the price of nine J2083.4; servingwomen carried in bottle D55.2.4. — Are there nine or t. geese (horses) J2031.2, J2032; cannibals eat t. men, women, children G94.2; oath valid only with t. witnesses M110.2; prophecy: death in t. years M341.1.5.1; transformation every t. days D623; twenty commandments better than t. J2213.5.1.

Ten-headed giant F531.1.2.2.6; ogre G361.1.5; serpent B15.1.2.9.

Ten thousand. — Transformation: ox-demon becomes t. feet long D412.2.7.

Tenant advised by landlord to steal J1179.8; -less houses at border of otherworld F147.1.

Tenderness. — Sleeping with head in wife's lap t. sign T299.1.

Tent with revolving door F782.6; house folded and swallowed as means of carrying it F923; torn down, man killed K959.3. — Eager warriors go through t. wall W212.1; extraordinary t. F775, F845; magic t. *D1138; seduction by showing wares in t. K1332.2; sinking of t. pole by magic D55.1.1.2; sky as t. A702.2; taking boy to enemy's t. H1418; twins born in t. T581.10.

Termagent. — Devil marries old maid t. G303.12.3.

Termite. — Helpful t. B481.2.

Terrapin hatching from bedbug eggs J1772.1.1. — Enmity between deer and t. A2494.12.7.

Terrestrial. — Journey to t. otherworlds F110ff.; riddles of t. distance H681ff.

Terrible. — Devil destroys hunting party with t. wind G303.20.2; devil disappears amid t. (rattle) G303.17.2.7, (stench) G303.17.2.8; river in paradise with t. roar F162.2.8.

Terrified. — Ogre (large animal) t. K1710ff.

Terrifying experience on Hallowe'en H1423.2. — Ugly ogre t. women who flee and are drowned G476.

Terror. — Curse of everlasting t. M403; hair turns gray from t. F1041.7.

Test for demons in corpses E431.0.1; of hero before otherworld journey H1250; of legitimacy of children: exposure to asps T642; for troll child F455.10.1. — Animal helps person pass t. B599.2; cannibal cuts captive's finger to t. fatness G82.1; false bride fails magician's t. K1911.3.3.2; fly helps suitor pass t. B587.2; girl as umpire in suitor t. K1227.8; husband transforms himself to t. his wife's faithfulness *T235; substitute specimen for laboratory t. K1858; to t. a favorite, a king says that he is going to retire from the world J1634; transformation to t. heroes D645; vigilance t. H1450ff.

Tests H (entire chapter); of character H1550ff. — Decisions based on experimental t. J1176; extraordinary companions help hero in suitor t. F601.2; false bride fails when husband t. her K1911.3.3; strong hero t. weapons F611.3.3; suitor t. *H310ff.

Testament of the dog J1607; of Virgin Mary V283; willing rewards and punishments (conventional ending of story) Z78. — Forged t. dupes host K455.8.2.

Testicle. — Beaver sacrifices t. to save life J351.1; cobold from boar's t. F481.0.1.1.

Testicles. — Enormous t. F547.7; nature of animal's t. A2365.1; why elephant has t. inside *A2365.1.1.

Testifying. — Heavenly voice t. for accused H216.2.

Testimony of fool J2667; gradually weakened J1151.3; of witness cleverly discredited J1151.

Testing money by throwing it into stream J1931; saint by sham death Q591.1.1; of witches G277. — God t. mortal A185.13; judgment by t. love J1171.

Thanks after eating C283. — All questions to be answered "T." C495.3; punishment for neglecting t. to gods Q223.2.

Thanked. — Fairies leave when t. F381.13.

Thankful fool *J2550—J2599.

Thanking fairy for gift tabu F348.5.2. — Tabu: t. (under certain circumstances) C493.

Thatched. — Castles t. with gold F163.1.3.

Thatching of birds' wings F165.5, F171.6.6; roof with feathers H1104.1.2; tail to roof so as to catch dupe K1021.1. — Burning t. protection against witch G272.17; ineffectual t. of house H619.4.

Theft, see also **Stealing, Thief;** of ambrosia A153.1; to avoid starvation forgiven U25; from fairies F350ff.; of fire *A1415; of light *A1411; by magic D2087; of moon *A758; from ogre G610ff.; punished *Q212; of seasons A1151; of sun *A721.1; as a task H1151; by trained animal K366; from troll F455.6.4; from witch G279.2. — Attention drawn by helpful animal's t. of food from wedding table: recognition follows H151.2; boy boasts, advertises father's t. J2355.2; blame for t. fastened on dupe K401; charms against t. D1389.2; fairy takes revenge for t. F361.2; false accusation of t. K2127; feet cut off as punishment for t. Q451.2.2; jewel present brings false accusation of t. K2104; judge wants to know how the t. was committed J2372; magic detection of t. D1817.0.1; man must labor as punishment for t. of fire A1346.1; master asked to help in the t. J2136.5.6.1; penalty for t. A1581.2; return from dead to punish t. of part of corpse E235.4; riddling answer betrays t. H582.1; ring proves t. H84.4; sham wise man declares who committed the t. (robbers) K1956.3; skill in t. granted after prayer V59.1; spurned woman accuses man of t. K2111.2; wolf punished for t.: kings honored U11.2.1.

Thefts K300—K439; and cheats *K300—K499. — Dupe imitates trickster's t. and is caught K1026; hypocrisy concerning t. K2095; origin of t. A1341.3; retorts concerning t. J1390ff.; Russians like t. A1674.2.

Theodora masks as monk and lives chastely in monastery Q537.1.

Theological questions answered by propounding simple questions in science J1291.2.

Theophilus goes to hell for return of his contract H1273.1.

Theoretical. — Practical vs. t. knowledge J251.

Theories. — Absurd scientific t. J2260—J2299.

Theseus and the bent tree released so as to tear him to pieces H1522.1; and giant robber with club G102.

Thetis F423.1.

Thick hair F555.4. — Armor ordered thin in front and t. in back J673.1.

Thief, see also **Highwayman, Robber;** asks any punishment except having two wives T251.1.6; beaten for not giving robbery warning J1191.6;

believes detective mind reader, confesses J1141.1.9; breaks foot climbing wall, sues owner Z49.11.2; -catcher caught by own club K1605; caught by man hiding in chest K751.2; claims he's taken only gifts J1161.11; coughs, watchmen blinded K2062.2.6; crushed to death by fragments of his boring N339.15; cursed M414.10; detected by feeling beard J1141.1.2; as discoverer J2223; climbing rope discovered and rope cut *K1622; detected (by building straw fire) J1143, (by psalter and key) H251.3.2, (by sieve and shears) H251.3.3, (when he pawns stolen goods) N276; in disguise *K311ff.; hears owner singing, thinks self detected N611.4; imagines is being laughed at, confesses N275.4; kept at sea in magic boat Q559.10; lives with twenty cats B292.6.1; makes a lame excuse J1391; masked as devil bought off by owner K152; mistakes leopard for calf J1758.4; to be pardoned if he can steal without being caught M56; posing as corpse detected by pricking his feet J1149.7; rendered unable to remove stolen goods Q551.2.3; reveals self in church J1141.15; robs own purse J2527; shows up owner's unjust claim J1213; suspected of crawling through hole must take off clothes J1141.7; -tailor cuts piece of own coat X221.1; threatened with divine punishment, confesses J1141.14; tries to feed watch dog and stop his mouth K2062; trusted to guard goods K346; warned what not to steal J2091. — Apparently pious man a t. K2058.1; brownie twitches t. F482.5.4.2; careless t. caught J2136.5; cattle t. struck by lightning Q552.1.8.1; cauldron t. detected J1661.1.10; clever t. may keep booty J1211.2; coward gives purse to t. W121.6; crucified t. in passion play complains of thirst J2041.1; ghost scares t. E293.1; god as t. A177; killed paramour alleged to be t. K1569.9; king plays t. H1557.6; lake bursts forth to drown t. A920.1.3; magic cloth betrays t. D1318.8.1; master t. *K301ff.; numskull convinced that he is a t. J2318; numskull as t. J2461.1.7; one-eyed t. J1661.1.8; owner assists t. J1392; pleading with t. fails, stones succeed J1088; priest shouts at t. J1261.2.6; punishment: devil carries off t. Q554.1; return from dead to capture t. E235.7; return from dead to prevent flight of t. E375; return from dead to warn t. E236.3; ruler protects t. W11.10; shadow mistaken for t. J1790.2; sheep t. confesses in church N275.5.1; skillful t. F676; story told to discover t. J1177; stick with money in it breaks and betrays t. H251.3.4; tabus of t. C572; waiting at the well for the t. J2214.3; waiting for the t. to return for the bolster J2214.3.2; waiting in the graveyard for the t. J2214.3.1; why wolf is t. A2455.1; wizard detects t. D1817.0.1.1ff.

Thief's corpse carried through streets J1142.4; money scales borrowed J1141.6. — Divining rod indicates t. house D1314.2.3; ear of stolen animal protrudes from t. mouth Q552.4; ghost prevents t. flight E375.

Thieves attempting to steal from church rendered powerless Q222.5.4; cannot quit plundering U138.2; claim walls so thin, house too great temptation J1165.1; deceived by overhearing conversation J1517; dig field, drain tank for gold K2316; flee man costumed as devil J1786.1;

make invoice of stolen goods J2214.3.3; magically petrified on entering house D2072.5.1; quarrel over booty: owner comes W151.8; waylay goddess in disguise K1811.0.2. — Ass warns of t. J2413.1.1; country of t. F709.3; dying like Christ: between two t. X313; escape from t. by reporting high prices elsewhere K576; god of t. A457; magic club brings t. D1427.6; millers as t. X211; why millers are t. P443.1; murder revealed to t. climbing into bank N615; numskull bridegroom unwittingly detects t. N611.3; poisoned cakes intended for husband eaten by t. N659.1; pupil surpasses t. in stealing L142.1; ridding city of t. H1199.9; river rises to prevent t. escape F932.8.3; tortoise and dog partners as t. B294.7; water for t. in king's garden H1471.1; wild hunt harmful to t. E501.18.1.2.

Thieves' nocturnal habits J1394.

Thievery, see also **Stealing;** habit can't be broken U138; a predestined lot M359.10. — Death as punishment for t. Q411.13.

Thieving contest K305.1; household spirit F480.3; spirit F419.2. — Magic t. object D1605.

Thigh as hiding place F1034.3. — Birth from man's t. T541.5; child incubated in man's t. T578.1; dirk stuck into t. in order to keep from sleeping H1482; tabu to eat t. vein C221.3.6.

Thimble. — Bailing out pond with t. H1113.1; tailor puts on t. as protection from slug J2623; thumbling hides under t. F535.1.1.10.1.

Thin. — Armor ordered t. in front and thick in back J673.1; lie: remarkably t. person X924.

Thinking, see also **Thought;** of God protects against devil G303.16.2.1.1; of good or evil tabu on magic journey D2121.6. — Consolation by t. of some one good aspect of a situation J865; husband forbids wife's t. J1511.8; man from deity's body from his mere t. A1211.0.1; person summoned by t. of him D2074.2.1; sinner t. of God saved V525.

Third, see also **Three.** — By t. day unusual sight has ceased to attract attention J1075.1; dead returns t. day after burial E586.2; heart breaks at t. drink from silver canister F1041.1.1.1; money lost twice, recovered t. time N183; mother's curse on t. son causes eclipse A737.2; obstinate wife: the t. egg T255.4; speech magically recovered when t. person guesses secret transaction D2025.3.

Thirst from breaking tabu C949.5; magically disappears D2033. — Contest in enduring t. H1544; why crane suffers t. *A2435.4.2; death by t. for breaking tabu C924; drunkard refuses cure of fever if it is to take away his t. J343.1; enemies magically feel t. D2091.6; great t. J1322; great t. of dead E489.11; husband lets wife die of t. S62.4; king's son to die from t. M341.2.26; madness from t. F1041.8.4; magic insatiable t. D2063.3; magic object causes constant t. D1373.0.1; magic object produces immunity from hunger and t. D1349.1; origin of t. A1345.1; patient will take care of own t. J1322.1; unremittent t. as punishment Q501.7; why raven suffers t. *A2435.4.3.

Thirsty cattle fight over well B266.1. — Adulterers tricked into riding t. mules drowned K1567; hanged man t. E422.0.1; pun involving t. and Thursday X111.15.

Thirteen as magic number D1273.1.6; as unlucky number N135.1; as name of victorious youngest son L10.1.1; rivers of balm in otherworld F162.2.7. — Formulistic number: t. Z71.9; string with t. knots in child's mouth G271.10.

Thirtieth. — Full moon and t. of the month H582.1.1.

Thirty days' respite from unwelcome marriage T151.2; girls fall in love with young man T27.1; Years War destroys home of dwarfs F451.4.4.2. — Formulistic number: t. Z71.11; God avenges murder after t. years Q211.0.1; man claims to be t. for many years J1218; prophecy: man hanging himself at t. M341.1.4.4; riddle: tree with twelve branches, each with t. leaves, black and white H721.1; talking statue, when destroyed, cannot be replaced for t. thousand years D1661.1; woman requires t. men T146.2.

Thirty-two as formulistic number Z71.16.5.

Thirty-six as formulistic number Z71.8.7.

Thisbe and Pyramus T41.1.

Thistle serves as milk-cup for Virgin Mary A2711.4.2. — Chain tale: conflict between fowl and t. Z41.3; fright when t. catches clothes J2625.

Thistles and nettles are the devil's vegetables G303.10.13. — Devil loses his grain and gets t. K249.1; origin of t. *A2688.1; punishment for first murder: t. A2631.1.

Thong of leather cut out from back as punishment Q451.8. — Magic t. D1209.6.

Thongs. — Sled t. cut to prevent pursuit K637.

Thor battles Midgard serpent at end of world A1082.3; carries giant across stream F531.3.1.3; slays foster father P271.8. — Luring T. into giants' power H1173; rowan helps T. out of river A2711.5; sisters curse child had by T. M437.2.

Thor's — Magic of T. temple D838.3.

Thorn -brake as refuge R311.1.1; fence surrounds food-plants K1038; growing in wound becomes tree F971.3; removed from cobra's throat N647; removed from lion's paw B381; removed from monkey's tail B381.2; removed from wolf's paws B381.1. — Ass begs wolf to pull t. out of foot before eating him *K566; bringing t. leaves without tearing them H1046.2; charm removes t. D1513; cowl in t.-brake symbol of Christ V124.1; cutting white t. tree fatal C518.2; devil carries a t. stick G303.4.8.5; disenchantment by removal of enchanting t. D765.1.2; feeling t. point through clothes F647.9.2; magic t. *D958, D976, D1393.5; man becomes t. D213.5; origin of t. tree from Joseph's staff A2624.1; saint transfers t. from foot D2161.4.2.3; saint digs canal while riding t. tree D2121.14; sleep t. D1364.2.

Thorns believed not to sting at night J1819.1; around nipples F546.4;

planted to kill birds K959.5; on plants A2736. A2752. — Death from t. in rice M341.2.16; evil spirit in spite puts bark and t. on tree A2736; food with t. hidden as test H1515.3; loser of shooting wager to go naked into t. for a bird N55.1; man put into moon for stealing t. A751.1.4; mountain of t. F759.6; riddle: fencing t. with thorns H583.2.5; roses lose t. for saint V222.14; stepmother feeds children t. S31.4; tongue with t. F544.2.4; trail magically covered with t. D2089.9.1.

Thornbush blamed by fox for wounding him J656.1. — Bat, diver, and t. shipwrecked A2275.5.3; laurel and olive tree scorn t. as umpire in their dispute as to who is most useful J411.7; magic t. points out road D1313.14; origin of t. A2688.1.1; pine and t. dispute as to their usefulness J242.2.

Thought, see also **Thinking;** is swiftest (riddle) H632.1. — Devil carries man through the air as swift as t. G303.9.5.4; magic journey as swift as t. *D2122.3; magic results from power of t. *D1777.

Thoughts must be on fairies in fairyland F378.3. — Devils do not know or understand t. of men G303.13.1; fairies read men's t. F256; friends reading each others' t. P310.9; good t. rewarded, bad punished Q6; journey to upper world by keeping t. continually on heaven *F64; magic knowledge of another's t. D1819.1; magic ring permits owner to learn person's secret t. D1316.4; saint can perceive another's t. V223.3; test: guessing person's t. H524.

Thoughtless. — Transformation through t. wish of father D521.1.

Thousand at one shot K1741.2; -headed serpent B15.1.2.10.3; -year old ogre G631.1. — Giant eats a t. cattle F531.3.4.1; giants live to be eighteen t. years old F531.6.4.2; life prolonged t. years D1855.5; man with t. arms F516.2.3; penance: hanging for a t. years head downward over a fire of chaff Q522.6; phoenix renews youth when a t. years old B32.1.1; talking statue when destroyed cannot be replaced for thirty t. years D1661.1.

Thousand-leg. — Enmity between elephant and t. A2494.11.1.

Thrall cursed to sit on chest, be restless M455.3; as sacrifice V12.6. — Curse of t. M411.13.

Thralls. — King not to settle quarrel of t. C563.4; origin of t. P177.

Thread awarded to disputant who knows what it was wound on J1179.6; bridge to otherworld F152.1.7; as a clue to find way out of labyrinth R121.5; cut by arrow F661.12; entering needle suggests intercourse J86, Z186; from lotus stalks on Vishnu's navel H1289.4.1; made to appear as a large log carried by a cock D2031.2; sold to lizard J1852.1.1; transformed to bridge D454.4.1; under dumb man's tongue cut F954.1. — Daw fleeing from captivity caught in trees by t. around foot N255.5; deception: climbing silk t. tossed upward in air K1871.1; dwarfs suspend large millstone on thin t. F451.5.4.2; goddesses descend by t. A189.10; jumping over magic t. H412.7.1; magic ball of t. indicates road D1313.1.1; magic t. *D1184ff., (gives illusion of drinking from spring, not sea) H1142.2.1, (from heaven) D811.2.1, (from yogi's garment) D1400.1.18; oath by touching sacred t. M114.6; recognition of disenchanted person by t. in his teeth H64.1; red t. on neck of person who has been decapitated and resuscitated *E12.1; Rome hanging by t. (lie) X1561; scarlet t. death omen J2311.1.4; sewing contest won by deception: the long t. K47.1; silk t. stretches to sea F642.6; speaking t. D1610.28; why spider has t. in back of body *A2356.2.8; tailor married to princess betrays trade by calling for needle and t. H38.2.1; test of resourcefulness: putting t. through coils of snail shell H506.4; trail of t. R135.0.5; traveling till two skeins of t. are unwound (task) H1125.1; weaving shirt from piece of t. H1022.2.2.

Threads. — Ants carry silk t. to prisoner, who makes rope and escapes R121.4; cotton already spun into t. A1346.2.1; extraordinary t. F877; self-weaving t. D1601.13.1; weaving cloth from two t. H1022.1.

Threading needle test in convent H509.1.

Threat to throw on fire causes changeling to cry out and betray his nature F321.1.1.6.—Bluffing t. K1771; seduction through t. K1397; ugly cobbler's continual t. to throw his last at people X241.

Threats overcome witch G275.15; to person as suitor test H1406.

Threatened. — Child t. with ogre *C25.1; when changeling is t. with burning, child is returned F321.1.4.5.

Threatening. — Dwarfs t. mortals F451.5.2.8; fairies t. sheep watcher F361.11; goat's t. song K1767; man behind tree t. his debtor K1971.2; princess t. amorous king T322.2; sham-dead t. bier bearers J2311.5.1; sham physician cures people by t. them with death K1955.1; son t. father to be recognized P233.7; sun's intense heat t. all life A727.1; suppliant t. image V123.1.

Three, see also **Third**; blasts on horn before sunrise to rescue prisoner from mound R112.1; blows received for every one given J221.3.2; -bodied goddess A123.1.1; -breasted woman F546.2; brothers contest in wishing H507.3.1; brothers take turns using mule J1914.2; caskets H511.1; creators A2.1; days' tournament R222; deformed witches invited to wedding in exchange for help *M233; -eyed person F512.2.1.1; -faced (god) A123.2.1.1, (person) F511.1.2; first cries to God A1344.1; -fold (magic sleep) *D1971, (oath) M115.1; foolish wishes J2071; giants with one eye *G121.1; gods bring up earth A811.2; Graces A468; -headed (animals) B15.1.2.2, (dragon) B11.2.3.2, (person) F511.0.2.2, (ogre) G361.1.2, (woman) F511.0.2.2; heavens A651.1.1; -horned animals B15.3.1; hunchback brothers drowned K2322; joint depositors may have their money back when all demand it J1161.1; lovers mourn dead girl T92.14; lower worlds A651.2.2; as magic number D1273.1.1; magical musical strains D1275.1.1; -night watch over grave to guard man from devil H1463; reasons for not giving alms J2225; reasons for refusing credit J1552.2; redeeming kisses D735.2; roses fall as sign of unfaithfulness H432.1.1; sevens in 1777 drive dwarfs out of the land F451.9.1.3;

sins of the hermit J485; stupid things: riddle H871.1; suns shine in sky F961.1.3.2; -tailed turtle B15.7.6; teachings of the fox (bird) *K604; victims of love T92.2; witch sisters G201; women have but one (eye among them) F512.1.2, (tooth among them) F513.1.1; worlds of dead E480.2; wells under t. roots of earth-tree A878.1.2; women humiliate importunate lover K1218.4.1; year eating tabu C231.6; -year old child as protection against devil G303.16.19.6; young men arrested tell who they are H581ff. — Child of t. fathers born with t. stripes T563.1; cup with two and t. handles J2665.1; dead awaken after t. days to new life and great wisdom E489.1; death's t. messengers J1051; deceptive bargain: t. wishes K175; devil as t. gentlemen G303.3.1.11; disenchantment by t. nights' silence under punishment D758.1; dividing four coins among t. persons J1241.2; equivocal inscriptions at parting of t. roads N122.0.1; eye with t. pupils F541.3.2; execution avoided by using t. wishes J1181.1; fairies give t. gifts F341.1; fairies' t. cornered hats F236.3.1; formulistic number: t. *Z71.1; giant t. spans between brows and t. yards between shoulders F531.2.2; giant with t. arms F531.1.6.7.1; girl may remain virgin for t. days after marriage T165; god in t. forms A132.0.1.2; heroine's t.-fold flight from ball R221; king given t. wheels to control his anger J571.2; magician assigned t. places at a table J1141.2; magic fan produces rain when waved t. times D1542.1.4; making shirt from piece of linen t. inches square (task) H1022.4; men with two faces, t. legs, and seven arms F526.5; modest choice: t. casket type L211; mother of world bears t. sons A1282.1; one eye of the t. giants stolen G612; one of the old maid's t. teeth breaks off X754; oracle that the first of t. sons to kiss his mother will be king J1652; person with t. bodies F524.1; porter's revenge for t. wise counsels J1511.6; prophecy: t.-fold death M341.2.4; prophecy: princess will wed t. men in one M306.3; person with t. hearts F559.7.1; person with t. rows of teeth F513.1.2.1; prophecy: death in t. years, three months M341.1.2.4; quest for t. (feathers of marvelous bird) H1331.1.2, (hairs from devil's beard) H1273.2, (persons as stupid as his wife) H1312.1; quest in hell for t. dragon feathers H1274; resuscitation after t. days E162.1; riding t. times around the hill to free captive confined within R112.2; Schlaraffenland lies t. miles beyond Christmas X1712.1; selling t. old women (task) H1153; skillful axe-man makes spearshafts with t. chippings F666.1; snake disenchanted by being allowed to wrap itself t. times around person's neck D759.8; son of t. dogs B635.4.1; student is helped by the devil when he can answer t. questions in rhyme G303.22.3; suitor test: winning horse-race t. times H331.5.3; test of cleverness: uttering t. wise words H505; test: sleeping by princess t. nights without looking at her or disturbing her H1472; theft from t. old women who have but a single eye among them *K333.2; transformation by encircling object t. times D563; beggar in disguise obtains alms t. times from same person K1982; tree bears fruit t. times yearly F811.18; vanquished ogre grants hero's t. wishes G665; wager: who can call t. tree names first N51; water-goddess allows body of drowning to come up t. times F420.5.2.1.4; woman becomes clean only after t. washings and the use of t. pounds of soap W115.2; woman ravished by t. brothers bears triplets T586.3.1.

Three hundred. — Cup of t. colors F866.1; eating t. fat oxen H1141.2; mermaid lives for t. years B81.13.12; river piles up to t. miles F932.8.6; man t. years old has infrequent intercourse T317.0.1; sacrifice to live t. years V17.6; woman with t. sixty-five children *L435.2.1; wood of sixty trees nourishing t. men apiece F812.2.

Three hundred sixty-five Z72.6. — House with t. windows and doors F782.1.

Three-legged dogs in wild hunt *E501.4.1.6; ghost of horse E423.1.3.1, *E521.1.2; god A123.6.1; pot sent to walk home J1881.1.3; quadrupeds *B15.6.1. — Fairies ride on t. horses *F241.1.3; treasure is found when t. cat shrieks over a grave N542.2.

Three thousand parables of Solomon J80.1. — Tree coiling leaves t. miles high with golden cock on top F811.2.3.1.

Thresher. — Lie: remarkable t. X1001.

Threshing contest K42.1; grain: granary roof used as t. flail K1422; in heaven H84.3. — Dead person t. E567; extraordinary t.-floor F896; woman t. corn in moon A751.8.2.

Threshold. — Bridal couple put one foot inside t. T137.2.1; father tells son not to drag him past t. J121.2; water from foot-washing sprinkled on t. as protection against witch G272.13.

Thrice killed corpse K2151. — Think t. before you speak J2516.1; wild hunt goes t. around pond E501.14.3.

Thrift W216; as bride test H381ff.; -less wife as accursed H659.18.1.

Throat. — Animal killed by forcing ball into t. K951.5; bone removed from animal's t. B382; frog rises from person's stomach into t. every spring B784.0.1; murder by cutting t. S118.2; ogre killed by throwing hot stones (metal) into his t. G512.3.1; punishment: cutting t. Q421.3; stones in t. to lay ghost E441.2; wine shows through woman's white t. F647.6.

Throbbing of right eye a favorable omen D1812.5.2.1.

Throne. — Answering questions only when on t. J1189.1; crown fits successor to t. H36.2.1; eagle regains t. for king B589.1; earth created from snow under divine t. A835.1; extraordinary t. F785ff.; god on t. A137.15; god's t. A152ff.; goddess' t. shakes when worshipper ill A189.5; heaven as God's t. A133.2.2; impostor's letter authorizes t. for him K1952.6; king forces follower onto t. to be killed K1845.2; lifting of goddess's t. D1654.17; magic t. *D1156; mythical animals surround God's t. B7.2; negro takes refuge under princess's t. R314; son usurps father's t. P236.4; succession to t. lost in gambling N2.5.1; sun sits on t. A731.1; tailor occupies God's t. for a day P441.1.

Thrones in otherworld F166.6. — Fairies' four flying t. F282.3.

Throstle giving all attention to sweet fruits is caught by bird catcher J651.1.

Through. — Chastity ordeal: passing t. fire H412.4; magic sight by looking t. keyhole D1821.3.6; magic sight by looking t. ring D1821.3.5; one animal jumps t. body of another F916; stream runs t. house F715.4; suitor contest: riding t. fire H331.1.5.

Throw at a rich man J1602. — Impostors t. hero into pit K1931.4; mountain-men t. person over church roof F460.4.4.3; ugly cobbler continually threatens to t. his last at people X241; wrestling match won by deception: where to t. the ogre K12.1.

Thrower. — Lie: remarkable t. X943; remarkable stone-t. F636.4.

Throwing ball to princess suitor test H331.16; contest won by deception K18; little stones to express love H316.5; stone at own reflection J1791.5.2; stone, not pebble, at girl J2461.9. — Adulteress t. object out window to distract husband K1514.15; animal characteristics from t. members at ancient animal A2215ff.; captor t. away trickster K649.12; deceptive land purchase: bounds fixed by t. object K185.6; devil t. stones A977.2; disenchantment by t. stone D712.3.2; divination by t. objects into water D1812.5.0.6; escape by t. objects far away K622.2; fatal game: t. from cliff K854; lost object found by t. spade at ghost D1816.2.1; magic book conjured away by t. it on stream D2176.4; magic journey by t. knife into whirlwind *D2121.8; man t. opponent into air F624.8; murder by t. from height S127; ogre killed by t. hot stones (metal) into his throat G512.3.1; poltergeist t. objects F473.1; spirit t. back shots fired at it F473.6.5; strong man t. stone F624.2.0.1; transformation by t. object D571; transformation to fish by t. into sea D586.

Thrown. — Ashes of dead t. on water to prevent return E431.9; dupe t. over precipice K891.5.3; footstool t. from heaven F1037; great rock t. by giant F531.3.2ff.; hat t. into air indicates route D1313.2; hero an abortion t. into the bushes T572.2.3; land t. down from heaven A953; magic object t. ahead carries owner with it D1526; magic staff t. causes wild animals to stand still D1442.4; magic sickness because girl has t. away her consecrated wafer *D2064.1; needles t. so that one enters eye of the other F661.7; object t. into air causes enemies to fight over it K1082.2; one strong man t. by another from walls F628.2.2; person t. to ground by wild hunt E501.18.5; suitor test: apple t. indicates princess's choice H316; true bride's children t. away K1911.2.3; water t. on corpse to prevent return E431.2.

Thrush teaches dove to build nest A2271.1. — Color of t. *A2411.12.1.1; creation of t. A1912.1.

Thrush's beautiful voice *A2423.2.1; wedding B282.12.

Thrushbeard, King T76.

Thugs. — Wisdom from t. J178.

Thumb cut and salt put on it in order to remain awake H1481; of knowledge D1811.1.1. — Child nourished by sucking t. of a god T611.1.1;

devil's t. G303.4.3; elves' half t. F232.7; magic knowledge from touching "knowledge tooth" with t. D1810.3; soul in t. E714.7.1.

Thumbs. — Saints confirm covenant by cutting off t. M201.4; why toad has no t. A2375.2.9.

Thumbling F535.1; born as result of hasty wish of parents T553; frightens off robbers K335.1.6.2; swallowed by animals F911.3.1.

Thunder drums of the dead A1142.9.1; at king's birth F960.1.1.1; said to be the rolling of hero's brother's wagon K1718.1; slays devils A162.3.2; spirits A1142.5.1.2, A284.3; sword sought H1337.1; weapon A157.1, A992.2. — Brother as t., sister as lightning R321.1; creator's voice makes the t. A1142.1; curse: to be stricken by t. M447; deserted children become t. S378; devil retreats into hell amid t. and lightning G303.17.2.5; dragon's liver of t. H1332.6; dupe deceived concerning the t.: finally killed by it K1177; extraordinary t. F968; giant's snoring as t. F531.3.8.1; giants killed by t. F531.6.12.4; god of t. A284; god's voice causes t. A139.5.2; hearing t. on setting forth a good omen D1812.5.2.3; impregnation by t. T528; man becomes t. D281.3; man saves devil from t. Q45.2.1; mountain-folk afraid of t. F460.2.1; not far from heaven to earth for t. there can be heard here H682.1.6; origin of t. A1142; rainbow as bow of t.-god A791.1; Socrates and Xanthippe: "after t. rain" T251.4; turtle holds with jaws till t. sounds B761.

Thunders. — Journey to the Land of the T. F117.

Thunderbird A284.2.

Thunderbolt as gods' weapon A157.1.1; magically produced D2149.1; prevents intimacy of saint's communities F968.2. — Death by t. as punishment Q552.1; dragon swallows t. intended for hero B529.2; origin of t. A1142.0.1; where t. fell sacred A992.2.

Thundergod. — Combat between t., devil A162.3; hammer of t. A157.7; man as helper of t. A189.1.1.

Thunderstorm. — Devil is followed by t. G303.6.3.1; woman hoists skirt to raise t. D2141.0.10.

Thursday birthday turns person into nightmare F471.1.5; as lucky day N127.3. — God speaks to saint each T. A182.3.0.3; Maundy T. tabu C235; pun on T. and thirsty X111.15; saint goes to heaven every T. Q172.8.1, A182.3.0.3.1.

Tick. — Bed-t. full of harp strings H1129.7.

Tickling. — Fairies t. mortals to death F363.6; origin of t. sensation A1319.11; resuscitation by t. E18; swallowed person t. serpent's throat F912.3.1.

Tidal wave (from breaking tabu) C984.4, (marks person's death place) A913.1. — Magic t. wave D2151.3.1.

Tide held back D2151.1.2f.; inquires whether moon is up J1292. — Army drowned by incoming t. N339.7; controlling t. as suitor task H335.6.1; deceptive drinking contest: rising and falling t. K82.1.1; devil extends t. up river G303.9.2.5; king vainly forbids t. to rise L414; spirit of t.-crack F429.1.

Tides. — Magic object controls t. D1545.1; magic object indicates t. D1324; origin of t. A913.

Tidings brought to the king: You said it, not I J1675.2.1.

Tied animal persuades another to take his place K842.3. — Deception into allowing oneself to be t. K713.1; fairies t. together by hair F239.1; importunate lover t. to tree K1218.7; marvelous runner keeps leg t. up F681.1; moon t. to sun A735.1; owner's hair t. while thief escapes with goods K338; rowing in a boat which is t. up J2164.2; sun t. to earth by beams of light A733.4; sun t. to sky A721.5.

Tiens-bon-là D1413.7, K1217.

Tiger as animals' king B240.13; attacks man pulling his thorn W154.3.2; beaten, fears man J17.1; becomes person D312.2; carries person B557.10; carries wood for saint B292.11; as child's nurse B535.0.8; and crane quarrel J428; crossing river with vat K1183; disguises as human being K1822.4; eats cow friend J427; enticed away, victims escape K629.2.1; enticed into coffin K714.2.2; enticed into pit by boar K735.6; flatters crow, kills her K815.9; formerly cooked its food A2435.1.2; frees man on promise to keep secret M295.1; frightened by clashing knives K2345.1; frightened of leak J2633; frightened off from prey K547.7ff.; frightened by wind K1727; gives man food for deer bait K361.3; -god A132.10; as god's messenger A165.2.1.1.2; guides lost man home: hence men do not eat tigers B563.4.1.1; has family of jaguars B672; to help foxes divide their young K579.5.2; hides guests in jar K649.1.2; hides woman from other tigers B525.1; in human form B651.9; -husband disenchanted D789.9; -killing tree K1715.6; lives on self-cooking food F989.22.2; made to frighten men L482.4; as magician B191.3; mistaken for horse, saddled N691.1.2; mistaken for other animal J1758; murders son of first couple A1277.3; persuaded to eat own eyes K1025.2; persuaded to enter house, locked in K737.2; plows for man B292.4.2; pretends to be girls' mother K2011.2; returns rope, tail cut off W154.11; seizes bridal couple Q557.7; settles jackals' argument K555.3; -shaped cake fulfills death prophecy M341.2.10.1; in sheep's clothing stolen by sheep-thief K1621; -slayer recognized by tiger parts H105.5.1; -slayers must not eat plant C226.0.1; son of human mother scratches, licks her U128; spares man returning to be eaten W37.2; spirit and man sons of same mother T554.1; stupid J1706.1; substituted for girl tears lecher Q243.6; substituted for woman in box: kills villain K1674; as suitor B621.3; sweeps temple for saint B256.7; thinks dog's tail a gun J1772.12; thinks water dropping sound of monster K1725.2; trip to underworld F98.1. — Abandoned son exposed to t. H105.5.4; abduction by t. R13.1.4; abduction by t.-man R16.4; axe becomes t. D1594.5; bee vitalizes t. D1594.3; being devoured by t. as punishment Q415.5; blind t. recognizes hypocrite F655.2; boar wins duel with t. K97.1; boys threaten to harness t. K1714; buffalo helps t. quench fire: white mark left on buffalo's neck where tiger held on while being ducked in water A2211.12; buffaloes save hero from t. B524.1.5.1; child borne off by t., which is caught by griffin, which is killed by lioness, who rears child with her whelps N215; coffin to prevent t. ghost E431.20; association of t. and crane J428; association of cow and t.: tiger eats cow as soon as she is hungry J427; cow thief grabs t. by mistake N392; creation of t. A1815; daughter promised to t. S232; devastating t. B16.2.2, G358; dog in disguise to frighten t. K1810.2; duel of buffalo and t. B264.3; enmity of t. and (cat) A2494.1.6, (dog) A2494.4.9, (hen) A2494.13.10.5, (boar) A2494.10.2, (man) A2494.10.1; false ascetic in partnership with t. K2058.2; fool rides t. J1758.1.1; four-eyed t. B15.4.1.2; friendship of t. and (buffalo) A2493.3, (cat) A2493.18, (cow, calf and cub) A2493.24, (deer) A2493.17, (jackal) A2493.11.3, A2493.11.5, A2493.14.1, (lion) A2493.30; ghost as t. E423.2.10; giant t. B871.2.2; girl eaten by t. reincarnated E613.0.6; headless king and tailless t. friends J876; helpful t. B431.3; hero cared for by t. A511.2.2.2; honest brahmin spared by t. Q151.10; horse arches neck to kick t. from rear A2351.6; hostile t. killed B16.2.2.1; husband promises t. a cow, wife frightens t. away K235.1.1; jackal and t. and business partners A2493.11.3; killing t. demons H335.3.6; killing t. by throwing hatchet in mouth K951.1.1.1; kindness to t. rewarded Q51.2; magic t. B181.3; man falling from tree frightens away t. N696.1; man gradually reincarnated as t. E695; man-t. B26; man transformed to t. D112.2; man-killing t. must not touch animals C549.1; man and t. in contest: winner to live in town A2250.1.1; marriage to wer-t. N399.3; marriage to t. B601.9; monkey jumps through body of t. F916.1; monkey gives t. sore-producing ointment K1043.1; monkey lures t. into tree, sets it afire K812.3; mythical t. B19.10; numskull's outcry overawes t. N691.1; old woman, t. flee each other K2323.3; ox- demon transformed to t. D412.2.3; quarreling couple were previously t. and dog T256.0.1; sham-dead t. betrayed by live penis K607.3.1; sham-warrior's boasting scares t. K1951.3.2; stripes of t. A2413.4; speaking t. B211.2.2.1; stick, rope frighten off t. K2336; strong man kills t. F628.1.1.1; tailless t. J876; tortoise escapes t. captor K563.1; treasure from t. B103.0.8; trickster's basket for t. partner K2033; trickster eats food left by t. K372.1; trickster to give t. wings K1013.4; two-headed t. B15.1.2.1.2; unborn child promised to t. S222.3; wer-t. D112.2.1; why t. does not attack wildboar until latter is old: result of duel A2257.1; witch rides on t. G241.1.7; why man and t. enemies A2281.1.1; why t. can't come down tree head foremost A2577; why t. lacks some qualities of cats A2581; why t. lives in jungle A2433.3.21; woman carried off by t. N392.2; woman marries t. G11.6.2.

Tiger's enemies A2494.10; fear of crabs exploited K1715.13; food A2435.3.9; paw mark on moon A751.5.4; short sight in day: good sight at night A2491.4. — Animal's tail tied to t. J2132.5.1; buffalo refuses t. dinner invitation J425.2; cat drives fish into t. mouth X1114.2; crab on t. tail J1762.3; crane pecks out t. eyes S165.2; escape by posing as t.

preceptor K601.1; fox drinks t. milk K362.5.1; fox sleeps with t. wife
K1354.2.3; god in t. skin A131.4; groom called "t. son" H151.15; hedgehog jumps into t. mouth L315.13; jackal escapes t. house K563.1; numskull on t. back injured J2132.4; origin of marks on t. face A2330.4;
quest for t. milk H1361.1; trickster eats all of t. cubs but one K933.

Tigers build bridge B299.8.1; dance B293.3; in hell A671.2.14; not discussed lest tiger-son return C441.1; stand on each other to reach man in
tree X1133.5. — Army of t. B268.9; buffaloes fail god: now killed by t.
A2231.12; divine twins cared for by mother of t. B241.2.8.1; ghosts of
those eaten by t. E419.12; girl rescued from t. R111.1.13; hero exterminates race of t. A531.3; king of t. B241.2.8; land of t. B221.6; man-t.
killed by one arrow F679.5.3; ogre changes men into t. G11.6.1; procuring four t. to guard palace H1154.3.7.1; seeds cast on lions and t.
render them helpless D1410.1; why slayers of t. must not eat certain
plants C226.0.1; why t. don't kill women who run away from husbands
A2499.1.

Tigress bears men-children B631.6; becomes mortar D421.4.1; grateful for
opening of abscess B386; swallows baby F914.3. — Mortar transformed
to t. D444.8; tasks to get t. H939.3; woman assists t. as midwife B387.

Tigress's. — Kid puts t. cub in his place: she eats it K1611.5.

Tile transformed to gold D475.1.7. — Taking t. from her house reveals
witch G257.4.

Tilling. — Magic t. D1620.2.7; rats t. soil for master B292.9.3.

Timber. — Good t. given for useless J2093.4.

Time, see also **When;** of appearance of wild hunt E501.11ff.; of death
postponed D1855; favorable for unearthing treasure N555; of giving
curse M412; personified Z122; renders all things commonplace J1075;
tabu C750ff.; is wisest (riddle) H659.9.1. — Absurd theories concerning
t. J2276; animal characteristic because creator runs short of t.
A2286.1.0.1; calculation of t. A1485; changing course of t. H1026;
compulsion to go to certain place at certain t. C666; disenchantment at
end of specified t. D791.1; no t. for lying today X905.4; lake forbidden
at certain t. C615.1; learning to read in extraordinarily short t. F695.3;
not to eat at certain t. C230ff.; goddess divides t. between upper and
lower worlds A316; invulnerability for limited t. D1845; journey to
Mother of T. F118, H1285; no t., no birth, no death in otherworld F172;
passage of t. U200ff.; primeval water to subside in a specified t. A810.2;
prophecy: death at certain t. M341.1; prophecy: hero's birth at certain
t. M311.0.2; resuscitation after great length of t. E162.0.1; resuscitation
impossible after certain length of t. E162; return from death for definite t. E166; river says, "T. has come but not the man" D1311.11.1;
supernatural lapse of t. in fairyland F377; tabu: doing thing after
certain t. C752; tabu: speaking before certain t. C402; tabu: one forbidden t. C630ff.; test of t. H1583; unlearned person wastes t. J252; women
have no t. to help God A1372.8.

Times. — Fairies visible only at certain t. F235.2; otherworld dwellings open only at certain t. F165.2.

Timid animal consoled when he sees others more timid J881. — Brave soldier and t. cabinet-maker as companions P444.1; dwarfs are bashful or t. F451.3.6.5, F451.5.19; more t. than the hare J881.1; why animal is t. A2534.

Timpan. — Bird plays t. B297.1.1.

Tin becomes silver D475.3.2; sail F841.2.6. — Hot t. under horse's tail K1181.

Tinder. — Magic t. *D1175.1; origin of t. A1414.5.

Tinsa. — Why t. bark is white A2751.4.4; why t. tree has no bark at bottom of trunk A2751.2.3.

Tint. — Gold t. as royalty sign H71.6.2.

Tiny, see also **Little, Small;** bow F836.4; fairy F239.4.3; wood-spirit F441.5.1.

Tir Tairngire Island F111.2.1.

Tired as if he had walked J1946. — Boat gets t. J1884; fighting though t. J356; hero t. of man, sends death A1335.9.1.

Titans. — Winds as children of t. A1123.

Tithes. — Ass insists upon payment of t. B259.1; monks persuade wives that they must pay t. as one tenth the number of times of their marital intimacies J2344.1; payment of t. P531.

Tithing. — Origin of t. A1548.

Tithonus given eternal life without eternal youth M416.2.

Title. — "Aforesaid" as t. J1749.1; his proper t. (swine) J1286.

Titmouse allowed to sing before sacrifice K551.3.7; ruffles feathers to enlarge himself J955.1.2.1; whistles for dogs to frighten fox K869.1. — Creation of t. A1918; crow refuses to marry 100-year-old t. B282.22.1; cumulative tale: t., what are you eating? Z39.4.1; friendship of fox and t. A2493.10; man transformed to t. D151.6; wedding of t. B282.8, (and crow) B282.22; why t. has no tongue A2344.2.4.

Toad, see also **Frog;** asks magpie in tree to throw down a chestnut (cumulative tale) Z43.1; carries man B559.1; carries mortars F982.6; carries tree F982.7; causes eclipses A737.3; considered venomous B776.2; controls rice paddies' flooding D2149.5; exchanges ugly daughter for lizard's K476.5; as follower of the devil G303.10.2; mistaken for food, eaten J1761.7; plays drum B297.1.2; receives water from frog K231.8; refuses to weep over its dead children: dries up when dead *A2231.8; remains still when he hears footsteps (defense) A2461.2; swallows woman's earthenware F911.6.1; trades his tail for mole's eyes A2247.5; transformed to man D396; as witch's familiar B225.4. — Cat transformed to t. D412.1.2; child shares food with t. B391.2; consecrated bread kept in mouth and fed to t. produces love D1355.10.1; contest lost by t., won by lizard A1319.12.1; daydreaming t. run over J2061.4; devil in form of t. G303.3.3.7.1; devil roasts t. G303.25.14.2; why t. dries up when dead A2231.8, A2468.2; dragon as modified t. B11.2.1.5; dying t. comforts his paramour J865; why t. has red eyes A2332.5.4; fairy in form of t. F234.1.5; helpful t. B493.2; laughing t. B214.3.1; lizard wins contest with t. A2250.2; magic t. B177.1; man grateful not hideous as t. W27.1; man transformed to t. D196; marriage to t. B645.1; meat transformed to t. D444.2; origin of t. A2161; ornaments of t. F827.3; over-hasty t. (lie) X1862; poisonous t. sits on food of undutiful children Q557.1; princess sick because t. has swallowed her consecrated wafer *V34.2; soul in form of t. E736.2; soul in t. E715.5.1; speaking t. B211.7.2; how t. lost tail A2378.2.7; undutiful son punished by t. clinging to face Q551.1; weeping t. B214.4.1; whistling t. B214.2.1; why t. has no thumbs A2375.2.9; why t. lives in cold place A2433.6.7; witch bone from t. G224.11.1; witch in form of t. G211.6.1; woman bears t. T554.8.1.

Toad's blood venomous B776.5.1; croak A2426.4.2; wedding B284.2. — Cause of t. hop A2441.4.3.

Toads in hell A671.2.8; suck blood B766.3; on way to otherworld F144.1. — Blood becomes t. D447.3.1; community of t. B226.1; curse: t. from mouth M431.2; during the day dwarfs appear in form of t. or other vermin F451.2.0.5; man kills serpents, t., dragons with own hands F628.1.3.1; war between t. and frogs B263.1; witch gives birth to t. G243.3.1; why t. have warts A2412.5.2.

Toadstools. — Fairy bread turns to t. F343.19.1.

Tobacco from grave of (bad woman) A2611.2, (virgin) A2611.2.1; pipe, and match debate usefulness to smoker J461.3; -spirit F445.1.1. — Dwarfs dislike t. smoke F451.3.6.3; earth from primeval water mixed with seeds of t. A814.7; girl eats only kola nuts and t. F561.5; magic t. plant D965.17, (hides treasure) D1463.4; origin of t. *A2691.2; parson takes a chew of t. during the sermon X445.2; person lives by smoking t. F561.4; quest for magic t. H1333.2.2; recognition by t.-pipe H147; reincarnation as t. plant E631.5.1; why men like t. A2854; wind raised by blowing into t. pipe D2142.1.6.1; woman reborn as t. plant E694.2.

Toboggan test H1536.

Tod des Hühnchens Z32.1.1.

Today. — Origin of t. A1178.

Today's catch traded for tomorrow's J321.1.1. — Is t. sun same as yesterday's? J2272.2.

Toe. — Child's missing t. proves legitimacy T318; feet backward prevent t. stubbing F517.1.5.1; identification of man by his little t. H79.2; magic t. D995.1; mistaking own t. for snake's head J1838; recognition by missing t. H57.3; sixth t. cut off as execution proof K512.2.4.1; stumping t. a bad omen D1812.5.1.31.

Toes mistaken for ghosts, shot off J1782.8. — Backward-pointing t. F441.4.4; devil's footprints without t. G303.4.5.3.2; feet with unusual number of t. F551.2; Jesus drives evil spirits into hogs: hence "t." on back of foreleg A2287.1.1; ladder of t. F848.2; mutilation by cutting off t. S162.3; stepping on t. as reminder of lying X904.1.

Toenail. — Hero creates companion from t. A511.1.4.4; man from creator's t. A1211.5.1.

Toenails. — Cutting t. of cannibal woman G519.1.2.

Toilet. — Girl makes t. and calls help K551.5; respite from death until t. is made permits escape K551.7; tabu: attending t. needs C720ff.

Token. — Betrothal t. sent bridegroom's parents T61.4.4; bride to suitor giving greatest love t. H315.2; disguise by carrying false t. K1839.8; life-t. *E761ff.; object stolen as infidelity t. T247; paramour leaves t. with girl to give their son *T645; victim lured by false t. K839.2.

Tokens from a dream F1068.1; of royalty (nobility) left with exposed child S334. — False t. of woman's unfaithfulness K2112.1; god recognized by t. H45.4; identification by t. *H80—H149; return from dead to return and ask back love t. E311.

Toll fraudulently collected K157.1.

Tollkeeper. — Ass as t. B292.13.

Tom-Tit-Tot *C432.1.

Tom-tom beats out king's news P14.20; frightens off ogre K547.6.

Tomb, see also **Grave;** gate magically enlarged D482.5.2; robbed, man buried alive escapes R212.1.1. — Curative waters touching holy t. D1500.1.18.1.1; deer lick saint's t. daily B251.2.6; friends clasp hands through t. P319.5; king refuses fine t. J912.2; lover finds lady in t. apparently dead T37; lover at t. takes poison T37.1; magic t. D1148, (kills) D1402.32; man buried alive with king escapes from the t. R212.1; numskull objects to unhealthy place for his t. J1937.2; resuscitation by vigil at t. E62; riddle: what was the walking t. with the living tenant H821; test: vigil at t. H1460ff.; words from t. E545.0.1.

Tombs. — Saints' t. distill oil V229.2.9.

Tommy Knockers F456.1.

Tomorrow. — Debt to be paid "t." K231.12; inscription "Come t." rots: devil claims soul K231.12.1.

Tomorrow's — Today's fish catch traded for t. J321.1.1.

Tomtit's. — Hornbill borrows t. bill A2241.9.

Ton. — Strong man lifts t. of rye F624.5.

Tongs. — Automatic fire t. D1601.24; gods wrought t. A1402.

Tongue debates with other bodily members J461.1.3; cut off as punishment Q451.4; of dead lawyer found to be lacking P422.1.1; as path to sky F57.2; as proof that man has been murdered H105.2; protusion for breaking tabu C948.3; transformed to other object D457.14. — "Ave" on the t. V254.3; books in church read without man's t. F1055; camel's t. as "one pound of flesh" payment K255.4; cobra writes letter on prince's t. B165.1.3; crocodile punished for attacking man: has only half t. A2239.7; cut-out t. magically restored D2161.3.6.1; dragon-t. proof H105.1; dupe wishing to learn to play flute puts t. in split bamboo

K1111.0.1.1; fools try to use buffalo t. as a knife J1971; forked t. reveals disguised snake K1822.3; goat's t. pierced, so is witch's G252.2; gold under t. restores speech D1507.8; leek under t. of dead protects D1389.12; magic object under dead girl's t. D849.6; magic t. D992.5; magic animal t. D1011.6; magic speaking t. D1610.5.1; magpie tells man he is to die next day: no t. and long tail A2236.4; minstrel throws wife into sea: her t. the heaviest thing on board T251.1.5; mutilation: cutting (tearing) out t. *S163; origin of t. A1316.5; origin and nature of animal's t. A2344; person without t. F513.2; punishment for cutting off bird's t. Q285.1.1; punishment: t. protrudes from sinner's mouth Q551.8.6; remarkable t. F544.2; ring under dead girl's t. D765.1.1.1; saint with t. of fire V229.11; sharp instrument as t. deceives ogre G572.2; stretching t. as punishment Q451.4.10; substituted t. E782.5; symbolic meaning of spiced t. H604; talkative wife's t. paralysed D2072.0.5.3; tempted man bites out his t. and spits it in temptress's face T333.1; thread under dumb man's t. cut F954.1; victim persuaded to hold out his t.: cut off K825; woman's t. swells for lying Q583.4.

Tongues. — Animals duped into turning t. upside down K1064; confusion of t. *A1333; dogs with fiery t. in wild hunt E501.4.1.2; enemies' t. as trophies S139.2.2.1.1; ghosts as dogs with glowing t. and eyes E421.3.6; magic knowledge of strange t. *D1815; riddle: seven t. in a head H793.

Tongue-tied heretic Q551.7.1.1.

Tonsure. — Druidic t. P427.1.4.

Tool for unlawful work sticks to user Q551.2.5.

Tools magically sharpened D2199.2. — Acquisition of t. A1446; fairies borrow t. F391.3; giants throw t. back and forth F531.3.2.3; god fashions t. A1402; iron t. become earth D479.2; lie: remarkable t. X1024; witch scatters t. at night G265.1; worship of t. V1.9.

Toolmaker. — God compared to t. J1262.6.

Tooth falls out if charm is incorrectly applied D1273.0.5; transformed to fox D477.6; transformed to axe head D457.8. — Bed made from t. F787.4; blue t. identifies man H79.8; brake where saint loses t. bursts into flame V222.2; cannibal has long t. and long nail G88; dead man's t. as cure for toothache D1502.2.1; heathen to desert spot where saint lost t. M364.5; knocking out slave's t. entitles him to freedom P178.1; knowledge t. D1810.3, (detects crime) K1817.3, (reveals events in distant place) D1813.3; luck residing in t. N101.4; N113.2.2; magic animal t. D1011.4; magic t. *D1009.2; mortal wound from killed enemy's t. N339.16; prince gives away own t. W11.7; recognition by broken t. H57.1; three women have but one t. among them F513.1.1; why frog lacks t. A2239.8; wife persuades her husband to have good t. pulled J2324.

Teeth blackened for breaking tabu C985.2; of slain cyclops H105.5.2. — Animal's strong t. B747; child born with all t. T585.5; children's t. on edge after fathers eat sour grapes U18; contest: pulling on steak with t. K64; corpse asks golden t. be sold E443.2.1.1; devil's t. G303.4.1.5;

giant with t. like those of saw F531.1.6.2; fairies work with t. F271.0.2; false t. overawe Indians K547.2; filing away chain with t. R121.10; giant polishes t. with tree F621.2.2; god with gold t. A125.3; goddess with pig's t. A131.8; huldra with long t. F460.1.6; lion suitor allows his t. to be pulled and claws cut J642.1; love through seeing marks of lady's t. in fruit which she has bitten T11.4.4; magic lost when t. gone D1741.8; man's t. like axeheads F531.2.12; man created from sown dragon t. A1265; monster with golden t. B101.5; mutilation: knocking out t. S164; no t. as excuse for not drinking J1391.6; ogress whets t. to kill captive G83.1; one of the old maid's three t. breaks off X754; origin and nature of animal's t. A2345; origin of t. A1316.6; person un- usual as to his t. F513.1; plowing with t. F1099.6.1; pulling out two t. for price of one J2213.7; recognition of disenchanted person by thread in his t. H64.1; red t. as sign of royalty H71.9; remarkable t. F544.3; return from dead to punish t. theft E235.4.6; revenant with chip of resin between t. E422.1.7; servant allowed anything he can take with t. J1161.10; sheep's t. J1391.3; soldier with severed hands fights with t. P461.1; sorcerer's power lost when his t. are knocked out D1741.8; sowing dragon's t. (task) H1024.5; successful suitor must have gold t. H312.2; sword between t. tokens defeat P555.1; warriors use t. F1084.2; why animal lacks t. A2345.7; wife carried up tree to the sky in bag in husband's t. J2133.5.1; witch drinks boiling oil to beautify t. G525.1; witch with extraordinary t. G214; women's vaginal t. A1313.3.1, F547.1.1; woodspirits' t. on stomachs F441.4.6.

Toothache. — False remedy for t. K1015; magic object cures t. D1502.2; witch causes t. G263.4.1.

Toothed penis F547.3.3; private parts F547.1. — Diamond-t. ogre G363.3.

Top. — Men hang down in a chain until t. man spits on his hands J2133.5; mountain with marvelous objects at t. F759.1; sun and moon placed in t. of tree A714.2.

Topographical features of the earth A900ff.; lies X1500. — Lie: hero responsible for t. features X958.

Topsy-turvy land X1505.

Tora as God's adviser A44. — Creation on condition Israel accept T. A74.1; extraordinary events at T. giving F960.10; neglect of T. punished Q223.10.1; oath by T. M114.1.1; study of T. as religious service V97.

Torch within enemy's camp signal for attack K2369.8. — Dead man wanders with t. E594; dwarf has silver miner's t. bright as the sun F451.7.4; life bound up with burning t. E765.1.2.

Torches. — Eyeballs become t. D457.11.2; god with spears as t. A137.14.2; lightning as t. of invisible dancer A1141.7.1; trickster bluffs old woman with t. K335.0.10.

Tormented. — Bull who cannot catch him t. by mouse L315.2; old man who has laid aside his humility t. by devil Q331.1; spirit t. by exorciser F405.14.

Tormenting by magic D2063.1; woman by chaste sleeping together T354. — Demons t. men G302.9.2; devils t. sinners in hell E755.2.7.

Torn garment proves man innocent of rape J1174.5. — Living t. to pieces by dead E267; murderer t. limb from limb Q469.12.

Tornado sunsets A1148.

Tortoise, see also **Turtle;** as animals' king B240.5; breaks elephant's back N335.7; carried, eaten by eagle J657.2; catches ogre helping him K1111.3; cheats leopard of meat K476.1.2; as creator's companion A36; cursed for going under water while ferrying rice-goddess A2231.7.3; and dog partners and thieves B294.7; escapes tiger captor K563.2; given hard shell for ferrying rice-goddess A2223.6; as God's footstool A139.2; lets self be carried by eagle J657.2; has no liver or teeth B723; jumps on, kills rhinoceros N622.1; leads elephant into trap K730.4; left in tree S143.2.1; outwits fowler, gets ruby K439.7.1; shell dug up, man dies E765.4.7; speaks and loses his hold on the stick J2357; as wooer B622.3. — Captured goose warns t. B143.1.6; creation of t. A2147; earth rests on t., serpent, elephant A844.6; enmity between panther, antelope, and t. A2494.12.1; fight between ape and t. B264.5; food of t. A2435.6.1; friendship between antelope, woodpecker, and t. A2493.32; giant t. B875.4; god as t. A132.15; hare and t. race: sleeping hare K11.3; helpful t. B491.5; why t. has humpy back *A2356.2.9; why t. lives in logs in stream A2433.6.1.1; magic t. fed with salt gives pearls B103.1.6; magic t. shell produces pearls D1469.14; man disguises as t. K1823.1; man transformed to t. D193; marriage to t. B604.2; ogre captured by t. G514.8.1; partridge's voice borrowed from t. A2241.3; prophetic t. B148.1; reincarnation as t. E614.4; storm frees marooned t. N662; why t. is amphibious A2214.5; why t. has short tail A2216.4, A2378.4.4; why t. has no voice A2421.4, A2422.4; woman bears t. T554.5.

Tortoise's foolish association with peacock J684.3. — Markings on t. back A2412.5.1; monkeys steal t. salt K343.4; origin of t. shell *A2312.1; why t. neck is outstretched to sky: is looking for his wife, the star A2351.5.

Torture *S180ff.; feigned K512.3; as punishment Q450.1. — Ascetic's self-t. V462.5; instruments of t. transformed to lotus flowers D454.16; magic objects enable one to withstand inquisitorial t. D1394.2; prisoner kills his watchers who enter to t. him K655; prophecy of t. M359.4; secret learned by t. N482; self-t. to secure holiness V464; servant undergoes t. for master P361.8; unremitting t. as punishment Q501ff.; virginity saved despite t. T320.1.1.

Tortured. — Ogre t. by not being allowed to sleep G585.

Tossing. — God t. created things into air A67.

Totem. — Eating t. animal forbidden C221.2; killing t. animal tabu C841.7; using t. tree for bed tabu C848.

Totems. — Animal t. B2.

Totemistic gods A113.

Toucan. — Man becomes t. D169.3; why beak of t. is black A2343.2.2.

Touch. — Birthmark removed at t. of dead man's hand E542.2; blood springs from corpse at t. of murderer's finger D1318.5.2; child's t. resuscitates E149.3; devil's t. marks G303.4.8.10; disenchantment by t. D782; Midas's golden t. D565.1, J2072.1; not to t. possessions of god C51; sight or t. of woman as source of sin T336; transformed animal refuses to t. meat of that animal D686.

Touched. — Keeping first thing t. K285; living man t. by dead man E542.

Touching corpse before burial E431.15; fruit tabu C621.2; head as acceptance sign P675; supernatural husband C32.2.3. — Devil t. body, not soul G303.25.18; disenchantment by t. water D766.1.2; don't sit on bed without t. it first J21.34.2; giant immortal while t. land of his birth D1854; king never t. earth P14.5; magic cure by t. D2161.4.16; magic knowledge from t. "knowledge tooth" with thumb D1810.3; magic powers from t. D1799.4; magic strength by t. earth *D1833; magic wishing-ring loses power by t. water D877.1; resuscitation by t. body E11.3; strength of witches depends on their t. earth G221.2; tabu: t. *C500—C549; tabu: t. deity's image with dirty hands C51.7; transformation by t. D565; vow against t. certain thing M172.

Tournament, see also **Contest;** with bride H332.1.4. — Devil accompanies knight to t. G303.8.9.1; hearing masses causes triumph in t. V41.2; suitor contest: t. H331.2; test of valor: t. H1561.1; three days' t. R222; Virgin substitutes in t. K1841.2.

Tournaments P561.

Tove's magic ring T85.4.1.

Tow transformed to person D439.1. — Husband made to believe that yarn has changed to t. through his carelessness J2325; paramour burned in barrel of t. K1554.1.

Tower of Babel F772.1, D2004.9.1, F941.3.1, Z71.6.4; neither too large, too high C771.1.1; in otherworld F163.7; to upper world F58. — Birds fly into t. of fire B172.10.1; dwarfs build t. F451.3.4.1.1; not to build too high a t. *C771.1; captivity in t. R41.2; confinement in t. to avoid fulfillment of prophecy M372; extraordinary t. F772; giant breaks from t. prison R211.1; girl's long hair as ladder into t. F848.1; fool gives three explanations of how the t. was built J2711; hill as unfinished t. like Nimrod's A963.8; magic t. D1149.2; measuring the t. by piling up hampers J2133.6.1; moving church t. J2328; princess builds t. of skulls of unsuccessful suitors *S110.3; quest for axe which sticks in beam outside a t. H1338; securing eggs from atop glass t. H1114.1; suitor contest: riding to fourth story of t. H331.1.2; virgin imprisoned in t. to prevent knowledge of men *T381.

Town crier frightened by grave robber K335.0.8; of fools J1703; mouse and country mouse J211.2; people transformed into witches G263.3.1. — Birds indicate building site of t. B155.2.3; why cock lives in t. A2433.4.2; why elephant does not live in t. A2433.3.15; ghosts punish intruders into ghost t. E241; how was t. burned? J2062.3; man and tiger in contest:

winner to live in t. A2250.1.1; punishment: sending out of t. on donkeys
Q473.5; tabued pot broken: t. appears C917.1.

Toy. — Giant's t. F531.5.3.

Track. — Bear knows if person looks at his t. D1813.0.1; life token: t.
fills with blood E761.1.3; thumbling lost in animal t. F535.1.1.5; transformation by drinking from animal's t. D555.1.

Tracks. — Covering t. immobilizes witch G273.7; fox sees all t. going
into lion's den but none coming out J644.1; hunter wants to be shown
lion t., not lion himself W121.1; person of remarkable sight finds t. of
swine stolen seven years before his birth F642.2; sticking objects into t.
pains witch G271.4.6; wild huntsmen leave fiery t. E501.7.6.3.

Tracker. — Skillful t. F677.

Tracking. — Dogs t. down law-breakers B578.

Trade involving eggs, needles and rum W154.26.1. — Devil fails to learn
t. G303.13.4; don't be greedy in making a t. J21.26; fairies must t.
whenever it is demanded of them F255.1; learning a t. in bed W111.5.9;
noble person saves self from difficulties by knowledge of a t. P51; origin
of t. between two places A1471.1; prince learning t. H335.0.2.2, P31;
son insists on following father's t. P401; sons meet after learning t. M271;
tailor married to princess betrays t. by calling for needle and thread
H38.2.1; youth learns robbery as a t.: boasts of it K301.1.

Trades and professions P400—P499. — God of t. A450ff.; parents murder
sons mentioning lowly t. S311.1; stupid sons use t. to harm father J2499.7.

Trader. — Barber wants to become t. J513.2.

Tradesmen of hell A677. — Humor dealing with t. X200—X299; treacherous officers and t. K2240ff.

Trading magic object away D871; wives T292.1. — Farmer cheated in t.
horses with devil G303.25.12.

Traditions. — Christian t. concerning Jews *V360ff.; forgotten t. J1445;
robber innocent because he is merely following t. of his ancestors J1179.4.

Tragedy. — Ghost haunts love t. scene E334.2.3; reenactment of t. E337.2;
trees wither at t. F979.23.

Tragic love T80ff. — Sun eclipses to avoid t. happenings A737.10.

Trail leads to abandoned person R135; magically closed D2089.9; of
stolen goods made to lead to dupe K401.1.1. — Faster one walks, longer
the t. D1783.3; tokens left as t. H86; walking backwards leaves misleading
t. K534.3.

Train of angels V242.1; leaves overpolite travelers J2183.2; of troubles
from (lost horseshoe nail) N258, (sparrow's vengeance) N261. — Devil in
woman's t. G303.8.9; phantom t. E535.4.

Traits of character W (entire chapter). — Fanciful t. of animal *B700—
B799.

Traitor thrown into pit, chased from country Q417.2. — Burning as
punishment for t. Q414.0.5.

Traitor's ashes thrown into lake, wind raised D2142.1.4.1.

Traitors, see **Treachery** *K2200—K2299.

Tramp. — Carrying the plow horse so as not to t. up the field J2163; transformation to t. D24.4, D659.12.

Trampling (kicking) to death by horses as punishment Q416.1. — Murder by t. S116.6.

Trance. — Body in t. while soul is absent E721.2; journey to heaven in t. F11.1; wizard detects thief by t. D1817.0.1.6.

Transferred. — Animal bodily members t. to person E780.2; curse t. to another person or thing M422; disease t. to another person or thing by magic object D1500.3; fish t. from tank to river B375.1.2; milk t. from another's cow by magic D2083.3; sickness t. to animal D2064.3; stolen object t. to innocent person K401.2.3; wish foolishly t. to wife J2075; witch power t. G224.10.

Transferring. — Cure by t. disease (to animal) *D2161.4.1, (to dead) E595.

Transform. — Hero's power to t. girl to carnation brings about recognition H151.7; ogre teaches smith how to t. sand in his smithy G651; witch's hair has power to bind or to t. G221.1.1.

Transformation D0—D699; animal to person D300—D399; and dis-enchantment at will D630ff.; for breaking tabu C960ff.; combat D615; as fitting punishment Q584; flight D671; of giant into mouse by trickery K722; of man to animal D100—D199, (as punishment) Q584.2; of god to guise of mortal D42; of man to different man D10—D99; of man to object D200—D299; of man to woman D12; of one animal to another D410ff.; in order to eat own kind G12; to old man to escape recognition D1891; of people by dwarfs F451.3.3.3; by saint before druid H1573.3.3; of woman to a man D11; by witch *G263; of witch into snake when she bathes G245.1. — Animal characteristics from t. A2260ff.; animal cries a lament over animal's t. A2275.2; creation of animals through t. *A1710ff.; creation of plants by t. A2610ff.; dragon's power of self-t. B11.5.1; means of t. D500—D599; plants characteristics from t. A2731ff.; murder through t. K928; periodic t. D620ff.; punishment: t. to deer which is devoured by dogs Q415.1.1; punishment: t. of lovers into lion and lioness for desecrating temple Q551.3; repeated t. D610ff.; request for immortality punished by t. into tree Q338.1; river from t. A934.11; rocks from t. of people to stone A974; seduction on promise of magic t. K1315.3.2; self t. (of fairy) F272, (of hero) A527.3.1.

Transformed brother as bird N733.4; fairy F234; golden pumpkin J1531.1; person as helper N819.2; person is swallowed and reborn in new form *E607.2; person sleeps before girl's door, at foot of bed, in bed K1361.1; prince killed N324.1; wife rescues husband R152.5. — Abduction by t. person R16; adulteress t. to mare and stirruped Q493.1; animal t. to man wants to marry woman B650.1; animals t. from other animals B318; animals from men t. for discourtesy to God (Jesus) *A1715.2; animals in otherworld pass in and out of church and are t. to human beings

*F171.5; ashes t. to insects, snakes to protect hero K2351.2.2; bad women from t. hog and goose A1371.3; cat from t. eagle A1811.1; devil's horses are t. men G303.7.1.2; devil's money t. to ashes G303.21.1; dog to avoid seeing husband t. K2371.4; extraordinary companions are t. animals F601.6; fairy t. as punishment F386.4; fairy t. to fly allows self to be swallowed by woman and reborn as fairy F392; ghost t. into animal E453; giant as t. man F531.6.1.2; husband t. (by adulteress) K2213.6, (to get rid of him) K1535; identification by feather taken from hero when he was t. to bird H78.2; Io t. to cow with gadfly ceaselessly pursuing Q501.6; man t. to beast becomes leader of herd B241.3; man had rather remain t. to mule than to live with his shrewish wife T251.1.3; man t. to animal kept as pet by heroine T33; man t. to horse and ridden by witch G241.2.1; male t. in womb to female T577.1; maltreated children t. S365; man's human wife t. by fairy mistress F302.5.2; not to mention original form of t. person C441; ogre captured while t. to animal G514.4; person t. to moon A747; recognition of person t. to animal H62; recognition of t. person among identical companions H161; sister faithful to t. brother P253.2; stolen animal magically t. K406.3; sun and moon beget stones and birds: these t. to first parents A1271.2; tabu: wife seeing t. husband C32.1.1; thief claims to have been t. into an ass K403; true bride t. by false K1911.2.1; wedding party t. into wolves by old beggar T155; woman t. to animal bears animal T554.0.1.

Transformer transformed Q584.1.

Transformers D683.1. — Original creator followed by t. A72.

Transforming monkeys to humans T68.5. — Adulteress t. man to stone K1535.1; dupe t. self into animal, can't change back K1062; fairy t. self F234.0.1; husband tests wife's faithfulness by t. himself *T235; jealous wife t. rival to dog T257.2.2; princess t. self to woo T55.11; sorceress t. new husband each day T113.1; witch t. man to object G263.2; wood-spirits t. men into animals F441.6.2.

Transfusion. — Son sold for blood t. S268.2.

Transition formulas Z10.3.

Translation to otherworld without dying F2.

Transmutation of the quail J1269.5.

Transparent body F529.5, (of pregnant woman) T579.8.1; stone F809.7.

Transplanting feather from one bird to another F668.3.

Transportation during magic sleep D1976.1; to or from upper world F60ff. — Gods with unusual t. A136ff.; magic object affords miraculous t. *D1520ff.; magic t. *D2120ff.; sham magician claims t. by demons K1963.6.

Transporting. — Ghost t. human E599.12; spirit t. people F414.

Trap. — Animal (grateful for rescue from t.) B364.1, (rescues from t.) B545; birds discuss the t. J655.1; chasing a hare into every t. in a high tree (task) H1024.3; contest in jumping into a t. K17.3; deceiver falls into own t. K1600—K1699; getting bait from t. by luring in another animal K1115.1; maiden in t. gives self to rescuer Q53.3.1; man enters girl's room through t.-door concealed in floor K1348.1; musician in wolf t. B848.1; paramour falls in t. K1574.1; perilous (t. bridge) *F842.2.1, (t. gate) F842.2.1.1; pitch-t. for fleeing girl J1146.1; small animals dupe larger into t. L315.15; trickster takes an oath by touching t. K1115; wait till I'm taken from t., then eat me K553.1.1.

Traps. — Origin of fish t. A1457.5.

Trapped. — Ogre t. in box (cage) G514.1; victim t. *K730ff., (by ogre) G421; wife and paramour t. with magic armor K1563.

Trapping contest won by deception K32. — Suitor contest: t. H331.9; wounding by t. with sharp knives (glass) S181.

Trappings. — Ass envies horse in fine t. J212.1.

Trash magically becomes food D2105.3.1. — Treasure box filled with t.: joint owners quarrel K2131.4.

Travel to wedding T133. — Devil and the wind t. together G303.6.3.3; forbidden t. direction C614.1; futility of distant t. J1076; transformation to t. fast D644.

Traveler meets ghost E332.2. — Devil (gentleman) invites t. into his wagon G303.7.1.2.2; devil invites t. to feast G303.25.17.1; devil as ribald t. G303.3.1.3.1; ghost misleads t. E272.5; man helps t. and makes riddling remarks H586.1; sham t. K1969.1; woman entertaining every t. H152.1.1.

Travelers draw swords in advance J2255; find exposed baby, save her S354.2; to other world not to look back C331.2; pursued by misfortune N251.4. — Brownie murders t. F363.2; deaf peasant: t. ask the way X111.2; devil as crow misleads t. G303.9.9.17; fairies lead t. astray F369.7; god of t. A491; hawthorn protects t. D1385.2.3; jokes about t. X583; ogress devours t. from cave G94.1; phantom t. E510; riddle: who are real t.? (sun, moon) H726.

Traveling prolongs life thousand years D1855.5; stones F809.5; till iron shoes are worn out *H1125; tooth F544.3.6. — Curse: woman not t. far M459.1; advice on t. with money J21.39; animal t. extraordinary distance B744; devil's t. G303.7ff.; dragon t. on sea or land B11.4.4; fairies t. through air F282; ghost t. swiftly E599.5; girl rescued by t. through air *R111.3.1; ghost t. under ground E591; magic horse t. on sea or land *B184.1.4; numskulls go t. J1711; riddling remarks of t. companion interpreted by girl at end of journey H586ff.; sunken bell t. on sea bottom V115.1.1; tabu: t. beyond spot where feat of skill was performed before duplicating it C888; wife t. for years seeking husband's cure T215.7.

Tray. — Cannibal with winnowing t. and pestle G11.12; stealing t. from king's bedside H1151.3.1.

Treacherous disposal of true bride by false K1911.2; impostors K1930ff.; murder during hunt K917; persons *K2200—K2299; philosophers P485.1; priests prolong mass to let enemy destroy city K2354; river F932.8.4;

servants assign tasks H919.1; soldier suggests task H919.5. — Counselor killed in own t. game K1626.2; king's son has t. foster brother P273.1.2.

Treachery *K2000ff.; punished *Q261. — Bird reveals t. B131.2; confessing all t. wins bride H331.11; death as punishment for t. Q411.4; demons goad man to t. G302.9.9; detection of t. K2060ff.; elder brothers banished for t. Q431.2; gods' t. brings death to man A1335.14; horse reveals t. B133.2; lovers separated by t. T84.

Treacle. — Lover made to fall into t. pit K1218.1.3.2.

Tread. — Plants from t. of holy person A2621ff.

Treading. — Magic sight by t. on another's foot *D1821.1.

Treason punished Q217. — King's advisor falsely accused of t. K2126.1.

Treasonable. — Innocent man compelled to write t. letter K2156.

Treasure buried with dead V67.3; and jewels in otherworld F166.1; animal *B100ff.; cast down crushes besiegers K2353; chest breaks avaricious man's neck Q272.2; disappears C401.3, D1555.3, N553.2; falls from mouth *D1454.2; -finders who murder one another K1685; given away or sold for trifle J2093; given away by saint restored V411.5; -guarding snake H335.3.4; hidden in tree's roots D2157.3.2; -laying bird B103.2.1; -producing animals B103ff.; as reward Q111.6; reward for selling lizard thread J1852.1.1; struck from phantom's hand F585.4; transformed to ducks D449.3; trove N500—N599. — Accidental acquisition of t. N630ff.; animal gives t. to man B583; animals guard t. B576.2; animal shows man t. B562.1; demon brings t. to benefactors G514.0.1; discovery of t. brings luck N135.2.1; dog indicates hidden t. *B153; doves show monk t. B562.1.3; dream of marking t. X31; dream of t. on the bridge N531.1; drowning in attempt to save t. J2146.2; druid causes t. loss P427.0.2; dupe digging t. from ant hill K1125; dwarfs direct mortals to t. F451.5.1.9; dragon feeds on t. B11.6.3; dragon guards t. *B11.6.2; dwarfs possess t. F451.7.1; eater of magic fish to spit up t. M312.3.1; entrusting t. as honesty test H1555.1; escaping robbers by promising to show them t. K567.2; fairy lured away by t. F381.5; fairies' t. F244; father's counsel: find t. within a foot of the ground H588.7; fool hides t. and leaves sign J2091.1; foolish dog finds t. and dies rather than leave it J1061.3; ghost laid when t. is unearthed E451.5; ghost points out t. E545.12; ghost steals t. E593.5; ghosts protect t. E291; giant's t. F531.6.7; hand-of-glory indicates location of t. D1314.5; hanging for silence about t. Q413.7; helpful animal discovers t. B562.1; hero hides in t. box, secures own share K677.1; hero leaves bedmate keys to t. chamber T645.4; hogs root up t. for saint B562.1.1; inexhaustible t. D2100.1; introducing t. animal into flock K2131.5; island covered with t. F731; jewels aid in search for t. D1314.8; magic object furnishes t. *D1450ff.; magic plant (flower) shows location of t. D1314.7; magic t. D2100ff., (as reward) Q142; magic t. animal killed D876; magic t. gives miraculous powers D1561.2.2; magic wand locates hidden t. *D1314.2; man finds t. he refused as gift N224; mandrake shows location of t. D1314.7.1;

miser transported to t.-wood F414.2; miser's t. stolen J1061.4; money or
t. given by dwarfs F451.5.1.5; mountain of t. F752; object transformed
to t. D475; pseudo-t.-producing objects sold K111; quest for t. in
hell H1275; refusal to tell of Rhine t. K239; return from dead
to reveal hidden t. E371; return from dead to seek t. E372;
return from dead to uncover t. E415.1.2; robbers' hidden t. stolen
K439.10; sacrifice made when t. is found V13; sale of false t.
K120ff.; not to speak while searching for t. C401.3; serpent demon
guards t. G354.1.1; sham priest claims can discover t. K1961.1.4; snake's
hoarded t. E765.4.6; spirit in hornet form guards t. F403.2.3.1; starving
woman to death for t. K2116.2.2; storm from calling up spirits to help
find buried t. D2141.0.2; swamp spirit guards t. F494.1.1; task: raising
a buried t. H1181; tax on t. P531.2; test of honesty: man entrusted with
t. H1555.1; thief persuades owner of goods to dive for t. K341.4; troll's
t. obtained by casting steel F455.6.4.2; underground t. chambers F721.4.

Treasures. — Dragon from transformed man lying on his t. B11.1.3;
dwarfs dig for t. F451.6.9; giants fight about t. F531.6.8.3.1; journey
to get lower world t. F81.5; not to touch t. of otherworld C542; preferring princess to t. H511.1.2; saint scratches earth, t. appear D2157.1.1.

Treasurer. — Treacherous t. K2249.2.

Treasury. — Animal gets t. keys K341.18; means of entering house or t.
K310ff.; mismanagement of king's t. a mortal offense P13.2.

Treatment of husband's good eye K1516.1. — Cobold avenges uncivil t.
F481.1; disenchantment by rough t. D710ff.; resuscitation by rough t.
*E10ff.

Treaty. — Making t. tabu C751.5; satirizing as punishment for breaking t.
Q499.4.1.

Tree aids escape from lower world F101.5; alleged to produce clothes
K118.1; appealed to as arbitrator D1311.4.1; appears to save saint from
abyss V222.10; bends to certain person D1648ff.; beside holy well
V134.0.1; blooms out of season D2145.2.2.2; bows before prince H71.10.1;
of cakes D2106.3; consumed by anchorite's breath D2082.2; cursed for
serving as cross A2721.2.1; cut down with axe for which it furnished
a handle J162; cut down to get victim in top K983.1; by day, man by
night D621.2; from which one cannot descend D1413.1; -destroying
monsters G346.3.1; dies when owner dies E766.2; with extraordinary
fruit F811.7; feeds abandoned children S376; follows murderer N271.9;
grateful D1658.1.5; grows from rod used in saint's birth T584.0.5; grows
out of horse and gives rider shade X1130.2.2; guarded by dragon
H1333.6; guarded by ghosts H1151.10; half green and half in flame in
otherworld garden F162.1.2.4; in hell made of living heads of the dead
A671.2.3; of immortality D1346.4; from innocent man's blood E631.0.5;
inside seventh series of forts H1333.5.0.2; on which Judas hanged himself cursed A2721.5; of knowledge J165, (eaten by serpent) B123.1.1; of
Life *E90ff., (in otherworld) F162.3.1; magically withers D2082.0.2;

opens and conceals fugitive D1393.1; points way to fugitive but misdirects enemy D1393.4; produced by magic D951, D2178.8; protects
D1380.2; protects Jesus from rain: is green all year A2711.4; pulled
down in order to give it water to drink J1973; -pulling contest K46;
refuge *R311; as repository of fire A1414.7.1; with silver branches
D1461.0.2; from sinner's grave E631.0.6; -spirits C43.2; springs back to
kill enemies K1112.1; supports sky A665.4; transformed (to animal)
D441.1, (to other object) D451.1, (to person) D431.2, (to stone) D471.6;
-trunks laid crosswise of the sledge J1964; as underworld roadway
F95.5; to upper world *F54; warns of danger *D1317.20; as wife
T461.3. — Abandonment on stretching t. K1113; abandonment in t.
S143.2; all-yielding t. in otherworld F162.1.3.1; animals emerge from t.
A1793; animals in t. cause its breathing X1116; bending the t. K1112;
big t. thought to be snake J1771.1; birth from a t. T543.1; blindness
cured by striking t. F952.4; boy in the hollow t. X1854.1; bonga lives
in t. F216.2; buckeye (or other t.) selected as repository for fire
A1414.7.1; branching t. as roadway for souls E750.2.3; bringing
marvelous t. suitor test H355.3; captivity in t. R49.1; capture between
t. branches K742; capture by hiding in hollow t. K763; caste from
catching t. A1651.2; castle in t. top F771.2.2; chopping down large t.
with blunt (fragile) instrument (task) H1115; child abandoned in hollow
t. S143.1; child born in t. T581.3; city inside a t. F765; climbing t. leads
to adventures N776.1; conception from embracing magic t. T532.1.2;
corpses exposed in t. V61.10; creation of man from t. A1251; creator
rests on t. or stake A813.3; crow seems to have caused t. to fall J953.11;
cure by passing patient under cleft of t. D2161.4.5; cutting down t.
tabu C518; cutting t. branches tabu C513.1; cutting t. with one stroke
H1562.1.1; cutting down t. without scratching for stinging insects (task)
H1184; dead t. comes to life *E2; death magically bound to t. Z111.2;
death respite for hero to climb t.: flies away K551.24; deceptive contest
in carrying a t.: riding K71; deceptive land purchase: as much land as
can be shadowed by a t. K185.10; deity born from t. A114.4; deity
lives in t. A151.7.1; demon imprisoned in t. R181.1; demon lives in t.
F402.6.1; devils haunt t. G303.15.4; disease transferred to t. D2161.4.2.4;
disenchantment by shaking t. D789.7; don't plant thorny t. H588.20;
door falls on robbers from t. K335.1.1.1; deer persuaded to butt head
into t. *K1058; devil pulls up t. to goad his oxen G303.9.2.1; disenchantment from leaf by breaking it from t. D711.5; disenchantment
from t. form by embrace of lover D735.3; dogs rescue fleeing master
from t. refuge *B524.1.2; dragon lives beneath t. B11.3.7; dream of
sprouting t. indicates hero's birth M312.0.4.1; dupe lured into t., killed
K983ff.; dupe induced to stand under falling t. K982; dupe persuaded
to climb tall t. K1113.1; dupe tricked into entering hollow t. K714.3;
dwarf caught by beard in cleft of t. F451.6.1; earth from t. grown in
primeval water A814.4; earth-t. A878; escape by catching hold of t.

limbs K685; escape from deluge on t. A1021.0.4, A1023; escape from deluge in hollow t. A1021.0.5; escape by falling from t. K558.1; escape from lower world on miraculously growing t. F101.5; everlasting t. in otherworld F162.3.3; extraordinary t. F811ff.; fairy harper enclosed in yew t. F386.1; fairy imprisoned in t. F386.1; fairies dance under t. F261.3.1; feather becomes t. D457.7; felled t. (raises itself again) *D1602.2, (restored) C43.3, (restored by reassembling all cut parts) E30.1; felling t. resuscitates incarnated being E29.4.1; fire burns up whole t. H1129.5; female spirit of particular t. (hamadryad) F441.2.3; first woman's mate from t. A1275.6; flight on a t., which ogre tries to cut down *R251; following a luminous t. in the desert K1886.1.1; forbidden t. *C621; fox burns t. in which eagle has his nest E315.3; frog becomes t. D428.1.1; fruit of magic t. exhilarating D1359.3.3; fruitful t. chosen J241; future hero found atop t. L111.2.3; future heroine found in hollow t. L111.2.1.1; getting fruit from the top of a tall t. without cutting the t. (task) H1038; ghost laid under t. E437.5; ghosts haunt t. E276; giant bird alighting on t. causes it to tremble B31.6.2.1; giant bird pulls up oak t. B31.6.2; giant with t. for herding-stick G152.1; girl rescued from t. R111.25; girl with t. carried to moon A751.8.5; girl summons fairy lover by lying under t. F301.1.1.3; god as t. trunk A139.81; God finds devil sitting under t. G303.1.2.1; god's home under t. of life A151.7.1.1; gods emerge from t. A115.7; goddess as t. A139.8.5; gullible husband behind t. K1533; harming t. before burning tabu C519.1; helpful t.-spirit N815.0.1; hero returning with berries sent back for t. H1241.1.1; horse made to appear as t. trunk D2031.7; importunate lover tied to t. K1218.7; impostor acting as God in t. unmasked K1971.12; jealous father sends son to upper world on stretching t. *S11.2; king (prince) finds maiden in t. and marries her N711.1; lecherous trickster seduces women from t. and loses them K1387; life bound up with t. E765.3.3; life recreated from t. A1006.9; lost wind found in hollow t. A1122.3; not to lie under t. *C516; life token (knife stuck in t. rusts) E761.4.1, (t. fades) *E761.3; light seen from t. lodging place at night leads to adventure N776; magic belt carries t. away D1539.2; magic belt destroys t. K525.8.1; magic feather causes chips from t. to return as fast as cut D1565.1; magic formula causes t. to open D1556.1; magic glance reduces t. to ashes D2082.1; magic healing hazel t. D1500.1.3.1; magic knife stuck in t. causes wine to flow D1472.2.11; magic knowledge of t. language D1815.4; magic object acquired by rapping on t. D859.1; magic object causes t. to spring up D1576; magic speaking t. betrays secret *D1316.5; magic spell makes t. grow D1487.3; magic song causes chips from t. to return D1565.1.1; magic t. *D950ff., (supplies food) D1472.1.3; man allowed to pick out t. to be hanged on K558; man behind t. speaks and pretends to be God K1971; man has t. for wife T461.3; man transformed to t. D215ff., G263.2.2; man in t. above illicit lovers comments on their child K1271.5; men in t. sing, clap, fall down and die J2133.5.3; man-devouring t. H1163; mankind from mating of t. and vine A1221.4; marriage with a t. T117.5; men wait in vain for nuts to fall from t. J2066.3; marvelous t. survives deluge A1029.1; miraculous growth of t. D2157.4; why monkey lives in t. A2433.3.19; monster's blood makes t. and surroundings poisonous D1563.2.2; murder by crushing beneath t. S116.5; murder by springing bent t. S135; night spent in t. F1045; numskull cuts off t.-limb on which he sits J2133.4; numskull sticks his head in the branches of a t. J2131.5.3; numskull to water roots of t. J2126; numskull tries to shake birds from t. like fruit J1909.3; objects falling from t. frighten off those below N696; object falls on robbers from t. K335.1.1; ogre bribes boy not to cut down certain t. N699.5; ogre's secret overheard from t. G661.1; oil on t. prevents pursuit K619.2; oracular t. *D1311.4; origin of sacred t. for crucifixion of Christ A2632.2; why parrot lives in t. A2433.4.4; picking all nuts from tall t. (task) H1121; placing frogs in a t. (task) H1024.2; plow in t. J2465.12; plane t. tests perjury H251.3.1; plucking fruits from t. unique ability H31.12; provisions received from magic t. D1470.2.1; pseudo-magic cake t. K112.3; pursued sweetheart becomes t. D642.3.1; quest for marvelous t. H1333.1, H1331.1; quest for singing t. H1333.1.1; question (propounded on quest): why does not a certain t. flourish H1292.2; reading from book makes fallen t. stand D1571.3; reason for withering of t. N452.1.1; recognition by tear falling from t. H151.14.1; reincarnation in t. growing from grave *E631ff.; reincarnation as t. spirit E653.2; rejuvenation by fruit of magic t. D1338.3.3; residence in a t. F562.2; return from lower world by being slung by bent t. F101.2; riddle: how many leaves are on the t. H705; riddle: t. with leaves white on one side and black on other H721.2; riddle: t. with twelve branches, each with thirty leaves, black and white H721.1; sacrifice to t. V11.1; saint's girdle causes t. to fall in right direction D1549.2; saints cause t. worshipped by pagans to fall P623.0.5; sawing iron t. H1115.2; sea released from t.-top A924.3; secrets of animals (demons) accidentally overheard from t. hiding place N451.1; self-opening t.-trunk D1556; shape of t. A2785; shoes carried into the t. J1521.1; singing t. D1615.1; sitting between heaven and earth (in a t.) H583.3.2; snake's venom kills t. B765.11; soul hidden in t. E712.1; soul of t. E701.3; souls of dead imprisoned in t. E755.4.1; speaking t. *D1610.2; spear becomes t. D454.9.1.1; spring from sacred t. shot by arrow A941.7.2; why squirrel lives in t. A2433.3.9; stolen sheep's tails severed and put in t. K404.3; strong man: t.-puller F621; strong man fells t. with one blow of axe F614.8; strong man uproots t. and uses it as a weapon F614.2; sun and moon (made from t.) A717, (placed in top of t.) A714.2; symbolism of World T. H619.3; tabu to cut t. where deity lives C93.6; tabu to steal from sacred t. C91.2; tabu: striking deity's t. C51.1.12; tasks performed by means of secrets overheard from t. *H963; test of strength: pulling up t. by roots H1562.1; thief tells his pursuer that the thief has gone to heaven by way of a t. K341.9; thorn growing in wound becomes a t. F971.3; thorn t. roots used by saint to dig canal D2121.14; tiger-killing t. K1715.6; not to touch t. C510ff.; transformation to t. C961.3.2, (as punishment) Q551.3.5.2; transformation: stretching t. *D482.1; transformation by stretching and swaying t. D1520.1.1; transformation: t. to stone D471.6; treasure buried under t. N511.1.9; tree-spirit persuades man spare t. F441.2.0.1; trickster hides in hollow t. K1971.1.1; trickster in t. advises that t. and fruit belong to him K1971.11; ungrateful wanderer pulls nut t. to pieces to get the nuts W154.6; unique ability to cut t. H31.6; vow not to touch certain t. M172.2; water from cut in t. D927.1.1; wager: who can call three t. names first N51; what is the t. that became flesh H823; wife carried up t. to the sky in bag in husband's teeth J2133.5.1; why certain t. is tall A2778.1; why fruit of t. not eaten? H1292.2.1; wild hunt disappears with movement of t. tops E501.16.2; wisdom acquired by hanging in a t. J162; wish for t. as husband realized C15.2; witch lives in t. G234; witch as t. G212.4; witches ride t. G242.4; withering of t. bad omen D1812.5.1.20; wolf transformed to t. D421.1.1; world t. felled by hunters A773.5.

Trees bear first buds to commemorate reign of primitive hero A2771.5; bewitched G265.10; could speak in golden age A1101.1.2; cut down to gather fruit J2126.1; falling reveals Savior's will D1311.4.0.2; killed by magic D2082; from lovers' graves resemble them E631.0.1.1; magically made fruitless D2082.0.1; prostrate selves E761.3.4; unbent F973.1; wither from breaking tabu C998. — Birth t. *T589.3; blinded trickster directed by t. *D1313.4; bramble chosen king of t. P11.0.2.1; city girl: do turnips grow in the ground or on t.? J1731.1; concurrently blooming, bearing t. in otherworld F162.1.3; counting palm t. within view of palace H1118.3; creator's servant puts t. to hold earth together A857.3; not to cut sacred t. C51.2.2; dead t. blossom at saint's command D2157.3; deceptive bargain with ogre: buying t. K186; why t. do not talk A2791.1; druids can pass through t. D1932; enigma on uprooting old t., planting new H599.5; extraordinary behavior of t. and plants F970ff.; extraordinary t. F810ff.; fairies live in t. by stream F216.1; father's counsel: dress up the trunks of t. H588.6; felled t. return to their places C939.3; five t. of paradise A661.3; flesh-eating spirits live in t. G312.3; giants carry t. F531.3.10; giant lies underground with t. growing all over his body F531.2.6; horse which will not go over t. K134.1; killing t. threaten hero H1522; lies about t. X1470; magic forests and t. D940ff.; magic object revivifies t. D1571; magic results from sacrifices at t. D1766.2.1; magic spear-head cuts down t. D1564.4.1; mother curses self, children into t. D525.1; ogres live in t. G637; origin of t. *A2681ff.; person of remarkable sight can see through hearts of t. F642.3.1; plants and t. miraculously unbent F973; riddle about t. not fading until they wither H852; skillful axe-man cuts down t. with single stroke F666ff.; soldiers of fairy king are t. by day and men by night F252.3.1; speaking and bleeding t. E631.0.4; stars are t. growing on clouds A769.1; strong hero practices up-rooting t. F611.3.1; strong man throws t. on roof and breaks it F614.6; symbolic names of three t. Z183.1; tabu: cutting certain t. C43.2; tears of Adam and Eve leaving paradise become t. A2612.1; why big t. have small fruit A2771.9; why t. remain fixed A2774; worship of t. V1.7.

Trembling mountain F1006.3; of pipal leaves A2762.3. — Earth t. at Crucifixion V211.2.3.1; worlds t. at rebirth F960.1.5.

Trench. — Ghost summoned by pouring blood of sacrifices into t. E382.

Trénther. — King's t. P14.15.

Trespasser's defence: standing on his own land J1161.3.

Trespassers. — Fairies take revenge on t. on ground they claim as theirs F361.4.

Trespassing sacred precincts forbidden C93ff. — Vow against t. M186.

Tresses. — Lai of the T. K1512.

Triad. — God as a t. A109.1.

Triads Z71.1.0.1.

Trial among animals (cumulative tale) Z49.6; by combat H218; by ordeal subverted by carrying magic object D1394.1; rehearsed before stick in the ground as judge J161. — Magic objects help hero in t. D1394ff.; rich man's t. in heaven Q172.2.1.

Triangle plot and its solutions T92.1.

Triangular hailstones F962.5.3. — Why dung of ass is t. A2385.1.

Tribal customs established by diviner A150.1. — Origin of t. subdivisions A1640ff.

Tribe born from fire A1268.1; descended from lone woman-survivor A1006.7; of one-eyed, one-footed, one-handed men F525.3. — Bringing sickness to t. H1199.2.1; cannibal t. G11.18; curse on t. M463; divining rod sinks at place where t. shall settle D1314.2.1; promise not to wed into certain t. M258.2; wandering of t. as punishment Q502.3.

Tribes. — Culture from ancestor of t. A1405; distribution of t. A1620ff.; king evades gift to hostile t. K234.1; origin of various t. A1610ff.; paths open in sea for Israel's t. F931.9.3; treacherous t. K2299.2; wandering of t. A1630ff.

Tribunal of the gods A169.1.

Tribute paid in enchanted snow K236.3; as punishment Q595.4.1; slaves must not know Irish P172; taken from fairies by fiend at stated periods F257; of youths regularly sent to foreign king S262.2. — Every third year t. period Z72.5; paying t. to save life, money J223; payment of t. P531; queen must pay t. to victorious queen P24; remitting t. until Luan K2314.2.1; reward for remitting t. Q42.7; tasks as t. H928.

Trick: cadaver arm placed in person's room N384.0.1.1; overawes ogre G572; solves sleeping problem H573.2. — Answer to riddle found by t. H573; cat's only t. J1662; entrance into girl's (man's) room (bed) by t. K1340ff.; heaven entered by t. K2371.1; king asks for new t. H1182.2; magic object acquired by t. D830ff.; series of t. exchanges Z47; underground monster fettered by t. A1071.1; woman persuaded (or wooed) by t. *K1350ff.

Tricks, see also **Deception**. — Occupational t. J2347; ogre killed through other t. G519; ogre outwitted by t. G501.

Tricked. — Girl t. into man's room (or power) K1330ff.; gods t. into help in escaping one's fate K2371.2; ogre t. into carrying his prisoners home in bag on his own back G561.

Tricking enemy by hiding behind hero F601.4.1. — Fairy t. mortal F369.4; man t. saint stricken dead Q591.1.1; parents t. children into forest S345.

Trickster, see also **Clever persons**; appears as Death J217.0.1.1; chooses his gift J1282; concealed in sacred tree advises that he is to marry the princess K1971.10; eats scratch-berries J2134.1; elopes with girl instead of lover T92.4.3; feigns death and eats ripe fruit from the tree K1867.1; gets caught on a fishhook J2136.2; goes around king, gets gem for going around kingdom J1289.14; joins bulrushes in a dance J1883; leads water to sea, ends flood A1028.1; makes two friends each suspicious of the other's intentions *K2131ff.; masks as doctor and punishes his cheaters K1825.1.3; outwits adulteress and paramour K1570ff.; outwits king, forces expensive gift J1593; pinched by shell-fish (crab) J2136.4; potter reborn as crab E692.3; puts on buffalo skull: gets head caught J2131.5.1; shifts married couples in bed K1318; travels, fish burn up J2173.7. — Animal as t. J1117; blinded t. directed by trees *D1313.4; culture hero as t. A521; god as t. A177.1; husband to wife about t.-seducer: "Let him have what he wants" K1354.2.1; liar outdoes t. X909.2.

Trickster's daughter inherits his skill J1111.2; false creations fail him J2186; greed while hunting causes him to be deserted J2751; interrupted feast revenged J1564.1. — Animals killed by t. breaking wind F981.3; sleeping t. feast stolen J2173.1.

Tricksters persuade women to share intimacy K1315.6.1.

Trident. — Magic t. D1102.

Tried. — Animal t. out as messenger B291.0.1; ghosts t. in court E573.

Trifle. — Consolation by a t. J860ff.; not lying for a t. X905; treasure given away or sold for t. J2093ff.

Trinity. — Names of persons in the T. X435.4; physician willing to believe four persons in T. J817.2.

Trinkets seller discovers true bride H151.15.

Triple tax N635.

Triplet. — Mother hides t. sons R153.4.2.

Triplets exposed S314; as heroes T687; killed by tribe at birth T586.3.2. — Extraordinary companions are t. F605.1; woman ravished by three brothers bears t. T586.3.1.

Tripping. — Bridge t. up bridal party if king is not marrying equal H31.2.1; woman t. over skirt Q331.2.3.

Triumph of the weak L300—L399. — Hearing masses causes t. in tournament V41.2.

Trivial. — Subject exiled for t. remark U38.

Trojans deceived by wooden horse K754.1; warned against attacking Greeks J652.4.1.

Troll lets two goats pass, waiting for biggest K553.2; as mountain-spirit F455; makes self small D55.2.2; as ogre *G304. — Disguise as t. aids escape K649.7.3; fat t. Z33.4; sunlight turns giant or t. to stone *F531.6.12.2; transformation by t. D683.3.

Troll's life in his brother's forehead E714.3.1. — Stealing t. golden horse (task) H1151.9.

Trolls F455ff.; live in range of hills F214. — Fallen angels become t. V236.1; hero fights t. H945.2; curse concerning names of t. M427; guessing names of t. H516; magic horseshoe keeps off t. D1385.9.

Trolls' horses water at peasant's well F241.1.2.1.

Troll-woman with beard G219.2. — Strong hero son of man and t. F611.1.13.

Trophy. — Head of murdered man as t. S139.2.1.1.

Trouble. — Beginnings of t. for man A1330ff.; magic t.-making D2097; makers of t. K2130ff.; quest for t. H1376.5; strong men make t. G512.0.1; task: having a shirt made by a woman free from t. and worry H1195; woman makes t. between man and wife K1085.

Troubles escape when forbidden casket is opened C915.1. — Distress over imagined t. of unborn child J2063; king chooses personal t., saves realm J221.2; peasant as priest preaches on the t. of laymen K1961.1.1; small injustices permitted rather than cause t. of state J221; train of t. from (lost horseshoe nail) N258, (sparrow's vengeance) N261.

Troubled liquid as life token E761.6ff.

Troublesome fairies F399.4.

Trough. — Victim lured into t. K838.

Trousers, see also **Breeches.** — Friar's t. on adulteress's bed K1273, K1526; hiding in plowman's t. J2631; magic t. *D1055, (render invisible) D1361.36, (render invulnerable) D1344.9.2.

Trout shams death, fisherman passes by K522.4.1. — Man becomes t. D179.1; stripes on t. A2413.7.

Truce. — Girl's favors traded for t. T455.4.

True. — Tests for t. lover H421.

Truest dreams at daybreak D1812.3.3.1.

Trumpet blown before house of one sentenced to death P612. — Brass (copper) statue at city gates blows on t. at stranger's approach *D1317.9.1; end of world announced by t. A1093; magic t. *D1221; resuscitation by blowing t. E55.3.

Trumpet-bird. — Color of t. A2411.2.1.15.

Trumpeter's false defense J1465.

Trunk. — Boat of tree t. F841.1.11; elephant killed by cutting off t. K825.2; ogre monstrous as to t. G366; origin of animal's t. A2350ff.; princess sent to beggar in t. N712.1.

Trunks. — Father's counsel: dress up the t. of trees, cover the road H588.6; keeping the rain from the t. J2129.6.

Trust. — Lack of t. in God punished Q221.6; not to t. the over-holy J21.18.

Truth best policy J751.1; in drink U180ff.; given in vision D1810.8.1; personified Z121; -speaking rewarded Q68.1; is strongest H631.5; -telling animals B130ff.; -telling dog killed to hide murder B339.1. — Act of t. H252; bird of t. B131; cleverness in detection of t. J1140ff.; disenchantment proves t. D797; fool given t. on his back J551.2; husband discredited by absurd t. J1151.1.2; intemperate zeal in t.-telling J551; Isle of T. F129.4.2; lies closely resembling t. H509.5.1; magic epistle assures wearer will utter t. D1316.9; magic object reveals t. *D1316ff.; peace more important than t. in marriage T203; quest for Bird of T. H1331.1.1; son tells king t., banished J551.6; speaking spittle reveals t. D1316.3; tests of t. H200—H299; wager that falsehood is better than t. N61; what is most difficult to find, to lose? T. H659.19.

Truths. — Flattering lies vs. unflattering t. J267; quest for bag of t. *H1376.4; unpleasant t. must be withheld from the great J815; uttering three t. cleverness test H505.1.

Truthful monk refuses to cheat even for his order V461.2.

Truthfulness as clerical virtue V461.4.1. — Wager on t. of servant N25.

Tryst. — Husband overhears wife's t., appeased K1533.

Trysting tabu C194.

Tuatha Dé Danann A1611.5.4.3; cause island illusion K1886.7.1; as demons G303.1.7; overcome by invaders F211.0.2.1. — Children of T. fostered by Milesians P273.4; jewels of T. F244.1.

Tub drips at high tide, holds water at low A913.4, D1324.1.1; -full of water in sea H696.1.3. — Abandoned wife hidden under a t. S445; bottomless t. holds water D2199.1; cynical philosopher lives in t. J152.1; dropped t. neither breaks, spills F1081; husband in hanging t. to escape coming flood K1522; magic t. *D1171.14; people in otherworld pour water into t. full of holes *F171.6.2; rejuvenation by burning and throwing bones into t. of milk D1886.1; rejuvenation by magic t. D1338.10.

Tubs. — Putting out t. to see if it is raining J2716.2; witch rides on t. G241.4.1.

Tube. — Magic t. *D1255.

Tuber. — Love charm from t. D1355.21.1.

Tuesday as auspicious day N127.1. — Making war on T. tabu C641.1.

Tug-of-war K22.

Tugging contest, loser's neck severed H1562.7.

Tulip. — Fairies care for t. bed F339.2.

Tumble-bug rolls in dung A2457.1.

Tumbler as monk dances while others chant psalms V92.

Tumor. — Magician's power in t. D1711.0.2.

Tune. — Hail produced by whistling t. D2143.4.1.

Tunic. — Fire spares saint's t. F964.2; magic t. *D1052.

Tunnel entrance to guarded maiden's chamber K1344; of crystal four miles long F721.1.1. — Death in t. to underground world J2137.7; mole as trickster killed in his own t. K1642.

Tunnels. — Mighty digger of t. F639.1.1.

Tunny. — Magic t. saves hero B175.2.

Tupilac G377.

Turban on tree far away H1355.3. — Long t. F821.5; numskull warns prospective buyer that t. is too short J2088; remove t. as last duty J2516.7.

Turf laid on breast of dead to prevent return E431.6. — Magic t. *D934, (from church-roof teaches animal languages) D1301.1.

Turkey envious of peacock W195.1. — Color of t. A2411.2.6.5; disguise as t.-girl K1816.5; why t. has red eyes A2332.5.5; helpful t. B469.7; man becomes t. D166.3; object mistaken for t. J1771.3; speaking t. B211.3.1; treasure-producing t. B103.0.1; wedding of t. and peacock B282.1; why brush t. nests on ground A2431.8.1.

Turkey's gobble misunderstood J1811.3; nest A2431.8.

Turkeys. — Why there are wild t. in a certain Pueblo town A2434.3.2.

Turkish ambassador misunderstands Christian ceremonies J1825.

Turks. — Princess gives self to T. to save people T455.7.

Turmeric smeared on bridal couple T135.12. — Man becomes t. plant D213.3; origin of t. A2686.5.

Turned. — Boneless man t. over to produce seasons A1152; boy t. out of doors by father S322.1.5; dogs t. loose on those whom wild huntsman meets E501.15.6.2; insect on back grateful for being t. over B364.3; magic t. against makers D1784; water t. to blood as life token E761.1.1.

Turning aside tabu C834; back after beginning tabu C833.3; jug wrong side out H1023.9.1; the plate around J1562.1; right-handwise brings luck N131.2; stream's course as task H1138.1. — Fairy spell averted by t. coat F385.1; mill t. backwards D2089.4; princess's t. to suitor indicates her choice H315; tabu: t. away from poets C872; transformation by t. magic hood D568; wife resuscitated by t. her around E181.1.

Turnip. — Carriage of t. F861.4.1; chain tale: pulling up t. Z49.9.

Turnips called bacon: cat called rabbit J1511.2. — City girl thinks t. grow on trees J1731.1; lies about t. X1431.

Turquoise gives miraculous speed D1521.5.1. — House of t. F771.1.5.3.

Turtle, see also **Tortoise;** allowed to pick flowers before death, escapes K551.26; carrying man across stream, threatens him J1172.4; carrying man through water upsets him because of a broken promise M205.1.1; carries person across river B551.5; holds with jaws till it thunders B761; induced to rob in a man's garden K1022.5; king B245.2; persuades an animal to swallow him: causes the animal's death and escapes K582.1; released: grateful B375.8; taken for island J1761.1.1. — Why t. beats with forelegs when caught A2466.2; color of t. A2411.5.1; creation of t. A2147; drowning punishment for t. K581.1; friendship between t. and heron A2493.12; friendship between t. and wallaby A2493.12.1; giant t. B875.3;

hedgehog and crab jump from boat after t. J2133.11; helpful t. B491.5; how t. got snake-like head A2247.2, A2320.2; magic adhesion to t. D2171.3.3; magic sea-t. sucks men to bottom B177.3; man-devouring t. B16.5.4; man transformed to t. D193; marriage to t. B604.2.1; scorpion in spite of himself stings the t. carrying him across stream U124; thieving t. K366.6; three-tailed t. B15.7.6; why t. lays eggs on beach A2433.6.12.

Turtle's war-party F1025.2. — Bowl placed on t. back: hence his shell A2215.3; earth from t. back A815; earth rests on t. back A844.1.

Turtles. — Marriage of jackals and t. J414.3.

Turtledove. — Why t. is sad A2521.1.

Tusita world A697.2.

Tusk. — Earth supported on boar's t. A844.9; magic wishing ivory t.: when struck on ground (only once) provides treasure D1470.1.37.

Tusks in ogre's mouth G363.2. — Boar with nine t. in each jaw B15.7.8; how elephant got its t. A2345.6; man-eater hangs carcasses on t. G88.2; stealing elephant's t. (task) H1151.6; wildboar sharpens t. when no enemy is in sight J674.1; witch with twisted t. G214.4.

Twelfth. — Death prophesied on t. day of life M341.1.2.2; tree blossoms on T. Night F971.5.2.1; wild hunt appears between Christmas and T. Night E501.11.2.2.

Twelve Apostles of Ireland V292.2; berserks F610.3.3; -eyed person F512.2.1.3; -headed dragon B11.2.3.5; -headed serpent B15.1.2.10.1; iron pillars steady the earth A841.3; -legged bird B15.6.3.3.2, (in cow's bag) B15.7.9.1, (symbolizes guilt) H619.5; as magic number D1273.1.5; months' pregnancy T574.1; stones unite in one D491.6; -year-old captures town F611.3.2.6; years' fight suitor test H328.6. — Appetite of t. men given with the gift of t. men's strength M416.1; baby to marry t.-year-old to avoid death prophecy M341.0.3; choice: t. famine years or t. hours' rain J229.13; cow gives t. measures of milk for t. apostles B251.2.10; creator establishes t. winds, each a different color A1129.1.1; devil's t. wings G303.4.2.2; disenchantment if t. men will not leave castle for year D759.4; eagle with t. wings B15.7.16; filling t. bed-ticks with feathers (task) H1129.2; formulistic number: t. Z71.8; hail-storm leaves t. chief rivers in Ireland A934.6; king deflowers all t.-year old girls T161.0.1; moon is wife to t. sun brothers A753.1.4.2; prophecy of marriage when t. years old M369.2.3; riddle: tree with t. branches, each with thirty leaves, black and white H721.1; stealing t. horses out of stall (task) H1151.2; strong hero suckled by mermaid and given strength of t. men F611.2.2; sun shines for t. days and nights after death of holy person F961.1.5.1; walking around grave t. times raises ghost E386.4.

Twenty commandments better than ten J2213.5.1; heavens A651.1.0.1. — Man granted t. years more life K551.22.2; punishment not given those under t. Q403

Twenty-first. — Prophecy: death on t. birthday M341.1.4.3.1.

Twenty-five as formulistic number Z71.16.3; years of chaste love T317.5. — Prophecy: death when t. years old M341.1.4.3.

Twenty-four as formulistic number Z71.8.6. — Magic carving knife serves t. men at meat simultaneously D1583.

Twenty-nine. — King is worth t. pieces of silver H711.1.

Twenty-one as formulistic number Z71.16.13.

Twenty-seven. — Giant takes space of t. men F531.2.9.

Twenty-six as formulistic number Z71.16.4.

Twenty thousand. — Recognition of own cow in herd of t. H163.

Twenty-two as formulistic number Z71.16.14.

Twice the wish to the enemy J2074, X111.6. — Money lost t.: recovered third time N183; not to strike monster t. *C742; take, but only t. C762.5.

Twig, born of a woman, is planted and becomes a girl T543.0.1; bows down, releases relics D1648.1.2.2. — Forest from t. F979.8; magic t. *D953, (locates hidden treasure) D1314.2; not to break t. C513; prince buys t. from her mother T52.1; oracular t. D1311.4.0.1.

Twigs. — Elder t. reveal witch G257.6; floors in dwarf home are covered with pine t. F451.4.3.5; oracular t. work only if man has fasted D1733.3.1.1; quarreling sons and the bundle of t. J1021; sight of magic t. gives foreknowledge of day's events D1311.4.0.1.1.

Twilight. — Coming at t. (neither by day nor by night) H1057; origin of t. A1179.1.

Twin, see also **Pair;** culture heroes A515.1.1; destroyers of monsters Z211; first parents A1273; gods A116; goddesses A116.2. — Cure by surviving t. D2161.5.6; husband's t. brother mistaken by woman for her husband K1311.1; jealous and overhasty man kills his rescuing t. brother N342.3; magic pills bring t. sons D1347.3.1; mother hides t. sons R153.4.2; one t. thrown into river to avoid evils of t. birth M371.0.2; sun and moon as t. brothers A736.3.1.

Twins T685; born at end of footrace T581.8; born in tent T581.10; exposed S314; freed from dead mother's body T584.2.1.1; quarrel before birth in mother's womb T575.1.3. — Albino t. cannibals G11.11.1; birth of t. T587, (prophesied) M369.7.1; divine t. cared for by mother-of-tigers B241.2.8.1; divine t. make bow, arrow A527.1.1; extraordinary companions are t. F601.5; medicine causes t. D1501.8; queen changes own t. for slave's son K1921.3; recognition of t. by golden chain under their skin H61.1; separation of t. through being carried off by beast N312; Siamese t. F523; test: which of t. is elder N255; waters created by divine t. A910.5.

Twine. — Twisting t.: trickster cuts it K1433.

Twining branches grow from graves of lovers E631.0.1.

Twisted witch G219.6. — Dwarf's feet t. backward F451.2.2.1.

Twister. — Remarkable t. X948.

Twisting twine K1433. — Murder by t. out intestines S139.1.

Two beams of fire shoot from devil's eyes G303.4.1.2.3; devils come to a dance-loving maid and play when she bathes G303.10.4.2; -edged knife D1313.8; eggs J1341.4; -faced person F511.1.1, F526.5; -facedness

W171ff.; -fold death F901.2; for the price of one J2083.2; giants with one axe throw it back and forth to each other G151; -headed, see following heading; -legged horse in wild hunt E501.4.2.6; lower worlds A651.21; monks renew their appetites J1606; presents to the king: the beet and the horse J2415.1; ravens follow wild huntsman E501.4.4; sheep kill a fox who has licked up the blood they have spilled in a fight J624.1; suns shine in sky F961.1.3.1. — Bad omen for t. bridal processions to meet D1812.5.1.8; cup with t. and three handles J2665.1; devil's thumb the size of t. fists G303.4.3.2; devil in wagon drawn by t. black horses carries off impious people G303.7.3.1; devil has t. horns G303.4.1.6.1; devil gives Eve t. grains of corn G303.9.4.1; dog between t. castles J2183.1; devil builds t. islands in a lake G303.9.1.9; devil compels t. miners to follow him G303.9.5.3; disenchantment by cutting person in t. D711.2; disenchantment by drinking milk of queen who has borne t. boys D764.1; eye with t. pupils F541.3.1; Fortuna with t. faces N111.2.2; ghost in t. places at once E599.9; god with t. faces A123.2.1.1; why horse has only t. eyes A2332.2.1; man fishes up t. blind women from a well F1065; milk of t. king's children protects hero in dragon fight D1385.14; murder by cutting in t. S118.1; skillful marksman shoots left eye of fly at t. miles F661.5.3; stealing t. horns of a savage bull H1151.7; tabu: staying t. nights in one place until certain event is brought to pass C761.4.1; task: traveling till t. skeins of thread are unwound H1125.1; troll drives t. he-goats G304.3.2.2; weaving cloth from t. threads H1022.1; youth sees half of t. quadrupeds H583.1.1.

Two-headed animal B15.1.2.1; child T551.2; dragon B11.2.3.6; ghost E422.1.1.1; man is only one man J1176.4; ogre G361.1.1; person F511.0.2.1.

Two hundred. — Disenchantment after t. years D791.1.4.

Two million stars in heaven H702.1.1.

Tying sun with stone chain H1023.23. — Escape by t. rope to post K638; jealous wife t. husband to her T257.11.

Types. — Different t. of men from one original type A1227.

Typhon F526.1.

Tyrannizing. — Ogre t. over fairyland G464.

Tyranny. — Care against future t. J643.

Tyrant. — Daughter killed to save her from t. T314.1; fear cruel t. will be succeeded by worse J215.2.1; if I were a t. you would not say so J1281; king as t. P12.2.1; suicide to make t. stop bloodshed J173.

Ubiquitous beggar in disguise obtains alms three times from same person *K1982; person D2031.18.

Ugliest girl chosen as bride L213.2.

Ugliness. — Cause of animal's u. *A2402ff.; extraordinary u. F576; frog as beauty doctor unable to cure his own u. J1062.1; humor of u. X137.

Ugly, see also **Hideous;** child becomes poet L112.9; by day, fair by night D621.3; disguise K1815.2; duckling L140ff.; face doesn't mean ugly soul U119.4; feet F551.4; fish borrows handsome fish's skin K1918.1; god

A139.14; husband's advances repulsed J1541.3; man becomes handsome D52.2; ogre terrifies women G476; picture makes girl refuse suitor T11.2.0.1; preferred to pretty sister L145; but wise son M93; woman sees beautiful woman reflected in water and thinks it is herself J1791.6.1. — Animal's u. voice A2423.1; better send an u. woman to the devil than a pretty one J229.4; bride refuses to sleep with u. groom T166.1; devil appears in the form of a man who is repugnantly u. G303.3.1.4; devil helps u. man win wife G303.22.7; druid makes self appear u. on one side, beautiful on other D2031.4.1; dwarfs are u. F451.2.0.1; fairy promises to make u. man beautiful F341.2.1; fairy son u. F233.4; father with handsome son and u. daughter J244.1; first wife u. but diligent T145.7; girl with u. name K1984.3; god with u. bodies A123.1.3; God makes serpent u. A2286.0.1; hero assumes u. guise A527.3.1.1; holy man embraces man who calls him u. J921; man does not court u. woman J1074.2; man magically made u. D1872.1; why peacock has u feet. A2375.2.2; princess calls her suitors u. names T76; trolls u. F455.2.2; useful and u. preferred to expensive and beautiful J245.

Ulcer from moon's rays F647.7. — Curing incurable u. H1199.2.2; death by u. for destroying churches Q558.17.

Ulcers. — Magic ointment cures u. D1512.1; origin of u. A1337.1; satire causes face u. D1402.15.3.

Ulysses, see also **Odysseus;** returns home in humble disguise K1815.1. — Palamides, having injured U., seeks advice from him J646.1.

Umbilical cord connects heaven and earth A625.2.1; cord not to be cut with iron C531.1. — Child helps mother in severing u. cord T584.8.

Umbrella. — Earth under u. A653; magic u. D1194; tree as strong man's u. F621.3; using u. under trees H591.2.

Umbrellas welcome bride A1555.3.

Umpire awards own coat to thief K419.3. — Girl as u. in suitor test K1227.8; magic object acquired by acting as u. for fighting heirs *D832; mortal as u. of gods' quarrel A187.2; laurel and olive tree scorn thornbush as u. in their dispute as to who is most useful J411.7; respite while captor acts as u. between captives K579.5; thief as u. in contest K342; unjust u. (misappropriates disputed goods) K452, (as trickster's confederate) K451.

Umpiring dispute in exchange for safety guarantee M222. — Strangers u. beauty contest H1596.2.

Unable, see also **Impossible, Inability;** to rid oneself of cobold F481.3. — Castle revolving at night so that one is u. to find entrance F771.2.6.2; cuckold's knife u. to carve boar's head H425.1; death sentence escaped by propounding riddle king (judge) is u. to solve *H542; demon has to serve girl whom he is u. to persuade to break vow of chastity G303.16.19.5; devil u. (to eat in an inn) G303.4.8.4, (to endure cross made by straps of knapsack) G303.16.3.2, (to enter house with horseshoe over the door) *G303.16.17, (to take one who has read the Pater Noster) G303.16.2.1;

fairies can set down an object once but are u. to raise it again F255.2; forms into which the devil is u. to change G303.3.6ff.; giant ogre u. to cross water *G131; giant so large that horse is u. to carry him F531.2.7; headless person u. to smell or hear F511.0.1.2; human hands u. to complete devil's unfinished work G303.14; mortals, informed by those benefitted, u. to find abode of dwarf F451.5.12.1; mortals u. to cross river F141.1.2; mountain-men u. to enter house till light is quenched F460.2.3; ogre u. to cross stream *G638; ogre u. to endure daylight G632; ogre u. to work evil after cockcrow G636; one is freed if he can set a task the devil is u. to perform G303.16.19.3; trolls u. to endure church bells *G304.2.4.1; witch u. (to cross stream) *G273.4, (to rise from chair with four-leaf clover under it) G254, (to rise if ring lies under her chair) G254.1.

Unacquainted. — Otherworld people u. with fire F167.8.

Unarmed. — Enemies taken u. spared W11.5.11.

Unattainable. — Never try to reach the u. J21.14.

Unavailing attempt to get rid of slippers N211.2.

Unawares. — Enemies taken u. spared W11.5.11.

Unbalanced. — Not everyone lives in the same place since earth would become u. J2274.1.

Unbaptized child reincarnated as bird E613.0.2; child's mother cannot rest in grave E412.2.2; children (as fairies) *F251.3, (as nightmares) F471.1.3. (in wild hunt) *E501.2.7, (pursued in wild hunt) *E501.5.4; person cannot rest in grave *E412.2. — Devil takes u. child out of cradle and lays wooden log in its place G303.9.9.4; fairies pursue u. children F360.1; fairies steal u. child F321.3.1; reincarnation of u. child as bird E613.0.2.

Unbeliever loses argument with hermit V351.2. — Ghost chides u. E367.5.

Unbent. — Aesop with the u. bow J553.1; plants and trees miraculously u. F973.

Unblessed. — Nun eating u. lettuce eats a demon G303.16.2.3.4; trolls live on u. food F455.4.2.3.

Unborn child affected by mother's broken tabu C993; children promised in marriage T61.5.3; son's soul issues from mother's mouth E726.2. — Abode of u. souls E706; curse on u. child: stillborn M441.1; distress over imagined troubles of u. child J2063; friar adds missing member to u. child K1363.2; heart of u. child renders person invisible D1361.8; journey to the Land of the U. F115; magic blood of u. child D1003.3; magic heart of u. child *D997.1.1; prophecy: future greatness of u. child M311; prophecy: u. child to bring evil on land M356.3; prophecy: u. child to be deformed M355; recognition of man u. child will slay D1812.4.1; riddle of the u. H792; room in hell for souls of u. A678; sham physician predicts sex of u. child K1955.3; three crimes in killing sheep with two u. lambs J1169.9; treasure discovered by hand of u. child N533.3; wagers on u. children N16.

Unbound. — Witch known by hose u. on one leg G255.

Unbreakable chain F863.1.

Uncanny. — Gambling with u. being N4.2; spying on u. persons Q411.14.

Unceasingly. — Person walks u. for year F1032.

Uncertainty about own identity *J2010ff.

Uncharitable king loses power Q494.1.1. — Reward of the u. V420ff.; ruler learns lesson from u. king J56.1.

Uncharitableness punished Q286.

Uncharitably. — Destruction (disappearance) of property u. refused Q585.1.

Unchaste. — Brother flogs u. sister to death Q458.2.1; father kills u. daughter S322.1.3; magic object points out u. woman H411.

Unchastity tests H400—H459.

Unchristened, see Unbaptized.

Uncivil. — Cobold avenges u. answer (or treatment) F481.1.

Uncle P293; slanders niece to appropriate patrimony K361.5; sleeps with nephew's beloved H1556.4.4. — Accidental meeting of nephew and u. N738; boy induces u. to climb tree X905.4.1; cruel u. S71; nephew kills u. S74.1; sending to older u. F571.2.1; sun and moon as u. and nephew A711.1; treacherous u. K2217.

Uncles. — Quest for lost u. H1385.11; throwing cakes into faces of u. H35.5.

Uncleanliness tabu C891.

Unclothed, see also Naked. — Curse: caste to remain u. M464; sight of u. women calms rage K774.2.

Unconfessed person cannot rest in grave E411.0.2.2.

Unconfirmed children can see trolls F455.5.4.2.

Unconscious prophecy M300.2. — Applying hot iron to revive u. man J2119.7.

Unconsecrated host V31.

Uncooked, see also Raw. — Why tigers eat u. food A2435.3.9.2.

Uncut field is already harvested (belongs to spendthrift) H586.4.

Undefeated. — Opponents agree not to fight, remain u. M237.1.

Under. — Chastity ordeal: passing u. magic rod H412.1; fairyland u. (hollow knoll) *F211, (water) F212; ghost travels u. ground E591; God finds the devil u. (stone) G303.1.2.2, (tree) G303.1.2.1; magic sight by looking u. one's (arm) D1821.3.1, (legs) D1821.3.3; magic u.-water journey D2126; man can breathe nine days u. water F691; man lives u. river F725.4; mankind ascends from u. the earth A1232.

Underclothing. — Magic u. D1058.

Underfed warhorse fails in war J1914.1. — Retort from u. servant (child) J1341ff.

Underground city F764; house F771.3.5; otherworld F160.0.1; passage *F721.1, (gives entrance to closed chamber) K315.0.1, (magically opens) D1555, (to paramour's house) K1523; people from children which Eve hid from God *F251.4; spirits *F450ff.; treasure chambers F721.4. — Abduction through u. passage R25; church sinks; song heard from u.

F941.2.1; death from attempt to visit u. world J2137.7; dwarf as u. spirit *F451ff.; dwarfs live u. F451.4.1ff.; dwarfs warm heath by u. fire F451.5.1.15; earthquake spirit lives u. F438.1; escape from execution pyre through u. passage R215.1; escape through u. passage R211.3; expelled dwarfs plan to dig u. bed for Rhine F451.5.22; extraordinary u. disappearance F940ff.; fairies' u. palace F222.1; fettering of u. monster *A1071; giant lies u. with trees growing all over his body F531.2.6; journey to u. animal kingdom *F127; lies about u. channels X1545; magic horse goes u. *B184.1.2; magic object found in u. room D845; magic power of seeing things u. D1825.4.1; magic u. journey *D2131; man falls u. F949.2; why mole lives u. A2433.3.20; rivers with marvelous u. connections F715.3; saint hides fugitive u. K2319.3; treasure in u. chamber N512; why crab lives u. A2433.6.3.3; why gods live u. A189.13; why porcupine lives u. A2433.3.22; wisdom learned in u. J179.2.

Under-king P13.0.1. — Military rights of u. P551.8.1.

Undersea river F715.3.1.

Understand. — Devils do not u. thoughts of men G303.13.1; "I don't u." J1802.1.

Understanding poem test H509.4.3. — Animal u. human speech B212.

Undertaker. — Calling u. with doctor J2516.9.

Undertaking quest H1220ff. — Intemperance in u. labor J557.

Underwater, see also **Submarine;** bridge F842.2.3.2; castle of jewels F771.1.5.4; causeway F842.2.4; entrance to lower world F93.0.2; otherworld F160.0.1.1; tree F811.4.2. — Disenchantment by following enchanted woman through lake to u. castle D759.5; extraordinary u. disappearance F940ff.; golden u. tower F772.2.3; water-goddess's u. home F420.7.1.

Underworld, see also **Hell;** F80—F100. — Children said to come from u. T589.6.3; deity emerges from u. A115.4; god of the u. *A300ff.; goddess of u. A300.1; magic salve from u. causes blindness D1331.2.2.1; mankind from bones of dead brought from u. A1232.1; physical features of u. F80.1; sun coaxed back from u. A739.6; sun, moon remain half time in u. A722.10.

Underworldlings. — Youths grind in mill of u. F106.

Undesirable children exposed, desirable preserved S311; girls keep up appearances to deceive suitors K1984.

Undesired. — Elopement to prevent u. marriage R225.2; escape from u. lover *T320ff.

Undeveloped. — First men u. A1225.

Undiminished. — Fairy food u. by eating F243.4.

Undressing. — Dead u. V68.4; marriage so girl won't be ashamed u. J2521.3; woman u., reveals guilt J1141.1.8.

Undutiful children P236; son punished by toad clinging to face Q551.1. — Poisonous toad sits on food of u. children Q557.1.

Unearthing treasure E451.5, *N550ff.

Unearthly. — Sexual intercourse with u. beings forbidden C112.

Unequal marriage T121; returns: man at lady's funeral has repartee with priest J1264.8. — Marriage with equal or with u. J414.

Unequals in love *T91. — Association of equals and u. J410ff.

Unerring spear D1653.1.2.

Unexpected encounters N700—N799.

Unextinguishable fire at end of earth A871.0.2.

Unfading garlands D1652.7.

Unfaithful, see also **Faithless;** husband (loses magic wife) C31.12, (persecutes wife) S413; wives become edible animals A1422.0.1. — Choice: staying at home with loving wife or going to tavern and having u. wife J229.1; husband refuses to believe wife u. J2342; king sees how male stork kills his u. wife and follows its example T252.2.1; man u. on wedding night T245; man with u. wife comforted J882; shooting stars are u. wives A788.5; swallowing hot coals because husband u. T81.8; wife refuses to become u. even though husband is T217; would-be u. wife T92.1.2.

Unfaithfulness, see also **Adultery;** tokened by ring H94.0.1. — Birth of twins an indication of u. in wife T587.1; dream warns emperor of wife's u. *D1813.1.1; false tokens of woman's u. K2112.1; king overlooks wife's u. rather than to cause troubles of state J221.1; man with unfaithful wife comforted when he sees the queen's u. J882.1; wife shields husband's u. T222.

Unfavorable prophecies M340ff.; traits of character *W100—W199.

Unfinished tales Z12. — Devil's u. work cannot be completed by human hands G303.14; fairies leave work u. when overseen F361.3.1; hill as u. tower A963.8; reincarnation to complete u. work E606.2.

Ungracious. — Plant punished for u. answer to holy person A2721.3.

Ungrateful, see also **Ingratitude;** animal returned to captivity J1172.3; cannibal G85; children punished Q281.1; dwarf F451.5.2.1; hero kills helpful animal B336; river passenger kills carrier from within K952.1; son punished by having a son equally ungrateful Q588; son reproved by naïve action of his own son: preparing for old age (the half-carpet) J121; wife T261. — Grateful animals: u. man W154.8; man u. for rescue by animal W154.2.2; supplying food to u. stepmother rewarded Q65.1.

Ungrowing. — Growing and u. (grass) F817.1, (trees) F811.12.

Ungulata. — Creation of u. A1870ff., A1889.

Ungulate. — Man transformed to u. D114.

Unhappiness. — Foreknowledge of son's u. D1812.0.4; man never knowing u. swallowed by earth L424.

Unhappy. — Why weavers are the most u. of men P445.1.

Unicorn *B13; as creator's companion A36; thrown from ark and drowned: hence they no longer exist A2214.3.

Uniform. — Magic u. *D1052.1; spirit of new born child in u. N121.1.1.

Unimportant. — Choice: important and u. work J370ff.

Uninhabited. — Ghosts banished to glaciers and u. places E437.1.

Unintentional curse or blessing takes effect M404; good deed seen as salvation V512.2; injuries bring unfortunate consequences N385.

Unique exceptions *Z300—Z399; oath binding M115; prohibitions and compulsions *C600—C699; weapon got by misrepresentation K362.0.1. — Disenchantment possible under u. condition D791; engraving shield with u. pattern H1199.4; ghost visible to u. person E421.1.1; quests for the u. H1300ff.; recognition by u. ability H31; recognition by u. manner of performing an act H35.

United. — First couple organically u. A1225.1; outcast wife at last u. with husband and children S451.

Uniting against a common enemy J624.

Unity of God A102.10. — National u. by expelling all foreign elements P711.6; strength in u. J1020ff.

Universality of death learned from watching animals J52.1.

Universe A600ff.; as increasing, decreasing paradox answer H1075. — Earlier u. opposite of present A633; size of u. A658ff.

Unjust, see also **Injustice;** judges punished Q265.1.1; official outwitted by peasant who quarrels with him *K1657; umpire (as trickster's confederate) K451, (misappropriates disputed goods) K452. — Animals' u. decision against man: man always unjust to them J1172.3.2; child in mother's womb reveals u. judgment T575.1.1.3; confession induced by bringing an u. action against accused J1141.4; concealed confederate as u. witness K451.3; judgment as rebuke to u. plaintiff J1172; laughing fish reveals u. judgment *D1318.2.1; series of clever u. decisions: plaintiff voluntarily withdraws J1173; stone bursts as sign of u. judgment *D1318.1.1; thief shows up owner's u. claim J1213.

Unkind. — Choices: king strangers, u. relatives J390ff.

Unkindness punished *Q280ff.

Unknown helper turns out to be known R169.11; knight R222; paramour *T475; prince (chosen chief of children in play) *P35, (shows his kingly qualities in dealing with his playmates) H41.5. — Bringing the devil an u. animal K216.2; combat of u. brothers brings about recognition H151.10; dwarfs emigrate to u. place F451.9.2.1; fools and the u. animal J1736; hero is served at table by his u. son: recognition of his wife follows H151.11; heroine taunted with her u. past S412; infant indicates his u. father by handing him an apple H481.1; king assigns tasks to his u. son H921; love through sight of something belonging to u. princess T11.4; mother sends son to find u. father H1216; object u. in a country sold for a fortune N411; prophecy of future greatness fulfilled when hero returns home u. N682; quest for u. (objects or places) H1382, (person) H1381, (woman) H1381.3; sacrifice to u. god V11.9.1; test: guessing u. propounder's name H521; test as to who is u. father of a child H480ff.

Unloading horse tabu C884.1.

Unlucky accidents *N300—N399; days N128; hunt X1110.1; to look at childless person T591.2. — Magpie sits outside ark jabbering, is u. A2542.1.1; thirteen as u. number N135.1.

Unmasked. — Jay in peacock's (pigeon's) skin u. J951.2; robbers accidentally u. by sham wise man K1956.1.

Unmasking. — Recognition by u. H181.

Unnatural children eat parent G71; cruelty S (entire chapter); parents eat children G72

Unpaid servant refuses to blame master J571.8.

Unpeeling. — Devil u. woman's skin G303.20.5.

Unpierceable. — Magic u. helmet D1381.10.3; magic u. skin protects against attack D1381.3.2.

Unpleasant truths must be withheld from the great J815; women A1372.7. — Ignoring the u. J1086.

Unpromising hero (heroine) L100—L199; hero last to try task H991; hero as rescuer R169.10; hero wins quest H1242.1; magic object chosen *L215.

Unquiet dead sinner taken to priest for absolution E411.0.2; grave *E410ff.

Unraveling in short time (task) H1094.

Unreasonable demands of pregnant women T571. — Not to make u. requests C773.1.

Unremitting torture as punishment Q501ff.

Unrepentent drunkard J1321.

Unrequited. — Death from u. love T81.2.

Unrestrained. — Why animals are u. A2526.

Unrestricted intercourse in marriage A1352.1. — Princess's u. choice of husband T131.0.1.

Unruly hero L114.3.

Unscathed. — Books u. by fire, water F883.1.4; passing through sea u. F931.9.

Unscrupulous business conduct turned against usurer J56.

Unseen hands serve hero in deserted castle H1239.2. — Dwarfs emigrate u. but heard F451.9.6.

Unseparated fingers F552.1.4.

Unshriven man restored to life in order to confess V23.1. — Wild huntsman wanders because of u. death *E501.3.4.

Unsolved problem: enigmatic ending of tale H620ff.

Unsophisticated hero L122.

Unspelling quest H1385.0.1.

Unstable bridge to land of dead E481.2.1.2; security J1383.

Unsuccessful attempt by enemy to kill helpful animal B335.3. — Devil's u. creation produces certain animals A1755; paramour poses as u. K1517.5.

Unthriftiness punished Q323.

Untiring object D1657ff.

Untouchable's contract with hungry god M242.2.

Untouchables C551. — Attitude to u. A1651.0.1.

Untrained colt result of master's neglect J143.

Untroubled. — Preciousness of u. sleep J1081.

Untying. — Disenchantment by u. enchanting knot D765.2; eating food without u. container H506.7; paramour u. horse for husband to chase K1514.14.

Unusual, see also **Extraordinary;** animal as riding-horse *B557; draft-animal B558; manner of life F560ff.; marriage *T110ff. — Abnormally born child has u. powers T550.2; animals with u. limbs or members B15ff.; castle of u. material F771.1; death of the little hen described with u. words Z32.2.1; devil performs deeds of u. strength *G303.9.2; feet with u. number of toes F551.2; hands with u. number of fingers F552.1.1; murder revealed by u. names of boys N271.2; people of u. residence F562ff.; person u. as to his head F511ff.; relationship riddles rising from u. marriages of relatives H795; riddles based on u. circumstances H790ff.; witch rides on u. animal G241.1ff.

Unveiling of Ishtar F85. — Image of Virgin veiling and u. itself D1623.1.

Unwashed. — Coming neither washed nor u. (task) H1062; tabu: touching deity's image with u. hands C51.7.

Unwed mother's drowning of child D1314.2.4.

Unwelcome bird (insect) proves to be messenger B291.0.2. — Hidden man behind image gives u. answer to suppliant: image blamed K1971.8; magic object protects from u. lover *D1386; treatment of u. guests J1563.6; vow to die rather than marry u. suitor M149.2; year's respite from u. marriage T151.

Unwise. — Kindness u. when it imperils one's food supply J715; wise and u. conduct J200—J1099.

Unwitting encounters N700—N799; marriage to cannibal *G81. — Tasks assigned at own u. suggestion H917.

Unwittingly. — Brothers u. fight each other N733.1; children u. promised (sold) S240ff.; father u. buys daughter who has been sold into slavery N732.1; human flesh eaten u. *G60ff.; incest u. committed *N365; magic object eaten u. D859.4; man u. sells soul to devil M211.1; money u. given away N351; "Old Saddle" name of an estate, which the king u. gives away K193.1; person u. killed N320ff.

Unworthy person rewarded, worthy not J1364, U14. — Man considering self u. to receive host given it by God himself V39.1; sacrament effective even from u. priest V39.3; woman deserts husband for u. lover T232.

Unwound. — Traveling till two skeins of thread are u. (task) H1125.1.

Uphill. — Saint's bachall leads stream u. D1549.3.2; unnecessary choice: to go u. or downhill J463.

Upper lip (curls over nostril; lower hangs down to neck) F544.1.1, (reaching heaven; lower, earth) F531.1.4.1; world F10—F79. — Access to u. world *F50ff.; fish carries man to u. world B551.1.0.1; god of the u. world A200ff.; goddess divides time between u. and lower worlds A316; hero returns to u. world A566; inhabitant of u. world visits earth F30ff.; journey to u. world *F10ff.; nature of the u. world *A660ff.; quest to

the u. world H1260ff.; refuge in u. world R323; river connecting earth
and u. and lower worlds A657; series of u. worlds A651.1; tear from u.
world of mortals falls on departed in lower world E361.1; tree in u. world
A652.3; where horse got his u. teeth A2345.1; woman enticed to u. world
on a stretching tree K1339.2.

Uprightness rewarded Q54.

Uprooted. — Plant shrieks when u. F992; tree u. and used as weapon by
strong man F614.2.

Uprooting man-eating tree H1163. — Sky window from digging or u.
plant (tree) in upper world *F56.1; strong hero practices u. trees F611.3.1.

Upside-down tree F811.15. — Nose turned u. F543.3.

Upstairs. — Persistent beggar invited u. J1331.

Upstream. — Obstinate wife sought for u. T255.2.

Uriah letter *K978.

Urinalysis reveals coition as illness cure J1149.4; reveals illegitimacy
F956.2. — Sham physician pretends to diagnose from u. K1955.2; substitute specimen in u. K1858.1.

Urinary. — Magic object cures u. disease D1502.6.

Urinating on fire tabu C99.1.1, C891.3. — Bull's u. thought to be bleeding
J1818.1; child's u. turns gold to ashes J2325.1; donkeys u. when others
begin A2495.3; fugitive u. from tree: pursuers think it rain, leave N696;
goat u. gold for master K366.5; resuscitation by u. E29.6; tabu to face sun
while u. C99.1; witch exorcised by preventing her u. G271.4.7.

Urine diagnosis to tell where a man comes from J1734.1; melting rocks
F559.8.1; waters tree F979.14. — Conception from drinking u. T512.2;
dupe drinks u. K1044.1; flood from u. A1012.2; god's u. used to make
pig A1871.0.1; goddess with red u. A139.9.1; lake from u. of horse A920.1.6;
lamps burn with u. F964.3.1; magic u. D1002.1, (of animal) D1027; magician's u. drunk D1721.4; ocean from u. A923.1; origin of u. A1317; rain
from u. A1131.1.1; river from u. of goddess (giantess) A933; serpent's u.
gives longevity D1345.1; spring from horse's u. A941.1.1; sun, moon as
spangles from creator's forehead falling into his u. A714.6; transformation by u. D562.2; why butterflies haunt u.-impregnated place A2433.5.6.

Urn. — Fish recovers u. from sea B548.2.5; magic u. D1171.15, (supplies
drink) D1472.1.25; soul hidden in u. E712.3.

Useful. — Choice between u. and ornamental J240ff.; riddle: what is most
u.? H659.11; senseless debate of the mutually u. J461ff.

Usurer *P435; blackmailed by daughter's suitor K443.11; cannot rest in
grave E411.4; charges for rope cut to save him from hanging W154.1.1;
encourages sermons against usury, so that his competitors will cease
activity X516; gets plague for boasting Q558.3. — Devil comes for u.
Q273.1; oxen bear dead u. to gallows to be buried N277; wife saves
u. J155.5.

Usurer's practices turned against him J56. — Ass carries u. body to the
gallows instead of to the church *B151.1.1.2.1.

Usurers. — Charity of u. ineffective V431; jokes concerning u. X510ff.; only u. to carry body of usurer to grave V62.2.

Usurper imposes burdensome taxes P12.3.

Usurping. — Impostors abandoning their companion and u. his place K1931; son u. throne P236.4.

Usury punished *Q273. — Going to mass before committing u. K2097; magician rebukes u. D1810.0.2.1.

Utensil transformed to person D434.1.

Utensils. — Magic u. and implements *D1170ff.; mortal repairs fairies' u. F338; punishment for desecrating holy u. Q222.6; recognition by overheard conversation with u. H13.2.5.

Uxorcide punished Q211.3. — Quartering in effigy for u. Q596.1.

Uxorious king (burned to death) N339.5, (neglects duties) P12.11.

Uxoriousness punished Q394.

Vætter F450.0.1.

Vagabonds banished P471.1.

Vagina dentata A1313.3.1, F547.1.1. — Extraordinary v. F547.5, F856.1; river from v. of first woman A933.2; seduction on pretence of repairing v. K1315.2.3; speaking v. D1610.6.1; why lover thinks v. is toothed K1222.

Vain, see also **Vanity;** attempts to (escape fulfillment of prophecy) M370ff., (kill hero) *H1510ff. — Why animal is v. A2527; wisdom found among v. words J263.

Vainglory. — Abbot avoids v. J916.

Valentine's Day for bird assembly B232.1.

Valhalla A661.1. — Souls of warriors go to V. E754.2.0.1.

Valkyries A485.2; ride through air and water A171.1.2.

Valley fills with gold at command D2102.2; of fire F756.1; from which no false lover can escape until it has been entered by true lover H421.1; of giants G105; like paradise F756.2.1. — Creator's giant servant makes v. and mountain A857.2; captivity in sunken v. R42; disenchanted v. rises D799.2; enchanted v. D7; otherworld as v. F160.2; peacock shows rivers way to v. A934.12; perilous v. in land of dead E750.2.2; perilous v. on way to otherworld F151.1.1; river v. licked out by giant beast A951.1.

Valleys. — Extraordinary v. and plains F756; lies about v. X1521; magic knowledge of language of v. D1815.6; origin of v. A983.

Valor personified Z124. — Quest to undertake feats of v. H1223; tests of v. H1561.

Valuable neglected for the interesting J345; object becomes worthless C967. — Worthless object substituted for v. K331.3.

Value depends upon real use J1061; -less oath M110.1; of religious exercises V4. — Riddles of v. H710ff.

Values. — Real and apparent v. J230—J299.

Vampire *E251; goddess A139.4.

Vanish. — Magic journey by making distance v. D2121.4; words of Christian comfort cause devil and his crew to v. G303.16.4.

Vanished. — Animal helps quest for v. wife B543.0.1; quest for v. daughter H1385.2; vow to find v. sister M155.2.

Vanishing ghost E599.8; ghost hitchhiker E332.3.3.1; person D2188.2. — Witches v. from prison G249.9; woman v. on breaking of tabu C926.

Vanity, see also **Vain;** W116; punished Q331.2. — Old racehorse in mill laments v. of youth J14; tar and feathers as punishment for v. Q475.1.

Vanquished king gives daughter to hero T68.4; ogre grants hero's three wishes G665.

Vapor. — Universe from congealed v. A621.

Variance. — Jokers set household at v. K2134.1.

Vasa Mortis B46.

Vase. — Emeralds from broken v. A978.3; magic v. *D1171.7; treasure discovered by clairvoyant v. N533.1.

Vassals' obligations to king P50.0.1.

Vat. — Bottomless v. holds water D2199.1; father's counsel: on wishing to drink wine go to the v. and drink it H588.4; paramour in v.: disguise as vat-buyer K1517.3; tiger crossing river with v. K1183.

Vaticinium M312.2.

Vault. — River arches over saint's body like a v. F932.2; sky as solid v. A702.2.

Vaulting. — Flight by v. on stick R252.

Veal thief set free after sending "Calf" K579.7.

Vegetable comes to life at woman's prayer T549.1; form transformed to (animal) D441, (person) D431; lamb B95ff.; supporting life without other food D1472.1.4. — Birth from v. T543.7; conception from eating v. T511.3; death v. must be eaten C662; eating certain v. tabu C224; lie: great v. X1401; magic knowledge of v. language D1815.5; magic v. *D983, (as food) D1034; man made from v. substance A1250ff.; man transformed to v. form D210ff.; person returns to original v. form when tabu is broken C963.3; transformation by eating v. D551.2.

Vegetables which mature in miraculously short time F815.1. — Acquisition of v. A1423; extraordinary v. F816; lies about v. X1420; magic fruits and v. D980ff.; origin of v. A2686ff.; sundry characteristics of grains and v. A2793; thistles and nettles as devil's v. G303.10.13.

Vegetation. — God of v. A430ff.

Vehicle. — Magic amphibian v. D1533; magic self-moving v. D1523ff.

Vehicles of the gods A156.5. — Acquisition of v. A1436.

Veil as chastity index H431.3. — Angels give pious woman heavenly v. V241.5; bird carries off jeweled v., separates lovers N352.1; birth with v. brings luck T589.4; holy water destroys v. over well D1562.6; identification by v. H115; magic v. *D1061, (renders invisible) D1361.33; saint's v. quells volcano D1549.6.

Veils of fire, ice before door of heaven A661.0.1.1.2. — Evil eye covered with seven v. D2071.0.1; image of Virgin v. and unveils itself D1623.1;

why women wear v. A1599.3; woman's beauty shows through seven v. F574.1.2; woman v. self as expression of surprise P671.

Veiled wife taken to paramour K1583.

Veiling. — Disguise by v. face K1821.3.

Veins. — Man's v. made from vines A1260.1.5; punishment: opening own v. and bleeding to death Q427.

Venality. — Repartee concerning clerical v. J1263.2.

Venereal. — Prostitute with v. disease sent to king Q244.3.

Vengeance, see also **Revenge;** for destroying fairy-mound P17.0.3. — Escape from v. caused by broken oaths M106; ghost demands v. E234.0.1; god's v. A194.2; quest undertaken for v. H1228; train of troubles for sparrow's v. N261.

Venom. — Animal v. causes swelling X1205; dragon spews v. B11.2.11.1; giant made of v. F531.6.1.6; man spews v. F582.2; origin of serpent's v. A2367.3.1; poisonous snakes have no v. B765.9; saint orders serpent to withdraw v. D2156.5.1; snake's v. kills tree B765.11; snake's v. poisons tree D1563.2.2.2.

Venomous, see also **Poisonous;** animals B776; man F582.3; sheep destroy enemy B776.1. — Dragon's blood v. B11.2.13.1; dragon with v. breath guards tree B11.6.10; reward: no v. creature ever to hurt man or posterity Q45.1.3; weapons magically v. D1402.7.0.1; why hairy caterpillar is v. A2532.2; why animals are v. A2532ff.; why water serpents are not v. A2531.1.

Ventures. — Lucky business v. *N410—N439.

Venus (goddess) has girl choose among suitors N817.1; jealous of Psyche, Cupid's love W181.6; as sin personified Z127.1. — Mountain of V. F131.1; sabbath from feast to V. A1541.4.1.

Venus (planet) as land of dead E481.8.3. — Origin of V. A781.

Venusberg F131.1.

Verbal. — Clever v. retorts J1250—J1499.

Vergil in basket K1211; as magician D1711.2.

Verità. — Bocca della V. H251.1.

Veritas. — In vino v. U180ff.

Vermicelli. — Magic v. D1039.1.

Veronica's — Saint V. miraculous napkin F950.1, V121.

Verse, see also **Poetry.** — Changeling addresses woman in v. and thus betrays maturity F321.1.1.3; contest in v. making H509.4.1.1; double-meaning v. aids theft K232.1; recognition by song's v. H12.2.

Versemaker, see also **Poet.** — Devil as v. G303.13.4.

Vessel full of nail-scrapings H1129.8; left under mound in sand, lost J1922.3; to be mended leads to adventure N783. — Alleged inexhaustible v. K117; cloak becomes v. D454.3.4.2; carrying water in a leaky v. (task) H1023.2.1.2; creation in covered v. A1295; deception into v. K717; drinking from v. only with certain tube Z323; embarkation in leaky v. as punishment Q466; extraordinary v. F881; fairy causes v. to remain full

F335.1; giant issues from tiny v. G161; magic spell causes v. to burst D1591; magic twigs from buried v. D953.1.1; magic v. *D1171, (furnishes money) D1452; prayer restores shattered v. V52.5; saint's breath restores shattered v. D1565.4; theft of v. from water-deity F352.2; truth-testing v. H251.3.12; wind raised by troubling v. of water D2142.1.4.

Vessels. — Burial in v. E431.18; copper v. are steaming under earth A857.1; devil piles sand in ocean so that v. may run aground G303.9.9.5; earth swallows temple v. F948.1.1; gigantic v. F881.1; king's earthen v. among gold J913; not to profane hallowed clothes and v. C93.2.

Vestments V131. — Color symbolism of mass v. Z140.3.

Vesuvius. — Skillful bowman shoots crater of V. open F661.6.

Veterinarian becomes doctor: does not have to pay for killing people J1438.

Vexing. — Devil v. friars caused to repent by singing "Te sanctum dominum" G303.24.3; maid v. suitor by pretence T77.

Vices. — Clerical v. *V465ff.; dwarfs dislike human v. F451.5.16.

Victim kills swallower from within F912. — Blood springs from murderer's finger when he touches v. D1318.5.1; cannibal fattens v. *G82ff.; disenchantment by blowing on v. D778; disguised flayer dresses in skin of his v. K1941; gods create earth from their dead v. A831.8; ogre carries v. in bag (basket) G441; ogre in animal form lures v. into captivity G403; tasks assigned at suggestion contained in letter borne by the v. H918; vampire brought to life through endurance of punishment by her v. E251.2.1.

Victim's — Ogre sucks v. finger and drinks all his blood G332.1; resuscitation by biting v. bone E29.1.

Victims. — Bodies of v. in front of ogre's house G691; three v. of love T92.2.

Victor demands defeated's daughter T104.2; forgives vanquished ruler J829.3. — Conquered warrior kills v. K235.4; giant becomes friend of v. G510.3; incognito king in court of v. K1812.5; famine punishes oppression of v. Q552.3.2.

Victorious ally feared J684.4; youngest child *L0. — King to be v. as long as rides muzzled gelding N125.3.

Victory by army leaders' single combat H217.1; personified Z132.1; as reward for piety Q156. — Animals help in military v. K2351; boaster of v. over a weaker person reprimanded J978; charm gives v. in fight D1400.1.10; curse of loss of v. for opposition to holy person remitted Q576.1; eagle as omen of v. B147.2.1.2; general gives king v. credit W11.8; king's presence necessary for v. P19.1; magic belt assures v. D1381.18; magic object gives v. D1400.1; magic spear gives omen of v. D1311.17.1; Norse spirits prophesy v. M301.13; prayer before battle brings v. V52.3; prisoners released in celebration of v. P14.1; prophecy: ruler's death to insure v. M362; prophecy of v. against odds M323; reward for getting v.-

stone Q112.0.4; saint's blessing brings v. D2163.8; warrior flees for future v. K2378.2.

Victuals, see **Food.**

Vidua K2213.1.

Vigil, see also **Watch;** with hands in shape of cross V462.4.2; of husband at wife's grave calls her forth E385. — Continuous prayer sustains man through frightful v. V52.2; magic object acquired as reward for v. D855.1; resuscitation by v. at tomb E62; not to speak during v. C401.1; test: speechless v. in church H1451; vow of v. at frightful place all night M156.

Vigilance. — Dupe persuaded to relax v.: seized K827; man killed on night when fairy guardian relaxes v. F311.2.1; tests of v. H1450—H1499.

Village disappears by magic D2095.1; dormitory A1559.1; of lion-men D112.1.1; of men only F566.1; as part of dowry T52.9; sinks in earth C984.7; of tiger-men D112.2.1.2; under lake F725.5.1; vanishes D2188.3; where cock crows, dog barks, mithian bellows B155.2.1. — Bought behind the v. J1169.2; building v. in one night H1104.2; countryman expects to find persons from his own v. when he travels to another land J1742.1; curse on v.: descendants remain few M461.1; fairy curses v. M411.16; lie: whole v. lifted X941.1; slain enemy's head must not enter v. C845.1; wise judgments settle v. quarrels J1170.1; your child's killer is in the v. M306.5.

Villages in otherworld F168. — Origin of v. A991.

Villain accidentally slain by own order K1612.1; nemesis Q581.

Villains and traitors *K2200—K2299.

Villainy. — What is greatest v.? H659.7.4.

Vindication by champion H218.0.1.

Vine as sky-rope F51.1.2. — Escape from land of dead upon v. R219.2; extraordinary v. F815.7; god of the v. A433.3; man becomes v. D213.4; mankind from mating of tree and v. A1221.4; why v.-leaves are hand-shaped A2761.2.

Vines. — Man's veins made from v. A1260.1.5.

Vinegar. — Life token: wine turns to v. E761.6.5.

Vineyard magically in fruit at Nativity D2145.2.2.1. — Father is in v. doing good and bad H583.2; magic v. D962; setting out v. in one night (task) H1103; tearing up the v. K1416.

Vineyards. — Beasts that destroy v. B16.0.1; dream brings treasure: trade v. with neighbor N531.2.

Vino. — In v. veritas U180ff.

Vintages. — Bluff: the rare v. K1786.

Viol. — The great noise from the bass-v. X1866.

Violated, see also **Raped;** woman's child exposed S312.2. — Groans of woman being v. C885.2.

Violating. — Captain hangs own son for v. order M13.2; mortal v. fairy F304.4; tabu: v. woman C118; transformation for v. vow D661.3.

Violence of temper W185; to woman during pregnancy tabu C152.1. — Disenchantment by v. D712; immunity from death by v. Q154; mildness triumphs over v. L350ff.

Violent treatment exorcises witch G271.5. — Buttons burst as consequence of v. emotion F1041.6; victim of v. death cannot rest in grave E411.10.

Violets. — Water with scent of v. F716.2.

Violin. — Fox stumbles over v. J864.1; magic v. *D1233; origin of v. A1461.1; resuscitation by playing v. E55.4.

Violinist. — Devil abducts v. for hell G303.9.5.8.

Viper eats squirrel's children A2426.1.2.1; as magician's familiar G225.7.2. — Child born with v. in heart T557; enmity between cobra and v. A2494.16.3; ruining garden to get rid of v. J2103.2.1.

Vipers. — Plowing field of v. (task) H1188.

Virgin daughter of culture hero A592.2; in monastery becomes abbot K1837.7; suffers no labor pains V211.1.4; tests men with hot iron H221.2.1. — Birth from v. T547; culture hero incarnated through birth from v. A511.3; decree that hero must wed only a v. M51; disenchantment by naked v. undergoing frightful journey at midnight D759.3; earth as v. mother of Adam A1234.1; false v. K1912; girl may remain v. for three days after marriage T165; girl remains v. after suitors killed T311.3; imprisoned v. to prevent knowledge of men *T381; male v. demigod A504; magic power to see whether girl is v. *D1825.4.2; praying to the nearer v. J2495.1; savage elephant lulled to sleep by v. D1964.1; tobacco from grave of v. A2611.2.1; vow: man will love only a v. M133.

Virgins condemned to wander at death E750.1.1; as guardians of doors of heaven A661.0.15.

Virgin Mary *V250ff.; appears to lady neglecting mass, takes taper Q223.7.1; produces spring A941.5.0.1; shielded in childbirth from on-lookers' gaze Q57.1; shows Jesus to nun D1766.1.2; threatens to leave heaven V254.6. — Contest arranged by V. A1372.7; devil as V. G303.3.2.5; flowers from under feet of V. A2621.1; girl claims she is second V. J1264.6; hazel shelters V. A2711.4.1; image of V. chastises clerk Q552.7; intervention of V. cheats devil G303.16.1, K218.4; Jewess to bear child must entreat V. T580.1; plant named for service to V. A2711.4.3; prayer to V. protects against plague D1586.2; seven joys of V. Z71.5.6.5; sham miracle: painting of V. weeps K1972.2; tears of V. become daisies A2612.2; thistle as milk-cup for V. A2711.4.2.

Virginity personified Z139.8; saved despite torture T320.1.1. — Black nipples reveal v. loss T494; catching salmon proof of v. H411.16; girls must pay for young man's v. J1174.4; girl named Mary has v. spared by knight who has bought her T321.2; girl's v. spared by knight when he sees her surrounded by the Virgin and her train T321.3; girl's v. saved by emissary's kindness T324; ravished girl's v. restored by Virgin Mary T313; sacrifice of v. T301; suicide to save v. T326; vow of v. M132.

Virility test for husband H493. — Substitute in v. test K1848.1.

Virtue personified Z125. — Christian v. brings about conversion V331.10; lake of milk from v. of saint A920.1.13; ordinary rather than pious man brings out v. by comparison J417; pretended v. K2050ff.; saint's v. to save great numbers M364.3.2.

Virtues. — Clerical v. V461; devil instructs saint on v. G303.9.4.6.1.; eight v. Z71.16.1.2.

Virtuous man seduced by woman T338. — Reward for v. life Q112.0.5; woman advised that nagging will never make husband v. T253.2.

Vise. — Dupe puts hand (paws) into v. *K1111.

Vishnu lies in bed of river from reincarnated girl A934.11.1; torments aunt's lover K1578. — Deceptive land purchase: as much land as V. can lie upon K185.2; lotus plants from navel of V. A123.9, H1289.4.1.

Visibility of fairies F235; of trolls F455.5.

Visible sun is pet of real sun A722.12. — Child in mother's womb v. T575.4; devil's house is v. on the way to hell G303.8.3.3; devil v. to one who walks in minister's (or minister's wife's) holy shoes (galoshes) G303.6.2.4; devil made v. by sign of cross G303.16.3.6; ghost v. only to summoner E389.2; otherworld v. from high mountain F132.0.1.

Vision as evil omen D1812.5.1.2.1; of sacrament in form of young child V39.4. — Angel visits mortals in v. V235.0.1; birds dispute over day or night v. B299.2.1; devil produces v. to tempt believers G303.9.4.5.1; dragon's miraculous v. B11.5.3; father in v. reproves son P233.10; god has magic v. only from his throne A199.2; journey to otherworld as v. F1; land grant dependent on v. K185.12; seduction by alleged v. K1375; saint in v. demands prisoner's release R121.6.1; truth given in v. D1810.8.1.

Visions. — Religious v. V510ff.; resuscitated man tells v. of beyond E177.

Visit of angel to mortal V235; to deceased F81.1.2; to fairyland F370ff.; to foreign country suitor task H336.1; to land of the sun *F17; to lower world through hole made by lifting clumps of grass F92.1; to mountain-men F460.4.8; to star-world F15; to otherworld F0—F199; to water-goddess's home F420.7.1. — Adventures motivated by v. N787; clandestine v. of princess to hero betrayed by token H81.2; dead person pays periodic v. to earth E585; death respite for paying v. K551.13; do not v. your friends often: counsel proved wise by experience J21.9; dwarfs v. mortal's house F451.5.7; not to eat while on v. home C234; encounter with clever children (woman) dissuades man from v. J31; gods (saints) in disguise v. mortals K1811; mortal's v. to land of dwarfs F451.5.4; youth promised to ogre makes v. to his home G461; wife's long v. to parents inadvisable J21.47.1.

Visitation. — Mysterious v. as punishment Q554ff.

Visiting friends take everything from house of dying man W151.2. — Fairy v. mortals F393; god v. sick mortal A185.17; soul v. important places of lifetime E722.3.3.

Visitor. — Tabus on feasting v. C616.

Visitor's — Chief reads v. thoughts D1819.1.1; fool and the v. large nose J2512; witch eats up v. bow G269.6.

Visitors of sick stag eat up all his provisions so that he starves W151.2.1. — Saints have divine v. V227.

Vital bodily members E780ff.; heads *E783, N819.3; objects E770ff.; skin E785. — Skillful surgeon removes and replaces v. organs F668.1.

Vitals. — Creator makes clouds from own v. A705.1.1.

Vivification of image of animal D445; of mankind from stone image A1245.2; of picture D435.2.1; of statue *D435.1.1.

Vixen's. — Cat as v. husband B281.9.1.

Vocal. — Deceptive v. contests K84.

Vocation. — Wager: fortune made from capital or from working at v. N66.

Voice of eaten child comes from cannibal G72.4; from grave answers pet name E324.1; from heaven curses city Q556.0.2; from heaven testifies for accused H216.1; petrifies suitors D581.1. — Ass in lion's skin unmasked when he raises his v. J951.1; ass tries to get a cricket's v. J512.8; big v.: little creature (frogs, crickets) U113; devil comes out of man when monk recognizes the devil's v. in man G303.16.19.7; devil speaks with v. of he-goat G303.4.7; disguise by changing v. K1832; divination from sound of v. D1812.5.0.11; divine v. points out magic D849.7; druid's spell drowning fairy's v. F381.6; eye bursts from v. overstrain F1085; falling in love with v. T11.8; ghost's v. scares away treasure-seekers N576.1; god's v. A139.5; quality of animal's v. A2423ff.; hearing v. of God as reward Q144; how animal got v. A2421ff.; how animal lost v. A2422ff.; how far his v. will reach J1941; jackal inside carcass pretends his v. is God's K1973; madness on hearing prophetic v. F1041.8.8; magic carrying power of v. D1921; magic power from heavenly v. D1739.2; man with marvelous v. F688; murderer warned by God's v. that murder will be avenged M348; mysterious v. announces death of Pan F442.1; mysterious v. announces prohibition C601; ogre disguises v. to lure victim G413; peacock dissatisfied with her v. W128.4; peacock has snake carry devil into paradise: cursed with ugly v. and feet A2236.2.2; partridge's v. borrowed from tortoise A2241.3; petrification at woman's v. D529.1; picture of a v. H1013; recognition by v. *H79.3; recognition of captive's v. brings about rescue from ogre G556; recognition of good health by hearing v. H1582.1; remarkable v. F556; resuscitation by heavenly v. E136; supernatural v. points out criminal N278; swallows torment Christ on cross: lose v. A2231.2.2; truth-telling v. warns of poison D1317.4.1; what animal has one v. living, seven, dead? H842.3; where sparrow got v.: taught by lark A2271.2; why women have a treble v. A1372.4; woman's v. as source of sin T336.2.

Voices of dead heard from graveyard E401; from heaven (or from the air) F966; from unhatched eggs J646.2. — Heavenly v. proclaim hero's birth M311.0.4; not to heed persuasive v. C811.

Volcano fire as goddess's head A139.8.3. — Giant cooks on v. crater G171; gods' home in v. A151.1.3; saint's veil quells v. D1549.6; saint stops eruption of v. D2148.3.

Volcanoes' origin A966.

Voluntarily. — Magic object v. restored to giver D878; quests v. undertaken H1220ff.; tasks v. undertaken H945.

Voluntary exile as punishment for murder Q431.1. — Reasons for v. transformation *D640ff.; victim enticed into v. captivity or helplessness K710ff.

Volunteers. — No sinless v. for cremating dead H1558.12.

Völva prophesies at child's birth M301.2.2.

Vomit. — Hero proves himself a cannibal by trick v.-exchange K1721; release from curse by burning v. M429.1.

Vomited, see also **Disgorged;** magic object D826.1. — Animals v. up by creator A1792; gold v. D2102.1; heavenly bodies v. up by creator A700.2; stolen magic object v. up D884; swallowed children v. by earth R142.

Vomiting V229.2.2; iron F1041.20; out heart as punishment Q552.21. — Abortion by v. up embryo T572.2.1; animal v. treasure B103.4ff.; burning bodies v. F1099.5; flood from whale's v. A1013.1; magic dog v. any required liquor B182.1.1; swallowing mouse without v. H1567.1.1; theft detected by enforced v. J1144.1.

Vow, see also **Oath;** to visit shrine V113.0.2. — Demon has to serve girl whom he cannot persuade to break v. of chastity G303.16.19.5; ghost laid when v. is fulfilled E451.3; girl pleads chastity v. to repel lover T322.4; punishment for violating v. D661.3; tabu: not to fulfill v. C68; wife keeps v. not to rewed T291.1.

Vows *M100—M199. — Clerical v. *V470ff.

Voyage, see **Journey.**

Voyagers may ask landsman first question P682.2.

Voyaging. — Christ's message to v. clerics V211.10.1.

Vulcan tutors youth F107.

Vulnerability. — Secret of unique v. disclosed N476, (by hero's wife) K2213.4.1; unique v. Z310ff.

Vulnerable. — Alliances which make both parties more v. J681; hound strikes unique v. spot N335.5.

Vulture as bird of ill omen B147.2.2.6; cures blindness B511.5.1; eats those to be reborn as human beings E697; as messenger B291.1.8; places baby in queen's lap F589.6.1.1; scouts after world-fire A1039.1. — Why v. is bald A2317.7; creation of v. A1931; helpful v. B455.1; lion and wild boar make peace rather than slay each other for benefit of v. J218.1; marriage to v. B602.4; man transformed to v. D152.3; return from lower world on v. F101.3.1; speaking v. B211.3.8.

Vulture's chicks will not eat murdered hero B159.4. — Carrion as v. food A2435.4.5.1; quest for v. egg figured with golden letters H1332.2.

Vultures. — King of v. B242.2.11; why v. are bald A2317.3.1.

Vulva, see also Vagina; hair becomes mantis F547.5.9. — Eye in v. F547.5.3; speaking v. D1610.6.1.

Waberlohe D1380.1.

Wading. — Giant w. the ocean F531.3.1; hero w. across sea F1057.

Wafer. — Consecrated w. kept in mouth in order to be a witch G281; not to lose consecrated w. *C55; penny baked in the w. J1582.1; tabu to shoot at consecrated w. C55.2.

Wafted. — Person w. to sky F61.

Wager, see also **Gambling;** greatest liar to get his supper free K455.7; involves spilling water on fops X32; that sheep are hogs K451.2; who shall rise last? J2511.1. — Bull wins master's w. B587.3; deceptive w. K264; devil helps journeyman win w. with master G303.22.8; guessing with life as w. H512; man and wife w. as to who shall speak first J2511; "never w. more than a groat": counsel proved wise by experience J21.8; wives w. as to who can best fool her husband K1545.

Wagers *N0—N99.

Wagering. — Man w. he can run with his head off J322.1; Satan w. with God over mortal G303.9.8.7; woman w. that she can seduce anchorite T337.

Wages: as much as he can carry K1732; successive harvests from grain of rice Z21.1.1. — Deceptive w. K256; high w. bring expensive living J342; sun earns day's w. for his daily work (riddle) H715.1.

Wagon accompanies wild hunt E501.10.3; bewitched G265.8.3.2; of jewels F861.3; paralyzed by witch D2072.0.2.1.1; refuses to move D1654.5; run back and forth to simulate artillery K2368.1.1; and sleigh figures for summer and winter H1058; stops creaking and fool thinks it is dead J1872.0.1. — Bluff: thunder said to be the rolling of hero's brother's w. K1718.1; carrying w. axle which has broken a wheel (task) H1183; child promised to devil for help on road with broken w. S225; corpse in coffin refuses to be moved in w. D1654.9; covering the whole w. with tar K1425; deer hitched to w. B558.4; devil drives horse and w. G303.7.3ff.; devil invites traveler into his w. G303.7.1.2.2; devil in form of wheel on w. G303.3.4.1; extraordinary w. F861ff.; ghosts in glowing w. E421.3.5; ghostly w. E535.2; grain-thief's w. falls into ditch: duped owner helps him K405.1; hay w. and the gate J1411; hen hitched to w. B558.3; living smith must repair w. belonging to wild hunt E501.15.5; magic w. *D1113; mice hitched to w. B558.5; people in otherworld hitch horses both before and behind w. F171.6.4; spirit makes wheels come off w. F473.6.6; spirit shoves w. into ditch F473.6.7; stretching, shrinking harness pulls w. uphill X1785.1; thumbling drives w. by sitting in horse's ear F535.1.1.1; trickster throws fish off the w. K371.1.

Wagons. — Dwarfs have steeds and w. F451.7.6; ghost upsets farmers' w. E299.3.

Wagtail. — Why w. moves tail up and down A2479.1.

Wailing of the dead E547. — Thieves' w. drowns abducted woman's outcries K419.8.

Waist. — Ant thrown from heaven: hence narrow w. A2214.2; origin and nature of animal's w. A2355ff.; penance: iron band forged round a man's w. Q522.5; sea as w.-deep H681.4.2.

Wait. — Bravest know how to w. J572.1; curious wife: w. and see T258.

Waiter. — Escape disguise as w. K521.4.4.

Waiting to announce choice of boon M204.1; for God to provide J2215.4; twenty-two years to see a beauty T24.7; at the well for the thief J2214.3; for the thief to return for the bolster J2214.3.2; in the graveyard for the thief J2214.3.1. — Drunk man w. for his house to come to him X815; foolish w. J2066; numskull w. for river to run down J1967.

Wakes, see **Funerals.**

Waking contest *H1450.1; from magic sleep *D1978. — Dead wife w. husband E322.2; disenchantment by proper person w. from magic sleep *D762; long w. follows long sleep F564.3.1; nut falls w. man about to be bitten by snake N652; ring w. from magic sleep D1364.0.1.

Walk. — Animal's gait or w. A2441; crow tries to imitate partridge's w. J512.6; do not w. half a mile with a man without asking his name J21.11; first w. by Adam A1392; dwarfs w. stooped F451.2.0.3; ghosts w. at certain times E587; magic power to w. on water *D2125.1; faster the w., longer the trail D1783.3; father's counsel: w. not in sunshine from your house to your shop H588.1; man who does not know how to pray so holy that he can w. on water V51.1; why children learn to w. late A1321.1.

Walked. — As tired as if he had w. J1946.

Walking around grave to raise ghost E386.4; backward around church at midnight G224.8; backward to leave misleading trail K534.3; ghost laid *E440ff.; on grass-blades without bending them F973.2; on head in otherworld F167.4; upon water without getting wet D1841.4.3. — Art of w. on stilts A1491; boy lives on ox never w. on ground F562.1; child at first w. resuscitates E149.2; child w. at birth T585.8; dead w. on grass, mud E489.9; dead w. on water G299.1; fairies teach under-water w. F345.1; fool w. on water P192.3; ghost w. through solids E572; giant's w. contest F531.5.11.1; lazy boy claims not w. W111.2.8; magic from maiden w. naked in public *D1796; magic w. on water *D2125.1; man w. faster than horse F681.9; ordeal by rope-w. H225; ordeals by w. H225; penance: w. on all-fours like beast Q523.2; person w. unceasingly for year F1032; power of w. to nearest water F651; sand enables w. on water D1524.1.4; woman has worn out carriage-load of shoes with w. F1015.1.2.

Walking-sticks. — Riddle about mares and w. H586.8.

Wall about otherworld F148; accuses the crowbar J1966; around grave to keep in ghost E431.14; broken by saint's kick V229.14; of cakes separates enemies D2163.6.2; collapses: who is guilty? Z49.11.1; of fire surrounds island F744; opens, closes to let saint through D1552.6; as path to upper world F57.4; of snow around hut in answer to prayer D2143.6.2; of water magically warded off D2151.0.3. — Burial in church w. cheats devil K219.4; coffin carried through hole in w. to prevent return of dead E431.4; communication of lovers through hole in w. T41.1; devil tries to w. in too large a piece of ground in a night and fails G303.13.3; drawing lover out of w. H412.6; eagle saves man from falling w. B521.2.1; garden w. that cannot be overleapt D1675; going through w. suitor test H312.7; horse jumps over high w. F989.1; life story painted on w. H11.1.2; magic horn blows down w. D1562.3; safety in shadow of w. N253; tearing down huge w. H1116.3; treasure found in ruined w. N511.1.6.1; treasure hidden within w. N517.2; waves form high w. around otherworld isle F141.3; woman suckles imprisoned relative through prison w. R81.

Walls of crystal in otherworld *F169.2; magically enclose enemy D2091.16; overthrown by magic D2093; thrown up by chariot wheels R5.1. — Devil as builder of w. G303.9.1.4; heaven surrounded by w. A661.0.9; house's w. so thin thieves must break in J1165.1; inscription on w. for condensed education J168; jewelled w. F165.3.2; shout makes w. fall F688.4; strong man throws another from w. F628.2.2.

Wallaby. — Friendship between turtle and w. A2493.12.1.

Wallet containing night and day A1172.2; from which one cannot escape D1413.9.1. — Sham miracle: w. changes to wasps K1975.1.

Walling up as a punishment Q455ff.

Wallowing. — Hog w. in mud after bath U123.

Wallpaper. — Spirit tears off w. F473.6.1.

Walrus. — Giant w. B871.2.6; hero kills w. F628.1.4.3; man transformed to w. D127.4; origin of w. A1838; soul in w. E715.4.3; strong man throws w. F624.1.2; where w. got his tusks A2247, A2345.4.

Wampaus as monster with huge dog tracks F401.3.3.1.

Wand transformed to other object D451.6.1; transforms D572.4. — King's w. P19.4.0.1; magic w. *D1254.1, (locates hidden treasure) *D1314.2; quest for magic w. H1342.0.1.

Wands of life and death D1663.1.

Wanderer. — Disguise as w. K1817.

Wanderers in shade of plane tree blame it for not bearing fruit W154.7.

Wandering islands F737; Jew Q502.1; ghost makes attack E261; prostitutes J1351.1; as punishment Q502ff.; of tribes A1630ff. — Child's stomach split to cure w. J1842.4; children w. into ogre's house G401; couple w. until they find new seat of race M455.4; dead man w. with torch E594; first man w. until he finds mate A1275.7; gods w. on earth K1811; person w. for 150 years F1032.1; sinner w. between heaven and earth E411.0.4; soul w. E750.1, (from body in sleep) E721.1, (till corpse decays) E722.3.2; uncharitable pope w. after death V425; wild huntsman's w. E501.17.7, E501.3ff.; witch recognized by seeing w. soul return G251.

Waning. — Magic waxing and w. of strength D1836; moon's w. A755.4, (caused by her sickness) A755.3, (caused by menstrual period) A755.7.

Want. — In time of plenty provide for w. J711; man never knowing w. swallowed by earth L424.

Wanted. — What is w., not what is asked J1311.

War of birds and quadrupeds *B261; -club H125.3; cry F418.1; between fairies F277.0.1; between fairies, giants F364.3; between fairies, mortals F364; horse J954.1, J1914.1; -making punished Q305; personified Z132; prisoners fettered Q434.2; prisoners shut up between stones Q433.13; of pygmies and cranes F535.5.1; of spirits in sky causes thunder A1142.6.1; with the sun Q739.2; between wild and domestic animals *B262. — Ass jealous of w. horse until he sees him wounded L452.2; dead predict w. E545.16.1; fairy incites mortals to w. F369.4.1; foreign king wages w. to enforce demand for princess in marriage T104; god of w. A485; goddess of w. as hag A125.1; hero leaves cradle for w. T585.7; lake to quell fairy w. A920.1.7.1; making w. tabu C641; men report false attack to bring about w. K1087.0.1; mortals aid fairies in w. F394.2; origin of w. A1599.11.1; origin of w. among men A1341; prophecies concerning w. M356.1; queen persuades king to w. so sons may have territory P23; rejected suitor wages w. T104.1; ruler diverts attention from misgovernment by beginning a w. K2381; sham threat of w. holds ships back K1771.7; stolen cows cause w. K300.1; tabu broken, w. lost C936; tabus concerning w. C845; test of sex of man masking as girl: w. trumpet sounded H1578.2; Thirty-Years W. destroys home of dwarfs F451.4.4.2; turtle's w.-party F1025.2; wild hunt as omen of w. E501.20.1.1; wives preventing w. J1112.4.

Warbler's — Garden w. song A2272.1.3, A2426.2.2.

Warding. — Animal w. off spirits B785; fires burnt in streets w. off witches G272.4; magic object w. off disease D1500.2ff.

Wares. — Seduction by showing w. in tent K1332.2.

Warehouse. — Cat in the w. J1175.1; hero threatens to haul away w. with rope K1745; where is the w. (cumulative tale) Z49.5.

Warfare of animals B260ff.; as tribal characteristic A1600ff.

Warm body restored E152. — Animals or objects kept w. J1873; beggar tells the bishop how to stay w. K151; dwarf wants to w. self at fire F451.5.7.1; dwarfs w. heath by underground fire F451.5.1.15; fairies w. themselves *F266; guest who could not keep w. J1563.1; seduction by entering woman's room to get w. K1361.3; why earth becomes w. and wet: underground vessels steaming A857.1; why sea is w. A1119.2.

Warmed. — Castle w. by love F771.13; cauldron w. by breath of nine maidens F686.1.

Warming hands across river J1945; man far away J1191.7; stove with wool J1873.3 — Ghosts w. selves E578.1; resuscitation by w. E133; saint carries fire in hands for w. guests D1841.3.2.3.1.

Warmth. — Magic object furnishes w. D1481; seduction: how to store up w. K1399.3.

Warn. — Devil appears to minister's serving man to w. of impending disaster to house G303.6.2.6; pupil returns from dead to w. master of futility of his studies E368.

Warned. — Boys w. by dogs' names to escape K649.5; buyer w. by fool that turban for sale is too short J2088; hero w. of danger by horse *B133.1; lover w. against husband by wife's parody incantation K1546; murderer w. by God's voice that murder will be avenged M348; thief w. what not to steal J2091.

Warner. — Ghostly w. of wild hunt's approach E501.6.

Warning in dreams D1810.8.3; by talking to trees K649.6. — Animal w. (of fatal danger) B521, (hero of enemy trap) B335.6; bird gives w. B143.1; danger w. restores speech F954.5; death w. prophesied M341.0.1; dog as animal of w. B134.3; dream w. against marriage C168; ghost w. the living E363.3; knockers' appearance as accident w. F456.1.2.2.4; leaf sent down stream as w. to one below H135; magic object w. of danger *D1317ff.; mermaid w. of bad weather B81.7; moon w. of assassin F961.3.3; sister w. brothers P253.6; son w. mother P231.2; son w. animal mother B631.0.1; spirit gives w. F403.2.3.2; sun w. of assassin F961.1.4; token as w. H82.5; wife's wise w. T299.2.

Warnings. — Attention to w. J1050ff.; inattention to w. J652.

Warrant. — Tokens sent to jailor as w. of king's authority H82.1.

Warrior attack as valor test H1561.7; buries oversized armor to prove prowess K1969.2; chieftain of underworld A308; combats when spear consents F834.7; deceived into attacking pillar-stone K1845.1; destroyed for asking princess's hand P41.1; fighting foster brother P273.2.1; flees for sake of future victory K2378.2; gives steed to enemy W11.5.9; having lost a city claims that he did not wish to sell it for a higher price J875; offered long life if he delays battle D1857.2; retires to cloister Q520.6; reveals camping place J2366; of special strength F610.3; will not fight where brother slain P251.2. — Admission test to w. band H1566; conquered w. kills victor K235.4; fairies bear dead w. to fairyland F399.1; fairy gives w. equipment F343.10; girl's favors traded for truce with w. T455.4; mask for w. with ruined face K521.2.3; messengers announce successive misfortunes to w. as he sets out for war N252.1; old w. longs for more adventure H1221.1; oldest w. as preferred suitor T92.13; sham w. K1951; supernatural substitute for pious w. K3.2.1; woman in love with dying w. T89.1; women bind w. by hair K713.1.8; women lure w. for confederate to kill K822; wounded w. continues fighting W33.1; wrestling with giant w. H1166.1.

Warrior's deceptive fight in "single" combat K2319.2; equipment magically furnished D2107; marriage for night to insure heir before being slain next day T156.1. — Fire from w. fingers F683.1.1.

Warriors P551; battle leader as valor test H1561.8; boastfully face strong enemy H945.1; discovered about to murder own chief N657; hidden in battlefield pit K2369.2; hidden on oxen driven into enemy's camp

K2357.15; identically equipped Z210.0.1; surrender after chief's death
R75.2; tabu in hero's land C566.5; use teeth F1084.2; whitewash weapons
as disguise K1839.6. — Band of professional w. P551.0.1; describing
approaching w. by senses J1661.3; eager w. go through tent wall W212.1;
ghostly w. recount lives E497; giants as w. F531.6.9; helpful spirit w.
dwell in rocks and hills F450.1.1; mad w. fly into clouds F1041.8.7;
physical reactions of w. in battle F1041.16.6; professional w. A1658; sex
activity tabu for w. C566.6; slain w. revive nightly E155.1; souls of w.
go to Valhalla E754.2.0.1; spring aids demigod's w. A941.4.2.1; tailors
cowards as w. X223; test for sham-dead w. H248.4; transformed fairy w.
F383.5; why snipe messenger for w. A2261.6; women w. F565.

Warts. — Why toads have w. A2412.5.2.

Wart-hog's burrow A2432.7.

Wash. — Ghost asks to w. shirt E412.3.2.1; giants sit on mountain and w.
feet in stream below F531.3.9; horse advises hero not to w. B521.1.1;
numskull tries to w. black hen white J1909.6; paramour hidden under
w. K1521.3.

Washed. — Black wool w. white H1023.6; coming neither w. nor unwashed (task) H1062; dead w. V68.1; death respite until mouth w.
K551.4.6; mermaid is w. up on beach B81.13.2; negro tries in vain to be
w. white J511.1; sleeping maids w. by dwarf F451.5.1.13; wine w. in the
Rhine J1312.2.

Washerman makes foolish minister J677; as minister thinks about washing
U129.3; rescues abandoned child R131.8.3. — Escape disguise as w.
K521.4.3.1.

Washers at ford disaster omen D1812.5.1.1.6.

Washerwoman. — Brahmin in love with w. T91.7.1; seducer disguised as
w. K1321.1.2.

Washing the child (in boiling water) J2465.4; enormous number of clothes
(and other articles) in short time (task) H1096; of feet by unseen hands
F171.7; grandmother (in boiling water) K1462; hair on sabbath tabu
C631.3; hairs from salt J2173.9; Jew as devil's task G303.16.19.3.3; in
magic bowl produces immunity from old age D1349.2.2; off ascetic's dirt
takes twelve years V462.14; quilt without soap H1023.6.1; room (floods
it) J2465.6. — Cure by w. in dew D2161.4.14.3; escape by w. clothes
K551.4.5; face wiped dry after w. A1599.4; fairies w. their clothes F271.9;
flowers drop on w. hands D2193; guilty detected by w. basin J1149.11;
man w. blindfolded F1017; Pilate w. hands on Mt. Pilatus E411.8; princess dupes giant into w. in death water G527; punishment for w. clothes
in holy well Q559.9; restrictions on w. murdered body Q559.3; vow
against w. M126; water from saint's w. curative D1500.1.18.1.2; why
women keep w. themselves A1372.10; wife w. face in dunghill puddle
H473.4.

Washings. — Woman becomes clean only after three w. W115.2.

Washington's Birthday: bees washed J1743.3.

Wasp released: grateful B376; seeking fame stings courtiers W116.5; steals yeast from old woman A1429.2; teaches man house-building A1445.2.2; twits butterfly with coming from chrysalis J312.1. — Burning w. nest J2102.5; demon as w. F401.3.4.1; devil as w. G303.3.3.4.3; enmity of spider and w. A2494.14.2; getting honey from w.-nest K1023; why w. has nest A2432.2; sexton arranges w.-nest so that parson sits on it X411.3; soul in form of w. E734.4; spider invites w. to rest on her white curtain K815.2; wedding of w. B285.7; witch recognized by seeing w. enter her mouth while asleep *G251.1.

Wasps as alleged interpreters of foreign language K137.1. — Army of w. B268.8.3; bridegroom driven from bridal chamber by w. T171; ground swallows demoniac w. F949.1.1; helpful w. B481.4; sham miracle: wallet (bee-hive) changes to w. K1975.1; snake rids himself of w. J2102.2.

Waste. — Demons live in w. mound F402.6.2; magic poem (satire) causes king to w. away D1402.15.

Wasted. — Bride test: making dress from w. flax H381.1; entire fortune w. before profligate begins his own adventures W131.1.

Wastefulness of God J2215.1; tabu C851. — Food disappears because of w. Q585.4; God punishes man's w. A2723.2; king reproached for w. J1289.15.

Wasting. — Ghost's body w. away E422.1.9.

Watch, see also **Vigil;** for devastating monster H1471; mistaken for the devil's eye J1781.2; runs indefinitely when lost X1755.1. — Hero keeps w. over earth A572; night w. with magic cats H1411.2.1; tailor asks soldier mount w. in his place P441.4; vow to w. at frightful place all night M156.

Watches. — Princess speaking all w. of night H343.0.1.

Watch-dog enticed away K318. — Dog created as w. for Jesus A1831.1; man in place of w. J1511.12; wild animal sold as w. K133; woman bitten by own w. K1651.

Watcher. — Buttocks as magic w. D1317.1; money exacted from w. who permits theft of wooden cow supposed to be real K443.4; sleepless w. magically put to sleep D1961; trickster entices wolves out of a stable by music: exacts money from their w. for his carelessness K443.5.

Watchers permitting theft blackmailed K443.3. — Actual rescuer, not w., gets woman J1179.12; master thief puts w. to sleep and cuts off their hair K331.2.1; money exacted from w. who permit chest to be stolen K443.3.1; prisoner kills his w. who enter to torture him K655.

Watchful. — Monster with magic w. eye put to sleep D1961.

Watching fairy at work tabu F348.8; fairies makes them leave F381.10. — Animal characteristics from contest in w. A2256; not w. sleeping princess long enough D759.9; tabu: w. game without aiding loser C882.

Watchman asleep as enemy approaches N396; of the gods A165.4. — Escape by teaching song to w. K606.0.2; giant's w. F531.6.16.1; owl as w. goes to sleep: does not see by day A2233.3; philosophical w. J2377; suitor outwits w. to meet lady T46; trickster w. exchanges gold for worthless bag K126.

Watchmen. — Coughing thief blinds w. D2062.2.6; demons as gods' w. A165.4.1; escape by singing w. to sleep K606.1.2.1; images to resemble w. K1883.8.

Water, see also **Fountains, Holy water, River, Springs, Stream, Wells;** barrier to otherworld *F141; becomes bloody D474.2; becomes rocks D471.10; becomes wine D477.1; from belly A1013; is best (riddle) H648.2; -bird A2442.2.6; boils when angry warrior is immersed in it F1041.16.6.6; -bottle H1023.2.2; cannibal G11.5; cannot be drawn to wash murdered body Q559.3; deity Q221.8; demon G424; disturbances at world's end A1063; -dragon D399.1; dripping off person becomes agates D475.4.8; drowns girl filling pitcher D1432.1; entrance to lower world F93; enters into giant's boots from above F531.3.1.1; that has neither fallen from heaven nor sprung from earth (horse's sweat) H1073; fairy (carries off woman) F322.0.1, (dies out of water) F321.1.5, (as foster mother) F311.3.1; fairies F212.0.1; falling on head death omen J2311.1.3; features A910ff.; fowl D169.1; from foot-washing sprinkled on threshold as protection against witch G272.13; freezes to form mountains A969.5; -gods S264.1.2; goddess A420.1, V1.6.2.0.1; gushes where strong man digs F639.1.2; -hen A2332.5.3, A2356.2.5; -hole D928; -horse B401.1; kept by monster so that mankind cannot use it A1111; of life *E80ff., F162.6.2; lighter than wood F716.2; from magic well causes person to dance D1415.1; -miller P443.0.1; -ousel A2411.2.1.2; pot A2320.6; from saint's washing as remedy D1500.1.18.4; -snakes A2531.1, A2532.1.1. B244.1.1, J2137.4; stands still before prince H71.10.2; -supply controlled by water spirit F420.4.9; for thieves in king's garden H1471.1; thrown on corpse to prevent return E431.2; transformed D478, (to milk) D478.1, (to money) D475.2.2; turns to blood as life token E761.1.1; turns into wine on Old Christmas M211.1.1; vanishes when man tries to drink D1647.1; -wheel A1441.3; of youth D1338.1.2; without father or mother (stagnant) H599.1. — Acquisition of w. A1429.3; adventures from seeking w. N785; angel created from w. A52.1.4; angel shows where to dig for w. V232.3.1; animal carries man across w. B551ff.; animals given drinking w. B391.4; animals that inhabit w. A2433.2.2; ashes of dead thrown on w. to prevent return E431.9; attempt to cross w. despite devil C12.5.8; audacious w. and continent husband T315.2.1; axe dropped in w.: modest choice Q3.1; ball falling into w. puts person into ogre's power G423; bathing in boiling w. without cooling it H1023.24; birth from w. T546; bitter w. grateful for being praised D1658.1.3; book dropped in w. by saint not wet F930.1; bringing w. from distant fountain more quickly than witch (task) H1109.1; when calf will not drink, peasant woman throws w. on its back J1903.1; cannibal sent for w. which magically recedes from him: victim escapes K605.1; cannibal sent for w. with vessel full of holes: victim escapes K605; captivity under w. R46; carrying w. jugs suitor test

H331.10; carrying w. in a sieve (task) H1023.2; casting into w. sack (barrel) as punishment Q467.1; cast-off wife thrown into w. S432; changeling thrown into w. and thus banished F321.1.4.1; clothes carry owner over w. D1524.2; cold w. warmed by saint D2144.3.1; collecting all drops of w. H1144.1; conception from drinking w. T512.3; contest in remaining under w. H1543; corpses thrown in w. E431.9.2; creator sent for w.: meantime animals assume their present forms A1713; why crabs live in w. A2433.6.3.1; cricket hears w. hiss on hot iron: learns his song A2272.1.2; dead spirits walk on w. G299.1; deity rewards animal for bringing him w. A2221.11; devil cannot cross running w. G303.16.19.13; devil as stream of w. G303.3.4.11; devil creates devils by casting w. behind himself G303.1.4.1; devil lives in w. G303.8.8; disenchantment by bathing (immersing) in w. D766.1; disenchantment by throwing object into w. D789.5; disenchantment by w. D766.1.1; divination by throwing objects into w. D1812.5.0.6; divination by w. *D1311.3.1.1; dragon controls w. supply B11.7.1; drinking bitter w. as chastity test H411.4.1; drops of w. make hollow in stone J67; druids dry up enemy's w. D2091.8.1; dupe crowded into the w.: drowns K892; dwarfs carry w. F451.3.4.8; earth rises from w. so saint can cross D2125.0.1; enigma on w. as only food H588.21; extraordinary bodies of w. F710ff.; fairies made visible through use of magic w. F235.4.4; fairies teach mortal to walk under w. F345.1; fairies' palace undestroyed by w. F222.1.1; fairyland under w. F212; falcon brings w. of life B172.5; falling in love with reflection in w. T11.5; famished wolf asks sheep to bring him w. K2061.5; fearless hero frightened by being awakened by cold w. H1441; fettered monster kept just out of reach of w. A1074.5; filling bottomless w.-tube H1023.2.4; fire and w. mixed to make sacrifice J1952; fish carries man across w. B551.1; flies try to drink w. from elephant's ears J971; fool can live under w. P192.4; fool can walk on w. P192.3; foot touching w. frees king abducted by fairies N661; fool fills self with w. before feast J2178; forbidden body of w. C615ff.; fountain produced from drop of w. D1567.7; four rivers, rising in paradise, w. world A871.2; frog-woman disenchanted by sight of w. D789.3.1; ghost kills by spewing w. E268; ghost laid in w. E437.2; ghost laid by pushing into w. E446.5; ghost summoned by holy w. E386.1; giant killed by own death w. G527; giants live under w. F531.6.2.2; glass of w. breakfast for farmer's help W152.12.1; god of w. A420ff.; god's promise not to destroy world by w. A1011.3, A1113; going on w. tabu C751.4; head of corpse thrown on w. to prevent return E431.9.1; holy w. *V132; how much w. in river? H696.1.4; identification by hair found floating on w. H75.1; impounded w. A1111; land of dead across w. *E481.2; learn to swim before going into w. J2226; lies about w. features X1540; looking at w. tabu C315.3; not to let ball fall into w. *C41.2; literal numskull throws w. on roasting pig J2461.1.3; magic cow from w. world B184.2.2.2; magic body of w. *D910ff.; magic healing w. *D1500.1.18; magic horse from w. world B184.1.3; magic land and w. vehicle D1533.1; magic name brings w. D1766.7.2; magic object enables person to cross w. *D1524ff.; magic object permits man to walk on w. D1524.1; magic power in w. D1718.1; magic power to walk on w. *D2125.1; magic results from contact with w. D1788.1; magic ring loses power on w. D877.1; magic sight by looking into glass of w. D1821.3.7.1; magic staff draws w. from stone D1549.5; magic w. *D1242.1, (protects) D1380.5; man can breathe nine days under w. F691; man proof against boiling w. D1841.2; man made from w. A1261; man stays under w. for long period X1737; man transformed to w. D283; man who does not know how to pray so holy that he walks on w. V51.1; man will not move in bed when w. drops in his eyes W111.1.3; mankind emerges from w. A1232.2.1; mare from w. world offended, disappears C918; mermaid entices people into w. B81.3.1; milk sack transformed to sheet of w. D494.5.1; monkey jumps into w. after butterfly J2133.10; moon is w. slung into sky A741.1; much w. compressed into small ditch D491.3; why muskrats live in w. A2433.3.10; numskull buys w. at market J2478; ogre draws victims under w. G336; ogre magically produces w. N812.6; ogress lives in w. G639; origin of fresh w. welling up in sea A925.4; origin of scum on stagnant w. A2847; ordeal by w. H222ff.; otherworlds under and beyond w. F141.0.1; oversalting food of giant so that he must go outside for w. K337; why oyster lives in salt w. A2433.6.2; people in otherworld pour w. into tub full of holes *F171.6.2; permission refused to drink from w. tank W155.5; person lives on w. for year F1033.1; person thrown into the w. and abandoned *S142; picking up w. thrown on ground no harder than undoing of slander J84; poisonous w. created by devil A63.7.1; pouring w. into his inkwell J1176.1; pouring w. on fire witch protection G272.8; power to walk to nearest w. F651; primeval w. A810ff.; princess stepping in w. tabu C567.2; prisoner has drunk w. furnished by the king and thus become king's guest J1183.1; quest for marvelous w. H1321; question (on quest): when will a certain w. animal be freed from an annoyance? H1292.9; rain produced by pouring w. *D2143.1.1; reflection in w. thought to be original of thing reflected J1791; reincarnation as w. E636; remarkable pourer of w. F636.3; remarkable power to walk straight to nearest w. F651; remedy for lack of w. in certain place overheard in conversation of animals (demons) N452.1; repression of lust through sitting in w. T317.1; residence in w. F562.3; resuscitation by w. E80.3; riddle: how much w. is in the sea? H696.1; rock becomes w. D452.1.10; sacrifice to secure w. supply S263.3; saint unhurt by boiling w. D1841.2.1; sea w. mixes with fresh at world's end A1063.2; serpent releases swallowed up w. supply *F914.1; sex changes after w. crossing D10.2; separation of persons caused by looking for w. N311; sitting in w. as penance Q541.1; sky consists of w. A702.1; Solomon refuses w. of immortality for himself J369.1; soul of w. E701.2; sound of w. mistaken for monster K1725.2; special power of chaste woman (carrying w. in a sieve) *H413.3; (making ball of w.) H413.2; spirit drinks w. supply dry G346.4; standing in w. for forty days as penance Q541.2; statues animated by w. or wind F855.2; stealing magic healing w. H1151.21; stone sheds w. at perjury H251.2.2; stroke of staff brings w. from rock *D1567.6; supplying w. in land where it is lacking (task) H1138; tabu broken, w. withdrawn from lake C939.1; tabu to enter w. during menses C141.3; tabus on drinking w. C273; task: carrying w. in leaky vessel H1023.2.1; touching w. tabu C532; touching w. in fairyland tabu F378.2; transformation by applying w. D562.1; transformation by crossing w. D574; transformation by touching w. D565.6; transformation to pool of w. D283.1; transformation when one expresses astonishment at smith drawing w. in an eggshell D512.1; transformation: w. to milk C479.7; treasure hidden under w. N513; tree pulled down in order to give it w. to drink J1973; trolls' horses w. at peasant's well F241.1.2.1; troubled w. as life token E761.6.1; true bride pushed into w. by false K1911.2.2; use of w. after call of nature tabu C725.1; vari-colored w. in well F718.2; victim pushed into w. K925.1; walking upon w. without wetting self D1841.4.3; wall of w. controlled D2151.0.3; wild hunt appears by body of w. E501.12.4; wine needs no further w. J125.1; wind raised by troubling vessel of w. D2142.1.4; wisdom from dream: the leper with the cup of w. J157.1; woman with newly-drawn w. good omen D1812.5.2.2.1; woman pushes lover into w. K1645.

Waters follow footsteps of one throwing flower D1547.2; made to dry up D2151.0.2; magically divide and close *D1551ff.; magically pursue man D1432; react to poet's words F996; rise to drown wrongdoer F930.2; turn aside for holy man D1841.4.3.1. — Cupbearer of the gods controls w. A165.3.2; escape from drowning by drying up all w. D2165.2; establishment of present order: w. A1110ff.; extraordinary occurrences concerning seas or w. F930ff.; fairies defile w. F369.2; magic control of w. *D2151ff.; magic w. and medicines *D1240ff.; quest for glass of all w. H1377.1; saint regulates temperature of w. D2151.0.1; wild huntsman w. his horse *E501.15.7; woman created from offerings on the w. A1275.5.

Watercress. — Conception from eating w. T511.2.2.

Waterfall as otherworld barrier F141.4. — Dragon's home beneath w. B11.3.1.2; giant's home beneath w. F531.6.2.2.3; ogre draws girl over w. G426; throwing into w. as punishment Q467.4.

Watermelon. — Lie: large w. X1411.1.1.

Water-monster G308.2; allows saint to place cauldron on head K2314.2.1; attacks man B877.1.1; tries to pull horse into water K1022.2.1. — Horned w. B68.

Water-monsters lick saint's feet B251.2.6.1.

Waternut. — Resuscitation with w. E181.1.1.

Waterskin. — Rain from w. in sky A1131.4.1; thunder from w. dragged along sky A1142.8.

Water-spirit. — Helpful w. N815.0.2; mythical horse belonging to w. B19.3.2; reincarnation as w. E653.1; sacrifice to w. S263.3.

Water-spirits *F420ff. — Magic object summons w. D1421.2; not to offend w. *C41.

Watersprite transformed to flood D283.3.

Watered milk sold K287; wine J1312.

Watering cow by pouring water over it J2465.1.1. — Contest in causing mouth w. H509.2; crawling on knees and w. a dry staff until it blooms Q521.1.1.

Wattle. — Building home w. at a time J67.1; silver w. F163.3.4, (in otherworld dwelling) F165.3.4.

Waumpaus F401.3.3.1.

Wave. — "He who throws himself against w. is overthrown" J21.52.9; homesick w. J1875.3; magic w. D911.1; man becomes ocean w. D283.5; roaring w. good omen D1812.5.2.7; saint rides blessed w. D2125.1.1.1; sand w. advances upon city Q552.14.3; singing of w. gives supernatural information D1310.7; tidal w. C984.4, (marks death place) A913.1.

Waves answer roar of magic shield D1549.10; blown by mighty blower F622.2; break caul of abandoned child N655; as daughters or widows of sea-god A423; form high wall around otherworld isle F141.3; as sea-god's horses Z118.2; as tresses of sea-god's wife Z118.1. — Binding w. of the sea (task) H1137; count only the w. before you J311.1; counting the w. H1144.2; dashing w. don't touch saint D2151.3.2; deformity cured by w. F959.2.1; extraordinary behavior of w. F931.4; fairy chariot rides w. F242.1.2; fiery, then icy w. around Judas E489.7; god drives chariot over w. A171.0.1; homeland sinks beneath w. F944.2; magic control of w. D2151.3; magic transportation by w. D2125.1.1; origin of sea w. A925.1, A1116; rabbits afraid of w. J1812.2; roaring of w. ill omen D1812.5.1.24; Virgin Mary saves devotee from w. V268.2.

Waving. — Resuscitation by w. magic object E74.

Wax figure comes to life D435.1.4; turned into earth D479.6. — Bees build church of w. to contain consecrated host B259.4; building w. replica of castle H1133.6; castle of w., shining like gold F771.1.8; creation of bee to provide w. for candles in church A2012.1; ears stopped with w. to avoid enchanting song J672.1; hare (jackal) makes horns of w. and poses as horned animal K1991; hero rides on w. elephant B557.11.1; resuscitation by w. from deer's ear E115.

Waxing of moon A755.4. — Magic w. and waning of strength D1836; sacrifice allows moon's w. A755.3.1.

Way, see also **Path;** to otherworld hard to find F150.1; short yet long J21.5.3; through the world is longest (riddle) H644.1. — Bird shows w. (by dropping feathers every seven steps) *B151.2.0.1, (by singing) B151.2.0.3; devil's house is visible on the w. to hell G303.8.3.3; false bride takes true bride's place on the w. to the wedding K1911.1.1; marking w. in unfamiliar country J765; short, dangerous vs. long, sure w. J266; women refuse to show God the w. A1372.8.

Wazir fulfills prophecy, murders rajah M370.1.1.

Weak fatally interfere in quarrel J2143; fear company of strong J425; son condemned to be brothers' servant M438.5. — Association of strong and w. J420ff.; dwarfs are w. F451.3.9; foolishness of alliances with w. J682; only w.-minded person may unearth a treasure N551.1; three w. things are strongest Z71.1.14; triumph of w. L300—L399; wise fear of w. for strong J613.

Weakest. — Defences by strengthening one's own w. spot J672.

Weakness from seeing nude woman C942.3. — Clever use of human w. J1672; fairy music causes w. F262.3.7; fairies cause w. F362.3; magic object gives w. *D1336ff.; magic w. *D1837; phantom women cause w. F585.3; sickness or w. for breaking tabu *C940ff.; spies' false report of enemies' w. K2363; spirit causes w. F402.1.6; unique source of w. Z312.3.

Wealth, see also **Treasure;** can't be taken with you after death J912.3; gained by seeming to be in the king's confidence K1782; hidden to keep son from gambling N94; marries weaver to princess N141.4; is most important J707; and poverty U60ff.; is relative: beggar with horse, wife, or dog considered rich by poorer beggar U65; sacrificed for freedom, virtue J347; or wisdom more important? N141.2. — Acquisition of w. J706; animal's advice leads man to w. B562; animal helps man to w. and greatness *B580ff.; not to boast of w. C451; cannibal offers w. to save life G683; choice: free poverty or enslaved w. J211; consecrated bread brings w. D1465.1.1; contest of wisdom, w. J185; devil in each stone of church built with ill-gotten w. G303.8.4.2; diligence and economy bring w. J706.1; dispute of w., wisdom J461.7; enjoyment preferred to w. J484; girl gives up w. to flee lecherous man T320.5; giving away all one's w. J211.1.1; god of w. A473, (in bad company) J451.3; goodness preferred to w. J247; magic object as w. D1470ff.; magic w. D2100ff.; man aspiring to greater w. loses all N251.2; penniless bride pretends to w. K1911.5; pretended w. wins girl's love K1917.5; pseudo-magic w.-providing objects sold K111ff.; reasons for condemning w. Z71.1.16; secret w. betrayed by money left in borrowed money-scales *N478; show of w. induces enemy to surrender city K2365.2; uncharitable king loses w. Q595.3; wife sacrificed to procure w. S263.6.

Wealthy man as helper N835; suitor disguised as beggar tests bride H384.1.1. — Forget God, become w. J556.2; how to become w. J706.1.

Weaning children A1566.

Weapon as chastity index H435; miraculously removed from wound F959.3.4; transformed D454.9. — Accidental death through misdirected w. N337; bringing enemy without w. M234.2; death from falling on own w. N339.8; don't uncover w. in assembly J21.2.4; extraordinary w. F830ff.; father gives son w. to kill him with S22.3; girl asks lover for w., uses it against him K1218.5; god with w. A137.14; identification by broken w. H101; identification by matching w., wound H101.1; immovable w. D1654.4; infallible w. D1653.1ff.; king pays for imaginary w. K499.7; lightning w. of the gods A285.1; magic object renders w. useless

*D1414ff.; magic sickness from w. in head D2064.7; man as w. F628.2.7; man pinned in bed by w. caught in quilt N386.2; prophecy: death by particular w. M341.2.0.1; stick becomes w. D451.6.3; strong man uproots tree and uses it as w. F614.2; suitor test: lifting strong princess's giant w. H345.1; tabu: fire, w., dog together C887; thunder from God beating his w. A1142.5.1; unique deadly w. Z312; unique w. obtained through misrepresentation K362.0.1; vow not to flee from w. M155.3; walking on w. edge F679.3.

Weapons, see also **Arms;** P553; disguised to enter enemy's camp K2357.5; of the gods A157; from horse's bones B338; join in keen F994.2; confined by flying bits of hair in furious battle F1084.0.2; magically blown from hands D2086.3; magically dulled D2086; magically venomous D1402.7.0.1; procured for boy at birth T602. — Acquisition of w. A1459.1; broken w. magically restored D2163.1; concealed w. sent king kill servant K929.11; deception by hiding w. K818.4; destruction of enemy's w. J621; dwarfs make w. for gods F451.10.4; father dies in fire while taking down w. N339.8.1; feigned ignorance of hero's w. K1792.2; foolishness of surrendering w. J642; giant's enormous w. F531.4.5; hero wields many w. at once F628.5; hero's extraordinary w. A524.2; identification by w. H125; indentions on rocks from w. A972.5.4; identions on rock from w. of robbers A972.3.1.1; invisible w. D1655.1; invulnerability from w. D1841.5; iron disappears, w. cannot be made D2089.1; magic w. *D1080ff.; moon's wooden w. A759.1; origin of w. A1459.1; precocious child demands w. T615.5; princess hangs up w. of dead lover as continual reminder T85.2; prophecy: w. killing man to recount deed M359.1; reincarnated person identifies former w. H19.1.1; river in hell filled with w. A671.2.2.2, A672.3; seeing man not killed by w. tabu C319.2; stones become w. D452.1.11; strong hero tests w. F611.3.3; substituted w. win combat K97.2; sun's iron w. A739.9; tabus concerning w. C835.2ff.; thunder from w. of sky warriors A1142.6.1; women not to touch man's w. C181.3; worship of w. V1.9.2.

Wearing apparel for menses C146. — Bride test: w. deceased wife's clothes H363.1; clothes never w. out F821.8; correct w. of clothes suitor test H312.6; magic strength from w. ribbon D1835.4; penance: w. friar's cord on skin Q522.7.

Weary. — Death because people w. of life A1335.9.

Weasel as conjurer B191.1; induces cuckoo to give away secret, kills it K815.10; paints self to deceive mice J951.4. — Enmity of hyena and w. A2494.3.3; fairy as w. F234.1.14; man transformed to w. D124.1; snake and w. stop fighting in order to catch mouse W151.4; tabu to eat w. C221.1.1.6; wedding of mouse and w. B281.2.1; why w. is part black A2411.1.2.1.1; why w. is white with dark tip to tail A2411.1.2.1; soul in form of w. E731.4.

Weasel's. — Why tip of w. tail is black A2378.8.3.

Weather auguries D1812.0.15; changed on confession of deed D2140.3; in otherworld F161; signs D1812.5.0.15; to please one only J1041.1. — Ass predicts w. B141.3; control of w. by saint's prayers D2140.1; effect of the four winds on w. A1127.1; establishment of w. phenomena *A1130ff.; extraordinary sky and w. phenomena F790ff.; farmer as w. predictor L144.2; fault-finding with God over w. Q312.4; favorable w. reward for good law Q176; futility of w. prophecies M398; good w. for one foul for another U148; god of w. A280ff.; hot w. from hole in hell A1137; lies about w. X1600; liveable w. from rain-god, wind-god A287.0.1; magic object controls w. D1548; magic w. phenomena *D900ff.; making w. calm as suitor task H335.6; man who asks for good w. given a box full of hornets J2327; origin of wintry w. A1135; pursuers aided by magic w. R236; sacrifice for good w. V17.4; saint as w. prophet V223.6.1; sham wise man predicting w. K1956.9; shaman's wife controls w. D2140.2; slight inconvenience in w., large gain J355; soul as w. phenomena E744ff.; wild hunt as w. omen E501.20.3; witch produces clear w. G283.4; witches have control over w. G283.

Weaver hero L113.3; laments old poverty L217.1; married to princess N141.4; married to princess betrays identity H38.2.4; outwits tax J1289.13; poses as deity K1969.4.1; poses as king to seduce K1315.14; prefers master with one hedgehog J229.8.1; throws himself into the ranks and holds them (riddle) H581.3. — Thieves set up w. as prince K1952.7.

Weavers P445. — Fairies as w. F271.4.2; jokes on w. X251.

Weaver-bird. — Enmity of woodpecker and w. A2494.13.8; why head of w. is small A2320.1.1.

Weaving cloth from two threads (task) H1022.1; of the Fates A463.1.1; large amount by specified time H1092.0.1; love charms D1355.18.1; magic cloth H383.2.2; mantle from single sheep's wool H1022.4.2; silk shirt from hair (task) H1021.6; shirt from piece of thread H1022.2.2; shoes on pilgrimage tabu C99.2. — Contest in w. A2091.1; dead person w. E562; dwarfs w. F455.3.4; false bride unable to finish w. H35.3.1; goddess of w. A451.3.1; husband behind saint's statue advises wife about w. K1971.4; origin of w. A1453.2; prayers w. garment for Virgin V276.1.

Web. — Extraordinary w. of guts F847; man so small he dances in spider w. F535.2.3; spider spins w. across sky F989.21; spider-w. sky-rope F51.1.1; suitors put off till w. is woven K1227.2.

Webs. — Islands from w. woven by primeval spiders A955.7; origin of floating w. in summer A2815.

Wedding, see also **Bride, Marriage;** ceremony T135; of dead E495; dress to go through ring H355.6; funeral on same day V65.3; to guard as condition of release K612; of mortal and fairy F303; tabus C117. — Attention drawn by helpful animal's theft of food from w. table H151.2; big w. X1071; bridegroom's ignorance on w. night J1744.1; brothers reunited at w. N733.5; chains involving w. Z31.1; child born on w. night J1276.2.1; curse on w. night M412.2; dead lover appears at w. E214.1; deaf peasant: w. invitation X111.4; deity assists at w. A185.5; devil plays fiddle at w. G303.9.8.2; devil's w. feast for woman who hanged herself

G303.25.17.3; drunk man at w. X813; dupe persuaded to play for w. party K844; dwarfs invisibly attend w. or christening feasts of mortals F451.5.17; escape by deceptive w. preparations K536.1; fairy slighted at son's w. F361.1.2.1; fairy runs away from w. F301.8; fairy w. F264; false bride takes true bride's place on way to w. K1911.1.1; feigned w. feast to deceive cuckold K1527; giant invited to plentiful w. feast F531.6.8.4.1; girl hidden to postpone w. R53.3; groom killed on w. night N339.4; hero in menial disguise at heroine's w. K1816.0.3.1; husband returns home just in time to forestall wife's w. to another N681; invisible troll attends w. F455.5.2; lenders never refuse money for w. V411.4; liquor at first w. feast A1427.0.3; lover steals bride from w. with unwelcome suitor K1371.1; man unfaithful on w. night T245; old beggar transforms w. party into wolves T155; origin of w. ceremony A1555.1; prince invites angel to w. C13.1; prophecy: death on w. day M341.1.1; prophecy of particular perils to prince on w. journey M352; quest to bring Soma to w. H1285.1; son named successor at w. P17.0.2.1; suitor sent from one relation to another for consent to w. Z31.1; sun and moon hero's w. presents A759.2; thief bribed to leave w. J1392.5; three deformed witches invited to w. in exchange for help *M233; transformation of w. party to marble statues D231.2.1.

Weddings. — Animal w. *B280ff.; dwarfs celebrate w. and christenings of their own F451.6.3.2; happenings at w. *T150ff.; matchmakers arrange w. T53.0.1; spirits borrow at w. F417.1.

Wedge test H1532. — Dupe puts hand (paws) in w. K1111; magic cranberry opens w. and frees hero D1564.5.

Wednesday as auspicious day N127.2; unlucky day N128.2. — Pun on Wesley and W. X111.15.

Wednesdays. — Fountain gives water on W. and Fridays F716.1.

Wee. — There was a w. w. woman who had a w. w. cow, etc. Z39.2.

Weed. — Crossing w.-filled stream H1197.

Weeds for divination D1311.13.2; spoil harvest of too rich men L482.2. — Magic w. D965.18; origin of w. A2688ff.

Weeding garden from rocking chair W111.5.13.

Week. — Forgetful man counts days of w. Z24; horse bought for each w. day (one for each day of year) H1117; message after w. J2192.1; mortal wins fairies' gratitude by joining in their song and completing it by adding names of days of w. F331.3; seven w. days have passed since time of Adam (riddle) H706.1; tabu: feasting for a w. C230.1; transformation each w. D622.

Weep. — Crane will not w. at crucifixion A2231.2.1; dwarfs w. F451.6.7; only one person refuses to w. at hero's death Z351; toad refuses to w. over its dead children: dries up when dead A2231.8.

Weeping animal B214.4; bitch K1351; coin J1875.4; dead man E551; of future suicide in mother's womb T575.1.2; ghost E402.1.1.6; horse B301.4.2, B736.2; man turned into owl: still bewails A2261.5; rocks F801;

at sins of the world U15.1; statue D1625; tabus G482; for thief J1142.4; -willow's curse A2776.2. — Animals w. B736ff.; ascetic w. V462.3; birds w. in sympathy B303.1; dead father stops daughter's w. E327.1; disenchantment by w. jug of tears D753.2; disguise as w. woman K1836.4; divinity w. A194.1; ghost summoned by w. E381; god summoned by w. A189.2; hardness of heart prevents w. W155.3; horse w. for saint's death B301.4.1.1; illiterate pretends to be w. over book K1795; magic w. object D1618; parson preaches so that half congregation is w. and half laughing X416; people w. at child's birth P617; prodigious w. of saint F1051; queen shames cowards for w. W121.4; resuscitation by w. E58; return from dead to stop w. *E361; Satan w. G303.9.8.10; sham miracle: w. painting of Virgin K1972.2; soul w. as it leaves body E722.2.7; not too much w. for dead *C762.2.

Weevil. — Reincarnation as w. E616.4.

Weigh. — How much does the moon w. (riddle) H691.1.2.

Weighed. — Souls w. at Judgment Day E751.1; stolen meat and w. cat J1611.

Weighing elephant as test of resourcefulness H506.1; fire H1145.1; mountain as task H1149.8; princess against flower H455; witch against Bible H234. — Fortune w. man's balance N111.3.2; princess can't marry anyone w. more than she T69.2.2.

Weight of bodily member chosen rather than its loss J341. — Castration to put on w. J1919.5.3; great w. of witch's corpse G259.4; light w. person F584; magic suspension of w. D1691; riddles of w. H691ff.; "Time" overpowered when w. is taken from his clock Z122.1; trickster threatens to throw w. into cloud K1746.

Weights. — Handling w. loudly enough to outwit robbers K432.2; origin of w. and measures A1471.2; reduced prices but false w. K286; use of false w. punished Q274.3.

Weighted order-cards J1382.2. — Penance: pilgrimage with hands and loins w. with iron Q522.4.

Weinsberg. — Women of W. J1545.4.1.

Welcome to the clothes J1561.3. — Birds w. saint B251.2.5; enigmatic w. of host H595; fish w. saint B251.2.2; umbrellas w. bride A1555.3.

Welfare. — Wraith investigates w. of absent person E723.4.6.

Well entrance to lower world F93.0.2.1; in hell A671.4; indicates life span D1663.5; of life and death D1663.3; located under sea F718.1; magically transported D2136.7; man made to believe that he is sick J2317; in midst of earth from which rivers spring A875.2; of oil runs into river F932.4; polluted by blood D1563.2.2.1; produced by magic D926.1; as refuge R317; rises to aid holy person F933.1.3; rises for sheep only for rightful owner H251.3.9.2; in sea F711.4.2; shines at night D1645.9. — Abandonment in w. S146.1; animal rescues man from w. B547.1; animals refuse to help dig w. and are punished A2233.1; boy protected by Virgin survives week in w. V268.1; bringing w. to king (task) H1023.25; bringing whole w. K1741.3; captivity in w. R41.3.4; child put down into w. instead of bucket

J2175.3; children said to come from w. T589.6.4; cursing by means of w. D2175.1; demons live in w. F402.6.3; devil drinks church w. dry G303.9.9.14; devil's w. G303.10.19; dragon dips wounds in holy w., is healed B11.12.1.2; drawing bucket of w. water without rope H1023.20; drinking from fairyland w. tabu F378.4; dupe sent to w., pushed in K831.1.1; dupe tricked into w. K735.5, K1078; extraordinary w. F718; fairyland entered through w. F212.1; forbidden w. C623; frogs decide not to jump into w. J752.1; ghost haunts w. E285; girl drowned in w. as river's origin A934.10; goats driven into w. J1959.1; holy water destroys veil over w. D1562.6; inexhaustible w. D1652.15; location of w. indicated by bell D1314.4.1; looking at w. tabu C315.4; magic healing w. D1500.1.1.1; magic stones from holy w. D1382.1.0.1; magic w. *D926; magic wisdom from drinking of w. D1811.1.2; man falling into w. kills cobra N624; man fishes up two blind women from w. F1065; miraculous w. yields milk, beer, wine D925.0.2; mother cuts off heads of w. to cure sick (riddle) H583.4.3; numskull tries to dig up w. J1933; object dropped into w. leads to adventures N777.2; one should let w. enough alone J513; otherworld at bottom of w. F133.5; penance: being locked in w. and key thrown into water Q544; person follows magic receding w. D1420.2; person pushed into w. rescued R131.3.3.1; prophecy inscribed on w. M302.6; pushing into w. as punishment Q465.3; queen pushes husband into w. K2213.2.1; rescue from w. R141; rivers from mythical w. A934.8; saint warns against poisoned w. V223.2; saving self from falling into w. J21.34; sick hung in w. to cool off J2412.6; stargazer falls into w. J2133.8; swans from fowl fed in Urd's w. A1981.0.1; thief sent into w. by trickster K345.2; trickster cheats rescuers into digging his w. K474; troll's horses water at peasant's w. F241.1.2.1; waiting at w. for thief J2214.3; water cannot be drawn from w. to wash murdered body Q559.3; wethers leap from w. B184.6.1; wolf descends into w. in one bucket and rescues fox in other K651; wolf tries to drink w. dry to get cheese J1791.3.1; world at bottom of w. F725.9.

Wells break forth at Christ's birth A941.5.0.2; in otherworld F162.5. — Cursing w. D1792.2; father's counsel: the four w. H588.8; first w. dug A1429.3.1; magic control of w. D2151.6; magic results from sacrifices at trees and w. D1766.2.1; ogre polluting w. G584; plague from Jews' poisoning w. V362; sacred w. V134; selling old oil w. for post holes X1761.1; three w. under three roots of earth-tree A878.1.2; why water from w. not drunk? H1292.1.1.

Welsh. — Fairies are W. cursed by St. Patrick F251.13.

Wen. — Hero breaking w. causes wall to fall X959.1.

Wench. — Devil as black w. G303.3.1.12.3; rakshasa in form of w. G369.1.5.

Wer-bear D113.2.1.

Wer-crocodile D194.0.1.

Wer-tiger D112.2.1. — Marriage to w. N399.3.

Wer-tigers. — Village of w. B221.6.1.

Werwolf *D113.1.1; recognized by man's clothes H64.2; with thread in teeth H64.1. — Boy saved by w. R169.3; magic axe keeps out w. D1385.5.2; not to look at w. C311.1.4; transformation to w. on Fridays D622.1.

Werwolves hold mass *V49.1.

Wesley. — Pun on W. and Wednesday X111.15.

West forbidden direction C614.13; wind exhausted from fleeing deity A1127.2. — Castle east of sun and w. of moon F771.3.2; divinity's departure for w. A561; female god invoked in w. A183.1; land of dead in w. E481.6.2; otherworld in w. A692.1, F136.2; sun travels from w. to east F961.1.2.

Westward. — Mountains push water w. A914.

Wet. — Ascetic sleeps in w. sheet V462.5.1.2; book dropped in water by saint not w. F930.1; feeding pigs w. meal J2465.1; man proof against w. from rain D1841.4.1; person proof against w. from snow D1841.4.2; resuscitation by w. cloth on corpse E80.2; why earth becomes warm and w.: underground vessels steaming A857.1.

Wet-nurse. — Own mother as exposed child's w. S351.0.1.

Wet-nurses. — Diabolical child kills his w. T614.

Wether. — Purple w. B731.9.

Wethers leap from well B184.6.1.

Wetting. — Adam created five devils by w. five fingers with dew and shaking them behind him G303.1.5; dipping water without w. dipper H1046.1; ferrying across river without w. feet H1046; magic causes bed w. D1379.4.

Whale boat *R245; carrying man shakes him off when struck M205.1.1.1; fights monster pursuing saint B523.2; with golden teeth B101.5; husband makes wife impervious to sea D1841.4.5; as messenger B291.4.3; raises back to help voyaging clerics land B256.12; thought to be an island J1761.1; transformed to skull D421.7.1. — Artificial w. made as stratagem K922; disenchantment by eating w. D764.5; dolphin and w. scorn crab as peacemaker J411.6; giant w. B874.3ff.; helpful w. B472; killing sacred w. Q211.6.2; man kills w. which carried him across sea W154.5.1.1; man transformed to w. D127.3; marriage to w. B603; origin of w. A2135; people pelt each other with w. meat J2195; Jonah and the w. the walking tomb with the living tenant H821; raven inside w. F911.2.1; reincarnation as w. E617.4; witch killed as w. G252.1; witch rides on w. G241.1.5; witch as w. G211.7.1.

Whale's — Ascetic lives on w. back V462.10; flood from w. vomit A1013.1; foxes killed in w. house K728; magic object in w. heart D849.5.1.

Whales disgorge gold B583.1; rescue drowning king who planned their death W154.9.1. — Giant eats w. F531.3.4.3; giant fishes w. F531.3.12.2; monster w. of human parentage G308.8; why some w. die on land: first whale did so A2211.4.

What should I have done (said)? J2461.

Wheat dough eaten by bitch becomes nobleman A1656.1; rice and dal dispute superiority J461.5; transformed to barley D451.2.2; undamaged by swift runner F681.12. — Bare hillside becomes w. field at Christ's presence V211.1.8.3; birth from w. T543.6.1; why grain of w. is divided A2793.2; inexhaustible w. D1652.1.3.3, (sack) D1472.1.22.2; magic w. *D1033.2; martyrs called red w. Z141.2.1; mill will not grind stolen w. D1318.15; numskull feeds his w. to frogs J1851.1.2; oats become w. D451.2.3; saint causes w. to ripen prematurely D2157.2.2; shower of w. F962.6.1; why w. must be planted one year, harvested the next A2793.2.1.

Wheel buried in doorstep to prevent deviltry D1385.10; followed to otherworld F159.3; symbol A137.3.1. — Carrying a wagon axle which has broken a w. (task) H1183; celestial bodies attached to w. in heaven A702.3.1; destructive rolling w. D1207.1; devil in form of w. on wagon G303.3.4.1; devil helps man place cart w. when it becomes unfastened G303.22.4; earth w.-shaped and boundless A875; Fortune's w. N111.3; get up and put your shoulder to the w. J1034; ghost as glowing w. E421.3.1; giant rolls like w. F531.6.17.6; glowing w. thought to be devil J1781.3; god with w. A137.3; Ixion lashed to revolving w. Q501.5; magic w. *D1207, (at otherworld door) F165.1.0.2; man transformed to w. D256; origin of water w. A1441.3; punishment: breaking upon a w. Q423; revolving w. at otherworld entrance F156.3; slaughter from w. rolling over Europe M341.2.20; victim bound to bladed w. S181.1.

Wheels. — Divination from sound of chariot w. D1812.5.0.12; dupe waits for rear w. to overtake front w. J2066.7; fiery w. in hell A671.2.4.6; god's throne on w. A152.3; king given three w. to control his anger J571.2; ship on w. F841.3.2; spirit makes w. come off wagon F473.6.6.

Wheelbarrow too large to leave shed J2199.2. — Fright at creaking of w. J2615; mad w. J1887.

Whelp leaps through hound F916.2. — King's vision of w. V515.2.1.1; magic w. kills hound B182.1.3.1.

Whetstone among best of stones (riddle) H659.3.1.

Whetting knife: whole blade whetted away K1418. — Devil's aid invoked in w. scythe C12.3; ogress w. teeth to kill captive G83.1; razor w. itself D1601.8.

Whimbrel sends mate to death in cave K813.1.

Whining. — Father kills sons for w. S11.3.3.2.

Whip. — Caves from w. in ground A2825; ghost beats man with w. E261.5; god creates the devil by striking a stone with his w. G303.1.1.4; lie: remarkable user of w. X1002; lightning as god's w. A1141.4; magic w. *D1208; serpent as saint's w. B292.12; sham-dead roused with w. J2311.12; snake cracks self like w. B765.10; snake mistaken for w. J1761.6.1.

Whips. — Origin of horse-w. A1459.1.5; person beaten by w. for breaking tabu C982.

Whipping causes changeling to betray his nature F321.1.1.7; ogre to death G512.8.4; reproves quarrelsome wife T256.3. — Anticipatory w. by schoolmaster J2175.1; tabu on w. magic horse C762.3.

Whirled. — Prisoner w. away in fire R122.1.

Whirlpool. — Devil disappears in w. G303.17.2.2; ebb-tide goes to great w. A913.3; magic calming of w. D2151.4; rubies in w. D1467.2.

Whirlpools. — Nine w. of world Z71.6.2.

Whirlwind as ghost's vehicle E581.1. — Abduction by w. R17; devil as w. G303.3.4.4.1; devil comes in w. G303.6.3.2; god of w. A282.1; magic journey by throwing knife into w. *D2121.8; man transformed to w. D281.1.1; reincarnation as w. E641; soul as w. E744.3; troll rides in w. *F455.3.3.2; troll as w. F455.2.9; witch flies as w. G242.2.

Whiskers. — Cock's w. (cumulative tale) Z43; husband's w. gone, mistaken for lover J1485.1; wooer strokes w., "All of these are mine" K1917.7.

Whiskey, see also **Liquor, Wine.** — Dead man asks for w. E556.1.1; deceptive contest in drinking w. K82.3; origin of w. A1427.2.

Whispers. — Answering dead in w. E545.23.

Whispering in church attracts devil G303.24.1.8.

Whistle heralds devil's coming G303.6.3.5; for Senate ruler's son J553.2. — Alleged resuscitating w. sold K113.2; ghost summoned by blast on w. E384.3; magic w. *D1225, (vitalizes cockroach) D1594.6; one to blow w. J1382.1; one must not w. after sunset, else devil will go along with one G303.16.18; origin of w. A1461.5; priest, devil quarrel over w. M216.2.

Whistlers. — Seven w. are souls of Jews who crucified Christ A1715.3.

Whistling animals B214.2; at mass X442; in mine brings ill luck F456.1.2.1.1; tabu C480.1, C483.1. — Animal w. B214; fairies w. F262.7; ghost raised by w. E384.2; hail produced by w. tune D2143.4.1; maid w. as she brings in dessert W152.12.3; ogre w. G653; respite from death while captor is w. K551.3.2; snake w. B765.15; wind raised by w. D2142.1.6.

White god A124.2; horse in wild hunt E501.4.2.1; as magic color D1293.3; man made to believe that he is negro J2013.1; mango tree F811.3.2; mare thought to be church J1761.2; rat transformed to white-winged elephant D411.2.1; sea F711.3.1; sheep comes to upper world, black to lower F67; sheep-skin used as source of light J1961; woman as guardian of treasure N572.1; woman bears black child T562. — Black beans, w. soup J1291.1; black sheep turn w. F985.1; creation of w. horse A1881.1; why deer has w. mark on nose A2335.2.1; devil as w. stallion G303.3.3.5.3; devil in shape of w. bull G303.3.3.12; dwarf cave has ceiling of mineral w. as snow F451.4.3.3; dwarfs clad in w. F451.2.7.4; dwarfs have silvery w. hair F451.2.4.2; why end of fox's tail is w.

A2378.8.1; explaining "w." to blind man U173; fairies in w. clothes
F236.1.3; fairies ride w. horses F241.1.1.1; Fortuna half w., half black
N111.2.3; ghost in w. E422.4.3; ghost as w. horse E423.1.3.4; glorified
w. garment F821.6; magic leaves turn w. bird black D1337.2.1; magic
w. cow B184.2.0.1; mermaid's w. skin B81.9.5.1; mountain-men in w.
caps F460.1.4.1; negro tries in vain to be washed w. J511.1; no w. man
near, so belongings safe J1373; objects on one side of palisade in
otherworld garden black, on other w. F162.1.2.3; one cheek w., other
red F545.3.1; origin of w. man A1614.9; peasants fed w. bread demand
rye bread to which they are accustomed U135; person in w. mistaken
for ghost J1782.6; pill transformed to a w. rabbit D444.3; pretty w.
hands F552.3; purely w. boar H1331.2.1; red as blood, w. as snow
Z65.1; revenant as lady in w. E425.1.1; riddle (black and w. horses
chasing each other) H722.2, (king in red: courtiers in w.) H731.1,
(king in w., courtiers in w.) H731.2, (w. field, black seed) H741;
series: w. cock, red cock, black cock Z65.2; son forgets to spread
w. sails, prearranged signal of his safety N344; soul as black or w.
spirit over coffin E722.1.1; soul as w. E722.1.2; symbolic color: w.
Z142; treasure found by sprinkling ground with blood of w. cock
D2101.1; troops of black, w., and red soldiers F873.1; wild huntsman
with black fur cap and w. staff E501.8.6; wild huntsmen dressed in w.
E501.8.3; wish for wife red as blood, w. as snow, black as raven T11.6.

Whiter. — Angel w. than swan (riddle) H663.

Whitest. — Successful suitor must have w. hands H312.4.

Whitefish. — Enmity of w. and pike A2494.15.1.

Whitewashing weapons as disguise K1839.6.

Whitsuntide V70.2.

Whittington's cat N411.1; fortune foretold M312.

Whole. — Animals eaten by fairies become w. again *F243.3.1; build
shelter for the w. year J741; journey to otherworld where people are
made w. F125; with his w. heart: devil carries off judge M215.

Whore, see **Prostitute.**

Wicked burned in heaven E755.1.2; flatter death J814.4; son blinded
Q451.7.5; son confined on island Q433.9; souls eaten E752.9; woman
unable to endure presence of host at mass V39.2. — Animals leave w.,
go to pious master B292.0.2; devil carries off w. people R11.2.1;
failure of crops during reign of w. king Q552.3; return from dead to
slay w. person E232; supernatural manifestations at death of w. person
*Q550.1; two w. men put to fiery test, ask for third K528.3.

Wicket. — Going through w. gate tabu C614.2.

Widened. — River magically w. D2151.2.6.

Widow in armor routs would-be ravisher T320.3.1; may not remarry
T131.4; of ogre's victim at ogre's house G691.2; refuses second marriage
so her brother can not kill a second husband J482.1.2. — Bridegroom
buys w. cloth for bride Z140.4; buying w. cloth: his wife must be

widow J2301.2; devil marries w. who maltreats him G303.12.2; faithless w. T231; ghost visits w. and new husband E321.4; hypocritical, oversensitive w. K2052.4; killing self to make wife w. J2106; king advised to marry maid rather than w. J482; lifting power of w. prepared for suttee H479.1; marriage to rich master's w. N251.3; rich lord who robs poor w. of her cow chokes on first mouthful Q552.6.

Widow's meal J355.1; son as hero L111.3. — Ogre assumes form of w. husband K1919.2; rich man seizes poor w. cow U35.

Widows. — England must be full of w. J2214.11; why w. do not remarry T291.

Widowed. — Woman w. twenty-two times F1073.

Widower marries wife's sister P263.1; tells of his courtship, marriage, and death of his wife, all in a week Z24.1. — Cynic's comment on w. remarrying J1442.12.

Wife, see also **Adulteress, Marriage, Woman;** accused of plan to escape weeps and threatens suicide so as to allay suspicion and escape K579.1; as adviser J155.4; assigns husband tasks H934.1; banished S411; betraying husband likened to poison H592.2; behind tree advises husband (about his marital duties) K1971.6.1, (against having his wife work) K1971.4.1; brings bad luck N134.1.2; carried up tree to sky in bag in husband's teeth J2133.5.1; chooses father's side in feud P211; chosen instead of fairy mistress J414.1; confesses for husband V29.5; cures self by calling husband F950.2.1; curses husband, devil takes him C12.5.7; dead of neglect torments husband E221.5; demands parrot who has accused her B335.4; deceives husband with substituted bedmate K1843; dies so that husband's death may be postponed T211.1; dies of fright after husband relates her adultery J1147.1; dies on hearing of her husband's death F1041.1.1.2.2; disguised as fakir makes husband do her bidding K1814.3; dismisses maid who is husband's mistress and reforms husband J1112.2; drinks blood of slain husband P214; flees husband R227; follows written instructions J2516.3.1; forces husband to kill faithful dog B335.1.1; in disguise wooed by her faithless husband K1814; hangs self on tree: friends ask for shoot of tree J1442.11; and husband poison each other K1613.2; imprisoned to preserve chastity T381.0.2; makes gift to husband's mistress and reforms wayward husband J1112.1; makes her husband believe that he is dead J2311.0.1; misunderstands husband's remark, confesses N275.3; more merciful than blood relations P212; multiplies secret J2353; must be returned pregnant to first husband J1173.1; persuades husband (that she has returned immediately) J2315, (to have good tooth pulled) J2324; of philanderer gets revenge by having an affair herself K1510.2; purchased T52.5; rescues husband R152; rescuing husband from supernatural H923.1; resuscitated by turning around, placing head on brick E181.1; sacrificed to procure wealth S263.6; scares robbers, says husband is home D2031.6.3; substitutes for mistress K1223.3; substitutes for princess jailed with husband K1814.2; suicide believing husband dead N343.2.1; sold unwillingly by husband T292; surprises husband in adultery K1271.3.1; takes mistress's place in husband's bed K1843.2; takes servant's place and discovers husband's adultery K1585; tells way to otherworld F174.1; tempts husband as another woman H1556.4.2.1; tests H460ff.; ties husband to bed so lover can kill him K713.1.7; transformed to mistress D659.7; who saw double X121; as wager N2.6; your own only when with you J21.47. — Abandoned w. recognized H152.3; abducted w. leaves needle sign H119.2; advice on choosing w. as equal J21.31; animal as confederate of adulterous w. B598; animal helps quest for vanished w. B543.0.1; animal-husband killed, w. throws self into pyre B691; animal-w. eats husband G79.1; animal wins w. for his master B582.1.1; animals created while god Mahadeo quarrels with his w. A1758; bear makes woman his w. B601.1.1; boasting coward shown up by w. who masks as highwayman and robs him K1837.1; burial of living husband or w. with dead spouse S123.2; cast-forth w. (buried up to waist for seven years and despitefully used) Q456.1.1, (must sit at horse-block of palace and tell story to each newcomer and offer to carry him inside) Q482.4; chaste woman refers lover to his w. K1231.1; chaste woman sends man's own w. as substitute K1223.2.1; child promised: "what your w. has under her belt" S242.1; church his w. J1264.1; clever w. J1112, (gets money from those who attempt to seduce her) K443.2, (prevents husband's disinheritance) J1521.2.1; concealed w. N741.1; creator's w. A37.3; criminal's w. and children sold into slavery Q437.1; calumniated w. K2110.1; dead w. (haunts husband on second marriage) *E221.1; death of w. for breaking tabu C920.2; debtor's w. demanded T52.8; deceased w. marriage test H363; deceptive division of shared w. K171.7; deity's w. creates mosquitoes to drive husband from jungle A2034.1; departing husband assigns his w. tasks H922; deposit money secured by false order to banker's w. K362.6; deserted w. chokes departing husband K951.0.1; devil (gets into ark by hiding in shadow of w. of Noah) G303.23.1, (helps ugly man win w.) G303.22.7, (takes man's w.) C12.5.6, (tries to get man to kill his w.) G303.9.4.3; devil's w. G303.11.1; discovery w. is witch G250.1; disguised husband visits his w. K1813; disguised w. makes husband buy kiss K1814.4; disenchantment by w. D791.2.2; don't send w. on visit to parents J21.47.1; dove helps deity draw w. into net B582.2.5; dream of marriage with another's w. T11.3.2; druid discovers abducted w. D1816.5.1; eavesdropping w. hidden in bushes killed unwittingly by husband N322.2; exchanging w. with ox J2081.3; fairy lover abducts fairy w. of mortal F301.6; fairy mistress and mortal w. F302.5; fairy offers to disenchant mortal w. if man will marry her F302.3.2.2; fairy w. (converted into woman) F302.5.2.1, (deserts mortal husband for repulsive lover) F302.2.1; fairies steal man's w. and carry her to fairyland F322; faithful w. T210.1; false w. identified by breasts H79.6; familiar spirit reveals infidelity of man's w.

F403.2.3.5; father's counsel: marry a new w. every week H588.3; first w. insists husband take second T282.1; forcing w. tabu C164; forgotten w. recalled as she gives beggar food D2006.1.10; fortune of lucky w. N251.5; fox brings human w. fox-food H48.2; future w. met during magic sleep D1976.2; future w. revealed in dream D1812.3.3.9; god swallows his pregnant w. to prevent birth of son whom he fears M376; god swallows his w. and incorporates her into his own being F911.1.1; good w. makes domestic life H659.21; help from ogre's w. G530.1; hero hidden and ogre deceived by his w. G532; hero wakened from magic sleep by w. who has purchased place in his bed from false bride *D1978.4; hero's w. rescued by friend R169.5.1; horse lays head in lap of dead master's w. B301.4.3.1; host surrenders his w. to his guest P325; husband eats w. G77; husband magically forgets w. D2003.1; husband refuses to believe w. unfaithful J2342; husband and w. *P210ff., (burn their mouths) J1478, (disguised and brother and sister) K1839.14, (each receive money from different persons to bury the other, who is supposed to be dead) K482.1; husband answers behind statue when w. wants to know how to fool him K1971.1; husband arrives home just as w. is to marry another *N681; husband as God behind tree forces his w. to confess adultery *K1971.5; husband behind saint's statue advises w. to spin and weave K1971.4; husband fondles second w. in presence of first as punishment for adultery Q484; husband refuses to murder his wife for high honors, w. agrees to murder husband H492.1; husband substitutes leaky vessel so that his w. and paramour are drowned Q466.1; impoverished nobleman offers w. to ruler W11.7.1; jealous w. tells sister to look below: pushes her over cliff K832.1; jealous w. of god A164.7; judgment: man belongs to third w. J1171.3.1; king demands subject's w. P15.2; king gives own w. as reward P14.13; knight unsuccessfully tempted by host's w. T331.2; lazy w. W111.3ff.; lazy w. taken naked in bundle of straw to a wedding Q495.1; loss of w. for breaking tabu C932; love for captive w. rewarded Q56.1; love image grants w. D1595.1; lover humiliated after leaving w. T75.4; Lot's w., having had father and mother, is not dead like other mortals (riddle) H815; Lot's w. transformed to pillar of salt for breaking tabu C961.1; magic object stolen (by hero's w.) D861.5, (by rival for w.) D861.4; magic object from w. D815.8; man disregards priest's warning that he will seduce his w. J652.3; man betrayed into killing his w. K940.2; man calls w. "my swallow": she becomes swallow D511.1; man commends w. to devil (devil takes charge seriously) C12.4; man disguised as w. K521.4.1.4; man rescues his w. from fairyland F322.2; man to bring w. purse-full of sense *J163.2; man sends his naked w. on all-fours in tar and feathers K216.2; man with unfaithful w. comforted J882; man wins w. for friend P310.7; mistress sends man's own w. as substitute without his knowledge K1223.2; moon as w. to twelve sun brothers A753.1.4.2; mortal saves fairy's w. F337; mountain with w. F755.5; mountain w. has breasts so long that she throws them over her shoulder *F460.1.2; must surrender w. to sovereign J1511.19; not to offend (animal w.) C35, (supernatural w.) *C31ff.; obtaining w. on otherworld quest H1256; ogre's w. burned in his own oven G512.3.2.1; ogre's w. killed through other tricks G519.1; ogre's w. jealous G674; old w. provokes sparrow to speak, drop new wife K929.10; origin of w. self-sacrifice A1545.5.1; paramour hidden in chest taken to own w. K1216; peasant w. asks king riddles H561.1.0.1; persecuted w. *S410ff.; plant w. T117.10; polygamy so head w. may be quickly replaced T145.8; poor girl chosen as w. L143.1; poorly dressed woman chosen as w. L213.1; pregnant w. left in friend's charge H1558.9; priest's dead w. found alive J1179.10; prince envious of hero's w. assigns hero tasks H931.1; promise to lend w. for a day M267; propounder's w. helps solve riddle H574; punishment for banishing w. at paramour's wish Q248; punishment for stealing a w. Q252.1; punishment: winning as w. and then killing Q411.1; predestined w. T22.2; queen says man's condition dependent on w. S411.2.1; quest accomplished with aid of w. H1233.2.1; quest assigned by w. through appeal to husband's love for her H1212.2; quest for lost w. H1237; quest for three persons as stupid as his w. H1312.1; quest for vanished w. H1385.3; rainbow king's w. A791.5; rescue by captor's w. *R162; resuscitation of w. by husband giving up half his remaining life *E165; retorts between husband and w. J1540ff.; reward: any boon that may be asked: king's w. demanded Q115.1; second w. orders husband to persecute first S413.2; second w. serving as menial Q482.1.1; senior w. ugly but digilent, second beautiful but lazy T145.7; serpent directed by beautiful w. J155.1.1; sight of deformed witches causes man to release his w. from spinning duty J51; speaking beans rebuke w. for misdeed D1619.1; squaring accounts by shaving w. J2082; star-w. gives birth to human T111.2.1.1; not to steal w. of god C51.2.3; stupid w. J1701; sun and moon as husband and w. A736.1.4.2; supernatural w. summoned by bell T111.0.2; tabu: giving garment back to supernatural w. C31.10; tabu: stealing god's w. C51.2.3; talkative w. discredited J1151.1.1; task left by departing husband for w. to accomplish H1187; task performed with help of supernatural w. H974; tasks assigned before man may rescue w. from spirit world H923; tasks assigned by w. and paramour H916.3; thief disguised as owner's w. K311.8.1; treacherous w. abandoned by lover Q261.2.1; treacherous w. *K2213; tree as w. T461.3; trickster exacts beautiful w. from curious spectators K443.6.1; unborn daughter promised to snake as w. S222.2; unrestricted intercourse between husband and w. A1352.1; unexpected meeting of husband and w. N741; vanished w. rescued R133; vow never to be jealous of one's w. M137; why tortoise looks towards sky: seeks his w., a star A2351.5; wild boar once faithless w. A1422.3; wish for star w. C15.1.1; woman given to devastating monster as w. to appease it S262.1.

Wife's absurd actions deceive ghost E432.2; attendants on trip chase wrong man as suspected lover and miss real lover K1549.6; equivocal oath K1513; nose cut off, husband resuscitated E165.2; ring proof of unfaithfulness H94.0.1. — Caesar's scorn of his w. advice leads to disaster J155.3; dead w. friendly return E322ff.; death from hearing of w. death F1041.1.2.2.3; disguised husband wins faithless w. love K1813.1; dream warns emperor of w. faithlessness *D1813.1.1; exiled w. dearest possession J1545.4; ghost protects w. estate E236.6; husband attracted by w. power of healing: recognition follows H151.8; husband concealed in w. ear F1034.1; husband disguised as woman answers w. riddle H582.3; husband learns of w. fidelity N455.6; husband unwittingly instrumental in w. adultery K1544; king overlooks w. unfaithfulness rather than to cause troubles of state J221.1; man attempts to kill faithful serpent at w. instigation B335.1; man murdered at w. side K959.2.3; man undertakes to do his w. work J2431; moon eats w. corpse G27; painting on w. stomach chastity index H439.1.1; putting out w. eyes J2462.3; reward for w. fidelity Q83.1; searching for rival to w. beauty H1301.1.3; talkative w. tongue paralysed D2072.0.5.3; tasks imposed because of w. foolish boast H916.1.

Wives exchanged T141.2; with hair thought to be witches J1786.6; killed for large corpse-price K941.1.1. — Animals tested as w.: none accepted B600.1.1; begging for any punishment except two w. K583.1; characteristics of w. and husbands *T250ff.; common w. of man debate as to which has helped him most J461.2; custom of purchasing w. A1555.2; deceptive agreement to kill w. K944; friends agree to beating w. K1394; gullible wife believes report that each man may have many w. J1546; hero granted free access to men's w. A591; king has amours with great men's w. so as to learn secrets from them J155.2; king's seven w. pregnant seven years Z71.5.7; Krishna's three w. A164.3.1; limited number of w. for king P18.2; man sees w. in their former incarnations E601.1; many w. T145; Pleiades six repudiated w. A773.2; repeated transformations to deceive w. D616; shooting stars are unfaithful w. A788.5; supernatural w. carry off hero F174; unfaithful w. become edible animals A1422.0.1; various animals tried out as w. B600.1; wagers on w. or servants N10ff.; woman murders son's w. Q211.4.2.

Wig. — Exposure to ridicule when w. snatched off X52.1; taking off w. overawes Indians K547.2; transformation by w. D537.4.

Wild animal (finds his liberty better than tame animal's ease) L451, (sold as watch-dog) K133; animals (herded) B845, (lose their ferocity) A2531.0.1; beast transformed to person D310ff.; Hunt *E501ff.; man (captured and tamed) R1, (lives alone in wood like a beast) F567, (of noble birth) P55, (becomes normal) D92, (as king of animals) B240.3, (as prophet) M301.1, (as ravisher of women) T471.2, (released from captivity aids hero) G671, (son of woman and satyr who overpowers her) F611.1.3, (of superhuman strength) F619.1, (as wood spirit) F441.3. — Bridling a w. horse (task) H1154.3.1; devil as w. goose

G303.3.3.8; disappointed lover becomes w. man in woods T93.1; god of w. animals A443; helpful w. (beasts) B430ff., (duck) B469.4.1, (hog, boar) B443.5, (ox) B443.7; hero in service of w. man G672; magic object received from w. man D812.9; magic wisdom possessed by w. man D1719.2; Milky Way is the W. Hunt A778.1.1; man transformed to w. beast (mammal) D110ff.; person keeps w. pigs as if domesticated B845.1; reincarnation as w. animal E612; revenant as w. animal E423.2ff.; saint's bachall subdues w. animals D1442.3; smith promises to make horse w. K1181; strong hero sent for w. animals F615.2; strong man sent for w. horses brings them back F615.2.3; unexpected meeting with w. man N764; war between domestic and w. animals B262; why w. animals lose ferocity A2294.

Wild boar captured in church K731; given permission to squeal before wolf eats him K551.3.4; sharpens tusks when no enemy is in sight J674.1. — Blind w. in wild hunt E501.4.3.2; fairy in form of w. F234.1.3.1; great w. X1233.1.2; haunt of w. tabu C619.2; man reincarnated as w. E611.3.1; vow to kill w. alone at night M155.1; why tiger does not attack w. until latter is old: result of duel A2257.1.

Wildcat. — Enmity of hyena and w. A2494.3.5; how w. got mashed face A2213.2.1, A2330.1.

Wildcats. — Lies about w. X1212; why w. eat chickens A2435.3.15.

Wild goats. — Herdsman neglects his she-goats in favor of w. J345.1.

Wild goose's flight A2442.2.7.

Wilderness full of beasts as fear test H1408. — Garden becomes w. F975; penance in w. Q520.5.

Wilhelm Tell F661.3.

Wiliwili tree's shape A2785.1.

Will. — Against his w. J1285; angels to execute God's w. A52.0.1; choice of kings by divine w. *P11.1; ghost foils counterfeiting of w. E236.4.1; giants large or small at w. F531.6.5.2; hare's last w. U242.1; last w. unfulfilled, ghost returns E236.4; magic comb changes person's size at w. D1377.1; magic runes control person's w. D1379.1.1; rascal in dead man's bed makes dead man's w. K1854.1; servant impersonates dead master, makes false w. K1854; sons falsifying father's w., deceived K1628; transformation and disenchantment at w. D630ff.

Will-o'-the-Wisp F491. — Origin of w. A2817; soul as w. E742.2.

Willow. — Man marries spirit of w. tree F441.2.3.1.1; origin of weeping w. A2632.1, A2681.1; why bark of red w. is thin A2751.2.2; why w. bears fruit when fruit trees bear A2771.6; why w. flowers do not bear fruit A2771.10.

Willow-grouse's. — Origin of w. crest A2321.9.

Wind blows persons into woman's eye X941.4; continually blows from cave F757.2; cursed for hot breath L351.2; drives buffaloes for god A199.4; personified Z115; produced by magic D2142ff.; -spirit A1128.2; sued for damages Z115.1. — Animals killed by trickster's breaking w. F981.3; ass finds hidden w. B133.0.1.1; blowing w. as life token

E761.7.8; bringing back flour scattered by w. (task) H1136.1; cannibal breaks w. as means of attack G93; conception from w. T524; contest in enduring cold: w. overcomes frost H1541.2; contest of w. and sun L351; demon ship sails against the w. F411.3; devil (as w.) G303.3.4.4, (and the w. travel together) G303.6.3.3, (carries man through the air as swift as w.) G303.9.5.4, (destroys hunting party with terrible w.) G303.20.2; directions on quest given by sun, moon, w. and stars H1232; divination from sound of w. D1311.22; divination from w. D1812.5.0.15.1; dragon-king transformed to gust of w. D429.2.1; extraordinary w. at world's end A1067; extraordinary behavior of w. F963; fool frightened by stirring of the w. J2622; forgotten w. J755.1; gathering w. in fists H1136.2; god of w. A139.8.4, A282, A287.0.1, A1126; goddess of w. A282.0.1; great w. because of broken tabu C984.1; jinn appears from w. G307.1.1; lost w. found in hollow tree: has been banished and is needed by men A1122.3; love like w. in hot sun H592.1.1; magic object controls w. *D1543ff.; magic object from w. D814.1; magic w. *D906, (against fugitive) R236.4, (blows open church doors for pope's body) Q147.2, (causes arms to fall from warriors' hands) D1414.3; magic red w. devastates country D1408.2; man can keep together feathers in great w. F673; man turned to stone for cursing w. Q551.3.4.2; man's breath made from w. A1260.1.5; measuring gust of w. H1145.2; marvelous runner outstrips March w. F681.2; man transformed to w. D281.1; primeval earth hardened by w. A856.1; regulation of w. A1128; reeds bend before w. J832; sacrifice to w. V11.5; soul borne away on w. E722.2.2; spider thinks that it has held back the w. J953.9; stag becomes w. D421.5.1; statues animated by water or w. F855.2; strong hero engendered by the w. F611.1.9; sun, moon as offspring of goddess and w. A715.2; thief's excuse: the big w. J1391.1; tiger frightened by w. K1727; what is moistest? South w. H659.8; wild hunt disappears with blast of w. E501.16.3.

Winds guard otherworld F150.2.3. — Bag of w. C322.1; bringing w. from the whole world (task) H1136; culture hero tames w. in caves *A532; establishment of w. A1120ff.; flaming w. in hell A671.2.4.12; Indra separates w. trying to unite A1142.7; lies about w. X1610; regulation of w. A1128; saint controls w. D2140.1.1; witch raises w. G283.1.

Windbreak. — Spear as w. F834.6.

Winding. — Witch w. yarn G244.1.

Windmill thought to be holy cross J1789.1.

Window. — Breaking w. to let cold out J1819.2; couple found "living in darkness", cut w. J1738.6; princess pulled through prison w. by hand and freed R121.1; sky w. F56.

Windows in firmament shed light A1171.2; in heaven A661.0.6; in otherworld F165.3.5. — Extraordinary doors and w. F782ff.; ghost breaks w. E299.4; magic w. *D1145; wild hunt avoided by keeping in house with w. closed E501.17.5.3; sunlight carried into house without w. in baskets J2123; witches open w. G249.8.

Windpipe. — Murder by putting clod in person's w. K951.4.

Wine cellar entered by removing lock K317.2; -distilling wood F811.5.2; from flowers F979.9; issues from Christ's wound V211.5.1; personified Z139.3; as reward Q135; touched by heathen tabu C272.1; transformed to other object D477.0.1; used to bathe relics V221.0.1.2; needs no further water J125.1; -spilling host rebuked J1511.5. — Acquisition of w. A1428; carrying w. in basket X1756.1; at communion witches spit out w. over shoulder G285.1; country without w. F708.3; can drink only one kind of w. at a time J1511.15; consecrated w. (as magic cure) D1500.10.2, (used to discover treasure) N533.4; doctor forbids patient w., drinks himself J1433; dog turns water to w. B119.1; drinking w.-cellar empty (task) H1142.1; drinking w. tabu C272; dwarf's palm w. F451.3.4.9; everlasting w. odor D1612.13; first humans from drops of w. A1211.6; fool (lets w. run in cellar) J2176, (tries to dry-up spilt w. with meal) J2176.1; father's counsel: on wishing to drink w. go to vat and drink it H588.4; fountain gives w. on feast days F716.1; fountain tasting of w. F716.1.1; four characteristics of w. A2851; host offers to send his guest a cask of w. which he has praised M206.1; host with overstock of sour w. spreads rumor of dragon at his house K484.2; identification by ring dropped in pitcher of w. H94.3; lake filled with palm w. A920.1.16; life token: w. turns to vinegar E761.6.5; magic knife stuck in tree causes w. to flow D1472.2.11; magic w. D1046; man strikes stone: w. flows D1472.1.2.1; man who only tasted w. W123.1; marvelous sensitiveness (w. shows through woman's white throat) F647.6, (w. tastes of corpse) F647.1; miser saves w. until it is strong W153.4; murder by leaving poisoned w. K929.1; odor of w. cask J34; other people's w. tastes best J1442.5; palace surrounded by rivers of w., rosewater, and honey F771.7; pig turns water into w. B184.3.2.2; priests drinking only one w. at a time J1511.15; repartee concerning w. J1310ff.; riddle: drink this w. which bird took to nest H806; river of w. F771.2.4.1; rivers of w. in otherworld *F162.2.2; rock produces w. D1472.1.2.2; sea aroma like w. F711.5; test: guessing nature of devil's w. glass H523.6; transformation: brine becomes w. D477.2; transformation by drinking w. D555.2; transformation by smelling w. D564.4; trickster sells mother's w. K499.1; trickster spits in w., given it K355.1; water becomes w. D477.1; water sold as w. in partitioned cask K476.3; well of w. D925.0.2, F162.5.1, F718.3; what is strongest? W. H631.8; where did he get w. J1321.1.

Wines. — Sickness ascribed to quarreling w. J1891.1.

Wing. — Music of bird's w. D2011.1.1.

Wings cut from flying mountains A1185; of dragon B11.2.6; of sun A726.2. — Angels' w. protect earth A1128.1; animal characteristics: w. A2377; ants ask God for w.: wind blows them away A2232.9; bird

gives shelter with w. B538.1; bird with w. of silver B101.1.1; birds beat
water with w. to honor saint B251.2.5; devil's w. G303.4.2; escape from
execution pyre by means of w. *R215; fairy comes into man's power when
he steals her w. *F302.4.2; flight on artificial w. *F1021.1; forest-spirits
with w. F441.4.4; fox's plan detected by crickets: cricket w. in his excrement K2061.10; hero enters maiden's tower by means of artificial w.
K1346; house in otherworld thatched with w. of birds F165.5; magic
birds cause sleep by shaking w. B172.9; magic object causes w. to
grow on person D1375.3; magic w. *D1022; origin of flying-fish's w.
A2136; owl's w. borrowed from rat A2241.2; person with w. F522;
raven singes feet: why its w. clap A2218.6; river contained under cock's
w. *D915.2; swan maiden finds her hidden w. and resumes her form
D361.1.1; thank God that camels have no w. J2564; thunder clouds
from w. of mountains A1142.4; trickster to give tiger w. K1013.4; winds
caused by flapping w. A1125.

Winged bull B43; chariot F861.2; dogs in wild hunt E501.4.1.7; elephant
B557.11.2; god A131.7; horse B41.1; serpent as boat: passengers within
F911.3.2; ship F841.3.1.

Wing-cornucopia B115.2.

Winking both at buyer and seller W171.1; club F835.1.

Winner. — Stakes not claimed by w. N2.0.2.

Winning, see also **Gambling;** of contest to be king P11.2; with devil's aid
G303.22.7, M217; first game to play for higher stakes K2378.1; soul
from devil in card game E756.2. — Animal w. contest for man B587;
despised boy w. race L176; magic object effects gambler's w. D1407ff.,
man granted power of w. at cards N221; punishment: w. as wife and
then killing Q411.1; suitor test: w. horse-race three times H331.5.3.

Winnings. — Bargain: to divide all w. *M241.

Winnowing peas devil's task G303.16.19.3.1; rice as royalty test H41.8.
— Animal shows w. fans as ears K1715.12; cannibal with w. tray,
pestle G11.12; origin of w. fan A1446.5.4; paramour pretends to be
returning w. basket K1517.11; witch aids w. grain G283.1.2.4.

Winter becomes summer at saint's funeral F960.2.6; magically produced
D2145.1. — Between summer and w. (i.e. between wagon and sledge)
H583.7, H1058; bringing berries (fruit, roses) in w. (task) H1023.3;
cold in w. A1135.1; continuous w. destroys race A1040ff.; cuckoo to
sing in w. H1023.3.1.1; daw waits in vain for the figs to ripen in w.
J2066.2; flowers bloom in w. F971.5; garden blooming in w. D1664,
H352, M261.1; genealogy of w. A1154; hospitality for whole w. P320.1;
for the long w. K362.1; fruit magically grows in w. *D2145.2.2; grasshopper builds no house for w. A2233.4; origin of w. weather A1135;
summer and w. garden D1664; storks become men in Egypt in w.
D624.1; wild hunt appears in w. E501.11.2.1.

Winters. — Year with two w. X1603.

Wiped. — Face w. dry after washing A1599.4.

Wiping hands on lame son S12.7.

Wisdom, see also **Knowledge;** from animals *J130ff.; as bride test H388; came before learning J1217.2; from children J120ff.; chosen above all else J231; from education J140ff.; from experience J10ff.; from fools J156; as God's companion A195.2; from inference J30ff.; from necessity J100ff.; from observation J50ff.; from old man J151ff.; from parable *J80ff.; personified Z128, Z139.8; or wealth more powerful? N141.2. — Acquisition and possession of w. J0—J199; Adam's seventy-two kinds of w. D1811.0.1; animals give w. *B160ff.; animals with magic w. B120— B169; book gives w. J2238; dead awaken after three days to new life and great w. E489.1; dispute of wealth, w. J461.7; found mortar taken to king reveals peasant girl's w. H561.1.2; god of w. A461; goddess of w. A461.1; magic object gives supernatural w. *D1300ff.; magic w. *D1811ff., (of extraordinary companion) D1719.4, (follows long sleep) F564.3.3, (possessed by wild man) D1719.2; man's w. puts all animals in his power A1421.1.1; moon's w. A753.3.4; origin of human w. A1481; precocious w. T615.3; quest for w. H1376.8; saint offered any gift chooses w. L212.1; seven grades of w. Z71.5.6.4; Solomon proves inferiority of woman's w. J80.1.1; stopping up mouth, ears to keep in w. J1977; streams of w. flow from magic well D1300.3.1; sun's w. A738.2.2; test of w. H501.

Wise animals B120ff.; carving of fowl H601; cleric as solver of riddles H561.8; and foolish J (entire chapter); giant as foster father of hero N812.1; eagle in earth-tree A878.3.4; man (acknowledges his ignorance) J911, (disguised as buffoon) K1818.3.1, (disguised as monk outdebates heretic) K3.4, (before entering a quarrel considers how it will end) J611, (humble in death) J912; man's advice scorned J2051; men (disguise as peasants) K1816.9.1, (of Gotham) J1700ff., (humble selves) J917, (predict rainstorm: wrong) J1714.3.1; but ugly son M93; and unwise conduct J200—J1000; woman as helper N828; words of dying father J154. — Animal gives w. example to man J133ff.; association of w. men with fools J1714; counsels proved w. by experience *J21ff.; dwarfs w. F451.3.12.3; fool passes as w. man by remaining silent N685; giants w. F531.6.17.7; king sends w. man to give rival advice K1994; land where everyone is w. F129.6; marvelously w. man F645; porter's revenge for three w. counsels J1511.6; sham w. man K1956, N611; test of cleverness: uttering three w. words H505.

Wisest. — Riddle: what is w. H659.9.

Wish for animal husband realized C26; for exalted husband realized *N201; granted before hearing it M223; for supernatural husband realized C15; for wife red as blood, white as snow, black as raven T11.6. — Conception from w. T513, (of another) T513.1; curse given to negate good w. M416; fairy ransoms self with w. F341.2; grateful fish grants mad hero his w. B375.1.1; magic last w. before death D1715.1; monster born because of hasty (inconsiderate) w. of parents

*C758.1; overheard w. realized N699.6; reward: any w. that may be asked Q115; river rises to prevent body's being carried over it against dying man's w. F932.8.1; summoning by w. D2074.2.3; transformation through w. D521; thumbling born as result of hasty w. of parents T553.

Wishes for good fortune realized N202. — Absurd w. J2070ff.; all princess's w. granted for month H313.1; deceptive bargain: three w. K175; execution evaded by using three w. J1181.1; fairies give fulfillment of w. F341; fairies make good w. for newborn child F312.1.1; fernseed makes w. come true C401.5; ghost laid when w. granted E459.3; selling soul for granting of w. M211.9; three foolish w. J2071; transformation to likeness of ruler: man so uses the last of three w. granted to him D41.1; vanquished ogre grants hero's three w. G665.

Wishing tree in otherworld F162.3.2. — Contest in w. H507.3; girl summons fairy lover by w. for him F301.1.1.1; heaven entered by trick: "w. sack" thrown in K2371.1.3; magic object from w. D852; magic results produced by w. *D1761ff.; magic w.-drum works only for owner D1651.7.2; magic w.-girdle supplies food D1472.2.1; magic w. object *D1470.1ff.; magic w.-ring loses power by touching water D877.1.

Wisp of hay transformed to bridge D451.5.7. — Magic w. D1282.2, (causes insanity) D1367.4.

Wit combat H507ff., (among sisters for dowry) H507.4; jokes over unfavorable decision J835; or learning more important? N141.1. — Hermes distributes w. L301; man buys a pennyworth of w. J163.1; one basket of w. better than twelve carloads J1662.1.

Witch *G200; abducts hero R10.4; assigns tasks H935; bone controls animals D1442.8; on broomstick G242.1; burns child's legs, magically heals them D2161.3.1; causes milk to curdle D2083.2.2; controls winds D2142.0.1; deceptively gets boy into sack K711.4; delays person's death D1855.1; in animal form G211ff.; draws rain, snow from clouds D2143.1.9; drinks boiling oil to beautify teeth G525.1; enchants bride D2062.4.1; flies with magic aids D1531.5ff.; foster mother P272.1; frightened by victim cleaving boulder K547.13; helps recover magic D885.1; imprisoned in boulder D2078.1; keeps water from boiling D2137.1; overcome or escaped G270ff.; paralyzes (mule) D2072.0.2.4, (pigs) D2072.0.2.5, (wagon) D2072.0.2.1.1; plays on jew's harp, disarmed K606.1.4; poses as beggar to steal child K764; possesses magic objects D801.1; prevents person from drinking D2072.0.5.1; produces lightning D2149.1.1; sells power to control winds D2142.0.1.1; sits atop mast D2142.0.1.2; suckles child T611.3; transforms self to hare so as to suck cows D655.2; of upper world A205; woman's son by demigod A592.1. — Allegorical game of w., devil, maiden, church Z178; beheading w. H1191.1; blinding a w. (task) H1191; bringing water from distant fountain more quickly than w. (task) H1109.1; cannibal w. G11.3; catching w. in king's garden H1191.2; child divides last loaf with w. Q42.1.1; dogs warn against w. B521.3.1; king marries w. P18.1; lending to w. tabu C784.1; man becomes w. D97; not to eat food of w.

C242; form of w. G210ff.; magic adhesion to w. *D2171.2; magic object received from w. D812.6; pipal protects against w. D1385.2.4; quest for w. stepmother H1397.1; salt bullet kills w. D1385.4.1; seeing w. tabu C311.1.6; selling to w. tabu C782.2; snow from feathers or clothes of a w. A1135.2.1; theft from w. revenged Q212.1; transformation by w. D683.2; weighing w. against Bible H234; woman promises her unborn child to appease offended w. S222.1.

Witch's aid in reaping contest F1038.2; curse M411.12; ghost chases man E261.4.1; horse-switch blossoms F971.1.2; house at border of otherworld F147.3; sabbath G243. — Breaking w. back tests strength H1562.8; curse: prince to fall in love with w. daughter M436; drawing w. blood annuls her spells D1741.2.1; earthquake at w. death F960.2.5.2, Q552.25.2; following w. fire into her power G451; mongoose leads to w. house G402.2; pasturing w. cattle, her daughters H1199.12.2; sickness of princess dependent on w. fire *D2064.2; stealing w. beautiful clothing H1151.23.

Witches G200—G299; make cows give bloody milk D2083.2.1; induce love D1901; pursued in wild hunt E501.5.1.3; steal in house D2087.7; in wild hunt E501.2.3. — Boy overhears w., gets their magic B838.9; characteristics of w. G220ff.; devil appears at meetings of w. G303.6.2.2; evil deeds of w. G260ff.; habitat of w. G230ff.; habits of w. G240ff.; magic horseshoe keeps off w. D1385.9; magic knowledge of w. D1810.0.5; maidens rescued from w. R111.1.8; men think hairy wives w. J1786.6; power of w. to see distant sights D1825.9; raja magically protected from w. D1400.1.22; recognition of w. G250ff.; secret remedy overheard in conversation of w. N452; sight of deformed w. causes man to release wife from spinning duty J51; silver bullet protects against w. D1385.4; three deformed w. invited to wedding in exchange for help *M233.

Witchcraft learning leaves man shadowless F1038.1. — Burning cut hair to prevent w. D2176.5; burning for w. Q414.0.10; churchyard mould in hat prevents w. D1385.11; charm prevents w. D1385.13; disease caused by w. A1337.0.3; door stuck by w. D1654.15; glen of w. F756.4; innocent woman accused of w. K2123; money to be regained by w. C401.3.1; origin of w. A1599.10.

Witchhazel protects against witches G272.22.

Withe at otherworld entrance F150.3.2. — Putting w. about sand Z63; recognition by carving on w. H35.4.1.

Withered. — Making w. flowers green H1023.3.2.

Withering by magic D2082.0.2; trees after tabu broken C998; of tree bad omen D1812.5.1.20. — Bird's breath w. B33.1.1, B777; flowers magically kept from w. D2167.3; hand w. after oath broken M101.4; hand w. as punishment Q559.5.2; oath w. tree M115.1.1; reason for tree's w. N452.1.1; trees w. at tragedy F979.23; witch w. arm G269.11.2.

Withershins circuit for ill luck D1791.2.

Witness always to answer "No" J1141.13. — False w. to free friend P315.2; heavens bear w. for man F961.0.5; no argument good without w. K1655.1; women disqualified as court w. A1589.1.

Witnesses bigger thieves than culprit U119.1.2. — No w. to robbery J1191.6; opposing w. have pockets filled with dung K1291.

Wizard burned, saint saved H1573.3.4; calms storm D2141.0.8.1; gives man illusion that he has been away long D2012.2; makes pupil think himself emperor W154.28. — Charm sung over flesh chewed by w. has magic power D1273.0.3; fire burns up, crackles as w. passes G229.8; magic object received from w. D812.6; storm at death of w. D2141.0.4.

Wizard's magic detection of thief D1817.0.1.1ff.; prophecy on cockfight D1814.1.1.

Wizardry. — Witches' w. cauldron G249.5.

Woe. — Idleness begets w. J21.50; quest for king's w. H1378.2.

Wolf, see also **Werwolf;** abducts person R13.1.5; acts as judge before eating the rams K579.5.1; almost locked up in the stable by the shepherd J2172.2.1; as animals' king B240.10; approaches too near to horse: kicked in face K1121; attracted to own children B751.6; bites off devil's heels G303.4.5.7; boy recovered by human parents B635.2; carries man B557.15; as commander orders all booty divided, but keeps his own U37; as dog's guest sings J581.1; boasts of having eaten horses J2351.4; brings cake from the window sill K1022.4; cut open and filled with stones as punishment Q426; defends master's child against serpent B524.1.4; does not mind dust from flock of sheep J352.1; eats devil G303.17.3.3; eats horse from rear, kicked to death K553.4; excuses killing goose by reference to saints K2055.1; executed for thefts B275.1.3; falls out of nest: cause of straight back A2211.3; flees from the wolf-head K1715.3; freezes internally from eating cold flesh J2284; as giants' dog F531.4.11.1; as God's dog A1833.3; granted patent of nobility A2546.2; hard to hold by eyebrows H659.2.1; harnessed (lie) X1216.1; in hell A671.2.6; -hounds C564.3; in human form B651.6; is the devil's craftiest enemy G303.25.1; kept at door until children have been christened K551.8; keeps well-fed leeches J215.1.3; loses interest in the sermon when he sees flock of sheep U125; makes fire as mock sunrise K1886.3; measured for clothes K551.20; not good living or dead (riddle) H841.4; objects to lion stealing sheep from him although he has himself stolen it U21.4; as ogre G352.1; offers (to act as midwife for sow) K2061.6, (to act as shepherd) *K2061.1; overeats in cellar K1022.1; persuaded to put head through jar K1022.7; persuades lamb to bring him drink: lamb to be food K815.11; poses as grandmother and kills child *K2011; poses as ram to cheat ewe K828.3; proposes abolition of dog guards for sheep K2061.1.1; punished by being married K583; punished for father's misdeeds J1863.2; punished for theft, kings honored U11.2.1; puts flour on his paw to disguise himself K1839.1; puts head in camel's mouth : killed J2131.5.5; returns sheep stolen from

saint B256.11; scorns salt meat in false expectation of other booty
J2066.4; sold as (goat) K132, (watchdog) K133.1; spares man livestock
after man aids him B381.1; steals old maid (she keeps him for husband) X755; substitutes for calf D2156.8; swears by God B251.7.1; -tail
blankets B538.2; thought to be (colt) J1752, (log of wood) J1761.5;
tied to cow's horns K1022.2; transformed to man D313.2; transformed
to object D421.1; tries (in vain to be doctor) J512.5, (to eat bowstring)
J514.2, (to drink well dry to get cheese) J1791.3.1, (to entice goat down
from high place) K2061.4, (to make friends with lion: killed) J411.5;
unjustly accuses lamb and eats him U31; waits in vain for nurse to
throw away child J2066.5; who wanted to make bread Z49.5.2; and
wolverine fight over girl B621.8; worship V1.8.5. — Alliance of dog
and w. B267.1; ass punished for stealing mouthful of grass: lion and w.
forgiven for eating sheep U11.1; blind man who feels young w.
recognizes his savage nature J33; camel lures w., crushes him K839.5;
cats unite against w. J1025.2; crane pulls bone from wolf's throat: w.
refuses payment W154.3; creation of w. A1833; curse: w. to carry off
man's genitals M442.2; death respite until w. reads horse's passport
K551.18; devil in form of w. G303.3.3.2.1; disdain of w. for dog
J953.5; dog tries to imitate w. J2413.5; dogs of w. color join wolves
J2137.2; dog refuses to help w. K231.1.3; eagle warns shepherds that
w. is eating sheep J715.1; enmity between lion and w. A2494.7.2; fairy
as w. F234.1.13; famished w. asks sheep to bring him water K2061.5;
fat w. (cumulative tale) Z33.4; fetter for Fenris w. F864.1; food of w.
A2435.3.4; fox persuades w. (to eat own brains) K1025.1, (to lie on
haycock in order to be painted) K1013.2; friendship between w. and ass
A2493.15; future hero found in w. den L111.2.4; ghost as w. E423.2.7;
giant as w. F531.1.8.1; giant w. overcome by hero B16.2.4; girl suckled
by w. has wolf's nail T611.10.1; god assumes form of w. D113.1.2; gods
battle Fenris w. A1082.2.1; hero suckled by w. A511.2.2.1; hidden w.
gives himself away by talking J2351.2; hungry w. envies fat dog until
he sees marks of his collar L451.3; why w. has straight back A2356.2.2;
helpful w. *B435.3; intruding w. (falls down chimney and kills himself)
J2133.7, K891.1; kid perched on house jeers at w. J974; lamb prefers to
be sacrificed in temple than to be eaten by w. J216.2; lion, bear, and
w. resuscitate master B515; lion kills w. who has killed mistress's sheep
B591.1; why w. lives in woods A2433.3.14; Loki's son transformed to
w. Q551.3.2.1; magic w. heart D1015.1.4; man in barrel grabs w. by
tail and is drawn out of danger X1133.3; man dreams wife attacked
by w.: so happens T255.7; man-w. B29.5; man transformed to w.
*D113.1; man turns w. inside out (lie) X1124.2; marriage to w. B601.16;
musician in w. trap B848.1; mysterious w. enters church and kills
blaspheming priest Q554.4; presumptious w. among lions J952.1;
prisoner escapes by using w. K649.10; prophecy: death by w. M341.2.6;
queen hides her child and accuses w. of eating it S332; reincarnation as

from sky A21.1; in finery in church thinks people are standing up to see her when they rise at gospel-reading J953.8; will not follow donkey on safe path: attacked by robbers J133.4; free from trouble, worry H1195; frightens devil G303.16.19.17.1; gives jewel for salad J2093.2; gives self to riddle solver H551.2; as guardian of treasure N572; from half-drop of wine A1211.6; with horseshoe on one foot F551.1.2.1; induces men to fight over her K1086; instructs in art of arms P461.4; as leader of wild hunt E501.1.8; with lovers carried in cloak F1034.2.1; lured into forest, captured K788; masks as lawyer (judge) and frees her husband K1825.2; in the moon A751.8; plans to eat her children G72.1; satirist M402.1; seeks unknown father of her child H1381.2.1; is strongest (riddle) H631.4; subservient to husband A1571.2; in tar and feathers does not know herself J2012.3; transformed to (cat) D142.0.1, (flower) D212, (flower, recognized) H63.1, (fruit) D211ff., (island) D284, (man) D11, (pool of water) A920.1.11, D283.1, (skein of silk) D264, (tree) D215ff.; with two husbands is to be killed J1171.3; from water world B81.0.2; won and then scorned T72.
— Animals from severed fingers of w. A1724.1.1; bearded w. F545.1.5; black tribe because w. put on fire A1614.8; blood as remedy for barrenness in w. D1347.2; boy behind tree tells w. about bad food he gets K1971.3; boy who had never seen w.: the Satans T371; brothers construct a w. — whose is she? Z16.1; burr-w. G311; bush by day, w. by night D621.2.1; cannibal w. devours raw buffalo H46.1; capture through wiles of w. K778; changeling addresses w. in verse and thus betrays his maturity F321.1.1.3; contract made by w. without husband void P525.2; country no w. may enter F566.1.1; creation of monkeys: old w. thrown into fire A1861.2; creation of w. from coconut A1253.2.1; death from sight of beautiful w. F1041.1.6; defeating certain old w. (task) H1149.3; devil appears when w. looks at herself in mirror after sunset G303.6.1.4; devil bargains to help man win w. M217; devil disguised as w. G303.12.6; devil in serpent form tempts first w. (Satan and Eve) A63.6; devil takes the place of w. who went to spend night with a priest G303.25.11; devil as w. G303.3.1.12; disguise as w. to enter enemy's camp K2357.8; disguise of w. in man's clothes *K1837; diving for reflection of beautiful w. J1791.6; earth gives birth to w. A1234.4; encounter with clever w. dissuades man from visit J31; every w. has her price U66.1; evil w. in glass case as last commodity K216.1; fairy as beautiful young w. F234.2.5; fairies take human midwife to attend fairy w. F372.1; fifteen characteristics of good w. Z71.6.11.1; first man catches w. in his snare A1275.10; flame indicates presence of beautiful w. F1061.1; forthputting w. imposes tabu C901.1.3.1; goddess of war in shape of w. A125.1.1; ground dries up when first w. cuts self, bleeds A856.2; guilt detected by query on possessing w. J1149.6; helping old w. tabu G745.1; impossible for w. to bear animals J1191.5.1; madness from seeing beautiful w. *F1041.8.1; magic object (draws w.

to man) D1426, (makes w. masterful) D1359.1, (received from cat-w.) D825.1, (received from old w.) D821; magician carries w. in glass coffin *D2185; man breaking oath to w. cannot be king M205.3; man creates w. from butter, sour milk, and curds A1275.5; man excels w. A1376; man made to appear to pursuers as w. carrying babe D2031.6.1; man not to look at w. C312; man-eating w. G11.6; man disguised as w. admitted to women's quarters: seduction K1321.1; man looks at copulating snakes: transformed to w. D513.1; man reincarnated as w. E605.1.2; man transformed to w. *D12; monotony of being restricted to one's favorite food (or w.) J81.0.1; mortal w. seduced by a god K1301; never have to do with w. unless wed to her J21.30; old w. F571.3, (as creator) A15.1.1, (and her pig) Z41, (builds air castle about the horse she is finally to get from sale of pail of milk) J2061.2.1, (guards gods' islands) A955.12, (guards post supporting earth: she causes earthquakes) A843, (helper) N825.3, (as prophet) M301.2, (gives chickens to devils) G303.25.6, (has control of frost) D2143.5.1, (helps on quest) H1233.1.1, (intercepts letter and takes girl's place in man's bed) K1317.2.1, (ruler of dead in lower world) E481.1.1, (supports earth on head) A842.2; only one w. on island F112.0.1.1; primeval w. cut in pieces A642.1; refusing to help w. tabu C686.1; reincarnation: w. reborn as man E605.1.1; remarkably beautiful w. F575.1; remarkably strong w. F610.0.1; race always to have illustrious w. M317; reincarnation: w. to bird, nettles, stone, woman E648.1; revenant as w. E425.1; saved soul of w. assists her husband's soul in battle against demons E756.5; seduction by man disguising as w. K1321; self-righteous w. punished L435.2; slaying w. with spear tabu C835.2.4; stupid w. swims on the roof J1972; sun a fat w. walking across sky A738.1.2; sun as w. A736.2; sun and moon born from a w. A715.1; supplies from toe of old w. D1470.2.4; tabu: eating before w. C231.3; tabu to violate w. C118; tasks performed with help of old w. H971.1; to which man does w. belong? J1153.2; there was once a w. (cumulative tale) Z49.4; transformation to seduce w. *D658; transformation to likeness of another w. D40.2; treacherous dark w. K2260.2; treacherous old w. K2293; vow to marry a certain w. M146; where devil can't reach, he sends an old w. G303.10.5; there was a wee wee w. Z39.2; wild animal will not harm chaste w. B771.0.1; wild hunter pursues a w. E501.5.1; wild w. F567.1.

Woman's garments cut off: does not know herself J2012.2. — Devil (buys w. hair) G303.25.13, (in w. train) G303.8.9; disguise of man in w. dress *K1836; dog betrays w. infidelity *B134.1; first w. mate from tree A1275.6; fish from w. severed fingers A2102; lake-serpent in w. form B91.5.2.1; Solomon proves inferiority of w. wisdom J80.1.1.

Women adorn heads, immoral below K2051.4; as best painters H659.16; disguised as ascetics escape enemy K521.9; disqualified as court witnesses A1589.1; druids P427.0.3; lead man on, then blackmail him K443.9; lure warrior aside, confederate kills him K822; poets P427.7.4;

as prime source of sin T334.1; scorned in love T71; tabu on certain island C619.4; transformed to bitches B297.2.1; transformed into flowers A2611.0.4.1; warriors F565. — Abusing w. tabu C867.1; animals punished for assaulting w. A2239.5; are there more men or w.? H708; why w. are bad A1371; birth of fifty w. prophesied M301.5.2; creation of flea: to give w. work A2032.2; death from excess of w. T99.1; don't shed blood of w. J21.2.5; dwarf w. bear children F451.3.5.5; fatal enticements of phantom w. F585.1; fox had rather meet one hen than fifty w. J488; god does not address w. A182.3.0.4; hell of w. F83; hero refuses to slay w. W11.5.12; journey to Land of W. F112; land where w. live separate from men F566.2; law requiring military service of w. P551.6; louse created to give w. work A2051.1; magic door invisible to w. D1982.1; man fishes up two blind w. from well F1065; men captive in Land of W. R7; ogre eats w. G11.6.1; origin of w. in Ireland A1611.5.4.1; portion of otherworld for w. F167.14.1; quest: what is it w. most desire H1388.1; riddle: why are there more w. than men? H774; sacred places closed to w. C51.1.10; selling three old w. (task) H1153; sterility among w. A1358; strong w. F565.2; tabu on assembly of w. C853.2; tabu confined to w. C181; tabu: w. leaving hero's land C566.3; ten w. carried in a bottle D55.2.4; three w. have among them but one (eye) F512.1.2, (tooth) F513.1.1; theft from three old w. who have but a single eye among them *K333.2; ugly ogre terrifies w. who flee, drown G476; wisdom (knowledge) from w. J155; why tigers don't kill w. who run away after quarreling with their husbands A2499.1; why witches are w. G286.1.

Women's — Besieged w. dearest possession J1545.4.1; magic protection against w. spells D1385.16.3; pope tests w. obedience: not to look into box H1557.4.

Womb. — Child in w. gives quest directions H1232.5; child speaks in mother's w. T575.1ff.; first humans from Mother Earth's w. A1234.1.1; hero enters w. of sleeping woman and is reborn T539.1; hero born by splitting mother's w. T584.7; hero in w. guides mother's direction A511.1.2.2; rebirth by crawling into w. E607.2.2; saint in w. renders woman invisible D1361.39; woman without w. F597.

Wonder that man who has been buying butcher's meat for seven years can still be alive X231; voyages F110.1. — Changeling betrays his age when his w. is excited F321.1.1.1; discovering new w. before eating C287; quest for unknown w. H1382.4.

Wonders. — Plain of w. F756.3.

Wood automatically burns D1649.4; at borders of otherworld F143; dealer prays for raja's death W153.13; enduring forever F812.7; which fire cannot consume F812.8; -gatherer K312.2; heaved on mother's head, kills her K1466; neither crooked nor straight H1378.1; turned to grain D476.1.3. — Bear builds house of w.: fox of ice J741.1; bleeding w. as Doomsday sign A1002.2.2; bundle of w. magically acts as riding horse D1523.3; child promised to w.-spirit S213; creation of man from w. A1252; cross of Christ made of four kinds of w.V211.4.1; devil exorcised by burning w. G303.16.14.2.1; expensive w. burned to make charcoal J2094; fairies give man w. that turns to gold F342.1; father cuts w. which was burnt last year (to pay old debts) H583.2.4; fish created from w. A2101; fool whose house is burning puts w. on the fire J2162.2; ghosts gather w. for hell fires E755.2.4; gift w. must be split W111.5.10; golden w. for knife H1359.1; island of rare w. F732; lake petrifies w. F934.3; lover unloads w. on door to keep husband out K1514.9; man in otherworld loaded down with w. F171.6.1; magic object (found in w.) D849.4, (provides w.) D1488; magic pebble splits w. D1564.1; Mahadeo turns w. chips into insects A2002.1; man proof against iron, stone, and w. D1841.1; magic stick of w. D956; object transformed to w. D473; not to offend w.-spirit C43; origin of w. carving A1465.5; piece of w. revives memory D2006.1.8; power of self-transformation received from w.-spirit D630.1; scavenger carrying w. bad omen D1812.5.1.29; serpent acts as rope to collect w. B579.5; special flavor of forest w. F812.6; splitting w. suitor contest H331.12; stacking w. from felled forest in one day H1095.2; sticks of w. become animals D441.7; strong hero w.-spirit's son F611.1.15; sword magically changes to w. when executioner is to decapitate innocent person H215.1; transformation to w. C961.3; treasure buried in w.-shed N511.1.5; why w. combustible A2782; wild hunt pursues w. spirit E501.5.3; wild man as w. spirit F441.3; wine-distilling w. F811.5.2; wolf thought to be log of w. J1761.5; woman becomes w. on breaking tabu C961.3; woman charms w. stick, hides in it D1393.1.1; wound closed with w. F959.3.2.

Woods, see also **Forests.** — Animals that live in w. A2433.2.1; devil in the w. G303.8.13; elk lives in w. A2433.3.13; king (prince) finds maiden in w. and marries her N711.1; ogre attacks intruders in house in w. G475.1; precept of the lion to his sons: honor the w. J22.2; wild hunt appears in w. E501.12.1; why wolf lives in w. A2433.3.14.

Woodcutter hero L113.5. — Disguise as w. K1816.3; queen forced to serve w. Q482.2.2.

Woodcutter's. — Disguise as cobbler to woo w. daughter K1816.10.1.

Woodcutters. — Mice win war with w. L318.

Wooden anchor would hold if it were only large, thinks the fool J2212.3; coat F821.1.4; image V127. — City populated by w. automata D1628; crippled cat catches mice with w. leg X1211.2; devil takes an unbaptized child and substitutes a w. log G303.9.9.4; disguise in w. covering K1821.9; dwarf rides through air on w. horse F451.6.2.2; earth supported on w. cross A843.1; from w. spring iron bucket makes stones from which water flows (riddle) H765; marvelous sensitiveness: fainting from noise of w. pestle and mortar F647.8; moon's w. weapons A759.1; penance: killing oneself with w. knife Q522.2; ship built with a w. saw J2171.1.1; Trojan w. horse K754.1; worship of w. idol V1.11.3.

wife only good w. hits her with a prayer book J1541.1; negligent priests
buried under bags filled with w. omitted from service V5.2; poet's confounding w. J1684; power in w., herbs, and stones J1581.2; quest for
unknown magic w. H1382.1; quest to lower world for lost w. H1276;
religious w. or exercises interpreted with absurd literalness J2495;
sham parson repeats same expression over and over or says few w. of
Latin K1961.1.2; similar w. mistaken for each other J1805.1; test of
cleverness: uttering three wise w. H505; unuttered w. heard F1099.3.

Work brings happiness J21.50; of day magically overthrown at night
*D2192. — Angel shows value of w. H605; animal council assigns place
and w. to all B238; animal's daily w. A2450ff.; any w. touched automatically done D1935; boasts about brother's, father's w. capacity J2353.1;
changeling shows supernatural power to w. and thus betrays maturity
F321.1.1.4; choices: important and unimportant w. J370ff.; creation of
flea: to give women w. A2032.2; dead cannot rest until certain w. is
finished E415; deceptive labor bargain: one partner is to do all the w.
K178; devils help people at w. G303.9.3.3; dissatisfied exchange w.
U136.1; dwarfs interfere with mortal's w. F451.5.2.5; fairies leave w.
unfinished when overseen F361.3.1; god teaches people to w. A1403; intemperance in w. J553; keeping up certain w. all night (task) H1128;
king demands w. from guests P337; lazy woman resumes her w. J1011;
life without w. A1346.2.2; magic w. paralysis D2072.5; make-believe
eating, make-believe w. J1511.1; man must w. as punishment for
theft of fire A1346.1; man undertakes to do his wife's w. J2431; men
exchange w.: each cheated J2431.1; merit for charity lost by asking w.
in return V438; monk discouraged by large amount of w. to be done
persuaded to undertake but small amount each day J557.1; monk fails
to escape w. J215.4; necessity of w. J702; people taught by God to w.
C53.1; punishment: man to do woman's w. Q482.6; watching fairy at
w. tabu F348.8; wife behind tree advises husband against having his
wife w. K1971.4.1; will w. when beaten J1545.1; what kind of w.
occupies most men (riddle) H659.6; who does more w.? Husband or
wife? J1545.3.1; world's w. dependent on inequalities of fortunes
A1599.8.

Works. — Creator's w. survive him A77; devil comes and w. with man
who continues to work after night G303.22.9; devil w. backward
G303.13.2; why negro w. A1671.1.

Worked. — Ox lent by fairies must not be w. after sunset F391.1.1.

Working ghost E596.1. — Animal characteristics: punishment for w. on
holy day A2231.3; familiars w. for witch G225.0.3; miraculous w.
of the host V34; peasants punished for w. on feast day Q559.4; punishment for w. on holy day Q551.2.2; riddles about w. H588.11; stepmother w. stepdaughter to death S322.7; suitors w. for chaste wife
K1218.12.

Workmen of hell A677; rescue abandoned child R131. — Dwarfs as w.
F451.3.4ff.; gods as w. A140ff.

World at bottom of pond F725.8; calamities A1000—A1099; -columns A841; -cords A841.1; -eclipse A1046; as egg A655; -fire A1030ff.; parents A625; -soul A612.1. — Adulteress to lover, "I can see whole w." K1271.4; bringing winds from the whole w. (task) H1136; China first land in our w. A802; colors corresponding to the four w. quarters Z140.2; devil's disappearance from w. G303.17; formula for other w. "Where no man goes or crow flies" Z91; god promises never again to destroy w. by water A1113; god of the w. of the dead *A310ff.; journey of soul to w. of dead on reindeer E750.3; land of dead in lower w. *E481.1; magic knowledge from queen of other w. D1810.1; measuring the w. A1186; nun forgets to hail Mary and goes into the w. to sin V254.5; nut hits cock in head: he thinks w. is coming to an end Z43.3; prophecy of w. catastrophe M357; quest to other w. H1250ff.; renewal of w. after w. calamity A1006; rejuvenation by going to other w. and having digestive tract removed D1889.5; Satan builds another w. G303.9.1.15; sight of old home reawakens memory and brings about return from other w. *D2006.2; submarine and subterranean w. F720ff.; tear from upper w. of mortals falls on departed in lower w. E361.1.

World's — Castle at w. end F771.3.1; giants live at w. end F531.6.2.5; four gods at w. quarters support sky A665.2.1.1; quest for w. end H1371.1.

Worlds above and below A651.3. — Hierarchy of w. A651; miscellaneous w. A690ff.; nine w. tremble at rebirth F960.1.5.

World-tree *A652. — Pleiades from hunters who felled w. A773.5; spring from beneath w. A941.7.1; symbolism of roots, branches of w. H619.3.

Worldly man puts religious man out of countenance J1217.

Worm from caul born with child B714; swallowed at conception eats unborn child T579.6; transformed to other animal D418.2; transformed to person D392. — Why w. is blind A2284.3, A2332.6.4; cat's tail mistaken for w. J1759.5; conception from swallowing w. (in drink of water) T511.5.2; demon's corpse turns to w. H47; dragon from w. B11.1.3.1; earth excreted by w. A828.1; earth from w. scratched by creator's nails A828; fairy as w. F234.1.7; helpful w. B491.4; man with w. in head F511.0.7; man transformed to w. (often snake) D192; multi-colored w. B731.10; mythical w. B99.2; origin of w. A2182; prophetic w. B145.3; quest for large-headed w. H1331.8; reincarnation as w. E618; seeing w. in loaf F642.3.2; transformation: demon (in human form) to w. D192.0.1; venomous w. B776.6; why thousand-legged w. avoids sun A2433.6.9.

Worm's flesh makes courageous D1358.1.2. — Horse fed with w. milk B710.2.1.

Worms. — Child born holding w. T552.2.2; lies about w. X1346; lost soul gnawed by w. E752.7; man eaten by w. as punishment Q415.3;

mankind descended from w. A1224.2; transformation to mass of w. Q551.3.2.5.

Wormwood. — Chain tale: w. rocking me to sleep Z41.7.

Worn-out broom at head of wild hunt E501.10.2; shoes as proof of long journey *H241. — Shoes miraculously w. F1015.1ff.; time measured by w. iron shoes *H1583.1; traveling till iron shoes are w. H1125.

Worry personified Z139.5. — Removing chance for w. J1396.

Worse. — Contentment with evil master for fear of w. successor J229.8; escape from one misfortune into w. N255.

Worship V0—V99. — Ancestor w. V1.3; animals praise or w. B251; devils w. host G303.24.2; intemperance in w. J564; intercourse before w. tabu C119.1.5; objects of w. V1ff.; origin of w. A1546; why Jews don't w. idols A1544.0.1.

Worshipped. — Kings w. after death P16.6.

Worshipper in trouble, goddess's throne shakes A189.5.

Worshipping. — Chain tale: brahmin w. himself Z42.3; death for w. idols Q558.12; magic results from w. D1766.10; resuscitation by w. body E63.1; sun w. God by night A722.11; witches w. demon G243.4; woman w. devil G303.9.4.10.

Worst. — Quest for w. meat H1305.1.1; what are best and w. stones (riddle) H659.3.

Worth. — Choice between w. and appearance J260ff.; what six things are not w. doing (riddle) H871.

Worthiness. — Test of w. for friendship H1558.0.1.

Worthless goods alleged to be valuable ones transformed K249.4; object substituted for valuable while owner sleeps K331.3; stones preferred to pearls J2093.3.1. — Lover pays husband w. money K1581.10; magic object exchanged for w. D871.1; robber mistakenly carries off w. goods and leaves valuable K421; sale of w. (articles) K110—K149, (services) K150ff., (animals) K130ff.; trading silver for w. cup J2096.

Worthy. — Biblical w. as giant F531.0.1; woman named "W." at communion X453.

Wound healed only by inflicter *D2161.4.10.2; healed by same spear that caused it D2161.4.10.1; masked by other wound K1872.4; received in dream F1068.2. — Birth from w. F541.2; curing w. by treating object causing it D1782.2; curse of clergy causes man to die of w. D2061.2.4.2; curse: w. not to heal M431.5; giant has w.-healing balm F531.6.5.3; identification by matching weapon, w. H101.1; insult worse than w. W185.6; lover's w. breaks while he is in bed with mistress N386; magic cure of w. D2161.2; magic object heals w. D1503ff.; miraculous cure of w. F959.3; no man with w. to be sacrificed C57.1.2; only one person able to heal w. D2161.4.10.0.1; physician describes person inflicting w. F956.4; recognition by means of ring enclosed in w. H61.3; recognition by w. H56; sham death to w. enemies K911.1; sister hidden in thigh w. F1034.3.1; surgeon can tell who inflicted w. F668.4; thorn growing in w. becomes a tree F971.3.

Wounds inflicted by certain man always fatal F693. — Beetles, barley as false remedy for w. K1016; bleeding w. don't stop hero H1507; dragon dips w. in holy well, is healed B11.12.1.2; dupe rubs salt on w. K1045.2; five w. of Christ V211.5, Z71.3.2; inflicters rather than receivers of w. chosen J481; inflaming warrior's w. K2014; king pretends to heal, really inflames ally's w. K2014.1; lovers' meeting: heroine heals hero's w. T32; magic arrow makes five w. D2092.0.1; magic girdle protects from all w. D1381.14; martyrs' w. emit milk V229.2.6; recognition by w. received in common H16.2; scratching contest: man's wife shows w. K83.1; sharing his w. J1621.

Wounded chieftain deceptively granted land K185.7.3; fairies F254.4; hero cured in peasant's house P411.3; hero restored by peasant R169.14; soldiers healed by druid P427.5.1; warrior continues fighting W33.1. — Animal cares for w. master B536; bride w. accidentally on way home T152; culture hero can be w. A526.1; curse by w. animal M411.19.1; fairy music brings sleep to w. F262.6; fairy w. by mortal F389.3; princess, w. prince abandoned in jungle T89.1.1; refusal to fight w. enemy W215.2; woman told father w., leaves, is robbed K343.1.2.

Wounding *S180ff.; animal without killing it tabu C841.0.2; self to accuse another of murder K2116.3; self from grief F1041.21.6.1. — Disenchantment by w. D712.6; foreknowledge of w. D1812.0.3; iron blessed by saint incapable of w. D1674; magic sickness from w. sick person D2064.6; symbolic w. of king Z182; trickster w. self to accuse others K2153.

Woven, see **Weaving.**

Wraiths separate from body E723ff.

Wrap. — Snake disenchanted by being allowed to w. itself three times around person's neck D759.8.

Wrapped. — Abandoned child w. in straw S336; child w. in altar coverings V135.1; coming w. in net (neither naked nor clad) H1054.1; ship w. with featherbeds and canvas F1031.

Wrapping. — Boy born in cloth w. T581.11; night from deity w. self in dark mantle A1174.4.

Wrath, see **Anger.**

Wreath. — Love through finding lady's w. T11.4.3.

Wrecked man saved on coffer of jewels becomes rich N226.

Wrecking of ship, see **Shipwreck.**

Wren as druid of the birds B242.1.2.1; helps mankind A1348.1; king of birds B242.1.2. — Fly, w., fox live with cleric B256.10; helpful w. B451.3; in burrowing contest w. goes into mouse hole K17.1.1; why w. is disliked A2522.6; why w. does not migrate A2482.3.

Wren's food A2435.4.11; wedding B282.9. — Crow's house full of w. eggs H1129.9.

Wrestler boasts he can carry mountain K1741.4. — Lie: remarkable w. X973; mighty w. F617.

Wrestling before food given strangers W213; with giant warrior H1166.1; match won by deception K12; ogre G317; as strength test H1562.9; to test son's legitimacy H218.2; with witch G275.9. — Devil and God w. at time of creation A63.3; earthquake as giant's w. F531.3.8.5.1; fairies w. with mortals F364.2; giants w. with each other F531.6.8.3.3; suitor contest: w. H331.6.

Wright. — Monk becomes w. P426.3.1.

Wrinkling. — Hills from earth w. up its feet A969.4.

Wrist. — Hand without w. F552.4.

Writer sent to heaven J225.7. — Bad w. who praises himself reprimanded J953.2.1.

Writing of Jews explained A1689.6; letter slowly because recipient can't read fast J2242.2; tablets transformed to bundle D454.11; tabu on sabbath C631.5. — Dead man w. E557; devil w. faults of man on goat skin G303.24.1.2; devil w. names of supplicants G303.6.1.2.1; genie called by w. his name on papers and burning them *D2074.2.4; ghost w. on wall E557.1; guessing magic w. H517; heavenly hand w. on wall F1036; indelible w. D1654.3.1.1; magic w. makes foster brothers enemies P273.2.4; origin of w. A1484; resuscitation by w. deity's name E75; scribe can't read own w. P425.1.

Writings. — Bird can recite sacred w. B122.3; deity authenticates sacred w. A199.6; extraordinary w. F883; magic w. *D1266.1; sacred w. V151.

Written charm renders invulnerable D1344.4. — Charm w. in blood has magic power *D1273.0.1; wife follows w. instructions J2516.3.1.

Wrong person killed N338.— Choice: apparent injustice over greater w. J225; countertask: turning jug w. side out H1923.9.1; fugitive slave takes w. road and is caught N382; one w. and five hundred good deeds J1605.

Wrongdoer. — Spring breaks forth against w. F933.6; waters drowning w. F930.2.

Wronged wife goes to wronged husband T233. — Curse by w. man M411.23; succession to fall to line that has been w. P17.7.

Wry-mouthed family X131.

Xanthippe and Socrates: "after thunder rain" T251.4.

Xylophone. — Chameleon plays x. B297.1.2.

Yak. — Magic y. tail D1029.2.1; resuscitation by y. tail E64.16.1; speaking y. B211.1.5.4.

Yaksa. — Sex exchanged with y. D592.1.

Yam cutting symbolizes daughter for marriage H611.3. — Not to heed magic y. that says not to take it up C811.2; magic y. D983.2.

Yams. — Origin of y. A1423.1, A2686.4.3; people in otherworld stand on their heads and pound y. with their heads F167.4.1; why some y. are good, some bad A2741.2, A2793.3; why y. are small and plentiful A2794.2.

Yard. — Filling y. with manure (task) H1129.1; shepherd shuts up lion in y. with livestock J2172.2.

Yards. — Giant three spans between brows and three y. between shoulders F531.2.2.

Yarn. — Husband made to believe that y. has changed to tow through his carelessness J2325; numskull ties y. around stove to keep heat from escaping J1942; pursuit of rolling ball of y. H1226.4; witch winds y. G244.1.

Yawning mouth paralyzed open D2072.0.5.2.

Yawns. — Contagious y. J1448; criminal accidentally detected: "that is the first": sleepy woman counting her y. N611.2; dupe made to believe that trickster becomes wolf when he y. three times, flees and leaves his clothes behind him K335.0.4.1.

Year added to life by eating fruit of magic tree D1338.3.3.1; and day Z72.1; seems hours in otherworld F377.2. — Bringing as many horses as there are days in y. (task) H1117; build shelter for whole y. J741; customs for the y. established A1502; disenchantment if twelve men will not leave castle for y. D759.4; door to fairyland opens once a y. F211.1.1; effects of wild hunt remedied by seeing it y. later in same place E501.19.1; formulas based on y. Z72; king for y. provides for future J711.3; kings exchange forms and kingdoms for y. D45.1; magic cauldron boils a y. D1601.10.2; magic weakness for five days each y. D1837.1.1; mermaid appears once each y. B81.12.2; one lie a y. X901; person walks unceasingly for y. F1032; prophetic dream loses force after a y. D1812.3.3.4; riddle of y. H721ff.; sinners endure hell for a y. Q560.3; strong man's labor contract: blow at end of y. F613.1; take y. to do errand: servant does J2461.4; wild hunt as omen of plentiful y. E501.20.2; windows and doors for every day in the y. F782.1.

Year's respite granted before death K551.22.1; respite for unwelcome marriage T151.

Years not counted J181; are days in Tusita world A697.2.1; seem moments while man listens to song of bird D2011.1; thought days *D2011. — Dead person visits earth every seven y. E585.1; disenchantment at end of seven y. D791.1.1; lost soul to serve as porter in hell for seven y. E755.2.3; magic pill on which one feeds self for y. D1652.1.8; moments thought y. D2012; person of remarkable sight finds tracks of swine stolen seven y. before his birth F642.2; seven y. of service imposed on suitor H317.1; talking statue, when destroyed, cannot be replaced for thirty thousand y. D1661.1.

Yearly tasks C684ff.; transformation D624. — Devil to help gambler in exchange for one task y. M214; ghost visits earth y. E585.4; wild hunt appears y. at same moment E501.11.3.2.

Yeast as an afterthought J1962. — Origin of y. A1429.2.

Yelling. — Monk y. to repel temptress T331.9.

Yellow lucky color Z148. — Blue, red, y. horses in fairyland F241.1.1.3; fairies' y. hair, clothing F233.5; why canary's eggs are y. A2391.1; why coyote has y. eyes A2332.5.1.

"Yes" C495.2.2.1. — Answering only "y." and "no" J1255.

Yesterday I was a herdsman and now I am an abbot H685.1. — Origin of y. A1178.

Yesterday's — Is today's sun same as y.? J2272.2.

Yew rod used for divination D1311.15.1. — Fairy harper in y. tree F386.1, F262.3.1.2; magic y. tree *D950.14; riddle about y. H852; sacred y. V1.7.1.3.

Yggdrasil A652. — Magic fruit from Y. D1501.4.

Yield. — God decreases plant's y. to punish man A2723.2; temporary advantage gained by pretending to y. in combat K2378.

Yielding. — Sea y. whatever people desire F931.9.2.

Ymir A642, A831.2. — Giants as sons of Y. F531.6.1.7; clouds from brain of Y. A1133.1; giants drowned in blood of Y. F531.6.12.8.1; origin of sky from skull of Y. A701.2.

Yogi advises king to use yogi blood; yogi killed J818.1; advises sacrifice of sister S260.1.2. — Contest between a y. and Musselman V351.5; thief disguised as y. K311.4.1.

Yoke. — Children in moon with y. and bucket A751.7; driving horses over ashen y. tabu C833.4; gold y. in magic tilling D1620.2.7; magic y. D1101.6, (impenetrable) D1381.10.4.

Yoked. — Old ox y. with young one J441.1; wild animals y. by saint B558.6.

Yoking stags H1154.3.6; together lion and wild boar (task) H1149.1. — Bhuiya y. cow and bullock together A1689.1; origin of custom of y. oxen A1441.2.

York. — Origin of Y. rose: from blood of War of the Roses A2656.2.

You are mine and I am yours (marriage formula) T135.1.

Young knight substitutes for old in tournament K3.2; not to precede old P633; queen murders old husband K2213.12; ravens drowned for promising father aid J267.1; wife loves young man T92.1.1. — Angel in form of y. man J225.0.3; animal neglects its y. B751.5; animal's fanciful treatment of their y. B751; animal grateful for rescue of its y. B365; army of y. men P551.1; association of y. and old J440ff.; do not go where an old man has a y. wife J21.3; man with obedient wife looks y. T254.3; old man in love with y. woman J1221; otherworld people ever y. F167.9; wisdom from y. man J175.

Younger brother asks older for health secret H596.1.1; child may not marry before elder T131.2. — Clever y. generation J1122; kingship given to y. brother P17.8; only y. son of lion keeps father's precepts and is successful J22ff.; prophecy: y. son will get throne M314.3; treacherous y. brother K2211.0.2.

Youngest brother (alone succeeds on quest) H1242, (rescues his elder brothers) R155.1, (shares wealth with older ones) W11.14, (surpasses elder as thief) K308; judge first to give decision P516; sister rescues elder R157.1. — Hero loves y. of seventy princesses T27.2; prophecy: y. brother to rule M312.2.2; victorious y. child *L0—L99; vigil for dead father: y. son alone endures frightful experiences H1462.1.

Youth, see also **Rejuvenation;** abducted by fairy F325; lamed by man whose daughter he refuses to marry Q451.2.1; made lame: had kicked his mother J225.1; meets devil in woods G303.8.13.1; promised to ogre visits his home G461; saved from death sentence R169.6; serves ogre G452; trusts self to horse over which he has no control J657.1; will answer only on throne: once there, orders king killed J1189.1. — Age and y. in love T91.4; betrayal through pretended fountain of y. K116.1; choice: suffering in y. or old age J214; conclusion: y. and age are alike J2214.2; devil (advises y. to enjoy himself and not to think of God) G303.9.7.2, (promises to help mistreated apprentice if y. will meet him by night in lonely spot) G303.22.12, (tempts y. to deny Virgin) G303.9.4.8; eagle renews y. B758; eternal y. D1883; foolish y. in love with ugly old mistress J445.1; fountain of y. D1338.1.1; god of y. A474.1; gods of y. and age A474; immortality useless without y. D1850.1; king and clever y. H561.4; land of y. D1338.7, F116.1; mature married woman in love with callow y. T91.4.1; old racehorse in mill laments vanity of y. J14; phoenix renews y. *B32.1; prophecy: either y. or mother will die M341.5; quest for the water of y. H1321.3; riddle about hastily passing y. H767.1; sun from head of sacrificed y. A718.1; token sent with y. H82.6; water of y. D1338.1.2.

Youths clever thieves K305.3; grind in mill of underworldlings F106; wear false beards K1821.4. — Devil appears among y. who jest while they say their evening prayers G303.6.2.3.

Yule. — King killed at Y. feast K913.1; vow taking at Y. festival M119.3.

Zabi's — Why z. eyes narrow: laughs so hard A2332.3.2.

Zacharias Z71.1.5.

Zadig J1661.1.1.

Zeal: temperate and intemperate J550ff.

Zebra. — Man transformed to z. D115.1; stripes of z. A2413.1; how z. got its mane A2322.3; why z. is continually eating A2478.1.

Zebra's. — Why z. ears long A2325.5; why z. mouth is large A2341.2.2.

Zenith. — Hero resides in z. A572.1.

Zeus, see also **Jove, Jupiter;** gives man modesty but it leaves when love enters T1; has embassy of dogs imprisoned for fouling his court *Q433.3; refuses wedding present from snake J411.2; smites Capaneus while he is climbing a ladder L472. — Casket with Good Luck in it given to men by Z. N113.1.1; dungbeetle keeps destroying eagle's eggs:

eagle at last goes to sky and lays eggs in lap of Z. L315.7; frogs demand live king from Z. J643.1; snake complains to Z. that people step on him J623.1.

Zise. — Feast for Z. A1541.2.1.

Zither string breaks as life token E761.5.2.

Ziz as birds' king B242.1.10. — Bird Z. B31.1.0.1.

Zodiac grows up: the Kid becomes the Goat J2212.6 — Zones of earth ·corresponding to Z. A881.

Zögernder Dieb J2136.5.1.

Zuñi. — Why Z. girls rub flour on their faces as they grind A1687.1.

THE END

ADDITIONS AND CORRECTIONS

(See also at end of Volume 5.)

VOLUME 1.

P. 380, 12 lines
  from bottom.   *For* B131.1 *read* B131.1.1.

P. 509, line 20.   *For* D243.1 *read* C243.1.

VOLUME 3.

P. 219, 3 lines
  from bottom.   *For* inexhaustible *read* inexhaustibly.

P. 409, line 13 (H363).   *For* 610B *read* 510B.

P. 501, line 5.   *For* 47 *read* 471.

VOLUME 4.

P. 90, line 36.   *For* V21 *read* U21.

P. 91, 11 lines
  from bottom.   *For* pleasant *read* peasant.

P. 108, line 24 (J1364).   *For* that *read* than.

VOLUME 5.

P. 365, line 31.   *For* naivité *read* naiveté

P. 369, line 35 (T251.8).   *For* heating *read* beating

P. 377, after line 5.   *Add* T317.0.1. *Life shortened by incontinence:* 300-year old man has had intercourse every two years. India: Thompson-Balys.

Note the following Cross-References:
A123.2.1.1—N111.2.2;   A123.9—H1289.4.1;   A185.6.1.1—Q147.3, E722.2.12; A692.1—F136.2;   A751.8.6—A1142.5.1.1;   A1313.3.1—F547.1.1;   A1346.2— A1420.4; A1423.1—A2686.4.1, A2686.4.3; A2211.14—K952.1.2; A2435.6.2.1— Q452; B15.7.3—B101.1.1;   B33.1.1—B777;   B143.1.3—H1578.1.6;   B765.3— D2161.4.10.2.2;   B765.11—D1563.2.2.2;   B771—H1155;   D215—G263.2.2; D473.1—D2086.1.1; D925.0.2—F162.5.1, F718.3; D1442—H1155; D1524.1.2.1 —K185.13; D1533.1.1—D1552.4; E629.1—E693.3; E643.1—F1075; F162.5.1— F718.3;   F262.3.1.2—F386.1.1;   F647.4—K2051.1;   F769.1—J21.52.1, X1503.3; F933.13.2—H251.3.9.2;   F1041.21.6—P678.1;   G254.1—Q551.2.7;   H252.1— M119.7; H583.7—H1058; H946.1—J1805.2.1; J86—Z186; J761.3—T455.3.1; J1149.2—K341.11;   J1162.3—K448;   J1805.1.1—J2489.8, K1462.2;   J1842.2— X372.4.1;   J2014—J2316.1;   K533—K1834;   K565.2—K1022.1.1,   K1973; K1023—X411.3;   K1321.1.1—K1514.16;   N317—N741.2;   T117.5—T461.3; T512.5—T533.

Note the following Inadvertant Duplications:
B301.1.2 and B301.7.1; B524.1.12 and B549.5; D452.3.1 and D476.1.11; D491.6 and F1009.4; D951 and D2178.8; F963.3 and Q147.2; H1553.5 and W185.4; J677 and U129.3; J1162.3 and K448; J1197 and U21.5; J1369.5 and J1714.5; J1603 and X372.3; V211.5 and Z271.3.2.